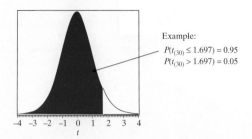

Example:
$P(t_{(30)} \leq 1.697) = 0.95$
$P(t_{(30)} > 1.697) = 0.05$

Table 2 Percentiles of the *t*-distribution

df	$t_{(0.90,df)}$	$t_{(0.95,df)}$	$t_{(0.975,df)}$	$t_{(0.99,df)}$	$t_{(0.995,df)}$
1	3.078	6.314	12.706	31.821	63.657
2	1.886	2.920	4.303	6.965	9.925
3	1.638	2.353	3.182	4.541	5.841
4	1.533	2.132	2.776	3.747	4.604
5	1.476	2.015	2.571	3.365	4.032
6	1.440	1.943	2.447	3.143	3.707
7	1.415	1.895	2.365	2.998	3.499
8	1.397	1.860	2.306	2.896	3.355
9	1.383	1.833	2.262	2.821	3.250
10	1.372	1.812	2.228	2.764	3.169
11	1.363	1.796	2.201	2.718	3.106
12	1.356	1.782	2.179	2.681	3.055
13	1.350	1.771	2.160	2.650	3.012
14	1.345	1.761	2.145	2.624	2.977
15	1.341	1.753	2.131	2.602	2.947
16	1.337	1.746	2.120	2.583	2.921
17	1.333	1.740	2.110	2.567	2.898
18	1.330	1.734	2.101	2.552	2.878
19	1.328	1.729	2.093	2.539	2.861
20	1.325	1.725	2.086	2.528	2.845
21	1.323	1.721	2.080	2.518	2.831
22	1.321	1.717	2.074	2.508	2.819
23	1.319	1.714	2.069	2.500	2.807
24	1.318	1.711	2.064	2.492	2.797
25	1.316	1.708	2.060	2.485	2.787
26	1.315	1.706	2.056	2.479	2.779
27	1.314	1.703	2.052	2.473	2.771
28	1.313	1.701	2.048	2.467	2.763
29	1.311	1.699	2.045	2.462	2.756
30	1.310	1.697	2.042	2.457	2.750
31	1.309	1.696	2.040	2.453	2.744
32	1.309	1.694	2.037	2.449	2.738
33	1.308	1.692	2.035	2.445	2.733
34	1.307	1.691	2.032	2.441	2.728
35	1.306	1.690	2.030	2.438	2.724
36	1.306	1.688	2.028	2.434	2.719
37	1.305	1.687	2.026	2.431	2.715
38	1.304	1.686	2.024	2.429	2.712
39	1.304	1.685	2.023	2.426	2.708
40	1.303	1.684	2.021	2.423	2.704
50	1.299	1.676	2.009	2.403	2.678
∞	1.282	1.645	1.960	2.326	2.576

Source: This table was generated using the SAS® function TINV

The Rules of Summation

$$\sum_{i=1}^{n} x_i = x_1 + x_2 + \cdots + x_n$$

$$\sum_{i=1}^{n} a = na$$

$$\sum_{i=1}^{n} ax_i = a \sum_{i=1}^{n} x_i$$

$$\sum_{i=1}^{n} (x_i + y_i) = \sum_{i=1}^{n} x_i + \sum_{i=1}^{n} y_i$$

$$\sum_{i=1}^{n} (ax_i + by_i) = a \sum_{i=1}^{n} x_i + b \sum_{i=1}^{n} y_i$$

$$\sum_{i=1}^{n} (a + bx_i) = na + b \sum_{i=1}^{n} x_i$$

$$\bar{x} = \frac{\sum_{i=1}^{n} x_i}{n} = \frac{x_1 + x_2 + \cdots + x_n}{n}$$

$$\sum_{i=1}^{n} (x_i - \bar{x}) = 0$$

$$\sum_{i=1}^{2} \sum_{j=1}^{3} f(x_i, y_j) = \sum_{i=1}^{2} [f(x_i, y_1) + f(x_i, y_2) + f(x_i, y_3)]$$
$$= f(x_1, y_1) + f(x_1, y_2) + f(x_1, y_3)$$
$$+ f(x_2, y_1) + f(x_2, y_2) + f(x_2, y_3)$$

Expected Values & Variances

$$E(X) = x_1 f(x_1) + x_2 f(x_2) + \cdots + x_n f(x_n)$$
$$= \sum_{i=1}^{n} x_i f(x_i) = \sum_{x} x f(x)$$

$$E[g(X)] = \sum_{x} g(x) f(x)$$

$$E[g_1(X) + g_2(X)] = \sum_{x} [g_1(x) + g_2(x)] f(x)$$
$$= \sum_{x} g_1(x) f(x) + \sum_{x} g_2(x) f(x)$$
$$= E[g_1(X)] + E[g_2(X)]$$

$$E(c) = c$$
$$E(cX) = cE(X)$$
$$E(a + cX) = a + cE(X)$$
$$\text{var}(X) = \sigma^2 = E[X - E(X)]^2 = E(X^2) - [E(X)]^2$$
$$\text{var}(a + cX) = E[(a + cX) - E(a + cX)]^2 = c^2 \text{var}(X)$$

Marginal and Conditional Distributions

$$f(x) = \sum_{y} f(x, y) \quad \text{for each value } X \text{ can take}$$

$$f(y) = \sum_{x} f(x, y) \quad \text{for each value } Y \text{ can take}$$

$$f(x|y) = P[X = x | Y = y] = \frac{f(x, y)}{f(y)}$$

If X and Y are independent random variables, then $f(x,y) = f(x)f(y)$ for each and every pair of values x and y. The converse is also true.

If X and Y are independent random variables, then the conditional probability density function of X given that

$$Y = y \text{ is } f(x|y) = \frac{f(x, y)}{f(y)} = \frac{f(x)f(y)}{f(y)} = f(x)$$

for each and every pair of values x and y. The converse is also true.

Expectations, Variances & Covariances

$$\text{cov}(X, Y) = E[(X - E[X])(Y - E[Y])]$$
$$= \sum_{x} \sum_{y} [x - E(X)][y - E(Y)] f(x, y)$$

$$\rho = \frac{\text{cov}(X,Y)}{\sqrt{\text{var}(X)\text{var}(Y)}}$$

$$E(c_1 X + c_2 Y) = c_1 E(X) + c_2 E(Y)$$
$$E(X + Y) = E(X) + E(Y)$$

$$\text{var}(aX + bY + cZ) = a^2 \text{var}(X) + b^2 \text{var}(Y) + c^2 \text{var}(Z)$$
$$+ 2ab\,\text{cov}(X,Y) + 2ac\,\text{cov}(X,Z) + 2bc\,\text{cov}(Y,Z)$$

If X, Y, and Z are independent, or uncorrelated, random variables, then the covariance terms are zero and:

$$\text{var}(aX + bY + cZ) = a^2 \text{var}(X)$$
$$+ b^2 \text{var}(Y) + c^2 \text{var}(Z)$$

Normal Probabilities

If $X \sim N(\mu, \sigma^2)$, then $Z = \dfrac{X - \mu}{\sigma} \sim N(0, 1)$

If $X \sim N(\mu, \sigma^2)$ and a is a constant, then

$$P(X \geq a) = P\left(Z \geq \frac{a - \mu}{\sigma}\right)$$

If $X \sim N(\mu, \sigma^2)$ and a and b are constants, then

$$P(a \leq X \leq b) = P\left(\frac{a - \mu}{\sigma} \leq Z \leq \frac{b - \mu}{\sigma}\right)$$

Assumptions of the Simple Linear Regression Model

SR1 The value of y, for each value of x, is $y = \beta_1 + \beta_2 x + e$

SR2 The average value of the random error e is $E(e) = 0$ since we assume that $E(y) = \beta_1 + \beta_2 x$

SR3 The variance of the random error e is $\text{var}(e) = \sigma^2 = \text{var}(y)$

SR4 The covariance between any pair of random errors, e_i and e_j is $\text{cov}(e_i, e_j) = \text{cov}(y_i, y_j) = 0$

SR5 The variable x is not random and must take at least two different values.

SR6 (optional) The values of e are normally distributed about their mean $e \sim N(0, \sigma^2)$

Least Squares Estimation

If b_1 and b_2 are the least squares estimates, then
$$\hat{y}_i = b_1 + b_2 x_i$$
$$\hat{e}_i = y_i - \hat{y}_i = y_i - b_1 - b_2 x_i$$

The Normal Equations
$$N b_1 + \Sigma x_i b_2 = \Sigma y_i$$
$$\Sigma x_i b_1 + \Sigma x_i^2 b_2 = \Sigma x_i y_i$$

Least Squares Estimators
$$b_2 = \frac{\Sigma(x_i - \bar{x})(y_i - \bar{y})}{\Sigma (x_i - \bar{x})^2}$$
$$b_1 = \bar{y} - b_2 \bar{x}$$

Principles of Econometrics

Fourth Edition

International Student version

R. Carter Hill
Louisiana State University

William E. Griffiths
University of Melbourne

Guay C. Lim
University of Melbourne

WILEY

John Wiley & Sons, Inc.

Carter Hill dedicates this work to his wife, Melissa Waters

Bill Griffiths dedicates this work to JoAnn, Jill, David, Wendy, Nina, and Isabella

Guay Lim dedicates this work to Tony Meagher

Brief Contents

Preface

Principles of Econometrics, 4th edition, is an introductory book for undergraduate students in economics and finance, as well as for first-year graduate students in economics, finance, accounting, agricultural economics, marketing, public policy, sociology, law, and political science. It is assumed that students have taken courses in the principles of economics, and elementary statistics. Matrix algebra is not used, and calculus concepts are introduced and developed in the appendices.

A brief explanation of the title is in order. This work is a revision of *Principles of Econometrics*, 3rd edition, by Hill, Griffiths, and Lim (Wiley, 2008), which was a revision of *Undergraduate Econometrics*, 2nd edition, by Hill, Griffiths, and Judge (Wiley, 2001). The earlier title was chosen to clearly differentiate the book from other more advanced books by the same authors. We made the title change because the book is appropriate not only for undergraduates, but also for first-year graduate students in many fields, as well as MBA students. Furthermore, naming it *Principles of Econometrics* emphasizes our belief that econometrics should be part of the economics curriculum, in the same way as the principles of microeconomics and the principles of macroeconomics. Those who have been studying and teaching econometrics as long as we have will remember that *Principles of Econometrics* was the title that Henri Theil used for his 1971 classic, which was also published by John Wiley and Sons. Our choice of the same title is not intended to signal that our book is similar in level and content. Theil's work was, and remains, a unique treatise on advanced graduate level econometrics. Our book is an introductory-level econometrics text.

Book Objectives

Principles of Econometrics is designed to give students an understanding of why econometrics is necessary, and to provide them with a working knowledge of basic econometric tools so that

- They can apply these tools to modeling, estimation, inference, and forecasting in the context of real-world economic problems.
- They can evaluate critically the results and conclusions from others who use basic econometric tools.
- They have a foundation and understanding for further study of econometrics.
- They have an appreciation of the range of more advanced techniques that exist and that may be covered in later econometric courses.

The book is *not* an econometrics cookbook, nor is it in a theorem-proof format. It emphasizes motivation, understanding, and implementation. Motivation is achieved by introducing very simple economic models and asking economic questions that the student can answer. Understanding is aided by lucid description of techniques, clear interpretation, and appropriate applications. Learning is reinforced by doing, with clear worked examples in the text and exercises at the end of each chapter.

Overview of Contents

This fourth edition retains the spirit and basic structure of the third edition. Chapter 1 introduces econometrics and gives general guidelines for writing an empirical research paper and for locating economic data sources. The Probability Primer preceding Chapter 2 summarizes essential properties of random variables and their probability distributions, and reviews summation notation. The simple linear regression model is covered in Chapters 2–4, while the multiple regression model is treated in Chapters 5–7. Chapters 8 and 9 introduce econometric problems that are unique to cross-sectional data (heteroskedasticity) and time-series data (dynamic models), respectively. Chapters 10 and 11 deal with random regressors, the failure of least squares when a regressor is endogenous, and instrumental variables estimation, first in the general case, and then in the simultaneous equations model. In Chapter 12 the analysis of time-series data is extended to discussions of nonstationarity and cointegration. Chapter 13 introduces econometric issues specific to two special time-series models, the vector error correction and vector autoregressive models, while Chapter 14 considers the analysis of volatility in data and the ARCH model. In Chapters 15 and 16 we introduce microeconometric models for panel data, and qualitative and limited dependent variables. In appendices A, B, and C we introduce math, probability, and statistical inference concepts that are used in the book.

Summary of Changes and New Material

This edition includes a great deal of new material, including new examples and exercises using real data, and some significant reorganizations. Important new features include:

- Chapter 1 includes a discussion of data types, and sources of economic data on the Internet. Tips on writing a research paper are given up front so that students can form ideas for a paper as the course develops.
- The Probability Primer precedes Chapter 2. This primer reviews the concepts of random variables, and how probabilities are calculated given probability density functions. Mathematical expectation and rules of expected values are summarized for discrete random variables. These rules are applied to develop the concept of variance and covariance. Calculations of probabilities using the normal distribution are illustrated.
- Chapter 2 is expanded to include brief introductions to nonlinear relationships and the concept of an indicator (or dummy) variable. A new section has been added on interpreting a standard error. An appendix has been added on Monte Carlo simulation and is used to illustrate the sampling properties of the least squares estimator.
- Estimation and testing of linear combinations of parameters is now included in Chapter 3. An appendix is added using Monte Carlo simulation to illustrate the properties of interval estimators and hypothesis tests. Chapter 4 discusses in detail nonlinear relationships such as the log-log, log-linear, linear-log, and polynomial models. Model interpretations are discussed and examples given, along with an introduction to residual analysis.
- The introductory chapter on multiple regression (Chapter 5) now includes material on standard errors for both linear and nonlinear functions of coefficients, and how they are used for interval estimation and hypothesis testing. The treatment of

polynomial and log-linear models given in Chapter 4 is extended to the multiple regression model; interaction variables are included and marginal effects are described. An appendix on large sample properties of estimators has been added.

- Chapter 6 contains a new section on model selection criteria and a reorganization of material on the F-test for joint hypotheses.

- Chapter 7 now deals exclusively with indicator variables. In addition to the standard material, we introduce the linear probability model and treatment effect models, including difference and difference-in-difference estimators.

- Chapter 8 has been reorganized so that testing for heteroskedasticity precedes estimation with heteroskedastic errors. A section on heteroskedasticity in the linear probability model has been added.

- Chapter 9 on regression with stationary time series data has been restructured to emphasize autoregressive distributed lag models and their special cases: finite distributed lags, autoregressive models, and the AR(1) error model. Testing for serial correlation using the correlogram and Lagrange multiplier tests now precedes estimation. Two new macroeconomic examples, Okun's law and the Phillips curve, are used to illustrate the various models. Sections on exponential smoothing and model selection criteria have been added, and the section on multiplier analysis has been expanded.

- Chapter 10 on endogeneity problems has been streamlined, using real data examples in the body of the chapter as illustrations. New material on assessing instrument strength has been added. An appendix on testing for weak instruments introduces the Stock-Yogo critical values for the Cragg-Donald F-test. A Monte Carlo experiment is included to demonstrate the properties of instrumental variables estimators.

- Chapter 11 now includes an appendix describing two alternatives to two-stage least squares: the limited information maximum likelihood and the k-class estimators. The Stock-Yogo critical values for LIML and k-class estimator are provided. Monte Carlo results illustrate the properties of LIML and the k-class estimator.

- Chapter 12 now contains a section on the derivation of the short-run error correction model.

- Chapter 13 now contains an example and exercise using data which includes the recent global financial crisis.

- Chapter 14 now contains a revised introduction to the ARCH model.

- Chapter 15 has been restructured to give more prominence to the fixed effects and random effects models. New sections on cluster-robust standard errors and the Hausman-Taylor estimator have been added.

- Chapter 16 includes more on post-estimation analysis within choice models. The average marginal effect is explained and illustrated. The "delta method" is used to create standard errors of estimated marginal effects and predictions. An appendix gives algebraic detail on the "delta method."

- Appendix A now introduces the concepts of derivatives and integrals. Rules for derivatives are given, and the Taylor series approximation explained. Both derivatives and integrals are explained intuitively using graphs and algebra, with each in separate sections.

- Appendix B includes a discussion and illustration of the properties of both discrete and continuous random variables. Extensive examples are given, including integration techniques for continuous random variables. The change-of-variable technique for deriving the probability density function of a function of a continuous random variable is discussed. The method of inversion for drawing random values is discussed and illustrated. Linear congruential generators for uniform random numbers are described.

- Appendix C now includes a section on kernel density estimation.
- Brief answers to selected problems, along with all data files, will now be included on the book website at www.wiley.com/college/hill.

Computer Supplement Books

The following books are offered by John Wiley and Sons as computer supplements to *Principles of Econometrics*:

- *Using EViews for Principles of Econometrics,* 4th edition, by Griffiths, Hill and Lim [ISBN 978-1-11803207-7 or at www.coursesmart.com]. This supplementary book presents the EViews 7.1 [www.eviews.com] software commands required for the examples in *Principles of Econometrics* in a clear and concise way. It includes many illustrations that are student friendly. It is useful not only for students and instructors who will be using this software as part of their econometrics course, but also for those who wish to learn how to use EViews.

- *Using Stata for Principles of Econometrics*, 4th edition, by Adkins and Hill [ISBN 978-1-11803208-4 or at www.coursesmart.com]. This supplementary book presents the Stata 11.1 [www.stata.com] software commands required for the examples in *Principles of Econometrics*. It is useful not only for students and instructors who will be using this software as part of their econometrics course, but also for those who wish to learn how to use Stata. Screen shots illustrate the use of Stata's drop-down menus. Stata commands are explained and the use of "do-files" illustrated.

- *Using SAS for Econometrics* by Hill and Campbell [ISBN 978-1-11803209-1 or at www.coursesmart.com]. This stand-alone book gives SAS 9.2 [www.sas.com] software commands for econometric tasks, following the general outline of *Principles of Econometrics*. It includes enough background material on econometrics so that instructors using any textbook can easily use this book as a supplement. The volume spans several levels of econometrics. It is suitable for undergraduate students who will use "canned" SAS statistical procedures, and for graduate students who will use advanced procedures as well as direct programming in SAS's matrix language; the latter is discussed in chapter appendices.

- *Using Excel for Principles of Econometrics*, 4th edition, by Briand and Hill [ISBN 978-1-11803210-7 or at www.coursesmart.com]. This supplement explains how to use Excel to reproduce most of the examples in *Principles of Econometrics*. Detailed instructions and screen shots are provided explaining both the computations and clarifying the operations of Excel. Templates are developed for common tasks.

- *Using GRETL for Principles of Econometrics*, 4th edition, by Adkins. This free supplement, readable using Adobe Acrobat, explains how to use the freely available statistical software GRETL (download from http://gretl.sourceforge.net). Professor Adkins explains in detail, using screen shots, how to use GRETL to replicate the examples in *Principles of Econometrics*. The manual is freely available at www.learneconometrics.com/gretl.html.

Resources for Students

Available at both the Book Companion Site for the International Student Version, and at the author website, principlesofeconometrics.com, are
- Data files
- Answers to selected exercises

Data Files

Data files for the book are provided in a variety of formats at the Book Companion Site. These include
- ASCII format (*.dat). These are text files containing only data.
- Definition files (*.def). These are text files describing the data file contents, with a listing of variable names, variable definitions, and summary statistics.
- EViews (*.wf1) workfiles for each data file
- Excel 2007 (*.xlsx) workbooks for each data file, including variable names in the first row
- Stata (*.dta) data files
- SAS (*.sas7bdat) data files
- GRETL (*.gdt) data files

Resources for Instructors

For instructors, also available at the Book Companion Site are
- An Instructor's Resources Guide with complete solutions, in both Microsoft Word and *.pdf formats, to *all* exercises in the text
- PowerPoint Presentation Slides
- Supplementary exercises with solutions

Author Website

The authors' website—principlesofeconometrics.com—includes
- Individual data files in each format, as well as Zip files containing data in compressed format
- Book errata
- Links to other useful websites, including RATS and SHAZAM computer resources for *Principles of Econometrics*, and tips on writing research papers
- Answers to selected exercises
- Hints and resources for writing

Acknowledgments

Several colleagues have helped us improve our book. We owe very special thanks to Genevieve Briand and Gawon Yoon, who have provided detailed and helpful comments on every part of the book. Also, we have benefited from comments made by Christian Kleiber, Daniel Case, Eric Hillebrand, Silvia Golem, Leandro M. Magnusson, Tom Means, Tong Zeng, Michael Rabbitt, Chris Skeels, Robert Dixon, Robert Brooks, Shuang Zhu, Jill Wright, and the many reviewers who have contributed feedback and suggestions over the years. Individuals who have pointed out errors of one sort or another are recognized in the errata listed at principlesofeconometrics.com.

Finally, authors Hill and Griffiths want to acknowledge the gifts given to them over the past 40 years by mentor, friend, and colleague George Judge. Neither this book, nor any of the other books in whose writing we have shared, would have ever seen the light of day without his vision and inspiration.

R. Carter Hill
William E. Griffiths
Guay C. Lim

Contents

Chapter 4 Prediction, Goodness-of-Fit, and Modeling Issues   130

Chapter 5 The Multiple Regression Model   167

Chapter 6 Further Inference in the Multiple Regression Model   221

Chapter 13 Vector Error Correction and Vector Autoregressive Models

Chapter 14 Time-Varying Volatility and ARCH Models

Chapter *1*

An Introduction to Econometrics

1.1 Why Study Econometrics?

Econometrics is fundamental for economic measurement. However, its importance extends far beyond the discipline of economics. Econometrics is a set of research tools also employed in the business disciplines of accounting, finance, marketing and management. It is used by social scientists, specifically researchers in history, political science, and sociology. Econometrics plays an important role in such diverse fields as forestry and agricultural economics. This breadth of interest in econometrics arises in part because economics is the foundation of business analysis and is the core social science. Thus research methods employed by economists, which includes the field of econometrics, are useful to a broad spectrum of individuals.

Econometrics plays a special role in the training of economists. As a student of economics, you are learning to "think like an economist." You are learning economic concepts such as opportunity cost, scarcity, and comparative advantage. You are working with economic models of supply and demand, macroeconomic behavior, and international trade. Through this training you become a person who better understands the world in which we live; you become someone who understands how markets work, and the way in which government policies affect the marketplace.

If economics is your major or minor field of study, a wide range of opportunities is open to you upon graduation. If you wish to enter the business world, your employer will want to know the answer to the question, "What can you do for me?" Students taking a traditional economics curriculum answer, "I can think like an economist." While we may view such a response to be powerful, it is not very specific, and may not be very satisfying to an employer who does not understand economics.

The problem is that a gap exists between what you have learned as an economics student and what economists actually do. Very few economists make their livings by studying economic theory alone, and those who do are usually employed by universities. Most economists, whether they work in the business world or for the government, or teach in universities, engage in economic analysis that is in part "empirical." By this we mean that they use economic data to estimate economic relationships, test economic hypotheses, and predict economic outcomes.

Studying econometrics fills the gap between being "a student of economics" and being "a practicing economist." With the econometric skills you will learn from this book, including how to work with econometric software, you will be able to elaborate on your answer to the employer's question above by saying "I can predict the sales of your product."

"I can estimate the effect on your sales if your competition lowers its price by \$1 per unit." "I can test whether your new ad campaign is actually increasing your sales." These answers are music to an employer's ears, because they reflect your ability to think like an economist and to analyze economic data. Such pieces of information are keys to good business decisions. Being able to provide your employer with useful information will make you a valuable employee and increase your odds of getting a desirable job.

On the other hand, if you plan to continue your education by enrolling in graduate school or law school, you will find that this introduction to econometrics is invaluable. If your goal is to earn a master's or Ph.D. degree in economics, finance, accounting, marketing, agricultural economics, sociology, political science, or forestry, you will encounter more econometrics in your future. The graduate courses tend to be quite technical and mathematical, and the forest often gets lost in studying the trees. By taking this introduction to econometrics you will gain an overview of what econometrics is about and develop some "intuition" about how things work before entering a technically oriented course.

1.2 **What Is Econometrics About?**

At this point we need to describe the nature of econometrics. It all begins with a theory from your field of study—whether it is accounting, sociology or economics—about how important variables are related to one another. In economics we express our ideas about relationships between economic variables using the mathematical concept of a function. For example, to express a relationship between income and consumption, we may write

$$CONSUMPTION = f(INCOME)$$

which says that the level of consumption is *some* function, $f(\bullet)$, of income.

The demand for an individual commodity—say, the Honda Accord—might be expressed as

$$Q^d = f(P,\ P^s,\ P^c,\ INC)$$

which says that the quantity of Honda Accords demanded, Q^d, is a function $f(P,\ P^s,\ P^c,\ INC)$ of the price of Honda Accords P, the price of cars that are substitutes P^s, the price of items that are complements P^c (like gasoline), and the level of income INC.

The supply of an agricultural commodity such as beef might be written as

$$Q^s = f(P,\ P^c,\ P^f)$$

where Q^s is the quantity supplied, P is the price of beef, P^c is the price of competitive products in production (e.g., the price of hogs), and P^f is the price of factors or inputs (e.g., the price of corn) used in the production process.

Each of the above equations is a general economic model that describes how we visualize the way in which economic variables are interrelated. Economic models of this type *guide our economic analysis*.

For most economic decision or choice problems, it is not enough to know that certain economic variables are interrelated, or even the direction of the relationship. In addition, we must understand the magnitudes involved. That is, we must be able to say **how much** a change in one variable affects another.

Econometrics is about how we can use theory and data from economics, business, and the social sciences, along with tools from statistics, to answer "how much" questions.

1.2.1 SOME EXAMPLES

As a case in point, consider the problem faced by a central bank. In the United States, this is the Federal Reserve System, with Ben Bernanke as chairman of the Federal Reserve Board (FRB). When prices are observed to rise, suggesting an increase in the inflation rate, the FRB must make a decision about whether to dampen the rate of growth of the economy. It can do so by raising the interest rate it charges its member banks when they borrow money (the discount rate) or the rate on overnight loans between banks (the federal funds rate). Increasing these rates sends a ripple effect through the economy, causing increases in other interest rates, such as those faced by would-be investors, who may be firms seeking funds for capital expansion or individuals who wish to buy consumer durables like automobiles and refrigerators. This has the economic effect of increasing costs, and consumers react by reducing the quantity of the durable goods demanded. Overall, aggregate demand falls, which slows the rate of inflation. These relationships are suggested by economic theory.

The real question facing Chairman Bernanke is "*How much* should we increase the discount rate to slow inflation and yet maintain a stable and growing economy?" The answer will depend on the responsiveness of firms and individuals to increases in the interest rates and to the effects of reduced investment on gross national product (GNP). The key elasticities and multipliers are called **parameters**. The values of economic parameters are unknown and must be estimated using a sample of economic data when formulating economic policies.

Econometrics is about how to best estimate economic parameters given the data we have. "Good" econometrics is important, since errors in the estimates used by policymakers such as the FRB may lead to interest rate corrections that are too large or too small, which has consequences for all of us.

Every day, decision-makers face "how much" questions similar to those facing Chairman Bernanke:

- A city council ponders the question of how much violent crime will be reduced if an additional million dollars is spent putting uniformed police on the street.

- The owner of a local Pizza Hut must decide how much advertising space to purchase in the local newspaper, and thus must estimate the relationship between advertising and sales.

- Louisiana State University must estimate how much enrollment will fall if tuition is raised by $300 per semester, and thus whether its revenue from tuition will rise or fall.

- The CEO of Proctor & Gamble must estimate how much demand there will be in ten years for the detergent Tide, and how much to invest in new plant and equipment.

- A real estate developer must predict by how much population and income will increase to the south of Baton Rouge, Louisiana, over the next few years, and whether it will be profitable to begin construction of a gambling casino and golf course.

- You must decide how much of your savings will go into a stock fund, and how much into the money market. This requires you to make predictions of the level of economic activity, the rate of inflation, and interest rates over your planning horizon.

- A public transportation council in Melbourne, Australia, must decide how an increase in fares for public transportation (trams, trains, and buses) will affect the number of travelers who switch to car or bike, and the effect of this switch on revenue going to public transportation.

To answer these questions of "how much," decision-makers rely on information provided by empirical economic research. In such research, an economist uses economic theory and reasoning to construct relationships between the variables in question. Data on these variables are collected and econometric methods are used to estimate the key underlying parameters and to make predictions. The decision-makers in the above examples obtain their "estimates" and "predictions" in different ways. The Federal Reserve Board has a large staff of economists to carry out econometric analyses. The CEO of Proctor & Gamble may hire econometric consultants to provide the firm with projections of sales. You may get advice about investing from a stock broker, who in turn is provided with econometric projections made by economists working for the parent company. Whatever the source of your information about "how much" questions, it is a good bet that there is an economist involved who is using econometric methods to analyze data that yield the answers.

In the next section, we show how to introduce parameters into an economic model, and how to convert an economic model into an econometric model.

1.3 **The Econometric Model**

What is an econometric model, and where does it come from? We will give you a general overview, and we may use terms that are unfamiliar to you. Be assured that before you are too far into this book, all the terminology will be clearly defined. In an econometric model we must first realize that economic relations are not exact. Economic theory does not claim to be able to predict the specific behavior of any individual or firm, but rather describes the *average* or *systematic* behavior of *many* individuals or firms. When studying car sales we recognize that the *actual* number of Hondas sold is the sum of this systematic part and a random and unpredictable component e that we will call a **random error**. Thus, an **econometric model** representing the sales of Honda Accords is

$$Q^d = f(P, \ P^s, \ P^c, \ INC) + e$$

The random error e accounts for the many factors that affect sales that we have omitted from this simple model, and it also reflects the intrinsic uncertainty in economic activity.

To complete the specification of the econometric model, we must also say something about the form of the algebraic relationship among our economic variables. For example, in your first economics courses quantity demanded was depicted as a *linear* function of price. We extend that assumption to the other variables as well, making the systematic part of the demand relation

$$f(P, \ P^s, \ P^c, \ INC) = \beta_1 + \beta_2 P + \beta_3 P^s + \beta_4 P^c + \beta_5 INC$$

The corresponding econometric model is

$$Q^d = \beta_1 + \beta_2 P + \beta_3 P^s + \beta_4 P^c + \beta_5 INC + e$$

The coefficients $\beta_1, \beta_2, \ldots, \beta_5$ are unknown **parameters** of the model that we estimate using economic data and an econometric technique. The functional form represents a hypothesis about the relationship between the variables. In any particular problem, one challenge is to determine a functional form that is compatible with economic theory and the data.

In every econometric model, whether it is a demand equation, a supply equation, or a production function, there is a systematic portion and an unobservable random component. The systematic portion is the part we obtain from economic theory, and includes an assumption about the functional form. The random component represents a "noise" component, which obscures our understanding of the relationship among variables, and which we represent using the random variable e.

We use the econometric model as a basis for **statistical inference**. Using the econometric model and a sample of data, we make inferences concerning the real world, learning something in the process. The ways in which statistical inference are carried out include

- **Estimating** economic parameters, such as elasticities, using econometric methods.
- **Predicting** economic outcomes, such as the enrollment in two-year colleges in the United States for the next ten years.
- **Testing** economic hypotheses, such as the question of whether newspaper advertising is better than store displays for increasing sales.

Econometrics includes all of these aspects of statistical inference. As we proceed through this book, you will learn how to properly estimate, predict, and test, given the characteristics of the data at hand.

1.4 How Are Data Generated?

In order to carry out statistical inference we must have data. Where do data come from? What type of real processes generate data? Economists and other social scientists work in a complex world in which data on variables are "observed" and rarely obtained from a controlled experiment. This makes the task of learning about economic parameters all the more difficult. Procedures for using such data to answer questions of economic importance are the subject matter of this book.

1.4.1 EXPERIMENTAL DATA

One way to acquire information about the unknown parameters of economic relationships is to conduct or observe the outcome of an experiment. In the physical sciences and agriculture, it is easy to imagine controlled experiments. Scientists specify the values of key control variables and then observe the outcome. We might plant similar plots of land with a particular variety of wheat, then vary the amounts of fertilizer and pesticide applied to each plot, observing at the end of the growing season the bushels of wheat produced on each plot. Repeating the experiment on N plots of land creates a sample of N observations. Such controlled experiments are rare in business and the social sciences. A key aspect of experimental data is that the values of the explanatory variables can be fixed at specific values in repeated trials of the experiment.

One business example comes from marketing research. Suppose we are interested in the weekly sales of a particular item at a supermarket. As an item is sold it is passed over a scanning unit to record the price and the amount that will appear on your grocery bill. But at the same time, a data record is created, and at every point in time the price of the item and the prices of all its competitors are known, as well as current store displays and coupon usage. The prices and shopping environment are controlled by store management, so this "experiment" can be repeated a number of days or weeks using the same values of the "control" variables.

There are some examples of planned experiments in the social sciences, but they are rare because of the difficulties in organizing and funding them. A notable example of a planned experiment is Tennessee's Project Star.[1] This experiment followed a single cohort of elementary school children from kindergarten through the third grade, beginning in 1985 and ending in 1989. In the experiment children were randomly assigned within schools into three types of classes: small classes with 13–17 students, regular-sized classes with 22–25 students, and regular-sized classes with a full-time teacher aide to assist the teacher. The objective was to determine the effect of small classes on student learning, as measured by student scores on achievement tests. We will analyze the data in Chapter 7, and show that small classes significantly increase performance. This finding will influence public policy towards education for years to come.

1.4.2   NONEXPERIMENTAL DATA

An example of nonexperimental data is survey data. The Public Policy Research Lab at Louisiana State University (www.survey.lsu.edu/) conducts telephone and mail surveys for clients. In a telephone survey, numbers are selected randomly and called. Responses to questions are recorded and analyzed. In such an environment, data on all variables are collected simultaneously, and the values are neither fixed nor repeatable. These are nonexperimental data.

Such surveys are carried out on a massive scale by national governments. For example, the Current Population Survey (CPS)[2] is a monthly survey of about 50,000 households conducted by the U.S. Bureau of the Census. The survey has been conducted for more than 50 years. The CPS web site says "CPS data are used by government policymakers and legislators as important indicators of our nation's economic situation and for planning and evaluating many government programs. They are also used by the press, students, academics, and the general public." In Section 1.8 we describe some similar data sources.

1.5 Economic Data Types

Economic data comes in a variety of "flavors." In this section we describe and give an example of each. In each example, be aware of the different data characteristics, such as the following:

  1. Data may be collected at various levels of aggregation:
     - *micro*—data collected on individual economic decision-making units such as individuals, households, and firms.

---

[1] See www.heros-inc.org/star.htm for program description, public use data, and extensive literature.
[2] www.census.gov/cps/

- *macro*—data resulting from a pooling or aggregating over individuals, households, or firms at the local, state, or national levels.

2. Data may also represent a flow or a stock:

   - *flow*—outcome measures over a period of time, such as the consumption of gasoline during the last quarter of 2010.
   - *stock*—outcome measured at a particular point in time, such as the quantity of crude oil held by Exxon in its U.S. storage tanks on November 1, 2010, or the asset value of the Wells Fargo Bank on July 1, 2009.

3. Data may be quantitative or qualitative:

   - *quantitative*—outcomes such as prices or income that may be expressed as numbers or some transformation of them, such as real prices or per capita income.
   - *qualitative*—outcomes that are of an "either-or" situation. For example, a consumer either did or did not make a purchase of a particular good, or a person either is or is not married.

1.5.1   TIME-SERIES DATA

A **time-series** is data collected over discrete intervals of time. Examples include the annual price of wheat in the United States and the daily price of General Electric stock shares. Macroeconomic data are usually reported in monthly, quarterly, or annual terms. Financial data, such as stock prices, can be recorded daily, or at even higher frequencies. The key feature of time-series data is that the same economic quantity is recorded at a regular time interval.

For example, the annual real gross domestic product (GDP) is depicted in Figure 1.1. A few values are given in Table 1.1. For each year, we have the recorded value. The data are annual, or yearly, and have been "deflated" by the Bureau of Economic Analysis to billions of real 2005 dollars.

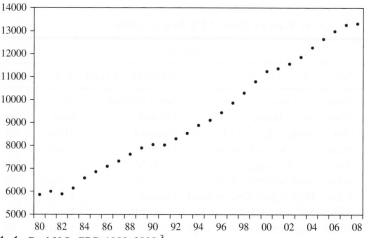

FIGURE *1.1*   Real U.S. GDP, 1980–2008.[3]

---

[3] Source: www.bea.gov/national/index.htm#personal.

Table 1.1 **Annual GDP (Billions of Real 2005 Dollars)**

Year	GDP
2001	11347.2
2002	11553.0
2003	11840.7
2004	12263.8
2005	12638.4
2006	12976.2
2007	13254.1
2008	13312.2

1.5.2 CROSS-SECTION DATA

A cross-section of data is collected across sample units in a particular time period. Examples are income by counties in California during 2009 or high school graduation rates by state in 2008. The "sample units" are individual entities and may be firms, persons, households, states, or countries. For example, the Current Population Survey reports results of personal interviews on a monthly basis, covering such items as employment, unemployment, earnings, educational attainment, and income. In Table 1.2 we report a few observations from the August, 2009 survey on the variables *RACE, EDUCATION, MARITIAL STATUS, SEX, HOURS* (usual number of hours worked), and *WAGE* (hourly wage rate).[4] There are many detailed questions asked of the respondents.

1.5.3 PANEL OR LONGITUDINAL DATA

A "panel" of data, also known as "longitudinal" data, has observations on individual micro-units who are followed over time. For example, the Panel Study of Income Dynamics

Table 1.2 **Cross Section Data: CPS August 2009**

			Variables			
Individual	*RACE*	*EDUCATION*	*MARITAL_STATUS*	*SEX*	*HOURS*	*WAGE*
1	White	10th Grade	Never Married	Male	2	8.00
2	White	Assoc Degree	Married	Male	40	10.81
3	Other	Some College No Degree	Divorced	Male	38	10.23
4	White	High School Grad or GED	Married	Female	32	11.50
5	White	Some College No Degree	Never Married	Male	50	12.50
6	White	High School Grad or GED	Divorced	Female	20	7.00
7	White	High School Grad or GED	Married	Female	10	8.00
8	White	5th or 6th Grade	Never Married	Female	15	9.30
9	White	High School Grad or GED	Married	Female	40	20.00

---

[4] In the actual raw data the outcomes for each individual are given in numerical codes, which then have the identifiers similar to those that we show.

(PSID)[5] describes itself as "a nationally representative longitudinal study of nearly 9000 U.S. families. Following the same families and individuals since 1969, the PSID collects data on economic, health, and social behavior." Other national panels exist and many are described at "Resources for Economists," at www.rfe.org.

To illustrate, data from two rice farms[6] are given in Table 1.3. The data are annual observations on rice farms (or firms) over the period 1990–1997.

The key aspect of panel data is that we observe each micro-unit, here a farm, for a number of time periods. Here we have amount of rice produced, area planted, labor input and fertilizer use. If we have the same number of time period observations for each micro-unit, which is the case here, we have a **balanced panel**. Usually the number of time series observations is small relative to the number of micro-units, but not always. The Penn World Table[7] provides purchasing power parity and national income accounts converted to international prices for 189 countries for some or all of the years 1950–2007.

1.6 **The Research Process**

Econometrics is ultimately a research tool. Students of econometrics plan to do research or they plan to read and evaluate the research of others, or both. This section provides a frame of reference and guide for future work. In particular, we show you the role of econometrics in research.

Research is a process, and like many such activities, it flows according to an orderly pattern. Research is an adventure, and can be *fun!* Searching for an answer to your question,

Table 1.3 **Panel Data from Two Rice Farms**

FIRM	YEAR	PROD	AREA	LABOR	FERT
1	1990	7.87	2.50	160	207.5
1	1991	7.18	2.50	138	295.5
1	1992	8.92	2.50	140	362.5
1	1993	7.31	2.50	127	338.0
1	1994	7.54	2.50	145	337.5
1	1995	4.51	2.50	123	207.2
1	1996	4.37	2.25	123	345.0
1	1997	7.27	2.15	87	222.8
2	1990	10.35	3.80	184	303.5
2	1991	10.21	3.80	151	206.0
2	1992	13.29	3.80	185	374.5
2	1993	18.58	3.80	262	421.0
2	1994	17.07	3.80	174	595.7
2	1995	16.61	4.25	244	234.8
2	1996	12.28	4.25	159	479.0
2	1997	14.20	3.75	133	170.0

---

[5] http://psidonline.isr.umich.edu/

[6] These data were used by O'Donnell, C.J. and W.E. Griffiths (2006), Estimating State-Contingent Production Frontiers, *American Journal of Agricultural Economics*, 88(1), 249–266.

[7] http://pwt.econ.upenn.edu/

seeking new knowledge, is very addictive—for the more you seek, the more new questions you will find.

A research project is an opportunity to investigate a topic that is important to you. Choosing a good research topic is essential if you are to complete a project successfully. A starting point is the question, "What are my interests?" Interest in a particular topic will add pleasure to the research effort. Also, if you begin working on a topic, other questions will usually occur to you. These new questions may put another light on the original topic, or may represent new paths to follow that are even more interesting to you. The idea may come after lengthy study of all that has been written on a particular topic. You will find that "inspiration is 99% perspiration." That means that after you dig at a topic long enough, a new and interesting question will occur to you. Alternatively, you may be led by your natural curiosity to an interesting question. Professor Hal Varian[8] suggests that you look for ideas outside academic journals—in newspapers, magazines, etc. He relates a story about a research project that developed from his shopping for a new TV set.

By the time you have completed several semesters of economics classes, you will find yourself enjoying some areas more than others. For each of us, specialized areas such as health economics, economic development, industrial organization, public finance, resource economics, monetary economics, environmental economics, and international trade hold a different appeal. If you find an area or topic in which you are interested, consult the *Journal of Economic Literature* (*JEL*) for a list of related journal articles. The *JEL* has a classification scheme that makes isolating particular areas of study an easy task. Alternatively, type a few descriptive words into your favorite search engine and see what pops up.

Once you have focused on a particular idea, begin the research process, which generally follows steps like these:

1. Economic theory gives us a way of thinking about the problem. Which economic variables are involved, and what is the possible direction of the relationship(s)? Every research project, given the initial question, begins by building an economic model and listing the questions (hypotheses) of interest. More questions will occur during the research project, but it is good to list those that motivate you at the project's beginning.

2. The working economic model leads to an econometric model. We must choose a functional form and make some assumptions about the nature of the error term.

3. Sample data are obtained and a desirable method of statistical analysis chosen, based on initial assumptions and an understanding of how the data were collected.

4. Estimates of the unknown parameters are obtained with the help of a statistical software package, predictions are made, and hypothesis tests are performed.

5. Model diagnostics are performed to check the validity of assumptions. For example, were all of the right-hand-side explanatory variables relevant? Was an adequate functional form used?

6. The economic consequences and the implications of the empirical results are analyzed and evaluated. What economic resource allocation and distribution results are implied, and what are their policy-choice implications? What remaining questions might be answered with further study or with new and better data?

---

[8] "How to Build an Economic Model in Your Spare Time," *The American Economist*, 41(2), Fall 1997, pp. 3–10.

These steps provide some direction for what must be done. However, research always includes some surprises that may send you back to an earlier point in your research plan or that may even cause you to revise it completely. Research requires a sense of urgency, which keeps the project moving forward, the patience not to rush beyond careful analysis, and the willingness to explore new ideas.

1.7 Writing An Empirical Research Paper

Research provides you the reward of new knowledge, but it is incomplete until a research paper or report is written. The process of writing forces the distillation of ideas. In no other way will your depth of understanding be so clearly revealed. When you have difficulty explaining a concept or thought, it may mean that your understanding is incomplete. Thus, writing is an integral part of research. We provide this section as a building block for future writing assignments. Consult it as needed. You will find other tips on writing economics papers on the book website, http://principlesofeconometrics.com.

1.7.1 WRITING A RESEARCH PROPOSAL

After you have selected a specific topic, it is a good idea to write up a brief project summary, or proposal. Writing it will help to focus your thoughts about what you really want to do. Show it to your colleagues or instructor for preliminary comments. The abstract should be short, usually no longer than 500 words, and should include

1. A concise statement of the problem
2. Comments on the information that is available, with one or two key references
3. A description of the research design that includes
   (a) the economic model
   (b) the econometric estimation and inference methods
   (c) data sources
   (d) estimation, hypothesis testing and prediction procedures, including econometric software version
4. The potential contribution of the research

1.7.2 A FORMAT FOR WRITING A RESEARCH REPORT

Economic research reports have a standard format in which the various steps of the research project are discussed and the results interpreted. The following outline is typical.

1. *Statement of the Problem* The place to start your report is with a summary of the questions you wish to investigate as well as why they are important and who should be interested in the results. This introductory section should be nontechnical and should motivate the reader to continue reading the paper. It is also useful to map out the contents of the following sections of the report. This is the first section to work on, and also the last. In today's busy world, the reader's attention must be garnered very quickly. A clear, concise, well-written introduction is a must, and is arguably the most important part of the paper.

2. *Review of the Literature* Briefly summarize the relevant literature in the research area you have chosen, and clarify how your work extends our knowledge. By all means, cite the works of others who have motivated your research, but keep it brief. You do not have to survey everything that has been written on the topic.

3. *The Economic Model* Specify the economic model that you used, and define the economic variables. State the model's assumptions, and identify hypotheses that you wish to test. Economic models can get complicated. Your task is to explain the model clearly, but as briefly and simply as possible. Don't use unnecessary technical jargon. Use simple terms instead of complicated ones when possible. Your objective is to display the quality of your thinking, not the extent of your vocabulary.

4. *The Econometric Model* Discuss the econometric model that corresponds to the economic model. Make sure you include a discussion of the variables in the model, the functional form, the error assumptions, and any other assumptions that you make. Use notation that is as simple as possible, and do not clutter the body of the paper with long proofs or derivations; these can go into a technical appendix.

5. *The Data* Describe the data you used, as well as the source of the data and any reservations you have about their appropriateness.

6. *The Estimation and Inference Procedures* Describe the estimation methods you used and why they were chosen. Explain hypothesis testing procedures and their usage. Indicate the software used and the version, such as Stata 11.1 or EViews 7.1.

7. *The Empirical Results and Conclusions* Report the parameter estimates, their interpretation, and the values of test statistics. Comment on their statistical significance, their relation to previous estimates, and their economic implications.

8. *Possible Extensions and Limitations of the Study* Your research will raise questions about the economic model, data, and estimation techniques. What future research is suggested by your findings, and how might you go about performing it?

9. *Acknowledgments* It is appropriate to recognize those who have commented on and contributed to your research. This may include your instructor, a librarian who helped you find data, or a fellow student who read and commented on your paper.

10. *References* An alphabetical list of the literature you cite in your study, as well as references to the data sources you used.

Once you've written the first draft, use your computer's software spelling checker to check for errors. Have a friend read the paper, make suggestions for clarifying the prose, and check your logic and conclusions. Before you submit the paper, you should eliminate as many errors as possible. Your work should look good. Use a word processor, and be consistent with font sizes, section headings, style of footnotes, references, and so on. Often software developers provide templates for term papers and theses. A little searching for a good paper layout before beginning is a good idea. Typos, missing references, and incorrect formulas can spell doom for an otherwise excellent paper. Some do's and don'ts are summarized nicely, and with good humor, by Deidre N. McClosky in *Economical Writing*, 2nd edition (Prospect Heights, IL: Waveland Press, Inc., 1999).

While it is not a pleasant topic to discuss, you should be aware of the rules of **plagiarism**. You must not use someone else's words as if they were your own. If you are unclear about what you can and cannot use, check with the style manuals listed in the next paragraph, or consult your instructor.

The paper should have clearly defined sections and subsections. The equations, tables and figures should be numbered. References and footnotes should be formatted in an acceptable fashion. A style guide is a good investment. Two classics are:

- *The Chicago Manual of Style*, 15th edition, is available online and in other formats.
- *A Manual for Writers of Research Papers, Theses, and Dissertations: Chicago Style for Students and Researchers*, 7th edition, by Kate L. Turabian; revised by Wayne C. Booth, Gregory G. Colomb, and Joseph M Williams (2007, University of Chicago Press).

1.8 Sources of Economic Data

Economic data are much easier to obtain since the development of the World Wide Web. In this section we direct you to some places on the Internet where economic data are accessible. During your study of econometrics, browse some of the sources listed to gain some familiarity with data availability.

1.8.1 Links to Economic Data on the Internet

There are a number of fantastic sites on the World Wide Web for obtaining economic data.

Resources for Economists (RFE)
www.rfe.org is a primary gateway to resources on the Internet for economists. This excellent site is the work of Bill Goffe. Here you will find links to sites for economic data and to sites of general interest to economists. The **Data** link has these broad data categories:

- *U.S. Macro and Regional Data* Here you will find links to various data sources such as the Bureau of Economic Analysis, Bureau of Labor Statistics, *Economic Reports of the President*, and the Federal Reserve Banks.
- *Other U.S. Data* Here you will find links to the U.S. Census Bureau, as well as links to many panel and survey data sources. The gateway to U.S. government agencies is FedStats [www.fedstats.gov/]. Once there, click on *Agencies* to see a complete list of U.S. government agencies and links to their homepages.
- *World and Non-U.S. Data* Here there are links to world data, such as at the CIA Factbook and the Penn World Tables, as well as international organizations such as the Asian Development Bank, the International Monetary Fund, the World Bank, and so on. There are also links to sites with data on specific countries and sectors of the world.
- *Finance and Financial Markets* Here there are links to sources of U.S. and world financial data on variables such as exchange rates, interest rates, and share prices.
- *Journal Data and Program Archives* Some economic journals post data used in articles. Links to these journals are provided here. (Many of the articles in these journals will be beyond the scope of undergraduate economics majors.)

National Bureau of Economic Research (NBER)
www.nber.org/data/ provides access to a great amount of data. There are headings for

- *Macro Data*
- *Industry Data*
- *International Trade Data*
- *Individual Data*
- *Hospital Data*
- *Demographic and Vital Statistics*
- *Patent and Scientific Papers Data*
- *Other Data*

EconEdLink

www.econedlink.org/datalinks/ is provided by the Council for Economic Education. It provides links to data and their explanation.

Economagic

Some Web sites make extracting data relatively easy. For example, Economagic [www .economagic.com/] is an excellent and easy-to-use source of macro time series (some 100,000 series available). The data series are easily viewed in a copy and paste format, or graphed.

1.8.2   INTERPRETING ECONOMIC DATA

In many cases it is easier to obtain economic data than it is to understand the meaning of the data. It is essential when using macroeconomic or financial data that you understand the definitions of the variables. Just what is the index of leading economic indicators? What is included in personal consumption expenditures? You may find the answers to some questions like these in your textbooks. Another resource you might find useful is *A Guide to Everyday Economic Statistics*, 6th edition, by Gary E. Clayton and Martin Gerhard Giesbrecht, (Boston: Irwin/McGraw-Hill 2003). This slender volume examines how economic statistics are constructed, and how they can be used.

1.8.3   OBTAINING THE DATA

Finding a data source is not the same as obtaining the data. Although there are a great many easy-to-use websites, "easy-to-use" is a relative term. The data will come packaged in a variety of formats. It is also true that there are many, many variables at each of these websites. A primary challenge is identifying the specific variables that you want, and what exactly they measure. The following examples are illustrative.

The Federal Reserve Bank of St. Louis[9] has a system called **FRED** (Federal Reserve Economic Data). Under "Categories" there are links to Banking, Business/Fiscal, and so on. Select Gross Domestic Product (GDP) and its Components.[10] Select "Download Data." There are three ZIP (compressed) files available, one containing the data in Excel format, another as space-delimited text, and a third comma-separated text. If the data are downloaded in either of the text formats, they must be read into your statistical software before

---

[9] http://research.stlouisfed.org/fred2/
[10] http://research.stlouisfed.org/fred2/categories/18

analysis. For these steps you need specific knowledge for the software available to you. Accompanying *Principles of Econometrics, 4e*, are computer manuals for Excel, EViews, Stata, and SAS to aid this process. See the publisher website www.wiley.com/go/global/hill, or the book website at http://principlesofeconometrics.com for a description of these aids.

The Current Population Survey (www.census.gov/cps/) has a tool called **Data Ferrett**. This tool will help you find and download data series that are of particular interest to you. There are tutorials that guide you through the process. Variable descriptions, as well as the specific survey questions, are provided to aid in your selection. It is somewhat like an Internet shopping site. Desired series are "ticked" and added to a "Shopping Basket." Once you have filled your basket, you download the data to use with specific software. Other Web-based data sources operate in this same manner. One example is the Panel Study of Income Dynamics (PSID).[11]

The Penn World Tables[12] offer data downloads in Excel spreadsheets, as comma-separated text files, and in SAS (a particular software) format.

You can expect to find massive amounts of readily available data at the various sites we have mentioned, but there is a learning curve. You should not expect to find, download and process the data without considerable work effort. Being skilled with Excel and statistical software is a must if you plan to regularly use these data sources.

---

[11] http://psidonline.isr.umich.edu/
[12] http://pwt.econ.upenn.edu/

Probability Primer

Learning Objectives

> **REMARK:** *Learning Objectives* and *Keywords* sections will appear at the beginning of each chapter. We urge you to think about, and possibly write out answers to the questions, and make sure you recognize and can define the keywords. If you are unsure about the questions or answers consult your instructor. When examples are requested in *Learning Objectives* sections, you should think of examples *not* in the book.

Based on the material in this primer you should be able to

1. Explain the difference between a random variable and its values, and give an example.

2. Explain the difference between discrete and continuous random variables, and give examples of each.

3. State the characteristics of a probability density function (*pdf*) for a discrete random variable, and give an example.

4. Compute probabilities of events, given a discrete probability function.

5. Explain the meaning of the following statement: "The probability that the discrete random variable takes the value 2 is 0.3."

6. Explain how the *pdf* of a continuous random variable is different from the *pdf* of a discrete random variable.

7. Show, geometrically, how to compute probabilities given a *pdf* for a continuous random variable.

8. Explain, intuitively, the concept of the mean, or expected value, of a random variable.

9. Use the definition of expected value for a discrete random variable to compute expectations, given a *pdf* $f(x)$ and a function $g(X)$ of X.

10. Define the variance of a discrete random variable, and explain in what sense the values of a random variable are more spread out if the variance is larger.

11. Use a joint *pdf* (table) for two discrete random variables to compute probabilities of joint events and to find the (marginal) *pdf* of each individual random variable.

12. Find the conditional *pdf* for one discrete random variable given the value of another and their joint *pdf*.

13. Work with single and double summation notation.

14. Give an intuitive explanation of statistical independence of two random variables, and state the conditions that must hold to prove statistical independence. Give

examples of two independent random variables and two dependent random variables.

15. Define the covariance and correlation between two random variables, and compute these values given a joint probability function of two discrete random variables.

16. Find the mean and variance of a sum of random variables.

17. Use Table 1, Cumulative Probabilities for the Standard Normal Distribution, and your computer software to compute probabilities involving normal random variables.

Keywords

cdf	expected value	probability density
conditional expectation	experiment	function
conditional *pdf*	indicator variable	random variable
conditional probability	joint probability density	standard deviation
continuous random variable	function	standard normal
correlation	marginal distribution	distribution
covariance	mean	statistical independence
cumulative distribution	normal distribution	summation operations
function	*pdf*	variance
discrete random variable	probability	

We assume that you have had a basic probability and statistics course. In this primer we review some essential probability concepts. Section P.1 defines discrete and continuous random variables. Probability distributions are discussed in Section P.2. Section P.3 introduces joint probability distributions, defines conditional probability and statistical independence. In Section P.4 we digress and discuss operations with summations. In Section P.5 we review the properties of probability distributions, paying particular attention to expected values and variances. Section P.6 summarizes important facts about the normal probability distribution. In Appendix B, "Probability Concepts," are enhancements and additions to this material.

P.1 Random Variables

Benjamin Franklin is credited with the saying "The only things certain in life are death and taxes." While not the original intent, this bit of wisdom points out that almost everything we encounter in life is uncertain. We do not know how many games our football team will win next season. You do not know what score you will make on the next exam. We don't know what the stock market index will be tomorrow. These events, or outcomes, are uncertain, or random. Probability gives us a way to talk about possible outcomes.

A **random variable** is a variable whose value is unknown until it is observed; in other words it is a variable that is not perfectly predictable. Each random variable has a set of possible values it can take. If W is the number of games our football team wins next year, then W can take the values $0, 1, 2, \ldots, 13$, if there are a maximum of 13 games. This is a **discrete random variable** since it can take only a limited, or **countable**, number of values. Other examples of discrete random variables are the number of computers owned by a randomly selected household, and the number of times you will visit your physician next year. A special case occurs when a random variable can only be one of two possible values—for example, in a phone survey, if you are asked if you are a college graduate or not, your answer can only be "yes" or "no." Outcomes like this can be characterized by an **indicator variable** taking the values one if yes, or zero if no. Indicator variables are discrete and are used to represent qualitative characteristics such as gender (male or female), or race (white or nonwhite).

The U.S. GDP is yet another example of a random variable, because its value is unknown until it is observed. In the fourth quarter of 2010 it is calculated to be $14,453.8 billion dollars. What the value will be in the second quarter of 2015 is unknown, and it cannot be predicted perfectly. GDP is measured in dollars and it *can* be counted in whole dollars, but the value is so large that counting individual dollars serves no purpose. For practical purposes GDP can take any value in the interval zero to infinity, and it is treated as a **continuous random variable**. Other common macroeconomic variables, like interest rates, investment, and consumption are also treated as continuous random variables. In finance, stock market indices, like the Dow Jones Industrial Index, are also treated as continuous. The key attribute of these variables that makes them continuous is that they can take any value in an interval.

P.2 Probability Distributions

Probability is usually defined in terms of **experiments**. Let us illustrate this in the context of a simple experiment. Consider the values in Table P.1 to be a population of interest.

If we were to select one cell from the table at random (imagine cutting the table into 10 equally sized pieces of paper, stirring them up, and drawing one of the slips without looking), that would constitute a **random experiment**. Based on this random experiment we can define several random variables. For example, let the random variable X be the numerical value showing on a slip that we draw. (We use uppercase letters like X to represent random variables in this primer). The term **random variable** is a bit odd, as it is actually a rule for assigning numerical values to experimental outcomes. In the context of Table P.1 the rule says, "Perform the experiment (stir the slips, and draw one) and for the slip that you obtain assign X to be the number showing." The values that X can take are denoted by corresponding lower case letters, x, and in this case the values of X are $x = 1, 2, 3,$ or 4.

For the experiment using the population in Table P.1, we can create a number of random variables. Let Y be a discrete random variable designating the color of the slip, with $Y = 1$ denoting a shaded slip and $Y = 0$ denoting a slip with no shading (white). The numerical values that Y can take are $y = 0, 1$.

Consider X, the numerical value on the slip. If the slips are equally likely to be chosen after shuffling, then in a large number of experiments (i.e., shuffling and drawing one of the ten slips), 10% of the time we would observe $X = 1$, 20% of the time $X = 2$, 30% of the time $X = 3$, and 40% of the time $X = 4$. These are probabilities that the specific values will occur. We would say, for example, $P(X = 3) = 0.3$. This interpretation is tied to the **relative frequency** of a particular outcome's occurring in a **large** number of random experiments.

We summarize the probabilities of possible outcomes using a **probability density function** (*pdf*). The *pdf* for a discrete random variable indicates the probability of each possible value occurring. For a discrete random variable X the value of the probability density function $f(x)$ is the probability that the random variable X takes the value x,

Table P. 1   **A Population**

1	2	3	4	4
2	3	3	4	4

$f(x) = P(X = x)$. Because $f(x)$ is a probability, it must be true that $0 \leq f(x) \leq 1$ and, if X takes n possible values $x_1, \ldots, x_n$, then the sum of their probabilities must be one

$$f(x_1) + f(x_2) + \cdots + f(x_n) = 1 \qquad (P.1)$$

For discrete random variables the *pdf* might be presented as a table, such as in Table P.2.

As shown in Figure P.1, the probability density function may also be represented as a bar graph, with the height of the bar representing the probability with which the corresponding value occurs.

The **cumulative distribution function** (*cdf*) is an alternative way to represent probabilities. The *cdf* of the random variable X, denoted $F(x)$, gives the probability that X is less than or equal to a specific value x. That is,

$$F(x) = P(X \leq x) \qquad (P.2)$$

Using the probabilities in Table P.2, we find that $F(1) = P(X \leq 1) = 0.1$, $F(2) = P(X \leq 2) = 0.3$, $F(3) = P(X \leq 3) = 0.6$, and $F(4) = P(X \leq 4) = 1$. For example, using the *pdf* $f(x)$ we compute the probability that X is less than or equal to 2 as

$$F(2) = P(X \leq 2) = P(X = 1) + P(X = 2) = 0.1 + 0.2 = 0.3$$

Table P.2 **Probability Density Function of X**

X	$f(x)$
1	0.1
2	0.2
3	0.3
4	0.4

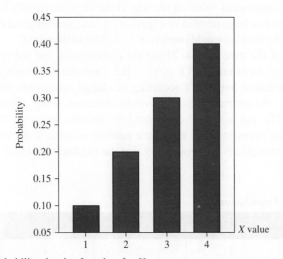

FIGURE P.1 Probability density function for X.

Since the sum of the probabilities $P(X = 1) + P(X = 2) + P(X = 3) + P(X = 4) = 1$, we can compute the probability that X is greater than 2 as

$$P(X > 2) = 1 - P(X \leq 2) = 1 - F(2) = 1 - 0.3 = 0.7$$

An important difference between the *pdf* and *cdf* for X is revealed by the question, "Using the probability distribution in Table P.2, what is the probability that $X = 2.5$?" This probability is zero because X cannot take this value. The question "What is the probability that X is less than or equal to 2.5?" does have an answer.

$$F(2.5) = P(X \leq 2.5) = P(X = 1) + P(X = 2) = 0.1 + 0.2 = 0.3$$

The cumulative probability can be calculated for any x between $-\infty$ and $+\infty$.

Continuous random variables can take any value in an interval and have an uncountable number of values. Consequently the probability of any specific value is zero. For continuous random variables we talk about outcomes being in a certain range. Figure P.2 illustrates the *pdf* $f(x)$ of a continuous random variable X that takes values of x from 0 to infinity. The shape is representative of the distribution for an economic variable like an individual's income or wages. Areas under the curve represent probabilities that X falls in an interval. The cumulative distribution function $F(x)$ is defined as in (P.2). For this distribution,

$$P(100 \leq X \leq 200) = F(200) - F(100) = 0.90291 - 0.72747 = 0.17544 \qquad \text{(P.3)}$$

How are these areas obtained? The integral from calculus gives the area under a curve. We will not compute many integrals in this book.[1] Instead we will use the computer and compute *cdf* values and probabilities using software commands.

P.3 Joint, Marginal and Conditional Probabilities

Working with more than one random variable requires a **joint probability density function**. For the population in Table P.1 we defined two random variables, X the numeric value of a

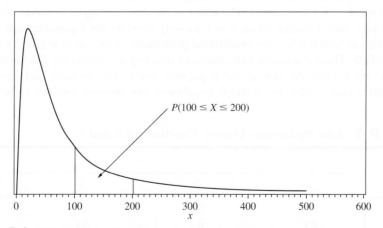

FIGURE **P.2** Probability density function for a continuous random variable.

---

[1] See Appendix A.4 for a brief explanation of integrals, and illustrations using integrals to compute probabilities in Appendix B.2.1.

randomly drawn slip, and the indicator variable Y that equals 1 if the selected slip is shaded, and 0 if it is not shaded.

Using the joint probability density function for X and Y we can say "The probability of selecting a shaded 2 is 0.10." This is a joint probability because we are talking about the probability of two events occurring simultaneously; the selection takes the value $X = 2$ **and** the slip is shaded so that $Y = 1$. We can write this as

$$P(X = 2 \text{ and } Y = 1) = P(X = 2, Y = 1) = f(x = 2, y = 1) = 0.1$$

The entries in Table P.3 are probabilities $f(x, y) = P(X = x, Y = y)$ of joint outcomes. Like the *pdf* of a single random variable, the sum of the joint probabilities is 1.

P.3.1   MARGINAL DISTRIBUTIONS

Given a joint probability density function, we can obtain the probability distributions of individual random variables, which are also known as **marginal distributions**. In Table P.3, we see that a shaded slip can be obtained with the values 1, 2, 3 and 4. The probability that we select a shaded slip is the sum of the probabilities that we obtain a shaded 1, a shaded 2, a shaded 3 and a shaded 4. The probability that $Y = 1$ is

$$P(Y = 1) = f_Y(1) = 0.1 + 0.1 + 0.1 + 0.1 = 0.4$$

This is the sum of the probabilities across the second row of the table. Similarly the probability of drawing a white slip is the sum of the probabilities across the first row of the table, and $P(Y = 0) = f_Y(0) = 0 + 0.1 + 0.2 + 0.3 = 0.6$. The probabilities $P(X = x)$ are computed similarly by summing down, across the values of Y. The joint and marginal distributions are often reported as in Table P.4.[2]

P.3.2   CONDITIONAL PROBABILITY

What is the probability that a randomly chosen slip will take the value 2 **given that** it is shaded? This question is about the **conditional probability** of the outcome $X = 2$ *given* that the outcome $Y = 1$ has occurred. The effect of the conditioning is to reduce the set of possible outcomes. Conditional on $Y = 1$ we only consider the 4 possible slips that are shaded. One of them is a 2, so the **conditional probability** of the outcome $X = 2$ *given* that $Y = 1$ is 0.25. There is a one in four chance of selecting a 2 given only the shaded slips. Conditioning reduces the size of the population under consideration, and conditional probabilities characterize the reduced population. For discrete random variables the

Ta b l e P. 3   **Joint Probability Density Function for X and Y**

y	x			
	1	2	3	4
0	0	0.1	0.2	0.3
1	0.1	0.1	0.1	0.1

---

[2] Similar calculations for continuous random variables use integration. See Appendix B.2.3 for an illustration.

Table P. 4 **Joint and Marginal Probabilities**

y/x	1	2	3	4	$f(y)$
0	0	0.1	0.2	0.3	0.6
1	0.1	0.1	0.1	0.1	0.4
$f(x)$	0.1	0.2	0.3	0.4	

probability that the random variable X takes the value x *given* that $Y = y$ is written $P(X = x|Y = y)$. This conditional probability is given by the **conditional** *pdf* $f(x|y)$

$$f(x|y) = P(X = x|Y = y) = \frac{P(X = x, Y = y)}{P(Y = y)} = \frac{f(x, y)}{f_Y(y)} \tag{P.4}$$

where $f_Y(y)$ is the marginal *pdf* of Y.

Using the marginal probability $P(Y = 1) = 0.4$, the conditional *pdf* of X given $Y = 1$ is obtained by using (P.4) for each value of X. For example,

$$\begin{aligned}
f(x = 2|y = 1) &= P(X = 2|Y = 1) \\
&= \frac{P(X = 2, Y = 1)}{P(Y = 1)} = \frac{f(x = 2, y = 1)}{f_Y(1)} \\
&= \frac{0.1}{0.4} = 0.25
\end{aligned}$$

A key point to remember is that by conditioning we are considering only the subset of a population for which the condition holds. Probability calculations are then based on the "new" population. We can repeat this process for each value of X to obtain the complete conditional probability density function given in Table P.5.

P.3.3   STATISTICAL INDEPENDENCE

When selecting a shaded slip from Table P.1, the probability of selecting each possible outcome, $x = 1, 2, 3$ and 4 is 0.25. In the population of shaded slips the numeric values are **equally likely**. The probability of randomly selecting $X = 2$ from the entire population, from the marginal *pdf*, is $P(X = 2) = f_X(2) = 0.2$. This is different from the conditional probability. Knowing that the slip is shaded tells us something about the probability of obtaining $X = 2$. Such random variables are **dependent** in a statistical sense. Two random variables are **statistically independent** if the conditional probability that $X = x$ given that $Y = y$, is the same as the unconditional probability that $X = x$. This means, if X and Y are independent random variables, then

Table P. 5 **Conditional Probability of X given $Y = 1$**

x	1	2	3	4
$f(x|y = 1)$	0.25	0.25	0.25	0.25

$$P(X = x | Y = y) = P(X = x) \tag{P.5}$$

Equivalently, if X and Y are independent, then the conditional *pdf* of X given $Y = y$ is the same as the unconditional, or marginal, *pdf* of X alone,

$$f(x|y) = \frac{f(x, y)}{f_Y(y)} = f_X(x) \tag{P.6}$$

Solving (P.6) for the joint *pdf*, we can also say that X and Y are statistically independent if their joint *pdf* factors into the product of their marginal *pdf*'s

$$P(X = x, Y = y) = f(x, y) = f_X(x)f_Y(y) = P(X = x) \times P(Y = y) \tag{P.7}$$

If (P.5) or (P.7) is true for each and every pair of values x and y, then X and Y are statistically independent. This result extends to more than two random variables. The rule allows us to check the independence of random variables X and Y in Table P.4. If (P.7) is violated for any pair of values, then X and Y are not statistically independent. Consider the pair of values $X = 1$ and $Y = 1$.

$$P(X = 1, Y = 1) = f(1, 1) = 0.1 \neq f_X(1)f_Y(1) = P(X = 1) \times P(Y = 1) = 0.1 \times 0.4$$
$$= 0.04$$

The joint probability is 0.1 and the product of the individual probabilities is 0.04. Since these are not equal, we can conclude that X and Y are not statistically independent.

P.4 A Digression: Summation Notation

Throughout this book we will use a **summation sign**, denoted by the Greek symbol Σ, to shorten algebraic expressions. Suppose the random variable X takes the values $x_1, x_2, \ldots,$ x_{15}. The sum of these values is $x_1 + x_2 + \cdots + x_{15}$. Rather than write this sum out each time we will represent it as $\sum_{i=1}^{15} x_i$, so that $\sum_{i=1}^{15} x_i = x_1 + x_2 + \cdots + x_{15}$. If we sum n terms, a general number, then the summation will be $\sum_{i=1}^{n} x_i = x_1 + x_2 + \cdots + x_n$. In this notation

- The symbol Σ is the capital Greek letter sigma, and means "the sum of."
- The letter i is called the **index of summation**. This letter is arbitrary and may also appear as t, j, or k.
- The expression $\sum_{i=1}^{n} x_i$ is read "the sum of the terms x_i, from i equal one to n."
- The numbers 1 and n are the **lower limit** and **upper limit** of summation.

The following rules apply to the summation operation.

Sum 1. The sum of n values $x_1, \ldots, x_n$ is

$$\sum_{i=1}^{n} x_i = x_1 + x_2 + \cdots + x_n$$

Sum 2. If a is a constant then

$$\sum_{i=1}^{n} a x_i = a \sum_{i=1}^{n} x_i$$

Sum 3. If a is a constant then

$$\sum_{i=1}^{n} a = a + a + \cdots + a = na$$

Sum 4. If X and Y are two variables, then

$$\sum_{i=1}^{n} (x_i + y_i) = \sum_{i=1}^{n} x_i + \sum_{i=1}^{n} y_i$$

Sum 5. If X and Y are two variables, then

$$\sum_{i=1}^{n} (a x_i + b y_i) = a \sum_{i=1}^{n} x_i + b \sum_{i=1}^{n} y_i$$

Sum 6. The arithmetic mean (average) of n values of X is

$$\bar{x} = \frac{\sum_{i=1}^{n} x_i}{n} = \frac{x_1 + x_2 + \cdots + x_n}{n}$$

Sum 7. A property of the average is that

$$\sum_{i=1}^{n} (x_i - \bar{x}) = \sum_{i=1}^{n} x_i - \sum_{i=1}^{n} \bar{x} = \sum_{i=1}^{n} x_i - n\bar{x} = \sum_{i=1}^{n} x_i - \sum_{i=1}^{n} x_i = 0$$

Sum 8. We often use an abbreviated form of the summation notation. For example, if $f(x)$ is a function of the values of X,

$$\sum_{i=1}^{n} f(x_i) = f(x_1) + f(x_2) + \cdots + f(x_n)$$
$$= \sum_{i} f(x_i) \quad (\text{``Sum over all values of the index } i\text{''})$$
$$= \sum_{x} f(x) \quad (\text{``Sum over all possible values of } X\text{''})$$

Sum 9. Several summation signs can be used in one expression. Suppose the variable Y takes n values and X takes m values, and let $f(x, y) = x + y$. Then the **double summation** of this function is

$$\sum_{i=1}^{m} \sum_{j=1}^{n} f(x_i, y_j) = \sum_{i=1}^{m} \sum_{j=1}^{n} (x_i + y_j)$$

To evaluate such expressions work from the innermost sum outward. First set $i = 1$ and sum over all values of j, and so on. That is,

$$\sum_{i=1}^{m} \sum_{j=1}^{n} f(x_i, y_j) = \sum_{i=1}^{m} \left[f(x_i, y_1) + f(x_i, y_2) + \cdots + f(x_i, y_n) \right]$$

The *order* of summation does not matter, so

$$\sum_{i=1}^{m} \sum_{j=1}^{n} f(x_i, y_j) = \sum_{j=1}^{n} \sum_{i=1}^{m} f(x_i, y_j)$$

P.5 Properties of Probability Distributions

Figures P.1 and P.2 give us a picture of how frequently values of the random variables will occur. Two key features of a probability distribution are its center (location) and width (dispersion). A key measure of the center is the **mean**, or **expected value**. Measures of dispersion are **variance**, and its square root, the **standard deviation**.

P.5.1   EXPECTED VALUE OF A RANDOM VARIABLE

The **mean** of a random variable is given by its **mathematical expectation**. If X is a discrete random variable taking the values $x_1, \ldots, x_n$, then the mathematical expectation, or **expected value**, of X is

$$E(X) = x_1 P(X = x_1) + x_2 P(X = x_2) + \cdots + x_n P(X = x_n) \tag{P.8}$$

The expected value, or mean, of X is a weighted average of its values, the weights being the probabilities that the values occur. The mean is often symbolized by μ or μ_X. It is the average value of the random variable in an infinite number of repetitions of the underlying experiment. The mean of a random variable is the **population mean**. We use Greek letters for **population parameters** because later on we will use data to estimate these real world unknowns. In particular, keep separate the population mean μ and the arithmetic (or sample) mean $\bar{x}$ that we introduced in Section P.4 as Sum 6. This can be particularly confusing when a conversation includes the term "mean" without the qualifying term "population" or "arithmetic." Pay attention to the usage context.

For the population in Table P.1, the expected value of X is

$$E(X) = 1 \times P(X = 1) + 2 \times P(X = 2) + 3 \times P(X = 3) + 4 \times P(X = 4)$$
$$= (1 \times 0.1) + (2 \times 0.2) + (3 \times 0.3) + (4 \times 0.4) = 3$$

For a discrete random variable the probability that X takes the value x is given by its *pdf* $f(x)$, $P(X = x) = f(x)$. The expected value in (P.8) can be written equivalently as

$$\mu_X = E(X) = x_1 f(x_1) + x_2 f(x_2) + \cdots + x_n f(x_n)$$
$$= \sum_{i=1}^{n} x_i f(x_i) = \sum_{x} x f(x) \tag{P.9}$$

Using (P.9), the expected value of X, the numeric value on a randomly drawn slip from Table P.1 is

$$\mu_X = E(X) = \sum_{x=1}^{4} xf(x) = (1 \times 0.1) + (2 \times 0.2) + (3 \times 0.3) + (4 \times 0.4) = 3$$

What does this mean? Draw one "slip" at random from Table P.1, and observe its numerical value X. This constitutes an experiment. If we repeat this experiment many times, the values $x = 1$, 2, 3, and 4 will appear 10%, 20%, 30%, and 40% of the time, respectively. The arithmetic average of all the numerical values will approach $\mu_X = 3$, as the number of draws becomes large. The key point is that **the expected value of the random variable is the average value that occurs in many repeated trials of an experiment**.

For continuous random variables, the interpretation of the expected value of X is unchanged—it is the average value of X if many values are obtained by repeatedly performing the underlying random experiment.[3]

P.5.2 CONDITIONAL EXPECTATION

Many economic questions are formulated in terms of **conditional expectation**, or the **conditional mean**. One example is, "What is the mean (expected value) wage of a person who has 16 years of education?" In expected value notation, what is $E(WAGE|$ $EDUCATION = 16)$? For a discrete random variable the calculation of conditional expected value uses (P.9) with the conditional probability density function $f(x|y)$ replacing $f(x)$, so that

$$\mu_{X|Y} = E(X|Y = y) = \sum_{x} xf(x|y)$$

Using the population in Table P.1, what is the expected numerical value of X given that $Y = 1$, the slip is shaded? The conditional probabilities $f(x|Y = 1)$ are given in Table P.5. The conditional expectation of X is

$$E(X|Y = 1) = \sum_{x=1}^{4} xf(x|1) = 1 \times f(1|1) + 2 \times f(2|1) + 3 \times f(3|1) + 4 \times f(4|1)$$
$$= 1(0.25) + 2(0.25) + 3(0.25) + 4(0.25) = 2.5$$

The average value of X in many repeated trials of the experiment of drawing from the shaded slips is 2.5. This example makes a good point about expected values in general, namely that the expected value of X does not have to be a value that X can take. The expected value of X is **not** the value that you expect to occur in any single experiment.

P.5.3 RULES FOR EXPECTED VALUES

Functions of random variables are also random. If $g(X)$ is a function of the random variable X, then $g(X)$ is also random. If X is a discrete random variable, then the expected value of $g(X)$ is obtained using calculations similar to those in (P.9)

---

[3] Since there are now an uncountable number of values to sum, mathematically we must replace the "summation over all possible values" in (P.9) by the "integral over all possible values." See Appendix B.2.2 for a brief discussion.

$$E[g(X)] = \sum_x g(x)f(x) \qquad \text{(P.10)}$$

For example, if a is a constant, then $g(X) = aX$ is a function of X, and

$$
\begin{aligned}
E(aX) = E[g(X)] &= \sum_x g(x)f(x) \\
&= \sum_x axf(x) = a\sum_x xf(x) \\
&= aE(X)
\end{aligned}
$$

Similarly, if a and b are constants, then we can show that

$$E(aX + b) = aE(X) + b \qquad \text{(P.11)}$$

If $g_1(X)$ and $g_2(X)$ are functions of X, then

$$E[g_1(X) + g_2(X)] = E[g_1(X)] + E[g_2(X)] \qquad \text{(P.12)}$$

This rule extends to any number of functions. Remember the phrase **"the expected value of a sum is the sum of the expected values."**

P.5.4 VARIANCE OF A RANDOM VARIABLE

The **variance** of a discrete or continuous random variable X is the expected value of

$$g(X) = [X - E(X)]^2$$

The variance of a random variable is important in characterizing the scale of measurement and the spread of the probability distribution. We give it the symbol σ^2, or σ_X^2, read "sigma squared." The variance σ^2 has a Greek symbol because it is a population parameter. Algebraically, letting $E(X) = \mu$, using the rules of expected values and the fact that $E(X) = \mu$ is not random, we have

$$
\begin{aligned}
\text{var}(X) = \sigma_X^2 = E(X - \mu)^2 \\
= E(X^2 - 2\mu X + \mu^2) = E(X^2) - 2\mu E(X) + \mu^2 \qquad \text{(P.13)} \\
= E(X^2) - \mu^2
\end{aligned}
$$

The calculation $\text{var}(X) = E(X^2) - \mu^2$ is usually simpler than $\text{var}(X) = E(X - \mu)^2$, but the solution is the same. For the population in Table P.1, we have shown that $E(X) = \mu = 3$. Using (P.10), the expectation of the random variable $g(X) = X^2$ is

$$
\begin{aligned}
E(X^2) = \sum_{x=1}^{4} g(x)f(x) = \sum_{x=1}^{4} x^2 f(x) \\
= [1^2 \times 0.1] + [2^2 \times 0.2] + [3^2 \times 0.3] + [4^2 \times 0.4] = 10
\end{aligned}
$$

Then, the variance of the random variable X is

$$\text{var}(X) = \sigma_X^2 = E(X^2) - \mu^2 = 10 - 3^2 = 1$$

The square root of the variance is called the **standard deviation**; it is denoted by σ or sometimes as σ_X if more than one random variable is being discussed. It also measures the spread or dispersion of a probability distribution and has the advantage of being in the same units of measure as the random variable.

A useful property of variances is the following. Let a and b be constants, then

$$\text{var}(aX + b) = a^2 \text{var}(X) \tag{P.14}$$

An additive constant like b changes the mean (expected value) of a random variable, but it does not affect its dispersion (variance). A multiplicative constant like a affects the mean, and it affects the variance by the **square** of the constant.

To see this, let $Y = aX + b$. Using (P.11)

$$E(Y) = \mu_Y = aE(X) + b = a\mu_X + b$$

Then

$$\text{var}(aX + b) = \text{var}(Y) = E\left[(Y - \mu_Y)^2\right] = E\left[\left(aX + b - (a\mu_X + b)\right)^2\right]$$

$$= E\left[(aX - a\mu_X)^2\right] = E\left[a^2(X - \mu_X)^2\right]$$

$$= a^2 E\left[(X - \mu_X)^2\right] = a^2 \text{var}(X)$$

The variance of a random variable is the *average* squared difference between the random variable X and its mean value μ_X. The larger the variance of a random variable, the more "spread out" the values of the random variable are. Figure P.3 shows two probability density functions for a continuous random variable, both with mean $\mu = 3$. The distribution with the smaller variance (the solid curve) is less spread out about its mean.

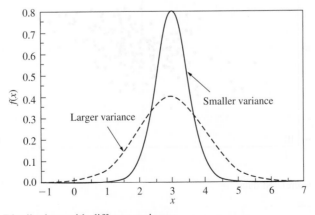

FIGURE *P.3* Distributions with different variances.

P.5.5   EXPECTED VALUES OF SEVERAL RANDOM VARIABLES

Let X and Y be random variables. The rule "the expected value of the sum is the sum of the expected values" applies. Then[4]

$$E(X + Y) = E(X) + E(Y) \tag{P.15}$$

Similarly

$$E(aX + bY + c) = aE(X) + bE(Y) + c \tag{P.16}$$

The product of random variables is not as easy. $E(XY) = E(X)E(Y)$ **if** X and Y are independent. These rules can be extended to more random variables.

P.5.6   COVARIANCE BETWEEN TWO RANDOM VARIABLES

The **covariance** between X and Y is a measure of linear association between them. Think about two continuous variables, such as heights and weights of children. We expect that there is an association between height and weight, with taller than average children tending to weigh more than the average. The product of X minus its mean times Y minus its mean is

$$(X - \mu_X)(Y - \mu_Y) \tag{P.17}$$

In Figure P.4 we plot values (x and y) of X and Y that have been constructed so that $E(X) = E(Y) = 0$.

The x and y values of X and Y fall predominantly in quadrants I and III, so that the arithmetic average of the values $(x - \mu_X)(y - \mu_Y)$ is positive. We define the covariance between two random variables as the expected (population average) value of the product in (P.17),

$$\text{cov}(X, Y) = \sigma_{XY} = E[(X - \mu_X)(Y - \mu_Y)] = E(XY) - \mu_X \mu_Y \tag{P.18}$$

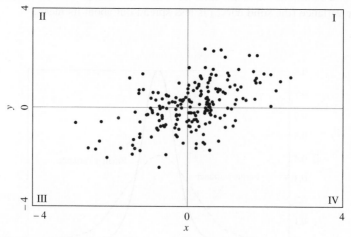

FIGURE P.4   Correlated data.

---

[4] These results are proven in Appendix B.1.4.

The covariance σ_{XY} of the random variables underlying Figure P.4 is positive, which tells us that when the values x are greater than μ_X then the values y also tend to be greater than μ_Y; and when the values x are below μ_X then the values y also tend to be less than μ_Y. If the random variables' values tend primarily to fall in quadrants II and IV, then $(x - \mu_X)(y - \mu_Y)$ will tend to be negative and σ_{XY} will be negative. If the random variables' values are spread evenly across the four quadrants, and show neither positive nor negative association, then the covariance is zero. The sign of σ_{XY} tells us whether the two random variables X and Y are positively associated or negatively associated.

Interpreting the actual value of σ_{XY} is difficult because X and Y may have different units of measurement. Scaling the covariance by the standard deviations of the variables eliminates the units of measurement, and defines the **correlation** between X and Y

$$\rho = \frac{\text{cov}(X, Y)}{\sqrt{\text{var}(X)}\sqrt{\text{var}(Y)}} = \frac{\sigma_{XY}}{\sigma_X \sigma_Y} \tag{P.19}$$

As with the covariance, the correlation ρ between two random variables measures the degree of *linear* association between them. However, unlike the covariance, the correlation must lie between -1 and 1. Thus the correlation between X and Y is 1 or -1 if X is a perfect positive or negative linear function of Y. If there is *no linear* association between X and Y, then $\text{cov}(X, Y) = 0$ and $\rho = 0$. For other values of correlation the magnitude of the absolute value $|\rho|$ indicates the "strength" of the linear association between the values of the random variables. In Figure P.4 the correlation between X and Y is $\rho = 0.5$.

To illustrate the calculation, reconsider the population in Table P.1 with joint probability density function given in Table P.4. The expected value of XY is

$$\begin{aligned}
E(XY) = \sum_{y=0}^{1} \sum_{x=1}^{4} xyf(x, y) &= (1 \times 0 \times 0) + (2 \times 0 \times 0.1) + (3 \times 0 \times 0.2) \\
&\quad + (4 \times 0 \times 0.3) + (1 \times 1 \times 0.1) + (2 \times 1 \times 0.1) \\
&\quad + (3 \times 1 \times 0.1) + (4 \times 1 \times 0.1) \\
&= 0.1 + 0.2 + 0.3 + 0.4 \\
&= 1
\end{aligned}$$

The random variable X has expected value $E(X) = \mu_X = 3$ and the random variable Y has expected value $E(Y) = \mu_Y = 0.4$. Then the covariance between X and Y is

$$\text{cov}(X, Y) = \sigma_{XY} = E(XY) - \mu_X\mu_Y = 1 - 3 \times (0.4) = -0.2$$

The correlation between X and Y is

$$\rho = \frac{\text{cov}(X, Y)}{\sqrt{\text{var}(X)}\sqrt{\text{var}(Y)}} = \frac{-0.2}{\sqrt{1} \times \sqrt{0.24}} = -0.4082$$

If X and Y are independent random variables then their covariance and correlation are zero. The converse of this relationship is **not** true. Independent random variables X and Y have zero covariance, indicating that there is no linear association between them. However, just because the covariance or correlation between two random variables is zero **does not** mean that they are necessarily independent. There may be more complicated nonlinear associations such as $X^2 + Y^2 = 1$.

In (P.15) we obtain the expected value of a sum of random variables. We obtain similar rules for variances. If a and b are constants, then

$$\text{var}(aX + bY) = a^2\text{var}(X) + b^2\text{var}(Y) + 2ab\text{cov}(X, Y) \qquad (\text{P.20})$$

A significant point to note is that the variance of a sum is **not** just the sum of the variances. There is a covariance term present. Two special cases of (P.20) are

$$\text{var}(X + Y) = \text{var}(X) + \text{var}(Y) + 2\text{cov}(X, Y) \qquad (\text{P.21})$$

$$\text{var}(X - Y) = \text{var}(X) + \text{var}(Y) - 2\text{cov}(X, Y) \qquad (\text{P.22})$$

To show that (P.22) is true, let $Z = X - Y$. Using the rules of expected value

$$E(Z) = \mu_Z = E(X) - E(Y) = \mu_X - \mu_Y$$

The variance of $Z = X - Y$ is obtained using the basic definition of variance, with some substituting,

$$
\begin{aligned}
\text{var}(X - Y) = \text{var}(Z) &= E\left[(Z - \mu_Z)^2\right] = E\left[\left(X - Y - (\mu_X - \mu_Y)\right)^2\right] \\
&= E\left\{[(X - \mu_X) - (Y - \mu_Y)]^2\right\} \\
&= E\left\{(X - \mu_X)^2 + (Y - \mu_Y)^2 - 2(X - \mu_X)(Y - \mu_Y)\right\} \\
&= E\left[(X - \mu_X)^2\right] + E\left[(Y - \mu_Y)^2\right] - 2E[(X - \mu_X)(Y - \mu_Y)] \\
&= \text{var}(X) + \text{var}(Y) - 2\text{cov}(X, Y)
\end{aligned}
$$

If X and Y are independent, or if $\text{cov}(X, Y) = 0$, then

$$\text{var}(aX + bY) = a^2\text{var}(X) + b^2\text{var}(Y) \qquad (\text{P.23})$$

$$\text{var}(X \pm Y) = \text{var}(X) + \text{var}(Y) \qquad (\text{P.24})$$

These rules extend to more random variables.

P.6 The Normal Distribution

In the previous sections we discussed random variables and their probability density functions in a general way. In real economic contexts some specific probability density functions have been found to be very useful. The most important is the normal distribution. If X is a normally distributed random variable with mean μ and variance σ^2, it can be symbolized as $X \sim N(\mu, \sigma^2)$. The *pdf* of X is given by the impressive formula

$$f(x) = \frac{1}{\sqrt{2\pi\sigma^2}}\exp\left[\frac{-(x - \mu)^2}{2\sigma^2}\right], \quad -\infty < x < \infty \qquad (\text{P.25})$$

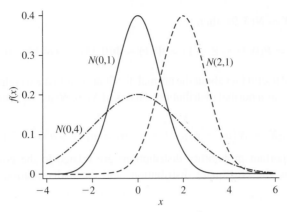

FIGURE P.5   Normal probability density functions $N(\mu, \sigma^2)$.

where $\exp(a)$ denotes the exponential[5] function e^a. The mean μ and variance σ^2 are the parameters of this distribution and determine its center and dispersion. The range of the continuous normal random variable is from minus infinity to plus infinity. Pictures of the normal probability density functions are given in Figure P.5 for several values of the mean and variance. Note that the distribution is symmetric and centered at μ.

Like all continuous random variables, probabilities involving normal random variables are found as areas under the probability density function. For calculating probabilities both computer software and statistical tables values make use of the relation between a normal random variable and its "standardized" equivalent. A **standard normal random variable** is one that has a normal probability density function with mean 0 and variance 1. If $X \sim N(\mu, \sigma^2)$, then

$$Z = \frac{X - \mu}{\sigma} \sim N(0, 1) \tag{P.26}$$

The *cdf* for the standardized normal variable Z is so widely used that it is given its own special symbol, $\Phi(z) = P(Z \leq z)$. Computer programs, and Table 1 at the end of this book, give values of $\Phi(z)$. To calculate normal probabilities remember that the distribution is symmetric, so that $P(Z > a) = P(Z < -a)$, and $P(Z > a) = P(Z \geq a)$, since the probability of any one point is zero for a continuous random variable. If $X \sim N(\mu, \sigma^2)$ and a and b are constants, then

$$P(X \leq a) = P\left(\frac{X - \mu}{\sigma} \leq \frac{a - \mu}{\sigma}\right) = P\left(Z \leq \frac{a - \mu}{\sigma}\right) = \Phi\left(\frac{a - \mu}{\sigma}\right) \tag{P.27}$$

$$P(X > a) = P\left(\frac{X - \mu}{\sigma} > \frac{a - \mu}{\sigma}\right) = P\left(Z > \frac{a - \mu}{\sigma}\right) = 1 - \Phi\left(\frac{a - \mu}{\sigma}\right) \tag{P.28}$$

$$P(a \leq X \leq b) = P\left(\frac{a - \mu}{\sigma} \leq Z \leq \frac{b - \mu}{\sigma}\right) = \Phi\left(\frac{b - \mu}{\sigma}\right) - \Phi\left(\frac{a - \mu}{\sigma}\right) \tag{P.29}$$

---

[5] See Appendix A.1.2 for a review of exponents.

For example, if $X \sim N(3,9)$, then

$$P(4 \leq X \leq 6) = P(0.33 \leq Z \leq 1) = \Phi(1) - \Phi(0.33) = 0.8413 - 0.6293 = 0.2120$$

An interesting and useful fact about the normal distribution is that a weighted sum of normal random variables has a normal distribution. That is, if $X_1 \sim N(\mu_1, \sigma_1^2)$ and $X_2 \sim N(\mu_2, \sigma_2^2)$ then

$$Y = a_1 X_1 + a_2 X_2 \sim N\left(\mu_Y = a_1\mu_1 + a_2\mu_2, \sigma_Y^2 = a_1^2\sigma_1^2 + a_2^2\sigma_2^2 + 2a_1a_2\sigma_{12}\right) \quad \text{(P.30)}$$

A number of important probability distributions are related to the normal distribution. The t-distribution, the chi-square distribution, and the F-distribution are discussed in Appendix B.

P.7 Exercises

Answers to exercises marked * appear on the web page www.wiley.com/go/global/hill.

P.1*   You are organizing an outdoor concert for next week and believe attendance will depend on the weather. You consider the following possibilities are appropriate:

Weather	Probability = $f(x)$	Attendance = X
Terrible weather	0.2	500
Mediocre weather	0.6	1000
Great weather	0.2	2000

(a) Let X denote the attendance. Why is X a random variable?
(b) What is the expected attendance?
(c) Suppose that each ticket costs $5 and that the total cost of giving the concert is a fixed $2,000. Let Y = profit = total sales revenue – total cost = $5X - 2000$. What is the expected profit?
(d) If the variance of attendance is $\sigma_X^2 = 240,000$, find the variance of profit Y.

P.2   As you walk into your econometrics exam, a friend bets you $10 that she will outscore you on the exam. Let X be a random variable denoting your winnings. X can take the values 10, 0 if there is a tie, or -10. You know that the probability distribution for $X, f(x)$, depends on whether she studied for the exam or not. Let $Y = 0$ if she studied and $Y = 1$ if she did not study. Consider the following joint distribution table.

		Y		
$f(x,y)$		0	1	$f(x)$
	-10	0.18	?	?
X	0	0	?	0.3
	10	?	0.45	?
$f(y)$		?	0.75	

(a) Fill in the missing elements in the table.
(b) Compute $E(X)$. Should you take the bet?

   (c) What is the probability distribution of your winnings if you **know** that she did not study?

   (d) Find your expected winnings **given that** she did not study.

P.3* A firm's marketing manager believes that total sales X can be modeled using a normal distribution with mean $\mu = \$2.5$ million and standard deviation $\sigma = \$300,000$. What is the probability that the firm's sales will exceed \$3 million? Draw a sketch to illustrate your calculation.

P.4 In the U.S. the North and South are quite different. Below is the joint probability distribution of political affiliation ($R =$ Republican, $I =$ Independent and $D =$ Democrat) for a Northern city and a Southern city.

	Political Affiliation (*PA*)		
	R	*I*	*D*
Southern	0.24	0.04	0.12
Northern	0.18	0.12	0.30

   (a) What is the probability of selecting a Republican given that we sample from the Northern city? Show your calculation.

   (b) Are political affiliation and region of residence statistically independent random variables? Explain.

   (c) Assign the values $R = 0, I = 2$ and $D = 5$ to political affiliation (*PA*). That is, if a citizen is selected at random, the variable *PA* can take the values 0, 2 and 5. Find the mathematical expectation of the random variable *PA*.

   (d) Find the expected value of $X = 2PA + 2PA^2$, where *PA* is the random variable political affiliation.

P.5* Before the 2009 Super Bowl there was a coin flip to determine who kicked off and who received. The NFC (National Football Conference) had won 11 prior coin flips.

   (a) Given that the NFC had won 11 straight flips, what is the probability that they would win the 12th flip? Explain.

   (b) Before the 2010 Super Bowl (won by the New Orleans Saints) the NFC won the coin toss for the 13th consecutive time. What is the probability that the NFC will win the next two consecutive tosses?

P.6 At supermarkets in a Midwestern city the sales of canned tuna varies from week to week. Marketing researchers have determined that there is a relationship between sales of canned tuna and the price of canned tuna. Specifically, *SALES* = 40710 − 430*PRICE* where *SALES* are cans sold per week and *PRICE* is measured in cents per can. Suppose *PRICE* over the year can be considered (approximately) a normal random variable with mean $\mu = 75$ cents and standard deviation $\sigma = 5$ cents. That is *PRICE* ~ $N(75, 25)$.

   (a) What is the numerical expected value of *SALES*? Show your work.

   (b) What is the numerical value of the variance of *SALES*? Show your work.

   (c) Find the probability that more than 6,300 cans are sold in a week. Draw a sketch illustrating the calculation.

P.7* "Charley Chicken" and "Bradley Bee" are brands of canned tuna. During a week a certain amount of advertising appears for these products. There may be no advertising, one form of advertising (newspaper coupon), or two forms (coupon and a special store display). Let C denote the level of advertising for Charley Chicken. It can take the values $c = 0, 1$ or 2. Let B denote the level of advertising of Bradley Bee; B can take the values $b = 0, 1$ or 2. Suppose the following table represents the joint probability distribution of the advertising levels for these two brands of canned tuna.

		B		
		0	1	2
C	0	0.05	0.05	0.05
	1	0.05	0.20	0.15
	2	0.05	0.25	0.15

(a) What is the marginal probability distribution of Charley Chicken advertising, C?
(b) What is the expected value of C? Show your work.
(c) What is the variance of C? Show your work.
(d) Are the two companies' advertising strategies statistically independent? Explain.
(e) Bradley Bee pays its advertising firm \$5,000 per week plus \$1,000 for each level of advertising B. What is the probability distribution of Bradley Bee's advertising outlay, A?
(f) What is the correlation between Bradley Bee's advertising level (B) and its advertising expenditure (A)? Explain.

P.8   Let X be a discrete random variable that is the value shown on a single roll of a fair die.
(a) Represent the probability density function $f(x)$ in tabular form.
(b) What is the probability that $X = 4$? That $X = 4$ or $X = 5$?
(c) What is the expected value of X? Explain the meaning of $E(X)$ in this case.
(d) Find the expected value of X^2.
(e) Find the variance of X.
(f) Obtain a die. Roll it 20 times and record the values obtained. What is the average of the first 5 values? The first 10? What is the average of the 20 rolls?

P.9   Let X be a continuous random variable whose probability density function is

$$f(x) = \begin{cases} \frac{2}{3} - \frac{2}{9}x & 0 \le x \le 3 \\ 0 & otherwise \end{cases}$$

(a) Sketch the probability density function $f(x)$. Is the area under the curve equal to one?
(b) Geometrically calculate the probability that X falls between 0 and ½.
(c) Geometrically calculate the probability that X falls between ¼ and ³/₄.

P.10 Suppose that X and Y are random variables with expected values $\mu_X = \mu_Y = \mu$ and variances $\sigma_X^2 = \sigma_Y^2 = \sigma^2$. Let $Z = (X + Y)/2$.
(a) Find $E(Z)$.
(b) Find $\text{var}(Z)$ assuming that X and Y are statistically independent.
(c) Find $\text{var}(Z)$ assuming that $\text{cov}(X, Y) = 0.5\sigma^2$.

P.11* The length of life (in years) of a personal computer is approximately normally distributed with mean 3.4 years and variance 1.6 years.
  (a) What fraction of computers will fail in the first year?
  (b) What fraction of computers will last 4 years or more?
  (c) What fraction of computers will last at least 2 years?
  (d) What fraction of computers will last more than 2.5 years but less than 4 years?
  (e) If the manufacturer adopts a warranty policy in which only 5% of the computers have to be replaced, what will be the length of the warranty period?

P.12 Based on many years of experience, an instructor in econometrics has determined that the probability distribution of X, the number of students absent on Mondays, is as follows:

x	0	1	2	3	4	5	6	7
$f(x)$	0.02	0.03	0.26	0.34	0.22	0.08	0.04	0.01

  (a) Sketch the probability function of X.
  (b) Find the probability that on a given Monday either 2, or 3 or 4 students will be absent.
  (c) Find the probability that on a given Monday more than 3 students are absent.
  (d) Compute the expected value of the random variable X. Interpret this expected value.
  (e) Compute the variance and standard deviation of the random variable X.
  (f) Compute the expected value and variance of $Y = 7X + 3$.

P.13* Suppose a certain mutual fund has an annual rate of return that is approximately normally distributed with mean (expected value) 5% and standard deviation 4%. Use Table 1, the table of cumulative probabilities for the standard normal distribution, for parts (a)–(c).
  (a) Find the probability that your 1-year return will be negative.
  (b) Find the probability that your 1-year return will exceed 15%.
  (c) If the mutual fund managers modify the composition of its portfolio, they can raise its mean annual return to 7%, but will also raise the standard deviation of returns to 7%. Answer parts (a) and (b) in light of these decisions. Would you advise the fund managers to make this portfolio change?
  (d) Verify your computations in (a)–(c) using your computer software.

P.14 An investor holding a portfolio consisting of two stocks invests 25% of assets in Stock A and 75% into Stock B. The return R_A from Stock A has a mean of 4% and a standard deviation of $\sigma_A = 8\%$. Stock B has an expected return $E(R_B) = 8\%$ with a standard deviation of $\sigma_B = 12\%$. The portfolio return is $P = 0.25R_A + 0.75R_B$.
  (a) Compute the expected return on the portfolio.
  (b) Compute the standard deviation of the returns on the portfolio assuming that the two stocks' returns are perfectly positively correlated.
  (c) Compute the standard deviation of the returns on the portfolio assuming that the two stocks' returns have a correlation of 0.5.
  (d) Compute the standard deviation of the returns on the portfolio assuming that the two stocks' returns are uncorrelated.

P.15* Let $x_1 = 7$, $x_2 = 2$, $x_3 = 4$, $x_4 = -7$, $y_1 = 5$, $y_2 = 2$, $y_3 = 3$, $y_4 = 12$. Calculate the following:

(a) $\displaystyle\sum_{i=1}^{2} x_i$

(b) $\displaystyle\bar{x} = \sum_{i=1}^{4} x_i \Big/ 4$ [Note: $\bar{x}$ is called the arithmetic average or arithmetic mean.]

(c) $\displaystyle\sum_{i=1}^{4} (x_i - \bar{x})$

(d) $\displaystyle\sum_{i=1}^{4} (x_i - \bar{x})^2$

(e) $\displaystyle\sum_{i=1}^{4} (x_i - \bar{x})(y_i - \bar{y})$ where $\bar{y} = \displaystyle\sum_{i=1}^{4} y_i \Big/ 4$

(f) $\displaystyle\frac{\left(\sum_{i=1}^{4} x_i y_i\right) - 4 \times \bar{x} \times \bar{y}}{\left(\sum_{i=1}^{4} x_i^2\right) - 4 \times \bar{x}^2}$

P.16   Express each of the following sums in summation notation:
    (a) $x_1 + x_2 + x_3 + x_4$
    (b) $x_2 + x_3$
    (c) $x_1 y_1 + x_2 y_2 + x_3 y_3 + x_4 y_4$
    (d) $x_1 y_3 + x_2 y_4 + x_3 y_5 + x_4 y_6$
    (e) $x_3 y_3^2 + x_4 y_4^2$
    (f) $(x_1 - y_1) + (x_2 - y_2) + (x_3 - y_3)$

P.17*   Write out each of the following sums and compute where possible.

    (a) $\displaystyle\sum_{i=1}^{4} (a + bx_i)$

    (b) $\displaystyle\sum_{i=1}^{3} i^2$

    (c) $\displaystyle\sum_{x=0}^{3} (x^2 + 2x + 2)$

    (d) $\displaystyle\sum_{x=2}^{4} f(x + 2)$

    (e) $\displaystyle\sum_{x=0}^{2} f(x, y)$

    (f) $\displaystyle\sum_{x=2}^{4} \sum_{y=1}^{2} (x + 2y)$

P.18   Let X take 4 values $x_1 = 1$, $x_2 = 3$, $x_3 = 5$, $x_4 = 3$.
    (a) Calculate the arithmetic average $\bar{x} = \sum_{i=1}^{4} x_i \Big/ 4$

    (b) Calculate $\sum_{i=1}^{4} (x_i - \bar{x})$
    (c) Calculate $\sum_{i=1}^{4} (x_i - \bar{x})^2$
    (d) Calculate $\left(\sum_{i=1}^{4} x_i^2\right) - 4\bar{x}^2$

    (e) Show algebraically that $\displaystyle\sum_{i=1}^{n} (x_i - \bar{x})^2 = \left(\sum_{i=1}^{n} x_i^2\right) - n\bar{x}^2$

P.19   Show that $\displaystyle\sum_{i=1}^{n} (x_i - \bar{x})(y_i - \bar{y}) = \left(\sum_{i=1}^{n} x_i y_i\right) - n\bar{x}\bar{y}$

Chapter *2*

The Simple Linear Regression Model

Learning Objectives

> **REMARK:** *Learning Objectives* and *Keywords* sections will appear at the beginning of each chapter. We urge you to think about, and possibly write out answers to the questions, and make sure you recognize and can define the keywords. If you are unsure about the questions or answers consult your instructor. When examples are requested in *Learning Objectives* sections, you should think of examples *not* in the book.

Based on the material in this chapter you should be able to

1. Explain the difference between an estimator and an estimate, and why the least squares estimators are random variables, and why least squares estimates are not.

2. Discuss the interpretation of the slope and intercept parameters of the simple regression model, and sketch the graph of an estimated equation.

3. Explain the theoretical decomposition of an observable variable y into its systematic and random components, and show this decomposition graphically.

4. Discuss and explain each of the assumptions of the simple linear regression model.

5. Explain how the least squares principle is used to fit a line through a scatter plot of data. Be able to define the least squares residual and the least squares fitted value of the dependent variable and show them on a graph.

6. Define the elasticity of y with respect to x and explain its computation in the simple linear regression model when y and x are not transformed in any way, and when y and/or x have been transformed to model a nonlinear relationship.

7. Explain the meaning of the statement "If regression model assumptions SR1–SR5 hold, then the least squares estimator b_2 is unbiased." In particular, what exactly does "unbiased" mean? Why is b_2 biased if an important variable has been omitted from the model?

8. Explain the meaning of the phrase "sampling variability."

9. Explain how the factors σ^2, $\sum(x_i - \bar{x})^2$, and N affect the precision with which we can estimate the unknown parameter β_2.

10. State and explain the Gauss–Markov theorem.

11. Use the least squares estimator to estimate nonlinear relationships and interpret the results.

Keywords

assumptions	heteroskedastic	quadratic model
asymptotic	homoskedastic	random error term
BLUE	independent variable	regression model
biased estimator	indicator variable	regression parameters
degrees of freedom	least squares estimates	repeated sampling
dependent variable	least squares estimators	sampling precision
deviation from the mean	least squares principle	sampling properties
form	least squares residuals	scatter diagram
econometric model	linear estimator	simple linear regression function
economic model	log-linear model	specification error
elasticity	nonlinear relationship	unbiased estimator
Gauss–Markov theorem	prediction	

Economic theory suggests many relationships between economic variables. In microeconomics you considered demand and supply models in which the quantities demanded and supplied of a good depend on its price. You considered "production functions" and "total product curves" that explained the amount of a good produced as a function of the amount of an input, such as labor, that is used. In macroeconomics you specified "investment functions" to explain that the amount of aggregate investment in the economy depends on the interest rate and "consumption functions" that related aggregate consumption to the level of disposable income.

Each of these models involves a relationship between economic variables. In this chapter we consider how to use a sample of economic data to quantify such relationships. As economists, we are interested in questions such as the following: If one variable (e.g., the price of a good) changes in a certain way, *by how much* will another variable (the quantity demanded or supplied) change? Also, given that we know the value of one variable, can we *forecast* or *predict* the corresponding value of another? We will answer these questions by using a **regression model**. Like all models the regression model is based on assumptions. In this chapter we hope to be very clear about these assumptions, as they are the conditions under which the analysis in subsequent chapters is appropriate.

2.1 An Economic Model

In order to develop the ideas of regression models we are going to use a simple, but important, economic example. Suppose that we are interested in studying the relationship between household income and expenditure on food. Consider the "experiment" of randomly selecting households from a particular population. The population might consist of households within a particular city, state, province, or country. For the present, suppose that we are interested only in households with an income of $1,000 per week. In this experiment we randomly select a number of households from this population and interview them. We ask the question, "How much did you spend per person on food last week?" Weekly food expenditure, which we denote as *y*, is a *random variable* since the value is unknown to us until a household is selected and the question is asked and answered.

> **REMARK:** In the Probability Primer and Appendices B and C we distinguished random variables from their values by using uppercase (Y) letters for random variables and lowercase (y) letters for their values. We *will not* make this distinction any longer because it leads to complicated notation. We will use lowercase letters, like 'y,' to denote random variables as well as their values, and we will make the interpretation clear in the surrounding text.

The continuous random variable y has a probability density function (which we will abbreviate as *pdf*) that describes the probabilities of obtaining various food expenditure values. *If you are rusty or uncertain about probability concepts see the Probability Primer and Appendix B at the end of this book for a comprehensive review.* The amount spent on food per person will vary from one household to another for a variety of reasons: some households will be devoted to gourmet food, some will contain teenagers, some will contain senior citizens, some will be vegetarian, and some will eat at restaurants more frequently. All of these factors and many others, including random, impulsive buying, will cause weekly expenditures on food to vary from one household to another, even if they all have the same income. The *pdf* $f(y)$ describes how expenditures are "distributed" over the population and might look like Figure 2.1.

The *pdf* in Figure 2.1a is actually a conditional probability density function since it is "conditional" upon household income. If x = weekly household income = \$1,000, then the conditional *pdf* is $f(y|x = \$1,000)$. The *conditional mean*, or *expected value*, of y is $E(y|x = \$1,000) = \mu_{y|x}$ and is our population's mean weekly food expenditure per person.

> **REMARK:** The expected value of a random variable is called its "mean" value, which is really a contraction of *population mean*, the center of the probability distribution of the random variable. This is *not* the same as the *sample mean*, which is the arithmetic average of numerical values. Keep the distinction between these two usages of the term "mean" in mind.

The *conditional variance* of y is $\text{var}(y|x = \$1,000) = \sigma^2$, which measures the dispersion of household expenditures y about their mean $\mu_{y|x}$. The parameters $\mu_{y|x}$ and σ^2, if they were known, would give us some valuable information about the population we are considering. If we knew these parameters, and if we knew that the conditional distribution $f(y|x = \$1,000)$ was *normal*, $N(\mu_{y|x}, \sigma^2)$, then we could calculate probabilities that y falls in specific intervals using properties of the normal distribution. That is, we could compute the

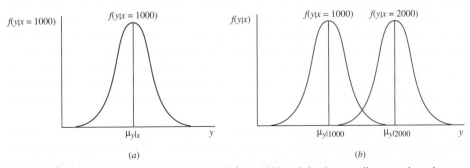

FIGURE **2.1**   (*a*) Probability distribution $f(y|x = 1000)$ of food expenditure y given income $x = \$1,000$. (*b*) Probability distributions of food expenditure y given incomes $x = \$1,000$ and $x = \$2,000$.

proportion of the household population that spends between \$50 and \$75 per person on food, given \$1,000 per week income.

As economists we are usually more interested in studying relationships between variables, in this case the relationship between y = weekly food expenditure per person and x = weekly household income. Economic theory tells us that expenditure on economic goods depends on income. Consequently we call y the "dependent variable" and x the "independent" or "explanatory" variable. In econometrics, we recognize that real-world expenditures are random variables, and we want to use data to learn about the relationship.

An econometric analysis of the expenditure relationship can provide answers to some important questions, such as: If weekly income goes up by \$100, **how much** will average weekly food expenditures rise? Or, could weekly food expenditures fall as income rises? How much would we predict the weekly per person expenditure on food to be for a household with an income of \$2,000 per week? The answers to such questions provide valuable information for decision makers.

> Using ... per person food spending information ... one can determine the similarities and disparities in the spending habits of households of differing sizes, races, incomes, geographic areas, and other socioeconomic and demographic features. This information is valuable for assessing existing market conditions, product distribution patterns, consumer buying habits, and consumer living conditions. Combined with demographic and income projections, this information may be used to anticipate consumption trends. The information may also be used to develop typical market baskets of food for special population groups, such as the elderly. These market baskets may, in turn, be used to develop price indices tailored to the consumption patterns of these population groups. [Blisard, Noel, Food Spending in American Households, 1997–1998, Electronic Report from the Economic Research Service, U.S. Department of Agriculture, Statistical Bulletin Number 972, June 2001]

From a business perspective, if we are managers of a supermarket chain (or restaurant, or health food store, etc.) we must consider long-range plans. If economic forecasters are predicting that local income will increase over the next few years, then we must decide whether, and how much, to expand our facilities to serve our customers. Or, if we plan to open franchises in high-income and low-income neighborhoods, then forecasts of expenditures on food per person, along with neighborhood demographic information, give an indication of how large the stores in those areas should be.

In order to investigate the relationship between expenditure and income we must build an **economic model** and then a corresponding **econometric model** that forms the basis for a quantitative or *empirical* economic analysis. In our food expenditure example, economic theory suggests that average weekly per person household expenditure on food, represented mathematically by the conditional mean $E(y|x) = \mu_{y|x}$, depends on household income x. If we consider households with different levels of income, we expect the average expenditure on food to change. In Figure 2.1b we show the probability density functions of food expenditure for two different levels of weekly income, \$1,000 and \$2,000. Each conditional *pdf* $f(y|x)$ shows that expenditures will be distributed about a mean value $\mu_{y|x}$, but the mean expenditure by households with higher income is larger than the mean expenditure by lower income households.

In most economics textbooks "consumption" or "expenditure" functions relating consumption to income are depicted as *linear relationships*, and we will begin by assuming the same thing. The mathematical representation of our economic model of household food expenditure, depicted in Figure 2.2, is

$$E(y|x) = \mu_{y|x} = \beta_1 + \beta_2 x \qquad (2.1)$$

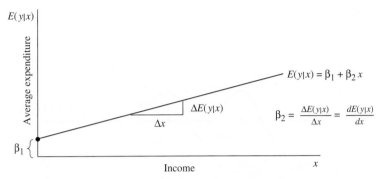

FIGURE 2.2 The economic model: a linear relationship between average per person food expenditure and income.

The conditional mean $E(y|x)$ in (2.1) is called a **simple regression function**. It is called *simple* regression not because it is easy, but because there is only one explanatory variable on the right-hand side of the equation. The unknown **regression parameters** β_1 and β_2 are the intercept and slope of the regression function, respectively. *If you need a review of the geometry, interpretation, and algebra of linear functions see Appendix A.2 at the end of the book.* In our food expenditure example the intercept β_1 represents the mean per person weekly household expenditure on food by a household with no weekly income, $x =$ \$0. If income is measured in dollars, then the slope β_2 represents the change in $E(y|x)$ given a \$1 change in weekly income; it could be called the marginal propensity to spend on food. Algebraically,

$$\beta_2 = \frac{\Delta E(y|x)}{\Delta x} = \frac{dE(y|x)}{dx} \tag{2.2}$$

where Δ denotes "change in" and $dE(y|x)/dx$ denotes the "derivative" of $E(y|x)$ with respect to x. We will not use derivatives to any great extent in this book, and if you are not familiar with the concept, you can think of "d" as a "stylized" version of Δ and go on. See Appendix A.3 for a discussion of derivatives.

The economic model (2.1) summarizes what theory tells us about the relationship between weekly household income (x) and expected household expenditure on food, $E(y|x)$. The parameters of the model, β_1 and β_2, are quantities that help characterize economic behavior in the population we are considering and are called **population parameters**. In order to use data we must now specify an *econometric model* that describes how the data on household income and expenditure are obtained, and that guides the econometric analysis.

2.2 **An Econometric Model**

The model $E(y|x) = \beta_1 + \beta_2 x$ describes economic behavior, but it is an abstraction from reality. If we take a random sample of households with weekly income $x =$ \$1,000, we know the actual expenditure values will be scattered around the mean value $E(y|x = 1000) = \mu_{y|x=1000} = \beta_1 + \beta_2(1000)$, as shown in Figure 2.1. If we were to sample household expenditures at other levels of income, we would expect the sample values to be scattered around their mean value $E(y|x) = \beta_1 + \beta_2 x$. In Figure 2.3 we arrange bell-shaped figures like Figure 2.1, depicting the *pdfs* of food expenditure $f(y|x)$, along the regression line for *each* level of income.

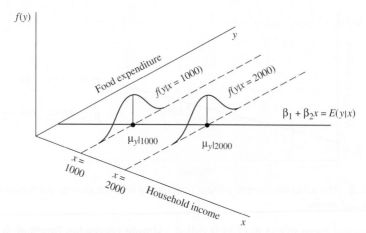

FIGURE **2.3** The probability density functions for y at two levels of income.

This figure shows that at each level of income the mean, or average, value of household expenditure is given by the regression function $E(y|x) = \beta_1 + \beta_2 x$. It also shows that we assume values of household expenditures on food will be distributed around the mean value $E(y|x) = \beta_1 + \beta_2 x$ at each level of income. This regression function is the foundation of an econometric model for household food expenditure.

In order to make the econometric model complete we have to make some assumptions.

> **REMARK:** You will hear a great deal about **assumptions** in this chapter and in the remainder of the book. Assumptions are the "if" part of an "if–then" type statement. If the assumptions we make are true, then certain things follow. And, as importantly, if the assumptions do not hold, then the conclusions we draw may not hold. Part of the challenge of econometric analysis is making realistic assumptions and then checking that they hold.

In Figure 2.1a we assumed that the *dispersion* of the values y about their mean is $\text{var}(y|x = \$1{,}000) = \sigma^2$. We must make a similar assumption about the dispersion of values at each level of income. The basic assumption is that the dispersion of values y about their mean is the same for all levels of income x. That is, $\text{var}(y|x) = \sigma^2$ for all values of x. In Figure 2.1b the *pdf*s for two different incomes have different means, but they have identical variances. This assumption is also illustrated in Figure 2.3, as we have depicted the "spread" of each of the distributions, like Figure 2.1, to be the same.

The constant variance assumption $\text{var}(y|x) = \sigma^2$ implies that at each level of income x we are *equally* uncertain about how far values of y might fall from their mean value, $E(y|x) = \beta_1 + \beta_2 x$, and the uncertainty does not depend on income or anything else. Data satisfying this condition are said to be **homoskedastic**. If this assumption is violated, so that $\text{var}(y|x) \neq \sigma^2$ for all values of income x, the data are said to be **heteroskedastic**.

We have described the sample as *random*. This description means that when data are collected they are *statistically independent*. If y_i and y_j denote the per person food expenditures of two randomly selected households, then knowing the *value* of one of these (random) variables tells us nothing about the probability that the other will take a particular value or range of values.

Mathematicians spend their lives (we exaggerate slightly) trying to prove the same theorem with weaker and weaker sets of assumptions. This mindset spills over to econometricians to some degree. Consequently, econometric models often make an assumption that is weaker than statistical independence. If y_i and y_j are the expenditures of two randomly selected households, then we will assume that their *covariance* is zero, or $\text{cov}(y_i, y_j) = 0$. This is a weaker assumption than statistical independence (since independence implies zero covariance, but zero covariance does not imply independence); it implies only that there is no systematic *linear* association between y_i and y_j. Refer to the Probability Primer, Sections P.3.3 and P.5.6 for more discussion of this difference.

In order to carry out a regression analysis, we must make two assumptions about the values of the variable x. The idea of regression analysis is to measure the effect of changes in one variable, x, on another, y. In order to do this x must take at least two values within the sample of data. If all the observations on x within the sample take the same value, say $x = \$1,000$, then regression analysis fails. Secondly, we will assume that the x-values are given, and not random. All our results will be conditional on the given x-values. More will be said about this assumption soon.

Finally, it is sometimes assumed that the values of y are *normally* distributed. The usual justification for this assumption is that in nature the "bell-shaped" curve describes many phenomena, ranging from IQs to the length of corn stalks to the birth weights of Australian male children. It is reasonable, sometimes, to assume that an economic variable is normally distributed about its mean. We will say more about this assumption later, but for now we will make it an "optional" assumption, since we do not need to make it in many cases, and it is a very strong assumption when it is made.

These ideas, taken together, define our **econometric model**. They are a collection of assumptions that describe the data.

ASSUMPTIONS OF THE SIMPLE LINEAR REGRESSION MODEL-I

- The mean value of y, for each value of x, is given by the linear regression function

$$E(y|x) = \beta_1 + \beta_2 x$$

- For each value of x, the values of y are distributed about their mean value, following probability distributions that all have the same variance,

$$\text{var}(y|x) = \sigma^2$$

- The sample values of y are all uncorrelated and have zero covariance, implying that there is no linear association among them,

$$\text{cov}(y_i, y_j) = 0$$

This assumption can be made stronger by assuming that the values of y are all statistically independent.

- The variable x is not random and must take at least two different values.
- (*optional*) The values of y are normally distributed about their mean for each value of x,

$$y \sim N\left[(\beta_1 + \beta_2 x), \sigma^2\right]$$

2.2.1 INTRODUCING THE ERROR TERM

It is convenient to describe the assumptions of the simple linear regression model in terms of y, which in general is called the **dependent variable** in the regression model. However, for statistical purposes it is useful to characterize the assumptions another way.

The essence of regression analysis is that any observation on the dependent variable y can be decomposed into two parts: a systematic component and a random component. The systematic component of y is its mean, $E(y|x) = \beta_1 + \beta_2 x$, which itself is not random since it is a mathematical expectation. The random component of y is the difference between y and its conditional mean value $E(y|x)$. This is called a **random error term**, and it is defined as

$$e = y - E(y|x) = y - \beta_1 - \beta_2 x \qquad (2.3)$$

If we rearrange (2.3) we obtain the **simple linear regression model**

$$y = \beta_1 + \beta_2 x + e \qquad (2.4)$$

The dependent variable y is explained by a component that varies systematically with the **independent variable** x and by the random error term e.

Equation (2.3) shows that y and the error term e differ only by the term $E(y|x) = \beta_1 + \beta_2 x$, which is not random. Since y is random, so is the error term e. Given what we have already assumed about y, the properties of the random error e can be derived directly from (2.3). The expected value of the error term, given x, is

$$E(e|x) = E(y|x) - \beta_1 - \beta_2 x = 0$$

The mean value of the error term, given x, is zero.

Since y and e differ only by a constant (i.e., a factor that is not random), their variances must be identical and equal to σ^2. Thus the probability density functions for y and e are identical except for their location, as shown in Figure 2.4. Note that the center of the *pdf* for the error term, $f(e)$, is zero, which is its expected value, $E(e|x) = 0$.

We can now discuss a bit more the simplifying assumption that x is not random. The assumption that x is not random means that its value is known. In statistics such x-values are said to be "fixed in repeated samples." If we could perform controlled experiments, as described in Chapter 1, the same set of x-values could be used over and over, so that only the outcomes y are random. As an example, suppose that we are interested in how price affects the number of Big Macs sold weekly at the local McDonald's. The franchise owner can set the price (x) and then observe the number of Big Macs sold (y) during the week. The

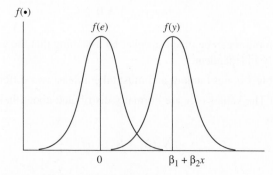

FIGURE **2.4** Probability density functions for e and y.

following week the price could be changed, and again the data on sales collected. In this case $x =$ the price of a Big Mac is not random, but fixed.

The number of cases in which the x-values are fixed is small in the world of business and economics. When we survey households we obtain the data on variables like food expenditure per person and household income at the same time. Thus y and x are both random in this case; their values are unknown until they are actually observed. However, making the assumption that x is given, and not random, does not change the results we will discuss in the following chapters. The additional benefit from the assumption is notational simplicity. Since x is treated as a constant nonrandom term, we no longer need the conditioning notation "|". So, instead of $E(e|x) = 0$ you will see $E(e) = 0$. There are some important situations in which treating x as fixed is not acceptable, and these will be discussed in Chapter 10.

It is customary in econometrics to state the assumptions of the regression model in terms of the random error e. For future reference the assumptions are named SR1–SR6, "SR" denoting "simple regression." Remember, since we are treating x as fixed, and not random, henceforth we will *not* use the "conditioning" notation $y|x$.

ASSUMPTIONS OF THE SIMPLE LINEAR REGRESSION MODEL-II

SR1. The value of y, for each value of x, is

$$y = \beta_1 + \beta_2 x + e$$

SR2. The expected value of the random error e is

$$E(e) = 0$$

which is equivalent to assuming that

$$E(y) = \beta_1 + \beta_2 x$$

SR3. The variance of the random error e is

$$\text{var}(e) = \sigma^2 = \text{var}(y)$$

The random variables y and e have the same variance because they differ only by a constant.

SR4. The covariance between any pair of random errors e_i and e_j is

$$\text{cov}(e_i, e_j) = \text{cov}(y_i, y_j) = 0$$

The stronger version of this assumption is that the random errors e are statistically independent, in which case the values of the dependent variable y are also statistically independent.

SR5. The variable x is not random and must take at least two different values.

SR6. (*optional*) The values of e are normally distributed about their mean

$$e \sim N(0, \sigma^2)$$

if the values of y are normally distributed, and vice versa.

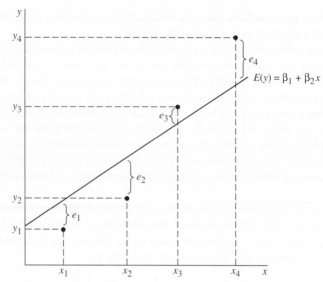

FIGURE 2.5 The relationship among y, e, and the true regression line.

The random error e and the dependent variable y are both random variables, and as we have shown the properties of one can be determined from the properties of the other. There is, however, one interesting difference between them: y is "observable" and e is "unobservable." If the regression parameters β_1 and β_2 were *known*, then for any value of y we could calculate $e = y - (\beta_1 + \beta_2 x)$. This is illustrated in Figure 2.5. Knowing the regression function $E(y) = \beta_1 + \beta_2 x$, we could separate y into its fixed and random parts. However, β_1 and β_2 *are never known*, and it is impossible to calculate e.

What comprises the error term e? The random error e represents all factors affecting y other than x. These factors cause individual observations y to differ from the mean value $E(y) = \beta_1 + \beta_2 x$. In the food expenditure example, what factors can result in a difference between household expenditure per person y and its mean, $E(y)$?

1. We have included income as the only explanatory variable in this model. Any *other* economic factors that affect expenditures on food are "collected" in the error term. Naturally, in any economic model, we want to include all the important and relevant explanatory variables in the model, so the error term e is a "storage bin" for unobservable and/or unimportant factors affecting household expenditures on food. As such, it adds noise that masks the relationship between x and y.

2. The error term e captures any approximation error that arises because the *linear* functional form we have assumed may be only an approximation to reality.

3. The error term captures any elements of random behavior that may be present in each individual. Knowing all the variables that influence a household's food expenditure might not be enough to perfectly predict expenditure. Unpredictable human behavior is also contained in e.

If we have omitted some important factor, or made any other serious **specification error**, then assumption SR2 $E(e) = 0$ will be violated, which will have serious consequences.

Table 2.1 **Food Expenditure and Income Data**

Observation (household)	Food expenditure ($)	Weekly income ($100)
i	y_i	x_i
1	115.22	3.69
2	135.98	4.39
	⋮	
39	257.95	29.40
40	375.73	33.40
	Summary statistics	
Sample mean	283.5735	19.6048
Median	264.4800	20.0300
Maximum	587.6600	33.4000
Minimum	109.7100	3.6900
Std. Dev.	112.6752	6.8478

2.3 **Estimating the Regression Parameters**

The economic and econometric models we developed in the previous section are the basis for using a sample of data to *estimate* the intercept and slope parameters, β_1 and β_2. For illustration we examine typical data on household food expenditure and weekly income from a random sample of 40 households. Representative observations and summary statistics are given in Table 2.1. We control for household size by considering only three-person households. The values of y are weekly food expenditures for a three-person household, in dollars. Instead of measuring income in dollars, we measure it in units of $100, because a $1 increase in income has a numerically small effect on food expenditure. Consequently, for the first household, the reported income is $369 per week with weekly food expenditure of $115.22. For the 40th household, weekly income is $3,340 and weekly food expenditure is $375.73. The complete data set of observations is in the file *food.dat*.

> **REMARK:** In this book, ASCII, or plain text, data files are referenced as *.dat; e.g., *food.dat*. Files in other formats will have the same name, but a different extension, such as *food.wf1, food.dta,* and so on. The corresponding data definition file will be *food.def*. These files are located at the book Web sites (www.wiley.com/go/global/hill) and http://principlesofeconometrics.com.

We assume that the expenditure data in Table 2.1 satisfy the assumptions SR1–SR5. That is, we assume that the expected value of household food expenditure is a linear function of income. This assumption about the expected value of y is equivalent to assuming that the random error has expected value zero, implying that we have not omitted any important factors. The variance of y, which is the same as the variance of the random error e, is assumed to be constant, implying that we are equally uncertain about the relationship between y and x for all observations. The values of y for different households are assumed to be uncorrelated with each other, which follows if we obtained the data by

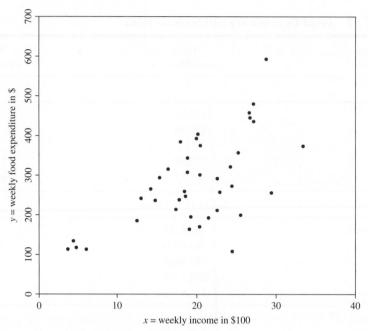

FIGURE 2.6   Data for the food expenditure example.

random sampling. The values of x were actually obtained by random sampling, but we will make the analysis conditional on the x values in the sample, which allows us to treat them as nonrandom values that are fixed in repeated samples. At the end of the day, this simplification does not change the analysis.

Given this theoretical model for explaining the sample observations on household food expenditure, the problem now is how to use the sample information in Table 2.1, specific values of y_i and x_i, to estimate the unknown regression parameters β_1 and β_2. These parameters represent the unknown intercept and slope coefficients for the food expenditure–income relationship. If we represent the 40 data points as (y_i, x_i), $i = 1, \ldots, N = 40$, and plot them, we obtain the **scatter diagram** in Figure 2.6.

> **REMARK:** It will be our notational convention to use i subscripts for cross-sectional data observations, with the number of sample observations being N. For time-series data observations we use the subscript t and label the total number of observations T. In purely algebraic or generic situations, we may use one or the other.

Our problem is to estimate the location of the mean expenditure line $E(y) = \beta_1 + \beta_2 x$. We would expect this line to be somewhere in the middle of all the data points since it represents population mean, or average, behavior. To estimate β_1 and β_2 we could simply draw a freehand line through the middle of the data and then measure the slope and intercept with a ruler. The problem with this method is that different people would draw different lines, and the lack of a formal criterion makes it difficult to assess the accuracy of the method. Another method is to draw a line from the expenditure at the smallest income level, observation $i = 1$, to the expenditure at largest income level, $i = 40$. This approach does provide a formal rule. However, it may not be a very good rule because it ignores information on the exact position of the remaining 38 observations. It would be better if we could devise a rule that uses all the information from all the data points.

2.3.1 THE LEAST SQUARES PRINCIPLE

To estimate β_1 and β_2 we want a rule, or formula, that tells us how to make use of the sample observations. Many rules are possible, but the one that we will use is based on the **least squares principle**. This principle asserts that to fit a line to the data values we should make the sum of the squares of the vertical distances from each point to the line as small as possible. The distances are squared to prevent large positive distances from being canceled by large negative distances. This rule is arbitrary, but very effective, and is simply one way to describe a line that runs through the middle of the data. The intercept and slope of this line, the line that best fits the data using the least squares principle, are b_1 and b_2, the least squares estimates of β_1 and β_2. The fitted line itself is then

$$\hat{y}_i = b_1 + b_2 x_i \qquad (2.5)$$

The vertical distances from each point to the fitted line are the **least squares residuals**. They are given by

$$\hat{e}_i = y_i - \hat{y}_i = y_i - b_1 - b_2 x_i \qquad (2.6)$$

These residuals are depicted in Figure 2.7a.

Now suppose we fit another line, *any other line*, to the data. Denote the new line as

$$\hat{y}_i^* = b_1^* + b_2^* x_i$$

where b_1^* and b_2^* are any other intercept and slope values. The residuals for this line, $\hat{e}_i^* = y_i - \hat{y}_i^*$, are shown in Figure 2.7b. The least squares estimates b_1 and b_2 have the property that the sum of their squared residuals is *less than* the sum of squared residuals for *any* other line. That is, if

$$SSE = \sum_{i=1}^{N} \hat{e}_i^2$$

is the sum of squared least squares residuals from (2.6) and

$$SSE^* = \sum_{i=1}^{N} \hat{e}_i^{*2} = \sum_{i=1}^{N} (y_i - \hat{y}_i^*)^2$$

is the sum of squared residuals based on any other estimates, then

$$SSE < SSE^*$$

no matter how the other line might be drawn through the data. The least squares principle says that the estimates b_1 and b_2 of β_1 and β_2 are the ones to use, since the line using them as intercept and slope fits the data best.

The problem is to find b_1 and b_2 in a convenient way. Given the sample observations on y and x, we want to find values for the unknown parameters β_1 and β_2 that minimize the "sum of squares" function

$$S(\beta_1, \beta_2) = \sum_{i=1}^{N} (y_i - \beta_1 - \beta_2 x_i)^2$$

This is a straightforward calculus problem, the details of which are given in Appendix 2A, at the end of this chapter. The formulas for the least squares estimates of β_1 and β_2 that give the minimum of the sum of squared residuals are

---

THE LEAST SQUARES ESTIMATORS

$$b_2 = \frac{\sum(x_i - \bar{x})(y_i - \bar{y})}{\sum(x_i - \bar{x})^2} \qquad (2.7)$$

$$b_1 = \bar{y} - b_2\bar{x} \qquad (2.8)$$

---

where $\bar{y} = \sum y_i/N$ and $\bar{x} = \sum x_i/N$ are the sample means of the observations on y and x.

The formula for b_2 reveals why we had to assume [SR5] that the values of x_i were not the same value for all observations. If $x_i = 5$, for example, for all observations, then b_2 is mathematically undefined and does not exist since the numerator and denominator of (2.7) are zero!

If we plug the sample values y_i and x_i into (2.7) and (2.8), then we obtain the least squares *estimates* of the intercept and slope parameters β_1 and β_2. It is interesting, however, and very

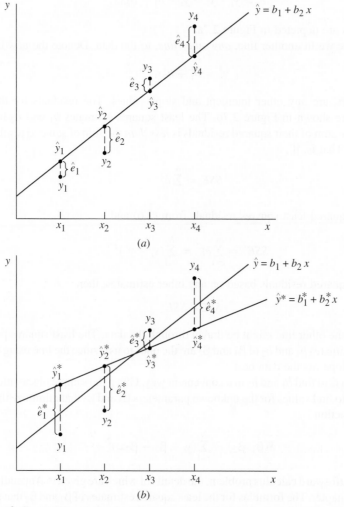

FIGURE 2.7 (*a*) The relationship among y, $\hat{e}$, and the fitted regression line. (*b*) The residuals from another fitted line.

important, that the formulas for b_1 and b_2 are perfectly general and can be used no matter what the sample values turn out to be. This should ring a bell. When the formulas for b_1 and b_2 are taken to be rules that are used whatever the sample data turn out to be, then b_1 and b_2 are random variables. When actual sample values are substituted into the formulas, we obtain numbers that are the observed values of random variables. To distinguish these two cases we call the rules or general formulas for b_1 and b_2 the **least squares estimators**. We call the numbers obtained when the formulas are used with a particular sample **least squares estimates**.

- Least squares *estimators* are general formulas and are *random variables*.
- Least squares *estimates* are numbers that we obtain by applying the general formulas to the observed data.

The distinction between *estimators* and *estimates* is a fundamental concept that is essential to understand everything in the rest of this book.

2.3.2 ESTIMATES FOR THE FOOD EXPENDITURE FUNCTION

Using the least squares estimators (2.7) and (2.8), we can obtain the least squares estimates for the intercept and slope parameters β_1 and β_2 in the food expenditure example using the data in Table 2.1. From (2.7), we have

$$b_2 = \frac{\Sigma(x_i - \bar{x})(y_i - \bar{y})}{\Sigma(x_i - \bar{x})^2} = \frac{18671.2684}{1828.7876} = 10.2096$$

and from (2.8)

$$b_1 = \bar{y} - b_2\bar{x} = 283.5735 - (10.2096)(19.6048) = 83.4160$$

A convenient way to report the values for b_1 and b_2 is to write out the *estimated* or *fitted* regression line, with the estimates rounded appropriately:

$$\hat{y}_i = 83.42 + 10.21x_i$$

This line is graphed in Figure 2.8. The line's slope is 10.21, and its intercept, where it crosses the vertical axis, is 83.42. The least squares fitted line passes through the middle of the data in a very precise way, since one of the characteristics of the fitted line based on the least squares parameter estimates is that it passes through the point defined by the sample means, $(\bar{x}, \bar{y}) = (19.6048, 283.5735)$. This follows directly from rewriting (2.8) as $\bar{y} = b_1 + b_2\bar{x}$. Thus the "point of the means" is a useful reference value in regression analysis.

2.3.3 INTERPRETING THE ESTIMATES

Once obtained, the least squares estimates are interpreted in the context of the economic model under consideration. The value $b_2 = 10.21$ is an estimate of β_2. Recall that x, weekly household income, is measured in $100 units. The regression slope β_2 is the amount by which expected weekly expenditure on food per household increases when household weekly income increases by $100. Thus, we estimate that if weekly household income goes up by $100, expected weekly expenditure on food will increase by approximately $10.21. A supermarket executive with information on likely changes in the income and the number

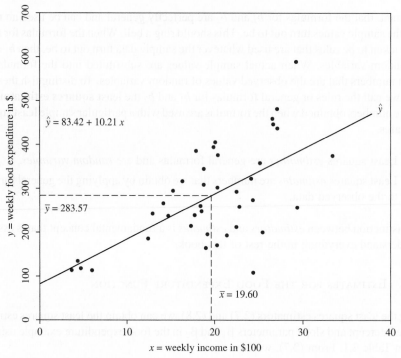

FIGURE 2.8 The fitted regression.

of households in an area could estimate that it will sell $10.21 more per typical household per week for every $100 increase in income. This is a very valuable piece of information for long-run planning.

Strictly speaking, the intercept estimate $b_1 = 83.42$ is an estimate of the weekly food expenditure for a household with zero income. In most economic models we must be very careful when interpreting the estimated intercept. The problem is that we usually do not have any data points near $x = 0$, something that is true for the food expenditure data shown in Figure 2.8. If we have no observations in the region where income is zero, then our estimated relationship may not be a good approximation to reality in that region. So, although our estimated model suggests that a household with zero income is expected to spend $83.42 per week on food, it might be risky to take this estimate literally. This is an issue that you should consider in each economic model that you estimate.

2.3.3a Elasticities
Income elasticity is a useful way to characterize the responsiveness of consumer expenditure to changes in income. See Appendix A.2.2 for a discussion of elasticity calculations in a linear relationship. The elasticity of a variable y with respect to another variable x is

$$\varepsilon = \frac{\text{percentage change in } y}{\text{percentage change in } x} = \frac{\Delta y/y}{\Delta x/x} = \frac{\Delta y}{\Delta x} \cdot \frac{x}{y}$$

In the linear economic model given by (2.1) we have shown that

$$\beta_2 = \frac{\Delta E(y)}{\Delta x}$$

so the elasticity of mean expenditure with respect to income is

$$\varepsilon = \frac{\Delta E(y)/E(y)}{\Delta x/x} = \frac{\Delta E(y)}{\Delta x} \cdot \frac{x}{E(y)} = \beta_2 \cdot \frac{x}{E(y)} \tag{2.9}$$

To estimate this elasticity we replace β_2 by $b_2 = 10.21$. We must also replace "x" and "$E(y)$" by something, since in a linear model the elasticity is different on each point upon the regression line. Most commonly the elasticity is calculated at the "point of the means" $(\bar{x}, \bar{y}) = (19.60, 283.57)$ because it is a representative point on the regression line. If we calculate the income elasticity at the point of the means we obtain

$$\hat{\varepsilon} = b_2 \, \frac{\bar{x}}{\bar{y}} = 10.21 \times \frac{19.60}{283.57} = 0.71$$

This *estimated* income elasticity takes its usual interpretation. We estimate that a 1% increase in weekly household income will lead, on average, to a 0.71% increase in weekly household expenditure on food, when x and y take their sample mean values, $(\bar{x}, \bar{y}) = (19.60, 283.57)$. Since the estimated income elasticity is less than one, we would classify food as a "necessity" rather than a "luxury," which is consistent with what we would expect for an average household.

2.3.3b Prediction
The estimated equation can also be used for prediction or forecasting purposes. Suppose that we wanted to predict weekly food expenditure for a household with a weekly income of $2,000. This prediction is carried out by substituting $x = 20$ into our estimated equation to obtain

$$\hat{y}_i = 83.42 + 10.21x_i = 83.42 + 10.21(20) = 287.61$$

We *predict* that a household with a weekly income of $2,000 will spend $287.61 per week on food.

2.3.3c Computer Output
Many different software packages can compute least squares estimates. Every software package's regression output looks different and uses different terminology to describe the output. Despite these differences, the various outputs provide the same basic information, which you should be able to locate and interpret. The matter is complicated somewhat by the fact that the packages also report various numbers whose meaning you may not know. For example, using the food expenditure data, the output from the software package EViews is shown in Figure 2.9.

In the EViews output the parameter estimates are in the "Coefficient" column, with names "C," for constant term (the estimate b_1), and *INCOME* (the estimate b_2). Software programs typically name the estimates with the name of the variable as assigned in the computer program (we named our variable *INCOME*) and an abbreviation for "constant." The estimates that we report in the text are rounded to two significant digits. The other numbers that you can recognize at this time are $SSE = \sum \hat{e}_i^2 = 304505.2$, which is called "Sum squared resid," and the sample mean of y, $\bar{y} = \sum y_i/N = 283.5735$, which is called "Mean dependent var."

We leave discussion of the rest of the output until later.

Dependent Variable: *FOOD_EXP*
Method: Least Squares
Sample: 1 40
Included observations: 40

	Coefficient	Std. Error	*t*-Statistic	Prob.
C	83.41600	43.41016	1.921578	0.0622
INCOME	10.20964	2.093264	4.877381	0.0000
R-squared	0.385002	Mean dependent var		283.5735
Adjusted R-squared	0.368818	S.D. dependent var		112.6752
S.E. of regression	89.51700	Akaike info criterion		11.87544
Sum squared resid	304505.2	Schwarz criterion		11.95988
Log likelihood	−235.5088	Hannan-Quinn criter		11.90597
F-statistic	23.78884	Durbin-Watson stat		1.893880
Prob(F-statistic)	0.000019			

FIGURE **2.9**   EViews regression output.

2.3.4   OTHER ECONOMIC MODELS

We have used the household expenditure on food versus income relationship as an example to introduce the ideas of simple regression. The simple regression model can be applied to estimate the parameters of many relationships in economics, business, and the social sciences. The applications of regression analysis are fascinating and useful. For example,

- If the hourly wage rate of electricians rises by 5%, how much will new house prices increase?
- If the cigarette tax increases by $1, how much additional revenue will be generated in the state of Louisiana?
- If the central banking authority raises interest rates by one-half a percentage point, how much will consumer borrowing fall within six months? How much will it fall within one year? What will happen to the unemployment rate in the months following the increase?
- If we increase funding on preschool education programs in 2012, what will be the effect on high school graduation rates in 2024? What will be the effect on the crime rate by juveniles in 2019 and subsequent years?

The range of applications spans economics and finance, as well as most disciplines in the social and physical sciences. Any time you ask **how much** a change in one variable will affect another variable, regression analysis is a potential tool.

2.4 Assessing the Least Squares Estimators

Using the food expenditure data we have estimated the parameters of the regression model $y_i = \beta_1 + \beta_2 x_i + e_i$ using the least squares formulas in (2.7) and (2.8). We obtained the least squares estimates $b_1 = 83.42$ and $b_2 = 10.21$. It is natural, but, as we shall argue, misguided, to ask the question "How good are these estimates?" This question is not answerable. We will never know the true values of the population parameters β_1 or β_2, so we cannot say how close $b_1 = 83.42$ and $b_2 = 10.21$ are to the true values. The least squares estimates are numbers that may or may not be close to the true parameter values, and we will never know.

Rather than asking about the quality of the estimates we will take a step back and examine the quality of the least squares estimation procedure. The motivation for this approach is this: if we were to collect another sample of data, by choosing another set of 40 households to survey, we would have obtained *different* estimates b_1 and b_2, even if we had carefully selected households with the same incomes as in the initial sample. This **sampling variation** is unavoidable. Different samples will yield different estimates because household food expenditures, $y_i, i = 1, \ldots, 40$, are random variables. Their values are not known until the sample is collected. Consequently, when viewed as an estimation procedure, b_1 and b_2 are also random variables, because their values depend on the random variable y. In this context we call b_1 and b_2 the **least squares estimators**.

We can investigate the properties of the estimators b_1 and b_2, which are called their **sampling properties**, and deal with the following important questions:

1. If the least squares estimators b_1 and b_2 are random variables, then what are their expected values, variances, covariances, and probability distributions?

2. The least squares principle is only *one* way of using the data to obtain estimates of β_1 and β_2. How do the least squares estimators compare with other procedures that might be used, and how can we compare alternative estimators? For example, is there another estimator that has a higher probability of producing an estimate that is close to β_2?

The answers to these questions will depend critically on whether the assumptions SR1–SR5 are satisfied. In later chapters we will discuss how to check whether the assumptions we make hold in a specific application, and what we might do if one or more assumptions are shown not to hold.

> **REMARK:** We will summarize the properties of the least squares estimators in the next several sections. "Proofs" of important results appear in the appendices to this chapter. In many ways it is good to see these concepts in the context of a simpler problem before tackling them in the regression model. Appendix C covers the topics in this chapter, and the next, in the familiar and algebraically easier problem of estimating the mean of a population.

2.4.1 THE ESTIMATOR b_2

Formulas (2.7) and (2.8) are used to compute the least squares estimates b_1 and b_2. However, they are not well suited for examining theoretical properties of the estimators. In this section we rewrite the formula for b_2 to facilitate its analysis. In (2.7), b_2 is given by

$$b_2 = \frac{\sum (x_i - \bar{x})(y_i - \bar{y})}{\sum (x_i - \bar{x})^2}$$

This is called the **deviation from the mean form** of the estimator because the data have their sample means subtracted. Using assumption SR1 and a bit of algebra (Appendix 2C), we can write b_2 as a **linear estimator**,

$$b_2 = \sum_{i=1}^{N} w_i y_i \qquad (2.10)$$

where

$$w_i = \frac{x_i - \bar{x}}{\sum(x_i - \bar{x})^2} \qquad (2.11)$$

The term w_i depends only on x_i that are not random, so that w_i is not random either. Any estimator that is a weighted average of y_i's, as in (2.10), is called a **linear estimator**. This is an important classification that we will speak more of later. Then, with yet more algebra (Appendix 2D) we can express b_2 in a theoretically convenient way,

$$b_2 = \beta_2 + \sum w_i e_i \qquad (2.12)$$

where e_i is the random error in the linear regression model $y_i = \beta_1 + \beta_2 x_i + e_i$. This formula is not useful for computations, because it depends on β_2, which we do not know, and on the e_is, which are unobservable. However, for understanding the sampling properties of the least squares estimator, (2.12) is very useful.

2.4.2   THE EXPECTED VALUES OF b_1 AND b_2

The estimator b_2 is a random variable since its value is unknown until a sample is collected. What we will show is that if our model assumptions hold, then $E(b_2) = \beta_2$; that is, the expected value of b_2 is equal to the true parameter β_2. When the expected value of *any* estimator of a parameter equals the true parameter value, then that estimator is **unbiased**. Since $E(b_2) = \beta_2$, the least squares estimator b_2 is an unbiased estimator of β_2. The intuitive meaning of unbiasedness comes from the repeated sampling interpretation of mathematical expectation. If many samples of size N are collected, and the formula for b_2 is used to estimate β_2 in each of those samples, then if our assumptions are valid, the average value of the estimates b_2 obtained from all the samples will be β_2.

We will show that this result is true so that we can illustrate the part played by the assumptions of the linear regression model. In (2.12), what parts are random? The parameter β_2 is not random. It is a population parameter we are trying to estimate. If assumption SR5 holds, then x_i is not random. Then w_i is not random either, as it depends only on the values of x_i. The only random factors in (2.12) are the random error terms e_i. We can find the expected value of b_2 using the fact that the expected value of a sum is the sum of the expected values:

$$
\begin{aligned}
E(b_2) &= E(\beta_2 + \sum w_i e_i) = E(\beta_2 + w_1 e_1 + w_2 e_2 + \cdots + w_N e_N) \\
&= E(\beta_2) + E(w_1 e_1) + E(w_2 e_2) + \cdots + E(w_N e_N) \\
&= E(\beta_2) + \sum E(w_i e_i) \\
&= \beta_2 + \sum w_i E(e_i) = \beta_2
\end{aligned} \qquad (2.13)
$$

The rules of expected values are fully discussed in the Probability Primer, Section P.5, and Appendix B.1.1 at the end of the book. In the last line of (2.13) we use two assumptions. First, $E(w_i e_i) = w_i E(e_i)$, because w_i is not random, and constants can be factored out of expected values. Second, we have relied on the assumption that $E(e_i) = 0$. If $E(e_i) \neq 0$, then $E(b_2) \neq \beta_2$, in which case b_2 is a biased estimator of β_2. Recall that e_i contains, among other things, factors affecting y_i that are omitted from the economic model. If we have omitted anything that is important, we would expect that $E(e_i) \neq 0$ and $E(b_2) \neq \beta_2$. Thus, having an economic model that is correctly specified, in the sense that it includes all relevant explanatory variables, is a must in order for the least squares estimators to be unbiased.

The unbiasedness of the estimator b_2 is an important sampling property. When sampling repeatedly from a population the least squares estimator is "correct," on average, and this is one desirable property of an estimator. This statistical property by itself does not mean that b_2 is a good estimator of β_2, but it is part of the story. The unbiasedness property depends on having *many* samples of data from the same population. The fact that b_2 is unbiased does not imply *anything* about what might happen *in just one sample*. An individual estimate (a number) b_2 may be near to, or far from, β_2. Since β_2 is *never* known we will never know, given only one sample, whether our estimate is "close" to β_2 or not. Thus the estimate $b_2 = 10.21$ may be close to β_2 or not.

The least squares estimator b_1 of β_1 is also an unbiased estimator, and $E(b_1) = \beta_1$ if the model assumptions hold.

2.4.3 REPEATED SAMPLING

To illustrate the concept of unbiased estimation in a slightly different way, we present in Table 2.2 least squares estimates of the food expenditure model from 10 random samples (*table2_2.dat*) of size $N = 40$ from the same population with the same incomes as the households given in Table 2.1. In practice we would use all available observations in one big sample of size 400 to estimate the regression model. Here we have broken up the data into samples of size 40 to illustrate **repeated sampling** properties. Note the variability of the least squares parameter estimates from sample to sample. This **sampling variation** is due to the fact that we obtained 40 *different* households in each sample, and their weekly food expenditure varies randomly.

The property of unbiasedness is about the *average* values of b_1 and b_2 if *many* samples of the same size are drawn from the same population. The average value of b_1 in these 10 samples is $\bar{b}_1 = 78.74$. The average value of b_2 is $\bar{b}_2 = 9.68$. If we took the averages of estimates from many samples, these averages would approach the true parameter values β_1 and β_2. Unbiasedness does not say that an estimate from any one sample is close to the true parameter value, and thus we cannot say that an *estimate* is unbiased. We can say that the least squares estimation procedure (or the least squares estimator) is unbiased.

Ta b l e 2 . 2 **Estimates from 10 Samples**

Sample	b_1	b_2
1	131.69	6.48
2	57.25	10.88
3	103.91	8.14
4	46.50	11.90
5	84.23	9.29
6	26.63	13.55
7	64.21	10.93
8	79.66	9.76
9	97.30	8.05
10	95.96	7.77

2.4.4 THE VARIANCES AND COVARIANCE OF b_1 AND b_2

Table 2.2 shows that the least squares estimates of β_1 and β_2 vary from sample to sample. Understanding this variability is a key to assessing the reliability and sampling precision of an estimator. We now obtain the variances and covariance of the estimators b_1 and b_2. Before presenting the expressions for the variances and covariance, let us consider why they are important to know. The variance of the random variable b_2 is the average of the squared distances between the possible values of the random variable and its mean, which we now know is $E(b_2) = \beta_2$. The variance of b_2 is defined as

$$\text{var}(b_2) = E[b_2 - E(b_2)]^2$$

It measures the spread of the probability distribution of b_2. In Figure 2.10 are graphs of two possible probability distributions of b_2, $f_1(b_2)$ and $f_2(b_2)$, that have the same mean value but different variances.

The probability density function $f_2(b_2)$ has a smaller variance than $f_1(b_2)$. Given a choice, we are interested in estimator precision and would prefer that b_2 have the *pdf* $f_2(b_2)$ rather than $f_1(b_2)$. With the distribution $f_2(b_2)$, the probability is more concentrated around the true parameter value β_2, giving, relative to $f_1(b_2)$, a higher probability of getting an estimate that is close to β_2. Remember, getting an estimate close to β_2 is our objective.

The variance of an estimator measures the *precision* of the estimator in the sense that it tells us how much the estimates can vary from sample to sample. Consequently, we often refer to the **sampling variance** or **sampling precision** of an estimator. The smaller the variance of an estimator is, the greater the sampling precision of that estimator. One estimator is more precise than another estimator if its sampling variance is less than that of the other estimator.

We will now present and discuss the variances and covariance of b_1 and b_2. Appendix 2E contains the derivation of the variance of the least squares estimator b_2. If the regression model assumptions SR1–SR5 are correct (assumption SR6 is not required), then the variances and covariance of b_1 and b_2 are

$$\text{var}(b_1) = \sigma^2 \left[\frac{\sum x_i^2}{N \sum (x_i - \bar{x})^2} \right] \tag{2.14}$$

$$\text{var}(b_2) = \frac{\sigma^2}{\sum (x_i - \bar{x})^2} \tag{2.15}$$

$$\text{cov}(b_1, b_2) = \sigma^2 \left[\frac{-\bar{x}}{\sum (x_i - \bar{x})^2} \right] \tag{2.16}$$

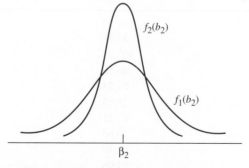

FIGURE 2.10 Two possible probability density functions for b_2.

At the beginning of this section we said that for unbiased estimators, smaller variances are better than larger variances. Let us consider the factors that affect the variances and covariance in (2.14)–(2.16).

1. The variance of the random error term, σ^2, appears in each of the expressions. It reflects the dispersion of the values y about their expected value $E(y)$. The greater the variance σ^2, the greater is that dispersion, and the greater is the uncertainty about where the values of y fall relative to their mean $E(y)$. When σ^2 is larger, the information we have about β_1 and β_2 is less precise. In Figure 2.3 the variance is reflected in the spread of the probability distributions $f(y|x)$. The *larger* the variance term σ^2, the *greater is* the uncertainty in the statistical model, and the *larger* the variances and covariance of the least squares estimators.

2. The sum of squares of the values of x about their sample mean, $\sum(x_i - \bar{x})^2$, appears in each of the variances and in the covariance. This expression measures how *spread out* about their mean are the sample values of the independent or explanatory variable x. The more they are spread out, the larger the sum of squares. The less they are spread out, the smaller the sum of squares. You may recognize this sum of squares as the numerator of the sample variance of the x-values. See Appendix C.4. The *larger* the sum of squares, $\sum(x_i - \bar{x})^2$, the *smaller* the variances of the least squares estimators and the more *precisely* we can estimate the unknown parameters. The intuition behind this is demonstrated in Figure 2.11. In panel (b) is a data scatter in which the values of x are widely spread out along the x-axis. In panel (a) the data are "bunched." Which data scatter would you prefer given the task of fitting a line by hand? Pretty clearly, the data in panel (b) do a better job of determining where the least squares line must fall, because they are more spread out along the x-axis.

3. The larger the sample size N, the *smaller* the variances and covariance of the least squares estimators; it is better to have *more* sample data than *less*. The sample size N appears in each of the variances and covariance because each of the sums consists of N terms. Also, N appears explicitly in $\mathrm{var}(b_1)$. The sum of squares term $\sum(x_i - \bar{x})^2$

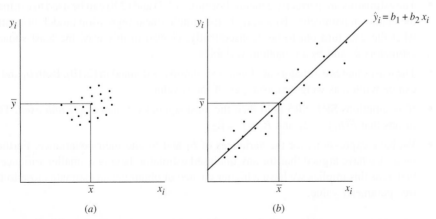

FIGURE 2.11   The influence of variation in the explanatory variable x on precision of estimation: (*a*) low x variation, low precision: (*b*) high x variation, high precision.

gets larger as N increases because each of the terms in the sum is positive or zero (being zero if x happens to equal its sample mean value for an observation). Consequently, as N gets larger, both $var(b_2)$ and $cov(b_1, b_2)$ get smaller, since the sum of squares appears in their denominator. The sums in the numerator and denominator of $var(b_1)$ both get larger as N gets larger and offset one another, leaving the N in the denominator as the dominant term, ensuring that $var(b_1)$ also gets smaller as N gets larger.

4. The term $\sum x_i^2$ appears in $var(b_1)$. The larger this term is, the larger the variance of the least squares estimator b_1. Why is this so? Recall that the intercept parameter β_1 is the expected value of y given that $x = 0$. The farther our data are from $x = 0$, the more difficult it is to interpret β_1, as in the food expenditure example, and the more difficult it is to accurately estimate β_1. The term $\sum x_i^2$ measures the squared distance of the data from the origin, $x = 0$. If the values of x are near zero then $\sum x_i^2$ will be small, and this will reduce $var(b_1)$. But if the values of x are large in magnitude, either positive or negative, the term $\sum x_i^2$ will be large and $var(b_1)$ will be larger, other things being equal.

5. The sample mean of the x-values appears in $cov(b_1, b_2)$. The absolute magnitude of the covariance *increases* with an increase in magnitude of the sample mean $\bar{x}$, and the covariance has a *sign* opposite to that of $\bar{x}$. The reasoning here can be seen from Figure 2.11. In panel (b) the least squares fitted line must pass through the point of the means. Given a fitted line through the data, imagine the effect of increasing the estimated slope b_2. Since the line must pass through the point of the means, the effect must be to lower the point where the line hits the vertical axis, implying a reduced intercept estimate b_1. Thus, when the sample mean is positive, as shown in Figure 2.11, there is a negative covariance between the least squares estimators of the slope and intercept.

2.5 The Gauss–Markov Theorem

What can we say about the least squares estimators b_1 and b_2 so far?

- The estimators are perfectly general. Formulas (2.7) and (2.8) can be used to estimate the unknown parameters β_1 and β_2 in the simple linear regression model, no matter what the data turn out to be. Consequently, viewed in this way, the least squares estimators b_1 and b_2 are random variables.

- The least squares estimators are *linear* estimators, as defined in (2.10). Both b_1 and b_2 can be written as weighted averages of the y_i values.

- If assumptions SR1–SR5 hold then the least squares estimators are *unbiased*. This means that $E(b_1) = \beta_1$ and $E(b_2) = \beta_2$.

- We have expressions for the variances of b_1 and b_2 and their covariance. Furthermore, we have argued that for any unbiased estimator, having a smaller variance is better, as this implies we have a higher chance of obtaining an estimate close to the true parameter value.

Now we will state and discuss the famous Gauss–Markov theorem, which is proven in Appendix 2F.

> **GAUSS–MARKOV THEOREM:** Under the assumptions SR1–SR5 of the linear regression model, the estimators b_1 and b_2 have the smallest variance of all linear and unbiased estimators of β_1 and β_2. They are the **best linear unbiased estimators (BLUE)** of β_1 and β_2.

Let us clarify what the Gauss–Markov theorem does, and does not, say.

1. The estimators b_1 and b_2 are "best" when compared to similar estimators, those that are linear and unbiased. The theorem does *not* say that b_1 and b_2 are the best of all *possible* estimators.

2. The estimators b_1 and b_2 are best within their class because they have the minimum variance. When comparing two linear and unbiased estimators, we *always* want to use the one with the smaller variance, since that estimation rule gives us the higher probability of obtaining an estimate that is close to the true parameter value.

3. In order for the Gauss–Markov theorem to hold, assumptions SR1–SR5 must be true. If any of these assumptions are *not* true, then b_1 and b_2 are *not* the best linear unbiased estimators of β_1 and β_2.

4. The Gauss–Markov theorem does *not* depend on the assumption of normality (assumption SR6).

5. In the simple linear regression model, if we want to use a linear and unbiased estimator, then we have to do no more searching. The estimators b_1 and b_2 are the ones to use. This explains why we are studying these estimators (we would not have you study *bad* estimation rules, would we?) and why they are so widely used in research, not only in economics but in all social and physical sciences as well.

6. The Gauss–Markov theorem applies to the least squares estimators. It *does not* apply to the least squares *estimates* from a single sample.

2.6 The Probability Distributions of the Least Squares Estimators

The properties of the least squares estimators that we have developed so far do not depend in any way on the normality assumption SR6. If we also make this assumption, that the random errors e_i are normally distributed with mean zero and variance σ^2, then the probability distributions of the least squares estimators are also normal. This conclusion is obtained in two steps. First, based on assumption SR1, if e_i is normal then so is y_i. Second, the least squares estimators are linear estimators, of the form $b_2 = \Sigma w_i y_i$, and sums of normal random variables are normally distributed themselves. Consequently, *if* we make the normality assumption (assumption SR6 about the error term), then the least squares estimators are normally distributed.

$$b_1 \sim N\left(\beta_1, \frac{\sigma^2 \Sigma x_i^2}{N\Sigma(x_i - \bar{x})^2}\right) \tag{2.17}$$

$$b_2 \sim N\left(\beta_2, \frac{\sigma^2}{\Sigma(x_i - \bar{x})^2}\right) \tag{2.18}$$

As you will see in Chapter 3, the normality of the least squares estimators is of great importance in many aspects of statistical inference.

What if the errors are not normally distributed? Can we say anything about the probability distribution of the least squares estimators? The answer is, sometimes, yes.

A CENTRAL LIMIT THEOREM: If assumptions SR1–SR5 hold, and if the sample size N is **sufficiently large**, then the least squares estimators have a distribution that approximates the normal distributions shown in (2.17) and (2.18).

The million-dollar question is "How large is sufficiently large?" The answer is that there is no specific number. The reason for this vague and unsatisfying answer is that "how large" depends on many factors, such as what the distributions of the random errors look like (are they smooth? symmetric? skewed?) and what the x_i values are like. In the simple regression model, some would say that $N = 30$ is sufficiently large. Others would say that $N = 50$ would be a more reasonable number. The bottom line is, however, that these are rules of thumb, and that the meaning of "sufficiently large" will change from problem to problem. Nevertheless, for better or worse, this *large sample*, or *asymptotic*, result is frequently invoked in regression analysis. This important result is an application of a central limit theorem, like the one discussed in Appendix C.3.4. If you are not familiar with this important theorem, you may want to review it now.

2.7 **Estimating the Variance of the Error Term**

The variance of the random error term, σ^2, is the one unknown parameter of the simple linear regression model that remains to be estimated. The variance of the random error e_i is

$$\text{var}(e_i) = \sigma^2 = E[e_i - E(e_i)]^2 = E(e_i^2)$$

if the assumption $E(e_i) = 0$ is correct. Since the "expectation" is an average value we might consider estimating σ^2 as the average of the squared errors,

$$\hat{\sigma}^2 = \frac{\sum e_i^2}{N}$$

This formula is unfortunately of no use since the random errors e_i are *unobservable*! However, although the random errors themselves are unknown, we do have an analog to them—namely, the least squares residuals. Recall that the random errors are

$$e_i = y_i - \beta_1 - \beta_2 x_i$$

From (2.6) the least squares residuals are obtained by replacing the unknown parameters by their least squares estimates:

$$\hat{e}_i = y_i - \hat{y}_i = y_i - b_1 - b_2 x_i$$

It seems reasonable to replace the random errors e_i by their analogs, the least squares residuals, so that

$$\hat{\sigma}^2 = \frac{\Sigma \hat{e}_i^2}{N}$$

This estimator, though quite satisfactory in large samples, is a *biased* estimator of σ^2. But there is a simple modification that produces an unbiased estimator:

$$\hat{\sigma}^2 = \frac{\Sigma \hat{e}_i^2}{N - 2} \qquad (2.19)$$

The 2 that is subtracted in the denominator is the number of *regression parameters* (β_1, β_2) in the model, and this subtraction makes the estimator $\hat{\sigma}^2$ unbiased, so that $E(\hat{\sigma}^2) = \sigma^2$.

2.7.1 ESTIMATING THE VARIANCES AND COVARIANCE OF THE LEAST SQUARES ESTIMATORS

Having an unbiased estimator of the error variance means we can *estimate* the variances of the least squares estimators b_1 and b_2, as well as the covariance between them. Replace the unknown error variance σ^2 in (2.14)–(2.16) with $\hat{\sigma}^2$ to obtain

$$\widehat{\text{var}(b_1)} = \hat{\sigma}^2 \left[\frac{\Sigma x_i^2}{N \Sigma (x_i - \bar{x})^2} \right] \qquad (2.20)$$

$$\widehat{\text{var}(b_2)} = \frac{\hat{\sigma}^2}{\Sigma (x_i - \bar{x})^2} \qquad (2.21)$$

$$\widehat{\text{cov}(b_1, b_2)} = \hat{\sigma}^2 \left[\frac{-\bar{x}}{\Sigma (x_i - \bar{x})^2} \right] \qquad (2.22)$$

The square roots of the estimated variances are the "standard errors" of b_1 and b_2. These quantities are used in hypothesis testing and confidence intervals. They are denoted as $\text{se}(b_1)$ and $\text{se}(b_2)$

$$\text{se}(b_1) = \sqrt{\widehat{\text{var}(b_1)}} \qquad (2.23)$$

$$\text{se}(b_2) = \sqrt{\widehat{\text{var}(b_2)}} \qquad (2.24)$$

2.7.2 CALCULATIONS FOR THE FOOD EXPENDITURE DATA

Let us make some calculations using the food expenditure data. The least squares estimates of the parameters in the food expenditure model are shown in Figure 2.9. First we will compute the least squares residuals from (2.6) and use them to calculate the estimate of the error variance in (2.19). In Table 2.3 are the least squares residuals for the first five households in Table 2.1.

Recall that we have estimated that for the food expenditure data the fitted least squares regression line is $\hat{y} = 83.42 + 10.21x$. For each observation we compute the least

Table 2.3   **Least Squares Residuals**

x	y	$\hat{y}$	$\hat{e} = y - \hat{y}$
3.69	115.22	121.09	−5.87
4.39	135.98	128.24	7.74
4.75	119.34	131.91	−12.57
6.03	114.96	144.98	−30.02
12.47	187.05	210.73	−23.68

squares residual $\hat{e}_i = y_i - \hat{y}_i$. Using the residuals for all $N = 40$ observations we estimate the error variance to be

$$\hat{\sigma}^2 = \frac{\Sigma \hat{e}_i^2}{N - 2} = \frac{304505.2}{38} = 8013.29$$

The numerator, 304505.2, is the sum of squared least squares residuals, reported as "Sum squared resid" in Figure 2.9. The denominator is the number of sample observations, $N = 40$, minus the number of estimated regression parameters, 2; the quantity $N - 2 = 38$ is often called the "degrees of freedom" for reasons that will be explained in Chapter 3. In Figure 2.9, the value $\hat{\sigma}^2$ is not reported. Instead, EViews software reports $\hat{\sigma} = \sqrt{\hat{\sigma}^2} = \sqrt{8013.29} = 89.517$, labeled "S.E. of regression," which stands for "standard error of the regression."

It is typical for software not to report the estimated variances and covariance unless requested. However, all software packages automatically report the standard errors. For example, in the EViews output shown in Figure 2.9 the column labeled "Std. Error" contains $se(b_1) = 43.410$ and $se(b_2) = 2.093$. The entry called "S.D. dependent var" is the sample standard deviation of y, that is $\left[\Sigma(y_i - \bar{y})^2/(N - 1)\right]^{1/2} = 112.6752$.

The full set of estimated variances and covariances for a regression is usually obtained by a simple computer command, or option, depending on the software being used. They are arrayed in a rectangular array, or matrix, with variances on the diagonal and covariances in the "off-diagonal" positions.

$$\begin{bmatrix} \widehat{var(b_1)} & \widehat{cov(b_1, b_2)} \\ \widehat{cov(b_1, b_2)} & \widehat{var(b_2)} \end{bmatrix}$$

For the food expenditure data the estimated covariance matrix of the least squares estimators is

	C	$INCOME$
C	1884.442	−85.90316
$INCOME$	−85.90316	4.381752

where C stands for the "constant term," which is the estimated intercept parameter in the regression, or b_1; similarly, the software reports the variable name $INCOME$ for the column relating to the estimated slope b_2. Thus

$$\widehat{var(b_1)} = 1884.442, \quad \widehat{var(b_2)} = 4.381752, \quad \widehat{cov(b_1, b_2)} = -85.90316$$

The standard errors are

$$se(b_1) = \sqrt{\widehat{\text{var}(b_1)}} = \sqrt{1884.442} = 43.410$$

$$se(b_2) = \sqrt{\widehat{\text{var}(b_2)}} = \sqrt{4.381752} = 2.093$$

These values will be used extensively in Chapter 3.

2.7.3 INTERPRETING THE STANDARD ERRORS

The standard errors of b_1 and b_2 are measures of the **sampling variability** of the least squares estimates b_1 and b_2 in **repeated samples**. As illustrated in Table 2.2, when we collect different samples of data the parameter estimates change from sample to sample. The estimators b_1 and b_2 are general formulas that are used whatever the sample data turns out to be. That is, the estimators are random variables. As such, they have probability distributions, means, and variances. In particular, if assumption SR6 holds, and the random error terms e_i are normally distributed, then $b_2 \sim N\left(\beta_2, \text{var}(b_2) = \sigma^2/\sum(x_i - \bar{x})^2\right)$. This probability density function $f(b_2)$ is shown in Figure 2.12.

The estimator variance, $\text{var}(b_2)$, or its square root $\sigma_{b_2} = \sqrt{\text{var}(b_2)}$, which we might call the true standard deviation of b_2, measure the sampling variation of the estimates b_2, and determine the width of the *pdf* in Figure 2.12. The bigger σ_{b_2} is the more variation in the least squares estimates b_2 we see from sample to sample. If σ_{b_2} is large then the estimates might change a great deal from sample to sample. The parameter σ_{b_2} would be a valuable number to know, because if it were large relative to the parameter β_2 we would know that the least squares estimator is not precise, and the estimate that we obtain may be far from the true value β_2 that we are trying to estimate. On the other hand, if σ_{b_2} is small relative to the parameter β_2, we know that the least squares estimate will fall near β_2 with high probability. Recall that for the normal distribution, 99.9% of values fall within the range of three standard deviations from the mean, so that 99.9% of the least squares estimates will fall in the range $\beta_2 - 3\sigma_{b_2}$ to $\beta_2 + 3\sigma_{b_2}$.

To put this in another context, in Table 2.2 we report estimates from 10 samples of data. We noted in Section 2.4.3 that the average values of those estimates are $\bar{b}_1 = 78.74$ and $\bar{b}_2 = 9.68$. The question we address with the standard error is "How much variation about their means do the estimates exhibit from sample to sample?" For those 10 samples the sample standard deviations are $std.dev.(b_1) = 30.80$ and $std.dev.(b_2) = 2.16$. What we would

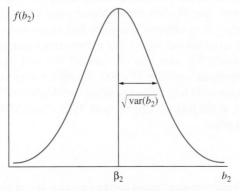

FIGURE **2.12** The probability density function of the least squares estimator b_2.

really like is the values of the standard deviations for a **very large** number of samples. Then we would know how much variation the least squares estimates exhibit from sample to sample. Unfortunately, we do not have a large number of samples, and because we do not know the true value of the variance of the error term σ^2 we cannot know the true value of σ_{b_2}.

Then what do we do? We estimate σ^2, and then estimate σ_{b_2} using

$$\text{se}(b_2) = \sqrt{\widehat{\text{var}(b_2)}} = \sqrt{\frac{\hat{\sigma}^2}{\Sigma(x_i - \bar{x})^2}}$$

The standard error of b_2 is thus an estimate of what the standard deviation of many estimates b_2 would be in a very large number of samples, and is an indicator of the width of the *pdf* of b_2 shown in Figure 2.12. Using our one sample of data, *food.dat*, the standard error of b_2 is 2.093, as shown in the computer output in Figure 2.9. This value is reasonably close to *std. dev.* $(b_2) = 2.16$ from the 10 samples in Table 2.2. To put this to a further test, in Appendix 2G we perform a simulation experiment, called a **Monte Carlo experiment**, in which we create many artificial samples to demonstrate the properties of the least squares estimator and how well se(b_2) reflects the true sampling variation in the estimates.

2.8 Estimating Nonlinear Relationships

The world is not linear. Economic variables are not always related by straight-line relationships; in fact, many economic relationships are represented by curved lines, and are said to display **curvilinear** forms. Fortunately, the simple linear regression model $y = \beta_1 + \beta_2 x + e$ is much more flexible than it looks at first glance, because the variables y and x can be transformations, involving logarithms, squares, cubes or reciprocals, of the basic economic variables, or they can be indicator variables that take only the values zero and one. Including these possibilities means the simple linear regression model can be used to account for nonlinear relationships between variables.[1]

Nonlinear relationships can sometimes be anticipated. Consider a model from real estate economics in which the price (*PRICE*) of a house is related to the house size measured in square feet (*SQFT*). As a starting point we might consider the linear relationship

$$PRICE = \beta_1 + \beta_2 SQFT + e \tag{2.25}$$

In this model, β_2 measures the increase in expected price given an additional square foot of living area. In the linear specification the expected price per additional square foot is constant. However it may be reasonable to assume that larger and more expensive homes have a higher value for an additional square foot of living area than smaller, less expensive, homes. How can we build this idea into our model? We will illustrate the use of two approaches: first, a **quadratic** equation in which the explanatory variable is $SQFT^2$; and second, a **log-linear** equation in which the dependent variable is ln (*PRICE*). In each case we will find that the slope of the relationship between *PRICE* and *SQFT* is not constant, but changes from point to point.

---

[1] The term **linear** in "linear regression" means that the parameters are not transformed in any way. In a linear regression model the parameters must not be raised to powers or transformed, so expressions like $\beta_1 \beta_2$ or $\beta_2^{\beta_1}$ are not permitted.

2.8.1 QUADRATIC FUNCTIONS

The quadratic function $y = a + bx^2$ is a parabola.[2] The y-intercept is a. The shape of the curve is determined by b; if $b > 0$, then the curve is U-shaped; and if $b < 0$, then the curve has an inverted-U shape. The slope of the function is given by the derivative[3] $dy/dx = 2bx$, which changes as x changes. The elasticity, or the percentage change in y given a 1% change in x, is $\varepsilon = slope \times x/y = 2bx^2/y$. If a and b are greater than zero, the curve resembles Figure 2.13.

2.8.2 USING A QUADRATIC MODEL

A **quadratic** model for house prices includes the **squared** value of *SQFT*, giving

$$PRICE = \alpha_1 + \alpha_2 SQFT^2 + e \tag{2.26}$$

This is a simple regression model, $y = \alpha_1 + \alpha_2 x + e$, with $y = PRICE$ and $x = SQFT^2$. Here we switch from using β to denote the parameters to using α, because the parameters of (2.26) are not comparable to the parameters of (2.25). In (2.25) β_2 is a slope, but α_2 is not a slope. Because $SQFT > 0$, the house price model will resemble the right side of the curve in Figure 2.13. Using ^ to denote estimated values, the least squares estimates $\hat{\alpha}_1$ and $\hat{\alpha}_2$, of α_1 and α_2, are calculated using the estimators in (2.7) and (2.8), just as before. The fitted equation is $\widehat{PRICE} = \hat{\alpha}_1 + \hat{\alpha}_2 SQFT^2$. It has slope

$$\frac{d\left(\widehat{PRICE}\right)}{dSQFT} = 2\hat{\alpha}_2 SQFT \tag{2.27}$$

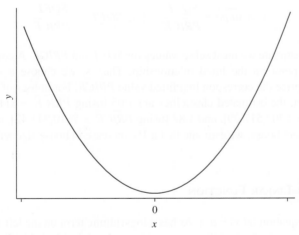

FIGURE *2.13*   A quadratic function.

---

[2] This is a special case of the more general quadratic function $y = a + bx + cx^2$.
[3] See Appendix A.3.1, Derivative Rules 1–5.

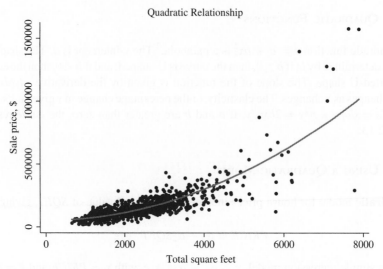

FIGURE **2.14**   A fitted quadratic relationship.

If $\hat{\alpha}_2 > 0$, then larger houses will have larger slope, and a larger estimated price per additional square foot.

The file *br.dat* contains data on 1080 houses sold in Baton Rouge, LA during mid-2005. Using these data the estimated quadratic equation is $\widehat{PRICE} = 55776.56 + 0.0154SQFT^2$. The data scatter and fitted quadratic relationship are shown in Figure 2.14.

The estimated slope is $\widehat{slope} = 2(0.0154)SQFT$ (estimated price per additional square foot), which for a 2000-square-foot house is \$61.69, for a 4000-square-foot house it is \$123.37, and for a 6000-square-foot house it is \$185.05. The elasticity of house price with respect to house size is the percentage increase in estimated price given a 1% increase in house size. Like the slope, the elasticity changes at each point. In our example

$$\hat{\varepsilon} = \widehat{slope} \times \frac{SQFT}{PRICE} = (2\hat{\alpha}_2 SQFT) \times \frac{SQFT}{PRICE}$$

To compute an estimate we must select values for *SQFT* and *PRICE*. A common approach is to choose a point on the fitted relationship. That is, we choose a value for *SQFT* and choose for price the corresponding fitted value $\widehat{PRICE}$. For houses of 2000, 4000 and 6000 square feet, the estimated elasticities are 1.05 [using $\widehat{PRICE} = \$117,461.77$], 1.63 [using $\widehat{PRICE} = \$302,517.39$], and 1.82 [using $\widehat{PRICE} = \$610,943.42$], respectively. For a 2000-square-foot house, we estimate that a 1% increase in house size will increase price by 1.05%.

2.8.3   A LOG-LINEAR FUNCTION

The log-linear equation $\ln(y) = a + bx$ has a logarithmic term on the left-hand side of the equation and an untransformed (linear) variable on the right-hand side. Both its slope and elasticity change at each point and are the same sign as b. Using the antilogarithm we see that $\exp[\ln(y)] = y = \exp(a + bx)$, so that the log-linear function is an exponential function. The function requires $y > 0$. The slope[4] at any point is $dy/dx = by$, which for $b > 0$ means that

---

[4] See Appendix A.3.1, Derivative Rule 7.

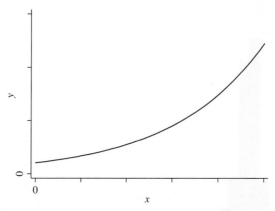

FIGURE **2.15** A log-linear function.

the marginal effect increases for larger values of y. An economist might say that this function is increasing at an increasing rate, as shown in Figure 2.15.

The elasticity, the percentage change in y given a 1% increase in x, at a point on this curve is $\varepsilon = slope \times x/y = bx$.

Using the slope expression, we can solve for a **semi-elasticity**, which tells us the percentage change in y given a 1-unit increase in x. Divide both sides of the slope dy/dx by y, then multiply by 100 to obtain

$$\eta = \frac{100(dy/y)}{dx} = 100b \tag{2.28}$$

In this expression the numerator $100(dy/y)$ is the percentage change in y; dx represents the change in x. If $dx = 1$, then a 1-unit change in x leads to a $100b$ percentage change in y. This interpretation can sometimes be quite handy.

2.8.4 Using a Log–Linear Model

The use of logarithms is very common in economic modeling. The **log-linear** model uses the logarithm of a variable as the dependent variable, and an independent, explanatory variable, that is not transformed, such as[5]

$$\ln(PRICE) = \gamma_1 + \gamma_2 SQFT + e \tag{2.29}$$

What effects does this have? First, the logarithmic transformation can regularize data that is skewed with a long tail to the right. In Figure 2.16(a) we show the histogram of $PRICE$ and in Figure 2.16(b) the histogram of $\ln(PRICE)$. The median house price in this sample is $130,000, and 95% of house prices are below $315,000, but there are 24 houses out of the 1080 with prices above $500,000, and an extreme value of $1,580,000. The extremely skewed distribution of $PRICE$ becomes more symmetric, if not bell-shaped, after taking the logarithm. Many economic variables, including prices, incomes, and wages, have skewed distributions, and the use of logarithms in models for such variables is common.

---

[5] Once again we use different symbols for the parameters of this model, γ_1 and γ_2, as a reminder that these parameters are not directly comparable to β's in (2.25) or α's in (2.26).

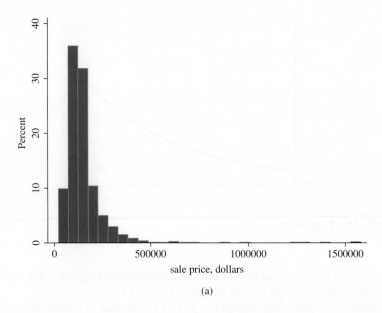

(a)

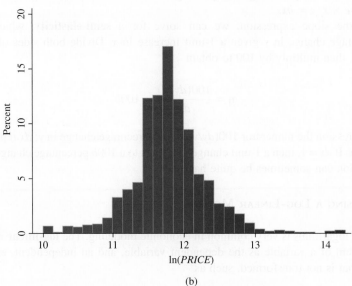

(b)

FIGURE 2.16 (a) Histogram of *PRICE* (b) Histogram of ln(*PRICE*).

Second, using a log-linear model allows us to fit regression curves like that shown in Figure 2.15. Using the Baton Rouge data, the fitted log-linear model is

$$\widehat{\ln(PRICE)} = 10.8386 + 0.0004113SQFT$$

To obtain predicted price take the anti-logarithm,[6] which is the exponential function

$$\widehat{PRICE} = \exp[\widehat{\ln(PRICE)}] = \exp(10.8386 + 0.0004113SQFT)$$

---

[6] In Chapter 4 we present an improved predictor for this model.

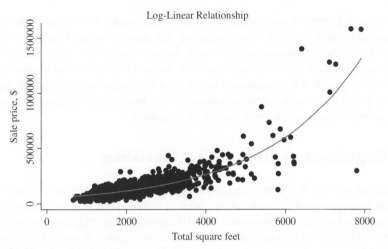

Log-Linear Relationship

FIGURE 2.17 The fitted log-linear model.

The fitted value of *PRICE* is shown in Figure 2.17.

The slope of the log-linear model is

$$\frac{d\left(\widehat{PRICE}\right)}{dSQFT} = \hat{\gamma}_2 \,\widehat{PRICE} = 0.0004113\widehat{PRICE}$$

For a house with a predicted *PRICE* of $100,000, the estimated increase in *PRICE* for an additional square foot of house area is $41.13, and for a house with a predicted *PRICE* of $500,000, the estimated increase in *PRICE* for an additional square foot of house area is $205.63. The estimated elasticity is $\hat{\varepsilon} = \hat{\gamma}_2 \, SQFT = 0.0004113SQFT$. For a house with 2000-square-feet, the estimated elasticity is 0.823: a 1% increase in house size is estimated to increase selling price by 0.823%. For a house with 4000 square feet, the estimated elasticity is 1.645: a 1% increase in house size is estimated to increase selling price by 1.645%. Using the "semi-elasticity" defined in (2.28) we can say that, for a one-square-foot increase in size, we estimate a price increase of 0.04%. Or, perhaps more usefully, we estimate that a 100-square-foot increase will increase price by approximately 4%.

2.8.5 CHOOSING A FUNCTIONAL FORM

For the Baton Rouge house price data, should we use the quadratic functional form, or the log-linear functional form? This is not an easy question. Economic theory tells us that house price should be related to the size of the house, and perhaps that larger, more expensive homes have a higher price per square foot of living area. But economic theory does not tell us what the exact algebraic form of the relationship should be. We should do our best to choose a functional form that is consistent with economic theory, that fits the data well, and that is such that the assumptions of the regression model are satisfied. In real-world problems it is sometimes difficult to achieve all these goals. Furthermore, we will never truly know the correct functional relationship, no matter how many years we study econometrics. The truth is out there, but we will never know it. In applications of econometrics we must simply do the best we can to choose a satisfactory functional form.

At this point we mention one dimension of the problem used for evaluating models with the same dependent variable. By comparing the sum of squared residuals (*SSE*) of alternative models, or, equivalently, $\hat{\sigma}^2$ or $\hat{\sigma}$, we can choose the model that is a better fit to the data. Smaller values of these quantities mean a smaller sum of squared residuals and a better model fit. This comparison is **not** valid for comparing models with dependent variables y and $\ln(y)$, or when other aspects of the models are different. We study the choice among functions like these further in Chapter 4.

2.9 Regression with Indicator Variables

An indicator variable is a binary variable that takes the values zero or one; it is used to represent a nonquantitative characteristic, such as gender, race, or location. For example, in the data file *utown.dat* we have a sample of 1000 observations on house prices (*PRICE*, in thousands of dollars) in two neighborhoods. One neighborhood is near a major university and called University Town. Another similar neighborhood, called Golden Oaks, is a few miles away from the university. The indicator variable of interest is

$$UTOWN = \begin{cases} 1 & \text{house is in University Town} \\ 0 & \text{house is in Golden Oaks} \end{cases}$$

The histograms of the prices in these two neighborhoods, shown in Figure 2.18, are revealing. The mean of the distribution of house prices in University Town appears to be larger than the mean of the distribution of house prices from Golden Oaks. The sample mean of the 519 house prices in University Town is 277.2416, whereas the sample mean of the 481 Golden Oaks houses is 215.7325.

If we include *UTOWN* in a regression model as an explanatory variable, what do we have? The simple regression model is

$$PRICE = \beta_1 + \beta_2 UTOWN + e$$

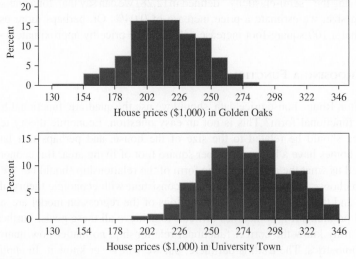

FIGURE 2.18 Distributions of house prices.

If the regression assumptions SR1–SR5 hold, then the least squares estimators in (2.7) and (2.8) can be used to estimate the unknown parameters β_1 and β_2.

When an indicator variable is used in a regression, it is important to write out the regression function for the different values of the indicator variable.

$$E(PRICE) = \beta_1 + \beta_2\, UTOWN = \begin{cases} \beta_1 + \beta_2 & \text{if } UTOWN = 1 \\ \beta_1 & \text{if } UTOWN = 0 \end{cases}$$

In this case, we find that the "regression function" reduces to a model that implies that the population mean house prices in the two subdivisions are different. The parameter β_2 is not a slope in this model. Here β_2 is the difference between the population means for house prices in the two neighborhoods. The expected price in University Town is $\beta_1 + \beta_2$, and the expected price in Golden Oaks is β_1. In our model there are no factors other than location affecting price, and the indicator variable splits the observations into two populations.

The estimated regression is

$$\widehat{PRICE} = b_1 + b_2 UTOWN = 215.7325 + 61.5091\, UTOWN$$

$$= \begin{cases} 277.2416 & \text{if } UTOWN = 1 \\ 215.7325 & \text{if } UTOWN = 0 \end{cases}$$

We see that the estimated price for the houses in University Town is \$277,241.60, which is also the sample mean of the house prices in University Town. The estimated price for houses outside University Town is \$215,732.50, which is the sample mean of house prices in Golden Oaks.

In the regression model approach we estimate the regression intercept β_1, which is the expected price for houses in Golden Oaks, where $UTOWN = 0$, and the parameter β_2 which is the difference between the population means for house prices in the two neighborhoods. The least squares estimators b_1 and b_2 in this indicator variable regression can be shown to be

$$b_1 = \overline{PRICE}_{\text{Golden Oaks}}$$
$$b_2 = \overline{PRICE}_{\text{University Town}} - \overline{PRICE}_{\text{Golden Oaks}}$$

where $\overline{PRICE}_{\text{Golden Oaks}}$ is the sample mean (average) price of houses in Golden Oaks and $\overline{PRICE}_{\text{University Town}}$ is the sample mean price of houses from University Town.

In the simple regression model, an indicator variable on the right-hand side gives us a way to estimate the differences between population means. This is a common problem in statistics, and the direct approach using samples means is discussed in Appendix C.7.2. Indicator variables are used in regression analysis very frequently in many creative ways. See Chapter 7 for a full discussion.

2.10 Exercises

Answers to exercises marked * appear on the web page www.wiley.com/go/global/hill.

2.10.1 PROBLEMS

2.1 Consider the following five observations. You are to do all the parts of this exercise using only a calculator.

x	y	$x - \bar{x}$	$(x - \bar{x})^2$	$y - \bar{y}$	$(x - \bar{x})(y - \bar{y})$
0	6				
1	5				
2	3				
3	1				
4	0				
$\sum x_i =$	$\sum y_i =$	$\sum (x_i - \bar{x}) =$	$\sum (x_i - \bar{x})^2 =$	$\sum (y_i - \bar{y}) =$	$\sum (x_i - \bar{x})(y_i - \bar{y}) =$

(a) Complete the entries in the table. Put the sums in the last row. What are the sample means $\bar{x}$ and $\bar{y}$?

(b) Calculate b_1 and b_2 using (2.7) and (2.8) and state their interpretation.

(c) Compute $\sum_{i=1}^{5} x_i^2$, $\sum_{i=1}^{5} x_i y_i$. Using these numerical values, show that

$$\sum (x_i - \bar{x})^2 = \sum x_i^2 - N\bar{x}^2 \quad \text{and} \quad \sum (x_i - \bar{x})(y_i - \bar{y}) = \sum x_i y_i - N\overline{xy}$$

(d) Use the least squares estimates from part (b) to compute the fitted values of y, and complete the remainder of the table below. Put the sums in the last row.

x_i	y_i	$\hat{y}_i$	$\hat{e}_i$	$\hat{e}_i^2$	$x_i \hat{e}_i$
0	6				
1	5				
2	3				
3	1				
4	0				
$\sum x_i =$	$\sum y_i =$	$\sum \hat{y}_i =$	$\sum \hat{e}_i =$	$\sum \hat{e}_i^2 =$	$\sum x_i \hat{e}_i =$

(e) On graph paper, plot the data points and sketch the fitted regression line $\hat{y}_i = b_1 + b_2 x_i$.

(f) On the sketch in part (e), locate the point of the means $(\bar{x}, \bar{y})$. Does your fitted line pass through that point? If not, go back to the drawing board, literally.

(g) Show that for these numerical values $\bar{y} = b_1 + b_2 \bar{x}$.

(h) Show that for these numerical values $\bar{\hat{y}} = \bar{y}$, where $\bar{\hat{y}} = \sum \hat{y}_i / N$.

(i) Compute $\hat{\sigma}^2$.

(j) Compute $\widehat{\text{var}(b_2)}$.

2.2 A household has weekly income of \$2,000. The mean weekly expenditure for households with this income is $E(y|x = \$2,000) = \mu_{y|x=\$2,000} = \$200$, and expenditures exhibit variance $\text{var}(y|x = \$2,000) = \sigma^2_{y|x=\$2,000} = 100$.

(a) Assuming that weekly food expenditures are normally distributed, find the probability that a household with this income spends between \$180 and \$215 on food in a week. Include a sketch with your solution.

(b) Find the probability that a household with this income spends more than \$250 on food in a week. Include a sketch with your solution.

(c) Find the probability in part (a) if the variance of weekly expenditures is $\text{var}(y|x = \$2,000) = \sigma^2_{y|x=\$2,000} = 81$.

(d) Find the probability in part (b) if the variance of weekly expenditures is $\text{var}(y|x = \$2,000) = \sigma^2_{y|x=\$2,000} = 81$.

2.3* Graph the following observations of x and y on graph paper.

x	1	2	3	4	5	6
y	10	8	5	5	2	3

(a) Using a ruler, draw a line that fits through the data. Measure the slope and intercept of the line you have drawn.

(b) Use formulas (2.7) and (2.8) to compute, using only a hand calculator, the least squares estimates of the slope and the intercept. Plot this line on your graph.

(c) Obtain the sample means of $\bar{y} = \sum y_i/N$ and $\bar{x} = \sum x_i/N$. Obtain the predicted value of y for $x = \bar{x}$ and plot it on your graph. What do you observe about this predicted value?

(d) Using the least squares estimates from (b), compute the least squares residuals $\hat{e}_i$. Find their sum.

(e) Calculate $\sum x_i \hat{e}_i$.

2.4 We have defined the simple linear regression model to be $y = \beta_1 + \beta_2 x + e$. Suppose however that we knew, for a fact, that $\beta_1 = 0$.

(a) What does the linear regression model look like, algebraically, if $\beta_1 = 0$?

(b) What does the linear regression model look like, graphically, if $\beta_1 = 0$?

(c) If $\beta_1 = 0$ the least squares "sum of squares" function becomes $S(\beta_2) = \sum_{i=1}^{N} (y_i - \beta_2 x_i)^2$. Using the data,

x	1	2	3	4	5	6
y	4	6	7	7	9	11

plot the value of the sum of squares function for enough values of β_2 for you to locate the approximate minimum. What is the significance of the value of β_2 that minimizes $S(\beta_2)$? (*Hint*: Your computations will be simplified if you algebraically expand $S(\beta_2) = \sum_{i=1}^{N} (y_i - \beta_2 x_i)^2$ by squaring the term in parentheses and carrying the summation operator through.)

(d)◆ Using calculus, show that the formula for the least squares estimate of β_2 in this model is $b_2 = \sum x_i y_i / \sum x_i^2$. Use this result to compute b_2 and compare this value to the value you obtained geometrically.

(e) Using the estimate obtained with the formula in (d), plot the fitted (estimated) regression function. On the graph locate the point $(\bar{x}, \bar{y})$. What do you observe?

(f) Using the estimates obtained with the formula in (d), obtain the least squares residuals, $\hat{e}_i = y_i - b_2 x_i$. Find their sum.

(g) Calculate $\sum x_i \hat{e}_i$.

2.5 A small business hires a consultant to predict the value of weekly sales of their product if their weekly advertising is increased to $750 per week. The consultant takes a record of how much the firm spent on advertising per week and the corresponding weekly sales over the past six months. The consultant writes "Over the past six months the average weekly expenditure on advertising has been $500 and average weekly sales have been $10,000. Based on the results of a simple linear regression, I predict sales will be $12,000 if $750 per week is spent on advertising."

(a) What is the estimated simple regression used by the consultant to make this prediction?

(b) Sketch a graph of the estimated regression line. Locate the average weekly values on the graph.

2.6* A soda vendor at Louisiana State University football games observes that more sodas are sold the warmer the temperature at game time is. Based on 32 home games covering five years, the vendor estimates the relationship between soda sales and temperature to be $\hat{y} = -240 + 8x$, where $y =$ the number of sodas she sells and $x =$ temperature in degrees Fahrenheit,

(a) Interpret the estimated slope and intercept. Do the estimates make sense? Why, or why not?

(b) On a day when the temperature at game time is forecast to be 80°F, predict how many sodas the vendor will sell.

(c) Below what temperature are the predicted sales zero?

(d) Sketch a graph of the estimated regression line.

2.7 You have the results of a simple linear regression based on state-level data and the District of Columbia, a total of $N = 52$ observations.

(a) The estimated error variance $\hat{\sigma}^2 = 2.04672$. What is the sum of the squared least squares residuals?

(b) The estimated variance of b_2 is 0.00088. What is the standard error of b_2? What is the value of $\sum(x_i - \bar{x})^2$?

(c) Suppose the dependent variable $y_i =$ the state's mean income (in thousands of dollars) of males who are 18 years of age or older and x_i the percentage of males 18 years or older who are high school graduates. If $b_2 = 0.15$, interpret this result.

(d) Suppose $\bar{x} = 68.143$ and $\bar{y} = 14.071$, what is the estimate of the intercept parameter?

(e) Given the results in (b) and (d), what is $\sum x_i^2$?

(f) For the state of Arkansas the value of $y_i = 12.274$ and the value of $x_i = 58.3$. Compute the least squares residual for Arkansas. (*Hint*: Use the information in parts (c) and (d).).

2.8♦ Professor E.Z. Stuff has decided that the least squares estimator is too much trouble. Noting that two points determine a line, Dr. Stuff chooses two points from a sample of size N and draws a line between them, calling the slope of this line the EZ estimator of β_2 in the simple regression model. Algebraically, if the two points are (x_1, y_1) and (x_2, y_2), the EZ estimation rule is

$$b_{EZ} = \frac{y_2 - y_1}{x_2 - x_1}$$

Assuming that all the assumptions of the simple regression model hold:

(a) Show that b_{EZ} is a "linear" estimator.

(b) Show that b_{EZ} is an unbiased estimator.

(c) Find the variance of b_{EZ}.

(d) Find the probability distribution of b_{EZ}.

(e) Convince Professor Stuff that the EZ estimator is not as good as the least squares estimator. No proof is required here.

2.10.2 COMPUTER EXERCISES

2.9* The owners of a motel discovered that a defective product was used in its construction. It took seven months to correct the defects, during which 14 rooms in the

100-unit motel were taken out of service for 1 month at a time. The motel lost profits due to these closures, and the question of how to compute the losses was addressed by Adams (2008).[7] For this exercise use the data in *motel.dat*.

(a) The occupancy rate for the damaged motel is *MOTEL_PCT*, and the competitor occupancy rate is *COMP_PCT*. On the same graph, plot these variables against *TIME*. Which had the higher occupancy before the repair period? Which had the higher occupancy during the repair period?

(b) Plot *MOTEL_PCT* against *COMP_PCT*. Does there seem to be a relationship between these two variables? Explain why such a relationship might exist.

(c) Estimate a linear regression with $y = MOTEL\_PCT$ and $x = COMP\_PCT$. Discuss the result.

(d) Compute the least squares residuals from the regression results in (c). Plot these residuals against time. Does the model overpredict, underpredict, or accurately predict the motel's occupancy rate during the repair period?

(e) Consider a linear regression with $y = MOTEL\_PCT$ and $x = RELPRICE$, which is the ratio of the price per room charged by the motel in question relative to its competitors. What sign do you predict for the slope coefficient? Why? Does the sign of the estimated slope agree with your expectation?

(f) Consider the linear regression with $y = MOTEL\_PCT$ and $x = REPAIR$, which is an indicator variable, taking the value 1 during the repair period and 0 otherwise. Discuss the interpretation of the least squares estimates. Does the motel appear to have suffered a loss of occupancy, and therefore profits, during the repair period?

(g) Compute the average occupancy rate for the motel and competitors when the repairs were not being made (call these $\overline{MOTEL_0}$ and $\overline{COMP_0}$), and when they were being made ($\overline{MOTEL_1}$ and $\overline{COMP_1}$). During the nonrepair period, what was the difference between the average occupancies, $\overline{MOTEL_0} - \overline{COMP_0}$? Does this comparison seem to support the motel's claims of lost profits during the repair period?

(h) Estimate a linear regression model with $y = MOTEL\_PCT - COMP\_PCT$ and $x = REPAIR$. How do the results of this regression relate to the result in part (g)?

2.10 The capital asset pricing model (CAPM) is an important model in the field of finance. It explains variations in the rate of return on a security as a function of the rate of return on a portfolio consisting of all publicly traded stocks, which is called the *market* portfolio. Generally the rate of return on any investment is measured relative to its opportunity cost, which is the return on a risk free asset. The resulting difference is called the *risk premium*, since it is the reward or punishment for making a risky investment. The CAPM says that the risk premium on security j is *proportional* to the risk premium on the market portfolio. That is,

$$r_j - r_f = \beta_j(r_m - r_f),$$

where r_j and r_f are the returns to security j and the risk-free rate, respectively, r_m is the return on the market portfolio, and β_j is the jth security's "*beta*" value. A stock's *beta* is important to investors since it reveals the stock's volatility. It measures the sensitivity of security j's return to variation in the whole stock market. As such, values of *beta* less than 1 indicate that the stock is "defensive" since its variation is

[7] A. Frank Adams (2008) "When a 'Simple' Analysis Won't Do: Applying Economic Principles in a Lost Profits Case," *The Value Examiner*, May/June 2008, 22–28. The authors thank Professor Adams for the use of his data.

less than the market's. A *beta* greater than 1 indicates an "aggressive stock." Investors usually want an estimate of a stock's *beta* before purchasing it. The CAPM model shown above is the "economic model" in this case. The "econometric model" is obtained by including an intercept in the model (even though theory says it should be zero) and an error term,

$$r_j - r_f = \alpha_j + \beta_j(r_m - r_f) + e$$

(a) Explain why the econometric model above is a simple regression model like those discussed in this chapter.

(b) In the data file *capm4.dat* are data on the monthly returns of six firms (Microsoft, GE, GM, IBM, Disney, and Mobil-Exxon), the rate of return on the market portfolio (*MKT*), and the rate of return on the risk free asset (*RISKFREE*). The 132 observations cover January 1998 to December 2008. Estimate the CAPM model for each firm, and comment on their estimated *beta* values. Which firm appears most aggressive? Which firm appears most defensive?

(c) Finance theory says that the intercept parameter α_j should be zero. Does this seem correct given your estimates? For the Microsoft stock, plot the fitted regression line along with the data scatter.

(d) Estimate the model for each firm under the assumption that $\alpha_j = 0$. Do the estimates of the *beta* values change much?

2.11 The file *br2.dat* contains data on 1080 houses sold in Baton Rouge, Louisiana, during mid-2005. The data include sale price, the house size in square feet, its age, whether it has a pool or fireplace or is on the waterfront. Also included is an indicator variable *TRADITIONAL* indicating whether the house style is traditional or not.[8] Variable descriptions are in the file *br2.def*.

(a) Plot house price against house size for houses with traditional style.

(b) For the traditional-style houses estimate the linear regression model $PRICE = \beta_1 + \beta_2 SQFT + e$. Interpret the estimates. Draw a sketch of the fitted line.

(c) For the traditional-style houses estimate the quadratic regression model $PRICE = \alpha_1 + \alpha_2 SQFT^2 + e$. Compute the marginal effect of an additional square foot of living area in a home with 1000 square feet of living space. Compute the elasticity of *PRICE* with respect to *SQFT* for a home with 1000 square feet of living space. Graph the fitted line. On the graph, sketch the line that is tangent to the curve for a 1000-square-foot house.

(d) For the regressions in (b) and (c) compute the least squares residuals and plot them against *SQFT*. Do any of our assumptions appear violated?

(e) One basis for choosing between these two specifications is how well the data are fit by the model. Compare the sum of squared residuals (*SSE*) from the models in (b) and (c). Which model has a lower *SSE*? How does having a lower *SSE* indicate a "better-fitting" model?

(f) For the traditional-style houses estimate the log-linear regression model $\ln(PRICE) = \gamma_1 + \gamma_2 SQFT + e$. Interpret the estimates. Graph the fitted line, and sketch the tangent line to the curve for a house with 1000 square feet of living area.

---

[8] The data file *br.dat* offers a wider range of style listings. Try this data set for a more detailed investigation of the effect of style.

(g) How would you compute the sum of squared residuals for the model in (f) to make it comparable to those from the models in (b) and (c)? Compare this sum of squared residuals to the *SSE* from the linear and quadratic specifications. Which model seems to fit the data best?

2.12* The file *stockton4.dat* contains data on 1500^9 houses sold in Stockton, CA during 1996–1998. Variable descriptions are in the file *stockton4.def*.

  (a) Plot house selling price against house living area for all houses in the sample.

  (b) Estimate the regression model $SPRICE = \beta_1 + \beta_2 LIVAREA + e$ for all the houses in the sample. Interpret the estimates. Draw a sketch of the fitted line.

  (c) Estimate the quadratic model $SPRICE = \alpha_1 + \alpha_2 LIVAREA^2 + e$ for all the houses in the sample. What is the marginal effect of an additional 100 square feet of living area for a home with 1500 square feet of living area?

  (d) In the same graph, plot the fitted lines from the linear and quadratic models. Which seems to fit the data better? Compare the sum of squared residuals (*SSE*) for the two models. Which is smaller?

  (e) Estimate the regression model in (c) using only houses that are on large lots. Repeat the estimation for houses that are not on large lots. Interpret the estimates. How do the estimates compare?

  (f) Plot house selling price against *AGE*. Estimate the linear model $SPRICE = \delta_1 + \delta_2 AGE + e$. Interpret the estimated coefficients. Repeat this exercise using the log-linear model $\ln(SPRICE) = \theta_1 + \theta_2 AGE + e$. Based on the plots and visual fit of the estimated regression lines, which of these two models would you prefer? Explain.

  (g) Estimate a linear regression $SPRICE = \eta_1 + \eta_2 LGELOT + e$ with dependent variable *SPRICE* and independent variable the indicator *LGELOT* which identifies houses on larger lots. Interpret these results.

2.13 A longitudinal experiment was conducted in Tennessee beginning in 1985 and ending in 1989. A single cohort of students was followed from kindergarten through third grade. In the experiment children were randomly assigned within schools into three types of classes: small classes with 13–17 students, regular-sized classes with 22–25 students, and regular-sized classes with a full-time teacher aide to assist the teacher. Student scores on achievement tests were recorded as well as some information about the students, teachers, and schools. Data for the kindergarten classes are contained in the data file *star.dat*.

  (a) Using children who are in either a regular-sized class or a small class, estimate the regression model explaining students' combined aptitude scores as a function of class size, $TOTALSCORE_i = \beta_1 + \beta_2 SMALL_i + e_i$. Interpret the estimates. Based on this regression result, what do you conclude about the effect of class size on learning?

  (b) Repeat part (a) using dependent variables *READSCORE* and *MATHSCORE*. Do you observe any differences?

  (c) Using children who are in either a regular-sized class or a regular-sized class with a teacher aide, estimate the regression model explaining student's combined aptitude scores as a function of the presence of a teacher aide, $TOTALSCORE = \gamma_1 + \gamma_2 AIDE + e$. Interpret the estimates. Based on this

---

[9] The data set *stockton3.dat* has 2,610 observations on these same variables.

regression result, what do you conclude about the effect on learning of adding a teacher aide to the classroom?

(d) Repeat part (c) using dependent variables *READSCORE* and *MATHSCORE*. Do you observe any differences?

2.14* Professor Ray C. Fair has for a number of years built and updated models that explain and predict the U.S. presidential elections. Visit his website at http://fairmodel.econ .yale.edu/vote2004/index2.htm. See in particular his paper entitled "A Vote Equation for the 2004 Election." The basic premise of the model is that the incumbent party's share of the two-party [Democratic and Republican] popular vote [incumbent means the party in power at the time of the election] is affected by a number of factors relating to the economy, and variables relating to the politics, such as how long the incumbent party has been in power, and whether the President is running for re-election. Fair's data, 33 observations for the election years from 1880 to 2008, are in the file *fair4.dat*. The dependent variable is *VOTE* = percentage share of the popular vote won by the incumbent party. Consider the explanatory variable *GROWTH* = growth rate in real per capita GDP in the first three quarters of the election year (annual rate). One would think that if the economy is doing well, and growth is high, the party in power would have a better chance of winning the election.

(a) Using the data for 1916–2008, plot a scatter diagram of *VOTE* against *GROWTH*. Does there appear to be positive association?

(b) Estimate the regression $VOTE = \beta_1 + \beta_2 GROWTH + e$ by least squares using the data from 1916 to 2008. Report and discuss the estimation result. Sketch, **by hand**, the fitted line on the data scatter from (a).

(c) Fit the regression in (b) using the data from 1916 to 2004. Predict the *VOTE* share for the incumbent party based on the actual 2008 value for *GROWTH*. How does the predicted vote for 2008 compare to the actual result?

(d) Economywide inflation may spell doom for the incumbent party in an election. The variable *INFLATION* is the growth in prices over the first 15 quarters of an administration. Using the data from 1916 to 2008, plot *VOTE* against *INFLATION*. Using the same sample, report and discuss the estimation results for the model $VOTE = \alpha_1 + \alpha_2 INFLATION + e$.

2.15 How much does education affect wage rates? The data file *cps4_small.dat* contains 1000 observations on hourly wage rates, education, and other variables from the 2008 Current Population Survey (CPS).

(a) Obtain the summary statistics and histograms for the variables *WAGE* and *EDUC*. Discuss the data characteristics.

(b) Estimate the linear regression $WAGE = \beta_1 + \beta_2 EDUC + e$ and discuss the results.

(c) Calculate the least squares residuals and plot them against *EDUC*. Are any patterns evident? If assumptions SR1–SR5 hold, should any patterns be evident in the least squares residuals?

(d) Estimate separate regressions for males, females, asians, and whites. Compare the results.

(e) Estimate the quadratic regression $WAGE = \alpha_1 + \alpha_2 EDUC^2 + e$ and discuss the results. Estimate the marginal effect of another year of education on wage for a person with 12 years of education, and for a person with 16 years of education. Compare these values to the estimated marginal effect of education from the linear regression in part (b).

(f) Plot the fitted linear model from part (b) and the fitted values from the quadratic model from part (e) in the same graph with the data on *WAGE* and *EDUC*. Which model appears to fit the data better?

(g) Construct a histogram of ln(*WAGE*). Compare the shape of this histogram to that for *WAGE* from part (a). Which appears more symmetric and bell-shaped?

(h) Estimate the log-linear regression $\ln(WAGE) = \gamma_1 + \gamma_2 EDUC + e$. Estimate the marginal effect of another year of education on wage for a person with 12 years of education, and for a person with 16 years of education. Compare these values to the estimated marginal effects of education from the linear regression in part (b) and the quadratic equation in part (e).

Appendix 2A Derivation of the Least Squares Estimates

Given the sample observations on y and x, we want to find values for the unknown parameters β_1 and β_2 that minimize the "sum of squares" function

$$S(\beta_1, \beta_2) = \Sigma_{i=1}^{N}(y_i - \beta_1 - \beta_2 x_i)^2 \tag{2A.1}$$

Since the points (y_i, x_i) have been observed, the sum of squares function S depends only on the unknown parameters β_1 and β_2. This function, which is a quadratic in terms of the unknown parameters β_1 and β_2, is a "bowl-shaped surface" like the one depicted in Figure 2A.1.

Our task is to find, out of all the possible values β_1 and β_2, the point (b_1, b_2) at which the sum of squares function S is a minimum. This minimization problem is a common one in calculus, and the minimizing point is at the "bottom of the bowl."

Those of you familiar with calculus and "partial differentiation" can verify that the partial derivatives of S with respect to β_1 and β_2 are

$$\frac{\partial S}{\partial \beta_1} = 2N\beta_1 - 2\Sigma y_i + 2(\Sigma x_i)\beta_2$$

$$\frac{\partial S}{\partial \beta_2} = 2(\Sigma x_i^2)\beta_2 - 2\Sigma x_i y_i + 2(\Sigma x_i)\beta_1 \tag{2A.2}$$

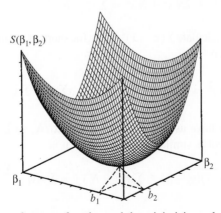

FIGURE $2A.1$ The sum of squares function and the minimizing values b_1 and b_2.

These derivatives are equations of the slope of the bowl-like surface in the directions of the axes. Intuitively, the "bottom of the bowl" occurs where the slope of the bowl, in the direction of each axis, $\partial S / \partial \beta_1$ and $\partial S / \partial \beta_2$, is zero.

Algebraically, to obtain the point (b_1, b_2) we set (2A.2) to zero and replace β_1 and β_2 by b_1 and b_2, respectively, to obtain

$$2[\Sigma y_i - Nb_1 - (\Sigma x_i)b_2] = 0$$

$$2[\Sigma x_i y_i - (\Sigma x_i)b_1 - (\Sigma x_i^2)b_2] = 0$$

Simplifying these gives equations usually known as the **normal equations**,

$$Nb_1 + (\Sigma x_i)b_2 = \Sigma y_i \tag{2A.3}$$

$$(\Sigma x_i)b_1 + (\Sigma x_i^2)b_2 = \Sigma x_i y_i \tag{2A.4}$$

These two equations have two unknowns b_1 and b_2. We can find the least squares estimates by solving these two linear equations for b_1 and b_2. To solve for b_2 multiply (2A.3) by Σx_i, multiply (2A.4) by N, then subtract the first equation from the second, and then isolate b_2 on the left-hand side.

$$b_2 = \frac{N \Sigma x_i y_i - \Sigma x_i \Sigma y_i}{N \Sigma x_i^2 - (\Sigma x_i)^2} \tag{2A.5}$$

This formula for b_2 is in terms of data sums, cross-products, and squares. The deviation from the mean form of the estimator is derived in Appendix 2B.

To solve for b_1, given b_2, divide both sides of (2A.3) by N and rearrange.

Appendix 2B Deviation from the Mean Form of b_2

The first step in the conversion of the formula for b_2 into (2.7) is to use some tricks involving summation signs. The first useful fact is that

$$\Sigma(x_i - \bar{x})^2 = \Sigma x_i^2 - 2\bar{x}\Sigma x_i + N\bar{x}^2 = \Sigma x_i^2 - 2\bar{x}\left(N\frac{1}{N}\Sigma x_i\right) + N\bar{x}^2$$
$$= \Sigma x_i^2 - 2N\bar{x}^2 + N\bar{x}^2 = \Sigma x_i^2 - N\bar{x}^2 \tag{2B.1}$$

Should you ever have to calculate $\Sigma(x_i - \bar{x})^2$, using the shortcut formula $\Sigma(x_i - \bar{x})^2 = \Sigma x_i^2 - N\bar{x}^2$ is much easier. Then

$$\Sigma(x_i - \bar{x})^2 = \Sigma x_i^2 - N\bar{x}^2 = \Sigma x_i^2 - \bar{x}\Sigma x_i = \Sigma x_i^2 - \frac{(\Sigma x_i)^2}{N} \tag{2B.2}$$

To obtain this result we have used the fact that $\bar{x} = \Sigma x_i / N$, so $\Sigma x_i = N\bar{x}$.

The second useful fact is similar to the first, and it is

$$\Sigma(x_i - \bar{x})(y_i - \bar{y}) = \Sigma x_i y_i - N\bar{x}\bar{y} = \Sigma x_i y_i - \frac{\Sigma x_i \Sigma y_i}{N} \tag{2B.3}$$

This result is proven in a similar manner.

If the numerator and denominator of b_2 in (2A.5) are divided by N, then using (2B.1)–(2B.3) we can rewrite b_2 in *deviation from the mean form* as

$$b_2 = \frac{\sum(x_i - \bar{x})(y_i - \bar{y})}{\sum(x_i - \bar{x})^2}$$

This formula for b_2 is one that you should remember, as we will use it time and time again in the next few chapters.

Appendix 2C b_2 Is a Linear Estimator

In order to derive (2.10) we make a further simplification using another property of sums. The sum of any variable about its average is zero; that is,

$$\sum(x_i - \bar{x}) = 0$$

Then, the formula for b_2 becomes

$$b_2 = \frac{\sum(x_i - \bar{x})(y_i - \bar{y})}{\sum(x_i - \bar{x})^2} = \frac{\sum(x_i - \bar{x})y_i - \bar{y}\sum(x_i - \bar{x})}{\sum(x_i - \bar{x})^2}$$

$$= \frac{\sum(x_i - \bar{x})y_i}{\sum(x_i - \bar{x})^2} = \sum\left[\frac{(x_i - \bar{x})}{\sum(x_i - \bar{x})^2}\right]y_i = \sum w_i y_i$$

where w_i is the constant given in (2.11).

Appendix 2D Derivation of Theoretical Expression for b_2

To obtain (2.12) replace y_i in (2.10) by $y_i = \beta_1 + \beta_2 x_i + e_i$ and simplify:

$$b_2 = \sum w_i y_i = \sum w_i(\beta_1 + \beta_2 x_i + e_i)$$

$$= \beta_1\sum w_i + \beta_2\sum w_i x_i + \sum w_i e_i$$

$$= \beta_2 + \sum w_i e_i$$

We used two more summation tricks to simplify this. First, $\sum w_i = 0$; this eliminates the term $\beta_1\sum w_i$. Secondly, $\sum w_i x_i = 1$, so $\beta_2\sum w_i x_i = \beta_2$, and (2.10) simplifies to (2.12).

The term $\sum w_i = 0$ because

$$\sum w_i = \sum\left[\frac{(x_i - \bar{x})}{\sum(x_i - \bar{x})^2}\right] = \frac{1}{\sum(x_i - \bar{x})^2}\sum(x_i - \bar{x}) = 0$$

where in the last step we used the fact that $\sum(x_i - \bar{x}) = 0$.

To show that $\sum w_i x_i = 1$ we again use $\sum(x_i - \bar{x}) = 0$. Another expression for $\sum(x_i - \bar{x})^2$ is

$$\sum(x_i - \bar{x})^2 = \sum(x_i - \bar{x})(x_i - \bar{x})$$

$$= \sum(x_i - \bar{x})x_i - \bar{x}\sum(x_i - \bar{x})$$

$$= \sum(x_i - \bar{x})x_i$$

Consequently,

$$\sum w_i x_i = \frac{\sum (x_i - \bar{x}) x_i}{\sum (x_i - \bar{x})^2} = \frac{\sum (x_i - \bar{x}) x_i}{\sum (x_i - \bar{x}) x_i} = 1$$

Appendix 2E Deriving the Variance of b_2

The starting point is (2.12), $b_2 = \beta_2 + \sum w_i e_i$. The least squares estimator is a random variable whose variance is defined to be

$$\text{var}(b_2) = E[b_2 - E(b_2)]^2$$

Substituting in (2.12) and using the unbiasedness of the least squares estimator, $E(b_2) = \beta_2$, we have

$$
\begin{aligned}
\text{var}(b_2) &= E(\beta_2 + \sum w_i e_i - \beta_2)^2 \\
&= E\left(\sum w_i e_i\right)^2 \\
&= E\left(\sum w_i^2 e_i^2 + 2\sum\sum_{i \neq j} w_i w_j e_i e_j\right) \qquad \text{(square of bracketed term)} \\
&= \sum w_i^2 E(e_i^2) + 2\sum\sum_{i \neq j} w_i w_j E(e_i e_j) \quad \text{(because } w_i \text{ not random)} \\
&= \sigma^2 \sum w_i^2 \\
&= \frac{\sigma^2}{\sum (x_i - \bar{x})^2}
\end{aligned}
$$

The next to last line is obtained by using two assumptions: First,

$$\sigma^2 = \text{var}(e_i) = E[e_i - E(e_i)]^2 = E(e_i - 0)^2 = E(e_i^2)$$

Second, $\text{cov}(e_i, e_j) = E[(e_i - E(e_i))(e_j - E(e_j))] = E(e_i e_j) = 0$. Then, the very last step uses the fact that

$$\sum w_i^2 = \sum \left[\frac{(x_i - \bar{x})^2}{\left\{ \sum (x_i - \bar{x})^2 \right\}^2} \right] = \frac{\sum (x_i - \bar{x})^2}{\left\{ \sum (x_i - \bar{x})^2 \right\}^2} = \frac{1}{\sum (x_i - \bar{x})^2}$$

Alternatively, we can employ the rule for finding the variance of a sum. If X and Y are random variables, and a and b are constants, then

$$\text{var}(aX + bY) = a^2 \text{var}(X) + b^2 \text{var}(Y) + 2ab\, \text{cov}(X, Y)$$

Appendix B.4 reviews all the basic properties of random variables. In the second line below we use this rule extended to more than two random variables. Then,

$$
\begin{aligned}
\text{var}(b_2) &= \text{var}(\beta_2 + \sum w_i e_i) = \text{var}(\sum w_i e_i) & \text{(since } \beta_2 \text{ is a constant)} \\
&= \sum w_i^2 \text{var}(e_i) + \sum\sum_{i \neq j} w_i w_j \, \text{cov}(e_i, e_j) & \text{(generalizing the variance rule)} \\
&= \sum w_i^2 \text{var}(e_i) & \text{(using } \text{cov}(e_i, e_j) = 0) \\
&= \sigma^2 \sum w_i^2 & \text{(using } \text{var}(e_i) = \sigma^2) \\
&= \frac{\sigma^2}{\sum (x_i - \bar{x})^2}
\end{aligned}
$$

Carefully note that the derivation of the variance expression for b_2 depends on assumptions SR3 and SR4. If $cov(e_i, e_j) \neq 0$, then we cannot drop out all those terms in the double summation. If $var(e_i) \neq \sigma^2$ for all observations, then σ^2 cannot be factored out of the summation. If either of these assumptions fails to hold then $var(b_2)$ is *something else* and is not given by (2.15). The same is true for the variance of b_1 and the covariance.

Appendix 2F Proof of the Gauss–Markov Theorem

We will prove the Gauss–Markov theorem for the least squares estimator b_2 of β_2. Our goal is to show that in the class of linear and unbiased estimators the estimator b_2 has the smallest variance. Let $b_2^* = \Sigma k_i y_i$ (where k_i are constants) be any other linear estimator of β_2. To make comparison to the least squares estimator b_2 easier, suppose that $k_i = w_i + c_i$, where c_i is another constant and w_i is given in (2.11). While this is tricky, it is legal, since for any k_i that someone might choose we can find c_i. Into this new estimator substitute y_i and simplify, using the properties of w_i in Appendix 2D

$$
\begin{aligned}
b_2^* = \Sigma k_i y_i &= \Sigma(w_i + c_i)y_i = \Sigma(w_i + c_i)(\beta_1 + \beta_2 x_i + e_i) \\
&= \Sigma(w_i + c_i)\beta_1 + \Sigma(w_i + c_i)\beta_2 x_i + \Sigma(w_i + c_i)e_i \\
&= \beta_1 \Sigma w_i + \beta_1 \Sigma c_i + \beta_2 \Sigma w_i x_i + \beta_2 \Sigma c_i x_i + \Sigma(w_i + c_i)e_i \\
&= \beta_1 \Sigma c_i + \beta_2 + \beta_2 \Sigma c_i x_i + \Sigma(w_i + c_i)e_i
\end{aligned}
\tag{2F.1}
$$

since $\Sigma w_i = 0$ and $\Sigma w_i x_i = 1$.

Take the mathematical expectation of the last line in (2F.1), using the properties of expectation and the assumption that $E(e_i) = 0$:

$$
\begin{aligned}
E(b_2^*) &= \beta_1 \Sigma c_i + \beta_2 + \beta_2 \Sigma c_i x_i + \Sigma(w_i + c_i)E(e_i) \\
&= \beta_1 \Sigma c_i + \beta_2 + \beta_2 \Sigma c_i x_i
\end{aligned}
\tag{2F.2}
$$

In order for the linear estimator $b_2^* = \Sigma k_i y_i$ to be unbiased, it must be true that

$$
\Sigma c_i = 0 \text{ and } \Sigma c_i x_i = 0
\tag{2F.3}
$$

These conditions must hold in order for $b_2^* = \Sigma k_i y_i$ to be in the class of *linear* and *unbiased estimators*. So we will assume that conditions (2F.3) hold and use them to simplify expression (2F.1):

$$
b_2^* = \Sigma k_i y_i = \beta_2 + \Sigma(w_i + c_i)e_i
\tag{2F.4}
$$

We can now find the variance of the linear unbiased estimator b_2^* following the steps in Appendix 2E and using the additional fact that

$$
\Sigma c_i w_i = \Sigma \left[\frac{c_i(x_i - \bar{x})}{\Sigma(x_i - \bar{x})^2} \right] = \frac{1}{\Sigma(x_i - \bar{x})^2} \Sigma c_i x_i - \frac{\bar{x}}{\Sigma(x_i - \bar{x})^2} \Sigma c_i = 0
$$

Use the properties of variance to obtain

$$
\begin{aligned}
\mathrm{var}(b_2^*) &= \mathrm{var}[\beta_2 + \Sigma(w_i + c_i)e_i] = \Sigma(w_i + c_i)^2 \mathrm{var}(e_i) \\
&= \sigma^2 \Sigma(w_i + c_i)^2 = \sigma^2 \Sigma w_i^2 + \sigma^2 \Sigma c_i^2 \\
&= \mathrm{var}(b_2) + \sigma^2 \Sigma c_i^2 \\
&\geq \mathrm{var}(b_2)
\end{aligned}
$$

The last line follows since $\Sigma c_i^2 \geq 0$ and establishes that for the family of linear and unbiased estimators b_2^*, each of the alternative estimators has variance that is greater than or equal to that of the least squares estimator b_2. The *only* time that $\mathrm{var}(b_2^*) = \mathrm{var}(b_2)$ is when all the $c_i = 0$, in which case $b_2^* = b_2$. Thus there is no *other linear and unbiased estimator of* β_2 that is better than b_2, which proves the Gauss–Markov theorem.

Appendix 2G Monte Carlo Simulation

The statistical properties of the least squares estimators are well known if the assumptions in Section 2.1 hold. In fact, we know that the least squares estimators are the best linear unbiased estimators of the regression parameters under these assumptions. And if the random errors are normal, then we know that the estimators themselves have normal distributions in **repeated experimental trials**. The meaning of "repeated trials" is difficult to grasp. **Monte Carlo** simulation experiments use random number generators to replicate the random way that data are obtained. In Monte Carlo simulations we specify a **data generation process** and create samples of artificial data. Then we "try out" estimation methods on the data we have created. We create **many** samples of size N and examine the **repeated sampling properties** of the estimators. In this way, we can study how statistical procedures behave under ideal, as well as not so ideal, conditions. This is important because economic, business, and social science data are not always (indeed, not usually) as nice as the assumptions we make.

The data generation process for the simple linear regression model is given by

$$
y_i = E(y_i|x_i) + e_i = \beta_1 + \beta_2 x_i + e_i, \quad i = 1, \ldots, N
$$

Each value of the dependent variable y_i is obtained, or generated, by adding a random error e_i to the regression function $E(y_i|x_i)$. To simulate values of y_i we create values for the systematic portion of the regression relationship $E(y_i|x_i)$ and add to it the random error e_i. This is analogous to a physical experiment in which variable factors are set at fixed levels and the experiment run. The outcome is different in each experimental trial because of random uncontrolled errors.

2G.1 The Regression Function

The regression function $E(y_i|x_i) = \beta_1 + \beta_2 x_i$ is the systematic portion of the regression relationship. To create these values we must select

1. A sample size N. From the discussion in Section 2.4.4 we know that the larger the sample size is, the greater is the precision of estimation of the least squares estimators

b_1 and b_2. Following the numerical examples in the book, we choose $N = 40$. This is not a large sample, but assuming SR1–SR5 are true, the least squares estimators' properties hold for any sample of size $N > 2$ in the simple regression model. In more complex situations, varying the sample size to see how estimators perform is an important ingredient of the simulation.

2. We must choose x_i values. We maintain the assumption of values of the explanatory variable that are fixed in repeated experimental trials. Following the depiction in Figure 2.1[10] we set the values $x_1, x_2, \ldots, x_{20} = 10$ and $x_{21}, x_{22}, \ldots, x_{40} = 20$, using the chapter assumption that x is measured in 100s. Does it matter how we choose the x_i values? Yes, it does. The variances and covariances of the least squares estimators depend on the variation in x_i, $\sum(x_i - \bar{x})^2$, how far the values are from 0, as measured by $\sum x_i^2$, and on the sample mean $\bar{x}$. Thus, if the values x_i change, the precision of estimation of the least squares estimators will change.

3. We must choose β_1 and β_2. Interestingly, for the least squares estimator under assumptions SR1–SR5, the actual magnitudes of these parameters do not matter a great deal. The estimator variances and covariances do not depend on them. The difference between the least squares estimator and the true parameter value, $E(b_2)$–β_2 given in (2.13) does not depend on the magnitude of β_2, only on the x_i values and the random errors e_i. To roughly parallel the regression results we obtained in Figure 2.9, we set $\beta_1 = 100$ and $\beta_2 = 10$.

Given the values above we can create $N = 40$ values $E(y_i|x_i) = \beta_1 + \beta_2 x_i$. These values are

$$E(y_i|x_i = 10) = 100 + 10x_i = 100 + 10 \times 10 = 200, \quad i = 1, \ldots, 20$$
$$E(y_i|x_i = 20) = 100 + 10x_i = 100 + 10 \times 20 = 300, \quad i = 21, \ldots, 40$$

2G.2 THE RANDOM ERROR

To be consistent with assumptions SR2–SR4 the random errors should have mean zero, constant variance $\text{var}(e_i \,|\, x_i) = \sigma^2$ and be uncorrelated with one another, so that $\text{cov}(e_i, e_j) = 0$. Researchers in the field of numerical analysis have studied how to simulate random numbers from a variety of probability distributions, such as the normal distribution. Of course the computer-generated numbers cannot be truly random, because they are generated by a computer code. The random numbers created by computer software are "pseudorandom," in that they behave like random numbers. The numbers created will begin to recycle after about 10^{13} values are drawn, which is plenty for our uses. Each software vender uses its own version of a random number generator. Consequently, you should not expect to obtain exactly the same numbers that we have, and your replication will produce slightly different results, even though the major conclusions will be the same. See Appendix B.4 for a discussion of how random numbers are created.

Following assumption SR6 we assume the random error terms have a normal distribution with mean 0 and a homoskedastic variance $\text{var}(e_i \,|\, x_i) = \sigma^2$. The variance σ^2 affects the precision of estimation through the variances and covariances of the least squares estimators

---

[10] This design is used in Chapter 2.4 of Briand, G. & Hill, R. C. (2010). *Using Excel 2007 for Principles of Econometrics*. John Wiley and Sons.

in (2.14)–(2.16). The bigger the value of σ^2, the bigger the variances and covariances of the least squares estimators, and the more spread out the probability distribution of the estimators, as shown in Figure 2.10. We choose $\text{var}(e_i \mid x_i) = \sigma^2 = 2500$, which also means that $\text{var}(y_i \mid x_i) = \sigma^2 = 2500$.

2G.3   THEORETICALLY TRUE VALUES

Using the values above we plot the theoretically true probability density functions for y_i in Figure 2G.1. The solid curve on the left is $N(200, 2500 = 50^2)$. The first 20 simulated observations will follow this probability density function. The dashed curve on the right is $N(300, 2500 = 50^2)$, which is the probability density function for the second 20 observations.

Given the parameter $\sigma^2 = 2500$ and the x_i values we can compute the true variances of the estimators

$$\text{var}(b_1) = \sigma^2 \left[\frac{\sum x_i^2}{N \sum (x_i - \bar{x})^2} \right] = 2500 \left[\frac{10000}{40 \times 1000} \right] = 625$$

$$\text{var}(b_2) = \frac{\sigma^2}{\sum (x_i - \bar{x})^2} = \frac{2500}{1000} = 2.50$$

$$\text{cov}(b_1, b_2) = \sigma^2 \left[\frac{-\bar{x}}{\sum (x_i - \bar{x})^2} \right] = 2500 \left[\frac{-15}{1000} \right] = -37.50$$

The true standard deviation of b_2 is $\sqrt{\text{var}(b_2)} = \sqrt{2.50} = 1.5811$. The true probability density function of b_2 is $N(\beta_2 = 10, \text{var}(b_2) = 2.5)$. Using the cumulative probabilities for the standard normal distribution in Table 1 at the end of this book, we find that 98% of values from a normal distribution fall within 2.33 standard deviations of the mean. Applying this rule to the estimates b_2 we have $\beta_2 \pm 2.33 \times \sqrt{\text{var}(b_2)} = 10 \pm 2.33 \times 1.5811 = [6.316, 13.684]$. We expect almost all values of b_2 (98% of them) to fall in the range

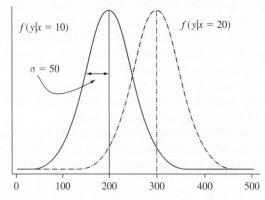

$f(y|x = 10)$ $f(y|x = 20)$

$\sigma = 50$

0	100	200	300	400	500

FIGURE 2G.1   The true probability density functions of the data.

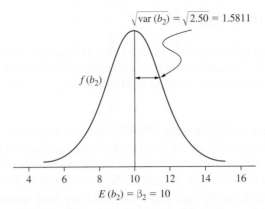

FIGURE **2G.2**   The true probability density functions of the estimator b_2.

6.32–13.68. The plot of the true probability density function of the estimator b_2 is shown in Figure 2G.2.

2G.4   CREATING A SAMPLE OF DATA

Most software will automatically create random values, z_i, from the standard normal distribution, $N(0, 1)$. To obtain a random value from a $N(0, \sigma^2)$ distribution, we multiply z_i by the standard deviation σ. That is $e_i = \sigma \times z_i$. Given values z_i from the standard normal distribution, we obtain the $N = 40$ sample values from the chosen data generation process as

$$y_i = E(y_i|x_i = 10) + e_i = 200 + 50 \times z_i \quad i = 1, \dots, 20$$
$$y_i = E(y_i|x_i = 20) + e_i = 300 + 50 \times z_i \quad i = 21, \dots, 40$$

One sample of data is in the file *mc1.dat*. Using these values we obtain the least squares estimates

$$\hat{y} = 75.7679 + 11.9683x_i$$
$$(\text{se}) \quad (25.7928) \quad (1.6313)$$

and the estimate $\hat{\sigma} = 51.5857$. The estimated variances and covariances of b_1 and b_2 are

	b1	b2
b1	665.2699	−39.9162
b2	−39.9162	2.6611

For this one sample the parameter estimates are reasonably near their true values. However, what happens in one sample does not prove anything. The repeated sampling properties of the least squares estimators are about what happens in many samples of data, from the same data generation process.

2G.5 MONTE CARLO OBJECTIVES

What do we hope to achieve with a Monte Carlo experiment? After the Monte Carlo experiment we will have many least squares estimates. If we obtain $M = 1000$ samples[11], we will have 1000 estimates $b_{1,1}, \ldots, b_{1,M}$, 1000 estimates $b_{2,1}, \ldots, b_{2,M}$ and 1000 estimates $\hat{\sigma}_1^2, \ldots, \hat{\sigma}_M^2$.

- We would like to verify that under SR1–SR5 the least squares estimators are unbiased. The estimator b_2 is unbiased if $E(b_2) = \beta_2$. Since an expected value is an average in many repeated experimental trials, we should observe that the average value of all the slope estimates, $\bar{b}_2 = \sum_{m=1}^{M} b_{2,m}/M$, is close to $\beta_2 = 10$.

- We would like to verify that under SR1–SR5 the least squares estimators have sampling variances given by (2.14) and (2.16). The estimator variances measure the sampling variation in the estimates. The sampling variation of the estimates in the Monte Carlo simulation can be measured by their sample variance. For example, the sample variance of the estimates $b_{2,1}, \ldots, b_{2,M}$ is $s_{b_2}^2 = \sum_{m=1}^{M} (b_{2,m} - \bar{b}_2)^2/(M - 1)$. This value should be close to $\mathrm{var}(b_2) = 2.50$, and the standard deviation s_{b_2} should be close to the true standard deviation of the regression estimates 1.5811.

- We would like to verify that the estimator of the error variance (2.19) is an unbiased estimator of $\sigma^2 = 2500$, or that $\hat{\sigma}^2 = \sum_{m=1}^{M} \hat{\sigma}_m^2/M$ is close to the true value.

- Because we have assumed the random errors are normal, SR6, we expect the least squares estimates to have a normal distribution.

2G.6 MONTE CARLO RESULTS

The numerical results of the Monte Carlo experiment are shown Table 2G.1. The averages (or "Sample Means") of the 1000 Monte Carlo estimates are close to their true values.

For example, the average of the slope estimates is $\bar{b}_2 = \sum_{m=1}^{M} b_{2,m}/M = 10.0143$, compared to the true value $\beta_2 = 10$. The sample variance of the estimates $s_{b_2}^2 = \sum_{m=1}^{M} (b_{2,m} - \bar{b}_2)^2/(M - 1) = 2.3174$ compared to the true value $\mathrm{var}(b_2) = 2.50$. The standard deviation of the estimates is $s_{b_2} = 1.5223$, compared to the true standard deviation $\sqrt{\mathrm{var}(b_2)} = \sqrt{2.50} = 1.5811$. The theoretical 1st and 99th percentiles of b_2 are [6.316, 13.684], which is reflected by the estimates [6.3811, 13.5620]. If the number of Monte Carlo samples is

Table 2G.1 **Summary of 1,000 Monte Carlo Samples**

	Mean	Variance	Std. Dev.	Minimum	Maximum	1st Pct.	99th Pct.
b_1 (100)	99.7581	575.3842	23.9872	25.8811	174.6061	42.1583	156.0710
b_2 (10)	10.0143	2.3174	1.5223	5.1401	14.9928	6.3811	13.5620
$\hat{\sigma}^2$ (2,500)	2489.935	329909.9	574.3778	1024.191	5200.785	1360.764	4031.641

---

[11] $M = 1000$ is a moderate number of Monte Carlo samples. Depending upon the purpose of the Monte Carlo, the number of samples may have to be larger. More will be said about this in an appendix to Chapter 3.

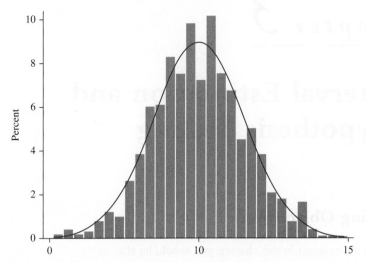

FIGURE $2G.3$ The sampling distribution of b_2 in 1000 Monte Carlo samples.

increased to $M = 10,000$, then the empirical Monte Carlo average values are even closer to the true parameters.

As for the normality of the estimates, we see from the histogram in Figure 2G.3, that the actual values follow the superimposed normal distribution very closely.

Chapter *3*

Interval Estimation and Hypothesis Testing

Learning Objectives

Based on the material in this chapter, you should be able to

1. Discuss how "repeated sampling theory" relates to interval estimation and hypothesis testing.

2. Explain why it is important for statistical inference that the least squares estimators b_1 and b_2 are normally distributed random variables.

3. Explain the "level of confidence" of an interval estimator, and exactly what it means in a repeated sampling context, and give an example.

4. Explain the difference between an interval estimator and an interval estimate. Explain how to interpret an interval estimate.

5. Explain the terms null hypothesis, alternative hypothesis, and rejection region, giving an example and a sketch of the rejection region.

6. Explain the logic of a statistical test, including why it is important that a test statistic have a known probability distribution if the null hypothesis is true.

7. Explain the term *p*-value and how to use a *p*-value to determine the outcome of a hypothesis test; provide a sketch showing a *p*-value.

8. Explain the difference between one-tail and two-tail tests. Explain, intuitively, how to choose the rejection region for a one-tail test.

9. Explain Type I error and illustrate it in a sketch. Define the level of significance of a test.

10. Explain the difference between economic and statistical significance.

11. Explain how to choose what goes in the null hypothesis, and what goes in the alternative hypothesis.

Keywords

alternative hypothesis	interval estimation	*p*-value
confidence intervals	level of significance	rejection region
critical value	linear hypothesis	test of significance
degrees of freedom	null hypothesis	test statistic
hypotheses	one-tail tests	two-tail tests
hypothesis testing	point estimates	Type I error
inference	probability value	Type II error

In Chapter 2 we used the least squares estimators to develop **point estimates** for the parameters in the simple linear regression model. These estimates represent an **inference** about the regression function $E(y) = \beta_1 + \beta_2 x$ describing a relationship between economic variables. *Infer* means "to conclude by reasoning from something known or assumed." This dictionary definition describes statistical inference as well. We have assumed a relationship between economic variables and made various assumptions (SR1–SR5) about the regression model. Based on these assumptions, and given empirical estimates of regression parameters, we want to make inferences about the population from which the data were obtained.

In this chapter we introduce additional tools of statistical inference: **interval estimation** and **hypothesis testing**. Interval estimation is a procedure for creating ranges of values, sometimes called **confidence intervals**, in which the unknown parameters are likely to be located. Hypothesis tests are procedures for comparing conjectures that we might have about the regression parameters to the parameter estimates we have obtained from a sample of data. Hypothesis tests allow us to say that the data are compatible, or are not compatible, with a particular conjecture or hypothesis.

The procedures for hypothesis testing and interval estimation depend very heavily on assumption SR6 of the simple linear regression model and the resulting normality of the least squares estimators. If assumption SR6 does not hold, then the sample size must be sufficiently large so that the distributions of the least squares estimators are *approximately* normal. In this case the procedures we develop in this chapter can be used but are also approximate. In developing the procedures in this chapter we will be using the "Student's" *t*-distribution. You may want to refresh your memory about this distribution by reviewing Appendix B.3.7. Also, it is sometimes helpful to see the concepts we are about to discuss in a simpler setting. In Appendix C we examine statistical inference, interval estimation, and hypothesis testing in the context of estimating the mean of a normal population. You may want to review this material now, or read it along with this chapter as we proceed.

3.1 Interval Estimation

In Chapter 2 we estimated that household food expenditure would rise by $10.21 given a $100 increase in weekly income. The estimate $b_2 = 10.21$ is a *point* estimate of the unknown population parameter β_2 in the regression model. Interval estimation proposes a range of values in which the true parameter β_2 is likely to fall. Providing a range of values gives a sense of what the parameter value might be, and the precision with which we have estimated it. Such intervals are often called **confidence intervals**. We prefer to call them **interval estimates** because the term "confidence" is widely misunderstood and misused. As we will see, our confidence is in the procedure we use to obtain the intervals, not in the intervals themselves. This is consistent with how we assessed the properties of the least squares estimators in Chapter 2.

3.1.1 THE *t*-DISTRIBUTION

Let us assume that assumptions SR1–SR6 hold for the simple linear regression model. In this case we know that the least squares estimators b_1 and b_2 have normal distributions, as discussed in Section 2.6. For example, the normal distribution of b_2, the least squares estimator of β_2, is

$$b_2 \sim N\left(\beta_2, \frac{\sigma^2}{\sum(x_i - \bar{x})^2}\right)$$

A standardized normal random variable is obtained from b_2 by subtracting its mean and dividing by its standard deviation:

$$Z = \frac{b_2 - \beta_2}{\sqrt{\sigma^2 / \Sigma(x_i - \bar{x})^2}} \sim N(0, 1) \qquad (3.1)$$

The standardized random variable Z is normally distributed with mean 0 and variance 1. Using a table of normal probabilities (Table 1 at the end of the book), we know that

$$P(-1.96 \leq Z \leq 1.96) = 0.95$$

Substituting (3.1) into this expression, we obtain

$$P\left(-1.96 \leq \frac{b_2 - \beta_2}{\sqrt{\sigma^2 / \Sigma(x_i - \bar{x})^2}} \leq 1.96\right) = 0.95$$

Rearranging gives us

$$P\left(b_2 - 1.96\sqrt{\sigma^2 / \Sigma(x_i - \bar{x})^2} \leq \beta_2 \leq b_2 + 1.96\sqrt{\sigma^2 / \Sigma(x_i - \bar{x})^2}\right) = 0.95$$

This defines an interval that has probability 0.95 of containing the parameter β_2. The two endpoints $\left(b_2 \pm 1.96\sqrt{\sigma^2 / \Sigma(x_i - \bar{x})^2}\right)$ provide an interval estimator. In repeated sampling, 95% of the intervals constructed this way will contain the true value of the parameter β_2. This easy derivation of an interval estimator is based on both assumption SR6 *and* our knowing the variance of the error term σ^2.

Although we do not know the value of σ^2, we can estimate it. The least squares residuals are $\hat{e}_i = y_i - b_1 - b_2 x_i$, and our estimator of σ^2 is $\hat{\sigma}^2 = \Sigma \hat{e}_i^2 / (N - 2)$. Replacing σ^2 by $\hat{\sigma}^2$ in (3.1) creates a random variable we can work with, but this substitution changes the probability distribution from standard normal to a t-distribution with $N - 2$ degrees of freedom,

$$t = \frac{b_2 - \beta_2}{\sqrt{\hat{\sigma}^2 / \Sigma(x_i - \bar{x})^2}} = \frac{b_2 - \beta_2}{\sqrt{\widehat{\text{var}(b_2)}}} = \frac{b_2 - \beta_2}{\text{se}(b_2)} \sim t_{(N-2)} \qquad (3.2)$$

The ratio $t = (b_2 - \beta_2)/\text{se}(b_2)$ has a t-distribution with $N - 2$ degrees of freedom, which we denote as $t \sim t_{(N-2)}$. A similar result holds for b_1, so in general we can say, if assumptions SR1–SR6 hold in the simple linear regression model, then

$$t = \frac{b_k - \beta_k}{\text{se}(b_k)} \sim t_{(N-2)} \quad \text{for} \quad k = 1, 2 \qquad (3.3)$$

This equation will be the basis for interval estimation and hypothesis testing in the simple linear regression model. The statistical argument of how we go from (3.1) to (3.2) is in Appendix 3A, at the end of this chapter.

When working with the t-distribution, remember that it is a bell-shaped curve centered at zero. It looks like the standard normal distribution, except that it is more spread out, with a larger variance and thicker tails. The shape of the t-distribution is controlled by a single parameter called the **degrees of freedom**, often abbreviated as *df*. We use the notation $t_{(m)}$ to specify a t-distribution with m degrees of freedom. In Table 2 at the end of the book (and inside

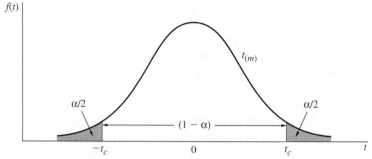

FIGURE **3.1** Critical values from a t-distribution.

the front cover) are percentile values of the t-distribution for various degrees of freedom. For m degrees of freedom the 95th percentile of the t-distribution is denoted $t_{(0.95, m)}$. This value has the property that 0.95 of the probability falls to its left, so $P\left[t_{(m)} \leq t_{(0.95, m)}\right] = 0.95$. For example, if the degrees of freedom are $m = 20$, then, from Table 2, $t_{(0.95, 20)} = 1.725$. Should you encounter a problem requiring percentiles that we do not give, you can interpolate for an approximate answer, or use your computer software to obtain an exact value.

3.1.2 OBTAINING INTERVAL ESTIMATES

From Table 2 we can find a "critical value" t_c from a t-distribution such that $P(t \geq t_c) = P(t \leq -t_c) = \alpha/2$, where α is a probability often taken to be $\alpha = 0.01$ or $\alpha = 0.05$. The critical value t_c for degrees of freedom m is the percentile value $t_{(1-\alpha/2, m)}$. The values t_c and $-t_c$ are depicted in Figure 3.1.

Each shaded "tail" area contains $\alpha/2$ of the probability, so that $1 - \alpha$ of the probability is contained in the center portion. Consequently, we can make the probability statement

$$P(-t_c \leq t \leq t_c) = 1 - \alpha \tag{3.4}$$

For a 95% confidence interval the critical values define a central region of the t-distribution containing probability $1 - \alpha = 0.95$. This leaves probability $\alpha = 0.05$ divided equally between the two tails, so that $\alpha/2 = 0.025$. Then the critical value $t_c = t_{(1-0.025, m)} = t_{(0.975, m)}$. In the simple regression model the degrees of freedom are $m = N - 2$, so expression (3.4) becomes

$$P\left[-t_{(0.975, N-2)} \leq t \leq t_{(0.975, N-2)}\right] = 0.95$$

We find the percentile values $t_{(0.975, N-2)}$ in Table 2.

Now, let us see how we can put all these bits together to create a procedure for interval estimation. Substitute t from (3.3) into (3.4) to obtain

$$P\left[-t_c \leq \frac{b_k - \beta_k}{\text{se}(b_k)} \leq t_c\right] = 1 - \alpha$$

Rearrange this expression to obtain

$$P[b_k - t_c\text{se}(b_k) \leq \beta_k \leq b_k + t_c\text{se}(b_k)] = 1 - \alpha \tag{3.5}$$

The interval endpoints $b_k - t_c\text{se}(b_k)$ and $b_k + t_c\text{se}(b_k)$ are random because they vary from sample to sample. These endpoints define an **interval estimator** of β_k. The probability statement in (3.5) says that the interval $b_k \pm t_c \text{se}(b_k)$ has probability $1 - \alpha$ of containing the true but unknown parameter β_k.

When b_k and $\text{se}(b_k)$ in (3.5) are estimated values (numbers), based on a given sample of data, then $b_k \pm t_c \text{se}(b_k)$ is called a $100(1 - \alpha)\%$ **interval estimate** of β_k. Equivalently it is called a $100(1 - \alpha)\%$ **confidence interval**. Usually $\alpha = 0.01$ or $\alpha = 0.05$, so that we obtain a 99% confidence interval or a 95% confidence interval.

The interpretation of confidence intervals requires a great deal of care. The properties of the interval estimation procedure are based on the notion of repeated sampling. If we were to select *many* random samples of size N, compute the least squares estimate b_k and its standard error $\text{se}(b_k)$ for each sample, and then construct the interval estimate $b_k \pm t_c \text{se}(b_k)$ for each sample, then $100(1 - \alpha)\%$ of all the intervals constructed would contain the true parameter β_k. In Appendix 3C we carry out a Monte Carlo simulation to demonstrate this repeated sampling property.

Any *one* interval estimate, based on one sample of data, may or may not contain the true parameter β_k, and because β_k is unknown, we will never know whether it does or does not. When "confidence intervals" are discussed, remember that our confidence is in the *procedure* used to construct the interval estimate; it is *not* in any one interval estimate calculated from a sample of data.

3.1.3 AN ILLUSTRATION

For the food expenditure data, $N = 40$ and the degrees of freedom are $N - 2 = 38$. For a 95% confidence interval $\alpha = 0.05$. The critical value $t_c = t_{(1-\alpha/2, N-2)} = t_{(0.975, 38)} = 2.024$ is the 97.5 percentile from the t-distribution with 38 degrees of freedom. For β_2 the probability statement in (3.5) becomes

$$P[b_2 - 2.024\text{se}(b_2) \leq \beta_2 \leq b_2 + 2.024\text{se}(b_2)] = 0.95 \tag{3.6}$$

To construct an interval estimate for β_2 we use the least squares estimate $b_2 = 10.21$ and its standard error

$$\text{se}(b_2) = \sqrt{\widehat{\text{var}(b_2)}} = \sqrt{4.38} = 2.09$$

Substituting these values into (3.6) we obtain a "95% confidence interval estimate" for β_2:

$$b_2 \pm t_c \text{se}(b_2) = 10.21 \pm 2.024(2.09) = [5.97, 14.45]$$

That is, we estimate "with 95% confidence" that from an additional \$100 of weekly income households will spend between \$5.97 and \$14.45 on food.

Is β_2 actually in the interval [5.97, 14.45]? We do not know, and we will never know. What we *do* know is that when the procedure we used is applied to many random samples of data from the same population, then 95% of all the interval estimates constructed using this procedure will contain the true parameter. The interval estimation procedure "works" 95% of the time. What we can say about the interval estimate based on our one sample is that, given the reliability of the procedure, we would be "surprised" if β_2 is not in the interval [5.97, 14.45].

What is the usefulness of an interval estimate of β_2? When reporting regression results we always give a point estimate, such as $b_2 = 10.21$. However, the point estimate alone gives no sense of its reliability. Thus, we might also report an interval estimate. Interval estimates incorporate both the point estimate and the standard error of the estimate, which is a measure of the variability of the least squares estimator. The interval estimate includes an allowance for the sample size as well, because for lower degrees of freedom the t-distribution critical value t_c is larger. If an interval estimate is wide (implying a large standard error), it suggests that there is not much information in the sample about β_2. If an interval estimate is narrow, it suggests that we have learned more about β_2.

What is "wide" and what is "narrow" depend on the problem at hand. For example, in our model $b_2 = 10.21$ is an estimate of how much weekly household food expenditure will rise given a \$100 increase in weekly household income. A CEO of a supermarket chain can use this estimate to plan future store capacity requirements, given forecasts of income growth in an area. However, no decision will be based on this one number alone. The prudent CEO will carry out a sensitivity analysis by considering values of β_2 around 10.21. The question is "Which values?" One answer is provided by the interval estimate [5.97, 14.45]. Though β_2 may or may not be in this interval, the CEO knows that the procedure used to obtain the interval estimate "works" 95% of the time. If varying β_2 within the interval has drastic consequences on company sales and profits, then the CEO may conclude that there is insufficient evidence upon which to make a decision and order a new and larger sample of data.

3.1.4 THE REPEATED SAMPLING CONTEXT

In Section 2.4.3 we illustrated the sampling properties of the least squares estimators by showing what would happen if we collected 10 additional samples of size $N = 40$ from the same population that gave us the food expenditure data. The data are in the file *table2_2.dat*. In Table 3.1 we present the least squares estimates, the estimates of σ^2, and the coefficient standard errors from each sample. Note the sampling variation illustrated by these estimates. This variation is due to the simple fact that we obtained 40 *different* households in each sample. The 95% confidence interval estimates for the parameters β_1 and β_2 are given in Table 3.2 for the same samples.

Sampling variability causes the center of each of the interval estimates to change with the values of the least squares estimates, and it causes the widths of the intervals to change with the standard errors. If we ask the question "How many of these intervals contain the true parameters, and which ones are they?" we must answer that we do not know. But since 95% of all interval estimates constructed this way contain the true parameter values, we would expect perhaps nine or 10 of these intervals to contain the true but unknown parameters.

Note the difference between point estimation and interval estimation. We have used the least squares estimators to obtain point estimates of unknown parameters. The estimated

Table 3.1 **Least Squares Estimates from 10 Random Samples**

Sample	b_1	se(b_1)	b_2	se(b_2)	$\hat{\sigma}^2$
1	131.69	40.58	6.48	1.96	7002.85
2	57.25	33.13	10.88	1.60	4668.63
3	103.91	37.22	8.14	1.79	5891.75
4	46.50	33.33	11.90	1.61	4722.58
5	84.23	41.15	9.29	1.98	7200.16
6	26.63	45.78	13.55	2.21	8911.43
7	64.21	32.03	10.93	1.54	4362.12
8	79.66	29.87	9.76	1.44	3793.83
9	97.30	29.14	8.05	1.41	3610.20
10	95.96	37.18	7.77	1.79	5878.71

Table 3.2   **Interval Estimates from 10 Random Samples**

Sample	$b_1 - t_c\text{se}(b_1)$	$b_1 + t_c\text{se}(b_1)$	$b_2 - t_c\text{se}(b_2)$	$b_2 + t_c\text{se}(b_2)$
1	49.54	213.85	2.52	10.44
2	−9.83	124.32	7.65	14.12
3	28.56	179.26	4.51	11.77
4	−20.96	113.97	8.65	15.15
5	0.93	167.53	5.27	13.30
6	−66.04	119.30	9.08	18.02
7	−0.63	129.05	7.81	14.06
8	19.19	140.13	6.85	12.68
9	38.32	156.29	5.21	10.89
10	20.69	171.23	4.14	11.40

variance $\widehat{\text{var}(b_k)}$, for $k = 1$ or 2, and its square root $\sqrt{\widehat{\text{var}(b_k)}} = \text{se}(b_k)$ provide information about the sampling variability of the least squares estimator from one sample to another. Interval estimators are a convenient way to report regression results because they combine point estimation with a measure of sampling variability to provide a range of values in which the unknown parameters might fall. When the sampling variability of the least squares estimator is relatively small, then the interval estimates will be relatively narrow, implying that the least squares estimates are "reliable." If the least squares estimators suffer from large sampling variability, then the interval estimates will be wide, implying that the least squares estimates are "unreliable."

3.2 Hypothesis Tests

Many business and economic decision problems require a judgment as to whether or not a parameter is a specific value. In the food expenditure example, it may make a good deal of difference for decision purposes whether β_2 is greater than 10, indicating that a $100 increase in income will increase expenditure on food by more than $10. Also, based on economic theory, we believe that β_2 should be positive. One check of our data and model is whether this theoretical proposition is supported by the data.

Hypothesis testing procedures compare a conjecture we have about a population to the information contained in a sample of data. Given an economic and statistical model, **hypotheses** are formed about economic behavior. These hypotheses are then represented as statements about model parameters. Hypothesis tests use the information about a parameter that is contained in a sample of data, its least squares point estimate, and its standard error, to draw a conclusion about the hypothesis.

In each and every hypothesis test five ingredients must be present:

COMPONENTS OF HYPOTHESIS TESTS

1. A null hypothesis H_0
2. An alternative hypothesis H_1
3. A test statistic
4. A rejection region
5. A conclusion

3.2.1 THE NULL HYPOTHESIS

The null hypothesis, which is denoted by H_0 (*H-naught*), specifies a value for a regression parameter, which for generality we denote as β_k, for $k = 1$ or 2. The null hypothesis is stated as $H_0 : \beta_k = c$, where c is a constant, and is an important value in the context of a specific regression model. A null hypothesis is the belief we will maintain until we are convinced by the sample evidence that it is not true, in which case we *reject* the null hypothesis.

3.2.2 THE ALTERNATIVE HYPOTHESIS

Paired with every null hypothesis is a logical alternative hypothesis H_1 that we will accept if the null hypothesis is rejected. The alternative hypothesis is flexible and depends to some extent on economic theory. For the null hypothesis $H_0 : \beta_k = c$ the three possible alternative hypotheses are

- $H_1 : \beta_k > c$. Rejecting the null hypothesis that $\beta_k = c$ leads us to accept the conclusion that $\beta_k > c$. Inequality alternative hypotheses are widely used in economics because economic theory frequently provides information about the *signs* of relationships between variables. For example, in the food expenditure example we might well test the null hypothesis $H_0 : \beta_2 = 0$ against $H_1 : \beta_2 > 0$ because economic theory strongly suggests that necessities like food are normal goods, and that food expenditure will rise if income increases.

- $H_1 : \beta_k < c$. Rejecting the null hypothesis that $\beta_k = c$ in this case leads us to accept the conclusion that $\beta_k < c$.

- $H_1 : \beta_k \neq c$. Rejecting the null hypothesis that $\beta_k = c$ in this case leads us to accept the conclusion that β_k takes a value either larger or smaller than c.

3.2.3 THE TEST STATISTIC

The sample information about the null hypothesis is embodied in the sample value of a test statistic. Based on the value of a test statistic we decide either to reject the null hypothesis or not to reject it. A test statistic has a special characteristic: its probability distribution is completely *known* when the null hypothesis is true, and it has some *other* distribution if the null hypothesis is not true.

It all starts with the key result in (3.3), $t = (b_k - \beta_k)/\mathrm{se}(b_k) \sim t_{(N-2)}$. **If** the null hypothesis $H_0 : \beta_k = c$ is *true*, **then** we can substitute c for β_k and it follows that

$$t = \frac{b_k - c}{\mathrm{se}(b_k)} \sim t_{(N-2)} \tag{3.7}$$

If the null hypothesis is *not true*, then the t-statistic in (3.7) does *not* have a t-distribution with $N - 2$ degrees of freedom. This point is elaborated in Appendix 3B.

3.2.4 THE REJECTION REGION

The rejection region depends on the form of the alternative. It is the range of values of the test statistic that leads to *rejection* of the null hypothesis. It is possible to construct a rejection region only if we have

- A test statistic whose distribution is known when the null hypothesis is true
- An alternative hypothesis
- A level of significance

The rejection region consists of values that are *unlikely* and that have low probability of occurring when the null hypothesis is true. The chain of logic is "If a value of the test statistic is obtained that falls in a region of low probability, then it is unlikely that the test statistic has the assumed distribution, and thus it is unlikely that the null hypothesis is true." If the alternative hypothesis is true, then values of the test statistic will tend to be unusually large or unusually small. The terms "large" and "small" are determined by choosing a probability α, called the **level of significance** of the test, which provides a meaning for "an *unlikely* event." The level of significance of the test α is usually chosen to be 0.01, 0.05 or 0.10.

If we reject the null hypothesis when it is true, then we commit what is called a **Type I error**. The level of significance of a test *is* the probability of committing a Type I error, so $P(\text{Type I error}) = \alpha$. Any time we reject a null hypothesis it is possible that we have made such an error—there is no avoiding it. The good news is that we can specify the amount of Type I error we will tolerate by setting the level of significance α. If such an error is costly, then we make α small. If we do not reject a null hypothesis that is false, then we have committed a **Type II error**. In a real-world situation we cannot control or calculate the probability of this type of error, because it depends on the unknown true parameter β_k. For more about Type I and Type II errors, see Appendix C.6.9.

3.2.5   A Conclusion

When you have completed testing a hypothesis, you should state your conclusion. Do you reject the null hypothesis, or do you not reject the null hypothesis? As we will argue below, you should avoid saying that you "accept" the null hypothesis, which can be very misleading. Also, we urge you to make it standard practice to say what the conclusion means in the economic context of the problem you are working on and the economic significance of the finding. Statistical procedures are not ends in themselves. They are carried out for a reason and have meaning, which you should be able to explain.

3.3   Rejection Regions for Specific Alternatives

In this section we hope to be very clear about the nature of the rejection rules for each of the three possible alternatives to the null hypothesis $H_0 : \beta_k = c$. As noted in the previous section, to have a rejection region for a null hypothesis, we need a test statistic, which we have; it is given in (3.7). Second, we need a specific alternative, $\beta_k > c$, $\beta_k < c$, or $\beta_k \neq c$. Third, we need to specify the level of significance of the test. The level of significance of a test, α, is the probability that we reject the null hypothesis when it is actually true, which is called a Type I error.

3.3.1   One-Tail Tests with Alternative "Greater Than" $(>)$

When testing the null hypothesis $H_0 : \beta_k = c$, if the *alternative* hypothesis $H_1 : \beta_k > c$ is true, then the value of the t-statistic (3.7) tends to become larger than usual for the t-distribution. We will reject the null hypothesis if the test statistic is larger than the critical value for the level of significance α. The critical value that leaves probability α in the right

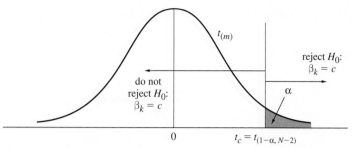

FIGURE 3.2 Rejection region for a one-tail test of $H_0 : \beta_k = c$ against $H_1 : \beta_k > c$.

tail is the $(1-\alpha)$-percentile $t_{(1-\alpha, N-2)}$, as shown in Figure 3.2. For example, if $\alpha = 0.05$ and $N - 2 = 30$, then from Table 2 the critical value is the 95th percentile value $t_{(0.95,30)} = 1.697$.

The rejection rule is

> When testing the null hypothesis $H_0 : \beta_k = c$ against the alternative hypothesis $H_1 : \beta_k > c$, reject the null hypothesis and accept the alternative hypothesis if $t \geq t_{(1-\alpha, N-2)}$.

The test is called a "one-tail" test because unlikely values of the t-statistic fall only in one tail of the probability distribution. If the null hypothesis is true, then the test statistic (3.7) has a t-distribution, and its value would tend to fall in the center of the distribution, to the left of the critical value, where most of the probability is contained. The level of significance α is chosen so that if the null hypothesis is true, then the probability that the t-statistic value falls in the extreme right tail of the distribution is small; an event that is unlikely to occur by chance. If we obtain a test statistic value in the rejection region, we take it as evidence *against* the null hypothesis, leading us to conclude that the null hypothesis is unlikely to be true. Evidence against the null hypothesis is evidence in support of the alternative hypothesis. Thus if we reject the null hypothesis then we conclude that the alternative is true.

If the null hypothesis $H_0 : \beta_k = c$ is *true,* then the test statistic (3.7) has a t-distribution and its values fall in the nonrejection region with probability $1 - \alpha$. If $t < t_{(1-\alpha, N-2)}$, then there is no statistically significant evidence against the null hypothesis, and we do not reject it.

3.3.2 ONE-TAIL TESTS WITH ALTERNATIVE "LESS THAN" ($<$)

If the alternative hypothesis $H_1 : \beta_k < c$ is true, then the value of the t-statistic (3.7) tends to become smaller than usual for the t-distribution. We reject the null hypothesis if the test statistic is smaller than the critical value for the level of significance α. The critical value that leaves probability α in the left tail is the α-percentile $t_{(\alpha, N-2)}$, as shown in Figure 3.3.

When using Table 2 to locate critical values, recall that the t-distribution is symmetric about zero, so that the α-percentile $t_{(\alpha, N-2)}$ is the negative of the $(1-\alpha)$-percentile $t_{(1-\alpha, N-2)}$. For example, if $\alpha = 0.05$ and $N - 2 = 20$, then from Table 2 the 95th percentile of the t-distribution is $t_{(0.95,20)} = 1.725$ and the 5th percentile value is $t_{(0.05,20)} = -1.725$.

The rejection rule is:

> When testing the null hypothesis $H_0 : \beta_k = c$ against the alternative hypothesis $H_1 : \beta_k < c$, reject the null hypothesis and accept the alternative hypothesis if $t \leq t_{(\alpha, N-2)}$.

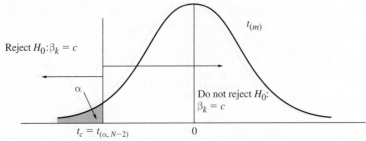

FIGURE 3.3   The rejection region for a one-tail test of $H_0 : \beta_k = c$ against $H_1 : \beta_k < c$.

The nonrejection region consists of t-statistic values greater than $t_{(\alpha, N-2)}$. When the null hypothesis is true, the probability of obtaining such a t-value is $1 - \alpha$, which is chosen to be large. Thus if $t > t_{(\alpha, N-2)}$ then do not reject $H_0 : \beta_k = c$.

Remembering where the rejection region is located may be facilitated by the following trick:

> **MEMORY TRICK:** The rejection region for a one-tail test is in the direction of the arrow in the alternative. If the alternative is $>$, then reject in the right tail. If the alternative is $<$, reject in the left tail.

3.3.3 Two-Tail Tests with Alternative "Not Equal To" ($\neq$)

When testing the null hypothesis $H_0 : \beta_k = c$, if the alternative hypothesis $H_1 : \beta_k \neq c$ is true, then the value of the t-statistic (3.7) tends to become either larger *or* smaller than usual for the t-distribution. To have a test with level of significance α we define the critical values so that the probability of the t-statistic falling in either tail is $\alpha/2$. The left-tail critical value is the percentile $t_{(\alpha/2, N-2)}$ and the right-tail critical value is the percentile $t_{(1-\alpha/2, N-2)}$. We reject the null hypothesis that $H_0 : \beta_k = c$ in favor of the alternative that $H_1 : \beta_k \neq c$ if the test statistic $t \leq t_{(\alpha/2, N-2)}$ or $t \geq t_{(1-\alpha/2, N-2)}$, as shown in Figure 3.4. For example, if $\alpha = 0.05$ and $N - 2 = 30$, then $\alpha/2 = 0.025$ and the left-tail critical value is the 2.5-percentile value $t_{(0.025, 30)} = -2.042$; the right-tail critical value is the 97.5-percentile $t_{(0.975, 30)} = 2.042$. The right-tail critical value is found in Table 2, and the left-tail critical value is found using the symmetry of the t-distribution.

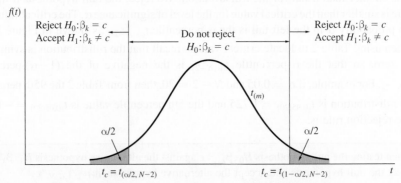

FIGURE 3.4   Rejection region for a test of $H_0 : \beta_k = c$ against $H_1 : \beta_k \neq c$.

Since the rejection region is composed of portions of the t-distribution in the left and right tails, this test is called a **two-tail test**. When the null hypothesis is true, the probability of obtaining a value of the test statistic that falls in *either* tail area is "small." The sum of the tail probabilities is α. Sample values of the test statistic that are in the tail areas are incompatible with the null hypothesis and are evidence against the null hypothesis being true. On the other hand, if the null hypothesis $H_0 : \beta_k = c$ is true, then the probability of obtaining a value of the test statistic t in the central nonrejection region is high. Sample values of the test statistic in the central nonrejection area are compatible with the null hypothesis and are not taken as evidence against the null hypothesis being true. Thus the rejection rule is

> When testing the null hypothesis $H_0 : \beta_k = c$ against the alternative hypothesis $H_1 : \beta_k \neq c$, reject the null hypothesis and accept the alternative hypothesis if $t \leq t_{(\alpha/2, N-2)}$ **or** if $t \geq t_{(1-\alpha/2, N-2)}$.

We do not reject the null hypothesis if $t_{(\alpha/2, N-2)} < t < t_{(1-\alpha/2, N-2)}$.

3.4 **Examples of Hypothesis Tests**

We illustrate the mechanics of hypothesis testing using the food expenditure model. We give examples of right-tail, left-tail, and two-tail tests. In each case we will follow a prescribed set of steps, closely following the list of required components for all hypothesis tests listed at the beginning of Section 3.2. A standard procedure for all hypothesis-testing problems and situations is

> **STEP-BY-STEP PROCEDURE FOR TESTING HYPOTHESES**
> 1. Determine the null and alternative hypotheses.
> 2. Specify the test statistic and its distribution if the null hypothesis is true.
> 3. Select α and determine the rejection region.
> 4. Calculate the sample value of the test statistic.
> 5. State your conclusion.

3.4.1   RIGHT-TAIL TESTS

3.4.1a   One-Tail Test of Signficance
Usually our first concern is whether there is a relationship between the variables, as we have specified in our model. If $\beta_2 = 0$ then there is no linear relationship between food expenditure and income. Economic theory suggests that food is a normal good, and that as income increases food expenditure will also increase, and thus that $\beta_2 > 0$. The least squares estimate of β_2 is $b_2 = 10.21$, which is certainly greater than zero. However, simply observing that the estimate has the right sign does not constitute scientific proof. We want to determine whether there is convincing, or *significant*, statistical evidence that would lead us to conclude that $\beta_2 > 0$. When testing the null hypothesis that a parameter is zero, we are asking if the estimate b_2 is significantly different from zero, and the test is called a **test of significance**.

A statistical test procedure cannot prove the truth of a null hypothesis. When we fail to reject a null hypothesis, all the hypothesis test can establish is that the information in a sample of data is *compatible* with the null hypothesis. Conversely, a statistical test can lead us to *reject* the null hypothesis, with only a small probability α of rejecting the null hypothesis when it is actually true. Thus rejecting a null hypothesis is a stronger conclusion than failing to reject it. For this reason the null hypothesis is usually stated in such a way that if our theory is correct, then we will reject the null hypothesis. In our example, economic theory implies that there should be a positive relationship between income and food expenditure. We would like to establish that there is statistical evidence to support this theory using a hypothesis test. With this goal we set up the null hypothesis that there is *no* relation between the variables, $H_0 : \beta_2 = 0$. In the alternative hypothesis we put the conjecture that we would like to establish, $H_1 : \beta_2 > 0$. If we then reject the null hypothesis we can make a direct statement, concluding that β_2 is positive, with only a small (α) probability that we are in error.

The steps of this hypothesis test are as follows:

1. The null hypothesis is $H_0 : \beta_2 = 0$. The alternative hypothesis is $H_1 : \beta_2 > 0$.

2. The test statistic is (3.7). In this case $c = 0$, so $t = b_2/\mathrm{se}(b_2) \sim t_{(N-2)}$ if the null hypothesis is true.

3. Let us select $\alpha = 0.05$. The critical value for the right-tail rejection region is the 95th percentile of the t-distribution with $N - 2 = 38$ degrees of freedom, $t_{(0.95,38)} = 1.686$. Thus we will reject the null hypothesis if the calculated value of $t \geq 1.686$. If $t < 1.686$, we will not reject the null hypothesis.

4. Using the food expenditure data, we found that $b_2 = 10.21$ with standard error $\mathrm{se}(b_2) = 2.09$. The value of the test statistic is

$$t = \frac{b_2}{\mathrm{se}(b_2)} = \frac{10.21}{2.09} = 4.88$$

5. Since $t = 4.88 > 1.686$, we reject the null hypothesis that $\beta_2 = 0$ and accept the alternative that $\beta_2 > 0$. That is, we reject the hypothesis that there is no relationship between income and food expenditure, and conclude that there is a *statistically significant* positive relationship between household income and food expenditure.

The last part of the conclusion is important. When you report your results to an audience, you will want to describe the outcome of the test in the context of the problem you are investigating, not just in terms of Greek letters and symbols.

What if we had not been able to reject the null hypothesis in this example? Would we have concluded that economic theory is wrong and that there is no relationship between income and food expenditure? No. Remember that failing to reject a null hypothesis **does not** mean that the null hypothesis is true.

3.4.1b One-Tail Test of an Economic Hypothesis

Suppose that the economic profitability of a new supermarket depends on households spending more than \$5.50 out of each additional \$100 weekly income on food and that construction will not proceed unless there is strong evidence to this effect. In this case the conjecture we want to establish, the one that will go in the alternative hypothesis, is that $\beta_2 > 5.5$. If $\beta_2 \leq 5.5$, then the supermarket will be unprofitable and the owners would not want to build it. The least squares estimate of β_2 is $b_2 = 10.21$, which is greater than 5.5. What we want to determine is whether there is convincing statistical evidence that would lead us to conclude, based on the available data, that $\beta_2 > 5.5$. This judgment is based not only on the estimate b_2, but also on its precision as measured by $\mathrm{se}(b_2)$.

What will the null hypothesis be? We have been stating null hypotheses as equalities, such as $\beta_2 = 5.5$. This null hypothesis is too limited, because it is theoretically possible that $\beta_2 < 5.5$. It turns out that the hypothesis testing procedure for testing the null hypothesis that $H_0 : \beta_2 \leq 5.5$ against the alternative hypothesis $H_1 : \beta_2 > 5.5$ is *exactly the same* as testing $H_0 : \beta_2 = 5.5$ against the alternative hypothesis $H_1 : \beta_2 > 5.5$. The test statistic and rejection region are exactly the same. For a right-tail test you can form the null hypothesis in either of these ways depending upon the problem at hand.

The steps of this hypothesis test are as follows:

1. The null hypothesis is $H_0 : \beta_2 \leq 5.5$. The alternative hypothesis is $H_1 : \beta_2 > 5.5$.

2. The test statistic $t = (b_2 - 5.5)/\text{se}(b_2) \sim t_{(N-2)}$ if the null hypothesis is true.

3. Let us select $\alpha = 0.01$. The critical value for the right-tail rejection region is the 99th percentile of the t-distribution with $N - 2 = 38$ degrees of freedom, $t_{(0.99,38)} = 2.429$. We will reject the null hypothesis if the calculated value of $t \geq 2.429$. If $t < 2.429$, we will not reject the null hypothesis.

4. Using the food expenditure data, $b_2 = 10.21$ with standard error $\text{se}(b_2) = 2.09$. The value of the test statistic is

$$t = \frac{b_2 - 5.5}{\text{se}(b_2)} = \frac{10.21 - 5.5}{2.09} = 2.25$$

5. Since $t = 2.25 < 2.429$ we do not reject the null hypothesis that $\beta_2 \leq 5.5$. We are *not* able to conclude that the new supermarket will be profitable and will not begin construction.

In this example we have posed a situation where the choice of the level of significance α becomes of great importance. A construction project worth millions of dollars depends on having *convincing* evidence that households will spend more than \$5.50 out of each additional \$100 income on food. Although the "usual" choice is $\alpha = 0.05$, we have chosen a conservative value of $\alpha = 0.01$ because we seek a test that has a low chance of rejecting the null hypothesis when it is actually true. Recall that the level of significance of a test defines what we mean by an unlikely value of the test statistic. In this example, if the null hypothesis is true, then building the supermarket will be unprofitable. We want the probability of building an unprofitable market to be very small, and therefore we want the probability of rejecting the null hypothesis when it is true to be very small. In each real-world situation, the choice of α must be made on an assessment of *risk* and the *consequences* of making an incorrect decision.

A CEO unwilling to make a decision based on the above evidence may well order a new and larger sample of data to be analyzed. Recall that as the sample size increases, the least squares estimator becomes more precise (as measured by estimator variance) and consequently hypothesis tests become more powerful tools for statistical inference.

3.4.2 LEFT-TAIL TESTS

For completeness we will illustrate a test with the rejection region in the left tail. Consider the null hypothesis that $\beta_2 \geq 15$ and the alternative hypothesis $\beta_2 < 15$. Recall our memory trick for determining the location of the rejection region for a t-test. The rejection region is in the direction of the arrow $<$ in the alternative hypothesis. That tells us that the rejection region is in the left tail of the t-distribution. The steps of this hypothesis test are as follows:

1. The null hypothesis is $H_0 : \beta_2 \geq 15$. The alternative hypothesis is $H_1 : \beta_2 < 15$.

2. The test statistic $t = (b_2 - 15)/\text{se}(b_2) \sim t_{(N-2)}$ if the null hypothesis is true.

3. Let us select $\alpha = 0.05$. The critical value for the left-tail rejection region is the 5th percentile of the t-distribution with $N - 2 = 38$ degrees of freedom, $t_{(0.05,38)} = -1.686$. We will reject the null hypothesis if the calculated value of $t \leq -1.686$. If $t > -1.686$ we will not reject the null hypothesis. A left-tail rejection region is illustrated in Figure 3.3.

4. Using the food expenditure data, $b_2 = 10.21$ with standard error $\text{se}(b_2) = 2.09$. The value of the test statistic is

$$t = \frac{b_2 - 15}{\text{se}(b_2)} = \frac{10.21 - 15}{2.09} = -2.29$$

5. Since $t = -2.29 < -1.686$, we reject the null hypothesis that $\beta_2 \geq 15$ and accept the alternative that $\beta_2 < 15$. We conclude that households spend less than \$15 from each additional \$100 income on food.

3.4.3 Two-Tail Tests

3.4.3a Two-Tail Test of an Economic Hypothesis

A consultant voices the opinion that based on other similar neighborhoods the households near the proposed market will spend an additional \$7.50 per additional \$100 income. In terms of our economic model, we can state this conjecture as the null hypothesis $\beta_2 = 7.5$. If we want to test whether this is true or not, then the alternative is that $\beta_2 \neq 7.5$. This alternative makes no claim about whether β_2 is greater than 7.5 or less than 7.5, simply that it is not 7.5. In such cases we use a two-tail test, as follows:

1. The null hypothesis is $H_0 : \beta_2 = 7.5$. The alternative hypothesis is $H_1 : \beta_2 \neq 7.5$.

2. The test statistic $t = (b_2 - 7.5)/\text{se}(b_2) \sim t_{(N-2)}$ if the null hypothesis is true.

3. Let us select $\alpha = 0.05$. The critical values for this two-tail test are the 2.5-percentile $t_{(0.025,38)} = -2.024$ and the 97.5-percentile $t_{(0.975,38)} = 2.024$. Thus we will reject the null hypothesis if the calculated value of $t \geq 2.024$ **or** if $t \leq -2.024$. If $-2.024 < t < 2.024$ we will not reject the null hypothesis.

4. For the food expenditure data $b_2 = 10.21$ with standard error $\text{se}(b_2) = 2.09$. The value of the test statistic is

$$t = \frac{b_2 - 7.5}{\text{se}(b_2)} = \frac{10.21 - 7.5}{2.09} = 1.29$$

5. Since $-2.204 < t = 1.29 < 2.204$ we do not reject the null hypothesis that $\beta_2 = 7.5$. The sample data are consistent with the conjecture households will spend an additional \$7.50 per additional \$100 income on food.

We must avoid reading into this conclusion more than it means. We **do not** conclude from this test that $\beta_2 = 7.5$, only that the data are not incompatible with this parameter value. The data are also compatible with the null hypotheses $H_0 : \beta_2 = 8.5$ ($t = 0.82$), $H_0 : \beta_2 = 6.5$ ($t = 1.77$), and $H_0 : \beta_2 = 12.5$ ($t = -1.09$). A hypothesis test **cannot** be used to prove that a null hypothesis is true.

There is a trick relating two-tail tests and confidence intervals that is sometimes useful. Let c be a value within a $100(1 - \alpha)\%$ confidence interval, so that if $t_c = t_{(1-\alpha/2, N-2)}$, then

$$b_k - t_c \text{se}(b_k) \leq c \leq b_k + t_c \text{se}(b_k)$$

If we test the null hypothesis $H_0 : \beta_k = c$ against $H_1 : \beta_k \neq c$, when c is inside the confidence interval, then we will *not* reject the null hypothesis at the level of significance α. If c is outside the confidence interval, then the two-tail test will reject the null hypothesis. We do not advocate using confidence intervals to test hypotheses, they serve a different purpose, but if you are given a confidence interval, this trick is handy.

3.4.3b Two-Tail Test of Significance

While we are confident that a relationship exists between food expenditure and income, models are often proposed that are more speculative, and the purpose of hypothesis testing is to ascertain whether a relationship between variables exists or not. In this case the null hypothesis is $\beta_2 = 0$; that is, no linear relationship exists between x and y. The alternative is $\beta_2 \neq 0$, which would mean that a relationship exists, but that there may be either a positive or negative association between the variables. This is the most common form of a **test of significance**. The test steps are as follows:

1. The null hypothesis is $H_0 : \beta_2 = 0$. The alternative hypothesis is $H_1 : \beta_2 \neq 0$.

2. The test statistic $t = b_2/\text{se}(b_2) \sim t_{(N-2)}$ *if the null hypothesis is true.*

3. Let us select $\alpha = 0.05$. The critical values for this two-tail test are the 2.5-percentile $t_{(0.025,38)} = -2.024$ and the 97.5-percentile $t_{(0.975,38)} = 2.024$. We will reject the null hypothesis if the calculated value of $t \geq 2.024$ *or* if $t \leq -2.024$. If $-2.024 < t < 2.024$, we will not reject the null hypothesis.

4. Using the food expenditure data, $b_2 = 10.21$ with standard error $\text{se}(b_2) = 2.09$. The value of the test statistic is $t = b_2/\text{se}(b_2) = 10.21/2.09 = 4.88$.

5. Since $t = 4.88 > 2.024$ we reject the null hypothesis that $\beta_2 = 0$ and conclude that there is a statistically significant relationship between income and food expenditure.

Two points should be made about this result. First, the value of the t-statistic we computed in this two-tail test is the same as the value computed in the one-tail test of significance in Section 3.4.1a. The difference between the two tests is the rejection region and the critical values. Second, the two-tail test of significance is something that should be done each time a regression model is estimated, and consequently computer software automatically calculates the t-values for null hypotheses that the regression parameters are zero. Refer back to Figure 2.9. Consider the portion that reports the estimates:

Variable	Coefficient	Std. Error	*t*-Statistic	Prob.
C	83.41600	43.41016	1.921578	0.0622
INCOME	10.20964	2.093264	4.877381	0.0000

Note that there is a column labeled t-Statistic. This is the t-statistic value for the null hypothesis that the corresponding parameter is zero. It is calculated as $t = b_k/\text{se}(b_k)$. Dividing the least squares estimates (Coefficient) by their standard errors (Std. Error) gives the t-statistic values (t-Statistic) for testing the hypothesis that the parameter is zero. The t-statistic value for the variable *INCOME* is 4.877381, which is relevant for testing the null hypothesis $H_0 : \beta_2 = 0$. We have rounded this value to 4.88 in our discussions.

The t-value for testing the hypothesis that the intercept is zero equals 1.92. The $\alpha = 0.05$ critical values for these two-tail tests are $t_{(0.025,38)} = -2.024$ and $t_{(0.975,38)} = 2.024$ whether we are testing a hypothesis about the slope or intercept, so we fail to reject the null hypothesis that $H_0 : \beta_1 = 0$ given the alternative $H_1 : \beta_1 \neq 0$.

The final column, labeled "Prob." is the subject of the next section.

> **REMARK:** "Statistically significant" does not necessarily imply "economically significant." For example, suppose the CEO of a supermarket chain plans a certain course of action *if* $\beta_2 \neq 0$. Furthermore, suppose a large sample is collected from which we obtain the estimate $b_2 = 0.0001$ with $se(b_2) = 0.00001$, yielding the t-statistic $t = 10.0$. We would reject the null hypothesis that $\beta_2 = 0$ and accept the alternative that $\beta_2 \neq 0$. Here $b_2 = 0.0001$ is statistically different from zero. However, 0.0001 may not be "economically" different from zero, and the CEO may decide not to proceed with the plans. The message here is that one must think carefully about the importance of a statistical analysis before reporting or using the results.

3.5 The p-Value

When reporting the outcome of statistical hypothesis tests, it has become standard practice to report the **p-value** (an abbreviation for **probability value**) of the test. If we have the p-value of a test, p, we can determine the outcome of the test by comparing the p-value to the chosen level of significance, α, *without* looking up or calculating the critical values. The rule is

> **p-VALUE RULE:** Reject the null hypothesis when the p-value is less than, or equal to, the level of significance α. That is, if $p \leq \alpha$ then reject H_0. If $p > \alpha$ then do not reject H_0.

If you have chosen the level of significance to be $\alpha = 0.01$, 0.05, 0.10, or any other value, you can compare it to the p-value of a test and then reject, or not reject, without checking the critical value. In written works reporting the p-value of a test allows the reader to apply his or her own judgment about the appropriate level of significance.

How the p-value is computed depends on the alternative. If t is the calculated value of the t-statistic, then

- if $H_1 : \beta_k > c$, $p =$ probability to the right of t
- if $H_1 : \beta_k < c$, $p =$ probability to the left of t
- if $H_1 : \beta_k \neq c$, $p = $ *sum* of probabilities to the right of $|t|$ *and* to the left of $-|t|$

> **MEMORY TRICK:** The direction of the alternative indicates the tail(s) of the distribution in which the p-value falls.

3.5.1 p-VALUE FOR A RIGHT-TAIL TEST

In Section 3.4.1b we tested the null hypothesis $H_0 : \beta_2 \leq 5.5$ against the one-sided alternative $H_1 : \beta_2 > 5.5$. The calculated value of the t-statistic was

$$t = \frac{b_2 - 5.5}{\text{se}(b_2)} = \frac{10.21 - 5.5}{2.09} = 2.25$$

In this case, since the alternative is "greater than" ($>$), the p-value of this test is the probability that a t-random variable with $N - 2 = 38$ degrees of freedom is greater than 2.25, or $p = P\big[t_{(38)} \geq 2.25\big] = 0.0152$.

This probability value cannot be found in the usual t-table of critical values, but it is easily found using the computer. Statistical software packages, and spreadsheets such as Excel, have simple commands to evaluate the *cumulative distribution function* (*cdf*) (see Appendix B.1) for a variety of probability distributions. If $F_X(x)$ is the *cdf* for a random variable X, then for any value $x = c$ the cumulative probability is $P[X \leq c] = F_X(c)$. Given such a function for the t-distribution, we compute the desired p-value

$$p = P\big[t_{(38)} \geq 2.25\big] = 1 - P\big[t_{(38)} \leq 2.25\big] = 1 - 0.9848 = 0.0152$$

Following the p-value rule we conclude that at $\alpha = 0.01$ we do not reject the null hypothesis. If we had chosen $\alpha = 0.05$, we would reject the null hypothesis in favor of the alternative.

The logic of the p-value rule is shown in Figure 3.5. The probability of obtaining a t-value greater than 2.25 is 0.0152, $p = P\big[t_{(38)} \geq 2.25\big] = 0.0152$. The 99th percentile $t_{(0.99,38)}$, which is the critical value for a right-tail test with level of significance of $\alpha = 0.01$, must fall to the right of 2.25. This means that $t = 2.25$ does not fall in the rejection region if $\alpha = 0.01$ and we will not reject the null hypothesis at this level of significance. This is consistent with the *p-value rule*: When the p-value (0.0152) is greater than the chosen level of significance (0.01), we do not reject the null hypothesis.

On the other hand, the 95th percentile $t_{(0.95,38)}$, which is the critical value for a right-tail

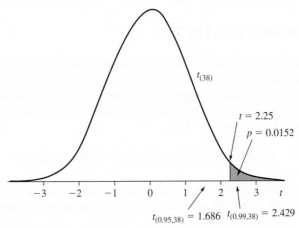

FIGURE **3.5** The p-value for a right-tail test.

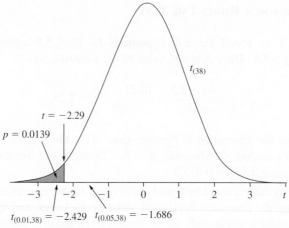

FIGURE 3.6 The p-value for a left-tail test.

test with $\alpha = 0.05$, must be to the left of 2.25. This means that $t = 2.25$ falls in the rejection region, and we reject the null hypothesis at the level of significance $\alpha = 0.05$. This is consistent with the *p-value rule*: When the p-value (0.0152) is less than or equal to the chosen level of significance (0.05) we will reject the null hypothesis.

3.5.2 *p*-Value for a Left-Tail Test

In Section 3.4.2 we carried out a test with the rejection region in the left tail of the t-distribution. The null hypothesis was $H_0 : \beta_2 \geq 15$, and the alternative hypothesis was $H_1 : \beta_2 < 15$. The calculated value of the t-statistic was $t = -2.29$. To compute the p-value for this left-tail test, we calculate the probability of obtaining a t-statistic to the left of -2.29. Using your computer software you will find this value to be $P\left[t_{(38)} \leq -2.29\right] = 0.0139$. Following the p-value rule we conclude that at $\alpha = 0.01$ we do not reject the null hypothesis. If we choose $\alpha = 0.05$, we will reject the null hypothesis in favor of the alternative. See Figure 3.6 to see this graphically. Locate the 1st and 5th percentiles. These will be the critical values for left-tail tests with $\alpha = 0.01$ and $\alpha = 0.05$ levels of significance. When the p-value (0.0139) is greater than the level of significance ($\alpha = 0.01$), then the t-value -2.29 is not in the test rejection region. When the p-value (0.0139) is less than or equal to the level of significance ($\alpha = 0.05$), then the t-value -2.29 is in the test rejection region.

3.5.3 *p*-Value for a Two-Tail Test

For a two-tail test, the rejection region is in the two tails of the t-distribution, and the p-value is similarly calculated in the two tails of the distribution. In Section 3.4.3a we tested the null hypothesis that $\beta_2 = 7.5$ against the alternative hypothesis $\beta_2 \neq 7.5$. The calculated value of the t-statistic was $t = 1.29$. For this two-tail test, the p-value is the combined probability to the right of 1.29 and to the left of -1.29:

$$p = P\left[t_{(38)} \geq 1.29\right] + P\left[t_{(38)} \leq -1.29\right] = 0.2033$$

This calculation is depicted in Figure 3.7. Once the p-value is obtained its use is unchanged. If we choose $\alpha = 0.05$, $\alpha = 0.10$, or even $\alpha = 0.20$, we will fail to reject the null hypothesis because $p > \alpha$.

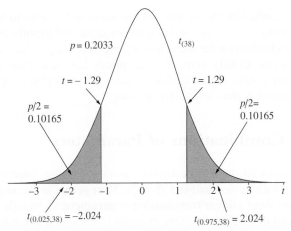

FIGURE **3.7** The p-value for a two-tail test of significance.

At the beginning of this section we stated the following rule for computing p-values for two-tail tests: if $H_1 : \beta_k \neq c$, $p = sum$ of probabilities to the right of $|t|$ *and* to the left of $-|t|$. The reason for the use of absolute values in this rule is that it will apply equally well if the value of the t-statistic turns out to be positive or negative.

3.5.4 p-VALUE FOR A TWO-TAIL TEST OF SIGNIFICANCE

All statistical software computes the p-value for the two-tail test of significance for each coefficient when a regression analysis is performed. In Section 3.4.3b we discussed testing the null hypothesis $H_0 : \beta_2 = 0$ against the alternative hypothesis $H_1 : \beta_2 \neq 0$. For the calculated value of the t-statistic $t = 4.88$ the p-value is

$$p = P\left[t_{(38)} \geq 4.88\right] + P\left[t_{(38)} \leq -4.88\right] = 0.0000$$

Your software will automatically compute and report this p-value for a two-tail test of significance. Refer back to Figure 2.9 and consider just the portion reporting the estimates:

Variable	Coefficient	Std. Error	t-Statistic	Prob.
C	83.41600	43.41016	1.921578	0.0622
INCOME	10.20964	2.093264	4.877381	0.0000

Next to each t-statistic value is the two-tail p-value, which is labeled "Prob." by the EViews software. Other software packages will use similar names. When inspecting computer output we can immediately decide if an estimate is statistically significant (statistically different from zero using a two-tail test) by comparing the p-value to whatever level of significance we care to use. The estimated intercept has p-value 0.0622, so it is not statistically different from zero at the level of significance $\alpha = 0.05$, but it is statistically significant if $\alpha = 0.10$.

The estimated coefficient for income has a *p*-value that is zero to four places. Thus $p \leq \alpha = 0.01$ or even $\alpha = 0.0001$, and thus we reject the null hypothesis that income has no effect on food expenditure at these levels of significance. The *p*-value for this two-tail test of significance is not actually zero. If more places are used, then $p = 0.00001946$. Regression software usually does not print out more than four places, because in practice levels of significance less than $\alpha = 0.001$ are rare.

3.6 Linear Combinations of Parameters

So far we have discussed statistical inference (point estimation, interval estimation, and hypothesis testing) for a single parameter, β_1 or β_2. More generally, we may wish to estimate and test hypotheses about a **linear combination of parameters** $\lambda = c_1\beta_1 + c_2\beta_2$, where c_1 and c_2 are constants that we specify. One example is if we wish to estimate the **expected** value of a dependent variable $E(y)$ when x takes some specific value, such as $x = x_0$. In this case $c_1 = 1$ and $c_2 = x_0$, so that, $\lambda = c_1\beta_1 + c_2\beta_2 = \beta_1 + x_0\beta_2 = E(y|x = x_0)$.

Under assumptions SR1–SR5 the least squares estimators b_1 and b_2 are the best linear unbiased estimators of β_1 and β_2. It is also true that $\hat{\lambda} = c_1b_1 + c_2b_2$ is the best linear unbiased estimator of $\lambda = c_1\beta_1 + c_2\beta_2$. The estimator $\hat{\lambda}$ is unbiased because

$$E(\hat{\lambda}) = E(c_1b_1 + c_2b_2) = c_1E(b_1) + c_2E(b_2) = c_1\beta_1 + c_2\beta_2 = \lambda$$

To find the variance of $\hat{\lambda}$, recall from the Probability Primer, Section P.5.6, that if X and Y are random variables, and if a and b are constants, then the variance $\mathrm{var}(aX + bY)$ is given in equation (P.20) as

$$\mathrm{var}(aX + bY) = a^2\mathrm{var}(X) + b^2\mathrm{var}(Y) + 2ab\mathrm{cov}(X, Y)$$

In the estimator $(c_1b_1 + c_2b_2)$, both b_1 and b_2 are random variables, as we do not know what their values will be until a sample is drawn and estimates calculated. Applying (P.20) we have

$$\mathrm{var}(\hat{\lambda}) = \mathrm{var}(c_1b_1 + c_2b_2) = c_1^2\mathrm{var}(b_1) + c_2^2\mathrm{var}(b_2) + 2c_1c_2\mathrm{cov}(b_1, b_2) \tag{3.8}$$

The variances and covariances of the least squares estimators are given in (2.14)–(2.16). We estimate $\mathrm{var}(\hat{\lambda}) = \mathrm{var}(c_1b_1 + c_2b_2)$ by replacing the unknown variances and covariances with their estimated variances and covariances in (2.20)–(2.22). Then

$$\widehat{\mathrm{var}(\hat{\lambda})} = \widehat{\mathrm{var}(c_1b_1 + c_2b_2)} = c_1^2\widehat{\mathrm{var}(b_1)} + c_2^2\widehat{\mathrm{var}(b_2)} + 2c_1c_2\widehat{\mathrm{cov}(b_1, b_2)} \tag{3.9}$$

The standard error of $\hat{\lambda} = c_1b_1 + c_2b_2$ is the square root of the estimated variance,

$$\mathrm{se}(\hat{\lambda}) = \mathrm{se}(c_1b_1 + c_2b_2) = \sqrt{\widehat{\mathrm{var}(c_1b_1 + c_2b_2)}} \tag{3.10}$$

If in addition SR6 holds, or if the sample is large, the least squares estimators b_1 and b_2 have normal distributions. It is also true that linear combinations of normally distributed variables are normally distributed, so that

$$\hat{\lambda} = c_1b_1 + c_2b_2 \sim N[\lambda, \mathrm{var}(\hat{\lambda})]$$

Where $\text{var}(\hat{\lambda})$ is given in (3.8). You may be thinking of how long such calculations will take using a calculator, but don't worry. Most computer software will do the calculations for you. Now it's time for an example.

3.6.1 ESTIMATING EXPECTED FOOD EXPENDITURE

An executive might ask of the research staff, "Give me an estimate of average weekly food expenditure by households with $2,000 weekly income." Interpreting the executive's word "average" to mean "expected value," for the food expenditure model this means estimating

$$E(FOOD\_EXP|INCOME) = \beta_1 + \beta_2 INCOME$$

Recall that we measured income in $100 units in this example, so a weekly income of $2,000 corresponds to $INCOME = 20$. The executive is requesting an estimate of

$$E(FOOD\_EXP|INCOME = 20) = \beta_1 + \beta_2 20$$

which is a linear combination of the parameters.

Using the 40 observations in *food.dat*, in Chapter 2.3.2 we obtained the fitted regression,

$$\overline{FOOD\_EXP} = 83.4160 + 10.2096 INCOME$$

The point estimate of average weekly food expenditure for a household with $2,000 income is

$$\overline{E(FOOD\_EXP|INCOME = 20)} = b_1 + b_2 20 = 83.4160 + 10.2096(20) = 287.6089$$

We estimate that the expected food expenditure by a household with $2,000 income is $287.61 per week.

3.6.2 AN INTERVAL ESTIMATE OF EXPECTED FOOD EXPENDITURE

If assumption SR6 holds, then the estimator $\hat{\lambda}$ has a normal distribution. We can form a standard normal random variable as

$$Z = \frac{\hat{\lambda} - \lambda}{\sqrt{\text{var}(\hat{\lambda})}} \sim N(0, 1)$$

Replacing the true variance in the denominator with the estimated variance we form a t-statistic

$$t = \frac{\hat{\lambda} - \lambda}{\sqrt{\widehat{\text{var}}(\hat{\lambda})}} = \frac{\hat{\lambda} - \lambda}{\text{se}(\hat{\lambda})} = \frac{(c_1 b_1 + c_2 b_2) - (c_1 \beta_1 + c_2 \beta_2)}{\text{se}(c_1 b_1 + c_2 b_2)} \sim t_{(N-2)} \tag{3.11}$$

If t_c is the $1 - \alpha/2$ percentile value from the $t_{(N-2)}$ distribution, then $P(-t_c \leq t \leq t_c) = 1 - \alpha$. Substitute (3.11) for t and rearrange to obtain

$$P[(c_1b_1 + c_2b_2) - t_c\text{se}(c_1b_1 + c_2b_2) \leq c_1\beta_1 + c_2\beta_2 \leq$$
$$(c_1b_1 + c_2b_2) + t_c\text{se}(c_1b_1 + c_2b_2)] = 1 - \alpha$$

Thus a $100(1 - \alpha)\%$ interval estimate for $c_1\beta_1 + c_2\beta_2$ is

$$(c_1b_1 + c_2b_2) \pm t_c\text{se}(c_1b_1 + c_2b_2)$$

In Chapter 2.7.2 we obtained the estimated covariance matrix

$$\begin{bmatrix} \widehat{\text{var}(b_1)} & \widehat{\text{cov}(b_1, b_2)} \\ \widehat{\text{cov}(b_1, b_2)} & \widehat{\text{var}(b_2)} \end{bmatrix} = \begin{array}{c|cc} & C & INCOME \\ \hline C & 1884.442 & -85.9032 \\ INCOME & -85.9032 & 4.3818 \end{array}$$

To obtain the standard error for $\widehat{E(FOOD\_EXP|INCOME} = 20) = b_1 + b_2 20$ we first calculate the estimated variance

$$\widehat{\text{var}(b_1 + 20b_2)} = \widehat{\text{var}(b_1)} + 20^2 \times \widehat{\text{var}(b_2)} + 2 \times 20 \times \widehat{\text{cov}(b_1, b_2)}$$
$$= 1884.442 + 20^2 \times 4.3818 + 2 \times 20 \times (-85.9032)$$
$$= 201.0169$$

Given $\widehat{\text{var}(b_1 + 20b_2)} = 201.0169$[1] the corresponding standard error is

$$\text{se}(b_1 + 20b_2) = \sqrt{\widehat{\text{var}(b_1 + 20b_2)}} = \sqrt{201.0169} = 14.1780$$

A 95% interval estimate of $\widehat{E(FOOD\_EXP|INCOME} = 20) = \beta_1 + \beta_2 20$ is $(b_1 + b_2 20) \pm t_{(0.975,38)}\text{se}(b_1 + b_2 20)$ or

$$[287.6089 - 2.024(14.1780), \ 287.6089 + 2.024(14.1780)] = [258.91, 316.31]$$

We estimate with 95% confidence that the expected food expenditure by a household with \$2,000 income is between \$258.91 and \$316.31.

3.6.3 TESTING A LINEAR COMBINATION OF PARAMETERS

So far we have tested hypotheses involving only one regression parameter at a time. That is, our hypotheses have been of the form $H_0 : \beta_k = c$. A more **general linear hypothesis** involves both parameters and may be stated as

$$H_0 : c_1\beta_1 + c_2\beta_2 = c_0 \tag{3.12a}$$

---

[1] The value 201.0169 was obtained using computer software. If you do the calculation by hand using the provided numbers you obtain 201.034. Do not be alarmed if you obtain small differences like this occasionally, as it most likely is the difference between a computer generated solution and a hand-calculation.

where c_0, c_1 and c_2 are specified constants, with c_0 being the hypothesized value. Despite the fact that the null hypothesis involves both coefficients, it still represents a single hypothesis to be tested using a t-statistic. Sometimes it is written equivalently in implicit form as

$$H_0 : (c_1\beta_1 + c_2\beta_2) - c_0 = 0 \tag{3.12b}$$

The alternative hypothesis for the null hypothesis in (3.12a) might be

(i) $H_1 : c_1\beta_1 + c_2\beta_2 \neq c_0$ leading to a two-tail t-test

(ii) $H_1 : c_1\beta_1 + c_2\beta_2 > c_0$ leading to a right-tail t-test [Null may be "$\leq$"]

(iii) $H_1 : c_1\beta_1 + c_2\beta_2 < c_0$ leading to a left-tail t-test [Null may be "$\geq$"]

If the implicit form is used, the alternative hypothesis is adjusted as well.

The test of the hypothesis (3.12) uses the t-statistic

$$t = \frac{(c_1b_1 + c_2b_2) - c_0}{\text{se}(c_1b_1 + c_2b_2)} \sim t_{(N-2)} \text{ if the null hypothesis is true} \tag{3.13}$$

The rejection regions for the one- and two-tail alternatives (i)–(iii) are the same as those described in Section 3.3, and conclusions are interpreted the same way as well.

The form of the t-statistic is very similar to the original specification in (3.7). In the numerator $(c_1b_1 + c_2b_2)$ is the best linear unbiased estimator of $(c_1\beta_1 + c_2\beta_2)$, and if the errors are normally distributed, or if we have a large sample, this estimator is normally distributed as well.

3.6.4 TESTING EXPECTED FOOD EXPENDITURE

The food expenditure model introduced in Chapter 2.1 and used as an illustration throughout provides an excellent example of how the linear hypothesis in (3.12) might be used in practice. For most medium and larger cities there are forecasts of income growth for the coming year. A supermarket or food retail store of any type will consider this before a new facility is built. Their question is, if income in a locale is projected to grow at a certain rate, how much of that will be spent on food items? An executive might say, based on years of experience, "I expect that a household with $2,000 weekly income will spend, on average, more than $250 a week on food." How can we use econometrics to test this conjecture?

The regression function for the food expenditure model is

$$E(FOOD\_EXP|INCOME) = \beta_1 + \beta_2 INCOME$$

The executive's conjecture is that

$$E(FOOD\_EXP|INCOME = 20) = \beta_1 + \beta_2 20 > 250$$

To test the validity of this statement we use it as the alternative hypothesis

$$H_1 : \beta_1 + \beta_2 20 > 250, \text{ or } H_1 : \beta_1 + \beta_2 20 - 250 > 0$$

The corresponding null hypothesis is the logical alternative to the executive's statement

$$H_0 : \beta_1 + \beta_2 20 \leq 250, \text{ or } H_0 : \beta_1 + \beta_2 20 - 250 \leq 0$$

Notice that the null and alternative hypothesis are in the same form as the general linear hypothesis with $c_1 = 1$, $c_2 = 20$, and $c_0 = 250$.

The rejection region for a right-tail test is illustrated in Figure 3.2. For a right-tail test at the $\alpha = 0.05$ level of significance the t-critical value is the 95th percentile of the $t_{(38)}$ distribution, which is $t_{(0.95,38)} = 1.686$. If the calculated t-statistic value is greater than 1.686, we will reject the null hypothesis and accept the alternative hypothesis, which in this case is the executive's conjecture.

Computing the t-statistic value

$$t = \frac{(b_1 + 20b_2) - 250}{se(b_1 + 20b_2)}$$

$$= \frac{(83.4160 + 20 \times 10.2096) - 250}{14.1780}$$

$$= \frac{287.6089 - 250}{14.1780} = \frac{37.6089}{14.1780} = 2.65$$

Since $t = 2.65 > t_c = 1.686$, we reject the null hypothesis that a household with weekly income of \$2,000 will spend \$250 per week or less on food, and conclude that the executive's conjecture that such households spend more than \$250 is correct, with the probability of Type I error 0.05.

In Section 3.6.1 we estimated that a household with \$2,000 weekly income will spend \$287.6089, which is greater than the executive's speculated value of \$250. However, simply observing that the estimated value is greater than \$250 is not a statistical test. It might be numerically greater, but is it **significantly** greater? The t-test takes into account the precision with which we have estimated this expenditure level and also controls the probability of Type I error.

3.7 Exercises

Answers to exercises marked * appear at www.wiley.com/go/global/hill.

3.7.1 PROBLEMS

3.1   Using the regression output for the food expenditure model shown in Figure 2.9:
(a) Construct a 95% interval estimate for β_1 and interpret.
(b) Test the null hypothesis that β_1 is zero against the alternative that it is not at the 5% level of significance without using the reported p-value. What is your conclusion?
(c) Draw a sketch showing the p-value 0.0622 shown in Figure 2.9, the critical value from the t-distribution used in (b), and how the p-value could have been used to answer (b).
(d) Test the null hypothesis that β_1 is zero against the alternative that it is positive at the 5% level of significance. Draw a sketch of the rejection region and compute the p-value. What is your conclusion?

(e) Explain the differences and similarities between the "level of significance" and the "level of confidence."

(f) The results in (d) show that we are 95% confident that β_1 is positive. True, or false? If false, explain.

3.2 The general manager of an engineering firm wants to know whether a technical artist's experience influences the quality of his or her work. A random sample of 24 artists is selected and their years of work experience and quality rating (as assessed by their supervisors) recorded. Work experience (*EXPER*) is measured in years and quality rating (*RATING*) takes a value of 1 through 7, with 7 = excellent and 1 = poor. The simple regression model $RATING = \beta_1 + \beta_2 EXPER + e$ is proposed. The least squares estimates of the model, and the standard errors of the estimates, are

$$\widehat{RATING} = 3.204 + 0.076\,EXPER$$
$$(se) \qquad (0.709) \quad (0.044)$$

(a) Sketch the estimated regression function. Interpret the coefficient of *EXPER*.

(b) Construct a 90% confidence interval for β_2, the slope of the relationship between quality rating and experience. In what are you 90% confident?

(c) Test the null hypothesis that β_2 is zero against the alternative that it is not using a two-tail test and the $\alpha = 0.10$ level of significance. What do you conclude?

(d) Test the null hypothesis that β_2 is zero against the one-tail alternative that it is positive at the $\alpha = 0.10$ level of significance. What do you conclude?

(e) For the test in part (c), the *p*-value is 0.0982. If we choose the probability of a Type I error to be $\alpha = 0.05$, do we reject the null hypothesis, or not, just based on an inspection of the *p*-value? Show, in a diagram, how this *p*-value is computed.

3.3* In an estimated simple regression model, based on 24 observations, the estimated slope parameter is 0.310 and the estimated standard error is 0.082.

(a) Test the hypothesis that the slope is zero against the alternative that it is not, at the 1% level of significance.

(b) Test the hypothesis that the slope is zero against the alternative that it is positive at the 1% level of significance.

(c) Test the hypothesis that the slope is zero against the alternative that it is negative at the 5% level of significance. Draw a sketch showing the rejection region.

(d) Test the hypothesis that the estimated slope is 0.5, against the alternative that it is not, at the 5% level of significance.

(e) Obtain a 99% interval estimate of the slope.

3.4 Consider a simple regression in which the dependent variable *MIM* = mean income of males who are 18 years of age or older, in thousands of dollars. The explanatory variable *PMHS* = percent of males 18 or older who are high school graduates. The data consist of 51 observations on the 50 states plus the District of Columbia. Thus *MIM* and *PMHS* are "state averages." The estimated regression, along with standard errors and *t*-statistics, is

$$\widehat{MIM} = \quad (a) \quad + \quad 0.180PMHS$$
$$(se) \quad (2.174) \qquad (b)$$
$$(t) \quad (1.257) \qquad (5.754)$$

(a) What is the estimated equation intercept? Show your calculation. Sketch the estimated regression function.

(b) What is the standard error of the estimated slope? Show your calculation.

(c) What is the *p*-value for the two-tail test of the hypothesis that the equation intercept is zero? Draw a sketch to illustrate.

(d) State the economic interpretation of the estimated slope. Is the sign of the coefficient what you would expect from economic theory?

(e) Construct a 99% confidence interval estimate of the slope of this relationship.

(f) Test the hypothesis that the slope of the relationship is 0.2 against the alternative that it is not. State in words the meaning of the null hypothesis in the context of this problem.

3.7.2 COMPUTER EXERCISES

3.5 A life insurance company wishes to examine the relationship between the amount of life insurance held by a family and family income. From a random sample of 20 households, the company collected the data in the file *insur.dat*. The data are in units of thousands of dollars.

(a) Estimate the linear regression with dependent variable *INSURANCE* and independent variable *INCOME*. Write down the fitted model and draw a sketch of the fitted function. Identify the estimated slope and intercept on the sketch. Locate the point of the means on the plot.

(b) Discuss the relationship you estimated in (a). In particular,

   (i) What is your estimate of the resulting change in the amount of life insurance when income increases by $1,000?

   (ii) What is the standard error of the estimate in (i), and how do you use this standard error for interval estimation and hypothesis testing?

(c) One member of the management board claims that for every $1,000 increase in income, the amount of life insurance held will go up by $5,000. Choose an alternative hypothesis and explain your choice. Does your estimated relationship support this claim? Use a 5% significance level.

(d) Test the hypothesis that as income increases the amount of life insurance increases by the same amount. That is, test the hypothesis that the slope of the relationship is one.

(e) Write a short report (200–250 words) summarizing your findings about the relationship between income and the amount of life insurance held.

3.6* In Exercise 2.9 we considered a motel that had discovered that a defective product was used during construction. It took seven months to correct the defects, during which approximately 14 rooms in the 100-unit motel were taken out of service for one month at a time. The data are in *motel.dat*.

(a) In the linear regression model $MOTEL\_PCT = \beta_1 + \beta_2 COMP\_PCT + e$, test the null hypothesis $H_0 : \beta_2 \leq 0$ against the alternative hypothesis $H_1 : \beta_2 > 0$ at the $\alpha = 0.01$ level of significance. Discuss your conclusion. Include in your answer a sketch of the rejection region and a calculation of the *p*-value.

(b) Consider a linear regression with $y = MOTEL\_PCT$ and $x = RELPRICE$, which is the ratio of the price per room charged by the motel in question relative to its competitors. Test the null hypothesis that there is no relationship between these variables against the alternative that there is an inverse relationship between them, at the $\alpha = 0.01$ level of significance. Discuss your conclusion. Include in your answer a sketch of the rejection region, and a calculation of the *p*-value. In this exercise follow and **show** all the test procedure steps suggested in Chapter 3.4.

(c) Consider the linear regression $MOTEL\_PCT = \delta_1 + \delta_2 REPAIR + e$, where $REPAIR$ is an indicator variable taking the value 1 during the repair period and 0 otherwise. Test the null hypothesis $H_0 : \delta_2 \geq 0$ against the alternative hypothesis $H_1 : \delta_2 < 0$ at the $\alpha = 0.05$ level of significance. Explain the logic behind stating the null and alternative hypotheses in this way. Discuss your conclusions.

(d) Using the model given in part (c), construct a 95% interval estimate for the parameter δ_2 and give its interpretation. Have we estimated the effect of the repairs on motel occupancy relatively precisely, or not? Explain.

(e) Consider the linear regression model with $y = MOTEL\_PCT - COMP\_PCT$ and $x = REPAIR$, that is $(MOTEL\_PCT - COMP\_PCT) = \gamma_1 + \gamma_2 REPAIR + e$. Test the null hypothesis that $\gamma_2 = 0$ against the alternative that $\gamma_2 < 0$ at the $\alpha = 0.01$ level of significance. Discuss the meaning of the test outcome.

(f) Using the model in part (e), construct and discuss the 95% interval estimate of γ_2.

3.7 Consider the capital asset pricing model (CAPM) in Exercise 2.10. Use the data in *capm4.dat* to answer each of the following:

(a) Test at the 5% level of significance the hypothesis that each stock's "*beta*" value is 1 against the alternative that it is not equal to 1. What is the economic interpretation of a *beta* equal to 1?

(b) Test at the 5% level of significance the null hypothesis that Mobil-Exxon's "*beta*" value is greater than or equal to 1 against the alternative that it is less than 1. What is the economic interpretation of a *beta* less than 1?

(c) Test at the 5% level of significance the null hypothesis that Microsoft's "*beta*" value is less than or equal to 1 against the alternative that it is greater than 1. What is the economic interpretation of a *beta* more than 1?

(d) Construct a 95% interval estimate of Microsoft's "*beta*." Assume that you are a stockbroker. Explain this result to an investor who has come to you for advice.

(e) Test (at a 5% significance level) the hypothesis that the intercept term in the CAPM model for each stock is zero, against the alternative that it is not. What do you conclude?

3.8 The file *br2.dat* contains data on 1080 houses sold in Baton Rouge, Louisiana during mid-2005. The data include sale price and the house size in square feet. Also included is an indicator variable *TRADITIONAL* indicating whether the house style is traditional or not.

(a) For the traditional-style houses estimate the linear regression model $PRICE = \beta_1 + \beta_2 SQFT + e$. Test the null hypothesis that the slope is zero against the alternative that it is positive, using the $\alpha = 0.05$ level of significance. Follow and show all the test steps described in Chapter 3.4.

(b) Using the linear model in (a), test the null hypothesis (H_0) that the expected price of a house of 1000 square feet is equal to, or less than, \$100,000. What is the appropriate alternative hypothesis? Use the $\alpha = 0.05$ level of significance. Obtain the p-value of the test and show its value on a sketch. What is your conclusion?

(c) Based on the estimated results from part (a), construct a 99% interval estimate of the expected price of a house of 1000 square feet.

(d) For the traditional-style houses, estimate the quadratic regression model $PRICE = \alpha_1 + \alpha_2 SQFT^2 + e$. Test the null hypothesis that the marginal effect of an additional square foot of living area in a home with 1000 square feet of living space is \$75 against the alternative that the effect is less than \$75. Use the

$\alpha = 0.05$ level of significance. Repeat the same test for a home of 2000 square feet of living space. Discuss your conclusions.

(e) For the traditional-style houses, estimate the log-linear regression model $\ln(PRICE) = \gamma_1 + \gamma_2 SQFT + e$. Test the null hypothesis that the marginal effect of an additional square foot of living area in a home with 1000 square feet of living space is \$75 against the alternative that the effect is less than \$75. Use the $\alpha = 0.05$ level of significance. Repeat the same test for a home of 2000 square feet of living space. Discuss your conclusions.

3.9* Reconsider the presidential voting data (*fair4.dat*) introduced in Exercise 2.14. Use the data from 1916 to 2008 for this exercise.

(a) Using the regression model $VOTE = \beta_1 + \beta_2 GROWTH + e$, test (at a 5% significance level) the null hypothesis that economic growth has no effect on the percentage vote earned by the incumbent party. Select an alternative hypothesis and a rejection region. Explain your choice.

(b) Using the regression model in part (a), construct a 95% interval estimate for β_2, and interpret.

(c) Using the regression model $VOTE = \beta_1 + \beta_2 INFLATION + e$, test the null hypothesis that inflation has no effect on the percentage vote earned by the incumbent party. Select an alternative hypothesis, a rejection region, and a significance level. Explain your choice.

(d) Using the regression model in part (c), construct a 95% interval estimate for β_2, and interpret.

(e) Test the null hypothesis that if $INFLATION = 0$ the expected vote in favor of the incumbent party is 50%, or more. Select the appropriate alternative. Carry out the test at the 5% level of significance. Discuss your conclusion.

(f) Construct a 95% interval estimate of the expected vote in favor of the incumbent party if $INFLATION = 2\%$. Discuss the interpretation of this interval estimate.

3.10 Reconsider Exercise 2.13, which was based on the experiment with small classes for primary school students conducted in Tennessee beginning in 1985. Data for the kindergarten classes is contained in the data file *star.dat*.

(a) Using children who are in either a regular-sized class or a small class, estimate the regression model explaining students' combined aptitude scores as a function of class size, $TOTALSCORE = \beta_1 + \beta_2 SMALL + e$. Test the null hypothesis that β_2 is zero, or negative, against the alternative that this coefficient is positive. Use the 5% level of significance. Compute the *p*-value of this test, and show its value in a sketch. Discuss the social importance of this finding.

(b) For the model in part (a), construct a 95% interval estimate of β_2 and discuss.

(c) Repeat part (a) using dependent variables *READSCORE* and *MATHSCORE*. Do you observe any differences?

(d) Using children who are in either a regular-sized class or a regular-sized class with a teacher aide, estimate the regression model explaining students' combined aptitude scores as a function of the presence or absence of a teacher aide, $TOTALSCORE = \gamma_1 + \gamma_2 AIDE + e$. Test the null hypothesis that γ_2 is zero or negative against the alternative that this coefficient is positive. Use the 5% level of significance. Discuss the importance of this finding.

(e) For the model in part (d), construct a 95% interval estimate of γ_2 and discuss.

(f) Repeat part (d) using dependent variables *READSCORE* and *MATHSCORE*. Do you observe any differences?

3.11 How much does experience affect wage rates? The data file *cps4_small.dat* contains 1000 observations on hourly wage rates, experience and other variables from the 2008 Current Population Survey (CPS).

(a) Estimate the linear regression $WAGE = \beta_1 + \beta_2 EXPER + e$ and discuss the results. Using your software plot a scatter diagram with *WAGE* on the vertical axis and *EXPER* on the horizontal axis. Sketch in by hand, or using your software, the fitted regression line.

(b) Test the statistical significance of the estimated slope of the relationship at the 1% level. Use a one-tail test.

(c) Repeat part (a) for the sub-samples consisting of (i) females, (ii) males, (iii) asians, and (iv) white males. What differences, if any, do you notice?

(d) For each of the estimated regression models in (a) and (c), calculate the least squares residuals and plot them against *EXPER*. Are any patterns evident?

3.12 Is the relationship between experience and wages constant over one's lifetime? To investigate we will fit a quadratic model using the data file *cps4_small.dat*, which contains 1,000 observations on hourly wage rates, experience and other variables from the 2008 Current Population Survey (CPS).

(a) Create a new variable called $EXPER30 = EXPER - 30$. Construct a scatter diagram with *WAGE* on the vertical axis and *EXPER30* on the horizontal axis. Are any patterns evident?

(b) Estimate by least squares the quadratic model $WAGE = \gamma_1 + \gamma_2 (EXPER30)^2 + e$. Are the coefficient estimates statistically significant? Test the null hypothesis that $\gamma_2 \geq 0$ against the alternative that $\gamma_2 < 0$ at the $\alpha = 0.01$ level of significance. What conclusion do you draw?

(c) Using the estimation in part (b), compute the estimated marginal effect of experience upon wage for a person with 10 years' experience, 30 years' experience, and 50 years' experience. Are these slopes significantly different from zero at the $\alpha = 0.01$ level of significance?

(d) Construct 99% interval estimates of each of the slopes in part (c). How precisely are we estimating these values?

(e) Using the estimation result from part (b) create the fitted values $\widehat{WAGE} = \hat{\gamma}_1 + \hat{\gamma}_2 (EXPER30)^2$, where the ^ denotes least squares estimates. Plot these fitted values and *WAGE* on the vertical axis of the same graph against *EXPER30* on the horizontal axis. Are the estimates in part (c) consistent with the graph?

(f) Estimate the linear regression $WAGE = \beta_1 + \beta_2 EXPER30 + e$ and the linear regression $WAGE = \alpha_1 + \alpha_2 EXPER + e$. What differences do you observe between these regressions and why do they occur? What is the estimated marginal effect of experience on wage from these regressions? Based on your work in parts (b)–(d), is the assumption of constant slope in this model a good one? Explain.

(g) Use the larger data *cps4.dat* (4838 observations) to repeat parts (b), (c), and (d). How much has the larger sample improved the precision of the interval estimates in part (d)?

3.13* Is the relationship between experience and ln(wages) constant over one's lifetime? To investigate we will fit a logarithmic model using the data file *cps4_small.dat*, which contains 1000 observations on hourly wage rates, experience and other variables from the 2008 Current Population Survey (CPS).

(a) Create a new variable called $EXPER30 = EXPER - 30$. Construct a scatter diagram with $\ln(WAGE)$ on the vertical axis and $EXPER30$ on the horizontal axis. Are any patterns evident?

(b) Estimate by least squares the quadratic model $\ln(WAGE) = \gamma_1 + \gamma_2(EXPER30)^2 + e$. Are the coefficient estimates statistically significant? Test the null hypothesis that $\gamma_2 \geq 0$ against the alternative that $\gamma_2 < 0$ at the $\alpha = 0.05$ level of significance. What conclusion do you draw?

(c) Using the estimation in part (b), compute the estimated marginal effect of experience upon wage for a person with 10 years of experience, 30 years of experience, and 50 years of experience. [Hint: If $\ln(y) = a + bx^2$ then $y = \exp(a + bx^2)$, and $dy/dx = \exp(a + bx^2) \times 2bx = 2bxy$]

(d) Using the estimation result from part (b) create the fitted values $\widehat{WAGE} = \exp\left(\hat{\gamma}_1 + \hat{\gamma}_2(EXPER30)^2\right)$, where the ^ denotes least squares estimates. Plot these fitted values and $WAGE$ on the vertical axis of the same graph against $EXPER30$ on the horizontal axis. Are the estimates in part (c) consistent with the graph?

3.14 Data on the weekly sales of a major brand of canned tuna by a supermarket chain in a large midwestern U.S. city during a mid-1990s calendar year are contained in the file *tuna.dat*. There are 52 observations on the variables. The variable $SAL1 =$ unit sales of brand no. 1 canned tuna, $APR1 =$ price per can of brand no. 1 canned tuna, $APR2$, $APR3 =$ price per can of brands nos. 2 and 3 of canned tuna.

(a) Create the relative price variables $RPRICE2 = APR1/APR2$ and $RPRICE3 = APR1/APR3$. What do you anticipate the relationship between sales ($SAL1$) and the relative price variables to be? Explain your reasoning.

(b) Estimate the log-linear model $\ln(SAL1) = \beta_1 + \beta_2 RPRICE2 + e$. Interpret the estimate of β_2. Construct and interpret a 95% interval estimate of the parameter.

(c) Test the null hypothesis that the slope of the relationship in (b) is zero. Create the alternative hypothesis based on your answer to part (a). Use the 1% level of significance and draw a sketch of the rejection region. Is your result consistent with economic theory?

(d) Estimate the log-linear model $\ln(SAL1) = \gamma_1 + \gamma_2 RPRICE3 + e$. Interpret the estimate of γ_2. Construct and interpret a 95% interval estimate of the parameter.

(e) Test the null hypothesis that the slope of this relationship is zero. Create the alternative hypothesis based on your answer to part (a). Use the 1% level of significance and draw a sketch of the rejection region. Is your result consistent with economic theory?

3.15 What is the relationship between crime and punishment? This important question has been examined by Cornwell and Trumbull[2] using a panel of data from North Carolina. The cross sections are 90 counties, and the data are annual for the years 1981–1987. The data are in the file *crime.dat*.

(a) Using the data from 1987, estimate the log-linear regression relating the log of the crime rate to the probability of an arrest, $LCRMRTE = \beta_1 + \beta_2 PRBARR + e$. The probability of arrest is measured as the ratio of arrests to offenses. If we increase the probability of arrest by 10%, what will be the effect on the crime rate? What is a 95% interval estimate of this quantity?

---

[2] "Estimating the Economic Model of Crime with Panel Data," *Review of Economics and Statistics*, 76, 1994, 360–366. The data were kindly provided by the authors.

   (b) Test the null hypothesis that there is no relationship between the crime rate and the probability of arrest against the alternative that there is an inverse relationship. Use the 1% level of significance.

   (c) Repeat parts (a) and (b) using the probability of conviction (*PRBCONV*) as the explanatory variable. The probability of conviction is measured as the ratio of convictions to arrests.

Appendix 3A Derivation of the t-Distribution

Interval estimation and hypothesis testing procedures in this chapter involve the t-distribution. Here we develop the key result.

   The first result that is needed is the normal distribution of the least squares estimator. Consider, for example, the normal distribution of b_2 the least squares estimator of β_2, which we denote as

$$b_2 \sim N\left(\beta_2, \frac{\sigma^2}{\Sigma(x_i - \bar{x})^2}\right)$$

A standardized normal random variable is obtained from b_2 by subtracting its mean and dividing by its standard deviation:

$$Z = \frac{b_2 - \beta_2}{\sqrt{\text{var}(b_2)}} \sim N(0, 1) \tag{3A.1}$$

That is, the standardized random variable Z is normally distributed with mean 0 and variance 1.

   The second piece of the puzzle involves a chi-square random variable. If assumption SR6 holds, then the random error term e_i has a normal distribution, $e_i \sim N(0, \sigma^2)$. Again, we can standardize the random variable by dividing by its standard deviation so that $e_i/\sigma \sim N(0, 1)$. The square of a standard normal random variable is a chi-square random variable (see Appendix B.5.2) with one degree of freedom, so $(e_i/\sigma)^2 \sim \chi^2_{(1)}$. If all the random errors are independent, then

$$\Sigma\left(\frac{e_i}{\sigma}\right)^2 = \left(\frac{e_1}{\sigma}\right)^2 + \left(\frac{e_2}{\sigma}\right)^2 + \cdots + \left(\frac{e_N}{\sigma}\right)^2 \sim \chi^2_{(N)} \tag{3A.2}$$

Since the true random errors are unobservable, we replace them by their sample counterparts, the least squares residuals $\hat{e}_i = y_i - b_1 - b_2 x_i$, to obtain

$$V = \frac{\Sigma\hat{e}_i^2}{\sigma^2} = \frac{(N-2)\hat{\sigma}^2}{\sigma^2} \tag{3A.3}$$

The random variable V in (3A.3) does not have a $\chi^2_{(N)}$ distribution, because the least squares residuals are *not* independent random variables. All N residuals $\hat{e}_i = y_i - b_1 - b_2 x_i$ depend on the least squares estimators b_1 and b_2. It can be shown that only $N - 2$ of the least squares residuals are independent in the simple linear regression model. Consequently, the random variable in (3A.3) has a chi-square distribution with $N - 2$ degrees of freedom. That is, when multiplied by the constant $(N - 2)/\sigma^2$, the random variable $\hat{\sigma}^2$ has a *chi-square distribution with $N - 2$ degrees of freedom*,

$$V = \frac{(N-2)\hat{\sigma}^2}{\sigma^2} \sim \chi^2_{(N-2)} \tag{3A.4}$$

We have *not* established the fact that the chi-square random variable V is statistically independent of the least squares estimators b_1 and b_2, but it is. The proof is beyond the scope of this book. Consequently, V and the standard normal random variable Z in (3A.1) are independent.

From the two random variables V and Z we can form a t-random variable. A t-random variable is formed by dividing a standard normal random variable, $Z \sim N(0, 1)$, by the square root of an *independent* chi-square random variable, $V \sim \chi^2_{(m)}$, that has been divided by its degrees of freedom, m. That is,

$$t = \frac{Z}{\sqrt{V/m}} \sim t_{(m)}$$

The t-distribution's shape is completely determined by the degrees of freedom parameter, m, and the distribution is symbolized by $t_{(m)}$. See Appendix B.5.3. Using Z and V from (3A.1) and (3A.4), respectively, we have

$$t = \frac{Z}{\sqrt{V/(N-2)}}$$

$$= \frac{(b_2 - \beta_2) \Big/ \sqrt{\sigma^2/\Sigma(x_i - \bar{x})^2}}{\sqrt{\dfrac{(N-2)\hat{\sigma}^2/\sigma^2}{N-2}}} \tag{3A.5}$$

$$= \frac{b_2 - \beta_2}{\sqrt{\dfrac{\hat{\sigma}^2}{\Sigma(x_i - \bar{x})^2}}} = \frac{b_2 - \beta_2}{\sqrt{\widehat{\text{var}(b_2)}}} = \frac{b_2 - \beta_2}{\text{se}(b_2)} \sim t_{(N-2)}$$

The last line is the key result that we state in (3.2), with its generalization in (3.3).

Appendix 3B Distribution of the t-Statistic under H_1

To examine the distribution of the t-statistic in (3.7) when the null hypothesis is not true, suppose that the true $\beta_2 = 1$. Following the steps in (3A.5) in Appendix 3A we would find that

$$t = \frac{b_2 - 1}{\text{se}(b_2)} \sim t_{(N-2)}$$

If $\beta_2 = 1$ and $c \neq 1$ then the test statistic in (3.7) does not have a t-distribution since, in its formation, the numerator of (3A.5) is *not* standard normal. It is not standard normal because the incorrect value $\beta_2 = c$ is subtracted from b_2.

If $\beta_2 = 1$ and we *incorrectly* hypothesize that $\beta_2 = c$, then the numerator in (3A.5) that is used in forming (3.7) has the distribution

$$\frac{b_2 - c}{\sqrt{\text{var}(b_2)}} \sim N\left(\frac{1-c}{\sqrt{\text{var}(b_2)}}, 1\right) \tag{3B.1}$$

where

$$\text{var}(b_2) = \frac{\sigma^2}{\sum(x_i - \bar{x})^2}$$

Since its mean is not zero, the distribution of the variable in (3B.1) is not standard normal, as required in the formation of a t-random variable.

Appendix 3C Monte Carlo Simulation

In Appendix 2G we introduced a Monte Carlo simulation to illustrate the repeated sampling properties of the least squares estimators. In this appendix we use the same framework to illustrate the repeated sampling performances of interval estimators and hypothesis tests.

Recall that the **data generation process** for the simple linear regression model is given by

$$y_i = E(y_i|x_i) + e_i = \beta_1 + \beta_2 x_i + e_i, \quad i = 1, \ldots, N$$

The Monte Carlo parameter values are $\beta_1 = 100$ and $\beta_2 = 10$. The value of x_i is 10 for the first 20 observations and 20 for the remaining 20 observations, so that the regression functions are

$$E(y_i|x_i = 10) = 100 + 10x_i = 100 + 10 \times 10 = 200, \quad i = 1, \ldots, 20$$
$$E(y_i|x_i = 20) = 100 + 10x_i = 100 + 10 \times 20 = 300, \quad i = 21, \ldots, 40$$

The random errors are independently and normally distributed with mean 0 and variance $\text{var}(e_i|x_i) = \sigma^2 = 2,500$, or $e_i \sim N(0, 2500)$.

When studying the performance of hypothesis tests and interval estimators it is necessary to use enough Monte Carlo samples so that the percentages involved are estimated precisely enough to be useful. For tests with probability of Type I error $\alpha = 0.05$ we should observe true null hypotheses being rejected 5% of the time. For 95% interval estimators we should observe that 95% of the interval estimates contain the true parameter values. We use $M = 10,000$ Monte Carlo samples so that the experimental error is very small. See Appendix 3C.3 for an explanation.

3C.1 REPEATED SAMPLING PROPERTIES OF INTERVAL ESTIMATORS

In Appendix 2G.4 we created one sample of data that is in the file *mc1.dat*. The least squares estimates using these data values are

$$\hat{y} = 75.7679 + 11.9683x$$
$$(\text{se}) \quad (25.7928) \quad (1.6313)$$

A 95% interval estimate of the slope is $b_2 \pm t_{(0.975,38)}\text{se}(b_2) = [8.6660, 15.2707]$. We see that for this sample, the 95% interval estimate contains the true slope parameter value $\beta_2 = 10$.

We repeat the process of estimation and interval estimation 10,000 times. In these repeated samples 95.18% of the interval estimates contain the true parameter. Table 3C.1 contains results for the Monte Carlo samples 101–120 for illustration purposes. The estimates are *B2*, the standard error is *SE*, the lower bound of the 95% interval estimate is *LB* and the upper

Table 3C.1 **Results of 10000 Monte Carlo Simulations**

SAMPLE	B2	SE	TSTAT	REJECT	LB	UB	COVER
101	8.3181	1.5024	−1.1195	0	5.2767	11.3595	1
102	10.9564	1.5488	0.6175	0	7.8210	14.0918	1
103	13.3644	1.7085	1.9692	1	9.9057	16.8230	1
104	9.7406	1.8761	−0.1383	0	5.9425	13.5386	1
105	12.3402	1.6275	1.4379	0	9.0454	15.6350	1
106	11.9019	1.6031	1.1864	0	8.6567	15.1472	1
107	8.7278	1.2252	−1.0383	0	6.2475	11.2081	1
108	9.0732	1.6978	−0.5459	0	5.6361	12.5102	1
109	9.5502	1.4211	−0.3165	0	6.6734	12.4270	1
110	9.2007	1.4895	−0.5366	0	6.1854	12.2161	1
111	11.0090	1.5221	0.6629	0	7.9277	14.0903	1
112	12.7234	1.4783	1.8423	1	9.7308	15.7160	1
113	11.8995	1.7587	1.0801	0	8.3393	15.4597	1
114	12.9712	1.4679	2.0242	1	9.9997	15.9427	1
115	10.6347	1.6320	0.3889	0	7.3309	13.9385	1
116	10.0045	1.4179	0.0031	0	7.1341	12.8748	1
117	11.2658	1.5584	0.8123	0	8.1110	14.4206	1
118	11.4842	1.4449	1.0272	0	8.5592	14.4093	1
119	9.6915	1.7422	−0.1771	0	6.1647	13.2183	1
120	11.6990	1.5132	1.1228	0	8.6358	14.7623	1

bound is *UB*. The variable *COVER* = 1 if the interval estimate contains the true parameter value. All of these intervals contain the true parameter value $\beta_2 = 10$.

The lesson is, that in many repeated samples from the data generation process, and if assumptions SR1–SR6 hold, the procedure for constructing 95% interval estimates "works" 95% of the time.

3C.2 REPEATED SAMPLING PROPERTIES OF HYPOTHESIS TESTS

The null hypothesis $H_0 : \beta_2 = 10$ is true. If we use the one-tail alternative $H_0 : \beta_2 > 0$, the null hypothesis is rejected if the test statistic $t = (b_2 - 10)/\text{se}(b_2) > 1.685954$, which is the 95th percentile of the *t*-distribution with 38 degrees of freedom.[3] For the sample *mc1.dat* the calculated value of the *t*-statistic is 1.21, so we fail to reject the null hypothesis, which in this case is the correct decision.

We repeat the process of estimation and hypothesis testing 10,000 times. In these repeated samples, 4.73% of the tests reject the null hypothesis that the parameter value is 10. In Table 3C.1, the *t*-statistic value is *TSTAT* and *REJECT* = 1 if the null hypothesis is rejected. We see that samples 103, 112 and 114 incorrectly reject the null hypothesis.

The lesson is that in many repeated samples from the data generation process, and if assumptions SR1–SR6 hold, the procedure for testing a true null hypothesis at significance level $\alpha = 0.05$ rejects the true null hypothesis 5% of the time. Or, stated positively, the test procedure does not reject the true null hypothesis 95% of the time.

---

[3] We use a *t*-critical value with more decimals, instead of the tabled value 1.686, to ensure accuracy in the Monte Carlo experiment.

3C.3   CHOOSING THE NUMBER OF MONTE CARLO SAMPLES

A 95% confidence interval estimator should contain the true parameter value 95% of the time in repeated samples. The M repeated samples in a Monte Carlo experiment are independent experimental trials in which the probability of a "success," an interval containing the true parameter value, is $P = 0.95$. The number of successes follows a **binomial** distribution. The **proportion** of successes $\hat{P}$ in M trials is a random variable with expectation P and variance $P(1 - P)/M$. If the number of Monte Carlo samples M is large, a 95% interval estimate of the proportion of Monte Carlo successes is $P \pm 1.96\sqrt{P(1 - P)/M}$. If $M = 10,000$, this interval is [0.9457, 0.9543]. We chose $M = 10,000$ so that this interval would be narrow, giving us confidence that *if* the true probability of success is 0.95 we will obtain a Monte Carlo average close to 0.95 with a "high" degree of confidence. Our result, that 95.18% of our interval estimates contain the true parameter β_2 is "within" the margin of error for such Monte Carlo experiments. On the other hand, if we had used $M = 1000$ Monte Carlo samples, the interval estimate of the proportion of Monte Carlo successes would be, [0.9365, 0.9635]. With this wider interval, the proportion of Monte Carlo successes could be quite different from 0.95, casting a shadow of doubt on whether our method was working as advertised or not.

Similarly, for a test with probability of rejection $\alpha = 0.05$, the 95% interval estimate of the proportion of Monte Carlo samples leading to rejection is $\alpha \pm 1.96\sqrt{\alpha(1 - \alpha)/M}$. If $M = 10,000$ this interval is [0.0457, 0.0543]. That our Monte Carlo experiments rejected the null hypothesis 4.73% of the time is within this margin of error. If we had chose $M = 1000$, then the proportion of Monte Carlo rejections is estimated to be in the interval [0.0365, 0.0635], which again leaves just a little too much wiggle room for comfort.

The point is that if fewer Monte Carlo samples are chosen the "noise" in the Monte Carlo experiment can lead to a percent of successes or rejections that has too wide a margin of error for us to tell whether the statistical procedure, interval estimation, or hypothesis testing, is "working" properly or not.[4]

---

[4] Other details concerning Monte Carlo simulations can be found in *Microeconometrics: Methods and Applications*, by A. Colin Cameron and Pravin K. Trivedi, (Cambridge University Press, 2005). The material is advanced.

Chapter 4

Prediction, Goodness-of-Fit, and Modeling Issues

Learning Objectives

Based on the material in this chapter, you should be able to

1. Explain how to use the simple linear regression model to predict the value of y for a given value of x.

2. Explain, intuitively and technically, why predictions for x values further from $\bar{x}$ are less reliable.

3. Explain the meaning of *SST*, *SSR*, and *SSE*, and how they are related to R^2.

4. Define and explain the meaning of the coefficient of determination.

5. Explain the relationship between correlation analysis and R^2.

6. Report the results of a fitted regression equation in such a way that confidence intervals and hypothesis tests for the unknown coefficients can be constructed quickly and easily.

7. Describe how estimated coefficients and other quantities from a regression equation will change when the variables are scaled. Why would you want to scale the variables?

8. Appreciate the wide range of nonlinear functions that can be estimated using a model that is linear in the parameters.

9. Write down the equations for the log-log, log-linear, and linear-log functional forms.

10. Explain the difference between the slope of a functional form and the elasticity from a functional form.

11. Explain how you would go about choosing a functional form and deciding that a functional form is adequate.

12. Explain how to test whether the equation "errors" are normally distributed.

13. Explain how to compute a prediction, a prediction interval, and a goodness-of-fit measure in a log-linear model.

Keywords

coefficient of determination	Jarque–Bera test	log-normal distribution
correlation	kurtosis	prediction
data scale	least squares predictor	prediction interval
forecast error	linear model	R^2
forecast standard error	linear relationship	residual
functional form	linear-log model	skewness
goodness-of-fit	log-linear model	
growth model	log-log model	

In Chapter 3 we focused on making statistical inferences, constructing confidence intervals, and testing hypotheses about regression parameters. Another purpose of the regression model, and the one we focus on first in this chapter, is **prediction**. A prediction is a forecast of an unknown value of the dependent variable y given a particular value of x. A **prediction interval**, much like a confidence interval, is a range of values in which the unknown value of y is likely to be located. Examining the **correlation** between sample values of y and their predicted values provides a **goodness-of-fit** measure called R^2 that describes how well our model fits the data. For each observation in the sample the difference between the actual value of y and the predicted value is a **residual**. Diagnostic measures constructed from the residuals allow us to check the adequacy of the **functional form** used in the regression analysis and give us some indication of the validity of the regression assumptions. We will examine each of these ideas and concepts in turn.

4.1 Least Squares Prediction

In Section 2.3.3b we briefly introduced the idea that the least squares estimates of the linear regression model provide a way to predict the value of y for any value of x. The ability to predict is important to business economists and financial analysts who attempt to forecast the sales and revenues of specific firms; it is important to government policy makers who attempt to predict the rates of growth in national income, inflation, investment, saving, social insurance program expenditures, and tax revenues; and it is important to local businesses who need to have predictions of growth in neighborhood populations and income so that they may expand or contract their provision of services. Accurate predictions provide a basis for better decision making in every type of planning context. In this section, we explore the use of linear regression as a tool for prediction.

Given the simple linear regression model and assumptions SR1–SR6, let x_0 be a value of the explanatory variable. We want to predict the corresponding value of y, which we call y_0. In order to use regression analysis as a basis for prediction, we must assume that y_0 and x_0 are related to one another by the same regression model that describes our sample of data, so that, in particular, SR1 holds for these observations

$$y_0 = \beta_1 + \beta_2 x_0 + e_0 \tag{4.1}$$

where e_0 is a random error. We assume that $E(y_0) = \beta_1 + \beta_2 x_0$ and $E(e_0) = 0$. We also assume that e_0 has the same variance as the regression errors, $var(e_0) = \sigma^2$, and e_0 is

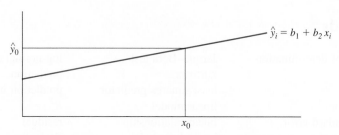

FIGURE 4.1 A point prediction.

uncorrelated with the random errors that are part of the sample data, so that $\text{cov}(e_0, e_i) = 0$ $i = 1, 2, \ldots, N$.

The task of **predicting** y_0 is related to the problem of **estimating** $E(y_0) = \beta_1 + \beta_2 x_0$ which we discussed in Chapter 3.6. The outcome $y_0 = E(y_0) + e_0 = \beta_1 + \beta_2 x_0 + e_0$ is composed of two parts, the systematic, nonrandom part $E(y_0) = \beta_1 + \beta_2 x_0$ and a random component e_0. We estimate the systematic portion using $\widehat{E(y_0)} = b_1 + b_2 x_0$ and add an "estimate" of e_0 equal to its expected value, which is zero. Therefore $\hat{y}_0 = \widehat{E(y_0)} + 0 = b_1 + b_2 x_0$. Despite the fact that we use the same statistic for both $\hat{y}_0$ and $\widehat{E(y_0)}$, we distinguish between them because, although $E(y_0) = \beta_1 + \beta_2 x_0$ is not random, the outcome y_0 is random. Consequently, as we will see, there is a difference between the **interval estimate** of $E(y_0) = \beta_1 + \beta_2 x_0$ and the **prediction interval** for y_0.

Following from the discussion in the previous paragraph, the **least squares predictor** of y_0 comes from the fitted regression line

$$\hat{y}_0 = b_1 + b_2 x_0 \tag{4.2}$$

That is, the predicted value $\hat{y}_0$ is given by the point on the least squares fitted line where $x = x_0$, as shown in Figure 4.1. How good is this prediction procedure? The least squares estimators b_1 and b_2 are random variables—their values vary from one sample to another. It follows that the least squares predictor $\hat{y}_0 = b_1 + b_2 x_0$ must also be random. To evaluate how well this predictor performs, we define the **forecast error**, which is analogous to the least squares residual,

$$f = y_0 - \hat{y}_0 = (\beta_1 + \beta_2 x_0 + e_0) - (b_1 + b_2 x_0) \tag{4.3}$$

We would like the forecast error to be small, implying that our forecast is close to the value we are predicting. Taking the expected value of f, we find

$$
\begin{aligned}
E(f) &= \beta_1 + \beta_2 x_0 + E(e_0) - [E(b_1) + E(b_2) x_0] \\
&= \beta_1 + \beta_2 x_0 + 0 - [\beta_1 + \beta_2 x_0] \\
&= 0
\end{aligned}
$$

which means, on average, the forecast error is zero, and $\hat{y}_0$ is an **unbiased predictor** of y_0. However, unbiasedness does not necessarily imply that a particular forecast will be close to the actual value. The probability of a small forecast error also depends on the variance of the forecast error. Although we will not prove it, $\hat{y}_0$ is the **best linear unbiased predictor** (**BLUP**) of y_0 if assumptions SR1–SR5 hold. This result is reasonable given that the least squares estimators b_1 and b_2 are best linear unbiased estimators.

Using (4.3) and what we know about the variances and covariance of the least squares estimators, we can show (see Appendix 4A at the end of this chapter) that the variance of the forecast error is

$$\text{var}(f) = \sigma^2 \left[1 + \frac{1}{N} + \frac{(x_0 - \bar{x})^2}{\Sigma (x_i - \bar{x})^2} \right] \qquad (4.4)$$

Notice that some of the elements of this expression appear in the formulas for the variances of the least squares estimators and affect the precision of prediction in the same way that they affect the precision of estimation. We would prefer that the variance of the forecast error be small, which would increase the probability that the prediction $\hat{y}_0$ is close to the value y_0 we are trying to predict. Note that the variance of the forecast error is smaller when

   i.   the overall uncertainty in the model is smaller, as measured by the variance of the random errors σ^2

  ii.   the sample size N is larger

 iii.   the variation in the explanatory variable is larger

 iv.   the value of $(x_0 - \bar{x})^2$ is small

The new addition is the term $(x_0 - \bar{x})^2$, which measures how far x_0 is from the center of the x-values. The more distant x_0 is from the center of the sample data the larger the forecast variance will become. Intuitively, this means that we are able to do a better job predicting in the region where we have more sample information, and we will have less accurate predictions when we try to predict outside the limits of our data.

In practice we replace σ^2 in (4.4) by its estimator $\hat{\sigma}^2$ to obtain

$$\widehat{\text{var}(f)} = \hat{\sigma}^2 \left[1 + \frac{1}{N} + \frac{(x_0 - \bar{x})^2}{\Sigma (x_i - \bar{x})^2} \right]$$

The square root of this estimated variance is the **standard error of the forecast**

$$\text{se}(f) = \sqrt{\widehat{\text{var}(f)}} \qquad (4.5)$$

Defining the critical value t_c to be the $100(1 - \alpha/2)$-percentile from the t-distribution, we can obtain a $100(1 - \alpha)\%$ **prediction interval** as

$$\hat{y}_0 \pm t_c \text{se}(f) \qquad (4.6)$$

See Appendix 4A for some details related to the development of this result.

Following our discussion of $\text{var}(f)$ in (4.4), the farther x_0 is from the sample mean $\bar{x}$, the larger the variance of the prediction error will be, and the less reliable the prediction is likely to be. In other words, our predictions for values of x_0 close to the sample mean $\bar{x}$ are more reliable than our predictions for values of x_0 far from the sample mean $\bar{x}$. This fact shows up in the size of our prediction intervals. The relationship between point and interval predictions for different values of x_0 is illustrated in Figure 4.2. A point prediction is given by the fitted least squares line $\hat{y}_0 = b_1 + b_2 x_0$. The prediction interval takes the form of two bands around the fitted least squares line. Because the forecast variance increases the farther x_0 is from the sample mean $\bar{x}$, the confidence bands are their narrowest when $x_0 = \bar{x}$, and they increase in width as $|x_0 - \bar{x}|$ increases.

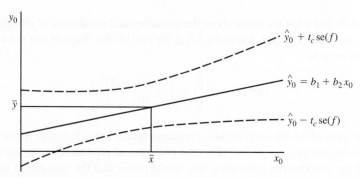

FIGURE 4.2 Point and interval prediction.

4.1.1 PREDICTION IN THE FOOD EXPENDITURE MODEL

In Section 2.3.3b we predicted that a household with $x_0 = \$2,000$ weekly income would spend $287.61 on food using the calculation

$$\hat{y}_0 = b_1 + b_2 x_0 = 83.4160 + 10.2096(20) = 287.6089$$

Now we are able to attach a "confidence interval" to this prediction. The estimated variance of the forecast error is

$$\widehat{\text{var}(f)} = \hat{\sigma}^2 \left[1 + \frac{1}{N} + \frac{(x_0 - \bar{x})^2}{\Sigma(x_i - \bar{x})^2} \right]$$

$$= \hat{\sigma}^2 + \frac{\hat{\sigma}^2}{N} + (x_0 - \bar{x})^2 \frac{\hat{\sigma}^2}{\Sigma(x_i - \bar{x})^2}$$

$$= \hat{\sigma}^2 + \frac{\hat{\sigma}^2}{N} + (x_0 - \bar{x})^2 \widehat{\text{var}(b_2)}$$

In the last line we have recognized the estimated variance of b_2 from (2.21). In Section 2.7.2 we obtained the values $\hat{\sigma}^2 = 8013.2941$ and $\widehat{\text{var}(b_2)} = 4.3818$. For the food expenditure data, $N = 40$ and the sample mean of the explanatory variable is $\bar{x} = 19.6048$. Using these values we obtain the standard error of the forecast $\text{se}(f) = \sqrt{\widehat{\text{var}(f)}} = \sqrt{8214.31} = 90.6328$. If we select $1 - \alpha = 0.95$, then $t_c = t_{(0.975,38)} = 2.0244$ and the 95% prediction interval for y_0 is

$$\hat{y}_0 \pm t_c \text{se}(f) = 287.6069 \pm 2.0244(90.6328) = [104.1323, 471.0854]$$

Our prediction interval suggests that a household with $2,000 weekly income will spend somewhere between $104.13 and $471.09 on food. Such a wide interval means that our point prediction $287.61 is not very reliable. We have obtained this wide prediction interval for the value of $x_0 = 20$ that is close to the sample mean $\bar{x} = 19.60$. For values of x that are more extreme, the prediction interval would be even wider. The unreliable predictions may be slightly improved if we collect a larger sample of data, which will improve the precision with which we estimate the model parameters. However, in this example the magnitude of the estimated error variance $\hat{\sigma}^2$ is very close to the estimated variance of the forecast error $\widehat{\text{var}(f)}$, indicating that the primary uncertainty in the forecast comes from large uncertainty in the model. This should not be a surprise, since we are predicting household behavior, which is a complicated phenomenon, on the basis of a single household characteristic, income. Although income is a key factor in explaining food expenditure, we can imagine that many other household demographic characteristics may play a role. To more accurately predict food expenditure we may need to include these additional factors into the regression model. Extending the simple regression model to include other factors will begin in Chapter 5.

4.2 **Measuring Goodness–of–Fit**

Two major reasons for analyzing the model

$$y_i = \beta_1 + \beta_2 x_i + e_i \tag{4.7}$$

are to explain how the dependent variable (y_i) changes as the independent variable (x_i) changes, and to predict y_0 given an x_0. These two objectives come under the broad headings of estimation and prediction. Closely allied with the prediction problem discussed in the previous section is the desire to use x_i to explain as much of the variation in the dependent variable y_i as possible. In the regression model (4.7) we call x_i the "explanatory" variable because we hope that its variation will "explain" the variation in y_i.

To develop a measure of the variation in y_i that is explained by the model, we begin by separating y_i into its explainable and unexplainable components. We have assumed that

$$y_i = E(y_i) + e_i \tag{4.8}$$

where $E(y_i) = \beta_1 + \beta_2 x_i$ is the explainable, "systematic" component of y_i, and e_i is the random, unsystematic and unexplainable component of y_i. While both of these parts are unobservable to us, we can estimate the unknown parameters β_1 and β_2 and, analogous to (4.8), decompose the value of y_i into

$$y_i = \hat{y}_i + \hat{e}_i \tag{4.9}$$

where $\hat{y}_i = b_1 + b_2 x_i$ and $\hat{e}_i = y_i - \hat{y}_i$.

In Figure 4.3 the "point of the means" $(\bar{x}, \bar{y})$ is shown, with the least squares fitted line passing through it. This is a characteristic of the least squares fitted line whenever the regression model includes an intercept term. Subtract the sample mean $\bar{y}$ from both sides of the equation to obtain

$$y_i - \bar{y} = (\hat{y}_i - \bar{y}) + \hat{e}_i \tag{4.10}$$

As shown in Figure 4.3 the difference between y_i and its mean value $\bar{y}$ consists of a part that is "explained" by the regression model $\hat{y}_i - \bar{y}$ and a part that is unexplained $\hat{e}_i$.

The breakdown in (4.10) leads to a decomposition of the total sample variability in y into explained and unexplained parts. Recall from your statistics courses (see Appendix C.4) that if we have a sample of observations $y_1, y_2, \ldots, y_N$, two descriptive measures are the sample mean $\bar{y}$ and the sample variance

$$s_y^2 = \frac{\sum(y_i - \bar{y})^2}{N - 1}$$

The numerator of this quantity, the sum of squared differences between the sample values y_i and the sample mean $\bar{y}$, is a measure of the total variation in the sample values. If we square

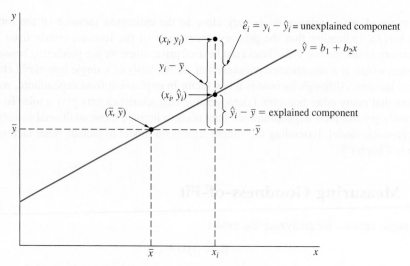

FIGURE 4.3 Explained and unexplained components of y_i.

and sum both sides of (4.10), and use the fact that the cross-product term $\Sigma(\hat{y}_i - \bar{y})\hat{e}_i = 0$ (see Appendix 4B), we obtain

$$\Sigma(y_i - \bar{y})^2 = \Sigma(\hat{y}_i - \bar{y})^2 + \Sigma\hat{e}_i^2 \tag{4.11}$$

Equation (4.11) gives us a decomposition of the "total sample variation" in y into explained and unexplained components. Specifically, these "sums of squares" are

1. $\Sigma(y_i - \bar{y})^2 = $ total sum of squares $= SST$: a measure of *total variation* in y about the sample mean.

2. $\Sigma(\hat{y}_i - \bar{y})^2 = $ sum of squares due to the regression $= SSR$: that part of total variation in y, about the sample mean, that is explained by, or due to, the regression. Also known as the "explained sum of squares."

3. $\Sigma\hat{e}_i^2 = $ sum of squares due to error $= SSE$: that part of total variation in y about its mean that is not explained by the regression. Also known as the unexplained sum of squares, the residual sum of squares, or the sum of squared errors.

Using these abbreviations (4.11) becomes

$$SST = SSR + SSE$$

This decomposition of the total variation in y into a part that is explained by the regression model and a part that is unexplained allows us to define a measure, called the **coefficient of determination**, or R^2, that is the proportion of variation in y explained by x within the regression model.

$$R^2 = \frac{SSR}{SST} = 1 - \frac{SSE}{SST} \tag{4.12}$$

The closer R^2 is to 1, the closer the sample values y_i are to the fitted regression equation $\hat{y}_i = b_1 + b_2 x_i$. If $R^2 = 1$, then all the sample data fall exactly on the fitted least squares line, so $SSE = 0$, and the model fits the data "perfectly." If the sample data for y and x are uncorrelated and show no linear association, then the least squares fitted line is "horizontal," and identical to $\bar{y}$, so that $SSR = 0$ and $R^2 = 0$. When $0 < R^2 < 1$, it is interpreted as "the proportion of the variation in y about its mean that is explained by the regression model."

4.2.1 CORRELATION ANALYSIS

In Appendix B.1.5 we discuss the **covariance** and **correlation** between two random variables x and y. The correlation coefficient ρ_{xy} between x and y is defined in (B.21) as

$$\rho_{xy} = \frac{\text{cov}(x, y)}{\sqrt{\text{var}(x)}\sqrt{\text{var}(y)}} = \frac{\sigma_{xy}}{\sigma_x \sigma_y} \tag{4.13}$$

In Appendix B we did not discuss *estimating* the correlation coefficient. We will do so now to develop a useful relationship between the sample correlation coefficient and R^2.

Given a sample of data pairs $(x_i, y_i), i = 1, \ldots, N$, the sample correlation coefficient is obtained by replacing the covariance and standard deviations in (4.13) by their sample analogs:

$$r_{xy} = \frac{s_{xy}}{s_x s_y}$$

where

$$s_{xy} = \Sigma(x_i - \bar{x})(y_i - \bar{y})/(N - 1)$$

$$s_x = \sqrt{\Sigma(x_i - \bar{x})^2/(N - 1)}$$

$$s_y = \sqrt{\Sigma(y_i - \bar{y})^2/(N - 1)}$$

The sample correlation coefficient r_{xy} has a value between -1 and 1, and it measures the strength of the linear association between observed values of x and y.

4.2.2 CORRELATION ANALYSIS AND R^2

There are two interesting relationships between R^2 and r_{xy} in the simple linear regression model.

1. The first is that $r_{xy}^2 = R^2$. That is, the square of the sample correlation coefficient between the sample data values x_i and y_i is algebraically equal to R^2 in a simple regression model. Intuitively this relationship makes sense: r_{xy}^2 falls between zero and one and measures the strength of the linear association between x and y. This interpretation is not far from that of R^2: the proportion of variation in y about its mean explained by x in the linear regression model.

2. The second, and more important, relation is that R^2 can also be computed as the square of the sample correlation coefficient between y_i and $\hat{y}_i = b_1 + b_2 x_i$. That is, $R^2 = r_{y\hat{y}}^2$. As such it measures the linear association, or goodness-of-fit, between the sample data and their predicted values. Consequently R^2 is sometimes called a measure of "goodness-of-fit." This result is valid not only in simple regression models but also in multiple regression models that we introduce in Chapter 5. Furthermore, as you will see in Section 4.4, the concept of obtaining a goodness-of-fit measure by predicting y as well as possible and finding the squared correlation

coefficient between this prediction and the sample values of y can be extended to situations in which the usual R^2 does not strictly apply.

4.2.3 THE FOOD EXPENDITURE EXAMPLE

Look at the food expenditure example in Section 2.3.2, and in particular the data scatter and fitted regression line in Figure 2.8, and the computer output Figure 2.9. Go ahead. I will wait until you get back. The question we would like to answer is "How well does our model fit the data?" To compute the R^2 we can use the sums of squares

$$SST = \Sigma(y_i - \bar{y})^2 = 495132.160$$
$$SSE = \Sigma(y_i - \hat{y}_i)^2 = \Sigma\hat{e}_i^2 = 304505.176$$

Then

$$R^2 = 1 - \frac{SSE}{SST} = 1 - \frac{304505.176}{495132.160} = 0.385$$

We conclude that 38.5% of the variation in food expenditure (about its sample mean) is explained by our regression model, which uses only income as an explanatory variable. Is this a good R^2? We would argue that such a question is not useful. Although finding and reporting R^2 provides information about the relative magnitudes of the different sources of variation, debates about whether a particular R^2 is "large enough" are not particularly constructive. Microeconomic household behavior is very difficult to explain fully. With cross-sectional data R^2 values from 0.10 to 0.40 are very common even with much larger regression models. Macroeconomic analyses using time-series data, which often trend together smoothly over time, routinely report R^2 values of 0.90 and higher. You should *not* evaluate the quality of the model based only on how well it predicts the sample data used to construct the estimates. To evaluate the model it is as important to consider factors such as the signs and magnitudes of the estimates, their statistical and economic significance, the precision of their estimation, and the ability of the fitted model to predict values of the dependent variable that were not in the estimation sample. Other model diagnostic issues will be discussed in the next section.

Correlation analysis leads to the same conclusions and numbers, but it is worthwhile to consider this approach in more detail. The sample correlation between the y and x sample values is

$$r_{xy} = \frac{s_{xy}}{s_x s_y} = \frac{478.75}{(6.848)(112.675)} = 0.62$$

The correlation is positive, indicating a positive association between food expenditure and income. The sample correlation measures the strength of the linear association, with a maximum value of 1. The value $r_{xy} = 0.62$ indicates a non-negligible but less than perfect fit. As expected $r_{xy}^2 = 0.62^2 = 0.385 = R^2$.

4.2.4 REPORTING THE RESULTS

In any paper where you write the results of a simple regression, with only one explanatory variable, these results can be presented quite simply. The key ingredients are the coefficient estimates, the standard errors (or t-values), an indication of statistical significance, and R^2.

Also, when communicating regression results, avoid using symbols like x and y. Use abbreviations for the variables that are readily interpreted, defining the variables precisely in a separate section of the report. For the food expenditure example, we might have the variable definitions:

$FOOD\_EXP$ = weekly food expenditure by a household of size 3, in dollars

$INCOME$ = weekly household income, in $100 units

Then the estimated equation results are

$$FOOD\_EXP = 83.42 + 10.21\,INCOME \qquad R^2 = 0.385$$
$$\text{(se)} \qquad (43.41)^* \quad (2.09)^{***}$$

Report the standard errors below the estimated coefficients. The reason for showing the standard errors is that an approximate 95% interval estimate (if the degrees of freedom $N - 2$ are greater than 30) is $b_k \pm 2 \times se$. The reader may then divide the estimate by the standard error to obtain the value of the t-statistic if desired. Furthermore, testing other hypotheses is facilitated by having the standard error present. To test the null hypothesis $H_0 : \beta_2 = 8.0$, we can quickly construct the t-statistic $t = [(10.21 - 8)/2.09]$ and proceed with the steps of the test procedure.

Asterisks are often used to show the reader the statistically significant (that is, significantly different from zero using a two-tail test) coefficients, with explanations in a table footnote:

* indicates significant at the 10% level

** indicates significant at the 5% level

*** indicates significant at the 1% level

The asterisks are assigned by checking the p-values from the computer output, as in Figure 2.9.

4.3 Modeling Issues

4.3.1 THE EFFECTS OF SCALING THE DATA

Data we obtain are not always in a convenient form for presentation in a table or use in a regression analysis. When the *scale* of the data is not convenient, it can be altered without changing any of the real underlying relationships between variables. For example, the real personal consumption in the United States, as of the 4th quarter of 2009, was $9291.7 *billion* annually. That is, written out, $9,291,700,000,000. While we *could* use the long form of the number in a table or in a regression analysis, there is no advantage to doing so. By choosing the units of measurement to be "billions of dollars," we have taken a long number and made it comprehensible. What are the effects of scaling the variables in a regression model?

Consider the food expenditure model. In Table 2.1 we report weekly expenditures in *dollars* but we report income in $100 units, so a weekly income of $2,000 is reported as $x = 20$. Why did we scale the data in this way? If we had estimated the regression using income in dollars, the results would have been

$$FOOD\_EXP = 83.42 + 0.1021\,INCOME(\$) \quad R^2 = 0.385$$
$$\text{(se)} \qquad (43.41)^*(0.0209)^{***}$$

There are two changes. First, the estimated coefficient of income is now 0.1021. The interpretation is "If weekly household income increases by \$1 then we estimate that weekly food expenditure will increase by about 10 cents." There is nothing mathematically wrong with this, but it leads to a discussion of changes that are so small as to seem irrelevant. An increase in income of \$100 leads to an estimated increase in food expenditure of \$10.21, as before, but these magnitudes are more easily discussed.

The other change that occurs in the regression results when income is in dollars is that the standard error becomes smaller, by a factor of 100. Since the estimated coefficient is smaller by a factor of 100 also, this leaves the t-statistic and all other results unchanged.

Such a change in the units of measurement is called *scaling the data*. The choice of the scale is made by the researcher to make interpretation meaningful and convenient. The choice of the scale does not affect the measurement of the underlying relationship, but it does affect the interpretation of the coefficient estimates and some summary measures. Let us list the possibilities:

1. **Changing the scale of x**: In the linear regression model $y = \beta_1 + \beta_2 x + e$, suppose we change the units of measurement of the explanatory variable x by dividing it by a constant c. In order to keep intact the equality of the left- and right-hand sides, the coefficient of x must be multiplied by c. That is, $y = \beta_1 + \beta_2 x + e = \beta_1 + (c\beta_2)(x/c) + e = \beta_1 + \beta_2^* x^* + e$, where $\beta_2^* = c\beta_2$ and $x^* = x/c$. For example, if x is measured in dollars, and $c = 100$, then x^* is measured in hundreds of dollars. Then β_2^* measures the expected change in y given a \$100 increase in x, and β_2^* is 100 times larger than β_2. When the scale of x is altered, the only other change occurs in the standard error of the regression coefficient, but it changes by the same multiplicative factor as the coefficient, so that their ratio, the t-statistic, is unaffected. All other regression statistics are unchanged.

2. **Changing the scale of y**: If we change the units of measurement of y, but not x, then all the coefficients must change in order for the equation to remain valid. That is, $y/c = (\beta_1/c) + (\beta_2/c)x + (e/c)$ or $y^* = \beta_1^* + \beta_2^* x + e^*$. In this rescaled model β_2^* measures the change we expect in y^* given a 1-unit change in x. Because the error term is scaled in this process the least squares residuals will also be scaled. This will affect the standard errors of the regression coefficients, but it will not affect t-statistics or R^2.

3. If the scale of y and the scale of x are changed by the same factor, then there will be no change in the reported regression results for b_2, but the estimated intercept and residuals will change; t-statistics and R^2 are unaffected. The interpretation of the parameters is made relative to the new units of measurement.

4.3.2 Choosing a Functional Form

In our ongoing example, we have assumed that the mean household food expenditure is a linear function of household income. That is, we assumed the underlying economic relationship to be $E(y) = \beta_1 + \beta_2 x$, which implies that there is a linear, straight-line relationship between $E(y)$ and x. Why did we do that? Although the world is not "linear," a straight line is a good approximation to many nonlinear or curved relationships over narrow ranges. Also, in your principles of economics classes you may have begun with straight lines for supply, demand, and consumption functions, and we wanted to ease you into the more "artistic" aspects of econometrics.

The starting point in all econometric analyses is economic theory. What does economics really say about the relation between food expenditure and income, holding all else constant? We expect there to be a positive relationship between these variables because food is a normal good. But nothing says the relationship must be a straight line. In fact, we do *not* expect that as household income rises, food expenditures will continue to rise indefinitely at the same constant rate. Instead, as income rises, we expect food expenditures to rise, but we expect such expenditures to increase at a decreasing rate. This is a phrase that is used many times in economics classes. What it means graphically is that there is not a straight-line relationship between the two variables. For a curvilinear relationship like that in Figure 4.4, the **marginal effect** of a change in the explanatory variable is measured by the slope of the tangent to the curve at a particular point. The marginal effect of a change in x is greater at the point (x_1, y_1) than it is at the point (x_2, y_2). As x increases, the value of y increases, but the slope is becoming smaller. This is the meaning of "increasing at a decreasing rate." In the economic context of the food expenditure model, the marginal propensity to spend on food is greater at lower incomes, and as income increases the marginal propensity to spend on food declines.

The simple linear regression model is much more flexible than it appears at first glance. By *transforming* the variables y and x we can represent many curved, nonlinear relationships and still use the linear regression model. In Chapter 2.8 we introduced the idea of using **quadratic** and **log-linear** functional forms. In this and subsequent sections, we introduce you to an array of other possibilities and give some examples.

Choosing an algebraic form for the relationship means choosing *transformations* of the original variables. This is not an easy process, and it requires good analytic geometry skills and some experience. It may *not* come to you easily. The variable transformations that we begin with are

1. Power: If x is a variable, then x^p means raising the variable to the power p; examples are quadratic (x^2) and cubic (x^3) transformations.

2. The natural logarithm: If x is a variable, then its natural logarithm is $\ln(x)$.

Using just these two algebraic transformations there are amazing varieties of "shapes" that we can represent, as shown in Figure 4.5.

A difficulty introduced when transforming variables is that regression result interpretations change. For each different functional form, shown in Table 4.1, the expressions for both the slope and elasticity change from the linear relationship case. This is so because

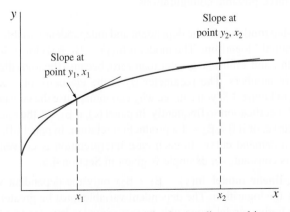

FIGURE **4.4** A nonlinear relationship between food expenditure and income.

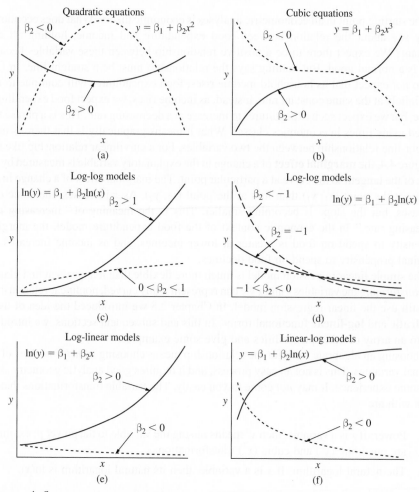

FIGURE **4.5** Alternative functional forms.

the variables are related nonlinearly. What this means for the practicing economist is that great attention must be given to result interpretation whenever variables are transformed. Because you may be less familiar with logarithmic transformations, let us summarize the interpretation in three possible configurations.

1. In the **log-log model** both the dependent and independent variables are transformed by the "natural" logarithm. The model is $\ln(y) = \beta_1 + \beta_2 \ln(x)$. In order to use this model both y and x must be greater than zero, because the logarithm is defined only for positive numbers. The parameter β_2 is the elasticity of y with respect to x. Referring to Figure 4.5, you can see why economists use the constant elasticity, log-log model specification so frequently. In panel (c), if $\beta_2 > 1$ the relation could depict a supply curve, or if $0 < \beta_2 < 1$ a production relation. In panel (d), if $\beta_2 < 0$ it could represent a demand curve. In each case interpretation is convenient because the elasticity is constant. An example is given in Section 4.6.

2. In the **log-linear model** $\ln(y) = \beta_1 + \beta_2 x$ only the dependent variable is transformed by the logarithm. The dependent variable must be greater than zero to use this form. In this model a one-unit increase in x leads to (approximately) a $100 \times \beta_2\%$ change in y. The log-linear form is common; it was introduced in Chapter

Table 4.1 **Some Useful Functions, their Derivatives, Elasticities and Other Interpretation**

Name	Function	Slope $= dy/dx$	Elasticity
Linear	$y = \beta_1 + \beta_2 x$	β_2	$\beta_2 \dfrac{x}{y}$
Quadratic	$y = \beta_1 + \beta_2 x^2$	$2\beta_2 x$	$(2\beta_2 x)\dfrac{x}{y}$
Cubic	$y = \beta_1 + \beta_2 x^3$	$3\beta_2 x^2$	$(3\beta_2 x^2)\dfrac{x}{y}$
Log-Log	$\ln(y) = \beta_1 + \beta_2 \ln(x)$	$\beta_2 \dfrac{y}{x}$	β_2
Log-Linear	$\ln(y) = \beta_1 + \beta_2 x$	$\beta_2 y$	$\beta_2 x$
	or, a 1 unit change in x leads to (approximately) a $100\,\beta_2\%$ change in y		
Linear-Log	$y = \beta_1 + \beta_2 \ln(x)$	$\beta_2 \dfrac{1}{x}$	$\beta_2 \dfrac{1}{y}$
	or, a 1% change in x leads to (approximately) a $\beta_2/100$ unit change in y		

2.8.3–2.8.4 and will be further discussed in Section 4.5. Note its possible shapes in Figure 4.5(e). If $\beta_2 > 0$ the function increases at an increasing rate; its slope is larger for larger values of y. If $\beta_2 < 0$, the function decreases, but at a decreasing rate.

3. In the **linear-log model** $y = \beta_1 + \beta_2 \ln(x)$ the variable x is transformed by the natural logarithm. See Figure 4.5(f). The slope of this function is $\Delta y / \Delta x = \beta_2/x$, and it changes at every point. We can interpret β_2 by rewriting the slope expression as

$$\frac{\Delta y}{100(\Delta x/x)} = \frac{\beta_2}{100}$$

The term $100(\Delta x/x)$ is the *percentage change in x*. Thus, in the linear-log model we can say that a 1% increase in x leads to a $\beta_2/100$-*unit* change in y. An example of this functional form is given in the next section.

4.3.3 A LINEAR–LOG FOOD EXPENDITURE MODEL

Suppose that in the food expenditure model, we wish to choose a functional form that is consistent with Figure 4.4. One option is the linear-log functional form. A linear-log equation has a linear, untransformed term on the left-hand side and a logarithmic term on the right-hand side, or $y = \beta_1 + \beta_2 \ln(x)$. Because of the logarithm, this function requires $x > 0$. It is an increasing or decreasing function, depending upon the sign of β_2. The slope of the function is β_2/x, so that as x increases, the slope decreases in absolute magnitude. If $\beta_2 > 0$, then the function increases at a decreasing rate. If $\beta_2 < 0$, then the function decreases at a decreasing rate. The function shapes are depicted in Figure 4.5(f). The elasticity of y with respect to x in this model is $\varepsilon = slope \times x/y = \beta_2/y$.

There is a convenient interpretation using approximations to changes in logarithms. Consider a small increase in x from x_0 to x_1. Then $y_0 = \beta_1 + \beta_2 \ln(x_0)$ and $y_1 = \beta_1 + \beta_2 \ln(x_1)$. Subtracting the former from the latter, and using the approximation developed in Appendix A, (A.3), gives

$$\Delta y = y_1 - y_0 = \beta_2[\ln(x_1) - \ln(x_0)]$$

$$= \frac{\beta_2}{100} \times 100[\ln(x_1) - \ln(x_0)]$$

$$\cong \frac{\beta_2}{100}(\%\Delta x)$$

The change in y, represented in its units of measure, is approximately $\beta_2/100$ times the percentage change in x.

Using a linear-log equation for the food expenditure relation results in the regression model

$$FOOD\_EXP = \beta_1 + \beta_2 \ln(INCOME) + e$$

For $\beta_2 > 0$ this function is increasing, but at a decreasing rate. As $INCOME$ increases the slope $\beta_2/INCOME$ decreases. In this context the slope is the marginal propensity to spend on food from additional income. Similarly, the elasticity, $\beta_2/FOOD\_EXP$, becomes smaller for larger levels of food expenditure. These results are consistent with the idea that at high incomes, and large food expenditures, the effect of an increase in income on food expenditure is small.

The estimated linear-log model using the food expenditure data is

$$\widehat{FOOD\_EXP} = -97.19 + 132.17 \ln(INCOME) \qquad R^2 = 0.357$$
$$\text{(se)} \qquad (84.24) \quad (28.80)^{***}$$

(4.14)

The fitted model is shown in Figure 4.6.

As anticipated, the fitted function is not a straight line. The fitted linear-log model is consistent with our theoretical model that anticipates declining marginal propensity to spend additional income on food. For a household with \$1,000 weekly income, we estimate that the household will spend an additional \$13.22 on food from an additional \$100 income, whereas we estimate that a household with \$2,000 per week income will spend an additional \$6.61 from an additional \$100 income. The marginal effect of income on food expenditure is smaller at higher levels of income. This is a change from the linear, straight-line relationship we originally estimated, in which the marginal effect of a change in income of \$100 was \$10.21 for all levels of income.

Alternatively, we can say that a 1% increase in income will increase food expenditure by approximately \$1.32 per week, or that a 10% increase in income will increase food expenditure by approximately \$13.22. Although this interpretation is conveniently simple to state, the diminishing marginal effect of income on food expenditure is somewhat

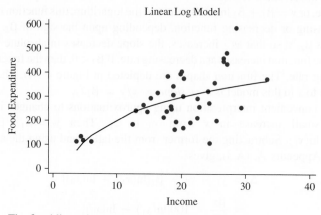

FIGURE **4.6**   The fitted linear-log model.

disguised, though still implied. At $1,000 per week income, a 10% increase is $100, while at $2,000 income a 10% increase is $200. At higher levels of income a larger dollar increase in income is required to elicit an additional $13.22 expenditure on food.

In terms of how well the model fits the data, we see that $R^2 = 0.357$ for the linear-log model, as compared to $R^2 = 0.385$ for the linear, straight-line relationship. Since these two models have the same dependent variable, *FOOD_EXP*, and each model has a single explanatory variable, a comparison of R^2 values is valid. However there is a very small difference in the fit of the two models, and in any case a model should not be chosen only on the basis of model fit with R^2 as the criterion.

REMARK: Given alternative models, that involve different transformations of the dependent and independent variables, and some of which have similar shapes, what are some guidelines for choosing a functional form?

1. Choose a shape that is consistent with what economic theory tells us about the relationship.
2. Choose a shape that is sufficiently flexible to "fit" the data.
3. Choose a shape so that assumptions SR1–SR6 are satisfied, ensuring that the least squares estimators have the desirable properties described in Chapters 2 and 3.

Although these objectives are easily stated, the reality of model building is much more difficult. You must recognize that we **never** know the "true" functional relationship between economic variables; also, the functional form that we select, no matter how elegant, is only an approximation. Our job is to choose a functional form that satisfactorily meets the three objectives stated above.

4.3.4 USING DIAGNOSTIC RESIDUAL PLOTS

When specifying a regression model, we may inadvertently choose an inadequate or incorrect functional form. Even if the functional form is adequate, one or more of the regression model assumptions may not hold. There are two primary methods for detecting such errors. First, examine the regression results. Finding an incorrect sign or a theoretically important variable that is not statistically significant may indicate a problem. Second, evidence of specification errors can reveal themselves in an analysis of the least squares residuals. We should ask whether there is any evidence that assumptions SR3 (homoskedasticity), SR4 (no serial correlation), and SR6 (normality) are violated. Usually heteroskedasticity might be suspected in cross-sectional data analysis, and serial correlation is a potential time series problem. In both cases diagnostic tools focus on the least squares residuals. In Chapters 8 and 9 we will provide formal tests for homoskedasticity and serial correlation. In addition to formal tests, residual plots of all types are useful as diagnostic tools. In this section residual analysis reveals potential heteroskedasticity and serial correlation problems, and also flawed choices of functional forms.

What should a scatter plot of least squares residuals look like if all model assumptions hold? The idea of simulation, or Monte Carlo simulation, is introduced in Appendix 2G and Appendix 3C. Here we simulate 300 data pairs (x, y), using the model $y = 1 + x + e$, where x is simulated, using a random number generator, to be evenly, or uniformly, distributed

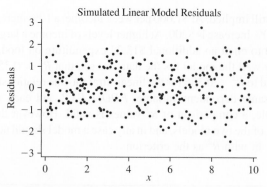

FIGURE **4.7** Randomly scattered residuals.

between zero and 10. The error term *e* is simulated to be uncorrelated, homoskedastic, and from a standard normal distribution, or $e \sim N(0, 1)$. These simulated observations can be found in *ch4sim1.dat*. We apply the least squares estimator and compute the least squares residuals. In a graphical residual analysis the least squares residuals are plotted against *x*, *y*, or the predicted *y*. In a time series framework, the residuals can be plotted against "time." If all the model assumptions hold, as they do here for the simulated data, the residuals plot should resemble Figure 4.7, where we have plotted the residuals against *x* values. The residual pattern is random, with no obvious trends or shapes. This is what we hope to see when residuals are plotted. The existence of patterns is an indication of an assumption violation or another problem.

4.3.4a Heteroskedastic Residual Pattern
The least squares residuals from the linear-log food expenditure model in (4.14) are plotted in Figure 4.8. These exhibit an expanding variation pattern with more variation in the residuals as *INCOME* becomes larger, which may suggest heteroskedastic errors. A similar residual plot is implied by Figure 2.8.

We must conclude that at this point we do not have a satisfactory model for the food expenditure data. The linear and linear-log models have different shapes, and different implied marginal effects. The two models fit the data equally well, but both models exhibit least squares residual patterns consistent with heteroskedastic errors. This example will be considered further in Chapter 8.

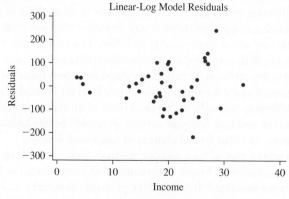

FIGURE **4.8** Residuals from linear-log food expenditure model.

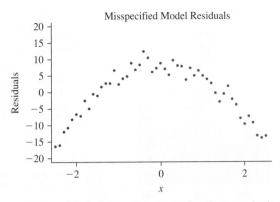

FIGURE **4.9**   Least squares residuals from a linear equation fit to quadratic data.

4.3.4b   Detecting Model Specification Errors

To give one other example, suppose that the functional relationship between y and x is quadratic, like the dashed curve shown in Figure 4.5(a), and yet we decide to fit a straight-line regression model. Again we simulate data, this time using as the true model $y = 15 - 4x^2 + e$, with $e \sim N(0, 4)$. These data are in the file *ch4sim2.dat*. The plot of the least squares residuals from a linear relationship is presented in Figure 4.9.

The well-defined quadratic pattern in the least squares residuals indicates that something is wrong with the linear model specification. The linear model has "missed" a curvilinear aspect of the relationship. An alternative interpretation could be that there is perhaps some dependence in the regression errors. Recall Assumption SR4, that the regression errors are assumed to be uncorrelated. The least squares residuals in Figure 4.9 show a long group of negative residuals, then a group of positive ones, then negative again. If the regression errors are uncorrelated, we do not expect such patterns if our model is well specified. This reveals that analyzing residual patterns is often not a clear-cut process. Model misspecifications and error assumption violations commingle, leading to multiple potential interpretations from analysis of least squares residuals. Nevertheless, residual diagnostics are a key aspect of regression analysis.

4.3.5   Are the Regression Errors Normally Distributed?

Recall that hypothesis tests and interval estimates for the coefficients rely on the assumption that the errors, and hence the dependent variable y, are normally distributed. Though our tests and confidence intervals are valid in large samples whether the data are normally distributed or not, it is nevertheless desirable to have a model in which the regression errors are normally distributed, so that we do not have to rely on large sample approximations. If the errors are not normally distributed, we might be able to improve our model by considering an alternative functional form or transforming the dependent variable. As noted in the last "Remark," when choosing a functional form, one of the criteria we might examine is whether a model specification satisfies regression assumptions, and in particular, whether it leads to errors that are normally distributed (SR6). How do we check out the assumption of normally distributed errors?

We cannot observe the true random errors, so we must base our analysis of their normality on the least squares residuals, $\hat{e}_i = y_i - \hat{y}_i$. Most computer software will create a histogram of the residuals for this purpose and may also give statistics that can be used to formally test a null hypothesis that the residuals (and thus the true errors) come from a normal distribution.

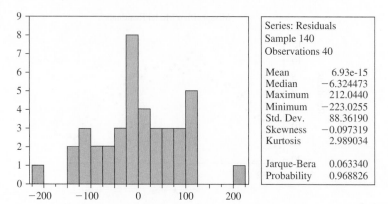

FIGURE 4.10   EViews output: residuals histogram and summary statistics for food expenditure example.

The relevant EViews output for the food expenditure example, using the linear relationship with no transformation of the variables, appears in Figure 4.10. What does this histogram tell us? First, notice that it is centered at zero. This is not surprising, because the mean of the least squares residuals is always zero if the model contains an intercept, as shown in Appendix 4B. Second, it seems symmetrical, but there are some large gaps, and it does not really appear bell-shaped. However, merely checking the shape of the histogram, especially when the number of observations is relatively small, is not a statistical "test."

There are many tests for normality. The **Jarque–Bera test** for normality is based on two measures, skewness and kurtosis. In the present context, **skewness** refers to how symmetric the residuals are around zero. Perfectly symmetric residuals will have a skewness of zero. The skewness value for the food expenditure residuals is −0.097. **Kurtosis** refers to the "peakedness" of the distribution. For a normal distribution the kurtosis value is 3. For more on skewness and kurtosis see Appendices B.1.2 and C.4.2. From Figure 4.10, we see that the food expenditure residuals have a kurtosis of 2.99. The skewness and kurtosis values are close to the values for the normal distribution. So, the question we have to ask is whether 2.99 is sufficiently different from 3, and −0.097 sufficiently different from zero, to conclude the residuals are not normally distributed. The Jarque–Bera statistic is given by

$$JB = \frac{N}{6}\left(S^2 + \frac{(K-3)^2}{4}\right)$$

where N is the sample size, S is skewness, and K is kurtosis. Thus, large values of the skewness, and/or values of kurtosis quite different from 3, will lead to a large value of the Jarque–Bera statistic. When the residuals are normally distributed, the Jarque–Bera statistic has a chi-squared distribution with two degrees of freedom. We reject the hypothesis of normally distributed errors if a calculated value of the statistic exceeds a critical value selected from the chi-squared distribution with two degrees of freedom. The 5% critical value from a χ^2-distribution with two degrees of freedom is 5.99, and the 1% critical value is 9.21.

Applying these ideas to the food expenditure example, we have

$$JB = \frac{40}{6}\left(-0.097^2 + \frac{(2.99-3)^2}{4}\right) = 0.063$$

Because $0.063 < 5.99$ there is insufficient evidence from the residuals to conclude that the normal distribution assumption is unreasonable at the 5% level of significance. The same conclusion could have been reached by examining the p-value. The p-value appears in Figure 4.10 described as "Probability." Thus, we also fail to reject the null hypothesis on the grounds that $0.9688 > 0.05$.

For the linear-log model of food expenditure reported in Section 4.3.3, the Jarque-Bera test statistic value is 0.1999 with a p-value of 0.9049. We cannot reject the null hypothesis that the regression errors are normally distributed, and this criterion does not help us choose between the linear and linear-log functional forms for the food expenditure model.

4.4 Polynomial Models

In Chapter 2.8.1–2.8.2 we introduced the use of quadratic polynomials to capture curvilinear relationships. Economics students will have seen many average and marginal cost curves (U-shaped) and average and marginal product curves (inverted-U shaped) in their studies. Higher order polynomials, such as cubic equations, are used for total cost and total product curves. A familiar example to economics students is the total cost curve, shaped much like the solid curve in Figure 4.5(b). In this section, we review quadratic and cubic equations and give an empirical example.

4.4.1 QUADRATIC AND CUBIC EQUATIONS

The general form of a quadratic equation $y = a_0 + a_1 x + a_2 x^2$ includes a constant term a_0, a linear term $a_1 x$, and a squared term $a_2 x^2$. Similarly, the general form of a cubic equation is $y = a_0 + a_1 x + a_2 x^2 + a_3 x^3$. In Chapter 5.6 we consider multiple regression models using the general forms of quadratic and cubic equations. For now, however, because we are working with "simple" regression models that include only one explanatory variable, we consider the quadratic and cubic forms, $y = \beta_1 + \beta_2 x^2$ and $y = \beta_1 + \beta_2 x^3$, respectively. The properties of the simple quadratic function are discussed in Chapter 2.8.1.

The simple cubic equation $y = \beta_1 + \beta_2 x^3$ has possible shapes shown in Figure 4.5(b). Using Derivative Rules 4 and 5 from Appendix A, the derivative, or slope, of the cubic equation is $dy/dx = 3\beta_2 x^2$. The slope of the curve is always positive if $\beta_2 > 0$, except when $x = 0$, yielding a direct relationship between y and x like the solid curve shown in Figure 4.5 (b). If $\beta_2 < 0$ then the relationship is an inverse one like the dashed curve in Figure 4.5(b). The slope equation shows that the slope is zero only when $x = 0$. The term a is the y-intercept. The elasticity of y with respect to x is $\varepsilon = slope \times x/y = 3\beta_2 x^2 \times x/y$. Both the slope and elasticity change along the curve.

4.4.2 AN EMPIRICAL EXAMPLE

Figure 4.11 describes a plot of average wheat yield (in tonnes per hectare—a hectare is about 2.5 acres, and a tonne is a metric ton that is 1000 kg or 2205 lb—we are speaking Australian here!) for the Greenough Shire in Western Australia, against time. The observations are for the period 1950–1997, and time is measured using the values $1, 2, \ldots, 48$. These data can be found in the file *wa_wheat.dat*. Notice in Figure 4.11 that wheat yield fluctuates quite a bit, but overall, it tends to increase over time, and the increase is at an increasing rate, particularly toward the end of the time period. An increase in yield is expected because of technological improvements, such as the development of varieties of wheat that are higher yielding and more resistant to pests and diseases. Suppose that we are interested in measuring the effect of technological improvement on yield. Direct data on changes in

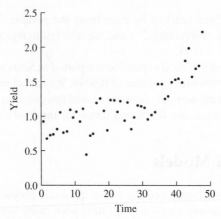

FIGURE 4.11   Scatter plot of wheat yield over time.

technology are not available, but we can examine how wheat yield has changed over time as a consequence of changing technology. The equation of interest relates *YIELD* to *TIME*, where *TIME* = 1, ... , 48. One problem with the linear equation

$$YIELD_t = \beta_1 + \beta_2 TIME_t + e_t$$

is that it implies that yield increases at the same constant rate β_2, when, from Figure 4.11, we expect this rate to be increasing. The least squares fitted line (standard errors in parentheses) is

$$\widehat{YIELD}_t = 0.638 + 0.0210 \ TIME_t \qquad R^2 = 0.649$$
$$\text{(se)} \qquad (0.064) \ (0.0022)$$

The residuals from this regression are plotted against time in Figure 4.12. Notice that there is a concentration of positive residuals at each end of the sample and a concentration of negative residuals in the middle. These concentrations are caused by the inability of a straight line to capture the fact that yield is increasing at an increasing rate. What alternative can we try? Two possibilities are $TIME^2$ and $TIME^3$. It turns out that $TIME^3$ provides the better fit, and so we consider instead the functional form

$$YIELD_t = \beta_1 + \beta_2 TIME_t^3 + e_t$$

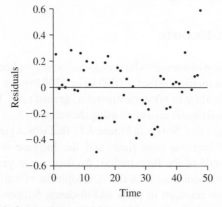

FIGURE 4.12   Residuals from a linear yield equation.

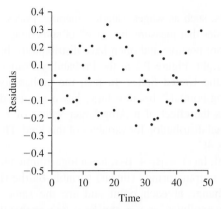

FIGURE **4.13** Residuals from a cubic yield equation.

The slope of the expected yield function is $3\beta_2 TIME^2$. Thus, so long as the estimate of β_2 turns out to be positive, the function will be increasing. Furthermore, the slope is increasing as well. Thus the function itself is "increasing at an increasing rate." Before estimating the cubic equation, note that the values of $TIME^3$ can get very large. This variable is a good candidate for scaling. If we define $TIMECUBE_t = TIME_t^3/1000000$ the estimated equation is

$$\widehat{YIELD}_t = 0.874 + 9.68\,TIMECUBE_t \qquad R^2 = 0.751$$
$$(\text{se}) \quad\;\; (0.036)\;\;(0.822)$$

The residuals from this cubic equation are plotted in Figure 4.13. The predominance of positive residuals at the ends and negative residuals in the middle no longer exists. Furthermore, the R^2 value has increased from 0.649 to 0.751, indicating that the equation with $TIMECUBE$ fits the data better than the one with just $TIME$. Both these equations have the same dependent variable and the same number of explanatory variables (only 1). In these circumstances the R^2 can be used legitimately to compare goodness of fit. What lessons have we learned from this example? First, a plot of the original dependent variable series y against the explanatory variable x is a useful starting point for deciding on a functional form in a simple regression model. Secondly, examining a plot of the residuals is a useful device for uncovering inadequacies in any chosen functional form. Runs of positive and/or negative residuals can suggest an alternative. In this example, with time-series data, plotting the residuals against time was informative. With cross-sectional data, using plots of residuals against both independent and dependent variables is recommended. Ideally we will see no patterns, and the residual histogram and Jarque–Bera test will not rule out the assumption of normality. As we travel through the book, you will discover that patterns in the residuals can also mean many other specification inadequacies, such as omitted variables, heteroskedasticity, and autocorrelation. Thus, as you become more knowledgeable and experienced, you should be careful to consider other options. For example, wheat yield in Western Australia is heavily influenced by rainfall. Inclusion of a rainfall variable might be an option worth considering. Also, it makes sense to include $TIME$ and $TIME^2$ in addition to $TIME^3$. A further possibility is the constant growth rate model that we consider in the next section.

4.5 Log-Linear Models

Econometric models that employ natural logarithms are very common. We first introduced the log-linear model in Chapter 2.8.3. Logarithmic transformations are often used for variables that are monetary values, such as wages, salaries, income, prices, sales, and expenditures, and in general for variables that measure the "size" of something. These variables have the characteristic that they are positive and often have distributions that are positively skewed, with a long tail to the right. Figure P.2 in the Probability Primer is representative of the income distribution in the United States. In fact, the probability density function $f(x)$ shown is called the "log-normal," because $\ln(x)$ has a normal distribution. Because the transformation $\ln(x)$ has the effect of making larger values of x less extreme, $\ln(x)$ will often be closer to a normal distribution for variables of this kind. The log-normal distribution is discussed in Appendix 4C.

The log-linear model, $\ln(y) = \beta_1 + \beta_2 x$, has a logarithmic term on the left-hand side of the equation and an untransformed (linear) variable on the right-hand side. Both its slope and elasticity change at each point and are the same sign as β_2. Using the antilogarithm we obtain $\exp[\ln(y)] = y = \exp(\beta_1 + \beta x)$, so that the log-linear function is an exponential function. The function requires $y > 0$. The slope at any point is $\beta_2 y$, which for $\beta_2 > 0$ means that the marginal effect increases for larger values of y. An economist might say that this function is increasing at an increasing rate. The shapes of the log-linear model are shown in Figure 4.5(e), and its derivative and elasticity given in Table 4.1. To make discussion relevant in a specific context, the slope can be evaluated at the sample mean $\bar{y}$, or the elasticity $\beta_2 x$ can be evaluated at the sample mean $\bar{x}$, or other interesting values can be chosen.

An easier interpretation can be obtained by using the properties of logarithms. In the log-linear model, a one-unit increase in x leads, approximately, to a $100\beta_2\%$ change in y. This interpretation was given in Chapter 2, (2.28), and used in the discussions and examples in Chapters 2.8.3–2.8.4.

Using the properties of logarithms, we can see this another way. Consider an increase in x from x_0 to x_1. The change in the log-linear model is from $\ln(y_0) = \beta_1 + \beta_2 x_0$ to $\ln(y_1) = \beta_1 + \beta_2 x_1$. Subtracting the first equation from the second gives $\ln(y_1) - \ln(y_0) = \beta_2(x_1 - x_0) = \beta_2 \Delta x$. Multiply by 100, and use the approximation introduced in Appendix A, (A.3) to obtain

$$100[\ln(y_1) - \ln(y_0)] \cong \%\Delta y = 100\beta_2(x_1 - x_0) = (100\beta_2) \times \Delta x$$

A 1-unit increase in x leads approximately, to, a $100 \times \beta_2\%$ change in y.

4.5.1 A GROWTH MODEL

Earlier in this chapter, in Section 4.4.2, we considered an empirical example in which the production of wheat was tracked over time, with improvements in technology leading to wheat production increasing at an increasing rate. Another way to represent such a relationship is using a log-linear model. To see how, suppose that due to advances in technology the yield of wheat produced (tonnes per hectare) is growing at approximately a constant rate per year. Specifically, suppose that the yield in year t is $YIELD_t = (1 + g)YIELD_{t-1}$, with g being the fixed growth rate in 1 year. By substituting repeatedly we obtain $YIELD_t = YIELD_0(1 + g)^t$. Here $YIELD_0$ is the yield in year "0," the year before the sample begins, so it is probably unknown. Taking logarithms, we obtain

$$\ln(YIELD_t) = \ln(YIELD_0) + [\ln(1 + g)] \times t$$
$$= \beta_1 + \beta_2 t$$

This is simply a log-linear model with dependent variable $\ln(YIELD_t)$ and explanatory variable t, or time. We expect growth to be positive, so that $\beta_2 > 0$, in which case the plot of *YIELD* against time looks like the upward-sloping curve in Figure 4.5(c), which closely resembles the scatter diagram in Figure 4.11.

Estimating the log-linear model for yield, we obtain

$$\widehat{\ln(YIELD_t)} = -0.3434 + 0.0178t$$
$$(\text{se}) \qquad (0.0584) \quad (0.0021)$$

The estimated coefficient $b_2 = \widehat{\ln(1+g)} = 0.0178$. Using the property that $\ln(1+x) \cong x$ if x is small [see Appendix A, (A.4) and the discussion following it], we estimate that the growth rate in wheat yield is approximately $\hat{g} = 0.0178$, or about 1.78% per year, over the period of the data.

4.5.2 A WAGE EQUATION

The relationship between wages and education is a key relationship in labor economics (and, no doubt, in your mind). Suppose that the rate of return to an extra year of education is a constant r. That is, in the first year after an additional year of education, your wage rate rises from an initial value $WAGE_0$ to $WAGE_1 = (1+r)WAGE_0$. For an extra two years of education, this becomes $WAGE_2 = (1+r)^2 WAGE_0$, and so on. Taking logarithms, we have a relationship between $\ln(WAGE)$ and years of education (*EDUC*)

$$\ln(WAGE) = \ln(WAGE_0) + [\ln(1+r)] \times EDUC$$
$$= \beta_1 + \beta_2 EDUC$$

An additional year of education leads to an approximate $100\beta_2\%$ increase in wages.

Data on hourly wages, years of education, and other variables are in the file *cps4_small. dat*. These, data consist of 1000 observations from the 2008 Current Population Survey (CPS). The CPS is a monthly survey of about 50000 households conducted in the United States by the Bureau of the Census for the Bureau of Labor Statistics. The survey has been conducted for more than 50 years. Using this data, the estimated log-linear model is

$$\widehat{\ln(WAGE)} = 1.6094 + 0.0904 \times EDUC$$
$$(\text{se}) \qquad (0.0864) \quad (0.0061)$$

We estimate that an additional year of education increases the wage rate by approximately 9%. A 95% interval estimate for the value of an additional year of education is 7.8% to 10.2%.

4.5.3 PREDICTION IN THE LOG-LINEAR MODEL

You may have noticed that when reporting regression results in this section, we did not include an R^2 value. In a log-linear regression the R^2 value automatically reported by statistical software is the percent of the variation in $\ln(y)$ explained by the model. However, our objective is to explain the variations in y, not $\ln(y)$. Furthermore, the fitted regression line predicts $\widehat{\ln(y)} = b_1 + b_2 x$, whereas we want to predict y. The problems of obtaining a useful measure of goodness-of-fit and prediction are connected, as we discussed in Section 4.2.2.

How shall we obtain the predicted value of y? A first inclination might be to take the antilog of $\widehat{\ln(y)} = b_1 + b_2 x$. For the natural logarithm the antilog is the exponential function, so that a natural choice for prediction is

$$\hat{y}_n = \exp(\widehat{\ln(y)}) = \exp(b_1 + b_2 x)$$

In the log-linear model this is not necessarily the best we can do. Using properties of the log-normal distribution it can be shown (see Appendix 4C) that an alternative predictor is

$$\hat{y}_c = \widehat{E(y)} = \exp(b_1 + b_2 x + \hat{\sigma}^2/2) = \hat{y}_n e^{\hat{\sigma}^2/2}$$

If the sample size is large, the "corrected" predictor $\hat{y}_c$ is, on average, closer to the actual value of y and should be used. In small samples (less than 30) the "natural" predictor may actually be a better choice. The reason for this incongruous result is that the estimated value of the error variance $\hat{\sigma}^2$ adds a certain amount of "noise" when using $\hat{y}_c$, leading it to have increased variability relative to $\hat{y}_n$ that can outweigh the benefit of the correction in small samples.

The effect of the correction can be illustrated using the wage equation. What would we predict the wage to be for a worker with 12 years of education? The predicted value of $\ln(WAGE)$ is

$$\widehat{\ln(WAGE)} = 1.6094 + 0.0904 \times EDUC = 1.6094 + 0.0904 \times 12 = 2.6943$$

Then the value of the natural predictor is $\hat{y}_n = \exp(\widehat{\ln(y)}) = \exp(2.6943) = 14.7958$. The value of the corrected predictor, using $\hat{\sigma}^2 = 0.2773$ from the regression output, is

$$\hat{y}_c = \widehat{E(y)} = \hat{y}_n e^{\hat{\sigma}^2/2} = 14.7958 \times 1.1487 = 16.9964$$

We predict that the wage for a worker with 12 years of education will be \$14.80 per hour if we use the natural predictor, and \$17.00 if we use the corrected predictor. In this case the sample is large ($N = 1000$), so we would use the corrected predictor. Among the 1000 workers there are 328 with 12 years of education. Their average wage is \$15.99, so the corrected predictor is consistent with the sample of data.

How does the correction affect our prediction? Recall that $\hat{\sigma}^2$ must be greater than zero and $e^0 = 1$. Thus, the effect of the correction is always to increase the value of the prediction, because $e^{\hat{\sigma}^2/2}$ is always greater than one. The natural predictor tends to systematically underpredict the value of y in a log-linear model, and the correction offsets the downward bias in large samples. The "natural" and "corrected" predictions are shown in Figure 4.14.

4.5.4 A GENERALIZED R^2 MEASURE

It is a general rule that the squared simple correlation between y and its fitted value $\hat{y}$, where $\hat{y}$ is the "best" prediction one can obtain, is a valid measure of goodness-of-fit that we can use as an R^2 in many contexts. As we have seen, what we may consider the "best" predictor can change depending upon the model under consideration. That is, a general goodness-of-fit measure, or general R^2, is

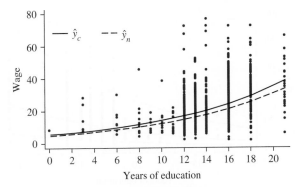

FIGURE **4.14**   The natural and corrected predictors of wage.

$$R_g^2 = [\text{corr}(y, \hat{y})]^2 = r_{y\hat{y}}^2$$

In the wage equation $R_g^2 = [\text{corr}(y, \hat{y}_c)]^2 = 0.4312^2 = 0.1859$, as compared to the reported $R^2 = 0.1782$ from the regression of $\ln(WAGE)$ on $EDUC$. (In this case since the corrected and natural predictors differ only by a constant factor, the correlation is the same for both.) These R^2 values are small, but we repeat our earlier message: R^2 values tend to be small with microeconomic, cross-sectional data, because the variations in individual behavior are difficult to fully explain.

4.5.5   PREDICTION INTERVALS IN THE LOG-LINEAR MODEL

We have a corrected predictor $\hat{y}_c$ for y in the log-linear model. It is the "point" predictor, or point forecast, that is relevant if we seek the single number that is our best prediction of y. If we prefer a prediction or forecast interval for y, then we must rely on the natural predictor $\hat{y}_n$.[1] Specifically we follow the procedure outlined in Section 4.1, and then take antilogs. That is, compute $\widehat{\ln(y)} = b_1 + b_2 x$ and then $\widehat{\ln(y)} \pm t_c \text{se}(f)$, where the critical value t_c is the $100(1-\alpha/2)$-percentile from the t-distribution and se(f) is given in (4.5). Then a $100(1-\alpha)\%$ prediction interval for y is

$$\left[\exp\left(\widehat{\ln(y)} - t_c \text{se}(f)\right), \exp\left(\widehat{\ln(y)} + t_c \text{se}(f)\right)\right]$$

For the wage data, a 95% prediction interval for the wage of a worker with 12 years of education is

$$[\exp(2.6943 - 1.96 \times 0.5270), \exp(2.6943 + 1.96 \times 0.5270)] = [5.2604, 41.6158]$$

The interval prediction is \$5.26–\$41.62, which is so wide that it is basically useless. What does this tell us? Nothing we did not already know. Our model is not an accurate predictor of individual behavior in this case. In later chapters we will see if we can improve this model by adding additional explanatory variables, such as experience, that should be relevant. The prediction interval is shown in Figure 4.15.

---

[1] See Appendix 4A. The corrected predictor includes the estimated error variance, making the t-distribution no longer relevant in (4A.1).

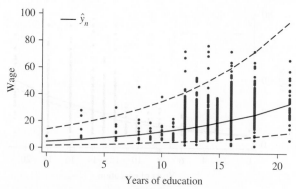

FIGURE 4.15 The 95% prediction interval for wage.

4.6 Log–Log Models

The log–log function, $\ln(y) = \beta_1 + \beta_2 \ln(x)$, is widely used to describe demand equations and production functions. The name "log–log" comes from the fact that the logarithm appears on both sides of the equation. In order to use this model, all values of y and x must be positive. The slopes of these curves change at every point, but the elasticity is constant and equal to β_2. A useful way to think about the log–log function comes from closer inspection of its slope $dy/dx = \beta_2(y/x)$. Rearrange this so that $\beta_2 = (dy/y)/(dx/x)$. Thus, the slope of the log–log function exhibits constant *relative* change, whereas the linear function displays constant absolute change. The log–log function is a transformation of the equation $y = Ax^{\beta_2}$, with $\beta_1 = \ln(A)$. The various shape possibilities for log–log models are depicted in Figure 4.5(c), for $\beta_2 > 0$ and Figure 4.5(d), for $\beta_2 < 0$.

If $\beta_2 > 0$, then y is an increasing function of x. If $\beta_2 > 1$, then the function increases at an increasing rate. That is, as x increases the slope increases as well. If $0 < \beta_2 < 1$, then the function is increasing, but at a decreasing rate; as x increases, the slope decreases.

If $\beta_2 < 0$, then there is an inverse relationship between y and x. If, for example, $\beta_2 = -1$, then $y = Ax^{-1}$ or $xy = A$. This curve has "unit" elasticity. If we let $y =$ quantity demanded and $x =$ price, then $A =$ total revenue from sales. For every point on the curve $xy = A$, the area under the curve A (total revenue for the demand curve) is constant. By definition, unit elasticity implies that a 1% increase in x (price, for example) is associated with a 1% decrease in y (quantity demanded), so that the product xy (price times quantity) remains constant.

4.6.1   A Log-Log Poultry Demand Equation

The log–log functional form is frequently used for demand equations. Consider, for example, the demand for edible chicken, which the U.S. Department of Agriculture calls "broilers." The data for this exercise is in the file *newbroiler.dat*, which is adapted from the data provided by Epple and McCallum (2006).[2] The scatter plot of $Q =$ per capita consumption of chicken, in pounds, versus $P =$ real price of chicken is shown in Figure 4.16 for 52 annual observations, 1950–2001. It shows the characteristic hyperbolic shape that was displayed in Figure 4.5(d).

---

[2] "Simultaneous Equation Econometrics: The Missing Example," *Economic Inquiry*, 44(2), 374–384.

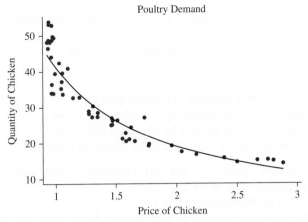

FIGURE **4.16** Quantity and Price of Chicken.

The estimated log-log model is

$$\widehat{\ln(Q)} = 3.717 - 1.121 \times \ln(P) \qquad R_g^2 = 0.8817$$

$$(\text{se}) \quad (0.022) \quad (0.049) \tag{4.15}$$

We estimate that the price elasticity of demand is 1.121: a 1% increase in real price is estimated to reduce quantity consumed by 1.121%.

The fitted line shown in Figure 4.16 is the "corrected" predictor discussed in Section 4.5.3. The corrected predictor $\hat{Q}_c$ is the natural predictor $\hat{Q}_n$ adjusted by the factor $\exp(\hat{\sigma}^2/2)$. That is, using the estimated error variance $\hat{\sigma}^2 = 0.0139$, the predictor is

$$\hat{Q}_c = \hat{Q}_n e^{\hat{\sigma}^2/2} = \exp\left(\widehat{\ln(Q)}\right) e^{\hat{\sigma}^2/2} = \exp(3.717 - 1.121 \times \ln(P)) e^{0.0139/2}$$

The goodness-of-fit statistic $R_g^2 = 0.8817$ is the generalized R^2 discussed in Section 4.5.4. It is the squared correlation between the predictor $\hat{Q}_c$ and the observations Q

$$R_g^2 = \left[corr(Q, \hat{Q}_c)\right]^2 = [0.939]^2 = 0.8817$$

4.7 Exercises

Answer to exercises marked * appear www.wiley.com/go/global/hill.

4.7.1 Problems

4.1* (a) Supposing that a simple regression has quantities $\sum(y_i - \bar{y})^2 = 631.63$ and $\sum\hat{e}_i^2 = 182.85$, find R^2.

(b) Suppose that a simple regression has quantities $N = 20$, $\sum y_i^2 = 5930.94$, $\bar{y} = 16.035$, and $SSR = 666.72$, find R^2.

(c) Suppose that a simple regression has quantities $R^2 = 0.7911$, $SST = 552.36$, and $N = 20$, find $\hat{\sigma}^2$.

4.2* Consider the following estimated regression equation (standard errors in parentheses):

$$\hat{y} = 5.83 + 0.869x \quad R^2 = 0.756$$
$$(\text{se}) \ (1.23) \ (0.117)$$

Rewrite the estimated equation that would result if
(a) All values of x were divided by 20 before estimation
(b) All values of y were divided by 50 before estimation
(c) All values of y and x were divided by 20 before estimation

4.3 Using the data in Exercise 2.1 and only a calculator (show your work) compute
(a) The predicted value of y for $x_0 = 5$
(b) The se(f) corresponding to part (a)
(c) A 95% prediction interval for y given $x_0 = 5$
(d) A 95% prediction interval for y given $x = \bar{x}$. Compare the width of this interval to the one computed in part (c)

4.4 The general manager of an engineering firm wants to know whether a technical artist's experience influences the quality of his or her work. A random sample of 50 artists is selected and their years of work experience and quality rating (as assessed by their supervisors) recorded. Work experience (*EXPER*) is measured in years and quality rating (*RATING*) takes a value in the interval one to four, with 4 = very good and 1 = very poor. Two models are estimated by least squares. The estimates and standard errors are

Model 1 :

$$\widehat{RATING} = 3.4464 - 0.001459(EXPER - 35)^2 \quad N = 50$$
$$(\text{se}) \quad (0.0375) \ (0.0000786)$$

Model 2 :

$$\widehat{RATING} = 1.4276 + 0.5343 \ln(EXPER) \quad N = 49$$
$$(\text{se}) \quad (0.1333) \ (0.0433)$$

(a) For each model, sketch the estimated regression function for $EXPER = 10$ to 40 years.
(b) Using each model, predict the rating of a worker with 20 years' experience.
(c) Using each model, find the marginal effect of another year of experience on the expected worker rating for a worker with 20 years' experience.
(d) Using each model, construct a 95% interval estimate for the marginal effect found in (c). Note that Model 2 has one fewer observations due to 1 worker having $EXPER = 0$.

4.5 Suppose you are estimating a simple linear regression model.
(a) If you multiply all the x values by 20, but not the y values, what happens to the parameter values β_1 and β_2? What happens to the least squares estimates b_1 and b_2? What happens to the variance of the error term?
(b) Suppose you are estimating a simple linear regression model. If you multiply all the y values by 50, but not the x values, what happens to the parameter values

β_1 and β_2? What happens to the least squares estimates b_1 and b_2? What happens to the variance of the error term?

4.6   The fitted least squares line is $\hat{y}_i = b_1 + b_2 x_i$.

(a) Algebraically, show that the fitted line passes through the point of the means, $(\bar{x}, \bar{y})$.

(b) Algebraically show that the average value of $\hat{y}_i$ equals the sample average of y. That is, show that $\bar{\hat{y}} = \bar{y}$, where $\bar{\hat{y}} = \Sigma \hat{y}_i / N$.

4.7   In a simple linear regression model suppose we know that the intercept parameter is zero, so the model is $y_i = \beta_2 x_i + e_i$. The least squares estimator of β_2 is developed in Exercise 2.4.

(a) What is the least squares predictor of y in this case?

(b) When an intercept is not present in a model, R^2 is often defined to be $R_u^2 = 1 - SSE/\Sigma y_i^2$, where SSE is the usual sum of squared residuals. Compute R_u^2 for the data in Exercise 2.4.

(c) Compare the value of R_u^2 in part (b) to the generalized $R^2 = r_{y\hat{y}}^2$, where $\hat{y}$ is the predictor based on the restricted model in part (a).

(d) Compute $SST = \Sigma(y_i - \bar{y})^2$ and $SSR = \Sigma(\hat{y}_i - \bar{y})^2$, where $\hat{y}$ is the predictor based on the restricted model in part (a). Does the sum of squares decomposition $SST = SSR + SSE$ hold in this case?

4.7.2 COMPUTER EXERCISES

4.8   The first three columns in the file *wa_wheat.dat* contain observations on wheat yield in the Western Australian shires Northampton, Chapman Valley, and Mullewa, respectively. There are 48 annual observations for the years 1950–1997. For the Chapman Valley shire, consider the three equations

$$y_t = \beta_1 + \beta_2 t + e_t$$
$$y_t = \alpha_1 + \alpha_2 \ln(t) + e_t$$
$$y_t = \gamma_1 + \gamma_2 t^2 + e_t$$

(a) Using data from 1950–1996, estimate each of the three equations.

(b) Taking into consideration (i) plots of the fitted equations, (ii) plots of the residuals, (iii) error normality tests, and (iv) values for R^2, which equation do you think is preferable? Explain.

4.9*   For each of the three functions in Exercise 4.8

(a) Find the predicted value and a 95% prediction interval for yield when $t = 48$. Is the actual value within the prediction interval?

(b) Find estimates of the slopes dy_t/dt at the point $t = 48$.

(c) Find estimates of the elasticities $(dy_t/dt)(t/y_t)$ at the point $t = 48$.

(d) Comment on the estimates you obtained in parts (b) and (c). What is their importance?

4.10   The file *london.dat* is a cross section of 1519 households drawn from the 1980–1982 British Family Expenditure Surveys. Data have been selected to include only households with one or two children living in Greater London. Self-employed and retired households have been excluded. Variable definitions are in the file *london.def*. The budget share of a commodity, say food, is defined as

$$WFOOD = \frac{\text{expenditure on food}}{\text{total expenditure}}$$

A functional form that has been popular for estimating expenditure functions for commodities is

$$WFOOD = \beta_1 + \beta_2 \ln(TOTEXP) + e$$

(a) Estimate this function for households with one child and households with two children. Report and comment on the results. (You may find it more convenient to use the files *lon1.dat* and *lon2.dat* that contain the data for the one and two children households, with 594 and 925 observations, respectively.)

(b) It can be shown that the expenditure elasticity for food is given by

$$\varepsilon = \frac{\beta_1 + \beta_2[\ln(TOTEXP) + 1]}{\beta_1 + \beta_2 \ln(TOTEXP)}$$

Find estimates of this elasticity for one- and two-child households, evaluated at average total expenditure in each case. Do these estimates suggest food is a luxury or a necessity? (*Hint*: Are the elasticities greater than one or less than one?)

(c) Analyze the residuals from each estimated function. Does the functional form seem appropriate? Is it reasonable to assume that the errors are normally distributed?

(d) Using the data on households with two children, *lon2.dat*, estimate budget share equations for fuel (*WFUEL*) and transportation (*WTRANS*). For each equation discuss the estimate of β_2 and carry out a two-tail test of statistical significance.

(e) Using the regression results from part (d), compute the elasticity ε for fuel and transportation first at the median of total expenditure (90), and then at the 95th percentile of total income (180). What differences do you observe? Are any differences you observe consistent with economic reasoning?

4.11* Reconsider the presidential voting data (*fair4.dat*) introduced in Exercises 2.14 and 3.9.

(a) Using the data from 1916 to 2008, estimate the regression model $VOTE = \beta_1 + \beta_2 GROWTH + e$. Based on these estimates, what is the predicted value of *VOTE* in 2008? What is the least squares residual for the 2008 election observation?

(b) Estimate the regression in (a) using the data from 1916–2004. Predict the value of *VOTE* in 2008 using the actual value of *GROWTH* for 2008, which was 0.22%. What is the prediction error in this forecast? Is it larger or smaller than the error computed in part (a)?

(c) Using the regression results from (b), construct a 95% prediction interval for the 2008 value of *VOTE* using the actual value of *GROWTH* = 0.22%. Is the actual 2008 outcome within the prediction interval?

(d) Using the estimation results in (b), what value of *GROWTH* would have led to a prediction that the incumbent party [Republicans] would have won 50.1% of the vote?

4.12 In Chapter 4.6 we considered the demand for edible chicken, which the U.S. Department of Agriculture calls "broilers." The data for this exercise are in the file *newbroiler.dat*.

(a) Using the 52 annual observations, 1950–2001, estimate the reciprocal model $Q = \alpha_1 + \alpha_2(1/P) + e$. Plot the fitted value of Q = per capita consumption of chicken, in pounds, versus P = real price of chicken. How well does the estimated relation fit the data?

(b) Using the estimated relation in part (a), compute the elasticity of per capita consumption with respect to real price when the real price is its median, $1.31, and quantity is taken to be the corresponding value on the fitted curve. [Hint: The derivative (slope) of reciprocal model $y = a + b(1/x)$ is $dy/dx = -b(1/x^2)$]. Compare this estimated elasticity to the estimate found in Chapter 4.6 where the log-log functional form was used.

(c) Estimate the poultry demand using the linear-log functional form $Q = \gamma_1 + \gamma_2 \ln(P) + e$. Plot the fitted values of Q = per capita consumption of chicken, in pounds, versus P = real price of chicken. How well does the estimated relation fit the data?

(d) Using the estimated relation in part (c), compute the elasticity of per capita consumption with respect to real price when the real price is its median, $1.31. Compare this estimated elasticity to the estimate from the log-log model and from the reciprocal model in part (b).

(e) Evaluate the suitability of the log-log, linear-log, and reciprocal models for fitting the poultry consumption data. Which of them would you select as best, and why?

4.13* The file *stockton2.dat* contains data on 880 houses sold in Stockton, CA, during mid-2005. Variable descriptions are in the file *stockton2.def*. These data were considered in Exercises 2.12 and 3.11.

(a) Estimate the log-linear model $\ln(PRICE) = \beta_1 + \beta_2 SQFT + e$. Interpret the estimated model parameters. Calculate the slope and elasticity at the sample means, if necessary.

(b) Estimate the log-log model $\ln(PRICE) = \beta_1 + \beta_2\ln(SQFT) + e$. Interpret the estimated parameters. Calculate the slope and elasticity at the sample means, if necessary.

(c) Compare the R^2-value from the linear model $PRICE = \beta_1 + \beta_2 SQFT + e$ to the "generalized" R^2 measure for the models in (b) and (c).

(d) Construct histograms of the least squares residuals from each of the models in (a), (b), and (c) and obtain the Jarque–Bera statistics. Based on your observations, do you consider the distributions of the residuals to be compatible with an assumption of normality?

(e) For each of the models (a)–(c), plot the least squares residuals against *SQFT*. Do you observe any patterns?

(f) For each model in (a)–(c), predict the value of a house with 2700 square feet.

(g) For each model in (a)–(c), construct a 95% prediction interval for the value of a house with 2700 square feet.

(h) Based on your work in this problem, discuss the choice of functional form. Which functional form would you use? Explain.

4.14 How much does education affect wage rates? This question will explore the issue further. The data file *cps4_small.dat* contains 1000 observations on hourly wage rates, education, and other variables from the 2008 Current Population Survey (CPS).

(a) Construct histograms of the *WAGE* variable and its logarithm, $\ln(WAGE)$. Which appears more normally distributed?

(b) Estimate the linear regression $WAGE = \beta_1 + \beta_2 EDUC + e$ and log-linear regression $\ln(WAGE) = \beta_1 + \beta_2 EDUC + e$. What is the estimated return to education in each model? That is, for an additional year of education, what percentage increase in wages can the average worker expect?

(c) Construct histograms of the residuals from the linear and log-linear models in (b), and the Jarque–Bera test for normality. Does one set of residuals appear more compatible with normality than the other?

(d) Compare the R^2 of the linear model to the "generalized" R^2 for the log-linear model. Which model fits the data better?

(e) Plot the least squares residuals from each model against *EDUC*. Do you observe any patterns?

(f) Using each model, predict the wage of a worker with 12 years of education. Compare these predictions to the actual average wage of all workers in the sample with 12 years of education.

(g) Based on the results in parts (a)–(f), which functional form would you use? Explain.

4.15 Does the return to education differ by race and gender? For this exercise, use the file *cps4.dat*. (This is a large file with 4,838 observations. If your software is a student version, you can use the smaller file *cps4_small.dat*.) In this exercise you will extract subsamples of observations consisting of (i) all males, (ii) all females, (iii) all whites, (iv) all asians, (v) white males, (vi) white females, (vii) asian males, and (viii) asian females.

(a) For each sample partition, obtain the summary statistics of *WAGE*.

(b) A variable's *coefficient of variation* is 100 times the ratio of its sample standard deviation to its sample mean. For a variable *y*, it is

$$CV = 100 \times \frac{s_y}{\bar{y}}$$

It is a measure of variation that takes into account the size of the variable. What is the coefficient of variation for *WAGE* within each sample partition?

(c) For each sample partition, estimate the log-linear model

$$\ln(WAGE) = \beta_1 + \beta_2 EDUC + e$$

What is the approximate percentage return to another year of education for each group?

(d) Does the model fit the data equally well for each sample partition?

(e) For each sample partition, test the null hypothesis that the rate of return to education is 10% against the alternative that it is not, using a two-tail test at the 5% level of significance.

4.16 In Chapter 4.3.5 and 4.4 we examined models for wheat yield in Western Australia over the period 1950–1997. The yield is "average wheat yield" in tonnes per hectare. These data can be found in the file *wa_wheat.dat*.

(a) How would you interpret the variable $RYIELD = 1/YIELD$?

(b) For each shire, plot the reciprocal of yield against time. What anomalies, if any, do you observe? Using your favorite Internet search engine, discover what conditions may have affected Australian wheat production during any unusual periods that you may find.

(c) Estimate the reciprocal of yield equation $RYIELD = \alpha_1 + \alpha_2 TIME + e$ for each shire. Interpret the estimated coefficient of *TIME* and test its significance using a one-tail test and a 5% level of significance.

(d) Plot the least squares residuals from part (c) against *TIME*. Locate the unusual observations using the least squares residuals.

(e) Discarding correct data is hardly ever a good idea, and we recommend that you not do it. Later in this book you will discover other methods for addressing such problems—such as adding addition explanatory variables—but for now let us experiment. For each shire, identify the most unusual observation (with the largest least squares residual). Re-estimate the reciprocal yield equations for each shire, omitting the most unusual data point. How sensitive are the regression results?

Appendix 4A Development of a Prediction Interval

The forecast error is $f = y_0 - \hat{y}_0 = (\beta_1 + \beta_2 x_0 + e_0) - (b_1 + b_2 x_0)$. To obtain its variance, let us first obtain the variance of $\hat{y}_0 = b_1 + b_2 x_0$. The variances and covariance of the least squares estimators are given in Section 2.4.4. Using them, we obtain

$$\text{var}(\hat{y}_0) = \text{var}(b_1 + b_2 x_0) = \text{var}(b_1) + x_0^2 \text{var}(b_2) + 2x_0 \text{cov}(b_1, b_2)$$

$$= \frac{\sigma^2 \sum x_i^2}{N \sum (x_i - \bar{x})^2} + x_0^2 \frac{\sigma^2}{\sum (x_i - \bar{x})^2} + 2x_0 \sigma^2 \frac{-\bar{x}}{\sum (x_i - \bar{x})^2}$$

Now we use a trick. Add the term $\sigma^2 N \bar{x}^2 / N \sum (x_i - \bar{x})^2$ after the first term (inside braces below) and subtract the same term at the end. Then combine the terms in brackets, as shown below:

$$\text{var}(\hat{y}_0) = \left[\frac{\sigma^2 \sum x_i^2}{N \sum (x_i - \bar{x})^2} - \left\{ \frac{\sigma^2 N \bar{x}^2}{N \sum (x_i - \bar{x})^2} \right\} \right]$$

$$+ \left[\frac{\sigma^2 x_0^2}{\sum (x_i - \bar{x})^2} + \frac{\sigma^2 (-2x_0 \bar{x})}{\sum (x_i - \bar{x})^2} + \left\{ \frac{\sigma^2 N \bar{x}^2}{N \sum (x_i - \bar{x})^2} \right\} \right]$$

$$= \sigma^2 \left[\frac{\sum x_i^2 - N \bar{x}^2}{N \sum (x_i - \bar{x})^2} + \frac{x_0^2 - 2x_0 \bar{x} + \bar{x}^2}{\sum (x_i - \bar{x})^2} \right]$$

$$= \sigma^2 \left[\frac{\sum (x_i - \bar{x})^2}{N \sum (x_i - \bar{x})^2} + \frac{(x_0 - \bar{x})^2}{\sum (x_i - \bar{x})^2} \right]$$

$$= \sigma^2 \left[\frac{1}{N} + \frac{(x_0 - \bar{x})^2}{\sum (x_i - \bar{x})^2} \right]$$

Taking into account that x_0 and the unknown parameters β_1 and β_2 are not random, you should be able to show that $\text{var}(f) = \text{var}(\hat{y}_0) + \text{var}(e_0) = \text{var}(\hat{y}_0) + \sigma^2$. A little factoring gives the result in (4.4). We can construct a standard normal random variable as

$$\frac{f}{\sqrt{\text{var}(f)}} \sim N(0, 1)$$

If the forecast error variance in (4.4) is estimated by replacing σ^2 by its estimator $\hat{\sigma}^2$,

$$\widehat{\text{var}(f)} = \hat{\sigma}^2 \left[1 + \frac{1}{N} + \frac{(x_0 - \bar{x})^2}{\Sigma(x_i - \bar{x})^2} \right]$$

then

$$\frac{f}{\sqrt{\widehat{\text{var}(f)}}} = \frac{y_0 - \hat{y}_0}{\text{se}(f)} \sim t_{(N-2)} \tag{4A.1}$$

where the square root of the estimated variance is the standard error of the forecast given in (4.5).

Using these results, we can construct an interval prediction procedure for y_0 just as we constructed confidence intervals for the parameters β_k. If t_c is a critical value from the $t_{(N-2)}$-distribution such that $P(t \geq t_c) = \alpha/2$, then

$$P(-t_c \leq t \leq t_c) = 1 - \alpha \tag{4A.2}$$

Substitute the t-random variable from (4A.1) into (4A.2) to obtain

$$P \left[-t_c \leq \frac{y_0 - \hat{y}_0}{\text{se}(f)} \leq t_c \right] = 1 - \alpha$$

Simplify this expression to obtain

$$P[\hat{y}_0 - t_c \text{se}(f) \leq y_0 \leq \hat{y}_0 + t_c \text{se}(f)] = 1 - \alpha$$

A $100(1-\alpha)\%$ confidence interval, or prediction interval, for y_0 is given by (4.6).

Appendix 4B The Sum of Squares Decomposition

To obtain the sum of squares decomposition in (4.11), we square both sides of (4.10)

$$(y_i - \bar{y})^2 = [(\hat{y}_i - \bar{y}) + \hat{e}_i]^2 = (\hat{y}_i - \bar{y})^2 + \hat{e}_i^2 + 2(\hat{y}_i - \bar{y})\hat{e}_i$$

Then sum

$$\Sigma(y_i - \bar{y})^2 = \Sigma(\hat{y}_i - \bar{y})^2 + \Sigma\hat{e}_i^2 + 2\Sigma(\hat{y}_i - \bar{y})\hat{e}_i$$

Expanding the last term, we obtain

$$\Sigma(\hat{y}_i - \bar{y})\hat{e}_i = \Sigma\hat{y}_i\hat{e}_i - \bar{y}\Sigma\hat{e}_i = \Sigma(b_1 + b_2 x_i)\hat{e}_i - \bar{y}\Sigma\hat{e}_i$$
$$= b_1\Sigma\hat{e}_i + b_2\Sigma x_i\hat{e}_i - \bar{y}\Sigma\hat{e}_i$$

Consider first the term $\Sigma\hat{e}_i$

$$\Sigma\hat{e}_i = \Sigma(y_i - b_1 - b_2 x_i) = \Sigma y_i - Nb_1 - b_2\Sigma x_i = 0$$

This last expression is zero because of the first normal equation, (2A.3). The first normal equation is valid *only if the model contains an intercept*. The sum of the least squares residuals is always zero *if* the model contains an intercept. It follows, then, that the *sample mean* of the least squares residuals is also zero (since it is the sum of the residuals divided by the sample size) if the model contains an intercept. That is, $\bar{\hat{e}} = \sum \hat{e}_i / N = 0$.

The next term $\sum x_i \hat{e}_i = 0$, because

$$\sum x_i \hat{e}_i = \sum x_i (y_i - b_1 - b_2 x_i) = \sum x_i y_i - b_1 \sum x_i - b_2 \sum x_i^2 = 0$$

This result follows from the second normal equation, (2A.4). This result always holds for the least squares estimator and does not depend on the model having an intercept. See Appendix 2A for discussion of the normal equations. Substituting $\sum \hat{e}_i = 0$ and $\sum x_i \hat{e}_i = 0$ back into the original equation, we obtain $\sum (\hat{y}_i - \bar{y}) \hat{e}_i = 0$.

Thus, if the model contains an intercept, it is guaranteed that $SST = SSR + SSE$. If, however, the model does not contain an intercept, then $\sum \hat{e}_i \neq 0$ and $SST \neq SSR + SSE$.

Appendix 4C The Log-Normal Distribution

Suppose that the variable y has a normal distribution, with mean μ and variance σ^2. By now you are familiar with this bell-shaped distribution. If we consider $w = e^y$, then $y = \ln(w) \sim N(\mu, \sigma^2)$ and w is said to have a **log-normal** distribution. The question then is, what are the mean and variance of w? Recall that the "expected value of a sum is the sum of the expected values." But unfortunately, the exponential function is nonlinear, and the expected value of nonlinear function of y is *not* just the same function of $E(y)$. That is, if $g(y)$ is some function of y, then in general $E[g(y)] \neq g[E(y)]$. So the expectation $E(w) = E(e^y) \neq e^{E(y)}$. Happily, the expected value and variance of w have been worked out, and are

$$E(w) = e^{\mu + \sigma^2/2}$$

and

$$\text{var}(w) = e^{2\mu + \sigma^2} \left(e^{\sigma^2} - 1 \right)$$

These results relate to the log-linear regression model in several ways. First, given the log-linear model $\ln(y) = \beta_1 + \beta_2 x + e$, if we assume that $e \sim N(0, \sigma^2)$, then

$$E(y_i) = E\left(e^{\beta_1 + \beta_2 x_i + e_i}\right) = E\left(e^{\beta_1 + \beta_2 x_i} e^{e_i}\right) = e^{\beta_1 + \beta_2 x_i} E(e^{e_i}) = e^{\beta_1 + \beta_2 x_i} e^{\sigma^2/2} = e^{\beta_1 + \beta_2 x_i + \sigma^2/2}$$

Consequently, if we want to predict $E(y)$, we should use

$$\widehat{E(y_i)} = e^{b_1 + b_2 x_i + \hat{\sigma}^2/2}$$

where b_1, b_2, and $\hat{\sigma}^2$ are from the log-linear regression.

The second implication comes from the growth and wage equations discussed in Section 4.4. For example, in the wage equation we estimated $\beta_2 = \ln(1 + r)$. Solving for r, we obtain $r = e^{\beta_2} - 1$. If assumption SR6 holds, then the least squares estimator is normally distributed $b_2 \sim N\big(\beta_2, \text{var}(b_2) = \sigma^2/\sum(x_i - \bar{x})^2\big)$. Then

$$E[e^{b_2}] = e^{\beta_2 + \text{var}(b_2)/2}$$

Therefore, an estimator of the rate of return r is

$$\hat{r} = e^{b_2 - \widehat{\text{var}(b_2)}/2} - 1$$

where $\widehat{\text{var}(b_2)} = \hat{\sigma}^2/\sum(x_i - \bar{x})^2$.

Chapter 5

The Multiple Regression Model

Learning Objectives

Based on the material in this chapter, you should be able to

1. Recognize a multiple regression model and be able to interpret the coefficients in that model.

2. Understand and explain the meanings of the assumptions for the multiple regression model.

3. Use your computer to find least squares estimates of the coefficients in a multiple regression model, and interpret those estimates.

4. Explain the meaning of the Gauss–Markov theorem.

5. Use your computer to obtain variance and covariance estimates, and standard errors, for the estimated coefficients in a multiple regression model.

6. Explain the circumstances under which coefficient variances (and standard errors) are likely to be relatively high, and those under which they are likely to be relatively low.

7. Find interval estimates for single coefficients and linear combinations of coefficients, and interpret the interval estimates.

8. Test hypotheses about single coefficients and about linear combinations of coefficients in a multiple regression model. In particular,
   (a) What is the difference between a one-tail and a two-tail test?
   (b) How do you compute the *p*-value for a one-tail test, and for a two-tail test?
   (c) What is meant by "testing the significance of a coefficient"?
   (d) What is the meaning of the *t*-values and *p*-values that appear in your computer output?
   (e) How do you compute the standard error of a linear combination of coefficient estimates?

9. Use your computer to compute the standard error of a nonlinear function of estimators. Use that standard error to find interval estimates and to test hypotheses about nonlinear functions of coefficients.

10. Estimate and interpret multiple regression models with polynomial and interaction variables.

11. Find point and interval estimates and test hypotheses for marginal effects in polynomial regressions and models with interaction variables.

12. Compute and explain the meaning of R^2 in a multiple regression model.

Keywords

BLU estimator	interval estimate	p-value
covariance matrix of	least squares estimates	polynomial
least squares estimator	least squares estimation	regression coefficients
critical value	least squares estimators	standard errors
delta method	linear combinations	sum of squared errors
error variance estimate	marginal effect	sum of squares of regression
error variance estimator	multiple regression model	testing significance
goodness-of-fit	nonlinear functions	total sum of squares
interaction variable	one-tail test	two-tail test

The model in Chapters 2–4 is called a simple regression model because the dependent variable *y* is related to only *one* explanatory variable *x*. Although this model is useful for a range of situations, in most economic models there are two or more explanatory variables that influence the dependent variable *y*. For example, in a demand equation the quantity demanded of a commodity depends on the price of that commodity, the prices of substitute and complementary goods, and income. Output in a production function will be a function of more than one input. Aggregate money demand will be a function of aggregate income and the interest rate. Investment will depend on the interest rate and on changes in income.

When we turn an economic model with more than one explanatory variable into its corresponding econometric model, we refer to it as a **multiple regression model**. Most of the results we developed for the simple regression model in Chapters 2–4 can be extended naturally to this general case. There are slight changes in the interpretation of the β parameters, the degrees of freedom for the *t*-distribution will change, and we will need to modify the assumption concerning the characteristics of the explanatory (*x*) variables. These and other consequences of extending the simple regression model to a multiple regression model are described in this chapter.

As an example for introducing and analyzing the multiple regression model, we begin with a model used to explain sales revenue for a fast-food hamburger chain with outlets in small U.S. cities.

5.1 Introduction

5.1.1 THE ECONOMIC MODEL

We will set up an economic model for a hamburger chain that we call Big Andy's Burger Barn.[1] Important decisions made by the management of Big Andy's include its pricing policy for different products and how much to spend on advertising. To assess the effect of different price structures and different levels of advertising expenditure, Big Andy's Burger Barn sets different prices, and spends varying amounts on advertising, in different cities.

---

[1] The data we use reflect a real fast-food franchise whose identity we disguise under the name Big Andy's.

Of particular interest to management is how sales revenue changes as the level of advertising expenditure changes. Does an increase in advertising expenditure lead to an increase in sales? If so, is the increase in sales sufficient to justify the increased advertising expenditure? Management is also interested in pricing strategy. Will reducing prices lead to an increase or decrease in sales revenue? If a reduction in price leads only to a small increase in the quantity sold, sales revenue will fall (demand is price-inelastic); a price reduction that leads to a large increase in quantity sold will produce an increase in revenue (demand is price-elastic). This economic information is essential for effective management.

The first step is to set up an economic model in which sales revenue depends on one or more explanatory variables. We initially hypothesize that sales revenue is linearly related to price and advertising expenditure. The economic model is

$$SALES = \beta_1 + \beta_2 PRICE + \beta_3 ADVERT \tag{5.1}$$

where $SALES$ represents monthly sales revenue in a given city, $PRICE$ represents price in that city, and $ADVERT$ is monthly advertising expenditure in that city. Both $SALES$ and $ADVERT$ are measured in terms of thousands of dollars. Because sales in bigger cities will tend to be greater than sales in smaller cities, we focus on smaller cities with comparable populations.

Since a hamburger outlet sells a number of products—burgers, fries, and shakes—and each product has its own price, it is not immediately clear what price should be used in (5.1). What we need is some kind of average price for all products and information on how this average price changes from city to city. For this purpose management has constructed a single price index $PRICE$, measured in dollars and cents, that describes overall prices in each city.

The remaining symbols in (5.1) are the unknown parameters β_1, β_2, and β_3 that describe the dependence of sales ($SALES$) on price ($PRICE$) and advertising ($ADVERT$). Mathematically, the intercept parameter β_1 is the value of the dependent variable when each of the independent, explanatory variables takes the value zero. However, in many cases this parameter has no clear economic interpretation. In this particular case, it is not realistic to have a situation in which $PRICE = ADVERT = 0$. Except in very special circumstances, we always include an intercept in the model, even if it has no direct economic interpretation. Omitting it can lead to a model that fits the data poorly and that does not predict well.

The other parameters in the model measure the change in the value of the dependent variable given a unit change in an explanatory variable, *all other variables held constant.* For example, in (5.1),

> β_2 = the change in monthly $SALES$ ($1,000) when the price index $PRICE$ is increased by one unit ($1) and advertising expenditure $ADVERT$ is held constant
>
> $$= \frac{\Delta SALES}{\Delta PRICE_{(ADVERT \text{ held constant})}} = \frac{\partial SALES}{\partial PRICE}$$

The symbol "∂" stands for "partial differentiation." Those of you familiar with calculus may have seen this operation. In the context above, the partial derivative of $SALES$ with respect to $PRICE$ is the rate of change of $SALES$ as $PRICE$ changes, with other factors, in this case $ADVERT$, held constant. Further details can be found in Section A.3.3 of Appendix A. We will occasionally use partial derivatives, but not to an extent that will disadvantage you if you have not had a course in calculus. Rules for differentiation are provided in Appendix A.3.1.

The sign of β_2 could be positive or negative. If an increase in price leads to an increase in sales revenue, then $\beta_2 > 0$, and the demand for the chain's products is price-inelastic. Conversely, a price-elastic demand exists if an increase in price leads to a decline in revenue, in which case $\beta_2 < 0$. Thus, knowledge of the *sign* of β_2 provides information on the price-elasticity of demand. The *magnitude* of β_2 measures the amount of change in revenue for a given price change.

The parameter β_3 describes the response of sales revenue to a change in the level of advertising expenditure. That is,

> β_3 = the change in monthly *SALES* ($1,000) when advertising expenditure *ADVERT* is increased by one unit ($1,000) and the price index *PRICE* is held constant
>
> $$= \frac{\Delta SALES}{\Delta ADVERT}_{(PRICE \text{ held constant})} = \frac{\partial SALES}{\partial ADVERT}$$

We expect the sign of β_3 to be positive. That is, we expect that an increase in advertising expenditure, unless the advertising is offensive, will lead to an increase in sales revenue. Whether or not the increase in revenue is sufficient to justify the added advertising expenditure, as well as the added cost of producing more hamburgers, is another question. With $\beta_3 < 1$, an increase of $1,000 in advertising expenditure will yield an increase in revenue that is less than $1,000. For $\beta_3 > 1$, it will be greater. Thus, in terms of the chain's advertising policy, knowledge of β_3 is very important.

The next step along the road to learning about β_1, β_2, and β_3 is to convert the economic model into an econometric model.

5.1.2 THE ECONOMETRIC MODEL

The economic model (5.1) describes the expected or average behavior of many individual franchises that make up the complete chain run by Big Andy's Burger Barn. Thus, we should write it as $E(SALES) = \beta_1 + \beta_2 PRICE + \beta_3 ADVERT$, where $E(SALES)$ is the "expected value" of sales revenue. Data for sales revenue, price, and advertising for different cities will not follow an exact linear relationship. Equation (5.1) describes not a line as in Chapters 2–4, but a *plane*. As illustrated in Figure 5.1, the plane intersects the vertical axis at β_1. The parameters β_2 and β_3 measure the slope of the plane in the directions of the "price axis" and the "advertising axis," respectively. Representative observations for sales revenue, price, and advertising for some cities are displayed in Table 5.1. The complete set of observations can be found in the file *andy.dat* and is represented by the dots in Figure 5.1. These data do not fall exactly on a plane, but instead resemble a "cloud."

To allow for a difference between observable sales revenue and the expected value of sales revenue, we add a **random error term**, $e = SALES - E(SALES)$. This random error represents all factors, other than price and advertising revenue, which cause sales revenue to differ from its expected value. These factors might include the weather, the behavior of competitors, a new Surgeon General's report on the deadly effects of fat intake, and so on, as well as differences in burger-buying behavior across cities. Including the error term gives the model

$$SALES = E(SALES) + e = \beta_1 + \beta_2 PRICE + \beta_3 ADVERT + e \qquad (5.2)$$

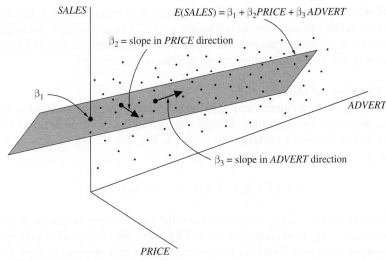

$SALES$

$E(SALES) = \beta_1 + \beta_2 PRICE + \beta_3 ADVERT$

$\beta_2 = $ slope in $PRICE$ direction

β_1

$ADVERT$

$\beta_3 = $ slope in $ADVERT$ direction

$PRICE$

FIGURE 5.1 The multiple regression plane.

The economic model in (5.1) describes the average, systematic relationship between the variables *SALES*, *PRICE*, and *ADVERT*. The expected value $E(SALES)$ is the nonrandom, systematic component, to which we add the random error e to determine *SALES*. Thus, *SALES* is a random variable. We do not know what the value of sales revenue will be until we observe it.

Table 5.1 **Observations on Monthly Sales, Price, and Advertising in Big Andy's Burger Barn**

City	*SALES* $1,000 units	*PRICE* $1 units	*ADVERT* $1,000 units
1	73.2	5.69	1.3
2	71.8	6.49	2.9
3	62.4	5.63	0.8
4	67.4	6.22	0.7
5	89.3	5.02	1.5
.	.	.	.
.	.	.	.
.	.	.	.
73	75.4	5.71	0.7
74	81.3	5.45	2.0
75	75.0	6.05	2.2
Summary statistics			
Sample mean	77.37	5.69	1.84
Median	76.50	5.69	1.80
Maximum	91.20	6.49	3.10
Minimum	62.40	4.83	0.50
Std. Dev.	6.49	0.52	0.83

The introduction of the error term and assumptions about its probability distribution turn the economic model into the **econometric model** in (5.2). The econometric model provides a more realistic description of the relationship between the variables as well as a framework for developing and assessing estimators of the unknown parameters.

5.1.2a The General Model

It is useful to digress for a moment and summarize how the concepts developed so far relate to the general case. In a general multiple regression model, a dependent variable y is related to a number of **explanatory variables** $x_2, x_3, \ldots, x_K$ through a linear equation that can be written as

$$y = \beta_1 + \beta_2 x_2 + \beta_3 x_3 + \cdots + \beta_K x_K + e \tag{5.3}$$

The coefficients $\beta_2, \beta_3, \ldots, \beta_K$ are unknown coefficients corresponding to the explanatory variables $x_2, x_3, \ldots, x_K$. A single parameter, call it β_k, measures the effect of a change in the variable x_k upon the expected value of y, all other variables held constant. In terms of partial derivatives,

$$\beta_k = \frac{\Delta E(y)}{\Delta x_k} \bigg|_{\text{other } xs \text{ held constant}} = \frac{\partial E(y)}{\partial x_k}$$

The parameter β_1 is the intercept term. We can think of it as being attached to a variable x_1 that is always equal to 1. That is, $x_1 = 1$. We use K to denote the number of unknown coefficients in (5.3).

The equation for sales revenue can be viewed as a special case of (5.3) where $K = 3$, $y = SALES$, $x_1 = 1$, $x_2 = PRICE$ and $x_3 = ADVERT$. Thus we rewrite (5.2) as

$$y = \beta_1 + \beta_2 x_2 + \beta_3 x_3 + e \tag{5.4}$$

In this chapter we introduce point and interval estimation in terms of this model with $K = 3$. The results hold generally for models with more explanatory variables ($K > 3$).

5.1.2b The Assumptions of the Model

To make the econometric model in (5.4) complete, assumptions about the probability distribution of the random errors e need to be made. The assumptions that we introduce for e are similar to those introduced for the simple regression model in Chapter 2. They are

1. $E(e) = 0$. Each random error has a probability distribution with zero mean. Some errors will be positive, some will be negative; over a large number of observations, they will average out to zero.

2. $\text{var}(e) = \sigma^2$. Each random error has a probability distribution with variance σ^2. The variance σ^2 is an unknown parameter and it measures the uncertainty in the statistical model. It is the same for each observation, so that for no observations will the model uncertainty be more, or less, nor is it directly related to any economic variable. Errors with this property are said to be **homoskedastic**.

3. $\text{cov}(e_i, e_j) = 0$. The covariance between the two random errors corresponding to any two different observations is zero. The size of an error for one observation has no bearing on the likely size of an error for another observation. Thus, any pair of errors is uncorrelated.

4. We will sometimes further assume that the random errors e have normal probability distributions. That is, $e \sim N(0, \sigma^2)$.

Because each observation on the dependent variable y depends on the random error term e, each y is also a random variable. The statistical properties of y follow from those of e. These properties are

1. $E(y) = \beta_1 + \beta_2 x_2 + \beta_3 x_3$. The expected (average) value of y depends on the values of the explanatory variables and the unknown parameters. It is equivalent to $E(e) = 0$. This assumption says that the average value of y changes for each observation and is given by the **regression function** $E(y) = \beta_1 + \beta_2 x_2 + \beta_3 x_3$.

2. $\text{var}(y) = \text{var}(e) = \sigma^2$. The variance of the probability distribution of y does not change with each observation. Some observations on y are not more likely to be further from the regression function than others.

3. $\text{cov}(y_i, y_j) = \text{cov}(e_i, e_j) = 0$. Any two observations on the dependent variable are uncorrelated. For example, if one observation is above $E(y)$, a subsequent observation is not more or less likely to be above $E(y)$.

4. We sometimes will assume that the values of y are normally distributed about their mean. That is, $y \sim N[(\beta_1 + \beta_2 x_2 + \beta_3 x_3), \sigma^2]$, which is equivalent to assuming that $e \sim N(0, \sigma^2)$.

In addition to the above assumptions about the error term (and hence about the dependent variable), we make two assumptions about the explanatory variables. The first is that the explanatory variables are not random variables. Thus we are assuming that the values of the explanatory variables are known to us prior to our observing the values of the dependent variable. This assumption is realistic for our hamburger chain, where a decision about prices and advertising is made for each city and values for these variables are set accordingly. For cases in which this assumption is untenable, our analysis will be conditional upon the values of the explanatory variables in our sample, or further assumptions must be made. This issue is taken up further in Chapters 9 and 10.

The second assumption is that any one of the explanatory variables is not an exact linear function of the others. This assumption is equivalent to assuming that no variable is redundant. As we will see, if this assumption is violated—a condition called **exact collinearity**—the least squares procedure fails.

To summarize, we construct a list of the assumptions for the general multiple regression model in (5.3)—much as we have done in the earlier chapters—to which we can refer as needed. We use the subscript i to denote the ith value of variables to be observed in a sample of size N.

ASSUMPTIONS OF THE MULTIPLE REGRESSION MODEL

MR1. $y_i = \beta_1 + \beta_2 x_{i2} + \cdots + \beta_K x_{iK} + e_i, \; i = 1, \ldots, N$

MR2. $E(y_i) = \beta_1 + \beta_2 x_{i2} + \cdots + \beta_K x_{iK} \Leftrightarrow E(e_i) = 0$

MR3. $\text{var}(y_i) = \text{var}(e_i) = \sigma^2$

MR4. $\text{cov}(y_i, y_j) = \text{cov}(e_i, e_j) = 0 \quad (i \neq j)$

MR5. The values of each x_{ik} are not random and are not exact linear functions of the other explanatory variables

MR6. $y_i \sim N[(\beta_1 + \beta_2 x_{i2} + \cdots + \beta_K x_{iK}), \sigma^2] \Leftrightarrow e_i \sim N(0, \sigma^2)$

5.2 **Estimating the Parameters of the Multiple Regression Model**

In this section we consider the problem of using the least squares principle to estimate the unknown parameters of the multiple regression model. We will discuss estimation in the context of the model in (5.4), which we repeat here for convenience, with i denoting the ith observation.

$$y_i = \beta_1 + \beta_2 x_{i2} + \beta_3 x_{i3} + e_i \tag{5.4}$$

This model is simpler than the full model, yet all the results we present carry over to the general case with only minor modifications.

5.2.1 LEAST SQUARES ESTIMATION PROCEDURE

To find an estimator for estimating the unknown parameters we follow the least squares procedure that was first introduced in Chapter 2 for the simple regression model. With the least squares principle we find those values of $(\beta_1, \beta_2, \beta_3)$ that minimize the sum of squared differences between the observed values of y_i and their expected values $E(y_i) = \beta_1 + x_{i2}\beta_2 + x_{i3}\beta_3$. Mathematically we minimize the sum of squares function $S(\beta_1, \beta_2, \beta_3)$, which is a function of the unknown parameters, given the data

$$
\begin{aligned}
S(\beta_1, \beta_2, \beta_3) &= \sum_{i=1}^{N} \Big(y_i - E(y_i) \Big)^2 \\
&= \sum_{i=1}^{N} \Big(y_i - \beta_1 - \beta_2 x_{i2} - \beta_3 x_{i3} \Big)^2
\end{aligned}
\tag{5.5}
$$

Given the sample observations y_i, minimizing the sum of squares function is a straightforward exercise in calculus. Details of this exercise are given in Appendix 5A at the end of this chapter. The solutions give us formulas for the least squares estimators for the β coefficients in a multiple regression model with two explanatory variables. They are extensions of those given in (2.7) and (2.8) for the simple regression model with one explanatory variable. There are three reasons for relegating these formulas to Appendix 5A instead of inflicting them on you here. First, they are complicated formulas that we do not expect you to memorize. Second, we never use these formulas explicitly; computer software uses the formulas to calculate least squares estimates. Third, we frequently have models with more than two explanatory variables, in which case the formulas become even more complicated. If you proceed with more advanced study in econometrics, you will discover that there is one relatively simple matrix algebra expression for the least squares estimator that can be used for all models, irrespective of the number of explanatory variables.

Although we always get the computer to do the work for us, it is important to understand the least squares principle and the difference between least squares estimators and least squares estimates. Looked at as a general way to use sample data, formulas for b_1, b_2, and b_3, obtained by minimizing (5.5), are estimation procedures, which are called the **least squares estimators** of the unknown parameters. In general, since their values are not known until the data are observed and the estimates calculated, the least squares estimators are random variables. Computer software applies the formulas to a specific sample of data producing **least squares estimates**, which are numeric values. To avoid too much notation, we use b_1, b_2, and b_3 to denote both the estimators and the estimates.

Table 5.2   **Least Squares Estimates for Sales Equation for Big Andy's Burger Barn**

Variable	Coefficient	Std. Error	t-Statistic	Prob.
C	118.9136	6.3516	18.7217	0.0000
PRICE	−7.9079	1.0960	−7.2152	0.0000
ADVERT	1.8626	0.6832	2.7263	0.0080

$R^2 = 0.4483$ $SSE = 1718.943$ $\hat{\sigma} = 4.8861$ $s_y = 6.48854.$

5.2.2   LEAST SQUARES ESTIMATES USING HAMBURGER CHAIN DATA

Table 5.2 contains the least squares results for the sales equation for Big Andy's Burger Barn. The least squares estimates are

$$b_1 = 118.91 \quad b_2 = -7.908 \quad b_3 = 1.863$$

Following Chapter 4.2.4, these estimates along with their standard errors and the equation's R^2 are typically reported in equation format as

$$\widehat{SALES} = 118.91 - 7.908\,PRICE + 1.863\,ADVERT \qquad R^2 = 0.448$$
$$\text{(se)} \qquad (6.35) \ (1.096) \qquad\qquad (0.683) \tag{5.6}$$

From the information in this equation one can readily construct interval estimates or test hypotheses for each of the β_k in a manner similar to that described in Chapter 3, but with a change in the number of degrees of freedom for the t-distribution. Like before, the t-values and p-values in Table 5.2 relate to testing $H_0 : \beta_k = 0$ against the alternative $H : \beta_k \neq 0$ for $k = 1, 2, 3$.

We proceed by first interpreting the estimates in (5.6). Then, to explain the degrees of freedom change that arises from having more than one explanatory variable, and to reinforce earlier material, we go over the sampling properties of the least squares estimator, followed by interval estimation and hypothesis testing.

What can we say about the coefficient estimates in (5.6)?

1. The negative coefficient on *PRICE* suggests that demand is price elastic; we estimate that, with advertising held constant, an increase in price of $1 will lead to a fall in monthly revenue of $7,908. Or, expressed differently, a reduction in price of $1 will lead to an increase in revenue of $7,908. If such is the case, a strategy of price reduction through the offering of specials would be successful in increasing sales revenue. We do need to consider carefully the magnitude of the price change, however. A $1 change in price is a relatively large change. The sample mean of price is 5.69 and its standard deviation is 0.52. A 10-cent change is more realistic, in which case we estimate the revenue change to be $791.

2. The coefficient on advertising is positive; we estimate that with price held constant, an increase in advertising expenditure of $1,000 will lead to an increase in sales revenue of $1,863. We can use this information, along with the costs of producing the additional hamburgers, to determine whether an increase in advertising expenditures will increase profit.

3. The estimated intercept implies that if both price and advertising expenditure were zero the sales revenue would be \$118,914. Clearly, this outcome is not possible; a zero price implies zero sales revenue. In this model, as in many others, it is important to recognize that the model is an approximation to reality in the region for which we have data. Including an intercept improves this approximation even when it is not directly interpretable.

In addition to providing information about how sales change when price or advertising change, the estimated equation can be used for prediction. Suppose Big Andy is interested in predicting sales revenue for a price of \$5.50 and an advertising expenditure of \$1,200. Including extra decimal places to get an accurate hand calculation, this prediction is

$$
\begin{aligned}
SALES &= 118.91 - 7.908 PRICE + 1.863 ADVERT \\
&= 118.914 - 7.9079 \times 5.5 + 1.8626 \times 1.2 \\
&= 77.656
\end{aligned}
$$

The predicted value of sales revenue for $PRICE = 5.5$ and $ADVERT = 1.2$ is \$77,656.

> **REMARK:** A word of caution is in order about interpreting regression results: The negative sign attached to price implies that reducing the price will increase sales revenue. If taken literally, why should we not keep reducing the price to zero? Obviously that would not keep increasing total revenue. This makes the following important point: Estimated regression models describe the relationship between the economic variables for values *similar* to those found in the sample data. Extrapolating the results to extreme values is generally not a good idea. Predicting the value of the dependent variable for values of the explanatory variables far from the sample values invites disaster. Refer to Figure 4.2 and the surrounding discussion.

5.2.3 ESTIMATION OF THE ERROR VARIANCE σ^2

There is one remaining parameter to estimate—the variance of the error term. For this parameter we follow the same steps that were outlined in Section 2.7. We know that

$$
\sigma^2 = \text{var}(e_i) = E(e_i^2)
$$

Thus, we can think of σ^2 as the expectation or population mean of the squared errors e_i^2. A natural estimator of this population mean is the sample mean $\hat{\sigma}^2 = \Sigma e_i^2/N$. However, the squared errors e_i^2 are unobservable, so we develop an estimator for σ^2 that is based on the squares of the least squares residuals. For the model in (5.4), these residuals are

$$
\hat{e}_i = y_i - \hat{y}_i = y_i - (b_1 + b_2 x_{i2} + b_3 x_{i3})
$$

An estimator for σ^2 that uses the information from $\hat{e}_i^2$ and has good statistical properties is

$$
\hat{\sigma}^2 = \frac{\Sigma_{i=1}^N \hat{e}_i^2}{N - K} \tag{5.7}
$$

where K is the number of β parameters being estimated in the multiple regression model. We can think of $\hat{\sigma}^2$ as an average of $\hat{e}_i^2$ with the denominator in the averaging process being

$N - K$ instead of N. It can be shown that replacing e_i^2 by $\hat{e}_i^2$ requires the use of $N - K$ instead of N for $\hat{\sigma}^2$ to be unbiased. Note that in Chapter 2, (2.19), where there was one explanatory variable and two coefficients, we had $K = 2$.

To appreciate further why $\hat{e}_i$ provide information about σ^2, recall that σ^2 measures the variation in e_i or, equivalently, the variation in y_i around the mean function $\beta_1 + \beta_2 x_{i2} + \beta_3 x_{i3}$. Since $\hat{e}_i$ are estimates of e_i, big values of $\hat{e}_i$ suggest σ^2 is large while small $\hat{e}_i$ suggest σ^2 is small. When we refer to "big" values of $\hat{e}_i$, we mean big positive ones or big negative ones. Using the squares of the residuals $\hat{e}_i^2$ means that positive values do not cancel with negative ones; thus, $\hat{e}_i^2$ provide information about the parameter σ^2.

In the hamburger chain example we have $K = 3$. The estimate for our sample of data in Table 5.1 is

$$\hat{\sigma}^2 = \frac{\sum_{i=1}^{75} \hat{e}_i^2}{N - K} = \frac{1718.943}{75 - 3} = 23.874$$

Go back and have a look at Table 5.2. There are two quantities in this table that relate to the above calculation. The first is the sum of squared errors

$$SSE = \sum_{i=1}^{N} \hat{e}_i^2 = 1718.943$$

The second is the square root of $\hat{\sigma}^2$, given by

$$\hat{\sigma} = \sqrt{23.874} = 4.8861$$

Both these quantities typically appear in the output from your computer software. Different software refer to it in different ways. Sometimes $\hat{\sigma}$ is referred to as the **standard error of the regression**. Sometimes it is called the **root mse** (short for mean squared error).

A major reason for estimating the error variance is to enable us to get an estimate of the unknown variances and covariances for the least squares estimators. We now consider those variances and covariances in the context of the overall properties of the least squares estimator.

5.3 **Sampling Properties of the Least Squares Estimator**

In a general context, the least squares estimators (b_1, b_2, b_3) are random variables; they take on different values in different samples, and their values are unknown until a sample is collected and their values computed. The sampling properties of a least squares estimator tell us how the estimates vary from sample to sample. They provide a basis for assessing the reliability of the estimates. In Chapter 2 we found that the least squares estimator was unbiased, and that there is no other linear unbiased estimator that has a smaller variance, if the model assumptions are correct. This result remains true for the *general* multiple regression model that we are considering in this chapter.

> **THE GAUSS–MARKOV THEOREM:** For the multiple regression model, if assumptions MR1–MR5 listed at the beginning of the chapter hold, then the least squares estimators are the best linear unbiased estimators (BLUE) of the parameters.

If we are able to assume that the errors are *normally distributed*, then y will also be a normally distributed random variable. The least squares estimators will also have normal probability distributions, since they are linear functions of y. If the errors are not normally distributed, then the least squares estimators are approximately normally distributed in large samples. What constitutes "large" is tricky. It depends on a number of factors specific to each application. Frequently, $N - K = 50$ will be large enough. See Appendices 5B.2 and 5B.3 for further details and a simulation experiment. Having least squares estimators with normal or approximately normal distributions is important for the construction of interval estimates and the testing of hypotheses about the parameters of the regression model.

5.3.1 THE VARIANCES AND COVARIANCES OF THE LEAST SQUARES ESTIMATORS

The variances and covariances of the least squares estimators give us information about the reliability of the estimators $b_1, b_2,$ and b_3. Since the least squares estimators are unbiased, the smaller their variances, the higher the probability that they will produce estimates "near" the true parameter values. For $K = 3$ we can express the variances and covariances in an algebraic form that provides useful insights into the behavior of the least squares estimator. For example, we can show that

$$\text{var}(b_2) = \frac{\sigma^2}{(1 - r_{23}^2)\sum_{i=1}^{N}(x_{i2} - \bar{x}_2)^2} \tag{5.8}$$

where r_{23} is the sample correlation coefficient between the values of x_2 and x_3; see Section 4.2.1. Its formula is given by

$$r_{23} = \frac{\sum(x_{i2} - \bar{x}_2)(x_{i3} - \bar{x}_3)}{\sqrt{\sum(x_{i2} - \bar{x}_2)^2\sum(x_{i3} - \bar{x}_3)^2}} \tag{5.9}$$

For the other variances and covariances, there are formulas of a similar nature. It is important to understand the factors affecting the variance of b_2:

1. Larger error variances σ^2 lead to larger variances of the least squares estimators. This is to be expected, since σ^2 measures the overall uncertainty in the model specification. If σ^2 is large, then data values may be widely spread about the regression function $E(y_i) = \beta_1 + \beta_2 x_{i2} + \beta_3 x_{i3}$ and there is less information in the data about the parameter values. If σ^2 is small, then data values are compactly spread about the regression function $E(y_i) = \beta_1 + \beta_2 x_{i2} + \beta_3 x_{i3}$, and there is more information about what the parameter values might be.

2. Larger sample sizes N imply smaller variances of the least squares estimators. A larger value of N means a larger value of the summation $\sum(x_{i2} - \bar{x}_2)^2$. Since this term appears in the denominator of (5.8), when it is large, $\text{var}(b_2)$ is small. This outcome is also an intuitive one; more observations yield more precise parameter estimation.

3. More variation in an explanatory variable around its mean, measured in this case by $\sum(x_{i2} - \bar{x}_2)^2$, leads to a smaller variance of the least squares estimator. To estimate β_2 precisely, we prefer a large amount of variation in x_{i2}. The intuition here is that if the variation or change in x_2 is small, it is difficult to measure the effect of that change. This difficulty will be reflected in a large variance for b_2.

4. A larger correlation between x_2 and x_3 leads to a larger variance of b_2. Note that $1 - r_{23}^2$ appears in the denominator of (5.8). A value of $|r_{23}|$ close to 1 means $1 - r_{23}^2$ will be small, which in turn means $\text{var}(b_2)$ will be large. The reason for this fact is that variation in x_{i2} about its mean adds most to the precision of estimation when it is not

connected to variation in the other explanatory variables. When the variation in one explanatory variable is connected to variation in another explanatory variable, it is difficult to disentangle their separate effects. In Chapter 6 we discuss "collinearity," which is the situation when the explanatory variables are correlated with one another. Collinearity leads to increased variances of the least squares estimators.

Although our discussion has been in terms of a model where $K = 3$, these factors affect the variances of the least squares estimators in the same way in larger models.

It is customary to arrange the estimated variances and covariances of the least squares estimators in a square array, which is called a matrix. This matrix has variances on its diagonal and covariances in the off-diagonal positions. It is called a **variance–covariance matrix** or, more simply, a **covariance matrix**. When $K = 3$, the arrangement of the variances and covariances in the covariance matrix is

$$\text{cov}(b_1, b_2, b_3) = \begin{bmatrix} \text{var}(b_1) & \text{cov}(b_1, b_2) & \text{cov}(b_1, b_3) \\ \text{cov}(b_1, b_2) & \text{var}(b_2) & \text{cov}(b_2, b_3) \\ \text{cov}(b_1, b_3) & \text{cov}(b_2, b_3) & \text{var}(b_3) \end{bmatrix}$$

Using the estimate $\hat{\sigma}^2 = 23.874$ and our computer software package, the estimated variances and covariances for b_1, b_2, and b_3 in the Big Andy's Burger Barn example are

$$\widehat{\text{cov}(b_1, b_2, b_3)} = \begin{bmatrix} 40.343 & -6.795 & -0.7484 \\ -6.795 & 1.201 & -0.0197 \\ -0.7484 & -0.0197 & 0.4668 \end{bmatrix} \tag{5.10}$$

Thus, we have

$$\widehat{\text{var}(b_1)} = 40.343 \quad \widehat{\text{cov}(b_1, b_2)} = -6.795$$

$$\widehat{\text{var}(b_2)} = 1.201 \quad \widehat{\text{cov}(b_1, b_3)} = -0.7484$$

$$\widehat{\text{var}(b_3)} = 0.4668 \quad \widehat{\text{cov}(b_2, b_3)} = -0.0197$$

Table 5.3 shows how this information is typically reported in the output from computer software.

Of particular relevance are the standard errors of b_1, b_2, and b_3; they are given by the square roots of the corresponding estimated variances. That is,

$$\text{se}(b_1) = \sqrt{\widehat{\text{var}(b_1)}} = \sqrt{40.3433} = 6.3516$$

$$\text{se}(b_2) = \sqrt{\widehat{\text{var}(b_2)}} = \sqrt{1.2012} = 1.0960$$

$$\text{se}(b_3) = \sqrt{\widehat{\text{var}(b_3)}} = \sqrt{0.4668} = 0.6832$$

Table 5.3 **Covariance Matrix for Coefficient Estimates**

	C	*PRICE*	*ADVERT*
C	40.3433	−6.7951	−0.7484
PRICE	−6.7951	1.2012	−0.0197
ADVERT	−0.7484	−0.0197	0.4668

Again, it is time to go back and look at Table 5.2. Notice that these values appear in the standard error column.

These standard errors can be used to say something about the range of the least squares estimates if we were to obtain more samples of 75 Burger Barns from different cities. For example, the standard error of b_2 is approximately $se(b_2) = 1.1$. We know that the least squares estimator is unbiased, so its mean value is $E(b_2) = \beta_2$. If b_2 is normally distributed, then based on statistical theory we expect 95% of the estimates b_2, obtained by applying the least squares estimator to other samples, to be within approximately two standard deviations of the mean β_2. Given our sample, $2 \times se(b_2) = 2.2$, so we estimate that 95% of the b_2 values would lie within the interval $\beta_2 \pm 2.2$. It is in this sense that the estimated variance of b_2, or its corresponding standard error, tells us something about the reliability of the least squares estimates. If the difference between b_2 and β_2 can be large, b_2 is not reliable; if the difference between b_2 and β_2 is likely to be small, then b_2 is reliable. Whether a particular difference is "large" or "small" will depend on the context of the problem and the use to which the estimates are to be put. This issue is considered again in later sections when we use the estimated variances and covariances to test hypotheses about the parameters and to construct interval estimates.

5.3.2 THE DISTRIBUTION OF THE LEAST SQUARES ESTIMATORS

We have asserted that, under the multiple regression model assumptions MR1–MR5, listed at the end of Section 5.1, the least squares estimator b_k is the best linear unbiased estimator of the parameter β_k in the model

$$y_i = \beta_1 + \beta_2 x_{i2} + \beta_3 x_{i3} + \cdots + \beta_K x_{iK} + e_i$$

If we add assumption MR6, that the random errors e_i have normal probability distributions, then the dependent variable y_i is normally distributed,

$$y_i \sim N\Big((\beta_1 + \beta_2 x_{i2} + \cdots + \beta_K x_{iK}), \sigma^2\Big) \Leftrightarrow e_i \sim N(0, \sigma^2)$$

Since the least squares estimators are linear functions of dependent variables, it follows that the least squares estimators are also normally distributed,

$$b_k \sim N\Big(\beta_k, \mathrm{var}(b_k)\Big)$$

That is, each b_k has a normal distribution with mean β_k and variance $\mathrm{var}(b_k)$. By subtracting its mean and dividing by the square root of its variance, we can transform the normal random variable b_k into the *standard normal variable Z*,

$$Z = \frac{b_k - \beta_k}{\sqrt{\mathrm{var}(b_k)}} \sim N(0, 1), \quad \text{for } k = 1, 2, \ldots, K \tag{5.11}$$

that has mean zero and a variance of 1. The variance of b_k depends on the unknown variance of the error term, σ^2, as illustrated in (5.8) for the $K = 3$ case. When we replace σ^2 by its estimator $\hat{\sigma}^2$, from (5.7), we obtain the estimated $\mathrm{var}(b_k)$ which we denote as

$\widehat{\text{var}(b_k)}$. Replacing $\text{var}(b_k)$ by $\widehat{\text{var}(b_k)}$ in (5.11) changes the $N(0,1)$ random variable to a t-random variable. That is,

$$t = \frac{b_k - \beta_k}{\sqrt{\widehat{\text{var}(b_k)}}} = \frac{b_k - \beta_k}{\text{se}(b_k)} \sim t_{(N-K)} \tag{5.12}$$

One difference between this result and that in Chapter 3, (3.2), is the degrees of freedom of the t-random variable. In Chapter 3, where there were two coefficients to be estimated, the number of degrees of freedom was $N - 2$. In this chapter there are K unknown coefficients in the general model, and *the number of degrees of freedom for t-statistics is $N - K$.*

The result in (5.12) extends to a linear combination of coefficients that was introduced in Chapter 3.6. Suppose that we are interested in estimating or testing hypotheses about a linear combination of coefficients that in the general case is given by

$$\lambda = c_1\beta_1 + c_2\beta_2 + \cdots + c_K\beta_K = \Sigma_{k=1}^{K} c_k\beta_k$$

Then,

$$t = \frac{\hat{\lambda} - \lambda}{\text{se}(\hat{\lambda})} = \frac{\Sigma c_k b_k - \Sigma c_k\beta_k}{\text{se}(\Sigma c_k b_k)} \sim t_{(N-K)} \tag{5.13}$$

This expression is a little intimidating, mainly because we have included all coefficients to make it general, and because hand calculation of $\text{se}(\Sigma c_k b_k)$ is onerous if more than 2 coefficients are involved. For example, if $K = 3$, then

$$\text{se}(c_1 b_1 + c_2 b_2 + c_3 b_3) = \sqrt{\widehat{\text{var}(c_1 b_1 + c_2 b_2 + c_3 b_3)}}$$

where

$$\widehat{\text{var}(c_1 b_1 + c_2 b_2 + c_3 b_3)} = c_1^2\,\widehat{\text{var}(b_1)} + c_2^2\,\widehat{\text{var}(b_2)} + c_3^2\,\widehat{\text{var}(b_3)} + 2c_1 c_2\widehat{\text{cov}(b_1, b_2)}$$
$$+ 2c_1 c_3\widehat{\text{cov}(b_1, b_3)} + 2c_2 c_3\widehat{\text{cov}(b_2, b_3)} \tag{5.14}$$

In many instances some of the c_k will be zero, which can simplify the expressions and the calculations considerably. If one c_k is equal to one, and the rest are zero, (5.13) simplifies to (5.12).

What happens if the errors are not normally distributed? Then the least squares estimator will not be normally distributed and (5.11), (5.12), and (5.13) will not hold exactly. They will, however, be approximately true in large samples. Thus, having errors that are not normally distributed does not stop us from using (5.12) and (5.13), but it does mean we have to be cautious if the sample size is not large. A test for normally distributed errors was given in Chapter 4.3.5. An example of errors that are not normally distributed can be found in Appendix 5B.3.

We now examine how the results in (5.12) and (5.13) can be used for interval estimation and hypothesis testing. The procedures are identical to those described in Chapter 3, except that the degrees of freedom change.

5.4 **Interval Estimation**

5.4.1   INTERVAL ESTIMATION FOR A SINGLE COEFFICIENT

Suppose we are interested in finding a 95% interval estimate for β_2, the response of sales revenue to a change in price at Big Andy's Burger Barn. Following the procedures described in Section 3.1, and noting that we have $N - K = 75 - 3 = 72$ degrees of freedom, the first step is to find a value from the $t_{(72)}$-distribution, call it t_c, such that

$$P(-t_c < t_{(72)} < t_c) = 0.95 \tag{5.15}$$

Using the notation introduced in Section 3.1, $t_c = t_{(0.975, N-K)}$ is the 97.5-percentile of the $t_{(N-K)}$-distribution (the area or probability to the left of t_c is 0.975), and $-t_c = t_{(0.025, N-K)}$ is the 2.5-percentile of the $t_{(N-K)}$-distribution (the area or probability to the left of $-t_c$ is 0.025). Consulting the t-table, we discover there is no entry for 72 degrees of freedom, but, from the entries for 70 and 80 degrees of freedom, it is clear that, correct to two decimal places, $t_c = 1.99$. If greater accuracy is required, your computer software can be used to find $t_c = 1.993$. Using this value, and the result in (5.12) for the second coefficient ($k = 2$), we can rewrite (5.15) as

$$P\left(-1.993 \le \frac{b_2 - \beta_2}{se(b_2)} \le 1.993\right) = 0.95$$

Rearranging this expression, we obtain

$$P\left(b_2 - 1.993 \times se(b_2) \le \beta_2 \le b_2 + 1.993 \times se(b_2)\right) = 0.95$$

The interval endpoints

$$\left(b_2 - 1.993 \times se(b_2), \ b_2 + 1.993 \times se(b_2)\right) \tag{5.16}$$

define a 95% interval estimator of β_2. If this interval estimator is used in many samples from the population, then 95% of them will contain the true parameter β_2. We can establish this fact before any data are collected, based on the model assumptions alone. Before the data are collected we have confidence in the **interval estimation procedure (estimator)** because of its performance when used repeatedly.

A 95% interval estimate for β_2 based on our particular sample is obtained from (5.16) by replacing b_2 and $se(b_2)$ by their values $b_2 = -7.908$ and $se(b_2) = 1.096$. Thus, our 95% interval estimate for β_2 is given by[2]

$$(-7.9079 - 1.9335 \times 1.096, 7.9079 + 1.9335 \times 1.096) = (-10.093, -5.723)$$

This interval estimate suggests that decreasing price by \$1 will lead to an increase in revenue somewhere between \$5,723 and \$10,093. Or, in terms of a price change whose magnitude is more realistic, a 10-cent price reduction will lead to a revenue increase between \$572 and \$1,009. Based on this information, and the cost of making and selling more burgers, Big Andy can decide whether to proceed with a price reduction.

---

[2] For this and the next calculation we used more digits so that it would match the more accurate computer output. You may see us do this occasionally.

Following a similar procedure for β_3, the response of sales revenue to advertising, we find a 95% interval estimate is given by

$$(1.8626 - 1.9935 \times 0.6832, \ 1.8626 + 1.9935 \times 0.6832) = (0.501, 3.225)$$

We estimate that an increase in advertising expenditure of $1,000 leads to an increase in sales revenue of between $501 and $3,225. This interval is a relatively wide one; it implies that extra advertising expenditure could be unprofitable (the revenue increase is less than $1,000) or could lead to a revenue increase more than three times the cost of the advertising. Another way of describing this situation is to say that the point estimate $b_3 = 1.8626$ is not very reliable, as its standard error (which measures sampling variability) is relatively large.

In general, if an interval estimate is uninformative because it is too wide, there is nothing immediate that can be done. A wide interval for the parameter β_3 arises because the estimated sampling variability of the least squares estimator b_3 is large. In the computation of an interval estimate, a large sampling variability is reflected by a large standard error. A narrower interval can only be obtained by reducing the variance of the estimator. Based on the variance expression in (5.8), one solution is to obtain more and better data exhibiting more independent variation. Big Andy could collect data from other cities and set a wider range of price and advertising combinations. It might be expensive to do so, however, and so he would need to assess whether the extra information is worth the extra cost. This solution is generally not open to economists, who rarely use controlled experiments to obtain data. Alternatively, we might introduce some kind of nonsample information on the coefficients. The question of how to use both sample and nonsample information in the estimation process is taken up in Chapter 6.

We cannot say, in general, what constitutes an interval that is too wide, or too uninformative. It depends on the context of the problem being investigated, and on how the information is to be used.

To give a general expression for an interval estimate, we need to recognize that the critical value t_c will depend on the degree of confidence specified for the interval estimate and the number of degrees of freedom. We denote the degree of confidence by $1 - \alpha$; in the case of a 95% interval estimate $\alpha = 0.05$ and $1 - \alpha = 0.95$. The number of degrees of freedom is $N - K$; in Big Andy's Burger Barn example this value was $75 - 3 = 72$. The value t_c is the percentile value $t_{(1-\alpha/2, N-K)}$, which has the property that $P[t_{(N-K)} \leq t_{(1-\alpha/2, N-K)}] = 1 - \alpha/2$. In the case of a 95% confidence interval, $1 - \alpha/2 = 0.975$; we use this value because we require 0.025 in each tail of the distribution. Thus, we write the general expression for a $100(1 - \alpha)\%$ confidence interval as

$$\left(b_k - t_{(1-\alpha/2, N-K)} \times \text{se}(b_k), \quad b_k + t_{(1-\alpha/2, N-K)} \times \text{se}(b_k) \right)$$

5.4.2 INTERVAL ESTIMATION FOR A LINEAR COMBINATION OF COEFFICIENTS

Big Andy wants to make next week a big sales week. He plans to increase advertising expenditure by $800 and drop the price by 40 cents. If the current price is $PRICE_0$ and the current advertising level is $ADVERT_0$, then the change in expected sales from Andy's planned strategy is

$$
\begin{aligned}
\lambda &= E(SALES_1) - E(SALES_0) \\
&= [\beta_1 + \beta_2(PRICE_0 - 0.4) + \beta_3(ADVERT_0 + 0.8)] \\
&\quad - [\beta_1 + \beta_2 PRICE_0 + \beta_3 ADVERT_0] \\
&= -0.4\,\beta_2 + 0.8\,\beta_3
\end{aligned}
$$

Andy would like a point estimate and a 90% interval estimate for λ.

A point estimate is given by

$$\hat{\lambda} = -0.4b_2 + 0.8b_3 = -0.4 \times (-7.9079) + 0.8 \times 1.8626 = 4.6532$$

Our estimate of the expected increase in sales from Big Andy's strategy is $4,653.

From (5.13), we can derive a 90% interval estimate for $\lambda = -0.4\beta_2 + 0.8\beta_3$ as

$$(\hat{\lambda} - t_c \times \text{se}(\hat{\lambda}), \ \hat{\lambda} + t_c \times \text{se}(\hat{\lambda}))$$
$$= \left((-0.4b_2 + 0.8b_3) - t_c \times \text{se}(-0.4b_2 + 0.8b_3), \right.$$
$$\left. (-0.4b_2 + 0.8b_3) + t_c \times \text{se}(-0.4b_2 + 0.8b_3) \right)$$

where $t_c = t_{(0.95, 72)} = 1.666$. To calculate the standard error $\text{se}(-0.4b_2 + 0.8b_3)$, we use the result in (5.14) with $c_1 = 0$, $c_2 = -0.4$ and $c_3 = 0.8$, and the covariance matrix of the coefficient estimates in Table 5.3:

$$\text{se}(-0.4\,b_2 + 0.8\,b_3) = \sqrt{\text{var}(-0.4\,b_2 + 0.8\,b_3)}$$
$$= \sqrt{(-0.4)^2 \,\text{var}(b_2) + (0.8)^2\,\text{var}(b_3) - 2 \times 0.4 \times 0.8 \times \text{cov}(b_2, b_3)}$$
$$= \sqrt{0.16 \times 1.2012 + 0.64 \times 0.4668 - 0.64 \times (-0.0197)}$$
$$= 0.7096$$

Thus, a 90% interval estimate is

$$(4.6532 - 1.666 \times 0.7096, \ 4.6532 + 1.666 \times 0.7096) = (3.471, \ 5.835)$$

We estimate, with 90% confidence, that the expected increase in sales from Big Andy's strategy will lie between $3,471 and $5,835.

5.5 Hypothesis Testing

As well as being useful for interval estimation, the t-distribution result in (5.12) provides the foundation for testing hypotheses about individual coefficients. As you discovered in Chapter 3, hypotheses of the form $H_0 : \beta_2 = c$ versus $H_1 : \beta_2 \neq c$, where c is a specified constant, are called two-tail tests. Hypotheses with inequalities such as $H_0 : \beta_2 \leq c$ versus $H_1 : \beta_2 > c$ are called one-tail tests. In this section we consider examples of each type of hypothesis. For a two-tail test, we consider testing the significance of an individual coefficient; for one-tail tests some hypotheses of economic interest are considered. Using the result in (5.13), one- and two-tail tests can also be used to test hypotheses about linear combinations of coefficients. An example of this type follows those for testing hypotheses about individual coefficients. We will follow the step-by-step procedure for testing hypotheses that was introduced in Section 3.4. To refresh your memory, here are the steps again:

> **STEP-BY-STEP PROCEDURE FOR TESTING HYPOTHESES**
>
> 1. Determine the null and alternative hypotheses.
> 2. Specify the test statistic and its distribution if the null hypothesis is true.
> 3. Select α and determine the rejection region.
> 4. Calculate the sample value of the test statistic and, if desired, the p-value.
> 5. State your conclusion.

At the time these steps were introduced, in Chapter 3, you had not discovered p-values. Knowing about p-values (see Section 3.5) means that steps 3–5 can be framed in terms of the test statistic and its value and/or the p-value. We will use both.

5.5.1   TESTING THE SIGNIFICANCE OF A SINGLE COEFFICIENT

When we set up a multiple regression model, we do so because we believe the explanatory variables influence the dependent variable y. If we are to confirm this belief, we need to examine whether or not it is supported by the data. That is, we need to ask whether the data provide any evidence to suggest that y is related to each of the explanatory variables. If a given explanatory variable, say x_k, has no bearing on y, then $\beta_k = 0$. Testing this null hypothesis is sometimes called a test of significance for the explanatory variable x_k. Thus, to find whether the data contain any evidence suggesting y is related to x_k, we test the null hypothesis

$$H_0 : \beta_k = 0$$

against the alternative hypothesis

$$H_1 : \beta_k \neq 0$$

To carry out the test, we use the test statistic (5.12), which, if the null hypothesis is true, is

$$t = \frac{b_k}{\text{se}(b_k)} \sim t_{(N-K)}$$

For the alternative hypothesis "not equal to," we use a two-tail test, introduced in Section 3.3.3, and reject H_0 if the computed t-value is greater than or equal to t_c (the critical value from the right side of the distribution) or less than or equal to $-t_c$ (the critical value from the left side of the distribution). For a test with level of significance α, $t_c = t_{(1-\alpha/2, N-K)}$ and $-t_c = t_{(\alpha/2, N-K)}$. Alternatively, if we state the acceptance–rejection rule in terms of the p-value, we reject H_0 if $p \leq \alpha$ and do not reject H_0 if $p > \alpha$.

In the Big Andy's Burger Barn example, we test, following our standard testing format, whether sales revenue is related to price:

1. The null and alternative hypotheses are $H_0 : \beta_2 = 0$ and $H_1 : \beta_2 \neq 0$.
2. The test statistic, if the null hypothesis is true, is $t = b_2/\text{se}(b_2) \sim t_{(N-K)}$.
3. Using a 5% significance level ($\alpha = 0.05$), and noting that there are 72 degrees of freedom, the critical values that lead to a probability of 0.025 in each tail of the distribution are $t_{(0.975, 72)} = 1.993$ and $t_{(0.025, 72)} = -1.993$. Thus we reject the null hypothesis if the calculated value of t from step 2 is such that $t \geq 1.993$ or $t \leq -1.993$.

If $-1.993 < t < 1.993$, we do not reject H_0. Stating the acceptance–rejection rule in terms of the p-value, we reject H_0 if $p \leq 0.05$ and do not reject H_0 if $p > 0.05$.

4. The computed value of the t-statistic is

$$t = \frac{-7.908}{1.096} = -7.215$$

From your computer software, the p-value in this case can be found as

$$P(t_{(72)} > 7.215) + P(t_{(72)} < -7.215) = 2 \times (2.2 \times 10^{-10}) = 0.000$$

Correct to three decimal places the result is p-value $= 0.000$.

5. Since $-7.215 < -1.993$, we reject $H_0 : \beta_2 = 0$ and conclude that there is evidence from the data to suggest that sales revenue depends on price. Using the p-value to perform the test, we reject H_0 because $0.000 < 0.05$.

For testing whether sales revenue is related to advertising expenditure, we have

1. $H_0 : \beta_3 = 0$ and $H_1 : \beta_3 \neq 0$.

2. The test statistic, if the null hypothesis is true, is $t = b_3/\text{se}(b_3) \sim t_{(N-K)}$.

3. Using a 5% significance level, we reject the null hypothesis if $t \geq 1.993$ or $t \leq -1.993$. In terms of the p-value, we reject H_0 if $p \leq 0.05$. Otherwise, we do not reject H_0.

4. The value of the test statistic is

$$t = \frac{1.8626}{0.6832} = 2.726$$

The p-value is given by

$$P(t_{(72)} > 2.726) + P(t_{(72)} < -2.726) = 2 \times 0.004 = 0.008$$

5. Because $2.726 > 1.993$, we reject H_0; the data support the conjecture that revenue is related to advertising expenditure. The same test outcome can be obtained using the p-value. In this case, we reject H_0 because $0.008 < 0.05$.

Note that the t-values -7.215 and 2.726 and their corresponding p-values 0.000 and 0.008 were reported in Table 5.2 at the same time that we reported the original least squares estimates and their standard errors. Hypothesis tests of this kind are carried out routinely by computer software, and their outcomes can be read immediately from the computer output that will be similar to Table 5.2.

Significance of a coefficient estimate is desirable—it confirms an initial prior belief that a particular explanatory variable is a relevant variable to include in the model. However, as mentioned in Section 3.4.3, statistical significance should not be confused with economic importance. If the estimated response of sales revenue to advertising had been $b_3 = 0.01$ with a standard error of $\text{se}(b_3) = 0.005$, then we would have concluded b_3 is significantly different from zero; but, since the estimate implies increasing advertising by \$1,000 increases revenue by only \$10, we would not conclude advertising is important. We should also be cautious about concluding that statistical significance implies precise estimation.

The advertising coefficient $b_3 = 1.8626$ was found to be significantly different from zero, but we also concluded the corresponding 95% interval estimate $(0.501, 3.224)$ was too wide to be very informative. In other words, we were not able to get a precise estimate of β_3.

5.5.2   One-Tail Hypothesis Testing for a Single Coefficient

In Section 5.1 we noted that two important considerations for the management of Big Andy's Burger Barn were whether demand was price-elastic or price-inelastic and whether the additional sales revenue from additional advertising expenditure would cover the costs of the advertising. We now are in a position to state these questions as testable hypotheses, and to ask whether the hypotheses are compatible with the data.

5.5.2a   Testing for Elastic Demand

With respect to demand elasticity, we wish to know whether

- $\beta_2 \geq 0$: a decrease in price leads to a change in sales revenue that is zero or negative (demand is price-inelastic or has an elasticity of unity)

- $\beta_2 < 0$: a decrease in price leads to an increase in sales revenue (demand is price-elastic)

If we are not prepared to accept that demand is elastic unless there is strong evidence from the data to support this claim, it is appropriate to take the assumption of an inelastic demand as our null hypothesis. Following our standard testing format, we first state the null and alternative hypotheses:

1. $H_0 : \beta_2 \geq 0$ (demand is unit-elastic or inelastic).
    $H_1 : \beta_2 < 0$ (demand is elastic).

2. To create a test statistic, we act as if the null hypothesis is the equality $\beta_2 = 0$. Doing so is valid because if we reject H_0 for $\beta_2 = 0$, we also reject it for any $\beta_2 > 0$. Then, assuming that $H_0 : \beta_2 = 0$ is true, from (5.12) the test statistic is $t = b_2/\mathrm{se}(b_2) \sim t_{(N-K)}$.

3. The rejection region consists of values from the t-distribution that are unlikely to occur if the null hypothesis is true. If we define "unlikely" in terms of a 5% significance level, then unlikely values of t are those less than the critical value $t_{(0.05,72)} = -1.666$. Thus, we reject H_0 if $t \leq -1.666$ or if the p-value < 0.05.

4. The value of the test statistic is

$$t = \frac{b_2}{\mathrm{se}(b_2)} = \frac{-7.908}{1.096} = -7.215$$

The corresponding p-value is $P\left(t_{(72)} < -7.215\right) = 0.000$.

5. Since $-7.215 < -1.666$, we reject $H_0 : \beta_2 \geq 0$ and conclude that $H_1 : \beta_2 < 0$ (demand is elastic) is more compatible with the data. The sample evidence supports the proposition that a reduction in price will bring about an increase in sales revenue. Since $0.000 < 0.05$, the same conclusion is reached using the p-value.

Note the similarities and differences between this test and the two-tail test of significance performed in Section 5.5.1. The calculated t-values are the same, but the critical t-values are different. Not only are the values themselves different, but with a two-tail test there are also two critical values, one from each side of the distribution. With a one-tail test there is only one critical value, from one side of the distribution. Also, the p-value from the one-tail test is usually half that of the two-tail test, although this fact is harder to appreciate from this example because both p-values are essentially zero.

5.5.2b Testing Advertising Effectiveness

The other hypothesis of interest is whether an increase in advertising expenditure will bring an increase in sales revenue that is sufficient to cover the increased cost of advertising. Since such an increase will be achieved if $\beta_3 > 1$, we set up the hypotheses:

1. $H_0 : \beta_3 \leq 1$ and $H_1 : \beta_3 > 1$.
2. Treating the null hypothesis as the equality $H_0 : \beta_3 = 1$, the test statistic that has the t-distribution when H_0 is true is, from (5.12),

$$t = \frac{b_3 - 1}{se(b_3)} \sim t_{(N-K)}$$

3. Choosing $\alpha = 0.05$ as our level of significance, the relevant critical value is $t_{(0.95, 72)} = 1.666$. We reject H_0 if $t \geq 1.666$ or if the p-value ≤ 0.05.
4. The value of the test statistic is

$$t = \frac{b_3 - \beta_3}{se(b_3)} = \frac{1.8626 - 1}{0.6832} = 1.263$$

The p-value of the test is $P(t_{(72)} > 1.263) = 0.105$.

5. Since $1.263 < 1.666$, we do not reject H_0. There is insufficient evidence in our sample to conclude that advertising will be cost effective. Using the p-value to perform the test, we again conclude that H_0 cannot be rejected, because $0.105 > 0.05$. Another way of thinking about the test outcome is as follows: Because the estimate $b_2 = 1.8626$ is greater than one, this estimate by itself suggests advertising will be effective. However, when we take into account the precision of estimation, measured by the standard error, we find that $b_2 = 1.8626$ is not significantly greater than one. In the context of our hypothesis-testing framework, we cannot conclude with a sufficient degree of certainty that $\beta_3 > 1$.

5.5.3 HYPOTHESIS TESTING FOR A LINEAR COMBINATION OF COEFFICIENTS

Big Andy's marketing adviser claims that dropping the price by 20 cents will be more effective for increasing sales revenue than increasing advertising expenditure by $500. In other words, she claims that $-0.2\beta_2 > 0.5\beta_3$. Andy does not wish to accept this proposition unless it can be verified by past data. He knows that the estimated change in expected sales from the price fall is $-0.2b_2 = -0.2 \times (-7.9079) = 1.5816$, and that the estimated change in expected sales from the extra advertising is $0.5b_3 = 0.5 \times 1.8626 = 0.9319$, so the marketer's claim appears to be correct. However, he wants to establish whether the difference $1.5816 - 0.9319$ could be attributable to sampling error, or whether it constitutes proof, at a 5% significance level, that $-0.2\,\beta_2 > 0.5\,\beta_3$. This constitutes a test about a linear combination of coefficients. Since $-0.2\,\beta_2 > 0.5\,\beta_3$ can be written as $-0.2\,\beta_2 - 0.5\,\beta_3 > 0$, we are testing a hypothesis about the linear combination $-0.2\,\beta_2 - 0.5\,\beta_3$.

Following our hypothesis testing steps, we have

1. $H_0 : -0.2\,\beta_2 - 0.5\,\beta_3 \leq 0$ (the marketer's claim is not correct)
    $H_1 : -0.2\,\beta_2 - 0.5\,\beta_3 > 0$ (the marketer's claim is correct)

2. Using (5.13) with $c_2 = -0.2$, $c_3 = 0.5$ and all other c_k's equal to zero, and assuming that the equality in H_0 holds $(-0.2\,\beta_2 - 0.5\,\beta_3 = 0)$, the test statistic and its distribution when H_0 is true is

$$t = \frac{-0.2\,b_2 - 0.5\,b_3}{\mathrm{se}(-0.2\,b_2 - 0.5\,b_3)} \sim t_{(72)}$$

3. For a one-tail test and a 5% significance level, the critical value is $t_{(0.95,\,72)} = 1.666$. We reject H_0 if $t \geq 1.666$ or if the p-value < 0.05.

4. To find the value of the test statistic, we first compute

$$\mathrm{se}(-0.2\,b_2 - 0.5\,b_3) = \sqrt{\widehat{\mathrm{var}}(-0.2\,b_2 - 0.5\,b_3)}$$

$$= \sqrt{\begin{array}{l}(-0.2)^2\,\widehat{\mathrm{var}}(b_2) + (-0.5)^2\,\widehat{\mathrm{var}}(b_3) \\ +2 \times (-0.2) \times (-0.5) \times \widehat{\mathrm{cov}}(b_2, b_3)\end{array}}$$

$$= \sqrt{0.04 \times 1.2012 + 0.25 \times 0.4668 + 0.2 \times (-0.0197)}$$

$$= 0.4010$$

Then, the value of the test statistic is

$$t = \frac{-0.2\,b_2 - 0.5\,b_3}{\mathrm{se}(-0.2\,b_2 - 0.5\,b_3)} = \frac{1.58158 - 0.9319}{0.4010} = 1.622$$

The corresponding p-value is $P(t_{(72)} > 1.622) = 0.055$.

5. Since $1.622 < 1.666$, we do not reject H_0. At a 5% significance level, there is not enough evidence to support the marketer's claim. Alternatively, we reach the same conclusion using the p-value, because $0.055 > 0.05$.

5.6 Polynomial Equations

The multiple regression model that we have studied so far has the form

$$y = \beta_1 + \beta_2 x_2 + \cdots + \beta_K x_K + e \tag{5.17}$$

It is a linear function of variables (the x's) and of the coefficients (the β's). However, (5.17) is much more flexible than it at first appears. Although the assumptions of the multiple regression model require us to retain the property of linearity in the β's, many different nonlinear functions of variables can be specified by defining the x's and/or y as transformations of original variables. Several examples of such transformations have already been encountered for the simple regression model. In Chapter 2 the quadratic model $y = \alpha_1 + \alpha_2 x^2 + e$ and the log-linear model $\ln(y) = \gamma_1 + \gamma_2 x + e$ were estimated. A detailed analysis of these and other nonlinear simple regression models — a linear-log model, a log-log model and a cubic model—was given in Chapter 4. The same kind of variable transformations and interpretations of their coefficients carry over to multiple regression models. In this section we are particularly interested in polynomial equations such as the quadratic $y = \beta_1 + \beta_2 x + \beta_3 x^2 + e$ or the cubic $y = \alpha_1 + \alpha_2 x + \alpha_3 x^2 + \alpha_4 x^3 + e$. When we studied these models as examples of the simple regression model, we were constrained by the need to have only one right-hand-side variable, such as $y = \beta_1 + \beta_3 x^2 + e$ or $y = \alpha_1 + \alpha_4 x^3 + e$. Now that we are working within the framework of the multiple regression model, we can consider unconstrained polynomials with all their terms included. Polynomials are a rich class of functions that can parsimoniously describe relationships that are curved, with one or more peaks and valleys. We begin with some examples from economics.

5.6.1   COST AND PRODUCT CURVES

In microeconomics you studied "cost" curves and "product" curves that describe a firm. Total cost and total product curves are mirror images of each other, taking the standard "cubic" shapes shown in Figure 5.2.

Average and marginal cost curves, and their mirror images, average and marginal product curves, take quadratic shapes, usually represented as shown in Figure 5.3.

The slopes of these relationships are not constant and cannot be represented by regression models that are "linear in the variables." However, these shapes are easily represented by polynomials. For example, if we consider the average cost relationship in Figure 5.3(a), a suitable regression model is

$$AC = \beta_1 + \beta_2 Q + \beta_3 Q^2 + e \tag{5.18}$$

This quadratic function can take the "U" shape we associate with average cost functions. For the total cost curve in Figure 5.2(a), a cubic polynomial is in order,

$$TC = \alpha_1 + \alpha_2 Q + \alpha_3 Q^2 + \alpha_4 Q^3 + e \tag{5.19}$$

These functional forms, which represent nonlinear shapes, can still be estimated using the least squares methods we have studied. The variables Q^2 and Q^3 are explanatory variables that are treated no differently from any others.

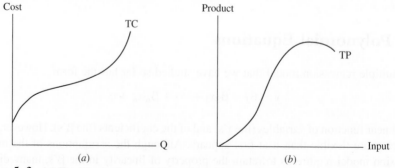

(a)   *(b)*

FIGURE 5.2   (a) Total cost curve and (b) total product curve.

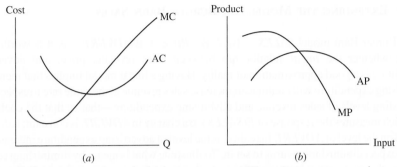

FIGURE **5.3** Average and marginal (*a*) cost curves and (*b*) product curves.

A difference in models of nonlinear relationships is in the interpretation of the parameters, which are not themselves slopes. To investigate the slopes, and how we can interpret the parameters, we need a little calculus. For the general polynomial function

$$y = a_0 + a_1 x + a_2 x^2 + a_3 x^3 + \cdots + a_p x^p$$

the slope or derivative of the curve is

$$\frac{dy}{dx} = a_1 + 2a_2 x + 3a_3 x^2 + \cdots + p a_p x^{p-1} \tag{5.20}$$

This slope changes depending on the value of *x*. Evaluated at a particular value, $x = x_0$, the slope is

$$\left.\frac{dy}{dx}\right|_{x=x_0} = a_1 + 2a_2 x_0 + 3a_3 x_0^2 + \cdots + p a_p x_0^{p-1} \tag{5.21}$$

For more on rules of derivatives, see Appendix A.3.1.

Using the general rule in (5.20), the slope of the average cost curve (5.18) is

$$\frac{dE(AC)}{dQ} = \beta_2 + 2\beta_3 Q$$

The slope of the average cost curve changes for every value of *Q* and depends on the parameters β_2 and β_3. For this U-shaped curve, we expect $\beta_2 < 0$ and $\beta_3 > 0$.

The slope of the total cost curve (5.19), which is the marginal cost, is

$$\frac{dE(TC)}{dQ} = \alpha_2 + 2\alpha_3 Q + 3\alpha_4 Q^2$$

The slope is a quadratic function of *Q*, involving the parameters α_2, α_3, and α_4. For a U-shaped marginal cost curve, we expect the parameter signs to be $\alpha_2 > 0$, $\alpha_3 < 0$, and $\alpha_4 > 0$.

Using polynomial terms is an easy and flexible way to capture nonlinear relationships between variables. As we have shown, care must be taken when interpreting the parameters of models that contain polynomial terms. Their inclusion does not complicate least squares estimation—with one exception. It is sometimes true that having a variable and its square or cube in the same model causes **collinearity** problems. (See Chapter 6.4.)

5.6.2 EXTENDING THE MODEL FOR BURGER BARN SALES

In the Burger Barn model $SALES = \beta_1 + \beta_2 PRICE + \beta_3 ADVERT + e$, it is worth questioning whether the *linear* relationship between sales revenue, price, and advertising expenditure is a good approximation of reality. Having a linear model implies that increasing advertising expenditure will continue to increase sales revenue at the same rate irrespective of the existing levels of sales revenue and advertising expenditure—that is, that the coefficient β_3, which measures the response of $E(SALES)$ to a change in $ADVERT$, is constant; it does not depend on the level of $ADVERT$. In reality, as the level of advertising expenditure increases, we would expect diminishing returns to set in. To illustrate what is meant by diminishing returns, consider the relationship between sales and advertising (assuming a fixed price) graphed in Figure 5.4. The figure shows the effect on sales of an increase of $200 in advertising expenditure when the original level of advertising is (a) $600 and (b) $1,600. Note that the units in the graph are thousands of dollars, so these points appear as 0.6 and 1.6. At the smaller level of advertising, sales increase from $72,400 to $74,000, whereas at the higher level of advertising, the increase is a much smaller one, from $78,500 to $79,000. The linear model with the constant slope β_3 does not capture the diminishing returns.

What is required is a model where the slope changes as the level of $ADVERT$ increases. One such model having this characteristic is obtained by including the squared value of advertising as another explanatory variable, making the new model

$$SALES = \beta_1 + \beta_2 PRICE + \beta_3 ADVERT + \beta_4 ADVERT^2 + e \qquad (5.22)$$

Adding the term $\beta_4 ADVERT^2$ to our original specification yields a model in which the response of expected revenue to a change in advertising expenditure depends on the level of advertising. Specifically, by applying the polynomial derivative rule in (5.20), and holding $PRICE$ constant, the response of $E(SALES)$ to a change in $ADVERT$ is

$$\frac{\Delta E(SALES)}{\Delta ADVERT}\bigg|_{(PRICE \text{ held constant})} = \frac{\partial E(SALES)}{\partial ADVERT} = \beta_3 + 2\beta_4 ADVERT \qquad (5.23)$$

The partial derivative sign "∂" is used in place of the derivative sign "d" that we used in (5.20) because $SALES$ depends on two variables, $PRICE$ and $ADVERT$, and we are holding $PRICE$ constant. See Appendix A.3.3 for further details about partial derivatives.

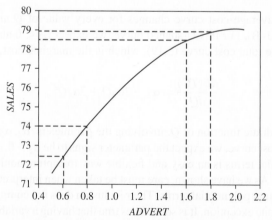

FIGURE *5.4* A model where sales exhibits diminishing returns to advertising expenditure.

We refer to $\partial E(SALES)/\partial ADVERT$ in (5.23) as the **marginal effect** of advertising on sales. In linear functions, the slope or marginal effect is constant. In nonlinear functions, it varies with one or more of the variables. To find the expected signs for β_3 and β_4, note that we expect the response of sales revenue to a change in advertising to be positive when $ADVERT = 0$. That is, we expect $\beta_3 > 0$. Also, to achieve diminishing returns, the response must decline as $ADVERT$ increases. That is, we expect $\beta_4 < 0$.

Using least squares to estimate (5.22) yields

$$\widehat{SALES} = 109.72 - 7.640\,PRICE + 12.151\,ADVERT - 2.768\,ADVERT^2 \tag{5.24}$$
$$(\text{se}) \quad (6.80) \quad (1.046) \qquad (3.556) \qquad\qquad (0.941)$$

What can we say about the addition of $ADVERT^2$ to the equation? Its coefficient has the expected negative sign and is significantly different from zero at a 5% significance level. Moreover, the coefficient of $ADVERT$ has retained its positive sign and continues to be significant. The estimated response of sales to advertising is

$$\frac{\partial \widehat{SALES}}{\partial ADVERT} = 12.151 - 5.536\,ADVERT$$

Substituting into this expression we find that when advertising is at its minimum value in the sample of \$500 ($ADVERT = 0.5$), the marginal effect of advertising on sales is 9.383. When advertising is at a level of \$2,000 ($ADVERT = 2$), the marginal effect is 1.079. Thus, allowing for diminishing returns to advertising expenditure has improved our model both statistically and in terms of meeting our expectations about how sales will respond to changes in advertising.

◆5.6.3 THE OPTIMAL LEVEL OF ADVERTISING: INFERENCE FOR A NONLINEAR COMBINATION OF COEFFICIENTS[3]

Economic theory tells us to undertake all those actions for which the marginal benefit is greater than the marginal cost. This optimizing principle applies to Big Andy's Burger Barn as it attempts to choose the optimal level of advertising expenditure. Recalling that $SALES$ denotes sales revenue or total revenue, the marginal benefit in this case is the marginal revenue from more advertising. From (5.23), the required marginal revenue is given by the marginal effect of more advertising $\beta_3 + 2\beta_4 ADVERT$. The marginal cost of \$1 of advertising is \$1 plus the cost of preparing the additional products sold due to effective advertising. If we ignore the latter costs, the marginal cost of \$1 of advertising expenditure is \$1. Thus, advertising should be increased to the point where

$$\beta_3 + 2\beta_4 ADVERT_0 = 1$$

with $ADVERT_0$ denoting the optimal level of advertising. Using the least squares estimates for β_3 and β_4 in (5.24), a point estimate for $ADVERT_0$ is

$$\widehat{ADVERT_0} = \frac{1 - b_3}{2b_4} = \frac{1 - 12.1512}{2 \times (-2.76796)} = 2.014$$

implying that the optimal monthly advertising expenditure is \$2,014.

---

[3] This section contains advanced material.

To assess the reliability of this estimate, we need a standard error and an interval estimate for $(1 - b_3)/2b_4$. This is a tricky problem, and one that requires the use of calculus to solve. What makes it more difficult than what we have done so far is the fact that it involves a **nonlinear function** of b_3 and b_4. Variances of nonlinear functions are hard to derive. Recall that the variance of a linear function, say, $c_3 b_3 + c_4 b_4$, is given by

$$\text{var}(c_3 b_3 + c_4 b_4) = c_3^2 \text{var}(b_3) + c_4^2 \text{var}(b_4) + 2 c_3 c_4 \text{cov}(b_3, b_4) \quad (5.25)$$

Finding the variance of $(1 - b_3)/2b_4$ is less straightforward. The best we can do is find an approximate expression that is valid in large samples. Suppose $\lambda = (1 - \beta_3)/2\beta_4$ and $\hat{\lambda} = (1 - b_3)/2b_4$; then, the approximate variance expression is

$$\text{var}(\hat{\lambda}) = \left(\frac{\partial \lambda}{\partial \beta_3}\right)^2 \text{var}(b_3) + \left(\frac{\partial \lambda}{\partial \beta_4}\right)^2 \text{var}(b_4) + 2\left(\frac{\partial \lambda}{\partial \beta_3}\right)\left(\frac{\partial \lambda}{\partial \beta_4}\right)\text{cov}(b_3, b_4) \quad (5.26)$$

This expression holds for all nonlinear functions of two estimators, not just $\hat{\lambda} = (1 - b_3)/2b_4$. Also, note that for the linear case, where $\lambda = c_3 \beta_3 + c_4 \beta_4$ and $\hat{\lambda} = c_3 b_3 + c_4 b_4$, (5.26) reduces to (5.25). Using (5.26) to find an approximate expression for a variance is called the **delta method**. For further details, consult Appendix 5B.5.

We will use (5.26) to estimate the variance of $\hat{\lambda} = \widehat{ADVERT_0} = (1 - b_3)/2b_4$, get its standard error, and use that to get an interval estimate for $\lambda = ADVERT_0 = (1 - \beta_3)/2\beta_4$. If the use of calculus in (5.26) frightens you, take comfort in the fact that most software will automatically compute the standard error for you.

The required derivatives are

$$\frac{\partial \lambda}{\partial \beta_3} = -\frac{1}{2\beta_4}, \quad \frac{\partial \lambda}{\partial \beta_4} = -\frac{1 - \beta_3}{2\beta_4^2}$$

To estimate $\text{var}(\hat{\lambda})$ we evaluate these derivatives at the least squares estimates b_3 and b_4.

Thus, for the estimated variance of the optimal level of advertising, we have

$$\widehat{\text{var}(\hat{\lambda})} = \left(-\frac{1}{2b_4}\right)^2 \widehat{\text{var}(b_3)} + \left(-\frac{1 - b_3}{2b_4^2}\right)^2 \widehat{\text{var}(b_4)} + 2\left(-\frac{1}{2b_4}\right)\left(-\frac{1 - b_3}{2b_4^2}\right)\widehat{\text{cov}(b_3, b_4)}$$

$$= \left(\frac{1}{2 \times 2.768}\right)^2 \times 12.646 + \left(\frac{1 - 12.151}{2 \times 2.768^2}\right)^2 \times 0.88477$$

$$+ 2\left(\frac{1}{2 \times 2.768}\right)\left(\frac{1 - 12.151}{2 \times 2.768^2}\right) \times 3.2887$$

$$= 0.016567$$

and

$$\text{se}(\hat{\lambda}) = \sqrt{0.016567} = 0.1287$$

We are now in a position to get a 95% interval estimate for $\lambda = ADVERT_0$. When dealing with a linear combination of coefficients in (5.13), and Section 5.4.2, we used the result $(\hat{\lambda} - \lambda)/\text{se}(\hat{\lambda}) \sim t_{(N-K)}$. This result can be used in exactly the same way for nonlinear functions, but a difference is that the result is only an approximate one for large samples, even when the errors are normally distributed. Thus, an approximate 95% interval estimate for $ADVERT_0$ is

$$\left(\hat{\lambda} - t_{(0.975, 71)}\text{se}(\hat{\lambda}), \quad \hat{\lambda} + t_{(0.975, 71)}\text{se}(\hat{\lambda})\right)$$
$$= (2.014 - 1.994 \times 0.1287, \quad 2.014 + 1.994 \times 0.1287)$$
$$= (1.757, \quad 2.271)$$

We estimate with 95% confidence that the optimal level of advertising lies between $1,757 and $2,271.

5.7 Interaction Variables

In the last section we saw how the inclusion of $ADVERT^2$ in the regression model for $SALES$ has the effect of making the marginal effect of $ADVERT$ on $SALES$ depend on the level of $ADVERT$. What if we wanted the marginal effect of one variable to depend on the level of another variable? How do we model this effect? To illustrate this idea we will consider a life-cycle model for pizza consumption. Suppose that we are economists for Gutbusters Pizza, and that we wish to study the effect of income and age on an individual's expenditure on pizza. For that purpose we take a random sample of 40 individuals, age 18 and older, and record their annual expenditure on pizza ($PIZZA$), their income in thousands of dollars ($INCOME$) and age (AGE). The first five observations are shown in Table 5.4. The full data set is contained in the file *pizza4.dat*.

As an initial model, let us consider

$$PIZZA = \beta_1 + \beta_2 AGE + \beta_3 INCOME + e \tag{5.27}$$

The implications of this specification are as follows:

1. $\partial E(PIZZA)/\partial AGE = \beta_2$: For a *given level of income*, the expected expenditure on pizza changes by the amount β_2 with an additional year of age. What would you expect here? Based on our casual observation of college students, who appear to consume massive quantities of pizza, we expect the sign of β_2 to be negative. With the effects of income removed, we expect that as a person ages his or her pizza expenditure will fall.

2. $\partial E(PIZZA)/\partial INCOME = \beta_3$: For individuals of a *given age*, an increase in income of $1,000 increases expected expenditures on pizza by β_3. Since pizza is probably a normal good, we expect the sign of β_3 to be positive. The parameter β_3 might be called the marginal propensity to spend on pizza.

Table 5.4 **Pizza Expenditure Data**

PIZZA	INCOME	AGE
109	19.5	25
0	39.0	45
0	15.6	20
108	26.0	28
220	19.5	25

Estimates of (5.27), with t-statistics in parentheses, are

$$\widehat{PIZZA} = 342.88 - 7.576AGE + 1.832INCOME$$

$$(t) \qquad\qquad (-3.27) \qquad (3.95)$$

The signs of the estimated parameters are as we anticipated. Both AGE and $INCOME$ have significant coefficients, based on their t-statistics.

These are the implications of the model in (5.27). However, is it reasonable to expect that, *regardless* of the age of the individual, an increase in income by \$1,000 should lead to an increase in pizza expenditure by \$1.83? Probably not. It would seem more reasonable to assume that as a person grows older, his or her marginal propensity to spend on pizza declines. That is, as a person ages, less of each extra dollar is expected to be spent on pizza. This is a case in which the effect of income depends on the age of the individual. That is, the effect of one variable is modified by another. One way of accounting for such interactions is to include an **interaction variable** that is the product of the two variables involved. Since AGE and $INCOME$ are the variables that interact, we will add the variable $(AGE \times INCOME)$ to the regression model. The result is

$$PIZZA = \beta_1 + \beta_2 AGE + \beta_3 INCOME + \beta_4(AGE \times INCOME) + e \qquad (5.28)$$

In this revised model, the effects of $INCOME$ and AGE are

1. $\partial E(PIZZA)/\partial AGE = \beta_2 + \beta_4 INCOME$: The effect of AGE now depends on income. As a person ages, his or her pizza expenditure is expected to fall, and, because β_4 is expected to be negative, the greater the income, the greater will be the fall attributable to a change in age.

2. $\partial E(PIZZA)/\partial INCOME = \beta_3 + \beta_4 AGE$: The effect of a change in income on expected pizza expenditure, which is the marginal propensity to spend on pizza, now depends on AGE. If our logic concerning the effect of aging is correct, then β_4 should be negative. Then, as AGE increases, the value of the partial derivative declines.

The estimated model (5.28) that includes the product $(AGE \times INCOME)$ is

$$\widehat{PIZZA} = 161.47 - 2.977AGE + 6.980\ INCOME - 0.1232\,(AGE \times INCOME)$$

$$(t) \qquad\qquad (-0.89) \qquad (2.47) \qquad\qquad (-1.85)$$

The estimated coefficient of the interaction term is negative and significant at the $\alpha = .05$ level using a one-tail test. The signs of other coefficients remain the same, but AGE, by itself, no longer appears to be a significant explanatory factor. This suggests that AGE affects pizza expenditure through its interaction with income—that is, on the marginal propensity to spend on pizza.

Using these estimates, let us estimate the marginal effect of age upon pizza expenditure for two individuals—one with \$25,000 income and one with \$90,000 income.

$$\frac{\widehat{\partial E(PIZZA)}}{\partial AGE} = b_2 + b_4 INCOME$$

$$= -2.977 - 0.1232INCOME$$

$$= \begin{cases} -6.06 & \text{for } INCOME = 25 \\ -14.07 & \text{for } INCOME = 90 \end{cases}$$

That is, we expect that an individual with $25,000 income will reduce pizza expenditures by $6.06 per year, whereas the individual with $90,000 income will reduce pizza expenditures by $14.07 per year.

5.7.1 LOG-LINEAR MODELS

In Chapter 4.5.1 we studied the simple log-linear model $\ln(y) = \beta_1 + \beta_2 x$ and discovered a useful interpretation of the coefficient of x: for a one-unit change in x the approximate percentage change in y is $100\beta_2\%$. This result extends naturally to the multiple regression model and to models with interaction and squared variables. Consider a wage equation where $\ln(WAGE)$ depends on years of education ($EDUC$) and years of experience ($EXPER$)

$$\ln(WAGE) = \beta_1 + \beta_2 EDUC + \beta_3 EXPER + e \tag{5.29}$$

In this model the approximate percentage change in $WAGE$ for an extra year of experience, with education held constant, is $100\beta_3\%$. Similarly, the approximate percentage change in $WAGE$ for an extra year of education, with experience held constant, is $100\beta_2\%$. If we believe the effect of an extra year of experience on wages will depend on the level of education, then we can add an interaction variable

$$\ln(WAGE) = \beta_1 + \beta_2 EDUC + \beta_3 EXPER + \beta_4 (EDUC \times EXPER) + e \tag{5.30}$$

In this case the effect of another year of experience, holding education constant, is roughly

$$\left. \frac{\Delta \ln(WAGE)}{\Delta EXPER} \right|_{EDUC \text{ fixed}} = \beta_3 + \beta_4 EDUC$$

Since 100 times the log difference is approximately the percentage difference (see Chapter 4.5), the approximate percentage change in wage given a one-year increase in experience is $100(\beta_3 + \beta_4 EDUC)\%$. Using the Current Population Survey data (*cps4_small.dat*), we estimate (5.30) to obtain

$$\widehat{\ln(WAGE)} = 1.392 + 0.09494\,EDUC + 0.00633\,EXPER$$
$$- 0.0000364\,(EDUC \times EXPER)$$

This result suggests that the greater the number of years of education, the less valuable is an extra year of experience. Similarly, the greater the number of years of experience, the less valuable is an extra year of education. For a person with 8 years of education, we estimate that an additional year of experience leads to an increase in wages of approximately $100(0.00633 - 0.0000364 \times 8)\% = 0.60\%$, whereas for a person with 16 years of education, the approximate increase in wages from an extra year of education is $100(0.00633 - 0.0000364 \times 16)\% = 0.57\%$.

If there is a quadratic term on the right-hand side, as in

$$\ln(WAGE) = \beta_1 + \beta_2 EDUC + \beta_3 EXPER + \beta_4 (EDUC \times EXPER) + \beta_5 EXPER^2 + e$$

then, using a little calculus, we find that a one-year increase in experience leads to an approximate percentage wage change of

$$\%\Delta WAGE \cong 100(\beta_3 + \beta_4 EDUC + 2\beta_5 EXPER)\%$$

The percentage wage change from an extra year of experience depends on both the level of education and the level of experience.

5.8 Measuring Goodness–of–Fit

For the simple regression model studied in Chapter 4, we introduced the coefficient of determination R^2 as a measure of the proportion of variation in the dependent variable that is explained by variation in the explanatory variable. In the multiple regression model the same measure is relevant and the same formulas are valid, but now we talk of the proportion of variation in the dependent variable explained by *all* the explanatory variables included in the linear model. The coefficient of determination is

$$R^2 = \frac{SSR}{SST} = \frac{\sum_{i=1}^{N}(\hat{y}_i - \bar{y})^2}{\sum_{i=1}^{N}(y_i - \bar{y})^2}$$

$$= 1 - \frac{SSE}{SST} = 1 - \frac{\sum_{i=1}^{N}\hat{e}_i^2}{\sum_{i=1}^{N}(y_i - \bar{y})^2} \tag{5.31}$$

where *SSR* is the variation in y "explained" by the model (sum of squares of regression), *SST* is the total variation in y about its mean (sum of squares total), and *SSE* is the sum of squared least squares residuals (errors) and is the portion of the variation in y that is not explained by the model.

The notation $\hat{y}_i$ refers to the predicted value of y for each of the sample values of the explanatory variables. That is,

$$\hat{y}_i = b_1 + b_2 x_{i2} + b_3 x_{i3} + \cdots + b_K x_{iK}$$

The sample mean $\bar{y}$ is both the mean of y_i and the mean of $\hat{y}_i$, so long as the model includes an intercept (β_1 in this case).

The value for *SSE* will be reported by almost all computer software, but sometimes *SST* is not reported. Recall, however, that the sample standard deviation for y, which is readily computed by most software, is given by

$$s_y = \sqrt{\frac{1}{N-1}\sum_{i=1}^{N}(y_i - \bar{y})^2} = \sqrt{\frac{SST}{N-1}}$$

and so

$$SST = (N-1)s_y^2$$

In the original model for Big Andy's Burger Barn (see Table 5.2), we find that $SST = 74 \times 6.488537^2 = 3115.482$ and $SSE = 1718.943$. Using these sums of squares, we have

$$R^2 = 1 - \frac{\sum_{i=1}^{N}\hat{e}_i^2}{\sum_{i=1}^{N}(y_i - \bar{y})^2} = 1 - \frac{1718.943}{3115.482} = 0.448$$

The interpretation of R^2 is that 44.8% of the variation in sales revenue is explained by the variation in price and by the variation in the level of advertising expenditure. It means that, *in our sample*, 55.2% of the variation in revenue is left unexplained and is due to variation in the error term or to variation in other variables that implicitly form part of the error term. Adding the square of advertising to the Burger Barn model (see (5.24)) increased the R^2 to 0.508. Thus an additional 6% of the variation in sales is explained by including this variable.

As mentioned in Section 4.2.2, the coefficient of determination is also viewed as a measure of the predictive ability of the model over the sample period or as a measure of how well the estimated regression fits the data. The value of R^2 is equal to the squared sample correlation coefficient between $\hat{y}_i$ and y_i. Since the sample correlation measures the linear association between two variables, if R^2 is high, it means that there is a close association between the values of y_i and the values predicted by the model, $\hat{y}_i$. In this case the model is said to "fit" the data well. If R^2 is low, there is not a close association between the values of y_i and the values predicted by the model, $\hat{y}_i$, and the model does not fit the data well.

One final note is in order. The intercept parameter β_1 is the y-intercept of the regression "plane," as shown in Figure 5.1. If, for theoretical reasons, you are *certain* that the regression plane passes through the origin, then $\beta_1 = 0$ and can be omitted from the model. While this is not a common practice, it does occur, and regression software includes an option that removes the intercept from the model. If the model does not contain an intercept parameter, then the measure R^2 given in (5.31) is no longer appropriate. The reason it is no longer appropriate is that without an intercept term in the model,

$$\sum_{i=1}^{N} (y_i - \bar{y})^2 \neq \sum_{i=1}^{N} (\hat{y}_i - \bar{y})^2 + \sum_{i=1}^{N} \hat{e}_i^2$$

or $SST \neq SSR + SSE$. To understand why, go back and check the proof in Appendix 4B of Chapter 4. In the sum of squares decomposition the cross-product term $\sum_{i=1}^{N}(\hat{y}_i - \bar{y})\hat{e}_i$ no longer disappears. Under these circumstances it does not make sense to talk of the proportion of total variation that is explained by the regression. Thus, when your model does not contain a constant, it is better not to report R^2, even if your computer displays one.

5.9 Exercises

Answers to exercises marked * appear at www.wiley.com/go/global/hill.

5.9.1 PROBLEMS

5.1* Consider the multiple regression model

$$y_i = x_{i1}\beta_1 + x_{i2}\beta_2 + x_{i3}\beta_3 + e_i$$

with the nine observations on y_i, x_{i1}, x_{i2} and x_{i3} given in Table 5.5.

Use a hand calculator to answer the following questions:
(a) Calculate the observations in terms of deviations from their means. That is, find
   $x_{i2}^* = x_{i2} - \bar{x}_2, x_{i3}^* = x_{i3} - \bar{x}_3,$ and $y_i^* = y_i - \bar{y}.$
(b) Calculate $\sum y_i^* x_{i2}^*, \sum x_{i2}^{*2}, \sum y_i^* x_{i3}^*, \sum x_{i2}^* x_{i3}^*,$ and $\sum x_{i3}^{*2}.$
(c) Use the expressions in Appendix 5A to find least squares estimates $b_1, b_2,$ and b_3.

Table 5.5   **Data for Exercise 5.1**

y_i	x_{i1}	x_{i2}	x_{i3}
1	1	0	1
2	1	1	-2
3	1	2	1
-1	1	-2	0
0	1	1	-1
-1	1	-2	-1
2	1	0	1
1	1	-1	1
2	1	1	0

    (d) Find the least squares residuals $\hat{e}_1, \hat{e}_2, \ldots, \hat{e}_9$.
    (e) Find the variance estimate $\hat{\sigma}^2$.
    (f) Use (5.9) to find the sample correlation between x_2 and x_3.
    (g) Find the standard error for b_2.
    (h) Find *SSE, SST, SSR,* and R^2.

5.2*   Use your answers to Exercise 5.1 to
    (a) Compute a 95% interval estimate for β_2
    (b) Test the hypothesis $H_0 : \beta_2 = 1$ against the alternative that $H_1 : \beta_2 \neq 1$

5.3   Consider the following model that relates the proportion of a household's budget spent on alcohol *WALC* to total expenditure *TOTEXP*, age of the household head *AGE*, and the number of children in the household *NK*.

$$WALC = \beta_1 + \beta_2 \ln(TOTEXP) + \beta_3 AGE + \beta_4 NK + e$$

The data in the file *london.dat* were used to estimate this model. See Exercise 4.10 for more details about the data. Note that only households with one or two children are being considered. Thus, *NK* takes only the values one or two. Output from estimating this equation appears in Table 5.6.

Table 5.6   **Output for Exercise 5.3**

Dependent Variable: *WALC*
Included observations: 1519

Variable	Coefficient	Std. Error	*t*-Statistic	Prob.
C	0.0091	0.0190		0.6347
ln(*TOTEXP*)	0.0276		6.6086	0.0000
AGE		0.0002	-6.9624	0.0000
NK	-0.0133	0.0033	-4.0750	0.0000

R-squared		Mean dependent var	0.0606
S.E. of regression		S.D. dependent var	0.0633
Sum squared resid	5.752896		

(a) Fill in the following blank spaces that appear in this table.
   (i) The t-statistic for b_1
   (ii) The standard error for b_2
   (iii) The estimate b_3
   (iv) R^2
   (v) $\hat{\sigma}$
(b) Interpret each of the estimates b_2, b_3, and b_4.
(c) Compute a 95% interval estimate for β_3. What does this interval tell you?
(d) Test the hypothesis that the budget proportion for alcohol does not depend on the number of children in the household. Can you suggest a reason for the test outcome?

5.4* The data set used in Exercise 5.3 is used again. This time it is used to estimate how the proportion of the household budget spent on transportation WTRANS depends on the log of total expenditure ln(TOTEXP), AGE, and number of children NK. The output is reported in Table 5.7.
(a) Write out the estimated equation in the standard reporting format with standard errors below the coefficient estimates.
(b) Interpret the estimates b_2, b_3, and b_4. Do you think the results make sense from an economic or logical point of view?
(c) Are there any variables that you might exclude from the equation? Why?
(d) What proportion of variation in the budget proportion allocated to transport is explained by this equation?
(e) Predict the proportion of a budget that will be spent on transportation, for both one- and two-children households, when total expenditure and age are set at their sample means, which are 98.7 and 36, respectively.

5.5 This question is concerned with the value of houses in towns surrounding Boston. It uses the data of Harrison, D., and D. L. Rubinfeld (1978), "Hedonic Prices and the Demand for Clean Air," *Journal of Environmental Economics and Management*, 5, 81–102. The output appears in Table 5.8. The variables are defined as follows:

VALUE = median value of owner-occupied homes in thousands of dollars
CRIME = per capita crime rate
NITOX = nitric oxide concentration (parts per million)
ROOMS = average number of rooms per dwelling
AGE = proportion of owner-occupied units built prior to 1940

Table 5.7 **Output for Exercise 5.4**

Dependent Variable: *WTRANS*
Included observations: 1519

Variable	Coefficient	Std. Error	t-Statistic	Prob.
C	−0.0315	0.0322	−0.9776	0.3284
ln(TOTEXP)	0.0414	0.0071	5.8561	0.0000
AGE	−0.0001	0.0004	−0.1650	0.8690
NK	−0.0130	0.0055	−2.3542	0.0187
R-squared	0.0247		Mean dependent var	0.1323
			S.D. dependent var	0.1053

Table 5.8   **Output for Exercise 5.5**

Dependent Variable: *VALUE*
Included observations: 506

Variable	Coefficient	Std. Error	*t*-Statistic	Prob.
C	28.4067	5.3659	5.2939	0.0000
CRIME	−0.1834	0.0365	−5.0275	0.0000
NITOX	−22.8109	4.1607	−5.4824	0.0000
ROOMS	6.3715	0.3924	16.2378	0.0000
AGE	−0.0478	0.0141	−3.3861	0.0008
DIST	−1.3353	0.2001	−6.6714	0.0000
ACCESS	0.2723	0.0723	3.7673	0.0002
TAX	−0.0126	0.0038	−3.3399	0.0009
PTRATIO	−1.1768	0.1394	−8.4409	0.0000

$DIST$ = weighted distances to five Boston employment centers
$ACCESS$ = index of accessibility to radial highways
TAX = full-value property-tax rate per \$10,000
$PTRATIO$ = pupil–teacher ratio by town

(a) Report briefly on how each of the variables influences the value of a home.
(b) Find 99% interval estimates for the coefficients of *CRIME* and *ACCESS*.
(c) Test the hypothesis that increasing the number of rooms by one increases the value of a house by \$5,000.
(d) Test as an alternative hypothesis H_1 that reducing the pupil–teacher ratio by 10 will increase the value of a house by more than \$8,000.

5.6   Suppose that from a sample of 63 observations, the least squares estimates and the corresponding estimated covariance matrix are given by

$$\begin{bmatrix} b_1 \\ b_2 \\ b_3 \end{bmatrix} = \begin{bmatrix} 2 \\ 3 \\ -1 \end{bmatrix}, \qquad \widehat{\text{cov}(b)} = \begin{bmatrix} 3 & -2 & 1 \\ -2 & 4 & 0 \\ 1 & 0 & 3 \end{bmatrix}$$

Test each of the following hypotheses and state the conclusion:
(a) $\beta_2 = 0$
(b) $\beta_1 + 2\beta_2 = 5$
(c) $\beta_1 - \beta_2 + \beta_3 = 4$

5.7   What are the standard errors of the least squares estimates b_2 and b_3 in the regression model $y = \beta_1 + \beta_2 x_2 + \beta_3 x_3 + e$ where $N = 202$, $SSE = 11.12389$, $r_{23} = -0.114255$, $\sum_{i=1}^{N}(x_{i2} - \bar{x}_2)^2 = 1210.178$, and $\sum_{i=1}^{N}(x_{i3} - \bar{x}_3)^2 = 30307.57$?

5.8*   An agricultural economist carries out an experiment to study the production relationship between the dependent variable *YIELD* = peanut yield (pounds per acre) and the production inputs

$NITRO$ = amount of nitrogen applied (hundreds of pounds per acre)
$PHOS$ = amount of phosphorus fertilizer (hundreds of pounds per acre)

A total $N = 27$ observations were obtained using different test fields. The estimated quadratic model, with an interaction term, is

$$\widehat{YIELD} = 1.385 + 8.011NITRO + 4.800PHOS - 1.944NITRO^2$$
$$- 0.778PHOS^2 - 0.567NITRO \times PHOS$$

(a) Find equations describing the marginal effect of nitrogen on yield and the marginal effect of phosporus on yield. What do these equations tell you?

(b) What are the marginal effects of nitrogen and of phosphorus when (i) $NITRO$ and $PHOS = 1$ and (ii) when $NITRO = 2$ and $PHOS = 2$? Comment on your findings.

(c) Test the hypothesis that the marginal effect of nitrogen is zero, when

(i) $PHOS = 1$ and $NITRO = 1$
(ii) $PHOS = 1$ and $NITRO = 2$
(iii) $PHOS = 1$ and $NITRO = 3$

Note: The following information may be useful:

$$\widehat{var}(b_2 + 2b_4 + b_6) = 0.233$$

$$\widehat{var}(b_2 + 4b_4 + b_6) = 0.040$$

$$\widehat{var}(b_2 + 6b_4 + b_6) = 0.233$$

(d) ◆[This part requires the use of calculus] For the function estimated, what levels of nitrogen and phosphorus give maximum yield? Are these levels the optimal fertilizer applications for the peanut producer?

5.9 When estimating wage equations, we expect that young, inexperienced workers will have relatively low wages and that with additional experience their wages will rise, but then begin to decline after middle age, as the worker nears retirement. This life-cycle pattern of wages can be captured by introducing experience and experience squared to explain the level of wages. If we also include years of education, we have the equation

$$WAGE = \beta_1 + \beta_2 EDUC + \beta_3 EXPER + \beta_4 EXPER^2 + e$$

(a) What is the marginal effect of experience on wages?

(b) What signs do you expect for each of the coefficients β_2, β_3, and β_4? Why?

(c) After how many years of experience do wages start to decline? (Express your answer in terms of β's.)

(d) The results from estimating the equation using 1000 observations in the file *cps4c_small.dat* are given in Table 5.9 on page 204. Find 95% interval estimates for

(i) The marginal effect of education on wages
(ii) The marginal effect of experience on wages when $EXPER = 2$
(iii) The marginal effect of experience on wages when $EXPER = 30$
(iv) The number of years of experience after which wages decline

5.9.2 COMPUTER EXERCISES

5.10 Use a computer to verify your answers to Exercise 5.1, parts (c), (e), (f), (g), and (h).

Table 5.9 **Wage Equation with Quadratic Experience**

Variable	Coefficient	Std. Error	t-Stat	Prob.
C	−13.4303	2.0285	−6.621	0.000
EDUC	2.2774	0.1394	16.334	0.000
EXPER	0.6821	0.1048	6.507	0.000
EXPER^2	−0.0101	0.0019	−5.412	0.000

Covariance Matrix for Least Squares Estimates

	C	EDUC	EXPER	EXPER^2
C	4.114757339	−0.215505842	−0.124023160	0.001822688
EDUC	−0.215505842	0.019440281	−0.000217577	0.000015472
EXPER	−0.124023160	−0.000217577	0.010987185	−0.000189259
EXPER^2	0.001822688	0.000015472	−0.000189259	0.000003476

5.11 (a) The file *lond_small.dat* contains a subset of 500 observations from the bigger file *london.dat*. Use the data in the file *lond_small.dat* to estimate budget share equations of the form

$$W = \beta_1 + \beta_2 \ln(TOTEXP) + \beta_3 AGE + \beta_4 NK + e$$

for all budget shares (food, fuel, clothing, alcohol, transportation, and other) in the data set. Report and discuss your results. In your discussion, comment on how total expenditure, age, and number of children influence the various budget proportions. Also comment on the significance of your coefficient estimates.

(b) Commodities are regarded as luxuries if $\beta_2 > 0$ and necessities if $\beta_2 < 0$. For each commodity group test $H_0 : \beta_2 \leq 0$ against $H_1 : \beta_2 > 0$ and comment on the outcomes.

5.12 The file *cocaine.dat* contains 56 observations on variables related to sales of cocaine powder in northeastern California over the period 1984–1991. The data are a subset of those used in the study Caulkins, J. P. and R. Padman (1993), "Quantity Discounts and Quality Premia for Illicit Drugs," *Journal of the American Statistical Association*, 88, 748–757. The variables are

PRICE = price per gram in dollars for a cocaine sale
QUANT = number of grams of cocaine in a given sale
QUAL = quality of the cocaine expressed as percentage purity
TREND = a time variable with 1984 = 1 up to 1991 = 8

Consider the regression model

$$PRICE = \beta_1 + \beta_2 QUANT + \beta_3 QUAL + \beta_4 TREND + e$$

(a) What signs would you expect on the coefficients β_2, β_3, and β_4?

(b) Use your computer software to estimate the equation. Report the results and interpret the coefficient estimates. Have the signs turned out as you expected?

(c) What proportion of variation in cocaine price is explained jointly by variation in quantity, quality, and time?

(d) It is claimed that the greater the number of sales, the higher the risk of getting caught. Thus, sellers are willing to accept a lower price if they can make sales in larger quantities. Set up H_0 and H_1 that would be appropriate to test this hypothesis. Carry out the hypothesis test.

(e) Test the hypothesis that the quality of cocaine has no influence on price against the alternative that a premium is paid for better-quality cocaine.

(f) What is the average annual change in the cocaine price? Can you suggest why price might be changing in this direction?

5.13 The file *br2.dat* contains data on 1,080 houses sold in Baton Rouge, Louisiana, during mid-2005. We will be concerned with the selling price (*PRICE*), the size of the house in square feet (*SQFT*), and the age of the house in years (*AGE*).

(a) Use all observations to estimate the following regression model and report the results

$$PRICE = \beta_1 + \beta_2 SQFT + \beta_3 AGE + e$$

(i) Interpret the coefficient estimates.

(ii) Find a 95% interval estimate for the price increase for an extra square foot of living space—that is, $\partial PRICE / \partial SQFT$.

(iii) Test the hypothesis that having a house a year older decreases price by 1000 or less ($H_0 : \beta_3 \geq -1000$) against the alternative that it decreases price by more than 1000 ($H_1 : \beta_3 < -1000$).

(b) Add the variables $SQFT^2$ and AGE^2 to the model in part (a) and re-estimate the equation. Report the results.

(i) Find estimates of the marginal effect $\partial PRICE / \partial SQFT$ for the smallest house in the sample, the largest house in the sample, and a house with 2000 *SQFT*. Comment on these values. Are they realistic?

(ii) Find estimates of the marginal effect $\partial PRICE / \partial AGE$ for the oldest house in the sample, the newest house in the sample, and a house that is 25 years old. Comment on these values. Are they realistic?

(iii) Find a 95% interval estimate for the marginal effect $\partial PRICE / \partial SQFT$ for a house with 2000 square feet.

(iv) For a house that is 20 years old, test the hypothesis

$$H_0 : \frac{\partial PRICE}{\partial AGE} \geq -1000 \text{ against } H_1 : \frac{\partial PRICE}{\partial AGE} < -1000$$

(c) Add the interaction variable $SQFT \times AGE$ to the model in part (b) and re-estimate the equation. Report the results. Repeat parts (i), (ii), (iii), and (iv) from part (b) for this new model. Use $SQFT = 2000$ and $AGE = 25$.

(d) From your answers to parts (a), (b), and (c), comment on the sensitivity of the results to the model specification.

5.14 The file *br2.dat* contains data on 1,080 houses sold in Baton Rouge, Louisiana, during mid-2005. We will be concerned with the selling price (*PRICE*), the size of the house in square feet (*SQFT*), and the age of the house in years (*AGE*). Define a new variable that measures house size in terms of hundreds of square feet, $SQFT100 = SQFT / 100$.

(a) Estimate the following equation and report the results:

$$\ln(PRICE) = \alpha_1 + \alpha_2 SQFT100 + \alpha_3 AGE + \alpha_4 AGE^2 + e$$

(b) Interpret the estimate for α_2.

(c) Find and interpret estimates for $\partial \ln(PRICE) / \partial AGE$ when $AGE = 2$ and $AGE = 15$.

(d) Find expressions for $\partial PRICE/\partial AGE$ and $\partial PRICE/\partial SQFT100$. (Ignore the error term.)

(e) Estimate $\partial PRICE/\partial AGE$ and $\partial PRICE/\partial SQFT100$ for a 15-year-old house with a living area of 2000 square feet.

(f) Find the standard errors of your estimates in (e).

(g) Find a 95% interval estimate for the marginal effect $\partial PRICE/\partial SQFT100$ for a 15-year-old house with 2000 square feet.

(h) For a 15-year-old house with 2000 square feet, test the hypothesis

$$H_0 : \frac{\partial PRICE}{\partial AGE} \geq -1000 \quad \text{against} \quad H_1 : \frac{\partial PRICE}{\partial AGE} < -1000$$

5.15* Reconsider the presidential voting data (*fair4.dat*) introduced in Exercise 2.14.

(a) Estimate the regression model

$$VOTE = \beta_1 + \beta_2 GROWTH + \beta_3 INFLATION + e$$

Report the results in standard format. Are the estimates for β_2 and β_3 significantly different from zero at a 10% significance level? Did you use one-tail tests or two-tail tests? Why?

(b) Assume the inflation rate is 4%. Predict the percentage vote for the incumbent party when the growth rate is (i) -3%, (ii) 0%, and (iii) 3%.

(c) Test, as an alternative hypothesis, that the incumbent party will get the majority of the expected vote when the growth rate is (i) -3%, (ii) 0%, and (iii) 3%. Use a 1% level of significance. If you were the president seeking re-election, why might you set up each of these hypotheses as an alternative rather than a null hypothesis?

5.16 Data on the weekly sales of a major brand of canned tuna by a supermarket chain in a large midwestern U.S. city during a mid-1990's calendar year are contained in the file *tuna.dat*. There are 52 observations on the variables. $SAL1 =$ unit sales of brand no. 1 canned tuna; $APR1 =$ price per can of brand no. 1 canned tuna; $APR2$, $APR3 =$ price per can of brands no. 2 and 3 of canned tuna.

(a) The prices $APR1$, $APR2$, and $APR3$ are expressed in dollars. Multiply the observations on each of these variables by 100 to express them in terms of cents; call the new variables $PR1$, $PR2$, and $PR3$. Estimate the following regression model and report the results:

$$SAL1 = \beta_1 + \beta_2 PR1 + \beta_3 PR2 + \beta_4 PR3 + e$$

(b) Interpret the estimates b_2, b_3, and b_4. Do they have the expected signs?

(c) Using suitable one-tail tests and a 5% significance level, test whether each of the coefficients b_2, b_3, and b_4 are significantly different from zero.

(d) Using a 5% significance level, test the following hypotheses:

(i) A 1-cent increase in the price of brand one reduces its sales by 300 cans.

(ii) A 1-cent increase in the price of brand two increases the sales of brand one by 300 cans.

(iii) A 1-cent increase in the price of brand three increases the sales of brand one by 300 cans.

(iv) The effect of a price increase in brand two on sales of brand one is the same as the effect of a price increase in brand three on sales of brand one. Does the outcome of this test contradict your findings from parts (ii) and (iii)?

(v) If prices of all 3 brands go up by 1 cent, there is no change in sales.

5.17 (a) Reconsider the model $SAL1 = \beta_1 + \beta_2 PR1 + \beta_3 PR2 + \beta_4 PR3 + e$ from Exercise 5.16. Estimate this model if you have not already done so, and find a 95% interval estimate for expected sales when $PR1 = 90$, $PR2 = 75$, and $PR3 = 75$. What is wrong with this interval?

(b) Estimate the alternative model $\ln(SAL1) = \alpha_1 + \alpha_2 PR1 + \alpha_3 PR2 + \alpha_4 PR3 + e$, and find a 95% interval estimate for expected log of sales when $PR1 = 90$, $PR2 = 75$, and $PR3 = 75$. Convert this interval into one for sales, and compare it with what you got in part (a).

(c) How does the interpretation of the coefficients in the model with $\ln(SAL1)$ as the dependent variable differ from that for the coefficients in the model with $SAL1$ as the dependent variable?

5.18 What is the relationship between crime and punishment? This important question has been examined by Cornwell and Trumbull[4] using a panel of data from North Carolina. The cross sections are 90 counties, and the data are annual for the years 1981–1987. The data are in the file *crime.dat*.

Using the data from 1987, estimate a regression relating the log of the crime rate *LCRMRTE* to the probability of an arrest *PRBARR* (the ratio of arrests to offenses), the probability of conviction *PRBCONV* (the ratio of convictions to arrests), the probability of a prison sentence *PRBPRIS* (the ratio of prison sentences to convictions), the number of police per capita *POLPC*, and the weekly wage in construction *WCON*. Write a report of your findings. In your report, explain what effect you would expect each of the variables to have on the crime rate and note whether the estimated coefficients have the expected signs and are significantly different from zero. What variables appear to be the most important for crime deterrence? Can you explain the sign for the coefficient of *POLPC*?

5.19 Use the data in *cps4_small.dat* to estimate the following wage equation

$$\ln(WAGE) = \beta_1 + \beta_2 EDUC + \beta_3 EXPER + \beta_4 HRSWK + e$$

(a) Report the results. Interpret the estimates for β_2, β_3, and β_4. Are these estimates significantly different from zero?

(b) Test the hypothesis that an extra year of education increases the wage rate by at least 10% against the alternative that it is less than 10%.

(c) Find a 99% interval estimate for the percentage increase in wage from working an additional hour per week.

(d) Re-estimate the model with the additional variables $EDUC \times EXPER$, $EDUC^2$, and $EXPER^2$. Report the results. Are the estimated coefficients significantly different from zero?

(e) For the new model, find expressions for the marginal effects $\partial \ln(WAGE)/\partial EDUC$ and $\partial \ln(WAGE)/\partial EXPER$.

---

[4] "Estimating the Economic Model of Crime with Panel Data," *Review of Economics and Statistics*, 76, 1994, 360–366. The data was kindly provided by the authors.

(f) Estimate the marginal effect $\partial \ln(WAGE)/\partial EDUC$ for two workers Jill and Wendy; Jill has 16 years of education and 2 years of experience, while Wendy has 12 years of education and 2 years of experience. What can you say about the marginal effect of education as education increases?

(g) Test, as an alternative hypothesis, that Jill's marginal effect of education is greater than that of Wendy. Use a 1% significance level.

(h) Estimate the marginal effect $\partial \ln(WAGE)/\partial EXPER$ for two workers Chris and Dave; Chris has 16 years of education and 2 years of experience, while Dave has 16 years of education and 20 years of experience. What can you say about the marginal effect of experience as experience increases?

(i) For someone with 16 years of education, find a 99% interval estimate for the number of years of experience after which the marginal effect of experience becomes negative.

5.20 In Section 5.6.3 we discovered that the optimal level of advertising for Big Andy's Burger Barn, $ADVERT_0$, satisfies the equation $\beta_3 + 2\beta_4 ADVERT_0 = 1$. Using a 5% significance level, test whether each of the following levels of advertising could be optimal: (a) $ADVERT_0 = 1.75$, (b) $ADVERT_0 = 1.9$, and (c) $ADVERT_0 = 2.3$. What are the p-values for each of the tests?

5.21 Each morning between 6:30AM and 8:00AM Bill leaves the Melbourne suburb of Carnegie to drive to work at the University of Melbourne. The time it takes Bill to drive to work (*TIME*) depends on the departure time (*DEPART*), the number of red lights that he encounters (*REDS*), and the number of trains that he has to wait for at the Murrumbeena level crossing (*TRAINS*). Observations on these variables for the 231 working days in 2006 appear in the file *commute.dat*. *TIME* is measured in minutes. *DEPART* is the number of minutes after 6:30AM that Bill departs.

(a) Estimate the equation

$$TIME = \beta_1 + \beta_2 DEPART + \beta_3 REDS + \beta_4 TRAINS + e$$

Report the results and interpret each of the coefficient estimates, including the intercept β_1.

(b) Find 95% interval estimates for each of the coefficients. Have you obtained precise estimates of each of the coefficients?

(c) Using a 5% significance level, test the hypothesis that each red light delays Bill by 3 minutes or more against the alternative that the delay is less than 3 minutes.

(d) Using a 10% significance level, test the hypothesis that each train delays Bill by 5 minutes.

(e) Using a 5% significance level, test the null hypothesis that leaving at 7:15 AM instead of 7:00 AM will make the trip at least 15 minutes longer (other things equal).

(f) Using a 5% significance level test the hypothesis that the minimum time it takes Bill is less than or equal to 15 minutes against the alternative that it is more than 15 minutes. What assumptions about the true values of β_2, β_3, and β_4 did you have to make to perform this test?

5.22 Reconsider the commuting time model estimated in Exercise 5.21 using the data file *commute.dat*

$$TIME = \beta_1 + \beta_2 DEPARTS + \beta_3 REDS + \beta_4 TRAINS + e$$

(a) Using a 5% significance level, test the hypothesis that the delay from a train is equal to 3 times the delay from a red light.

(b) Using a 5% significance level, test the null hypothesis that the delay from a train is at least 3 times greater than the delay from a red light against the alternative that it is less than 3 times greater.

(c) Worried that he may miss an important meeting if there are 3 trains, Bill leaves for work at 7:10AM instead of 7:15AM. Using a 5% significance level, test the null hypothesis that leaving 5 minutes earlier is enough time to allow for 3 trains against the alternative that it is not enough time.

(d) Suppose that Bill encounters no red lights and no trains. Using a 5% significance level, test the hypothesis that leaving Carnegie at 7:15AM is early enough to get him to the university before 8:00AM against the alternative it is not. (Carry out the test in terms of the expected time $E(TIME)$.)

5.23* Lion Forest has been a very successful golf professional. However, at age 45 his game is not quite what it used to be. He started the pro-tour when he was only 20 and he has been looking back examining how his scores have changed as he got older. In the file *golf.dat*, the first column contains his final score (relative to par) for 150 tournaments. The second column contains his age (in units of 10 years). There are scores for 6 major tournaments in each year for the last 25 years. Denoting his score by $SCORE$ and his age by AGE, estimate the following model and obtain the within-sample predictions:

$$SCORE = \beta_1 + \beta_2 AGE + \beta_3 AGE^2 + \beta_4 AGE^3 + e$$

(a) Test the null hypothesis that a quadratic function is adequate against the cubic function as an alternative. What are the characteristics of the cubic equation that might make it appropriate?

(b) Use the within-sample predictions to answer the following questions:
   (i) At what age was Lion at the peak of his career?
   (ii) When was Lion's game improving at an increasing rate?
   (iii) When was Lion's game improving at a decreasing rate?
   (iv) At what age did Lion start to play worse than he had played when he was 20 years old?
   (v) When could he no longer score less than par (on average)?

(c) When he is aged 70, will he be able to break 100? Assume par is 72.

5.24* The file *rice.dat* contains 352 observations on 44 rice farmers in the Tarlac region of the Philippines for the 8 years 1990 to 1997. Variables in the data set are tonnes of freshly threshed rice ($PROD$), hectares planted ($AREA$), person-days of hired and family labor ($LABOR$), and kilograms of fertilizer ($FERT$). Treating the data set as one sample with $N = 352$, proceed with the following questions:

(a) Estimate the production function

$$\ln(PROD) = \beta_1 + \beta_2 \ln(AREA) + \beta_3 \ln(LABOR) + \beta_4 \ln(FERT) + e$$

Report the results, interpret the estimates, and comment on the statistical significance of the estimates.

(b) Using a 1% level of significance, test the hypothesis that the elasticity of production with respect to land is equal to 0.5.

(c) Find a 95% interval estimate for the elasticity of production with respect to fertilizer. Has this elasticity been precisely measured?

(d) Using a 5% level of significance, test the hypothesis that the elasticity of production with respect to labor is less than or equal to 0.3 against the alternative that it is greater than 0.3. What happens if you reverse the null and alternative hypotheses?

5.25 Consider the following aggregate production function for the U.S. manufacturing sector:

$$Y = \alpha K^{\beta_2} L^{\beta_3} E^{\beta_4} M^{\beta_5} \exp\{e\}$$

where Y is gross output, K is capital, L is labor, E is energy, and M denotes other intermediate materials. The data underlying these variables are given in index form in the file *manuf.dat*.

(a) Show that taking logarithms of the production function puts it in a form suitable for least squares estimation.

(b) Estimate the unknown parameters of the production function and find the corresponding standard errors.

(c) Discuss the economic and statistical implications of these results.

Appendix 5A Derivation of Least Squares Estimators

In Appendix 2A we derived expressions for the least squares estimators b_1 and b_2 in the simple regression model. In this appendix we proceed with a similar exercise for the multiple regression model; we describe how to obtain expressions for b_1, b_2, and b_3 in a model with two explanatory variables. Given sample observations on y, x_2, and x_3, the problem is to find values for β_1, β_2, and β_3 that minimize

$$S(\beta_1, \beta_2, \beta_3) = \sum_{i=1}^{N} (y_i - \beta_1 - \beta_2 x_{i2} - \beta_3 x_{i3})^2$$

The first step is to partially differentiate S with respect to β_1, β_2, and β_3 and to set the first-order partial derivatives to zero. This yields

$$\frac{\partial S}{\partial \beta_1} = 2N\beta_1 + 2\beta_2 \Sigma x_{i2} + 2\beta_3 \Sigma x_{i3} - 2\Sigma y_i$$

$$\frac{\partial S}{\partial \beta_2} = 2\beta_1 \Sigma x_{i2} + 2\beta_2 \Sigma x_{i2}^2 + 2\beta_3 \Sigma x_{i2} x_{i3} - 2\Sigma x_{i2} y_i$$

$$\frac{\partial S}{\partial \beta_3} = 2\beta_1 \Sigma x_{i3} + 2\beta_2 \Sigma x_{i2} x_{i3} + 2\beta_3 \Sigma x_{i3}^2 - 2\Sigma x_{i3} y_i$$

Setting these partial derivatives equal to zero, dividing by 2, and rearranging yields

$$\begin{aligned} Nb_1 + \Sigma x_{i2} b_2 + \Sigma x_{i3} b_3 &= \Sigma y_i \\ \Sigma x_{i2} b_1 + \Sigma x_{i2}^2 b_2 + \Sigma x_{i2} x_{i3} b_3 &= \Sigma x_{i2} y_i \\ \Sigma x_{i3} b_1 + \Sigma x_{i2} x_{i3} b_2 + \Sigma x_{i3}^2 b_3 &= \Sigma x_{i3} y_i \end{aligned} \tag{5A.1}$$

The least squares estimators for b_1, b_2, and b_3 are given by the solution of this set of three *simultaneous equations*, known as the **normal equations**. To write expressions for this solution it is convenient to express the variables as deviations from their means. That is, let

$$y_i^* = y_i - \bar{y}, \quad x_{i2}^* = x_{i2} - \bar{x}_2, \quad x_{i3}^* = x_{i3} - \bar{x}_3$$

Then the least squares estimates b_1, b_2, and b_3 are

$$b_1 = \bar{y} - b_2 \bar{x}_2 - b_3 \bar{x}_3$$

$$b_2 = \frac{(\sum y_i^* x_{i2}^*)(\sum x_{i3}^{*2}) - (\sum y_i^* x_{i3}^*)(\sum x_{i2}^* x_{i3}^*)}{(\sum x_{i2}^{*2})(\sum x_{i3}^{*2}) - (\sum x_{i2}^* x_{i3}^*)^2}$$

$$b_3 = \frac{(\sum y_i^* x_{i3}^*)(\sum x_{i2}^{*2}) - (\sum y_i^* x_{i2}^*)(\sum x_{i3}^* x_{i2}^*)}{(\sum x_{i2}^{*2})(\sum x_{i3}^{*2}) - (\sum x_{i2}^* x_{i3}^*)^2}$$

For models with more than three parameters the solutions become quite messy without using matrix algebra; we will not show them. Computer software used for multiple regression computations solves normal equations like those in (5A.1) to obtain the least squares estimates.

Appendix 5B Large Sample Analysis

In the multiple regression model, if assumptions MR1–MR5 hold (or SR1–SR5 in the simple regression model) we are able to show that the least squares estimators are Best, Linear, Unbiased Estimators (BLUE). These properties are called "finite sample" properties because they do not depend on the sample size N, and will hold if the sample is any size $N > K$. In this section we discuss additional properties of the least squares estimator that can be established if samples are imagined becoming infinitely large. In econometrics and statistics these are called **asymptotic properties**, with the term asymptotic implying the analysis of limiting behavior, here as $N \to \infty$. First we describe and discuss the properties, and then extend the Monte Carlo simulations from Appendices 2G and 3C to illustrate them.

5B.1 Consistency

When choosing econometric estimators, we do so with the objective in mind of obtaining an estimate that is close to the true but unknown parameter with high probability. Consider the simple linear regression model $y_i = \beta_1 + \beta_2 x_i + e_i$, $i = 1, \ldots, N$. Suppose that for decision-making purposes we consider that obtaining an estimate of β_2 within "epsilon" of the true value is satisfactory. The probability of obtaining an estimate "close" to β_2 is

$$P(\beta_2 - \varepsilon \le b_2 \le \beta_2 + \varepsilon) \tag{5B.1}$$

An estimator is said to be **consistent** if this probability converges to 1 as the sample size $N \to \infty$. Or, using the concept of a limit, the estimator b_2 is consistent if

$$\lim_{N \to \infty} P(\beta_2 - \varepsilon \le b_2 \le \beta_2 + \varepsilon) = 1 \tag{5B.2}$$

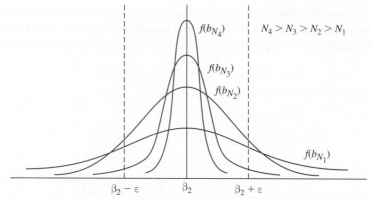

FIGURE *5B.1* An illustration of consistency.

What does this mean? In Figure 5B.1 we depict the probability density functions $f\left(b_{N_i}\right)$ for the least squares estimator b_2 based on samples sizes $N_4 > N_3 > N_2 > N_1$. As the sample size increases, the probability density function becomes narrower. Why is that so? First of all, the least squares estimator is unbiased if MR1–MR5 hold, so that $E(b_2) = \beta_2$. This property is true in samples of all sizes. As the sample size changes, the center of the *pdf*s remains at β_2. The variance of the least squares estimator b_2 in the simple regression model is given in (2.15), and for the multiple regression model in (5.8). In each case, we established that as the sample size N gets larger, the variance of the estimator b_2 becomes smaller. As N increases, the center of the *pdf* remains fixed at $E(b_2) = \beta_2$, and the variance decreases, resulting in probability density functions such as $f\left(b_{N_i}\right)$. The probability that b_2 falls in the interval $\beta_2 - \varepsilon \le b_2 \le \beta_2 + \varepsilon$ is the area under the *pdf* between these limits. As the sample size increases, the probability of b_2 falling within the limits increases toward 1. In large samples we can say that the least squares estimator will provide an estimate close to the true parameter with high probability.

The property of consistency applies to many estimators, even ones that are biased in finite samples. For example, the estimator $\hat{\beta}_2 = b_2 + 1/N$ is a biased estimator. The amount of the bias is

$$\text{bias}\left(\hat{\beta}_2\right) = E\left(\hat{\beta}_2\right) - \beta_2 = \frac{1}{N}$$

For the estimator $\hat{\beta}_2$ the bias converges to zero as $N \to \infty$. That is

$$\lim_{N \to \infty} \text{bias}\left(\hat{\beta}_2\right) = \lim_{N \to \infty} \left[E\left(\hat{\beta}_2\right) - \beta_2\right] = 0 \tag{5B.3}$$

In this case the estimator is said to be **asymptotically unbiased**. Consistency for an estimator can be established by showing that the estimator is either unbiased or asymptotically unbiased, and that its variance converges to zero as $N \to \infty$,

$$\lim_{N \to \infty} \text{var}\left(\hat{\beta}_2\right) = 0 \tag{5B.4}$$

Conditions (5B.3) and (5B.4) are intuitive, and sufficient to establish an estimator to be consistent.

Because the probability density function of a consistent estimator collapses around the true parameter, and the probability that an estimator b_2 will be close to the true parameter β_2 approaches one, the estimator b_2 is said to "converge in probability" to β_2, with the "in probability" part reminding us that it is the probability of being "close" in (5B.2) that is the key factor. Several notations are used for this type of convergence. One is $b_2 \overset{p}{\to} \beta_2$, with the p over the arrow indicating "probability." A second is $\underset{N\to\infty}{\text{plim}}(b_2) = \beta_2$, with "plim" being short for "probability limit."

5B.2 Asymptotic Normality

In most cases econometric estimators in models satisfying MR1–MR5 (SR1–SR5) can be shown to have an approximate normal distribution in large samples. As $N \to \infty$ the probability density function of the standardized estimator has a distribution that approaches the standard normal

$$\frac{b_k - \beta_k}{\sqrt{\text{var}(b_k)}} \overset{a}{\sim} N(0,1)$$

We say in this case that the estimator is asymptotically normal and generally write

$$b_k \overset{a}{\sim} N(\beta_k, \text{var}(b_k))$$

This result is similar to the Central Limit Theorem given in Appendix C.3.4.

The consequence of this powerful result is that we can apply t-tests, F-tests and the usual interval estimation and prediction interval procedures even if MR6 (SR6) does not hold, as long as the sample is sufficiently large. "How large?" is a tricky question, because we cannot provide a single number. In each application the answer depends on the nature of the data and the error term. The more complicated the model, the larger the sample likely to be required for the approximate normality to hold. In section 5B.3, we carry out some Monte Carlo simulations so that you can see for yourself how many observations are required before the normal approximation becomes satisfactory.

5B.3 Monte Carlo Simulation

In Appendices 2G and 3C, we introduced a Monte Carlo simulation to illustrate the repeated sampling properties of the least squares estimators. In this appendix we use the same framework to illustrate the repeated sampling performances of interval estimators and hypothesis tests when the errors are not normally distributed.

Recall that the **data generation process** for the simple linear regression model is given by

$$y_i = E(y_i|x_i) + e_i = \beta_1 + \beta_2 x_i + e_i, \quad i = 1, \ldots, N$$

The Monte Carlo parameter values are $\beta_1 = 100$ and $\beta_2 = 10$. The value of x_i is 10 for the first $N/2$ observations and 20 for the remaining $N/2$ observations, so that the regression functions are

$$E(y_i|x_i = 10) = 100 + 10x_i = 100 + 10 \times 10 = 200, \quad i = 1, \ldots, N/2$$
$$E(y_i|x_i = 20) = 100 + 10x_i = 100 + 10 \times 20 = 300, \quad i = (N/2) + 1, \ldots, N$$

Table 5B.1 **The least squares estimators, tests, and interval estimators**

N	$\overline{b}_1$	$\overline{b}_2$	$\overline{\hat{\sigma}^2}$	REJECT	COVER	CLOSE
20	99.4368	10.03317	2496.942	0.0512	0.9538	0.3505
40	100.0529	9.99295	2498.030	0.0524	0.9494	0.4824
100	99.7237	10.01928	2500.563	0.0518	0.9507	0.6890
200	99.8427	10.00905	2497.473	0.0521	0.9496	0.8442
500	100.0445	9.99649	2499.559	0.0464	0.9484	0.9746
1,000	100.0237	9.99730	2498.028	0.0517	0.9465	0.9980

In this appendix we modify the simulation in an important way. The random errors are independently distributed but with normalized chi-square distributions. In Figure B.7 the *pdf*s of several chi-square distributions are shown. We will use the $\chi^2_{(4)}$ in this simulation, which is skewed with a long tail to the right. Let $v_i \sim \chi^2_{(4)}$. The expected value and variance of this random variable are $E(v_i) = 4$ and $var(v_i) = 8$, respectively, so that $z_i = (v_i - 4)/\sqrt{8}$ has mean zero and variance one. The random errors we employ are $e_i = 50z_i$ so that $var(e_i|x_i) = \sigma^2 = 2500$, as in earlier appendices.

As before we use $M = 10000$ Monte Carlo simulations, using the sample sizes $N = 20$, 40 (as before), 100, 200, 500, and 1000. Our objectives are to illustrate that the least squares estimators of β_1, β_2, and the estimator $\hat{\sigma}^2$ are unbiased, and to investigate whether hypothesis tests and interval estimates perform as they should, even though the errors are not normally distributed. As in Appendix 3C we

- Test the null hypothesis $H_0 : \beta_2 = 10$ using the one-tail alternative $H_0 : \beta_2 > 0$. The critical value for the test is the 95th percentile of the *t*-distribution with $N - 2$ degrees of freedom, $t_{(0.95,N-2)}$. We report the percentage of rejections from this test (*REJECT*).

- Construct a 95% interval estimate for β_2 and report the percentage of the estimates (*COVER*) that contain the true parameter, $\beta_2 = 10$.

- Compute the percentage of the time (*CLOSE*) that the estimates b_2 are in the interval $\beta_2 \pm 1$, or between 9 and 11. Based on our theory, this percentage should increase toward 1 as N increases.

The Monte Carlo simulation results are summarized in Table 5B.1.

The unbiasedness of the least squares estimators is verified by the average values of the estimates' being very close to the true parameter values for all sample sizes. The percentage of estimates that are "close" to the true parameter value rises as the sample size N increases, verifying the consistency of the estimator. Because the rejection rates from the *t*-test are close to 0.05 and the coverage of the interval estimates is close to 95%, the approximate normality of the estimators is very good. To illustrate, in Figure 5B.2 we present the histogram of the estimates b_2 for $N = 40$. It is very bell-shaped, with the superimposed normal density function fitting it very well. The non-normality of the errors does not invalidate inferences in this model, even with only $N = 40$ sample observations.

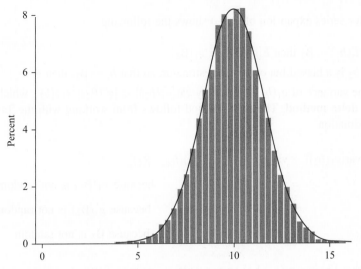

FIGURE 5B.2   Histogram of the estimates b_2 for $N = 40$.

◆5B.4   THE DELTA METHOD[5]

In Chapters 3.6, 5.3, 5.4, and 5.5 we discussed estimating and testing linear combinations of parameters. If the regression errors are normal, the results discussed there hold in finite samples. If the regression errors are not normal, then those results hold in large samples, as we discussed in the previous section. You will be surprised in the subsequent chapters how many times we become interested in **nonlinear functions** of regression parameters. For example, we may find ourselves interested in functions such as $g_1(\beta_2) = \exp(\beta_2/10)$ or $g_2(\beta_1, \beta_2) = \beta_1/\beta_2$. The first function $g_1(\beta_2)$ is a function of the single parameter β_2. Intuitively, we would estimate this function of β_2 using $g_1(b_2)$. The second function $g_2(\beta_1, \beta_2)$ is a function of two parameters, and, similarly, $g_2(b_1, b_2)$ seems like a reasonable estimator. Working with nonlinear functions of the estimated parameters requires additional tools, because even if the regression errors are normal, nonlinear functions of them are not normally distributed in finite samples, and usual variance formulas do not apply.

5B.4.1   Nonlinear Functions of a Single Parameter
The key to working with nonlinear functions of a single parameter is the Taylor series approximation discussed in Appendix A, Derivative Rule 9. It is stated there as

$$f(x) \cong f(a) + \frac{df(x)}{dx}\bigg|_{x=a} (x - a) = f(a) + f'(a)(x - a)$$

The value of a function at x is approximately equal to the value of the function at $x = a$, plus the derivative of the function evaluated at $x = a$, times the difference $x-a$. This approximation works well when the function is smooth and the difference $x-a$ is not too large. We will apply this rule to $g_1(b_2)$ replacing x with b_2 and a with β_2

$$g_1(b_2) \cong g_1(\beta_2) + g_1'(\beta_2)(b_2 - \beta_2) \tag{5B.5}$$

---

[5] This section contains advanced material.

This Taylor series expansion of $g_1(b_2)$ shows the following:

1. If $E(b_2) = \beta_2$ then $E[g_1(b_2)] \cong g_1(\beta_2)$.
2. If b_2 is a biased but consistent estimator, so that $b_2 \xrightarrow{p} \beta_2$, then $g_1(b_2) \xrightarrow{p} g_1(\beta_2)$.
3. The variance of $g_1(b_2)$ is given by $\text{var}[g_1(b_2)] \cong [g_1'(\beta_2)]^2 \text{var}(b_2)$, which is known as the **delta method**. The delta method follows from working with the Taylor series approximation

$$\text{var}[g_1(b_2)] \cong \text{var}[g_1(\beta_2) + g_1'(\beta_2)(b_2 - \beta_2)]$$

$$= \text{var}[g_1'(\beta_2)(b_2 - \beta_2)] \quad \text{because } g_1(\beta_2) \text{ is not random}$$

$$= [g_1'(\beta_2)]^2 \text{var}(b_2 - \beta_2) \quad \text{because } g_1'(\beta_2) \text{ is not random}$$

$$= [g_1'(\beta_2)]^2 \text{var}(b_2) \quad \text{because } \beta_2 \text{ is not random}$$

4. The estimator $g_1(b_2)$ has an approximate normal distribution in large samples,

$$g_1(b_2) \overset{a}{\sim} N\left[g_1(\beta_2), \; [g_1'(\beta_2)]^2 \text{var}(b_2)\right] \tag{5B.6}$$

The asymptotic normality of $g_1(b_2)$ means that we can test nonlinear hypotheses about β_2, such as $H_0 : g_1(\beta_2) = c$, and we can construct interval estimates of $g_1(\beta_2)$ in the usual way. To implement the delta method we replace β_2 by its estimate b_2 and the true variance $\text{var}(b_2)$ by its estimate $\widehat{\text{var}(b_2)}$ which, for the simple regression model, is given in (2.21).

5B.4.2 The Delta Method Illustrated
To illustrate the delta method calculations, we use one sample from the $N = 20$ simulation, stored as *mc2.dat*. For these data values the fitted regression is

$$\hat{y} = 87.44311 + 10.68456x$$
$$\text{(se)} \quad (33.8764) \quad (2.1425)$$

The nonlinear function we consider is $g_1(\beta_2) = \exp(\beta_2/10)$. In the simulation we know the value of $\beta_2 = 10$, so the value of the function is $g_1(\beta_2) = \exp(\beta_2/10) = e^1 = 2.71828$. To apply the delta method we need the derivative, $g_1'(\beta_2) = \exp(\beta_2/10) \times (1/10)$ (see Appendix A, Derivative Rule 7), and the estimated covariance matrix in Table 5B.2.

The estimated value of the nonlinear function is

$$g_1(b_2) = \exp(b_2/10) = \exp(10.68456/10) = 2.91088$$

Table 5B.2 **Estimated covariance matrix**

	b_1	b_2
b_1	1147.61330	−68.85680
b_2	−68.85680	4.59045

Table 5B.3 **Estimates and tests of $g_1(\beta_2) = \exp(\beta_2/10)$**

N	$\overline{\exp(b_2/10)}$	REJECT
20	2.79647	0.0556
40	2.75107	0.0541
100	2.73708	0.0485
200	2.72753	0.0503
500	2.72001	0.0522
1000	2.71894	0.0555

The estimated variance is

$$\widehat{\text{var}[g_1(b_2)]} = [g_1'(b_2)]^2 \widehat{\text{var}(b_2)}) = [\exp(b_2/10) \times (1/10)]^2 \widehat{\text{var}(b_2)}$$

$$= [\exp(10.68456/10) \times (1/10)]^2 4.59045 = 0.38896$$

and $\text{se}[g_1(b_2)] = 0.62367$. The 95% interval estimate is

$$g_1(b_2) \pm t_{(0.975,20-2)}\text{se}[g_1(b_2)] = 2.91088 \pm 2.10092 \times 0.62367 = [1.60061, \quad 4.22116]$$

5B.4.3 Monte Carlo Simulation of the Delta Method

In this Monte Carlo simulation, again using 10,000 samples, we compute the value of the nonlinear function estimator $g_1(b_2) = \exp(b_2/10)$ for each sample, and we test the true null hypothesis $H_0 : g_1(\beta_2) = \exp(\beta_2/10) = e^1 = 2.71828$ using a two-tail test at the 5% level of significance. We are interested in how well the estimator does in finite samples (recall that the random errors are not normally distributed and that the function is nonlinear), and how well the test performs. In Table 5B.3 we report the average of the parameter estimates for each sample size. Note that the mean estimate converges towards the true value as N becomes larger. The test at the 5% level of significance rejects the true null hypothesis about 5% of the time. The test statistic is

$$t = \frac{g_1(b_2) - 2.71828}{\text{se}[g_1(b_2)]} \sim t_{(N-2)}$$

The fact that the t-test rejects the correct percentage of the time implies not only that the estimates are well behaved, but that the standard error in the denominator is correct, and that the distribution of the statistic is "close" to its limiting standard normal distribution.

The histogram of the estimates for sample size $N = 40$ in Figure 5B.3 shows only the very slightest deviation from normality, which is why the t-test performs so well.

◆◆5B.5 THE DELTA METHOD EXTENDED[6]

When working with functions of two (or more) parameters, the approach is much the same, but the Taylor series approximation changes to a more general form. For a function of two parameters the Taylor series approximation is

---

[6] This section contains advanced material. For an advanced discussion (requires matrix algebra) of the general case see William Greene, *Econometric Analysis 6e*, (Upper Saddle River, NJ: Pearson Prentice-Hall, 2008), 1055–1056.

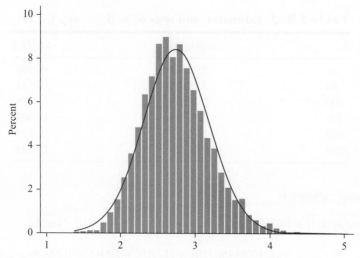

FIGURE *5B.3*   Histogram of $g_1(b_2) = \exp(b_2/10)$.

$$g_2(b_1, b_2) \cong g_2(\beta_1, \beta_2) + \frac{\partial g_2(\beta_1, \beta_2)}{\partial \beta_1}(b_1 - \beta_1) + \frac{\partial g_2(\beta_1, \beta_2)}{\partial \beta_2}(b_2 - \beta_2) \qquad (5B.7)$$

1. If $E(b_1) = \beta_1$ and $E(b_2) = \beta_2$ then $E[g_2(b_1, b_2)] \cong g_2(\beta_1, \beta_2)$.
2. If b_1 and b_2 are consistent estimators, so that $b_1 \xrightarrow{p} \beta_1$ and $b_2 \xrightarrow{p} \beta_2$, then $g_2(b_1, b_2) \xrightarrow{p} g_2(\beta_1, \beta_2)$.
3. The variance of $g_2(b_1, b_2)$ is given by the **delta method** as

$$\mathrm{var}[g_2(b_1, b_2)] \cong \left[\frac{\partial g_2(\beta_1, \beta_2)}{\partial \beta_1}\right]^2 \mathrm{var}(b_1) + \left[\frac{\partial g_2(\beta_1, \beta_2)}{\partial \beta_2}\right]^2 \mathrm{var}(b_2)$$
$$+ 2\left[\frac{\partial g_2(\beta_1, \beta_2)}{\partial \beta_1}\right]\left[\frac{\partial g_2(\beta_1, \beta_2)}{\partial \beta_2}\right]\mathrm{cov}(b_1, b_2) \qquad (5B.8)$$

4. The estimator $g_2(b_1, b_2)$ has an approximate normal distribution in large samples,

$$g_2(b_1, b_2) \overset{a}{\sim} N\big(g_2(\beta_1, \beta_2),\ \mathrm{var}[g_2(b_1, b_2)]\big) \qquad (5B.9)$$

The asymptotic normality of $g_2(b_1, b_2)$ means that we can test nonlinear hypotheses such as $H_0 : g_2(\beta_1, \beta_2) = c$, and we can construct interval estimates of $g_2(\beta_1, \beta_2)$ in the usual way. In practice we evaluate the derivatives at the estimates b_1 and b_2, and the variances and covariances by their usual estimates from equations like those for the simple regression model in (2.20)–(2.22).

5B.5.1   The Delta Method Illustrated: Continued

The nonlinear function of two parameters that we consider is $g_2(\beta_1, \beta_2) = \beta_1/\beta_2$. To employ the delta method we require the derivatives (see Appendix A, Derivative Rules 3 and 6)

Table 5B.4 **Estimates $g_2(b_1, b_2) = b_1/b_2$**

N	$\overline{b_1/b_2}$
20	11.50533
40	10.71856
100	10.20997
200	10.10097
500	10.05755
1000	10.03070

$$\frac{\partial g_2(\beta_1, \beta_2)}{\partial \beta_1} = \frac{1}{\beta_2}$$

and

$$\frac{\partial g_2(\beta_1, \beta_2)}{\partial \beta_2} = -\frac{\beta_1}{\beta_2^2}$$

The estimate $g_2(b_1, b_2) = b_1/b_2 = 87.44311/10.68456 = 8.18406$ and its estimated variance is

$$\overline{\text{var}[g_2(b_1, b_2)]} = \left[\frac{1}{b_2}\right]^2 \overline{\text{var}(b_1)} + \left[-\frac{b_1}{b_2^2}\right]^2 \overline{\text{var}(b_2)} + 2\left[\frac{1}{b_2}\right]\left[-\frac{b_1}{b_2^2}\right] \overline{\text{cov}(b_1, b_2)}$$

$$= 22.61857$$

The resulting 95% interval estimate for b_1/b_2 is $[-1.807712, \quad 18.17583]$. While all this seems incredibly complicated, most software packages will compute at least the estimates and standard errors automatically. And now that you understand the calculations, you can be confident when you use the "canned" routines.

5B.5.2 Monte Carlo Simulation of the Extended Delta Method

The mean estimates in Table 5B.4 show that there is some bias in the estimates for small samples sizes. However, the bias diminishes as the sample size increases and is close to the true value, 10, when $N = 100$.

The Monte Carlo simulated values of $g_2(b_1, b_2) = b_1/b_2$ are shown in Figure 5B.4a and 5B.4b from the experiments with $N = 40$, and $N = 200$. With sample size $N = 40$ there is pronounced skewness. With $N = 200$ the distribution of the estimates is much more symmetric and bell-shaped.

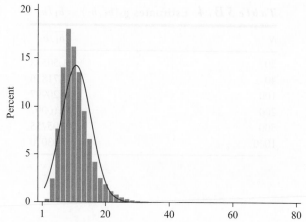

FIGURE 5B.4a   Histogram of $g_2(b_1, b_2) = b_1/b_2$, $N = 40$.

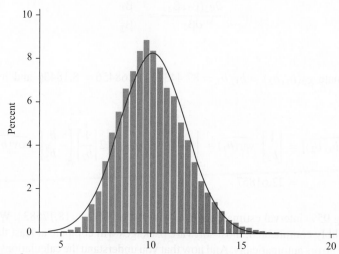

FIGURE 5B.4b   Histogram of $g_2(b_1, b_2) = b_1/b_2$, $N = 200$.

Chapter 6

Further Inference in the Multiple Regression Model

Learning Objectives

Based on the material in this chapter, you should be able to

1. Explain the concepts of restricted and unrestricted sums of squared errors and how they are used to test hypotheses.

2. Use the *F*-test to test single null hypotheses or joint null hypotheses.

3. Use your computer to perform an *F*-test.

4. Test the overall significance of a regression model, and identify the components of this test from your computer output.

5. From output of your computer software, locate (a) the sum of squared errors, (b) the *F*-value for the overall significance of a regression model, (c) the estimated covariance matrix for the least squares estimates, and (d) the correlation matrix for the explanatory variables.

6. Obtain restricted least squares estimates that include nonsample information in the estimation procedure.

7. Explain the properties of the restricted least squares estimator. In particular, how do its bias and variance compare with those of the unrestricted least squares estimator?

8. Explain the issues that need to be considered when choosing a regression model.

9. Explain what is meant by (a) an omitted variable and (b) an irrelevant variable. Explain the consequences of omitted and irrelevant variables for the properties of the least squares estimator.

10. Explain what the Akaike information criterion and the Schwarz criterion are used for.

11. Explain what is meant by collinearity and the consequences for least squares estimation.

12. Explain how RESET can pick up model misspecification.

Keywords

AIC	omitted variable	restricted *SSE*
auxiliary regressions	bias	SC
BIC	overall significance	single and joint null hypotheses
collinearity	prediction	testing many parameters
F-test	RESET	unrestricted model
irrelevant variable	restricted least	unrestricted *SSE*
nonsample information	squares	
omitted variable	restricted model	

Economists develop and evaluate theories about economic behavior. Hypothesis testing procedures are used to test these theories. In Chapter 5 we developed *t*-tests for null hypotheses consisting of a single restriction on one parameter β_k from the multiple regression model, and null hypotheses consisting of a single restriction that involves more than one parameter. In this chapter we extend our earlier analysis to testing a null hypothesis with two or more restrictions on two or more parameters. An important new development for such tests is the *F*-test.

The theories that economists develop sometimes provide **nonsample** information that can be used along with the information in a sample of data to estimate the parameters of a regression model. A procedure that combines these two types of information is called **restricted least squares**. It can be a useful technique when the data are not information-rich—a condition called collinearity—and the theoretical information is good. The restricted least squares procedure also plays a useful practical role when testing hypotheses. In addition to these topics, we discuss model specification for the multiple regression model, prediction, and the construction of prediction intervals. Model specification involves choosing a functional form and choosing a set of explanatory variables. In this chapter, we focus on issues related to variable choice. What happens if we omit a relevant variable? What happens if we include an irrelevant one? We also discuss the problems that arise if our data are not sufficiently rich because the variables are collinear or lack adequate variation.

The assumptions MR1–MR6 listed in Section 5.1 are adopted throughout this chapter. In particular, we assume the errors are normally distributed. This assumption is needed for the *t*- and *F*-test statistics to have their required distributions in samples of all sizes. If the errors are not normal, then the results presented in this chapter are still valid in the sense that they hold approximately if the sample size is large.

6.1 Testing Joint Hypotheses

In Chapter 5 we showed how to use one- and two-tail *t*-tests to test hypotheses involving

1. A single coefficient
2. A linear combination of coefficients
3. A nonlinear combination of coefficients

The test for a single coefficient was the most straightforward, requiring only the estimate of the coefficient and its standard error. For testing a linear combination of coefficients, computing the standard error of the estimated linear combination brought added complexity. It uses the variances and covariances of all estimates in the linear combination and can be computationally demanding if done on a hand calculator, especially if there are three or more coefficients in the linear combination. Software will perform the test automatically, however, yielding the standard error, the value of the t-statistic, and the p-value of the test.

For testing a nonlinear combination of coefficients, one must rely on large sample approximations for the test statistic and for the delta method used to compute the standard error. Derivatives of the nonlinear function and the covariance matrix of the coefficients are required, but as with a linear combination, software will perform the test automatically, computing the standard error for you, as well as the value of the t-statistic and its p-value. In Chapter 5 we gave an example of an interval estimate rather than a hypothesis test for a nonlinear combination, but that example—the optimal level of advertising—showed how to obtain all the ingredients needed for a test. For both hypothesis testing and interval estimation of a nonlinear combination, it is the standard error that requires more effort.

A characteristic of all the t tests in Chapter 5 is that they involve a single conjecture about one or more of the parameters—or, put another way, there is only one "equal sign" in the null hypothesis. In this chapter, we are interested in extending hypothesis testing to null hypotheses that involve multiple conjectures about the parameters. A null hypothesis with multiple conjectures, expressed with more than one equal sign, is called a **joint hypothesis**. An example of a joint hypothesis is testing whether a group of explanatory variables should be included in a particular model. Should variables on socioeconomic background, along with variables describing education and experience, be used to explain a person's wage? Does the quantity demanded of a product depend on the prices of substitute goods, or only on its own price? Economic hypotheses such as these must be formulated into statements about model parameters. To answer the first of the two questions, we set up a null hypothesis where the coefficients of all the socioeconomic variables are equal to zero. For the second question the null hypothesis would equate the coefficients of prices of all substitute goods to zero. Both are of the form

$$H_0 : \beta_4 = 0, \ \beta_5 = 0, \ \beta_6 = 0 \tag{6.1}$$

where β_4, β_5, and β_6 are the coefficients of the socioeconomic variables, or the coefficients of the prices of substitute goods. The joint null hypothesis in (6.1) contains three conjectures (three equal signs): $\beta_4 = 0$, $\beta_5 = 0$, and $\beta_6 = 0$. A test of H_0 is a joint test for whether all three conjectures hold simultaneously.

It is convenient to develop the test statistic for testing hypotheses such as (6.1) within the context of an example. We return to Big Andy's Burger Barn.

6.1.1 TESTING THE EFFECT OF ADVERTISING: THE *F*-TEST

The test used for testing a joint null hypothesis is the **F-test**. To introduce this test and concepts related to it, consider the Burger Barn sales model given in (5.22):

$$SALES = \beta_1 + \beta_2 PRICE + \beta_3 ADVERT + \beta_4 ADVERT^2 + e \tag{6.2}$$

Suppose now we wish to test whether *SALES* is influenced by advertising. Since advertising appears in (6.2) as both a linear term *ADVERT* and as a quadratic term *ADVERT*^{2}, advertising will have no effect on sales if $\beta_3 = 0$ *and* $\beta_4 = 0$; advertising will have an effect if $\beta_3 \neq 0$ or $\beta_4 \neq 0$ or if both β_3 and β_4 are nonzero. Thus, for this test our null and alternative hypotheses are

$$H_0 : \beta_3 = 0, \quad \beta_4 = 0$$

$$H_1 : \beta_3 \neq 0 \text{ or } \beta_4 \neq 0 \text{ or both are nonzero}$$

Relative to the null hypothesis $H_0 : \beta_3 = 0$, $\beta_4 = 0$, the model in (6.2) is called the **unrestricted model**; the restrictions in the null hypothesis have not been imposed on the model. It contrasts with the **restricted model**, which is obtained by assuming the parameter restrictions in H_0 are true. When H_0 is true, $\beta_3 = 0$ and $\beta_4 = 0$, and $ADVERT$ and $ADVERT^2$ drop out of the model. It becomes

$$SALES = \beta_1 + \beta_2 PRICE + e \tag{6.3}$$

The F-test for the hypothesis $H_0 : \beta_3 = 0$, $\beta_4 = 0$ is based on a comparison of the sums of squared errors (sums of squared least squares residuals) from the unrestricted model in (6.2) and the restricted model in (6.3). Our shorthand notation for these two quantities is SSE_U and SSE_R, respectively.

Adding variables to a regression reduces the sum of squared errors—more of the variation in the dependent variable becomes attributable to the variables in the regression and less of its variation becomes attributable to the error. In terms of our notation, $SSE_R - SSE_U \geq 0$. Using the data in the file *andy.dat* to estimate (6.2) and (6.3), we find that $SSE_U = 1532.084$ and $SSE_R = 1896.391$. Adding $ADVERT$ and $ADVERT^2$ to the equation reduces the sum of squared errors from 1896.391 to 1532.084.

What the F-test does is to assess whether this reduction is sufficiently large to be significant. If adding the extra variables has little effect on the sum of squared errors, then those variables contribute little to explaining variation in the dependent variable, and there is support for a null hypothesis that drops them. On the other hand, if adding the variables leads to a big reduction in the sum of squared errors, those variables contribute significantly to explaining the variation in the dependent variable, and we have evidence against the null hypothesis. The F-statistic determines what constitutes a large reduction or a small reduction in the sum of squared errors. It is given by

$$F = \frac{(SSE_R - SSE_U)/J}{SSE_U/(N - K)} \tag{6.4}$$

where J is the number of restrictions, N is the number of observations and K is the number of coefficients in the unrestricted model.

If the null hypothesis is true, then the statistic F has what is called an F-distribution with J numerator degrees of freedom and $N - K$ denominator degrees of freedom. Some details about this distribution are given in Appendix B.3.8, with its typical shape illustrated in Figure B.9; the reason why the expression in (6.4) has an F-distribution is given in an appendix to this chapter, Appendix 6A. **If the null hypothesis is not true,** then the difference between SSE_R and SSE_U becomes large, implying that the restrictions placed on the model by the null hypothesis significantly reduce the ability of the model to fit the data. A large value for $SSE_R - SSE_U$ means that the value of F tends to be *large*, so that we *reject* the null hypothesis if the value of the F-test statistic becomes too large. What is too large is decided by comparing the value of F to a critical value F_c, which leaves a probability α in the upper tail of the F-distribution with J and $N - K$ degrees of freedom. Tables of critical values for $\alpha = 0.01$ and $\alpha = 0.05$ are provided in Tables 4 and 5 at the end of the book. The rejection region $F > F_c$ is illustrated in Figure B.9.

Using the hypothesis testing steps introduced in Chapter 3, the F-test procedure for testing whether $ADVERT$ and $ADVERT^2$ should be excluded from the sales equation is as follows:

1. *Specify the null and alternative hypotheses:* The joint null hypothesis is $H_0 : \beta_3 = 0, \; \beta_4 = 0$. The alternative hypothesis is $H_1 : \beta_3 \neq 0$ or $\beta_4 \neq 0$ or both are nonzero.

2. *Specify the test statistic and its distribution if the null hypothesis is true:* Having two restrictions in H_0 means $J = 2$. Also, recall that $N = 75$, so the distribution of the F-test statistic when H_0 is true is

$$F = \frac{(SSE_R - SSE_U)/2}{SSE_U/(75 - 4)} \sim F_{(2,71)}$$

3. *Set the significance level and determine the rejection region:* Using $\alpha = 0.05$, the critical value from the $F_{(2,71)}$-distribution is $F_c = F_{(0.95, 2, 71)}$, giving a rejection region of $F \geq 3.126$. Alternatively, H_0 is rejected if p-value ≤ 0.05.

4. *Calculate the sample value of the test statistic and, if desired, the p-value:* The value of the F-test statistic is

$$F = \frac{(SSE_R - SSE_U)/J}{SSE_U/(N - K)} = \frac{(1896.391 - 1532.084)/2}{1532.084/(75 - 4)} = 8.44$$

   The corresponding p-value is $p = P(F_{(2,71)} > 8.44) = 0.0005$.

5. *State your conclusion:* Since $F = 8.44 > F_c = 3.126$, we reject the null hypothesis that both $\beta_3 = 0$ and $\beta_4 = 0$, and conclude that at least one of them is not zero. Advertising does have a significant effect upon sales revenue. The same conclusion is reached by noting that p-value $= 0.0005 < 0.05$.

You might ask where the value $F_c = F_{(0.95, 2, 71)} = 3.126$ came from. The F critical values in Tables 4 and 5 at the end of the book are reported for only a limited number of degrees of freedom. However, exact critical values such as the one for this problem can be obtained for any number of degrees of freedom using your econometric software.

6.1.2 TESTING THE SIGNIFICANCE OF THE MODEL

An important application of the F-test is for what is called testing the overall significance of a model. In Chapter 5.5.1 we tested whether the dependent variable y is related to a particular explanatory variable x_k using a t-test. In this section we extend this idea to a joint test of the relevance of *all* the included explanatory variables. Consider again the general multiple regression model with $(K - 1)$ explanatory variables and K unknown coefficients

$$y = \beta_1 + \beta_2 x_2 + \beta_3 x_3 + \cdots + \beta_K x_K + e \tag{6.5}$$

To examine whether we have a viable explanatory model, we set up the following null and alternative hypotheses:

$$H_0 : \beta_2 = 0, \; \beta_3 = 0, \; \cdots, \; \beta_K = 0$$
$$H_1 : \text{At least one of the } \beta_k \text{ is nonzero for } k = 2, 3, \ldots, K \tag{6.6}$$

The null hypothesis is a joint one because it has $K - 1$ components. It conjectures that each and every one of the parameters β_k, other than the intercept parameter β_1, are simultaneously zero. If this null hypothesis is true, none of the explanatory variables influence y, and thus our model is of little or no value. If the alternative hypothesis H_1 is true, then at least one of the parameters is not zero, and thus one or more of the explanatory variables should be included in the model. The alternative hypothesis does not indicate, however, which variables those might be. Since we are testing whether or not we have a viable explanatory model, the test for (6.6) is sometimes referred to as a **test of the overall significance of the regression model**. Given that the t-distribution can only be used to test a single null hypothesis, we use the F-test for testing the joint null hypothesis in (6.6). The unrestricted model is that given in (6.5). The restricted model, assuming the null hypothesis is true, becomes

$$y_i = \beta_1 + e_i \tag{6.7}$$

The least squares estimator of β_1 in this restricted model is $b_1^* = \sum_{i=1}^{N} y_i / N = \bar{y}$, which is the sample mean of the observations on the dependent variable. The *restricted* sum of squared errors from the hypothesis (6.6) is

$$SSE_R = \sum_{i=1}^{N} (y_i - b_1^*)^2 = \sum_{i=1}^{N} (y_i - \bar{y})^2 = SST$$

In this one case, in which we are testing the null hypothesis that all the model parameters are zero *except the intercept*, the restricted sum of squared errors is the total sum of squares (*SST*) from the full unconstrained model. The unrestricted sum of squared errors is the sum of squared errors from the unconstrained model—that is, $SSE_U = SSE$. The number of restrictions is $J = K - 1$. Thus, to test the overall significance of a model, *but not in general*, the F-test statistic can be modified and written as

$$F = \frac{(SST - SSE)/(K - 1)}{SSE/(N - K)} \tag{6.8}$$

The calculated value of this test statistic is compared to a critical value from the $F_{(K-1, N-K)}$ distribution. It is used to test the overall significance of a regression model. The outcome of the test is of fundamental importance when carrying out a regression analysis, and it is usually automatically reported by computer software as the F-value.

To illustrate, we test the overall significance of the regression, (6.2), used to explain Big Andy's sales revenue. We want to test whether the coefficients of *PRICE*, *ADVERT*, and *ADVERT*^{2} are all zero, against the alternative that at least one of these coefficients is not zero. Recalling that the model is $SALES = \beta_1 + \beta_2 PRICE + \beta_3 ADVERT + \beta_4 ADVERT^2 + e$, the hypothesis testing steps are as follows:

1. We are testing

$$H_0 : \quad \beta_2 = 0, \quad \beta_3 = 0, \quad \beta_4 = 0$$

against the alternative

$$H_1 : \quad \text{At least one of } \beta_2 \text{ or } \beta_3 \text{ or } \beta_4 \text{ is nonzero}$$

2. If H_0 is true, $F = \dfrac{(SST - SSE)/(4 - 1)}{SSE/(75 - 4)} \sim F_{(3, 71)}$.

3. Using a 5% significance level, we find the critical value for the F-statistic with $(3,71)$ degrees of freedom is $F_c = 2.734$. Thus, we reject H_0 if $F \geq 2.734$.

4. The required sums of squares are $SST = 3115.482$ and $SSE = 1532.084$ which give an F-value of

$$F = \frac{(SST - SSE)/(K - 1)}{SSE/(N - K)} = \frac{(3115.482 - 1532.084)/3}{1532.084/(75 - 4)} = 24.459$$

Also, p-value $= P(F \geq 24.459) = 0.0000$, correct to four decimal places.

5. Since $24.459 > 2.734$, we reject H_0 and conclude that the estimated relationship is a significant one. A similar conclusion is reached using the p-value. We conclude that at least one of *PRICE*, *ADVERT*, or *ADVERT*^{2} have an influence on sales. Note that this conclusion is consistent with conclusions that would be reached using separate t-tests for the significance of each of the coefficients in (5.24).

Go back and check the output from your computer software. Can you find the F-value 24.459 and the corresponding p-value of 0.0000 that form part of the routine output?

6.1.3   THE RELATIONSHIP BETWEEN t- AND F-TESTS

In Section 6.1.1, we tested whether advertising affects sales by using an F-test to test whether $\beta_3 = 0$ and $\beta_4 = 0$ in the model

$$SALES = \beta_1 + \beta_2 PRICE + \beta_3 ADVERT + \beta_4 ADVERT^2 + e \qquad (6.9)$$

Suppose now we want to test whether *PRICE* affects *SALES*. Following the same F-testing procedure, we have $H_0 : \beta_2 = 0$, $H_1 : \beta_2 \neq 0$, and the restricted model

$$SALES = \beta_1 + \beta_3 ADVERT + \beta_4 ADVERT^2 + e \qquad (6.10)$$

Estimating (6.9) and (6.10) gives $SSE_U = 1532.084$ and $SSE_R = 2683.411$, respectively. The required F-value is

$$F = \frac{(SSE_R - SSE_U)/J}{SSE_U/(N - K)} = \frac{(2683.411 - 1532.084)/1}{1532.084/(75 - 4)} = 53.355$$

The 5% critical value is $F_c = F_{(0.95, 1, 71)} = 3.976$. Thus, we reject $H_0 : \beta_2 = 0$.

You might be wondering why we have used an F-test to test $H_0 : \beta_2 = 0$ when we could have used the t-test for significance of an individual coefficient described in Chapter 5.5.1. There is only one conjecture in the null hypothesis. It is not a joint hypothesis. Will the two tests give the same result? What is the relationship between the t- and F-tests?

When testing a single "equality" null hypothesis (a single restriction) against a "not equal to" alternative hypothesis, either a t-test or an F-test can be used; the test outcomes will be identical. The reason for this correspondence is an exact relationship between the t- and F-distributions. The square of a t random variable with df degrees of freedom is an F random variable with 1 degree of freedom in the numerator and df degrees of freedom in the denominator. It has distribution $F_{(1,df)}$.

To use a t-test for testing $H_0 : \beta_2 = 0$ against $H_1 : \beta_2 \neq 0$, we return to (5.24), which presented the results from estimating (6.9). It is given by

$$\widehat{SALES} = 109.72 - 7.640\,PRICE + 12.151\,ADVERT - 2.768\,ADVERT^2$$
$$(\text{se}) \qquad (6.80)\ (1.046) \qquad\qquad (3.556) \qquad\qquad (0.941)$$

The t-value for testing $H_0 : \beta_2 = 0$ against $H_1 : \beta_2 \neq 0$ is $t = 7.640/1.045939 = 7.30444$. Its square is $t^2 = (7.30444)^2 = 53.355$, which is identical to the F-value calculated above. The 5% critical value for the t-test is $t_c = t_{(0.975,\,71)} = 1.9939$, whose square is $t_c^2 = 1.9939^2 = 3.976 = F_c$, the critical value for the F-test. Because of these exact relationships, the p-values for the two tests are identical, meaning that we will always reach the same conclusion whichever approach we take. However, there is no equivalence when using a one-tail t-test, since the F-test is not appropriate when the alternative is an inequality such as $>$ or $<$. The equivalence between t-tests and F-tests also does not carry over when a null hypothesis consists of more than a single restriction. Under these circumstances, where $J \geq 2$, the t-test cannot be used, but an F-test is available.

We can summarize the elements of an F-test as follows:

1. The null hypothesis H_0 consists of one or more equality restrictions on the model parameters β_k. The number of restrictions is denoted by J. When $J = 1$, the null hypothesis is called a single null hypothesis. When $J \geq 2$, it is called a joint null hypothesis. The null hypothesis may not include any "greater than or equal to" or "less than or equal to" hypotheses.

2. The alternative hypothesis states that one or more of the equalities in the null hypothesis is not true. The alternative hypothesis may not include any "greater than" or "less than" options.

3. The test statistic is the F-statistic in (6.4).

4. If the null hypothesis is true, F has the F-distribution with J numerator degrees of freedom and $N - K$ denominator degrees of freedom. The null hypothesis is *rejected* if $F > F_c$, where $F = F_{(1-\alpha, J, N-K)}$ is the critical value that leaves α percent of the probability in the upper tail of the F-distribution.

5. When testing a single equality null hypothesis, it is perfectly correct to use either the t- or F-test procedure: they are equivalent. In practice, it is customary to test single restrictions using a t-test. The F-test is usually reserved for joint hypotheses.

6.1.4   MORE GENERAL F-TESTS

So far we have discussed the F-test in the context of whether a variable or a group of variables could be excluded from the model. The conjectures made in the null hypothesis were that particular coefficients are equal to zero. The F-test can also be used for much more general hypotheses. Any number of conjectures ($\leq K$) involving linear hypotheses with equal signs can be tested. Deriving the restricted model implied by H_0 can be trickier, but the same general principles hold. The restricted sum of squared errors is still greater than the unrestricted sum of squared errors. In the restricted model, least squares estimates are obtained by minimizing the sum of squared errors subject to the restrictions on the parameters being true, and the unconstrained minimum (SSE_U) is always less than the constrained minimum (SSE_R). If SSE_U and SSE_R are substantially different, assuming that the null hypothesis is true significantly reduces the ability of the model to fit the data; in other words, the data do not support the null hypothesis, and it is rejected by the F-test. On the other hand, if the null hypothesis is true, we expect the data to be compatible with the conditions placed on the parameters. We expect little change in the sum of squared errors, in which case the null hypothesis will not be rejected by the F-test.

For an example we return to Chapter 5.6.3, where we found that the optimal amount for Andy to spend on advertising, $ADVERT_0$, is such that

$$\beta_3 + 2\beta_4 ADVERT_0 = 1 \tag{6.11}$$

Now suppose that Big Andy has been spending \$1,900 per month on advertising and he wants to know whether this amount could be optimal. Does the information from the estimated equation provide sufficient evidence to reject a hypothesis that \$1,900 per month is optimal? The null and alternative hypotheses for this test are

$$H_0 : \beta_3 + 2 \times \beta_4 \times 1.9 = 1 \qquad H_1 : \beta_3 + 2 \times \beta_4 \times 1.9 \neq 1$$

After carrying out the multiplication, these hypotheses can be written as

$$H_0 : \beta_3 + 3.8\beta_4 = 1 \qquad H_1 : \beta_3 + 3.8\beta_4 \neq 1$$

How do we obtain the restricted model implied by the null hypothesis? Note that when H_0 is true, $\beta_3 = 1 - 3.8\beta_4$. Substituting this restriction into the unrestricted model in (6.9) gives

$$SALES = \beta_1 + \beta_2 PRICE + (1 - 3.8\beta_4)ADVERT + \beta_4 ADVERT^2 + e$$

Collecting terms and rearranging this equation to put it in a form convenient for estimation yields

$$(SALES - ADVERT) = \beta_1 + \beta_2 PRICE + \beta_4(ADVERT^2 - 3.8ADVERT) + e \tag{6.12}$$

Estimating this model by least squares with dependent variable $y = SALES - ADVERT$ and explanatory variables $x_2 = PRICE$ and $x_3 = ADVERT^2 - 3.8ADVERT$ yields the restricted sum of squared errors $SSE_R = 1552.286$. The unrestricted sum of squared errors is the same as before, $SSE_U = 1532.084$. We also have one restriction ($J = 1$) and $N-K = 71$ degrees of freedom. Thus, the calculated value of the F-statistic is

$$F = \frac{(1552.286 - 1532.084)/1}{1532.084/71} = 0.9362$$

For $\alpha = 0.05$, the critical value is $F_c = 3.976$. Since $F = 0.9362 < F_c = 3.976$, we do not reject H_0. We conclude that Andy's conjecture, that an advertising expenditure of \$1,900 per month is optimal is compatible with the data.

Because there is only one conjecture in H_0, you can also carry out this test using the t-distribution. Check it out. For the t-value you should find $t = 0.9676$. The value $F = 0.9362$ is equal to $t^2 = (0.9676)^2$, obeying the relationship between t- and F-random variables that we mentioned previously. You will also find that the p-values are identical. Specifically,

$$p\text{-value} = P(F_{(1,71)} > 0.9362) = P(t_{(71)} > 0.9676) + P(t_{(71)} < -0.9676) = 0.3365$$

The result $0.3365 > 0.05$ leads us to conclude that $ADVERT_0 = 1.9$ is compatible with the data.

You may have noticed that our description of this test has deviated slightly from the step-by-step hypothesis testing format introduced in Chapter 3 and used so far in the book. The same ingredients were there, but the arrangement of them varied. From now on, we will be less formal about following these steps. By being less formal, we can expose you to the type of discussion you will find in research reports, but please remember that the steps were introduced for a purpose: to teach you good habits. Following the steps ensures that you include a description of all the relevant components of the test and that you think about the steps in the correct order. It is **not correct,** for example, to decide on the hypotheses or the rejection region **after** you observe the value of the statistic.

6.1.4a A One-Tail Test

Suppose that instead of wanting to test whether the conjecture "$ADVERT = 1.9$ is optimal" is supported by the data, Big Andy wants to test whether the optimal value of $ADVERT$ is greater than 1.9. If he has been spending $1,900 per month on advertising, and he does not want to increase this amount unless there is convincing evidence that the optimal amount is greater than $1,900, he will set up the hypotheses

$$H_0 : \beta_3 + 3.8\,\beta_4 \leq 1 \qquad H_1 : \beta_3 + 3.8\,\beta_4 > 1 \tag{6.13}$$

In this case, we can no longer use the F-test. Because $F = t^2$, the F-test cannot distinguish between the left and right tails as is needed for a one-tail test. We restrict ourselves to the t-distribution when considering alternative hypotheses that have inequality signs such as $<$ or $>$. If you proceed with a t-test for (6.13), your calculations will reveal $t = 0.9676$. The rejection region for a 5% significane level is as follows: Reject H_0 if $t \geq 1.667$. Because $0.9676 < 1.667$, we do not reject H_0. There is not enough evidence in the data to suggest that the optimal level of advertising expenditure is greater than $1,900.

6.1.5 USING COMPUTER SOFTWARE

Though it is possible and instructive to compute an F-value by using the restricted and unrestricted sums of squares, it is often more convenient to use the power of econometric software. Most software packages have commands that will automatically compute t- and F-values and their corresponding p-values when provided with a null hypothesis. You should check your software. Can you work out how to get it to test null hypotheses such as those we constructed? These tests belong to a class of tests called **Wald tests**; your software might refer to them in this way. Can you reproduce the answers we got for all the tests in Chapters 5 and 6?

We conclude this section with a joint test of two of Big Andy's conjectures. In addition to proposing that the optimal level of monthly advertising expenditure is $1,900, Big Andy is planning staffing and purchasing of inputs on the assumption that when $PRICE = \$6$ and $ADVERT = 1.9$, sales revenue will be $80,000 on average. That is, in the context of our model, and in terms of the regression coefficients β_k, the conjecture is

$$E(SALES) = \beta_1 + \beta_2 PRICE + \beta_3 ADVERT + \beta_4 ADVERT^2$$
$$= \beta_1 + 6\beta_2 + 1.9\,\beta_3 + 1.9^2\,\beta_4$$
$$= 80$$

Are the conjectures about sales and optimal advertising compatible with the evidence contained in the sample of data? We formulate the joint null hypothesis

$$H_0 : \beta_3 + 3.8\,\beta_4 = 1 \ and \ \beta_1 + 6\,\beta_2 + 1.9\,\beta_3 + 3.61\,\beta_4 = 80$$

The alternative is that at least one of these restrictions is not true. Because there are $J = 2$ restrictions to test jointly, we use an F-test. A t-test is not suitable. Note also that this is an example of a test with two restrictions that are more general than simply omitting variables. Constructing the restricted model requires substituting both of these restrictions into our extended model, which is left as an exercise. Using instead computer output obtained by supplying the two hypotheses directly to the software, we obtain a computed value for the F-statistic of 5.74 and a corresponding p-value of 0.0049. At a 5% significance level, the joint null hypothesis is rejected. As another exercise, use the least squares estimates to predict sales revenue for $PRICE = 6$ and $ADVERT = 1.9$. Has Andy been too optimistic about the level of sales, or too pessimistic?

6.2 The Use of Nonsample Information

In many estimation problems we have information over and above the information contained in the sample observations. This nonsample information may come from many places, such as economic principles or experience. When it is available, it seems intuitive that we should find a way to use it. If the nonsample information is correct, and if we combine it with the sample information, the precision with which we can estimate the parameters is improved.

To illustrate how we might go about combining sample and nonsample information, consider a model designed to explain the demand for beer. From the theory of consumer choice in microeconomics, we know that the demand for a good will depend on the price of that good, on the prices of other goods—particularly substitutes and complements—and on income. In the case of beer, it is reasonable to relate the quantity demanded (Q) to the price of beer (PB), the price of liquor (PL), the price of all other remaining goods and services (PR), and income (I). To estimate this demand relationship, we need a further assumption about the functional form. Using "ln" to denote the natural logarithm, we assume, for this case, that the log-log functional form is appropriate:

$$\ln(Q) = \beta_1 + \beta_2 \ln(PB) + \beta_3 \ln(PL) + \beta_4 \ln(PR) + \beta_5 \ln(I) \tag{6.14}$$

This model is a convenient one because it precludes infeasible negative prices, quantities, and income, and because the coefficients β_2, β_3, β_4, and β_5 are elasticities. See Chapter 4.6.

A relevant piece of nonsample information can be derived by noting that if all prices and income go up by the same proportion, we would expect there to be no change in quantity demanded. For example, a doubling of all prices and income should not change the quantity of beer consumed. This assumption is that economic agents do not suffer from "money illusion." Let us impose this assumption on our demand model and see what happens. Having all prices and income change by the same proportion is equivalent to multiplying each price and income by a constant. Denoting this constant by λ and multiplying each of the variables in (6.14) by λ yields

$$\begin{aligned}
\ln(Q) &= \beta_1 + \beta_2\ln(\lambda PB) + \beta_3\ln(\lambda PL) + \beta_4\ln(\lambda PR) + \beta_5\ln(\lambda I) \\
&= \beta_1 + \beta_2\ln(PB) + \beta_3\ln(PL) + \beta_4\ln(PR) + \beta_5\ln(I) \qquad (6.15) \\
&\quad + (\beta_2 + \beta_3 + \beta_4 + \beta_5)\ln(\lambda)
\end{aligned}$$

Comparing (6.14) with (6.15) shows that multiplying each price and income by λ will give a change in $\ln(Q)$ equal to $(\beta_2 + \beta_3 + \beta_4 + \beta_5)\ln(\lambda)$. Thus, for there to be no change in $\ln(Q)$ when all prices and income go up by the same proportion, it must be true that

$$\beta_2 + \beta_3 + \beta_4 + \beta_5 = 0 \qquad (6.16)$$

Thus, we can say something about how quantity demanded should not change when prices and income change by the same proportion, and this information can be written in terms of a specific restriction on the parameters of the demand model. We call such a restriction **nonsample information**. If we believe that this nonsample information makes sense, and hence that the parameter restriction in (6.16) holds, then it seems desirable to be able to obtain estimates that obey this restriction.

To obtain estimates that obey (6.16), we begin with the multiple regression model

$$\ln(Q) = \beta_1 + \beta_2\ln(PB) + \beta_3\ln(PL) + \beta_4\ln(PR) + \beta_5\ln(I) + e \qquad (6.17)$$

and a sample of data consisting of 30 years of annual data on beer consumption collected from a randomly selected household. These data are stored in the file *beer.dat*.

To introduce the nonsample information, we solve the parameter restriction $\beta_2 + \beta_3 + \beta_4 + \beta_5 = 0$ for one of the β_k's. Which one is not important mathematically, but for reasons explained below we solve for β_4:

$$\beta_4 = -\beta_2 - \beta_3 - \beta_5$$

Substituting this expression into the original model in (6.17) gives

$$\begin{aligned}
\ln(Q) &= \beta_1 + \beta_2\ln(PB) + \beta_3\ln(PL) + (-\beta_2 - \beta_3 - \beta_5)\ln(PR) + \beta_5\ln(I) + e \\
&= \beta_1 + \beta_2\big[\ln(PB) - \ln(PR)\big] + \beta_3\big[\ln(PL) - \ln(PR)\big] \\
&\quad + \beta_5\big[\ln(I) - \ln(PR)\big] + e \\
&= \beta_1 + \beta_2\ln\left(\frac{PB}{PR}\right) + \beta_3\ln\left(\frac{PL}{PR}\right) + \beta_5\ln\left(\frac{I}{PR}\right) + e \qquad (6.18)
\end{aligned}$$

We have used the parameter restriction to eliminate the parameter β_4, and in so doing, and using the properties of logarithms, we have constructed the new variables $\ln(PB/PR)$, $\ln(PL/PR)$, and $\ln(I/PR)$. The last line in (6.18) is our restricted model. To get least squares estimates that satisfy the parameter restriction, called **restricted least squares estimates**, we apply the least squares estimation procedure directly to the restricted model in (6.18). The estimated equation is

$$\widehat{\ln(Q)} = -4.798 - 1.2994\ln\left(\frac{PB}{PR}\right) + 0.1868\ln\left(\frac{PL}{PR}\right) + 0.9458\ln\left(\frac{I}{PR}\right) \qquad (6.19)$$
$$\text{(se)} \qquad\qquad (0.166) \qquad\qquad (0.284) \qquad\qquad (0.427)$$

Let the restricted least squares estimates in (6.19) be denoted by b_1^*, b_2^*, b_3^*, and b_5^*. To obtain an estimate for β_4, we use the restriction

$$b_4^* = -b_2^* - b_3^* - b_5^* = -(-1.2994) - 0.1868 - 0.9458 = 0.1668$$

By using the restriction *within* the model, we have ensured that the estimates obey the constraint, so that $b_2^* + b_3^* + b_4^* + b_5^* = 0$. Though it is always possible to obtain restricted estimates by substituting the constraints into the model, it may become messy if there are a number of restrictions or if the restrictions involve several parameters. Some software packages have commands that automatically compute the restricted least squares estimates when provided with the constraints. You should check out the commands available in your software.

What are the properties of this restricted least squares estimation procedure? First, the restricted least squares *estimator* is biased, $E(b_k^*) \neq \beta_k$, *unless* the constraints we impose are *exactly* true. This result makes an important point about econometrics. A good *economist* will obtain more reliable parameter estimates than a poor one, because a good economist will introduce better nonsample information. This is true at the time of model specification as well as later, when constraints might be applied to the model. Nonsample information is not restricted to constraints on the parameters; it is also used for model specification. *Good economic theory* is a very important ingredient in empirical research.

The second property of the restricted least squares estimator is that its variance is smaller than the variance of the least squares estimator, *whether the constraints imposed are true or not*. By combining nonsample information with the sample information, we reduce the variation in the estimation procedure caused by random sampling. This reduction in variance obtained by imposing restrictions on the parameters is not at odds with the Gauss–Markov theorem. The Gauss–Markov result that the least squares estimator is the best linear unbiased estimator applies to linear and unbiased estimators that use data alone, and no constraints on the parameters. Including additional information with the data gives the added reward of a reduced variance. If the additional nonsample information is correct, we are unambiguously better off; the restricted least squares estimator is unbiased and has lower variance. If the additional nonsample information is incorrect, the reduced variance comes at the cost of bias. This bias can be a big price to pay if it leads to estimates substantially different from their corresponding true parameter values. Evidence on whether or not a restriction is true can be obtained by testing the restriction along the lines of the previous section. In the case of this particular demand example, the test is left as an exercise.

6.3 Model Specification

In what has been covered so far, we have generally taken the role of the model as given. Questions have been of the following type: Given a particular regression model, what is the best way to estimate its parameters? Given a particular model, how do we test hypotheses about the parameters of that model? How do we construct interval estimates for the parameters of a model? What are the properties of estimators in a given model? Given that all these questions require knowledge of the model, it is natural to ask where the model comes from. In any econometric investigation, choice of the model is one of the first steps. In this section, we focus on the following questions: What are the important considerations when choosing a model? What are the consequences of choosing the wrong model? Are there ways of assessing whether a model is adequate?

Three essential features of model choice are (1) choice of functional form, (2) choice of explanatory variables (regressors) to be included in the model, and (3) whether the multiple regression model assumptions MR1–MR6, listed in Chapter 5, hold. Later chapters on heteroskedasticity, autocorrelation, and random regressors deal with violations of the assumptions. For choice of functional form and regressors, economic principles and logical reasoning play a prominent and vital role. We need to ask: What variables are likely to influence the dependent variable y? How is y likely to respond when these variables change: at a constant rate? at a decreasing rate? Is it reasonable to assume constant elasticities over the whole range of the data? The answers to these questions have a bearing on regressor choice and choice of a suitable functional form. Alternative functional forms were considered in Chapters 2.8, 4.3 to 4.6, and 5.6 to 5.7. We turn now to consider the consequences of choosing the wrong set of regressors and some questions about regressor choice.

6.3.1   OMITTED VARIABLES

It is possible that a chosen model may have important variables omitted. Our economic principles may have overlooked a variable, or lack of data may lead us to drop a variable even when it is prescribed by economic theory. To introduce the **omitted-variable problem**, we consider a sample of married couples such that both husbands and wives work. This sample was used by labor economist Tom Mroz in a classic paper on female labor force participation. The variables from this sample that we use in our illustration are stored in the file *edu_inc.dat*. The dependent variable is annual family income *FAMINC* defined as the combined income of husband and wife. We are interested in the impact of level of education—both the husband's years of education (*HEDU*) and the wife's years of education (*WEDU*)—on family income. The estimated relationship is

$$\widehat{FAMINC} = -5534 + 3132\,HEDU + 4523\,WEDU$$

$$\text{(se)} \quad (11230) \quad (803) \quad\quad (1066) \quad\quad\quad (6.20)$$

$$(p\text{-value}) \quad (0.622) \quad (0.000) \quad\quad (0.000)$$

We estimate that an additional year of education for the husband will increase annual income by \$3,132, and an additional year of education for the wife will increase income by \$4,523.

What happens if we now incorrectly omit wife's education from the equation? The estimated equation becomes

$$\widehat{FAMINC} = 26191 + 5155\,HEDU$$

$$\text{(se)} \quad\quad (8541) \quad (658) \quad\quad\quad\quad (6.21)$$

$$(p\text{-value}) \quad (0.002) \quad (0.000)$$

Relative to (6.20), omitting *WEDU* leads us to overstate the effect of an extra year of education for the husband by about \$2,000. This change in the magnitude of a coefficient is typical of the effect of incorrectly omitting a relevant variable. Omission of a relevant variable (defined as one whose coefficient is nonzero) leads to an estimator that is biased. Naturally enough, this bias is known as **omitted-variable bias**. To give a general expression for this bias for the case in which one explanatory variable is omitted from a model with two explanatory variables, we write the underlying model for (6.20) as

$$y = \beta_1 + \beta_2 x_2 + \beta_3 x_3 + e \quad\quad\quad (6.22)$$

Table 6.1 **Correlation Matrix for Variables Used in Family Income Example**

	FAMINC	HEDU	WEDU	KL6	X_5	X_6
FAMINC	1.000					
HEDU	0.355	1.000				
WEDU	0.362	0.594	1.000			
KL6	−0.072	0.105	0.129	1.000		
X_5	0.290	0.836	0.518	0.149	1.000	
X_6	0.351	0.821	0.799	0.160	0.900	1.000

where $y = FAMINC$, $x_2 = HEDU$, and $x_3 = WEDU$. Omitting x_3 from the equation is equivalent to imposing the restriction $\beta_3 = 0$. It can be viewed as an example of imposing an incorrect constraint on the parameters. As discussed in the previous section, the implications of an incorrect constraint are biased coefficient estimates, but a reduced variance. Let b_2^* be the least squares estimator for β_2 when x_3 is omitted from the equation. In an appendix to this chapter, Appendix 6B, we show that

$$\text{bias}(b_2^*) = E(b_2^*) - \beta_2 = \beta_3 \frac{\overline{\text{cov}(x_2, x_3)}}{\overline{\text{var}(x_2)}} \tag{6.23}$$

Knowing the sign of β_3 and the sign of the covariance between x_2 and x_3 tells us the direction of the bias. Also, while omitting a variable from the regression usually biases the least squares estimator, if the sample covariance (or sample correlation) between x_2 and the omitted variable x_3 is zero, then the least squares estimator in the misspecified model is still unbiased.

To analyze (6.23) in the context of our example, first note that $\beta_3 > 0$ because husband's education has a positive effect on family income. Also, from Table 6.1, $\overline{\text{cov}(x_2, x_3)} > 0$ because husband's and wife's levels of education are positively correlated. Thus, the bias exhibited in (6.21) is positive. There are, of course, other variables that could be included in (6.20) as explanators of family income. In the following equation we include *KL6*, the number of children less than six years old. The larger the number of young children, the fewer the number of hours likely to be worked; hence, a lower family income would be expected.

$$\begin{aligned}\widehat{FAMINC} &= -7755 + 3212\,HEDU + 4777\,WEDU - 14311\,KL6 \\ \text{(se)} &\quad\;\; (11163) \quad\;\; (797) \quad\quad\;\; (1061) \quad\quad\;\; (5004) \\ (p\text{-value}) &\quad\;\; (0.488) \quad\;\; (0.000) \quad\quad\; (0.000) \quad\quad\; (0.004)\end{aligned} \tag{6.24}$$

We estimate that a child under six reduces family income by \$14,311. Notice that compared to (6.20), the coefficient estimates for *HEDU* and *WEDU* have not changed a great deal. This outcome occurs because *KL6* is not highly correlated with the education variables. From a general modeling perspective, it means that useful results can still be obtained when a relevant variable is omitted if that variable is uncorrelated with the included variables and our interest is on the coefficients of the included variables. (Such instances can arise, for example, if data are not available for the relevant omitted variable.)

6.3.2 IRRELEVANT VARIABLES

The consequences of omitting relevant variables may lead you to think that a good strategy is to include as many variables as possible in your model. However, doing so will not only complicate your model unnecessarily, but may also inflate the variances of your estimates because of the presence of **irrelevant variables**. To see the effect of irrelevant variables, we add two artificially generated variables X_5 and X_6 to (6.24). These variables were constructed so that they are correlated with *HEDU* and *WEDU* (see Table 6.1) but are not expected to influence family income. The resulting estimated equation is

$$\widehat{FAMINC} = -7759 + 3340\,HEDU + 5869\,WEDU - 14200\,KL6 + 889X_5 - 1067X_6$$

$$(\text{se}) \quad (11195)\ (1250) \qquad (2278) \qquad\quad (5044) \qquad (2242) \quad (1982)$$

$$(p\text{-value}) \quad (0.500)\ (0.008) \qquad (0.010) \qquad\quad (0.005) \qquad (0.692) \quad (0.591)$$

What can we observe from these estimates? First, as expected, the coefficients of X_5 and X_6 have p-values greater than 0.05. They do indeed appear to be irrelevant variables. Also, the standard errors of the coefficients estimated for all other variables have increased, with p-values increasing correspondingly. The inclusion of irrelevant variables has reduced the precision of the estimated coefficients for other variables in the equation. This result follows because by the Gauss–Markov theorem, the least squares estimator of the correct model is the minimum variance linear unbiased estimator.

6.3.3 CHOOSING THE MODEL

The possibilities of omitted-variable bias or inflated variances from irrelevant variables mean that it is important to specify an appropriate set of explanatory variables. Unfortunately, doing so is often not an easy task. There is no one set of mechanical rules that can be applied to come up with the best model. What is needed is an intelligent application of both theoretical knowledge and the outcomes of various statistical tests. Better choices come with experience. What is important is to recognize ways of assessing whether a model is reasonable or not. Some points worth keeping in mind are as follows:

1. Choose variables and a functional form on the basis of your theoretical and general understanding of the relationship.

2. If an estimated equation has coefficients with unexpected signs, or unrealistic magnitudes, they could be caused by a misspecification such as the omission of an important variable.

3. One method for assessing whether a variable or a group of variables should be included in an equation is to perform significance tests. That is, t-tests for hypotheses such as $H_0: \beta_3 = 0$ or F-tests for hypotheses such as $H_0: \beta_3 = \beta_4 = 0$. Failure to reject hypotheses such as these can be an indication that the variable(s) are irrelevant. However, it is important to remember that failure to reject a null hypothesis can also occur if the data are not sufficiently rich to disprove the hypothesis. More will be said about poor data in the next section. For the moment we note that, when a variable has an insignificant coefficient, it can either be (a) discarded as an irrelevant variable or (b) retained because the theoretical reason for its inclusion is a strong one.

4. At different times in the history of econometrics and statistics, various model selection criteria have been introduced based on maximizing R^2 or minimizing the sum of squared errors (*SSE*) subject to a penalty for too many variables. We will describe three of these in Section 6.3.4: an adjusted R^2, the Akaike information criterion (AIC), and the Schwarz criterion (SC), also known as the Bayesian information criterion (BIC).

5. The adequacy of a model can be tested using a general specification test known as RESET. This test is described in Section 6.3.5.

6.3.4   MODEL SELECTION CRITERIA

In this section we consider three model selection criteria: $\overline{R}^2$, AIC, and SC (BIC). Throughout the section you should keep in mind that we are not recommending blind application of any of these criteria; they should be treated as devices that provide additional information about the relative merits of alternative models, and they should be used in conjunction with the other considerations listed in Section 6.3.3 and the introduction to Section 6.3.

A common feature of the criteria we describe is that they are suitable only for comparing models with the same dependent variable, not models with different dependent variables like y and $\ln(y)$. More general versions of the AIC and SC, based on likelihood functions,[1] are available for models with transformations of the dependent variable, but we do not consider them here.

6.3.4a   The Adjusted Coefficient of Determination
In Chapters 4 and 5 we introduced the coefficient of determination $R^2 = 1 - SSE/SST$ as a measure of goodness of fit. It shows the proportion of variation in a dependent variable explained by variation in the explanatory variables. Since it is desirable to have a model that fits the data well, there can be a tendency to think that the best model is the one with the highest R^2. Although this line of thinking is legitimate if we are comparing models with the same number of explanatory variables, it breaks down when we are adding or deleting variables. The problem is that R^2 can be made large by adding more and more variables, even if the variables added have no justification. Algebraically, it is a fact that as variables are added the sum of squared errors SSE goes down, and thus R^2 goes up. If the model contains $N - 1$ variables, then $R^2 = 1$.

An alternative measure of goodness of fit called the adjusted-R^2, denoted as $\overline{R}^2$, has been suggested to overcome this problem. It is computed as

$$\overline{R}^2 = 1 - \frac{SSE/(N - K)}{SST/(N - 1)} \tag{6.25}$$

This measure does not always go up when a variable is added, because of the degrees of freedom term $N - K$ in the numerator. As the number of variables K increases, SSE goes down, but so does $N - K$. The effect on $\overline{R}^2$ depends on the amount by which SSE falls. While solving one problem, this corrected measure of goodness of fit unfortunately introduces other problems. It loses its interpretation; $\overline{R}^2$ is no longer the proportion of explained variation. Also, it can be shown that if a variable is added to an equation, say with coefficient β_K, then $\overline{R}^2$ will increase if the t-value for testing the hypothesis $H_0 : \beta_K = 0$ is greater than one. Thus, using $\overline{R}^2$ as a device for selecting the appropriate set of explanatory variables is like using a hypothesis test for significance of a coefficient with a critical value of one, a value much less than that typically used with 5% and 10% levels of significance. Because of these complications, we prefer to report the unadjusted R^2 as a goodness-of-fit measure, and caution is required if $\overline{R}^2$ is used for model selection. Nevertheless, you should be familiar with $\overline{R}^2$. You will see it in research reports and on the output of software packages.

---

[1] An introduction to maximum likelihood estimation can be found in Appendix C8.

6.3.4b Information Criteria

Selecting variables to maximize $\overline{R}^2$ can be viewed as selecting variables to minimize *SSE*, subject to a penalty for introducing too many variables. Both the AIC and the SC work in a similar way, but with different penalties for introducing too many variables. The **Akaike information criterion (AIC)** is given by

$$\text{AIC} = \ln\left(\frac{SSE}{N}\right) + \frac{2K}{N} \tag{6.26}$$

and the **Schwarz criterion (SC)**, also known as the **Bayesian information criterion (BIC)**, is given by

$$\text{SC} = \ln\left(\frac{SSE}{N}\right) + \frac{K\ln(N)}{N} \tag{6.27}$$

In each case, the first term becomes smaller as extra variables are added, reflecting the decline in the *SSE*, but the second term becomes larger, because K increases. Because $K\ln(N)/N > 2K/N$ for $N \geq 8$, in reasonable sample sizes the SC penalizes extra variables more heavily than does the AIC. Using these criteria, the model with the smallest AIC, or the smallest SC, is preferred.

To get values of the more general versions of these criteria based on maximized values of the likelihood function, you need to add $[1 + \ln(2\pi)]$ to (6.26) and (6.27). It is good to be aware of this fact in case your computer software reports the more general versions. However, although it obviously changes the AIC and SC values, adding a constant does not change the choice of variables that minimize the criteria.

6.3.4c An Example

To illustrate the different criteria, we have computed the R^2, $\overline{R}^2$, AIC, and SC for the different family income equations that were estimated earlier in this section. They are presented in Table 6.2. Notice that adding more variables always increases the R^2, whether they are relevant or not. The $\overline{R}^2$ increases when relevant variables are added, but declines in the last case when the irrelevant variables *X5* and *X6* are added. The AIC and SC are smallest for the model with variables *HEDU*, *WEDU*, and *KL6*. Thus, in this case, but not necessarily in general, maximizing $\overline{R}^2$, minimizing AIC, and minimizing SC all lead to selection of the same model.

6.3.5 RESET

Testing for model misspecification is a way of asking whether our model is adequate, or whether we can improve on it. It could be misspecified if we have omitted important

Table 6.2 Goodness-of-Fit and Information Criteria for Family Income Example

Included Variables	R^2	$\overline{R}^2$	AIC	SC
HEDU	0.1258	0.1237	21.262	21.281
HEDU, WEDU	0.1613	0.1574	21.225	21.253
HEDU, WEDU, KL6	0.1771	0.1714	21.211	21.248
HEDU, WEDU, KL6, X5, X6	0.1778	0.1681	21.219	21.276

variables, included irrelevant ones, chosen a wrong functional form, or have a model that violates the assumptions of the multiple regression model. RESET (REgression Specification Error Test) is designed to detect omitted variables and incorrect functional form. It proceeds as follows.

Suppose that we have specified and estimated the regression model

$$y = \beta_1 + \beta_2 x_2 + \beta_3 x_3 + e$$

Let (b_1, b_2, b_3) be the least squares estimates, and let

$$\hat{y} = b_1 + b_2 x_2 + b_3 x_3 \tag{6.28}$$

be the predicted values of y. Consider the following two artificial models:

$$y = \beta_1 + \beta_2 x_2 + \beta_3 x_3 + \gamma_1 \hat{y}^2 + e \tag{6.29}$$

$$y = \beta_1 + \beta_2 x_2 + \beta_3 x_3 + \gamma_1 \hat{y}^2 + \gamma_2 \hat{y}^3 + e \tag{6.30}$$

In (6.29) a test for misspecification is a test of $H_0: \gamma_1 = 0$ against the alternative $H_1: \gamma_1 \neq 0$. In (6.30), testing $H_0: \gamma_1 = \gamma_2 = 0$ against $H_1: \gamma_1 \neq 0$ and/or $\gamma_2 \neq 0$ is a test for misspecification. In the first case a t- or an F-test can be used. An F-test is required for the second equation. Rejection of H_0 implies that the original model is inadequate and can be improved. A failure to reject H_0 says that the test has not been able to detect any misspecification.

To understand the idea behind the test, note that $\hat{y}^2$ and $\hat{y}^3$ will be polynomial functions of x_2 and x_3. If you square and cube both sides of (6.28), you will get terms such as x_2^2, x_3^3, $x_2 x_3$, $x_2 x_3^2$, and so on. Since polynomials can approximate many different kinds of functional forms, if the original functional form is not correct, the polynomial approximation that includes $\hat{y}^2$ and $\hat{y}^3$ may significantly improve the fit of the model. If it does, this fact will be detected through nonzero values of γ_1 and γ_2. Furthermore, if we have omitted variables and these variables are correlated with x_2 and x_3, then they are also likely to be correlated with terms like x_2^2 and x_3^2, so some of their effect may be picked up by including the terms $\hat{y}^2$ and/or $\hat{y}^3$. Overall, the general philosophy of the test is: If we can significantly improve the model by artificially including powers of the predictions of the model, then the original model must have been inadequate.

Applying the two forms of RESET in (6.29) and (6.30) to the family income equation in (6.24) yields the following results:

$$H_0: \gamma_1 = 0 \qquad F = 5.984 \quad p\text{-value} = 0.015$$

$$H_0: \gamma_1 = \gamma_2 = 0 \quad F = 3.123 \quad p\text{-value} = 0.045$$

In both cases the null hypothesis of no misspecification is rejected at a 5% significance level. So although this equation was a useful one for illustrating the effect of omitted-variable bias, it could be improved upon as a model for explaining family income. Perhaps age and experience could be included in the model, along with whether the household is in a city or the country. Perhaps the linear functional form is inappropriate.

Although RESET is often useful for picking up poorly specified models, keep in mind that it will not always discriminate between alternative models. For example, if two different functional forms are being considered for a particular relationship, it is possible for RESET to reject neither of them.

6.4 Poor Data, Collinearity, and Insignificance

Most economic data that are used for estimating economic relationships are nonexperimental. Indeed, in most cases they are simply "collected" for administrative or other purposes. They are not the result of a planned experiment in which an experimental design is specified for the explanatory variables. In controlled experiments the right-hand-side variables in the model can be assigned values in such a way that their individual effects can be identified and estimated with precision. When data are the result of an uncontrolled experiment, many of the economic variables may move together in systematic ways. Such variables are said to be **collinear**, and the problem is labeled **collinearity**. In this case there is no guarantee that the data will be "rich in information," nor that it will be possible to isolate the economic relationship or parameters of interest.

As an example, consider the problem faced by the marketing executives at Big Andy's Burger Barn when they try to estimate the increase in sales revenue attributable to advertising that appears in newspapers *and* the increase in sales revenue attributable to coupon advertising. Suppose that it has been common practice to coordinate these two advertising devices, so that at the same time that advertising appears in the newspapers there are flyers distributed containing coupons for price reductions on hamburgers. If variables measuring the expenditures on these two forms of advertising appear on the right-hand side of a sales revenue equation such as (5.2), then the data on these variables will show a systematic, positive relationship; intuitively, it will be difficult for such data to reveal the separate effects of the two types of ads. Although it is clear that total advertising expenditure increases sales revenue, because the two types of advertising expenditure move together, it may be difficult to sort out their separate effects on sales revenue.

As a second example, consider a production relationship explaining output over time as a function of the amounts of various quantities of inputs employed. There are certain factors of production (inputs), such as labor and capital, that are used in *relatively fixed proportions*. As production increases, the changing amounts of two or more such inputs reflect equiproportionate increases. Proportional relationships between variables are the very sort of systematic relationships that epitomize "collinearity." Any effort to measure the individual or separate effects (marginal products) of various mixes of inputs from such data will be difficult.

It is not just relationships between variables in a sample of data that make it difficult to isolate the separate effects of individual explanatory variables. If the values of an explanatory variable do not vary or change much within a sample of data, then it is clearly difficult to use that data to estimate a coefficient that describes the effect of change in that variable. It is hard to estimate the effect of change if there has been no change.

6.4.1 The Consequences of Collinearity

The consequences of collinearity and/or lack of variation depend on whether we are examining an extreme case in which estimation breaks down or a bad, but not extreme, case in which estimation can still proceed but our estimates lack precision. In Section 5.3.1, we considered the model

$$y_i = \beta_1 + \beta_2 x_2 + \beta_3 x_3 + e_i$$

and wrote the variance of the least squares estimator for β_2 as

$$\text{var}(b_2) = \frac{\sigma^2}{\left(1 - r_{23}^2\right) \sum_{i=1}^{N} (x_2 - \bar{x}_2)^2} \tag{6.31}$$

where r_{23} is the correlation between x_2 and x_3. Exact or extreme collinearity exists when x_2 and x_3 are perfectly correlated, in which case $r_{23} = 1$ and var(b_2) goes to infinity. Similarly, if x_2 exhibits no variation $\sum(x_2 - \bar{x}_2)^2$ equals zero and var(b_2) again goes to infinity. In this case x_2 is collinear with the constant term. In general, w*henever there are one or more **exact** linear relationships among the explanatory variables, then the condition of exact collinearity exists. In this case the least squares estimator is not defined.* We *cannot* obtain estimates of β_k's using the least squares principle. One of our least squares assumptions MR5, which says that the values of x_{ik} are not exact linear functions of the other explanatory variables, is violated.

The more usual case is one in which correlations between explanatory variables might be high, but not exactly one; variation in explanatory variables may be low but not zero; or linear dependencies between more than two explanatory variables could be high but not exact. These circumstances do *not* constitute a violation of least squares assumptions. By the Gauss–Markov theorem, the least squares estimator is still the best linear unbiased estimator. We might still be unhappy, however, if the best we can do is constrained by the poor characteristics of our data. From (6.31) we can see that when r_{23} is close to one or $\sum(x_2 - \bar{x}_2)^2$ is close to zero, the variance of b_2 will be large. A large variance means a large standard error, which means the estimate may not be significantly different from zero and an interval estimate will be wide. The sample data have provided relatively imprecise information about the unknown parameters. The effects of this imprecise information can be summarized as follows:

1. When estimator standard errors are large, it is likely that the usual *t*-tests will lead to the conclusion that parameter estimates are not significantly different from zero. This outcome occurs despite possibly high R^2- or F-values indicating significant explanatory power of the model as a whole. The problem is that collinear variables do not provide enough information to estimate their separate effects, even though theory may indicate their importance in the relationship.

2. Estimators may be very sensitive to the addition or deletion of a few observations, or to the deletion of an apparently insignificant variable.

3. Despite the difficulties in isolating the effects of individual variables from such a sample, accurate forecasts may still be possible if the nature of the collinear relationship remains the same within the out-of-sample observations. For example, in an aggregate production function where the inputs labor and capital are nearly collinear, accurate forecasts of output may be possible for a particular ratio of inputs but not for various mixes of inputs.

6.4.2 AN EXAMPLE

The file *cars.dat* contains observations on the following variables for 392 cars:

MPG = miles per gallon
CYL = number of cylinders
ENG = engine displacement in cubic inches
WGT = vehicle weight in pounds

Suppose we are interested in estimating the effect of *CYL, ENG,* and *WGT* on *MPG*. All the explanatory variables are related to the power and size of the car. Although there are exceptions, overall we would expect the values for *CYL, ENG*, and *WGT* to be large for large cars and small for small cars. They are variables that are likely to be highly correlated and whose separate effect on *MPG* may be difficult to estimate. A regression of *MPG* on *CYL* yields

$$\widehat{MPG} = 42.9 - 3.558 \, CYL$$

$$\text{(se)} \qquad (0.83) \quad (0.146)$$

$$(p\text{-value}) \quad (0.000) \quad (0.000)$$

We estimate that an additional cylinder reduces the gasoline consumption by 3.6 miles per gallon, and the significance of its coefficient suggests that it is an important variable. Now, observe what happens when *ENG* and *WGT* are included. The estimated model becomes

$$\widehat{MPG} = 44.4 - 0.268 \, CYL - 0.0127 ENG - 0.00571 \, WGT$$

$$\text{(se)} \qquad (1.5) \quad (0.413) \qquad (0.0083) \qquad (0.00071)$$

$$(p\text{-value}) \quad (0.000) \quad (0.517) \qquad (0.125) \qquad (0.000)$$

The estimated coefficient on *CYL* has changed dramatically, and although we know that number of cylinders and engine size are important variables, when considered separately, their coefficients are not significantly different from zero at a 5% significance level. The null hypotheses $H_0 : \beta_2 = 0$ and $H_0 : \beta_3 = 0$ are not rejected by separate *t*-tests, where β_2 is the coefficient of *CYL* and β_3 is the coefficient of *ENG*. What is happening is that the high correlation between *CYL* and *ENG* ($r = 0.95$) is making it difficult to accurately estimate the effects of each variable. When we test the null hypothesis $H_0 : \beta_2 = \beta_3 = 0$ against the alternative $H_1 : \beta_2 \neq 0$ and/or $\beta_3 \neq 0$, we obtain an *F*-value of 4.30 with corresponding *p*-value of 0.014. The null hypothesis is firmly rejected. The data are telling us that together *CYL* and *ENG* influence *MPG*, but it is difficult to sort out the influence of each. If one coefficient is free to take any value, the data are not good enough to prove that the other coefficient must be nonzero. Should you drop one of the insignificant variables, say, *CYL*? Doing so will reduce the variances of the remaining estimates, but given that *CYL* is an important variable that is highly correlated with *ENG* and *WGT*, it is also likely to introduce omitted-variable bias.

6.4.3 IDENTIFYING AND MITIGATING COLLINEARITY

Because nonexact collinearity is not a violation of least squares assumptions, it does not make sense to go looking for a problem if there is no evidence that one exists. If you have estimated an equation where the coefficients are precisely estimated and significant, they have the expected signs and magnitudes, and they are not sensitive to adding or deleting a few observations, or an insignificant variable, then there is no reason to try and identify or mitigate collinearity. If there are highly correlated variables, they are not causing you a problem. However, if you have a poorly estimated equation that does not live up to expectations, it is useful to establish why the estimates are poor.

One simple way to detect collinear relationships is to use sample correlation coefficients between pairs of explanatory variables. These sample correlations are descriptive measures of linear association. However, in some cases in which collinear relationships involve more than two of the explanatory variables, the collinearity may not be detected by examining pairwise correlations. In such instances, a second simple and effective procedure for identifying the presence of collinearity is to estimate the so-called auxiliary regressions.

In these least squares regressions, the left-hand-side variable is one of the *explanatory* variables and the right-hand-side variables are all the remaining explanatory variables. For example, a general auxiliary regression for x_2 is

$$x_2 = a_1 x_1 + a_3 x_3 + \cdots + a_K x_K + error$$

If R^2 from this artificial model is high, above 0.80, say, the implication is that a large portion of the variation in x_2 is explained by variation in the other explanatory variables. In Section 5.3.1 we made the point that it is variation in a variable that is *not* associated with any other explanatory variable that is valuable for improving the precision of the least squares estimator b_2. If R^2 from the auxiliary regression is not high, then the variation in x_2 is not explained by the other explanatory variables, and the estimator b_2's precision is not affected by this problem.

The collinearity problem is that the data do not contain enough "information" about the individual effects of explanatory variables to permit us to estimate all the parameters of the statistical model precisely. Consequently, one solution is to obtain more information and include it in the analysis. One form the new information can take is more, and better, sample data. Unfortunately, in economics, this is not always possible. Cross-sectional data are expensive to obtain, and, with time-series data, one must wait for the data to appear. Alternatively, if new data are obtained via the same nonexperimental process as the original sample of data, then the new observations may suffer the same collinear relationships and provide little in the way of new, independent information. Under these circumstances the new data will help little to improve the precision of the least squares estimates.

A second way of adding new information is to introduce, as we did in Section 6.2, *nonsample* information in the form of restrictions on the parameters. This nonsample information may then be combined with the sample information to provide restricted least squares estimates. The good news is that using nonsample information in the form of linear constraints on the parameter values reduces estimator sampling variability. The bad news is that the resulting restricted estimator is *biased* unless the restrictions are *exactly* true. Thus it is important to use good nonsample information, so that the reduced sampling variability is not bought at a price of large estimator biases.

6.5 Prediction

The prediction or forecasting problem for a linear model with one explanatory variable was covered in depth in Section 4.1. That material extends naturally to the more general model that has more than one explanatory variable.

To describe the extensions, consider a model with an intercept term and two explanatory variables x_2 and x_3. That is,

$$y_i = \beta_1 + x_2 \beta_2 + x_3 \beta_3 + e \tag{6.32}$$

where the e_i are uncorrelated random variables with mean 0 and variance σ^2. Given a set of values for the explanatory variables, say, $(1, x_{02}, x_{03})$, the prediction problem is to predict the value of the dependent variable y_0, which is given by

$$y_0 = \beta_1 + x_{02} \beta_2 + x_{03} \beta_3 + e_0$$

If the data are time-series data, $(1, x_{02}, x_{03})$ will be future values for the explanatory variables; for cross-section data they represent values for an individual or some other economic unit that was not sampled. We are assuming that the parameter values determining y_0 are the same as those in the model (6.32) describing how the original sample of data was generated. Also, we assume the random error e_0 to be uncorrelated with each of the sample errors e_i and to have the same mean zero and variance σ^2. Under these assumptions, the best linear unbiased predictor of y_0 is given by

$$\hat{y}_0 = b_1 + x_{02}b_2 + x_{03}b_3$$

where b_k's are the least squares estimators. This predictor is unbiased in the sense that the average value of the forecast or prediction error is zero. That is, if $f = (y_0 - \hat{y}_0)$ is the forecast error, then $E(f) = 0$. The predictor is best in the sense that the variance of the forecast error for all other linear and unbiased predictors of y_0 is not less than var$(y_0 - \hat{y}_0)$.

The variance of forecast error var$(y_0 - \hat{y}_0)$ contains two components. One component occurs because b_1, b_2, and b_3 are estimates of the true parameters, and the other component is a consequence of the unknown random error e_0. The expression for var$(y_0 - \hat{y}_0)$ is given by

$$
\begin{aligned}
\text{var}(f) &= \text{var}[(\beta_1 + \beta_2 x_{02} + \beta_3 x_{03} + e_0) - (b_1 + b_2 x_{02} + b_3 x_{03})] \\
&= \text{var}(e_0 - b_1 - b_2 x_{02} - b_3 x_{03}) \\
&= \text{var}(e_0) + \text{var}(b_1) + x_{02}^2 \text{var}(b_2) + x_{03}^2 \text{var}(b_3) \\
&\quad + 2x_{02} \, \text{cov}(b_1, b_2) + 2x_{03} \, \text{cov}(b_1, b_3) + 2x_{02}x_{03} \, \text{cov}(b_2, b_3)
\end{aligned}
\tag{6.33}
$$

To obtain var(f) we recognized that the unknown parameters and the values of the explanatory variables are constants, and that e_0 is uncorrelated with the sample data and thus is uncorrelated with the least squares estimators (b_1, b_2, b_3). The remaining terms in the last line of (6.33) are obtained using the rule for calculating the variance of a weighted sum in (P.20) of the Probability Primer.

Each of the terms in the expression for var(f) involves σ^2. To obtain the estimated variance of the forecast error $\widehat{\text{var}(f)}$, we replace σ^2 with its estimator $\hat{\sigma}^2$. The standard error of the forecast is given by se$(f) = \sqrt{\widehat{\text{var}(f)}}$. If the random errors e_i and e_0 are normally distributed, or if the sample is large, then

$$\frac{f}{\text{se}(f)} = \frac{y_0 - \hat{y}_0}{\sqrt{\widehat{\text{var}(y_0 - \hat{y}_0)}}} \sim t_{(N-K)}$$

Following the steps we have used many times, a $100(1-\alpha)\%$ interval predictor for y_0 is $\hat{y}_0 \pm t_c \text{se}(f)$, where t_c is a critical value from the $t_{(N-K)}$-distribution.

Thus, the methods for prediction in the model with $K = 3$ are straightforward extensions of the results from the simple linear regression model. For $K > 3$, the methods extend in a similar way.

6.5.1 AN EXAMPLE

As an example we find a 95% prediction interval for *SALES* at Big Andy's Burger Barn when $PRICE_0 = 6, ADVERT_0 = 1.9$, and $ADVERT_0^2 = 3.61$. These are the values considered by Big Andy in Section 6.1.5. The point prediction is

$$
\begin{aligned}
\widehat{SALES}_0 &= 109.719 - 7.640 \, PRICE_0 + 12.1512 \, ADVERT_0 - 2.768 \, ADVERT_0^2 \\
&= 109.719 - 7.640 \times 6 + 12.1512 \times 1.9 - 2.768 \times 3.61 \\
&= 76.974
\end{aligned}
$$

With the settings proposed by Big Andy, we forecast that sales will be \$76,974.

Table 6.3 **Covariance Matrix for Andy's Burger Barn Model**

	b_1	b_2	b_3	b_4
b_1	46.227019	−6.426113	−11.600960	2.939026
b_2	−6.426113	1.093988	0.300406	−0.085619
b_3	−11.600960	0.300406	12.646302	−3.288746
b_4	2.939026	−0.085619	−3.288746	0.884774

To obtain a prediction interval, we first need to compute the estimated variance of the forecast error. Extending (6.33) to accommodate four unknown coefficients, and using the covariance matrix values in Table 6.3, we have

$$
\begin{aligned}
\widehat{\mathrm{var}(f)} &= \hat{\sigma}^2 + \widehat{\mathrm{var}(b_1)} + x_{02}^2 \widehat{\mathrm{var}(b_2)} + x_{03}^2 \widehat{\mathrm{var}(b_3)} + x_{04}^2 \widehat{\mathrm{var}(b_4)} \\
&\quad + 2x_{02}\,\widehat{\mathrm{cov}(b_1,b_2)} + 2x_{03}\,\widehat{\mathrm{cov}(b_1,b_3)} + 2x_{04}\,\widehat{\mathrm{cov}(b_1,b_4)} \\
&\quad + 2x_{02}x_{03}\,\widehat{\mathrm{cov}(b_2,b_3)} + 2x_{02}x_{04}\,\widehat{\mathrm{cov}(b_2,b_4)} + 2x_{03}x_{04}\,\widehat{\mathrm{cov}(b_3,b_4)} \\
&= 21.57865 + 46.22702 + 6^2 \times 1.093988 + 1.9^2 \times 12.6463 + 3.61^2 \times 0.884774 \\
&\quad + 2 \times 6 \times (-6.426113) + 2 \times 1.9 \times (-11.60096) + 2 \times 3.61 \times 2.939026 \\
&\quad + 2 \times 6 \times 1.9 \times 0.300406 + 2 \times 6 \times 3.61 \times (-0.085619) \\
&\quad + 2 \times 1.9 \times 3.61 \times (-3.288746) \\
&= 22.4208
\end{aligned}
$$

The standard error of the forecast error is $\mathrm{se}(f) = \sqrt{22.4208} = 4.7351$, and the relevant t-value is $t_{(0.975,\,71)} = 1.9939$, giving a 95% prediction interval of

$$
(76.974 - 1.9939 \times 4.7351,\ 76.974 + 1.9939 \times 4.7351) = (67.533,\ 86.415)
$$

We predict, with 95% confidence, that Big Andy's settings for price and advertising expenditure will yield *SALES* between \$67,533 and \$86,415.

It is useful to distinguish between forecasting *SALES* in a given week, and estimating average sales over a number of weeks, given particular settings of *PRICE* and *ADVERT*. The point forecast and the point estimate are both the same

$$
\widehat{SALES_0} = \widehat{E(SALES_0)} = 76.974
$$

However, the standard error for $\widehat{E(SALES_0)}$ is much less than that for the forecast error from forecasting for a single week, $f = SALES_0 - \widehat{SALES_0}$. The difference arises because $\widehat{\mathrm{var}(f)}$ includes an estimate of the error variance $\hat{\sigma}^2$, and it is this value that contributes most to $\widehat{\mathrm{var}(f)}$. Using the expression for $\widehat{\mathrm{var}(f)}$ and the results given above, we can write

$$
\mathrm{se}\left(\widehat{E(SALES_0)}\right) = \sqrt{\widehat{\mathrm{var}(f)} - \hat{\sigma}^2} = \sqrt{22.4208 - 21.5786} = 0.9177
$$

Thus, a 95% interval estimate for $\widehat{E(SALES_0)}$ is

$$
(76.974 - 1.9939 \times 0.9177,\ 76.974 + 1.9939 \times 0.9177) = (75.144,\ 78.804)
$$

With 95% confidence we estimate that average sales over many weeks will lie between $75,144 and $78,804, but in any single week we forecast sales will be between $67,533 and $86,415.

6.6 Exercises

Answers to exercises marked * appear at www.wiley.com/go/global/hill.

6.6.1 PROBLEMS

6.1   When using $N = 40$ observations to estimate the model

$$y = \beta_1 + \beta_2 x + \beta_3 z + e$$

you obtain $SSE = 979.830$ and $s_y = 13.45222$. Find
(a) R^2
(b) The value of the F-statistic for testing $H_0: \beta_2 = \beta_3 = 0$ (Do you reject or fail to reject H_0?)

6.2   Consider again the model in Exercise 6.1. After augmenting this model with the squares and cubes of predictions $\hat{y}^2$ and $\hat{y}^3$, we obtain $SSE = 696.5357$. Use RESET to test for misspecification.

6.3* Consider the model
$$y = \beta_1 + x_2\beta_2 + x_3\beta_3 + e$$

and suppose that application of least squares to 20 observations on these variables yields the following results $\left(\widehat{\text{cov}(b)} \text{ denotes the estimated covariance matrix}\right)$:

$$\begin{bmatrix} b_1 \\ b_2 \\ b_3 \end{bmatrix} = \begin{bmatrix} 0.96587 \\ 0.69914 \\ 1.7769 \end{bmatrix}, \quad \widehat{\text{cov}(b)} = \begin{bmatrix} 0.21812 & 0.019195 & -0.050301 \\ 0.019195 & 0.048526 & -0.031223 \\ -0.050301 & -0.031223 & 0.037120 \end{bmatrix}$$

$$\hat{\sigma}^2 = 2.5193 \qquad R^2 = 0.9466$$

(a) Find the total variation, unexplained variation, and explained variation for this model.
(b) Find 95% interval estimates for β_2 and β_3.
(c) Use a t-test to test the hypothesis $H_0: \beta_2 \geq 1$ against the alternative $H_1: \beta_2 < 1$.
(d) Use your answers in part (a) to test the joint hypothesis $H_0: \beta_2 = 0, \beta_3 = 0$.
(e) Test the hypothesis $H_0: 2\beta_2 = \beta_3$.

6.4   Consider the wage equation

$$\ln(WAGE) = \beta_1 + \beta_2 EDUC + \beta_3 EDUC^2 + \beta_4 EXPER + \beta_5 EXPER^2$$
$$+ \beta_6 (EDUC \times EXPER) + \beta_7 HRSWK + e$$

where the explanatory variables are years of education, years of experience and hours worked per week. Estimation results for this equation, and for modified versions of it obtained by dropping some of the variables, are displayed in Table 6.4. These results are from the 1000 observations in the file *cps4c_small.dat*.
(a) Using an approximate 5% critical value of $t_c = 2$, what coefficient estimates are not significantly different from zero?
(b) What restriction on the coefficients of Eqn (A) gives Eqn (B)? Use an F-test to test this restriction. Show how the same result can be obtained using a t-test.

(c) What restrictions on the coefficients of Eqn (A) give Eqn (C)? Use an F-test to test these restrictions. What question would you be trying to answer by performing this test?

(d) What restrictions on the coefficients of Eqn (B) give Eqn (D)? Use an F-test to test these restrictions. What question would you be trying to answer by performing this test?

(e) What restrictions on the coefficients of Eqn (A) give Eqn (E)? Use an F-test to test these restrictions. What question would you be trying to answer by performing this test?

(f) Based on your answers to parts (a) to (e), which model would you prefer? Why?

(g) Compute the missing AIC value for Eqn (D) and the missing SC value for Eqn (A). Which model is favored by the AIC? Which model is favored by the SC?

6.5* Consider the wage equation

$$\ln(WAGE) = \beta_1 + \beta_2 EDUC + \beta_3 EDUC^2 + \beta_4 EXPER + \beta_5 EXPER^2 + \beta_6 HRSWK + e$$

(a) Suppose you wish to test the hypothesis that a year of education has the same effect on ln ($WAGE$) as a year of experience. What null and alternative hypotheses would you set up?

(b) What is the restricted model, assuming that the null hypothesis is true?

(c) Given that the sum of squared errors from the restricted model is $SSE_R = 254.1726$, test the hypothesis in (a). (For SSE_U use the relevant value from Table 6.4. The sample size is $N = 1,000$.)

Table 6.4 **Wage Equation Estimates for Exercises 6.4 and 6.5**

Variable	Coefficient Estimates and (Standard Errors)				
	Eqn (A)	Eqn (B)	Eqn (C)	Eqn (D)	Eqn (E)
C	1.055	1.252	1.573	1.917	0.904
	(0.266)	(0.190)	(0.188)	(0.080)	(0.096)
EDUC	0.0498	0.0289	0.0366		0.1006
	(0.0397)	(0.0344)	(0.0350)		(0.0063)
$EDUC^2$	0.00319	0.00352	0.00293		
	(0.00169)	(0.00166)	(0.00170)		
EXPER	0.0373	0.0303		0.0279	0.0295
	(0.0081)	(0.0048)		(0.0054)	(0.0048)
$EXPER^2$	−0.000485	−0.000456		−0.000470	−0.000440
	(0.000090)	(0.000086)		(0.000096)	(0.000086)
$EXPER \times EDUC$	−0.000510				
	(0.000482)				
HRSWK	0.01145	0.01156	0.01345	0.01524	0.01188
	(0.00137)	(0.00137)	(0.00136)	(0.00151)	(0.00136)
SSE	222.4166	222.6674	233.8317	280.5061	223.6716
AIC	−1.489	−1.490	−1.445		−1.488
SC		−1.461	−1.426	−1.244	−1.463

6.6   RESET suggests augmenting an existing model with the squares of the predictions $\hat{y}^2$, or with their squares and cubes $(\hat{y}^2, \hat{y}^3)$. What would happen if you augmented the model with the predictions themselves $\hat{y}$?

6.7   Table 6.5 contains output for the two models

$$y = \beta_1 + \beta_2 x + \beta_3 w + e$$
$$y = \beta_1 + \beta_2 x + e$$

obtained using $N = 35$ observations. RESET applied to the second model yields F-values of 17.98 (for $\hat{y}^2$) and 8.72 (for $\hat{y}^2$ and $\hat{y}^3$). The correlation between x and w is $r_{xw} = 0.975$. Discuss the following questions:
(a) Should w be included in the model?
(b) What can you say about omitted-variable bias?
(c) What can you say about the existence of collinearity and its possible effect?

6.8   In Section 6.1.5 we tested the joint null hypothesis

$$H_0: \beta_3 + 3.8\,\beta_4 = 1 \quad \text{and} \quad \beta_1 + 6\,\beta_2 + 1.9\,\beta_3 + 3.61\,\beta_4 = 80$$

in the model

$$SALES = \beta_1 + \beta_2 PRICE + \beta_3 ADVERT + \beta_4 ADVERT^2 + e$$

By substituting the restrictions into the model and rearranging variables, show how the model can be written in a form in which least squares estimation will yield restricted least squares estimates.

6.6.2   COMPUTER EXERCISES

6.9   In Exercise 5.25 we expressed the model

$$Y = \alpha K^{\beta_2} L^{\beta_3} E^{\beta_4} M^{\beta_5} \exp\{e\}$$

in terms of logarithms and estimated it using data in the file *manuf.dat*. Use the data and results from Exercise 5.25 to test the following hypotheses:
(a) $H_0: \beta_2 = 0$ against $H_1: \beta_2 \neq 0$.
(b) $H_0: \beta_2 = 0, \beta_3 = 0$ against $H_1: \beta_2 \neq 0$ and/or $\beta_3 \neq 0$.
(c) $H_0: \beta_2 = 0, \beta_4 = 0$ against $H_1: \beta_2 \neq 0$ and/or $\beta_4 \neq 0$.
(d) $H_0: \beta_2 = 0, \beta_3 = 0, \beta_4 = 0$ against $H_1: \beta_2 \neq 0$ and/or $\beta_3 \neq 0$ and/or $\beta_4 \neq 0$.
(e) $H_0: \beta_2 + \beta_3 + \beta_4 + \beta_5 = 1$ against $H_1: \beta_2 + \beta_3 + \beta_4 + \beta_5 \neq 1$.
(f) Analyze the impact of collinearity on this model.

Table 6.5   **Output for Exercise 6.7**

Variable	Coefficient	Std. Error	t-value	Coefficient	Std. Error	t-value
C	3.6356	2.763	1.316	−5.8382	2.000	−2.919
X	−0.99845	1.235	−0.8085	4.1072	0.3383	12.14
W	0.49785	0.1174	4.240			

6.10* Use the sample data for beer consumption in the file *beer.dat* to

(a) Estimate the coefficients of the demand relation (6.14) using only sample information. Compare and contrast these results to the restricted coefficient results given in (6.19).

(b) Does collinearity appear to be a problem?

(c) Test the validity of the restriction that implies that demand will not change if prices and income go up in the same proportion.

(d) Use model (6.19) to construct a 95% prediction interval for Q when $PB = 3.00, PL = 10, PR = 2.00$, and $I = 50000$. (*Hint*: Construct the interval for $\ln(Q)$ and then take antilogs.)

(e) Repeat part (d) using the unconstrained model from part (a). Comment.

6.11 Consider production functions of the form $Q = f(L, K)$, where Q is the output measure and L and K are labor and capital inputs, respectively. A popular functional form is the Cobb–Douglas equation

$$\ln(Q) = \beta_1 + \beta_2 \ln(L) + \beta_3 \ln(K) + e$$

(a) Use the data in the file *cobb.dat* to estimate the Cobb–Douglas production function. Is there evidence of collinearity?

(b) Re-estimate the model with the restriction of constant returns to scale—that is, $\beta_2 + \beta_3 = 1$—and comment on the results.

6.12* Using data in the file *beer.dat*, apply RESET to the two alternative models

$$\ln(Q) = \beta_1 + \beta_2 \ln(PB) + \beta_3 \ln(PL) + \beta_4 \ln(PR) + \beta_5 \ln(I) + e$$

$$Q = \beta_1 + \beta_2 PB + \beta_3 PL + \beta_4 PR + \beta_5 I + e$$

Which model seems to better reflect the demand for beer?

6.13 The file *toodyay.dat* contains 48 annual observations on a number of variables related to wheat yield in the Toodyay Shire of Western Australia, for the period 1950–1997. Those variables are

Y = wheat yield in tonnes per hectare,
t = trend term to allow for technological change,
RG = rainfall at germination (May–June),
RD = rainfall at development stage (July–August), and
RF = rainfall at flowering (September–October).

The unit of measurement for rainfall is centimeters. A model that allows for the yield response to rainfall to be different for the three different periods is

$$Y = \beta_1 + \beta_2 t + \beta_3 RG + \beta_4 RD + \beta_5 RF + e$$

(a) Estimate this model. Report the results and comment on the signs and significance of the estimated coefficients.

(b) Test the hypothesis that the response of yield to rainfall is the same irrespective of whether the rain falls during germination, development, or flowering.

(c) Estimate the model under the restriction that the three responses to rainfall are the same. Comment on the results.

6.14 Following on from the example in Section 6.3, the file *hwage.dat* contains another subset of the data used by labor economist Tom Mroz. The variables with which we are concerned are

HW = husband's wage in 2006 dollars
HE = husband's education attainment in years
HA = husband's age
CIT = a variable equal to one if living in a large city, otherwise zero

(a) Estimate the model

$$HW = \beta_1 + \beta_2 HE + \beta_3 HA + e$$

What effects do changes in the level of education and age have on wages?

(b) Does RESET suggest that the model in part (a) is adequate?

(c) Add the variables HE^2 and HA^2 to the original equation and re-estimate it. Describe the effect that education and age have on wages in this newly estimated model.

(d) Does RESET suggest that the model in part (c) is adequate?

(e) Reestimate the model in part (c) with the variable CIT included. What can you say about the level of wages in large cities relative to outside those cities?

(f) Do you think CIT should be included in the equation?

(g) For both the model estimated in part (c) and the model estimated in part (e), evaluate the following four derivatives:

(i) $\dfrac{\partial HW}{\partial HE}$ for $HE = 5$ and $HE = 10$

(ii) $\dfrac{\partial HW}{\partial HA}$ for $HA = 30$ and $HA = 40$

Does the omission of CIT lead to omitted-variable bias? Can you suggest why?

6.15 The file *stockton4.dat* contains data on 1500 houses sold in Stockton, California, during 1996–1998. Variable descriptions are in the file *stockton4.def*.

(a) Estimate the following model and report the results:

$$SPRICE = \beta_1 + \beta_2 LIVAREA + \beta_3 AGE + \beta_4 BEDS + \beta_5 BATHS + e$$

(b) Xiaohui wants to buy a house. She is considering two that have the same living area, the same number of bathrooms, and the same number of bedrooms. One is five years old and the other is fifteen years old. What price difference can she expect between the two houses? What is a 95% interval estimate for this difference?

(c) Wanling's house has a living area of 2000 square feet. She is planning to extend her living room by 500 square feet. What is the expected increase in price she will get from this extension? Test as an alternative hypothesis that the increase in price will be more than $25,000. Use $\alpha = 0.05$.

(d) Xueyan's house has a living area of 1500 square feet. She is planning to add another bedroom of size 500 square feet. What is the expected increase in price she will get from this extension? Find a 95% interval estimate for the expected price increase.

(e) Does RESET suggest that the model is a reasonable one?

6.16 Reconsider the data and model estimated in Exercise 6.15.

(a) Add the variables $LIVAREA^2$ and AGE^2 to the model, re-estimate it, and report the results.

(b) Does an F-test suggest that the addition of $LIVAREA^2$ and AGE^2 has improved the model? Use $\alpha = 0.05$.

(c) Answer parts (b)–(e) of Exercise 6.15 using the new specification.

6.17 The file *stockton4.dat* contains data on 1500 houses sold in Stockton, CA during 1996–1998. Variable descriptions are in the file *stockton4.def*.

(a) Estimate the following model and report the results

$$\ln(SPRICE) = \beta_1 + \beta_2 LIVAREA + \beta_3 LIVAREA^2 + \beta_4 AGE + \beta_5 AGE^2$$
$$+ \beta_6 BEDS + e$$

(b) Using a 5% significance level, test whether living area helps explain selling price.

(c) Using a 5% significance level, test whether age helps explain selling price.

(d) Predict the price of 5-year-old house with a living area of 2000 square feet, and three bedrooms. Find predictions using both (1) the natural predictor, and (2) the corrected predictor. (See Chapter 4.5.3.)

(e) Find a 95% prediction interval for a house with the characteristics specified in (d).

(f) After extending her living area by 200 square feet, Wanling's 10-year old, 3-bedroom house has a living area of 2500 square feet. Ignoring the error term, estimate the price of Wanling's house after the extension.

(g) Test, as an alternative hypothesis, that the extension to Wanling's living area has increased the price of the house by more than $25,000. Use $\alpha = 0.05$.

(h) Does RESET suggest that the model is a reasonable one?

6.18 The file *stockton4.dat* contains data on 1,500 houses sold in Stockton, CA during 1996–1998. Variable descriptions are in the file *stockton4.def*.

(a) Estimate the following model

$$\ln(SPRICE) = \beta_1 + \beta_2 LIVAREA + \beta_3 LIVAREA^2 + \beta_4 AGE + \beta_5 AGE^2$$
$$+ \beta_6 BEDS + \beta_7 (LIVAREA \times BEDS) + \beta_8 (LIVAREA^2 \times BEDS)$$
$$+ \beta_9 (AGE \times BEDS) + \beta_{10} (AGE^2 \times BEDS) + e$$

Report the estimated relationship between $\ln(SPRICE)$, $LIVAREA$ and AGE for two-, three- and four-bedroom houses.

(b) Test the null hypothesis $H_0: \beta_6 = 0$, $\beta_8 = 0$, $\beta_9 = 0$, $\beta_{10} = 0$. Use $\alpha = 0.05$.

(c) Estimate the model implied by the test result in (b). Report the estimated relationship between $\ln(SPRICE)$, $LIVAREA$ and AGE for two-, three- and four-bedroom houses.

(d) Which of the two models in parts (a) and (c) is favored by, (1) the AIC? (2) the SC?

6.19 Reconsider the commuting time model estimated in Exercise 5.21 using the data file *commute.dat*:

$$TIME = \beta_1 + \beta_2 DEPART + \beta_3 REDS + \beta_4 TRAINS + e$$

Find 95% interval estimates for the time Bill arrives at the University when:

(a) He leaves Carnegie at 7:15 AM and encounters four red lights and one train.

(b) He leaves Carnegie at 7:45 AM and encounters ten red lights and two trains.

6.20* Reconsider the production function for rice estimated in Exercise 5.24 using data in the file *rice.dat*:

$$\ln(PROD) = \beta_1 + \beta_2 \ln(AREA) + \beta_3 \ln(LABOR) + \beta_4 \ln(FERT) + e$$

(a) Using a 5% level of significance, test the hypothesis that the elasticity of production with respect to land is equal to the elasticity of production with respect to labor.

(b) Using a 10% level of significance, test the hypothesis that the production function exhibits constant returns to scale—that is, $H_0: \beta_2 + \beta_3 + \beta_4 = 1$.

(c) Using a 5% level of significance, jointly test the two hypotheses in parts (a) and (b)—that is, $H_0: \beta_2 = \beta_3$ and $\beta_2 + \beta_3 + \beta_4 = 1$.

(d) Find restricted least squares estimates for each of the restricted models implied by the null hypotheses in parts (a), (b) and (c). Compare the different estimates and their standard errors.

6.21* Re-estimate the model in Exercise 6.20 with (i) *FERT* omitted, (ii) *LABOR* omitted, and (iii) *AREA* omitted. In each case, discuss the effect of omitting a variable on the estimates of the remaining two elasticities. Also, in each case, check to see if RESET has picked up the omitted variable.

6.22* In Chapter 5.7 we used the data in file *pizza4.dat* to estimate the model

$$PIZZA = \beta_1 + \beta_2 AGE + \beta_3 INCOME + \beta_4 (AGE \times INCOME) + e$$

(a) Test the hypothesis that age does not affect pizza expenditure—that is, test the joint hypothesis $H_0: \beta_2 = 0$, $\beta_4 = 0$. What do you conclude?

(b) Construct point estimates and 95% interval estimates of the marginal propensity to spend on pizza for individuals of ages 20, 30, 40, 50, and 55. Comment on these estimates.

(c) Modify the equation to permit a "life-cycle" effect in which the marginal effect of income on pizza expenditure increases with age, up to a point, and then falls. Do so by adding the term $(AGE^2 \times INCOME)$ to the model. What sign do you anticipate on this term? Estimate the model and test the significance of the coefficient for this variable. Did the estimate have the expected sign?

(d) Using the model in (c), construct point estimates and 95% interval estimates of the marginal propensity to spend on pizza for individuals of ages 20, 30, 40, 50 and 55. Comment on these estimates. In light of these values, and of the range of age in the sample data, what can you say about the quadratic function of age that describes the marginal propensity to spend on pizza?

(e) For the model in part (c), are each of the coefficient estimates for AGE, $(AGE \times INCOME)$ and $(AGE^2 \times INCOME)$ significantly different from zero at a 5% significance level? Carry out a joint test for the significance of these variables. Comment on your results.

(f) Check the model used in part (c) for collinearity. Add the term $(AGE^3 \times INCOME)$ to the model in (c) and check the resulting model for collinearity.

6.23 Use the data in *cps4_small.dat* to estimate the following wage equation:

$$\ln(WAGE) = \beta_1 + \beta_2 EDUC + \beta_3 EDUC^2 + \beta_4 EXPER$$
$$+ \beta_5 EXPER^2 + \beta_6 (EDUC \times EXPER) + e$$

(a) Find 95% interval estimates for:

   (i) The approximate percentage change in *WAGE* from an extra year of education for someone with 12 years of education and 2 years of experience.

   (ii) The approximate percentage change in *WAGE* from an extra year of experience for someone with 12 years of education and 2 years of experience.

   (iii) The approximate percentage change in *WAGE* from an extra year of education for someone with 16 years of education and 10 years of experience.

   (iv) The approximate percentage change in *WAGE* from an extra year of experience for someone with 16 years of education and 10 years of experience.

(b) Test the joint hypothesis that the change in (i) is 10% and the change in (ii) is 4%.

(c) Test the joint hypothesis that the change in (iii) is 12%, and the change in (iv) is 1%.

(d) Test the joint hypothesis that the change in (i) is 10%, the change in (ii) is 4%, the change in (iii) is 12%, and the change in (iv) is 1%.

(e) Find and report restricted least squares estimates under the assumption that the joint hypothesis in (c) is true.

6.24 Data on the weekly sales of a major brand of canned tuna by a supermarket chain in a large midwestern U.S. city during a mid-1990s calendar year are contained in the file *tuna.dat*. There are 52 observations on the variables. The variable $SAL1$ = unit sales of brand no. 1 canned tuna, $APR1$ = price per can of brand no. 1 canned tuna, $APR2$, $APR3$ = price per can of brands nos. 2 and 3 of canned tuna.

(a) Interpret the coefficients in the following equation. What are their expected signs?

$$\ln(SAL1) = \beta_1 + \beta_2 \ln(APR1) + \beta_3 \ln(APR2) + \beta_4 \ln(APR3) + e$$

(b) Estimate the equation and report the results. Do the estimates have the expected signs? Are they significantly different from zero at a 5% significance level?

(c) The marketing manager for no. 1 brand of tuna claims that it is the price of brand 1 relative to the prices of brands 2 and 3 that is important. She suggests the model

$$\ln(SAL1) = \alpha_1 + \alpha_2 \ln\left(\frac{APR1}{APR2}\right) + \alpha_3 \ln\left(\frac{APR1}{APR3}\right) + e$$

Show that this model is a restricted version of the original model where $\beta_2 + \beta_3 + \beta_4 = 0$, with $\alpha_2 = -\beta_3$ and $\alpha_3 = -\beta_4$.

(d) Using a 10% significance level, test whether the data supports the marketing manager's claim.

(e) Estimate the restricted model given in part (c). Report the results. Interpret the estimates. Are the estimates significantly different from zero?

(f) Which brand, no. 2 or no. 3, is the strongest competitor to brand no. 1? Why?

(g) Does a hypothesis test confirm your answer to part (f)? Do the test twice: once using the model in part (a) and once using the model in part (c).

6.25 Consider again the data in the file *tuna.dat* used in Exercise 6.24. Carry out the following data transformations:

$SALES = SAL1/1000 = $ sales measured in thousands of units
$PR1 = APR1 \times 100 = $ price of brand no. 1 in cents
$PR2 = APR2 \times 100 = $ price of brand no. 2 in cents
$PR3 = APR3 \times 100 = $ price of brand no. 3 in cents

(a) Estimate each of the following three equations and explain the relationship between the estimated coefficients:

$$SAL1 = \beta_1 + \beta_2 APR1 + \beta_3 APR2 + \beta_4 APR3 + e$$
$$SAL1 = \alpha_1 + \alpha_2 PR1 + \alpha_3 PR2 + \alpha_4 PR3 + e$$
$$SALES = \gamma_1 + \gamma_2 PR1 + \gamma_3 PR2 + \gamma_4 PR3 + e$$

(b) Estimate each of the following equations and explain the relationship between the estimated coefficients:

$$\ln(SAL1) = \beta_1 + \beta_2 APR1 + \beta_3 APR2 + \beta_4 APR3 + e$$
$$\ln(SAL1) = \alpha_1 + \alpha_2 PR1 + \alpha_3 PR2 + \alpha_4 PR3 + e$$
$$\ln(SALES) = \gamma_1 + \gamma_2 PR1 + \gamma_3 PR2 + \gamma_4 PR3 + e$$

(c) Estimate each of the following equations and explain the relationship between the estimated coefficients:

$$\ln(SAL1) = \beta_1 + \beta_2 \ln(APR1) + \beta_3 \ln(APR2) + \beta_4 \ln(APR3) + e$$
$$\ln(SAL1) = \alpha_1 + \alpha_2 \ln(PR1) + \alpha_3 \ln(PR2) + \alpha_4 \ln(PR3) + e$$
$$\ln(SALES) = \gamma_1 + \gamma_2 \ln(PR1) + \gamma_3 \ln(PR2) + \gamma_4 \ln(PR3) + e$$

Appendix 6A Chi-Square and *F*-tests: More Details

This appendix has two objectives. The first is to explain why the statistic

$$F = \frac{(SSE_R - SSE_U)/J}{SSE_U/(N - K)} \tag{6A.1}$$

has an $F_{(J, N-K)}$-distribution when a specified null hypothesis is true. The other is to introduce a χ^2 (chi-square) statistic that is also used for testing null hypotheses containing single or joint hypotheses about the coefficients in a regression relationship. You may already have noticed and wondered about computer output that gives a χ^2-value and corresponding *p*-value in addition to the *F*-value and its *p*-value.

The starting point is the following result that holds when the null hypothesis being tested is true

$$V_1 = \frac{(SSE_R - SSE_U)}{\sigma^2} \sim \chi^2_{(J)} \tag{6A.2}$$

In other words, V_1 has a χ^2-distribution with J degrees of freedom. If σ^2 was known, V_1 could be used to test the null hypothesis. There are two ways of overcoming the problem of an unknown σ^2: one leads to the F-statistic in (6A.1); the other yields the χ^2-statistic you may have been wondering about. Considering the second one first, one way to obtain a workable test statistic is to replace σ^2 in (6A.2) with its estimate $\hat{\sigma}^2$ from the unrestricted model. If sample size is sufficiently large, it will be approximately true that

$$\hat{V}_1 = \frac{(SSE_R - SSE_U)}{\hat{\sigma}^2} \sim \chi^2_{(J)} \tag{6A.3}$$

This statistic can be used to test hypotheses about the unknown regression coefficients. At a 5% significance level we reject H_0 if $\hat{V}_1$ is greater than the critical value $\chi^2_{(0.95, J)}$, or if the p-value $P[\chi^2_{(J)} > \hat{V}_1]$ is less than 0.05.

To describe the second way of eliminating the unknown σ^2 we introduce the result

$$V_2 = \frac{(N - K)\hat{\sigma}^2}{\sigma^2} \sim \chi^2_{(N-K)} \tag{6A.4}$$

This result is the multiple regression extension of the simple regression result given in (3A.4) of the appendix to Chapter 3. We are now in a position to use the result that the ratio of two independent χ^2 random variables, each divided by their respective degrees of freedom, is an F random variable. That is, from (B.49) in Appendix B at the end of the book,

$$F = \frac{V_1/m_1}{V_2/m_2} \sim F(m_1, m_2)$$

In the context of our problem,

$$F = \frac{\dfrac{(SSE_R - SSE_U)}{\sigma^2} \Big/ J}{\dfrac{(N - K)\hat{\sigma}^2}{\sigma^2} \Big/ (N - K)} \tag{6A.5}$$

$$= \frac{(SSE_R - SSE_U)/J}{\hat{\sigma}^2} \sim F_{(J, N-K)}$$

The two σ^2's in V_1 and V_2 cancel. Also, although we have not done so, it is possible to prove that V_1 and V_2 are independent.

Noting that $\hat{\sigma}^2 = SSE_U/(N - K)$, we can see that (6A.5) and (6A.1) are identical. The F-statistic in (6A.5) is the one we have used throughout this chapter for testing hypotheses.

What is the relationship between $\hat{V}_1$ and F given in (6A.3) and (6A.5), respectively? A moment's thought reveals that

$$F = \frac{\hat{V}_1}{J}$$

The F-value is equal to the χ^2-value divided by the number of restrictions in the null hypothesis. We can confirm this relationship by reexamining some examples.

When testing $H_0: \beta_3 = \beta_4 = 0$ in the equation

$$SALES = \beta_1 + \beta_2 PRICE + \beta_3 ADVERT + \beta_4 ADVERT^2 + e$$

we obtain

$$F = 8.44 \quad p\text{-value} = 0.0005$$

$$\chi^2 = 16.88 \quad p\text{-value} = 0.0002$$

Because there are two restrictions ($J = 2$), the F-value is half the χ^2-value. The p-values are different because the tests are different.

For testing $H_0 : \beta_3 + 3.8\beta_4 = 1$ (see Section 6.1.4), we obtain

$$F = 0.936 \quad p\text{-value} = 0.3365$$

$$\chi^2 = 0.936 \quad p\text{-value} = 0.3333$$

The F- and χ^2-values are equal because $J = 1$, but again the p-values are different.

Appendix 6B   Omitted–Variable Bias: A Proof

Consider the model

$$y_i = \beta_1 + \beta_2 x_{i2} + \beta_3 x_{i3} + e_i$$

Suppose that we incorrectly omit x_3 from the model and estimate instead

$$y_i = \beta_1 + \beta_2 x_{i2} + v_i$$

where $v_i = \beta_3 x_{i3} + e_i$. Then, the estimator used for β_2 is

$$b_2^* = \frac{\sum(x_{i2} - \bar{x}_2)(y_i - \bar{y})}{\sum(x_{i2} - \bar{x}_2)^2} = \beta_2 + \sum w_i v_i \tag{6B.1}$$

where

$$w_i = \frac{(x_{i2} - \bar{x}_2)}{\sum(x_{i2} - \bar{x}_2)^2}$$

The second equality in (6B.1) follows from Appendix 2D in Chapter 2. Substituting for v_i in (6B.1) yields

$$b_2^* = \beta_2 + \beta_3 \sum w_i x_{i3} + \sum w_i e_i$$

Hence, the mean of b_2^* is

$$
\begin{aligned}
E(b_2^*) &= \beta_2 + \beta_3 \sum w_i x_{i3} \\
&= \beta_2 + \beta_3 \frac{\sum(x_{i2} - \bar{x}_2) x_{i3}}{\sum(x_{i2} - \bar{x}_2)^2} \\
&= \beta_2 + \beta_3 \frac{\sum(x_{i2} - \bar{x}_2)(x_{i3} - \bar{x}_3)}{\sum(x_{i2} - \bar{x}_2)^2} \\
&= \beta_2 + \beta_3 \frac{\widehat{\text{cov}}(x_2, x_3)}{\widehat{\text{var}}(x_2)} \neq \beta_2
\end{aligned}
$$

Thus, the restricted estimator is biased. Knowing the sign of β_3 and the sign of the covariance between x_2 and x_3 tells us the direction of the bias. Also, although omitting a variable from the regression usually biases the least squares estimator, if the sample covariance (or the simple correlation) between x_2 and the omitted variable x_3 is zero, then the least squares estimator in the misspecified model is still unbiased. In Section 2.2, we suggested that omitting an important factor will lead to violation of the assumption SR2 $E(e) = 0$ and that such a violation can have serious consequences. We can now be more precise about that statement. Omitting an important variable that is correlated with variables included in the equation yields an error that we have called v_i in the above discussion. This error will have a nonzero mean, and the consequences are biased estimates for the coefficients of the remaining variables in the model.

Chapter 7

Using Indicator Variables

Learning Objectives

Based on the material in this chapter you should be able to explain

1. The difference between qualitative and quantitative economic variables.

2. How to include a 0–1 indicator variable on the right-hand side of a regression, how this affects model interpretation, and give an example.

3. How to interpret the coefficient on an indicator variable in a log-linear equation.

4. How to include a slope-indicator variable in a regression, how this affects model interpretation, and give an example.

5. How to include a product of two indicator variables in a regression, and how this affects model interpretation, giving an example.

6. How to model qualitative factors with more than two categories (like region of the country), and how to interpret the resulting model, giving an example.

7. The consequences of ignoring a structural change in parameters during part of the sample.

8. How to test the equivalence of two regression equations using indicator variables.

9. How to estimate and interpret a regression with an indicator dependent variable.

10. The difference between a randomized controlled experiment and a natural experiment.

Keywords

annual indicator variables	exact collinearity	natural experiment
Chow test	hedonic model	quasi-experiment
dichotomous variable	indicator variable	reference group
difference estimator	interaction variable	regional indicator variable
differences-in-differences estimator	intercept indicator variable	seasonal indicator variables
dummy variable	linear probability model	slope-indicator variable
dummy variable trap	log-linear models	treatment effect

7.1 Indicator Variables

Indicator variables, which were first introduced in Chapter 2.9, allow us to construct models in which some or all regression model parameters, including the intercept, change for some observations in the sample. To make matters specific, let us consider an example from real estate economics. Buyers and sellers of homes, tax assessors, real estate appraisers, and mortgage bankers are interested in predicting the current market value of a house. A common way to predict the value of a house is to use a **hedonic model**, in which the price of the house is explained as a function of its characteristics, such as its size, location, number of bedrooms, age, and so on. The idea is to break down a good into its component pieces, and then estimate the value of each characteristic.[1]

For the present, let us assume that the size of the house, measured in square feet, *SQFT*, is the only relevant variable in determining house price, *PRICE*. Specify the regression model as

$$PRICE = \beta_1 + \beta_2 SQFT + e \tag{7.1}$$

In this model β_2 is the value of an additional square foot of living area, and β_1 is the value of the land alone.

In real estate the three most important words are "location, location, and location." How can we take into account the effect of a property's being in a desirable neighborhood, such as one near a university, or near a golf course? Thought of this way, location is a "qualitative" characteristic of a house.

Indicator variables are used to account for qualitative factors in econometric models. They are often called **dummy**, **binary** or **dichotomous** variables, because they take just two values, usually one or zero, to indicate the presence or absence of a characteristic or to indicate whether a condition is true or false. They are also called **dummy variables**, to indicate that we are creating a numeric variable for a qualitative, non-numeric characteristic. We use the terms *indicator variable* and *dummy variable* interchangeably. Using zero and one for the values of these variables is arbitrary, but very convenient, as we will see. Generally, we define an indicator variable D as

$$D = \begin{cases} 1 & \text{if characteristic is present} \\ 0 & \text{if characteristic is not present} \end{cases} \tag{7.2}$$

Thus, for the house price model, we can define an indicator variable, to account for a desirable neighborhood, as

$$D = \begin{cases} 1 & \text{if property is in the desirable neighborhood} \\ 0 & \text{if property is not in the desirable neighborhood} \end{cases}$$

Indicator variables can be used to capture changes in the model intercept, or slopes, or both. We consider these possibilities in turn.

---

[1] Such models have been used for many types of goods, including personal computers, automobiles and wine. This famous idea was introduced by Sherwin Rosen (1978) "Hedonic Prices and Implicit Markets," *Journal of Political Economy*, 82, 357–369. The ideas are summarized and applied to asparagus and personal computers in Ernst Berndt (1991) *The Practice of Econometrics: Classic and Contemporary*, Reading, MA: Addison-Wesley, Chapter 4.

7.1.1   Intercept Indicator Variables

The most common use of indicator variables is to modify the regression model intercept parameter. Adding the indicator variable D to the regression model, along with a new parameter δ, we obtain

$$PRICE = \beta_1 + \delta D + \beta_2 SQFT + e \qquad (7.3)$$

The effect of the inclusion of an indicator variable D into the regression model is best seen by examining the regression function, $E(PRICE)$, in the two locations. If the model in (7.3) is correctly specified, then $E(e) = 0$ and

$$E(PRICE) = \begin{cases} (\beta_1 + \delta) + \beta_2 SQFT & \text{when } D = 1 \\ \beta_1 + \beta_2 SQFT & \text{when } D = 0 \end{cases} \qquad (7.4)$$

In the desirable neighborhood $D = 1$, and the intercept of the regression function is $(\beta_1 + \delta)$. In other areas the regression function intercept is simply β_1. This difference is depicted in Figure 7.1, assuming that $\delta > 0$.

Adding the indicator variable D to the regression model causes a parallel shift in the relationship by the amount δ. In the context of the house price model the interpretation of the parameter δ is that it is a **location premium**, the difference in house price due to the houses being located in the desirable neighborhood. An indicator variable like D that is incorporated into a regression model to capture a shift in the intercept as the result of some qualitative factor is called an **intercept indicator variable**, or an **intercept dummy variable**. In the house price example, we expect the price to be higher in a desirable location, and thus we anticipate that δ will be positive.

The least squares estimator's properties are not affected by the fact that one of the explanatory variables consists only of zeros and ones—D is treated as any other explanatory variable. We can construct an interval estimate for δ, or we can test the significance of its least squares estimate. Such a test is a statistical test of whether the neighborhood effect on house price is "statistically significant." If $\delta = 0$, then there is no location premium for the neighborhood in question.

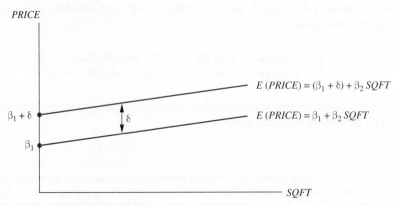

FIGURE **7.1**   An intercept indicator variable.

7.1.1a Choosing the Reference Group

The convenience of the values $D = 0$ and $D = 1$ is seen in (7.4). The value $D = 0$ defines the **reference group**, or **base group**, of houses that are not in the desirable neighborhood. The expected price of these houses is simply $E(PRICE) = \beta_1 + \beta_2 SQFT$. Using (7.3) we are comparing the house prices in the desirable neighborhood to those in the base group.

A researcher can choose whichever neighborhood is most convenient, for expository purposes, to be the reference group. For example, we can define the indicator variable LD to denote the less desirable neighborhood:

$$LD = \begin{cases} 1 & \text{if property is not in the desirable neighborhood} \\ 0 & \text{if property is in the desirable neighborhood} \end{cases}$$

This indicator variable is defined just the opposite from D, and $LD = 1 - D$. If we include LD in the model specification

$$PRICE = \beta_1 + \lambda LD + \beta_2 SQFT + e$$

then we make the reference group, $LD = 0$, the houses in the desirable neighborhood.

You may be tempted to include both D and LD in the regression model to capture the effect of each neighborhood on house prices. That is, you might consider the model

$$PRICE = \beta_1 + \delta D + \lambda LD + \beta_2 SQFT + e$$

In this model the variables D and LD are such that $D + LD = 1$. Since the intercept variable $x_1 = 1$, we have created a model with **exact collinearity**, and as explained in Section 6.4, the least squares estimator is not defined in such cases. This error is sometimes described as falling into the **dummy variable trap**. By including only one of the indicator variables, either D or LD, the omitted variable defines the reference group, and we avoid the problem.[2]

7.1.2 SLOPE-INDICATOR VARIABLES

Instead of assuming that the effect of location on house price causes a change in the intercept of the hedonic regression (7.1), let us assume that the change is in the slope of the relationship. We can allow for a change in a slope by including in the model an additional explanatory variable that is equal to the product of an indicator variable and a continuous variable. In our model the slope of the relationship is the value of an additional square foot of living area. If we assume that this is one value for homes in the desirable neighborhood, and another value for homes in other neighborhoods, we can specify

$$PRICE = \beta_1 + \beta_2 SQFT + \gamma(SQFT \times D) + e \tag{7.5}$$

The new variable $(SQFT \times D)$ is the product of house size and the indicator variable, and is called an **interaction variable**, as it captures the interaction effect of location and size on house price. Alternatively, it is called a **slope-indicator variable** or a **slope dummy variable**, because it allows for a change in the slope of the relationship. The slope-indicator variable takes a value equal to $SQFT$ for houses in the desirable neighborhood, when $D = 1$, and it is zero for homes in other neighborhoods. Despite its unusual nature, a slope-indicator

---

[2] Another way to avoid the dummy variable trap is to omit the intercept from the model.

variable is treated just like any other explanatory variable in a regression model. Examining the regression function for the two different locations best illustrates the effect of the inclusion of the slope-indicator variable into the economic model,

$$E(PRICE) = \beta_1 + \beta_2 SQFT + \gamma(SQFT \times D) = \begin{cases} \beta_1 + (\beta_2 + \gamma)SQFT & \text{when } D = 1 \\ \beta_1 + \beta_2 SQFT & \text{when } D = 0 \end{cases}$$

In the desirable neighborhood, the price per additional square foot of a home is $(\beta_2 + \gamma)$; it is β_2 in other locations. We would anticipate $\gamma > 0$ if price per additional square foot is higher in the more desirable neighborhood. This situation is depicted in Figure 7.2a.

Another way to see the effect of including a slope-indicator variable is to use calculus. The partial derivative of expected house price with respect to size (measured in square feet), which gives the slope of the relation, is

$$\frac{\partial E(PRICE)}{\partial SQFT} = \begin{cases} \beta_2 + \gamma & \text{when } D = 1 \\ \beta_2 & \text{when } D = 0 \end{cases}$$

If the assumptions of the regression model hold for (7.5), then the least squares estimators have their usual good properties, as discussed in Section 5.3. A test of the hypothesis that the value of an additional square foot of living area is the same in the two locations is carried

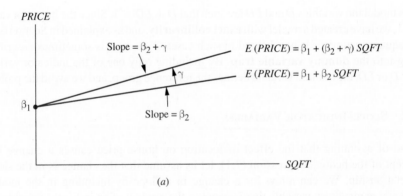

(a)

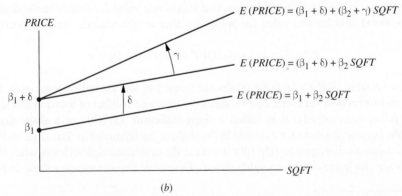

(b)

FIGURE 7.2   (a) A slope-indicator variable. (b) Slope- and intercept-indicator variables.

Table 7.1 **Representative Real Estate Data Values**

PRICE	SQFT	AGE	UTOWN	POOL	FPLACE
205.452	23.46	6	0	0	1
185.328	20.03	5	0	0	1
248.422	27.77	6	0	0	0
287.339	23.67	28	1	1	0
255.325	21.30	0	1	1	1
301.037	29.87	6	1	0	1

out by testing the null hypothesis $H_0 : \gamma = 0$ against the alternative $H_1 : \gamma \neq 0$. In this case, we might test $H_0 : \gamma = 0$ against $H_1 : \gamma > 0$, since we expect the effect to be positive.

If we assume that house location affects *both* the intercept and the slope, then both effects can be incorporated into a single model. The resulting regression model is

$$PRICE = \beta_1 + \delta D + \beta_2 SQFT + \gamma(SQFT \times D) + e \qquad (7.6)$$

In this case the regression functions for the house prices in the two locations are

$$E(PRICE) = \begin{cases} (\beta_1 + \delta) + (\beta_2 + \gamma)SQFT & \text{when } D = 1 \\ \beta_1 + \beta_2 SQFT & \text{when } D = 0 \end{cases}$$

In Figure 7.2b we depict the house price relations assuming that $\delta > 0$ and $\gamma > 0$.

7.1.3 AN EXAMPLE: THE UNIVERSITY EFFECT ON HOUSE PRICES

A real estate economist collects information on 1000 house price sales from two similar neighborhoods, one called "University Town" bordering a large state university, and one a neighborhood about three miles from the university. A few of the observations are shown in Table 7.1. The complete data file is *utown.dat*.

House prices are given in $1,000; size (*SQFT*) is the number of hundreds of square feet of living area. For example, the first house sold for $205,452 and has 2346 square feet of living area. Also recorded are the house *AGE* (in years), location (*UTOWN* = 1 for homes near the university, 0 otherwise), whether the house has a pool (*POOL* = 1 if a pool is present, 0 otherwise) and whether the house has a fireplace (*FPLACE* = 1 if a fireplace is present, 0 otherwise). The economist specifies the regression equation as

$$PRICE = \beta_1 + \delta_1 UTOWN + \beta_2 SQFT + \gamma(SQFT \times UTOWN)$$
$$+ \beta_3 AGE + \delta_2 POOL + \delta_3 FPLACE + e \qquad (7.7)$$

We anticipate that all the coefficients in this model will be positive except β_3, which is an estimate of the effect of age, or depreciation, on house price. Note that *POOL* and *FPLACE* are intercept dummy variables. By introducing these variables we are asking whether, and by how much, these features change house price. Because these variables stand alone, and are not interacted with *SQFT*, we are assuming that they affect the regression intercept, but not the slope. The estimated regression results are shown in Table 7.2. The goodness-of-fit statistic is $R^2 = 0.8706$, indicating that the model fits the data well. The slope-indicator

Table 7.2 **House Price Equation Estimates**

Variable	Coefficient	Std. Error	*t*-Statistic	Prob.
C	24.5000	6.1917	3.9569	0.0001
UTOWN	27.4530	8.4226	3.2594	0.0012
SQFT	7.6122	0.2452	31.0478	0.0000
SQFT×UTOWN	1.2994	0.3320	3.9133	0.0001
AGE	−0.1901	0.0512	−3.7123	0.0002
POOL	4.3772	1.1967	3.6577	0.0003
FPLACE	1.6492	0.9720	1.6968	0.0901

$R^2 = 0.8706$ $\qquad$ $SSE = 230184.4$

variable is $SQFT \times UTOWN$. Based on one-tail *t*-tests of significance,[3] at the $\alpha = 0.05$ level we reject zero null hypotheses for each of the parameters and accept the alternatives that they are positive, except for the coefficient on AGE, which we accept to be negative. In particular, based on these *t*-tests, we conclude that houses near the university have a significantly higher base price, and that their price per additional square foot is significantly higher than in the comparison neighborhood.

The estimated regression function for the houses near the university is

$$\widehat{PRICE} = (24.5 + 27.453) + (7.6122 + 1.2994)SQFT - 0.1901AGE$$
$$+ 4.3772POOL + 1.6492FPLACE$$

$$= 51.953 + 8.9116SQFT - 0.1901AGE + 4.3772POOL + 1.6492FPLACE$$

For houses in other areas, the estimated regression function is

$$\widehat{PRICE} = 24.5 + 7.6122SQFT - 0.1901AGE + 4.3772POOL + 1.6492FPLACE$$

Based on the regression results in Table 7.2, we estimate that

- The location premium for lots near the university is $27,453
- The change in expected price per additional square foot is $89.12 for houses near the university and $76.12 for houses in other areas
- Houses depreciate $190.10 per year
- A pool increases the value of a home by $4,377.20
- A fireplace increases the value of a home by $1,649.20

7.2 Applying Indicator Variables

Indicator variables can be used to ask and answer a rich variety of questions. In this section we consider some common applications.

---

[3] Recall that the *p*-value for a one-tail test is half of the reported two-tail *p*-value.

7.2.1 Interactions Between Qualitative Factors

We have seen how indicator variables can be used to represent qualitative factors in a regression model. Intercept indicator variables for qualitative factors are *additive*. That is, the effect of each qualitative factor is added to the regression intercept, and the effect of any indicator variable is independent of any other qualitative factor. Sometimes, however, we might question whether the effects of qualitative factors are independent.

For example, suppose we are estimating a wage equation, in which an individual's wages are explained as a function of their experience, skill, and other factors related to productivity. It is customary to include indicator variables for race and gender in such equations. If we have modeled productivity attributes well, and if wage determination is not discriminatory, then the coefficients of the race and gender indicator variables should not be significant. Including just race and gender indicator variables, however, will not capture interactions between these qualitative factors. Is there a differential in wages for black women? Separate indicator variables for being "black" and "female" will not capture this extra interaction effect. To allow for such a possibility, consider the following specification, in which for simplicity we use only education ($EDUC$) as a productivity measure:

$$WAGE = \beta_1 + \beta_2 EDUC + \delta_1 BLACK + \delta_2 FEMALE$$
$$+ \gamma(BLACK \times FEMALE) + e \qquad (7.8)$$

where $BLACK$ and $FEMALE$ are indicator variables, and thus so is their interaction. These are intercept dummy variables, because they are not interacted with any continuous explanatory variable. They have the effect of causing a parallel shift in the regression, as in Figure 7.1. When multiple dummy variables are present, and especially when there are interactions between indicator variables, it is important for proper interpretation to write out the regression function, $E(WAGE)$, for each indicator variable combination:

$$E(WAGE) = \begin{cases} \beta_1 + \beta_2 EDUC & WHITE-MALE \\ (\beta_1 + \delta_1) + \beta_2 EDUC & BLACK-MALE \\ (\beta_1 + \delta_2) + \beta_2 EDUC & WHITE-FEMALE \\ (\beta_1 + \delta_1 + \delta_2 + \gamma) + \beta_2 EDUC & BLACK-FEMALE \end{cases}$$

In this specification, white males are the reference group, because this is the group defined when all indicator variables take the value zero, in this case $BLACK = 0$ and $FEMALE = 0$. The parameter δ_1 measures the effect of being black, relative to the reference group; the parameter δ_2 measures the effect of being female, and the parameter γ measures the effect of being black and female.

Using CPS data (*cps4_small.dat*) from 2008, we obtain the results in Table 7.3. Holding the effect of education constant, we estimate that black males earn $4.17 per hour less than

Table 7.3 **Wage Equation with Race and Gender**

Variable	Coefficient	Std. Error	*t*-Statistic	Prob.
C	−5.2812	1.9005	−2.7789	0.0056
EDUC	2.0704	0.1349	15.3501	0.0000
BLACK	−4.1691	1.7747	−2.3492	0.0190
FEMALE	−4.7846	0.7734	−6.1863	0.0000
BLACK × FEMALE	3.8443	2.3277	1.6516	0.0989

$R^2 = 0.2089$ $\qquad SSE = 130194.7$

white males, white females earn \$4.78 less than white males, and black females earn \$5.11 less than white males. The coefficients of *EDUC, BLACK,* and *FEMALE* are all significantly different from zero using individual *t*-tests. The interaction effect between *BLACK* and *FEMALE* is not estimated very precisely using this sample of 1000 observations, and it is not statistically significant.[4]

Suppose we are asked to test the joint significance of all the qualitative factors. How do we test the hypothesis that neither race nor gender affects wages? We do it by testing the joint null hypothesis $H_0: \delta_1 = 0$, $\delta_2 = 0$, $\gamma = 0$ against the alternative that at least one of the tested parameters is not zero. If the null hypothesis is true, race and gender fall out of the regression, and thus have no effect on wages.

To test this hypothesis, we use the *F*-test procedure that is described in Section 6.1. The test statistic for a joint hypothesis is

$$F = \frac{(SSE_R - SSE_U)/J}{SSE_U/(N - K)}$$

where SSE_R is the sum of squared least squares residuals from the "restricted" model in which the null hypothesis is assumed to be true, SSE_U is the sum of squared residuals from the original, "unrestricted," model, J is the number of joint hypotheses, and $N - K$ is the number of degrees of freedom in the unrestricted model. If the null hypothesis is true, then the test statistic F has an *F*-distribution with J numerator degrees of freedom and $N - K$ denominator degrees of freedom, $F_{(J, N-K)}$. We reject the null hypothesis if $F \geq F_c$, where F_c is the critical value, illustrated in Figure B.9 of Appendix B, for the level of significance α. To test the $J = 3$ joint null hypotheses $H_0: \delta_1 = 0$, $\delta_2 = 0$, $\gamma = 0$, we obtain the unrestricted sum of squared errors $SSE_U = 130194.7$ from the model reported in Table 7.3. The restricted sum of squares is obtained by estimating the model that assumes that the null hypothesis is true, leading to the fitted model

$$\widehat{WAGE} = -6.7103 + 1.9803 EDUC$$
$$\text{(se)} \quad (1.9142) \quad (0.1361)$$

which has $SSE_R = 135771.1$. The degrees of freedom $N - K = 1000 - 5 = 995$ come from the unrestricted model. The value of the *F*-statistic is

$$F = \frac{(SSE_R - SSE_U)/J}{SSE_U/(N - K)} = \frac{(135771.1 - 130194.7)/3}{130194.7/995} = 14.21$$

The 1% critical value (i.e., the 99th percentile value) is $F_{(0.99,3,995)} = 3.80$. Thus, we conclude that race and/or gender affect the wage equation.

7.2.2 QUALITATIVE FACTORS WITH SEVERAL CATEGORIES

Many qualitative factors have more than two categories. An example is the variable region of the country in our wage equation. The CPS data record worker residence within

---

[4] Estimating this model using the larger data set *cps4.dat*, which contains 4838 observations, yields a coefficient estimate of 4.6534 with a *t*-value of 4.4318. Recall from Sections 2.4.4 and 5.3.1 that larger sample sizes lead to smaller standard errors, and thus to more precise estimation. Labor economists tend to use large data sets so that complex effects and interactions can be estimated precisely. We use the smaller data set as a text example so that results can be replicated using student versions of software.

one of the four regions: northeast, midwest, south, and west. Again, using just the simple wage specification for illustration, we can incorporate indicator variables into the wage equation as

$$WAGE = \beta_1 + \beta_2 EDUC + \delta_1 SOUTH + \delta_2 MIDWEST + \delta_3 WEST + e \qquad (7.9)$$

Notice that we have not included the indicator variables for all regions. Doing so would have created a model in which exact collinearity exists. Since the regional categories are exhaustive, the sum of the regional indicator variables is $NORTHEAST + SOUTH + MIDWEST + WEST = 1$. Thus, the "intercept variable" $x_1 = 1$ is an exact linear combination of the region indicators. Recall, from Chapter 6.4, that the least squares estimator is not defined in such cases. Failure to omit one indicator variable will lead to your computer software's returning a message saying that least squares estimation fails. This error is the **dummy variable trap** that we mentioned in Section 7.1.1a.

The usual solution to this problem is to omit one indicator variable, which defines a **reference group**, as we shall see by examining the regression function,

$$E(WAGE) = \begin{cases} (\beta_1 + \delta_3) + \beta_2 EDUC & WEST \\ (\beta_1 + \delta_2) + \beta_2 EDUC & MIDWEST \\ (\beta_1 + \delta_1) + \beta_2 EDUC & SOUTH \\ \beta_1 + \beta_2 EDUC & NORTHEAST \end{cases}$$

The omitted indicator variable, *NORTHEAST*, identifies the reference group for the equation, to which workers in other regions are compared. It is the group that remains when the regional indicator variables *WEST*, *MIDWEST*, and *SOUTH* are set to zero. Mathematically it does not matter which indicator variable is omitted; the choice can be made that is most convenient for interpretation. The intercept parameter β_1 represents the base wage for a worker with no education who lives in the northeast. The parameter δ_1 measures the expected wage differential between southern workers relative to those in the northeast; δ_2 measures the expected wage differential between midwestern workers and those in the northeast.

Using the CPS data *cps4_small.dat*, let us take the specification in Table 7.3 and add the regional dummies *SOUTH*, *MIDWEST*, and *WEST*. The results are in Table 7.4. Based on those results we can say that workers in the midwest earn significantly less per hour than

Table 7.4 **Wage Equation with Regional Indicator Variables**

Variable	Coefficient	Std. Error	t-Statistic	Prob.
C	−4.8062	2.0287	−2.3691	0.0180
EDUC	2.0712	0.1345	15.4030	0.0000
BLACK	−3.9055	1.7863	−2.1864	0.0290
FEMALE	−4.7441	0.7698	−6.1625	0.0000
BLACK × FEMALE	3.6250	2.3184	1.5636	0.1182
SOUTH	−0.4499	1.0250	−0.4389	0.6608
MIDWEST	−2.6084	1.0596	−2.4616	0.0140
WEST	0.9866	1.0598	0.9309	0.3521

$R^2 = 0.2189$ $SSE = 128544.2$

workers in the northeast, holding constant the factors education, race, and gender. We estimate that workers in the midwest earn $2.61 less per hour than workers in the northeast.

How would we test the hypothesis that there are no regional differences? This would be a joint test of the null hypothesis that the coefficients of the regional indicators are all zero. In the context of the CPS data, $SSE_U = 128544.2$ for the wage equation in Table 7.4. Under the null hypothesis the model in Table 7.4 reduces to that in Table 7.3 where $SSE_R = 130194.7$. This yields an F-statistic value of 4.2456. The $\alpha = 0.01$ critical value [99th percentile] is $F_{(0.99,3,992)} = 3.8029$. At the 1% level of significance, we reject the null hypothesis and conclude that there are significant regional differences.[5]

7.2.3 TESTING THE EQUIVALENCE OF TWO REGRESSIONS

In the Section 7.1.2 we introduced both intercept and slope-indicator variables into the hedonic equation for house price. The result was given in (7.6)

$$PRICE = \beta_1 + \delta D + \beta_2 SQFT + \gamma(SQFT \times D) + e$$

The regression functions for the house prices in the two locations are

$$E(PRICE) = \begin{cases} \alpha_1 + \alpha_2 SQFT & D = 1 \\ \beta_1 + \beta_2 SQFT & D = 0 \end{cases}$$

where $\alpha_1 = \beta_1 + \delta$ and $\alpha_2 = \beta_2 + \gamma$. Figure 7.2b shows that by introducing both intercept and slope-indicator variables we have essentially assumed that the regressions in the two neighborhoods are completely different. We could obtain the estimates for (7.6) by estimating separate regressions for each of the neighborhoods. In this section we generalize this idea, which leads to the **Chow test**, named after econometrician Gregory Chow. The Chow test is an F-test for the equivalence of two regressions.

By including an intercept indicator variable and an interaction variable for *each* additional variable in an equation, we allow all coefficients to differ based on a qualitative factor. Consider again the wage equation in (7.8)

$$WAGE = \beta_1 + \beta_2 EDUC + \delta_1 BLACK + \delta_2 FEMALE + \gamma(BLACK \times FEMALE) + e$$

We might ask "Are there differences between the wage regressions for the south and for the rest of the country?" If there are no differences, then the data from the south and other regions can be pooled into one sample, with no allowance made for differing slope or intercept. How can we test this? We can carry out the test by creating intercept and slope-indicator variables for *every* variable in the model, and then jointly testing the significance of the indicator variable coefficients using an F-test. That is, we specify the model

$$\begin{aligned} WAGE = \beta_1 &+ \beta_2 EDUC + \delta_1 BLACK + \delta_2 FEMALE + \gamma(BLACK \times FEMALE) \\ &+ \theta_1 SOUTH + \theta_2(EDUC \times SOUTH) + \theta_3(BLACK \times SOUTH) \\ &+ \theta_4(FEMALE \times SOUTH) + \theta_5(BLACK \times FEMALE \times SOUTH) + e \end{aligned} \qquad (7.10)$$

In (7.10) we have twice the number of parameters and variables than in (7.8). We have added five new variables, the *SOUTH* intercept indicator variable and interactions between *SOUTH* and the other four variables, and corresponding parameters. Estimating (7.10)

---

[5] Using the larger CPS data file *cps4.dat*, the $F = 9.3613$, which is also significant at the 1% level.

Table 7.5   **Comparison of Fully Interacted to Separate Models**

Variable	(1) Full sample Coefficient	Std. Error	(2) Nonsouth Coefficient	Std. Error	(3) South Coefficient	Std. Error
C	−6.6056	2.3366	−6.6056	2.3022	−2.6617	3.4204
EDUC	2.1726	0.1665	2.1726	0.1640	1.8640	0.2403
BLACK	−5.0894	2.6431	−5.0894	2.6041	−3.3850	2.5793
FEMALE	−5.0051	0.8990	−5.0051	0.8857	−4.1040	1.5806
BLACK × FEMALE	5.3056	3.4973	5.3056	3.4457	2.3697	3.3827
SOUTH	3.9439	4.0485				
EDUC × SOUTH	−0.3085	0.2857				
BLACK × SOUTH	1.7044	3.6333				
FEMALE × SOUTH	0.9011	1.7727				
BLACK × FEMALE × SOUTH	−2.9358	4.7876				
SSE	129984.4		89088.5		40895.9	
N	1000		704		296	

is equivalent to estimating (7.8) twice—once for the southern workers and again for workers in the rest of the country. To see this, examine the regression functions

$$
E(WAGE) = \begin{cases} \beta_1 + \beta_2 EDUC + \delta_1 BLACK + \delta_2 FEMALE \\ + \gamma(BLACK \times FEMALE) & SOUTH = 0 \\ (\beta_1 + \theta_1) + (\beta_2 + \theta_2)EDUC + (\delta_1 + \theta_3)BLACK \\ + (\delta_2 + \theta_4)FEMALE + (\gamma + \theta_5)(BLACK \times FEMALE) & SOUTH = 1 \end{cases}
$$

Note that each variable has a separate coefficient for southern and nonsouthern workers.

In column (1) of Table 7.5 we report the estimates and standard errors for the fully interacted model (7.10), using the full sample. The base model (7.8) is estimated once for workers outside the south [column (2)] and again for southern workers [column (3)]. Note that the coefficient estimates on the nonsouth data in (2) are identical to those using the full sample in (1). The standard errors differ because the estimates of the error variance, σ^2, differ. The coefficient estimates using only southern workers are obtained from the full model by adding the indicator variable interaction coefficients θ_i to the corresponding nonsouth coefficients. For example, the coefficient estimate for BLACK in column (3) is obtained as $(\hat{\delta}_1 + \hat{\theta}_3) = -5.0894 + 1.7044 = -3.3850$. Similarly the coefficient on FEMALE in (3) is $(\hat{\delta}_2 + \hat{\theta}_4) = -5.0051 + 0.9011 = -4.1040$. Furthermore, note that the sum of squared residuals for the full model in column (1) is the sum of the SSE from the two separate regressions

$$SSE_{full} = SSE_{nonsouth} + SSE_{south} = 89088.5 + 40895.9 = 129984.4$$

Using this indicator variable approach, we can test for a southern regional difference. We estimate (7.10) and test the joint null hypothesis

$$H_0 : \theta_1 = \theta_2 = \theta_3 = \theta_4 = \theta_5 = 0$$

against the alternative that at least one $\theta_i \neq 0$. This is the Chow test. If we reject this null hypothesis, we conclude that there is some difference in the wage equation in the southern region relative to the rest of the country. The test can also be thought of as comparing the estimates in the nonsouth and south in columns (2) and (3) in Table 7.5.

The test ingredients are the unrestricted $SSE_U = 129984.4$ from the full model in Table 7.5 (or the sum of the SSEs from the two separate regressions), and the restricted $SSE_R = 130194.7$ from Table 7.3. The test statistic for the $J = 5$ hypotheses is

$$F = \frac{(SSE_R - SSE_U)/J}{SSE_U/(N - K)} = \frac{(130194.7 - 129984.4)/5}{129984.4/990} = 0.3203$$

The denominator degrees of freedom come from the unrestricted model, $N - K = 1000 - 10$. The 10% critical value is $F_c = 1.85$, and thus we fail to reject the hypothesis that the wage equation is the same in the southern region and the remainder of the country at the 10% level of significance.[6] The p-value of this test is $p = 0.9009$.

> **REMARK:** The usual F-test of a joint hypothesis relies on the assumptions MR1–MR6 of the linear regression model. Of particular relevance for testing the equivalence of two regressions is assumption MR3, that the variance of the error term, $var(e_i) = \sigma^2$, is the same *for all* observations. If we are considering possibly different slopes and intercepts for parts of the data, it might also be true that the error variances are different in the two parts of the data. In such a case, the usual F-test is not valid. Testing for equal variances is covered in Chapter 8.2.3, and the question of pooling in this case is covered in Chapter 8.4.2. For now, be aware that we are assuming constant error variances in the calculations above.

7.2.4   CONTROLLING FOR TIME

The earlier examples we have given apply indicator variables to cross-sectional data. Indicator variables are also used in regressions using time-series data, as the following examples illustrate.

7.2.4a   Seasonal Indicators

Summer means outdoor cooking on barbeque grills. What effect might this have on the sales of charcoal briquettes, a popular fuel for grilling? To investigate, let us define a model with dependent variable y_t = the number of 20-pound bags of Royal Oak charcoal sold in week t at a supermarket. Explanatory variables would include the price of Royal Oak, the price of competitive brands (Kingsford and the store brand), the prices of complementary goods (charcoal lighter fluid, pork ribs and sausages), and advertising (newspaper ads and coupons). While these standard demand factors are all relevant, we may also find strong seasonal effects. All other things being equal, more charcoal is sold in the warm summer months than in other seasons. Thus we may want to include either monthly indicator variables (for example, $AUG = 1$ if month is August, $AUG = 0$ otherwise) or seasonal indicator variables (in North America, $SUMMER = 1$ if month = June, July, or August; $SUMMER = 0$ otherwise) into the regression. In addition to these seasonal effects, holidays are special occasions for cookouts. In the United States these are Memorial Day (last Monday in May), Independence Day (July 4), and Labor Day (first Monday in September).

---

[6] Using the larger data file *cps4.dat* $F = 1.2568$.

Additional sales can be expected in the week before these holidays, meaning that indicator variables for each should be included into the regression.

7.2.4b   Year Indicators

In the same spirit as seasonal indicator variables, annual indicator variables are used to capture year effects not otherwise measured in a model. The real estate model discussed earlier in this chapter provides an example. Real estate data are available continuously, every month, every year. Suppose we have data on house prices for a certain community covering a 10-year period. In addition to house characteristics, such as those employed in (7.7), the overall price level is affected by demand factors in the local economy, such as population change, interest rates, unemployment rate, and income growth. Economists creating "cost-of-living" or "house price" indexes for cities must include a component for housing that takes the pure price effect into account. Understanding the price index is important for tax assessors, who must reassess the market value of homes in order to compute the annual property tax. It is also important to mortgage bankers and other home lenders, who must reevaluate the value of their portfolio of loans with changing local conditions, as well as to homeowners trying to sell their houses, and to potential buyers as they attempt to agree upon a selling price.

The simplest method for capturing these price effects is to include annual indicator variables (for example, $D99 = 1$ if year $= 1999$; $D99 = 0$ otherwise) into the hedonic regression model. An example can be found in Exercise 7.4.

7.2.4c   Regime Effects

An economic regime is a set of structural economic conditions that exist for a certain period. The idea is that economic relations may behave one way during one regime, but may behave differently during another. Economic regimes may be associated with political regimes (conservatives in power, liberals in power), unusual economic conditions (oil embargo, recession, hyperinflation), or changes in the legal environment (tax law changes). An investment tax credit[7] was enacted in 1962 in an effort to stimulate additional investment. The law was suspended in 1966, reinstated in 1970, and eliminated in the Tax Reform Act of 1986. Thus we might create an indicator variable

$$ITC_t = \begin{cases} 1 & \text{if } t = 1962 - 1965, \ 1970 - 1986 \\ 0 & otherwise \end{cases}$$

A macroeconomic investment equation might be

$$INV_t = \beta_1 + \delta ITC_t + \beta_2 GNP_t + \beta_3 GNP_{t-1} + e_t$$

If the tax credit was successful, then $\delta > 0$.

7.3 Log-Linear Models

In Section 4.5 and Appendix 4C we examined the log-linear model in some detail. In this section we explore the interpretation of indicator variables in log-linear models. Some additional detail is provided in Appendix 7A.

---

[7] Intriligator, Bodkin and Hsiao, *Econometric Models, Techniques and Applications*, 2nd edition, Upper Saddle River, NJ: Prentice-Hall, 1996, p. 53.

Let us consider the log-linear model

$$\ln(WAGE) = \beta_1 + \beta_2 EDUC + \delta FEMALE \tag{7.11}$$

What is the interpretation of the parameter δ? *FEMALE* is an intercept dummy variable, creating a parallel shift of the log-linear relationship when $FEMALE = 1$. That is

$$\ln(WAGE) = \begin{cases} \beta_1 + \beta_2 EDUC & MALES\ (FEMALE = 0) \\ (\beta_1 + \delta) + \beta_2 EDUC & FEMALES\ (FEMALE = 1) \end{cases}$$

But what about the fact that the dependent variable is $\ln(WAGE)$? Does that have an effect? The answer is yes—and there are two solutions.

7.3.1   A ROUGH CALCULATION

First, take the difference between $\ln(WAGE)$ of females and males:

$$\ln(WAGE)_{FEMALES} - \ln(WAGE)_{MALES} = \delta$$

Recall from Appendix A.1.6 and (A.3) that 100 times the log difference, 100δ, is approximately the percentage difference. Using the data file *cps4_small.dat*, the estimated log-linear model (7.11) is

$$\widehat{\ln(WAGE)} = 1.6539 + 0.0962 EDUC - 0.2432 FEMALE$$
$$(se) \qquad\quad (0.0844) \quad (0.0060) \qquad\quad (0.0327)$$

Thus, we estimate that there is a 24.32% differential between male and female wages. This is quick and simple, but as shown in Table A.2 there is close to a 10% approximation error with so large a difference.

7.3.2   AN EXACT CALCULATION

We can overcome the approximation error by doing a little algebra. The wage difference is

$$\ln(WAGE)_{FEMALES} - \ln(WAGE)_{MALES} = \ln\left(\frac{WAGE_{FEMALES}}{WAGE_{MALES}}\right) = \delta$$

using the property of logarithms that $\ln(x) - \ln(y) = \ln(x/y)$. These are natural logarithms, and the anti-log is the exponential function,

$$\frac{WAGE_{FEMALES}}{WAGE_{MALES}} = e^{\delta}$$

Subtract 1 from each side (in a tricky way) to obtain

$$\frac{WAGE_{FEMALES}}{WAGE_{MALES}} - \frac{WAGE_{MALES}}{WAGE_{MALES}} = \frac{WAGE_{FEMALES} - WAGE_{MALES}}{WAGE_{MALES}} = e^{\delta} - 1$$

The percentage difference between wages of females and males is $100(e^\delta - 1)\%$. From this, we estimate the wage differential between males and females to be

$$100(e^{\hat\delta} - 1)\% = 100(e^{-0.2432} - 1)\% = -21.59\%$$

Using the delta method from Appendix 5B.4, the approximate standard error for this estimate is 2.57%, which is a calculation that may be provided by your software, making this exact calculation more than one standard error different from the approximate value of -24.32%.

7.4 The Linear Probability Model

Economics is sometimes described as the "theory of choice." Many of the choices we make in life are "either—or" in nature. A few examples include

- A consumer who must choose between Coke and Pepsi
- A married woman who must decide whether to enter the labor market or not
- A bank official must choose to accept a loan application or not
- A high school graduate must decide whether to attend college or not
- A member of Parliament, a Senator, or a Representative must vote for or against a piece of legislation

To analyze and predict such outcomes using an econometric model, we represent the choice using an indicator variable, the value one if one alternative is chosen and the value zero if the other alternative is chosen. Because we are attempting to explain choice between two alternatives, the indicator variable will be the **dependent** variable rather than an independent variable in a regression model.

To begin, let us represent the variable indicating a choice as

$$y = \begin{cases} 1 & \text{if first alternative is chosen} \\ 0 & \text{if second alternative is chosen} \end{cases}$$

If we observe the choices that a random sample of individuals makes, then y is a random variable. If p is the probability that the first alternative is chosen, then $P[y = 1] = p$. The probability that the second alternative is chosen is $P[y = 0] = 1 - p$. The probability function for the binary indicator variable y is

$$f(y) = p^y(1 - p)^{1-y}, \quad y = 0, 1$$

The indicator variable y is said to follow a Bernoulli[8] distribution. The expected value of y is $E(y) = p$, and its variance is $\text{var}(y) = p(1 - p)$.

We are interested in identifying factors that might affect the probability p using a linear regression function, or, in this context, a **linear probability model**,

$$E(y) = p = \beta_1 + \beta_2 x_2 + \cdots + \beta_K x_K$$

---

[8] After Swiss mathematician Jacob Bernoulli, 1654–1705.

Proceeding as usual, we break the observed outcome y into a systematic portion, $E(y)$, and an unpredictable random error, e, so that the econometric model is

$$y = E(y) + e = \beta_1 + \beta_2 x_2 + \cdots + \beta_K x_K + e$$

One difficulty with using this model for choice behavior is that the usual error term assumptions cannot hold. The outcome y only takes two values, implying that the error term e also takes only two values, so that the usual "bell-shaped" curve describing the distribution of errors does not hold. The probability functions for y and e are

y value	e value	Probability
1	$1 - (\beta_1 + \beta_2 x_2 + \cdots + \beta_K x_K)$	p
0	$-(\beta_1 + \beta_2 x_2 + \cdots + \beta_K x_K)$	$1 - p$

The variance of the error term e is

$$\text{var}(e) = p(1 - p) = (\beta_1 + \beta_2 x_2 + \cdots + \beta_K x_K)(1 - \beta_1 - \beta_2 x_2 - \cdots - \beta_K x_K)$$

This error is not homoskedastic, so the usual formula for the variance of the least squares estimator is incorrect. A second problem associated with the linear probability model is that predicted values, $\widehat{E(y)} = \hat{p}$, can fall outside the $(0, 1)$ interval, meaning that their interpretation as probabilities does not make sense. Despite these weaknesses, the linear probability model has the advantage of simplicity, and it has been found to provide good estimates of the marginal effects of changes in explanatory variables x_k on the choice probability p, as long as p is not too close to zero or one.[9]

7.4.1 A MARKETING EXAMPLE

A shopper is deciding between Coke and Pepsi. Define the variable *COKE*:

$$COKE = \begin{cases} 1 & \text{if Coke is chosen} \\ 0 & \text{if Pepsi is chosen} \end{cases}$$

The expected value of this variable is $E(COKE) = p_{COKE}$ = probability that Coke is chosen. What factors might enter the choice decision? The relative price of Coke to Pepsi (*PRATIO*) is a potential factor. As the relative price of Coke rises, we should observe a reduced probability of its choice. Other factors influencing the consumer might be the presence of store displays for these products. Let *DISP_COKE* and *DISP_PEPSI* be indicator variables taking the value one if the respective store display is present and zero if it is not. We expect that the presence of a Coke display will increase the probability of a Coke purchase, and the presence of a Pepsi display will decrease the probability of a Coke purchase.

---

[9] See Chapter 16 for nonlinear models of choice, called probit and logit, which ensure that predicted probabilities fall between zero and one. These models require the use of more complex estimators and methods of inference.

The data file *coke.dat*[10] contains "scanner" data on 1140 individuals who purchased Coke or Pepsi. In this sample 44.7% of the customers chose Coke. The estimated regression model is

$$\widehat{E(COKE)} = \hat{p}_{COKE} = 0.8902 - 0.4009 PRATIO + 0.0772 DISP\_COKE - 0.1657 DISP\_PEPSI$$

(se)   (0.0655) (0.0613)   (0.0344)   (0.0356)

Assuming for the moment that the standard errors are reliable,[11] all the coefficients are significantly different from zero at the $\alpha = 0.05$ level. Recall that $PRATIO = 1$ if the prices of Coke and Pepsi are equal, and that $PRATIO = 1.10$ would represent a case in which Coke was 10% more expensive than Pepsi. Such an increase is estimated to reduce the probability of purchasing Coke by 0.04. A store display for Coke is estimated to increase the probability of a Coke purchase by 0.077, and a Pepsi display is estimated to reduce the probability of a Coke purchase by 0.166. The concerns about predicted probabilities falling outside (0, 1) are well founded in general, but in this example only 16 of the 1140 sample observations resulted in predicted probabilities less than zero, and there were no predicted probabilities greater than one.

7.5 Treatment Effects

Consider the question "Do hospitals make people healthier?" Angrist and Pischke[12] report the results of a National Health Interview Survey that included the question "During the past 12 months, was the respondent a patient in a hospital overnight?" Also asked was "Would you say your health in general is excellent, very good, good, fair or poor?" Using the number 1 for poor health and 5 for excellent health, those *who had not* gone to the hospital had an average health score of 3.93, and those *who had been* to the hospital had an average score of 3.21. That is, individuals who had been to the hospital had poorer health than those who had not.

Principles of economics books warn in the first chapter[13] about the faulty line of reasoning known as **post hoc, ergo propter hoc**, which means that one event's preceding another does not necessarily make the first the cause of the second. Going to the hospital does not *cause* the poorer health status. Those who were less healthy *chose* to go to the hospital because of an illness or injury, and at the time of the survey were still less healthy than those who had not gone to the hospital. Another way to say this is embodied in the warning that "**correlation** is not the same as **causation**." We observe that those who had been in a hospital are less healthy, but observing this association does not imply that going to the hospital causes a person to be less healthy. Still another way to describe the problem we face in this example is to say that data exhibit a **selection bias**, because some people chose (or **self-selected**) to go to the hospital and the others did not. When membership in the treated group is in part determined by choice, then the sample is *not* a random sample. There are systematic factors, in this case health status, contributing to the composition of the sample.

---

[10] Obtained from the ERIM public data base, James M. Kilts Center, University of Chicago Booth School of Business. *Scanner data* is information recorded at the point of purchase by an electronic device reading a barcode.

[11] The estimates and standard errors are not terribly dissimilar from those obtained using more advanced options discussed in Chapters 8 and 16.

[12] *Mostly Harmless Econometrics: An Empiricist's Guide*, Princeton, 2009, pp. 12–13.

[13] See, for example, Campbell R. McConnell and Stanley L. Brue, *Economics, Twelfth Edition*, McGraw-Hill, 1993, pp. 8–9.

A second example of selection bias may bring the concept closer to home. Are you reading this great book because you are enrolled in an econometrics class? Is the course required, or not? If your class is an "elective," then you and your classmates are *not a random sample* from the broader student population. It is our experience that students taking econometrics as an elective have an ability level and quantitative preparation that is higher, on average, than a random sample from the university population. We also observe that a higher proportion of undergraduate students who take econometrics enroll in graduate programs in economics or related disciplines. Is this a causal relationship? In part, it certainly is, but also your abilities and future plans for graduate training may have drawn you to econometrics, so that the high success rate of our students is in part attributed to **selection bias**.

Selection bias is also an issue when asking

- "How much does an additional year of education increase the wages of married women?" The difficulty is that we are able to observe a woman's wages only if she chooses to join the labor force, and thus the observed data is not a random sample.

- "How much does participation in a job-training program increase wages?" If participation is voluntary, then we may see a greater proportion of less skilled workers taking advantage of such a program.

- "How much does a dietary supplement contribute to weight loss?" If those taking the supplement are among the severely overweight, then the results we observe may not be "typical."

In each of these cases selection bias interferes with a straightforward examination of the data, and makes more difficult our efforts to measure a **causal effect**, or **treatment effect**.

In some situations, usually those involving the physical or medical sciences, it is clearer how we might study causal effects. For example, if we wish to measure the effect of a new type of fertilizer on rice production, we can **randomly** assign identical rice fields to be treated with a new fertilizer (the **treatment group**), with the others being treated with an existing product (the **control group**). At the end of the growing period we compare the production on the two types of fields. The key here is that we perform a **randomized controlled experiment**. By randomly assigning subjects to treatment and control groups, we ensure that the differences we observe will result from the treatment. In medical research the effectiveness of a new drug is measured by such experiments. Test subjects are randomly assigned to the control group, who receive a placebo drug, and the treatment group, who receive the drug being tested. By random assignment of treatment and control groups, we prevent any selection bias from occurring.

As economists we would like to have the type of information that arises from randomized controlled experiments to study the consequences of social policy changes, such as changes in laws, or changes in types and amounts of aid and training we provide the poor. The ability to perform randomized controlled experiments is limited because the subjects are people, and their economic well-being is at stake. However, there are some examples. Before we proceed, we will examine the statistical consequences of selection bias for the measurement of treatment effects.

7.5.1 The Difference Estimator

In order to understand the measurement of treatment effects, consider a simple regression model in which the explanatory variable is a dummy variable, indicating whether a particular individual is in the treatment or control group. Let y be the outcome variable, the measured characteristic the treatment is designed to effect. In the rice production example, y would be the output of rice on a particular rice field. Define the indicator variable d as

$$d_i = \begin{cases} 1 & \text{individual in treatment group} \\ 0 & \text{individual in control group} \end{cases} \tag{7.12}$$

The effect of the treatment on the outcome can be modeled as

$$y_i = \beta_1 + \beta_2 d_i + e_i, \quad i = 1, \ldots, N \tag{7.13}$$

where e_i represents the collection of other factors affecting the outcome. The regression functions for the treatment and control groups are

$$E(y_i) = \begin{cases} \beta_1 + \beta_2 & \text{if in treatment group, } d_i = 1 \\ \beta_1 & \text{if in control group, } d_i = 0 \end{cases}$$

This is the same model we used in Chapter 2.9 to study the effect of location on house prices. The **treatment effect** that we wish to measure is β_2. The least squares estimator of β_2 is

$$b_2 = \frac{\sum\limits_{i=1}^{N} (d_i - \bar{d})(y_i - \bar{y})}{\sum\limits_{i=1}^{N} (d_i - \bar{d})^2} = \bar{y}_1 - \bar{y}_0 \tag{7.14}$$

where $\bar{y}_1 = \sum_{i=1}^{N_1} y_i / N_1$ is the sample mean of the N_1 observations on y for the treatment group $(d = 1)$ and $\bar{y}_0 = \sum_{i=1}^{N_0} y_i / N_0$ is the sample mean of the N_0 observations on y for the control group $(d = 0)$. In this treatment/control framework the estimator b_2 is called the **difference estimator**, because it is the difference between the sample means of the treatment and control groups.[14]

7.5.2 ANALYSIS OF THE DIFFERENCE ESTIMATOR

The statistical properties of the difference estimator can be examined using the same strategy employed in Chapter 2.4.2. We can rewrite the difference estimator as

$$b_2 = \beta_2 + \frac{\sum_{i=1}^{N} (d_i - \bar{d})(e_i - \bar{e})}{\sum_{i=1}^{N} (d_i - \bar{d})^2} = \beta_2 + (\bar{e}_1 - \bar{e}_0)$$

In the middle equality, the factor added to β_2 has the same form as the difference estimator in (7.14), with e_i replacing y_i—hence the final equality. The difference estimator b_2 equals the true treatment effect β_2 plus the difference between the averages of the unobserved factors affecting the outcomes y for the treatment group $(\bar{e}_1)$ and for the control group $(\bar{e}_0)$. In order for the difference estimator to be unbiased, $E(b_2) = \beta_2$, it must be true that

$$E(\bar{e}_1 - \bar{e}_0) = E(\bar{e}_1) - E(\bar{e}_0) = 0$$

---

[14] See Appendix 7B for an algebraic derivation.

In words, the expected value of all the factors affecting the outcome, other than the treatment, must be **equal** for the treatment and control groups.

If we allow individuals to "self-select" into treatment and control groups, then $E(\bar{e}_1) - E(\bar{e}_0)$ is the selection bias in the estimation of the treatment effect. For example, we observed that those who had not gone to the hospital (control group) had an average health score of 3.93, and those who had been to the hospital (treatment group) had an average health score of 3.21. The estimated effect of the treatment is $(\bar{y}_1 - \bar{y}_0) = 3.21 - 3.93 = -0.72$. The estimator bias in this case arises because the pre-existing health conditions for the treated group, captured by $E(\bar{e}_1)$, are poorer than the pre-existing health of the control group, captured by $E(\bar{e}_0)$, so that in this example there is a negative bias in the difference estimator.

We can anticipate that anytime some individuals **select** treatment there will be factors leading to this choice that are systematically different from those leading individuals in the control group to not select treatment, resulting in a selection bias in the difference estimator. How can we eliminate the self-selection bias? The solution is to **randomly** assign individuals to treatment and control groups, so that there are no systematic differences between the groups, except for the treatment itself. With random assignment, and the use of a large number of experiment subjects, we can be sure that $E(\bar{e}_1) = E(\bar{e}_0)$ and $E(b_2) = \beta_2$.

7.5.3   APPLICATION OF DIFFERENCE ESTIMATION: PROJECT STAR

Medical researchers use white mice to test new drugs, because these mice, surprisingly, are genetically similar to humans. Mice that are bred to be identical are randomly assigned to treatment and control groups, making estimation of the treatment effect of a new drug on the mice a relatively straightforward and reproducible process. Medical research on humans is strictly regulated, and volunteers are given incentives to participate, then randomly assigned to treatment and control groups. Randomized controlled experiments in the social sciences are equally attractive from a statistician's point of view, but are rare because of the difficulties in organizing and funding them. A notable example of a randomized experiment is Tennessee's Project STAR.[15]

A longitudinal experiment was conducted in Tennessee beginning in 1985 and ending in 1989. A single cohort of students was followed from kindergarten through third grade. In the experiment children were randomly assigned within schools into three types of classes: small classes with 13–17 students, regular-sized classes with 22–25 students, and regular-sized classes with a full-time teacher aide to assist the teacher. Student scores on achievement tests were recorded, as was some information about the students, teachers, and schools. Data for the kindergarten classes is contained in the data file *star.dat*.

Let us first compare the performance of students in small classes versus regular classes.[16] The variable *TOTALSCORE* is the combined reading and math achievement scores and *SMALL* $= 1$ if the student was assigned to a small class, and zero if the student is in a regular class. In Tables 7.6a and 7.6b are summary statistics for the two types of classes. First, note that on all measures **except** *TOTALSCORE* the variable means reported are very similar. This is because students were randomly assigned to the classes, so that there should be no patterns evident. The average value of *TOTALSCORE* in the regular classes is 918.0429 and in small classes it is 931.9419, a difference of 13.899 points. The test scores are higher in the

---

[15] See www.heros-inc.org/star.htm for program description, public use data and extensive literature.

[16] Interestingly there is no significant difference in outcomes comparing a regular class to a regular class with an aide. For this example all observations for students in the third treatment group are dropped.

Table 7.6a **Summary Statistics for Regular-Sized Classes**

Variable	Mean	Std. Dev.	Min	Max
TOTALSCORE	918.0429	73.1380	635	1229
SMALL	0.0000	0.0000	0	0
TCHEXPER	9.0683	5.7244	0	24
BOY	0.5132	0.4999	0	1
FREELUNCH	0.4738	0.4994	0	1
WHITE_ASIAN	0.6813	0.4661	0	1
TCHWHITE	0.7980	0.4016	0	1
TCHMASTERS	0.3651	0.4816	0	1
SCHURBAN	0.3012	0.4589	0	1
SCHRURAL	0.4998	0.5001	0	1

$N = 2005$

Table 7.6b **Summary Statistics for Small Classes**

Variable	Mean	Std. Dev.	Min	Max
TOTALSCORE	931.9419	76.3586	747	1253
SMALL	1.0000	0.0000	1	1
TCHEXPER	8.9954	5.7316	0	27
BOY	0.5150	0.4999	0	1
FREELUNCH	0.4718	0.4993	0	1
WHITE_ASIAN	0.6847	0.4648	0	1
TCHWHITE	0.8625	0.3445	0	1
TCHMASTERS	0.3176	0.4657	0	1
SCHURBAN	0.3061	0.4610	0	1
SCHRURAL	0.4626	0.4987	0	1

$N = 1738$

smaller classes. The difference estimator obtain using regression will yield the same estimate, along with significance levels.

The model of interest is

$$TOTALSCORE = \beta_1 + \beta_2 SMALL + e \qquad (7.15)$$

The regression results are in column (1) of Table 7.7. The estimated "treatment effect" of putting kindergarten children into small classes is 13.899 points, the same as the difference in sample means computed above, on their achievement score total; the difference is statistically significant at the 0.01 level.

7.5.4 THE DIFFERENCE ESTIMATOR WITH ADDITIONAL CONTROLS

Because of the random assignment of the students to treatment and control groups, there is no selection bias in the estimate of the treatment effect. However, if additional factors might affect the outcome variable, they can be included in the regression specification. For example, it is possible that a teacher's experience leads to greater learning and higher achievement test scores. Adding *TCHEXPER* to the base model we obtain

Table 7.7   **Project STAR: Kindergarden**

	(1)	(2)	(3)	(4)
C	918.0429***	907.5643***	917.0684***	908.7865***
	(1.6672)	(2.5424)	(1.4948)	(2.5323)
SMALL	13.8990***	13.9833***	15.9978***	16.0656***
	(2.4466)	(2.4373)	(2.2228)	(2.2183)
TCHEXPER		1.1555***		0.9132***
		(0.2123)		(0.2256)
SCHOOL EFFECTS	No	No	Yes	Yes
N	3743	3743	3743	3743
adj. R^2	0.008	0.016	0.221	0.225
SSE	20847551	20683680	16028908	15957534

Standard errors in parentheses
Two-tail p-values: * $p < 0.10$, ** $p < 0.05$, *** $p < 0.01$

$$TOTALSCORE = \beta_1 + \beta_2 SMALL + \beta_3 TCHEXPER + e \qquad (7.16)$$

The least squares/difference estimates of (7.16) are in column (2) of Table 7.7. We estimate that each additional year of teaching experience increases the test score performance by 1.156 points, which is statistically significant at the 0.01 level. This increases our understanding of the effect of small classes. The results show that the effect of small classes is the same as the effect of approximately 12 years of teaching experience.

Note that adding *TCHEXPER* to the regression changed the estimate of the effect of *SMALL* classes very little. This is exactly what we would expect if *TCHEXPER* is uncorrelated with *SMALL*. The simple correlation between *SMALL* and *TCHEXPER* is only −0.0064. Recall that omitting a variable that is uncorrelated with an included variable does not change the estimated coefficient of the included variable. Comparing the models in columns (1) and (2) of Table 7.7, the model in (1) omits the significant variable *TCHEXPER*, but there is little change in the estimate of β_2 introduced by omitting this nearly uncorrelated variable. Furthermore, we can expect, in general, to obtain a difference estimator with smaller standard errors if we are able to include additional controls. In (7.15), any and all factors other than small class size are included in the error term. By taking some of those factors out of the error term and including them in the regression, the variance of the error term σ^2 is reduced, which reduces estimator variance.

7.5.4a School Fixed Effects

It may be that assignment to treatment groups is related to one or more observable characteristics. That is, treatments are randomly assigned *given* an external factor. Prior to a medical experiment concerning weight loss, participants may fall into the "overweight" category and the "obese" category. Of those in the overweight group 30% are randomly assigned for treatment, and of the obese group 50% are randomly assigned for treatment. Given pretreatment status, the treatment is randomly assigned. If such conditioning factors are omitted and put into the error term in (7.15) or (7.16), then these factors are correlated with the treatment variable and the least squares estimator of the treatment effect is biased and inconsistent. The way to adjust to "conditional" randomization is to include the conditioning factors into the regression.

In the STAR data, another factor that we might consider affecting the outcome is the school itself. The students were randomized *within* schools (conditional randomization), but not *across* schools. Some schools may be located in wealthier school districts that can pay higher salaries, thus attracting better teachers. The students in our sample are enrolled in 79 different schools. One way to account for school effects is to include an indicator variable for each school. That is, we can introduce 78 new indicators:

$$SCHOOL\_j = \begin{cases} 1 & \text{if student is in school } j \\ 0 & \text{otherwise} \end{cases}$$

This is an "intercept" indicator variable, allowing the expected total score to differ for each school. The model including these indicator variables is

$$TOTALSCORE_i = \beta_1 + \beta_2 SMALL_i + \beta_3 TCHEXPER_i + \sum_{j=2}^{79} \delta_j SCHOOL\_j_i + e_i \quad (7.17)$$

The regression function for a student in school j is

$$E(TOTALSCORE_i) = \begin{cases} (\beta_1 + \delta_j) + \beta_3 TCHEXPER_i & \text{student in regular class} \\ (\beta_1 + \delta_j + \beta_2) + \beta_3 TCHEXPER_i & \text{student in small class} \end{cases}$$

The expected score for a student in a regular class for a teacher with no experience is adjusted by the fixed amount δ_j. This **fixed effect** controls for some differences in the schools that are not accounted for by the regression model.

Columns (3) and (4) in Table 7.7 contain the estimated coefficients of interest, but not the 78 indicator variable coefficients. The joint F-test of the hypothesis that all $\delta_j = 0$ consists of $J = 78$ hypotheses with $N - K = 3663$ degrees of freedom. The F-value $= 14.118$ is significant at the 0.001 level. We conclude that there are statistically significant individual differences among schools. The important coefficients on *SMALL* and *TCHEXPER* change a little. The estimated effect of being in a small class increases to 16.0656 achievement test points in model (4), as compared to 13.9833 points in the corresponding model (2). It appears that some effect of small classes was masked by unincorporated individual school differences. This effect is small however, as the 95% interval estimate for the coefficient of *SMALL* [11.7165, 20.4148] in model (4) includes 13.9833. Similarly, the estimated effect of teacher experience is slightly different in the models with and without the school fixed effects.

7.5.4b Linear Probability Model Check of Random Assignment
In Tables 7.6a and 7.6b we examined the summary statistics for the data sorted by whether pupils were in a regular class or a small class. Except for total score, we did not find much difference in the sample means of the variables examined. Another way to check for random assignment is to regress *SMALL* on these characteristics and check for any significant coefficients, or an overall significant relationship. If there is random assignment, we should not find any significant relationships. Because *SMALL* is an indicator variable, we use the linear probability model discussed in Section 7.4. The estimated linear probability model is

$$\widehat{SMALL} = 0.4665 + 0.0014 BOY + 0.0044 WHITE\_ASIAN - 0.0006 TCHEXPER$$
$$(t) \qquad\qquad (0.09) \qquad\quad (0.22) \qquad\qquad\qquad (-0.42)$$
$$- 0.0009 FREELUNCH$$
$$(-0.05)$$

First, note that none of the right-hand-side variables are statistically significant. Second, the overall F statistic for this linear probability model is 0.06 with a $p = 0.99$. There is no evidence that students were assigned to small classes based on any of these criteria. Also, recall that the linear probability model is so named because $E(SMALL)$ is the probability of observing $SMALL = 1$ in a random draw from the population. If the values of all the potential explanatory factors are zero, the estimated intercept gives the estimated probability of observing a child in a small class to be 0.4665, with 95% interval estimate [0.4171, 0.5158]. We cannot reject the null hypothesis that the intercept equals 0.5, which is what it should be if students are allocated by a "flip" of a coin. *The importance of this, again, is that by randomly assigning students to small classes we can estimate the "treatment" effect using the simple difference estimator in* (7.15). The ability to isolate the important class size effect is a powerful argument in favor of randomized controlled experiments.

7.5.5 The Differences-in-Differences Estimator

Randomized controlled experiments are rare in economics because they are expensive and involve human subjects. **Natural experiments**, also called **quasi-experiments**, rely on observing real-world conditions that approximate what would happen in a randomized controlled experiment. Treatment appears *as if* it were randomly assigned. In this section we consider estimating treatment effects using "before and after" data.

Suppose that we observe two groups before and after a policy change, with the **treatment group** being affected by the policy, and the **control group** being unaffected by the policy. Using such data, we will examine any change that occurs to the control group and compare it to the change in the treatment group.

The analysis is explained by Figure 7.3. The outcome variable y might be an employment rate, a wage rate, a price, or so on. Before the policy change we observe the treatment group value $y = B$, and after the policy is implemented the treatment group value is $y = C$. Using only the data on the treatment group we cannot separate out the portion of the change from $y = B$ to $y = C$ that is due to the policy from the portion that is due to other factors that may affect the outcome. We say that the treatment effect is not "identified."

We can isolate the effect of the treatment by using a control group that is not affected by the policy change. Before the policy change, we observe the control group value $y = A$, and after the policy change, the control group value is $y = E$. In order to estimate the treatment effect using the four pieces of information contained in the points A, B, C, and E, we make

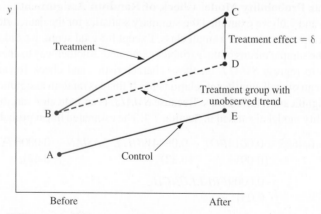

FIGURE 7.3 Difference-in-Differences Estimation.

the strong assumption that the two groups experience a **common trend**. In Figure 7.3, the dashed line $\overline{BD}$ represents what we imagine the treatment group growth would have been (the term **counterfactual** from psychology is sometimes used to describe this imagined outcome) in the absence of the policy change. The growth described by the dashed line $\overline{BD}$ is unobservable, and is obtained by assuming that the growth in the treatment group that is unrelated to the policy change is the same as the growth in the control group.

The treatment effect $\delta = \overline{CD}$ is the difference between the treatment and control values of y in the "after" period, after subtracting $\overline{DE}$, which is what the difference between the two groups would have been in the absence of the policy. Using the common growth assumption, the difference $\overline{DE}$ equals the initial difference $\overline{AB}$. Using the four observable points A, B, C, and E depicted in Figure 7.3, estimation of the treatment effect is based on data averages for the two groups in the two periods,

$$\hat{\delta} = (\hat{C} - \hat{E}) - (\hat{B} - \hat{A})$$

$$= (\bar{y}_{Treatment, After} - \bar{y}_{Control, After}) - (\bar{y}_{Treatment, Before} - \bar{y}_{Control, Before}) \qquad (7.18)$$

In (7.18), the sample means are

$\bar{y}_{Control, Before} = \hat{A}$ = sample mean of y for control group before policy implementation

$\bar{y}_{Treatment, Before} = \hat{B}$ = sample mean of y for treatment group before policy implementation

$\bar{y}_{Control, After} = \hat{E}$ = sample mean of y for control group after policy implementation

$\bar{y}_{Treatment, After} = \hat{C}$ = sample mean of y for treatment group after policy implementation

The estimator $\hat{\delta}$ is called a **differences-in-differences** (abbreviated as D-in-D, DD, or DID) estimator of the treatment effect.

The estimator $\hat{\delta}$ can be conveniently calculated using a simple regression. Define y_{it} to be the observed outcome for individual i in period t. Let $AFTER_t$ be an indicator variable that equals one in the period after the policy change ($t = 2$) and zero in the period before the policy change ($t = 1$). Let $TREAT_i$ be a dummy variable that equals one if individual i is in the treatment group and zero if the individual is in the control (non-treatment) group. Consider the regression model

$$y_{it} = \beta_1 + \beta_2 TREAT_i + \beta_3 AFTER_t + \delta(TREAT_i \times AFTER_t) + e_{it} \qquad (7.19)$$

The regression function is

$$E(y_{it}) = \begin{cases} \beta_1 & TREAT = 0, \ AFTER = 0 & [\text{Control before} = A] \\ \beta_1 + \beta_2 & TREAT = 1, \ AFTER = 0 & [\text{Treatment before} = B] \\ \beta_1 + \beta_3 & TREAT = 0, \ AFTER = 1 & [\text{Control after} = E] \\ \beta_1 + \beta_2 + \beta_3 + \delta & TREAT = 1, \ AFTER = 1 & [\text{Treatment after} = C] \end{cases}$$

In Figure 7.3, points $A = \beta_1$, $B = \beta_1 + \beta_2$, $E = \beta_1 + \beta_3$ and $C = \beta_1 + \beta_2 + \beta_3 + \delta$. Then,

$$\delta = (C - E) - (B - A) = [(\beta_1 + \beta_2 + \beta_3 + \delta) - (\beta_1 + \beta_3)] - [(\beta_1 + \beta_2) - \beta_1]$$

Using the least squares estimates b_1, b_2, b_3 and $\hat{\delta}$ from (7.19), we have

$$\hat{\delta} = \left[\left(b_1 + b_2 + b_3 + \hat{\delta} \right) - (b_1 + b_3) \right] - [(b_1 + b_2) - b_1]$$

$$= (\bar{y}_{Treatment, After} - \bar{y}_{Control, After}) - (\bar{y}_{Treatment, Before} - \bar{y}_{Control, Before})$$

7.5.6   Estimating the Effect of a Minimum Wage Change

Card and Krueger (1994)[17] provide an example of a natural experiment and the differences-in-differences estimator. On April 1, 1992, New Jersey's minimum wage was increased from \$4.25 to \$5.05 per hour, while the minimum wage in Pennsylvania stayed at \$4.25 per hour. Card and Krueger collected data on 410 fast food restaurants in New Jersey (the treatment group) and eastern Pennsylvania (the control group). The "before" period is February 1992, and the "after" period is November 1992. Using these data, they estimate the effect of the "treatment," raising the New Jersey minimum wage on employment at fast food restaurants in New Jersey. Their interesting finding, that there was no significant reduction[18] in employment, sparked a great debate and much further research.[19] In model (7.19) we will test the null and alternative hypotheses

$$H_0 : \delta \geq 0 \text{ versus } H_1 : \delta < 0 \tag{7.20}$$

The relevant Card and Krueger data is in the data file *njmin3.dat*. We use the sample means of *FTE*, the number of full-time-equivalent[20] employees, given in Table 7.8, to estimate the treatment effect δ using the differences-in-differences estimator.

In Pennsylvania, the control group, employment fell during the period February to November. Recall that the minimum wage level was changed in New Jersey, but not in Pennsylvania, so that employment levels in Pennsylvania were not affected. In New Jersey we see an increase in *FTE* in the same period. The differences-in-differences estimate of the change in employment due to the change in the minimum wage is

$$\begin{aligned}
\widehat{\delta} &= \left(\overline{FTE}_{NJ,After} - \overline{FTE}_{PA,After} \right) - \left(\overline{FTE}_{NJ,Before} - \overline{FTE}_{PA,Before} \right) \\
&= (21.0274 - 21.1656) - (20.4394 - 23.3312) \\
&= 2.7536
\end{aligned} \tag{7.21}$$

We estimate that *FTE* employment increased by 2.75 employees during the period in which the New Jersey minimum wage was increased. This positive effect is contrary to what is predicted by economic theory.

Table 7.8   **Full-time Equivalent Employees by State and Period**

Variable	N	mean	se
Pennsylvania (PA)			
Before	77	23.3312	1.3511
After	77	21.1656	0.9432
New Jersey (NJ)			
Before	321	20.4394	0.5083
After	319	21.0274	0.5203

---

[17] David Card and Alan Krueger (1994) "Minimum Wages and Employment: A Case Study of the Fast Food Industry in New Jersey and Pennsylvania," *The American Economic Review*, 84, 316–361. We thank David Card for letting us use the data.

[18] Remember that failure to reject a null hypothesis does not make it true!

[19] The issue is hotly contested and the literature extensive. See, for example, http://en.wikipedia.org/wiki/Minimum_wage, and the references listed, as a starting point.

[20] Card and Krueger calculate FTE = 0.5 × number of part time workers + number of full time workers + number of managers.

Rather than compute the differences-in-differences estimate using sample means, it is easier and more general to use the regression format. In (7.19) let $y = FTE$ employment, the treatment variable is the indicator variable $NJ = 1$ if observation is from New Jersey, and zero if from Pennsylvania. The time indicator is $D = 1$ if the observation is from November and zero if it is from February. The differences-in-differences regression is then

$$FTE_{it} = \beta_1 + \beta_2 NJ_i + \beta_3 D_t + \delta(NJ_i \times D_t) + e_{it} \qquad (7.22)$$

Using the 794 complete observations in *njmin3.dat*, the least squares estimates are reported in column (1) of Table 7.9. At the $\alpha = 0.05$ level of significance the rejection region for the left-tail test in (7.20) is $t \leq -1.645$, so we fail to reject the null hypothesis. We cannot conclude that the increase in the minimum wage in New Jersey reduced employment at New Jersey fast food restaurants.

As with randomized control experiments it is interesting to see the robustness of these results. In Table 7.9 column (2) we add indicator variables for fast food chain and whether

Table 7.9 **Difference-in-Differences Regressions**

	(1)	(2)	(3)
C	23.3312***	25.9512***	25.3205***
	(1.072)	(1.038)	(1.211)
NJ	−2.8918*	−2.3766*	−0.9080
	(1.194)	(1.079)	(1.272)
D	−2.1656	−2.2236	−2.2119
	(1.516)	(1.368)	(1.349)
D_NJ	2.7536	2.8451	2.8149
	(1.688)	(1.523)	(1.502)
KFC		−10.4534***	−10.0580***
		(0.849)	(0.845)
ROYS		−1.6250	−1.6934*
		(0.860)	(0.859)
WENDYS		−1.0637	−1.0650
		(0.929)	(0.921)
CO_OWNED		−1.1685	−0.7163
		(0.716)	(0.719)
SOUTHJ			−3.7018***
			(0.780)
CENTRALJ			0.0079
			(0.897)
PA1			0.9239
			(1.385)
N	794	794	794
R^2	0.007	0.196	0.221
adj. R^2	0.004	0.189	0.211

Standard errors in parentheses
Two-tail *p*-values: * $p < 0.05$, ** $p < 0.01$, *** $p < 0.001$

the restaurant was company-owned rather than franchise-owned. In column (3) we add indicator variables for geographical regions within the survey area. None of these changes alter the differences-in-differences estimate, and none lead to rejection of the null hypothesis in (7.20).

7.5.7 USING PANEL DATA

In the previous section's differences-in-differences analysis, we did not exploit one very important feature of Card and Krueger's data—namely, that the *same* fast food restaurants were observed on two occasions. We have "before" and "after" data on 384 of the 410 restaurants. These are called **paired data** observations, or **repeat data** observations, or **panel data** observations. In Chapter 1 we introduced the notion of a **panel** of data—we observe the same individual-level units over several periods. The Card and Krueger data includes $T = 2$ observations on $N = 384$ individual restaurants among the 410 restaurants surveyed. The remaining 26 restaurants had missing data on *FTE* either in the "before" or "after" period. There are powerful advantages to using panel data, some of which we will describe here. See Chapter 15 for a much more extensive discussion.

Using panel data we can control for **unobserved individual-specific characteristics**. There are characteristics of the restaurants that we do not observe. Some restaurants will have preferred locations, some may have superior managers, and so on. These unobserved individual specific characteristics are included in the error term of the regression (7.22). Let c_i denote any unobserved characteristics of individual restaurant i that do not change over time. Adding c_i to (7.22) we have

$$FTE_{it} = \beta_1 + \beta_2 NJ_i + \beta_3 D_t + \delta(NJ_i \times D_t) + c_i + e_{it} \qquad (7.23)$$

Whatever c_i might be, it contaminates this regression model. A solution is at hand *if* we have a panel of data. If we have $T = 2$ repeat observations we can *eliminate* c_i by analyzing the changes in *FTE* from period one to period two. Recall that $D_t = 0$ in period one, so $D_1 = 0$; and $D_t = 1$ in period two, so $D_2 = 1$. Subtract the observation for $t = 1$ from that for $t = 2$

$$FTE_{i2} = \beta_1 + \beta_2 NJ_i + \beta_3 1 + \delta(NJ_i \times 1) + c_i + e_{i2}$$
$$- \underline{FTE_{i1} = \beta_1 + \beta_2 NJ_i + \beta_3 0 + \delta(NJ_i \times 0) + c_i + e_{i1}}$$
$$\Delta FTE_i = \beta_3 + \delta NJ_i + \Delta e_i$$

where $\Delta FTE_i = FTE_{i2} - FTE_{i1}$ and $\Delta e_i = e_{i2} - e_{i1}$. Using the **differenced data**, the regression model of interest becomes

$$\Delta FTE_i = \beta_3 + \delta NJ_i + \Delta e_i \qquad (7.24)$$

Observe that the contaminating factor c_i has dropped out! Whatever those unobservable features might have been, they are now gone. The intercept β_1 and the coefficient β_2 have also dropped out, with the parameter β_3 becoming the new intercept. The most important parameter, δ, measuring the treatment effect is the coefficient of the indicator variable NJ_i, which identifies the treatment (New Jersey) and control group (Pennsylvania) observations.

The estimated model (7.24) is

$$\widehat{\Delta FTE} = -2.2833 + 2.7500NJ \quad R^2 = 0.0146$$
$$\text{(se)} \qquad (1.036) \quad (1.154)$$

The estimate of the treatment effect $\hat{\delta} = 2.75$ using the differenced data, which accounts for any unobserved individual differences, is very close to the differences-in-differences. Once again we fail to conclude that the minimum wage increase has reduced employment in these New Jersey fast food restaurants.

7.6 Exercises

Answers to exercises marked * appear at www.wiley.com/go/global/hill.

7.6.1 PROBLEMS

7.1 An economics department at a large state university keeps track of its majors' starting salaries. Does taking econometrics affect starting salary? Let SAL = salary in dollars, GPA = grade point average on a 4.0 scale, $METRICS = 1$ if student took econometrics, and $METRICS = 0$ otherwise. Using the data file *metrics.dat*, which contains information on 50 recent graduates, we obtain the estimated regression

$$\widehat{SAL} = 24200 + 1643GPA + 5033METRICS \quad R^2 = 0.74$$
$$\text{(se)} \qquad (1078) \quad (352) \qquad (456)$$

(a) Interpret the estimated equation.
(b) How would you modify the equation to see whether women had lower starting salaries than men? (Hint: Define an indicator variable $FEMALE = 1$, if female; zero otherwise.)
(c) How would you modify the equation to see if the value of econometrics was the same for men and women?

7.2* In September 1998, a local TV station contacted an econometrician to analyze some data for them. They were going to do a Halloween story on the legend of full moons' affecting behavior in strange ways. They collected data from a local hospital on emergency room cases for the period from January 1, 1998, until mid-August. There were 229 observations. During this time there were eight full moons and seven new moons (a related myth concerns new moons) and three holidays (New Year's Day, Memorial Day, and Easter). If there is a full-moon effect, then hospital administrators will adjust numbers of emergency room doctors and nurses, and local police may change the number of officers on duty.

Using the data in the file *fullmoon.dat* we obtain the regression results in the following table: T is a time trend ($T = 1,2,3,\ldots,229$) and the rest are indicator variables. $HOLIDAY = 1$ if the day is a holiday; 0 otherwise. $FRIDAY = 1$ if the day is a Friday; 0 otherwise. $SATURDAY = 1$ if the day is a Saturday; 0 otherwise. $FULLMOON = 1$ if there is a full moon; 0 otherwise. $NEWMOON = 1$ if there is a new moon; 0 otherwise.

Emergency Room Cases Regression—Model 1

Variable	Coefficient	Std. Error	t-Statistic	Prob.
C	93.6958	1.5592	60.0938	0.0000
T	0.0338	0.0111	3.0580	0.0025
HOLIDAY	13.8629	6.4452	2.1509	0.0326
FRIDAY	6.9098	2.1113	3.2727	0.0012
SATURDAY	10.5894	2.1184	4.9987	0.0000
FULLMOON	2.4545	3.9809	0.6166	0.5382
NEWMOON	6.4059	4.2569	1.5048	0.1338

$R^2 = 0.1736$ $SSE = 27108.82$

(a) Interpret these regression results. When should emergency rooms expect more calls?

(b) The model was reestimated omitting the variables *FULLMOON* and *NEW-MOON*, as shown below. Comment on any changes you observe.

(c) Test the joint significance of *FULLMOON* and *NEWMOON*. State the null and alternative hypotheses and indicate the test statistic you use. What do you conclude?

Emergency Room Cases Regression—Model 2

Variable	Coefficient	Std. Error	t-Statistic	Prob.
C	94.0215	1.5458	60.8219	0.0000
T	0.0338	0.0111	3.0568	0.0025
HOLIDAY	13.6168	6.4511	2.1108	0.0359
FRIDAY	6.8491	2.1137	3.2404	0.0014
SATURDAY	10.3421	2.1153	4.8891	0.0000

$R^2 = 0.1640$ $SSE = 27424.19$

7.3   Henry Saffer and Frank Chaloupka ("The Demand for Illicit Drugs," *Economic Inquiry*, 37(3), 1999, 401–411) estimate demand equations for alcohol, marijuana, cocaine, and heroin using a sample of size $N = 44,889$. The estimated equation for alcohol use after omitting a few control variables is shown in the chart at the top of page 289.

The variable definitions (sample means in parentheses) are as follows:

The dependent variable is the number of days alcohol was used in the past 31 days (3.49)

ALCOHOL PRICE—price of a liter of pure alcohol in 1983 dollars (24.78)
INCOME—total personal income in 1983 dollars (12,425)
GENDER—a binary variable = 1 if male (0.479)
MARITAL STATUS—a binary variable = 1 if married (0.569)
AGE 12–20—a binary variable = 1 if individual is 12–20 years of age (0.155)
AGE 21–30—a binary variable = 1 if individual is 21–30 years of age (0.197)
BLACK—a binary variable = 1 if individual is black (0.116)
HISPANIC—a binary variable = 1 if individual is Hispanic (0.078)

Demand for Illicit Drugs

Variable	Coefficient	t-statistic
C	4.099	17.98
ALCOHOL PRICE	−0.045	5.93
INCOME	0.000057	17.45
GENDER	1.637	29.23
MARITAL STATUS	−0.807	12.13
AGE 12–20	−1.531	17.97
AGE 21–30	0.035	0.51
BLACK	−0.580	8.84
HISPANIC	−0.564	6.03

(a) Interpret the coefficient of alcohol price.
(b) Compute the price elasticity at the means of the variables.
(c) Compute the price elasticity at the means of alcohol price and income, for a married hispanic male, age 21–30.
(d) Interpret the coefficient of income. If we measured income in $1,000 units, what would the estimated coefficient be?
(e) Interpret the coefficients of the indicator variables, as well as their significance.

7.4   In the file *stockton.dat* we have data from January 1991 to December 1996 on house prices, square footage, and other characteristics of 4682 houses that were sold in Stockton, California. One of the key problems regarding housing prices in a region concerns construction of "house price indexes," as discussed in Section 7.2.4b. To illustrate, we estimate a regression model for house price, including as explanatory variables the size of the house (*SQFT*), the age of the house (*AGE*), and annual indicator variables, omitting the indicator variable for the year 1991.

$$PRICE = \beta_1 + \beta_2 SQFT + \beta_3 AGE + \delta_1 D92 + \delta_2 D93 + \delta_3 D94 + \delta_4 D95$$
$$+ \delta_5 D96 + e$$

The results are as follows:

Stockton House Price Index Model

Variable	Coefficient	Std. Error	t-Statistic	Prob.
C	21456.2000	1839.0400	11.6671	0.0000
SQFT	72.7878	1.0001	72.7773	0.0000
AGE	−179.4623	17.0112	−10.5496	0.0000
D92	−4392.8460	1270.9300	−3.4564	0.0006
D93	−10435.4700	1231.8000	−8.4717	0.0000
D94	−13173.5100	1211.4770	−10.8739	0.0000
D95	−19040.8300	1232.8080	−15.4451	0.0000
D96	−23663.5100	1194.9280	−19.8033	0.0000

(a) Discuss the estimated coefficients on *SQFT* and *AGE*, including their interpretation, signs, and statistical significance.
(b) Discuss the estimated coefficients on the indicator variables.
(c) What would have happened if we had included an indicator variable for 1991?

7.6.2 COMPUTER EXERCISES

7.5* In (7.7) we specified a hedonic model for house price. The dependent variable was the price of the house in dollars. Real estate economists have found that for many data sets, a more appropriate model has the dependent variable ln(*PRICE*).
  (a) Using the data in the file *utown.dat,* estimate the model (7.7) using ln(*PRICE*) as the dependent variable.
  (b) Discuss the estimated coefficients on *SQFT* and *AGE*. Refer to Chapter 4.5 for help with interpreting the coefficients in this log-linear functional form.
  (c) Compute the percentage change in price due to the presence of a pool. Use both the rough approximation in Section 7.3.1 and the exact calculation in Section 7.3.2.
  (d) Compute the percentage change in price due to the presence of a fireplace. Use both the rough approximation in Section 7.3.1 and the exact calculation in Section 7.3.2.
  (e) Compute the percentage change in price of a 2500-square-foot home near the university relative to the same house in another location using the methodology in Section 7.3.2.

7.6 Data on the weekly sales of a major brand of canned tuna by a supermarket chain in a large midwestern U.S. city during a mid-1990s calendar year are contained in the file *tuna.dat*. There are 52 observations on the variables

SAL1 = unit sales of brand no. 1 canned tuna
APR1 = price per can of brand no. 1 canned tuna
APR2, APR3 = price per can of brands nos. 2 and 3 of canned tuna
DISP = an indicator variable that takes the value one if there is a store display for brand no. 1 during the week but no newspaper ad; zero otherwise
DISPAD = an indicator variable that takes the value one if there is a store display *and* a newspaper ad during the week; zero otherwise

(a) Estimate, by least squares, the log-linear model

$$\ln(SAL1) = \beta_1 + \beta_2 APR1 + \beta_3 APR2 + \beta_4 APR3 + \beta_5 DISP + \beta_6 DISPAD + e$$

(b) Discuss and interpret the estimates of β_2, β_3, and β_4.
(c) Are the signs and *relative* magnitudes of the estimates of β_5 and β_6 consistent with economic logic? Interpret these estimates using the approaches in Sections 7.3.1 and 7.3.2.
(d) Test, at the $\alpha = 0.05$ level of significance, each of the following hypotheses:
  (i) $H_0: \beta_5 = 0$, $H_1: \beta_5 \neq 0$
  (ii) $H_0: \beta_6 = 0$, $H_1: \beta_6 \neq 0$
  (iii) $H_0: \beta_5 = 0, \beta_6 = 0$; $H_1: \beta_5$ or $\beta_6 \neq 0$
  (iv) $H_0: \beta_6 \leq \beta_5$, $H_1: \beta_6 > \beta_5$
(e) Discuss the relevance of the hypothesis tests in (d) for the supermarket chain's executives.

7.7 Mortgage lenders are interested in determining borrower and loan factors that may lead to delinquency or foreclosure. In the file *lasvegas.dat* are 1000 observations on mortgages for single-family homes in Las Vegas, Nevada, during 2008. The variable of interest is *DELINQUENT*, an indicator variable $= 1$ if the borrower missed at least three payments (90 or more days late), but zero otherwise. Explanatory variables are *LVR* = the ratio of the loan amount to the value of the property; *REF* = 1 if purpose of the loan was a "refinance" and $= 0$ if loan was for a purchase; *INSUR* = 1 if mortgage carries mortgage insurance, zero otherwise; *RATE* = initial interest rate of the mortgage; *AMOUNT* = dollar value of mortgage (in \$100,000); *CREDIT* = credit score, *TERM* = number of years between disbursement of the loan and the date it is expected to be fully repaid, *ARM* = 1 if mortgage has an adjustable rate, and $= 0$ if mortgage has a fixed rate.

(a) Estimate the linear probability (regression) model explaining *DELINQUENT* as a function of the remaining variables. Are the signs of the estimated coefficients reasonable?

(b) Interpret the coefficient of *INSUR*. If *CREDIT* increases by 40 points, what is the estimated effect on the probability of a delinquent loan?

(c) Compute the predicted value of *DELINQENT* for the final (1000th) observation. Interpret this value.

(d) Compute the predicted value of *DELINQUENT* for all 1000 observations. How many were less than zero? How many were greater than 1? Explain why such predictions are problematic.

7.8 A motel's management discovered that a defective product was used in the motel's construction. It took seven months to correct the defects, during which time approximately 14 rooms in the 100-unit motel were taken out of service for one month at a time. The motel lost profits due to these closures, and the question of how to compute the losses was addressed by Adams (2008).[21] For this exercise, use the data in *motel.dat*.

(a) The occupancy rate for the damaged motel is *MOTEL_PCT*, and the competitor occupancy rate is *COMP_PCT*. On the same graph, plot these variables against *TIME*. Which had the higher occupancy before the repair period? Which had the higher occupancy during the repair period?

(b) Compute the average occupancy rate for the motel and competitors when the repairs were not being made (call these $\overline{MOTEL}_0$ and $\overline{COMP}_0$) and when they were being made ($\overline{MOTEL}_1$ and $\overline{COMP}_1$). During the nonrepair period, what was the difference between the average occupancies, $\overline{MOTEL}_0 - \overline{COMP}_0$? Assume that the damaged motel occupancy rate would have maintained the same relative difference in occupancy if there had been no repairs. That is, assume that the damaged motel's occupancy would have been $\overline{MOTEL}_1^* = \overline{COMP}_1 + (\overline{MOTEL}_0 - \overline{COMP}_0)$. Compute the "simple" estimate of lost occupancy $\overline{MOTEL}_1^* - \overline{MOTEL}_1$. Compute the amount of revenue lost during the seven-month period (215 days) assuming an average room rate of \$58.71 per night.

(c) Draw a revised version of Figure 7.3 that explains the calculation in part (b).

(d) Alternatively, consider a regression approach. A model explaining motel occupancy uses as explanatory variables the competitors' occupancy, the relative

───────────

[21] A. Frank Adams (2008) "When a 'Simple' Analysis Won't Do: Applying Economic Principles in a Lost Profits Case," *The Value Examiner*, May/June 2008, 22–28. The authors thank Professor Adams for the use of his data.

price (*RELPRICE*) and an indicator variable for the repair period (*REPAIR*). That is, let

$$MOTEL\_PCT_t = \beta_1 + \beta_2 COMP\_PCT_t + \beta_3 RELPRICE_t + \beta_4 REPAIR_t + e_t$$

Obtain the least squares estimates of the parameters. Interpret the estimated coefficients, as well as their signs and significance.

(e) Using the least squares estimate of the coefficient of *REPAIR* from part (d), compute an estimate of the revenue lost by the damaged motel during the repair period (215 days @ \$58.71 × b_4). Compare this value to the "simple" estimate in part (b). Construct a 99% interval estimate for the estimated loss. Is the estimated loss from part (b) within the interval estimate?

(f) Carry out the regression specification test RESET. Is there any evidence of model misspecification?

(g) Plot the least squares residuals against *TIME*. Are there any obvious patterns?

7.9* In the STAR experiment (Section 7.5.3), children were randomly assigned within schools into three types of classes: small classes with 13 to 17 students, regular-sized classes with 22–25 students, and regular-sized classes with a full-time teacher aide to assist the teacher. Student scores on achievement tests were recorded, as was some information about the students, teachers, and schools. Data for the kindergarten classes is contained in the data file *star.dat*.

(a) Calculate the average of *TOTALSCORE* for (i) students in regular-sized classrooms with full time teachers, but no aide; (ii) students in regular-sized classrooms with full time teachers, and an aide; and (iii) students in small classrooms. What do you observe about test scores in these three types of learning environments?

(b) Estimate the regression model $TOTALSCORE_i = \beta_1 + \beta_2 SMALL_i + \beta_3 AIDE_i + e_i$, where *AIDE* is a indicator variable equaling one for classes taught by a teacher and an aide and zero otherwise. What is the relation of the estimated coefficients from this regression to the sample means in part (a)? Test the statistical significance of β_3 at the 5% level of significance.

(c) To the regression in (b) add the additional explanatory variable *TCHEXPER*. Is this variable statistically significant? Does its addition to the model affect the estimates of β_2 and β_3?

(d) To the regression in (c) add the additional explanatory variables *BOY*, *FREELUNCH*, and *WHITE_ASIAN*. Are any of these variables statistically significant? Does their addition to the model affect the estimates of β_2 and β_3?

(e) To the regression in (d) add the additional explanatory variables *TCHWHITE*, *TCHMASTERS*, *SCHURBAN*, and *SCHRURAL*. Are any of these variables statistically significant? Does their addition to the model affect the estimates of β_2 and β_3?

(f) Discuss the importance of parts (c), (d), and (e) to our estimation of the "treatment" effects in part (b).

(g) Add to the models in (b) through (e) indicator variables for each school

$$SCHOOL\_j = \begin{cases} 1 & \text{if student is in school } j \\ 0 & \text{otherwise} \end{cases}$$

Test the joint significance of these school "fixed effects." Does the inclusion of these fixed effect indicator variables substantially alter the estimates of β_2 and β_3?

7.10 Many cities in California have passed Inclusionary Zoning policies (also known as below-market housing mandates) as an attempt to make housing more affordable. These policies require developers to sell some units below the market price on a percentage of the new homes built. For example, in a development of 10 new homes each with market value $850,000, the developer may have to sell 5 of the units at $180,000. Means et al. (2007)[22] examine the effects of such policies on house prices and number of housing units available using 1990 (before policy impact) and 2000 (after policy impact) census data on California cities. Use *means.dat* for the following exercises.

   (a) Using only the data for 2000, compare the sample means of *LNPRICE* and *LNUNITS* for cities with an Inclusionary Zoning policy, *IZLAW* = 1, to those without the policy, *IZLAW* = 0. Based on these estimates, what is the percentage difference in prices and number of units for cities with and without the law? [For this example, use the simple rule that $100[\ln(y_1) - \ln(y_0)]$ is the approximate percentage difference between y_0 and y_1.] Does the law achieve its purpose?

   (b) Use the existence of an Inclusionary Zoning policy as a "treatment." Consider those cities who did not pass such a law, *IZLAW* = 0, the "control" group. Draw a figure like Figure 7.3 comparing treatment and control groups *LNPRICE* and *LNUNITS*, and determine the "treatment effect." Are your conclusions about the effect of the policy the same as in (a)?

   (c) Use *LNPRICE* and *LNUNITS* in differences-in-differences regressions, with explanatory variables *D*, the indicator variable for year 2000; *IZLAW*, and the interaction of *D* and *IZLAW*. Is the estimate of the treatment effect statistically significant, and of the anticipated sign?

   (d) To the regressions in (c) add the control variable *LMEDHHINC*. Interpret the estimate of the new variable, including its sign and significance. How does the addition affect the estimates of the treatment effect?

   (e) To the regressions in (d) add the variables *EDUCATTAIN*, *PROPPOVERTY*, and *LPOP*. Interpret the estimates of these new variables, including their signs and significance. How do these additions affect the estimates of the treatment effect?

   (f) Write a 250-word essay discussing the essential results in parts (a) through (e). Include in your essay an economic analysis of the policy.

7.11 This question extends the analysis of Exercise 7.10. Read the introduction to that exercise if you have not done so. Each city in the sample may have unique, unobservable characteristics that affect *LNPRICE* and *LNUNITS*. Following the discussion in Section 7.5.6, use the differenced data to control for these unobserved effects.

   (a) Regress *DLNPRICE* and *DLNUNITS* on *IZLAW*. Compare the estimate of the treatment effect to those from the differences-in-differences regression of *LNPRICE* and *LNUNITS* on the explanatory variables *D*, the indicator variable for year 2000; *IZLAW*, and the interaction of *D* and *IZLAW*.

   (b)◆Explain, algebraically, why the outcome in (a) occurs.

   (c) To the regression in (a) add the variable *DLMEDHHINC*. Interpret the estimate of this new variable, including its sign and significance. How does the addition affect the estimates of the treatment effect?

[22] "Below-Market Housing Mandates as Takings: Measuring their Impact" Tom Means, Edward Stringham, and Edward Lopez, Independent Policy Report, November 2007. The authors wish to thank Tom Means for providing the data and insights into this exercise.

(d) To the regression in (c), add the variables *DEDUCATTAIN*, *DPROPPOVERTY*, and *DLPOP*. Interpret the estimates of these new variables, including their signs and significance. How do these additions affect the estimates of the treatment effect?

7.12 Use the data in the file *cps5.dat* to estimate the regression of ln(*WAGE*) on the explanatory variables *EDUC*, *EXPER*, *EXPER*^{2}, *FEMALE*, *BLACK*, *MARRIED*, *SOUTH*, *FULLTIME*, and *METRO*.

(a) Discuss the results of the estimation. Interpret *each* coefficient and comment on its sign and significance. Are things as you would expect?

(b)◆(large data set) Use the data *cps4.dat* to re-estimate the equation. What changes do you observe?

7.13◆ (large data set) Use the data file *cps4.dat* for the following:

(a) Estimate the model used in Table 7.4. (i) Test the null hypothesis that the interaction between *BLACK* and *FEMALE* is statistically significant. (ii) Test the null hypothesis that there is no regional effect.

(b) Estimate the model used in Table 7.4 using ln(*WAGE*) as the dependent variable rather than *WAGE*. (i) Discuss any important differences in results between the linear and log-linear specifications. (ii) Test the null hypothesis that the interaction between *BLACK* and *FEMALE* is statistically significant. (iii) Test the null hypothesis that there is no regional effect.

(c) Estimate the models used in Table 7.5. Carry out the test for the null hypothesis that there is no difference between wage equations for southern and nonsouthern workers.

(d) Estimate the models used in Table 7.5 using ln(*WAGE*) as the dependent variable rather than *WAGE*. (i) Discuss any important differences in results between the linear and log-linear specifications. (ii) Carry out the test for the null hypothesis that there is no difference between wage equations for southern and nonsouthern workers.

7.14* Professor Ray C. Fair's voting model was introduced in Exercise 2.14. He builds models that explain and predict the U.S. presidential elections. See his website at http://fairmodel.econ.yale.edu/vote2008/index2.htm. The basic premise of the model is that the incumbent party's share of the two-party (Democratic and Republican) popular vote (incumbent means the party in power at the time of the election) is affected by a number of factors relating to the economy, and variables relating to the politics, such as how long the incumbent party has been in power, and whether the president is running for reelection. Fair's data, 33 observations for the election years from 1880 to 2008, are in the file *fair4.dat*. The dependent variable is *VOTE* = percentage share of the popular vote won by the incumbent party.

The explanatory variables include

PARTY = 1 if there is a Democratic incumbent at the time of the election and −1 if there is a Republican incumbent.

PERSON = 1 if the incumbent is running for election and zero otherwise.

DURATION = 0 if the incumbent party has been in power for one term, one if the incumbent party has been in power for two consecutive terms, 1.25 if the incumbent party has been in power for three consecutive terms, 1.50 for four consecutive terms, and so on.

WAR = 1 for the elections of 1920, 1944, and 1948 and zero otherwise.

$GROWTH$ = growth rate of real per capita GDP in the first three quarters of the election year (annual rate).

$INFLATION$ = absolute value of the growth rate of the GDP deflator in the first 15 quarters of the administration (annual rate) except for 1920, 1944, and 1948, where the values are zero.

$GOODNEWS$ = number of quarters in the first 15 quarters of the administration in which the growth rate of real per capita GDP is greater than 3.2% at an annual rate except for 1920, 1944, and 1948, where the values are zero.

(a) Consider the regression model

$$VOTE = \beta_1 + \beta_2 GROWTH + \beta_3 INFLATION + \beta_4 GOODNEWS$$
$$+ \beta_5 PERSON + \beta_6 DURATION + \beta_7 PARTY + \beta_8 WAR + e$$

Discuss the anticipated effects of the dummy variables $PERSON$ and WAR.

(b) The binary variable $PARTY$ is somewhat different from the dummy variables we have considered. Write out the regression function $E(VOTE)$ for the two values of $PARTY$. Discuss the effects of this specification.

(c) Use the data for the period 1916–2004 to estimate the proposed model. Discuss the estimation results. Are the signs as expected? Are the estimates statistically significant? How well does the model fit the data?

(d) Predict the outcome of the 2008 election using the given 2008 data for values of the explanatory variables. Based on the prediction, would you have picked the outcome of the election correctly?

(e) Construct a 95% prediction interval for the outcome of the 2008 election.

(f) Using data values of your choice (you must explain them), predict the outcome of the 2012 election.

7.15   The data file *br2.dat* contains data on 1080 house sales in Baton Rouge, Louisiana, during July and August 2005. The variables are $PRICE$ ($), $SQFT$ (total square feet), $BEDROOMS$ (number), $BATHS$ (number), AGE (years), $OWNER$ (=1 if occupied by owner; zero if vacant or rented), $POOL$ (=1 if present), $TRADITIONAL$ (=1 if traditional style; 0 if other style), $FIREPLACE$ (=1 if present), and $WATERFRONT$ (=1 if on waterfront).

(a) Compute the data summary statistics and comment. In particular, construct a histogram of $PRICE$. What do you observe?

(b) Estimate a regression model explaining $\ln(PRICE/1000)$ as a function of the remaining variables. Divide the variable $SQFT$ by 100 prior to estimation. Comment on how well the model fits the data. Discuss the signs and statistical significance of the estimated coefficients. Are the signs what you expect? Give an exact interpretation of the coefficient of $WATERFRONT$.

(c) Create a variable that is the product of $WATERFRONT$ and $TRADITIONAL$. Add this variable to the model and reestimate. What is the effect of adding this variable? Interpret the coefficient of this interaction variable, and discuss its sign and statistical significance.

(d) It is arguable that the traditional-style homes may have a different regression function from the diverse set of nontraditional styles. Carry out a Chow test of the equivalence of the regression models for traditional versus nontraditional styles. What do you conclude?

(e) Using the equation estimated in part (c), predict the value of a traditional style house with 2000 square feet of area, that is 15 years old, that is owner-occupied at the time of sale, that has a fireplace, 3 bedrooms, and 2 baths, but no pool, and that is not on the waterfront.

7.16* Data on 1500 house sales from Stockton, California, are contained in the data file *stockton4.dat*. [Note: *stockton3.dat* is a larger version of the same data set, containing 2610 observations.] The houses are detached single-family homes that were listed for sale between October 1, 1996, and November 30, 1998. The variables are *PRICE* ($), *LIVAREA* (hundreds of square feet), *BEDS* (number of bedrooms), *BATHS* (number of bathrooms), *LGELOT* (= 1 if lot size is greater than 0.5 acres, zero otherwise), *AGE* (years), and *POOL* (= 1 if home has pool, zero otherwise).

(a) Examine the histogram of *PRICE*. What do you observe? Create the variable ln(*PRICE*) and examine its histogram. Comment on the difference.

(b) Estimate a regression of ln(*PRICE*/1000) on the remaining variables. Discuss the estimation results. Comment on the signs and significance of the variables *LIVAREA*, *BEDS*, *BATHS*, *AGE*, and *POOL*.

(c) Discuss the effect of large lot size on the selling price of a house.

(d) Introduce to the model an interaction variable *LGELOT*LIVAREA*. Estimate this model and discuss the interpretation, sign, and significance of the coefficient of the interaction variable.

(e) Carry out a Chow test of the equivalence of models for houses that are on large lots and houses that are not.

Appendix 7A Details of Log-Linear Model Interpretation

You may have noticed that in Section 7.3, while discussing the interpretation of the log-linear model, we omitted the error term, and we did not discuss the regression function *E(WAGE)*. To do so, we make use of the properties of the log-normal distribution in Appendix 4C. There we noted that for the log-linear model $\ln(y) = \beta_1 + \beta_2 x + e$, if the error term $e \sim N(0, \sigma^2)$, then the expected value of y is

$$E(y) = \exp(\beta_1 + \beta_2 x + \sigma^2/2) = \exp(\beta_1 + \beta_2 x) \times \exp(\sigma^2/2)$$

Starting from this equation we can explore the interpretation of dummy variables and interaction terms.

Let D be a dummy variable. Adding this to our log-linear model, we have $\ln(y) = \beta_1 + \beta_2 x + \delta D + e$ and

$$E(y) = \exp(\beta_1 + \beta_2 x + \delta D) \times \exp(\sigma^2/2)$$

If we let $E(y_1)$ and $E(y_0)$ denote the cases when $D = 1$ and $D = 0$, respectively, then we can compute their percentage difference as

$$\%\Delta E(y) = 100 \left[\frac{E(y_1) - E(y_0)}{E(y_0)} \right] \%$$

$$= 100 \left[\frac{\exp(\beta_1 + \beta_2 x + \delta) \times \exp(\sigma^2/2) - \exp(\beta_1 + \beta_2 x) \times \exp(\sigma^2/2)}{\exp(\beta_1 + \beta_2 x) \times \exp(\sigma^2/2)} \right] \%$$

$$= 100 \left[\frac{\exp(\beta_1 + \beta_2 x)\exp(\delta) - \exp(\beta_1 + \beta_2 x)}{\exp(\beta_1 + \beta_2 x)} \right] \% = 100[\exp(\delta) - 1] \%$$

The interpretation of dummy variables in log-linear models carries over to the regression function. The percentage difference in the *expected* value of y is $100[\exp(\delta) - 1]\%$.

Appendix 7B Derivation of the Differences Estimator

To verify the expression for the differences-in-differences estimator in (7.14), note that the numerator can be expressed as

$$\sum_{i=1}^{N} (d_i - \bar{d})(y_i - \bar{y}) = \sum_{i=1}^{N} d_i(y_i - \bar{y}) - \bar{d} \sum_{i=1}^{N} (y_i - \bar{y})$$

$$= \sum_{i=1}^{N} d_i(y_i - \bar{y}) \qquad \left[\text{using } \sum_{i=1}^{N} (y_i - \bar{y}) = 0\right]$$

$$= \sum_{i=1}^{N} d_i y_i - \bar{y} \sum_{i=1}^{N} d_i$$

$$= N_1 \bar{y}_1 - N_1 \bar{y}$$

$$= N_1 \bar{y}_1 - N_1 (N_1 \bar{y}_1 + N_0 \bar{y}_0)/N$$

$$= \frac{N_0 N_1}{N} (\bar{y}_1 - \bar{y}_0) \qquad [\text{using } N = N_1 + N_0]$$

The denominator of b_2 is

$$\sum_{i=1}^{N} (d_i - \bar{d})^2 = \sum_{i=1}^{N} d_i^2 - 2\bar{d} \sum_{i=1}^{N} d_i + \sum_{i=1}^{N} \bar{d}^2$$

$$= \sum_{i=1}^{N} d_i - 2\bar{d} N_1 + N\bar{d}^2 \qquad \left[\text{using } d_i^2 = d_i \text{ and } \sum_{i=1}^{N} d_i = N_1\right]$$

$$= N_1 - 2\frac{N_1}{N} N_1 + N \left(\frac{N_1}{N}\right)^2$$

$$= \frac{N_0 N_1}{N} \qquad [\text{using } N = N_0 + N_1]$$

Combining the expressions for numerator and denominator, we obtain the result for the difference estimator in (7.14).

Chapter 8

Heteroskedasticity

Learning Objectives

Based on the material in this chapter you should be able to

1. Explain the meaning of heteroskedasticity and give examples of data sets likely to exhibit heteroskedasticity.

2. Explain how and why plots of least squares residuals can reveal heteroskedasticity.

3. Specify a variance function and use it to test for heteroskedasticity with (a) a Breusch–Pagan test and (b) a White test.

4. Test for heteroskedasticity using a Goldfeldt–Quandt test applied to (a) two subsamples with potentially different variances and (b) a model where the variance is hypothesized to depend on an explanatory variable.

5. Describe and compare the properties of the least squares and generalized least squares estimators when heteroskedasticity exists.

6. Compute heteroskedasticity-consistent standard errors for least squares.

7. Describe how to transform a model to eliminate heteroskedasticity.

8. Compute generalized least squares estimates for heteroskedastic models where (a) the variance is known except for the proportionality constant σ^2, (b) the variance is a function of explanatory variables and unknown parameters, and (c) the sample is partitioned into two groups with different variances.

9. Explain why the linear probability model exhibits heteroskedasticity.

10. Compute generalized least squares estimates of the linear probability model.

Keywords

Breusch–Pagan test	homoskedasticity	variance function
generalized least squares	Lagrange multiplier test	weighted least squares
Goldfeld–Quandt test	linear probability model	White test
grouped data	mean function	
heteroskedasticity	residual plot	
heteroskedasticity-consistent standard errors	transformed model	

8.1 The Nature of Heteroskedasticity

In Chapter 2 the relationship between average or mean household expenditure on food $E(y)$ and household income x was described by the linear function

$$E(y) = \beta_1 + \beta_2 x \tag{8.1}$$

The unknown parameters β_1 and β_2 convey information about this expenditure function. The response parameter β_2 describes how mean household food expenditure changes when household income increases by one unit. The intercept parameter β_1 measures expenditure on food for a zero income level. Knowledge of these parameters aids planning by institutions such as government agencies or food retail chains. To estimate β_1 and β_2 we considered a sample of $N = 40$ households indexed by $i = 1, 2, \ldots, 40$, with the pair (y_i, x_i) denoting expenditure on food and income for the ith household.

In order to recognize that not all households with a particular income will have the same food expenditure, and in line with our general specification of the regression model, we let e_i be the difference between expenditure on food by the ith household y_i and mean expenditure on food for all households with income x_i. That is,

$$e_i = y_i - E(y_i) = y_i - \beta_1 - \beta_2 x_i \tag{8.2}$$

Thus, the model used to describe expenditure on food for the ith household is written as

$$y_i = \beta_1 + \beta_2 x_i + e_i \tag{8.3}$$

We can view $E(y_i) = \beta_1 + \beta_2 x_i$ as that part of food expenditure explained by income x_i and e_i as that part of food expenditure explained by other factors.

We begin this chapter by asking whether the mean function $E(y) = \beta_1 + \beta_2 x$ is better at explaining expenditure on food for low-income households than it is for high-income households. If you were to guess food expenditure for a low-income household and food expenditure for a high-income household, which guess do you think would be easier? Low-income households do not have the option of extravagant food tastes. Comparatively, they have few choices and are almost forced to spend a particular portion of their income on food. High-income households on the other hand could have simple food tastes or extravagant food tastes. They might dine on caviar or spaghetti, while their low-income counterparts have to take the spaghetti. Thus, income is relatively less important as an explanatory variable for food expenditure of high-income households. It is harder to guess their food expenditure.

Another way of describing what we have just said is to say that the probability of getting large positive or negative values for e is higher for high incomes than it is for low incomes. Factors other than income can have a larger impact on food expenditure when household income is high. How can we model this phenomenon? A random variable, in this case e, has a higher probability of taking on large values if its variance is high. Thus, we can capture the effect we are describing by having var(e) depend directly on income x. An equivalent statement is to say var(y) increases as x increases. Food expenditure y can deviate further from its mean $E(y) = \beta_1 + \beta_2 x$ when x is large. In such a case, when the variances for all observations are not the same, we say that **heteroskedasticity** exists. Alternatively, we say the random variable y and the random error e are **heteroskedastic**. Conversely, if all observations come from probability density functions with the same variance, we say that **homoskedasticity** exists, and y and e are **homoskedastic**.

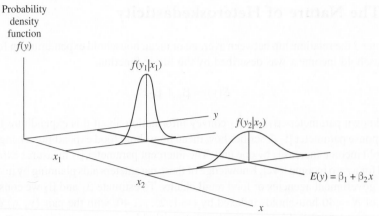

FIGURE **8.1**   Heteroskedastic errors.

The heteroskedastic assumption is illustrated in Figure 8.1. At $x = x_1$, the probability density function $f(y_1|x_1)$ is such that y_1 will be close to $E(y_1)$ with high probability. When we move to x_2, the probability density function $f(y_2|x_2)$ is more spread out; we are less certain about where y_2 might fall, and larger values are possible. When homoskedasticity exists, the probability density function for the errors does not change as x changes, as we illustrated in Figure 2.3.

Note that the existence of heteroskedasticity is a violation of one of our least squares assumptions that were listed in Section 5.1. When we previously considered the model in (8.3), we assumed that the e_i were uncorrelated random error terms with mean zero and constant variance σ^2. That is,

$$E(e_i) = 0 \quad \text{var}(e_i) = \sigma^2 \quad \text{cov}(e_i, e_j) = 0 \ \textit{for } i \neq j$$

The assumption we are questioning now is the constant variance assumption MR3 that states $\text{var}(y_i) = \text{var}(e_i) = \sigma^2$. Our discussion suggests that it should be replaced with an assumption of the form

$$\text{var}(y_i) = \text{var}(e_i) = h(x_i) \tag{8.4}$$

where $h(x_i)$ is a function of x_i that increases as x_i increases.

This chapter is concerned with the consequences of a variance assumption like (8.4). What are the consequences for the properties of least squares estimators? Is there a better estimation technique? How do we detect the existence of heteroskedasticity?

We can further illustrate the nature of heteroskedasticity, and at the same time demonstrate an informal way of detecting heteroskedasticity, by reexamining least squares estimation of the mean function $E(y_i) = \beta_1 + \beta_2 x_i$ and the corresponding least squares residuals. The least squares estimated equation from the observations in the file *food.dat* is

$$\hat{y} = 83.42 + 10.21\,x$$

A graph of this estimated function, along with all the observed expenditure-income points (y_i, x_i), appears in Figure 8.2. Notice that, as income (x) grows, the prevalence of data points that deviate further from the estimated mean function increases. There are more

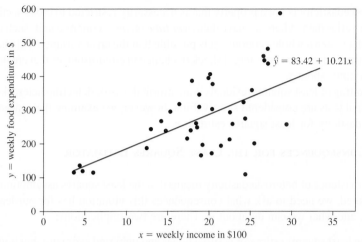

FIGURE **8.2**   Least squares estimated food expenditure function and observed data points.

points scattered further away from the line as x gets larger. Another way of describing this feature is to say that there is a tendency for the least squares residuals, defined by

$$\hat{e}_i = y_i - 83.42 - 10.21x_i$$

to increase in absolute value as income grows.

Since the observable least squares residuals ($\hat{e}_i$) are estimates of the unobservable errors (e_i), given by $e_i = y_i - \beta_1 - \beta_2 x_i$, Figure 8.2 also suggests that the unobservable errors tend to increase in absolute value as income increases. That is, the variation of food expenditure y around mean food expenditure $E(y)$ increases as income x increases. This observation is consistent with the hypothesis that we posed earlier: namely, that the mean food expenditure function is better at explaining food expenditure for low-income (spaghetti-eating) house-holds than it is for high-income households who might be spaghetti eaters or caviar eaters. We can capture the increasing variation of y around its mean by the heteroskedasticity assumption given in (8.4).

Heteroskedasticity is often encountered when using **cross-sectional data**. The term cross-sectional data refers to having data on a number of economic units such as firms or households, *at a given point in time*. The household data on income and food expenditure fall into this category. Other possible examples include data on costs, outputs, and inputs for a number of firms, and data on quantities purchased and prices for some commodity, or commodities, in a number of retail establishments. Cross-sectional data invariably involve observations on economic units of varying sizes. For example, data on house-holds will involve households with varying numbers of household members and different levels of household income. With data on a number of firms, we might measure the size of the firm by the quantity of output it produces. Frequently, the larger the firm, or the larger the household, the more difficult it is to explain the variation in some outcome variable y by the variation in a set of explanatory variables. Larger firms and households are likely to be more diverse and flexible with respect to the way in which values for y are determined. What this means for the linear regression model is that as the size of the economic unit becomes larger, there is more uncertainty associated with the outcomes y. This greater uncertainty is modeled by specifying an error variance that is larger, the larger the size of the economic unit.

Heteroskedasticity is not a property that is necessarily restricted to cross-sectional data. With time-series data, where we have data *over time* on *one* economic unit, such as a firm, a household, or even a whole economy, it is possible that the error variance will change. This would be true if there was an external shock or change in circumstances that created more or less uncertainty about *y*.

The plotting of least squares residuals is an informal way of detecting heteroskedasticity. More formal tests are considered shortly. First, however, we examine the consequences of heteroskedasticity for least squares estimation.

8.1.1   CONSEQUENCES FOR THE LEAST SQUARES ESTIMATOR

Since the existence of heteroskedasticity means that the least squares assumption $\text{var}(e_i) = \sigma^2$ is violated, we need to ask what consequences this violation has for our least squares estimator, and what we can do about it. There are two implications:

1. The least squares estimator is still a linear and unbiased estimator, but it is no longer best. There is another estimator with a smaller variance.

2. The standard errors usually computed for the least squares estimator are incorrect. Confidence intervals and hypothesis tests that use these standard errors may be misleading.

We consider the second implication first. What happens to the standard errors?

For the simple linear regression model without heteroskedasticity

$$y_i = \beta_1 + \beta_2 x_i + e_i \quad \text{var}(e_i) = \sigma^2 \tag{8.5}$$

we showed in Chapter 2 that the variance of the least squares estimator for b_2 is

$$\text{var}(b_2) = \frac{\sigma^2}{\sum_{i=1}^{N}(x_i - \bar{x})^2} \tag{8.6}$$

Now suppose the error variances for each observation are different, and that we recognize this difference by putting a subscript i on σ^2, so that we have

$$y_i = \beta_1 + \beta_2 x_i + e_i \quad \text{var}(e_i) = \sigma_i^2 \tag{8.7}$$

It is shown in Appendix 8A at the end of this chapter that the variance of the least squares estimator for β_2 under the heteroskedastic specification in (8.7) is

$$\text{var}(b_2) = \sum_{i=1}^{N} w_i^2 \sigma_i^2 = \frac{\sum_{i=1}^{N}\left[(x_i - \bar{x})^2 \sigma_i^2\right]}{\left[\sum_{i=1}^{N}(x_i - \bar{x})^2\right]^2} \tag{8.8}$$

where $w_i = (x_i - \bar{x})/\sum(x_i - \bar{x})^2$. Consequently, if we proceed to use the least squares estimator and its usual standard errors when $\text{var}(e_i) = \sigma_i^2$, we will be using an estimate of (8.6) to compute the standard error of b_2 when we should be using an estimate of (8.8).

To consider the first implication of using the least squares estimator, that it is no longer best in the sense that it is the minimum variance linear unbiased estimator, we need to describe how to obtain an alternative estimator that has the minimum variance property. We discover in Sections 8.4 and 8.5 that which estimator is best depends on the nature of the heteroskedasticity—how we specify the form of the variance function. Before considering the various options for alternative estimators, we examine how we might detect the presence of heteroskedasticity.

8.2 Detecting Heteroskedasticity

In our discussion of the food expenditure equation we used the nature of the economic problem and data to argue why heteroskedasticity of a particular form might be present. However, in this and in other equations that use other types of data, there will be uncertainty about whether a heteroskedastic assumption is warranted. It is natural to ask: How do I know if heteroskedasticity is likely to be a problem for my model and my set of data? Is there a way of detecting heteroskedasticity so that I know whether to investigate other estimation techniques? We consider three ways of investigating these questions. The first is the informal use of residual plots. The other two are more formal classes of statistical tests.

8.2.1 RESIDUAL PLOTS

One way of investigating the existence of heteroskedasticity is to estimate your model using least squares and to plot the least squares residuals. Examples of residual plots were given in Figures 4.7 and 4.8 of Chapter 4. If the errors are homoskedastic, there should be no patterns of any sort in the residuals. If the errors are heteroskedastic, they may tend to exhibit greater variation in some systematic way. For example, for the household food expenditure data, we suspect that the variance increases as incomes increases. A plot of the least-squares residuals against income appears in Figure 8.3. Notice how the absolute magnitudes of the residuals increase dramatically as income increases. This method of investigating heteroskedasticity can be followed for any simple regression. In a regression with more than one explanatory variable we can plot the least squares residuals against each explanatory variable, or against $\hat{y}_i$, to see if they vary in a systematic way.

8.2.2 LAGRANGE MULTIPLIER TESTS

In this section we consider a test for heteroskedasticity based on a **variance function**. To introduce the concept of a variance function, consider first the mean function $E(y_i)$ that, for the general multiple regression model, is given by

$$E(y_i) = \beta_1 + \beta_2 x_{i2} + \cdots + \beta_K x_{iK} \tag{8.9}$$

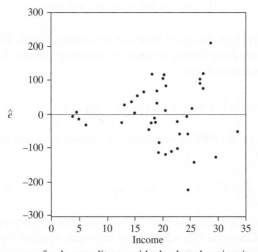

FIGURE 8.3 Least squares food expenditure residuals plotted against income.

The variance function is relevant when heteroskedasticity is a possibility. It is similar to (8.9) except that we relate the variance to a set of explanatory variables $z_{i2}, z_{i3}, \ldots, z_{iS}$ that are possibly different from $x_{i2}, x_{i3}, \ldots, x_{iK}$. A general form for the variance function is

$$\text{var}(y_i) = \sigma_i^2 = E\left(e_i^2\right) = h(\alpha_1 + \alpha_2 z_{i2} + \cdots + \alpha_S z_{iS}) \qquad (8.10)$$

This is a *general* form because we have not been specific about the function $h(\cdot)$. Notice that the variance of y_i changes for each observation depending on the values of the z's. In the mean and variance functions for the food expenditure example given in (8.1) and (8.4), respectively, there was only one x and one z, and they were both the same variable, household income.

One of the desirable features of the test that we develop is that it is valid for most functions $h(\cdot)$. There are many possible functions; two examples are an exponential function

$$h(\alpha_1 + \alpha_2 z_{i2} + \cdots + \alpha_S z_{iS}) = \exp(\alpha_1 + \alpha_2 z_{i2} + \cdots + \alpha_S z_{iS}) \qquad (8.11)$$

and a linear function

$$h(\alpha_1 + \alpha_2 z_{i2} + \cdots + \alpha_S z_{iS}) = \alpha_1 + \alpha_2 z_{i2} + \cdots + \alpha_S z_{iS} \qquad (8.12)$$

In this latter case one must be careful to ensure $h(\cdot) > 0$.

Notice what happens to the function $h(\cdot)$ when $\alpha_2 = \alpha_3 = \cdots = \alpha_S = 0$. It collapses to

$$h(\alpha_1 + \alpha_2 z_{i2} + \cdots + \alpha_S z_{iS}) = h(\alpha_1)$$

The term $h(\alpha_1)$ is a constant; in (8.11), $h(\alpha_1) = \alpha_1$, and in (8.12), $h(\alpha_1) = \exp(\alpha_1)$. The variance does not depend on any explanatory variables. In other words, when $\alpha_2 = \alpha_3 = \cdots = \alpha_S = 0$, heteroskedasticity is not present; the variance is constant. In terms of notation that you are familiar with, we can write $\sigma^2 = h(\alpha_1)$. Consequently, the null and alternative hypotheses for a test for heteroskedasticity based on the variance function are

$$H_0 : \alpha_2 = \alpha_3 = \cdots = \alpha_S = 0$$
$$H_1 : \text{not all the } \alpha_s \text{ in } H_0 \text{ are zero} \qquad (8.13)$$

The null and alternative hypotheses are the first components of a test. The next component is a test statistic. To obtain a test statistic we consider the linear variance function in (8.12) that we substitute into (8.10) to obtain

$$\text{var}(y_i) = \sigma_i^2 = E\left(e_i^2\right) = \alpha_1 + \alpha_2 z_{i2} + \cdots + \alpha_S z_{iS} \qquad (8.14)$$

Let $v_i = e_i^2 - E(e_i^2)$ be the difference between a squared error and its mean. Then, from (8.14), we can write

$$e_i^2 = E\left(e_i^2\right) + v_i = \alpha_1 + \alpha_2 z_{i2} + \cdots + \alpha_S z_{iS} + v_i \qquad (8.15)$$

Notice that the addition of v_i to the variance function serves a similar purpose to addition of e_i to the mean function. Specifically, adding e_i to the mean function $E(y_i)$ gives the general regression model that we have studied in earlier chapters:

$$y_i = E(y_i) + e_i = \beta_1 + \beta_2 x_{i2} + \cdots + \beta_K x_{iK} + e_i \qquad (8.16)$$

There is an important difference, however. In (8.16) the dependent variable y_i is observable. If we try to estimate (8.15), we find that the "dependent variable" e_i^2 is not observable because the true regression errors e_i are not known. We overcome this problem by replacing the e_i^2 with the squares of the least squares residuals $\hat{e}_i^2$, obtained from estimating (8.16). Thus, we write an operational version of (8.15) as

$$\hat{e}_i^2 = \alpha_1 + \alpha_2 z_{i2} + \cdots + \alpha_S z_{iS} + v_i \qquad (8.17)$$

Strictly speaking, replacing e_i^2 by $\hat{e}_i^2$ also changes the definition of v_i, but we will retain the same notation to avoid unnecessary complication.

The variance function test for heteroskedasticity uses quantities obtained from least squares estimation of (8.17). We are interested in discovering whether the variables $z_{i2}, z_{i3}, \ldots, z_{iS}$ help explain the variation in $\hat{e}_i^2$. Since the R^2 goodness-of-fit statistic from (8.17) measures the proportion of variation in $\hat{e}_i^2$ explained by the z's, it is a natural candidate for a test statistic. It can be shown that when H_0 is true, the sample size multiplied by R^2 has a chi-square (χ^2) distribution with $S-1$ degrees of freedom. That is,

$$\chi^2 = N \times R^2 \sim \chi^2_{(S-1)} \qquad (8.18)$$

It is likely that so far, your exposure to the χ^2-distribution has been limited. It was introduced in Appendix B.3.6, it was used for testing for normality in Chapter 4.3.5, and its relationship with the F-test was explored in an appendix to Chapter 6, Appendix 6A. It is a distribution that is used for testing many different kinds of hypotheses. Like an F random variable, a χ^2 random variable only takes positive values. Because a large R^2 value provides evidence against the null hypothesis (it suggests the z variables explain changes in the variance), the rejection region for the statistic in (8.18) is in the right tail of the distribution. Thus, for a 5% significance level, we reject H_0 and conclude that heteroskedasticity exists when $\chi^2 \geq \chi^2_{(0.95, S-1)}$.

There are several important features of this test:

- It is a large sample test. The result in (8.18) holds approximately in large samples when the null hypothesis is true.

- You will often see the test referred to as a **Lagrange multiplier test** or a **Breusch-Pagan test** for heteroskedasticity. Breusch and Pagan used the Lagrange multiplier principle (see Appendix C.8.4) to derive an earlier version of the test which was later modified by other researchers to the form in (8.18). The test values for these and other slightly different versions of the test, one of which is an F-test, are automatically calculated by a number of software packages. The one provided by your software may or may not be exactly the same as the $N \times R^2$ version in (8.18). The relationships between the different versions of the test are described in Appendix 8B. As you proceed through the book and study more econometrics, you will find that many Lagrange multiplier tests can be written in the form $N \times R^2$ where the R^2 comes from a convenient auxiliary regression related to the hypothesis being tested.

- We motivated the test in terms of an alternative hypothesis with the very general variance function $\sigma_i^2 = h(\alpha_1 + \alpha_2 z_{i2} + \cdots + \alpha_S z_{iS})$, yet we proceeded to carry out the test using the linear function $\hat{e}_i^2 = \alpha_1 + \alpha_2 z_{i2} + \cdots + \alpha_S z_{iS} + v_i$. One of the amazing features of the Breusch-Pagan test is that the value of the statistic computed from the linear function is valid for testing an alternative hypothesis of heteroskedasticity where the variance function can be of any form given by (8.10).

8.2.2a The White Test

One problem with the variance function test described so far is that it presupposes that we have knowledge of the variables appearing in the variance function if the alternative hypothesis of heteroskedasticity is true. In other words, it assumes we are able to specify $z_2, z_3, \ldots, z_S$. In reality we may wish to test for heteroskedasticity without precise knowledge of the relevant variables. With this point in mind, econometrician Hal White suggested defining the z's as equal to the x's, the squares of the x's, and possibly their cross-products. Frequently, the variables that affect the variance are the same as those in the mean function. Also, by using a quadratic function we can approximate a number of other possible variance functions. Suppose the mean function has two explanatory variables

$$E(y) = \beta_1 + \beta_2 x_2 + \beta_3 x_3$$

The White test without cross-product terms (interactions) specifies

$$z_2 = x_2 \quad z_3 = x_3 \quad z_4 = x_2^2 \quad z_5 = x_3^2$$

Including interactions adds one further variable, $z_6 = x_2 x_3$. If the mean function contains quadratic terms ($x_3 = x_2^2$ for example), then some of the z's are redundant and are deleted. The White test is performed as an F-test (see Appendix 8B for details) or using the $\chi^2 = N \times R^2$ test defined in (8.18).

8.2.2b Testing the Food Expenditure Example

To test for heteroskedasticity in the food expenditure example where the variance is potentially a function of income, we test $H_0 : \alpha_2 = 0$ against the alternative $H_1 : \alpha_2 \neq 0$ in the variance function $\sigma_i^2 = h(\alpha_1 + \alpha_2 x_i)$. We begin by estimating the function $\hat{e}_i^2 = \alpha_1 + \alpha_2 x_i + v_i$ by least squares, from which we obtain

$$R^2 = 1 - \frac{SSE}{SST} = 0.1846$$

and

$$\chi^2 = N \times R^2 = 40 \times 0.1846 = 7.38$$

Since there is only one parameter in the null hypothesis, the χ^2-test has one degree of freedom. The 5% critical value is 3.84. Because 7.38 is greater than 3.84, we reject H_0 and conclude that the variance depends on income.

For the White version of the test we estimate the equation $\hat{e}_i^2 = \alpha_1 + \alpha_2 x_i + \alpha_3 x_i^2 + v_i$ and test $H_0 : \alpha_2 = \alpha_3 = 0$ against $H_1 : \alpha_2 \neq 0$ or $\alpha_3 \neq 0$. In this case, including both the test and p-value, we have

$$\chi^2 = N \times R^2 = 40 \times 0.18888 = 7.555 \quad p\text{-value} = 0.023$$

The 5% critical value is $\chi^2_{(0.95, 2)} = 5.99$. Again, we conclude that heteroskedasticity exists with the variance dependent on income.

8.2.3 The Goldfeld-Quandt Test

The second test for heteroskedasticity is designed for two groups of data with possibly different variances. To introduce this case, consider a wage equation where earnings per hour (*WAGE*) depends on years of education (*EDUC*), years of experience (*EXPER*) and a dummy variable *METRO* that is equal to one for workers who live in a metropolitan area and zero for workers who live outside a metropolitan area. Using data in the file *cps2.dat* the least squares estimated equation for this model is

$$\widehat{WAGE} = -9.914 + 1.234EDUC + 0.133EXPER + 1.524METRO \tag{8.19}$$
$$\text{(se)} \quad (1.08) \quad (0.070) \quad (0.015) \quad (0.431)$$

The results suggest that education and experience have a positive effect on the level of wages and that given a particular level of education and experience, the average metropolitan wage is $1.50 per hour higher than the average wage in a rural area.

The question we now ask is: How does the variance of wages in a metropolitan area compare with the variance of wages in a rural area? Are the variances likely to be the same, or different? One might suspect that the greater range of different types of jobs in a metropolitan area might lead to city wages' having a higher variance. If the variance of metropolitan wages differs from the variance of rural wages, then we have heteroskedasticity. The variance is not constant for all observations. The Goldfeld-Quandt test is designed to test for this form of heteroskedasticity, where the sample can be partitioned into two groups—metropolitan and rural in this case—and we suspect the variance could be different in the two groups.

The test is based on a comparison of the error variances estimated from each group. Using the subscript *M* to denote metropolitan observations and the subscript *R* to denote rural observations, we can write separate equations for the two groups as

$$WAGE_{Mi} = \beta_{M1} + \beta_2 EDUC_{Mi} + \beta_3 EXPER_{Mi} + e_{Mi} \qquad i = 1, 2, \ldots, N_M \tag{8.20a}$$

$$WAGE_{Ri} = \beta_{R1} + \beta_2 EDUC_{Ri} + \beta_3 EXPER_{Ri} + e_{Ri} \qquad i = 1, 2, \ldots, N_R \tag{8.20b}$$

Note that *METRO* does not appear in the equations. Can you explain why?

Implicit in the above specification is the assumption that the coefficients for *EDUC* and *EXPER* (β_2 and β_3) are the same in both metropolitan and rural areas, but the intercepts differ. This assumption is in line with the estimated equation in (8.19) where the estimate for β_{R1} is $b_{R1} = -9.914$ and the estimate for β_{M1} is $b_{M1} = -9.914 + 1.524 = -8.39$.

We wish to test the null hypothesis $\sigma_M^2 = \sigma_R^2$, where $\sigma_M^2 = \text{var}(e_{Mi})$ and $\sigma_R^2 = \text{var}(e_{Ri})$. The alternative hypothesis will depend on whether we want to establish that the variances are different ($\sigma_M^2 \neq \sigma_R^2$) or, as suggested above, that metropolitan wages have a greater variance ($\sigma_M^2 > \sigma_R^2$). The test statistic is derived from a result in Appendix C.7.3 which, in the context of regression models, is

$$F = \frac{\hat{\sigma}_M^2 / \sigma_M^2}{\hat{\sigma}_R^2 / \sigma_R^2} \sim F_{(N_M - K_M, N_R - K_R)} \tag{8.21}$$

where $N_M - K_M$ and $N_R - K_R$ are the degrees of freedom for the two sub-sample regressions. Usually, and in our example, $K_M = K_R$. In words, (8.21) says: The F statistic that has a numerator equal to the ratio of one variance estimate to its true population value, and a denominator equal to the ratio of the other variance estimate to its population value, has an F distribution with $(N_M - K_M, N_R - K_R)$ degrees of freedom. The degrees of freedom are different to those for the result in Appendix C.7.3 because we are considering the error variances from two regression equations rather than the variances from two samples of data.

Suppose we want to test

$$H_0 : \sigma_M^2 = \sigma_R^2 \quad \text{against} \quad H_1 : \sigma_M^2 \neq \sigma_R^2 \tag{8.22}$$

When H_0 is true, (8.21) reduces to the test statistic

$$F = \frac{\hat{\sigma}_M^2}{\hat{\sigma}_R^2} \tag{8.23}$$

Given that (8.22) is a two-tail test, that $K_M = K_R = 3$, and, that in the file *cps2.dat* there are $N_M = 808$ metropolitan observations and $N_R = 192$ rural observations, the relevant lower and upper critical values for a 5% significance level are $F_{Lc} = F_{(0.025, 805, 189)} = 0.81$ and $F_{Uc} = F_{(0.975, 805, 189)} = 1.26$. We reject H_0 if $F < F_{Lc}$ or $F > F_{Uc}$.

Using least squares to estimate (8.20a) and (8.20b) separately yields variance estimates

$$\hat{\sigma}_M^2 = 31.824 \qquad \hat{\sigma}_R^2 = 15.243$$

The estimated error variance for the metropolitan wage equation is approximately double that for the rural wage equation. To decide whether this difference could be attributable to sampling error or is sufficiently large to conclude that $\sigma_M^2 \neq \sigma_R^2$, we compute

$$F = \frac{\hat{\sigma}_M^2}{\hat{\sigma}_R^2} = \frac{31.824}{15.243} = 2.09$$

Since $2.09 > F_{Uc} = 1.26$, we reject H_0 and conclude that the wage variances for the rural and metropolitan regions are not equal.

When following the above procedure, it does not matter whether you put the larger variance estimate in the numerator or the denominator of the F-statistic. However, if you always put the larger estimate in the numerator, you reject H_0 at a 5% level of significance if $F > F_{Uc} = F_{(0.975, N_M - K_M, N_R - K_R)}$. In other words, you must still recognize that it is a two-tail test by using $F_{Uc} = F_{(0.975, N_M - K_M, N_R - K_R)}$ and not $F_{Uc} = F_{(0.95, N_M - K_M, N_R - K_R)}$. For a one-tail test, the critical value changes. For $H_1 : \sigma_M^2 > \sigma_R^2$, we reject H_0 at a 5% level of significance if $F > F_c = F_{(0.95, 805, 189)} = 1.22$. Since we originally hypothesized that greater job variety in the metropolitan area might lead to a greater variance, one could argue that a one-tail test is appropriate.

8.2.3a The Food Expenditure Example

Although the Goldfeld-Quandt test is specifically designed for instances in which the sample divides naturally into two groups, it can also be used where, under H_1, the variance is a function of a single explanatory variable, say z_i. To perform the test under these circumstances, we order the observations according to z_i so that if heteroskedasticity exists, the first half of the sample will correspond to observations with lower variances and the last half of the sample will correspond to observations with higher variances. Then we split the sample into approximately two equal halves, carry out two separate least squares regressions that yield variance estimates, say $\hat{\sigma}_1^2$ and $\hat{\sigma}_2^2$, and proceed with the test as described previously.

Following these steps for the food expenditure example, with the observations ordered according to income x_i, and the sample split into two equal groups of 20 observations each, yields $\hat{\sigma}_1^2 = 3574.8$ and $\hat{\sigma}_2^2 = 12921.9$, from which we obtain

$$F = \frac{\hat{\sigma}_2^2}{\hat{\sigma}_1^2} = \frac{12921.9}{3574.8} = 3.61$$

Believing that the variances could increase, but not decrease with income, we use a one-tail test with 5% critical value $F_{(0.95, 18, 18)} = 2.22$. Since $3.61 > 2.22$, a null hypothesis of homoskedastcity is rejected in favor of the alternative that the variance increases with income.

8.3 Heteroskedasticity–Consistent Standard Errors

Suppose that hypothesis tests suggest that our model suffers from heteroskedasticity. What should we do about it? Recall that there are two problems with using the least squares estimator in the presence of heteroskedasticity: One is that the least squares estimator, although still being unbiased, is no longer best. The other is that the usual least squares standard errors are incorrect, which invalidates interval estimates and hypothesis tests. If we are prepared to accept the least squares estimator as a useful estimator, despite the fact it is not the minimum variance estimator, there is a way of correcting the standard errors so that our interval estimates and hypothesis tests are valid.

In Section 8.1.1, for the simple regression model $y_i = \beta_1 + \beta_2 x_i + e_i$ with heteroskedastic variance $\text{var}(e_i) = \sigma_i^2$, we indicated that the variance of the least squares estimator for β_2 is given by

$$\text{var}(b_2) = \frac{\sum\limits_{i=1}^{N} \left[(x_i - \bar{x})^2 \sigma_i^2 \right]}{\left[\sum\limits_{i=1}^{N} (x_i - \bar{x})^2 \right]^2} \tag{8.24}$$

A consistent estimator for this variance and similar variances in the multiple regression model has been suggested by econometrician Hal White.[1] The resulting standard errors (the standard error for b_2 and the standard errors for the least squares estimator of other coefficients in the multiple regression model) have become known as White's **heteroskedasticity-consistent standard errors**, or **heteroskedasticity robust standard errors**, or simply **robust standard errors**. The term "robust" is used because they are valid in large samples for both heteroskedastic and homoskedastic errors.

---

[1] See Appendix 5B for a discussion of consistency.

The White standard error for b_2 is obtainded from (8.24) by replacing σ_i^2 with the squares of the least squares residuals $\hat{e}_i = y_i - b_1 - b_2 x_i$, and including a degrees of freedom adjustment $N/(N-K)$, which is similar to that used for estimating σ^2 in the regression model with homoskedasticity. Noting that $K = 2$ in this case, the White variance estimator is given by

$$\widehat{\text{var}(b_2)} = \frac{N}{N-2} \frac{\sum\limits_{i=1}^{N}\left[(x_i - \bar{x})^2\, \hat{e}_i^{\,2}\right]}{\left[\sum\limits_{i=1}^{N}(x_i - \bar{x})^2\right]^2} \tag{8.25}$$

and the White standard error is given by the square root of this quantity. In multiple regression models the formulas are more complex, but the principle is the same. Replacing σ_i^2 with the squared residuals $\hat{e}_i^2$ leads to a consistent variance estimator. Large variances tend to lead to large values of the squared residuals.

Most regression packages include an option for calculating standard errors using White's estimator. If we do so for the food expenditure example, we obtain

$$\hat{y} = 83.42 + 10.21x$$
$$(27.46) \quad (1.81) \quad \text{(White se)}$$
$$(43.41) \quad (2.09) \quad \text{(incorrect se)}$$

In this case, ignoring heteroskedasticity and using incorrect standard errors, based on the usual formula in (8.6), tends to understate the precision of estimation; we tend to get confidence intervals that are wider than they should be. Specifically, following the result in (3.6) in Chapter 3, we can construct two corresponding 95% confidence intervals for β_2.

$$\text{White}: \quad b_2 \pm t_c \text{se}(b_2) = 10.21 \pm 2.024 \times 1.81 = [6.55, 13.87]$$
$$\text{Incorrect}: \quad b_2 \pm t_c \text{se}(b_2) = 10.21 \pm 2.024 \times 2.09 = [5.97, 14.45]$$

If we ignore heteroskedasticity, we estimate that β_2 lies between 5.97 and 14.45. When we recognize the existence of heteroskedasticity, our information is more precise, and we estimate that β_2 lies between 6.55 and 13.87. A word of caution is in order, however. This result is contrary to what typically happens in empirical work. The most frequent outcome is where the least squares standard errors overstate precision in the presence of heteroskedasticity. Our atypical result may be attributable to the relatively small sample of 40 observations.

White's estimator for the standard errors helps us avoid computing incorrect interval estimates or incorrect values for test statistics in the presence of heteroskedasticity. It does not address the other implication of heteroskedasticity, that the least squares estimator is no longer best. However, failing to address this issue may not be a grave sin. If you have a large sample size—many cross-sectional data sets have thousands of observations—the variance of the least squares estimator may still be sufficiently small to get precise estimates. Also, as we discover in the next section, to find an alternative estimator with a lower variance it is necessary to specify a suitable variance function. Using least squares with robust standard errors avoids the need to specify a suitable variance function.

8.4 Generalized Least Squares: Known Form of Variance

8.4.1 Variance Proportional to X

Consider again the food expenditure example with heteroskedasticity assumption,

$$y_i = \beta_1 + \beta_2 x_i + e_i$$
$$E(e_i) = 0, \quad \text{var}(e_i) = \sigma_i^2, \quad \text{cov}(e_i, e_j) = 0 \quad (i \neq j) \tag{8.26}$$

Although it is possible to obtain the White heteroskedasticity-consistent variance estimates by simply assuming that the error variances σ_i^2 can be different for each observation, to develop an estimator that is better than the least squares estimator we need to make a further assumption about how the variances σ_i^2 change with each observation. This further assumption becomes necessary because the best linear unbiased estimator in the presence of heteroskedasticity, an estimator known as the **generalized least squares** estimator, depends on the unknown σ_i^2. It is not practical to estimate N unknown variances $\sigma_1^2, \sigma_2^2, \ldots, \sigma_N^2$ with only N observations without making a restrictive assumption about how the σ_i^2 change. Thus, to make the generalized least squares estimator operational, some structure is imposed on σ_i^2.

Our earlier inspection of the least squares residuals for the food expenditure example suggested that the error variance increases as income increases. One possible assumption for the variance σ_i^2 that has this characteristic is

$$\text{var}(e_i) = \sigma_i^2 = \sigma^2 x_i \tag{8.27}$$

That is, we assume that the variance of the ith error term σ_i^2 is given by a positive unknown constant parameter σ^2 multiplied by the positive income variable x_i, so that $\text{var}(e_i)$ is proportional to income. As explained earlier, in economic terms this assumption implies that for low levels of income (x_i), food expenditure (y_i) will be clustered closer to the mean function $E(y_i) = \beta_1 + \beta_2 x_i$. Expenditure on food for low-income households will be largely explained by the level of income. At high levels of income, food expenditures can deviate more from the mean function. This means that there are likely to be many other factors, such as specific tastes and preferences, that reside in the error term, and that lead to a greater variation in food expenditure for high-income households.

8.4.1a Transforming the Model

The least squares estimator is not the best linear unbiased estimator when the errors are heteroskedastic. What is the best linear unbiased estimator under these circumstances? We approach this problem by *changing or transforming the model into one with homoskedastic errors*. Leaving the basic structure of the model intact, it is possible to turn the heteroskedastic error model into a homoskedastic error model. Once this transformation has been carried out, application of least squares to the transformed model gives a best linear unbiased estimator.

To demonstrate these facts, we begin by dividing both sides of the original model in (8.26) by $\sqrt{x_i}$

$$\frac{y_i}{\sqrt{x_i}} = \beta_1 \left(\frac{1}{\sqrt{x_i}} \right) + \beta_2 \left(\frac{x_i}{\sqrt{x_i}} \right) + \frac{e_i}{\sqrt{x_i}} \tag{8.28}$$

Now, define the following **transformed variables**

$$y_i^* = \frac{y_i}{\sqrt{x_i}}, \quad x_{i1}^* = \frac{1}{\sqrt{x_i}}, \quad x_{i2}^* = \frac{x_i}{\sqrt{x_i}} = \sqrt{x_i}, \quad e_i^* = \frac{e_i}{\sqrt{x_i}} \tag{8.29}$$

so that (8.28) can be rewritten as

$$y_i^* = \beta_1 x_{i1}^* + \beta_2 x_{i2}^* + e_i^* \tag{8.30}$$

The beauty of this transformed model is that the new transformed error term e_i^* is homoskedastic. The proof of this result is as follows:

$$\text{var}(e_i^*) = \text{var}\left(\frac{e_i}{\sqrt{x_i}}\right) = \frac{1}{x_i}\text{var}(e_i) = \frac{1}{x_i}\sigma^2 x_i = \sigma^2 \tag{8.31}$$

Also, the transformed error term will retain the properties of zero mean, $E(e_i^*) = 0$, and zero correlation between different observations, $\text{cov}(e_i^*, e_j^*) = 0$ for $i \neq j$. As a consequence, we can apply least squares to the transformed variables, y_i^*, x_{i1}^*, and x_{i2}^* to obtain the best linear unbiased estimator for β_1 and β_2. Note that the transformed variables y_i^*, x_{i1}^*, and x_{i2}^* are all observable; it is a straightforward matter to compute "the observations" on these variables. An important difference, however, is that the model no longer contains a constant term. The old x_{i1} is implicitly equal to one for all observations. The new transformed variable $x_{i1}^* = 1/\sqrt{x_i}$ is no longer constant. You will have to be careful to exclude a constant if your software automatically inserts one, but you can still proceed. The transformed model is linear in the unknown parameters β_1 and β_2. These are the original parameters that we are interested in estimating. They have not been affected by the transformation. In short, the transformed model is a linear model to which we can apply least squares estimation. The transformed model satisfies the conditions of the Gauss–Markov theorem, and the least squares estimators defined in terms of the transformed variables are BLUE.

To summarize, to obtain the best linear unbiased estimator for a model with hetero-skedasticity of the type specified in (8.27)

1. Calculate the transformed variables given in (8.29).
2. Use least squares to estimate the transformed model given in (8.30).

The estimator obtained in this way is called a generalized least squares estimator.

8.4.1b   Weighted Least Squares

One way of viewing the generalized least squares estimator is as a **weighted least squares** estimator. Recall that the least squares estimator yields values of β_1 and β_2 that minimize the sum of squared errors. In this case, we are minimizing the sum of squared transformed errors that is given by

$$\sum_{i=1}^{N} e_i^{*2} = \sum_{i=1}^{N} \frac{e_i^2}{x_i} = \sum_{i=1}^{N} \left(x_i^{-1/2} e_i\right)^2$$

The errors are **weighted** by $x_i^{-1/2}$, the reciprocal of $\sqrt{x_i}$. When $\sqrt{x_i}$ is small, the data contain more information about the regression function and the observations are weighted heavily.

When $\sqrt{x_i}$ is large, the data contain less information and the observations are weighted lightly. In this way we take advantage of the heteroskedasticity to improve parameter estimation.

Most software has a weighted least squares or generalized least squares option. If your software falls into this category, you do not have to worry about transforming the variables before estimation, nor do you have to worry about omitting the constant. The computer will do both the transforming and the estimating. If you do the transforming yourself—that is, you create y_i^*, x_{i1}^*, and x_{i2}^* and apply least squares—be careful not to include a constant in the regression. As noted before, there is no constant because $x_{i1}^* \neq 1$.

8.4.1c Food Expenditure Estimates

Applying the generalized (weighted) least squares procedure to our household expenditure data yields the following estimates:

$$\hat{y}_i = 78.68 + 10.45 x_i$$
$$\text{(se)} \quad (23.79) \quad (1.39) \tag{8.32}$$

That is, we estimate the intercept term as $\hat{\beta}_1 = 78.68$ and the slope coefficient that shows the response of food expenditure to a change in income as $\hat{\beta}_2 = 10.45$. These estimates are somewhat different from the least squares estimates $b_1 = 83.42$ and $b_2 = 10.21$ that did not allow for the existence of heteroskedasticity. It is important to recognize that the interpretations for β_1 and β_2 are the same in the transformed model in (8.30) as they are in the untransformed model in (8.26). *Transformation of the variables should be regarded as a device for converting a heteroskedastic error model into a homoskedastic error model, not as something that changes the meaning of the coefficients.*

The standard errors in (8.32), namely $\text{se}(\hat{\beta}_1) = 23.79$ and $\text{se}(\hat{\beta}_2) = 1.39$, are both lower than their least squares counterparts that were calculated from White's estimator, namely $\text{se}(b_1) = 26.77$ and $\text{se}(b_2) = 1.76$. Since generalized least squares is a better estimation procedure than least squares, we do expect the generalized least squares standard errors to be lower. This statement needs to be qualified in two ways, however. First, remember that standard errors are square roots of *estimated* variances; in a single sample the relative magnitudes of variances may not always be reflected by their corresponding variance estimates. Thus, lower standard errors do not always mean better estimation. Second, the reduction in variance has come at the cost of making an additional assumption, namely, that the variances have the structure given in (8.27).

The smaller standard errors have the advantage of producing narrower more informative confidence intervals. For example, using the generalized least squares results, a 95% confidence interval for β_2 is given by

$$\hat{\beta}_2 \pm t_c \text{se}(\hat{\beta}_2) = 10.451 \pm 2.024 \times 1.386 = [7.65, 13.26]$$

The least squares confidence interval computed using White's standard errors was [6.64, 13.78].

8.4.2 GROUPED DATA

Another form of heteroskedasticity is where the sample can be divided into two or more groups with each group having a different error variance. To describe the generalized least squares estimator relevant for this setup, we return to the wage equation introduced in Section 8.2.3 where the error variance for observations on metropolitan workers was found to be different from that for observations on rural workers. The equations for each group were given by

$$WAGE_{Mi} = \beta_{M1} + \beta_2 EDUC_{Mi} + \beta_3 EXPER_{Mi} + e_{Mi} \qquad i = 1, 2, \ldots, N_M \qquad (8.33a)$$

$$WAGE_{Ri} = \beta_{R1} + \beta_2 EDUC_{Ri} + \beta_3 EXPER_{Ri} + e_{Ri} \qquad i = 1, 2, \ldots, N_R \qquad (8.33b)$$

and the estimated error variances for each group were $\widehat{var(e_{Mi})} = \hat{\sigma}_M^2 = 31.824$ and $\widehat{var(e_{Ri})} = \hat{\sigma}_R^2 = 15.243$.

One set of estimates that recognizes that the error variances are different are the separate least squares estimates of (8.33a) and (8.33b) that turn out to be

$$b_{M1} = -9.052 \qquad b_{M2} = 1.282 \qquad b_{M3} = 0.1346$$
$$b_{R1} = -6.166 \qquad b_{R2} = 0.956 \qquad b_{R3} = 0.1260$$

However, a problem with these estimates is that we have two estimates for β_2 and two estimates for β_3 when in (8.33) we are assuming the effect of education and experience on wages is the same for both metropolitan and rural areas. Given that this assumption is correct, better estimates (ones with lower variances) can be obtained by combining both subsets of data and applying a generalized least squares estimator to the complete set of data, with recognition given to the existence of heteroskedasticity.

The strategy for obtaining generalized least squares estimates is the same as it was in the previous section. The variables are transformed by dividing each observation by the standard deviation of the corresponding error term. With the grouped data, that means that all metropolitan observations are divided by σ_M and all rural observations are divided by σ_R. Equations (8.33a) and (8.33b) become

$$\left(\frac{WAGE_{Mi}}{\sigma_M}\right) = \beta_{M1}\left(\frac{1}{\sigma_M}\right) + \beta_2\left(\frac{EDUC_{Mi}}{\sigma_M}\right) + \beta_3\left(\frac{EXPER_{Mi}}{\sigma_M}\right) + \left(\frac{e_{Mi}}{\sigma_M}\right)$$
$$i = 1, 2, \ldots, N_M \qquad (8.34a)$$

$$\left(\frac{WAGE_{Ri}}{\sigma_R}\right) = \beta_{R1}\left(\frac{1}{\sigma_R}\right) + \beta_2\left(\frac{EDUC_{Ri}}{\sigma_R}\right) + \beta_3\left(\frac{EXPER_{Ri}}{\sigma_R}\right) + \left(\frac{e_{Ri}}{\sigma_R}\right)$$
$$i = 1, 2, \ldots, N_R \qquad (8.34b)$$

The variances of the transformed error terms (e_{Mi}/σ_M) and (e_{Ri}/σ_R) are the same. They are both equal to one. Is this fact obvious to you? No? Go back to (8.31) and try out the same steps with the transformed errors in (8.34). When you are comfortable, it will be clear to you that the combined set of error terms is homoskedastic. Thus, application of least squares to the complete set of transformed observations yields best linear unbiased estimators.

There are two complications, however. The first is that σ_M and σ_R are unknown. We solve this problem by transforming the observations with their estimates $\hat{\sigma}_M$ and $\hat{\sigma}_R$. Doing so yields a **feasible generalized least squares** estimator that has good properties in large samples. The second complication relates to the fact that the metropolitan and rural intercepts are different. This complication will not necessarily be present in all models with grouped data, but it arises in this case because both the mean and variance of wage depend on the dummy variable *METRO*.

The different intercepts are accommodated by including *METRO* as we did in the original (8.19), but this time it is transformed in the same way as the other variables.

Collecting all these facts together, we can combine (8.34a) and (8.34b) and summarize the method for obtaining feasible generalized least squares estimates in the following way:

1. Obtain estimated $\hat{\sigma}_M$ and $\hat{\sigma}_R$ by applying least squares separately to the metropolitan and rural observations.

2. Let $\hat{\sigma}_i = \begin{cases} \hat{\sigma}_M & \text{when } METRO_i = 1 \\ \hat{\sigma}_R & \text{when } METRO_i = 0 \end{cases}$

3. Apply least squares to the transformed model

$$\left(\frac{WAGE_i}{\hat{\sigma}_i}\right) = \beta_{R1}\left(\frac{1}{\hat{\sigma}_i}\right) + \beta_2\left(\frac{EDUC_i}{\hat{\sigma}_i}\right) + \beta_3\left(\frac{EXPER_i}{\hat{\sigma}_i}\right) + \delta\left(\frac{METRO_i}{\hat{\sigma}_i}\right)$$
$$+ \left(\frac{e_i}{\hat{\sigma}_i}\right) \tag{8.35}$$

where $\beta_{M1} = \beta_{R1} + \delta$.

Following these steps using the data in the file *cps2.dat* yields the estimated equation

$$\widehat{WAGE} = -9.398 + 1.196EDUC + 0.132EXPER + 1.539METRO$$
$$\text{(se)} \qquad (1.02) \quad (0.069) \qquad (0.015) \qquad (0.346) \tag{8.36}$$

These coefficient estimates are similar in magnitude to those in (8.19), an outcome that is not surprising given that both least squares and generalized least squares are unbiased in the presence of heteroskedasticity. We would hope, however, that the greater precision of the generalized least squares estimator is reflected in smaller standard errors. The standard errors in (8.19) are not a good basis for comparison because they are incorrect under heteroskedasticity. Instead, we can compare those in (8.36) with the heteroskedasticity-consistent standard errors from least squares estimation using all observations, or the standard errors obtained by applying least squares separately to the metropolitan and rural observations. With separate least squares estimation, they are, for *EDUC*, se(b_{M2}) = 0.080 and se(b_{R2}) = 0.133, and for *EXPER*, se(b_{M3}) = 0.018 and se(b_{R3}) = 0.025. These values are larger than the corresponding ones in (8.36); using the larger combined set of observations has led to a reduction in the standard errors. The heteroskedasticity-consistent standard errors from least squares estimation using all observations are se(b_2) = 0.084, se(b_3) = 0.016, and se(b_4) = 0.345, which are slightly larger or comparable to those in (8.36).

8.5 Generalized Least Squares: Unknown Form of Variance

A characteristic of the two generalized least squares estimators considered in Section 8.4, was knowledge of the form of variance. In the first case where we assumed var(e_i) = $\sigma^2 x_i$, the only unknown parameter in the variance function was σ^2, and after transforming the model, we are able to estimate it in the usual way. In the other case we had two groups of observations with two different variances (σ_M^2 and σ_R^2), and we could estimate each of these variances by applying least squares separately to each of the groups. We now consider a more complex model where the variance function contains extra parameters that need to be estimated.

To motivate this model, we return to our earlier error variance specification for the food expenditure equation, $\text{var}(e_i) = \sigma^2 x_i$. You may have wondered why we chose this specification. There are many other possible variance functions that have the property that as x_i increases, the variance increases. Two examples are $\text{var}(e_i) = \sigma^2 x_i^2$ and $\text{var}(e_i) = \sigma^2 x_i^{1/2}$. Why not choose one of these functions? A more general specification that includes all these specifications as special cases is

$$\text{var}(e_i) = \sigma_i^2 = \sigma^2 x_i^\gamma \tag{8.37}$$

where γ is an unknown parameter.

How do we proceed with estimation with an assumption like (8.37)? Our earlier discussion suggests that we should transform our model by dividing the ith observation on each variable by $x_i^{\gamma/2}$. Doing so will lead to a transformed error term with constant variance σ^2. Do you understand why? Go back to (8.31) and redo the little proof in this equation with γ included.

Because γ is unknown, we must estimate it before we can proceed with the transformation. To do so it is convenient to consider a framework more general than (8.37). To introduce this framework, we take logs of (8.37) to yield

$$\ln(\sigma_i^2) = \ln(\sigma^2) + \gamma \ln(x_i)$$

Then, taking the exponential of both sides,

$$\sigma_i^2 = \exp\left[\ln(\sigma^2) + \gamma \ln(x_i)\right] = \exp(\alpha_1 + \alpha_2 z_i) \tag{8.38}$$

where $\alpha_1 = \ln(\sigma^2)$, $\alpha_2 = \gamma$, and $z_i = \ln(x_i)$. Writing the variance function in this form is convenient because it shows how the variance can be related to any explanatory variable z_i that may or may not be one of the variables in the mean function $E(y_i) = \beta_1 + \beta_2 x_i$. Also, if we believe the variance is likely to depend on more than one explanatory variable, say z_{i2}, $z_{i3}, \ldots, z_{iS}$, (8.38) can be extended to the function

$$\sigma_i^2 = \exp(\alpha_1 + \alpha_2 z_{i2} + \cdots + \alpha_S z_{iS}) \tag{8.39}$$

The exponential function is convenient because it ensures that we will get positive values for the variances σ_i^2 for all possible values of the parameters $\alpha_1, \alpha_2, \ldots, \alpha_S$. Note also that we suggested it as a possible variance function in (8.11) when testing for heteroskedasticity.

Returning to (8.38), we rewrite it as

$$\ln(\sigma_i^2) = \alpha_1 + \alpha_2 z_i \tag{8.40}$$

and now address the question of how to estimate α_1 and α_2. Recall how we get the least squares estimator for the mean function $E(y_i) = \beta_1 + \beta_2 x_i$. We expressed the observations y_i as

$$y_i = E(y_i) + e_i = \beta_1 + \beta_2 x_i + e_i$$

and then applied least squares. We can follow a similar strategy for estimating the variance function using the squares of the least squares residuals $\hat{e}_i^2$ as our observations. That is, we write

$$\ln(\hat{e}_i^2) = \ln(\sigma_i^2) + v_i = \alpha_1 + \alpha_2 z_i + v_i \tag{8.41}$$

and apply least squares. Regressing $\ln(\hat{e}_i^2)$ on a constant and z_i yields least squares estimates for α_1 and α_2.

Whether or not this procedure is a legitimate one depends on the properties of the new error term v_i that we introduced in (8.41). Does it have a zero mean? Is it uncorrelated and homoskedastic? The answer to these questions is no; $E(v_i) \neq 0$ and the v_i are both correlated and heteroskedastic. However, it can be shown that the least squares estimator for α_2 (and any other slope parameters that might be present) is unbiased in large samples. The least squares estimator for the intercept α_1 is asymptotically biased downward by the amount 1.2704, and thus the obvious "fix" is to use the intercept estimator $\hat{\hat{\alpha}}_1 = \hat{\alpha}_1 + 1.2704$. Interestingly, this correction has no effect on the generalized least squares estimates of the β coefficients because α_1 cancels out during the calculations.[2]

In the food expenditure example, with z_i defined as $z_i = \ln(x_i)$, the least squares estimate of (8.41) is

$$\widehat{\ln(\sigma_i^2)} = 0.9378 + 2.329z_i$$

Notice that the estimate $\hat{\alpha}_2 = \hat{\gamma} = 2.329$ is more than twice the value of $\gamma = 1$ that was an implicit assumption of the variance specification used in Section 8.4.1. It suggests that the earlier assumption could be too restrictive.

The next step is to transform the observations in such a way that the transformed model has a constant error variance. As suggested earlier, we could do so by dividing both sides of the equation $y_i = \beta_1 + \beta_2 x_i + e_i$ by $x_i^{\hat{\gamma}/2}$. However, in line with the more general specification in (8.39), we can obtain variance estimates from

$$\hat{\sigma}_i^2 = \exp(\hat{\alpha}_1 + \hat{\alpha}_1 z_i)$$

and then divide both sides of the equation by $\hat{\sigma}_i$. Both strategies ultimately lead to the same generalized least squares estimates for β_1 and β_2. Why does the second one work? Dividing (8.26) by σ_i yields

$$\left(\frac{y_i}{\sigma_i}\right) = \beta_1 \left(\frac{1}{\sigma_i}\right) + \beta_2 \left(\frac{x_i}{\sigma_i}\right) + \left(\frac{e_i}{\sigma_i}\right)$$

The variance of the transformed error is constant (homoskedastic) because

$$\text{var}\left(\frac{e_i}{\sigma_i}\right) = \left(\frac{1}{\sigma_i^2}\right)\text{var}(e_i) = \left(\frac{1}{\sigma_i^2}\right)\sigma_i^2 = 1 \tag{8.42}$$

Thus, to obtain a generalized least squares estimator for β_1 and β_2, using the estimates $\hat{\sigma}_i^2$ in place of the unknown σ_i^2, we define the transformed variables

$$y_i^* = \left(\frac{y_i}{\hat{\sigma}_i}\right) \quad x_{i1}^* = \left(\frac{1}{\hat{\sigma}_i}\right) \quad x_{i2}^* = \left(\frac{x_i}{\hat{\sigma}_i}\right) \tag{8.43}$$

and apply least squares to the equation

$$y_i^* = \beta_1 x_{i1}^* + \beta_2 x_{i2}^* + e_i^* \tag{8.44}$$

---

[2] The "fix" requires the errors e_i to be normally distributed. Further discussion of this advanced point can be found in *Econometric Methods with Applications in Business and Economics* (Oxford, 2004) by Heij, de Boer, Franses, Kloek and Van Dijk, p. 337.

To summarize these steps for the general case, suppose we are estimating the model

$$y_i = \beta_1 + \beta_2 x_{i2} + \cdots + \beta_K x_{iK} + e_i \tag{8.45}$$

where

$$\text{var}(e_i) = \sigma_i^2 = \exp(\alpha_1 + \alpha_2 z_{i2} + \cdots + \alpha_S z_{iS}) \tag{8.46}$$

The steps for obtaining a generalized least squares estimator for $\beta_1, \beta_2, \ldots, \beta_K$ are

1. Estimate (8.45) by least squares and compute the squares of the least squares residuals $\hat{e}_i^2$.
2. Estimate $\alpha_1, \alpha_2, \ldots, \alpha_S$ by applying least squares to the equation $\ln(\hat{e}_i^2) = \alpha_1 + \alpha_2 z_{i2} + \cdots + \alpha_S z_{iS} + v_i$.
3. Compute variance estimates $\hat{\sigma}_i^2 = \exp(\hat{\alpha}_1 + \hat{\alpha}_2 z_{i2} + \cdots + \hat{\alpha}_S z_{iS})$.
4. Compute the transformed observations defined by (8.43), including $x_{i3}^*, \ldots, x_{iK}^*$ if $K > 2$.
5. Apply least squares to (8.44), or to an extended version of (8.44), if $K > 2$.

Steps 4 and 5 can be replaced by weighted least squares with weights defined by $\hat{\sigma}_i^{-1}$ if your software automatically computes weighted least squares estimates. If you are very fortunate, you will have software that performs all five steps automatically.

Following these steps to obtain generalized least squares estimates for the food expenditure example yields

$$\begin{aligned} \hat{y} &= 76.05 + 10.63x \\ \text{(se)} \quad &\quad (9.71) \quad (0.97) \end{aligned} \tag{8.47}$$

Compared to the generalized least squares results for the variance specification $\sigma_i^2 = \sigma^2 x_i$, the estimates for β_1 and β_2 have not changed a great deal, but there has been a considerable drop in the standard errors that under the previous specification were $\text{se}(\hat{\beta}_1) = 23.79$ and $\text{se}(\hat{\beta}_2) = 1.39$.

As mentioned earlier, because standard errors are themselves estimates, we cannot conclude with certainty that allowing for a more general variance specification has improved the precision with which we have estimated β_1 and β_2. However, in this particular case it is distinctly possible that our improved results are attributable to better modeling and better estimation.

8.5.1 USING ROBUST STANDARD ERRORS

The generalized least squares estimators described in Sections 8.4 and 8.5 each require an assumption about the form of heteroskedasticity. If that assumption is correct, the generalized least squares estimator is minimum variance. If that assumption is wrong, then, like the least squares estimator, the generalized least squares estimator will not be minimum variance, and its standard errors will be incorrect. As discussed in Section 8.3, this problem can be avoided by using least squares with White standard errors where an assumption about the form of heteroskedasticity is not needed, but then the potential reduction in variance from generalized least squares will not be realized. Given that we cannot be sure about the form of the variance function, how do we solve this dilemma?

After correcting for heteroskedasticity via generalized least squares, one can test the residuals from the transformed model to see if any evidence of heteroskedasticity remains. If there is no evidence of remaining heteroskedasticity, then we can expect that generalized least squares has improved the precision of estimation, and that the chance of obtaining incorrect standard errors has been reduced. However, if we wish to err on the side of caution, or if further modeling fails to eliminate heteroskedasticity, we can use robust standard errors in conjunction with the generalized least squares estimator. Robust standard errors can be used not only to guard against the possible presence of heteroskedasticity when using least squares, they can be used to guard against the possible misspecification of a variance function when using generalized least squares.

8.6 Heteroskedasticity in the Linear Probability Model

In Chapter 7.4 we introduced the linear probability model for explaining choice between two alternatives. We can represent this choice by an indicator variable y that takes the value one with probability p if the first alternative is chosen, and the value zero with probability $1-p$ if the second alternative is chosen. An indicator variable with these properties is a Bernoulli random variable with mean $E(y) = p$ and variance $\text{var}(y) = p(1-p)$. Interest centers on measuring the effect of explanatory variables $x_2, x_3, \ldots, x_K$ on the probability p. In the linear probability model the relationship between p and the explanatory variables is specified as the linear function

$$E(y) = p = \beta_1 + \beta_2 x_2 + \cdots + \beta_K x_K$$

Defining the error e_i as the difference $y_i - E(y_i)$ for the ith observation, we have the model

$$y_i = E(y_i) + e_i = \beta_1 + \beta_2 x_{i2} + \cdots + \beta_K x_{iK} + e_i \tag{8.48}$$

This model can be estimated with least squares—an example was given in Section 7.4—but it suffers from heteroskedasticity because

$$\begin{aligned} \text{var}(y_i) = \text{var}(e_i) &= p_i(1 - p_i) \\ &= (\beta_1 + \beta_2 x_{i2} + \cdots + \beta_K x_{iK})(1 - \beta_1 - \beta_2 x_{i2} - \cdots - \beta_K x_{iK}) \end{aligned} \tag{8.49}$$

The error variance depends on the values of the explanatory variables. We can rectify this problem by applying the techniques described earlier in this chapter. Instead of using least squares standard errors, we can use heteroskedasticity-robust standard errors. Or, alternatively, we can apply a generalized least squares procedure.

The first step towards obtaining generalized least squares estimates is to estimate the variance in (8.49). An estimate of p_i can be obtained from the least squares predictions

$$\hat{p}_i = b_1 + b_2 x_{i2} + \cdots + b_K x_{iK} \tag{8.50}$$

giving an estimated variance of

$$\widehat{\text{var}(e_i)} = \hat{p}_i(1 - \hat{p}_i) \tag{8.51}$$

A word of caution is required at this point. It is possible that some of the $\hat{p}_i$ obtained from (8.50) will not lie within the interval $0 < \hat{p}_i < 1$. If that happens, the corresponding variance estimate in (8.51) will be negative or zero, a nonsensical outcome. Thus, before proceeding to calculate the estimated variances from (8.51), it is necessary to check the estimated probabilities from (8.50) to ensure that they lie between zero and one. For those observations that violate this requirement, one possible solution is to set $\hat{p}_i$'s greater than 0.99 equal to 0.99, and $\hat{p}_i$'s less than 0.01 equal to 0.01. Another possible solution is to omit the offending observations. Neither of these solutions is totally satisfactory. Truncating at 0.99 or 0.01 is arbitrary, and the results could be sensitive to the truncation point. Omitting observations means that we are throwing away information. It might be preferable to use least squares with robust standard errors—that should, at least, be one of the options that is tried.

Once positive variance estimates have been obtained using (8.51), with adjustments where necessary, generalized least squares estimates can be obtained by applying least squares to the transformed equation

$$\frac{y_i}{\sqrt{\hat{p}_i(1 - \hat{p}_i)}} = \beta_1 \frac{1}{\sqrt{\hat{p}_i(1 - \hat{p}_i)}} + \beta_2 \frac{x_{i2}}{\sqrt{\hat{p}_i(1 - \hat{p}_i)}} + \cdots + \beta_K \frac{x_{iK}}{\sqrt{\hat{p}_i(1 - \hat{p}_i)}} + \frac{e_i}{\sqrt{\hat{p}_i(1 - \hat{p}_i)}}$$

8.6.1 THE MARKETING EXAMPLE REVISITED

In Section 7.4.1 the choice of purchasing either Coke ($COKE = 1$) or Pepsi ($COKE = 0$) was modeled as depending on the relative price of Coke to Pepsi ($PRATIO$), and whether store displays for Coke and Pepsi were present ($DISP\_COKE = 1$ if a Coke display was present, otherwise 0; $DISP\_PEPSI = 1$ if a Pepsi display was present, otherwise zero). The file *coke. dat* contains 1140 observations on these variables. Table 8.1 contains the results for (1) least squares, (2) least squares with robust standard errors, (3) generalized least squares with variances below 0.01 truncated to 0.01, and (4) generalized least squares with observations not satisfying $0 < \hat{p}_i < 1$ omitted. For the generalized least squares estimates there were no observations for which $\hat{p}_i > 0.99$ and there were 16 observations where $\hat{p}_i < 0.01$; for these latter cases it was also true that $\hat{p}_i < 0$.

Since the variance function in (8.49) contains the x's, their squares, and their cross products, a suitable test for heteroskedasticity is the White test described in Section 8.2.2a. Applying this test to the residuals from the least-squares estimated equation yields

$$\chi^2 = N \times R^2 = 25.817 \qquad p\text{-value} = 0.0005$$

Table 8.1   **Linear Probability Model Estimates**

	LS	LS-robust	GLS-trunc	GLS-omit
C	0.8902	0.8902	0.6505	0.8795
	(0.0655)	(0.0652)	(0.0568)	(0.0594)
$PRATIO$	−0.4009	−0.4009	−0.1652	−0.3859
	(0.0613)	(0.0603)	(0.0444)	(0.0527)
$DISP\_COKE$	0.0772	0.0772	0.0940	0.0760
	(0.0344)	(0.0339)	(0.0399)	(0.0353)
$DISP\_PEPSI$	−0.1657	−0.1657	−0.1314	−0.1587
	(0.0356)	(0.0343)	(0.0354)	(0.0360)

leading us to reject a null hypothesis of homoskedasticity at a 1% level of significance. Note that, when carrying out this test, your software will omit the squares of *DISP_COKE* and *DISP_PEPSI*. Because these variables are indicator variables, $DISP\_COKE^2 = DISP\_COKE$ and $DISP\_PEPSI^2 = DISP\_PEPSI$, leaving a χ^2 test with 7 degrees of freedom.

Examining the estimates in Table 8.1, we see there is little difference in the four sets of standard errors. In this particular case the use of least squares standard errors does not seem to matter. The four sets of coefficient estimates are also similar with the exception of those from generalized least squares where the negative $\hat{p}$'s were truncated to 0.01. The weight on observations with variance $\widehat{\text{var}(e_i)} = 0.01(1 - 0.01) = 0.0099$ is a relatively large one. It appears that the large weights placed on those 16 observations are having a noticeable impact on the estimates. The signs are all as expected. Making Coke more expensive leads more people to purchase Pepsi. A Coke display encourages purchase of Coke, and a Pepsi display encourages purchase of Pepsi.

In Chapter 16 we study models which are specifically designed for modeling choice between two or more alternatives, and which do not suffer from the problems of the linear probability model.

8.7 Exercises

Answers to exercises marked * appear at www.wiley.com/go/global/hill.

8.7.1 PROBLEMS

8.1 Show that the variance of the least squares estimator given in (8.8) simplifies to that given in (8.6) when $\sigma_i^2 = \sigma^2$. That is,

$$\frac{\sum_{i=1}^{N}\left[(x_i - \bar{x})^2 \sigma_i^2\right]}{\left[\sum_{i=1}^{N}(x_i - \bar{x})^2\right]^2} = \frac{\sigma^2}{\sum_{i=1}^{N}(x_i - \bar{x})^2}$$

8.2 Consider the model $y_i = \beta_1 + \beta_2 x_i + e_i$ with heteroskedastic variance $\text{var}(e_i) = \sigma_i^2$ and its transformed homoskedastic version $y_i^* = \beta_1 \sigma_i^{-1} + \beta_2 x_i^* + e_i^*$ where $y_i^* = \sigma_i^{-1} y_i$, $x_i^* = \sigma_i^{-1} x_i$, and $e_i^* = \sigma_i^{-1} e_i$. The normal equations whose solution yields the generalized least squares estimators $\hat{\beta}_1$ and $\hat{\beta}_2$ are

$$\left(\sum \sigma_i^{-2}\right)\hat{\beta}_1 + \left(\sum \sigma_i^{-1} x_i^*\right)\hat{\beta}_2 = \sum \sigma_i^{-1} y_i^*$$
$$\left(\sum \sigma_i^{-1} x_i^*\right)\hat{\beta}_1 + \left(\sum x_i^{*2}\right)\hat{\beta}_2 = \sum x_i^* y_i^*$$

(a) Show that $\hat{\beta}_1$ and $\hat{\beta}_2$ can be written as

$$\hat{\beta}_2 = \frac{\dfrac{\sum \sigma_i^{-2} y_i x_i}{\sum \sigma_i^{-2}} - \left(\dfrac{\sum \sigma_i^{-2} y_i}{\sum \sigma_i^{-2}}\right)\left(\dfrac{\sum \sigma_i^{-2} x_i}{\sum \sigma_i^{-2}}\right)}{\dfrac{\sum \sigma_i^{-2} x_i^2}{\sum \sigma_i^{-2}} - \left(\dfrac{\sum \sigma_i^{-2} x_i}{\sum \sigma_i^{-2}}\right)^2}, \qquad \hat{\beta}_1 = \frac{\sum \sigma_i^{-2} y_i}{\sum \sigma_i^{-2}} - \left(\frac{\sum \sigma_i^{-2} x_i}{\sum \sigma_i^{-2}}\right)\hat{\beta}_2$$

(b) Show that $\hat{\beta}_1$ and $\hat{\beta}_2$ are equal to the least squares estimators b_1 and b_2 when $\sigma_i^2 = \sigma^2$ for all i. That is, the error variances are constant.

(c) Does a comparison of the formulas for $\hat{\beta}_1$ and $\hat{\beta}_2$ with those for b_1 and b_2 suggest an interpretation for $\hat{\beta}_1$ and $\hat{\beta}_2$?

8.3 Consider the simple regression model

$$y_i = \beta_1 + \beta_2 x_i + e_i$$

where the e_i are independent errors with $E(e_i) = 0$ and $\text{var}(e_i) = \sigma^2 x_i^2$. Suppose that you have the following five observations

$$y = (4, 3, 1, 0, 2) \quad x = (2, 1, 1, 1, 2)$$

Use a hand calculator to find generalized least squares estimates of β_1 and β_2.

8.4 A sample of 200 Chicago households was taken to investigate how far American households tend to travel when they take vacation. Measuring distance in miles per year, the following model was estimated

$$MILES = \beta_1 + \beta_2 INCOME + \beta_3 AGE + \beta_4 KIDS + e$$

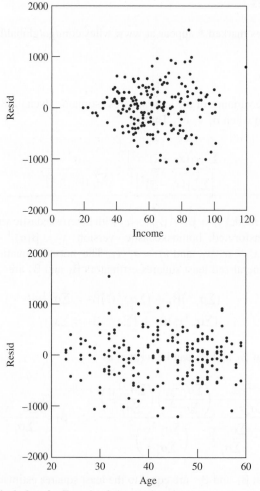

FIGURE **8.4** Residual plots for Exercise 8.4: vacation data.

The variables are self-explanatory except perhaps for *AGE*, the average age of the adult members of the household. The data are in the file *vacation.dat*.

(a) The equation was estimated by least squares and the residuals are plotted against age and income in Figure 8.4. What do these graphs suggest to you?

(b) Ordering the observations according to descending values of *INCOME*, and applying least squares to the first 100 observations, and again to the second 100 observations, yields the sums of squared errors

$$SSE_1 = 2.9471 \times 10^7 \quad SSE_2 = 1.0479 \times 10^7$$

Use the Goldfeld–Quandt test to test for heteroskedastic errors. Include specification of the null and alternative hypotheses.

(c) Table 8.2 contains three sets of estimates: those from least squares, those from least squares with White's standard errors, and those from generalized least squares under the assumption $\sigma_i^2 = \sigma^2 \times INCOME^2$.

   (i) How do vacation miles traveled depend on income, age, and the number of kids in the household?

   (ii) How do White's standard errors compare with the least squares standard errors? Do they change your assessment of the precision of estimation?

   (iii) Is there evidence to suggest the generalized least squares estimates are better estimates?

8.5 In Exercise 5.5 an equation used for the valuation of homes in towns surrounding Boston was estimated. Reestimating that equation with White's standard errors yields the output in Table 8.3.

(a) For the coefficients of *CRIME, ROOMS, AGE*, and *TAX*, compare 95% confidence intervals obtained using the standard errors from Exercise 5.5 with those from Table 8.3.

Ta b l e 8 . 2 **Output for Exercise 8.4**

Variable	Coefficient	Std. Error	*t*-value	*p*-value
Least squares estimates				
C	−391.55	169.78	−2.31	0.022
INCOME	14.20	1.80	7.89	0.000
AGE	15.74	3.76	4.19	0.000
KIDS	−81.83	27.13	−3.02	0.003
Least squares estimates with White standard errors				
C	−391.55	142.65	−2.74	0.007
INCOME	14.20	1.94	7.32	0.000
AGE	15.74	3.97	3.97	0.000
KIDS	−81.83	29.15	−2.81	0.006
Generalized least squares estimates				
C	−425.00	121.44	−3.50	0.001
INCOME	13.95	1.48	9.42	0.000
AGE	16.72	3.02	5.53	0.000
KIDS	−76.81	21.85	−3.52	0.001

Table 8.3 **Estimated Mean Function for Exercise 8.5**

Dependent Variable: *VALUE*
Observations: 506
Heteroskedasticity-Consistent Standard Errors

Variable	Coefficient	Std. Error	t-value	p-value
C	28.407	7.380	3.849	0.000
CRIME	−0.183	0.035	−5.283	0.000
NITOX	−22.811	4.360	−5.232	0.000
ROOMS	6.372	0.665	9.574	0.000
AGE	−0.048	0.011	−4.433	0.000
DIST	−1.335	0.190	−7.019	0.000
ACCESS	0.272	0.075	3.644	0.000
TAX	−0.013	0.003	−4.430	0.000
PTRATIO	−1.177	0.124	−9.522	0.000

$R^2 = 0.657$ $SSE = 14,652.22$ $SST = 42,716.29$

Table 8.4 **Estimated Variance Function for Exercise 8.6**

Dependent Variable: *EHAT_SQ*
Included observations: 506

Variable	Coefficient	Std. Error	t-value	p-value
C	1007.037	204.522	4.92	0.000
ROOMS	−305.311	63.088	−4.84	0.000
ROOMS^2	23.822	4.844	4.92	0.000
CRIME	2.285	1.242	1.84	0.067
CRIME^2	−0.039	0.019	−2.04	0.042
DIST	−4.419	2.466	−1.79	0.074

$R^2 = 0.08467$ $SSE = 5,038,458$ $SST = 5,504,525$

    (b) Do you think heteroskedasticity is likely to be a problem?
    (c) What misleading inferences are likely if the incorrect standard errors are used?

8.6 Continuing with the example in Exercise 8.5, Table 8.4 contains output for the following least squares regression

$$EHAT\_SQ = \alpha_1 + \alpha_2 ROOMS + \alpha_3 ROOMS^2 + \alpha_4 CRIME + \alpha_5 CRIME^2$$
$$+ \alpha_6 DIST + v$$

where *EHAT_SQ* denotes the squares of the least squares residuals from the mean function estimated in Exercise 8.5.
    (a) Discuss how each of the variables *ROOMS*, *CRIME*, and *DIST* influences the variance of house values.
    (b) Test for heteroskedasticity.

8.7* Consider the model

$$y_i = \beta_1 + \beta_2 x_i + e_i \quad E(e_i) = 0 \quad \text{var}(e_i) = \sigma_i^2 = \exp(\alpha z_i)$$

You have the following eight observations on y_i, x_i, and z_i:

y	1.1	−0.5	18.9	−0.9	6.4	1.8	4.5	−0.2
x	−0.5	−3	3.2	−1.8	3.4	−3.5	2.4	−0.2
z	3.3	0.3	7.0	4.7	1.9	6.8	2.3	6.4

Use a hand calculator to
(a) Find least squares estimates of β_1 and β_2.
(b) Find the least squares residuals.
(c) Estimate α.
(d) Find variance estimates $\hat{\sigma}_i^2$.
(e) Find generalized least squares estimates of β_1 and β_2. (*Hint*: Use the results in Exercise 8.2)

8.7.2 COMPUTER EXERCISES

8.8   The file *stockton96.dat* contains 940 observations on home sales in Stockton, CA in 1996. They are a subset of the data in the file *stockton.dat* used for Exercise 7.4.
(a) Use least squares to estimate a linear equation that relates house price *PRICE* to the size of the house in square feet *SQFT* and the age of the house in years *AGE*. Comment on the estimates.
(b) Suppose that you own two houses. One has 1600 square feet; the other has 2000 square feet. Both are 15 years old. What price do you estimate you will get for each house.
(c) Use the White test (with cross-product term included) to test for heteroskedasticity.
(d) Estimate α_1 and α_2 in the variance function $\sigma_i^2 = \exp(\alpha_1 + \alpha_2 SQFT)$.
(e) Using the variance assumption from part (d), find generalized least squares estimates for the parameters of the equation estimated by least squares in part (a). Comment on the results.
(f) Use the results from part (e) to estimate the prices you will get for your two houses.

8.9   (a) Using the estimates obtained in part (a) of Exercise 8.8 as the true parameter values, and assuming normally distributed errors, find the probability that (i) your 1600-square-foot house sells for more than \$115,000 and (ii) your 2000-square-foot house sells for less than \$110,000.
(b) After making the correction $\hat{\alpha}_1 = \hat{\alpha}_1 + 1.2704$, use the estimates obtained in parts (d) and (e) of Exercise 8.8 as the parameter values and, assuming normally distributed errors, find the probability that (i) your 1600-square-foot house sells for more than \$115,000 and (ii) your 2000-square-foot house sells for less than \$110,000.
(c) Comment on and compare the answers you obtained in parts (a) and (b).

8.10* (a) The purpose of this exercise is to test whether the variance specification $\sigma_i^2 = \sigma^2 x_i$ introduced in Section 8.4.1 has been adequate to eliminate heteroskedasticity in the food expenditure example in the text. Compute the squares of the residuals from the transformed model used to obtain the estimates in (8.32). Regress the squares of the residuals on x_i and test for heteroskedasticity.

(b) We now ask whether the variance specification $\sigma_i^2 = \sigma^2 x_i^\gamma$ introduced in Section 8.5 eliminates heteroskedasticity. Compute the squares of the residuals from the transformed model used to obtain the estimates in (8.47). Regress the squares of the residuals on x_i and test for heteroskedasticity.

8.11   Reconsider the household expenditure model that appears in the text, and the data for which are in the file *food.dat*. That is, we have the model

$$y_i = \beta_1 + \beta_2 x_i + e_i$$

where y_i is food expenditure for the ith household and x_i is income. Find generalized least squares estimates for β_1 and β_2 under the assumptions
   (i) $\text{var}(e_i) = \sigma^2 \sqrt{x_i}$
   (ii) $\text{var}(e_i) = \sigma^2 x_i^2$
   (iii) $\text{var}(e_i) = \sigma^2 \ln(x_i)$
Comment on the sensitivity of the estimates and their standard errors to the heteroskedastic specification. For each case, use the White $N \times R^2$ statistic and the residuals from the transformed model to test whether heteroskedasticity has been eliminated.

8.12   In the file *pubexp.dat* there are data on public expenditure on education (*EE*), gross domestic product (*GDP*), and population (*P*) for 34 countries in the year 1980. It is hypothesized that per capita expenditure on education is linearly related to per capita *GDP*. That is,

$$y_i = \beta_1 + \beta_2 x_i + e_i$$

where

$$y_i = \left(\frac{EE_i}{P_i} \right) \quad \text{and} \quad x_i = \left(\frac{GDP_i}{P_i} \right)$$

It is suspected that e_i may be heteroskedastic with a variance related to x_i.
(a) Why might the suspicion about heteroskedasticity be reasonable?
(b) Estimate the equation using least squares; plot the least squares function and the residuals. Is there any evidence of heteroskedasticity?
(c) Test for the existence of heteroskedasticity using a White test.
(d) Use White's formula for least squares variance estimates to find some alternative standard errors for the least squares estimates obtained in part (b). Use these standard errors and those obtained in part (b) to construct two alternative 90% confidence intervals for β_2. What can you say about the confidence interval that ignores the heteroskedasticity?
(e) Reestimate the equation under the assumption that $\text{var}(e_i) = \sigma^2 x_i$. Report the results. Construct a 90% confidence interval for β_2. Comment on its width relative to that of the confidence intervals found in part (d).

8.13* Consider the following cost function where C denotes cost and Q denotes output. Assume that $\text{var}(e_{1t}) = \sigma^2 Q_{1t}$. We use a subscript t because the observations are time-series data. They are stored in the file *cloth.dat*.

$$C_{1t} = \beta_1 + \beta_2 Q_{1t} + \beta_3 Q_{1t}^2 + \beta_4 Q_{1t}^3 + e_{1t}$$

(a) Find generalized least squares estimates of $\beta_1, \beta_2, \beta_3,$ and β_4.
(b) Test the hypothesis $\beta_1 = \beta_4 = 0$.

(c) What can you say about the nature of the average cost function if the hypothesis in (b) is true?

(d) Under what assumption about the error term would it be more appropriate to estimate the average cost function than the total cost function?

8.14* In the file *cloth.dat* there are 28 time-series observations on total cost (C) and output (Q) for two clothing manufacturing firms. It is hypothesized that both firms' cost functions are cubic and can be written as

$$\text{firm 1:} \quad C_{1t} = \beta_1 + \beta_2 Q_{1t} + \beta_3 Q_{1t}^2 + \beta_4 Q_{1t}^3 + e_{1t}$$
$$\text{firm 2:} \quad C_{2t} = \delta_1 + \delta_2 Q_{2t} + \delta_3 Q_{2t}^2 + \delta_4 Q_{2t}^3 + e_{2t}$$

where $E(e_{1t}) = E(e_{2t}) = 0$, $\text{var}(e_{1t}) = \sigma_1^2$, and $\text{var}(e_{2t}) = \sigma_2^2$. Also, e_{1t} and e_{2t} are independent of each other and over time.

(a) Estimate each function using least squares. Report and comment on the results. Do the estimated coefficients have the expected signs?

(b) Using a 10% significance level, test the hypothesis that $H_0: \sigma_1^2 = \sigma_2^2$ against the alternative that $H_1: \sigma_1^2 \neq \sigma_2^2$.

(c) Estimate both equations jointly, assuming that $\beta_1 = \delta_1$, $\beta_2 = \delta_2$, $\beta_3 = \delta_3$, and $\beta_4 = \delta_4$. Report and comment on the results.

(d) Test the hypothesis

$$H_0: \beta_1 = \delta_1, \; \beta_2 = \delta_2, \; \beta_3 = \delta_3 \text{ and } \beta_4 = \delta_4$$

Comment on the test outcome.

8.15* (a) Reconsider the wage equation that was estimated in Section 8.4.2. Instead of estimating the variances from two separate subsamples, one for metropolitan and the other for rural, estimate the two variances using the model

$$\sigma_i^2 = \exp(\alpha_1 + \alpha_2 METRO_i)$$

and one single combined sample. Are your variance estimates different from those obtained using two separate subsamples? Why?

(b) Find a new set of generalized least squares estimates for the mean function and compare them with those in (8.36).

(c) Find White standard errors for the least squares estimates of the mean function. How do they compare with the generalized least squares standard errors obtained in part (b)?

8.16 Consider the following model used to explain gasoline consumption per car in Germany and Austria for the period 1960–1978:

$$\ln(GAS) = \beta_1 + \beta_2 \ln(INC) + \beta_3 \ln(PRICE) + \beta_4 \ln(CARS) + e$$

where *INC* is per capita real income, *PRICE* is the real gasoline price, and *CARS* is the per capita stock of cars. Data on these variables appear in the file *gasga.dat*.

(a) Using separate least squares estimations, estimate the error variance for Germany σ_G^2, and the error variance for Austria σ_A^2.

(b) Test the hypothesis $H_0: \sigma_G^2 = \sigma_A^2$ against the alternative $H_1: \sigma_G^2 \neq \sigma_A^2$ at a 1% significance level.

(c) Find generalized least squares estimates of the coefficients β_1, β_2, β_3, β_4.

(d) Use the results in (c) to test the null hypothesis that demand is price inelastic ($\beta_3 \geq -1$) against the alternative that demand is elastic $\beta_3 < -1$.

8.17   The file *br2.dat* contains data on 1080 houses sold in Baton Rouge, Louisiana during mid-2005. We will be concerned with the selling price (*PRICE*), the size of the house in square feet (*SQFT*), and the age of the house in years (*AGE*). Define a new variable that measures house size in terms of hundreds of square feet, $SQFT100 = SQFT/100$.

(a) Find least squares estimates of the following equation and save the residuals:

$$\ln(PRICE) = \beta_1 + \beta_2 SQFT100 + \beta_3 AGE + \beta_4 AGE^2 + e$$

(b) Plot the least residuals against (i) *AGE* and (ii) *SQFT100*. Is there any evidence of heteroskedasticity?

(c) Test for heteroskedasticity using a Breusch-Pagan test and the variables *AGE* and *SQFT100*. Is there evidence of heteroskedasticity at a 1% level of significance?

(d) Estimate the variance function $\sigma_i^2 = \exp(\alpha_1 + \alpha_2 AGE_i + \alpha_3 SQFT100_i)$ and report the results. Use the robust standard error option and comment on the effects of *AGE* and *SQFT100* on the variance.

(e) Use the estimated variance function in (d) to find variance estimates $\hat{\sigma}_i^2$, $i = 1$, $2, \ldots$, 1080, and use those estimates to find generalized least squares estimates of the equation in (a).

(f) Use a table format to report estimates and standard errors for the model in part (a), from the following estimation techniques. Comment on any differences and similarities.

(i) Least squares

(ii) Least squares with heteroskedasticity-robust standard errors

(iii) Generalized least squares from part (e)

(iv) Generalized least squares from part (e), but with robust standard errors

(g) Do the transformed residuals from the transformed regression in part (e) show evidence of heteroskedasticity? Use a Breusch-Pagan test with variables *AGE* and *SQFT100*.

8.18   In Section 8.6.1 we estimated the linear probability model

$$COKE = \beta_1 + \beta_2 PRATIO + \beta_3 DISP\_COKE + \beta_4 DISP\_PEPSI + e$$

where $COKE = 1$ if a shopper purchased Coke and $COKE = 0$ if a shopper purchased Pepsi. The variable *PRATIO* was the relative price ratio of Coke to Pepsi, and *DISP_COKE* and *DISP_PEPSI* were indicator variables equal to one if the relevant display was present. Suppose now that we have 1140 observations on randomly selected shoppers from 50 different grocery stores. Each grocery store has its own settings for *PRATIO*, *DISP_COKE* and *DISP_PEPSI*. Let an (i, j) subscript denote the jth shopper at the ith store, so that we can write the model as

$$COKE_{ij} = \beta_1 + \beta_2 PRATIO_i + \beta_3 DISP\_COKE_i + \beta_4 DISP\_PEPSI_i + e_{ij}$$

Average this equation over all shoppers in the ith store so that we have

$$\overline{COKE}_{i\cdot} = \beta_1 + \beta_2 PRATIO_i + \beta_3 DISP\_COKE_i + \beta_4 DISP\_PEPSI_i + \bar{e}_{i\cdot}. \quad (8.52)$$

where

$$\bar{e}_{i\cdot} = \frac{1}{N_i} \sum_{j=1}^{N_i} e_{ij} \qquad \overline{COKE}_{i\cdot} = \frac{1}{N_i} \sum_{j=1}^{N_i} COKE_{ij}$$

and N_i is the number of sampled shoppers in the ith store.

(a) Explain why $\overline{COKE}_i$ is the proportion of shoppers from the ith store who bought Coke.

(b) Given that $E(COKE_{ij}) = p_i$ and $\text{var}(COKE_{ij}) = p_i(1 - p_i)$, show that

$$E(\overline{COKE}_{i\cdot}) = p_i \text{ and var}(\overline{COKE}_{i\cdot}) = \frac{p_i(1 - p_i)}{N_i}$$

(c) Interpret p_i and express it in terms of $PRATIO_i$, $DISP\_COKE_i$ and $DISP\_PEPSI_i$.

(d) Observations on the variables $\overline{COKE}_{i\cdot}$, $PRATIO_i$, $DISP\_COKE_i$, $DISP\_PEPSI_i$ and N_i appear in the file *coke_grouped.dat*. Find least squares estimates of (8.52). Comment on the results.

(e) Test for heteroskedasticity by applying the White test with cross-product terms to the least squares residuals. Explain why it makes sense to include the cross-product terms.

(f) Estimate p_i and $\text{var}(\overline{COKE}_{i\cdot})$ for each of the stores. Report the mean, standard deviation, maximum, and minimum values of the estimated p_i.

(g) Find generalized least squares estimates of (8.52). Comment on the results and compare them with those obtained in part (d).

8.19 (a) Using the data in *cps4_small.dat* estimate the following wage equation with least squares and heteroskedasticity-robust standard errors:

$$\ln(WAGE) = \beta_1 + \beta_2 EDUC + \beta_3 EXPER + \beta_4 EXPER^2$$
$$+ \beta_5(EXPER \times EDUC) + e$$

Report the results.

(b) Add *MARRIED* to the equation and re-estimate. Holding education and experience constant, do married workers get higher wages? Using a 1% significance level, test a null hypothesis that wages of married workers are less than or equal to those of unmarried workers against the alternative that wages of married workers are higher.

(c) Plot the residuals from part (a) against the two values of *MARRIED*. Is there evidence of heteroskedasticity?

(d) Estimate the model in part (a) twice—once using observations on only married workers and once using observations on only unmarried workers. Use the Goldfeld-Quandt test and a 1% significance level to test whether the error variances for married and unmarried workers are different.

(e) Find generalized least squares of the model in part (a). Compare the estimates and standard errors with those obtained in part (a).

(f) Find two 95% interval estimates for the marginal effect $\partial E(\ln(WAGE))/\partial EDUC$ for a worker with 12 years of education and 25 years of experience. Use the results from part (a) for one interval and the results from part (e) for the other interval. Comment on any differences.

8.20 Consider again the data in *cps4_small.dat* and the wage equation

$$\ln(WAGE) = \beta_1 + \beta_2 EDUC + \beta_3 EXPER + \beta_4 EXPER^2$$
$$+ \beta_5(EXPER \times EDUC) + e$$

    (a) Plot the least squares residuals against *EDUC* and against *EXPER*. What do they suggest?

    (b) Test for heteroskedasticity using a Breusch-Pagan test where the variance depends on *EDUC*, *EXPER* and *MARRIED*. What do you conclude at a 5% significance level?

    (c) Estimate a variance function that includes *EDUC*, *EXPER*, and *MARRIED* and use it to estimate the standard deviation for each observation.

    (d) Find generalized least squares estimates of the wage equation. Compare the estimates and standard errors with those obtained from least squares estimation with heteroskedasticity-robust standard errors.

    (e) Find two 95% interval estimates for the marginal effect $\partial E(\ln(WAGE))/\partial EXPER$ for a worker with 16 years of education and 20 years of experience. Use least squares with heteroskedasticity-robust standard errors for one interval and the results from part (d) for the other. Comment on any differences.

8.21   This exercise is a continuation of Exercise 8.20. Estimates from 8.20(c) and 8.20(d) should be used to answer the following questions.

    (a) Forecast the wage of a married worker with 18 years of education and 16 years of experience. Use both the natural predictor and the corrected predictor. (See Chapter 4.5.3.)

    (b) Find a 95% forecast interval for the wage of a married worker with 18 years of education and 16 years of experience. Ignore the uncertainty and sampling error from estimating the coefficients.

8.22   In Exercise 7.7 we considered a model designed to provide information to mortgage lenders. They want to determine borrower and loan factors that may lead to delinquency or foreclosure. In the file *lasvegas.dat* are 1000 observations on mortgages for single-family homes in Las Vegas, Nevada during 2008. The variable of interest is *DELINQUENT*, an indicator variable $= 1$ if the borrower missed at least three payments (90+ days late), but zero otherwise. Explanatory variables are *LVR* = the ratio of the loan amount to the value of the property; *REF* $= 1$ if purpose of the loan was a "refinance" and $= 0$ if loan was for a purchase; *INSUR* $= 1$ if mortgage carries mortgage insurance, zero otherwise; *RATE* = initial interest rate of the mortgage; *AMOUNT* = dollar value of mortgage (in $100,000); *CREDIT* = credit score, *TERM* = number of years between disbursement of the loan and the date it is expected to be fully repaid, *ARM* $= 1$ if mortgage has an adjustable rate, and $= 0$ if mortgage has a fixed rate.

    (a) Estimate the linear probability (regression) model explaining *DELINQUENT* as a function of the remaining variables. Use the White test with cross-product terms included to test for heteroskedasticity. Why did we include the cross-product terms?

    (b) Use the estimates from (a) to estimate the error variances for each observation. How many of these estimates are at least one? How many are at most zero? How many are less than 0.01?

    (c) Prepare a table containing estimates and standard errors from estimating the linear probability model in each of the following ways:

       (i) Least squares with conventional standard errors.

      (ii) Least squares with heteroskedasticity-robust standard errors.

      (iii) Generalized least squares omitting observations with variances less than 0.01.

(iv) Generalized least squares with variances less than 0.01 changed to 0.01.

(v) Generalized least squares with variances less than 0.00001 changed to 0.00001.

Discuss and compare the different results.

(d) Using the results from (iv), interpret each of the coefficients. Mention whether the signs are reasonable and whether they are significantly different from zero.

Appendix 8A Properties of the Least Squares Estimator

We are concerned with the properties of the least squares estimator for β_2 in the model

$$y_i = \beta_1 + \beta_2 x_i + e_i$$

where

$$E(e_i) = 0 \quad \text{var}(e_i) = \sigma_i^2 \quad \text{cov}(e_i, e_j) = 0 \quad (i \neq j)$$

Note that we are assuming the existence of heteroskedasticity. In Appendix 2D of Chapter 2, we wrote the least squares estimator for β_2 as

$$b_2 = \beta_2 + \Sigma w_i e_i \qquad (8A.1)$$

where

$$w_i = \frac{x_i - \bar{x}}{\Sigma(x_i - \bar{x})^2}$$

This expression is a useful one for exploring the properties of least squares estimation under heteroskedasticity. The first property that we establish is that of unbiasedness. This property was derived under homoskedasticity in (2.13). The same proof holds under heteroskedasticity because the only error term assumption that was used is $E(e_i) = 0$. We summarize the results here for completeness:

$$E(b_2) = E(\beta_2) + E(\Sigma w_i e_i)$$
$$= \beta_2 + \Sigma w_i E(e_i) = \beta_2$$

The next result is that the least squares estimator is no longer best. That is, although it is still unbiased, it is no longer *the best* linear unbiased estimator. We showed this result in Section 8.4 by considering alternative variance specifications and deriving alternative estimators that were best under these specifications.

The final consequence of using least squares under heteroskedasticity is that the usual formulas for the least squares standard errors are incorrect. To prove this result, we write, from (8A.1),

$$\text{var}(b_2) = \text{var}(\Sigma w_i e_i)$$
$$= \Sigma w_i^2 \text{var}(e_i) + \underset{i \neq j}{\Sigma \Sigma} w_i w_j \text{cov}(e_i, e_j)$$
$$= \Sigma w_i^2 \sigma_i^2$$
$$= \frac{\Sigma \left[(x_i - \bar{x})^2 \sigma_i^2 \right]}{\left[\Sigma (x_i - \bar{x})^2 \right]^2} \qquad (8A.2)$$

If the variances are all the same ($\sigma_i^2 = \sigma^2$), then the next-to-last line becomes $\sigma^2 \Sigma w_i^2$. This simplification is not possible under heteroskedasticity, so the result in (8A.2) is different to that derived in Appendix 2E. Specifically, it follows from (8A.2) that

$$\text{var}(b_2) \neq \frac{\sigma^2}{\Sigma(x_i - \bar{x})^2} \tag{8A.3}$$

Thus, if we use the least squares estimation procedure and ignore heteroskedasticity when it is present, we will be using an estimate of the right-hand-side of (8A.3) to obtain the standard error for b_2 when in fact we should be using an estimate of (8A.2). Using incorrect standard errors means that interval estimates and hypothesis tests will no longer be valid. Note that standard computer software for least squares regression will compute the estimated variance for b_2 based on (8A.3) unless told specifically to compute White standard errors.

Appendix 8B Lagrange Multiplier Tests for Heteroskedasticity

More insights into Lagrange multiplier and other variance function tests can be developed by relating them to the F-test introduced in (6.8) for testing the significance of a mean function. To put that test in the context of a variance function, consider (8.15)

$$\hat{e}_i^2 = \alpha_1 + \alpha_2 z_{i2} + \cdots + \alpha_S z_{iS} + v_i \tag{8B.1}$$

and assume that our objective is to test $H_0 : \alpha_2 = \alpha_3 = \cdots = \alpha_S = 0$ against the alternative that at least one α_s, for $s = 2, \ldots, S$, is nonzero. In Section 8.2.2 we considered a more general variance function than that in (8B.1), but we also pointed out that using the linear function in (8B.1) is valid for testing more general alternative hypotheses.

Adapting the F-value reported in (6.8) to test the overall significance of (8B.1), we have

$$F = \frac{(SST - SSE)/(S - 1)}{SSE/(N - S)} \tag{8B.2}$$

where

$$SST = \sum_{i=1}^{N} \left[\hat{e}_i^2 - \overline{\hat{e}^2} \right]^2 \quad \text{and} \quad SSE = \sum_{i=1}^{N} \hat{v}_i^2$$

are the total sum of squares and sum of squared errors from estimating (8B.1). Note that $\overline{\hat{e}^2}$ is the mean of the dependent variable in (8B.1), or, equivalently, the average of the squares of the least squares residuals from the mean function. At a 5% significance level, a valid test is to reject H_0 if the F-value is greater than a critical value given by $F_{(0.95, S-1, N-S)}$.

Two further tests, the original Breusch–Pagan test and its $N \times R^2$ version, can be obtained by modifying (8B.2). Please be patient as we work through these modifications. We begin by rewriting (8B.2) as

$$\chi^2 = (S - 1) \times F = \frac{SST - SSE}{SSE/(N - S)} \sim \chi^2_{(S-1)} \tag{8B.3}$$

The chi-square statistic $\chi^2 = (S-1) \times F$ has an approximate $\chi^2_{(S-1)}$-distribution in large samples. That is, multiplying an F-statistic by its numerator degrees of freedom gives another statistic that follows a chi-square distribution. The degrees of freedom of the chi-square distribution are $S-1$, the same as that for the numerator of the F-distribution. The background for this result is given in Appendix 6A.

Next, note that

$$\widehat{\text{var}(e_i^2)} = \widehat{\text{var}(v_i)} = \frac{SSE}{N-S} \tag{8B.4}$$

That is, the variance of the dependent variable is the same as the variance of the error, which can be estimated from the sum of squared errors in (8B.1). Substituting (8B.4) into (8B.3) yields

$$\chi^2 = \frac{SST - SSE}{\widehat{\text{var}(e_i^2)}} \tag{8B.5}$$

This test statistic represents the basic form of the Breusch–Pagan statistic. Its two different versions occur because of the alternative estimators used to replace $\widehat{\text{var}(e_i^2)}$.

If it is assumed that e_i is normally distributed, it can be shown that $\text{var}(e_i^2) = 2\sigma_e^4$, and the statistic for the first version of the Breusch–Pagan test is

$$\chi^2 = \frac{SST - SSE}{2\hat{\sigma}_e^4} \tag{8B.6}$$

Note that $\sigma_e^4 = (\sigma_e^2)^2$ is the square of the error variance from the mean function; unlike SST and SSE, its estimate comes from estimating (8.16). The result $\text{var}(e_i^2) = 2\sigma_e^4$ might be unexpected—here is a little proof so that you know where it comes from. When $e_i \sim N(0, \sigma_e^2)$, then $(e_i/\sigma_e) \sim N(0, 1)$, and $(e_i^2/\sigma_e^2) \sim \chi^2_{(1)}$. The variance of a $\chi^2_{(1)}$ random variable is 2. Thus,

$$\text{var}\left(\frac{e_i^2}{\sigma_e^2}\right) = 2 \quad \Rightarrow \quad \frac{1}{\sigma_e^4}\text{var}(e_i^2) = 2 \quad \Rightarrow \quad \text{var}(e_i^2) = 2\sigma_e^4$$

Using (8B.6), we reject a null hypothesis of homoskedasticity when the χ^2-value is greater than a critical value from the $\chi^2_{(S-1)}$ distribution.

For the second version of (8B.5) the assumption of normally distributed errors is not necessary. Because this assumption is not used, it is often called the robust version of the Breusch–Pagan test. The sample variance of the squared least squares residuals, the $\hat{e}_i^2$, is used as an estimator for $\text{var}(e_i^2)$. Specifically, we set

$$\widehat{\text{var}(e_i^2)} = \frac{1}{N}\sum_{i=1}^{N}\left[\hat{e}_i^2 - \overline{\hat{e}^2}\right]^2 = \frac{SST}{N} \tag{8B.7}$$

This quantity is an estimator for $\text{var}(e_i^2)$ under the assumption that H_0 is true. It can also be written as the total sum of squares from estimating the variance function divided by the sample size. Substituting (8B.7) into (8B.5) yields

$$\chi^2 = \frac{SST - SSE}{SST/N}$$

$$= N \times \left(1 - \frac{SSE}{SST}\right) \tag{8B.8}$$

$$= N \times R^2$$

where R^2 is the R^2 goodness-of-fit statistic from estimating the variance function. At a 5% significance level, a null hypothesis of homoskedasticity is rejected when $\chi^2 = N \times R^2$ exceeds the critical value $\chi^2_{(0.95, S-1)}$.

Software often reports the outcome of the White test described in Section 8.4.3a as an F-value or a χ^2-value. The F-value is from the statistic in (8B.4), with the z's chosen as the x's and their squares and possibly cross-products. The χ^2-value is from the statistic in (8B.8), with the z's chosen as the x's and their squares and possibly cross-products.

Chapter 9

Regression With Time-Series Data: Stationary Variables

Learning Objectives

Based on the material in this Chapter, you should be able to:

1. Explain why lags are important in models that use time-series data, and the ways in which lags can be included in dynamic econometric models.

2. Explain what is meant by a serially correlated time series, and how we measure serial correlation.

3. Specify, estimate, and interpret the estimates from a finite distribute lag model.

4. Explain the nature of regressions that involve lagged variables and the number of observations that are available.

5. Specify and explain how the multiple regression assumptions are modified to accommodate time series data.

6. Compute the autocorrelations for a time-series, graph the corresponding correlogram, and use it to test for serial correlation.

7. Use a correlogram of residuals to test for serially correlated errors.

8. Use a Lagrange multiplier test for serially correlated errors.

9. Compute HAC standard errors for least squares estimates. Explain why they are used.

10. Describe the properties of an AR(1) error.

11. Compute nonlinear least squares estimates for a model with an AR(1) error.

12. Test whether an ARDL(1, 1) model can be written as an AR(1) error model.

13. Specify and estimate autoregressive distributed lag models. Use serial correlation checks, significance of coefficients and model selection criteria to choose lag lengths.

14. Estimate an autoregressive model and choose a suitable lag length.

15. Use AR and ARDL models to compute forecasts, standard errors of forecasts and forecast intervals.

16. Explain what is meant by exponential smoothing. Use exponential smoothing to compute a forecast.

17. Compute delay, interim, and total multipliers for both ARDL and finite distributed lag models.

Keywords

AIC criterion
AR(1) error
AR(p) model
ARDL(p,q) model
autocorrelation
autoregressive
  distributed lags
autoregressive error
autoregressive model
BIC criterion
correlogram
delay multiplier
distributed lag weight

dynamic models
exponential smoothing
finite distributed lag
forecast error
forecast intervals
forecasting
HAC standard errors
impact multiplier
infinite distributed lag
interim multiplier
lag length
lag operator
lagged dependent variable

LM test
multiplier analysis
nonlinear least squares
out-of-sample forecasts
sample autocorrelations
serial correlation
standard error of
  forecast error
SC criterion
serial correlation
total multiplier
$T \times R^2$ form of *LM* test
within-sample forecasts

9.1 Introduction

When modeling relationships between variables, the nature of the data that have been collected has an important bearing on the appropriate choice of an econometric model. In particular, it is important to distinguish between cross-section data (data on a number of economic units at a particular point in time) and time-series data (data collected over time on one particular economic unit). Examples of both types of data were given in Chapter 1.5. When we say "economic units" we could be referring to individuals, households, firms, geographical regions, countries, or some other entity on which data is collected. Because cross-section observations on a number of economic units at a given time are often generated by way of a random sample, they are typically uncorrelated. The level of income observed in the Smiths' household, for example, does not affect, nor is it affected by, the level of income in the Jones's household. On the other hand, time-series observations on a given economic unit, observed over a number of time periods, are likely to be correlated. The level of income observed in the Smiths' household in one year is likely to be related to the level of income in the Smiths' household in the year before. Thus, one feature that distinguishes time-series data from cross-section data is the likely correlation between different observations. Our challenges for this chapter include testing for and modeling such correlation.

A second distinguishing feature of time-series data is its natural ordering according to time. With cross-section data there is no particular ordering of the observations that is better or more natural than another. One could shuffle the observations and then proceed with estimation without losing any information. If one shuffles time-series observations, there is a danger of confounding what is their most important distinguishing feature: the possible existence of dynamic relationships between variables. A dynamic relationship is one in which the change in a variable now has an impact on that same variable, or other variables, in one or more future time periods. For example, it is common for a change in the level of an explanatory variable to have behavioral implications for other variables beyond the time period in which it occurred. The consequences of economic decisions that result in changes in economic variables can last a long time. When the income tax rate is increased, consumers have less disposable income, reducing their expenditures on goods and services, which reduces profits of suppliers, which reduces the demand for productive inputs, which reduces the profits of the input suppliers, and so on. The effect of the tax increase ripples through the economy. These effects do not occur instantaneously but are spread, or **distributed**, over future time periods. As shown in Figure 9.1, economic actions or decisions taken at one point in time, t, have effects on the economy at time t, but also at times $t + 1$, $t + 2$, and so on.

9.1.1 DYNAMIC NATURE OF RELATIONSHIPS

Given that the effects of changes in variables are not always instantaneous, we need to ask how to model the dynamic nature of relationships. We begin by recognizing three different ways of doing so.

1. One way is to specify that a dependent variable y is a function of current and past values of an explanatory variable x. That is,

$$y_t = f(x_t, x_{t-1}, x_{t-2}, \cdots) \tag{9.1}$$

We can think of (y_t, x_t) as denoting the values for y and x in the current period; x_{t-1} means the value of x in the previous period; x_{t-2} is the value of x two periods ago, and so on. For the moment $f(\cdot)$ is used to denote any general function. Later we replace $f(\cdot)$ by a linear function, like those used so far in the book. Equations such as (9.1) say, for example, that the current rate of inflation y_t depends not just on the current interest rate x_t, but also on the rates in previous time periods $x_{t-1}, x_{t-2}, \ldots$. Turning this interpretation around as in Figure 9.1, it means that a change in the interest rate now will have an impact on inflation now and in future periods; it takes time for the effect of an interest rate change to fully work its way through the economy. Because of the existence of these lagged effects, (9.1) is called a **distributed lag model**.

2. A second way of capturing the dynamic characteristics of time-series data is to specify a model with a **lagged dependent variable** as one of the explanatory variables. For example,

$$y_t = f(y_{t-1}, x_t) \tag{9.2}$$

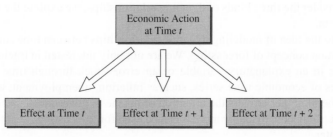

FIGURE *9.1* The distributed lag effect.

where again $f(\cdot)$ is a general function that we later replace with a linear function. In this case we are saying that the inflation rate in one period y_t will depend (among other things) on what it was in the previous period, y_{t-1}. Assuming a positive relationship, periods of high inflation will tend to follow periods of high inflation and periods of low inflation will tend to follow periods of low inflation. Or, in other words, inflation is positively correlated with its value lagged one period. A model of this nature is one way of modeling correlation between current and past values of a dependent variable. Also, we can combine the features of (9.1) and (9.2) so that we have a dynamic model with lagged values of both the dependent and explanatory variables, such as

$$y_t = f(y_{t-1}, x_t, x_{t-1}, x_{t-2}) \tag{9.3}$$

Such models are called **autoregressive distributed lag (ARDL)** models, with "autoregressive" meaning a regression of y_t on its own lag or lags.

3. A third way of modeling the continuing impact of change over several periods is via the error term. For example, using general functions $f(\cdot)$ and $g(\cdot)$, both of which are replaced later with linear functions, we can write

$$y_t = f(x_t) + e_t \qquad\qquad e_t = g(e_{t-1}) \tag{9.4}$$

where the function $e_t = g(e_{t-1})$ is used to denote the dependence of the error on its value in the previous period. In this case e_t is correlated with e_{t-1}; we say the errors are **serially correlated** or **autocorrelated**. Because (9.3) implies $e_{t+1} = g(e_t)$, the dynamic nature of this relationship is such that the impact of any unpredictable shock that feeds into the error term will be felt not just in period t, but also in future periods. The current error e_t affects not just the current value of the dependent variable y_t, but also its future values $y_{t+1}, y_{t+2}, \ldots$. As an example, suppose that a terrorist act creates fear of an oil shortage, driving up the price of oil. The terrorist act is an unpredictable shock that forms part of the error term e_t. It is likely to affect the price of oil in the future as well as during the current period.

In this chapter we consider these three ways in which dynamics can enter a regression relationship—lagged values of the explanatory variable, lagged values of the dependent variable, and lagged values of the error term. What we discover is that these three ways are not as distinct as one might at first think. Including a lagged dependent variable y_{t-1} can capture similar effects to those obtained by including a lagged error e_{t-1}, or a long history of past values of an explanatory variable, $x_{t-1}, x_{t-2}, \ldots$. Thus, we not only consider the three kinds of dynamic relationships, we explore the relationships between them.

Related to the idea of modeling dynamic relationships between time series variables is the important concept of forecasting. We are not only interested in tracing the impact of a change in an explanatory variable or an error shock through time. Forecasting future values of economic time series, such as inflation, unemployment, and exchange rates, is something that attracts the attention of business, governments, and the general public. Describing how dynamic models can be used for forecasting is another objective of this chapter.

9.1.2 Least Squares Assumptions

An important consequence of using time series data to estimate dynamic relationships is the possible violation of one of our least squares assumptions. Assumption MR4 specified in Chapter 5 states that different observations on y and on e are uncorrelated. That is,

$$\text{cov}(y_i, y_j) = \text{cov}(e_i, e_j) = 0 \quad \text{for } i \neq j$$

In this chapter, to emphasize that we are using time-series observations, we drop the i and j subscripts and use t and s instead, with t and s referring to two different time periods such as days, months, quarters, or years. Thus, the above assumption becomes

$$\text{cov}(y_t, y_s) = \text{cov}(e_t, e_s) = 0 \text{ for } t \neq s$$

The dynamic models in (9.2), (9.3) and (9.4) imply correlation between y_t and y_{t-1} or e_t and e_{t-1} or both, so they clearly violate assumption MR4. As mentioned below (9.4), when a variable is correlated with its past values, we say that it is autocorrelated or serially correlated. How to test for serial correlation, and its implications for estimation, are also covered in this chapter.

9.1.2a Stationarity

An assumption that we maintain throughout the chapter is that the variables in our equations are **stationary**. This assumption will take on more meaning in Chapter 12 when it is relaxed. For the moment we note that a stationary variable is one that is not explosive, nor trending, and nor wandering aimlessly without returning to its mean. These features can be illustrated with some graphs. Figures 9.2(a), 9.2(b) and 9.2(c) contain graphs of the observations on three different variables, plotted against time. Plots of this kind are routinely considered when examining time-series variables. The variable Y that appears in Figure 9.2(a) is considered stationary because it tends to fluctuate around a constant mean without wandering or trending. On the other hand, X and Z in Figures 9.2(b) and 9.2(c) possess characteristics of nonstationary variables. In Figure 9.2(b) X tends to wander, or is "slow turning," while Z in Figure 9.2(c) is trending. These concepts will be defined more precisely in Chapter 12. For now the important thing to remember is that this chapter is concerned with modeling and estimating dynamic relationships between stationary variables whose time series have similar characteristics to those of Y. That is, they neither wander nor trend.

9.1.3 Alternative Paths Through the Chapter

This chapter covers a great deal of material. Instructors teaching a one-semester course may not wish to cover all of it, and different instructors are likely to have different preferences for the sections they wish to cover. Figures 9.3(a) and 9.3(b) provide a guide to alternative ways of covering a limited amount of the material. Figure 9.3(a) is designed for instructors who wish to start with finite distributed lags. This starting point has the advantage of beginning with a model that is closest to those studied so far in Chapters 2 to 8. From there we recommend covering serial correlation—relevant definitions, concepts, and testing. At this point some instructors might like to proceed with the AR(1) error model; others might prefer to jump straight to ARDL models. The second path in Figure 9.3(b) is designed for instructors who wish to start the chapter with serial correlation. After covering definitions, concepts, and testing, they can proceed to the AR(1) error model or straight to ARDL models. Finite distributed lag models can be covered as a special case of ARDL models or omitted.

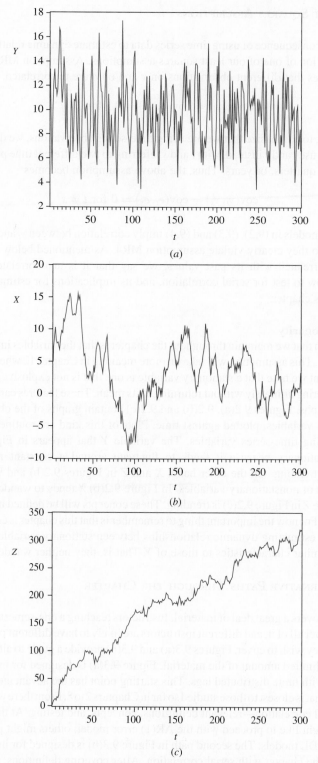

FIGURE 9.2 (a) Time series of a stationary variable; (b) time series of a nonstationary variable that is "slow-turning" or "wandering"; (c) time series of a nonstationary variable that "trends."

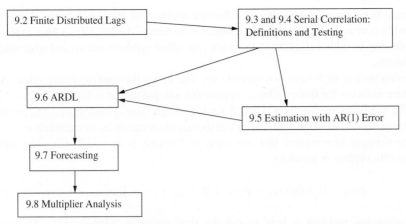

FIGURE **9.3** (a) Alternative paths through the chapter starting with finite distributed lags.

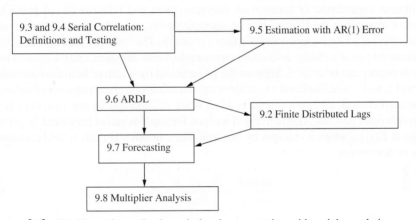

FIGURE **9.3** (b) Alternative paths through the chapter starting with serial correlation.

9.2 **Finite Distributed Lags**

The first dynamic relationship that we consider is that given in (9.1), $y_t = f(x_t, x_{t-1}, x_{t-2}, \cdots)$, with the additional assumptions that the relationship is linear, and, after q time periods, changes in x no longer have an impact on y. Under these conditions we have the multiple regression model

$$y_t = \alpha + \beta_0 x_t + \beta_1 x_{t-1} + \beta_2 x_{t-2} + \cdots + \beta_q x_{t-q} + e_t \tag{9.5}$$

The model in (9.5) can be treated in the same way as the multiple regression model studied in Chapters 5 and 6. Instead of having a number of explanatory variables, we have a number of different lags of the same explanatory variable. However, for the purpose of estimation, these different lags can be treated in the same way as different explanatory variables. It is convenient to change subscript notation on the coefficients: β_s is used to denote the coefficient of x_{t-s} and α is introduced to denote the intercept. Other explanatory variables can be added if relevant, in which case other symbols are needed to denote their coefficients.

Models such as (9.5) have two special uses. The first is **forecasting** future values of y. To introduce notation for future values, suppose our sample period is for $t = 1, 2, \ldots, T$. We use t for the index (rather than i) and T for the sample size (rather than N) to emphasize the time series nature of the data. Given that the last observation in our sample is at $t = T$, the first postsample observation that we want to forecast is at $t = T + 1$. The equation for this observation is given by

$$y_{T+1} = \alpha + \beta_0 x_{T+1} + \beta_1 x_T + \beta_2 x_{T-1} + \cdots + \beta_q x_{T-q+1} + e_{T+1} \qquad (9.6)$$

The forecasting problem is how to use the time series of x-values, $x_{T+1}, x_T, x_{T-1}, \ldots,$ x_{T-q+1} to forecast the value y_{T+1}, with special attention needed to obtain a value for x_{T+1}. We consider this problem in Section 9.7, within the context of a more general model.

The second special use of models like (9.5) is for **policy analysis**. Examples of policy analysis where the distributed-lag effect is important are the effects of changes in government expenditure or taxation on unemployment and inflation (fiscal policy), the effects of changes in the interest rate on unemployment and inflation (monetary policy), and the effect of advertising on sales of a firm's products. The timing of the effect of a change in the interest rate or a change in taxation on unemployment, inflation, and the general health of the economy can be critical. Suppose the government (or a firm or business) controls the values of x, and would like to set x to achieve a given value, or a given sequence of values, for y. The coefficient β_s gives the change in $E(y_t)$ when x_{t-s} changes by one unit, but x is held constant in other periods. Alternatively, if we look forward instead of backward, β_s gives the change in $E(y_{t+s})$ when x_t changes by one unit, but x in other periods is held constant. In terms of derivatives

$$\frac{\partial E(y_t)}{\partial x_{t-s}} = \frac{\partial E(y_{t+s})}{\partial x_t} = \beta_s \qquad (9.7)$$

To further appreciate this interpretation, suppose that x and y have been constant for at least the last q periods and that x_t is increased by one unit, then returned to its original level. Then, using (9.5) but ignoring the error term, the immediate effect will be an increase in y_t by β_0 units. One period later, y_{t+1} will increase by β_1 units, then y_{t+2} will increase by β_2 units and so on, up to period $t + q$, when y_{t+q} will increase by β_q units. In period $t + q + 1$ the value of y will return to its original level. The effect of a one-unit change in x_t is **distributed** over the current and next q periods, from which we get the term "distributed lag model." It is called a **finite distributed lag model of order q** because it is assumed that after a finite number of periods q, changes in x no longer have an impact on y. The coefficient β_s is called a **distributed-lag weight** or an **s-period delay multiplier**. The coefficient β_0 ($s = 0$) is called the **impact multiplier**.

It is also relevant to ask what happens if x_t is increased by one unit and then maintained at its new level in subsequent periods $(t + 1), (t + 2), \ldots$. In this case, the immediate impact will again be β_0; the total effect in period $t + 1$ will be $\beta_0 + \beta_1$, in period $t + 2$ it will be $\beta_0 + \beta_1 + \beta_2$, and so on. We add together the effects from the changes in all preceding periods. These quantities are called **interim multipliers**. For example, the two-period interim multiplier is $(\beta_0 + \beta_1 + \beta_2)$. The **total multiplier** is the final effect on y of the sustained increase after q or more periods have elapsed; it is given by $\sum_{s=0}^{q} \beta_s$.

9.2.1 Assumptions

When the simple regression model was first introduced in Chapter 2, it was written in terms of the mean of y conditional on x. Specifically, $E(y|x) = \beta_1 + \beta_2 x$, which led to the error term assumption $E(e|x) = 0$. Then, so that we could avoid the need to condition on x, and hence ease the notational burden, we made the simplifying assumption that the x's are not random. We maintained this assumption through Chapters 2–8, recognizing that although it is unrealistic for most data sets, relaxing it in a limited but realistic way would have had little impact on our results and on our choice of estimators and test statistics. Further consequences of relaxing it are explored in Chapter 10. However, because the time-series variables used in the examples in this chapter are random, it is useful to mention alternative assumptions under which we can consider the properties of least squares and other estimators.

In distributed lag models both y and x are typically random. The variables used in the example that follows are unemployment and output growth. They are both random. They are observed at the same time; we do not know their values prior to "sampling." We do not "set" output growth and then observe the resulting level of unemployment. To accommodate this randomness we assume that the x's are random and that e_t is independent of all x's in the sample—past, current, and future. This assumption, in conjunction with the other multiple regression assumptions, is sufficient for the least squares estimator to be unbiased and to be best linear unbiased conditional on the x's in the sample.[1] With the added assumption of normally distributed error terms, our usual t and F tests have finite sample justification. Accordingly, the multiple regression assumptions given in Chapter 5 can be modified for the distributed lag model as follows:

ASSUMPTIONS OF THE DISTRIBUTED LAG MODEL

TSMR1. $y_t = \alpha + \beta_0 x_t + \beta_1 x_{t-1} + \beta_2 x_{t-2} + \cdots + \beta_q x_{t-q} + e_t$
$$t = q + 1, \ldots, T$$

TSMR2. y and x are stationary random variables, and e_t is independent of current, past and future values of x.

TSMR3. $E(e_t) = 0$

TSMR4. $\text{var}(e_t) = \sigma^2$

TSMR5. $\text{cov}(e_t, e_s) = 0 \quad t \neq s$

TSMR6. $e_t \sim N(0, \sigma^2)$

9.2.2 An Example: Okun's Law

To illustrate and expand on the various distributed lag concepts, we introduce an economic model known as Okun's Law. In this model the change in the unemployment rate from one period to the next depends on the rate of growth of output in the economy:[2]

$$U_t - U_{t-1} = -\gamma(G_t - G_N) \tag{9.8}$$

---

[1] The complete independence of e and all x's is stronger than needed to establish good large sample properties. See Section 9.5 and Chapter 10.

[2] See O. Blanchard (2009), *Macroeconomics*, 5th edition, Upper Saddle River, NJ, Pearson Prentice Hall, p. 184.

where U_t is the unemployment rate in period t, G_t is the growth rate of output in period t, and G_N is the "normal" growth rate, which we assume is constant over time. The parameter γ is positive, implying that when the growth of output is above the normal rate, unemployment falls; a growth rate below the normal rate leads to an increase in unemployment. The normal growth rate G_N is the rate of output growth needed to maintain a constant unemployment rate. It is equal to the sum of labor force growth and labor productivity growth. We expect $0 < \gamma < 1$, reflecting that output growth leads to less than one-to-one adjustments in unemployment.[3]

To write (9.8) in the more familiar notation of the multiple regression model, we denote the change in unemployment by $DU_t = \Delta U_t = U_t - U_{t-1}$,[4] we set $\beta_0 = -\gamma$, and $\alpha = \gamma G_N$. Including an error term then yields

$$DU_t = \alpha + \beta_0 G_t + e_t \tag{9.9}$$

Recognizing that changes in output are likely to have a distributed-lag effect on unemployment—not all of the effect will take place instantaneously—we expand (9.9) to include lags of G_t

$$DU_t = \alpha + \beta_0 G_t + \beta_1 G_{t-1} + \beta_2 G_{t-2} + \cdots + \beta_q G_{t-q} + e_t \tag{9.10}$$

To estimate this relationship we use quarterly U.S. data on unemployment and the percentage change in gross domestic product (GDP) from quarter 2, 1985, to quarter 3, 2009. Output growth is defined as

$$G_t = \frac{GDP_t - GDP_{t-1}}{GDP_{t-1}} \times 100 \tag{9.11}$$

These data are stored in the file *okun.dat*. The time series for DU and G are graphed in Figures 9.4(a) and 9.4(b). The effects of the global financial crisis are clearly evident towards the end of the sample. At this time we note that the series appear to be stationary; tools for more rigorous assessment of stationarity are deferred until Chapter 12.

To fully appreciate how the lagged variables are defined and how their observations enter the estimation procedure, consider the spreadsheet in Table 9.1. This table contains the observations on U_t, its lag U_{t-1}, and its difference DU_t, as well as G_t and its lags up to G_{t-3}. Notice that for $t = 2$, $U_t = U_2 = 7.2$, $U_{t-1} = U_1 = 7.3$, and $DU_t = U_2 - U_1 = 7.2 - 7.3 = -0.1$. Similarly, for $t = 3$, $U_t = U_3 = 7.0$, $U_{t-1} = U_2 = 7.2$, and $DU_t = U_3 - U_2 = 7.0 - 7.2 = -0.2$. No observations are listed for U_{t-1} and DU_t for $t = 1$, because they would require a value for U_0 (1985Q1) which is not provided in this data set. For G_t, when $t = 2$, $G_{t-1} = G_1 = 1.4$. When $t = 3$, $G_{t-1} = G_2 = 2.0$ and $G_{t-2} = G_1 = 1.4$. When $t = 4$, $G_{t-1} = G_3 = 1.4$, $G_{t-2} = G_2 = 2.0$, and $G_{t-3} = G_1 = 1.4$. Because an observation for G_0 is not available, an observation is lost for each lag that is introduced. Using three lags of G ($q = 3$) means that only 95 of the original 98 observations are used for estimation.[5] In the general case with q lags, the observations used are those for $t = q + 1, q + 2, \ldots, T$.

---

[3] For more details see Blanchard (2009), *ibid*, Chapter 9.

[4] Using DU_t, instead of U_t, has two advantages. The first is that Okun's Law is stated in terms of the change in unemployment. The second is that DU_t, is stationary, but U_t, is not.

[5] Since G is defined as the percentage change in *GDP*, one might question whether an extra observation on G should be lost. However, the growth rate for 1985Q2 was obtained directly from Federal Reserve economic data.

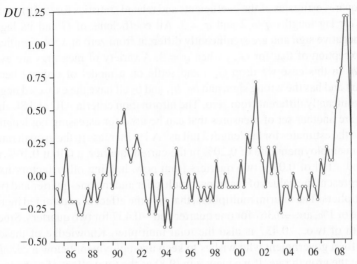

FIGURE **9.4**   (a) Time series for the change in the U.S. unemployment rate: 1985Q3 to 2009Q3.

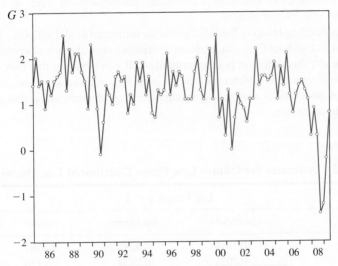

FIGURE **9.4**   (b) Time series for U.S. GDP growth: 1985Q2 to 2009Q3.

Table **9.1**   **Spreadsheet of Observations for Distributed Lag Model**

t	Quarter	U_t	U_{t-1}	DU_t	G_t	G_{t-1}	G_{t-2}	G_{t-3}
1	1985Q2	7.3	•	•	1.4	•	•	•
2	1985Q3	7.2	7.3	−0.1	2.0	1.4	•	•
3	1985Q4	7.0	7.2	−0.2	1.4	2.0	1.4	•
4	1986Q1	7.0	7.0	0.0	1.5	1.4	2.0	1.4
5	1986Q2	7.2	7.0	0.2	0.9	1.5	1.4	2.0
96	2009Q1	8.1	6.9	1.2	−1.2	−1.4	0.3	0.9
97	2009Q2	9.3	8.1	1.2	−0.2	−1.2	−1.4	0.3
98	2009Q3	9.6	9.3	0.3	0.8	−0.2	−1.2	−1.4

Least squares estimates of the coefficients and related statistics for (9.10) are reported in Table 9.2 for lag lengths $q = 2$ and $q = 3$. All coefficients of G and its lags have the expected negative sign and are significantly different from zero at a 5% significance level, with the exception of that for G_{t-3} when $q = 3$. A variety of measures are available for choosing q. In this case we drop G_{t-3} and settle on a model of order 2 because b_3 is insignificant and has the wrong sign, and b_0, b_1, and b_2 all have the expected negative signs and are significantly different from zero. The information criteria AIC and SC discussed in Chapter 6 are another set of measures that can be used for assessing lag length.

What do the estimates for lag length 2 tell us? A 1% increase in the growth rate leads to a fall in the unemployment rate of 0.20% in the current quarter, a fall of 0.16% in the next quarter, and a fall of 0.07% two quarters from now, holding other factors fixed. These changes represent the values of the impact multiplier and the one-quarter and two-quarter delay multipliers. The interim multipliers, that give the effect of a sustained increase in the growth rate of 1%, are -0.367 for one quarter and -0.437 for two quarters. Since we have a lag length of two, -0.437 is also the total multiplier. Knowledge of these values is important for a government who wishes to keep unemployment below a certain level by influencing the growth rate. If we view γ in (9.8) as the total effect of a change in output growth, then its estimate is $\hat{\gamma} = -\sum_{s=0}^{2} b_s = 0.437$. An estimate of the normal growth rate that is needed to maintain a constant unemployment rate is $\hat{G}_N = \hat{\alpha}/\hat{\gamma} = 0.5836/0.437 = 1.3\%$ per quarter.

A possibly puzzling result in Table 9.2 is that the estimated model with G_{t-3} has a slightly lower R^2 than that without G_{t-3}. Since adding a variable lowers the sum of squared errors and increases the R^2, this outcome is counterintuitive. It can occur in this case because the number of observations is different in each case. If we are using all of the data available, the number of observations changes as the number of lags changes unless specific provision is made to do otherwise.

Table 9.2 Estimates for Okun's Law Finite Distributed Lag Model

	Lag Length $q = 3$			
Variable	Coefficient	Std. Error	t-value	p-value
Constant	0.5810	0.0539	10.781	0.0000
G_t	−0.2021	0.0330	6.120	0.0000
G_{t-1}	−0.1645	0.0358	−4.549	0.0000
G_{t-2}	−0.0716	0.0353	−2.027	0.0456
G_{t-3}	0.0033	0.0363	0.091	0.9276
Observations = 95	$R^2 = 0.652$		$\hat{\sigma} = 0.1743$	
	Lag Length $q = 2$			
Variable	Coefficient	Std. Error	t-value	p-value
Constant	0.5836	0.0472	12.360	0.0000
G_t	−0.2020	0.0324	−6.238	0.0000
G_{t-1}	−0.1653	0.0335	−4.930	0.0000
G_{t-2}	−0.0700	0.0331	−2.115	0.0371
Observations = 96	$R^2 = 0.654$		$\hat{\sigma} = 0.1726$	

9.3 Serial Correlation

In the distributed lag model in the previous section we examined one feature of time-series data: how a dependent variable can be related to current and past values of an explanatory variable. The effect of a change in the value of an explanatory variable is distributed over a number of future periods. We noted that, if the specified assumptions hold, and, in particular, the equation errors are uncorrelated with each other and with x, the traditional least squares estimator and associated testing procedures can be used.

We turn now to another question: When is assumption TSMR5, $\text{cov}(e_t, e_s) = 0$ for $t \neq s$ likely to be violated, and how do we assess its validity? As mentioned in the introduction to this chapter, different observations in a cross-section data set, collected by way of a random sample, are typically uncorrelated. With time-series data, however, successive observations are likely to be correlated. If unemployment is high in this quarter, it is more likely to be high than low next quarter. Changes in variables such as unemployment, output growth, inflation and interest rates are usually more gradual than abrupt; their values in one period will depend on what happened in the previous period. This dependence means that output growth now, for example, will be correlated with output growth in the previous period. When a variable exhibits correlation over time, we say it is **autocorrelated** or **serially correlated**; we will use these two terms interchangeably. Both observable time-series variables such as DU and G, and the unobservable error e, can be autocorrelated. Autocorrelation in the error can arise from an autocorrelated omitted variable, or it can arise if a dependent variable y is autocorrelated and this autocorrelation is not adequately explained by the x's and their lags that are included in the equation.

To illustrate the concept of autocorrelation or serial correlation, we begin by considering the observations on output growth G that were used in the distributed lag model of the previous section. We describe methodology for measuring autocorrelation and for testing whether it is significantly different from zero. Then, later in this section, we apply the methodology to the error term in a regression equation. It is useful to assess the autocorrelation properties of both observable variables and the error term. For the observable variables, the properties are useful for the construction of autoregressive models that are considered later in this chapter. For the error term it is useful to check whether one of the least squares assumptions has been violated.

9.3.1 SERIAL CORRELATION IN OUTPUT GROWTH

To appreciate the nature of autocorrelation, consider the time-series graph of G in Figure 9.4(b). In a few instances G changes dramatically from one quarter to the next, but on average, high values of G_{t-1} are followed by high values of G_t, and low values of G_{t-1} are followed by low values of G_t, suggesting a positive correlation between observations that are one period apart. We can further illustrate this correlation by examining the scatter diagram in Figure 9.5 where pairs of observations (G_{t-1}, G_t) are plotted using the data from Table 9.1.[6] If G_t and G_{t-1} are uncorrelated, the observations would be scattered randomly throughout all four quadrants. The predominance of points in the NE and SW quadrants suggests G_t and G_{t-1} are positively correlated.

---

[6] This diagrammatic tool was introduced in Figure P.4 in the Probability Primer to explain the meaning of covariance and correlation.

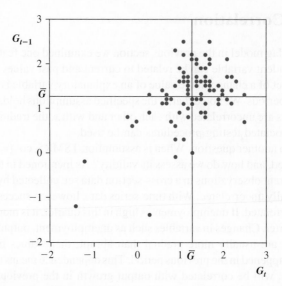

FIGURE **9.5** Scatter diagram for G_t and G_{t-1}.

9.3.1a Computing Autocorrelations

The correlations between a variable and its lags are called autocorrelations. How do we measure this kind of correlation? Recall from Chapter 4.2 that the population correlation between two variables x and y is given by

$$\rho_{xy} = \frac{\text{cov}(x, y)}{\sqrt{\text{var}(x)\text{var}(y)}}$$

Turning this formula into one that measures the correlation between G_t and G_{t-1}, we have

$$\rho_1 = \frac{\text{cov}(G_t, G_{t-1})}{\sqrt{\text{var}(G_t)\text{var}(G_{t-1})}} = \frac{\text{cov}(G_t, G_{t-1})}{\text{var}(G_t)} \tag{9.12}$$

The notation ρ_1 is used to denote the population correlation between observations that are one period apart in time, known also as the **population autocorrelation of order one**. The second equality in (9.12) holds because $\text{var}(G_t) = \text{var}(G_{t-1})$, a property of time series that are stationary.

The **first-order sample autocorrelation** for G is obtained from (9.12) by replacing $\text{cov}(G_t, G_{t-1})$ and $\text{var}(G_t)$ by their estimates

$$\overline{\text{cov}(G_t, G_{t-1})} = \frac{1}{T-1}\sum_{t=2}^{T}(G_t - \overline{G})(G_{t-1} - \overline{G}), \qquad \overline{\text{var}(G_t)} = \frac{1}{T-1}\sum_{t=1}^{T}(G_t - \overline{G})^2$$

where $\overline{G}$ is the sample mean $\overline{G} = T^{-1}\sum_{t=1}^{T}G_t$. The index of summation in the formula for $\overline{\text{cov}(G_t, G_{t-1})}$ starts at $t = 2$ because we do not observe G_0. Making the substitutions, and using r_1 to denote the sample autocorrelation at lag one, yields

$$r_1 = \frac{\sum_{t=2}^{T}(G_t - \overline{G})(G_{t-1} - \overline{G})}{\sum_{t=1}^{T}(G_t - \overline{G})^2} \tag{9.13}$$

More generally, **the k-th order sample autocorrelation** for a series y that gives the correlation between observations that are k periods apart (the correlation between y_t and y_{t-k}) is given by

$$r_k = \frac{\sum_{t=k+1}^{T}(y_t - \bar{y})(y_{t-k} - \bar{y})}{\sum_{t=1}^{T}(y_t - \bar{y})^2} \tag{9.14}$$

This formula is commonly used in the literature and in software and is the one we use to compute autocorrelations in this text, but it is worth mentioning variations of it that are sometimes used. Because $(T - k)$ observations are used to compute the numerator and T observations are used to compute the denominator, an alternative that leads to larger estimates in finite samples is

$$r_k' = \frac{\frac{1}{T-k}\sum_{t=k+1}^{T}(y_t - \bar{y})(y_{t-k} - \bar{y})}{\frac{1}{T}\sum_{t=1}^{T}(y_t - \bar{y})^2} \tag{9.15}$$

Another modification of (9.14) that has a similar effect is to use only $(T - k)$ observations in the denominator, so that it becomes $\sum_{t=k+1}^{T}(y_t - \bar{y})^2$.

Applying (9.14) to the series G yields, for the first four autocorrelations,

$$r_1 = 0.494 \quad r_2 = 0.411 \quad r_3 = 0.154 \quad r_4 = 0.200 \tag{9.16}$$

The autocorrelations at lags one and two are moderately high; those at lags three and four are much smaller—less than half the magnitude of the earlier ones. How do we test whether an autocorrelation is significantly different from zero? Let the kth order population autocorrelation be denoted by ρ_k. Then, when the null hypothesis $H_0 : \rho_k = 0$ is true, it turns out that r_k has an approximate normal distribution with mean zero and variance $1/T$. Thus, a suitable test statistic is

$$Z = \frac{r_k - 0}{\sqrt{1/T}} = \sqrt{T}r_k \sim N(0, 1) \tag{9.17}$$

The product of the square root of the sample size and the sample autocorrelation r_k has an approximate standard normal distribution. At a 5% significance level, we reject $H_0 : \rho_k = 0$ when $\sqrt{T}r_k \geq 1.96$ or $\sqrt{T}r_k \leq -1.96$.

For the series G, $T = 98$, and the values of the test statistic Z for the first four lags are

$$Z_1 = \sqrt{98} \times 0.494 = 4.89, \quad Z_2 = \sqrt{98} \times 0.414 = 4.10$$
$$Z_3 = \sqrt{98} \times 0.154 = 1.52, \quad Z_4 = \sqrt{98} \times 0.200 = 1.98$$

Thus, we reject the hypotheses $H_0 : \rho_1 = 0$ and $H_0 : \rho_2 = 0$, we have insufficient evidence to reject $H_0 : \rho_3 = 0$, and r_4 is on the borderline of being significant. We conclude that G, the quarterly growth rate in U.S. GDP, exhibits significant serial correlation at lags one and two.

9.3.1b The Correlogram
A useful device for assessing the significance of autocorrelations is a diagrammatic representation of the correlogram. The **correlogram,** also called the **sample autocorrelation function**, is the sequence of autocorrelations r_1, r_2, r_3, ... It shows the correlation

between observations that are one period apart, two periods apart, three periods apart, and so on. We indicated that an autocorrelation r_k will be significantly different from zero at a 5% significance level if $\sqrt{T}r_k \geq 1.96$ or if $\sqrt{T}r_k \leq -1.96$. Alternatively, we can say that r_k will be significantly different from zero if $r_k \geq 1.96/\sqrt{T}$ or $r_k \leq -1.96/\sqrt{T}$. By drawing the values $\pm1.96/\sqrt{T}$ as bounds on a graph that illustrates the magnitude of each of the r_k, we can see at a glance which correlations are significant.

A graph of the correlogram for G for the first 12 lags appears in Figure 9.6. The heights of the bars represent the correlations and the horizontal lines drawn at $\pm2/\sqrt{98} = \pm0.202$ are the significance bounds. We have used 2 rather than 1.96 as a convenient approximation. We can see at a glance that r_1 and r_2 are significantly different from zero, that r_4 and r_{12} are bordering on significance, and the remainder of the autocorrelations are not significantly different from zero.

Your software may not produce a correlogram that is exactly the same as Figure 9.6. It might have the correlations on the x-axis and the lags on the y-axis. It could use spikes instead of bars to denote the correlations, it might provide a host of additional information, and the width of its significance bounds might vary with different lags. So be prepared! Learn to isolate and focus on the information corresponding to that in Figure 9.5 and do not be disturbed if the output is slightly different. If the significance bounds vary, it is because they use a refinement of the large sample approximation $\sqrt{T}r_k \sim N(0, 1)$.

Before turning to the question of autocorrelated errors in a regression equation, we note a few facts related to the stationarity of a series. The formula used for computing auto-correlations assumes that the mean and variance of the series are constant over time, and that an autocorrelation depends on the time between observations, not on the actual time period. These are characteristics of a stationary time series—characteristics that are more precise than our earlier vague description of a stationary time series as one which neither trends nor wanders. These issues are explored in detail in Chapter 12.

9.3.2 SERIALLY CORRELATED ERRORS

The correlogram can also be used to check whether the multiple regression assumption $\text{cov}(e_t, e_s) = 0$ for $t \neq s$ is violated. To illustrate how to do so, we introduce another

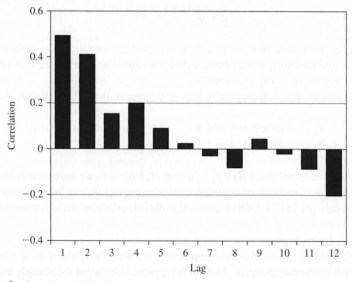

FIGURE **9.6** Correlogram for G.

example: the Phillips curve. A further test for serially correlated errors is considered in Section 9.4. In Section 9.5 we investigate the consequences of serial correlation for least squares estimates, and examine alternative ways of overcoming the problem. Autoregressive distributed lag models, which provide a very general way of allowing for serially correlated errors and at the same time accommodate the dynamic features of lagged y's and lagged x's, are considered in Section 9.6, where we re-examine both the Phillips curve and the model for Okun's Law.

9.3.2a A Phillips Curve

The Phillips curve has a long history in macroeconomics as a tool for describing the relationship between inflation and unemployment.[7] Our starting point is the model

$$INF_t = INF_t^E - \gamma(U_t - U_{t-1}) \tag{9.18}$$

where INF_t is the inflation rate in period t, INF_t^E denotes inflationary expectations for period t, $DU_t = U_t - U_{t-1}$ denotes the change in the unemployment rate from period $t - 1$ to period t, and γ is an unknown positive parameter. It is hypothesized that falling levels of unemployment $(U_t - U_{t-1} < 0)$ reflect excess demand for labor that drives up wages, which in turn drives up prices. Conversely, rising levels of unemployment $(U_t - U_{t-1} > 0)$ reflect an excess supply of labor that moderates wage and price increases. The expected inflation rate is included because workers will negotiate wage increases to cover increasing costs from expected inflation, and these wage increases will be transmitted into actual inflation. We initially assume that inflationary expectations are constant over time $(\beta_1 = INF_t^E)$, an assumption that we relax in Section 9.5. With this change, setting $\beta_2 = -\gamma$, and adding an error term, the Phillips curve can be written as the simple regression model

$$INF_t = \beta_1 + \beta_2 DU_t + e_t \tag{9.19}$$

The data used for estimating (9.19) are quarterly Australian data from 1987, Quarter 1 to 2009, Quarter 3. The data are stored in the file *phillips_aus.dat*. One observation is lost in the construction of $DU_t = U_t - U_{t-1}$, making the sample period from 1987Q2 to 2009Q3, a total of 90 observations. Inflation is calculated as the percentage change in the Consumer Price Index, with an adjustment in the third quarter of 2000 when Australia introduced a national sales tax. The adjusted time series is graphed in Figure 9.7(a); the time series for the change in the unemployment rate appears in Figure 9.7(b). While both of these graphs wander a bit, we will proceed under the assumption that they are stationary. More formal tests are set as exercises in Chapter 12.

To examine whether the errors in the Phillips curve in (9.19) are serially correlated, we first compute the least squares residuals

$$\hat{e}_t = INF_t - b_1 - b_2 DU_t \tag{9.20}$$

Because the e_t are unobserved, it is impossible to compute their autocorrelations. We rely instead on the correlogram of the residuals which is an estimate of the correlogram of the unobserved errors and hence provides evidence on whether or not the assumption

---

[7] For a historical review of the development of different versions, see Gordon, R. J. (2008), "The History of the Phillips Curve: An American Perspective," www.nzae.org.nz/conferences/2008/090708/nr1217302437.pdf. Keynote Address at the Australasian Meetings of the Econometric Society.

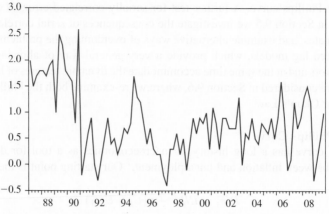

FIGURE 9.7 (a) Time series for Australian price inflation.

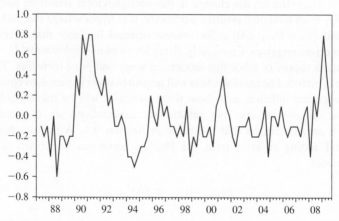

FIGURE 9.7 (b) Time series for the quarterly change in the Australian unemployment rate.

$\text{cov}(e_t, e_s) = 0$ is violated. Replacing y by $\hat{e}$ in (9.14), and recalling that the sample mean of the least squares residuals is zero, the k-th order autocorrelation for the residuals can be written as

$$r_k = \frac{\displaystyle\sum_{t=k+1}^{T} \hat{e}_t \hat{e}_{t-k}}{\displaystyle\sum_{t=1}^{T} \hat{e}_t^2} \tag{9.21}$$

The least squares estimated equation is

$$\widehat{INF} = 0.7776 - 0.5279DU \tag{9.22}$$
$$(\text{se}) \quad (0.0658) \quad (0.2294)$$

These preliminary estimates suggest that an increase in unemployment has the expected negative effect on inflation, and the estimate is significantly different from zero at a 5% significance level.

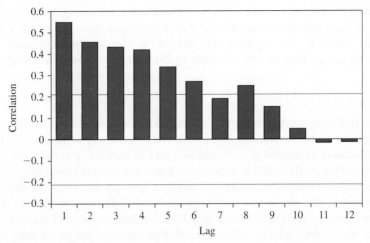

FIGURE *9.8* Correlogram for residuals from least-squares estimated Phillips curve.

Applying (9.21) to the residuals of the least-squares estimated equation in (9.22) yields the correlogram in Figure 9.8. Its significance bounds are $\pm 2/\sqrt{90} = 0.21$. There is strong evidence that the residuals are autocorrelated. The correlations at lags one through six and at lag eight are all significantly different from zero. The values at the first five lags are

$$r_1 = 0.549 \qquad r_2 = 0.456 \qquad r_3 = 0.433 \qquad r_4 = 0.420 \qquad r_5 = 0.339$$

We have found that the errors in the Phillips curve (9.19) are serially correlated. The implications of this correlation and what to do about it are considered in Sections 9.5 and 9.6. Before turning to these solutions, we consider two other tests for serially correlated errors.

9.4 Other Tests For Serially Correlated Errors

9.4.1 A Lagrange Multiplier Test

A second test that we consider for testing for serially correlated errors is derived from a general set of hypothesis testing principles that produce Lagrange[8] multiplier (*LM*) tests. In more advanced courses you will learn the origin of the term Lagrange multiplier. The general principle is described in Appendix C.8.4. An advantage of this test is that it readily generalizes to a **joint** test of correlations at more than one lag.

To introduce the test, suppose in the first instance that we want to test whether errors that are one period apart are correlated. In other words, is $\text{cov}(e_t, e_{t-1})$ equal to zero? Or is r_1 significantly different from zero? If e_t and e_{t-1} are correlated, then one way to model the relationship between them is to write

$$e_t = \rho e_{t-1} + v_t \tag{9.23}$$

---

[8] Joseph-Louis Lagrange (1736–1813) was an Italian born mathematician. Statistical tests using the so-called Lagrange multiplier principle were introduced into statistics by C. R. Rao in 1948.

where ρ is an unknown parameter and v_t is another random error term. We are saying that e_t depends on e_{t-1}, just like y depends on x in a regression equation where y and x are correlated. Now, if the equation of interest is the simple regression equation $y_t = \beta_1 + \beta_2 x_t + e_t$, then we can substitute (9.23) for e_t, which leads to the equation

$$y_t = \beta_1 + \beta_2 x_t + \rho e_{t-1} + v_t \tag{9.24}$$

Assuming that v_t is independent of e_{t-1}, one way to test whether e_t and e_{t-1} are correlated is to test the null hypothesis $H_0 : \rho = 0$. The obvious way to perform this test if e_{t-1} was observable is to regress y_t on x_t and e_{t-1} and to then use a t- or F-test to test the significance of the coefficient of e_{t-1}. However, because e_{t-1} is not observable, we replace it by the lagged least squares residuals $\hat{e}_{t-1}$ and then perform the test in the usual way.

Proceeding in this way seems straightforward, but to complicate matters, time-series econometricians have managed to do it in at least four different ways! Let $t = 1, 2, \ldots, 90$ denote the observations used to estimate the Phillips curve for the period from 1987Q2 to 2009Q3. Then, estimation of (9.24) requires a value for $\hat{e}_0$. Two common ways of overcoming the unavailability of $\hat{e}_0$ are (i) to delete the first observation and hence use a total of 89 observations and (ii) to set $\hat{e}_0 = 0$ and use all 90 observations. The results for the Phillips curve from these two alternatives are

(i) $t = 6.219$ $F = 38.67$ p-value $= 0.000$

(ii) $t = 6.202$ $F = 38.47$ p-value $= 0.000$

The results are almost identical. The null hypothesis $H_0 : \rho = 0$ is rejected at all conventional significance levels. We conclude that the errors are serially correlated.

As we discovered in Chapter 8, LM tests are such that they can frequently be written as the simple expression $T \times R^2$ where T is the number of sample observations and R^2 is the goodness-of-fit statistic from an auxiliary regression. To derive the relevant auxiliary regression for the autocorrelation LM test, we begin by writing the test equation from (9.24) as

$$y_t = \beta_1 + \beta_2 x_t + \rho \hat{e}_{t-1} + v_t \tag{9.25}$$

Noting that $y_t = b_1 + b_2 x_t + \hat{e}_t$, we can rewrite (9.25) as

$$b_1 + b_2 x_t + \hat{e}_t = \beta_1 + \beta_2 x_t + \rho \hat{e}_{t-1} + v_t$$

Rearranging this equation yields

$$\begin{aligned} \hat{e}_t &= (\beta_1 - b_1) + (\beta_2 - b_2)x_t + \rho \hat{e}_{t-1} + v_t \\ &= \gamma_1 + \gamma_2 x_t + \rho \hat{e}_{t-1} + v_t \end{aligned} \tag{9.26}$$

where $\gamma_1 = \beta_1 - b_1$ and $\gamma_2 = \beta_2 - b_2$. When testing for autocorrelation by testing the significance of the coefficient of $\hat{e}_{t-1}$, one can estimate (9.25) or (9.26). Both yield the same test result—the same coefficient estimate for $\hat{e}_{t-1}$ and the same t-value. The estimates for the intercept and the coefficient of x_t will be different, however, because in (9.26) we are estimating $(\beta_1 - b_1)$ and $(\beta_2 - b_2)$ instead of β_1 and β_2. The auxiliary regression from which the $T \times R^2$ version of the LM test is obtained is (9.26). Because $(\beta_1 - b_1)$ and $(\beta_2 - b_2)$ are centered around zero, if (9.26) is a regression with significant explanatory power, that power will come from $\hat{e}_{t-1}$.

If $H_0 : \rho = 0$ is true, then $LM = T \times R^2$ has an approximate $\chi^2_{(1)}$ distribution where T and R^2 are the sample size and goodness-of-fit statistic, respectively, from least squares estimation of (9.26). Once again there are two alternatives depending on whether the first observation is discarded, or $\hat{e}_0$ is set equal to zero. Labeling these two alternatives as (iii) and (iv), respectively, we obtain the following results for the Phillips curve:

(iii) $LM = (T - 1) \times R^2 = 89 \times 0.3102 = 27.61$

(iv) $LM = T \times R^2 = 90 \times 0.3066 = 27.59$

These values are much larger than 3.84, which is the 5% critical value from a $\chi^2_{(1)}$-distribution, leading us to reject the null hypothesis of no autocorrelation. Alternatively, we can reject H_0 by examining the p-value for $LM = 27.61$, which is 0.000.

There is no strong theoretical reason for choosing between the four representations of the test. The best one for you to use is that which is automatically computed by your software. We have described all four so that there will not be any mysteries in your computer output.

9.4.1a Testing Correlation at Longer Lags

The correlogram in Figure 9.8 suggested not just correlation between e_t and e_{t-1}, but also between e_t and $(e_{t-2}, e_{t-3}, e_{t-4}, e_{t-5}, e_{t-6})$. The LM test can be used to test for more complicated autocorrelation structures involving higher order lags by including the additional lagged errors in (9.25) or (9.26). An F-test can be used to test the relevance of their inclusion, or, a χ^2-test can be used for the $T \times R^2$ version of the test. The degrees of freedom for the χ^2-test and the numerator degrees of freedom for the F-test are the number of lagged residuals that are included. Slightly different results are obtained depending on whether one discards the initial observations where the lagged values of $\hat{e}_t$ are not available, or sets these values equal to zero. Suppose for the Phillips curve that we add $\hat{e}_{t-2}$, $\hat{e}_{t-3}$ and $\hat{e}_{t-4}$ to (9.26) and use the $T \times R^2$ version of the test. The results we obtain for (iii) omitting the first four observations and (iv) setting $e_0 = e_{-1} = e_{-2} = e_{-3} = 0$ are

(iii) $LM = (T - 4) \times R^2 = 86 \times 0.3882 = 33.4$

(iv) $LM = T \times R^2 = 90 \times 0.4075 = 36.7$

Because the 5% critical value from a $\chi^2_{(4)}$- distribution is 9.49, these LM values lead us to conclude that the errors are serially correlated.

9.4.2 THE DURBIN-WATSON TEST

The sample correlogram and the Lagrange multiplier test are two large sample tests for serially correlated errors. Their test statistics have their specified distributions in large samples. An alternative test, one that is exact in the sense that its distribution does not rely on a large sample approximation, is the Durbin-Watson test. It was developed in 1950 and for a long time was the standard test for $H_0 : \rho = 0$ in the error model $e_t = \rho e_{t-1} + v_t$. It is used less frequently today because its critical values are not available in all software packages, and one has to examine upper and lower critical bounds instead. Also, unlike the LM and correlogram tests, its distribution no longer holds when the equation contains a lagged dependent variable. Details are provided in Appendix 9A at the end of this chapter.

9.5 Estimation With Serially Correlated Errors

In the last two sections we described hypothesis tests for checking whether the least squares assumption $\text{cov}(e_t, e_s) = 0$ is violated. If it is violated, we say the errors are serially correlated. We now ask: What are the implications of serially correlated errors for least squares estimation? And how do we overcome the negative consequences of serially correlated errors? Three estimation procedures are considered:

1. Least squares estimation (Section 9.5.1)
2. An estimation procedure that is relevant when the errors are assumed to follow what is known as a first-order autoregressive model $e_t = \rho e_{t-1} + v_t$ (Section 9.5.2)
3. A general estimation strategy for estimating models with serially correlated errors

The general estimation strategy that will be introduced in Section 9.5.3 and considered in more depth in Section 9.6 is the estimation of an autoregressive distributed lag (ARDL) model which is designed to capture dynamics from all sources—lagged x's, lagged y's, and serially correlated errors.

Before considering each of the above estimation procedures, we need to introduce an extra assumption. We will encounter models with a lagged dependent variable, such as

$$y_t = \delta + \theta_1 y_{t-1} + \delta_0 x_t + \delta_1 x_{t-1} + v_t$$

In such cases the time-series assumption TSMR2 introduced in Section 9.2.1 is no longer valid. In the context of the above equation, this assumption says that v_t is not correlated with current, past, and future values of y_{t-1}, x_t and x_{t-1}. Since y_t is a future value of y_{t-1} and y_t depends directly on v_t, the assumption will be violated. We can, however, replace it with a weaker, more tenable assumption—namely, that v_t is uncorrelated with current and past values of the right-hand-side variables. Under this assumption, the least squares estimator is no longer unbiased, but it does have the desirable large sample property of consistency,[9] and, if the errors are normally distributed, it is best in a large sample sense. Thus, we replace TSMR2 with the following assumption.

> **ASSUMPTION FOR MODELS WITH A LAGGED DEPENDENT VARIABLE**
> TSMR2A: In the multiple regression model $y_t = \beta_1 + \beta_2 x_{t2} + \cdots + \beta_K x_{tK} + v_t$ where some of the x_{tk} may be lagged values of y, v_t is uncorrelated with all x_{tk} and their past values.

This assumption is the one maintained throughout the remainder of this chapter. Note that the v_t are assumed to be uncorrelated random errors with zero mean and constant variance and hence satisfy assumptions TSMR3, TSMR4, and TSMR5 that were previously written in terms of e_t.

---

[9] The property of consistency is discussed in Appendix 5B.

9.5.1 LEAST SQUARES ESTIMATION

First, suppose we proceed with least squares estimation without recognizing the existence of serially correlated errors. What are the consequences? They are essentially the same as ignoring heteroskedasticity should it exist.

1. The least squares estimator is still a linear unbiased estimator, but it is no longer best. If we are able to correctly model the autocorrelated errors, then there exists an alternative estimator with a lower variance. Having a lower variance means there is a higher probability of obtaining a coefficient estimate close to its true value. It also means that hypothesis tests have greater power and a lower probability of a Type II error.

2. The formulas for the standard errors usually computed for the least squares estimator are no longer correct, and hence confidence intervals and hypothesis tests that use these standard errors may be misleading.

Although the usual least squares standard errors are not the correct ones, it is possible to compute correct standard errors for the least squares estimator when the errors are autocorrelated. These standard errors are known as **HAC (heteroskedasticity and auto-correlation consistent) standard errors**, or **Newey-West standard errors**, and are analogous to the heteroskedasticity consistent standard errors introduced in Chapter 8. By using HAC standard errors with least squares, we can avoid having to specify the precise nature of the autocorrelated error model that is required for an alternative estimator with a lower variance. For the HAC standard errors to be valid, we need to assume that the autocorrelations go to zero as the time between observations increases (a condition necessary for stationarity), and we need a large sample, but it is not necessary to make a precise assumption about the autocorrelated error model.

To get a feel for how HAC standard errors are found, consider the simple regression model $y_t = \beta_1 + \beta_2 x_t + e_t$. From Appendix 8A the variance of the least squares estimator b_2 can be written as (with subscripts i and j replaced by t and s)

$$\text{var}(b_2) = \sum_t w_t^2 \text{var}(e_t) + \sum \sum_{t \neq s} w_t w_s \text{cov}(e_t, e_s)$$

$$= \sum_t w_t^2 \text{var}(e_t) \left[1 + \frac{\sum \sum_{t \neq s} w_t w_s \text{cov}(e_t, e_s)}{\sum_t w_t^2 \text{var}(e_t)} \right] \tag{9.27}$$

where $w_t = (x_t - \bar{x}) / \sum_t (x_t - \bar{x})^2$. When the errors are not correlated, $\text{cov}(e_t, e_s) = 0$, and the term in square brackets is equal to one. The resulting expression $\text{var}(b_2) = \sum_t w_t^2 \text{var}(e_t)$ is the one used to find heteroskedasticity-consistent (HC) standard errors. When the errors are correlated, the term in square brackets is estimated to obtain HAC standard errors. If we call the quantity in square brackets g and its estimate $\hat{g}$, then the relationship between the two estimated variances is

$$\widehat{\text{var}_{HAC}(b_2)} = \widehat{\text{var}_{HC}(b_2)} \times \hat{g} \tag{9.28}$$

The HAC variance estimate is equal to the HC variance estimate multiplied by an extra term that depends on the serial correlation in the errors.

This explanation is a simplified one because it treats x as nonrandom. If x is random and e_t is independent of all x values, as specified in assumption TSMR2, then essentially the same argument holds. More general arguments allow for correlation between e_t and the x values, as will occur if the model contains a lagged dependent variable, and they extend the results to the multiple regression model with more than one x. However, in all cases the end result is an expression like (9.28). Several alternative estimators for g are available. They differ depending on the number of lags for which autocorrelations are estimated and on the weights placed on the autocorrelations at each lag. Because a large number of alternatives are possible, you will discover that different software packages may yield different HAC standard errors; also, different options are possible within a given software package. The message is: Don't be disturbed if you see slightly different HAC standard errors computed for the same problem.

The least squares-estimated Phillips curve $INF_t = \beta_1 + \beta_2 DU_t + e_t$ with both sets of standard errors—the incorrect least squares ones that ignore autocorrelation, and the correct HAC ones that recognize the autocorrelation—are as follows:[10]

$$\widehat{INF} = 0.7776 - 0.5279DU$$

$$(0.0658) \quad (0.2294) \qquad \text{(incorrect se)} \qquad\qquad (9.29)$$

$$(0.1030) \quad (0.3127) \qquad \text{(HAC se)}$$

The HAC standard errors are larger than those from least squares, implying that if we ignore the autocorrelation, we will overstate the reliability of the least squares estimates. The t and p-values for testing $H_0 : \beta_2 = 0$ are

$$t = -0.5279/0.2294 = -2.301 \qquad p = 0.0238 \qquad \text{(from LS standard errors)}$$
$$t = -0.5279/0.3127 = -1.688 \qquad p = 0.0950 \qquad \text{(from HAC standard errors)}$$

With least squares standard errors, a two-tail test, and a 5% significance level, we reject $H_0 : \beta_2 = 0$. With HAC standard errors, we do not reject H_0. Thus, using incorrect standard errors can lead to misleading results. A similar conclusion can be reached by examining the 95% interval estimates for β_2 for each set of standard errors. Using $t_{(0.975, 88)} = 1.987$, those interval estimates are $(-0.984, -0.072)$ for least squares and $(-1.149, 0.094)$ for HAC standard errors. The narrower least squares interval leads to an exaggerated conclusion about the reliability of estimation.

9.5.2   ESTIMATING AN AR(1) ERROR MODEL

Using least squares with HAC standard errors overcomes the negative consequences that autocorrelated errors have for least squares standard errors. However, it does not address the issue of finding an estimator that is better, in the sense that it has a lower variance. One way to proceed is to make an assumption about the model that generates the autocorrelated errors, and to derive an estimator compatible with this assumption. In this section we examine one such assumption. To introduce it, we return to the Lagrange multiplier test for serially correlated errors, where correlation between e_t and e_{t-1} was modeled by writing e_t as dependent on e_{t-1} through the equation

---

[10] The HAC standard errors were computed by EViews 7.0 using a Bartlett kernel, a Newey-West fixed bandwidth of 4, and a degrees-of-freedom adjustment.

$$e_t = \rho e_{t-1} + v_t \tag{9.30}$$

If we assume the v_t are uncorrelated random errors with zero mean and constant variances,

$$E(v_t) = 0 \qquad \text{var}(v_t) = \sigma_v^2 \qquad \text{cov}(v_t, v_s) = 0 \quad \text{for } t \neq s \tag{9.31}$$

then (9.30) describes a **first-order autoregressive model** or a first-order autoregressive **process** for e_t. The term **AR(1) model** is used as an abbreviation for first-order autoregressive model. It is called an **autoregressive** model because it can be viewed as a regression model where e_t depends on its lagged value, inducing autocorrelation. It is called **first-order** because the right-hand-side variable is e_t lagged **one** period.

One way to estimate a regression equation with serially correlated errors is to assume that those errors follow an AR(1) model and to develop an estimation procedure relevant for that model. Other autocorrelated error models could be assumed. In particular, one could include more lags of e_t leading to, say, an AR(2) or an AR(3) model. However, for the moment we focus on the AR(1) error model because it has been a popular one in econometrics and is a good starting point.

9.5.2a Properties of an AR(1) Error

Before turning to estimation, it is useful to examine the properties of e_t when it follows an AR(1) process. In (9.31) we made assumptions about v_t that are the same as those made about e_t in Chapters 2–7. The question now is: How do the assumptions about v_t in (9.31), and the AR(1) error model, change the properties of e_t? We make one further assumption to ensure the e_t are stationary: namely, that ρ is less than one in absolute value. That is,

$$-1 < \rho < 1 \tag{9.32}$$

In Appendix 9B, we show that the mean and variance of e_t are

$$E(e_t) = 0 \qquad \text{var}(e_t) = \sigma_e^2 = \frac{\sigma_v^2}{1 - \rho^2} \tag{9.33}$$

The AR(1) error e_t has a mean of zero, and a variance that depends on the variance of v_t and the magnitude of ρ. The larger the degree of autocorrelation (the closer ρ is to $+1$ or -1), the larger the variance of e_t. Also, since $\sigma_v^2 / (1 - \rho^2)$ is constant over time, e_t is homoskedastic.

In Appendix 9B we also discover that the covariance between two errors that are k periods apart $(e_t$ and $e_{t-k})$ is

$$\text{cov}(e_t, e_{t-k}) = \frac{\rho^k \sigma_v^2}{1 - \rho^2}, \quad k > 0 \tag{9.34}$$

This expression shows how the properties of the e_t differ from those assumed in Chapters 2–7. In these earlier chapters we assumed that the covariance between errors for different observations was zero. It is now nonzero because of the existence of a lagged relationship between the errors from different time periods.

It is useful to describe the *correlation* implied by the covariance in (9.34). Using the correlation formula in (9.12), we have

$$\begin{aligned}
\rho_k = \text{corr}(e_t, e_{t-k}) &= \frac{\text{cov}(e_t, e_{t-k})}{\sqrt{\text{var}(e_t)\text{var}(e_{t-k})}} = \frac{\text{cov}(e_t, e_{t-k})}{\text{var}(e_t)} \\
&= \frac{\rho^k \sigma_v^2 / (1 - \rho^2)}{\sigma_v^2 / (1 - \rho^2)} \\
&= \rho^k
\end{aligned} \tag{9.35}$$

That is, $\rho_k = \rho^k$. The correlation between two errors that are k periods apart (ρ_k) is given by ρ raised to the power k. An interpretation or definition of the unknown parameter ρ can be obtained by setting $k = 1$. Specifically,

$$\rho_1 = \text{corr}(e_t, e_{t-1}) = \rho \tag{9.36}$$

Thus, ρ represents the correlation between two errors that are one period apart; it is the **first-order autocorrelation** for e, sometimes simply called the autocorrelation coefficient. Recall the concept of a correlogram that was introduced in Section 9.3. It consisted of the sequence of **sample** autocorrelations $r_1, r_2, r_3, \ldots$. The coefficient ρ is the **population** autocorrelation at lag one for a time series that can be described by an AR(1) model; r_1 is an estimate for ρ when we assume a series is AR(1).

Corresponding to the sample correlogram $r_1, r_2, r_3, \ldots$, we can also define a population correlogram as $\rho_1, \rho_2, \rho_3, \ldots$. From (9.35), the population correlogram for an AR(1) model is $\rho, \rho^2, \rho^3, \ldots$. Because $-1 < \rho < 1$, these autocorrelations decline geometrically as the lag increases, eventually becoming negligible. Since the AR(1) error model $e_t = \rho e_{t-1} + v_t$ only contains one lag of e, you might be surprised to find that autocorrelations at lags greater than one, although declining, are still nonzero. The correlation persists because each e_t depends on all past values of the errors v_t through the equation (see Appendix 9B)

$$e_t = v_t + \rho v_{t-1} + \rho^2 v_{t-2} + \rho^3 v_{t-3} + \cdots \tag{9.37}$$

We can relate these results to the errors from the Phillips curve. The sample correlogram for the first five lags was found to be

$$r_1 = 0.549 \qquad r_2 = 0.456 \qquad r_3 = 0.433 \qquad r_4 = 0.420 \qquad r_5 = 0.339$$

Without any assumptions about the model that generates the errors, these values are unrestricted estimates of the population autocorrelations ($\rho_1, \rho_2, \rho_3, \rho_4, \rho_5$). Now suppose the errors follow an AR(1) model where we have only one unknown parameter ρ. In this case,

$$\hat{\rho}_1 = \hat{\rho} = r_1 = 0.549$$

Imposing the structure of the AR(1) model leads to the following estimates at longer lags:

$$\hat{\rho}_2 = \hat{\rho}^2 = (0.549)^2 = 0.301$$
$$\hat{\rho}_3 = \hat{\rho}^3 = (0.549)^3 = 0.165$$
$$\hat{\rho}_4 = \hat{\rho}^4 = (0.549)^4 = 0.091$$
$$\hat{\rho}_5 = \hat{\rho}^5 = (0.549)^5 = 0.050$$

These values are considerably smaller than the unrestricted estimates of the correlogram, suggesting that the AR(1) assumption might not be adequate for the errors of the Phillips curve.

9.5.2b Nonlinear Least Squares Estimation

In this section we develop an estimator for the regression model with AR(1) errors. First, let us summarize the model and its assumptions. It is given by

$$y_t = \beta_1 + \beta_2 x_t + e_t \quad \text{with} \quad e_t = \rho e_{t-1} + v_t \tag{9.38}$$

and $-1 < \rho < 1$. Only one explanatory variable is included, to keep the discussion simple and to use the framework of the Phillips curve example. The v_t are uncorrelated random variables with mean zero and a constant variance σ_v^2 (see assumptions MR2, MR3, and MR4, stated in Section 5.1):

$$E(v_t) = 0 \qquad \text{var}(v_t) = \sigma_v^2 \qquad \text{cov}(v_t, v_s) = 0 \quad \text{for } t \neq s \tag{9.39}$$

Substituting $e_t = \rho e_{t-1} + v_t$ into $y_t = \beta_1 + \beta_2 x_t + e_t$ yields

$$y_t = \beta_1 + \beta_2 x_t + \rho e_{t-1} + v_t \tag{9.40}$$

From the regression equation the error in the previous period can be written as

$$e_{t-1} = y_{t-1} - \beta_1 - \beta_2 x_{t-1} \tag{9.41}$$

Multiplying (9.41) by ρ yields

$$\rho e_{t-1} = \rho y_{t-1} - \rho \beta_1 - \rho \beta_2 x_{t-1} \tag{9.42}$$

Substituting (9.42) into (9.40) yields

$$y_t = \beta_1(1 - \rho) + \beta_2 x_t + \rho y_{t-1} - \rho \beta_2 x_{t-1} + v_t \tag{9.43}$$

What have we done? We have transformed the original model in (9.38) with the auto-correlated error term e_t into a new model given by (9.43) that has an error term v_t that is uncorrelated over time. The advantage of doing so is that we can now proceed to find estimates for (β_1, β_2, ρ) that minimize the sum of squares of uncorrelated errors $S_v = \sum_{t=2}^{T} v_t^2$. Minimizing the sum of squares of the correlated errors $S_e = \sum_{t=1}^{T} e_t^2$ yields the least squares estimator that is not best and whose standard errors are not correct. However, minimizing the sum of squares of uncorrelated errors, S_v, yields an estimator that is best and whose standard errors are correct (in large samples). Note that this result is in line with earlier practice in the book. The least squares estimator used in Chapters 2–7 minimizes a sum of squares of uncorrelated errors.

There are, however, two important distinctive features about the transformed model in (9.43). To appreciate the first, note that the coefficient of x_{t-1} is equal to $-\rho\beta_2$ which is the negative product of ρ (the coefficient of y_{t-1}) and β_2 (the coefficient of x_t). This fact means that although (9.43) is a linear function of the variables x_t, y_{t-1} and x_{t-1}, it is not a linear function of the parameters (β_1, β_2, ρ). The usual linear least squares formulas cannot be obtained by using calculus to find the values of (β_1, β_2, ρ) that minimize S_v. Nevertheless, computer software can be used to find the estimates numerically. Numerical methods use a systematic procedure for trying a sequence of alternative parameter values until those which minimize the sum of squares function are found. Because these estimates are not computed from a linear formula but still minimize a sum of squares function, they are called

nonlinear least squares estimates. Estimates obtained in this way have the usual desirable properties in large samples under assumptions TSMR2A and TSMR3–5.

The second distinguishing feature about the model in (9.43) is that it contains the lagged dependent variable y_{t-1} as well as x_t and x_{t-1}, the current and lagged values of the explanatory variable. For this reason, the summation $S_v = \sum_{t=2}^{T} v_t^2$ begins at $t = 2$.

In the last section, we cast some doubt on whether the AR(1) error model was an appropriate one for capturing the residual autocorrelations in the Phillips curve example. Nevertheless, we will estimate the Phillips curve assuming AR(1) errors; later, we investigate whether a better model can be found. In this context, (9.43) becomes

$$INF_t = \beta_1(1 - \rho) + \beta_2 DU_t + \rho INF_{t-1} - \rho\beta_2 DU_{t-1} + v_t \tag{9.44}$$

Applying nonlinear least squares and presenting the estimates in terms of the original untransformed model, we have

$$\widehat{INF} = 0.7609 - 0.6944DU \qquad e_t = 0.557e_{t-1} + v_t$$
$$\text{(se)} \quad (0.1245) \ (0.2479) \qquad\qquad (0.090) \tag{9.45}$$

Comparing these estimates with those from least squares ($b_1 = 0.7776$, $b_2 = -0.5279$), we find that the estimate for β_1 is of similar magnitude, but that that for β_2 is a larger negative value, suggesting a greater impact of unemployment on inflation. The standard error $\text{se}(\hat{\beta}_2) = 0.2479$ is smaller than the corresponding HAC least squares standard error $[\text{se}(b_2) = 0.3127]$, suggesting a more reliable estimate, but the standard error for $\hat{\beta}_1$ is unexpectedly larger, something that we do not expect since we have used an estimation procedure with a lower variance. It must be kept in mind, however, that standard errors are themselves estimates of true underlying standard deviations. The estimate $\hat{\rho} = 0.557$ is similar but not exactly the same as the estimate $r_1 = 0.549$ obtained from the correlation between least squares residuals that are one quarter apart.

9.5.2c   Generalized Least Squares Estimation

In Chapter 8 we discovered that the problem of heteroskedasticity could be overcome by using an estimation procedure known as generalized least squares, and that a convenient way to obtain generalized least squares estimates is to first transform the model so that it has a new uncorrelated homoskedastic error term, and to then apply least squares to the transformed model. This same kind of approach can be pursued when the errors follow an AR(1) model. Indeed, it can be shown that nonlinear least squares estimation of (9.43) is equivalent to using an iterative generalized least squares estimator called the Cochrane-Orcutt procedure. Details are provided in Appendix 9C.

9.5.3   ESTIMATING A MORE GENERAL MODEL

The results for the Phillips curve example presented in (9.45) came from estimating the AR(1) error model written as the transformed model

$$y_t = \beta_1(1 - \rho) + \rho y_{t-1} + \beta_2 x_t - \rho\beta_2 x_{t-1} + v_t \tag{9.46}$$

Suppose now that we consider the model

$$y_t = \delta + \theta_1 y_{t-1} + \delta_0 x_t + \delta_1 x_{t-1} + v_t \tag{9.47}$$

How do (9.46) and (9.47) differ? What characteristics do they have in common? The first thing to notice is that they contain the same variables; in both cases y_t depends on x_t, x_{t-1} and y_{t-1}. There is a difference in the number of parameters, however. In (9.46) there are three unknown parameters, β_1, β_2, and ρ. In (9.47) there are four unknown parameters, δ, δ_0, δ_1, and θ_1. Also, the notation in (9.47) is new; we have used the symbols δ (delta) and θ (theta). The intercept is denoted by δ, the coefficients of x and its lag are denoted by subscripted δ's, and the coefficient of the lagged dependent variable y_{t-1} is given by a subscripted θ. This new notation will prove to be convenient in Section 9.6, where we discuss a general class of **autoregressive distributed lag (ARDL) models**. Equation (9.47) is a member of this class.

To establish the relationship between (9.46) and (9.47), note that (9.47) is the same as (9.46) if we set

$$\delta = \beta_1(1-\rho) \qquad \delta_0 = \beta_2 \qquad \delta_1 = -\rho\beta_2 \qquad \theta_1 = \rho \qquad (9.48)$$

From these relationships, it can be seen that (9.46) is a restricted version of (9.47) with the restriction $\delta_1 = -\theta_1\delta_0$ imposed. The restriction reduces the number of parameters from four to three and makes (9.47) equivalent to the AR(1) error model.

These observations raise a number of questions. Instead of estimating the AR(1) error model, would it be better to estimate the more general model in (9.47)? What technique should be used for estimating (9.47)? Is it possible to estimate (9.47) and then test the validity of the AR(1) error model by testing a null hypothesis $H_0 : \delta_1 = -\theta_1\delta_0$?

Considering estimation first, we note that (9.47) can be estimated by linear least squares providing that the v_t satisfy the usual assumptions required for least squares estimation— namely, that they have zero mean and constant variance and are uncorrelated. The presence of the lagged dependent variable y_{t-1} means that a large sample is required for the desirable properties of the least squares estimator to hold, but the least squares procedure is still valid providing that assumption TSMR2A holds. It is important for the v_t to be uncorrelated. If they are correlated, assumption TSMR2A will be violated, and the least squares estimator will be biased, even in large samples.

In the introduction to this chapter we observed that dynamic characteristics of time-series relationships can occur through lags in the dependent variable, lags in the explanatory variables, or lags in the error term. In this section we modeled a lag in the error term with an AR(1) process and showed that such a model is equivalent to (9.46), which, in turn, is a special case of (9.47). Notice that (9.46) and (9.47) do not have lagged error terms, but they do have a lagged dependent variable and a lagged explanatory variable. Thus, the dynamic features of a model implied by an AR(1) error can be captured by using instead a model with a lagged y and a lagged x. This observation raises issues about a general modeling strategy for dynamic economic relationships. Instead of explicitly modeling lags through an autocorrelated error, we may be able to capture the same dynamic effects by adding lagged variables y_{t-1} and x_{t-1} to the original linear equation.

Is it possible to test $H_0 : \delta_1 = -\theta_1\delta_0$ and hence decide whether the AR(1) model is a reasonable restricted version of (9.47) or whether the more general model in (9.47) would be preferable? The answer is yes: the test is similar to, but more complicated than, those considered in Chapter 5. Complications occur because the hypothesis involves an equation that is nonlinear in the parameters, and the delta method (see Appendix 5B) is needed to compute the standard error of products such as $\hat{\theta}_1\hat{\delta}_0$. Nevertheless, the test, known as a Wald test, can be performed using most software.

Applying the least squares estimator to (9.47) using the data for the Phillips curve example yields

$$\widehat{INF}_t = 0.3336 + 0.5593INF_{t-1} - 0.6882DU_t + 0.3200DU_{t-1}$$

$$\text{(se)} \quad (0.0899) \ (0.0908) \qquad\qquad (0.2575) \qquad (0.2499) \tag{9.49}$$

How do these results compare with those from the more restrictive AR(1) error model? Most of them turn out to be very similar. The equivalent estimates from the AR(1) error model are found by substituting the estimates in (9.45) into the expressions in (9.48). We find

$$\hat{\delta} = \hat{\beta}_1(1 - \hat{\rho}) = 0.7609 \times (1 - 0.5574) = 0.3368 \text{ which is similar to } 0.3336$$

$$\hat{\theta}_1 = \hat{\rho} = 0.5574 \text{ which is similar to } 0.5593$$

$$\hat{\delta}_0 = \hat{\beta}_2 = -0.6944 \text{ which is similar to } -0.6882$$

$$\hat{\delta}_1 = -\hat{\rho}\hat{\beta}_2 = -0.5574 \times (-0.6944) = 0.3871 \text{ which differs a little from } 0.3200$$

The closeness of these values and the relatively large standard error on the coefficient of DU_{t-1} suggest that a test of the restriction $H_0 : \delta_1 = -\theta_1\delta_0$ would not be rejected. More formally, using a Wald chi-square test yields a value of $\chi^2_{(1)} = 0.112$ with a corresponding p-value $= 0.738$. On the basis of this test, we conclude that the AR(1) error model is not too restrictive.

Specification and estimation of the more general model does have some advantages, however. It makes the dependence of y_t on its lag and that of x more explicit, and it can often provide a useful economic interpretation. The original economic model for the Phillips curve was

$$INF_t = INF_t^E - \gamma(U_t - U_{t-1}) \tag{9.50}$$

Comparing this model with the estimated one in (9.50), an estimate of the model for inflationary expectations is $INF_t^E = 0.3336 + 0.5593INF_{t-1}$; expectations for inflation in the current quarter are 0.33% plus 0.56 times last quarter's inflation rate. The effect of unemployment in (9.49) is $-0.6882(U_t - U_{t-1}) + 0.3200(U_{t-1} - U_{t-2})$, which is dynamically more complex than the original specification of $-\gamma(U_t - U_{t-1})$. Note, however, that the coefficient of DU_{t-1} is not significantly different from zero in (9.49). If DU_{t-1} is excluded from the equation, then the unemployment effect is consistent with the original equation. Re-estimation of the model after omitting DU_{t-1} yields

$$\widehat{INF}_t = 0.3548 + 0.5282INF_{t-1} - 0.4909DU_t$$

$$\text{(se)} \quad (0.0876) \ (0.0851) \qquad\qquad (0.1921) \tag{9.51}$$

In this model inflationary expectations are given by $INF_t^E = 0.3548 + 0.5282INF_{t-1}$ and a 1% rise in the unemployment rate leads to an approximate 0.5% fall in the inflation rate.

9.5.4 Summary of Section 9.5 and Looking Ahead

In Section 9.5 we have described three ways of overcoming the effect of serially correlated errors:

1. Estimate the model using least squares with HAC standard errors.
2. Use nonlinear least squares to estimate the model with a lagged x, a lagged y, and the restriction implied by an AR(1) error specification.

3. Use least squares to estimate the model with a lagged x and a lagged y, but without the restriction implied by an AR(1) error specification.

Using least squares with HAC standard errors is preferred if one does not wish to bother transforming the model to one with relevant lagged variables that have the effect of eliminating the serial correlation in the errors. The nonlinear model with the AR(1) error restriction is appropriate if the error has serial correlation that takes the form of an AR(1) process. For many years it was the most common method for correcting for autocorrelated errors. However, the third method—including appropriate lags of y and x without the AR(1) error restriction—is now generally preferred by applied econometricians. It is less restrictive than the AR(1) error model, the model with lags frequently has a useful economic interpretation, and it can be used to correct for more general forms of serially correlated errors than the AR(1) error model.

This last statement raises some unanswered questions. While including one lag of y and one lag of x will correct for serially correlated errors if they follow an AR(1) model, it might not solve the problem if the form of serial correlation is more complex. How do we check whether some serial correlation still remains? If we include a lagged y and a lagged x and the errors are still serially correlated, how do we proceed? Checking for serial correlation proceeds along the same lines as we have described in Section 9.4. We apply the same tests to the errors from the new model with lags. Also, if we have doubts about whether the errors in the new model are correlated, we can use HAC standard errors with this model. Alternatively, including more lags of y on the right side of the equation can have the effect of eliminating any remaining serial correlation in the errors. Models with a general number of lags of y and x are called autoregressive distributed lag models; we consider them in the next section.

9.6 Autoregressive Distributed Lag Models

An autoregressive distributed lag (ARDL) model is one that contains both lagged x_t's and lagged y_t's. In its general form, with p lags of y and q lags of x, an ARDL(p, q) model can be written as

$$y_t = \delta + \theta_1 y_{t-1} + \cdots + \theta_p y_{t-p} + \delta_0 x_t + \delta_1 x_{t-1} + \cdots + \delta_q x_{t-q} + v_t \tag{9.52}$$

The AR component of the name ARDL comes from the regression of y on lagged values of itself; the DL component comes from the distributed lag effect of the lagged x's. Two examples that we have encountered so far in (9.50) and (9.51) are

$$\text{ARDL(1,1): } \widehat{INF}_t = 0.3336 + 0.5593 INF_{t-1} - 0.6882 DU_t + 0.3200 DU_{t-1}$$

$$\text{ARDL(1,0): } \widehat{INF}_t = 0.3548 + 0.5282 INF_{t-1} - 0.4909 DU_t$$

The ARDL model has several advantages. It captures dynamic effects from lagged x's and lagged y's, and by including a sufficient number of lags of y and x, we can eliminate serial correlation in the errors. Moreover, an ARDL model can be transformed into one with only lagged x's which go back into the infinite past:

$$\begin{aligned} y_t &= \alpha + \beta_0 x_t + \beta_1 x_{t-1} + \beta_2 x_{t-2} + \beta_3 x_{t-3} + \cdots + e_t \\ &= \alpha + \sum_{s=0}^{\infty} \beta_s x_{t-s} + e_t \end{aligned} \tag{9.53}$$

Because it does not have a finite cut off point, this model is called an **infinite distributed lag model**. It contrasts with the finite distributed lag model we studied in Section 9.2, where the effect of the lagged x's was assumed to cut off to zero after q lags. Like before, the parameter β_s is the distributed lag weight or the s-period delay multiplier showing the effect of a change in x_t on y_{t+s}. The total or long-run multiplier showing the long-run effect of a sustained change in x_t is $\sum_{s=0}^{\infty}\beta_s$. For the transformation from (9.52) to (9.53) to be valid, the effect of a change must gradually die out. Thus, the values of β_s for large s will be small and decreasing, a property that is necessary for the infinite sum $\sum_{s=0}^{\infty}\beta_s$ to be finite. Estimates for the lag weights β_s can be found from estimates of the θ_k's and the δ_j's in (9.52), with the precise relationship between them depending on the values for p and q. This relationship is explored in Section 9.8.

The two main uses of ARDL models are for forecasting and multiplier analysis. Both are useful policy tools. We consider them in Sections 9.7 and 9.8, respectively. For the remainder of this section we consider *estimation* of (9.52). Because estimation is straight-forward—least squares is an appropriate estimation technique under assumptions TSMR1, TSMR2A, and TSMR3–5—the main concern for estimation is choice of the lag lengths p and q.

There are a number of different criteria for choosing p and q. Because they all do not necessarily lead to the same choice, there is a degree of subjective judgment that must be used. Four possible criteria are

1. Has serial correlation in the errors been eliminated? If not, then least squares will be biased in small and large samples. It is important to include sufficient lags, especially of y, to ensure that serial correlation does not remain. It can be checked using the correlogram or Lagrange multiplier tests.

2. Are the signs and magnitudes of the estimates consistent with our expectations from economic theory? Estimates which are poor in this sense may be a consequence of poor choices for p and q, but they could also be symptomatic of a more general modeling problem.

3. Are the estimates significantly different from zero, particularly those at the longest lags?

4. What values for p and q minimize information criteria such as the AIC and SC? Information criteria were first considered in Chapter 6. In the context of the ARDL model they involve choosing p and q to minimize the sum of squared errors (SSE) subject to a penalty that increases as the number of parameters increases. Increasing lag lengths increases the number of parameters, and, providing we use the same number of observations in each case,[11] it reduces the sum of squared errors; penalty terms are included with a view to capturing the essential lag effects without introducing an excessive number of parameters. The **Akaike information criterion (AIC)** is given by[12]

$$\text{AIC} = \ln\left(\frac{SSE}{T}\right) + \frac{2K}{T} \tag{9.54}$$

---

[11] Care must be taken to use the same number of observations. Unless special provision is made, the number of observations used will typically decline as the lag length increases.

[12] You will find slight but nonessential variations in the definitions of AIC and SC. For example, to get the values computed by EViews 7.0 you need to add $[1+\ln(2\pi)]$ to the expressions in (9.54) and (9.55). Adding or subtracting a constant does not change the lag length that minimizes AIC or SC.

where $K = p + q + 2$ is the number of coefficients that are estimated. The **Schwarz criterion (SC)**, also known as the **Bayes information criterion (BIC)**, is given by

$$SC = \ln\left(\frac{SSE}{T}\right) + \frac{K\ln(T)}{T} \qquad (9.55)$$

Because $K\ln(T)/T > 2K/T$ for $T \geq 8$, the SC penalizes additional lags more heavily than does the AIC.

We now apply the above criteria to our two examples—the Phillips curve and the equation for Okun's law—to see if we can improve on our earlier specifications.

9.6.1 THE PHILLIPS CURVE

Our starting point for the Phillips curve is the previously estimated ARDL(1,0) model

$$\widehat{INF}_t = 0.3548 + 0.5282INF_{t-1} - 0.4909DU_t, \quad obs = 90$$
$$(se) \quad (0.0876) \quad (0.0851) \qquad\quad (0.1921) \qquad\qquad (9.56)$$

We choose this model in preference to the ARDL(1,1) model because the coefficient of DU_{t-1} was not significantly different from zero. Also, to help avoid confusion that may arise because we are considering models with differing numbers of lags, we have indicated that 90 observations were used for estimation.

Checking first to see whether the errors from (9.56) are serially correlated, we obtain the correlogram for its residuals presented in Figure 9.9. Since these autocorrelations are not significantly different from zero, they provide no evidence of serial correlation. However, a further check using Lagrange multiplier tests provides conflicting evidence. Table 9.3 contains the p-values for the $LM = T \times R^2$ version of the LM test (with pre-sample errors set equal to zero) for autocorrelation of orders one to five. Using a 5% significance level, tests for orders one, four, and five reject a null hypothesis of no autocorrelation.

Taken together, these test results provide some evidence, but not overwhelming evidence, that serial correlation in the errors still exists; one lag of the dependent variable

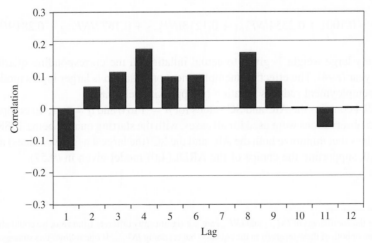

FIGURE **9.9** Correlogram for residuals from Phillips curve ARDL(1,0) model.

T a b l e 9 . 3   p-**values for** *LM* **Test for Autocorrelation**

Lag	p-value
1	0.0421
2	0.0772
3	0.1563
4	0.0486
5	0.0287

INF has not been sufficient to eliminate the autocorrelation. When additional lags of both *INF* and *DU* are tried, we find

1. Coefficients of extra lags of *DU* are never significantly different from zero at a 5% level of significance.

2. For $p = 2$, $q = 0$, the coefficients of INF_{t-1} and INF_{t-2} are significantly different from zero at a 5% significance level; for $p = 3$, $q = 0$, the coefficients of INF_{t-1} and INF_{t-3} are significant; and for $p = 4$, $q = 0$, the coefficients of INF_{t-1} and INF_{t-4} are significant. Coefficients of lags greater than 4 ($p \geq 5$) were not significant. Moreover, for $p = 2$ and $p = 3$ the *LM* test continued to suggest serial correlation in the errors. For $p = 4$ no correlation remained.

Thus, if we use significance of coefficients and elimination of serial correlation in the errors as our criteria for selecting lag lengths, our choice is the ARDL(4,0) model

$$\widehat{INF}_t = 0.1001 + 0.2354INF_{t-1} + 0.1213INF_{t-2} + 0.1677INF_{t-3}$$
$$\text{(se)} \quad (0.0983) \quad (0.1016) \qquad (0.1038) \qquad (0.1050)$$
$$+ 0.2819INF_{t-4} - 0.7902DU_t$$
$$(0.1014) \qquad (0.1885) \quad \text{obs} = 87 \tag{9.57}$$

In this model inflationary expectations are given by

$$INF_t^E = 0.1001 + 0.2354INF_{t-1} + 0.1213INF_{t-2} + 0.1677INF_{t-3} + 0.2819INF_{t-4}$$

A relatively large weight is given to actual inflation in the corresponding quarter of the previous year ($t-4$). The effect of unemployment on inflation is larger in this model. A 1% rise in unemployment reduces inflation by approximately 0.8%.

Table 9.4 contains the AIC and SC values for $p = 1$ to 6 and $q = 0, 1$. To compute these values, 85 observations were used for all cases, with the starting quarter being 1988, quarter 3. The values that minimize both the AIC and the SC (the largest negative values) are $p = 4$ and $q = 0$, supporting the choice of the ARDL(4,0) model given in (9.57).[13]

---

[13] Since the coefficients of INF_{t-2} and INF_{t-3} are not significantly different from zero, we could also consider dropping one or both of these terms from the equation but retaining INF_{t-4}. If one follows this strategy, the model that minimizes the AIC and the SC omits INF_{t-2} but keeps INF_{t-1}, INF_{t-3}, and INF_{t-4}.

Table 9.4 **AIC and SC Values for Phillips Curve ARDL Models**

p	q	AIC	SC	p	q	AIC	SC
1	0	−1.247	−1.160	1	1	−1.242	−1.128
2	0	−1.290	−1.176	2	1	−1.286	−1.142
3	0	−1.335	−1.192	3	1	−1.323	−1.151
4	0	−1.402	−1.230	4	1	−1.380	−1.178
5	0	−1.396	−1.195	5	1	−1.373	−1.143
6	0	−1.378	−1.148	6	1	−1.354	−1.096

9.6.2 Okun's Law

In Section 9.2.1 we estimated an equation for Okun's law. It was given by the following finite distributed lag model where the change in unemployment (DU) was related to GDP growth (G) and its lags

$$\widehat{DU}_t = 0.5836 - 0.2020G_t - 0.1653G_{t-1} - 0.0700G_{t-2}$$
$$(\text{se}) \quad (0.0472) \quad (0.0324) \quad (0.0335) \quad (0.0331)$$

$$\text{obs} = 96 \qquad (9.58)$$

In the more general ARDL context, this equation is an ARDL(0,2) model. It has no lags of DU and two lags of G. We now ask whether we can improve on this model. Does it suffer from serially correlated errors? If we include lagged values of DU, do those lags have coefficients that are significantly different from zero?

The correlogram for the residuals from (9.58) is displayed in Figure 9.10. It shows a significant autocorrelation at lag one, with the remaining autocorrelations being insignificant. This correlation is confirmed by the *LM* test whose *p*-value is 0.0004 for a test with lag order one and pre-sample residual set to zero. When DU_{t-1} is included with a view to eliminating the serial correlation, we find that its coefficient is significantly different from zero, but that for G_{t-2} becomes insignificant. The estimated equation is

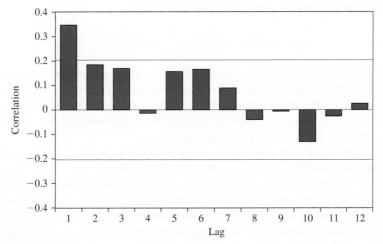

FIGURE 9.10 Correlogram for residuals from Okun's law ARDL(0,2) model.

Table 9.5   **AIC and SC Values for Okun's Law ARDL Models**

(p, q)	AIC	SC	(p, q)	AIC	SC	(p, q)	AIC	SC
(0,1)	−3.436	−3.356	(1,1)	−3.588	−3.480	(2,1)	−3.569	−3.435
(0,2)	−3.463	−3.356	(1,2)	−3.568	−3.433	(2,2)	−3.548	−3.387
(0,3)	−3.442	−3.308	(1,3)	−3.561	−3.400	(2,3)	−3.549	−3.361

$$\widehat{DU}_t = 0.3780 + 0.3501DU_{t-1} - 0.1841G_t - 0.0992G_{t-1}$$
$$\text{(se)} \quad (0.0578) \ (0.0846) \qquad (0.0307) \quad (0.0368) \qquad \text{obs} = 96 \qquad (9.59)$$

There is no evidence that the residuals from (9.59) are autocorrelated. Both the correlogram and *LM* test failed to reject null hypotheses of zero autocorrelations. Furthermore, when extra lags of *DU* and *G* are added to (9.59), their coefficients are not significantly different from zero at a 5% significance level. Thus, we are led to conclude that the ARDL(1,1) model in (9.59) is a suitable one for modeling the relationship between *DU* and *G*. As a final check we can examine what values of *p* and *q* minimize the AIC and SC criteria. Table 9.5 contains the AIC and SC values for possibly relevant lags. They support our choice of the ARDL(1,1) model; both criteria are at a minimum when $p = q = 1$. They were calculated using 95 observations with a starting period of 1986, quarter 1.

We examine how this model can be used for forecasting in Section 9.7. In Section 9.8 we derive multipliers showing the effect of a change in the growth rate of GDP on changes in the unemployment rate.

9.6.3 AUTOREGRESSIVE MODELS

The ARDL models in the previous section had an autoregressive component (lagged values of the dependent variable *y*) and a distributed lag component (an explanatory variable *x*, and its lags). One special case of an ARDL model is the finite distributed lag model that has no autoregressive component ($p = 0$). We studied this model in Section 9.2. It is also possible to have a pure autoregressive (AR) model with only lagged values of the dependent variable as the right-hand-side variables, and no distributed-lag component. Specifically, an auto-regressive model of order *p*, denoted AR(*p*), is given by

$$y_t = \delta + \theta_1 y_{t-1} + \theta_2 y_{t-2} + \cdots + \theta_p y_{t-p} + v_t \qquad (9.60)$$

In this model the current value of a variable y_t depends on its values in the last *p* periods and on a random error that is assumed to have a zero mean and a constant variance, and to be uncorrelated over time. The order of the model *p* is equal to the largest lag of *y* on the right side of the equation. Notice that there are no explanatory variables in (9.60). The value of y_t depends only on a history of its past values and no *x*'s.

In Section 9.5.2 we were concerned with an AR(1) error model $e_t = \rho e_{t-1} + v_t$ and its implications for estimating β_1 and β_2 in the regression model $y_t = \beta_1 + \beta_2 x_t + e_t$. What is now evident is that the AR class of models has wider applicability than its use for modeling dynamic error terms. It is also used for modeling observed values of a time series y_t. The main use of AR models is for forecasting. Multiplier analysis, where the effect on *y* of a change in *x* is traced through time, is no longer possible in the absence of an *x*. When (9.60) is used for forecasting, we are using the current and past values of a variable to forecast its future value. The model relies on correlations between values of the variable over time to help produce a forecast.

As an example, consider the data on growth of U.S. GDP from quarter 2, 1985 to quarter 3, 2009, stored in the file *okun.dat*. This series was graphed in Figure 9.4(b), and its correlogram is displayed in Figure 9.6. Go back and look at the correlogram. The correlation between G_t and G_{t-1} (observations that are one quarter apart) is 0.494, and the correlation between G_t and G_{t-2} (observations that are two quarters apart) is 0.411. Both are significantly different from zero. How many lags are needed—what value of p is required—for an AR model to capture these correlations? Recall from Section 9.5.2a that the population autocorrelations from an AR(1) model are given by $\rho_k = \rho^k$ where k is the order of the lag. In particular, $\rho_1 = \rho$ and $\rho_2 = \rho_1^2$. Thus, for an AR(1) model to be adequate for G, we would expect $r_2 = 0.411$ to be approximately equal to the square of $r_1 = 0.494$. However, $r_1^2 = (0.494)^2 = 0.244$, which is quite a bit smaller than 0.411. It is likely that the extra correlation will be captured by an AR(2) model, and so we begin with the estimated model

$$\widehat{G}_t = 0.4657 + 0.3770G_{t-1} + 0.2462G_{t-2}$$
$$\text{(se)} \quad (0.1433) \ (0.1000) \qquad (0.1029)$$

$$\text{obs} = 96 \qquad (9.61)$$

The coefficient of G_{t-2} is significantly different from zero at a 5% level, suggesting we do need at least two lags of G. To check whether two lags are adequate we follow the same steps that were used for selecting the lag orders in an ARDL model. The possibility of serially correlated errors is assessed using the correlogram of the residuals and *LM* tests. Extra lags of G are added to see if their coefficients are significantly different from zero. And we can check what value of p minimizes the AIC and SC criteria.

The correlogram for the residuals is displayed in Figure 9.11. With the exception of a slightly significant autocorrelation at lag 12, all autocorrelations are not significantly different from zero at a 5% level. Since the correlations at lags 1 to 11 are insignificant, we are inclined not to react strongly to the result at lag 12. Also, *LM* tests using various orders of lags did not reveal any residual autocorrelation, and when extra lags of G were added, their coefficients were not significantly different from zero. All these results point towards the AR(2) model in (9.61) as a suitable model.

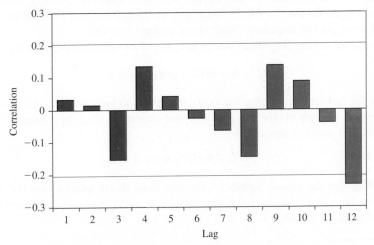

FIGURE **9.11** Correlogram for residuals from AR(2) model for GDP growth.

Table 9.6   **AIC and SC Values for AR Model of Growth in U.S. GDP**

Order (p)	1	2	3	4	5
AIC	−1.094	−1.131	−1.124	−1.133	−1.112
SC	−1.039	−1.049	−1.015	−0.997	−0.948

The AIC and SC values for lags up to five using a starting date of 1986, quarter 3 and 93 observations are given in Table 9.6. In this case the lag length that minimizes the AIC is different from that which minimizes the SC. Specifically, the SC suggests that we choose $p = 2$ and thus supports our earlier choice of an AR(2) model, whereas the AIC suggests a longer lag length of $p = 4$. The SC imposes a heavier penalty for the longer lag. You will find instances like this where different strategies for model choice lead to different outcomes, making some subjective judgment necessary. We will retain the AR(2) model and move to the next section where we show how to use it for forecasting.

9.7 Forecasting

Forecasting values of economic variables is a major activity for many institutions, including firms, banks, governments, and individuals. Accurate forecasts are important for decision-making on government economic policy, investment strategies, the supply of goods to retailers, and a multitude of other things that affect our everyday lives. Because of its importance, you will find that there are whole books and courses that are devoted to the various aspects of forecasting—methods and models for forecasting, ways of evaluating forecasts and their reliability, and practical examples. In this section we consider forecasting using three different models, an AR model, an ARDL model, and an exponential smoothing model. Our focus is on short-term forecasting, typically up to three periods into the future.

9.7.1 FORECASTING WITH AN AR MODEL

Suppose that it is the third quarter in 2009, you have estimated the AR(2) model in (9.61) using observations on growth in U.S. GDP up to and including that for 2009Q3, and you would like to forecast GDP growth for the next three quarters: 2009Q4, 2010Q1, and 2010Q2. How do we use the AR(2) model to give these forecasts? How do we calculate standard errors for our forecasts? What about forecast intervals?

We begin by writing the AR(2) model in terms of its unknown coefficients

$$G_t = \delta + \theta_1 G_{t-1} + \theta_2 G_{t-2} + v_t \tag{9.62}$$

Denoting the last sample observation as G_T, our task is to forecast G_{T+1}, G_{T+2}, and G_{T+3}. Using (9.62), we can obtain the equation that generates G_{T+1} by changing the time subscripts. The required equation is

$$G_{T+1} = \delta + \theta_1 G_T + \theta_2 G_{T-1} + v_{T+1}$$

Recognizing that the growth values for the two most recent quarters are $G_T = G_{2009Q3} = 0.8$, and $G_{T-1} = G_{2009Q2} = -0.2$, the forecast of $G_{T+1} = G_{2009Q4}$ obtained from the estimated equation in (9.61) is[14]

---

[14] We carry the coefficient estimates to five decimal places to avoid rounding error.

$$\hat{G}_{T+1} = \hat{\delta} + \hat{\theta}_1 G_T + \hat{\theta}_2 G_{T-1}$$
$$= 0.46573 + 0.37700 \times 0.8 + 0.24624 \times (-0.2) \qquad (9.63)$$
$$= 0.7181$$

Moving to the forecast for two quarters ahead, G_{2010Q1}, we have

$$\hat{G}_{T+2} = \hat{\delta} + \hat{\theta}_1 \hat{G}_{T+1} + \hat{\theta}_2 G_T$$
$$= 0.46573 + 0.37700 \times 0.71808 + 0.24624 \times 0.8 \qquad (9.64)$$
$$= 0.9334$$

There is an important difference in the way the forecasts $\hat{G}_{T+1}$ and $\hat{G}_{T+2}$ are obtained. It is possible to calculate $\hat{G}_{T+1}$ using only past observations on y. However, G_{T+2} depends on G_{T+1}, which is unobserved at time T. To overcome this problem, we replace G_{T+1} by its forecast $\hat{G}_{T+1}$ on the right side of (9.64). For forecasting G_{T+3}, the forecasts for both G_{T+2} and G_{T+1} are needed on the right side of the equation. Specifically,

$$\hat{G}_{T+3} = \hat{\delta} + \hat{\theta}_1 \hat{G}_{T+2} + \hat{\theta}_2 \hat{G}_{T+1}$$
$$= 0.46573 + 0.37700 \times 0.93343 + 0.24624 \times 0.71808 \qquad (9.65)$$
$$= 0.9945$$

The forecast growth rates for 2009Q4, 2010Q1, and 2010Q2 are approximately 0.72%, 0.93%, and 0.99%, respectively.

We are typically interested not just in point forecasts, but also in interval forecasts that give a likely range in which a future value could fall and that indicate the reliability of a point forecast. A 95% interval forecast for j periods into the future is given by $\hat{G}_{T+j} \pm t_{(0.975, \, df)} \hat{\sigma}_j$ where $\hat{\sigma}_j$ is the standard error of the forecast error and df is the number of degrees of freedom in the estimation of the AR model ($df = 93$ in our example). To get the standard errors, note that the first forecast error, occurring at time $T+1$, is

$$u_1 = G_{T+1} - \hat{G}_{T+1} = (\delta - \hat{\delta}) + (\theta_1 - \hat{\theta}_1)G_T + (\theta_2 - \hat{\theta}_2)G_{T-1} + v_{T+1}$$

The difference between the forecast $\hat{G}_{T+1}$ and the corresponding realized value G_{T+1} depends on the differences between the actual coefficients and the estimated coefficients and on the value of the unpredictable random error v_{T+1}. A similar situation arose in Chapters 4 and 6 when we were forecasting using the regression model. What we are going to do differently now is to ignore the error from estimating the coefficients. It is common to do so because the variance of the random error is usually large relative to the variances of the estimated coefficients, and the resulting variance estimator retains the property of consistency. This means we can write the forecast error for one quarter ahead as

$$u_1 = v_{T+1} \qquad (9.66)$$

For two quarters ahead, the forecast error gets more complicated because we have to allow for not only v_{T+2} but also for the error that occurs from using $\hat{G}_{T+1}$ instead of G_{T+1} on the right side of (9.64). Thus, the forecast error for two periods ahead is

$$u_2 = \theta_1(G_{T+1} - \hat{G}_{T+1}) + v_{T+2} = \theta_1 u_1 + v_{T+2} = \theta_1 v_{T+1} + v_{T+2} \qquad (9.67)$$

Table 9.7   **Forecasts and Forecast Intervals for GDP Growth**

Quarter	Forecast $\hat{G}_{T+j}$	Standard Error of Forecast Error ($\hat{\sigma}_j$)	Forecast Interval $(\hat{G}_{T+j} \pm 1.9858 \times \hat{\sigma}_j)$
2009Q4 ($j = 1$)	0.71808	0.55269	$(-0.379, 1.816)$
2010Q1 ($j = 2$)	0.93343	0.59066	$(-0.239, 2.106)$
2010Q2 ($j = 3$)	0.99445	0.62845	$(-0.254, 2.242)$

For three periods ahead the error can be shown to be

$$u_3 = \theta_1 u_2 + \theta_2 u_1 + v_{T+3} = (\theta_1^2 + \theta_2)v_{T+1} + \theta_1 v_{T+2} + v_{T+3} \tag{9.68}$$

Expressing the forecast errors in terms of the v_t's is convenient for deriving expressions for the forecast error variances. Because the v_t's are uncorrelated with constant variance σ_v^2, (9.66), (9.67), and (9.68) can be used to show that

$$\sigma_1^2 = \text{var}(u_1) = \sigma_v^2$$
$$\sigma_2^2 = \text{var}(u_2) = \sigma_v^2\left(1 + \theta_1^2\right)$$
$$\sigma_3^2 = \text{var}(u_3) = \sigma_v^2\left(\left(\theta_1^2 + \theta_2\right)^2 + \theta_1^2 + 1\right)$$

The standard errors of the forecast errors are obtained by replacing the unknown parameters in the above expressions by their estimates $(\hat{\theta}_1 = 0.37700, \hat{\theta}_2 = 0.24624, \hat{\sigma}_v = 0.55269)$ and then taking the square roots of the variance estimates $\hat{\sigma}_1^2, \hat{\sigma}_2^2$, and $\hat{\sigma}_3^2$. These standard errors appear in Table 9.7, along with the forecast intervals calculated using $t_{(0.975, 93)} = 1.9858$. The forecast intervals are relatively wide, including the possibility of negative as well as positive growth. The point forecasts by themselves do not convey the great deal of uncertainty that is associated with these forecasts. Notice also how the forecast standard errors and the widths of the intervals increase as we forecast further into the future, reflecting the additional uncertainty from doing so.

9.7.2 FORECASTING WITH AN ARDL MODEL

In the previous section we saw how an autoregressive model can be used for forecasting, delivering both point and interval forecasts for a variable of interest. Suppose now that we wish to use an ARDL model for forecasting. As an example, consider forecasting future unemployment using the Okun's Law ARDL(1,1) model that we estimated in Section 9.6.2:

$$DU_t = \delta + \theta_1 DU_{t-1} + \delta_0 G_t + \delta_1 G_{t-1} + v_t \tag{9.69}$$

Does using this model for forecasting, instead of a pure AR model, create any special problems? One obvious difference is that future values of G are required. The value of DU in the first post-sample quarter is

$$DU_{T+1} = \delta + \theta_1 DU_T + \delta_0 G_{T+1} + \delta_1 G_T + v_{T+1} \tag{9.70}$$

Before we can use this equation to forecast DU_{T+1}, a value for G_{T+1} is needed; forecasting further into the future will require more future values of G. These values may be independent forecasts or they might be from "what if" questions: If GDP growth in the next two quarters is $G^*_{T+1} = G^*_{T+2}$, what is our forecast for the level of unemployment?

Apart from the need to supply future values of G, the forecasting procedure for an ARDL model is essentially the same as that for a pure AR model. Providing we are content to construct forecast intervals that ignore any error in the specification of future values of G, adding a distributed lag component to the AR model does not require any special treatment. Point and interval forecasts are obtained in the same way.

There is, however, one special feature of the model in (9.69) that is worthy of further consideration. Recall that the dependent variable DU_t is the *change* in unemployment defined as $DU_t = U_t - U_{t-1}$. Does this have any implications for forecasting the *level* of unemployment given by U_t? To investigate this question, we rewrite (9.70) as

$$U_{T+1} - U_T = \delta + \theta_1(U_T - U_{T-1}) + \delta_0 G_{T+1} + \delta_1 G_T + v_{T+1}$$

Bringing U_T over to the right side and collecting terms yields

$$\begin{aligned} U_{T+1} &= \delta + (\theta_1 + 1)U_T - \theta_1 U_{T-1} + \delta_0 G_{T+1} + \delta_1 G_T + v_{T+1} \\ &= \delta + \theta^*_1 U_T + \theta^*_2 U_{T-1} + \delta_0 G_{T+1} + \delta_1 G_T + v_{T+1} \end{aligned} \qquad (9.71)$$

where $\theta^*_1 = \theta_1 + 1$ and $\theta^*_2 = -\theta_1$. For the purpose of computing point and interval forecasts, the ARDL(1,1) model for a *change* in unemployment can be written as an ARDL(2,1) model for the *level* of unemployment, with parameters θ^*_1 and θ^*_2. This result holds not only for ARDL models where a dependent variable is measured in terms of a change or difference, but also for pure AR models involving such variables. It is particularly relevant when nonstationary variables are differenced to achieve stationarity—a transformation that is considered further in Chapter 12.

Finally, we note that forecasting with a finite distributed lag model with no AR component can be carried out within the same framework as forecasting (prediction) in the linear regression model considered in Chapter 6. Instead of the right-hand-side variables' being a number of different x's, they comprise a number of lags on the same x.

9.7.3 EXPONENTIAL SMOOTHING

In Section 9.7.1 we saw how an autoregressive model can be used to forecast the future value of a variable by making use of past observations on that variable. Another popular model used for predicting the future value of a variable on the basis of its history is the exponential smoothing method. Like forecasting with an AR model, forecasting using exponential smoothing does not utilize information from any other variable.

To introduce this method, consider a sample of observations $(y_1, y_2, \ldots, y_{T-1}, y_T)$ where our objective is to forecast the next observation y_{T+1}. One possible forecasting method, and one that has some intuitive appeal, is to use the average of past information—say, the average of the last k observations. For example, if we adopt this method with $k = 3$, the proposed forecast is

$$\hat{y}_{T+1} = \frac{y_T + y_{T-1} + y_{T-2}}{3}$$

This forecasting rule is an example of a simple (equally-weighted) **moving average** model with $k = 3$. Note that when $k = 1$, all weight is placed on the most recent value and the forecast is $\hat{y}_{T+1} = y_T$.

Now let us extend the moving average idea by changing the equal weighting system where the weights are all $(1/k)$ to one where more weight is put on recent information—or, put another way, less weight is placed on observations further into the past. The exponential smoothing model is one such forecasting model; in this case, the weights decline exponentially as the observations get older. It has the form

$$\hat{y}_{T+1} = \alpha y_T + \alpha(1-\alpha)^1 y_{T-1} + \alpha(1-\alpha)^2 y_{T-2} + \cdots \tag{9.72}$$

The weight attached to y_{T-s} is given by $\alpha(1-\alpha)^s$. We assume that $0 < \alpha \le 1$, which means that the weights get smaller as s gets larger (as we go further into the past). Also, using results on the infinite sum of a geometric progression, it can be shown that the weights sum to one: $\sum_{s=0}^{\infty}\alpha(1-\alpha)^s = 1$.

Using information from the infinite past is not convenient for forecasting. Recognizing that

$$(1-\alpha)\hat{y}_T = \alpha(1-\alpha)y_{T-1} + \alpha(1-\alpha)^2 y_{T-2} + \alpha(1-\alpha)^3 y_{T-3} + \cdots \tag{9.73}$$

allows us to simplify the model. Notice that the terms on the right hand side of (9.73) also appear on the right-hand side of (9.72). This means we can replace an infinite sum by a single term, so that the forecast can be more conveniently presented as

$$\hat{y}_{T+1} = \alpha y_T + (1-\alpha)\hat{y}_T \tag{9.74}$$

That is, the forecast for next period is a weighted average of the forecast for the current period and the actual realized value in the current period.

The exponential smoothing method is a versatile forecasting tool, but one needs a value for the smoothing parameter α and a value for $\hat{y}_T$ to generate the forecast $\hat{y}_{T+1}$. The value of α can reflect one's judgment about the relative weight of current information; alternatively, it can be estimated from historical information by obtaining **within-sample forecasts**

$$\hat{y}_t = \alpha y_{t-1} + (1-\alpha)\hat{y}_{t-1} \quad t = 2, 3, \ldots, T \tag{9.75}$$

and choosing that value of α which minimizes the sum of squares of the **one-step forecast errors**

$$v_t = y_t - \hat{y}_t = y_t - (\alpha y_{t-1} + (1-\alpha)\hat{y}_{t-1}) \tag{9.76}$$

To compute $\sum_{t=2}^{T}v_t^2$ for a given value of α we need a starting value for $\hat{y}_1$. One option is to set $\hat{y}_1 = y_1$; another is to set $\hat{y}_1$ equal to the average of the first $(T+1)/2$ observations on y.[15] Once $\hat{y}_1$ has been set, (9.75) can be used recursively to generate a series of within-sample forecasts, and (9.76) can be used to generate a series of within-sample forecast errors.

The last value of the within-sample forecasts, generated, either with an α that reflects personal judgment or with one that minimizes $\sum_{t=2}^{T}v_t^2$, is $\hat{y}_T$, which is then used in (9.74) to generate a forecast for the first post-sample observation y_{T+1}. Forecasts for more than one period into the future are identical to that for period $T+1$. Can you see why?

For an illustration, we use the same quarterly data on U.S. GDP growth that was used for the AR model in Section 9.7.1. It runs from 1985Q2 to 2009Q3 and is stored in the file

---

[15] This second option is that used by the software EViews 7.0, and the one used in the example that follows.

okun.dat. Two values of α were chosen: α = 0.8, and the value that minimized the sum of squares of within-sample forecast errors—in this case, α = 0.38. The smaller the value of α, the greater the contribution of past observations to a forecast, and the smoother the series of within-sample forecasts is. With large values of α, the most recent observation is the major contributor to a forecast, and the series of forecasts more closely mimics the actual series. These characteristics are evident in Figures 9.12(a) and (b), where the actual series is graphed alongside the within-sample forecasts for α = 0.38 (Figure 9.12(a)), and α = 0.8 (Figure 9.12(b)). In both these figures, the solid line represents actual GDP growth and the dashed line represents the within-sample forecasts. In Figure 9.12(a), where α = 0.38, the smoothed series is much less volatile than the actual series. It retains a jagged appearance, but the peaks and troughs are much less extreme. In Figure 9.12(b), where α = 0.8, the peaks and troughs of the smoothed series are only slightly less pronounced, and the forecasts closely follow the actual series by one period reflecting the high weight placed on the most recent value.

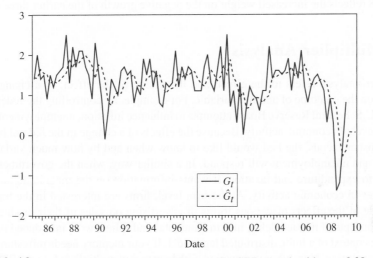

*FIGURE **9.12*** (a) Exponentially smoothed forecasts for GDP growth with α = 0.38.

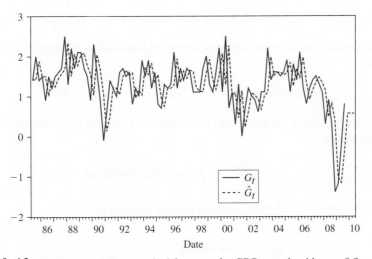

*FIGURE **9.12*** (b) Exponentially smoothed forecasts for GDP growth with α = 0.8.

The forecasts for 2009Q4 from each value of α are

$$\alpha = 0.38: \quad \hat{G}_{T+1} = \alpha G_T + (1 - \alpha)\hat{G}_T = 0.38 \times 0.8 + (1 - 0.38) \times (-0.403921)$$

$$= 0.0536$$

$$\alpha = 0.8: \quad \hat{G}_{T+1} = \alpha G_T + (1 - \alpha)\hat{G}_T = 0.8 \times 0.8 + (1 - 0.8) \times (-0.393578)$$

$$= 0.5613$$

The difference between these two forecasts can be explained by the different weights placed on the most recent values of past growth. GDP growth was positive in 2009Q3 $(G_{2009Q3} = 0.8)$ after three successive quarters of negative growth attributable to the global financial crisis $(G_{2009Q2} = -0.2, G_{2009Q1} = -1.2, G_{2008Q4} = -1.4)$. The 2009Q4 forecast that uses $\alpha = 0.8$ is higher than that for $\alpha = 0.38$ because it places a heavy weight on the most recent positive growth in 2009Q3. The forecast for low growth that comes from using $\alpha = 0.38$ reflects the increased weight on the negative growth of the earlier three quarters.

9.8 Multiplier Analysis

Multiplier analysis refers to the effect, and the timing of the effect, of a change in one variable on the outcome of another variable. For example, by controlling the federal funds rate, the U.S. Federal Reserve Board attempts to influence inflation, unemployment, and the general level of economic activity. Because the effects of a change in the federal funds rate are not instantaneous, the Fed would like to know when and by how much variables like inflation and unemployment will respond. In a similar way, when the government makes changes to expenditure and taxation, it wants information on the magnitude and timing of changes in economic activity. At the firm level, firms are interested in the timing and magnitude of the effects of various forms of advertising on sales of their products.

The concepts of impact, delay, interim, and total multipliers were introduced in Section 9.2 in the context of a finite distributed lag model. If your memory needs refreshing, please reread that section. Now we are concerned with how to find multipliers for an ARDL model of the form

$$y_t = \delta + \theta_1 y_{t-1} + \cdots + \theta_p y_{t-p} + \delta_0 x_t + \delta_1 x_{t-1} + \cdots + \delta_q x_{t-q} + v_t \tag{9.77}$$

The secret for doing so lies in our ability to transform it into an infinite distributed lag model written as

$$y_t = \alpha + \beta_0 x_t + \beta_1 x_{t-1} + \beta_2 x_{t-2} + \beta_3 x_{t-3} + \cdots + e_t \tag{9.78}$$

The multipliers defined for this model are similar to those for the finite distributed lag model. Specifically,

$$\beta_s = \frac{\partial y_t}{\partial x_{t-s}} = s \text{ period delay multiplier}$$

$$\sum_{j=0}^{s} \beta_j = s \text{ period interim multiplier}$$

$$\sum_{j=0}^{\infty} \beta_j = \text{total multiplier}$$

When we estimate an ARDL model, we obtain estimates of the θ's and δ's in (9.77). To obtain multipliers that are expressed in terms of the β's, we need to be able to compute estimates of the β's from those for the θ's and δ's. Describing how the β's can be derived from the θ's and δ's is the purpose of this section.

Our task is made easier if we can master some machinery known as the **lag operator**. The lag operator L has the effect of lagging a variable,

$$Ly_t = y_{t-1}$$

For lagging a variable twice, we have

$$L(Ly_t) = Ly_{t-1} = y_{t-2}$$

which we write as $L^2 y_t = y_{t-2}$. More generally, L raised to the power of s means lag a variable s times

$$L^s y_t = y_{t-s}$$

Now we are in a position to write the ARDL model in terms of lag operator notation. Equation (9.77) becomes

$$
\begin{aligned}
y_t = \delta &+ \theta_1 L y_t + \theta_2 L^2 y_t + \cdots + \theta_p L^p y_t + \delta_0 x_t + \delta_1 L x_t + \delta_2 L^2 x_t \\
&+ \cdots + \delta_q L^q x_t + v_t
\end{aligned}
\tag{9.79}
$$

Bringing the terms that contain y_t to the left side of the equation, and factoring out y_t and x_t yields

$$\left(1 - \theta_1 L - \theta_2 L^2 - \cdots - \theta_p L^p\right) y_t = \delta + \left(\delta_0 + \delta_1 L + \delta_2 L^2 + \cdots + \delta_q L^q\right) x_t + v_t \tag{9.80}$$

This algebra is starting to get heavy. To make our derivation manageable, consider the ARDL(1,1) model used to describe Okun's law. From the above results, the model

$$DU_t = \delta + \theta_1 DU_{t-1} + \delta_0 G_t + \delta_1 G_{t-1} + v_t \tag{9.81}$$

can be written as

$$(1 - \theta_1 L) DU_t = \delta + (\delta_0 + \delta_1 L) G_t + v_t \tag{9.82}$$

Now suppose that it is possible to define an inverse of $(1 - \theta_1 L)$, which we write as $(1 - \theta_1 L)^{-1}$, which is such that

$$(1 - \theta_1 L)^{-1} (1 - \theta_1 L) = 1$$

This concept is a bit abstract. Using it will seem like magic the first time that you encounter it. Stick with us. We have nearly reached the essential result. Multiplying both sides of (9.82) by $(1 - \theta_1 L)^{-1}$ yields

$$DU_t = (1 - \theta_1 L)^{-1} \delta + (1 - \theta_1 L)^{-1} (\delta_0 + \delta_1 L) G_t + (1 - \theta_1 L)^{-1} v_t \tag{9.83}$$

This representation is useful because we can equate it with the infinite distributed lag representation

$$DU_t = \alpha + \beta_0 G_t + \beta_1 G_{t-1} + \beta_2 G_{t-2} + \beta_3 G_{t-3} + \cdots + e_t$$

$$= \alpha + (\beta_0 + \beta_1 L + \beta_2 L^2 + \beta_3 L^3 + \cdots) G_t + e_t \tag{9.84}$$

For (9.83) and (9.84) to be identical, it must be true that

$$\alpha = (1 - \theta_1 L)^{-1} \delta \tag{9.85}$$

$$\beta_0 + \beta_1 L + \beta_2 L^2 + \beta_3 L^3 + \cdots = (1 - \theta_1 L)^{-1}(\delta_0 + \delta_1 L) \tag{9.86}$$

$$e_t = (1 - \theta_1 L)^{-1} v_t \tag{9.87}$$

Equation (9.85) can be used to derive α in terms of θ_1 and δ, and (9.86) can be used to derive the β's in terms of the θ's and δ's. To see how, first multiply both sides of (9.85) by $(1 - \theta_1 L)$ to obtain $(1 - \theta_1 L)\alpha = \delta$. Then, recognizing that the lag of a constant that does not change over time is the same constant ($L\alpha = \alpha$), we have

$$(1 - \theta_1)\alpha = \delta \quad \text{and} \quad \alpha = \frac{\delta}{1 - \theta_1}$$

Turning now to the β's, we multiply both sides of (9.86) by $(1 - \theta_1 L)$ to obtain

$$\delta_0 + \delta_1 L = (1 - \theta_1 L)(\beta_0 + \beta_1 L + \beta_2 L^2 + \beta_3 L^3 + \cdots)$$

$$= \beta_0 + \beta_1 L + \beta_2 L^2 + \beta_3 L^3 + \cdots$$

$$- \beta_0 \theta_1 L - \beta_1 \theta_1 L^2 - \beta_2 \theta_1 L^3 - \cdots \tag{9.88}$$

$$= \beta_0 + (\beta_1 - \beta_0 \theta_1)L + (\beta_2 - \beta_1 \theta_1)L^2 + (\beta_3 - \beta_2 \theta_1)L^3 + \cdots$$

Notice how we can do algebra with the lag operator. We have used the fact that $L^r L^s = L^{r+s}$.

Equation (9.88) holds the key to deriving the β's in terms of the θ's and the δ's. For both sides of this equation to mean the same thing (to imply the same lags), coefficients of like powers in the lag operator must be equal. To make what follows more transparent, we rewrite (9.88) as

$$\delta_0 + \delta_1 L + 0L^2 + 0L^3 = \beta_0 + (\beta_1 - \beta_0 \theta_1)L + (\beta_2 - \beta_1 \theta_1)L^2 + (\beta_3 - \beta_2 \theta_1)L^3 + \cdots \tag{9.89}$$

Equating coefficients of like powers in L yields

$$\delta_0 = \beta_0$$
$$\delta_1 = \beta_1 - \beta_0 \theta_1$$
$$0 = \beta_2 - \beta_1 \theta_1$$
$$0 = \beta_3 - \beta_2 \theta_1$$

and so on. Thus, the β's can be found from the θ's and the δ's using the recursive equations

$$\beta_0 = \delta_0$$
$$\beta_1 = \delta_1 + \beta_0 \theta_1 \tag{9.90}$$
$$\beta_j = \beta_{j-1} \theta_1 \quad \text{for} \quad j \geq 2$$

You are probably asking: Do I have to go through all this each time I want to derive some multipliers for an ARDL model? The answer is no. You can start from the equivalent of (9.88) which, in its general form, is

$$\delta_0 + \delta_1 L + \delta_2 L^2 + \cdots + \delta_q L^q = \left(1 - \theta_1 L - \theta_2 L^2 - \cdots - \theta_p L^p\right)$$
$$\times \left(\beta_0 + \beta_1 L + \beta_2 L^2 + \beta_3 L^3 + \cdots\right) \qquad (9.91)$$

Given the values p and q for your ARDL model, you need to multiply out the above expression, and then equate coefficients of like powers in the lag operator.

What are the values of the multipliers for our Okun's Law example?

$$\widehat{DU}_t = 0.3780 + 0.3501 DU_{t-1} - 0.1841 G_t - 0.0992 G_{t-1}$$

Using the relationships in (9.90), the impact multiplier and the delay multipliers for the first four quarters are given by

$$\hat{\beta}_0 = \hat{\delta}_0 = -0.1841$$

$$\hat{\beta}_1 = \hat{\delta}_1 + \hat{\beta}_0 \hat{\theta}_1 = -0.099155 - 0.184084 \times 0.350116 = -0.1636$$

$$\hat{\beta}_2 = \hat{\beta}_1 \hat{\theta}_1 = -0.163606 \times 0.350166 = -0.0573$$

$$\hat{\beta}_3 = \hat{\beta}_2 \hat{\theta}_1 = -0.057281 \times 0.350166 = -0.0201$$

$$\hat{\beta}_4 = \hat{\beta}_3 \hat{\theta}_1 = -0.020055 \times 0.350166 = -0.0070$$

An increase in GDP growth leads to a fall in unemployment, with its greatest effect being felt in the current and next quarters and a declining effect thereafter. The effect eventually declines to zero. This property—that the weights at long lags go to zero—is an essential one for the above analysis to be valid. The weights are displayed in Figure 9.13 for lags up to seven quarters.

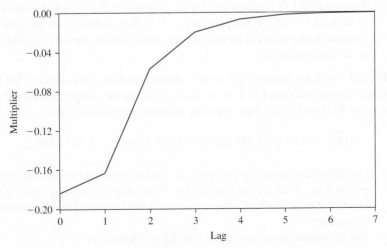

FIGURE **9.13** Delay multipliers from Okun's law ARDL(1,1) model.

Finally, we can estimate the total multiplier that is given by $\sum_{j=0}^{\infty}\beta_j$, and the normal growth rate that is needed to maintain a constant rate of unemployment, $G_N = -\alpha/\sum_{j=0}^{\infty}\beta_j$. The total multiplier can be found by summing those β's which are sufficiently large to contribute to the sum or by using results on the sum of an infinite geometric progression. For the latter approach, we can show that

$$\sum_{j=0}^{\infty}\hat{\beta}_j = \hat{\delta}_0 + \frac{\hat{\delta}_1 + \hat{\delta}_0\hat{\theta}_1}{1 - \hat{\theta}_1} = -0.184084 + \frac{-0.163606}{1 - 0.350116} = -0.4358$$

An estimate for α is given by $\hat{\alpha} = \hat{\delta}/(1 - \hat{\theta}_1) = 0.37801/0.649884 = 0.5817$ which leads to a normal growth rate of $\hat{G}_N = 0.5817/0.4358 = 1.3\%$ per quarter. These results are consistent with those that we found from the finite distributed lag model in Section 9.2. In that instance, we had -0.437 for the total multiplier and 1.3% for G_N.

9.9 Exercises

Answers to exercises marked * appear at www.wiley.com/go/global/hill.

9.9.1 PROBLEMS

9.1 Consider the following distributed lag model relating the percentage growth in private investment (INVGWTH) to the federal funds rate of interest (FFRATE):

$$INVGWTH_t = 4 - 0.4FFRATE_t - 0.8FFRATE_{t-1} - 0.6FFRATE_{t-2}$$
$$- 0.2FFRATE_{t-3}$$

(a) Suppose $FFRATE = 2\%$ for $t = 1, 2, 3, 4$. Use the above equation to forecast INVGWTH for $t = 4$.

(b) Suppose FFRATE is raised to 2.5% in period $t = 5$ and then returned to its original level of 2% for $t = 6, 7, 8, 9$. Use the equation to forecast INVGWTH for periods $t = 5, 6, 7, 8, 9$. Relate the changes in your forecasts to the values of the coefficients. What are the delay multipliers?

(c) Suppose FFRATE is raised to 2.5% for periods $t = 5, 6, 7, 8, 9$. Use the equation to forecast INVGWTH for periods $t = 5, 6, 7, 8, 9$. Relate the changes in your forecasts to the values of the coefficients. What are the interim multipliers? What is the total multiplier?

9.2 The file ex9_2.dat contains 105 weekly observations on sales revenue (SALES) and advertising expenditure (ADV) in millions of dollars for a large midwest department store in 2008 and 2009. The following relationship was estimated:

$$\widehat{SALES}_t = 25.34 + 1.842\,ADV_t + 3.802\,ADV_{t-1} + 2.265\,ADV_{t-2}$$

(a) Describe the relationship between sales and advertising expenditure. Include an explanation of the lagged relationship. When does advertising have its greatest impact? What is the total effect of a sustained $1 million increase in advertising expenditure?

(b) The estimated covariance matrix of the coefficients is

	C	ADV	ADV_{t-1}	ADV_{t-2}
C	2.5598	−0.7099	−0.1317	−0.7661
ADV	−0.7099	1.3946	−1.0406	0.0984
ADV_{t-1}	−0.1317	−1.0406	2.1606	−1.0367
ADV_{t-2}	−0.7661	0.0984	−1.0367	1.4214

Using a two-tail test and a 1% significance level, which lag coefficients are significantly different from zero? Do your conclusions change if you use a one-tail test? Do they change if you use a 5% significance level?

(c) Find 95% confidence intervals for the impact multiplier, the one-period interim multiplier, and the total multiplier.

9.3 Reconsider the estimated equation and covariance matrix in Exercise 9.2. The amounts spent on advertising in the last two weeks were $ADV_{104} = 1.313$ and $ADV_{105} = 1.358$. Suppose, as a marketing executive for the department store, that you have a total of $6 million to spend on advertising over the next three weeks, $t = 106, 107,$ and 108. Consider the following allocations of the $6 million:

$$ADV_{106} = 6, \quad ADV_{107} = 0, \quad ADV_{108} = 0$$
$$ADV_{106} = 0, \quad ADV_{107} = 6, \quad ADV_{108} = 0$$
$$ADV_{106} = 2, \quad ADV_{107} = 4, \quad ADV_{108} = 0$$

(a) For each allocation of the $6 million, forecast sales revenue for $t = 106, 107,$ and 108. Which allocation leads to the largest forecast for total sales revenue over the three weeks? Which allocation leads to the largest forecast for sales in week $t = 108$? Explain why these outcomes were obtained.

(b) Find 95% forecast intervals for ADV_{108} for each of the three allocations. The estimated error variance is $\hat{\sigma}v^2 = 2.3891$. If maximizing ADV_{108} is your objective, which allocation would you choose? Why?

9.4* The following least squares residuals come from a sample of size $T = 10$:

t	1	2	3	4	5	6	7	8	9	10
$\hat{e}_t$	0.28	−0.31	−0.09	0.03	−0.37	−0.17	−0.39	−0.03	0.03	1.02

(a) Use a hand calculator to compute the sample autocorrelations:

$$r_1 = \frac{\sum\limits_{t=2}^{T} \hat{e}_t \hat{e}_{t-1}}{\sum\limits_{t=1}^{T} \hat{e}_t^2} \qquad r_2 = \frac{\sum\limits_{t=3}^{T} \hat{e}_t \hat{e}_{t-2}}{\sum\limits_{t=1}^{T} \hat{e}_t^2}$$

(b) Test whether (i) r_1 is significantly different from zero and (ii) r_2 is significantly different from zero. Sketch the first two bars of the correlogram. Include the significance bounds.

9.5   The file *growth47.dat* contains 250 quarterly observations on U.S. GDP growth from quarter two, 1947, to quarter three, 2009. From these data, we calculate the following quantities:

$$\sum_{t=1}^{250}\left(G_t - \overline{G}\right)^2 = 333.8558 \qquad\qquad \sum_{t=2}^{250}\left(G_t - \overline{G}\right)\left(G_{t-1} - \overline{G}\right) = 162.9753$$

$$\sum_{t=3}^{250}\left(G_t - \overline{G}\right)\left(G_{t-2} - \overline{G}\right) = 112.4882 \qquad\qquad \sum_{t=4}^{250}\left(G_t - \overline{G}\right)\left(G_{t-3} - \overline{G}\right) = 30.5802$$

(a) Compute the first three autocorrelations (r_1, r_2 and r_3) for G. Test whether each one is significantly different from zero at a 5% significance level. Sketch the first three bars of the correlogram. Include the significance bounds.

(b) Given that $\sum_{t=2}^{250}\left(G_{t-1} - \overline{G}_{-1}\right)^2 = 333.1119$ and $\sum_{t=2}^{250}\left(G_t - \overline{G}_1\right)\left(G_{t-1} - \overline{G}_{-1}\right) = 162.974$, where $\overline{G}_1 = \sum_{t=2}^{250} G_t / 249 = 1.662249$ and $\overline{G}_{-1} = \sum_{t=2}^{250} G_{t-1} / 249 = 1.664257$, find least squares estimates of δ_1 and θ_1 in the AR(1) model $G_t = \delta + \theta_1 G_{t-1} + e_t$. Explain the difference between the estimate $\hat{\theta}_1$ and the estimate r_1 obtained in part (a).

9.6   Increases in the mortgage interest rate increase the cost of owning a house and lower the demand for houses. In this question we consider an equation where the monthly change in the number of new one-family houses sold in the U.S. depends on last month's change in the 30-year conventional mortgage rate. Let *HOMES* be the number of new houses sold (in thousands) and *IRATE* be the mortgage rate. Their monthly changes are denoted by $DHOMES_t = HOMES_t - HOMES_{t-1}$ and $DIRATE_t = IRATE_t - IRATE_{t-1}$. Using data from January 1992 to March 2010, we obtain the following least squares regression estimates:

$$\widehat{DHOMES_t} = -2.077 - 53.51 DIRATE_{t-1}$$
$$\text{(se)} \qquad\quad (3.498)\quad (16.98) \qquad\qquad \text{obs} = 218$$

(a) Interpret the estimate -53.51. Construct and interpret a 99% confidence interval for the coefficient of $DIRATE_{t-1}$.

(b) Let $\hat{e}_t$ denote the residuals from the above equation. Use the following estimated equation to conduct two separate tests for first-order autoregressive errors.

$$\hat{e}_t = -0.1835 - 3.210 DIRATE_{t-1} - 0.3306 \hat{e}_{t-1} \qquad R^2 = 0.1077$$
$$\text{(se)} \qquad\quad (16.087) \qquad\qquad\qquad (0.0649) \qquad\qquad \text{obs} = 218$$

(c) The model with AR(1) errors was estimated as

$$\widehat{DHOMES_t} = -2.124 - 58.61 DIRATE_{t-1} \qquad e_t = -0.3314 e_{t-1} + \hat{v}_t$$
$$\text{(se)} \qquad\quad (2.497)\quad (14.10) \qquad\qquad\qquad\qquad (0.0649)$$
$$\text{obs} = 217$$

Construct a 99% confidence interval for the coefficient of $DIRATE_{t-1}$, and comment on the effect of ignoring autocorrelation on inferences about this coefficient.

9.7* Consider the model

$$e_t = \rho e_{t-1} + v_t$$

(a) Suppose $\rho = 0.9$ and $\sigma_v^2 = 1$. What is (i) the correlation between e_t and e_{t-1}? (ii) the correlation between e_t and e_{t-4}? (iii) the variance σ_e^2?

(b) Repeat part (a) with $\rho = 0.4$ and $\sigma_v^2 = 1$. Comment on the difference between your answers for parts (a) and (b).

9.8 In Section 9.6, the following Phillips curve was estimated:

$$\widehat{INF}_t = 0.1001 + 0.2354\ INF_{t-1} + 0.1213\ INF_{t-2} + 0.1677\ INF_{t-3}$$
$$+ 0.2819\ INF_{t-4} - 0.7902\ DU_t$$

The last four sample values for inflation are $INF_{2009Q3} = 1.0$, $INF_{2009Q2} = 0.5$, $INF_{2009Q1} = 0.1$, and $INF_{2008Q4} = -0.3$. The unemployment rate in 2009Q3 was 5.8%. The estimated error variance for the above equation is $\hat{\sigma}_v^2 = 0.225103$.

(a) Given that the unemployment rates in the first three post-sample quarters are $U_{2009Q4} = 5.6$, $U_{2010Q1} = 5.4$, and $U_{2010Q2} = 5.0$, use the estimated equation to forecast inflation for 2009Q4, 2010Q1 and 2010Q2.

(b) Find the standard errors of the forecast errors for your forecasts in (a).

(c) Find 95% forecast intervals for $INF_{2009Q4}, INF_{2010Q1}$, and INF_{2010Q2}. How reliable are the forecasts you found in part (a)?

9.9 Consider the infinite lag representation

$$y_t = \alpha + \sum_{s=0}^{\infty} \beta_s x_{t-s} + e_t$$

for the ARDL model

$$y_t = \delta + \theta_1 y_{t-1} + \theta_2 y_{t-2} + \theta_3 y_{t-3} + \theta_4 y_{t-4} + \delta_0 x_t + v_t$$

(a) Show that

$$\alpha = \delta/(1 - \theta_1 - \theta_2 - \theta_3 - \theta_4)$$
$$\beta_0 = \delta_0$$
$$\beta_1 = \beta_0 \theta_1$$
$$\beta_2 = \beta_1 \theta_1 + \beta_0 \theta_2$$
$$\beta_3 = \beta_2 \theta_1 + \beta_1 \theta_2 + \beta_0 \theta_3$$
$$\beta_s = \beta_{s-1} \theta_1 + \beta_{s-2} \theta_2 + \beta_{s-3} \theta_3 + \beta_{s-4} \theta_4 \quad \text{for } s \geq 4$$

(b) Use the results in (a) to find estimates of the first 12 lag weights for the estimated Phillips curve in Exercise 9.8. Graph those weights and comment on the graph.

(c) What rate of inflation is consistent with a constant unemployment rate (where $DU = 0$ in all time periods)?

9.10* Quarterly data from 1960Q1 to 2009Q4, stored in the file *consumptn.dat*, were used to estimate the following relationship between growth in consumption of consumer durables in the U.S. (*DURGWTH*) and growth in personal disposable income (*INCGWTH*):

$$\widehat{DURGWTH_t} = 0.0103 - 0.1631 DURGWTH_{t-1} + 0.7422 INCGWTH_t$$
$$+ 0.3479 INCGWTH_{t-1}$$

(a) Given that $DURGWTH_{2009Q4} = 0.1$, $INCGWTH_{2009Q4} = 0.9$, $INCGWTH_{2010Q1} = 0.6$, and $INCGWTH_{2010Q2} = 0.8$, forecast $DURGWTH$ for 2010Q1 and 2010Q2.

(b) Find and comment on the implied lag weights for up to 12 quarters for the infinite distributed lag representation

$$DURGWTH_t = \alpha + \sum_{s=0}^{\infty} \beta_s INCGWTH_{t-s} + e_t$$

(c) Find values for the one- and two-quarter delay and interim multipliers, and the total multiplier. Interpret those values.

9.11 (a) Write the AR(1) error model $e_t = \rho e_{t-1} + v_t$ in lag operator notation.

   (b) Show that

$$(1 - \rho L)^{-1} = 1 + \rho L + \rho^2 L + \rho^3 L^3 + \cdots$$

and hence that

$$e_t = v_t + \rho v_{t-1} + \rho^2 v_{t-2} + \rho^3 v_{t-3} + \cdots$$

9.9.2 COMPUTER EXERCISES

9.12* Consider the Okun's Law finite distributed lag model that was estimated in Section 9.2 and the data for which appears in *okun.dat*.

   (a) Estimate the following model for $q = 0, 1, 2, 3, 4, 5$, and 6.

$$DU_t = \alpha + \sum_{s=0}^{q} \beta_s G_{t-s} + e_t$$

In each case use data from $t = 1986Q4$ to $t = 2009Q3$ to ensure that 92 observations are used for each estimation. Report the values of the AIC and SC selection criteria for each value of q. What lag length would you choose on the basis of the AIC? What lag length would you choose based on the SC?

   (b) Using the model that minimizes the AIC:

   (i) Find a 95% confidence interval for the impact multiplier.

   (ii) Test the null hypothesis that the total multiplier equals -0.5 against the alternative that it is greater than -0.5. Use a 5% significance level.

   (iii) Find a 95% confidence interval for the normal growth rate G_N. (*Hint*: Use your software to get the standard error for $\hat{G}_N = \hat{\alpha}/\hat{\gamma}$ where $\hat{\gamma} = -\sum_{s=0}^{q} b_s$. You can do so by pretending to test a hypothesis such as $H_0 : \alpha/\gamma = 1$.)

9.13 The file *ex9_13.dat* contains 157 weekly observations on sales revenue (*SALES*) and advertising expenditure (*ADV*) in millions of dollars for a large midwest department store for 2005–2007. (Exercise 9.2 used data on this store for 2008–2009.) The weeks are from December 28, 2004, to December 25, 2007. We denote them as $t = 1, 2, \ldots, 157$.

(a) Graph the series for *SALES* and *ADV*. Do they appear be trending or do they appear to fluctuate around a constant mean? On your graphs, draw horizontal lines at the means of the series.

(b) Estimate a finite distributed lag model of the form

$$SALES_t = \alpha + \sum_{s=0}^{q} \beta_s ADV_{t-s} + e_t$$

for $q = 0, 1, 2, 3, 4$, and 5. In each case use 152 observations $(t = 6, 7, \ldots, 157$ where $t = 6$ is February 1, 2005). Report the SC values and the total multipliers for each equation. Is the estimated total multiplier sensitive to choice of lag length?

(c) Comment on the estimated lag structure of the model that minimizes the SC. Does it seem sensible to you? Are all the estimates significantly different from zero at a 1% significance level? Use this model to answer the remaining parts of this question.

(d) Construct 99% interval estimates for the (i) one-week delay multiplier, (ii) one-week interim multiplier, (iii) two-week delay multiplier, and (iv) two-week interim multiplier.

(e) The CEO claims that increasing advertising expenditure by $1 million a week in each of the next three weeks will increase total sales over those three weeks by more than $5 million. Is there enough evidence in the data to support this claim?

(f) Forecast sales revenue for the first four post-sample weeks, $t = 158, 159, 160, 161$ when (i) nothing is spent on advertising for those four weeks, (ii) $6 million is spent in the first week ($t = 158$), and nothing is spent in the remaining three weeks, and (iii) $1 million is spent in each of the four weeks. Comment on the three different forecast paths.

9.14 One way of modeling supply response for an agricultural crop is to specify a model in which area planted (acres) depends on price. When the price of the crop's output is high, farmers plant more of that crop than when its price is low. Letting *AREA* denote area planted, and *PRICE* denote output price, and assuming a log-log (constant elasticity) functional form, a finite distributed lag area response model of this type can be written as

$$\ln(AREA_t) = \alpha + \sum_{s=0}^{q} \beta_s \ln(PRICE_{t-s}) + e_t$$

We use this model to explain the area of sugar cane planted in a region of the southeast Asian country of Bangladesh. Information on the delay and interim elasticities is useful for government planning. It is important to know whether existing sugar processing mills are likely to be able to handle predicted output, whether there is likely to be excess milling capacity, and whether a pricing policy linking production, processing, and consumption is desirable. Data comprising 34 annual observations on area and price are given in the file *bangla.dat*.

(a) Estimate this model assuming $q = 4$. What are the estimated delay and interim elasticities? Comment on the results.

(b) You will have discovered that the lag weights obtained in part (a) are not sensible. One way to try and overcome this problem is to insist that the weights lie on a straight line

$$\beta_s = \alpha_0 + \alpha_1 s \qquad s = 0, 1, 2, 3, 4$$

If $\alpha_0 > 0$ and $\alpha_1 < 0$, these weights will decline, implying that farmers place a larger weight on more recent prices when forming their expectations. Substitute $\beta_s = \alpha_0 + \alpha_1 s$ into the original equation and hence show that this equation can be written as

$$\ln(AREA_t) = \alpha + \alpha_0 z_{t0} + \alpha_1 z_{t1} + e_t$$

where $z_{t0} = \sum_{s=0}^{4} \ln(PRICE_{t-s})$ and $z_{t1} = \sum_{s=1}^{4} s \ln(PRICE_{t-s})$.

  (c) Create variables z_{t0} and z_{t1} and find least squares estimates of α_0 and α_1.
  (d) Use the estimates for α_0 and α_1 to find estimates for $\beta_s = \alpha_0 + \alpha_1 s$ and comment on them. Has the original problem been cured? Do the weights now satisfy a priori expectations?
  (e) How do the delay and interim elasticities compare with those obtained earlier?

9.15* Reconsider the sugar cane supply response problem that was introduced in Exercise 9.14. Using data in *bangla.dat*, estimate the following model with no lags

$$\ln(AREA_t) = \beta_1 + \beta_2 \ln(PRICE_t) + e_t$$

  (a) Find the correlogram for the residuals. What autocorrelations are significantly different from zero?
  (b) Perform an *LM* test for autocorrelated errors using one lagged residual and a 5% significance level.
  (c) Find two 95% confidence intervals for the elasticity of supply—one using least squares standard errors and one using HAC standard errors. What are the consequences for interval estimation when serially correlated errors are ignored?
  (d) Estimate the model under the assumption that the error is an AR(1) process. Is the estimate for ρ significantly different from zero at a 5% significance level? Compute a 95% confidence interval for the elasticity of supply. How does it compare with those obtained in part (c)?
  (e) Estimate an ARDL(1,1) model for sugar supply response. What restrictions are necessary on the coefficients of this model to make it equivalent to that in (d)? Test these restrictions using a 5% significance level. Do the residuals from this model show any evidence of serial correlation?

9.16* Consider further the ARDL(1,1) supply response model for sugar cane estimated in part (e) of Exercise 9.15.

$$\ln(AREA_t) = \delta + \theta_1 \ln(AREA_{t-1}) + \delta_0 \ln(PRICE_t) + \delta_1 \ln(PRICE_{t-1}) + v_t$$

  (a) Suppose the first two post-sample prices are $PRICE_{T+1} = 1$ and $PRICE_{T+2} = 0.8$. Use the estimated equation to forecast ln $(AREA)$ in years $T + 1$ and $T + 2$. What are the corresponding forecasts for $AREA$?
  (b) Find 95% forecast intervals for $AREA$ in years $T + 1$ and $T + 2$. Can we forecast area accurately?
  (c) Use the results in (9.90) and the estimated equation to find lag and interim elasticities for up to four years. Interpret these values.
  (d) Find the estimated total elasticity. What does this value tell you?

9.17 The file *growth47.dat* contains 250 quarterly observations on U.S. GDP growth (percentage change in GDP) from quarter 2, 1947, to quarter 3, 2009.

(a) Estimate an AR(2) model for GDP growth and check to see if the residuals are autocorrelated. What residual autocorrelations, if any, are significantly different from zero? Does an *LM* test with two lagged errors suggest serially correlated errors?

(b) Repeat part(a) using an AR(3) model.

(c) Use the estimated AR(3) model to find 95% forecast intervals for growth in 2009Q4, 2010Q1, and 2010Q2. Check to see if the actual growth figures fell within your forecast intervals. (You can find these figures on the Federal Reserve Economic Data (FRED) web page maintained by the Federal Reserve Bank of St. Louis).

9.18 You wish to compare the performance of an AR model and an exponential smoothing model for forecasting sales revenue one week into the future.

(a) Using the data in *ex9_13.dat*, estimate an AR(2) model for *SALES*. Check to see if the errors are serially correlated.

(b) Re-estimate the AR(2) model with the last four observations ($t = 154, 155, 156$, and 157) omitted. Use the estimated model to forecast *SALES* for $t = 154$ (one week ahead). Call the forecast $SALES^{AR}_{154}$.

(c) Re-estimate the AR(2) model with the last three observations ($t = 155, 156$, and 157) omitted. Use the estimated model to forecast *SALES* for $t = 155$ (one week ahead). Call the forecast $SALES^{AR}_{155}$.

(d) Continue the process described in parts (b) and (c) to obtain forecasts $SALES^{AR}_{156}$ and $SALES^{AR}_{157}$.

(e) Follow the same procedure with an exponential smoothing model. First with the last four observations omitted, then the last three, then the last two, and then the last one, find the smoothing parameter estimate which minimizes the sum of squares of the within-sample one-step forecast errors. In each case use the estimated smoothing parameter to forecast one week ahead, obtaining the forecasts $SALES^{ES}_{154}$, $SALES^{ES}_{155}$, $SALES^{ES}_{156}$ and $SALES^{ES}_{157}$.

(f) Find the mean-square prediction errors (MSPE) $\sum_{t=154}^{157} (SALES^{AR}_t - SALES_t)^2/4$ and $\sum_{t=154}^{157} (SALES^{ES}_t - SALES_t)^2/4$. On the basis of their MSPEs, which method has led to the most accurate forecasts?

9.19 In this exercise we explore further the relationship between houses sold and the mortgage rate that was introduced in Exercise 9.6. To familiarize yourself with the variables, go back and read the question for Exercise 9.6. Then, use the data in *homes.dat* to answer the following questions:

(a) Graph *HOMES, IRATE, DHOMES*, and *DIRATE*. Which variables appear to be trending? Which ones are not trending?

(b) Estimate the following model and report the results. Are all the estimates significantly different from zero at a 1% significance level?

$$DHOMES_t = \delta + \theta_1 DHOMES_{t-1} + \delta_1 DIRATE_{t-1}$$
$$+ \delta_2 DIRATE_{t-2} + v_t \tag{9.92}$$

(c) Test the hypothesis $H_0 : \theta_1 \delta_1 = -\delta_2$ against the alternative $H_1 : \theta_1 \delta_1 \neq -\delta_2$ at a 1% significance level. What does the outcome of this test tell you?

(d) Find the correlogram of the residuals from estimating (9.92). Does it show any evidence of serial correlation in the errors?

(e) Test for serially correlated errors in (9.92) using an *LM* test with two lagged errors.

(f) Estimate the following ARDL model:

$$DHOMES_t = \delta + \theta_1 DHOMES_{t-1} + \theta_5 DHOMES_{t-5} + \delta_1 DIRATE_{t-1} \\ + \delta_3 DIRATE_{t-3} + v_t \tag{9.93}$$

This is a special case of an ARDL(5,3) model where $\theta_2 = \theta_3 = \theta_4 = \delta_0 = \delta_2 = 0$. Is this equation an improvement over (9.92)? Why?

9.20 (a) Show that (9.93) can be written as

$$HOMES_t = \delta + (\theta_1 + 1)HOMES_{t-1} - \theta_1 HOMES_{t-2} + \theta_5 DHOMES_{t-5} \\ + \delta_1 DIRATE_{t-1} + \delta_3 DIRATE_{t-3} + v_t$$

(b) If you have not already done so, estimate (9.93). Use this estimated equation and the result in part (a) to forecast the number of new one-family houses sold in April, May, and June 2010, assuming the mortgage rate in those three months remains constant at 4.75%

(c) Find 99% forecast intervals for the three forecasts made in part (b).

9.21 In (9.59) we obtained the following estimated equation for Okun's Law

$$\widehat{DU_t} = 0.3780 + 0.3501DU_{t-1} - 0.1841G_t - 0.0992G_{t-1}$$
$$\text{(se)} \quad (0.0578) \quad (0.0846) \qquad (0.0307) \qquad (0.0368)$$

(a) Use the data in *okun.dat* to reproduce these estimates.

(b) Check the correlogram of the residuals. Are there any significant autocorrelations?

(c) Carry out *LM* tests for autocorrelation on the residuals for error lags up to four.

(d) Re-estimate the equation with variables DU_{t-2} and G_{t-2} added separately and then together. Are their coefficients significantly different from zero?

(e) What do you conclude about the specification in (9.59)?

9.22 An important relationship in macroeconomics is the consumption function. The file *consumptn.dat* contains quarterly data from 1960Q1 to 2009Q4 on the percentage changes in disposable personal income and personal consumption expenditures. We describe these variables as income growth (*INCGWTH*) and consumption growth (*CONGWTH*). To ensure that the same number of observations (197) are used for estimation in each of the models that we consider, use as your sample period 1960Q4 to 2009Q4. Where relevant, lagged variables on the right-hand side of equations can use values prior to 1960Q4.

(a) Graph the time series for *CONGWTH* and *INCGWTH*. Include a horizontal line at the mean of each series. Do the series appear to fluctuate around a constant mean?

(b) Estimate the model $CONGWTH_t = \delta + \delta_0 INCGWTH_t + v_t$. Interpret the estimate for δ_0. Check for serially correlated errors using the residual correlogram, and an *LM* test with two lagged errors. What do you conclude?

(c) Estimate the model $CONGWTH_t = \delta + \theta_1 CONGWTH_{t-1} + \delta_0 INCGWTH_t + v_t$. Is this model an improvement over that in part (b)? Is the estimate for θ_1

significantly different from zero? Have the values for the AIC and the SC gone down? Has serial correlation in the errors been eliminated?

(d) Add the variable $CONGWTH_{t-2}$ to the model in part (c) and re-estimate. Is this model an improvement over that in part (c)? Is the estimate for θ_2 (the coefficient of $CONGWTH_{t-2}$) significantly different from zero? Have the values for the AIC and the SC gone down? Has serial correlation in the errors been eliminated?

(e) Add the variable $INCGWTH_{t-1}$ to the model in part (d) and re-estimate. Is this model an improvement over that in part (d)? Is the estimate for δ_1 (the coefficient of $INCGWTH_{t-1}$) significantly different from zero? Have the values for the AIC and the SC gone down? Has serial correlation in the errors been eliminated?

(f) Does the addition of $CONGWTH_{t-3}$ or $INCGWTH_{t-2}$ improve the model in part (e)?

(g) Drop the variable $CONGWTH_{t-1}$ from the model in part (e) and re-estimate. Why might you consider dropping this variable? The model you should be estimating is

$$CONGWTH_t = \delta + \theta_2 CONGWTH_{t-2} + \delta_0 INCGWTH_t \\ + \delta_1 INCGWTH_{t-1} + v_t \tag{9.94}$$

Does this model have lower AIC and SC values than that in (e)? Is there any evidence of serially correlated errors?

9.23 If you have not already done so, use the data in *consumptn.dat* and the sample period 1960Q4 to 2009Q4 to estimate (9.94). Given that $INCGWTH_{2010Q1} = 0.6$, $INCGWTH_{2010Q2} = 0.8$, and $INCGWTH_{2010Q3} = 0.7$, find 90% forecast intervals for consumption growth in 2010Q1, 2010Q2, and 2010Q3. Comment on these intervals.

9.24 Consider the infinite lag representation of (9.94) that we write as

$$CONGWTH_t = \alpha + \sum_{s=0}^{\infty} \beta_s INCGWTH_{t-s} + e_t$$

(a) Derive expressions that can be used to calculate the β_s from $\theta_2, \delta_0,$ and δ_1.

(b) Find estimates for the one-, two-, and three-quarter delay and interim multipliers, and the total multiplier. Interpret these estimates.

9.25 In this question we investigate the effect of wage changes on the inflation rate. Such effects can be from the demand side or the supply side. On the supply side, we expect wage increases to increase costs of production and to drive up prices. On the demand side, wage increases mean greater disposable income, and a greater demand for goods and services that also pushes up prices. Irrespective of the line of reasoning, the relationship between wage changes and inflation is likely to be a dynamic one; it takes time for wage changes to impact on inflation. To investigate this dynamic relationship, we use quarterly data on U.S. inflation (*INF*) and wage growth (*WGWTH*) from 1970Q2 to 2010Q1. These data can be found in the file *infln_wage.dat*.

(a) Graph the time series for *INF* and *WGWTH*. Include a horizontal line at the mean of each series. Do the series appear to fluctuate around a constant mean?

(b) Estimate the model $INF_t = \delta + \delta_0 WGWTH_t + v_t$. Interpret the estimate for δ_0. Check for serially correlated errors using the residual correlogram, and an *LM* test with two lagged errors. What do you conclude?

(c) Estimate the model $INF_t = \delta + \theta_1 INF_{t-1} + \delta_0 WGWTH_t + v_t$. Find estimates for the impact multiplier and the total multiplier for the effect of a change in wage growth on inflation. How do these values compare with the estimate for δ_0 from part (b)? (*Hint*: Use (9.90) with $\delta_1 = 0$ and sum the geometric progression to get the total multiplier.)

(d) Did inclusion of INF_{t-1} in the model eliminate serial correlation in the errors? Report any significant residual autocorrelations from the equation in part (c) and the results from *LM* tests with two and three lagged residuals.

(e) Add first INF_{t-2}, and then INF_{t-3}, to the model in part (c). In each case report the results of correlogram and *LM* checks for serially correlated errors.

(f) Omit INF_{t-2} from the second model estimated in part (e), and estimate the resulting model

$$INF_t = \delta + \theta_1 INF_{t-1} + \theta_3 INF_{t-3} + \delta_0 WGWTH_t + v_t \qquad (9.95)$$

Why might you consider dropping INF_{t-2}? Did its omission lead to a fall in the AIC and SC? Try adding $WGWTH_{t-1}$. Does its inclusion improve the equation?

9.26 If you have not already done so, use the data in *infln_wage.dat* to estimate (9.95). Given that $WGWTH_{2010Q2} = 0.6$, $WGWTH_{2010Q3} = 0.5$, $WGWTH_{2010Q4} = 0.7$, and $WGWTH_{2011Q1} = 0.4$, find 95% forecast intervals for inflation in 2010Q2, 2010Q3, 2010Q4, and 2011Q1. Does knowing wage growth tell you much about future inflation?

9.27 Consider the infinite lag representation of (9.95) that we write as

$$INF_t = \alpha + \sum_{s=0}^{\infty} \beta_s WGWTH_{t-s} + e_t$$

(a) Derive expressions that can be used to calculate α and the β_s from θ_1, θ_3, δ, and δ_0.

(b) Estimate the rate of inflation when $WGWTH$ remains at $WGWTH = 0$. Use the estimates from (9.95) to test the hypothesis that the rate of inflation is zero when wage growth is zero.

(c) Estimate the rate of inflation when wage growth is constant at 0.2% per quarter.

(d) Graph the delay multipliers for lags up to 12 quarters. Comment on what this graph shows.

(e) Graph the interim multipliers for lags up to 12 quarters. Comment on what this graph shows.

(f) Suppose $WGWTH$ has been constant for a long period into the past. Then, in quarter $T + 1$ it increases by 0.1%, in quarter $T + 2$ it increases by another 0.1%, and in quarter $T + 3$ it returns to its original level. Estimate the amount by which inflation will change in quarters $T + 1$, $T + 2$, $T + 3$, $T + 4$, and $T + 5$.

Appendix 9A The Durbin–Watson Test

In Sections 9.3 and 9.4 two testing procedures for testing for autocorrelated errors, the sample correlogram and a Lagrange multiplier test, were considered. These are two large sample tests; their test statistics have their specified distributions in large samples. An alternative test, one that is exact in the sense that its distribution does not rely on a large sample approximation, is the Durbin-Watson test. It was developed in 1950 and for a long time was the standard test for $H_0 : \rho = 0$ in the AR(1) error model $e_t = \rho e_{t-1} + v_t$. It is used less frequently today because of the need to examine upper and lower bounds, as we describe below, and because its distribution no longer holds when the equation contains a lagged dependent variable.

It is assumed that the v_t are independent random errors with distribution $N(0, \sigma_v^2)$, and that the alternative hypothesis is one of positive autocorrelation. That is,

$$H_0 : \rho = 0 \qquad H_1 : \rho > 0$$

The statistic used to test H_0 against H_1 is

$$d = \frac{\sum\limits_{t=2}^{T} (\hat{e}_t - \hat{e}_{t-1})^2}{\sum\limits_{t=1}^{T} \hat{e}_t^2} \tag{9A.1}$$

where the $\hat{e}_t$ are the least squares residuals $\hat{e}_t = y_t - b_1 - b_2 x_t$. To see why d is a reasonable statistic for testing for autocorrelation, we expand (9A.1) as

$$
\begin{aligned}
d &= \frac{\sum\limits_{t=2}^{T} \hat{e}_t^2 + \sum\limits_{t=2}^{T} \hat{e}_{t-1}^2 - 2 \sum\limits_{t=2}^{T} \hat{e}_t \hat{e}_{t-1}}{\sum\limits_{t=1}^{T} \hat{e}_t^2} \\[2mm]
&= \frac{\sum\limits_{t=2}^{T} \hat{e}_t^2}{\sum\limits_{t=1}^{T} \hat{e}_t^2} + \frac{\sum\limits_{t=2}^{T} \hat{e}_{t-1}^2}{\sum\limits_{t=1}^{T} \hat{e}_t^2} - 2 \frac{\sum\limits_{t=2}^{T} \hat{e}_t \hat{e}_{t-1}}{\sum\limits_{t=1}^{T} \hat{e}_t^2} \\[2mm]
&\approx 1 + 1 - 2r_1
\end{aligned}
\tag{9A.2}
$$

The last line in (9A.2) holds only approximately. The first two terms differ from 1 through the exclusion of $\hat{e}_1^2$ and $\hat{e}_T^2$ from the first and second numerator summations, respectively. Thus, we have

$$d \approx 2(1 - r_1) \tag{9A.3}$$

If the estimated value of ρ is $r_1 = 0$, then the Durbin-Watson statistic $d \approx 2$, which is taken as an indication that the model errors are not autocorrelated. If the estimate of ρ happened to be $r_1 = 1$ then $d \approx 0$, and thus a low value for the Durbin-Watson statistic implies that the model errors are correlated, and $\rho > 0$.

The question we need to answer is: How close to zero does the value of the test statistic have to be before we conclude that the errors are correlated? In other words, what is a critical value d_c such that we reject H_0 when $d \le d_c$? Determination of a critical value and a rejection region for the test requires knowledge of the probability distribution of the test statistic under the assumption that the null hypothesis, $H_0 : \rho = 0$, is true. For a 5% significance level, knowledge of the probability distribution $f(d)$ under H_0 allows us to find d_c such that $P(d \le d_c) = 0.05$. Then, as illustrated in Figure 9A.1, we reject H_0 if $d \le d_c$ and fail to reject H_0 if $d > d_c$. Alternatively, we can state the test procedure in terms of the p-value of the test. For this one-tail test, the p-value is given by the area under $f(d)$ to the left of

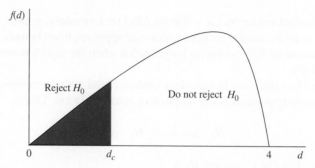

FIGURE **9A.1** Testing for positive autocorrelation.

the calculated value of d. Thus, if the p-value is less than or equal to 0.05, it follows that $d \leq d_c$, and H_0 is rejected. If the p-value is greater than 0.05, then $d > d_c$, and H_0 is accepted.

In any event, whether the test result is found by comparing d with d_c or by computing the p-value, the probability distribution $f(d)$ is required. A difficulty associated with $f(d)$, and one that we have not previously encountered when using other test statistics, is that this probability distribution depends on the values of the explanatory variables. Different sets of explanatory variables lead to different distributions for d. Because $f(d)$ depends on the values of the explanatory variables, the critical value d_c for any given problem will also depend on the values of the explanatory variables. This property means that it is impossible to tabulate critical values that can be used for every possible problem. With other test statistics, such as t, F, and χ^2, the tabulated critical values are relevant for all models.

There are two ways to overcome this problem. The first way is to use software that computes the p-value for the explanatory variables in the model under consideration. Instead of comparing the calculated d value with some tabulated values of d_c, we get our computer to calculate the p-value of the test. If this p-value is less than the specified significance level, $H_0 : \rho = 0$ is rejected, and we conclude that the errors are correlated.

In the Phillips curve example the calculated value for the Durbin-Watson statistic from the estimated equation in (9.22) is $d = 0.8873$. Is this value sufficiently close to zero (or sufficiently less than 2), to reject H_0 and conclude that autocorrelation exists? Using suitable software,[16] we find that

$$p\text{-value} = \Pr(d \leq 0.8873) = 0.0000$$

The p-value turns out to less than 10^{-6}, a value much less than a conventional 0.05 significance level; we conclude, therefore, that the equation's error is positively auto-correlated.

9A.1 THE DURBIN–WATSON BOUNDS TEST

In the absence of software that computes a p-value, a test known as the bounds test can be used to partially overcome the problem of not having general critical values. Durbin and Watson considered two other statistics d_L and d_U whose probability distributions do not depend on the explanatory variables and which have the property that

$$d_L < d < d_U$$

---

[16] The software packages SHAZAM and SAS, for example, will compute the exact Durbin-Watson p-value.

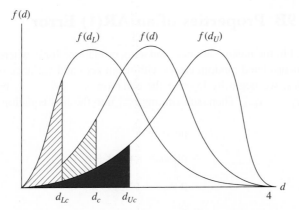

$FIGURE$ $9A.2$ Upper and lower critical value bounds for the Durbin-Watson test.

That is, irrespective of the explanatory variables in the model under consideration, d will be bounded by an upper bound d_U and a lower bound d_L. The relationship between the probability distributions $f(d_L), f(d)$, and $f(d_U)$ is depicted in Figure 9A.2. Let d_{Lc} be the 5% critical value from the probability distribution for d_L. That is, d_{Lc} is such that $P(d_L < d_{Lc}) = 0.05$. Similarly, let d_{Uc} be such that $P(d_U < d_{Uc}) = 0.05$. Since the probability distributions $f(d_L)$ and $f(d_U)$ do not depend on the explanatory variables, it is possible to tabulate the critical values d_{Lc} and d_{Uc}. These values do depend on T and K, but it is possible to tabulate the alternative values for different T and K.

Thus, in Figure 9A.2 we have three critical values. The values d_{Lc} and d_{Uc} can be readily tabulated. The value d_c, the one in which we are really interested for testing purposes, cannot be found without a specialized computer program. However, it is clear from the figure that if the calculated value d is such that $d < d_{Lc}$, then it must follow that $d < d_c$, and H_0 is rejected. Also, if $d > d_{Uc}$, then it follows that $d > d_c$, and H_0 is not rejected. If it turns out that $d_{Lc} < d < d_{Uc}$, then, because we do not know the location of d_c, we cannot be sure whether to accept or reject. These considerations led Durbin and Watson to suggest the following decision rules, known collectively as the Durbin-Watson *bounds test*:

If $d < d_{Lc}$, reject $H_0 : \rho = 0$ and accept $H_1 : \rho > 0$;

if $d > d_{Uc}$, do not reject $H_0 : \rho = 0$;

if $d_{Lc} < d < d_{Uc}$, the test is inconclusive.

The presence of a range of values where no conclusion can be reached is an obvious disadvantage of the test. For this reason it is preferable to have software which can calculate the required p-value if such software is available.

The critical bounds for the Phillips curve example for $T = 90$ are[17]

$$d_{Lc} = 1.635 \quad d_{Uc} = 1.679$$

Since $d = 0.8873 < d_{Lc}$, we conclude that $d < d_c$, and hence we reject H_0; there is evidence to suggest that the errors are serially correlated.

---

[17] These bounds can be found from the Dubin-Watson tables on the website www.principlesofeconometrics.com.

Appendix 9B Properties of an AR(1) Error

We are interested in the mean, variance, and autocorrelations for e_t where $e_t = \rho e_{t-1} + v_t$ and the v_t are uncorrelated random errors with mean zero and variance σ_v^2. To derive the desired properties, we begin by lagging the equation $e_t = \rho e_{t-1} + v_t$ by one period, to obtain $e_{t-1} = \rho e_{t-2} + v_{t-1}$. Then, substituting e_{t-1} into the first equation yields

$$
\begin{aligned}
e_t &= \rho e_{t-1} + v_t \\
&= \rho(\rho e_{t-2} + v_{t-1}) + v_t \\
&= \rho^2 e_{t-2} + \rho v_{t-1} + v_t
\end{aligned}
\tag{9B.1}
$$

Lagging $e_t = \rho e_{t-1} + v_t$ by two periods gives $e_{t-2} = \rho e_{t-3} + v_{t-2}$. Substituting this expression for e_{t-2} into (9B.1) yields

$$
\begin{aligned}
e_t &= \rho^2(\rho e_{t-3} + v_{t-2}) + \rho v_{t-1} + v_t \\
&= \rho^3 e_{t-3} + \rho^2 v_{t-2} + \rho v_{t-1} + v_t
\end{aligned}
\tag{9B.2}
$$

Repeating this process k times and rearranging the order of the lagged v's yields

$$
e_t = \rho^k e_{t-k} + v_t + \rho v_{t-1} + \rho^2 v_{t-2} + \cdots + \rho^{k-1} v_{t-k+1}
\tag{9B.3}
$$

If we view the process as operating for a long time into the past, then we can let $k \to \infty$. This makes the first and last terms, $\rho^k e_{t-k}$ and $\rho^{k-1} v_{t-k+1}$, go to zero, because $-1 < \rho < 1$. The result is

$$
e_t = v_t + \rho v_{t-1} + \rho^2 v_{t-2} + \rho^3 v_{t-3} + \cdots
\tag{9B.4}
$$

The regression error e_t can be written as a weighted sum of the current and past values of the uncorrelated error v_t. This is an important result. It means that all past values of the v's have an impact on the current error e_t and that this impact feeds through into y_t through the regression equation. Notice, however, that the impact of the past v's declines the further we go into the past. The weights that are attached to the lagged v's are ρ, ρ^2, ρ^3, ... Because $-1 < \rho < 1$, these weights decline geometrically as we consider past v's that are more distant from the current period. Eventually, they become negligible.

Equation (9B.4) can be used to find the properties of the e_t. Its mean is zero, because

$$
\begin{aligned}
E(e_t) &= E(v_t) + \rho E(v_{t-1}) + \rho^2 E(v_{t-2}) + \rho^3 E(v_{t-3}) + \cdots \\
&= 0 + \rho \times 0 + \rho^2 \times 0 + \rho^3 \times 0 + \cdots \\
&= 0
\end{aligned}
$$

To find the variance, we write

$$
\begin{aligned}
\text{var}(e_t) &= \text{var}(v_t) + \rho^2 \text{var}(v_{t-1}) + \rho^4 \text{var}(v_{t-2}) + \rho^6 \text{var}(v_{t-3}) + \cdots \\
&= \sigma_v^2 + \rho^2 \sigma_v^2 + \rho^4 \sigma_v^2 + \rho^6 \sigma_v^2 + \cdots \\
&= \sigma_v^2 (1 + \rho^2 + \rho^4 + \rho^6 + \cdots) \\
&= \frac{\sigma_v^2}{1 - \rho^2}
\end{aligned}
$$

In the above derivation zero covariance terms are ignored because the v's are uncorrelated. The result in the last line follows from rules for the sum of a geometric progression. Using shorthand notation, we have $\sigma_e^2 = \sigma_v^2/(1 - \rho^2)$; the variance of e depends on that for v and the value for ρ.

To find the covariance between two e's that are one period apart, we use (9B.4) and its lag to write

$$
\begin{aligned}
\text{cov}(e_t, e_{t-1}) &= E(e_t e_{t-1}) \\
&= E\big[\big(v_t + \rho v_{t-1} + \rho^2 v_{t-2} + \rho^3 v_{t-3} + \cdots\big) \\
&\qquad \big(v_{t-1} + \rho v_{t-2} + \rho^2 v_{t-3} + \rho^3 v_{t-4} \cdots\big)\big] \\
&= \rho E\big(v_{t-1}^2\big) + \rho^3 E\big(v_{t-2}^2\big) + \rho^5 E\big(v_{t-3}^2\big) + \cdots \\
&= \rho \sigma_v^2\big(1 + \rho^2 + \rho^4 + \cdots\big) \\
&= \frac{\rho \sigma_v^2}{1 - \rho^2}
\end{aligned}
$$

When the second line in the above derivation is expanded, only squared terms with the same subscript are retained. Because the v's are uncorrelated, the cross-product terms with different time subscripts will have zero expectation, and are dropped from the third line. To obtain the fourth line from the third line, we have used $E(v_{t-k}^2) = \text{var}(v_{t-k}) = \sigma_v^2$ for all lags k.

In a similar way, we can show that the covariance between errors that are k periods apart is

$$
\text{cov}(e_t, e_{t-k}) = \frac{\rho^k \sigma_v^2}{1 - \rho^2} \qquad k > 0
$$

Appendix 9C Generalized Least Squares Estimation

We are considering the simple regression model with AR(1) errors

$$
y_t = \beta_1 + \beta_2 x_t + e_t \qquad e_t = \rho e_{t-1} + v_t
$$

Our objective is to obtain the generalized least squares estimator for β_1 and β_2 by transforming the model so that it has a new uncorrelated homoskedastic error term, enabling us to apply least squares to the transformed model. To specify the transformed model we begin with (9.44), which is

$$
y_t = \beta_1 + \beta_2 x_t + \rho y_{t-1} - \rho \beta_1 - \rho \beta_2 x_{t-1} + v_t \tag{9C.1}
$$

and then rearrange it to give

$$
y_t - \rho y_{t-1} = \beta_1(1 - \rho) + \beta_2(x_t - \rho x_{t-1}) + v_t \tag{9C.2}
$$

After defining the following transformed variables

$$
y_t^* = y_t - \rho y_{t-1} \qquad x_{t2}^* = x_t - \rho x_{t-1} \qquad x_{t1}^* = 1 - \rho
$$

we can rewrite (9C.2) as

$$y_t^* = x_{t1}^* \beta_1 + x_{t2}^* \beta_2 + v_t \tag{9C.3}$$

We have formed a new model with transformed variables y_t^*, x_{t1}^*, and x_{t2}^* and, *importantly*, with an error term that is *not* the correlated e_t, but the uncorrelated v_t that we assumed to be distributed $(0, \sigma_v^2)$. We would expect application of least squares to (9C.3) to yield the best linear unbiased estimator for β_1 and β_2.

There are two additional problems that we need to solve, however:

1. Because lagged values of y_t and x_t had to be formed, only $(T-1)$ new observations were created by the transformation. We have values $(y_t^*, x_{t1}^*, x_{t2}^*)$ for $t = 2, 3, \ldots, T$, but we have no $(y_1^*, x_{11}^*, x_{12}^*)$.

2. The value of the autoregressive parameter ρ is not known. Since y_t^*, x_{t1}^* and x_{t2}^* depend on ρ, we cannot compute these transformed observations without estimating ρ.

Considering the second problem first, we can use the sample correlation r_1 defined in (9.21) as an estimator for ρ. Alternatively, (9C.1) can be rewritten as

$$y_t - \beta_1 - \beta_2 x_t = \rho(y_{t-1} - \beta_1 - \beta_2 x_{t-1}) + v_t \tag{9C.4}$$

which is the same as $e_t = \rho e_{t-1} + v_t$. After replacing β_1 and β_2 with the least squares estimates b_1 and b_1, least squares can be applied to (9C.4) to estimate ρ.

Equations (9C.3) and (9C.4) can be estimated iteratively. That is, we use $\hat{\rho}$ from (9C.4) to estimate β_1 and β_2 from (9C.3). We then use these new estimates for β_1 and β_2 in (9C.4) to re-estimate ρ, which we then use again in (9C.3) to re-estimate β_1 and β_2, and so on. This iterative procedure is known as the Cochrane-Orcutt estimator. On convergence it is identical to the nonlinear least squares estimator described in Section 9.3.2.

What about the problem of having $(T-1)$ instead of T transformed observations? One way to solve this problem is to ignore it and to proceed with estimation on the basis of the $(T-1)$ observations. That is the strategy adopted by the estimators we have considered so far. If T is large, it is a reasonable strategy. However, if we wish to improve efficiency by including a transformation of the first observation, we need to create a transformed error that has the same variance as the errors $(v_2, v_3, \ldots, v_T)$.

The first observation in the regression model is

$$y_1 = \beta_1 + x_1 \beta_2 + e_1$$

with error variance $\text{var}(e_1) = \sigma_e^2 = \sigma_v^2 / (1 - \rho^2)$. The transformation that yields an error variance of σ_v^2 is multiplication by $\sqrt{1 - \rho^2}$. The result is

$$\sqrt{1 - \rho^2} y_1 = \sqrt{1 - \rho^2} \beta_1 + \sqrt{1 - \rho^2} x_1 \beta_2 + \sqrt{1 - \rho^2} e_1$$

or

$$y_1^* = x_{11}^* \beta_1 + x_{12}^* \beta_2 + e_1^* \tag{9C.5}$$

where

$$y_1^* = \sqrt{1 - \rho^2}y_1 \qquad x_{11}^* = \sqrt{1 - \rho^2}$$
$$x_{12}^* = \sqrt{1 - \rho^2}x_1 \qquad e_1^* = \sqrt{1 - \rho^2}e_1$$

(9C.6)

To confirm that the variance of e_1^* is the same as that of the errors $(v_2, v_3, \ldots, v_T)$, note that

$$\text{var}(e_1^*) = (1 - \rho^2)\text{var}(e_1) = (1 - \rho^2)\frac{\sigma_v^2}{1 - \rho^2} = \sigma_v^2$$

We also require that e_1^* be uncorrelated with $(v_2, v_3, \ldots, v_T)$. This result will hold because each of the v_t does not depend on any past values for e_t. The transformed first observation in (9C.5) can be used with the remaining transformed observations in (9C.3) to obtained generalized least squares estimates that utilize all T observations. This procedure is sometimes known as the Prais-Winsten estimator.

Chapter *10*

Random Regressors and Moment-Based Estimation

Learning Objectives

Based on the material in this chapter you should be able to:

1. Explain why we might sometimes consider explanatory variables in a regression model to be random.

2. Explain the difference between finite sample and large sample properties of estimators.

3. Give an intuitive explanation of why correlation between a random x and the error term causes the least squares estimator to be inconsistent.

4. Describe the "errors-in-variables" problem in econometrics and its consequences for the least squares estimator.

5. Describe the properties of a good instrumental variable.

6. Discuss how the method of moments can be used to derive the least squares and instrumental variables estimators, paying particular attention to the assumptions upon which the derivations are based.

7. Explain why it is important for an instrumental variable to be highly correlated with the random explanatory variable for which it is an instrument.

8. Describe how instrumental variables estimation is carried out in the case of surplus instruments.

9. State the large-sample distribution of the instrumental variables estimator for the simple linear regression model, and how it can be used for the construction of interval estimates and hypothesis tests.

10. Describe a test for the existence of correlation between the error term and the explanatory variables in a model, explaining the null and alternative hypotheses, and the consequences of rejecting the null hypothesis.

Keywords

asymptotic properties	instrumental variable	random sampling
conditional expectation	instrumental variable	reduced form equation
endogenous variables	estimator	sample moments
errors-in-variables	just identified equations	simultaneous equations bias
exogenous variables	large sample properties	test of surplus moment conditions
finite sample properties	over identified equations	two-stage least squares estimation
first stage regression	population moments	weak instruments
Hausman test		

In this chapter we reconsider the linear regression model. We will initially discuss the simple linear regression model, but our comments apply to the general model as well. The usual assumptions are SR1–SR6, given in Chapter 2.2.1. In Chapter 8, we relaxed the assumption $\text{var}(e) = \sigma^2$ that the error variance is the same for all observations. In Chapter 9 we considered regressions with time-series data in which the assumption of serially uncorrelated errors, $\text{cov}(e_i, e_j) = 0$, for $i \neq j$, cannot be maintained.

In this chapter we relax the assumption that variable x is not random. You may have wondered about the validity of this assumption. In our original discussion of random variables in the Probability Primer, Section P.1, we said that a variable is random if its value is unknown until an experiment is performed. In an economist's nonexperimental world, the values of x and y are usually revealed at the same time, making x and y random in the same way. This was recognized in the time-series context in Chapter 9.2.2.

We have considered the variable x to be nonrandom for several reasons. First, when regression is based on data from controlled experiments, or if we are conditioning our results upon the sample we have, it is a proper assumption. Secondly, it simplifies the algebra of least squares. Thirdly, even if x is random, the properties of the least squares estimator still hold under slightly modified assumptions.

The purpose of this chapter is to discuss regression models in which x is random and correlated with the error term e. We will

- Discuss the conditions under which having a random x is not a problem, and how to test whether our data satisfies these conditions.

- Present cases in which the randomness of x causes the least squares estimator to fail. These are cases in which x is correlated with the error e.

- Provide estimators that have good properties even when x is random and correlated with the error e.

10.1 Linear Regression with Random x's

Let us modify the usual simple regression assumptions as follows:

A10.1 $y = \beta_1 + \beta_2 x + e$ correctly describes the relationship between y and x in the population, where β_1 and β_2 are unknown (fixed) parameters and e is an unobservable random error term.

A10.2   The data pairs $(x_i, y_i), i = 1, \ldots, N$, are obtained by **random sampling**. That is, the data pairs are collected from the same population, by a process in which each pair is independent of every other pair. Such data are said to be independent and identically distributed.

A10.3 $E(e|x) = 0$. The expected value of the error term e, **conditional** on any value of x, is zero.

A10.4   In the sample, x must take at least two different values.

A10.5 $\text{var}(e|x) = \sigma^2$. The variance of the error term, conditional on any x, is a constant σ^2.

A10.6   The distribution of the error term is normal.

There is only one new assumption in this list. That is, assumption A10.2 states that both y and x are obtained by a sampling process, and thus are random. Also, assuming that the pairs are independent implies that assumption SR4 holds as well. In the other assumptions, all we have done is bring back the explicit conditioning notation introduced in Chapter 2. Recognize that the random sampling assumption A10.2 is appropriate for cross-section data but not time-series data. The assumptions for time-series data were discussed in Chapter 9.

Because it plays a key role in the properties of the least squares estimator, let us clearly state the interpretation of A10.3, $E(e|x) = 0$. This assumption implies that we have (i) omitted no important variables, (ii) that we have used the correct functional form, and (iii) that there exist no factors that cause the error term e to be correlated with x.

Although the first two of these implications are intuitive, the third may not be.

- If $E(e|x) = 0$, then we can show that it is also true that x and e are uncorrelated, and that $\text{cov}(x, e) = 0$. Explanatory variables that are **not correlated with the error term** are called **exogenous variables**. This terminology is used in various disciplines, and means "determined outside of a system." For example, in a supply and demand model, changes in supply due to events like hurricanes or earthquakes are "exogenous." The econometric analysis of economic systems is considered in Chapter 11. There you will gain a deeper understanding of the term.

- Conversely, if x and e are correlated, then $\text{cov}(x, e) \neq 0$ and we can show that $E(e|x) \neq 0$. Explanatory variables that are **correlated with the error term** are called **endogenous variables**. This means "determined within a system." For example, in a supply and demand model, equilibrium price and quantity are endogenous.

Thus in addition to the usual specification errors of omitted variables and an incorrect functional form, assumption A10.3 eliminates correlation between a random explanatory variable x and the random error term e. We discuss the consequences of correlation between x and e in Section 10.1.3. In Section 10.2 we will explore some cases in which we can anticipate that correlation will exist between x and e. In each such case the usual least squares estimation procedure is no longer appropriate.

10.1.1   THE SMALL SAMPLE PROPERTIES OF THE LEAST SQUARES ESTIMATOR

In Chapter 2 we proved the Gauss-Markov theorem. The result that under the classical assumptions, and fixed x's, the least squares estimator is the best linear unbiased estimator, is a **finite sample**, or a **small sample**. What this means is that the result does not depend on the size of the sample. It holds in every sample, whether the sample size $N = 20, 50$, or 10,000.

The finite sample properties of the least squares estimator when x is random can be summarized as follows: Under assumptions A10.1–A10.6,[1]

1. The least squares estimator is unbiased.

2. The least squares estimator is the best linear unbiased estimator of the regression parameters, and the usual estimator of σ^2 is unbiased.

3. The distributions of the least squares estimators, conditional upon the x's, are normal, and their variances are estimated in the usual way. The usual interval estimation and hypothesis testing procedures are valid.

What these results say is that if x is random, as long as the data are obtained by random sampling and the other usual assumptions hold, no changes in our regression methods are required.

10.1.2 Large Sample Properties of the Least Squares Estimator

In Chapter 5, Appendices 5B.1–5B.2 we introduced "large sample," or "asymptotic" analysis. If you have not read those appendices, *please do so now*.

For the purposes of a "large sample" analysis of the least squares estimator, it is convenient to replace assumption A10.3 by

A10.3* $E(e) = 0$ and $\mathrm{cov}(x, e) = 0$

We can make this replacement because if assumption A10.3 is true, it follows that A10.3* is true. That is, $E(e|x) = 0 \Rightarrow \mathrm{cov}(x, e) = 0$ and $E(e|x) = 0 \Rightarrow E(e) = 0$. These relations are proven in Appendix 10A. Introducing assumption A10.3* is convenient because we want to investigate how to estimate models in which a random regressor x is correlated with the error term e—that is, when we violate the assumption that $\mathrm{cov}(x, e) = 0$. While it does not seem like much of a change, because A10.3* is actually a weaker assumption than A10.3, under A10.3* we cannot show that the least squares estimator is unbiased, or that any of the other finite sample properties hold.

What we can say is the following: Under assumptions A10.1, A10.2, A10.3*, A10.4, and A10.5, the least squares estimators

1. Are consistent. That is, they converge in probability to the true parameter values as $N \rightarrow \infty$.

2. Have approximate normal distributions in large samples, whether the errors are normally distributed or not. Furthermore, our usual interval estimators and test statistics are valid, if the sample is large.

3. If assumption A10.3* is *not* true, and in particular if $\mathrm{cov}(x,e) \neq 0$ so that x and e are correlated, then the least squares estimators are inconsistent. They do not converge to the true parameter values even in very large samples. Furthermore, none of our usual hypothesis testing or interval estimation procedures are valid.

---

[1] An advanced reference for these results is William Greene (2008) *Econometric Analysis, 6e*, Pearson Prentice-Hall, pp. 43–58.

When x is random, the relationship between x and e is the crucial factor when deciding whether least squares estimation is appropriate or not. If the error term e is correlated with x (or any x_k in the multiple regression model), then the least squares estimator fails. In the next section we explain why correlation between x and e leads to the failure of the least squares estimator.

10.1.3 Why Least Squares Estimation Fails

In this section we provide an intuitive explanation why the least squares estimator fails when $\text{cov}(x, e) \neq 0$. An algebraic proof is given in Appendix 10B. The regression model **data generation process** adds a random error e to the systematic regression function $E(y|x) = \beta_1 + \beta_2 x$ to obtain the observed outcome y. In Figure 10.1(a) are positively correlated x and e values. In Figure 10.1(b) the positively-sloped regression function $E(y|x) = \beta_1 + \beta_2 x$, the object of our analysis, is the solid line. For each value of x, add to $E(y|x) = \beta_1 + \beta_2 x$

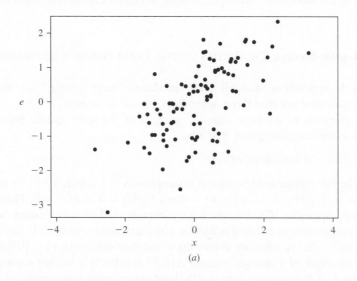

(a)

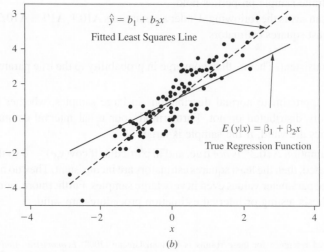

(b)

FIGURE 10.1 (a) Correlated x and e. (b) Plot of data, true and fitted regression functions.

the random error *e* to obtain *y* data values, $y = \beta_1 + \beta_2 x + e$, shown as dots in Figure 10.1(b). As you see, the true regression function does not pass through the middle of the data in this case, and that is because of the correlation between *x* and *e*. The *y* values for larger *x* values have positive errors *e*. The *y* values for smaller *x* values have negative errors *e*.

Least squares estimation leads to a fitted line passing through the middle of the data, shown as a dashed line in Figure 10.1(b). The slope of the fitted line (the estimate b_2) overestimates the true slope of the regression function, $\beta_2 > 0$. The least squares estimator attributes all variation in *y* to variation in *x*. In this case, however, the variation in *y* is from two sources: changes in *x* and changes in *e*; and these changes have a positive correlation. If we think about the effect of changes in *x* and *e* on *y*, we have

$$\Delta y = \beta_2 \Delta x + \Delta e$$
$$(+) \qquad (+) \quad (+)$$

If *x* and *e* are positively correlated and $\beta_2 > 0$, increases in the *x* and *e* values combine to increase *y*. In the least squares estimation process, all the change (increase) in *y* is attributed to the effect of the change (increase) in *x*, and thus the least squares estimator will overestimate β_2.

Throughout this chapter we use the relation between wages and years of education as an example. In this case the omitted variable "intelligence" is in the regression error, and it is likely to be positively correlated with the years of education a person receives, with more intelligent individuals choosing to obtain more years of education. When regressing wage on years of education, increases in wages are all attributed to increases in education by the least squares estimator. The effect of education is overstated because some of the increase in wages is also due to higher intelligence.

The statistical consequences of correlation between *x* and *e* is that the least squares estimator is biased—and this bias will not disappear no matter how large the sample. Consequently the least squares estimator is **inconsistent** when there is correlation between *x* and *e*. In the following section we describe some common situations in which there is correlation between *x* and *e*, causing the least squares estimator to fail.

10.2 Cases in Which *x* and *e* Are Correlated

There are several common situations in which the least squares estimator fails due to the presence of correlation between an explanatory variable and the error term. When an explanatory variable and the error term are correlated, the explanatory variable is said to be **endogenous**. This term comes from simultaneous equations models, which we will consider in Chapter 11, and means "determined within the system." Using this terminology when an explanatory variable is correlated with the regression error, one is said to have an "endogeneity problem."

10.2.1 MEASUREMENT ERROR

The **errors-in-variables** problem occurs when an explanatory variable is measured with error. If we measure an explanatory variable with error, then it is correlated with the error term, and the least squares estimator is inconsistent. As an illustration, consider the following important example. Let us assume that an individual's personal saving, like their consumption, is based on his or her "permanent" or long-run income. Let *y* = annual savings and let $x^* =$ the permanent annual income of a person. A simple regression model representing this relationship is

$$y = \beta_1 + \beta_2 x^* + v \tag{10.1}$$

We have asterisked (*) the permanent income variable because it is difficult, if not impossible, to observe. For the purposes of a regression, suppose that we attempt to measure permanent income using $x =$ current income. Current income is a measure of permanent income, but it does not measure permanent income exactly. It is sometimes called a **proxy variable**. To capture this feature, let us specify that

$$x = x^* + u \tag{10.2}$$

where u is a random disturbance, with mean 0 and variance σ_u^2. With this statement, we are admitting that observed current income only approximates permanent income, and consequently that we have measured permanent income with error. Furthermore, let us assume that u is independent of v and serially uncorrelated. When we use x in the regression in place of x^*, we do so by replacement. That is, substitute $x^* = x - u$ into (10.1) to obtain

$$
\begin{aligned}
y &= \beta_1 + \beta_2 x^* + v \\
&= \beta_1 + \beta_2 (x - u) + v \\
&= \beta_1 + \beta_2 x + (v - \beta_2 u) \\
&= \beta_1 + \beta_2 x + e
\end{aligned}
\tag{10.3}
$$

In (10.3) the explanatory variable x is random, from the assumption of measurement error in (10.2).

In order to estimate (10.3) by least squares, we must determine whether or not x is uncorrelated with the random disturbance e. The covariance between these two random variables, using the fact that $E(e) = 0$, is

$$
\begin{aligned}
\text{cov}(x, e) &= E(xe) = E[(x^* + u)(v - \beta_2 u)] \\
&= E(-\beta_2 u^2) = -\beta_2 \sigma_u^2 \neq 0
\end{aligned}
\tag{10.4}
$$

The least squares estimator b_2 is an *inconsistent* estimator of β_2 because of the correlation between the explanatory variable and the error term. Consequently, b_2 does not converge to β_2 in large samples. Furthermore, in large or small samples b_2 is *not* approximately normal with mean β_2 and variance $\text{var}(b_2) = \sigma^2 / \sum(x - \bar{x})^2$. When least squares fails in this way, is there another estimation approach that works? The answer is yes, as we will see in Section 10.3.

10.2.2   SIMULTANEOUS EQUATIONS BIAS

Another situation in which an explanatory variable is correlated with the regression error term arises in simultaneous equations models. While this terminology may not sound familiar, students of economics deal with such models from their earliest introduction to supply and demand. Recall that in a competitive market, the prices and quantities of goods are determined jointly by the forces of supply and demand. Thus if $P =$ equilibrium price and $Q =$ equilibrium quantity, we can say that P and Q are endogenous, because they are jointly determined within a simultaneous system of two equations, one equation for the supply curve and the other equation for the demand curve. Suppose that we write down the relation

$$Q = \beta_1 + \beta_2 P + e \tag{10.5}$$

We know that changes in price affect the quantities supplied and demanded. But it is also true that changes in quantities supplied and demanded lead to changes in prices. There is a feedback relationship between P and Q. Because of this feedback, which results because price and quantity are jointly, or simultaneously, determined, we can show that $cov(P, e) \neq 0$. The least squares estimation procedure will fail if applied to (10.5) because of an endogeneity problem, and the resulting bias (and inconsistency) is called the **simultaneous equations bias**. Supply and demand models permeate economic analysis, and we will treat simultaneous equations models fully in Chapter 11.

10.2.3 OMITTED VARIABLES

When an omitted variable is correlated with an included explanatory variable, then the regression error will be correlated with the explanatory variable, making it endogenous. The classic example is from labor economics. A person's wage is determined by in part his or her level of education. Let us specify a log-linear regression model explaining observed hourly wage as

$$\ln(WAGE) = \beta_1 + \beta_2 EDUC + \beta_3 EXPER + \beta_4 EXPER^2 + e \qquad (10.6)$$

with $EDUC$ = years of education and $EXPER$ = years of experience. What else affects wages? What have we omitted? This introspective experiment should be carried out each time a regression model is formulated. There are several factors we might think of, such as labor market conditions, region of the country, and union membership. However, labor economists are most concerned about the omission of a variable measuring ability. It is logical that a person's ability (and industriousness) may affect the quality of their work and their wage. These variables are components of the error term e, since we usually have no measure for them. The problem is that not only might ability affect wages, but more able individuals may also spend more years in school, causing a positive correlation between the error term e and the education variable $EDUC$, so that $cov(EDUC, e) > 0$. If this is true, then we can expect that the least squares estimator of the returns to another year of education will be positively biased, $E(b_2) > \beta_2$, and inconsistent, meaning that the bias will not disappear even in very large samples.

10.2.4 LEAST SQUARES ESTIMATION OF A WAGE EQUATION

We will use the data on married women in the file *mroz.dat* to estimate the wage model in (10.6). Using the $N = 428$ women in the sample who are in the labor force, the least squares estimates and their standard errors are

$$\ln(WAGE) = -0.5220 + 0.1075 \times EDUC + 0.0416 \times EXPER - 0.0008 \times EXPER^2$$
$$(se) \qquad (0.1986) \quad (0.0141) \qquad \qquad (0.0132) \qquad \qquad (0.0004)$$

We estimate that an additional year of education increases wages approximately 10.75%, holding everything else constant. If ability has a positive effect on wages, then this estimate is overstated, as the contribution of ability is attributed to the education variable.

The social and policy importance of the estimate 0.1075 can hardly be exaggerated. Countries invest a large portion of tax revenue to improve education. Why? It is an investment, and like any other investment investors (taxpaying citizens) expect a rate of return that is competitive with rates of returns for alternative projects. Based on the estimated equation above, additional years of schooling are estimated to increase wages by 10.75%, holding other factors fixed, meaning that individuals are more likely to be self-sufficient, enjoy a good quality of life, not requiring welfare or public health assistance, and less likely to engage in crime. Suppose, however, that 10.75% overestimates the returns to education for wage income. We might re-evaluate the investment in education and perhaps decide to spend tax dollars on bridges or parks instead of schools. Evaluating the social rate of return to education is a social policy problem. Regression estimates such as those above play heavily into the calculation. Consequently we must do all that we can, as econometricians, to obtain estimates using the best methods. In the next section we begin our examination of alternative estimation methods for models in which regression errors are correlated with regression variables.

10.3 Estimators Based on the Method of Moments

In the simple linear regression model $y = \beta_1 + \beta_2 x + e$, when x is random and $\text{cov}(x, e) = E(xe) \neq 0$, the least squares estimators are biased and inconsistent, with none of their usual nice properties holding. When faced with such a situation we must consider alternative estimation procedures. In this section we discuss the "method of moments" principle of estimation, which is an alternative to the least squares estimation principle. When all the usual assumptions of the linear model hold, the method of moments leads us to the least squares estimator. If x is random and correlated with the error term, the method of moments leads us to an alternative, called instrumental variables estimation or two-stage least squares estimation, that will work in large samples.

10.3.1 METHOD OF MOMENTS ESTIMATION OF A POPULATION MEAN AND VARIANCE

Let us begin with a simple case. The kth moment of a random variable Y is the expected value of the random variable raised to the kth power. That is,

$$E(Y^k) = \mu_k = k\text{th moment of } Y \tag{10.7}$$

Recall that an "expected value" is an average, over an infinite number of experimental outcomes. Consequently, the kth population moment in (10.7) can be estimated consistently using the sample (of size N) analog

$$\widehat{E(Y^k)} = \hat{\mu}_k = k\text{th sample moment of } Y = \sum y_i^k / N \tag{10.8}$$

The **method of moments** estimation procedure equates m population moments to m sample moments to estimate m unknown parameters. As an example, let Y be a random variable with mean $E(Y) = \mu$ and variance, given in the Probability Primer, equation (P.13):

$$\text{var}(Y) = \sigma^2 = E(Y - \mu)^2 = E(Y^2) - \mu^2 \tag{10.9}$$

In order to estimate the two population parameters μ and σ^2, we must equate two population moments to two sample moments. The first two population and sample moments of Y are

Population moments	Sample moments	
$E(Y) = \mu_1 = \mu$	$\hat{\mu} = \Sigma y_i / N$	(10.10)
$E(Y^2) = \mu_2$	$\hat{\mu}_2 = \Sigma y_i^2 / N$	

Note that for the first population moment μ_1, it is customary to drop the subscript and use μ to denote the mean of Y. With these two moments, we can solve for the unknown mean and variance parameters. Equate the first sample moment in (10.10) to the first population moment to obtain an estimate of the population mean,

$$\hat{\mu} = \Sigma y_i / N = \bar{y} \tag{10.11}$$

Then use (10.9), replacing the second population moment in (10.10) by its sample value and replacing first moment μ by (10.11)

$$\tilde{\sigma}^2 = \hat{\mu}_2 - \hat{\mu}^2 = \frac{\Sigma y_i^2}{N} - \bar{y}^2 = \frac{\Sigma y_i^2 - N\bar{y}^2}{N} = \frac{\Sigma(y_i - \bar{y})^2}{N} \tag{10.12}$$

The method of moments leads us to the sample mean as an estimator of the population mean. The method of moments estimator of the variance has N in its denominator, rather than the usual $N-1$, so it is not exactly the sample variance we are used to. But in large samples this will not make much difference. In general, method of moments estimators are consistent, and converge to the true parameter values in large samples, but there is no guarantee that they are "best" in any sense.

10.3.2 METHOD OF MOMENTS ESTIMATION IN THE SIMPLE LINEAR REGRESSION MODEL

The definition of a "moment" can be extended to more general situations. In the linear regression model $y = \beta_1 + \beta_2 x + e$, we usually assume that

$$E(e) = 0 \Rightarrow E(y - \beta_1 - \beta_2 x) = 0 \tag{10.13}$$

Furthermore, if x is fixed, or random but not correlated with e, then

$$E(xe) = 0 \Rightarrow E[x(y - \beta_1 - \beta_2 x)] = 0 \tag{10.14}$$

Equations (10.13) and (10.14) are moment conditions. If we replace the two population moments by the corresponding sample moments, we have two equations in two unknowns, which define the method of moments estimators for β_1 and β_2,

$$\frac{1}{N}\Sigma(y_i - b_1 - b_2 x_i) = 0$$

$$\frac{1}{N}\Sigma x_i(y_i - b_1 - b_2 x_i) = 0 \tag{10.15}$$

These two equations are equivalent to the least squares "normal" equations [see Chapter 2 Appendix A, (2A.3) and (2A.4)] and their solution yields the least squares estimators

$$b_2 = \frac{\Sigma(x_i - \bar{x})(y_i - \bar{y})}{\Sigma(x_i - \bar{x})^2}$$

$$b_1 = \bar{y} - b_2\bar{x}$$

Thus, under "nice" assumptions, the method of moments principle of estimation leads us to the same estimators for the simple linear regression model as the least squares principle.

10.3.3 INSTRUMENTAL VARIABLES ESTIMATION IN THE SIMPLE LINEAR REGRESSION MODEL

Problems for least squares arise when x is random and correlated with the random disturbance e, so that $E(xe) \neq 0$. This makes the moment condition in (10.14) invalid. Suppose, however, that there is another variable z such that

1. z does not have a direct effect on y, and thus it does not belong on the right-hand side of the model as an explanatory variable.
2. z is not correlated with the regression error term e. It is **exogenous**.
3. z is strongly (or at least not weakly) correlated with x, the endogenous explanatory variable.

A variable z with these properties is called an **instrumental variable**. This terminology arises because although z does not have a direct effect on y, having it will allow us to estimate the relationship between x and y. It is a *tool*, or instrument, that we are using to achieve our objective.

If such a variable z exists, then we can use it to form the moment condition

$$E(ze) = 0 \Rightarrow E[z(y - \beta_1 - \beta_2 x)] = 0 \tag{10.16}$$

Then we can use (10.13) and (10.16) to obtain estimates of β_1 and β_2. The sample moment conditions are

$$\frac{1}{N}\Sigma(y_i - \hat{\beta}_1 - \hat{\beta}_2 x_i) = 0$$

$$\frac{1}{N}\Sigma z_i(y_i - \hat{\beta}_1 - \hat{\beta}_2 x_i) = 0 \tag{10.17}$$

Solving these equations leads us to method of moments estimators, which are usually called the **instrumental variable (IV) estimators**,

$$\hat{\beta}_2 = \frac{N\Sigma z_i y_i - \Sigma z_i \Sigma y_i}{N\Sigma z_i x_i - \Sigma z_i \Sigma x_i} = \frac{\Sigma(z_i - \bar{z})(y_i - \bar{y})}{\Sigma(z_i - \bar{z})(x_i - \bar{x})}$$

$$\hat{\beta}_1 = \bar{y} - \hat{\beta}_2\bar{x} \tag{10.18}$$

These new estimators have the following properties:

- They are consistent, if z is exogenous, with $E(ze) = 0$ (see Appendix 10C).
- In large samples the instrumental variable estimators have approximate normal distributions. In the simple regression model

$$\hat{\beta}_2 \sim N\left(\beta_2, \frac{\sigma^2}{r_{zx}^2 \Sigma(x_i - \bar{x})^2}\right) \tag{10.19}$$

where r_{zx}^2 is the squared sample correlation between the instrument z and the random regressor x.

- The error variance is estimated using the estimator

$$\hat{\sigma}_{IV}^2 = \frac{\Sigma(y_i - \hat{\beta}_1 - \hat{\beta}_2 x_i)^2}{N - 2}$$

10.3.3a The Importance of Using Strong Instruments

Examine the variance expression in (10.19). The denominator includes the squared correlation between the instrument z and the endogenous variable x. We want to obtain an instrument z that is highly correlated with x to improve the efficiency of the instrumental variable estimator. If x and e are uncorrelated, so that least squares is still an option, we can compare the efficiency of the two estimators. Note that we can write the variance of the instrumental variables estimator of β_2 as

$$\text{var}(\hat{\beta}_2) = \frac{\sigma^2}{r_{zx}^2 \Sigma(x_i - \bar{x})^2} = \frac{\text{var}(b_2)}{r_{zx}^2}$$

Because $r_{zx}^2 < 1$ the variance of the instrumental variables estimator will always be larger than the variance of the least squares estimator, and thus it is said to be less *efficient*. Using the instrumental variables estimation procedure when it is not required leads to wider confidence intervals, and less precise inference, than if least squares estimation is used. If the correlation between z and x is 0.1, then the variance of the instrumental variables estimator is 100 times as large as the variance of the least squares estimator. If the correlation between z and x is 0.5, then the variance of the instrumental variables estimator is four times as large as the variance of the least squares estimator.

In recent years there has been a great deal of research on the behavior of the instrumental variables estimator when the instrument is weakly correlated with the endogenous variable x. When using a weak instrument, the instrumental variables estimator can be badly biased, even in large samples, and its distribution is not approximately normal. Thus point estimates can be substantially off, 95% confidence intervals may not work 95% of the time, and hypothesis tests using the $\alpha = 0.05$ level of significance may not have a probability of Type I error equal to 0.05. The bottom line is that when instruments are weak, instrumental variables estimation is not reliable.

10.3.4 Instrumental Variables Estimation in the Multiple Regression Model

To implement instrumental variables estimation in a multiple regression equation, we need an estimation formula that is more general than (10.18). To extend our analysis to a more general setting, consider the multiple regression model $y = \beta_1 + \beta_2 x_2 + \cdots + \beta_K x_K + e$. Suppose that among the explanatory variables we know, or suspect, that x_K is an endogenous variable correlated with the error term. The first $K - 1$ variables ($x_1 = 1, x_2, \ldots, x_{K-1}$) are exogenous variables that are uncorrelated with the error term e—they are "included" instruments. Instrumental variables estimation can be carried out using a two-step process, with a least squares regression in each step.

The **first stage regression** has the endogenous variable x_K on the left-hand side, and **all exogenous and instrumental variables** on the right-hand side. If we have L "external" instrumental variables that are from outside the model $z_1, z_2, \ldots, z_L$, then the first stage regression is

$$x_K = \gamma_1 + \gamma_2 x_2 + \cdots + \gamma_{K-1} x_{K-1} + \theta_1 z_1 + \cdots + \theta_L z_L + v_K \qquad (10.20)$$

where v_K is a random error term that is uncorrelated with all the right-hand side variables. Estimate the first-stage regression (10.20) by least squares and obtain the fitted value

$$\hat{x}_K = \hat{\gamma}_1 + \hat{\gamma}_2 x_2 + \cdots + \hat{\gamma}_{K-1} x_{K-1} + \hat{\theta}_1 z_1 + \cdots + \hat{\theta}_L z_L \qquad (10.21)$$

The fitted value $\hat{x}_K$ is a weighted average, or a linear combination, of all the exogenous and instrumental variables that we have available.

The **second stage regression** is based on the original specification with $\hat{x}_K$ replacing x_K,

$$y = \beta_1 + \beta_2 x_2 + \cdots + \beta_K \hat{x}_K + e^* \qquad (10.22)$$

where e^* is an error term. Least squares estimation of (10.22) is justified because in large samples e^* is uncorrelated with the explanatory variables, including $\hat{x}_K$. The least squares estimators from this equation, $\hat{\beta}_1, \ldots, \hat{\beta}_K$, are the **instrumental variables (IV)** estimators, and because they can be obtained by two least squares regressions, they are also popularly known as the **two-stage least squares (2SLS)** estimators. They are exactly the same. We will refer to them as *IV* or *2SLS* or *IV/2SLS* estimators. In the general case with more than one endogenous variable on the right-hand side, the steps are similar, and are discussed in Section 10.3.8.

We can use the standard formulas for estimator variances and covariances for the least squares estimator of (10.22), which we described in Chapter 5.3.1, with one modification. While we can use two least squares estimations to obtain proper estimates, least squares software does not produce correct standard errors and t-values. The *IV/2SLS* estimator of the error variance is based on the residuals from the original model, $y = \beta_1 + \beta_2 x_2 + \cdots + \beta_K x_K + e$,

$$\hat{\sigma}_{IV}^2 = \frac{\sum (y_i - \hat{\beta}_1 - \hat{\beta}_2 x_{2i} - \cdots - \hat{\beta}_K x_{Ki})^2}{N - K} \qquad (10.23)$$

Econometric software will automatically use the proper variance estimator if a two-stage least squares or instrumental variables estimation option is chosen. Using the *IV/2SLS* estimated standard errors from (10.22) we can carry out t-tests and construct interval estimates of parameters that are valid in large samples. Furthermore, the usual tests of joint hypotheses are valid in large samples *if* the instrumental variables are not weak.

10.3.4a Using Surplus Instruments in Simple Regression

Using the simple regression model the logic of the two-stage least squares estimation procedure can be clarified. With surplus instruments we could select just the number we need and discard the rest, but generally discarding information is not attractive. The *2SLS* method shows that we can use all the available instruments (assuming that they are strong) by forming a linear combination of them. In the simple regression $y = \beta_1 + \beta_2 x + e$, if x is endogenous, and we have L instruments, (10.21) becomes

$$\hat{x} = \hat{\gamma}_1 + \hat{\theta}_1 z_1 + \cdots + \hat{\theta}_L z_L$$

We have combined all the instruments into a single variable. Then use $\hat{x}$ as an instrumental variable for x. This leads to the two sample moment conditions

$$\frac{1}{N} \sum (y_i - \hat{\beta}_1 - \hat{\beta}_2 x_i) = 0$$

$$\frac{1}{N} \sum \hat{x}_i (y_i - \hat{\beta}_1 - \hat{\beta}_2 x_i) = 0$$

Solving these conditions, and using the fact that $\bar{\hat{x}} = \bar{x}$, we have

$$\hat{\beta}_2 = \frac{\sum (\hat{x}_i - \bar{\hat{x}})(y_i - \bar{y})}{\sum (\hat{x}_i - \bar{\hat{x}})(x_i - \bar{x})} = \frac{\sum (\hat{x}_i - \bar{x})(y_i - \bar{y})}{\sum (\hat{x}_i - \bar{x})(x_i - \bar{x})}$$

$$\hat{\beta}_1 = \bar{y} - \hat{\beta}_2 \bar{x}$$

We are forming a single "optimal" instrument from the L available instruments. This estimator is identical to the *IV/2SLS* estimator arising from (10.22).

10.3.4b Surplus Moment Conditions

In the simple regression model we need only one instrumental variable, yielding two moment conditions like (10.17), which we solve for the two unknown model parameters. Sometimes, however, we have more instrumental variables at our disposal than are necessary. In these circumstances we can use the two-stage procedure just described, where the information from all the instrumental variables is collected into one variable, $\hat{x}$. To see why this is necessary, suppose we have $L = 2$ instruments, z_1 and z_2. Compared to (10.17) we have the additional moment condition

$$E(z_2 e) = E[z_2 (y - \beta_1 - \beta_2 x)] = 0$$

Now we have three sample moment conditions:

$$\frac{1}{N} \sum (y_i - \hat{\beta}_1 - \hat{\beta}_2 x_i) = \hat{m}_1 = 0$$

$$\frac{1}{N} \sum z_{i1} (y_i - \hat{\beta}_1 - \hat{\beta}_2 x_i) = \hat{m}_2 = 0$$

$$\frac{1}{N} \sum z_{i2} (y_i - \hat{\beta}_1 - \hat{\beta}_2 x_i) = \hat{m}_3 = 0$$

We have three equations with only two unknowns. We could simply throw away one of the conditions (instruments) and use the remaining two to solve for the unknowns. However, throwing away good information is hardly ever a good idea. An alternative that uses all of the moment conditions is to choose values for $\hat{\beta}_1$ and $\hat{\beta}_2$ satisfying the three moment conditions as closely as possible. One way to do this is to use the least squares principle, choosing $\hat{\beta}_1$ and $\hat{\beta}_2$ to minimize the sum of squares $\hat{m}_1^2 + \hat{m}_2^2 + \hat{m}_3^2$. It is best, however, to use weighted least squares, putting the greatest weight on the moments with the smaller variances. While the exact details are beyond the scope of this book,[2] the values of $\hat{\beta}_1$ and $\hat{\beta}_2$ that minimize this weighted sum of squares are the *IV/2SLS* estimators.

10.3.5 ASSESSING INSTRUMENT STRENGTH USING THE FIRST STAGE MODEL

In Section 10.3.3a we emphasized the importance of strong instruments when estimating a simple regression model with an endogenous explanatory variable. There the assessment of the instrument's strength was based on the correlation between the endogenous variable x and the instrument z. In a multiple regression, measuring instrument strength is more complicated. The first stage regression is a key tool in assessing whether an instrument is "strong" or "weak" in the multiple regression setting.

10.3.5a   One Instrumental Variable

Suppose that x_K is endogenous and that we have available one external instrumental variable z_1. In terms of the notation above, $L = 1$. The first stage regression equation is

$$x_K = \gamma_1 + \gamma_2 x_2 + \cdots + \gamma_{K-1} x_{K-1} + \theta_1 z_1 + v_K \tag{10.24}$$

In a simple regression model, we can look for instrument strength in the correlation between the endogenous variable and the instrument. In the multiple regression model we must deal with the other exogenous variables $(x_2, \ldots, x_{K-1})$. The key to assessing the strength of the instrumental variable z_1 is the strength of its relationship to x_K *after* controlling for the effects of all the other exogenous variables. This, however, is exactly the purpose of multiple regression analysis. The coefficient θ_1 in the first stage regression (10.24) measures the effect of z_1 on x_K after accounting for the effects of the other variables. A numerical illustration of this property of multiple regression is given below in Section 10.3.7.

Not only must there be an effect of z_1 on x_K; it must also be a *statistically significant* effect. How significant? Very significant. To reject the hypothesis that the instrument z_1 is weak, the usual rule of thumb is that the F-test statistic for the null hypothesis $H_0 : \theta_1 = 0$ in (10.24) should be greater than 10. Using the relationship between the t- and F-tests, $t^2 = F$ described in Chapter 6.1.3, this translates into the absolute t-statistic for significance being greater than 3.16. The $F > 10$ rule has been refined by econometric researchers Stock and Yogo, and their analysis is discussed in Appendix 10E. When instrumental variables are weak, estimates and tests based on the resulting *IV* estimator are unreliable.

10.3.5b   More Than One Instrumental Variable

Suppose that x_K is endogenous and we have available external instrumental variables z_1, $z_2, \ldots, z_L$. For a single endogenous variable we need only a single instrument. Sometimes more instruments are available, and having more strong instruments may improve the instrumental variables estimator. The first stage regression equation is now

$$x_K = \gamma_1 + \gamma_2 x_2 + \cdots + \gamma_{K-1} x_{K-1} + \theta_1 z_1 + \cdots + \theta_L z_L + v_K \tag{10.25}$$

We require that *at least one* of the instruments be strong. Given the nature of the requirement, a joint F-test of the null hypothesis $H_0 : \theta_1 = 0, \theta_2 = 0, \ldots, \theta_L = 0$ in (10.25) is relevant, because the alternative is that at least one of the θ_i coefficients is nonzero. Once again the magnitude of the F statistic is relevant, and roughly the $F > 10$ rule

---

[2] A very advanced reference is Greene (2008), op. cit., Chapter 15.6.

applies. As noted above, this threshold is refined in Appendix 10E. If the F-test statistic value is sufficiently large, we reject the hypothesis that the instruments are "weak" and can proceed with instrumental variables estimation. If the F-value is not sufficiently large, then instrumental variables and two-stage least squares estimation is quite possibly worse than "ordinary" least squares.

10.3.6 INSTRUMENTAL VARIABLES ESTIMATION OF THE WAGE EQUATION

We continue the wage equation example from Section 10.2.4. We first consider the use of a single instrumental variable, and then add a "surplus" instrument.

To carry out an instrumental variable estimation, we require a variable that does not belong in the wage equation itself and that is correlated with $EDUC$, but that is uncorrelated with the omitted factors in the error term, here a person's ability, or intelligence. Such variables are difficult to obtain, but in Thomas Mroz's data, we have the number of years of education for the woman's mother. A mother's education ($MOTHEREDUC$) does itself not belong in the daughter's wage equation, and it is reasonable to propose that more educated mothers are more likely to have more educated daughters. We will assess this requirement using the method of Section 10.3.5a. The remaining question is whether a woman's ability and intelligence are correlated with her mother's education? To be valid instruments, these variables must be uncorrelated. We will assume so for purposes of illustration.

Before implementing $IV/2SLS$ estimation, we obtain the least squares estimates of the first stage equation for $EDUC$. The first stage equation has as explanatory variables all the exogenous variables in the original equation, plus any external instrumental variables. The least squares estimates are

$$\widehat{EDUC} = 9.7751 + 0.0489EXPER - 0.0013EXPER^2 + 0.2677MOTHEREDUC$$

$$\text{(se)} \quad (0.4249) \quad (0.0417) \qquad (0.0012) \qquad\qquad (0.0311) \qquad\qquad\qquad (10.26)$$

Note that the coefficient of $MOTHEREDUC$ is very significant, with a t-value of 8.6, corresponding to an F-test value of 73.95. This is important, as it indicates that our instrument is correlated with the variable we suspect to be endogenous, even after accounting for the other exogenous variables in the model.

To implement instrumental variables estimation using the two-stage least squares approach, we obtain the predicted values of education from the first stage equation, $\widehat{EDUC}$, and insert it into the log-linear wage equation to replace $EDUC$. Then estimate the resulting equation by least squares. While this two-step process yields proper $IV/2SLS$ estimates, as we discussed in Section 10.3.4, the accompanying standard errors and t-values are not correct. It is always best to use software commands designed for instrumental variables, or two-stage least squares, estimation. The instrumental variables estimates of the log-linear wage equation are

$$\widehat{\ln(WAGE)} = 0.1982 + 0.0493EDUC + 0.0449EXPER - 0.0009EXPER^2$$

$$\text{(se)} \qquad (0.4729) \quad (0.0374) \qquad\quad (0.0136) \qquad\quad (0.0004)$$

Note two changes as compared to the least squares estimates. First, the estimated return to education is 4.93%, which is lower than the least squares estimate of 10.75%. This is consistent with the fact that the least squares estimator tends to overestimate the effect of education if $EDUC$ is positively correlated with the omitted factors in the error term. Also notice that the standard error on the coefficient of education (0.0374) is over 2.5 times larger than the standard error reported with the least squares estimates (0.0141). This reflects the fact that even with a good instrumental variable, the *IV/2SLS* estimator is not efficient, as discussed in Section 10.3.3a. How can we improve the efficiency of the instrumental variables estimator? We can obtain a larger sample, if possible, or we can obtain more and stronger instrumental variables.

Let us add "father's education" as an additional instrumental variable. To test for weak instruments, we test the joint significance of the two proposed instruments *MOTHEREDUC* and *FATHEREDUC* using a standard *F*-test in the first stage regression. Since there is only one potentially endogenous variable in the wage equation, *EDUC*, the minimum number of instrumental variables is one. Given two instruments, we require that at least one of them be significant in the first stage equation. The first stage equation is

$$EDUC = \gamma_1 + \gamma_2 EXPER + \gamma_3 EXPER^2 + \theta_1 MOTHEREDUC + \theta_2 FATHEREDUC + v$$

The *F*-test null hypothesis is that both coefficients, θ_1 and θ_2, are zero, and if we reject this null hypothesis we conclude that at least one of them is nonzero. The first stage estimates are shown in Table 10.1.

In the first stage regression, the estimated coefficient of *MOTHEREDUC* is 0.1576 with a *t*-value of 4.39, and the estimated coefficient of *FATHEREDUC* is 0.1895 with a *t*-value of 5.62. The *F*-statistic value for the null hypothesis that both these coefficients are zero is 55.40. This value is greater than the rule-of-thumb threshold of 10. We conclude that at least one of the instruments is not weak. The *IV/2SLS* estimates are

$$\widehat{\ln(WAGE)} = 0.0481 + 0.0614EDUC + 0.0442EXPER - 0.0009EXPER^2$$
$$(se) \quad (0.4003) \ (0.0314) \qquad (0.0134) \qquad (0.0004) \tag{10.27}$$

Compared to the previous result using only *MOTHEREDUC* as an instrument, we see that there is an increase in the estimate of the return to education to 6.14%, and a slight reduction in the standard error. The estimated return to education is statistically significant now, whereas it was not when only the mother's education was used as an instrument.

10.3.7 PARTIAL CORRELATION

When introducing the multiple regression model, in Chapter 5.1.1, we stressed that the coefficients are the effect of a unit change in an explanatory, independent, variable on

Table 10.1   **First-Stage Equation**

Variable	Coefficient	Std. Error	*t*-Statistic	Prob.
C	9.1026	0.4266	21.3396	0.0000
EXPER	0.0452	0.0403	1.1236	0.2618
EXPER^2	−0.0010	0.0012	−0.8386	0.4022
MOTHEREDUC	0.1576	0.0359	4.3906	0.0000
FATHEREDUC	0.1895	0.0338	5.6152	0.0000

the expected outcome, holding all other things constant. In calculus terminology, the coefficients are **partial** derivatives. In Section 10.3.5a we discussed another perspective on the coefficients in a multiple regression model: they measure the effect of a unit change in an explanatory variable on the expected outcome after accounting for, or controlling for, the effects of all other variables. In this section we discuss this interpretation a bit further. It will benefit your understanding of regression analysis, and how we test for weak instruments in the first stage regression. Furthermore this idea will lead to a more general test for weak instrumental variables, which is introduced in the following section and discussed further in Appendix 10E.

Let us perform an experiment based on the first stage regression in (10.26). Compute the least squares residuals, say $RESID_E$, from the regression of $EDUC$ on $EXPER$ and $EXPER^2$. These residuals are $EDUC$ with the effects of $EXPER$ and $EXPER^2$ removed. Sometimes this process is called **netting out** or **partialling out** the effects of $EXPER$ and $EXPER^2$. Do the same thing for $MOTHEREDUC$, computing the least squares residuals $RESID_M$ from the regression of $MOTHEREDUC$ on $EXPER$ and $EXPER^2$. Finally, regress $RESID_E$ on $RESID_M$. The estimated coefficient is 0.2676908. The regression coefficient of $MOTHER$-$EDUC$ in (10.26) carried out to more decimal places is 0.2676908. They are the same, and it is not an accident. Regression coefficients can be thought of measuring the effect of one variable on another after removing, or partialling out, the effects of all other variables. The sample correlation between $RESID_E$ and $RESID_M$, 0.3854, is called the **partial correlation** coefficient. Partial correlations play an important role in testing for weak instrumental variables in the general model.

10.3.8 INSTRUMENTAL VARIABLES ESTIMATION IN A GENERAL MODEL

To extend our analysis to a more general setting, consider the multiple regression model $y = \beta_1 + \beta_2 x_2 + \cdots + \beta_K x_K + e$. Suppose that among the explanatory variables ($x_1 = 1$, $x_2, \ldots, x_K$) we know, or suspect, that several may be correlated with the error term e. Divide the variables into two groups, with the first G variables ($x_1 = 1, x_2, \ldots, x_G$) being exogenous variables that are uncorrelated with the error term e. The second group of $B = K-G$ variables $(x_{G+1}, x_{G+2}, \ldots, x_K)$ is correlated with the regression error, and thus they are endogenous. The multiple regression model, including all K variables, is then

$$y = \underbrace{\beta_1 + \beta_2 x_2 + \cdots + \beta_G x_G}_{G \ exogenous \ variables} + \underbrace{\beta_{G+1} x_{G+1} + \cdots + \beta_K x_K}_{B \ endogenous \ variables} + e \qquad (10.28)$$

In order to carry out *IV* estimation we must have at least as many instrumental variables as we have endogenous variables. Suppose we have L external instrumental variables, from outside the model, $z_1, z_2, \ldots, z_L$. Such notation is invariably confusing and cumbersome. It may help to keep things straight to think of $G = Good$ explanatory variables and $B = Bad$ explanatory variables and $L = Lucky$ instrumental variables, since we are lucky to have them. Then we have *The Good, the Bad, and the Lucky*.

It is a necessary condition for *IV* estimation that $L \geq B$. If $L = B$ then there are just enough instrumental variables to carry out *IV* estimation. The model parameters are said to be **just identified** or **exactly identified** in this case. The term **identified** is used to indicate that the model parameters can be consistently estimated. If $L > B$ then we have more instruments than are necessary for *IV* estimation, and the model is said to be **overidentified**.

To implement *IV/2SLS*, estimate B first-stage equations, one for each explanatory variable that is endogenous. On the left-hand side of the first-stage equations, we have an endogenous variable. On the right-hand side, we have *all* the exogenous variables, including the G explanatory variables that are exogenous, *and* the L instrumental variables, which also must be exogenous. The B first-stage equations are

$$x_{G+j} = \gamma_{1j} + \gamma_{2j}x_2 + \cdots + \gamma_{Gj}x_G + \theta_{1j}z_1 + \cdots + \theta_{Lj}z_L + v_j, \quad j = 1, \ldots, B \quad (10.29)$$

The first-stage parameters (γ's and θ's) take different values in each equation, which is why they have a "j" subscript. We have omitted the observation subscript for simplicity. Since the right-hand-side variables are all exogenous, we can estimate (10.29) by least squares. Then obtain the predicted values

$$\hat{x}_{G+j} = \hat{\gamma}_{1j} + \hat{\gamma}_{2j}x_2 + \cdots + \hat{\gamma}_{Gj}x_G + \hat{\theta}_{1j}z_1 + \cdots + \hat{\theta}_{Lj}z_L, \quad j = 1, \ldots, B$$

This comprises the first stage of two-stage least squares estimation.

In the second stage of estimation we apply least squares to

$$y = \beta_1 + \beta_2 x_2 + \cdots \beta_G x_G + \beta_{G+1}\hat{x}_{G+1} + \cdots + \beta_K \hat{x}_K + e^* \quad (10.30)$$

This two-stage estimation process leads to proper instrumental variables estimates, but it should not be done this way in applied work. Use econometric software designed for two-stage least squares or instrumental variables estimation so that standard errors, t-statistics, and other test statistics will be computed properly.

10.3.8a   Assessing Instrument Strength in a General Model

The F-test for weak instruments discussed in Section 10.3.5b is not valid for models having more than one endogenous variable on the right side of the equation. Consider the model in (10.28) with $B = 2$,

$$y = \beta_1 + \beta_2 x_2 + \cdots + \beta_G x_G + \beta_{G+1}x_{G+1} + \beta_{G+2}x_{G+2} + e \quad (10.31)$$

where $x_2, \ldots, x_G$ are exogenous and uncorrelated with the error term e, while x_{G+1} and x_{G+2} are endogenous. Suppose that we have two external instrumental variables z_1 and z_2, with z_1 being a good instrument for both x_{G+1} and x_{G+2}. The weak instrument F-test may be significant in each first-stage equation even if z_2 is an irrelevant instrument and not at all related to x_{G+1} or x_{G+2}. In such a case we might conclude that we have two valid instruments when we have only one.

The first-stage equations in this case are

$$x_{G+1} = \gamma_{11} + \gamma_{21}x_2 + \cdots + \gamma_{G1}x_G + \theta_{11}z_1 + \theta_{21}z_2 + v_1$$

$$x_{G+2} = \gamma_{12} + \gamma_{22}x_2 + \cdots + \gamma_{G2}x_G + \theta_{12}z_1 + \theta_{22}z_2 + v_2$$

The weak instrument F-test in the first equation is for the joint significance of θ_{11} and θ_{21}, $H_0 : \theta_{11} = 0, \ \theta_{21} = 0$, with the alternative hypothesis that at least *one* of these coefficients is not zero. If θ_{11} is statistically significant, then the joint null hypothesis may be rejected even if $\theta_{21} = 0$. Similarly in the second equation we can obtain a significant F-test outcome even if z_2 is irrelevant as an instrument for x_{G+2} as long as z_1 is statistically significant.

In this case we have two individually significant F-tests despite the fact that only one valid instrument z_1 is available, and thus the model in (10.31) is not identified.

The more general test required for this case, which builds on the concept of "partial correlation" in Section 10.3.7, is discussed in Appendix 10E.

10.3.8b Hypothesis Testing with Instrumental Variables Estimates

We may be interested in testing hypotheses about the regression parameters based on the two-stage least squares/instrumental variables estimates. When testing the null hypothesis $H_0: \beta_k = c$, use of the test statistic $t = (\hat{\beta}_k - c)/\text{se}(\hat{\beta}_k)$ is valid in large samples. We know that as $N \to \infty$, the $t_{(N-K)}$ distribution converges to the standard normal distribution $N(0, 1)$. If the degrees of freedom $N - K$ are large, then critical values from the two distributions will be very close. It is common, but not universal, practice to use critical values, and p-values, based on the $t_{(N-K)}$ distribution rather than the more strictly appropriate $N(0, 1)$ distribution. The reason is that tests based on the t-distribution tend to work better in samples of data that are not large.

Another issue is whether to use standard errors that are "robust" to the presence of heteroskedasticity (in cross-section data) or autocorrelation and heteroskedasticity (in time-series data). These options were described in Chapters 8 and 9 for the linear regression model, and they are also available in most software packages for IV estimation. Such corrections to standard errors require large samples in order to work properly.

When using software to test a joint hypothesis, such as $H_0: \beta_2 = c_2, \beta_3 = c_3$, the test may be based on the chi-square distribution with the number of degrees of freedom equal to the number of hypotheses (J) being tested. The test itself may be called a Wald test, or a likelihood ratio (LR) test, or a Lagrange multiplier (LM) test. These testing procedures are all asymptotically equivalent and are discussed in Appendix C.8.4. However, the test statistic reported may also be called an F-statistic with J numerator degrees of freedom and $N - K$ denominator degrees of freedom. This F-value is often calculated by dividing one of the chi-square tests statistics, such as the Wald statistic, by J. The motivation for using the F-test is to achieve better performance in small samples. Asymptotically, the tests will all lead to the same conclusion. See Chapter 6, Appendix 6A, for some related discussion. Once again, joint tests can be made "robust" to potential heteroskedasticity or autocorrelation problems, and this is an option with many software packages.

10.3.8c Goodness-of-Fit with Instrumental Variables Estimates

We discourage the use of measures like R^2 outside the context of least squares estimation. When there are endogenous variables on the right-hand side of a regression equation, the concept of measuring how well the variation in y is explained by the x variables breaks down, because as we discussed in Section 10.2, these models exhibit feedback. This logical problem is paired with a numerical one. If our model is $y = \beta_1 + \beta_2 x + e$, then the IV residuals are $\hat{e} = y - \hat{\beta}_1 - \hat{\beta}_2 x$. Many software packages will report the goodness-of-fit measure $R^2 = 1 - \Sigma \hat{e}_i^2 / \Sigma (y_i - \bar{y})^2$. Unfortunately, this quantity can be negative when based on IV estimates.

10.4 Specification Tests

We have shown that if an explanatory variable is correlated with the regression error term, the least squares estimator fails. If a strong instrumental variable is available, the IV estimator is consistent and approximately normally distributed in large samples. But if we use a weak instrument, or an instrument that is invalid in the sense that it is not uncorrelated with the regression error, then *IV* estimation can be as bad as, or worse than, using the least squares estimator. We addressed how to detect weak instruments in Section 10.3.5, and go into much greater detail on this problem in Appendix 10E. In this section we ask two other important questions that must be answered in each situation in which instrumental variables estimation is considered:

1. Can we test for whether *x* is correlated with the error term? This might give us a guide for when to use least squares and when to use *IV* estimators.

2. Can we test if our instrument is valid, and uncorrelated with the regression error, as required?

10.4.1   THE HAUSMAN TEST FOR ENDOGENEITY

In the previous sections we discussed the fact that the least squares estimator fails if there is correlation between an explanatory variable and the error term. We also provided an estimator, the instrumental variables estimator, that can be used when the least squares estimator fails. The question we address in this section is how to test for the presence of a correlation between an explanatory variable and the error term, so that we can use the appropriate estimation procedure.

The null hypothesis is $H_0 : \mathrm{cov}(x, e) = 0$ against the alternative that $H_1 : \mathrm{cov}(x, e) \neq 0$. The idea of the test is to compare the performance of the least squares estimator to an instrumental variables estimator. Under the null and alternative hypotheses, we know the following:

-   If the null hypothesis is true, both the least squares estimator b and the instrumental variables estimator $\hat{\beta}$ are consistent. Thus, in large samples the difference between them converges to zero. That is, $q = (b - \hat{\beta}) \to 0$. Naturally, if the null hypothesis is true, use the more efficient estimator, which is the least squares estimator.

-   If the null hypothesis is false, the least squares estimator is not consistent, and the instrumental variables estimator is consistent. Consequently, the difference between them does not converge to zero in large samples. That is, $q = (b - \hat{\beta}) \to c \neq 0$. If the null hypothesis is not true, use the instrumental variables estimator, which is consistent.

There are several forms of the test, usually called the **Hausman test** in recognition of econometrician Jerry Hausman's pioneering work on this problem, for these null and alternative hypotheses. One form of the test directly examines the differences between the least squares and instrumental variables estimates, as we have described above. Some computer software programs implement this test for the user, which can be computationally difficult to carry out.[3]

An alternative form of the test is very easy to implement, and is the one we recommend. See Appendix 10D for an explanation of the test's logic. In the regression $y = \beta_1 + \beta_2 x + e$, we wish to know whether *x* is correlated with *e*. Let z_1 and z_2 be instrumental variables for *x*. At minimum, one instrument is required for each variable that might be correlated with the error term. Then carry out the following steps:

---

[3] Some software packages compute Hausman tests with K, or $K - 1$, degrees of freedom, where K is the total number of regression parameters. This is incorrect. Use the correct degrees of freedom B, equal to the number of potentially endogenous right-hand-side variables. See (10.28).

1. Estimate the first-stage model $x = \gamma_1 + \theta_1 z_1 + \theta_2 z_2 + v$ by least squares, including on the right-hand side all instrumental variables and all exogenous variables not suspected to be endogenous, and obtain the residuals

    $$\hat{v} = x - \hat{\gamma}_1 - \hat{\theta}_1 z_1 - \hat{\theta}_2 z_2$$

    If more than one explanatory variable is being tested for endogeneity, repeat this estimation for each one.

2. Include the residuals computed in step 1 as an explanatory variable in the original regression, $y = \beta_1 + \beta_2 x + \delta\hat{v} + e$. Estimate this "artificial regression" by least squares, and employ the usual t-test for the hypothesis of significance:

    $$H_0 : \delta = 0 \quad (\text{no correlation between } x \text{ and } e)$$
    $$H_1 : \delta \neq 0 \quad (\text{correlation between } x \text{ and } e)$$

3. If more than one variable is being tested for endogeneity, the test will be an F-test of joint significance of the coefficients on the included residuals.

The t- and F-tests in steps two and three can be made robust if heteroskedasticity and/or autocorrelation are potential problems.

10.4.2 TESTING INSTRUMENT VALIDITY

A valid instrument z must be uncorrelated with the regression error term, so that $\text{cov}(z, e) = 0$. If this condition fails then the resulting moment condition, like (10.16), is invalid and the IV estimator will not be consistent. Unfortunately, not every instrument can be tested for validity. In order to compute the IV estimator for an equation with B possibly endogenous variables, we must have at least B instruments. The validity of this minimum number of required instruments cannot be tested. In the case in which we have $L > B$ instruments available, we can test the validity of the $L - B$ extra, or surplus, moment conditions.[4]

An intuitive approach is the following. From the set of L instruments, form groups of B instruments and compute the IV estimates using each different group. If all the instruments are valid, then we would expect all the IV estimates to be similar. Rather than do this, there is a test of the validity of the surplus moment conditions that is easier to compute. The steps are

1. Compute the IV estimates $\hat{\beta}_k$ using all available instruments, including the G variables $x_1 = 1, x_2, \ldots, x_G$ that are presumed to be exogenous, and the L instruments $z_1, \ldots, z_L$.

2. Obtain the residuals $\hat{e} = y - \hat{\beta}_1 - \hat{\beta}_2 x_2 - \cdots - \hat{\beta}_K x_K$.

3. Regress $\hat{e}$ on all the available instruments described in step one.

4. Compute NR^2 from this regression, where N is the sample size and R^2 is the usual goodness-of-fit measure.

5. If all of the surplus moment conditions are valid, then $NR^2 \sim \chi^2_{(L-B)}$.[5] If the value of the test statistic exceeds the $100(1 - \alpha)$th percentile (i.e., the critical value) from the

---

[4] Econometric jargon for surplus moment conditions is "overidentifying restrictions." A surplus of moment conditions means we have more than enough for identification, hence "overidentifying." Moment conditions like (10.16) can be thought of as restrictions on parameters.

[5] This test is valid if errors are homoskedastic and is sometimes called the Sargan test. If the errors are heteroskedastic, there is a more general test called Hansen's J-test that is provided by some software. A very advanced reference is Hayashi, *Econometrics*, Princeton, 2000, pp. 227–228.

$\chi^2_{(L-B)}$ distribution, then we conclude that at least one of the surplus moment conditions is not valid.

If we reject the null hypothesis that all the surplus moment conditions are valid, then we are faced with trying to determine which instrument(s) are invalid, and how to weed them out.

10.4.3   SPECIFICATION TESTS FOR THE WAGE EQUATION

In Section 10.3.6 we examined a ln($WAGE$) equation for married women, using the two instruments "mother's education" and "father's education" for the potentially endogenous explanatory variable education ($EDUC$).

To implement the Hausman test we first obtain the first-stage regression estimates, which are shown in Table 10.1. Using these estimates we calculate the least squares residuals $\hat{v} = EDUC - \widehat{EDUC}$. Insert the residuals in the ln($WAGE$) equation as an extra variable, and estimate the resulting augmented regression using least squares. The resulting estimates are shown in Table 10.2

The Hausman test of the endogeneity is based on the t-test of significance of the first-stage regression residuals, $\hat{v}$. If we reject the null hypothesis that the coefficient is zero, we conclude that education is endogenous. Note that the coefficient of the first-stage regression residuals ($VHAT$) is significant at the 10% level of significance using a two-tail test. While this is not strong evidence of the endogeneity of education, it is sufficient cause for concern to consider using instrumental variables estimation. Second, note that the coefficient estimates of the remaining variables, but not their standard errors, are identical to their instrumental variables estimates. This feature of the regression-based Hausman test is explained in Appendix 10D.

In order to be valid, the instruments $MOTHEREDUC$ and $FATHEREDUC$ should be uncorrelated with the regression error term. As discussed in Section 10.4.2, we cannot test the validity of both instruments only the "overidentifying" or surplus instrument. Since we have two instruments and only one potentially endogenous variable, we have $L - B = 1$ extra instrument. The test is carried out by regressing the residuals from the ln($WAGE$) equation, calculated using the instrumental variables estimates, on all available exogenous and instrumental variables. The test statistic is NR^2 from this artificial regression, and R^2 is the usual goodness-of-fit measure. If the surplus instruments are valid, then the test statistic has an asymptotic $\chi^2_{(1)}$ distribution, where the degrees of freedom are the number of surplus instruments. If the test statistic value is greater than the critical value from this distribution, then we reject the null hypothesis that the surplus instrument is valid. For the artificial regression $R^2 = 0.000883$, and the test statistic value is $NR^2 = 428 \times 0.000883 = 0.3779$.

Table 10.2   **Hausman Test Auxiliary Regression**

Variable	Coefficient	Std. Error	t-Statistic	Prob.
C	0.0481	0.3946	0.1219	0.9030
$EDUC$	0.0614	0.0310	1.9815	0.0482
$EXPER$	0.0442	0.0132	3.3363	0.0009
$EXPER^2$	−0.0009	0.0004	−2.2706	0.0237
$VHAT$	0.0582	0.0348	1.6711	0.0954

The 0.05 critical value for the chi-square distribution with one degree of freedom is 3.84, so we fail to reject the surplus instrument as valid. With this result we are reassured that our instrumental variables estimator for the wage equation is consistent.

10.5 Exercises

Answers to exercises marked * appear at www.wiley.com/go/global/hill.

10.5.1 PROBLEMS

10.1 Using state level data, a researcher wishes to examine the relationship between the median rent paid (*RENT*) as a function of median house values (*MDHOUSE* in $1,000). The percentage of the state population living in an urban area (*PCTURBAN*) is used as an additional control.

	(1) *RENT*	(2) *MDHOUSE*	(3) *MDHOUSE*	(4) *RENT*	(5) *RENT*	(6) *EHAT*
C	125.9	−18.67	7.225	120.7	120.7	−62.85
	(14.19)	(12.00)	(8.936)	(12.43)	(15.71)	(26.95)
PCTURBAN	0.525	0.182	0.616	0.0815	0.0815	−0.283
	(0.249)	(0.115)	(0.131)	(0.244)	(0.305)	(0.258)
MDHOUSE	1.521			2.240	2.240	
	(0.228)			(0.268)	(0.339)	
FAMINC		2.731				4.448
		(0.682)				(1.532)
REG2		−5.095				−6.768
		(4.122)				(9.262)
REG3		−1.778				4.847
		(4.073)				(9.151)
REG4		13.41				−18.77
		(4.048)				(9.096)
VHAT				−1.589		
				(0.398)		
N	50	50	50	50	50	50
R^2	0.669	0.691	0.317	0.754	0.599	0.226
SSE	20259.6	3767.6	8322.2	15054.0	24565.7	19019.9

Standard errors in parentheses

(a) The least squares estimates of the model are in column (1). Why might we be concerned that *MEDHOUSE*, the median price of houses, is endogenous in this regression?

(b) Four instruments are considered: median family income (*FAMINC* in $1,000) and region of the country (*REG1, REG2, REG3*). Using the models in columns (2) and (3), test if the instruments are weak.

(c) In column (4) the least squares residuals (*VHAT*) from the regression in column (2) are added as a regressor to the basic regression. The estimates are obtained using least squares. What is the usefulness of this regression? What does it indicate about the results in (1)?

(d) In column (5) are *IV/2SLS* estimates using the instruments listed in part (b). What differences do you observe between these results and the least squares results in column (1)? Note that the estimates (though not the standard errors) are the same in columns (4) and (5). Is this a mistake? Explain.

(e) In column (6) the residuals from the estimation in (5) are regressed upon the variables shown. What information is contained in these results?

10.2 The labor supply of married women has been a subject of a great deal of economic research. Consider the following supply equation specification

$$HOURS = \beta_1 + \beta_2 WAGE + \beta_3 EDUC + \beta_4 AGE + \beta_5 KIDSL6 + \beta_6 KIDS618$$
$$+ \beta_7 NWIFEINC + e$$

where *HOURS* is the supply of labor, *WAGE* is hourly wage, *EDUC* is years of education, *KIDSL6* is the number of children in the household who are less than six years old, *KIDS618* is the number between 6 and 18 years old, and *NWIFEINC* is household income from sources other than the wife's employment.

(a) Discuss the signs you expect for each of the coefficients.

(b) Explain why this supply equation cannot be consistently estimated by least squares regression.

(c) Suppose we consider the woman's labor market experience *EXPER* and its square, $EXPER^2$, to be instruments for *WAGE*. Explain how these variables satisfy the logic of instrumental variables.

(d) Is the supply equation identified? Explain.

(e) Describe the steps (not computer commands) you would take to obtain *2SLS* estimates.

10.5.2 COMPUTER EXERCISES

10.3 To examine the quantity theory of money, Brumm (2005) ["Money Growth, Output Growth, and Inflation: A Reexamination of the Modern Quantity Theory's Linchpin Prediction," *Southern Economic Journal*, 71(3), 661–667] specifies the equation

$$INFLAT = \beta_1 + \beta_2 MONEY + \beta_3 OUTPUT + e$$

where *INFLAT* is the growth rate of the general price level, *MONEY* is the growth rate of the money supply, and *OUTPUT* is the growth rate of national output. According to theory we should observe that $\beta_1 = 0$, $\beta_2 = 1$, and $\beta_3 = -1$. Dr. Brumm kindly provided us the data he used in his paper, which is contained in the file *brumm.dat*. It consists of 1995 data on 76 countries.

(a) Estimate the model by least squares, and test
  (i) the *strong* joint hypothesis that $\beta_1 = 0$, $\beta_2 = 1$, and $\beta_3 = -1$
  (ii) the *weak* joint hypothesis $\beta_2 = 1$ and $\beta_3 = -1$

(b) Examine the least squares residuals for the presence of heteroskedasticity related to the variable *MONEY*.

(c) Obtain robust standard errors for the model and compare them to the least squares standard errors.

(d) It is argued that *OUTPUT* may be endogenous. Four instrumental variables are proposed, *INITIAL* = initial level of real GDP, *SCHOOL* = a measure of the population's educational attainment, *INV* = average investment share of GDP, and *POPRATE* = average population growth rate. Using these instruments, obtain instrumental variables (*2SLS*) estimates of the inflation equation.

(e) Test the strong and weak hypotheses listed in (a) using the *IV* estimates. If your software permits, make the tests robust to heteroskedasticity.

(f) Use the Hausman test to check the endogeneity of *OUTPUT*. Because the regression errors may be heteroskedastic, use robust standard errors when estimating the auxiliary regression.

(g) Test the validity of the overidentifying restrictions.

(h) Test the relevance of the instruments using a joint F-test as described in Section 10.4.2. If your software permits, use a robust joint test.

10.4 The 25 values of x and e in *ivreg1.dat* were generated artificially. Use your computer software to carry out the following:

(a) Create the value of the dependent variable y from the model $y = \beta_1 + \beta_2 x + e = 1 + 1 \times x + e$ by the method described in Section 10.1.3.

(b) In the same graph, plot the value of y against x, and the regression function $E(y) = 1 + 1 \times x$. Do the data fall randomly about the regression function?

(c) Using the data on y created in part (a) and x, obtain the least squares estimates of the parameters β_1 and β_2. Compare the estimated values of the parameters to the true values.

(d) Plot the data and the fitted least squares regression line $\hat{y} = b_1 + b_2 x$. Compare this plot to the one in part (b).

(e) Compute the least squares residuals from the least squares regression in part (d). Find the sample correlation matrix of the variables x, e, and the least squares residuals $\hat{e} = y - b_1 - b_2 x$. Comment on the values of the correlations. Which of these correlations could you *not* compute using a sample of data collected from the real world?

10.5* Using your computer software, and the 50 observations on savings (y), income (x), and averaged income (z) in *savings.dat*,

(a) Estimate a least squares regression of savings on income.

(b) Estimate the relation between savings and income (x) using the instrumental variables estimator, with instrument z, using econometric software designed for instrumental variables, or two-stage least squares, estimation.

(c) Using the steps outlined in Section 10.4.1, carry out the Hausman test (via an artificial regression) for the existence of correlation between x and the random disturbance e.

(d) Use two least squares regressions to obtain the *IV* estimates in part (b). Compare the estimates, standard errors, and t-statistics to those in part (b) and comment on the differences.

10.6 The 500 values of x, y, z_1, and z_2 in *ivreg2.dat* were generated artificially. The variable $y = \beta_1 + \beta_2 x + e = 3 + 1 \times x + e$.

(a) The explanatory variable x follows a normal distribution with mean zero and variance $\sigma_x^2 = 2$. The random error e is normally distributed with mean zero and variance $\sigma_e^2 = 1$. The covariance between x and e is 0.9. Using the algebraic definition of correlation, determine the correlation between x and e.

(b) Given the values of y and x, and the values of $\beta_1 = 3$ and $\beta_2 = 1$, solve for the values of the random disturbances e. Find the sample correlation between x and e and compare it to your answer in (a).

(c) In the same graph, plot the value of y against x, and the regression function $E(y) = 3 + 1 \times x$. Note that the data do not fall randomly about the regression function.

(d) Estimate the regression model $y = \beta_1 + \beta_2 x + e$ by least squares using a sample consisting of the first $N = 10$ observations on y and x. Repeat using $N = 20$, $N = 100$, and $N = 500$. What do you observe about the least squares estimates? Are they getting closer to the true values as the sample size increases, or not? If not, why not?

(e) The variables z_1 and z_2 were constructed to have normal distributions with means zero and variances one, and to be correlated with x but uncorrelated with e. Using the full set of 500 observations, find the sample correlations between z_1, z_2, x, and e. Will z_1 and z_2 make good instrumental variables? Why? Is one better than the other? Why?

(f) Estimate the model $y = \beta_1 + \beta_2 x + e$ by instrumental variables using a sample consisting of the first $N=10$ observations and the instrument z_1. Repeat using $N=20, N=100$, and $N = 500$. What do you observe about the *IV* estimates? Are they getting closer to the true values as the sample size increases, or not? If not, why not?

(g) Estimate the model $y = \beta_1 + \beta_2 x + e$ by instrumental variables using a sample consisting of the first $N=10$ observations and the instrument z_2. Repeat using $N=20, N=100$, and $N=500$. What do you observe about the *IV* estimates? Are they getting closer to the true values as the sample size increases, or not? If not, why not? Comparing the results using z_1 alone to those using z_2 alone, which instrument leads to more precise estimation? Why is this so?

(h) Estimate the model $y=\beta_1 + \beta_2 x + e$ by instrumental variables using a sample consisting of the first $N=10$ observations and the instruments z_1 and z_2. Repeat using $N=20$, $N=100$, and $N=500$. What do you observe about the *IV* estimates? Are they getting closer to the true values as the sample size increases, or not? If not, why not? Is estimation more precise using two instruments than one, as in parts (f) and (g)?

10.7* A consulting firm run by Mr. John Chardonnay is investigating the relative efficiency of wine production at 75 California wineries. John sets up the production function

$$Q = \beta_1 + \beta_2 MGT + \beta_3 CAP + \beta_4 LAB + e$$

where Q is an index of wine output for a winery, taking into account both quantity and quality, MGT is a variable that reflects the efficiency of management, CAP is an index of capital input, and LAB is an index of labor input. Because he cannot get data on management efficiency, John collects observations on the number of years of experience ($XPER$) of each winery manager and uses that variable in place of MGT. The 75 observations are stored in the file *chard.dat*.

(a) Estimate the revised equation using least squares and comment on the results.

(b) Find corresponding interval estimates for wine output at wineries that have the sample average values for labor and capital and have managers with
  (i) 10 years experience
  (ii) 20 years experience
  (iii) 30 years experience.

(c) John is concerned that the proxy variable $XPER$ might be correlated with the error term. He decides to do a Hausman test, using the manager's age (AGE) as an instrument for $XPER$. Regress $XPER$ on AGE, CAP, and LAB, and save the residuals. Include these residuals as an extra variable in the equation you estimated in part (a), and comment on the outcome of the Hausman test.

(d) Use the instrumental variables estimator to estimate the equation

$$Q = \beta_1 + \beta_2 XPER + \beta_3 CAP + \beta_4 LAB + e$$

with *AGE*, *CAP*, and *LAB* as the instrumental variables. Comment on the results and compare them with those obtained in part (a).

(e) Find corresponding interval estimates for wine output at wineries that have the sample average values for labor and capital and have managers with

(i) 10 years experience

(ii) 20 years experience

(iii) 30 years experience

Compare these interval estimates with those obtained in part (b).

10.8 The labor supply of married women has been a subject of a great deal of economic research. A classic work[6] is that of Professor Tom Mroz, who kindly provided us his data. The data file is *mroz.dat* and the variable definitions are in the file *mroz.def*. The data file contains information on women who have worked in the previous year and those who have not. The variable indicating whether a woman worked is *LFP*, labor force participation, which takes the value 1 if a woman worked and 0 if she did not. Use only the data on women who worked for the following exercises. Consider the supply equation specification

$$HOURS = \beta_1 + \beta_2 \ln(WAGE) + \beta_3 EDUC + \beta_4 AGE + \beta_5 KIDSL6$$
$$+ \beta_6 KIDS618 + \beta_7 NWIFEINC + e$$

The variable *NWIFEINC* is defined as

$$NWIFEINC = FAMINC - WAGE \times HOURS$$

(a) Considering the woman's labor market experience *EXPER* and its square, $EXPER^2$, to be instruments for $\ln(WAGE)$, test the endogeneity of $\ln(WAGE)$ using the Hausman test.

(b) Estimate the first-stage equation

$$\ln(WAGE) = \pi_1 + \pi_2 EDUC + \pi_3 AGE + \pi_4 KIDSL6 + \pi_5 KIDS618$$
$$+ \pi_6 NWIFEINC + \pi_7 EXPER + \pi_8 EXPER^2 + v$$

using least squares estimation, and test the joint significance of *EXPER* and $EXPER^2$. Do these instruments seem adequate?

(c) In this problem we have one surplus instrument. Check the validity of the surplus instrument using the test suggested in Section 10.4.2. What do you conclude about the validity of the overidentifying variable?

(d) It is also possible in the supply equation that the woman's level of education is endogenous, due to the omission of ability from the model. Discuss the suitability of using as instruments the woman's mother's education (*MOTHEREDUC*), her father's education (*FATHEREDUC*), her husband's education (*HEDUC*), and the woman's number of siblings (*SIBLINGS*).

---

[6] Mroz, T. A. (1987) "The sensitivity of an empirical model of a married woman's hours of work to economic and statistical assumptions," *Econometrica*, 55, 765–800.

(e) Estimate the first-stage equations for *EDUC* and ln(*WAGE*) including all instruments in (b) and the potential instruments listed in (d). In each first-stage equation, test the joint significance of *EXPER*, *EXPER*^{2}, *MOTHEREDUC*, *FATHEREDUC*, *HEDUC*, and *SIBLINGS*.

(f) Use the results of (e) to carry out a Hausman test of the endogeneity of *EDUC* and ln(*WAGE*).

(g) Compute the *2SLS* estimates of the supply equation, assuming that *EDUC* and ln(*WAGE*) are endogenous. Discuss the estimates' signs and significance. Are there any surprises?

(h) Test the validity of the overidentifying instruments based on part (g).

(i) Write a 200-word summary of what you have discovered in this exercise about the labor supply of married women.

10.9 Consider a supply model for edible chicken, which the U.S. Department of Agriculture calls "broilers." The data for this exercise are in the file *newbroiler.dat*, which is adapted from the data provided by Epple and McCallum (2006).[7] The data are annual, 1950–2001, but in the estimations use data from 1960–1999. The supply equation is

$$\ln(QPROD_t) = \beta_1 + \beta_2 \ln(P_t) + \beta_3 \ln(PF_t) + \beta_4 TIME_t + \ln(QPROD_{t-1}) + e_t^s$$

where *QPROD* = aggregate production of young chickens, *P* = real price index of fresh chicken, *PF* = real price index of broiler feed, *TIME* = 1, ..., 52. This supply equation is dynamic, with lagged production on the right-hand side. This predetermined variable is known at time *t* and is treated as exogenous. *TIME*(= 1, 2, ..., 52) is included to capture technical progress in production. Some potential *external* instrumental variables are ln(Y_t) where *Y* is real per capita income; ln(PB_t) where *PB* is the real price of beef; *POPGRO* = percentage population growth from year $t − 1$ to t; ln($P_{t−1}$) = lagged log of real price of chicken; ln(*EXPTS*) = log of exports of chicken.

(a) Estimate the supply equation by least squares. Discuss the estimation results. Are the signs and significance what you anticipated?

(b) Estimate the supply equation using an instrumental variables estimator with all available instruments. Compare these results to those in (a).

(c) Test the endogeneity of ln(P_t) using the regression-based Hausman test described in Section 10.4.1.

(d) Check whether the instruments are adequate, using the test for weak instruments described in Section 10.3.5. What do you conclude?

(e) Do you suspect the validity of any instruments on logical grounds? If so, which ones, and why? Check the instrument validity using the test procedure described in Section 10.4.2.

Appendix 10A Conditional and Iterated Expectations

In this appendix we provide some results related to conditional expectations.

---

[7] "Simultaneous equation econometrics: The missing example," *Economic Inquiry*, 44(2), 374–384. We would like to thank Professor Bennett McCallum for his generous help.

10A.1 CONDITIONAL EXPECTATIONS

In the Probability Primer, Section P.3, we defined the conditional probability distribution. If X and Y are two random variables with joint probability distribution $f(x, y)$, then the conditional probability distribution of Y given X is $f(y|x)$. We can use this conditional *pdf* to compute the **conditional mean** of Y given X. That is, we can obtain the expected value of Y given that $X = x$. The conditional expectation $E(Y|X = x)$ is the average (or mean) value of Y given that X takes the value x. In the discrete case it is defined to be

$$E(Y|X = x) = \sum_y yP(Y = y|X = x) = \sum_y yf(y|x) \tag{10A.1}$$

Similarly we can define the **conditional variance** of Y given X. This is the variance of the conditional distribution of Y given X. In the discrete case it is

$$\text{var}(Y|X = x) = \sum_y \left[y - E(Y|X = x)\right]^2 f(y|x)$$

10A.2 ITERATED EXPECTIONS

The **law of iterated expectations** says that the expected value of Y is equal to the expected value of the conditional expectation of Y given X. That is,

$$E(Y) = E_X[E(Y|X)] \tag{10A.2}$$

What this means becomes clearer with the following demonstration that it is true in the discrete case. We will use two facts about probability distributions discussed in Appendix B.1.3. First, the marginal *pdf* of Y is $f(y) = \sum_x f(x, y)$ and second, the joint *pdf* of X and Y can be expressed as $f(x, y) = f(y|x)f(x)$ [see Appendix B, (B.14)]. Then,

$$E(Y) = \sum_y yf(y) = \sum_y y\left[\sum_x f(x, y)\right]$$

$$= \sum_y y\left[\sum_x f(y|x)f(x)\right]$$

$$= \sum_x \left[\sum_y yf(y|x)\right] f(x) \qquad \text{(by changing order of summation)}$$

$$= \sum_x E(Y|X = x)f(x)$$

$$= E_X[E(Y|X)]$$

In the final expression $E_X[\ ]$ means that the expectation of the term in brackets is taken assuming that X is random. So the expected value of Y can be found by finding its conditional expectation given X, and then taking the expected value of the result with respect to X.

Two other results can be shown to be true in the same way:

$$E(XY) = E_X[XE(Y|X)] \tag{10A.3}$$

and

$$\text{cov}(X, Y) = E_X[(X - \mu_X)E(Y|X)] \tag{10A.4}$$

10A.3 REGRESSION MODEL APPLICATIONS

The results above relate to assumption A10.3* made in Section 10.1.2. In the regression model $y = \beta_1 + \beta_2 x + e$, we have assumed that the conditional mean of y is $E(y|x) = \beta_1 + \beta_2 x$. Equivalently we have assumed that $E(e|x) = 0$. Conditional on x, the expected value of the error term is zero. Using the law of iterated expectations (10A.2), it then follows that the *unconditional* expectation of the error is also zero,

$$E(e) = E_x[E(e|x)] = E_x[0] = 0 \tag{10A.5}$$

Next, using (10A.3),

$$E(xe) = E_x[xE(e|x)] = E_x[x \times 0] = 0 \tag{10A.6}$$

and using (10A.4),

$$\text{cov}(x, e) = E_x[(x - \mu_x)E(e|x)] = E_x[(x - \mu_x)0] = 0 \tag{10A.7}$$

Thus, if $E(e|x) = 0$ it follows that $E(e) = 0$, $E(xe) = 0$, and $\text{cov}(x, e) = 0$. However, from (10A.7), if $E(e|x) \neq 0$ then $\text{cov}(x, e) \neq 0$.

Appendix 10B The Inconsistency of the Least Squares Estimator

Here we provide an algebraic proof that the least squares estimator is not consistent when $\text{cov}(x, e) \neq 0$. Our regression model is $y = \beta_1 + \beta_2 x + e$. Under A10.3* $E(e) = 0$, so that $E(y) = \beta_1 + \beta_2 E(x)$. Then,

- Subtract this expectation from the original equation,

$$y - E(y) = \beta_2[x - E(x)] + e$$

- Multiply both sides by $x - E(x)$,

$$[x - E(x)][y - E(y)] = \beta_2[x - E(x)]^2 + [x - E(x)]e$$

- Take expected values of both sides,

$$E[x - E(x)][y - E(y)] = \beta_2 E[x - E(x)]^2 + E\{[x - E(x)]e\},$$

or

$$\text{cov}(x, y) = \beta_2 \text{var}(x) + \text{cov}(x, e)$$

- Solve for β_2:

$$\beta_2 = \frac{\text{cov}(x, y)}{\text{var}(x)} - \frac{\text{cov}(x, e)}{\text{var}(x)} \qquad (10\text{B}.1)$$

Equation (10B.1) is the basis for showing when the least squares estimator is consistent, and when it is not.

If we can assume that $\text{cov}(x, e) = 0$, then

$$\beta_2 = \frac{\text{cov}(x, y)}{\text{var}(x)} \qquad (10\text{B}.2)$$

The least squares estimator can be expressed as

$$b_2 = \frac{\Sigma(x_i - \bar{x})(y_i - \bar{y})}{\Sigma(x_i - \bar{x})^2} = \frac{\Sigma(x_i - \bar{x})(y_i - \bar{y})/(N-1)}{\Sigma(x_i - \bar{x})^2/(N-1)} = \frac{\widehat{\text{cov}(x, y)}}{\widehat{\text{var}(x)}} \qquad (10\text{B}.3)$$

This shows that the least squares estimator b_2 is the sample analog of the population relationship in (10B.2). The sample variance and covariance converge to the true variance and covariance as the sample size N increases, so that the least squares estimator converges to β_2. That is, if $\text{cov}(x, e) = 0$ then

$$b_2 = \frac{\widehat{\text{cov}(x, y)}}{\widehat{\text{var}(x)}} \rightarrow \frac{\text{cov}(x, y)}{\text{var}(x)} = \beta_2$$

showing that the least squares estimator is consistent.

On the other hand, if x and e are correlated, then

$$\beta_2 = \frac{\text{cov}(x, y)}{\text{var}(x)} - \frac{\text{cov}(x, e)}{\text{var}(x)}$$

The least squares estimator now converges to

$$b_2 \rightarrow \frac{\text{cov}(x, y)}{\text{var}(x)} = \beta_2 + \frac{\text{cov}(x, e)}{\text{var}(x)} \neq \beta_2 \qquad (10\text{B}.4)$$

In this case b_2 is an inconsistent estimator of β_2 and the amount of bias that exists even asymptotically, when samples can be assumed to be very large, is $\text{cov}(x, e)/\text{var}(x)$. The direction of the bias depends on the sign of the covariance between x and e. If factors in the error are positively correlated with the explanatory variable x, then the least squares estimator will overestimate the true parameter.

Appendix 10C The Consistency of the *IV* Estimator

The demonstration that the instrumental variables estimator is consistent follows the logic used in Appendix 10B. The *IV* estimator can be expressed as

$$\hat{\beta}_2 = \frac{\Sigma(z_i - \bar{z})(y_i - \bar{y})/(N-1)}{\Sigma(z_i - \bar{z})(x_i - \bar{x})/(N-1)} = \frac{\widehat{\text{cov}(z, y)}}{\widehat{\text{cov}(z, x)}} \qquad (10\text{C}.1)$$

The sample covariance converges to the true covariance in large samples, so we can say

$$\hat{\beta}_2 \rightarrow \frac{\text{cov}(z, y)}{\text{cov}(z, x)} \tag{10C.2}$$

If the instrumental variable z is not correlated with x in both the sample data and the population, then the instrumental variable estimator fails, since that would mean a zero in the denominator of $\hat{\beta}_2$ in (10C.1) and (10C.2). Thus for an instrumental variable to be valid, it must be uncorrelated with the error term e but correlated with the explanatory variable x.

Now, follow the same steps that led to (10B.1). We obtain

$$\beta_2 = \frac{\text{cov}(z, y)}{\text{cov}(z, x)} - \frac{\text{cov}(z, e)}{\text{cov}(z, x)} \tag{10C.3}$$

If we can assume that $\text{cov}(z, e) = 0$, a condition we imposed on the choice of the instrumental variable z, then the instrumental variables estimator in (10C.2) converges in large samples to β_2,

$$\hat{\beta}_2 \rightarrow \frac{\text{cov}(z, y)}{\text{cov}(z, x)} = \beta_2 \tag{10C.4}$$

Thus if $\text{cov}(z, e) = 0$ and $\text{cov}(z, x) \neq 0$, then the instrumental variable estimator of β_2 is consistent, in a situation in which the least squares estimator is not consistent due to correlation between x and e.

Appendix 10D The Logic of the Hausman Test

In Section 10.4.1 we present a test for whether or not an explanatory variable is endogenous using an artificial regression. Let us explore how and why this test might work. The simple regression model is

$$y = \beta_1 + \beta_2 x + e \tag{10D.1}$$

If x is correlated with the error term e, then x is endogenous and the least squares estimator is biased and inconsistent.

An instrumental variable z must be correlated with x but uncorrelated with e in order to be valid. A correlation between z and x implies that there is a linear association between them (see the Probability Primer, Section P.5.6). This means that we can describe their relationship as a regression:

$$x = \pi_0 + \pi_1 z + v \tag{10D.2}$$

There is a correlation between x and z if, and only if, $\pi_1 \neq 0$. This regression is called a "first-stage" equation. The standard regression assumptions apply to (10D.2), in particular the error term v has mean zero, $E(v) = 0$. We can divide x into two parts, a systematic part and a random part, as

$$x = E(x) + v \tag{10D.3}$$

where $E(x) = \pi_0 + \pi_1 z$. If we knew π_0 and π_1, we could substitute (10D.3) into the simple regression model (10D.1) to obtain

$$
\begin{aligned}
y &= \beta_1 + \beta_2 x + e = \beta_1 + \beta_2[E(x) + v] + e \\
&= \beta_1 + \beta_2 E(x) + \beta_2 v + e
\end{aligned} \tag{10D.4}
$$

Now, suppose for a moment that $E(x)$ and v can be observed and are viewed as explanatory variables in the regression $y = \beta_1 + \beta_2 E(x) + \beta_2 v + e$. Will least squares work when applied to this equation? The explanatory variable $E(x)$ is not correlated with the error term e (or v). The problem, if there is one, comes from a correlation between v (the random part of x) and e. In fact, in the regression (10D.1), any correlation between x and e implies correlation between v and e, because $v = x - E(x)$.

We cannot exactly create the partition in (10D.3), because we do not know π_0 and π_1. However, we can consistently estimate the first-stage (10D.2) by least squares to obtain the fitted first-stage model $\hat{x} = \hat{\pi}_0 + \hat{\pi}_1 z$ and the residuals $\hat{v} = x - \hat{x}$, which we can rearrange to obtain an estimated analog of (10D.3),

$$
x = \hat{x} + \hat{v} \tag{10D.5}
$$

Substitute (10D.5) into the original (10D.1) to obtain

$$
\begin{aligned}
y &= \beta_1 + \beta_2 x + e = \beta_1 + \beta_2[\hat{x} + \hat{v}] + e \\
&= \beta_1 + \beta_2 \hat{x} + \beta_2 \hat{v} + e
\end{aligned} \tag{10D.6}
$$

To reduce confusion, let the coefficient of $\hat{v}$ be denoted as γ, so that (10D.6) becomes

$$
y = \beta_1 + \beta_2 \hat{x} + \gamma \hat{v} + e \tag{10D.7}
$$

If we omit $\hat{v}$ from (10D.7), the regression becomes

$$
y = \beta_1 + \beta_2 \hat{x} + e \tag{10D.8}
$$

The least squares estimates of β_1 and β_2 in (10D.8) *are* the *IV* estimates, as defined in (10.22). Then recall from Chapter 6.3.1, (6.23), that if we omit a variable from a regression that is uncorrelated with the included variable(s), there is no omitted variables bias, and in fact the least squares estimates are unchanged! This holds true in (10D.7) because the least squares residuals $\hat{v}$ are uncorrelated with $\hat{x}$ and the intercept variable. Thus the least squares estimates of β_1 and β_2 in (10D.7) and (10D.8) are identical, and are equal to the *IV* estimates. Consequently, the least squares estimators of β_1 and β_2 in (10D.7) are consistent whether or not x is exogenous, because they are the *IV* estimators.

What about γ? If x is exogenous, and hence v and e are uncorrelated, then the least squares estimator of γ in (10D.7) will also converge in large samples to β_2. However, if x is endogenous, then the least squares estimator of γ in (10D.7) will *not* converge to β_2 in large samples, because $\hat{v}$, like v, is correlated with the error term e. This observation makes it possible to test for whether x is exogenous by testing the equality of the estimates of β_2 and γ in (10D.7). If we reject the null hypothesis $H_0 : \beta_2 = \gamma$, then we reject the exogeneity of x, and conclude that it is endogenous.

Carrying out the test is made simpler by playing a trick on (10D.7). Add and subtract $\beta_2 \hat{v}$ to the right-hand side to obtain

$$
\begin{aligned}
y &= \beta_1 + \beta_2 \hat{x} + \gamma \hat{v} + e + \beta_2 \hat{v} - \beta_2 \hat{v} \\
&= \beta_1 + \beta_2 (\hat{x} + \hat{v}) + (\gamma - \beta_2) \hat{v} + e \qquad\qquad (10D.9) \\
&= \beta_1 + \beta_2 x + \delta \hat{v} + e
\end{aligned}
$$

Thus, instead of testing $H_0 : \beta_2 = \gamma$, we can simply use an ordinary t-test of the null hypothesis $H_0 : \delta = 0$ in (10D.9), which is exactly the test we described in Section 10.4.1. This is much easier, because ordinary software automatically prints out the t-statistic for this hypothesis test.

Appendix 10E Testing for Weak Instruments

As discussed in Section 10.3.8a, the F-test for weak instruments discussed in Section 10.3.5 is not valid for models with more than one endogenous variable on the right side of the equation.[8] Using **canonical correlations** there is a solution to the problem of identifying weak instruments when an equation has more than one endogenous variable. Canonical correlations are a generalization of the usual concept of a correlation between two variables and attempt to describe the association between two **sets** of variables. The association in which we are interested is the association between the pair of endogenous variables (x_{G+1}, x_{G+2}) and the pair of additional, external, instrumental variables (z_1, z_2) **after** controlling for the effect of the other G exogenous variables $x_1 \equiv 1, x_2, \dots, x_G$. We introduced this idea in Section 10.3.7. The effects of the G exogenous variables are "removed" by first regressing (x_{G+1}, x_{G+2}) and (z_1, z_2) on $x_1 \equiv 1$, $x_2, \dots, x_G$ and then computing the residuals ($\tilde{x}_{G+1}$, $\tilde{x}_{G+2}$) and ($\tilde{z}_1$, $\tilde{z}_2$). This process is often called **partialing out** or **netting out** the effect of $x_1 \equiv 1, x_2, \dots, x_G$.[9]

Suppose that $x_1^* = h_{11} \tilde{x}_{G+1} + h_{21} \tilde{x}_{G+2}$ is a linear combination of the "partialed out" endogenous variables ($\tilde{x}_{G+1}$, $\tilde{x}_{G+2}$) and $z_1^* = k_{11} \tilde{z}_1 + k_{21} \tilde{z}_2$ is a linear combination of the "partialed out" instrumental variables ($\tilde{z}_1$, $\tilde{z}_2$). Using **canonical correlation analysis**, we can determine values h_{11}, h_{21}, k_{11}, and k_{21}, resulting in the largest correlation between x_1^* and z_1^*.[10] It is called the **first** canonical correlation, r_1. Similarly, we can determine values h_{12}, h_{22}, k_{12}, and k_{22}, resulting in the second largest correlation between $x_2^* = h_{12} \tilde{x}_{G+1} + h_{22} \tilde{x}_{G+2}$ and $z_2^* = k_{12} \tilde{z}_1 + k_{22} \tilde{z}_2$, which is called the **second** canonical correlation, r_2—and so on.

If we have two variables in the first set of variables and two variables in the second set, then there are two canonical correlations, r_1 and r_2. If we have B variables in the first group (the endogenous variables with the effects of $x_1 \equiv 1, x_2, \dots, x_G$ removed) and $L \geq B$ variables in the second group (the group of instruments with the effects of $x_1 \equiv 1, x_2, \dots, x_G$ removed), then there are B possible canonical correlations, $r_1 \geq r_2 \geq \cdots \geq r_B$. If the

---

[8] The $F > 10$ rule of thumb comes from D. Staiger and J. H. Stock (1997) "Instrumental Variables with Weak Instruments," *Econometrica*, 65, pp. 557–586.

[9] See, for example, William Greene, *Econometric Analysis, 6th Edition*, Pearson Prentice Hall, 2008, pp. 25–29.

[10] Certain normalizations on h and k constants are necessary to make the solutions unique. The algebra and calculations are beyond the scope of this book. An online search will reveal many sources, but virtually all use matrix algebra and multidimensional calculus. Harold Hotelling did research in mathematical statistics and economic theory and introduced the concept of canonical correlation in a 1935 publication, "The most predictable criterion," in the *Journal of Educational Psychology*.

smallest canonical correlation $r_B = 0$, then we do not have enough relationships between the instruments and the endogenous variables, and **the equation is not identified**.

10E.1 A TEST FOR WEAK IDENTIFICATION

Using the smallest canonical correlation, we are able to test whether any relationship between the instruments and the endogenous variables is sufficiently strong for reliable econometric inferences.[11] Let N denote the sample size, B the number of right-hand-side endogenous variables, G the number of exogenous variables included in the equation (including the intercept), L the number of "external" instruments that are not included in the model, and r_B the minimum canonical correlation. A test for weak identification, the situation that arises when the instruments are correlated with the endogenous regressors but only weakly, is based on the **Cragg-Donald F-test statistic**[12]

$$\text{Cragg-Donald } F = [(N - G - B)/L] \times [r_B^2 / (1 - r_B^2)] \qquad (10\text{E}.1)$$

The Cragg-Donald statistic reduces to the usual weak instruments F-test when the number of endogenous variables is $B = 1$. Critical values for this test statistic have been tabulated by James Stock and Motohiro Yogo (2005),[13] so that we can test the null hypothesis that the instruments are weak against the alternative that they are not, for two particular consequences of weak instruments.

- **Relative Bias:** In the presence of weak instruments the amount of bias in the *IV* estimator can become large. Stock and Yogo consider the bias when estimating the coefficients of the endogenous variables. They examine the maximum *IV* estimator bias relative to the bias of the least squares estimator. Stock and Yogo give the illustration of estimating the return to education. If a researcher believes that the least squares estimator suffers a maximum bias of 10%, and if the relative bias is 0.1, then the maximum bias of the *IV* estimator is 1%.

- **Rejection Rate (Test Size):** When estimating a model with endogenous regressors, testing hypotheses about the coefficients of the endogenous variables is frequently of interest. If we choose the $\alpha = 0.05$ level of significance we expect that a true null hypothesis is rejected 5% of the time in repeated samples. If instruments are weak, then the actual rejection rate of the null hypothesis, also known as the **test size**, may be larger. Stock and Yogo's second criterion is the maximum rejection rate of a true null hypothesis if we choose $\alpha = 0.05$. For example, we may be willing to accept a maximum rejection rate of 10% for a test at the 5% level, but we may not be willing to accept a rejection rate of 20% for a 5% level test.

---

[11] The tests based on canonical correlations are neatly summarized in "Enhanced Routines for Instrumental Variables/Generalized Method of Moments Estimation and Testing," by Christopher F. Baum, Mark E. Schaffer, and Steven Stillman, *The Stata Journal* (2007), 7, pp. 465–506. Further discussion is provided by Alastair R. Hall, Glenn D. Rudebusch and David W. Wilcox (1996) "Judging Instrument Relevance in Instrumental Variables Estimation," *International Economic Review*, 37(2), pp. 283–298.

[12] Cragg, J. G. and S. G. Donald (1993) "Testing Identifiability and Specification in Instrumental Variable Models," *Econometric Theory*, 9, 222–240. D. Poskitt and C. Skeels (2009), "Assessing the magnitude of the concentration parameter in a simultaneous equations model," *The Econometrics Journal*, 12, pp. 26–44, showed that the Cragg-Donald statistic could be conveniently written in terms of the smallest canonical correlation.

[13] "Testing for Weak Instruments in Linear IV Regression," in *Identification and Inference for Econometric Models: Essays in Honor of Thomas Rothenberg*, eds, Donald W. K. Andrews and James H. Stock, *Cambridge University Press*, Chapter 5.

To test the null hypothesis that instruments are weak against the alternative that they are not, we compare the Cragg-Donald F-test statistic to a critical value chosen from Table 10E.1 or Table 10E.2.

1.   **First** choose either the maximum relative bias or maximum test size criterion. You must also choose the maximum relative bias or maximum test size you are willing to accept.

2a.   If you choose the maximum test size criterion, select from Table 10E.1 the critical value associated with a maximum test size of 0.10, 0.15, 0.20 or 0.25 for $B = 1$ or $B = 2$ endogenous variables using $L = 1$ to $L = 4$ instrumental variables.

2b.   If you choose the maximum relative bias criterion, select from Table 10E.2 the critical value associated with a maximum relative bias of 0.05, 0.10, 0.20 or 0.30 for $B = 1$ or $B = 2$ endogenous variables using $L = 3$ or $L = 4$ instrumental variables. There are no critical values using this criterion if $L < 3$.

3.   Reject the null hypothesis that the instruments are weak if the Cragg-Donald F-test statistic is larger than the tabled critical value. If the F-test statistic is not larger than the critical value, then do not reject the null hypothesis that the instruments are weak.

Table 10E.1   **Critical Values for the Weak Instrument Test Based on *IV* Test Size (5% level of significance)**[14]

L	$B = 1$ Maximum Test Size				$B = 2$ Maximum Test Size			
	0.10	0.15	0.20	0.25	0.10	0.15	0.20	0.25
1	16.38	8.96	6.66	5.53				
2	19.93	11.59	8.75	7.25	7.03	4.58	3.95	3.63
3	22.30	12.83	9.54	7.80	13.43	8.18	6.40	5.45
4	24.58	13.96	10.26	8.31	16.87	9.93	7.54	6.28

Table 10E.2   **Critical Values for the Weak Instrument Test Based on *IV* Relative Bias (5% level of significance)**[15]

L	$B = 1$ Maximum Relative Bias				$B = 2$ Maximum Relative Bias			
	0.05	0.10	0.20	0.30	0.05	0.10	0.20	0.30
3	13.91	9.08	6.46	5.39				
4	16.85	10.27	6.71	5.34	11.04	7.56	5.57	4.73

---

[14] These values are from Table 5.2, page 101, in Stock and Yogo (2005), *op cit*. The authors thank James Stock and Motohiro Yogo for permission to use these results. (Their tables are more extensive than the ones we provide.)

[15] These values are from Table 5.1, page 100, in James H. Stock and Motohiro Yogo (2005), *op cit*. In their paper Stock and Yogo explain that the $F > 10$ rule introduced by Staiger and Stock (1997), *op cit.*, is for $B = 1$ approximately the critical value for a maximum relative bias of 0.10 for all values of L. Their critical values can be considered refinements of the Staiger-Stock rule of thumb.

10E.2   EXAMPLES OF TESTING FOR WEAK IDENTIFICATION

In Section 10.2.4 we introduced an example of a wage equation for married working women using Thomas Mroz's data. Consider the following *HOURS* supply equation specification:

$$HOURS = \beta_1 + \beta_2 MTR + \beta_3 EDUC + \beta_4 KIDSL6 + \beta_5 NWIFEINC + e \qquad (10E.4)$$

The variable $NWIFEINC = (FAMINC - WAGE \times HOURS)/1000$ is household income attributable to sources other than the wife's income. The variable *MTR* is the marginal tax rate facing the wife, including Social Security taxes. In this equation we expect the signs of coefficients on *MTR*, *KIDSL6* and *NWIFEINC* to be negative, and the coefficient on *EDUC* is of uncertain sign. In this example we treat the marginal tax rate as endogenous.[16] Initially we treat *EDUC* as exogenous and use the wife's previous years of work experience, *EXPER*, as an instrumental variable for *MTR*.

Weak *IV* Example 1: Endogenous: *MTR*; Instrument: *EXPER*
Suppose that we choose the maximum test size criterion and are willing to accept a maximum test size of 0.15 for a 5% test. In Table 10E.1 we see that for $B = 1$ (one right-side endogenous variable) and $L = 1$ (one instrument) that the Stock-Yogo critical value is 8.96. The estimated first-stage equation for *MTR* is Model (1) of Table 10E.3. The *F*-statistic for the hypothesis that the coefficient of experience is zero is 30.61. The Cragg-Donald *F*-statistic is also 30.61 in this case. Since the Cragg-Donald *F*-test statistic is larger than the Stock-Yogo critical value 8.96, we reject the null hypothesis that the instruments are weak and accept the alternative that they are not weak. This conclusion is conditional upon the test criterion we have chosen and the maximum size selected. The relative bias criterion cannot be used in this case because it requires at least three instruments. The estimated coefficient of *MTR* in the estimated *HOURS* supply equation in Model (1) of Table 10E.4 is negative and significant at the 5% level.

Weak *IV* Example 2: *Endogenous: MTR; Instruments: EXPER, EXPER², LARGECITY*
For the sake of illustration, consider using the $L = 3$ instruments *EXPER*, $EXPER^2$, and the indicator variable *LARGECITY*, which $= 1$ if the city is large. Suppose we choose the maximum relative bias criterion and are willing to tolerate a maximum relative bias of 0.10. From Table 10E.2 the Stock-Yogo critical value is 9.08. If the Cragg-Donald *F*-test statistic is greater than this value, we reject the null hypothesis that the instruments are weak. The first-stage equation estimates are reported in Model (2) of Table 10E.3. The Cragg-Donald *F*-statistic is 13.22. We conclude that using this test the instruments are not weak. If, however, we are only willing to accept a 0.05 relative bias, then the Stock-Yogo critical value is 13.91. Since the Cragg-Donald *F*-statistic is less than this value, we cannot reject the null hypothesis that the instruments are weak. The estimated coefficient of *MTR* in the estimated *HOURS* supply equation in Model (2) of Table 10E.4 is negative and significant at the 5% level, although the magnitudes of all the coefficients are smaller in absolute value for this estimation than the model in Model (1). Qualitatively the estimates of Model (1) and Model (2), using $L = 1$ instrument and $L = 3$ instruments are much the same, with likely thanks to the strong instrument *EXPER*. This example illustrates the point that having more instrumental variables is not necessarily beneficial from the standpoint of weak instrument diagnostics.

---

[16] This idea is explored by Mroz (1987, p. 786).

Table 10E.3   **First-stage Equations**

MODEL Dependent/ independent	(1) *MTR*	(2) *MTR*	(3) *MTR*	(4) *EDUC*	(5) *MTR*	(6) *EDUC*
C	0.87930	0.88470	0.79907	8.71459	0.82960	8.17622
	(74.33)	(71.93)	(103.22)	(25.83)	(93.34)	(20.34)
EXPER	−0.00142	−0.00217			−0.00168	0.02957
	(−5.53)	(−2.65)			(−6.23)	(2.43)
EDUC	−0.00718	−0.00689				
	(−7.76)	(−7.45)				
KIDSL6	0.02037	0.02039	0.02189	0.61812	0.01559	0.72921
	(3.86)	(3.89)	(3.92)	(2.54)	(2.87)	(2.96)
NWIFEINC	−0.00551	−0.00539	−0.00565	0.04961	−0.00585	0.05304
	(−27.40)	(−26.35)	(−27.15)	(5.46)	(−28.96)	(5.81)
EXPER²		0.00002				
		(1.01)				
LARGECITY		−0.01163				
		(−2.70)				
MOTHEREDUC			−0.00111	0.15202	−0.00134	0.15601
			(−1.40)	(4.40)	(−1.76)	(4.54)
FATHEREDUC			−0.00180	0.16371	−0.00202	0.16754
			(−2.40)	(5.01)	(−2.81)	(5.15)
N	428	428	428	428	428	428
Weak IV F	30.61	13.22	8.14	49.02	18.86	35.03
Number IV L	1	3	2	2	3	3
Number Endog B	1	1	2	2	2	2

t statistics in parentheses.

Weak *IV* Example 3 *Endogenous: MTR, EDUC; Instruments: MOTHEREDUC, FATHEREDUC*

Now treat both marginal tax rate *MTR* and education *EDUC* as endogenous, so that $B = 2$. Following Section 10.3.6 we use mother's and father's education, *MOTHEREDUC* and *FATHEREDUC*, as instruments, so that $L = 2$. Suppose that we are willing to accept a maximum test size of 15% for a 5% test. From Table 10E.1 the critical value for the weak instrument test is 4.58. The first-stage equations for *MTR* and *EDUC* are Model (3) and Model (4) of Table 10E.3. These instruments are strong for *EDUC* as we have earlier seen, with the first-stage weak instrument *F*-test statistic 49.02. For *MTR* [Model (3)] these two instruments are less strong. *FATHEREDUC* is significant at the 5% level, and the first-stage weak instrument *F*-test statistic is 8.14, which has a *p*-value of 0.0003. While this does not satisfy the $F \geq 10$ rule of thumb, it is "close," and we may have concluded that these two instruments were adequately strong. The Cragg-Donald *F*-test statistic value is only 0.101, which is far below the critical value 4.58 for 15% maximum test size (for a 5% test on *MTR* and *EDUC*). We cannot reject the null hypothesis that the instruments are *weak*, despite the favorable first stage *F*-test values. The estimates of the *HOURS* supply equation, Model (3)

Table 10E.4   *IV* **Estimation of Hours Equation**

MODEL	(1)	(2)	(3)	(4)
C	17423.7211	14394.1144	−24491.5995	18067.8425
	(5.56)	(5.68)	(−0.31)	(5.11)
MTR	−18456.5896	−14934.3696	29709.4677	−18633.9223
	(−5.08)	(−5.09)	(0.33)	(−4.85)
EDUC	−145.2928	−118.8846	258.5590	−189.8611
	(−4.40)	(−4.28)	(0.32)	(−3.04)
KIDSL6	151.0229	58.7879	−1144.4779	190.2755
	(1.07)	(0.48)	(−0.46)	(1.20)
NWIFEINC	−103.8983	−85.1934	149.2325	−102.1516
	(−5.27)	(−5.32)	(0.31)	(−5.11)
N	428	428	428	428
CRAGG-DONALD F	30.61	13.22	0.10	8.60

t statistics in parentheses.

of Table 10E.4, shows parameter estimates that are wildly different from those in Model (1) and Model (2), and the very small *t*-statistic values imply very large standard errors, another consequence for instrumental variables estimation in the presence of weak instruments.

Weak *IV* Example 4 *Endogenous: MTR, EDUC; Instruments: MOTHEREDUC, FATHEREDUC, EXPER*

If we include the additional instrument *EXPER*, so that $L = 3$, we obtain the first stage estimates in Model (5) and Model (6) of Table 10E.3. Once again the first-stage weak instrument *F*-test statistic values appear strong, with values for *MTR* of 18.86 and for *EDUC* of 35.03. Using the $F > 10$ rule of thumb we would be comfortable that our instruments are strong. The Cragg-Donald *F*-test statistic value is 8.60 which tells a slightly different story. Our instruments are not quite as strong as the first-stage weak instrument *F*-test statistics imply. If we choose a maximum test size of 0.15, we can reject the null hypothesis of weak instruments. If, however, we are prepared to accept only a maximum 10% rejection rate for a 5% test, the critical value is 13.43, and we do not reject the null hypothesis that the instruments are weak. The instrumental variables estimates of the *HOURS* supply equation are Model (4) of Table 10E.4, and we see that they are more in line with Model (1) and Model (2) than those in Model (3).

10E.3   TESTING FOR WEAK IDENTIFICATION: CONCLUSIONS

If instrumental variables are "weak," then the instrumental variables, or two-stage least squares, estimator is unreliable. When there is a single endogenous variable, the first-stage *F*-test of the joint significance of the external instruments is an indicator of instrument strength. The $F > 10$ rule of thumb has been refined by Stock and Yogo, who provide tables of critical values for the null hypothesis "the instruments are weak" using two criteria: the bias of the *IV* estimator relative to the bias of the least squares estimator, and the maximum size of a 5% test of the coefficients of the endogenous variables. If there is more than one endogenous variable on the right-hand side of an equation, then the *F*-test statistics from the first stage equations do not provide reliable information about instrument strength. In this case the Cragg-Donald F-test statistic should be used to test for weak instruments, along with the Stock-Yogo tables of critical values.

Econometric research continues for alternatives to the $IV/2SLS$ estimator in the weak instrument case. Some progress has been made; these results are summarized in Appendix 11B. The discussion is deferred until the next chapter, as the advances have their genesis in discussions of estimation of simultaneous equations models.

Appendix 10F Monte Carlo Simulation

In this appendix we do two sorts of simulations. First, we generate a sample of artificial data and give numerical illustrations of the estimators and tests discussed in the chapter. In the chapter the illustrations used real data. The advantage gained here is that we can see how the estimators and tests perform using data we know comes from a particular data generation process. Secondly, we carry out a Monte Carlo simulation to illustrate the repeated sampling properties of the least squares and $IV/2SLS$ estimators under various conditions.

10F.1   ILLUSTRATIONS USING SIMULATED DATA

In this section we demonstrate, using a simulated sample of data, that the least squares estimator fails when $\text{cov}(x, e) \neq 0$, and that instrumental variables estimators "work" when conditions listed in Section 10.3.3 are satisfied. For the simulated data we specify a simple regression model in which the parameter values are $\beta_1 = 1$ and $\beta_2 = 1$. Thus, the systematic part of the regression model is $E(y) = \beta_1 + \beta_2 x = 1 + 1 \times x$. By adding to $E(y)$ an error term value, which will be a random number we create, we can create a sample value of y.

We want to explore the properties of the least squares estimator when x and e are correlated. Using random number generators, we create $N = 100$ pairs of x and e values, such that each has a normal distribution with mean zero and variance one. The population correlation between the x and e values is ρ_{xe}. We then create an artificial sample of y values by adding e to the systematic portion of the regression,

$$y = E(y) + e = \beta_1 + \beta_2 x + e = 1 + 1 \times x + e$$

The data values are contained in *ch10.dat*. The least squares estimates are

$$\hat{y}_{LS} = 0.9789 + 1.7034x$$
$$(\text{se}) \quad (0.088) \quad (0.090)$$

When x and e are positively correlated, the estimated slope tends to be too large—here, $b_2 = 1.7034$ compared to the true $\beta_2 = 1$. Furthermore, the systematic overestimation of the slope will not go away in larger samples, so the least squares estimators are not correct on average even in large samples. The least squares estimators are inconsistent.

In the process of creating the artificial data (*ch10.dat*) we also created two instrumental variables, both uncorrelated with the error term. The correlation between the first instrument z_1 and x is $\rho_{xz_1} = 0.5$, and the correlation between the second instrument z_2 and x is $\rho_{xz_2} = 0.3$. The IV estimates using z_1 are

$$\hat{y}_{IV\_z_1} = 1.1011 + 1.1924x$$
$$(\text{se}) \quad (0.109) \quad (0.195)$$

and the *IV* estimates using z_2 are

$$\hat{y}_{IV\_z2} = 1.3451 + 0.1724x$$
$$\text{(se)} \quad (0.256) \quad (0.797)$$

Using z_1, the stronger instrument, yields an estimate of the slope of 1.1924 with a standard error of 0.195, about twice the standard error of the least squares estimate. Using the weaker instrument z_2 produces a slope estimate of 0.1724, which is far from the true value, and a standard error of 0.797, about eight times as large as the least squares standard error. The results with the weaker instrument are far less satisfactory than the estimates based on the stronger instrument z_1.

Another problem that an instrument can have is that it is not uncorrelated with the error term as it is supposed to be. The variable z_3 is correlated with x, with correlation $\rho_{xz_3} = 0.5$, but it is correlated with the error term e, with correlation $\rho_{ez_3} = 0.3$. Thus, z_3 is not a valid instrument. What happens if we use instrumental variables estimation with the invalid instrument? The results are

$$\hat{y}_{IV\_z3} = 0.9640 + 1.7657x$$
$$\text{(se)} \quad (0.095) \quad (0.172)$$

As you can see, using the invalid instrument produces a slope estimate even further from the true value than the least squares estimate. Using an invalid instrumental variable means that the instrumental variables estimator will be inconsistent, just like the least squares estimator.

What is the outcome of two-stage least squares estimation using the two instruments z_1 and z_2? Obtain the first-stage regression of x on the two instruments z_1 and z_2,

$$\hat{x} = 0.1947 + 0.5700z_1 + 0.2068z_2$$
$$\text{(se) } (0.079) \quad (0.089) \quad (0.077)$$

(10F.1)

Using the predicted value $\hat{x}$ to replace x, then applying least squares to the modified equation, as in (10.22), we obtain the instrumental variables estimates

$$\hat{y}_{IV\_z1,z2} = 1.1376 + 1.0399x$$
$$\text{(se)} \quad (0.116) \quad (0.194)$$

(10F.2)

The standard errors are based on an estimated error variance as in (10.23). Using the two valid instruments yields an estimate of the slope of 1.0399, which, in this example, is close to the true value of $\beta_2 = 1$.

10F.1.1 The Hausman Test
To implement the Hausman test we estimate the first-stage equation, which is shown in (10F.1) using the instruments z_1 and z_2. Compute the residuals

$$\hat{v} = x - \hat{x} = x - 0.1947 - 0.5700z_1 - 0.2068z_2$$

Include the residuals as an extra variable in the regression equation and apply least squares,

$$\hat{y} = 1.1376 + 1.0399x + 0.9957\hat{v}$$
$$\text{(se)} \quad (0.080) \quad (0.133) \quad (0.163)$$

The t-statistic for the null hypothesis that the coefficient of $\hat{v}$ is zero is 6.11. The critical value comes from the t-distribution with 97 degrees of freedom and is 1.985, so we reject the null hypothesis that x is uncorrelated with the error term and correctly conclude that it is endogenous.

10F.1.2   Test for Weak Instruments

The test for weak instruments again begins with estimation of the first-stage regression. If we consider using just z_1 as an instrument, the estimated first-stage equation is

$$\hat{x} = 0.2196 + 0.5711z_1$$
$$(t) \qquad (6.24)$$

The t-statistic 6.24 corresponds to an F-value of 38.92, which is well above the guideline value of 10. If we use just z_2 as an instrument, the estimated first-stage equation is

$$\hat{x} = 0.2140 + 0.2090z_2$$
$$(t) \qquad (2.28)$$

While the t-statistic 2.28 indicates statistical significance at the 0.05 level, the corresponding F value is $5.21 < 10$, indicating that z_2 is a weak instrument. The first-stage equation using both instruments is shown in (10F.1), and the F-test for their joint significance is 24.28, indicating that we have at least one strong instrument.

10F.1.3   Testing the Validity of Surplus Instruments

If we use z_1 and z_2 as instruments, there is one extra. The number of instruments is $L = 2$ and the number of endogenous regressors is $B = 1$. The IV estimates are shown in (10F.2). Calculate the residuals from this equation and then regress them on an intercept, z_1 and z_2, to obtain $\hat{e} = 0.0189 + 0.0881z_1 - 0.1818z_2$. The R^2 from this regression is 0.03628, and $NR^2 = 3.628$. The 0.05 critical value for the chi-square distribution with one degree of freedom is 3.84, so we fail to reject the validity of the surplus moment condition.

If we use z_1, z_2, and z_3 as instruments, there are two surplus moment conditions. The IV estimates using these three instruments are $\hat{y}_{IV\_z_1,z_2,z_3} = 1.0626 + 1.3535x$. Obtaining the residuals and regressing them on the instruments yields

$$\hat{e} = 0.0207 - 0.1033z_1 - 0.2355z_2 + 0.1798z_3$$

The R^2 from this regression is 0.1311, and $NR^2 = 13.11$. The 0.05 critical value for the chi-square distribution with two degrees of freedom is 5.99, so we reject the validity of the two surplus moment conditions. This test does not identify the problem instrument, but since we first tested the validity of z_1 and z_2 and failed to reject their validity, and then found that adding z_3 led us to reject the validity of the surplus moment conditions, the instrument z_3 seems to be the culprit.

10F.2   THE REPEATED SAMPLING PROPERTIES OF *IV/2SLS*

To illustrate the repeated sampling properties of the least squares and *IV/2SLS* estimators, we use an experimental design based on the discussion in Appendix 10D. In the simple regression model $y = \beta_1 + \beta_2 x + e$, if x is correlated with the error term e, then x is endogenous and the least squares estimator is biased and inconsistent. An instrumental variable z must be correlated with x but uncorrelated with e in order to be valid. A correlation between z and x implies that there is a linear association between them. This means that we can describe their relationship as a regression $x = \pi_0 + \pi_1 z + v$. There is a correlation between x and z if, and only if, $\pi_1 \neq 0$. If we knew π_0 and π_1 we could substitute $E(x) = \pi_0 + \pi_1 z$ into the simple regression model to obtain $y = \beta_1 + \beta_2 E(x) + \beta_2 v + e$. Suppose for a moment that $E(x)$ and v can be observed and are viewed as explanatory variables in the regression $y = \beta_1 + \beta_2 E(x) + \beta_2 v + e$. The explanatory variable $E(x)$ is not correlated with the error term e (or v). Any correlation between x and e implies correlation between v and e because $v = x - E(x)$.

In the simulation[17] we use the data generation process $y = x + e$, so that the intercept parameter is 0 and the slope parameter is 1. The first-stage regression is $x = \pi z_1 + \pi z_2 + \pi z_3 + v$. Note that we have $L = 3$ instruments, each of which has an independent standard normal $N(0,1)$ distribution. The parameter π controls the instrument strength. If $\pi = 0$, the instruments are not correlated with x, and instrumental variables estimation will fail. The larger π becomes, the stronger the instruments become. Finally, we create the random errors e and v to have standard normal distributions with correlation ρ, which controls the endogeneity of x. If $\rho = 0$, then x is not endogenous. The larger ρ becomes, the stronger the endogeneity. We create 10,000 samples of size $N = 100$ and then try out least squares and *IV/2SLS* under several scenarios. We let $\pi = 0.1$ (weak instruments) and $\pi = 0.5$ (strong instruments). We let $\rho = 0$ (x exogenous) and $\rho = 0.8$ (x highly endogenous).

In Table 10F.1 the reported values are:

- $\overline{F}$ is the average first stage F: compare these values to 10. Note that the average value of F is about 2 when $\pi = 0.1$ indicating weak instruments. The average value of F is about 21 when $\pi = 0.5$ indicating strong instruments.

- $\overline{b}_2$ is the average of the least squares estimates of $\beta_2 = 1$. The least squares estimator is unbiased when $\rho = 0$, but when $\rho = 0.8$, the least squares estimator shows severe bias.

- $s.d.(b_2)$ is the sample standard deviation of the 10,000 Monte Carlo values of b_2. It tells us how much variation the least squares estimates exhibit in repeated sampling.

- $t(b_2)$ is the percentage of rejections of the true null hypothesis $\beta_2 = 1$ using the 0.05 level of significance t-test based on the least squares estimator. If there is no

Table 10F.1 **Monte Carlo Simulation Results**

ρ	π	$\overline{F}$	$\overline{b}_2$	$s.d.(b_2)$	$t(b_2)$	$t(H)$	$\overline{\hat{\beta}}_2$	$s.d.(\hat{\beta}_2)$	$t(\hat{\beta}_2)$
0.0	0.1	1.98	1.0000	0.1000	0.0499	0.0510	0.9941	0.6378	0.0049
0.0	0.5	21.17	0.9999	0.0765	0.0484	0.0518	0.9998	0.1184	0.0441
0.8	0.1	2.00	1.7762	0.0610	1.0000	0.3077	1.3311	0.9483	0.2886
0.8	0.5	21.18	1.4568	0.0610	1.0000	0.9989	1.0111	0.1174	0.0636

[17] This design is similar to that used by Jinyong Hahn and Jerry Hausman (2003) "Weak Instruments: Diagnosis and Cures in Empirical Economics," *American Economic Review*, 93(2), pp. 118–125.

endogeneity, the percent rejections is very close to the 0.05 value, but if there is strong endogeneity, the least squares estimator rejects the true null hypothesis 100% of the time. That is not good.

- $t(H)$ is the percentage rejections of the regression-based Hausman test for endogeneity using the 0.05 level of significance. If there is no endogeneity, the test rejects 5% of the time, which is what we expect. If there is strong endogeneity but weak instruments, $\pi = 0.1$, the test rejects only 31% of the time, failing to indicate the endogeneity problem. If instruments are not strong, nothing is going to work well. If the instruments are strong, then the test for endogeneity is very successful in detecting strong endogeneity.

- $\overline{\hat{\beta}}_2$ is the average of the instrumental variables estimates of $\beta_2 = 1$. The IV estimator is unbiased when $\rho = 0$. When endogeneity is strong, with weak instruments the IV estimator has a 33% bias, but when instruments are strong it has an average very close to the true value.

- $s.d.(\hat{\beta}_2)$ is the sample standard deviation of the IV estimates in the 10,000 Monte Carlo samples. If there is no endogeneity, note how large its standard deviation is relative to the least squares estimator. With weak instruments its standard deviation is six times that of the least squares estimator. Even with strong instruments, it is substantially larger. The IV estimator is **inefficient** relative to the least squares estimator when endogeneity is absent. When endogeneity is present, the effect of weak instruments shows up in the large standard deviation of the estimates. When instruments are stronger, the standard deviation of the IV estimates falls from 0.95 to 0.12, a substantial improvement.

- Finally, we see the rate of rejections of the true null hypothesis $\beta_2 = 1$ under the scenarios. When x is endogenous and the instruments are weak, the t-test rejects far too often, but it is better than the t-test based on the least squares estimator. Otherwise, the rejection rate is close to the 5% that we expect.

These results are based on a sample size of $N = 100$, which is neither large nor small. What results do you anticipate with larger or smaller samples?

Advice about what to do when there is uncertainty as to whether a regressor is endogenous or not is somewhat mixed. In Table 10.2, the Hausman test statistic p-value is 0.0954. The prevailing attitude is probably summarized by Jeffrey Wooldridge,[18] who says, "We find evidence of endogeneity of *EDUC* at the 10% significance level against a two-sided alternative, and so *2SLS* is probably a good idea (assuming that we trust the instruments.)" On the other hand, Patrik Guggenberger[19] advises, that if testing the coefficient of the endogenous regressor is the objective, then we should avoid considering the Hausman test result and use *2SLS*. On the other hand, if we consider how close the estimates are to the true value on average, the "mean square error," Chmelarova and Hill[20] advise that perhaps *IV/2SLS* should be used only if a Hausman pretest has a much smaller p-value. This result is revealed somewhat in the Monte Carlo simulation.

---

[18] *Econometric Analysis of Cross Section and Panel Data*, 2nd Edition, The MIT Press, 2010, p. 132.

[19] "The Impact of a Hausman Pretest on the Asymptotic Size of a Hypothesis Test," *Econometric Theory*, 2010, 26(2), pp. 369–382.

[20] "The Hausman Pretest Estimator," *Economics Letters*, 2010, Vol. 108, 96–99.

In the case in which $\rho = 0.8$ and $\pi = 0.1$, the mean square error for the least squares estimator is

$$\sum_{m=1}^{10000} (b_{2m} - \beta_2)^2 \Big/ 10000 = 0.6062$$

while for the *IV* estimator it is

$$\sum_{m=1}^{10000} (\hat{\beta}_{2m} - \beta_2)^2 \Big/ 10000 = 1.0088$$

In other words, in this experimental setting with strong endogeneity and weak instruments, the least squares estimator is, on average, closer to the true parameter value than the *IV* estimator.

Chapter *11*

Simultaneous Equations Models

Learning Objectives

Based on the material in this chapter you should be able to:

1. Explain why estimation of a supply and demand model requires an alternative to least squares.

2. Explain the difference between exogenous and endogenous variables.

3. Define the "identification" problem in simultaneous equations models.

4. Define the reduced form of a simultaneous equations model and explain its usefulness.

5. Explain why it is acceptable to estimate reduced-form equations by least squares.

6. Describe the two-stage least squares estimation procedure for estimating an equation in a simultaneous equations model, and explain how it resolves the estimation problem for least squares.

Keywords

endogenous variables	reduced-form equation	simultaneous equations
exogenous variables	reduced-form errors	structural parameters
identification	reduced-form parameters	two-stage least squares

For most of us, our first encounter with economic models comes through studying supply and demand models, in which the market price and quantity of goods sold are *jointly determined* by the equilibrium of supply and demand. In this chapter we consider econometric models for data that are jointly determined by two or more economic relations. These **simultaneous equations** models differ from those we have considered in previous chapters because in each model there are *two* or more dependent variables rather than just one.

Simultaneous equations models also differ from most of the econometric models we have considered so far, because they consist of a *set of equations*. For example, price and quantity are determined by the interaction of two equations, one for supply and the other for demand. Simultaneous equations models, which contain more than one dependent variable and more than one equation, require special statistical treatment. The least squares estimation procedure *is not* appropriate in these models, and we must develop new ways to obtain reliable estimates of economic parameters.

Some of the concepts in this chapter were introduced in Chapter 10. However, reading Chapter 10 is *not* a prerequisite for reading Chapter 11, which is self-contained. If you *have* read Chapter 10, you will observe that much of what you learned there will carry over to this chapter, including how simultaneous equations models fit into the big picture. If you *have not* read Chapter 10, referring back to portions of it will provide a deeper understanding of material presented in this chapter. This chapter on simultaneous equations is presented separately because its treatment was the first major contribution of econometrics to the wider field of statistics, and because of its importance in economic analysis.

11.1 A Supply and Demand Model

Supply and demand *jointly* determine the market price of a good and the quantity of it that is sold. Graphically, you recall that market equilibrium occurs at the intersection of the supply and demand curves, as shown in Figure 11.1. An econometric model that explains market price and quantity should consist of two equations, one for supply and the other for demand. It will be a simultaneous equations model, since both equations working together determine price and quantity. A very simple model might look like the following:

$$\text{Demand:} \quad Q = \alpha_1 P + \alpha_2 X + e_d \tag{11.1}$$

$$\text{Supply:} \quad Q = \beta_1 P + e_s \tag{11.2}$$

Based on economic theory we expect the supply curve to be positively sloped, $\beta_1 > 0$, and the demand curve to be negatively sloped, $\alpha_1 < 0$. In this model we assume that the quantity demanded (Q) is a function of price (P) and income (X). Quantity supplied is taken to be a function of only price. (We have omitted the intercepts to make the algebra easier. In practice, we would include intercept terms in these models.)

The point we wish to make very clear is that it takes *two* equations to describe the supply and demand equilibrium. The *two* equilibrium values, for price and quantity, P^* and Q^*, respectively, are determined at the same time. In this model the variables P and Q are called **endogenous** variables because their values are determined within the system we have created. The endogenous variables P and Q are *dependent* variables and both are random

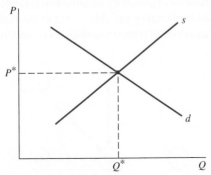

FIGURE *11.1* Supply and demand equilibrium.

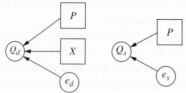

FIGURE **11.2**   Influence diagrams for two regression models.

variables. The income variable X has a value that is determined outside this system. Such variables are said to be **exogenous**, and these variables are treated like usual "x" explanatory variables.

Random errors are added to the supply and demand equations for the usual reasons, and we assume that they have the usual properties

$$E(e_d) = 0, \quad \text{var}(e_d) = \sigma_d^2$$
$$E(e_s) = 0, \quad \text{var}(e_s) = \sigma_s^2 \tag{11.3}$$
$$\text{cov}(e_d, e_s) = 0$$

Let us emphasize the difference between simultaneous equations models and regression models using influence diagrams. An "influence diagram" is a graphical representation of relationships between model components. In the previous chapters we would have modeled the supply and demand relationships as separate regressions, implying the influence diagrams in Figure 11.2. In this diagram the circles represent endogenous dependent variables and error terms. The squares represent exogenous explanatory variables. In regression analysis the direction of the influence is one-way: from the explanatory variable and the error term to the dependent variable. In this case there is no equilibrating mechanism that will lead quantity demanded to equal quantity supplied at a market-clearing price. For price to adjust to the market clearing equilibrium, there must be an influence running from P to Q and from Q to P.

Recognizing that price P and quantity Q are *jointly determined*, and that there is feedback between them, suggests the influence diagram in Figure 11.3. In the simultaneous equations model we see the two-way influence, or feedback, between P and Q because they are jointly determined. The random error terms e_d and e_s affect both P and Q, suggesting a correlation between each of the endogenous variables and each of the random error terms. As we will see, this leads to failure of the least squares estimator in simultaneous equations models. Income X is an exogenous variable that affects the endogenous variables, but there is no feedback from P and Q to X.

The fact that P is an endogenous variable on the right-hand side of the supply and demand equations means that we have an explanatory variable that is random. This is contrary to the usual assumption of "fixed explanatory variables," but as we explained in Chapter 10, this by itself does not mean that standard regression analysis is inappropriate. The real problem

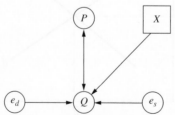

FIGURE **11.3**   Influence diagram for a simultaneous equations model.

is that the endogenous regressor P is correlated with the random errors, e_d and e_s, which has a devastating impact on our usual least squares estimation procedure, making the least squares estimator biased and inconsistent.

11.2 **The Reduced–Form Equations**

The two structural equations (11.1) and (11.2) can be solved to express the endogenous variables P and Q as functions of the exogenous variable X. This reformulation of the model is called the **reduced form** of the structural equation system. The reduced form is very important in its own right, and also helps us understand the structural equation system. To find the reduced form, we solve (11.1) and (11.2) simultaneously for P and Q.

To solve for P, set Q in the demand and supply equations to be equal,

$$\beta_1 P + e_s = \alpha_1 P + \alpha_2 X + e_d$$

Then solve for P,

$$P = \frac{\alpha_2}{(\beta_1 - \alpha_1)} X + \frac{e_d - e_s}{(\beta_1 - \alpha_1)} \tag{11.4}$$

$$= \pi_1 X + v_1$$

To solve for Q, substitute the value of P in (11.4) into either the demand or supply equation. The supply equation is simpler, so we will substitute P into (11.2) and simplify:

$$Q = \beta_1 P + e_s$$

$$= \beta_1 \left[\frac{\alpha_2}{(\beta_1 - \alpha_1)} X + \frac{e_d - e_s}{(\beta_1 - \alpha_1)} \right] + e_s$$

$$= \frac{\beta_1 \alpha_2}{(\beta_1 - \alpha_1)} X + \frac{\beta_1 e_d - \alpha_1 e_s}{(\beta_1 - \alpha_1)} \tag{11.5}$$

$$= \pi_2 X + v_2$$

The parameters π_1 and π_2 in (11.4) and (11.5) are called **reduced-form parameters**. The error terms v_1 and v_2 are called **reduced-form errors**.

The reduced-form equations can be estimated consistently by least squares. The explanatory variable X is determined outside this system. It is not correlated with the disturbances v_1 and v_2, which themselves have the usual properties of zero mean, constant variances, and zero covariance. Thus the least squares estimator is BLUE for the purposes of estimating π_1 and π_2.

The reduced-form equations are important for economic analysis. These equations relate the *equilibrium* values of the endogenous variables to the exogenous variables. Thus, if there is an increase in income X, π_1 is the expected increase in price, after market adjustments lead to a new equilibrium for P and Q. Similarly, π_2 is the expected increase in the equilibrium value of Q. (*Question*: how did we determine the directions of these changes?) Secondly, and using the same logic, the estimated reduced-form equations can be used to *predict* values of equilibrium price and quantity for different levels of income. Clearly CEOs and other market analysts are interested in the ability to forecast both prices and quantities sold of their products. It is the estimated reduced-form equations that make such predictions possible.

11.3 The Failure of Least Squares Estimation

In this section we explain why the least squares estimator should not be used to estimate an equation in a simultaneous equations model. For reasons that will become clear in the next section, we focus on the supply equation. In the supply equation (11.2), the endogenous variable P on the right-hand side of the equation is *correlated* with the error term e_s. We will give an intuitive explanation for the existence of this correlation here. An algebraic explanation is in Appendix 11A.

Suppose there is a small change, or blip, in the error term e_s, say Δe_s. Trace the effect of this change through the system. The blip Δe_s in the error term of (11.2) is directly transmitted to the equilibrium value of P. This follows from the reduced form (11.4) that has P on the left and e_s on the right. Every change in the supply equation error term e_s has a direct linear effect upon P. Since $\beta_1 > 0$ and $\alpha_1 < 0$, if $\Delta e_s > 0$, then $\Delta P < 0$. Thus, every time there is a change in e_s, there is an associated change in P in the opposite direction. Consequently, P and e_s are negatively correlated.

The failure of least squares estimation for the supply equation can be explained as follows: least squares estimation of the relation between Q and P gives "credit" to price (P) for the effect of changes in the error term (e_s). This occurs because we do not observe the change in the error term, but rather only the change in P resulting from its correlation with the error e_s. The least squares estimator of β_1 will *understate* the true parameter value in this model, because of the negative correlation between the endogenous variable P and the error term e_s. In large samples, the least squares estimator will tend to be negatively biased in this model. This bias persists even if the sample size goes to infinity, and thus the least squares estimator is inconsistent. This means that the probability distribution of the least squares estimator will ultimately "collapse" about a point that is not the true parameter value as the sample size $N \to \infty$. See Appendix 5B for a general discussion of "large sample" properties of estimators, and see Appendix 11A for an algebraic derivation. Here, we summarize by saying:

> The least squares estimator of parameters in a structural simultaneous equation is biased and inconsistent because of the correlation between the random error and the endogenous variables on the right-hand side of the equation.

11.4 The Identification Problem

In the supply and demand model given by (11.1) and (11.2),

- The parameters of the demand equation, α_1 and α_2, *cannot* be consistently estimated by *any* estimation method
- The slope of the supply equation, β_1, *can* be consistently estimated.

How are we able to make such statements? The answer is quite intuitive, and it can be illustrated graphically. What happens when income X changes? The demand curve shifts and a new equilibrium price and quantity are created. In Figure 11.4 we show the demand curves d_1, d_2, and d_3 and equilibria, at points a, b, and c, for three levels of income. As income changes, data on price and quantity will be observed around the

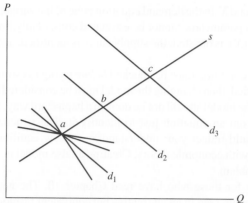

FIGURE **11.4** The effect of changing income.

intersections of supply and demand. The random errors e_d and e_s cause small shifts in the supply and demand curves, creating equilibrium observations on price and quantity that are scattered about the intersections at points a, b, and c.

The data values will trace out the *supply curve*, suggesting that we can fit a line through them to estimate the slope β_1. The data values fall along the supply curve because income is *present* in the demand curve and *absent* from the supply curve. As income changes, the demand curve shifts but the supply curve remains fixed, resulting in observations along the supply curve.

There are *no* data values falling along any of the demand curves, and there is no way to estimate their slope. Any one of an infinite number of demand curves passing through the equilibrium points could be correct. Given the data, there is no way to distinguish the true demand curve from all the rest. Through the equilibrium point a we have drawn a few demand curves, each of which *could* have generated the data we observe.

The problem lies with the model that we are using. There is no variable in the supply equation that will shift it relative to the demand curve. If we were to add a variable to the supply curve, say W, then each time W changed, the supply curve would shift, and the demand curve would stay fixed. The shifting of supply relative to a fixed demand curve (since W is *absent* from the demand equation) would create equilibrium observations along the demand curve, making it possible to estimate the slope of the demand curve and the effect of income on demand.

It is the *absence* of variables in one equation that are *present* in another equation that makes parameter estimation possible. A general rule, which is called a **necessary condition** for *identification* of an equation, is this:

> **A NECESSARY CONDITION FOR IDENTIFICATION:** In a system of M simultaneous equations, which jointly determine the values of M endogenous variables, at least $M - 1$ variables must be absent from an equation for estimation of its parameters to be possible. When estimation of an equation's parameters is possible, then the equation is said to be *identified*, and its parameters can be estimated consistently. If fewer than $M - 1$ variables are omitted from an equation, then it is said to be *unidentified*, and its parameters cannot be consistently estimated.

In our supply and demand model there are $M = 2$ equations, so we require at least $M - 1 = 1$ variable to be omitted from an equation to identify it. There are a total of three variables: P, Q, and X. In the demand equation none of the variables are omitted; thus it is unidentified and its parameters cannot be estimated consistently. In the supply equation, one variable, income (X), is omitted; the supply curve is identified, and its parameter can be estimated.

The identification condition must be checked *before* trying to estimate an equation. If an equation is not identified, then changing the model must be considered before it is estimated. However, changing the model should not be done in a haphazard way; no important variable should be omitted from an equation just to identify it. The structure of a simultaneous equations model should reflect your understanding of how equilibrium is achieved and should be consistent with economic theory. Creating a false model is not a good solution to the identification problem.

This paragraph is for those who have read Chapter 10. The necessary condition for identification can be expressed in an alternative but equivalent fashion. The two-stage least squares estimation procedure was developed in Chapter 10 and shown to be an instrumental variables estimator. This procedure is developed further in the next section. The number of instrumental variables required for estimation of an equation within a simultaneous equations model is equal to the number of right-hand-side endogenous variables. In a typical equation within a simultaneous equations model, several exogenous variables appear on the right-hand side. Thus instruments must come from those exogenous variables omitted from the equation in question. Consequently, identification requires that the number of excluded exogenous variables in an equation be at least as large as the number of included right-hand-side endogenous variables. This ensures an adequate number of instrumental variables.

11.5 Two–Stage Least Squares Estimation

The most widely used method for estimating the parameters of an identified structural equation is called **two-stage least squares**, which is often abbreviated as *2SLS*. The name comes from the fact that it can be calculated using two least squares regressions. We will explain how it works by considering the supply equation in (11.2). Recall that we cannot apply the usual least squares procedure to estimate β_1 in this equation, because the endogenous variable P on the right-hand side of the equation is correlated with the error term e_s.

The variable P is composed of a systematic part, which is its expected value $E(P)$, and a random part, which is the reduced-form random error v_1. That is,

$$P = E(P) + v_1 = \pi_1 X + v_1 \tag{11.6}$$

In the supply equation (11.2) the portion of P that causes problems for the least squares estimator is v_1, the random part. It is v_1 that causes P to be correlated with the error term e_s. Suppose we *knew* the value of π_1. Then we could replace P in (11.2) with (11.6) to obtain

$$
\begin{aligned}
Q &= \beta_1[E(P) + v_1] + e_s \\
&= \beta_1 E(P) + (\beta_1 v_1 + e_s)
\end{aligned}
\tag{11.7}
$$

In (11.7) the explanatory variable on the right-hand side is $E(P)$. It is not a random variable and it is not correlated with the error term. We could apply least squares to (11.7) to consistently estimate β_1.

Of course, we cannot use the variable $E(P) = \pi_1 X$ in place of P, since we do not know the value of π_1. However, we can *estimate* π_1 using $\hat{\pi}_1$ from the reduced-form equation for P. Then, a consistent estimator for $E(P)$ is

$$\hat{P} = \hat{\pi}_1 X$$

Using $\hat{P}$ as a replacement for $E(P)$ in (11.7) we obtain

$$Q = \beta_1 \hat{P} + e_* \tag{11.8}$$

In large samples, $\hat{P}$ and the random error e_* are uncorrelated, and consequently the parameter β_1 can be consistently estimated by applying least squares to (11.8).

Estimating (11.8) by least squares generates the so-called **two-stage least squares** estimator of β_1, which is consistent and normally distributed in large samples. To summarize, the *two stages* of the estimation procedure are

1. Least squares estimation of the reduced-form equation for P and the calculation of its predicted value, $\hat{P}$

2. Least squares estimation of the structural equation in which the right-hand-side endogenous variable P is replaced by its predicted value $\hat{P}$[1]

11.5.1 THE GENERAL TWO-STAGE LEAST SQUARES ESTIMATION PROCEDURE

The two-stage least squares estimation procedure can be used to estimate the parameters of any identified equation within a simultaneous equations system. In a system of M simultaneous equations, let the endogenous variables be $y_1, y_2, \ldots, y_M$. Let there be K exogenous variables, $x_1, x_2, \ldots, x_K$. Suppose the first structural equation within this system is

$$y_1 = \alpha_2 y_2 + \alpha_3 y_3 + \beta_1 x_1 + \beta_2 x_2 + e_1 \tag{11.9}$$

If this equation is identified, then its parameters can be estimated in the two steps:

1. Estimate the parameters of the reduced-form equations

$$y_2 = \pi_{12} x_1 + \pi_{22} x_2 + \cdots + \pi_{K2} x_K + v_2$$
$$y_3 = \pi_{13} x_1 + \pi_{23} x_2 + \cdots + \pi_{K3} x_K + v_3$$

by least squares and obtain the predicted values

$$\hat{y}_2 = \hat{\pi}_{12} x_1 + \hat{\pi}_{22} x_2 + \cdots + \hat{\pi}_{K2} x_K$$
$$\hat{y}_3 = \hat{\pi}_{13} x_1 + \hat{\pi}_{23} x_2 + \cdots + \hat{\pi}_{K3} x_K \tag{11.10}$$

---

[1] The discussion above is an intuitive explanation of the two-stage least squares estimator. For a general explanation of this estimation method, see Section 10.3. There we derive the two-stage least squares estimator and discuss its properties.

2. Replace the endogenous variables, y_2 and y_3, on the right-hand side of the structural (11.9) by their predicted values from (11.10)

$$y_1 = \alpha_2 \hat{y}_2 + \alpha_3 \hat{y}_3 + \beta_1 x_1 + \beta_2 x_2 + e_1^*$$

Estimate the parameters of this equation by least squares.

11.5.2   The Properties of the Two-Stage Least Squares Estimator

We have described how to obtain estimates for structural equation parameters in identified equations. The properties of the two-stage least squares estimator are as follows:

- The *2SLS* estimator is a biased estimator, but it is consistent.
- In large samples the *2SLS* estimator is approximately normally distributed.
- The variances and covariances of the *2SLS* estimator are unknown in small samples, but for large samples we have expressions for them that we can use as approximations. These formulas are built into econometric software packages, which report standard errors and *t*-values, just like an ordinary least squares regression program.
- If you obtain *2SLS* estimates by applying two least squares regressions using ordinary least squares regression software, the standard errors and *t*-values reported in the *second* regression are *not* correct for the *2SLS* estimator. Always use specialized *2SLS* or instrumental variables software when obtaining estimates of structural equations.

11.6 An Example of Two–Stage Least Squares Estimation

Truffles are a gourmet delight. They are edible fungi that grow below the ground. In France they are often located by collectors who use pigs to sniff out the truffles and "point" to them. Actually the pigs dig frantically for the truffles because pigs have an insatiable taste for them, as do the French, and they must be restrained from "pigging out" on them. Consider a supply and demand model for truffles:

$$\text{Demand:}\quad Q_i = \alpha_1 + \alpha_2 P_i + \alpha_3 PS_i + \alpha_4 DI_i + e_{di} \qquad (11.11)$$

$$\text{Supply:}\quad Q_i = \beta_1 + \beta_2 P_i + \beta_3 PF_i + e_{si} \qquad (11.12)$$

In the demand equation Q is the quantity of truffles traded in a particular French market-place, indexed by i, P is the market price of truffles, PS is the market price of a substitute for real truffles (another fungus much less highly prized), and DI is per capita monthly disposable income of local residents. The supply equation contains the market price and quantity supplied. Also it includes PF, the price of a factor of production, which in this case is the hourly rental price of truffle-pigs used in the search process. In this model we assume that P and Q are endogenous variables. The exogenous variables are PS, DI, PF, and the intercept.

11.6.1 IDENTIFICATION

Before thinking about estimation, check the identification of each equation. The rule for identifying an equation is that in a system of M equations at least $M - 1$ variables must be omitted from each equation in order for it to be identified. In the demand equation the variable PF is not included; thus the necessary $M - 1 = 1$ variable is omitted. In the supply equation both PS and DI are absent; more than enough to satisfy the identification condition. Note too that the variables that are omitted are different for each equation, ensuring that each contains at least one *shift* variable not present in the other. We conclude that each equation in this system is identified and can thus be estimated by two-stage least squares.

Why are the variables omitted from their respective equations? Because economic theory says that the price of a factor of production should affect supply but not demand, and that the price of substitute goods and income should affect demand and not supply. The specifications we used are based on the microeconomic theory of supply and demand.

11.6.2 THE REDUCED-FORM EQUATIONS

The reduced-form equations express each endogenous variable, P and Q, in terms of the exogenous variables PS, DI, PF, and the intercept, plus an error term. They are

$$Q_i = \pi_{11} + \pi_{21}PS_i + \pi_{31}DI_i + \pi_{41}PF_i + v_{i1}$$
$$P_i = \pi_{12} + \pi_{22}PS_i + \pi_{32}DI_i + \pi_{42}PF_i + v_{i2}$$

We can estimate these equations by least squares since the right-hand-side variables are exogenous and uncorrelated with the random errors v_{i1} and v_{i2}. The data file *truffles.dat* contains 30 observations on each of the endogenous and exogenous variables. The units of measurement are $ per ounce for price P, ounces for Q, $ per ounce for PS, and thousands of dollars for DI; PF is the hourly rental rate ($) for a truffle-finding pig. A few of the observations are shown in Table 11.1. The results of the least squares estimations of the reduced-form equations for Q and P are reported in Table 11.2.

In Table 11.2a we see that the estimated coefficients are statistically significant, and thus we conclude that the exogenous variables affect the quantity of truffles traded, Q, in this reduced-form equation. The $R^2 = 0.697$, and the overall F-statistic is 19.973, which has a p-value of less than 0.0001. In Table 11.2b the estimated coefficients are statistically

Table 11.1 **Representative Truffle Data**

OBS	P	Q	PS	DI	PF
1	29.64	19.89	19.97	2.103	10.52
2	40.23	13.04	18.04	2.043	19.67
3	34.71	19.61	22.36	1.870	13.74
4	41.43	17.13	20.87	1.525	17.95
5	53.37	22.55	19.79	2.709	13.71
		Summary Statistics			
Mean	62.72	18.46	22.02	3.53	22.75
Std. Dev.	18.72	4.61	4.08	1.04	5.33

Table 11.2a   **Reduced Form for Quantity of Truffles (Q)**

Variable	Coefficient	Std. Error	t-Statistic	Prob.
C	7.8951	3.2434	2.4342	0.0221
PS	0.6564	0.1425	4.6051	0.0001
DI	2.1672	0.7005	3.0938	0.0047
PF	−0.5070	0.1213	−4.1809	0.0003

Table 11.2b   **Reduced Form for Price of Truffles (P)**

Variable	Coefficient	Std. Error	t-Statistic	Prob.
C	−32.5124	7.9842	−4.0721	0.0004
PS	1.7081	0.3509	4.8682	0.0000
DI	7.6025	1.7243	4.4089	0.0002
PF	1.3539	0.2985	4.5356	0.0001

significant, indicating that the exogenous variables have an effect on market price P. The $R^2 = 0.889$ implies a good fit of the reduced-form equation to the data. The overall F-statistic value is 69.189 that has a p-value of less than 0.0001, indicating that the model has statistically significant explanatory power.

11.6.3   THE STRUCTURAL EQUATIONS

The reduced-form equations are used to obtain $\hat{P}$ that will be used in place of P on the right-hand side of the supply and demand equations in the second stage of two-stage least squares. From Table 11.2b we have

$$\hat{P} = \hat{\pi}_{12} + \hat{\pi}_{22}PS + \hat{\pi}_{32}DI + \hat{\pi}_{42}PF$$

$$= -32.512 + 1.708PS + 7.603DI + 1.354PF$$

The *2SLS* results are given in Tables 11.3a and 11.3b. The estimated demand curve results are in Table 11.3a. Note that the coefficient of price is negative, indicating that as the market price rises, the quantity demanded of truffles declines, as predicted by the law of demand. The standard errors that are reported are obtained from *2SLS* software. They and the t-values are valid in large samples. The p-value indicates that the estimated slope of the demand curve is significantly different from zero. Increases in the price of the substitute for truffles increase the demand for truffles, which is a characteristic of substitute goods. Finally the effect of income is positive, indicating that truffles are a normal good. All of these variables

Table 11.3a   ***2SLS* Estimates for Truffle Demand**

Variable	Coefficient	Std. Error	t-Statistic	Prob.
C	−4.2795	5.5439	−0.7719	0.4471
P	−0.3745	0.1648	−2.2729	0.0315
PS	1.2960	0.3552	3.6488	0.0012
DI	5.0140	2.2836	2.1957	0.0372

Table 11.3b   **2SLS Estimates for Truffle Supply**

Variable	Coefficient	Std. Error	t-Statistic	Prob.
C	20.0328	1.2231	16.3785	0.0000
P	0.3380	0.0249	13.5629	0.0000
PF	−1.0009	0.0825	−12.1281	0.0000

have statistically significant coefficients and thus have an effect upon the quantity demanded.

The supply equation results appear in Table 11.3b. As anticipated, increases in the price of truffles increase the quantity supplied, and increases in the rental rate for truffle-seeking pigs, which is an increase in the cost of a factor of production, reduces supply. Both of these variables have statistically significant coefficient estimates.

11.7 Supply and Demand at the Fulton Fish Market

The Fulton Fish Market has operated in New York City for over 150 years. The prices for fish are determined daily by the forces of supply and demand. Kathryn Graddy[2] collected daily data on the price of whiting (a common type of fish), quantities sold, and weather conditions during the period December 2, 1991, to May 8, 1992. These data are in the file *fultonfish.dat*. Fresh fish arrive at the market about midnight. The wholesalers, or dealers, sell to buyers for retail shops and restaurants. The first interesting feature of this example is to consider whether prices and quantities are *simultaneously* determined by supply and demand at all.[3] We might consider this a market with a fixed, perfectly inelastic supply. At the start of the day, when the market is opened, the supply of fish available for the day is fixed. If supply is fixed, with a vertical supply curve, then price is demand-determined, with higher demand leading to higher prices but no increase in the quantity supplied. If this is true, then the feedback between prices and quantities is eliminated. Such models are said to be **recursive** and the demand equation can be estimated by ordinary least squares rather than the more complicated two-stage least squares procedure.

However whiting fish can be kept for several days before going bad, and dealers can decide to sell less, and add to their inventory, or buffer stock, if the price is judged too low, in hope for better prices the next day. Or, if the price is unusually high on a given day, then sellers can increase the day's catch with additional fish from their buffer stock. Thus despite the perishable nature of the product, and the daily resupply of fresh fish, daily price is simultaneously determined by supply and demand forces. The key point here is that "simultaneity" does not require that events occur at a simultaneous moment in time.

Let us specify the demand equation for this market as

$$
\ln(QUAN_t) = \alpha_1 + \alpha_2\ln(PRICE_t) + \alpha_3 MON_t + \alpha_4 TUE_t + \alpha_5 WED_t \\
+ \alpha_6 THU_t + e_{dt}
\tag{11.13}
$$

---

[2] See Kathryn Graddy (2006) "The Fulton Fish Market," *Journal of Economic Perspectives*, 20(2), 207–220. The authors would like to thank Professor Graddy for permission to use the data from her study.

[3] The authors thank Peter Kennedy for this observation. See Kathryn Graddy and Peter E. Kennedy (2010) "When are supply and demand determined recursively rather than simultaneously?" *Eastern Economic Journal*, 36, pp. 188–197.

where $QUAN_t$ is the quantity sold, in pounds, and $PRICE_t$ is the average daily price per pound. Note that we are using the subscript "t" to index observations for this relationship because of the time series nature of the data. The remaining variables are indicator variables for the days of the week, with Friday being omitted. The coefficient α_2 is the price elasticity of demand, which we expect to be negative. The daily indicator variables capture day-to-day shifts in demand. The supply equation is

$$\ln(QUAN_t) = \beta_1 + \beta_2\ln(PRICE_t) + \beta_3 STORMY_t + e_{st} \tag{11.14}$$

The coefficient β_2 is the price elasticity of supply. The variable $STORMY$ is an indicator variable indicating stormy weather during the previous three days. This variable is important in the supply equation because stormy weather makes fishing more difficult, reducing the supply of fish brought to market.

11.7.1 IDENTIFICATION

Prior to estimation, we must determine whether the supply and demand equation parameters are identified. The necessary condition for an equation to be identified is that in this system of $M = 2$ equations, it must be true that at least $M - 1 = 1$ variable must be omitted from each equation. In the demand equation the weather variable $STORMY$ is omitted, and it does appear in the supply equation. In the supply equation, the four daily indicator variables that are included in the demand equation are omitted. Thus the demand equation shifts daily, while the supply remains fixed (since the supply equation does not contain the daily indicator variables), thus tracing out the supply curve, making it identified, as shown in Figure 11.4. Similarly, stormy conditions shift the supply curve relative to a fixed demand, tracing out the demand curve and making it identified.

11.7.2 THE REDUCED-FORM EQUATIONS

The reduced-form equations specify each endogenous variable as a function of all exogenous variables

$$\ln(QUAN_t) = \pi_{11} + \pi_{21}MON_t + \pi_{31}TUE_t + \pi_{41}WED_t + \pi_{51}THU_t \\ + \pi_{61}STORMY_t + v_{t1} \tag{11.15}$$

$$\ln(PRICE_t) = \pi_{12} + \pi_{22}MON_t + \pi_{32}TUE_t + \pi_{42}WED_t + \pi_{52}THU_t \\ + \pi_{62}STORMY_t + v_{t2} \tag{11.16}$$

These reduced-form equations can be estimated by least squares because the right-hand-side variables are all exogenous and uncorrelated with the reduced-form errors v_{t1} and v_{t2}. Using the Graddys' data (*fultonfish.dat*) we estimate these reduced-form equations and report them in Table 11.4. Estimation of the reduced-form equations is the first step of two-stage least squares estimation of the supply and demand equations. It is a requirement for successful two-stage least squares estimation that the estimated coefficients in the reduced form for the right-hand-side endogenous variable be statistically significant. We have specified the

Table 11.4a   **Reduced Form for ln(Quantity) Fish**

Variable	Coefficient	Std. Error	t-Statistic	Prob.
C	8.8101	0.1470	59.9225	0.0000
STORMY	−0.3878	0.1437	−2.6979	0.0081
MON	0.1010	0.2065	0.4891	0.6258
TUE	−0.4847	0.2011	−2.4097	0.0177
WED	−0.5531	0.2058	−2.6876	0.0084
THU	0.0537	0.2010	0.2671	0.7899

Table 11.4b   **Reduced Form for ln(Price) Fish**

Variable	Coefficient	Std. Error	t-Statistic	Prob.
C	−0.2717	0.0764	−3.5569	0.0006
STORMY	0.3464	0.0747	4.6387	0.0000
MON	−0.1129	0.1073	−1.0525	0.2950
TUE	−0.0411	0.1045	−0.3937	0.6946
WED	−0.0118	0.1069	−0.1106	0.9122
THU	0.0496	0.1045	0.4753	0.6356

structural equations (11.13) and (11.14) with ln(*QUAN*) as the left-hand-side variable and ln(*PRICE*) as the right-hand-side endogenous variable. Thus the key reduced-form equation is (11.16) for ln(*PRICE*). In this equation

- To identify the supply curve, the daily indicator variables must be jointly significant. This implies that at least one of their coefficients is statistically different from zero, meaning that there is at least one significant shift variable in the demand equation, which permits us to reliably estimate the supply equation.

- To identify the demand curve, the variable *STORMY* must be statistically significant, meaning that supply has a significant shift variable, so that we can reliably estimate the demand equation.

Why is this so? The identification discussion in Section 11.4 requires only the presence of shift variables, not their significance. The answer comes from a great deal of econometric research in the past decade, which shows that the two-stage least squares estimator performs very poorly if the shift variables are not strongly significant.[4] Recall that to implement two-stage least squares we take the predicted value from the reduced-form regression and include it in the structural equations in place of the right-hand-side endogenous variable. That is, we calculate

$$\widehat{\ln(PRICE_t)} = \hat{\pi}_{12} + \hat{\pi}_{22}MON_t + \hat{\pi}_{32}TUE_t + \hat{\pi}_{42}WED_t + \hat{\pi}_{52}THU_t + \hat{\pi}_{62}STORMY_t$$

where $\hat{\pi}_{k2}$ are the least squares estimates of the reduced-form coefficients, and then replace ln(*PRICE*) with $\widehat{\ln(PRICE)}$. To illustrate our point, let us focus on the problem

---

[4] See Chapter 10.3.5 for further discussion of this point.

of estimating the supply equation (11.14) and take the extreme case that $\hat{\pi}_{22} = \hat{\pi}_{32} = \hat{\pi}_{42} = \hat{\pi}_{52} = 0$, meaning that the coefficients on the daily indicator variables are all identically zero. Then

$$\widetilde{\ln(PRICE_t)} = \hat{\pi}_{12} + \hat{\pi}_{62}STORMY_t$$

If we replace $\ln(PRICE)$ in the supply equation (11.14) with this predicted value, there will be *exact* collinearity between $\widetilde{\ln(PRICE)}$ and the variable *STORMY*, which is already in the supply equation, and two-stage least squares will fail. If the coefficient estimates on the daily indicator variables are not exactly zero, but are jointly insignificant, it means there will be severe collinearity in the second stage, and although the two-stage least squares estimates of the supply equation can be computed, they will be unreliable. In Table 11.4b, showing the reduced-form estimates for (11.16), none of the daily indicator variables are statistically significant. Also, the joint F-test of significance of the daily indicator variables has p-value 0.65, so that we cannot reject the null hypothesis that all these coefficients are zero.[5] In this case the supply equation is not identified in practice, and we will not report estimates for it.

However, *STORMY* is statistically significant in Table 11.4b, meaning that the demand equation may be reliably estimated by two-stage least squares. An advantage of two-stage least squares estimation is that each equation can be treated and estimated separately, so the fact that the supply equation is not reliably estimable does not mean that we cannot proceed with estimation of the demand equation. The check of statistical significance of the sets of shift variables for the structural equations should be carried out each time a simultaneous equations model is formulated.

11.7.3 TWO-STAGE LEAST SQUARES ESTIMATION OF FISH DEMAND

Applying two-stage least squares estimation to the demand equation we obtain the results as given in Table 11.5. The price elasticity of demand is estimated to be -1.12, meaning that a 1% increase in fish price leads to about a 1.12% decrease in the quantity demanded; this estimate is statistically significant at the 5% level. The indicator variable coefficients are negative and statistically significant for Tuesday and Wednesday, meaning that demand is lower on these days relative to Friday.

Table 11.5 **2SLS Estimates for Fish Demand**

Variable	Coefficient	Std. Error	t-Statistic	Prob.
C	8.5059	0.1662	51.1890	0.0000
$\ln(PRICE)$	−1.1194	0.4286	−2.6115	0.0103
MON	−0.0254	0.2148	−0.1183	0.9061
TUE	−0.5308	0.2080	−2.5518	0.0122
WED	−0.5664	0.2128	−2.6620	0.0090
THU	0.1093	0.2088	0.5233	0.6018

---

[5] Even if the variables are jointly significant, there may be a problem. The significance must be "strong." An F-value <10 is cause for concern. This problem is the same as that of weak instruments in instrumental variables estimation. See Section 10.3.5.

11.8 Exercises

Answers to exercises marked * appear at www.wiley.com/go/global/hill.

11.8.1 PROBLEMS

11.1 Can you suggest a method for using the reduced-form (11.4) and (11.5) to obtain an estimate of the slope of the supply function $Q = \beta_1 P + e_s$? In particular, suppose that the estimated reduced-form equations are $\hat{P} = 18X$ and $\hat{Q} = 5X$. What is an estimated value of β_1? (*Hint:* look at the expressions for π_1 and π_2.)

11.2 Supply and demand curves as traditionally drawn in economics principles classes have price (P) on the vertical axis and quantity (Q) on the horizontal axis.
   (a) Take the estimates in Table 11.3 and on graph paper accurately sketch the supply and demand equations. For these sketches, set the values of the exogenous variables *DI*, *PS*, and *PF* to be $DI^* = 3.5$, $PF^* = 23$, and $PS^* = 22$.
   (b) What are the equilibrium values of P and Q from (a)?
   (c) Calculate the predicted equilibrium values of P and Q using the estimated reduced-form equations from Table 11.2, using the same values of the exogenous variables as those in (a). Compare these predicted equilibrium values to those in (b). Do they seem to agree, or not?
   (d) On the graph from part (a), show the consequences of increasing income from $DI^* = 3.5$ to $DI^{**} = 4.5$, holding the values of *PF* and *PS* at the values given in (a).
   (e) Calculate the change in equilibrium price P and quantity Q in (d) based on your sketch.
   (f) Using the results in part (e), calculate the income elasticity of demand implied by the shift in part (d). Calculate an estimate of the income elasticity of demand from the estimated reduced-form equation in Table 11.2a and compare to your graphical solution.

11.3 Suppose you want to estimate a wage equation for married women of the form

$$\ln(WAGE) = \beta_1 + \beta_2 HOURS + \beta_3 EDUC + \beta_4 EXPER + e$$

where *WAGE* is hourly wage, *HOURS* is the number of hours worked per week, *EDUC* is years of education, and *EXPER* is years of experience. Your classmate observes that higher wages can bring forth increased work effort, and that married women with young children may reduce their hours of work to take care of them, so that there may be an auxiliary relationship such as

$$HOURS = \alpha_1 + \alpha_2 \ln(WAGE) + \alpha_3 KIDS + u$$

where *KIDS* is the number of children under the age of six in the woman's household.
   (a) Can the wage equation be estimated satisfactorily using the least squares estimator? If not, why not?
   (b) Is the wage equation "identified"? What does the term *identification* mean in this context?
   (c) If you seek an alternative to least squares estimation for the wage equation, suggest an estimation procedure and how (step by step, and not a computer command) it is carried out.

11.4   Consider the following simultaneous equations model. Assume that x is exogenous.

$$y_1 = \beta x + e$$
$$y_2 = \alpha y_1 + u$$

(a) How would you estimate the parameter β? Is it identified?
(b) How would you estimate the parameter α? Is it identified?

11.8.2   COMPUTER EXERCISES

11.5   (a) Use your computer software for two-stage least squares or instrumental variables estimation, and the 30 observations in the file *truffles.dat* to obtain *2SLS* estimates of the system in (11.11) and (11.12). Compare your results to those in Table 11.3.

(b) Using the *2SLS* estimated equations, compute the price elasticity of supply and demand "at the means." The summary statistics for the data are given in Table 11.1. [*Hint*: See Appendix A, equation (A.8).] Comment on the signs and magnitudes of these elasticities.

11.6   Estimate (11.11) and (11.12) by least squares regression, ignoring the fact that they form a simultaneous system. Use the data in *truffles.dat*. Compare your results to those in Table 11.3. Do the signs of the least squares estimates agree with economic reasoning?

11.7* Supply and demand curves as traditionally drawn in economics principles classes have price (P) on the vertical axis and quantity (Q) on the horizontal axis.

(a) Rewrite the truffle demand and supply equations in (11.11) and (11.12) with price P on the left-hand side. What are the anticipated signs of the parameters in this rewritten system of equations?

(b) Using the data in the file *truffles.dat*, estimate the supply and demand equations that you have formulated in (a) using two-stage least squares. Are the signs correct? Are the estimated coefficients significantly different from zero?

(c) Estimate the price elasticity of demand "at the means" using the results from (b).

(d) On graph paper accurately sketch the supply and demand equations using the estimates from part (b). For these sketches set the values of the exogenous variables DI, PS, and PF to be $DI^* = 3.5$, $PF^* = 23$, and $PS^* = 22$.

(e) What are the equilibrium values of P and Q obtained in part (d)? Calculate the predicted equilibrium values of P and Q using the estimated reduced-form equations from Table 11.2, using the same values of the exogenous variables. How well do they agree?

(f) Estimate the supply and demand equations that you have formulated in (a) using ordinary least squares. Are the signs correct? Are the estimated coefficients significantly different from zero? Compare the results to those in part (b).

11.8* The labor supply of married women has been a subject of a great deal of economic research. A classic work[6] is that of Professor Tom Mroz, who kindly provided his data to us. The data file is *mroz.dat* and the variable definitions are in the file *mroz.def*. The data file contains information on women who have worked in the previous

---

[6] Mroz, T.A. (1987) "The sensitivity of an empirical model of a married woman's hours of work to economic and statistical assumptions," *Econometrica*, 55, 765–800.

year and those who have not. The variable indicating whether a woman worked is *LFP*, labor force participation, which takes the value 1 if a woman worked and 0 if she did not.

(a) Calculate the summary statistics for the variables: wife's age, number of children younger than six years old in the household, and the family income for the women who worked (*LFP* = 1) and those who did not (*LFP* = 0). Comment on any differences you observe.

(b) Consider the following supply equation specification

$$HOURS = \beta_1 + \beta_2 \ln(WAGE) + \beta_3 EDUC + \beta_4 AGE + \beta_5 KIDSL6$$
$$+ \beta_6 KIDS618 + \beta_7 NWIFEINC + e$$

The variable *NWIFEINC* is defined as

$$NWIFEINC = FAMINC - WAGE \times HOURS$$

What signs do you expect each of the coefficients to have, and why? What does *NWIFEINC* measure?

(c) Estimate the supply equation in (b) using least squares regression on *only the women who worked* (*LFP* = 1). You must create *NWIFEINC* and ln(*WAGE*). Did things come out as expected? If not, why not?

(d) Estimate the reduced-form equation by least squares for the women who worked

$$\ln(WAGE) = \pi_1 + \pi_2 EDUC + \pi_3 AGE + \pi_4 KIDSL6 + \pi_5 KIDS618$$
$$+ \pi_6 NWIFEINC + \pi_7 EXPER + \pi_8 EXPER^2 + v$$

Based on the estimated reduced form, what is the effect upon wage of an additional year of education?

(e) Check the identification of the supply equation, considering the availability of the extra instruments *EXPER* and its square.

(f) Estimate the supply equation by two-stage least squares, using software designed for this purpose. Discuss the signs and significance of the estimated coefficients.

11.9 This exercise examines a supply and demand model for edible chicken, which the U. S. Department of Agriculture calls "broilers." The data for this exercise is in the file *newbroiler.dat*, which is adapted from the data provided by Epple and McCallum (2006).[7]

(a) Consider the demand equation

$$\ln(Q_t) = \alpha_1 + \alpha_2 \ln(Y_t) + \alpha_3 \ln(P_t) + \alpha_4 \ln(PB_t) + e_{dt}$$

where Q = per capita consumption of chicken, in pounds; Y = real per capita income; P = real price of chicken; PB = real price of beef. What are the endogenous variables? What are the exogenous variables?

---

[7] "Simultaneous equation econometrics: The missing example," *Economic Inquiry*, 44(2), 374–384. We thank Professor Bennett McCallum for his generous help.

(b) The demand equation in (a) suffers from severe serial correlation. In the AR(1) model $e_{dt} = \rho e_{d,t-1} + v_{dt}$, the value of ρ is near 1. Epple and McCallum estimate the model in "first difference" form,

$$\ln(Q_t) = \alpha_1 + \alpha_2\ln(Y_t) + \alpha_3\ln(P_t) + \alpha_4\ln(PB_t) + e_{dt}$$
$$\underline{-[\ln(Q_{t-1}) = \alpha_1 + \alpha_2\ln(Y_{t-1}) + \alpha_3\ln(P_{t-1}) + \alpha_4\ln(PB_{t-1}) + e_{d,t-1}]}$$
$$\Delta\ln(Q_t) = \alpha_2\Delta\ln(Y_t) + \alpha_3\Delta\ln(P_t) + \alpha_4\Delta\ln(PB_t) + v_{dt}$$

(i) What changes do you notice after this transformation? (ii) Are the parameters of interest affected? (iii) If $\rho = 1$, have we solved the serial correlation problem? (iv) What is the interpretation of the "Δ" variables like $\Delta\ln(Q_t)$? (*Hint*: see Appendix A.1.6) (v) What is the interpretation of the parameter α_2? (vi) What signs do you expect for each of the coefficients? Explain.

(c) The supply equation is

$$\ln(QPROD_t) = \beta_1 + \beta_2\ln(P_t) + \beta_3\ln(PF_t) + \beta_4 TIME_t$$
$$+ \beta_5\ln(QPROD_{t-1}) + e_{st}$$

where $QPROD$ = aggregate production of young chickens, PF = nominal price index of broiler feed, $TIME$ = time index with 1950 = 1 to 2001 = 52. This supply equation is dynamic, with lagged production on the right-hand side. This predetermined variable is known at time t and is treated as exogenous. $TIME$ is included to capture technical progress in production. (i) What are the endogenous variables? (ii) What are the exogenous variables? (iii) What is the interpretation of the parameter β_2? (iv) What signs do you expect for each of the parameters?

(d) Is the order condition for identification satisfied for the demand equation in (b) (in differenced form) and the supply equation in (c)?

(e) Use the data from 1960 to 1999 to estimate the reduced-form equation for $\Delta\ln(P_t)$. (i) Discuss the estimated model, including the signs and significance of the estimated coefficients. (ii) Use the estimated reduced-form equation to predict the approximate percentage change in prices for the year 2000 and its 95% prediction (confidence) interval. Set $PF = 0.61765$ for year 2000. Is the actual value within the interval?

(f) Use the data from 1960 to 1999 to estimate the reduced form equation for $\ln(P_t)$. (i) Discuss the estimated model, including the signs and significance of the estimated coefficients. (ii) Use the estimated reduced-form equation to predict the real price for the year 2000 and its 95% prediction (confidence) interval. Set $PF = 0.61765$ for year 2000. Is the actual value within the interval?

(g) Use the data from 1960 to 1999 to estimate the two equations by two-stage least squares, using the exogenous variables in the system as instruments. (i) Discuss your results, paying particular attention to the signs, magnitudes, and significance of the estimated coefficients. (ii) Interpret the numerical magnitudes of the estimates for α_2 and β_2.

(h) Reestimate the supply equation using the log of exports, $\ln(EXPTS)$, as an additional instrumental variable. Discuss the logic of using this variable as an instrument? (*Hint*: What characteristics do good instruments have?)

11.10 Reconsider the example used in Section 11.7 on the supply and demand for fish at the Fulton Fish Market. The data are in the file *fultonfish.dat*.

(a) Carry out two-stage least squares estimation of the supply equation in (11.14). Comment on the signs and significance of the estimated coefficients. What is your estimate of the elasticity of supply?

(b) It is possible that bad weather on shore reduces attendance at restaurants, which in turn may reduce the demand for fish at the market. Add the variables *RAINY* and *COLD* to the demand equation in (11.13). Derive the algebraic reduced form for ln(*PRICE*) for this new specification.

(c) Estimate the reduced form you derived in (b) by least squares. Test the joint significance of the variables *MON, TUE, WED, THU, RAINY,* and *COLD*. Are these variables jointly significant at the $\alpha = 0.05$ level? Is the addition of *RAINY* and *COLD* to the demand sufficient to allow reliable two-stage least squares estimation of the supply equation? Explain.

(d) Obtain two-stage least squares estimates and ordinary least squares estimates of the augmented demand equation in part (b) and the supply equation (11.14). Discuss the estimates and their signs and significance. Are the estimates consistent with economic theory?

(e) Augment the supply equation with the variable *MIXED*, which indicates poor but not *STORMY* weather conditons. For the demand equation, use the augmented model in part (b). Derive the algebraic reduced form for ln(*PRICE*) for this new specification. Estimate this reduced form by least squares. Test the joint significance of the variables *MON, TUE, WED, THU, RAINY,* and *COLD*. Has this improved the chances of estimating the supply equation by two-stage least squares? Explain your answer.

(f) Estimate the supply and demand equations in (e) by two-stage least squares and ordinary least squares and discuss the results.

11.11 Reconsider the example used in Section 11.7 on the supply and demand for fish at the Fulton Fish Market. The data are in the file *fultonfish.dat*. In this exercise we explore the behavior of the market on days in which changes in fish inventories are large relative to those days on which inventory changes are small. Graddy and Kennedy (2006) anticipate that prices and quantities will demonstrate simultaneity on days with large changes in inventories, as these are days when sellers are demonstrating their responsiveness to prices. On days when inventory changes are small, the anticipation is that feedback between prices and quantities is broken, and simultaneity is no longer an issue.

(a) Use the subset of data for days in which inventory change is large, as indicated by the variable *CHANGE* = 1. Estimate the reduced-form (11.16) and test the significance of *STORMY*. Discuss the importance of this test for the purpose of estimating the demand equation by two-stage least squares.

(b) Obtain the least squares residuals $\hat{v}_{t2}$ from the reduced-form equation estimated in (a). Carry out a Hausman test[8] for the endogeneity of ln(*PRICE*) by adding $\hat{v}_{t2}$ as an extra variable to the demand equation in (11.13), estimating the resulting model by least squares, and testing the significance of $\hat{v}_{t2}$ using a standard t-test. If $\hat{v}_{t2}$ is a significant variable in this augmented regression then we may conclude that ln(*PRICE*) is endogenous. Based on this test, what do you conclude?

(c) Estimate the demand equation using two-stage least squares and ordinary least squares using the data when *CHANGE* = 1, and discuss these estimates. Compare them to the estimates in Table 11.5.

---

[8] This test is introduced in Section 10.4.1 and is further discussed in Appendix 10D.

(d) Estimate the reduced-form equation (11.16) for the data when $CHANGE = 0$. Compare these reduced-form estimates to those in (a) and those in Table 11.4b.

(e) Obtain the least squares residuals $\hat{v}_{t2}$ from the reduced-form equation estimated in (d). Carry out a Hausman test for the endogeneity of $\ln(PRICE)$, as described in part (b). Based on this test, what do you conclude?

(f) Obtain the two-stage least squares and the ordinary least squares estimates for the demand equation for the data when $CHANGE = 0$. Compare these estimates to each other and to the estimates in (c). Discuss the relationships between them.

Appendix 11A   An Algebraic Explanation of the Failure of Least Squares

Consider the supply and demand model in (11.1) and (11.2). To explain the failure of least squares estimation of the supply equation, let us first obtain the covariance between P and e_s.

$$
\begin{aligned}
\mathrm{cov}(P, e_s) &= E[P - E(P)][e_s - E(e_s)] \\
&= E(Pe_s) && \text{(since } E(e_s) = 0) \\
&= E[\pi_1 X + v_1]e_s && \text{(substitute for } P) \\
&= E\left[\frac{e_d - e_s}{\beta_1 - \alpha_1}\right]e_s && \text{(since } \pi_1 X \text{ is exogenous)} && \text{(11A.1)} \\
&= \frac{-E(e_s^2)}{\beta_1 - \alpha_1} && \text{(since } e_d, e_s \text{ assumed uncorrelated)} \\
&= \frac{-\sigma_s^2}{\beta_1 - \alpha_1} < 0
\end{aligned}
$$

What impact does the negative covariance in (11A.1) have on the least squares estimator? The least squares estimator of the supply equation (11.2) (which does not have an intercept term) is

$$
b_1 = \frac{\Sigma P_i Q_i}{\Sigma P_i^2} \tag{11A.2}
$$

Substitute for Q from the supply equation (11.2) and simplify,

$$
b_1 = \frac{\Sigma P_i(\beta_1 P_i + e_{si})}{\Sigma P_i^2} = \beta_1 + \Sigma\left(\frac{P_i}{\Sigma P_i^2}\right)e_{si} = \beta_1 + \Sigma h_i e_{si} \tag{11A.3}
$$

where $h_i = P_i/\Sigma P_i^2$. The expected value of the least squares estimator is

$$
E(b_1) = \beta_1 + \Sigma E(h_i e_{si}) \neq \beta_1
$$

The least squares estimator is biased because e_s and P are correlated, implying $E(h_i e_{si}) \neq 0$.

In large samples there is a similar failure. Multiply through the supply equation by price P, take expectations, and solve.

$$PQ = \beta_1 P^2 + P e_s$$

$$E(PQ) = \beta_1 E(P^2) + E(P e_s)$$

$$\beta_1 = \frac{E(PQ)}{E(P^2)} - \frac{E(P e_s)}{E(P^2)}$$

In large samples, as $N \to \infty$, sample analogs of expectations, which are averages, converge to the expectations. That is, $\sum Q_i P_i / N \to E(PQ)$, $\sum P_i^2 / N \to E(P^2)$. Consequently, because the covariance between P and e_s is negative, from (11A.1),

$$b_1 = \frac{\sum Q_i P_i / N}{\sum P_i^2 / N} \to \frac{E(PQ)}{E(P^2)} = \beta_1 + \frac{E(P e_s)}{E(P^2)} = \beta_1 - \frac{\sigma_s^2 / (\beta_1 - \alpha_1)}{E(P^2)} < \beta_1$$

The least squares estimator of the slope of the supply equation (11.2), in large samples, converges to a value less than β_1.

Appendix 11B *2SLS* Alternatives

There has always been great interest in alternatives to the standard *IV/2SLS* estimator. The search for better alternatives was energized by the discovery of the problems weak instruments pose for the usual *IV/2SLS* estimator. In this appendix we examine a few alternative estimators for a single equation with endogenous regressors. The equation might be part of a simultaneous equations system, or a standalone equation with an endogenous regressor, as we studied in Chapter 10. The limited information maximum likelihood (*LIML*) estimator was first derived by Anderson and Rubin in 1949.[9] It has played a "back seat" role relative to *2SLS* over the years, but this is no longer true. There is renewed interest in *LIML* in the presence of weak instruments. Several modifications of *LIML* have been suggested by Fuller (1977) and others. These estimators are unified in a common framework, along with *2SLS*, using the idea of a **k-class** of estimators. Later in this appendix we provide Stock-Yogo tables of critical values for weak instruments that apply to the *LIML* estimator and Fuller modifications. What is illustrated by these tables is that *LIML* suffers less from test size aberrations than the *2SLS* estimator, and that the Fuller modification suffers less from bias.

11B.1   THE *k*-CLASS OF ESTIMATORS

In a system of M simultaneous equations let the endogenous variables be $y_1, y_2, \ldots, y_M$. Let there be K exogenous variables, $x_1, x_2, \ldots, x_K$. Suppose the first structural equation within this system is

$$y_1 = \alpha_2 y_2 + \beta_1 x_1 + \beta_2 x_2 + e_1 \qquad (11B.1)$$

---

[9] Anderson, T.W. and H. Rubin (1949) "Estimation of the Parameters of a Single Equation in a Complete System of Stochastic Equations," *Annals of Mathematical Statistics*, 21, pp. 46–63.

If this equation is identified, then its parameters can be estimated. The variable y_2 is endogenous because it is correlated with the regression error term e_1. The endogenous variable y_2 has reduced form $y_2 = \pi_{12}x_1 + \pi_{22}x_2 + \cdots + \pi_{K2}x_K + v_2 = E(y_2) + v_2$. The source of the endogeneity of y_2 is not the systematic portion $E(y_2)$, which is not random. The random component v_2 is the source of the endogeneity problem. One way to think about developing an instrumental variable for y_2 is to remove, or "purge," v_2 from it. That is, use the instrumental variable $y_2 - v_2 = E(y_2)$. This instrument has the essential properties of an instrument: It is correlated with the endogenous variable y_2 and it is uncorrelated with the structural equation error e_1. The difficulty is that $E(y_2)$ is unknown. However, the parameters of the reduced form equation are consistently estimated by least squares, so that

$$\widehat{E(y_2)} = \hat{\pi}_{12}x_1 + \hat{\pi}_{22}x_2 + \cdots + \hat{\pi}_{K2}x_K \tag{11B.2}$$

The reduced form residuals are

$$\hat{v}_2 = y_2 - \widehat{E(y_2)}$$

In large samples the reduced-form estimators $\hat{\pi}_{k2}$ converge in probability to their true values. This means that in large samples we can substitute for $E(y_2)$ its estimated value

$$\widehat{E(y_2)} = y_2 - \hat{v}_2 \tag{11B.3}$$

The two-stage least squares estimator is an *IV* estimator using $\widehat{E(y_2)}$ as an instrument. Equation (11B.3) shows that the instrument used in *2SLS* can be thought of as the endogenous variable y_2 "purged" of the troublesome error term v_2.

The **k-class** of estimators is a unifying framework. A *k-class* estimator is an *IV* estimator using instrumental variable $y_2 - k\hat{v}_2$. It is called a *class* of estimators because it represents the least squares estimator if $k = 0$ and the *2SLS* estimator if $k = 1$. Why would we be interested in using values of k other than 1? Hopefully by adjusting this value we can improve upon the performance of the k-class estimator relative to the *2SLS* estimator.

11B.2 THE *LIML* ESTIMATOR

As noted earlier, the *LIML* estimator is one of the oldest estimators for an equation within a system of simultaneous equations, or any equation with an endogenous variable on the right-hand side. Rather than obtaining the *LIML* estimates by maximizing a likelihood function (see Appendix C.8 for an introduction to maximum likelihood estimation) we will exploit the fact that the *LIML* estimator is a member of the *k-class*.

The equation $y_1 = \alpha_2 y_2 + \beta_1 x_1 + \beta_2 x_2 + e_1$ is in **normalized form**, meaning that we have chosen one variable to appear as the dependent variable. In general the first equation can be written in **implicit form** as $\alpha_1 y_1 + \alpha_2 y_2 + \beta_1 x_1 + \beta_2 x_2 + e_1 = 0$. There is no rule that says y_1 has to be the dependent variable in the first equation. **Normalization** amounts to setting α_1 or α_2 to the value -1. One parameter α_i must be set to -1 so that we can identify the equation, but it does not matter which one. Let $y^* = \alpha_1 y_1 + \alpha_2 y_2$, then the unnormalized equation can be written $y^* + \beta_1 x_1 + \beta_2 x_2 + e_1 = 0$, or

$$y^* = -\beta_1 x_1 - \beta_2 x_2 - e_1 = \theta_1 x_1 + \theta_2 x_2 + \eta \tag{11B.4}$$

In (11B.1) the exogenous variables $x_3, \ldots, x_K$ were omitted. If we had included them, (11B.4) would be

$$y^* = \theta_1 x_1 + \cdots + \theta_K x_K + \eta \tag{11B.5}$$

The **least variance ratio** estimator chooses α_1 and α_2 so that the ratio of the sum of squared residuals from (11B.4) relative to the sum of squared residuals from (11B.5) is as small as possible. Define the ratio of sum of squared residuals from the two models as

$$\ell = \frac{SSE \text{ from regression of } y^* \text{ on } x_1, \ x_2}{SSE \text{ from regression of } y^* \text{ on } x_1, \ldots, x_K} \geq 1 \tag{11B.6}$$

We assume that the variables $x_3, \ldots, x_K$ were omitted from (11B.1) for a reason based in economic theory. The estimates of α_1 and α_2, one of which will be set to -1, should be chosen so to make the reduced regression (11B.4) fit the data as well as possible while still imposing the condition that $x_3, \ldots, x_K$ are omitted.

The algebra required for the solution is beyond the scope of this book.[10] The interesting result is that the minimum value of ℓ in (11B.6), call it $\hat{\ell}$, results in the *LIML* estimator when used as k in the *k-class* estimator. That is, use $k = \hat{\ell}$ when forming the instrument $y_2 - k\hat{v}_2$, and the resulting *IV* estimator is the *LIML* estimator.

11B.2.1 Fuller's Modified *LIML*
A modification suggested by Wayne Fuller (1977)[11] uses the *k-class* value

$$k = \hat{\ell} - \frac{a}{N - K} \tag{11B.7}$$

where K is the total number of instrumental variables (included and excluded exogenous variables) and N is the sample size. The value of a is a constant. Fuller says (1977, p. 951), "If one desires estimates that are nearly unbiased 'a' is set equal to 1. Presumably 'a' = 1 would be used when one is interested in testing hypotheses or setting approximate confidence intervals for the parameters." Fuller also showed that a value $a = 4$ leads to an estimator that minimizes the "mean square error" of estimation. If we are estimating some parameter δ using an estimator $\hat{\delta}$, then the mean square error of estimation is

$$MSE(\hat{\delta}) = E(\hat{\delta} - \delta)^2 = \text{var}(\hat{\delta}) + [E(\hat{\delta}) - \delta]^2 = \text{var}(\hat{\delta}) + [bias(\hat{\delta})]^2$$

Estimator *MSE* combines both variance and bias into a single measure.

11B.2.2 Advantages of *LIML*
A great deal of research has been devoted to the performance of the *LIML* estimator relative to the *2SLS* estimator when instruments are weak and/or there are a large number of instruments. Stock and Yogo (2005, p. 106), say, "Our findings support the view that *LIML* is far superior to (2)*SLS* when the researcher has weak instruments …" when using interval estimates' coverage rate as the criterion. Also "… the Fuller-k estimator is more robust to

---

[10] Advanced students should consider reading Peter Schmidt's *Econometrics*, 1976 (New York, NY: Marcel Dekker, Inc.) Chapter 4.

[11] Wayne Fuller, "Some Properties of a Modification of the Limited Information Estimator," *Econometrica*, 45, pp. 939–953.

weak instruments than (2)*SLS* when viewed from the perspective of bias." Some other findings are discussed by Mariano (2001):[12]

- For the *2SLS* estimator the amount of bias is an increasing function of the degree of over identification. The distributions of the *2SLS* and least squares estimators tend to become similar when overidentification is large. *LIML* has the advantage over *2SLS* when there are a large number of instruments.

- The *LIML* estimator converges to normality faster than the *2SLS* estimator and is generally more symmetric.

11B.2.3   Stock-Yogo Weak *IV* Tests for *LIML*

Tables 11B.1 and 11B.2 contain Stock-Yogo critical values for testing weak instruments. These tests are discussed in Chapter 10, Appendix E. Table 11B.1 contains the critical values using the criterion of maximum *LIML* test size for a 5% test. Note that for $L > 1$, *LIML* critical values are lower than the *2SLS* critical values in Table 10E.1. This means that the Cragg-Donald *F*-test statistic does not have to be as large for us to reject the null hypothesis that the instruments are weak when using *LIML* instead of *2SLS*. Table 11B.2 contains the

Table 11B.1   **Critical Values for the Weak Instrument Test Based on *LIML* Test Size (5% level of significance)**[13]

	B = 1 Maximum Test Size				*B* = 2 Maximum Test Size			
L	0.10	0.15	0.20	0.25	0.10	0.15	0.20	0.25
1	16.38	8.96	6.66	5.53				
2	8.68	5.33	4.42	3.92	7.03	4.58	3.95	3.63
3	6.46	4.36	3.69	3.32	5.44	3.81	3.32	3.09
4	5.44	3.87	3.30	2.98	4.72	3.39	2.99	2.79

Table 11B.2   **Critical Values for the Weak Instrument Test Based on Fuller-*k* Relative Bias (5% level of significance)**[14]

	B = 1 Maximum Relative Bias				*B* = 2 Maximum Relative Bias			
L	0.05	0.10	0.20	0.30	0.05	0.10	0.20	0.30
1	24.09	19.36	15.64	12.71				
2	13.46	10.89	9.00	7.49	15.50	12.55	9.72	8.03
3	9.61	7.90	6.61	5.60	10.83	8.96	7.18	6.15
4	7.63	6.37	5.38	4.63	8.53	7.15	5.85	5.10

---

[12] R. S. Mariano (2001) "Simultaneous Equation Model Estimators," in *The Companion to Theoretical Econometrics*, Badi Baltagi ed. (Oxford: Blackwell Publishing), pp. 139–142.

[13] These values are from Table 5.4, page 103, in Stock and Yogo (2005), *op. cit.* The authors thank James Stock and Motohiro Yogo for permission to use these results. Their tables are more extensive than the ones we provide. The significance level of the test for weak instruments is 5%.

[14] These values are from Table 5.3, page 102, in James H. Stock and Motohiro Yogo (2005), *op. cit.*

critical values for the test of weak instruments using the relative bias criterion for the Fuller modification of *LIML*, using $a = 1$. There is no similar table for *LIML*, because the *LIML* estimator does not have a finite expected value, and thus the concept of bias breaks down.

11B.2.3a   Testing for Weak Instruments with *LIML*   This illustration was introduced in Chapter 10 Appendix E, Section 10E.2.1. With the Mroz data we estimate the *HOURS* supply equation

$$HOURS = \beta_1 + \beta_2 MTR + \beta_3 EDUC + \beta_4 KIDSL6 + \beta_5 NWIFEINC + e \qquad (11B.8)$$

The reduced form estimates are in Table 10E.3. The *LIML* estimates are given in Table 11B.3. The models we consider are:

Model 1: endogenous: *MTR*; *IV: EXPER*

Model 2: endogenous: *MTR*; *IV: EXPER, EXPER², LARGECITY*

Model 3: endogenous: *MTR, EDUC*; *IV: MOTHEREDUC, FATHEREDUC*

Model 4: endogenous: *MTR, EDUC*; *IV: MOTHEREDUC, FATHEREDUC, EXPER*

First, for the just identified equations for which the number of instruments equals the number of endogenous variables in Models (1) and (3), the *LIML* estimates are identical to the *2SLS* estimators. This identity is always true for just-identified equations. For the overidentified Models (2) and (4), the estimated values $\hat{\ell}$ are close to 1, so that the estimates are not too far from the *2SLS* estimates.

The estimates are not the important aspect of this illustration. The Cragg-Donald *F*-test statistic is the same for all the estimators. For convenience its values for each equation are given at the bottom of Table 11B.3. In Model (2) we have $B = 1$ endogenous variable and

Table 11B.3   *LIML* **Estimations**

MODEL	(1)	(2)	(3)	(4)
C	17423.7211	16191.3338	−24491.5972	18587.9064
	(5.56)	(5.40)	(−0.31)	(5.05)
MTR	−18456.5896	−17023.8164	29709.4652	−19196.5172
	(−5.08)	(−4.90)	(0.33)	(−4.79)
EDUC	−145.2928	−134.5504	258.5590	−197.2591
	(−4.40)	(−4.26)	(0.31)	(−3.05)
KIDSL6	151.0229	113.5034	−1144.4778	207.5531
	(1.07)	(0.84)	(−0.46)	(1.27)
NWIFEINC	−103.8983	−96.2895	149.2325	−104.9415
	(−5.27)	(−5.11)	(0.32)	(−5.07)
N	428	428	428	428
$\hat{\ell}$	1.0000	1.0195	1.0000	1.0029
CRAGG-DONALD F	30.61	13.22	0.10	8.60
NUMBER IV L	1	3	2	3
NUMBER ENDOG B	1	1	2	2

t statistics in parentheses

$L = 3$ instruments. Using the *LIML* maximum size of 10% as our criterion, the Stock-Yogo critical value is 6.46. The Cragg-Donald F-test statistic 13.22 exceeds this value, so we reject the null hypothesis that the instruments are weak and conclude that they are not weak. This is not the conclusion we would have drawn based on *IV/2SLS* estimation. The critical value from Table 10E.1 is 22.30, and we would have not rejected the null hypothesis that the instruments are weak.

In Model (4) there are $B = 2$ endogenous variables and $L = 3$ instruments. Using the maximum size of 10% critical value from Table 11B.1 of 5.44, we reject the null hypothesis that the instruments are weak using the Cragg-Donald F-test statistic of 8.60. If we were using the *2SLS/IV* estimator, we would have not rejected the hypothesis that the instruments are weak because the critical value from Table 10E.1 is 13.43.

What is indicated by these examples is that the *LIML* estimator performs better, at least potentially, in the face of weak instruments. We cannot prove anything based on one result from one sample, which is why we present a Monte Carlo simulation experiment in Appendix 11B.3.

11B.2.3b   Testing for Weak Instruments with Fuller Modified *LIML*   Using the Fuller modification of *LIML*, and setting the constant $a = 1$, we obtain the estimates in Table 11B.4. All the results are at least somewhat different from the *2SLS/IV* estimations, because even for just-identified equations, the Fuller estimator is different from the *2SLS* estimator. The only extremely dramatic change now comes in Model (3), where coefficient signs become more in line with the other models, although still nothing is significant. In Model (4) if we adopt the criterion of 10% maximum relative bias, then the Stock-Yogo critical value is 8.96. The Cragg-Donald F-test statistic is 8.6, so we fail to reject the null hypothesis that the instruments are weak.

Table 11B.4   **Fuller ($a = 1$) Estimations**

MODEL	(1)	(2)	(3)	(4)
C	17108.0110	15924.1895	2817.5400	18156.7850
	(5.60)	(5.44)	(0.20)	(5.10)
MTR	−18089.5451	−16713.2345	−1304.8205	−18730.1617
	(−5.11)	(−4.93)	(−0.08)	(−4.84)
EDUC	−142.5409	−132.2218	−29.6043	−191.1248
	(−4.41)	(−4.27)	(−0.20)	(−3.05)
KIDSL6	141.4113	105.3703	−287.7915	193.2295
	(1.02)	(0.79)	(−0.65)	(1.21)
NWIFEINC	−101.9491	−94.6401	−12.0108	−102.6290
	(−5.31)	(−5.14)	(−0.15)	(−5.12)
N	428	428	428	428
k	0.9976	1.0172	0.9976	1.0005
FULLER a	1.0000	1.0000	1.0000	1.0000
NUMBER IV L	1	3	2	3
CRAGG-DONALD F	30.61	13.22	0.10	8.60
NUMBER ENDOG B	1	1	2	2

t statistics in parentheses

Table 11B.5 **Monte Carlo Simulation Results**

ρ	π	$\overline{F}$	$\overline{\hat{\beta}_2}$	$t(\hat{\beta}_2)$	$t(\hat{\beta}_{2,\text{liml}})$	$\overline{\hat{\beta}}_{2,\text{F}}$	$\text{mse}(\hat{\beta}_2)$	$\text{mse}(\hat{\beta}_{2,\text{F}})$
0.0	0.1	1.98	0.9941	0.0049	0.0049	0.9941	0.4068	0.0748
0.0	0.5	21.17	0.9998	0.0441	0.0473	0.9997	0.0140	0.0132
0.8	0.1	2.00	1.3311	0.2886	0.1347	1.3375	1.0088	0.3289
0.8	0.5	21.18	1.0111	0.0636	0.0509	1.0000	0.0139	0.0127

11B.3 Monte Carlo Simulation Results

In Appendix 10F.2 we carried out a Monte Carlo simulation to explore the properties of the *IV/2SLS* estimators. Here we employ the same experiment, adding aspects of the new estimators we have introduced in this appendix.

First, examine the percentage rejections of the true null hypothesis $\beta_2 = 1$ using a two-tail test at the 5% level of significance. The Monte Carlo rejection rate for the *IV/2SLS* estimator is in the column labeled $t(\hat{\beta}_2)$, and for the *LIML* estimator in the column $t(\hat{\beta}_{2,\text{liml}})$. The largest difference is in the case of strong endogeneity with weak instruments, in which the test based upon the two-stage least squares estimator rejects 28.86% of the time, while the test based on the *LIML* estimator rejects 13.47% of the time. Recall that a two-tail test at the 5% level of significance corresponds to determining whether the 95% interval estimate contains the hypothesized parameter value. In these Monte Carlo experiments, the 95% interval estimate based on the *LIML* estimator contains the true parameter 86.53% of the time, whereas the 95% interval estimate using *IV/2SLS* contains the true parameter only 71.14% of the time. This finding is consistent with Stock and Yogo's conclusion about coverage rates of the two interval estimation approaches.

In these experiments, there is little difference between the averages of the two-stage least squares estimates, $\overline{\hat{\beta}_2}$ and the Fuller modified $(a = 1)$ *LIML* estimates $\hat{\beta}_{2,\text{F}}$. A greater contrast shows up when comparing how close the estimates are to the true parameter value using the mean square error criterion. In Table 11B.5 we report the empirical mean square error for the *IV/2SLS* estimator, $\text{mse}(\hat{\beta}_2)$ and that for the Fuller modification of *LIML* with $a = 4$, $\text{mse}(\hat{\beta}_{2,\text{F}})$. Recall that the mean square error measures how close the estimates are to the true parameter value. For the *IV/2SLS* estimator, the empirical mean square error is

$$\text{mse}(\hat{\beta}_2) = \sum_{m=1}^{10000}(\hat{\beta}_{2m} - \beta_2)^2 / 10,000$$

The Fuller modified *LIML* has lower mean square error than the *IV/2SLS* estimator in each experiment, and when the instruments are weak, the improvement is large.

Chapter *12*

Regression with Time-Series Data: Nonstationary Variables

Learning Objectives

Based on the material in this chapter, you should be able to

1. Explain the differences between stationary and nonstationary time-series processes.
2. Describe the general behavior of an autoregressive process and a random walk process.
3. Explain why we need "unit root" tests, and state implications of the null and alternative hypotheses.
4. Explain what is meant by the statement that a series is "integrated of order one" or I(1).
5. Perform Dickey–Fuller and augmented Dickey–Fuller tests for stationarity.
6. Explain the meaning of a "spurious regression".
7. Explain the concept of cointegration and test whether two series are cointegrated.
8. Explain how to choose an appropriate model for regression analysis with time-series data.

Keywords

autoregressive process	order of integration	stochastic process
cointegration	random walk process	stochastic trend
Dickey–Fuller tests	random walk with drift	tau statistic
difference stationary	spurious regressions	trend stationary
mean reversion	stationary	unit root tests
nonstationary		

In 2003 the Nobel Prize in Economics[1] was awarded jointly to two distinguished econometricians: Professor Robert F. Engle "for methods of analyzing economic time series with time-varying volatility (ARCH)" and Professor Clive W. J. Granger "for

---

[1] For more details, see http://nobelprize.org/nobel_prizes/economics/.

methods of analyzing economic time series with common trends (cointegration)." The aim of this and the following two chapters is to discuss the background that prompted these contributions, and to show how the proposed methods have revolutionized the way we conduct econometrics with time-series data.

The analysis of time-series data is of vital interest to many groups, such as macro-economists studying the behavior of national and international economies, finance economists analyzing the stock market, and agricultural economists predicting supplies and demands for agricultural products. For example, if we are interested in forecasting the growth of gross domestic product or inflation, we look at various indicators of economic performance and consider their behavior over recent years. Alternatively, if we are interested in a particular business, we analyze the history of the industry in an attempt to predict potential sales. In each of these cases, we are analyzing time-series data.

We have already worked with time-series data in Chapter 9 and have discovered how regression models for these data often have special characteristics designed to capture their dynamic nature. We saw how including lagged values of the dependent variable or explanatory variables as regressors, or considering lags in the errors, can be used to model dynamic relationships. We also showed how autoregressive models can be used in fore-casting. However, an important assumption maintained throughout Chapter 9 was that the variables have a property called stationarity. It is time now to learn the difference between stationary and nonstationary variables. Many economic variables are nonstationary and, as you will learn, the consequences of nonstationary variables for regression modeling are profound.

The aim of this chapter is to describe how to estimate regression models involving nonstationary variables. The first step in this direction is to examine the time-series concepts of **stationarity** (and **nonstationarity**) and how we distinguish between them. **Cointegration** is another important related concept that has a bearing on our choice of a regression model. The seminal contributions of the Nobel laureates show that the econometric consequences of nonstationarity can be quite severe, and offer methods to overcome them.

12.1 Stationary and Nonstationary Variables

Plots of the time series of some important economic variables for the U.S. economy are displayed in Figure 12.1. The data for these figures can be found in the file *usa.dat*. The figures on the left-hand side are the real gross domestic product (a measure of aggregate economic production), the annual inflation rate (a measure of changes in the aggregate price level), the federal funds rate (the interest rate on overnight loans between banks), and the three-year bond rate (interest rate on a financial asset to be held for three years). Observe how the GDP variable displays upward trending behavior, while the inflation rate appears to "wander up and down" with no discernable pattern or trend. Similarly, both the federal funds rate and the bond rate show "wandering up and down" behavior. The figures on the right-hand side of Figure 12.1 are the changes of the corresponding variables on the left-hand side.

The change in a variable is an important concept that is used repeatedly in this chapter; it is worth dwelling on its definition. The change in a variable y_t, also known as its first difference, is given by $\Delta y_t = y_t - y_{t-1}$. Thus Δy_t is the change in the value of the variable y from period $t - 1$ to period t.

The time series of the changes on the right-hand side of Figure 12.1 display behavior that can be described as irregular ups and downs, or fluctuations. Note that while changes in the inflation rate and the two interest rates appear to fluctuate around a constant value, the

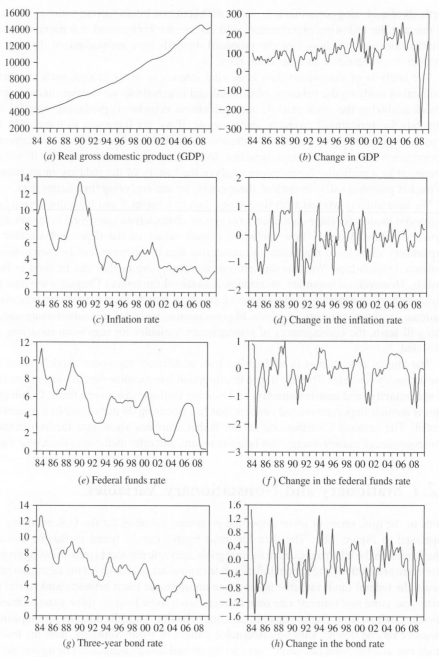

FIGURE 12.1 U.S. economic time series.

changes in the GDP variable appear to fluctuate around an upward trend, until the financial crisis. The first question we address in this chapter is: Which data series represent stationary variables and which are observations on nonstationary variables?

Formally, a time series y_t is stationary if its mean and variance are constant over time, and if the covariance between two values from the series depends only on the length of time separating the two values, and not on the actual times at which the variables are observed. That is, the time series y_t is stationary if for all values, and every time period, it is true that

Table 12.1   **Sample Means of Time Series Shown in Figure 12.1**

Variable	Sample periods	
	1984:2 to 1996:4	1997:1 to 2009:4
Real GDP (a)	5813.0	11458.2
Inflation rate (c)	6.9	3.2
Federal funds rate (e)	6.4	3.5
Bond rate (g)	7.3	4.0
Change in GDP (b)	82.7	120.3
Change in the inflation rate (d)	−0.16	0.02
Change in the federal funds rate (f)	−0.09	−0.10
Change in the bond rate (h)	−0.10	−0.09

$$E(y_t) = \mu \quad \text{(constant mean)} \tag{12.1a}$$

$$\text{var}(y_t) = \sigma^2 \quad \text{(constant variance)} \tag{12.1b}$$

$$\text{cov}(y_t, y_{t+s}) = \text{cov}(y_t, y_{t-s}) = \gamma_s \quad \text{(covariance depends on } s, \text{ not } t) \tag{12.1c}$$

The first condition, that of a constant mean, is the feature that has received the most attention. To appreciate this condition for stationarity, look at the plots shown in Figure 12.1 and their sample means shown in Table 12.1. The sample means for the changes in the two interest rates are similar across different sample periods, whereas the sample means for the variables in the original levels, as well as the changes in GDP and inflation, differ across sample periods. Thus, while the federal funds rate, and the bond rate display characteristics of nonstationarity, their changes display characteristics of stationarity. For inflation and GDP, both their levels and their changes display characteristics of nonstationarity. Non-stationary series with nonconstant means are often described as *not* having the property of **mean reversion**. That is, stationary series have the property of mean reversion.

Looking at the sample means of time-series variables is a convenient indicator as to whether a series is stationary or nonstationary, but this does not constitute a hypothesis test. A formal test is described in Section 12.3. However, before we introduce the test, it is useful to revisit the first-order autoregressive model that was introduced in Chapter 9.

12.1.1 THE FIRST-ORDER AUTOREGRESSIVE MODEL

Let y_t be an economic variable that we observe over time. In line with most economic variables, we assume that y_t is random, since we cannot perfectly predict it. We never know the values of random variables until they are observed. The econometric model generating a time-series variable y_t is called a **stochastic** or **random process**. A sample of observed y_t values is called a particular **realization** of the stochastic process. It is one of many possible paths that the stochastic process could have taken. Univariate time-series models are examples of stochastic processes where a single variable y is related to past values of itself and current and past error terms. In contrast to regression modeling, univariate time-series models do not contain any explanatory variables (no x's).

The autoregressive model of order one, the AR(1) model, is a useful univariate time-series model for explaining the difference between stationary and nonstationary series. It is given by

$$y_t = \rho y_{t-1} + v_t, \quad |\rho| < 1 \qquad (12.2a)$$

where the errors v_t are independent, with zero mean and constant variance σ_v^2, and may be normally distributed. In the context of time-series models, the errors are sometimes known as "shocks" or "innovations." As we will see, the assumption $|\rho| < 1$ implies that y_t is stationary. The AR(1) process shows that each realization of the random variable y_t contains a proportion ρ of last period's value y_{t-1} plus an error v_t drawn from a distribution with mean zero and variance σ_v^2. Since we are concerned with only one lag, the model is described as an autoregressive model of order one. In general an AR(p) model includes lags of the variable y_t up to y_{t-p}. An example of an AR(1) time series with $\rho = 0.7$, and independent $N(0,1)$ random errors is shown in Figure 12.2a. Note that the data have been artificially generated. Observe how the time series fluctuates around zero and has no trend-like behavior, a characteristic of stationary series.

The value "zero" is the constant mean of the series, and it can be determined by doing some algebra known as recursive substitution.[2] Consider the value of y at time $t = 1$, then its value at time $t = 2$ and so on. These values are

$$y_1 = \rho y_0 + v_1$$
$$y_2 = \rho y_1 + v_2 = \rho(\rho y_0 + v_1) + v_2 = \rho^2 y_0 + \rho v_1 + v_2$$
$$\vdots$$
$$y_t = v_t + \rho v_{t-1} + \rho^2 v_{t-2} + \cdots + \rho^t y_0$$

The mean of y_t is

$$E(y_t) = E(v_t + \rho v_{t-1} + \rho^2 v_{t-2} + \cdots) = 0$$

since the error v_t has zero mean and the value of $\rho^t y_0$ is negligible for a large t. The variance can be shown to be a constant $\sigma_v^2/(1 - \rho^2)$ while the covariance between two errors s periods apart γ_s can be shown to be $\sigma_v^2 \rho^s/(1 - \rho^2)$. Thus, the AR(1) model in (12.2a) is a classic example of a stationary process with a zero mean.

Real-world data rarely have a zero mean. We can introduce a nonzero mean μ by replacing y_t in (12.2a) with $(y_t - \mu)$ as follows:

$$(y_t - \mu) = \rho(y_{t-1} - \mu) + v_t$$

which can then be rearranged as

$$y_t = \alpha + \rho y_{t-1} + v_t, \quad |\rho| < 1 \qquad (12.2b)$$

---

[2] An alternative to recursive substitution when the variable is stationary is to use the lag operator algebra discussed in Chapter 9.8.

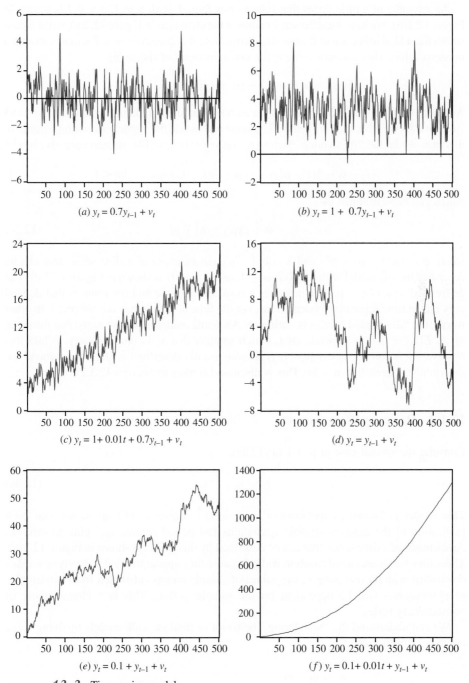

FIGURE *12.2* Time-series models.

where $\alpha = \mu(1 - \rho)$. That is, we can accommodate a nonzero mean in y_t by either working with the "de-meaned" variable $(y_t - \mu)$ or introducing the intercept term α in the autoregressive process of y_t as in (12.2b). Corresponding to these two ways, we describe the "de-meaned" variable $(y_t - \mu)$ as being stationary around zero, or the variable y_t as stationary around its mean value $\mu = \alpha/(1 - \rho)$.

An example of a time series that follows this model, with $\alpha = 1$, $\rho = 0.7$ is shown in Figure 12.2(b). We have used the same values of the error v_t as in Figure 12.2(a), so the figure shows the added influence of the constant term. Note that the series now fluctuates around a nonzero value. This nonzero value is the constant mean of the series

$$E(y_t) = \mu = \alpha/(1-\rho) = 1/(1-0.7) = 3.33$$

Another extension to (12.2a) is to consider an AR(1) model fluctuating around a linear trend $(\mu + \delta t)$. As we have seen in Figure 12.1, some real-world data appear to exhibit a trend. In this case, we let the "de-trended" series $(y_t - \mu - \delta t)$ behave like an autoregressive model

$$(y_t - \mu - \delta t) = \rho(y_{t-1} - \mu - \delta(t-1)) + v_t, \quad |\rho| < 1$$

which can be rearranged as

$$y_t = \alpha + \rho y_{t-1} + \lambda t + v_t \tag{12.2c}$$

where $\alpha = (\mu(1-\rho) + \rho\delta)$ and $\lambda = \delta(1-\rho)$. An example of a time series that can be described by this model with $\rho = 0.7$, $\alpha = 1$, and $\delta = 0.01$ is shown in Figure 12.2(c). The de-trended series $(y_t - \mu - \delta t)$ also has a constant variance and covariances that depend only on the time separating observations, not the time at which they are observed. In other words, the "de-trended" series is stationary. An astute reader may have noted that the mean of y_t, $E(y_t) = \mu + \delta t$ depends on t, which implies that y_t is nonstationary. While this observation is correct, when $|\rho| < 1$, y_t is more usually described as stationary around the deterministic trend line $\mu + \delta t$. This is discussed further in Section 12.5.2.

12.1.2   Random Walk Models

Consider the special case of $\rho = 1$ in (12.2a):

$$y_t = y_{t-1} + v_t \tag{12.3a}$$

This model is known as the random walk model. Equation (12.3a) shows that each realization of the random variable y_t contains last period's value y_{t-1} plus an error v_t. An example of a time series that can be described by this model is shown in Figure 12.2(d). These time series are called **random walks** because they appear to wander slowly upward or downward with no real pattern; the values of sample means calculated from subsamples of observations will be dependent on the sample period. This is a characteristic of nonstationary series.

We can understand the "wandering" behavior of random walk models by doing some recursive substitution.

$$y_1 = y_0 + v_1$$
$$y_2 = y_1 + v_2 = (y_0 + v_1) + v_2 = y_0 + \sum_{s=1}^{2} v_s$$
$$\vdots$$
$$y_t = y_{t-1} + v_t = y_0 + \sum_{s=1}^{t} v_s$$

The random walk model contains an initial value y_0 (often set to zero because it is so far in the past that its contribution to y_t is negligible) plus a component that is the sum of the past stochastic terms $\sum_{s=1}^{t} v_s$. This latter component is often called the **stochastic trend**. This term arises because a stochastic component v_t is added for each time t, and because it causes the time series to trend in unpredictable directions. If the variable y_t is subjected to a sequence of positive shocks, $v_t > 0$, followed by a sequence of negative shocks, $v_t < 0$, it will have the appearance of wandering upward, then downward.

We have used the fact that y_t is a sum of errors to explain graphically the nonstationary nature of the random walk. We can also use it to show algebraically that the conditions for stationarity do not hold. Recognizing that the v_t are independent, taking the expectation and the variance of y_t yields, for a fixed initial value y_0,

$$E(y_t) = y_0 + E(v_1 + v_2 + \cdots + v_t) = y_0$$

$$\text{var}(y_t) = \text{var}(v_1 + v_2 + \cdots + v_t) = t\sigma_v^2$$

The random walk has a mean equal to its initial value and a variance that increases over time, eventually becoming infinite. Although the mean is constant, the increasing variance implies that the series may not return to its mean, and so sample means taken for different periods are not the same.

Another nonstationary model is obtained by adding a constant term to (12.3a):

$$y_t = \alpha + y_{t-1} + v_t \tag{12.3b}$$

This model is known as the **random walk with drift**. Equation (12.3b) shows that each realization of the random variable y_t contains an intercept (the drift component α) plus last period's value y_{t-1} plus the error v_t. An example of a time series that can be described by this model (with $\alpha = 0.1$) is shown in Figure 12.2(e). Notice how the time-series data appear to be "wandering" as well as "trending" upward. In general, random walk with drift models show definite trends either upward (when the drift α is positive) or downward (when the drift α is negative).

Again, we can get a better understanding of this behavior by applying recursive substitution:

$$y_1 = \alpha + y_0 + v_1$$
$$y_2 = \alpha + y_1 + v_2 = \alpha + (\alpha + y_0 + v_1) + v_2 = 2\alpha + y_0 + \sum_{s=1}^{2} v_s$$
$$\vdots$$
$$y_t = \alpha + y_{t-1} + v_t = t\alpha + y_0 + \sum_{s=1}^{t} v_s$$

The value of y at time t is made up of an initial value y_0, the stochastic trend component $(\sum_{s=1}^{t} v_s)$, and now a **deterministic trend** component $t\alpha$. It is called a deterministic trend because a fixed value α is added for each time t. The variable y wanders up and down as well as increases by a fixed amount at each time t. The mean and variance of y_t are

$$E(y_t) = t\alpha + y_0 + E(v_1 + v_2 + v_3 + \cdots + v_t) = t\alpha + y_0$$
$$\text{var}(y_t) = \text{var}(v_1 + v_2 + v_3 + \cdots + v_t) = t\sigma_v^2$$

In this case both the constant mean and constant variance conditions for stationarity are violated.

We can extend the random walk model even further by adding a time trend:

$$y_t = \alpha + \delta t + y_{t-1} + v_t \tag{12.3c}$$

An example of a time series that can be described by this model (with $\alpha = 0.1; \delta = 0.01$) is shown in Figure 12.2(f). Note how the addition of a time-trend variable t strengthens the trend behavior. We can see the amplification using the same algebraic manipulation as before:

$$y_1 = \alpha + \delta + y_0 + v_1$$

$$y_2 = \alpha + \delta 2 + y_1 + v_2 = \alpha + 2\delta + (\alpha + \delta + y_0 + v_1) + v_2 = 2\alpha + 3\delta + y_0 + \sum_{s=1}^{2} v_s$$

$$\vdots$$

$$y_t = \alpha + \delta t + y_{t-1} + v_t = t\alpha + \left(\frac{t(t+1)}{2}\right)\delta + y_0 + \sum_{s=1}^{t} v_s$$

where we have used the formula for a sum of an arithmetic progression,

$$1 + 2 + 3 + \cdots + t = t(t+1)/2$$

The additional term has the effect of strengthening the trend behavior.

To recap, we have considered the autoregressive class of models and have shown that they display properties of stationarity when $|\rho| < 1$. We have also discussed the random walk class of models when $\rho = 1$. We showed that random walk models display properties of nonstationarity. Now, go back and compare the real-world data in Figure 12.1 with those in Figure 12.2. Ask yourself what models might have generated the different data series in Figure 12.1. In the next few sections we shall consider how to test which series in Figure 12.1 exhibit properties associated with stationarity, as well as which series exhibit properties associated with nonstationarity.

12.2 Spurious Regressions

The main reason why it is important to know whether a time series is stationary or nonstationary before one embarks on a regression analysis is that there is a danger of obtaining apparently significant regression results from unrelated data when nonstationary series are used in regression analysis. Such regressions are said to be **spurious**.

To illustrate the problem, let us take two independent random walks:

$$rw_1: y_t = y_{t-1} + v_{1t}$$

$$rw_2: x_t = x_{t-1} + v_{2t}$$

where v_{1t} and v_{2t} are independent $N(0,1)$ random errors. Two such series are shown in Figure 12.3(a)—the data are in the file *spurious.dat*. These series were generated independently and, in truth, have no relation to one another, yet when we plot them, as we have done in Figure 12.3(b), we see a positive relationship between them. If we estimate a simple regression of series one (rw_1) on series two (rw_2), we obtain the following results:

$$\widehat{rw_{1t}} = 17.818 + 0.842\, rw_{2t}, \quad R^2 = 0.70$$

$$(t) \qquad\qquad (40.837)$$

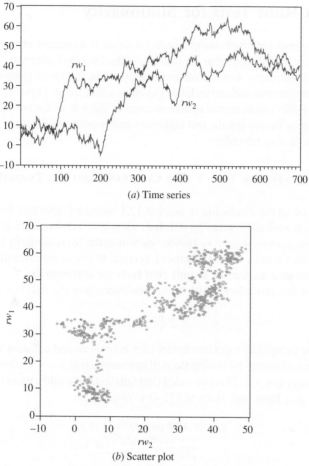

FIGURE 12.3 Time series and scatter plot of two random walk variables.

This result suggests that the simple regression model fits the data well ($R^2 = 0.70$), and that the estimated slope is significantly different from zero. In fact, the *t*-statistic is huge! These results are, however, completely meaningless, or spurious. The apparent significance of the relationship is false. It results from the fact that we have related one series with a stochastic trend to another series with another stochastic trend. In fact, these series have nothing in common, nor are they causally related in any way. Similar and more dramatic results are obtained when random walk with drift series are used in regressions. Typically the residuals from such regressions will be highly correlated. For this example, the *LM* test value to test for first-order autocorrelation (*p*-value in parenthesis) is 682.958 (0.000); a sure sign that there is a problem with the regression.

In other words, when nonstationary time series are used in a regression model, the results may spuriously indicate a significant relationship when there is none. In these cases the least squares estimator and least squares predictor do not have their usual properties, and *t*-statistics are not reliable. Since many macroeconomic time series are nonstationary, it is particularly important to take care when estimating regressions with macroeconomic variables.

How then can we test whether a series is stationary or nonstationary, and how do we conduct regression analysis with nonstationary data? The former is discussed in Section 12.3, while the latter is considered in Section 12.4.

12.3 Unit Root Tests for Stationarity

There are many tests for determining whether a series is stationary or nonstationary. The most popular one, and the one that we discuss, is the Dickey–Fuller test. As noted in our discussion of the autoregressive and random walk models, stochastic processes can include or exclude a constant term and can include or exclude a time trend. There are three variations of the Dickey–Fuller test designed to take account of the role of the constant term and the trend. We begin by describing the test equations and hypotheses for these three cases and then outline the testing procedure.

12.3.1   DICKEY–FULLER TEST 1 (NO CONSTANT AND NO TREND)

This test is based on the discussion in Section 12.1 where we note that the AR(1) process $y_t = \rho y_{t-1} + v_t$ is stationary when $|\rho| < 1$, but, when $\rho = 1$, it becomes the nonstationary random walk process $y_t = y_{t-1} + v_t$. Hence, one way to test for stationarity is to examine the value of ρ. In other words, we test whether ρ is equal to one or significantly less than one. Tests for this purpose are known as **unit root tests for stationarity**.

To formalize this procedure a little more, consider again the AR(1) model:

$$y_t = \rho y_{t-1} + v_t \tag{12.4}$$

where the v_t are independent random errors with zero mean and constant variance σ_v^2. We can test for nonstationarity by testing the null hypothesis that $\rho = 1$ against the alternative that $|\rho| < 1$, or simply $\rho < 1$. This one-sided (left tail) test is put into a more convenient form by subtracting y_{t-1} from both sides of (12.4) to obtain

$$y_t - y_{t-1} = \rho y_{t-1} - y_{t-1} + v_t$$
$$\Delta y_t = (\rho - 1)y_{t-1} + v_t$$
$$= \gamma y_{t-1} + v_t \tag{12.5a}$$

where $\gamma = \rho - 1$ and $\Delta y_t = y_t - y_{t-1}$. Then, the hypotheses can be written in terms of either ρ or γ:

$$H_0 : \rho = 1 \Leftrightarrow H_0 : \gamma = 0$$
$$H_1 : \rho < 1 \Leftrightarrow H_1 : \gamma < 0$$

Note that the null hypothesis is that the series is nonstationary. In other words, if we do not reject the null, we conclude that it is a nonstationary process; if we reject the null hypothesis that $\gamma = 0$, then we conclude that the series is stationary.

12.3.2   DICKEY–FULLER TEST 2 (WITH CONSTANT BUT NO TREND)

The second Dickey–Fuller test includes a constant term in the test equation:

$$\Delta y_t = \alpha + \gamma y_{t-1} + v_t \tag{12.5b}$$

The null and alternative hypotheses are the same as before. In this case, if we do not reject the null hypothesis that $\gamma = 0$ (or $\rho = 1$), we conclude that the series is nonstationary. If we reject the null hypothesis that $\gamma = 0$, we conclude that the series is stationary.

12.3.3 DICKEY–FULLER TEST 3 (WITH CONSTANT AND WITH TREND)

The third Dickey–Fuller test includes a constant and a trend in the test equation:

$$\Delta y_t = \alpha + \gamma y_{t-1} + \lambda t + v_t \tag{12.5c}$$

As before, the null and alternative hypotheses are $H_0 : \gamma = 0$ and $H_1 : \gamma < 0$. If we do not reject the null hypothesis that $\gamma = 0$ ($\rho = 1$), we conclude that the series is nonstationary. If we reject the null hypothesis that $\gamma = 0$, we conclude that the series is stationary.

12.3.4 THE DICKEY–FULLER CRITICAL VALUES

To test the hypothesis in all three cases, we simply estimate the test equation by least squares and examine the t-statistic for the hypothesis that $\gamma = 0$. Unfortunately this t-statistic no longer has the t-distribution that we have used previously to test zero null hypotheses for regression coefficients. A problem arises because when the null hypothesis is true, y_t is nonstationary and has a variance that increases as the sample size increases. This increasing variance alters the distribution of the usual t-statistic when H_0 is true. To recognize this fact, the statistic is often called a τ *(tau)* **statistic**, and its value must be compared to specially generated critical values. Note that critical values are generated for the three different tests because, as we have seen in Section 12.1, the addition of the constant term and the time-trend term changes the behavior of the time series.

Originally these critical values were tabulated by the statisticians Professor David Dickey and Professor Wayne Fuller. The values have since been refined, but in deference to the seminal work, unit root tests using these critical values have become known as **Dickey–Fuller tests**. Table 12.2 contains the critical values for the *tau* (τ) statistic for the three cases; they are valid in large samples for a one-tail test.

Note that the Dickey–Fuller critical values are more negative than the standard critical values (shown in the last row). This implies that the τ-statistic must take larger (negative) values than usual for the null hypothesis of nonstationarity $\gamma = 0$ to be rejected in favor of the alternative of stationarity $\gamma < 0$. Specifically, to carry out this one-tail test of significance, if τ_c is the critical value obtained from Table 12.2, we reject the null hypothesis of nonstationarity if $\tau \leq \tau_c$. If $\tau > \tau_c$ then we do not reject the null hypothesis that the series y_t is nonstationary. Expressed in a casual way, but one that avoids the proliferation of "double negatives," $\tau \leq \tau_c$ suggests that the series is stationary while $\tau > \tau_c$ suggests nonstationarity.

An important extension of the Dickey–Fuller test allows for the possibility that the error term is autocorrelated. Such autocorrelation is likely to occur if our earlier models did not have sufficient lag terms to capture the full dynamic nature of the process. Using the model with an intercept as an example, the extended test equation is

$$\Delta y_t = \alpha + \gamma y_{t-1} + \sum_{s=1}^{m} a_s \Delta y_{t-s} + v_t \tag{12.6}$$

where $\Delta y_{t-1} = (y_{t-1} - y_{t-2})$, $\Delta y_{t-2} = (y_{t-2} - y_{t-3}), \ldots$. We add as many lagged first difference terms as we need to ensure that the residuals are not autocorrelated. As we discovered in Section 9.6, including lags of the dependent variable can be used to eliminate autocorrelation in the errors. The number of lagged terms can be determined by examining the autocorrelation function (ACF) of the residuals v_t, or the significance of the estimated lag coefficients a_s. The unit root tests based on (12.6) and its variants (intercept excluded or trend included) are referred to as **augmented Dickey–Fuller tests**. The hypotheses for stationarity

Table 12.2   **Critical Values for the Dickey–Fuller Test**

Model	1%	5%	10%
$\Delta y_t = \gamma y_{t-1} + v_t$	−2.56	−1.94	−1.62
$\Delta y_t = \alpha + \gamma y_{t-1} + v_t$	−3.43	−2.86	−2.57
$\Delta y_t = \alpha + \lambda t + \gamma y_{t-1} + v_t$	−3.96	−3.41	−3.13
Standard critical values	−2.33	−1.65	−1.28

Note: These critical values are taken from R. Davidson and J. G. MacKinnon (1993), *Estimation and Inference in Econometrics*, New York: Oxford University Press, p. 708.

and nonstationarity are expressed in terms of γ in the same way and the test critical values are the same as those for the Dickey–Fuller test shown in Table 12.2. When $\gamma = 0$, in addition to saying that the series is nonstationary, we also say the series has a **unit root**. In practice, we always use the augmented Dickey–Fuller test (rather than the nonaugmented version) to ensure the errors are uncorrelated.

12.3.5   THE DICKEY FULLER TESTING PROCEDURES

Up to now, we have discussed a number of stationary and nonstationary processes as well as three Dickey-Fuller tests. How do we go about deciding which test to use? To understand the rationale for what we suggest, it is useful to first take a look at the design of the unit root tests.

The critical values for the three tests shown in Table 12.2 were derived from the following simulations:

- true process; $y_t = y_{t-1} + v_t, v_t \sim N(0, \sigma^2)$, test equation: $y_t = \rho y_{t-1} + v_t$
- true process; $y_t = y_{t-1} + v_t, v_t \sim N(0, \sigma^2)$, test equation: $y_t = \alpha + \rho y_{t-1} + v_t$
- true process; $y_t = \delta + y_{t-1} + v_t, v_t \sim N(0, \sigma^2)$, test equation: $y_t = \alpha + \rho y_{t-1} + \lambda t + v_t$

Now take a look at Table 12.3. Column one shows the stationary autoregressive models covered in Section 12.1.1, and column two shows the corresponding nonstationary processes when $\rho = 1$. As we can see the processes in column two correspond to the true processes underlying the Dickey-Fuller tests described in column three while the processes in column one are the test equations.

Table 12.3   **AR processes and the Dickey-Fuller Tests**

AR processes: $\|\rho\| < 1$	Setting $\rho = 1$	Dickey Fuller Tests
$y_t = \rho y_{t-1} + u_t$	$y_t = y_{t-1} + u_t$	Test with no constant and no trend
$y_t = \alpha + \rho y_{t-1} + v_t$ $\alpha = \mu(1-\rho)$	$y_t = y_{t-1} + v_t$ $\alpha = 0$	Test with constant and no trend
$y_t = \alpha + \rho y_{t-1} + \lambda t + v_t$ $\alpha = (\mu(1 - \rho) + \rho\delta)$ $\lambda = \delta(1 - \rho)$	$y_t = \delta + y_{t-1} + v_t$ $\alpha = \delta$ $\lambda = 0$	Test with constant and trend

This then suggests the following Dickey-Fuller testing procedure. First plot the time series of the variable and select a suitable Dickey-Fuller test based on a visual inspection of the plot.

- If the series appears to be wandering or fluctuating around a sample average of zero (see for example Figure 12.2(a) or Figure 12.2(d) with mean around zero), use test equation (12.5a).

- If the series appears to be wandering or fluctuating around a sample average which is nonzero (see for example Figure 12.2(b) or Figure 12.2(d) with a non-zero mean), use test equation (12.5b).

- If the series appears to be wandering or fluctuating around a linear trend (see, for example, Figure 12.5(c) or Figure 12.2(e)), use test equation (12.5c).

Second, proceed with one of the unit root tests described in Sections 12.3.1 to 12.3.3, bearing in mind that it is important to choose the correct critical values as they depend upon the test equation estimated, which, in turn, depends on the absence or presence of the constant and trend terms.

12.3.6   THE DICKEY–FULLER TESTS: AN EXAMPLE

As an example, consider the two interest rate series—the federal funds rate (F_t) and the three-year bond rate (B_t)—plotted in Figure 12.1(e) and 12.1(g), respectively. Both series exhibit wandering behavior, so we suspect that they may be nonstationary variables. When performing Dickey–Fuller tests, we need to decide whether to use (12.5a) with no constant, or (12.5b) that includes a constant term, or (12.5c) that includes a constant and a deterministic time trend t. As suggested earlier, (12.5b) is the appropriate test equation because the series fluctuate around a nonzero mean. We also have to decide on how many lagged difference terms to include on the right-hand side of the equation. Following procedures described in Sections 9.3 and 9.4, we find that the inclusion of one lagged difference term is sufficient to eliminate autocorrelation in the residuals in both cases. The results from estimating the resulting equations are

$$\widehat{\Delta F_t} = 0.173 - 0.045F_{t-1} + 0.561\Delta F_{t-1}$$
$$(tau) \qquad \quad (-2.505)$$

$$\widehat{\Delta B_t} = 2.90 - 0.056B_{t-1} + 0.237\Delta B_{t-1}$$
$$(tau) \qquad \quad (-2.703)$$

The *tau* value (τ) for the federal funds rate is -2.505, and the 5% critical value for *tau* (τ_c) is -2.86. Again, recall that to carry out this one-tail test of significance, we reject the null hypothesis of nonstationarity if $\tau \leq \tau_c$. If $\tau > \tau_c$ then we do not reject the null hypothesis that the series is nonstationary. In this case, since $-2.505 > -2.86$, we do not reject the null hypothesis that the series is nonstationary. Similarly, the *tau* value for the bond rate is greater than the 5% critical value of -2.86 and again we do not reject the null hypothesis that the series is nonstationary. Expressed another way, there is insufficient evidence to suggest F_t and B_t are stationary.

12.3.7   ORDER OF INTEGRATION

Up to this stage, we have discussed only whether a series is stationary or nonstationary. We can take the analysis another step forward and consider a concept called the "order of integration." Recall that if y_t follows a random walk, then $\gamma = 0$ and the first difference of y_t becomes

$$\Delta y_t = y_t - y_{t-1} = v_t$$

An interesting feature of the series $\Delta y_t = y_t - y_{t-1}$ is that it is stationary since v_t, being an independent $(0, \sigma_v^2)$ random variable, is stationary. Series like y_t, which can be made stationary by taking the first difference, are said to be **integrated of order one**, and denoted as **I(1)**. Stationary series are said to be integrated of order zero, **I(0)**. In general, the order of integration of a series is the minimum number of times it must be differenced to make it stationary.

For example, to determine the order of integration of F and B, we then ask the next question: is the first difference of the federal funds rate $(\Delta F_t = F_t - F_{t-1})$ stationary? Is the first difference of the bond rate $(\Delta B_t = B_t - B_{t-1})$ stationary? Their plots, in Figure 12.1(f) and 12.1(h), seem to suggest that they are stationary.

The results of the Dickey–Fuller test for a random walk applied to the first differences are given below:

$$\widehat{\Delta(\Delta F)}_t = -0.447(\Delta F)_{t-1}$$
$$(tau) \quad (-5.487)$$

$$\widehat{\Delta(\Delta B)}_t = -0.701(\Delta B)_{t-1}$$
$$(tau) \quad (-7.662)$$

where $\Delta(\Delta F)_t = \Delta F_t - \Delta F_{t-1}$ and $\Delta(\Delta B)_t = \Delta B_t - \Delta B_{t-1}$. Note that the null hypotheses are that the variables ΔF and ΔB are not stationary. Also, because the series ΔF and ΔB appear to fluctuate around zero, we use the test equation without the intercept term. Based on the large negative value of the *tau* statistic $(-5.487 < -1.94)$, we reject the null hypothesis that ΔF_t is nonstationary and accept the alternative that it is stationary. We similarly conclude that ΔB_t is stationary $(-7.662 < -1.94)$.

This result implies that while the level of the federal funds rate (F_t) is nonstationary, its first difference (ΔF_t) is stationary. We say that the series F_t is I(1) because it had to be differenced once to make it stationary [ΔF_t is I(0)]. Similarly we have also shown that the bond rate (B_t) is integrated of order one. In the next section we investigate the implications of these results for regression modeling.

12.4 Cointegration

As a general rule, nonstationary time-series variables should not be used in regression models, to avoid the problem of spurious regression. However, there is an exception to this rule. If y_t and x_t are nonstationary I(1) variables, then we expect their difference, or any linear combination of them, such as $e_t = y_t - \beta_1 - \beta_2 x_t$,[3] to be I(1) as well. However, there is an important case when $e_t = y_t - \beta_1 - \beta_2 x_t$ is a stationary I(0) process. In this case y_t and x_t are said to be **cointegrated**. Cointegration implies that y_t and x_t share similar stochastic trends, and, since the difference e_t is stationary, they never diverge too far from each other.

A natural way to test whether y_t and x_t are cointegrated is to test whether the errors $e_t = y_t - \beta_1 - \beta_2 x_t$ are stationary. Since we cannot observe e_t, we test the stationarity of the

---

[3] A linear combination of x and y is a new variable $z = a_0 + a_1 x + a_2 y$. Here we set the constants $a_0 = -\beta_1$, $a_1 = -\beta_2$, and $a_2 = 1$, and call z the series e.

Table 12.4 **Critical Values for the Cointegration Test**

Regression model	1%	5%	10%
(1) $y_t = \beta x_t + e_t$	−3.39	−2.76	−2.45
(2) $y_t = \beta_1 + \beta_2 x_t + e_t$	−3.96	−3.37	−3.07
(3) $y_t = \beta_1 + \delta t + \beta_2 x_t + e_t$	−3.98	−3.42	−3.13

Note: These critical values are taken from J. Hamilton (1994), *Time Series Analysis*, Princeton University Press, p. 766.

least squares residuals, $\hat{e}_t = y_t - b_1 - b_2 x_t$ using a Dickey–Fuller test. The test for co-integration is effectively a test of the stationarity of the residuals. If the residuals are stationary, then y_t and x_t are said to be cointegrated; if the residuals are nonstationary, then y_t and x_t are not cointegrated, and any apparent regression relationship between them is said to be spurious.

The test for stationarity of the residuals is based on the test equation

$$\Delta \hat{e}_t = \gamma \hat{e}_{t-1} + v_t \tag{12.7}$$

where $\Delta \hat{e}_t = \hat{e}_t - \hat{e}_{t-1}$. As before, we examine the t (or *tau*) statistic for the estimated slope coefficient. Note that the regression has no constant term because the mean of the regression residuals is zero. Also, since we are basing this test upon **estimated** values of the residuals, the critical values will be different from those in Table 12.2. The proper critical values for a test of cointegration are given in Table 12.4. The test equation can also include extra terms like $\Delta \hat{e}_{t-1}, \Delta \hat{e}_{t-2}, \ldots$ on the right-hand side if they are needed to eliminate autocorrelation in v_t.

There are three sets of critical values. Which set we use depends on whether the residuals $\hat{e}_t$ are derived from a regression equation without a constant term [like (12.8a)] or a regression equation with a constant term [like (12.8b)], or a regression equation with a constant and a time trend [like (12.8c)].

$$\text{Equation 1}: \quad \hat{e}_t = y_t - b x_t \tag{12.8a}$$

$$\text{Equation 2}: \quad \hat{e}_t = y_t - b_2 x_t - b_1 \tag{12.8b}$$

$$\text{Equation 3}: \quad \hat{e}_t = y_t - b_2 x_t - b_1 - \hat{\delta} t \tag{12.8c}$$

12.4.1 AN EXAMPLE OF A COINTEGRATION TEST

To illustrate, let us test whether $y_t = B_t$ and $x_t = F_t$, as plotted in Figure 12.1(e) and 12.1(g), are cointegrated. We have already shown that both series are nonstationary. The estimated least squares regression between these variables is

$$\hat{B}_t = 1.140 + 0.914 F_t, \quad R^2 = 0.881$$
$$(t) \quad (6.548)(29.421) \tag{12.9}$$

and the unit root test for stationarity in the estimated residuals $(\hat{e}_t = B_t - 1.140 - 0.914 F_t)$ is

$$\Delta \hat{e}_t = -0.225 \hat{e}_{t-1} + 0.254 \Delta \hat{e}_{t-1}$$
$$(tau) \quad (-4.196)$$

Note that this is the augmented Dickey–Fuller version of the test with one lagged term Δe_{t-1} to correct for autocorrelation. Since there is a constant term in (12.9), we use the equation (2) critical values in Table 12.4.

The null and alternative hypotheses in the test for cointegration are

$$H_0 \text{:the series are not cointegrated} \Leftrightarrow \text{residuals are nonstationary}$$

$$H_1 \text{:the series are cointegrated} \Leftrightarrow \text{residuals are stationary}$$

Similar to the one-tail unit root tests, we reject the null hypothesis of no cointegration if $\tau \leq \tau_c$, and we do not reject the null hypothesis that the series are not cointegrated if $\tau > \tau_c$. The *tau* statistic in this case is -4.196 which is less than the critical value -3.37 at the 5% level of significance. Thus, we reject the null hypothesis that the least squares residuals are nonstationary and conclude that they are stationary. This implies that the bond rate and the federal funds rate are cointegrated. In other words, there is a fundamental relationship between these two variables (the estimated regression relationship between them is valid and not spurious) and the estimated values of the intercept and slope are 1.140 and 0.914, respectively.

The result—that the federal funds and bond rates are cointegrated—has major economic implications! It means that when the Federal Reserve implements monetary policy by changing the federal funds rate, the bond rate will also change thereby ensuring that the effects of monetary policy are transmitted to the rest of the economy. In contrast, the effectiveness of monetary policy would be severely hampered if the bond and federal funds rates were spuriously related as this implies that their movements, fundamentally, have little to do with each other.

12.4.2 THE ERROR CORRECTION MODEL

In the previous section, we discussed the concept of cointegration as the relationship between I(1) variables such that the residuals are I(0). A relationship between I(1) variables is also often referred to as a long run relationship while a relationship between I(0) variables is often referred to as a short run relationship. In this section, we describe a dynamic relationship between I(0) variables, which embeds a cointegrating relationship, known as the short-run error correction model.

As discussed in Chapter 9, when one is working with time-series data, it is quite common, and in fact, is quite important to allow for dynamic effects. To derive the error correction model requires a bit of algebra, but we shall persevere as this model offers a coherent way to combine the long- and short-run effects.

Let us start with a general model that contains lags of y and x, namely the autoregressive distributed lag (ARDL) model introduced in Chapter 9, except that now the variables are nonstationary:

$$y_t = \delta + \theta_1 y_{t-1} + \delta_0 x_t + \delta_1 x_{t-1} + v_t$$

For simplicity, we shall consider lags up to order one, but the following analysis holds for any order of lags. Now recognize that if y and x are cointegrated, it means that there is a long-run relationship between them. To derive this exact relationship, we set $y_t = y_{t-1} = y, x_t = x_{t-1} = x$ and $v_t = 0$ and then, imposing this concept in the ARDL, we obtain

$$y(1 - \theta_1) = \delta + (\delta_0 + \delta_1)x$$

This equation can be rewritten as $y = \beta_1 + \beta_2 x$ where $\beta_1 = \delta/(1 - \theta_1)$ and $\beta_2 = (\delta_0 + \delta_1)/(1 - \theta_1)$. To repeat, we have now derived the implied cointegrating relationship between y and x; alternatively, we have derived the long-run relationship that holds between the two I(1) variables.

We will now manipulate the ARDL to see how it embeds the cointegrating relation. First, add the term, $-y_{t-1}$, to both sides of the equation:

$$y_t - y_{t-1} = \delta + (\theta_1 - 1)y_{t-1} + \delta_0 x_t + \delta_1 x_{t-1} + v_t.$$

Second, add the term $-\delta_0 x_{t-1} + \delta_0 x_{t-1}$ to the right-hand side to obtain

$$\Delta y_t = \delta + (\theta_1 - 1)y_{t-1} + \delta_0 (x_t - x_{t-1}) + (\delta_0 + \delta_1)x_{t-1} + v_t$$

where $\Delta y_t = y_t - y_{t-1}$. If we then manipulate the equation to look like

$$\Delta y_t = (\theta_1 - 1)\left(\frac{\delta}{(\theta_1 - 1)} + y_{t-1} + \frac{(\delta_0 + \delta_1)}{(\theta_1 - 1)}x_{t-1}\right) + \delta_0 \Delta x_t + v_t$$

where $\Delta x_t = x_t - x_{t-1}$, and do a bit more tidying, using the definitions β_1 and β_2, we get

$$\Delta y_t = -\alpha(y_{t-1} - \beta_1 - \beta_2 x_{t-1}) + \delta_0 \Delta x_t + v_t \qquad (12.10)$$

where $\alpha = (1 - \theta_1)$. As you can see, the expression in parenthesis is the cointegrating relationship. In other words, we have embedded the cointegrating relationship between y and x in a general ARDL framework.

Equation (12.10) is called an error correction equation because (a) the expression $(y_{t-1} - \beta_1 - \beta_1 x_{t-1})$ shows the deviation of y_{t-1} from its long run value, $\beta_1 + \beta_2 x_{t-1}$—in other words, the "error" in the previous period—and (b) the term (θ_1-1) shows the "correction" of Δy_t to the "error." More specifically, if the error in the previous period is positive so that $y_{t-1} > (\beta_0 + \beta_1 x_{t-1})$, then y_t should fall and Δy_t should be negative; conversely, if the error in the previous period is negative so that $y_{t-1} < (\beta_0 + \beta_1 x_{t-1})$, then y_t should rise and Δy_t should be positive. This means that if a cointegrating relationship between y and x exists, so that adjustments always work to "error-correct," then empirically we should also find that $(1 - \theta_1) > 0$, which implies that $\theta_1 < 1$. If there is no evidence of cointegration between the variables, then the term θ_1 would be insignificant.

The error correction model is a very popular model because it allows for the existence of an underlying or fundamental link between variables (the long-run relationship) as well as for short-run adjustments (i.e. changes) between variables, including adjustments to achieve the cointegrating relationship. It also shows that we can work with I(1) variables (y_{t-1}, x_{t-1}) and I(0) variables $(\Delta y_t, \Delta x_t)$ in the same equation provided that (y, x) are cointegrated, meaning that the term $(y_{t-1} - \beta_0 - \beta_1 x_{t-1})$ contains stationary residuals. In fact, this formulation can also be used to test for cointegration between y and x.

To illustrate, consider our earlier example of the bond and federal funds rates. The result from estimating (12.10) using nonlinear least squares is

$$\Delta \hat{B}_t = -0.142(B_{t-1} - 1.429 - 0.777F_{t-1}) + 0.842\Delta F_t - 0.327\Delta F_{t-1}$$
$$(t) \quad (2.857) \qquad\qquad\qquad\qquad (9.387) \quad (3.855)$$

Note first that we need two lags $(\Delta F_t, \Delta F_{t-1})$ to ensure that the residuals are purged of all serial correlation effects. Second, note that the estimate $\hat{\theta}_1 = -0.142 + 1 = 0.858$ is less than one, as expected.

We can now generate the estimated residuals:

$$\hat{e}_{t-1} = (B_{t-1} - 1.429 - 0.777 F_{t-1})$$

The result from applying the ADF test for stationarity is

$$\Delta\hat{e}_t = -0.169\hat{e}_{t-1} + 0.180\Delta\hat{e}_{t-1}$$
$$(t) \quad (-3.929)$$

As before, the null is that (B, F) are not cointegrated. Since the cointegrating relationship includes a constant term, the critical value is -3.37. Comparing the calculated value (-3.929) with the critical value, we reject the null hypothesis and conclude that (B, F) are cointegrated.

12.5 Regression When There Is No Cointegration

Thus far, we have shown that regression with I(1) variables is acceptable providing those variables are cointegrated, allowing us to avoid the problem of spurious results. We also know that regression with stationary I(0) variables, that we studied in Chapter 9, is acceptable. What happens when there is no cointegration between I(1) variables? In this case, the sensible thing to do is to convert the nonstationary series to stationary series and to use the techniques discussed in Chapter 9 to estimate dynamic relationships between the stationary variables. However, we stress that this step should be taken only when we fail to find cointegration between the I(1) variables. Regression with cointegrated I(1) variables makes the least squares estimator "super-consistent"[4] and, moreover, is economically useful to establish relationships between the levels of economic variables.

How we convert nonstationary series to stationary series, and the kind of model we estimate, depend on whether the variables are **difference stationary** or **trend stationary**. In the former case, we convert the nonstationary series to its stationary counterpart by taking first differences. In the latter case, we convert the nonstationary series to its stationary counterpart by de-trending. We now explore these issues.

12.5.1 FIRST DIFFERENCE STATIONARY

Consider a variable y_t that behaves like the random walk model:

$$y_t = y_{t-1} + v_t$$

This is a nonstationary series with a "stochastic" trend, but it can be rendered stationary by taking the first difference:

$$\Delta y_t = y_t - y_{t-1} = v_t$$

The variable y_t is said to be a **first difference stationary** series. Recall that this means that y is said to be integrated of order 1. Now suppose that Dickey–Fuller tests reveal that two variables, y and x, that you would like to relate in a regression, are first difference stationary,

---

[4]Consistency means that as $T \to \infty$ the least squares estimator converges to the true parameter value. See Appendix 5B. Super-consistency means that it converges to the true value at a faster rate.

I(1), and not cointegrated. Then, a suitable regression involving only stationary variables is one that relates changes in y to changes in x, with relevant lags included, and no intercept. For example, using one lagged Δy_t and a current and lagged Δx_t, we have

$$\Delta y_t = \theta \Delta y_{t-1} + \beta_0 \Delta x_t + \beta_1 \Delta x_{t-1} + e_t \tag{12.11a}$$

Now consider a series y_t that behaves like a random walk with drift,

$$y_t = \alpha + y_{t-1} + v_t$$

and note that y can be rendered stationary by taking the first difference:

$$\Delta y_t = \alpha + v_t$$

The variable y_t is also said to be a **first difference stationary** series, even though it is stationary around a constant term. Now suppose again that y and x are I(1) and not cointegrated. Then an example of a suitable regression equation, again involving stationary variables, is obtained by adding a constant to (12.11a). That is,

$$\Delta y_t = \alpha + \theta \Delta y_{t-1} + \beta_0 \Delta x_t + \beta_1 \Delta x_{t-1} + e_t \tag{12.11b}$$

In line with Section 9.7, the models in (12.11a) and (12.11b) are autoregressive distributed lag models with first-differenced variables. In general, since there is often doubt about the role of the constant term, the usual practice is to include an intercept term in the regression.

12.5.2 TREND STATIONARY

Consider a model with a constant term, a trend term, and a stationary error term:

$$y_t = \alpha + \delta t + v_t$$

The variable y_t is said to be **trend stationary** because it can be made stationary by removing the effect of the deterministic (constant and trend) components

$$y_t - \alpha - \delta t = v_t$$

A series like this is, strictly speaking, not an I(1) variable, but is described as stationary around a deterministic trend. Thus, if y and x are two trend-stationary variables, a possible autoregressive distributed lag model is

$$y_t^* = \theta y_{t-1}^* + \beta_0 x_t^* + \beta_1 x_{t-1}^* + e_t \tag{12.12}$$

where $y_t^* = y_t - \alpha_1 - \delta_1 t$ and $x_t^* = x_t - \alpha_2 - \delta_2 t$ are the de-trended data (the coefficients (α_1, δ_1) and (α_2, δ_2) can be estimated by least squares).

As an alternative to using the de-trended data for estimation, a constant term and a trend term can be included directly in the equation. For example, by substituting y_t^* and x_t^* into (12.12), it can be shown that estimating (12.12) is equivalent to estimating

$$y_t = \alpha + \delta t + \theta y_{t-1} + \beta_0 x_t + \beta_1 x_{t-1} + e_t$$

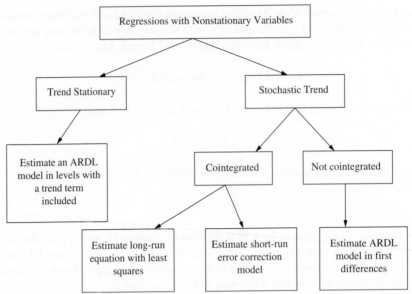

FIGURE *12.4* Regression with time-series data: nonstationary variables.

where $\alpha = \alpha_1(1 - \theta_1) - \alpha_2(\beta_0 + \beta_1) + \theta_1\delta_1 + \beta_1\delta_2$ and $\delta = \delta_1(1 - \theta_1) - \delta_2(\beta_0 + \beta_1)$. In practice, this is usually the preferred option as it is relatively more straightforward.

12.5.3 SUMMARY

- If variables are stationary, or I(1) and cointegrated, we can estimate a regression relationship between the levels of those variables without fear of encountering a spurious regression. In the later case, we can do this by estimating a least squares equation between the I(1) variables or by estimating a nonlinear least squares error correction model which embeds the I(1) variables.

- If the variables are I(1) and not cointegrated, we need to estimate a relationship in first differences, with or without the constant term.

- If they are trend stationary, we can either de-trend the series first and then perform regression analysis with the stationary (de-trended) variables or, alternatively, estimate a regression relationship that includes a trend variable. The latter alternative is typically applied.

These options are shown in Figure 12.4.

12.6 Exercises

12.6.1 Problems

12.1 (a) Consider an AR(1) model

$$y_t = \rho y_{t-1} + v_t, \quad |\rho| < 1$$

Rewrite y as a function of lagged errors. (*Hint*: perform recursive substitution.) What is the mean and variance of y? What is the covariance between y_t and y_{t-2}?

(b) Consider a random walk model

$$y_t = y_{t-1} + v_t$$

Rewrite y as a function of lagged errors. What is the mean and variance of y? What is the covariance between y_t and y_{t-2}?

12.2 Figure 12.5 (data file *unit.dat*) shows plots of four time series. Since W and Y appear to be fluctuating around a nonzero mean, a Dickey–Fuller test 2 (with constant but no trend) was performed on these variables. Since X and Z appear to be fluctuating around a trend, a Dickey–Fuller test 3 (with constant and trend) was performed for these two variables. The results are shown below.

$$\widehat{\Delta W_t} = 0.757 - 0.091 W_{t-1}$$
$$(tau) \qquad (-3.178)$$

$$\widehat{\Delta Y_t} = 0.031 - 0.039 Y_{t-1}$$
$$(tau) \qquad (-1.975)$$

$$\widehat{\Delta X_t} = 0.782 - 0.092 X_{t-1} + 0.009t$$
$$(tau) \qquad (-3.099)$$

$$\widehat{\Delta Z_t} = 0.332 - 0.036 Z_{t-1} + 0.005t$$
$$(tau) \qquad (-1.913)$$

Which series are stationary, and which are nonstationary?

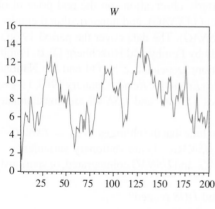

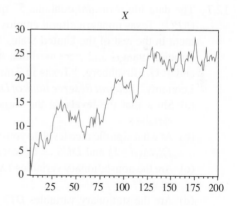

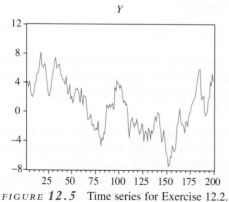

FIGURE 12.5 Time series for Exercise 12.2.

12.3   A time series process of the form $y_t = \alpha + y_{t-1} + v_t, v_t \sim N(0, \sigma^2)$ can be rearranged as $y_t - y_{t-1} = \Delta y_t = \alpha + v_t$. This shows that y_t is integrated of order one, since its first difference is stationary. Show that a time series of the form $y_t = 2y_{t-1} - y_{t-2} + \alpha + v_t$ is integrated of order two.

12.6.2   Computer Exercises

12.4   The data file *oil.dat* contains 88 annual observations on the price of oil (in 1967 constant dollars) for the period 1883–1970.
   (a) Plot the data. Do the data look stationary, or nonstationary?
   (b) Use a unit root test to demonstrate that the series is stationary.
   (c) What do you conclude about the order of integration of this series?

12.5   The data file *bond.dat* contains 102 monthly observations on AA railroad bond yields for the period January 1968 to June 1976.
   (a) Plot the data. Do railroad bond yields appear stationary, or nonstationary?
   (b) Use a unit root test to demonstrate that the series is nonstationary.
   (c) Find the first difference of the bond yield series and test for stationarity.
   (d) What do you conclude about the order of integration of this series?

12.6   The data file *oz.dat* contains quarterly data on disposable income and consumption in Australia from 1985:1 to 2005:2.
   (a) Test each of these series for stationarity.
   (b) What do you conclude about the "order of integration" of each of these series?
   (c) Is consumption cointegrated with, or spuriously related to, disposable income?

12.7   The data file *texas.dat* contains 57 quarterly observations on the real price of oil (*RPO*), Texas nonagricultural employment (*TXNAG*), and nonagricultural employment in the rest of the United States (*USNAG*). The data cover the period 1974Q1 through 1988Q1 and were used in a study by Fomby and Hirschberg [T. B. Fomby and J. G. Hirschberg, "Texas in Transition: Dependence on Oil and the National Economy," *Federal Reserve Bank of Dallas Economic Review,* January 1989, 11–28].
   (a) Show that the **levels** of the variables *TXNAG* and *USNAG* are nonstationary variables.
   (b) At what significance level do you conclude that the **changes** $DTX = TXNAG - TXNAG(-1)$ and $DUS = USNAG - USNAG(-1)$ are stationary variables?
   (c) Are the nonstationary variables *TXNAG* and *USNAG* cointegrated, or spuriously related?
   (d) Are the stationary variables *DTX* and *DUS* related?
   (e) What is the difference between (d) and (c)?

12.8   The data file *usa.dat* contains the data shown in Figure 12.1. Consider the two time series, real GDP and the inflation rate.
   (a) Are the series stationary, or nonstationary? Which Dickey–Fuller test (no constant, no trend; with constant, no trend; or with constant and with trend) did you use?
   (b) What do you conclude about the order of integration of these series?
   (c) Forecast GDP and inflation for 2010:1.

12.9   The data file *canada.dat* contains monthly Canadian/U.S. exchange rates for the period 1971:01 to 2006:12. Split the observations into two sample periods—a 1971:01–1987:12 sample period and a 1988:01–2006:12 sample period.
   (a) Perform a unit root test on the data for each sample period. Which Dickey–Fuller test did you use?
   (b) Are the results for the two sample periods consistent?

(c) Perform a unit root test for the full sample 1971:01–2006:12. What is the order of integration of the data?

12.10 The data file *csi.dat* contains the Consumer Sentiment Index (CSI), produced by the University of Michigan for the sample period 1978:01–2006:12.
(a) Perform all three Dickey–Fuller tests. Are the results consistent? If not, why not?
(b) Based on a graphical inspection of the data, which test should you have used?
(c) Does the CSI suggest that consumers "remember" and "retain" news information for a short time, or for a long time?

12.11 The data file *mexico.dat* contains real GDP for Mexico and the Unites States from the first quarter of 1980 to the third quarter of 2006. Both series have been standardized so that the average value in 2,000 is 100.
(a) Perform the test for cointegration between Mexico and the Unites States for all three test equations in (12.8). Are the results consistent?
(b) The theory of convergence in economic growth suggests the two GDPs should be proportional and cointegrated. That is, there should be a cointegrating relationship that does not contain an intercept or a trend. Do your results support this theory?
(c) If the variables are not cointegrated, what should you do if you are interested in testing the relationship between Mexico and the United States?

12.12 The file *inter2.dat* contains 300 observations of a generated I(2) process shown in Figure 12.6 below. Show that the variable called *inter2* is indeed an I(2) variable by conducting a number of unit root tests—first on the level of the data, then on the first difference and finally on the second difference.

12.13 Prices around the world tend to move together. The data file *ukpi.dat* contains information about the price indices in the United Kingdom and in the Euro Area (the United Kingdom is a member of the European Union, but not a member of the single European currency zone) for the period 1996:1–2009:12.
(a) Plot the data. Are the series I(1) or I(0)?
(b) Are prices in the UK and in the Euro Area cointegrated, or spuriously related? Use both the least squares and the error correction method to test this proposition.

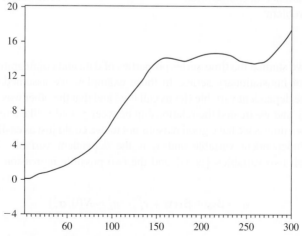

FIGURE *12.6* A generated I(2) process.

Chapter 13

Vector Error Correction and Vector Autoregressive Models

Learning Objectives

Based on the material in this chapter, you should be able to do the following:

1. Explain why economic variables are dynamically interdependent.
2. Explain the VEC model.
3. Explain the importance of error correction.
4. Explain the VAR model.
5. Explain the relationship between a VEC model and a VAR model.
6. Explain how to estimate the VEC and VAR models for the bivariate case.
7. Explain how to generate impulse response functions and variance decompositions for the simple case when the variables are not contemporaneously interdependent and the shocks are not correlated.

Keywords

dynamic relationships	impulse response functions
error correction	VAR model
forecast error variance decomposition	VEC model
identification problem	

In Chapter 12, we studied the time-series properties of data and cointegrating relationships between pairs of nonstationary series. In those examples, we assumed that one of the variables was the dependent variable (let us call it y_t) and that the other was the independent variable (say x_t), and we treated the relationship between y_t and x_t like a regression model. However, a priori, unless we have good reasons not to, we could just as easily have assumed that y_t is the independent variable and x_t is the dependent variable. Put simply, we are working with two variables $\{y_t, x_t\}$ and the two possible regression models relating them are

$$y_t = \beta_{10} + \beta_{11}x_t + e_t^y, \quad e_t^y \sim N(0, \sigma_y^2) \tag{13.1a}$$

$$x_t = \beta_{20} + \beta_{21} y_t + e_t^x, \quad e_t^x \sim N(0, \sigma_x^2) \tag{13.1b}$$

In this bivariate (two series) system there can be only one unique relationship between x_t and y_t, and so it must be the case that $\beta_{21} = 1/\beta_{11}$ and $\beta_{20} = -\beta_{10}/\beta_{11}$. A bit of terminology: for (13.1a) we say that we have normalized on y (meaning that the coefficient in front of y is set to 1), whereas for (13.1b) we say that we have normalized on x (meaning that the coefficient in front of x is set to 1).

Is it better to write the relationship as (13.1a) or (13.1b), or is it better to recognize that in many relationships, variables like y and x are simultaneously determined? The aim of this chapter is to explore the causal relationship between pairs of time-series variables. In doing so, we shall be extending our study of time-series data to take account of their dynamic properties and interactions. In particular, we will discuss the **vector error correction (VEC)** and **vector autoregressive (VAR)** models. We will learn how to estimate a VEC model when there is cointegration between I(1) variables, and how to estimate a VAR model when there is no cointegration. Note that this is an extension of the single-equation models examined in chapter 12.

Some important terminology emerges here. Univariate analysis examines a single data series. Bivariate analysis examines a pair of series. The term **vector** indicates that we are considering a number of series: two, three, or more. The term "vector" is a generalization of the univariate and bivariate cases.

13.1 VEC and VAR Models

Let us begin with two time-series variables y_t and x_t and generalize the discussion about dynamic relationships in Chapter 9 to yield a system of equations:

$$\begin{aligned} y_t &= \beta_{10} + \beta_{11} y_{t-1} + \beta_{12} x_{t-1} + v_t^y \\ x_t &= \beta_{20} + \beta_{21} y_{t-1} + \beta_{22} x_{t-1} + v_t^x \end{aligned} \tag{13.2}$$

The equations in (13.2) describe a system in which each variable is a function of its own lag and the lag of the other variable in the system. In this case, the system contains two variables y and x. In the first equation y_t is a function of its own lag y_{t-1} and the lag of the other variable in the system x_{t-1}. In the second equation x_t is a function of its own lag x_{t-1} and the lag of the other variable in the system y_{t-1}. Together the equations constitute a system known as a vector autoregression (VAR). In this example, since the maximum lag is of order 1, we have a VAR(1).

If y and x are stationary I(0) variables, the above system can be estimated using least squares applied to each equation. If, however, y and x are nonstationary I(1) and not cointegrated, then as discussed in Chapter 12, we work with the first differences. In this case, the VAR model is

$$\begin{aligned} \Delta y_t &= \beta_{11} \Delta y_{t-1} + \beta_{12} \Delta x_{t-1} + v_t^{\Delta y} \\ \Delta x_t &= \beta_{21} \Delta y_{t-1} + \beta_{22} \Delta x_{t-1} + v_t^{\Delta x} \end{aligned} \tag{13.3}$$

All variables are now I(0), and the system can again be estimated by least squares. To recap: the VAR model is a general framework to describe the dynamic interrelationship between stationary variables. Thus, if y and x are stationary I(0) variables, the system in (13.2) is used. On the other hand, if y and x are I(1) variables but are not cointegrated, we examine the interrelation between them using a VAR framework in first differences (13.3).

If y and x are I(1) and cointegrated, then we need to modify the system of equations to allow for the cointegrating relationship between the I(1) variables. We do this for two reasons. First, as economists, we like to retain and use valuable information about the cointegrating relationship, and second, as econometricians, we like to ensure that we use the best technique that takes into account the properties of the time-series data. Recall the chapter on simultaneous equations—the cointegrating equation is one way of introducing simultaneous interactions without requiring the data to be stationary. Introducing the cointegrating relationship leads to a model known as the VEC model. We turn now to this model.

Consider two nonstationary variables y_t and x_t that are integrated of order 1: $y_t \sim I(1)$ and $x_t \sim I(1)$ and which we have shown to be cointegrated, so that

$$y_t = \beta_0 + \beta_1 x_t + e_t \tag{13.4}$$

and $\hat{e}_t \sim I(0)$ where $\hat{e}_t$ are the estimated residuals. Note that we could have chosen to normalize on x. Whether we normalize on y or x is often determined from economic theory; the critical point is that there can be at most one fundamental relationship between the two variables.

The VEC model is a special form of the VAR for I(1) variables that are cointegrated. The VEC model is

$$\Delta y_t = \alpha_{10} + \alpha_{11}(y_{t-1} - \beta_0 - \beta_1 x_{t-1}) + v_t^y$$
$$\Delta x_t = \alpha_{20} + \alpha_{21}(y_{t-1} - \beta_0 - \beta_1 x_{t-1}) + v_t^x \tag{13.5a}$$

which we can expand as

$$y_t = \alpha_{10} + (\alpha_{11} + 1)y_{t-1} - \alpha_{11}\beta_0 - \alpha_{11}\beta_1 x_{t-1} + v_t^y$$
$$x_t = \alpha_{20} + \alpha_{21}y_{t-1} - \alpha_{21}\beta_0 - (\alpha_{21}\beta_1 - 1)x_{t-1} + v_t^x \tag{13.5b}$$

Comparing (13.5b) with (13.2) shows the VEC as a VAR where the I(1) variable y_t is related to other lagged variables (y_{t-1} and x_{t-1}) and where the I(1) variable x_t is also related to the other lagged variables (y_{t-1} and x_{t-1}). Note, however, that the two equations contain the common cointegrating relationship.

The coefficients α_{11}, α_{21} are known as error correction coefficients, so named because they show how much Δy_t and Δx_t respond to the cointegrating error $y_{t-1} - \beta_0 - \beta_1 x_{t-1} = e_{t-1}$. The idea that the error leads to a correction comes about because of the conditions put on α_{11}, α_{21} to ensure stability, namely $(-1 < \alpha_{11} \leq 0)$ and $(0 \leq \alpha_{21} < 1)$. To appreciate this idea, consider a positive error $e_{t-1} > 0$ that occurred because $y_{t-1} > (\beta_0 + \beta_1 x_{t-1})$. A negative error correction coefficient in the first equation (α_{11}) ensures that Δy falls, while the positive error correction coefficient in the second equation (α_{21}) ensures that Δx rises, thereby correcting the error. Having the error correction coefficients less than 1 in absolute value ensures that the system is not explosive. Note that the VEC is a generalization of the error-correction (single-equation) model discussed in Chapter 12. In the VEC (system) model, both y_t and x_t "error-correct."

The error correction model has become an extremely popular model because its interpretation is intuitively appealing. Think about two nonstationary variables, say consumption (let us call it y_t) and income (let us call it x_t), that we expect to be related (cointegrated). Now think about a change in your income Δx_t, say a pay raise! Consumption will most likely increase, but it may take you a while to change your consumption pattern in response to a change in your pay. The VEC model allows us to examine how much consumption will change in response to a change in the explanatory variable (the cointegration part, $y_t = \beta_0 + \beta_1 x_t + e_t$), as well as the speed of the change (the error correction part, $\Delta y_t = \alpha_{10} + \alpha_{11}(e_{t-1}) + v_t^y$ where e_{t-1} is the cointegrating error).

There is one final point to discuss—the role of the intercept terms. Thus far, we have introduced an intercept term in the cointegrating equation (β_0) as well as in the VEC (α_{10} and α_{20}). However, doing so can create a problem. To see why, we collect all the intercept terms and rewrite (13.5b) as

$$
\begin{aligned}
y_t &= (\alpha_{10} - \alpha_{11}\beta_0) + (\alpha_{11} + 1)y_{t-1} - \alpha_{11}\beta_1 x_{t-1} + v_t^y \\
x_t &= (\alpha_{20} - \alpha_{21}\beta_0) + \alpha_{21}y_{t-1} - (\alpha_{21}\beta_1 - 1)x_{t-1} + v_t^x
\end{aligned}
\tag{13.5c}
$$

If we estimate each equation by least squares, we obtain estimates of composite terms $(\alpha_{10} - \alpha_{11}\beta_0)$ and $(\alpha_{20} - \alpha_{21}\beta_0)$, and we are not able to disentangle the separate effects of β_0, α_{10}, and α_{20}. In the next section, we discuss a simple two-step least squares procedure that gets around this problem. However, the lesson here is to check whether, and where, an intercept term is needed.

13.2 Estimating a Vector Error Correction Model

There are many econometric methods to estimate the error correction model. Nonlinear (system) least squares is one method, but the most straightforward method is to use a two-step least squares procedure. First, use least squares to estimate the cointegrating relationship $y_t = \beta_0 + \beta_1 x_t + e_t$ and generate the lagged residuals $\hat{e}_{t-1} = y_{t-1} - b_0 - b_1 x_{t-1}$.

Second, use least squares to estimate the equations:

$$
\Delta y_t = \alpha_{10} + \alpha_{11}\hat{e}_{t-1} + v_t^y
\tag{13.6a}
$$

$$
\Delta x_t = \alpha_{20} + \alpha_{21}\hat{e}_{t-1} + v_t^x
\tag{13.6b}
$$

Note that all the variables in (13.6) (Δy, Δx and $\hat{e}$) are stationary (recall that for y and x to be cointegrated, the residuals $\hat{e}$ must be stationary). Hence, the standard regression analysis studied in earlier chapters may be used to test the significance of the parameters. The usual residual diagnostic tests may be applied.

We need to be careful here about how we combine stationary and nonstationary variables in a regression model. Cointegration is about the relationship between I(1) variables. The cointegrating equation does not contain I(0) variables. The corresponding VEC model, however, relates the change in an I(1) variable (the I(0) variables Δy and Δx) to other I(0) variables, namely the cointegration residuals $\hat{e}_{t-1}$; if required, other stationary variables may be added. In other words, we should not mix stationary and nonstationary variables: an I(0) dependent variable on the left-hand side of a regression equation should be "explained" by other I(0) variables on the right-hand side and an I(1) dependent variable on the left-hand side of a regression equation should be explained by other I(1) variables on the right-hand side.

13.2.1 EXAMPLE

In Figure 13.1 the quarterly real GDP of a small economy (Australia) and a large economy (United States) for the sample period 1970:1 to 2000:4 are displayed. Note that the series have been scaled so that both economies show a real GDP value of 100 in 2000. They appear in the file *gdp.dat*. It appears from the figure that both series are nonstationary and possibly cointegrated.

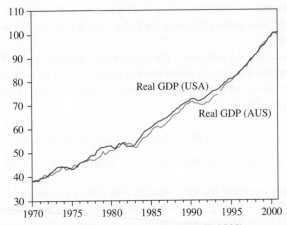

FIGURE **13.1**   Real gross domestic products (GDP = 100 in 2000).

Formal unit root tests of the series confirm that they are indeed nonstationary. To check for cointegration we obtain the fitted equation in (13.7) (the intercept term is omitted because it has no economic meaning):

$$\hat{A}_t = 0.985 U_t, \tag{13.7}$$

where A denotes real GDP for Australia and U denotes real GDP for the United States. Note that we have normalized on A because it makes more sense to think of a small economy responding to a large economy. The residuals derived from the cointegrating relationship $\hat{e}_t = A_t - 0.985 U_t$ are shown in Figure 13.2. Their first order autocorrelation is 0.870, and a visual inspection of the time series suggests that the residuals may be stationary.

A formal unit root test is performed, and the estimated unit root test equation is

$$\widehat{\Delta e_t} = -0.128 \hat{e}_{t-1} \tag{13.8}$$
$$(tau) \quad (-2.889)$$

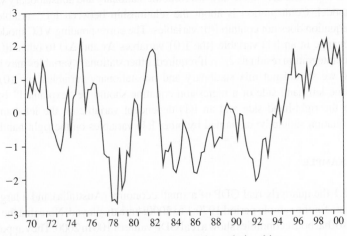

FIGURE **13.2**   Residuals derived from the cointegrating relationship.

Since the cointegrating relationship does not contain an intercept term [see Chapter 12, (12.8a)], the 5% critical value is -2.76. The unit root t-value of -2.889 is less than -2.76. We reject the null of no cointegration and we conclude that the two real GDP series are cointegrated. This result implies that economic activity in the small economy (Australia, A_t) is linked to economic activity in the large economy (United States, U_t). If U_t were to increase by one unit, A_t would increase by 0.985. But the Australian economy may not respond fully by this amount within the quarter. To ascertain how much it will respond within a quarter, we estimate the error correction model by least squares. The estimated VEC model for $\{A_t, U_t\}$ is

$$\widehat{\Delta A_t} = 0.492 - 0.099\hat{e}_{t-1}$$
$$(t) \qquad\qquad (2.077)$$

$$\widehat{\Delta U_t} = 0.510 + 0.030\hat{e}_{t-1}$$
$$(t) \qquad\qquad (0.789)$$

(13.9)

The results show that both error correction coefficients are of the appropriate sign. The negative error correction coefficient in the first equation (-0.099) indicates that ΔA falls (i.e., A_t falls or ΔA_t is negative) while the positive error correction coefficient in the second equation (0.030) indicates that ΔU rises (i.e., U_t rises or ΔU_t is positive), when there is a positive cointegrating error $(\hat{e}_{t-1} > 0$ or $A_{t-1} > 0.985 U_{t-1})$. This behavior (negative change in A and positive change in U) "corrects" the cointegrating error. The error correction coefficient (-0.099) is significant at the 5% level; it indicates that the quarterly adjustment of A_t will be about 10% of the deviation of A_{t-1} from its cointegrating value $0.985 U_{t-1}$. This is a slow rate of adjustment. However, the error correction coefficient in the second equation (0.030) is insignificant; it suggests that ΔU does not react to the cointegrating error. This outcome is consistent with the view that the small economy is likely to react to economic conditions in the large economy, but not vice versa.

13.3 Estimating a VAR Model

The VEC is a multivariate dynamic model that incorporates a cointegrating equation. It is relevant when, for the bivariate case, we have two variables, say y and x, that are both I(1), but are cointegrated. Now we ask: what should we do if we are interested in the interdependencies between y and x, but they are not cointegrated? In this case, we estimate a vector autoregressive (VAR) model as shown in (13.3).

As an example, consider Figure 13.3, which shows the log of real personal disposable income (denoted as Y) and log of real personal consumption expenditure (denoted as C) for the U.S. economy over the period 1960:1 to 2009:4. Both series appear to be nonstationary, but are they cointegrated? The data are in the file *fred.dat*.

The ADF tests for unit roots for C and Y (for the case with an intercept only) give values -1.995 and -2.741, respectively. Given a critical value of -2.876 at the 5% level of significance, we may conclude that the series are nonstationary. The test for cointegration for the case normalized on C is shown below:

$$\hat{e}_t = C_t + 0.404 - 1.035 Y_t$$
$$\Delta \hat{e}_t = -0.088\hat{e}_{t-1} - 0.299\Delta\hat{e}_{t-1}$$
$$(tau) \ (-2.873)$$

(13.10)

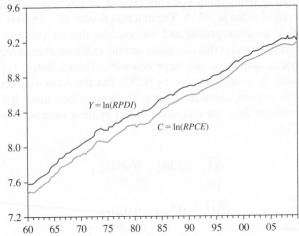

FIGURE **13.3** Real personal disposable income and real personal consumption expenditure (in logarithms).

This is a Case 2 test [see Chapter 12, (12.8b)], since the cointegrating relationship contains an intercept term. Note that an intercept term has been included here to capture the component of (log) consumption that is independent of disposable income. The 5% critical value of the test for stationarity in the cointegrating residuals is −3.37. Since the *tau* (unit root *t*-value) of −2.873 is greater than −3.37, it indicates that the errors are not stationary, and hence that the relationship between C (i.e., $\ln(RPCE)$) and Y (i.e., $\ln(RPDI)$) is spurious—that is, we have no cointegration. Thus, we would not apply a VEC model to examine the dynamic relationship between aggregate consumption C and income Y. Instead we would estimate a VAR model for the set of I(0) variables $\{\Delta C_t, \Delta Y_t\}$.

For illustrative purposes, the order of lag in this example has been restricted to one. In general, we should test for the significance of lag terms greater than one. The results are

$$\Delta \hat{C}_t = \;\; 0.005 + 0.215\Delta C_{t-1} + 0.149\Delta Y_{t-1}$$
$$(t) \qquad (6.969) \;\; (2.884) \qquad\quad (2.587) \qquad\qquad\qquad (13.11a)$$
$$\Delta \hat{Y}_t = \;\; 0.006 + 0.475\Delta C_{t-1} - 0.217\Delta Y_{t-1}$$
$$(t) \qquad (6.122) \;\; (4.885) \qquad\quad (2.889) \qquad\qquad\qquad (13.11b)$$

The first equation (13.11a) shows that the quarterly growth in consumption (ΔC_t) is significantly related to its own past value (ΔC_{t-1}) and also significantly related to the quarterly growth in the last period's income (ΔY_{t-1}). The second equation (13.11b) shows that ΔY_t is significantly negatively related to its own past value but significantly positively related to the last period's change in consumption. The constant terms capture the fixed component in the change in log consumption and the change in log income.

Having estimated these models, can we infer anything else? If the system is subjected to an income shock, what is the effect of the shock on the dynamic path of the quarterly growth in consumption and income? Will they rise, and if so, by how much? If the system is also subjected to a consumption shock, what is the contribution of an income versus a consumption shock on the variation of income? We turn now to some analysis suited to addressing these questions.

13.4 **Impulse Responses and Variance Decompositions**

Impulse response functions and variance decompositions are techniques that are used by macroeconometricians to analyze problems such as the effect of an oil price shock on inflation and GDP growth, and the effect of a change in monetary policy on the economy.

13.4.1 IMPULSE RESPONSE FUNCTIONS

Impulse response functions show the effects of shocks on the adjustment path of the variables. To help us understand this, we shall first consider a univariate series.

13.4.1a   The Univariate Case

Consider a univariate series $y_t = \rho y_{t-1} + v_t$ and subject it to a shock of size v in period one. Assume an arbitrary starting value of y at time zero: $y_0 = 0$. (Since we are interested in the dynamic path, the starting point is irrelevant.) At time $t = 1$, following the shock, the value of y will be: $y_1 = \rho y_0 + v_1 = v$. Assume that there are no subsequent shocks in later time periods $[v_2 = v_3 = \cdots = 0]$, at time $t = 2$, $y_2 = \rho y_1 = \rho v$. At time $t = 3$, $y_3 = \rho y_2 = \rho(\rho y_1) = \rho^2 v$, and so on. Thus the time-path of y following the shock is $\{v, \rho v, \rho^2 v, \ldots\}$. The values of the coefficients $\{1, \rho, \rho^2, \ldots\}$ are known as multipliers, and the time-path of y following the shock is known as the impulse response function.

To illustrate, assume that $\rho = 0.9$ and let the shock be unity: $v = 1$. According to the analysis, y will be $\{1, 0.9, 0.81, \ldots\}$, approaching zero over time. This impulse response function is plotted in Figure 13.4. It shows us what happens to y after a shock. In this case, y initially rises by the full amount of the shock and then it gradually returns to the value before the shock.

13.4.1b   The Bivariate Case

Now, let us consider an impulse response function analysis with two time series based on a bivariate VAR system of stationary variables:

$$y_t = \delta_{10} + \delta_{11}y_{t-1} + \delta_{12}x_{t-1} + v_t^y$$
$$x_t = \delta_{20} + \delta_{21}y_{t-1} + \delta_{22}x_{t-1} + v_t^x \tag{13.12}$$

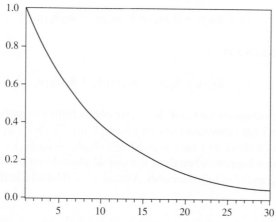

FIGURE *13.4* Impulse responses for an AR(1) model $y_t = 0.9\,y_{t-1} + e_t$ following a unit shock.

In this case, there are two possible shocks to the system—one to y and the other to x. Thus we are interested in four impulse response functions—the effect of a shock to y on the time-paths of y and x and the effect of a shock to x on the time-paths of y and x.

The actual mechanics of generating impulse responses in a system is complicated by the facts that (i) one has to allow for interdependent dynamics (the multivariate analog of generating the multipliers) and (ii) one has to identify the correct shock from unobservable data. Taken together, these two complications lead to what is known as the **identification problem**. In this chapter, we consider a special case where there is no identification problem.[1] This special case occurs when the system that is described in (13.12) is a true representation of the dynamic system—namely, y is related only to lags of y and x, and x is related only to lags of y and x. In other words, y and x are related dynamically, but not contemporaneously. The current value x_t does not appear in the equation for y_t and the current value y_t does not appear in the equation for x_t. Also, we need to assume that the errors v_t^x and v_t^y are independent of each other (contemporaneously uncorrelated). In addition, we assume that $v^y \sim N(0, \sigma_y^2)$ and $v^x \sim N(0, \sigma_x^2)$.

Consider the case when there is a one–standard deviation shock (alternatively called an **innovation**) to y so that at time $t = 1$, $v_1^y = \sigma_y$, and v_t^y is zero thereafter. Assume $v_t^x = 0$ for all t. It is traditional to consider a standard deviation shock (innovation) rather than a unit shock to overcome measurement issues. Assume $y_0 = x_0 = 0$. Also, since we are focusing on how a shock *changes* the paths of y and x, we can ignore the intercepts. Then

1. When $t = 1$, the effect of a shock of size σ_y on y is $y_1 = v_1^y = \sigma_y$, and the effect on x is $x_1 = v_1^x = 0$.

2. When $t = 2$, the effect of the shock on y is

$$y_2 = \delta_{11}y_1 + \delta_{12}x_1 = \delta_{11}\sigma_y + \delta_{12}0 = \delta_{11}\sigma_y$$

and the effect on x is

$$x_2 = \delta_{21}y_1 + \delta_{22}x_1 = \delta_{21}\sigma_y + \delta_{22}0 = \delta_{21}\sigma_y.$$

3. When $t = 3$, the effect of the shock on y is

$$y_3 = \delta_{11}y_2 + \delta_{12}x_2 = \delta_{11}\delta_{11}\sigma_y + \delta_{12}\delta_{21}\sigma_y$$

and the effect on x is

$$x_3 = \delta_{21}y_2 + \delta_{22}x_2 = \delta_{21}\delta_{11}\sigma_y + \delta_{22}\delta_{21}\sigma_y.$$

By repeating the substitutions for $t = 4, 5, \ldots$, we obtain further expressions. The impulse response of the shock (or innovation) to y on y is $\sigma_y\{1, \delta_{11}, (\delta_{11}\delta_{11} + \delta_{12}\delta_{21}), \ldots\}$ and the impulse response of a shock to y on x is $\sigma_y\{0, \delta_{21}, (\delta_{21}\delta_{11} + \delta_{22}\delta_{21}), \ldots\}$.

Now consider what happens when there is a one standard deviation shock to x so that at time $t = 1$, $v_1^x = \sigma_x$, and v_t^x is zero thereafter. Assume $v_t^y = 0$ for all t. In the first period after

---

[1] Appendix 13A introduces the general problem.

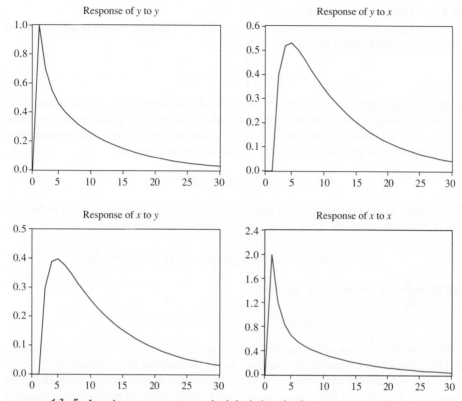

FIGURE *13.5* Impulse responses to standard deviation shock.

the shock, the effect of a shock of size σ_x on y is $y_1 = v_1^y = 0$, and the effect of the shock on x is $x_1 = v_t^x = \sigma_x$. Two periods after the shock, when $t = 2$, the effect on y is

$$y_2 = \delta_{11}y_1 + \delta_{12}x_1 = \delta_{11}0 + \delta_{12}\sigma_x = \delta_{12}\sigma_x$$

and the effect on x is

$$x_2 = \delta_{21}y_1 + \delta_{22}x_1 = \delta_{21}0 + \delta_{22}\sigma_x = \delta_{22}\sigma_x$$

Again, by repeated substitutions, we obtain the impulse response of a shock to x on y as $\sigma_x\{0, \delta_{12}, (\delta_{11}\delta_{12} + \delta_{12}\delta_{22}), \ldots\}$, and the impulse response of a shock to x on x as $\sigma_x\{1, \delta_{22}, (\delta_{21}\delta_{12} + \delta_{22}\delta_{22}), \ldots\}$. Figure 13.5 shows the four impulse response functions for numerical values: $\sigma_y = 1, \sigma_x = 2, \delta_{11} = 0.7, \delta_{12} = 0.2, \delta_{21} = 0.3$ and $\delta_{22} = 0.6$.

The advantage of examining impulse response functions (and not just VAR coefficients) is that they show the size of the impact of the shock plus the rate at which the shock dissipates, allowing for interdependencies.

13.4.2 FORECAST ERROR VARIANCE DECOMPOSITIONS

Another way to disentangle the effects of various shocks is to consider the contribution of each type of shock to the forecast error variance.

13.4.2a Univariate Analysis

Consider again the univariate series, $y_t = \rho y_{t-1} + v_t$. The best one-step-ahead forecast (alternatively the forecast one period ahead) is

$$y_{t+1}^F = E_t[\rho y_t + v_{t+1}]$$

where E_t is the expected value conditional on information at time t (i.e., we are interested in the mean value of y_{t+1} using what is known at time t). At time t the conditional expectation $E_t[\rho y_t] = \rho y_t$ is known, but the error v_{t+1} is unknown, and so its conditional expectation is zero. Thus the best forecast of y_{t+1} is ρy_t, and the forecast error is

$$y_{t+1} - E_t[y_{t+1}] = y_{t+1} - \rho y_t = v_{t+1}$$

The variance of the one-step forecast error is $\text{var}(v_{t+1}) = \sigma^2$. Suppose we wish to forecast two steps ahead; using the same logic, the two-step forecast becomes

$$y_{t+2}^F = E_t[\rho y_{t+1} + v_{t+2}] = E_t[\rho(\rho y_t + v_{t+1}) + v_{t+2}] = \rho^2 y_t$$

and the two-step forecast error becomes

$$y_{t+2} - E_t[y_{t+2}] = y_{t+2} - \rho^2 y_t = \rho v_{t+1} + v_{t+2}$$

In this case, the variance of the forecast error is $\text{var}(\rho v_{t+1} + v_{t+2}) = \sigma^2(\rho^2 + 1)$, showing that the variance of forecast error increases as we increase the forecast horizon.

In this univariate example, there is only one shock that leads to a forecast error. Hence the forecast error variance is 100% due to its own shock. The exercise of attributing the source of the variation in the forecast error is known as variance decomposition.

13.4.2b Bivariate Analysis

We can perform a variance decomposition for our special bivariate example where there is no identification problem. Ignoring the intercepts (since they are constants), the one–step ahead forecasts are

$$y_{t+1}^F = E_t[\delta_{11}y_t + \delta_{12}x_t + v_{t+1}^y] = \delta_{11}y_t + \delta_{12}x_t$$
$$x_{t+1}^F = E_t[\delta_{21}y_t + \delta_{22}x_t + v_{t+1}^x] = \delta_{21}y_t + \delta_{22}x_t$$

The corresponding one-step-ahead forecast errors and variances are

$$FE_1^y = y_{t+1} - E_t[y_{t+1}] = v_{t+1}^y \quad \text{var}(FE_1^y) = \sigma_y^2$$
$$FE_1^x = x_{t+1} - E_t[x_{t+1}] = v_{t+1}^x \quad \text{var}(FE_1^x) = \sigma_x^2$$

Hence in the first period, all variation in the forecast error for y is due to its own shock. Likewise, 100% of the forecast error for x can be explained by its own shock. Using the same technique, the two–step ahead forecast for y is

$$y_{t+2}^F = E_t[\delta_{11}y_{t+1} + \delta_{12}x_{t+1} + v_{t+2}^y]$$
$$= E_t[\delta_{11}(\delta_{11}y_t + \delta_{12}x_t + v_{t+1}^y) + \delta_{12}(\delta_{21}y_t + \delta_{22}x_t + v_{t+1}^x) + v_{t+2}^y]$$
$$= \delta_{11}(\delta_{11}y_t + \delta_{12}x_t) + \delta_{12}(\delta_{21}y_t + \delta_{22}x_t)$$

and that for x is

$$
\begin{aligned}
x_{t+2}^F &= E_t[\delta_{21}y_{t+1} + \delta_{22}x_{t+1} + v_{t+2}^x] \\
&= E_t[\delta_{21}(\delta_{11}y_t + \delta_{12}x_t + v_{t+1}^y) + \delta_{22}(\delta_{21}y_t + \delta_{22}x_t + v_{t+1}^x) + v_{t+2}^x] \\
&= \delta_{21}(\delta_{11}y_t + \delta_{12}x_t) + \delta_{22}(\delta_{21}y_t + \delta_{22}x_t)
\end{aligned}
$$

The corresponding two-step-ahead forecast errors and variances are (recall that we are working with the special case of independent errors)

$$
FE_2^y = y_{t+2} - E_t[y_{t+2}] = [\delta_{11}v_{t+1}^y + \delta_{12}v_{t+1}^x + v_{t+2}^y]
$$

$$
\mathrm{var}(FE_2^y) = \delta_{11}^2\sigma_y^2 + \delta_{12}^2\sigma_x^2 + \sigma_y^2
$$

$$
FE_2^x = x_{t+2} - E_t[x_{t+2}] = [\delta_{21}v_{t+1}^y + \delta_{22}v_{t+1}^x + v_{t+2}^x]
$$

$$
\mathrm{var}(FE_2^x) = \delta_{21}^2\sigma_y^2 + \delta_{22}^2\sigma_x^2 + \sigma_x^2
$$

We can decompose the total variance of the forecast error for y, $(\delta_{11}^2\sigma_y^2 + \delta_{12}^2\sigma_x^2 + \sigma_y^2)$, into that due to shocks to y, $(\delta_{11}^2\sigma_y^2 + \sigma_y^2)$, and that due to shocks to x, $(\delta_{12}^2\sigma_x^2)$. This decomposition is often expressed in proportional terms. The proportion of the two-step forecast error variance of y explained by its "own" shock is

$$
(\delta_{11}^2\sigma_y^2 + \sigma_y^2)/(\delta_{11}^2\sigma_y^2 + \delta_{12}^2\sigma_x^2 + \sigma_y^2)
$$

and the proportion of the two-step forecast error variance of y explained by the "other" shock is

$$
(\delta_{12}^2\sigma_x^2)/(\delta_{11}^2\sigma_y^2 + \delta_{12}^2\sigma_x^2 + \sigma_y^2)
$$

Similarly, the proportion of the two-step forecast error variance of x explained by its own shock is

$$
(\delta_{22}^2\sigma_x^2 + \sigma_x^2)/(\delta_{21}^2\sigma_y^2 + \delta_{22}^2\sigma_x^2 + \sigma_x^2)
$$

and the proportion of the forecast error of x explained by the other shock is

$$
(\delta_{21}^2\sigma_y^2)/(\delta_{21}^2\sigma_y^2 + \delta_{22}^2\sigma_x^2 + \sigma_x^2)
$$

For our numerical example with $\sigma_y = 1$, $\sigma_x = 2$, $\delta_{11} = 0.7$, $\delta_{12} = 0.2$, $\delta_{21} = 0.3$, and $\delta_{22} = 0.6$, we find that 90.303% of the two-step forecast error variance of y is due to y, and only 9.697% is due to x.

To sum up, suppose you were interested in the relationship between economic growth and inflation. A VAR model will tell you whether they are significantly related to each other; an impulse response analysis will show how growth and inflation react dynamically to shocks, and a variance decomposition analysis will be informative about the sources of volatility.

13.4.2c The General Case

The example above assumes that x and y are not contemporaneously related and that the shocks are uncorrelated. There is no identification problem, and the generation and interpretation of the impulse response functions and decomposition of the forecast error variance are straightforward. In general, this is unlikely to be the case. Contemporaneous interactions and correlated errors complicate the identification of the nature of shocks and hence the interpretation of the impulses and decomposition of the causes of the forecast error variance. This topic is discussed in greater detail in textbooks devoted to time-series analysis.[2] A description of how the identification problem can arise is given in Appendix 13A.

13.5 Exercises

13.5.1 PROBLEMS

13.1 Consider the following first-order VAR model of stationary variables:

$$y_t = \delta_{11} y_{t-1} + \delta_{12} x_{t-1} + v_t^y$$
$$x_t = \delta_{21} y_{t-1} + \delta_{22} x_{t-1} + v_t^x$$

Under the assumption that there is no contemporaneous dependence, determine the impulse responses, four periods after a standard deviation shock for
(a) y following a shock to y
(b) y following a shock to x
(c) x following a shock to y
(d) x following a shock to x

13.2 Consider the first-order VAR model in Exercise 13.1. Under the assumption that there is no contemporaneous dependence, determine
(a) the contribution of a shock to y on the variance of the three-step ahead forecast error for y
(b) the contribution of a shock to x on the variance of the three-step ahead forecast error for y
(c) the contribution of a shock to y on the variance of the three-step ahead forecast error for x
(d) the contribution of a shock to x on the variance of the three-step ahead forecast error for x

13.3 The VEC model is a special form of the VAR for I(1) variables that are cointegrated. Consider the following VEC model:

$$\Delta y_t = \alpha_{10} + \alpha_{11}(y_{t-1} - \beta_0 - \beta_1 x_{t-1}) + v_t^y$$

$$\Delta x_t = \alpha_{20} + \alpha_{21}(y_{t-1} - \beta_0 - \beta_1 x_{t-1}) + v_t^x$$

The VEC model may also be rewritten as a VAR, but the two equations will contain common parameters:

$$y_t = \alpha_{10} + (\alpha_{11} + 1)y_{t-1} - \alpha_{11}\beta_0 - \alpha_{11}\beta_1 x_{t-1} + v_t^y$$

$$x_t = \alpha_{20} + \alpha_{21} y_{t-1} - \alpha_{21}\beta_0 - (\alpha_{21}\beta_1 - 1)x_{t-1} + v_t^x$$

---

[2] One reference you might consider is Lütkepohl, H. (2005) *Introduction to Multiple Time Series Analysis*, Springer, Chapter 9.

(a) Suppose you were given the following results of an estimated VEC model:

$$\widehat{\Delta y_t} = 2 - 0.5(y_{t-1} - 1 - 0.7x_{t-1})$$

$$\widehat{\Delta x_t} = 3 + 0.3(y_{t-1} - 1 - 0.7x_{t-1})$$

Rewrite the model in the VAR form.

(b) Now suppose you were given the following results of an estimated VAR model, but you were also told that y and x are cointegrated.

$$\hat{y}_t = 0.7y_{t-1} + 0.3 + 0.24x_{t-1}$$

$$\hat{x}_t = 0.6y_{t-1} - 0.6 + 0.52x_{t-1}$$

Rewrite the model in the VEC form.

13.4 VAR and VEC models are popular forecasting models because they rely on the past history of observed outcomes to predict the expected future values.

(a) Consider the following estimated VAR model:

$$y_t = \hat{\delta}_{11}y_{t-1} + \hat{\delta}_{12}x_{t-1} + \hat{v}_{1t}$$

$$x_t = \hat{\delta}_{21}y_{t-1} + \hat{\delta}_{22}x_{t-1} + \hat{v}_{2t}$$

What are the forecasts for y_{t+1} and x_{t+1}?
What are the forecasts for y_{t+2} and x_{t+2}?

(b) Consider the following estimated VEC model:

$$\Delta y_t = \hat{\alpha}_{11}(y_{t-1} - \hat{\beta}_1 x_{t-1}) + \hat{v}_{1t}$$

$$\Delta x_t = \hat{\alpha}_{21}(y_{t-1} - \hat{\beta}_1 x_{t-1}) + \hat{v}_{2t}$$

What are the forecasts for y_{t+1} and x_{t+1}?
What are the forecasts for y_{t+2} and x_{t+2}?

13.5.2 COMPUTER EXERCISES

13.5 The data file *gdp.dat* contains quarterly data on the real GDP of Australia (*AUS*) and real GDP of the United States (*USA*) for the sample period 1970:1 to 2000:4.

(a) Are the series stationary or nonstationary?

(b) Test for cointegration allowing for an intercept term. You will find that the intercept is negative. Is this sensible? If not, repeat the test for cointegration excluding the constant term.

(c) Save the cointegrating residuals and estimate the VEC model.

13.6 The data file *fred.dat* contains the log of real personal disposable income (*Y*) and the log of real personal consumption expenditure (*C*) for the U.S. economy over the period 1960:1 to 2009:4.

(a) Are the series stationary, or nonstationary? In particular, test whether the series are trend stationary.

(b) Test for cointegration allowing for an intercept term. Are the series cointegrated?

(c) Estimate a VAR model for the set of I(0) variables $\{\Delta C_t, \Delta Y_t\}$. Pay particular attention to the order of lags.

13.7 The data file *vec.dat* contains 100 observations on two generated series of data, x and y. The variables are nonstationary and cointegrated without a constant term. Save the cointegrating residuals $(\hat{e})$ and estimate the VEC model. As a check, the results for the case normalized on y are

$$\widehat{\Delta y_t} = -0.576(\hat{e}_{t-1})$$
$$(t) \quad (-6.158)$$

$$\widehat{\Delta x_t} = 0.450(\hat{e}_{t-1})$$
$$(t) \quad (4.448)$$

(a) The residuals from the error correction model should not be autocorrelated. Are they?
(b) Note that one of the error correction terms is negative and the other is positive. Explain why this is necessary.

13.8 The data file *var.dat* contains 100 observations on two generated series of data, w and z. The variables are nonstationary but not cointegrated. Estimate a VAR model of changes in the variables. As a check, the results are (the intercept terms were not significant):

$$\widehat{\Delta w_t} = 0.743\Delta w_{t-1} + 0.214\Delta z_{t-1}$$
$$(t) \quad (11.403) \qquad (2.893)$$

$$\widehat{\Delta z_t} = -0.155\Delta w_{t-1} + 0.641\Delta z_{t-1}$$
$$(t) \quad (-2.293) \qquad (8.338)$$

(a) The residuals from the VAR model should not be autocorrelated. Is this the case?
(b) Determine the impulse responses for the first two periods. (You may assume the special condition that there is no contemporaneous dependence.)
(c) Determine the variance decompositions for the first two periods.

13.9 The quantity theory of money says that there is a direct relationship between the quantity of money in the economy and the aggregate price level. Put simply, if the quantity of money doubles, then the price level should also double. Figure 13.6 shows the percentage change in a measure of the quantity of money (M) and the

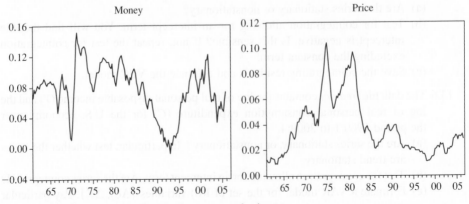

FIGURE **13.6** Percentage changes in money and price.

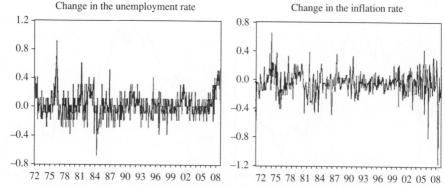

FIGURE **13.7** Changes in the unemployment and inflation rates.

percentage change in a measure of aggregate prices (P) for the United States between 1961:1 and 2005:4 (data file *qtm.dat*). A VEC model was estimated as follows:

$$\widehat{\Delta P_t} = -0.016(P_{t-1} - 1.004M_{t-1} + 0.039) + 0.514\Delta P_{t-1} - 0.005\Delta M_{t-1}$$
$$(t) \quad (2.127) \qquad (3.696) \qquad (1.714) \quad (7.999) \qquad (0.215)$$

$$\widehat{\Delta M_t} = 0.067(P_{t-1} - 1.004M_{t-1} + 0.039) - 0.336\Delta P_{t-1} - 0.340\Delta M_{t-1}$$
$$(t) \quad (3.017) \qquad (3.696) \qquad (1.714) \quad (1.796) \qquad (4.802)$$

(a) Identify the cointegrating relationship between P and M. Is the quantity theory of money supported?

(b) Identify the error-correction coefficients. Is the system stable?

(c) The above results were estimated using a system approach. Derive the co-integrating residuals and confirm that the series is indeed an I(0) variable.

(d) Estimate a VEC model using the cointegrating residuals. (Your results should be the same as above.)

13.10 Research into the Phillips curve is concerned with providing empirical evidence of a tradeoff between inflation and unemployment. Can an economy experience lower unemployment if it is prepared to accept higher inflation? Figure 13.7 plots the changes in a measure of the unemployment rate (DU) and the changes in a measure of inflation (DP) for the United States for the sample period 1970:07 to 2009:06 (data file *phillips.dat*). A VAR model was estimated as follows:

$$\Delta DU_t = 0.180DU_{t-1} - 0.046DP_{t-1}$$
$$(t) \quad (3.905) \qquad (0.909)$$

$$\Delta DP_t = -0.098DU_{t-1} + 0.373DP_{t-1}$$
$$(t) \quad (-2.522) \qquad (8.711)$$

(a) Is there evidence of an inverse relationship between the change in the unemployment rate (DU) and the change in the inflation rate (DP)?

(b) What is the response of DU at time $t + 1$ following a unit shock to DU at time t?

(c) What is the response of DP at time $t + 1$ following a unit shock to DU at time t?

(d) What is the response of DU at time $t + 2$?

(e) What is the response of DP at time $t + 2$?

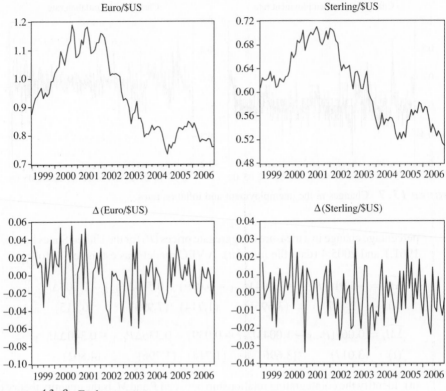

FIGURE **13.8** Exchange rates.

13.11 Figure 13.8 shows the time series for two exchange rates—the *EURO* per \$US and the *STERLING* per \$US (data file *sterling.dat*). Both the levels and the changes in the data are shown.
   (a) Which set of data would you consider using to estimate a VEC model, and which set to estimate a VAR? Why?
   (b) Apply the two-step approach suggested in this chapter to estimate a VEC model.
   (c) Estimate a VAR model paying attention to the order of the lag.

13.12 Financial analysts often debate the role of dividends in the determination of share prices. Figure 13.9 shows plots of the rate of change in dividends and price computed as

$$DV_t = 100 \ln(DN_t/DN_{t-1}), \qquad SP_t = 100 \ln(PN_t/PN_{t-1})$$

where *PN* is the Standard and Poor Composite Price Index; *DN* is the nominal dividends per share (source: Prescott, E. C. and Mehra, R. "The Equity Premium: A Puzzle," *Journal of Monetary Economics*, 15 March, 1985, pp. 145–161). The data are annual observations over the period 1889–1979. The data file is called *equity.dat*. Estimate a first-order VAR for *SP* and *DV* by applying least-squares to each equation:

$$SP_t = \beta_{10} + \beta_{11}SP_{t-1} + \beta_{12}DV_{t-1} + v_t^s$$
$$DV_t = \beta_{20} + \beta_{21}SP_{t-1} + \beta_{22}DV_{t-1} + v_t^d$$

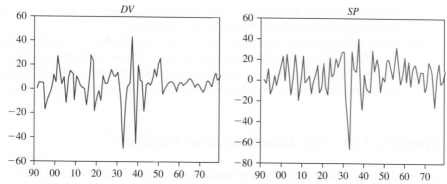

FIGURE **13.9** Change in dividends (*DV*) and share price (*SP*).

Estimate an ARDL for each equation:

$$SP_t = \alpha_{10} + \alpha_{11}SP_{t-1} + \alpha_{12}DV_{t-1} + \alpha_{13}DV_t + e_t^s$$

$$DV_t = \alpha_{20} + \alpha_{21}SP_{t-1} + \alpha_{22}DV_{t-1} + \alpha_{23}SP_t + e_t^d$$

Compare the two sets of results and note the importance of the contemporaneous endogenous variable (*SP*, *DV*) in each equation.

(a) Explain why least squares estimation of the VAR model with lagged variables on the right-hand side yields consistent estimates.

(b) Explain why least squares estimation of the model with lagged and contemporaneous variables on the right-hand side yields inconsistent estimates. (You might like to refer to the material in Chapter 11).

(c) What do you infer about the role of dividends in the determination of share prices?

13.13 The file *gfc.dat* contains data about economic activity in two major economies: the United States and the Euro Area (the group of countries in Europe where the Euro currency is the legal tender). Specifically, the data are the logs of their Gross Domestic Product (*GDP*), standardized so that the value of *GDP* is equal to 100 in 2000. The levels and the change in economic activity are shown in Figure 13.10 (a) and (b). The sample period is from 1995Q1 to 2009Q4 and includes the global financial crisis that began in September 2007.

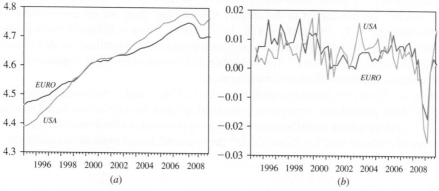

FIGURE **13.10** Logs of GDP (a) and change in logs of GDP (b).

(a) Based on a visual inspection of the data, what would you infer about the interactions between the GDPs in the two economies?
(b) Do the economies have a long-run relationship? Specify the econometric model and estimate the model. Plot the residuals and comment on their properties.
(c) Do the economies have a short-run relationship? Specify the econometric model and estimate the model. Plot the residuals and comment on their properties.

Appendix 13A The Identification Problem[3]

A bivariate dynamic system with contemporaneous interactions (also known as a structural model) is written as

$$y_t + \beta_1 x_t = \alpha_1 y_{t-1} + \alpha_2 x_{t-1} + e_t^y$$
$$x_t + \beta_2 y_t = \alpha_3 y_{t-1} + \alpha_4 x_{t-1} + e_t^x \qquad (13A.1)$$

which can be more conveniently expressed in matrix form as

$$\begin{bmatrix} 1 & \beta_1 \\ \beta_2 & 1 \end{bmatrix} \begin{bmatrix} y_t \\ x_t \end{bmatrix} = \begin{bmatrix} \alpha_1 & \alpha_2 \\ \alpha_3 & \alpha_4 \end{bmatrix} \begin{bmatrix} y_{t-1} \\ x_{t-1} \end{bmatrix} + \begin{bmatrix} e_t^y \\ e_t^x \end{bmatrix}$$

or rewritten in symbolic form as $BY_t = AY_{t-1} + E_t$, where

$$Y = \begin{bmatrix} y_t \\ x_t \end{bmatrix} \quad B = \begin{bmatrix} 1 & \beta_1 \\ \beta_2 & 1 \end{bmatrix} \quad A = \begin{bmatrix} \alpha_1 & \alpha_2 \\ \alpha_3 & \alpha_4 \end{bmatrix} \quad E_t = \begin{bmatrix} e_t^y \\ e_t^x \end{bmatrix}$$

A VAR representation (also known as reduced-form model) is written as

$$y_t = \delta_1 y_{t-1} + \delta_2 x_{t-1} + v_t^y$$
$$x_t = \delta_3 y_{t-1} + \delta_4 x_{t-1} + v_t^x \qquad (13A.2)$$

or in matrix form as: $Y_t = CY_{t-1} + V_t$, where

$$C = \begin{bmatrix} \delta_1 & \delta_2 \\ \delta_3 & \delta_4 \end{bmatrix} \quad V_t = \begin{bmatrix} v_t^y \\ v_t^x \end{bmatrix}$$

Clearly, there is a relationship between (13.A.1) and (13A.2): $C = B^{-1}A$ and $V_t = B^{-1}E_t$. The special case considered in the chapter assumes that there are no contemporaneous interactions ($\beta_1 = \beta_2 = 0$), making B an identity matrix. There is no identification problem in this case because the VAR residuals can be unambiguously "identified" as shocks to y or as shocks to x: $v^y = e^y, v^x = e^x$. The generation and interpretation of the impulse responses and variance decompositions are unambiguous.

In general, however, B is not an identity matrix, making v^y and v^x weighted averages of e^y and e^x. In this general case, impulse responses and variance decompositions based on v^y and v^x are not meaningful or useful because we cannot be certain about the source of the shocks. A number of methods exist for "identifying" the structural model from its reduced form.

---

[3] This appendix requires a basic understanding of matrix notation.

Chapter *14*

Time–Varying Volatility and ARCH Models

Learning Objectives

Based on the material in this chapter, you should be able to do the following:

1. Explain the difference between a constant and a time-varying variance of the error term.
2. Explain the term "conditionally normal."
3. Perform a test for ARCH effects.
4. Estimate an ARCH model.
5. Forecast volatility.
6. Explain the difference between ARCH and GARCH specifications.
7. Explain the distinctive features of a T-GARCH model and a GARCH-in-mean model.

Keywords

ARCH
ARCH-in-mean
conditional and unconditional forecasts
conditionally normal

GARCH
GARCH-in-mean
T-ARCH and T-GARCH
time-varying variance

In Chapter 12, our focus was on time-varying mean processes and macroeconomic time series. We were concerned with stationary and nonstationary variables, and, in particular, macroeconomic variables like GDP, inflation, and interest rates. The nonstationary nature of the variables implied that they had **means that change over time**. In this chapter we are concerned with stationary series, but with conditional variances that change over time. The model we focus on is called the autoregressive conditional heteroskedastic (ARCH) model.

Nobel Prize winner Robert Engle's original work on ARCH was concerned with the volatility of inflation. However, it was applications of the ARCH model to financial time series that established and consolidated the significance of his contribution. For this reason, the examples used in this chapter will be based on financial time series. As we will see, financial time series have characteristics that are well represented by models with dynamic variances. The particular aims of this chapter are to discuss the modeling of dynamic variances using the ARCH class of models of volatility, the estimation of these models, and their use in forecasting.

14.1 The ARCH Model

ARCH stands for **auto-regressive conditional heteroskedasticity**. We have covered the concepts of autoregressive and heteroskedastic errors in Chapters 9 and 8, respectively, so let us begin with a discussion of the concepts of conditional and unconditional means and variances of the error term.

Consider a model with an AR(1) error term

$$y_t = \phi + e_t \tag{14.1a}$$

$$e_t = \rho e_{t-1} + v_t, \quad |\rho| < 1 \tag{14.1b}$$

$$v_t \sim N(0, \sigma_v^2) \tag{14.1c}$$

For convenience of exposition, first perform some successive substitution to obtain e_t as the sum of an infinite series of the error term v_t. To do this, note that if $e_t = \rho e_{t-1} + v_t$, then $e_{t-1} = \rho e_{t-2} + v_{t-1}$ and $e_{t-2} = \rho e_{t-3} + v_{t-2}$, and so on. Hence $e_t = v_t + \rho v_{t-1} + \rho^2 v_{t-2} + \cdots + \rho^t e_0$ where the final term $\rho^t e_0$ is negligible.

The **unconditional mean** of the error is

$$E[e_t] = E[v_t + \rho v_{t-1} + \rho^2 v_{t-2} + \cdots] = 0$$

because $E[v_{t-j}] = 0$ for all j, whereas the **conditional mean** for the error is

$$E[e_t|I_{t-1}] = E[\rho e_{t-1}|I_{t-1}] + E[v_t] = \rho e_{t-1}$$

because the information set at time $t-1$, I_{t-1}, includes knowing ρe_{t-1}. Put simply, "unconditional" describes the situation when you have no information, whereas conditional describes the situation when you have information, up to a certain point in time.

The **unconditional variance** of the error is

$$
\begin{aligned}
E[e_t - 0]^2 &= E[v_t + \rho v_{t-1} + \rho^2 v_{t-2} + \cdots]^2 \\
&= E[v_t^2 + \rho^2 v_{t-1}^2 + \rho^4 v_{t-2}^2 + \cdots] \\
&= \sigma_v^2[1 + \rho^2 + \rho^4 + \cdots] = \frac{\sigma_v^2}{1 - \rho^2}
\end{aligned}
$$

because $E[v_{t-j}v_{t-i}] = \sigma_v^2$ when $i = j$; $E[v_{t-j}v_{t-i}] = 0$ when $i \neq j$ and the sum of a geometric series $[1 + \rho^2 + \rho^4 + \cdots]$ is $1/(1 - \rho^2)$. The **conditional variance** for the error is

$$E[(e_t - \rho e_{t-1})^2|I_{t-1}] = E[v_t^2|I_{t-1}] = \sigma_v^2$$

Note, as an aside, that since $[1/(1 - \rho^2)] > 1$, it follows that the unconditional variance $[\sigma_v^2/(1 - \rho^2)]$ is always greater than the conditional variance $[\sigma_v^2]$. This result is a general one; conditioning improves precision.

Now notice, for this model, that the conditional mean of the error varies over time, while the conditional variance does not. Suppose that instead of a conditional mean that changes over time we have a conditional variance that changes over time. To introduce this modification, consider a variant of the above model

$$y_t = \phi + e_t \tag{14.2a}$$

$$e_t | I_{t-1} \sim N(0, h_t) \tag{14.2b}$$

$$h_t = \alpha_0 + \alpha_1 e_{t-1}^2, \quad \alpha_0 > 0, \quad 0 \le \alpha_1 < 1 \tag{14.2c}$$

Equations (14.2b and 14.2c) describe the autoregressive conditional heteroskedastic (ARCH) class of models. The second equation (14.2b) says that the error term is **conditionally normal** $e_t | I_{t-1} \sim N(0, h_t)$ where I_{t-1} represents the information available at time $t-1$ with mean 0 and time-varying variance, denoted as h_t, following popular terminology. The third equation (14.2c) models h_t as a function of a constant term and the lagged error squared e_{t-1}^2.

The name — ARCH — conveys the fact that we are working with time-varying variances (heteroskedasticity) that depend on (are conditional on) lagged effects (autocorrelation). This particular example is an ARCH(1) model since the time-varying variance h_t is a function of a constant term (α_0) plus a term lagged once, the square of the error in the previous period ($\alpha_1 e_{t-1}^2$). The coefficients, α_0 and α_1, have to be positive to ensure a positive variance. The coefficient α_1 must be less than 1, or h_t will continue to increase over time, eventually exploding. Conditional normality means that the normal distribution is a function of known information at time $t-1$ i.e., when $t = 2$, $e_2 | I_1 \sim N(0, \alpha_0 + \alpha_1 e_1^2)$ and when $t = 3$, $e_3 | I_2 \sim N(0, \alpha_0 + \alpha_1 e_2^2)$, and so on. In this particular case, conditioning on I_{t-1} is equivalent to conditioning on the square of the error in the previous period e_{t-1}^2.

Note that while the conditional distribution of the error e_t is assumed to be normal, the unconditional distribution of the error e_t will not be normal. This is not an inconsequential consideration given that a lot of real-world data appear to be drawn from non-normal distributions.

We have noted that, conditional on e_{t-1}^2, the mean and variance of the error term e_t are zero and h_t, respectively. To find the mean and variance of the unconditional distribution of e_t, we note that, conditional on e_{t-1}^2, the standardized errors are standard normal. That is,

$$\left(\frac{e_t}{\sqrt{h_t}} \bigg| I_{t-1} \right) = z \sim N(0, 1)$$

Because this distribution does not depend on e_{t-1}^2, it follows that the unconditional distribution of $z = \left(e_t / \sqrt{h_t} \right)$ is also $N(0,1)$, and that z and e_{t-1}^2 are independent. Thus, we can write

$$E(e_t) = E(z_t) E \left(\sqrt{\alpha_0 + \alpha_1 e_{t-1}^2} \right)$$

and

$$E(e_t^2) = E(z_t^2) E(\alpha_0 + \alpha_1 e_{t-1}^2) = \alpha_0 + \alpha_1 E(e_{t-1}^2)$$

From the first of these equations we get $E(e_t) = 0$, because $E(z_t) = 0$. From the second of the equations we get $\text{var}(e_t^2) = E(e_t^2) = \alpha_0/(1 - \alpha_1)$, because $E(z_t^2) = 1$ and $E(e_t^2) = E(e_{t-1}^2)$.

The ARCH model has become a very important econometric model because it is able to capture stylized features of real-world volatility. Furthermore, in the context of the ARCH(1) model, knowing the squared error in the previous period e_{t-1}^2 improves our knowledge about the likely magnitude of the variance in period t. This is useful for situations when it is important to understand risk, as measured by the volatility of the variable.

14.2 Time-Varying Volatility

The ARCH model has become a popular one because its variance specification can capture commonly observed features of the time series of financial variables; in particular, it is useful for modeling **volatility** and especially changes in volatility over time. To appreciate what we mean by volatility and time-varying volatility, and how it relates to the ARCH model, let us look at some stylized facts about the behavior of financial variables—for example, the returns to stock price indices (also known as share price indices).

Figure 14.1 shows the time series of the monthly returns to a number of stock prices; namely, the US Nasdaq, the Australian All Ordinaries, the Japanese Nikkei, and the UK FTSE over the period 1988:01 to 2010:07 (data file *returns.dat*). The values of these series change rapidly from period to period in an apparently unpredictable manner; we say the series are volatile. Furthermore, there are periods when large changes are followed by further large changes and periods when small changes are followed by further small changes. In this case the series are said to display time-varying volatility as well as "clustering" of changes.

Figure 14.2 shows the histograms of the returns. All returns display non-normal properties. We can see this more clearly if we draw normal distributions (using the respective

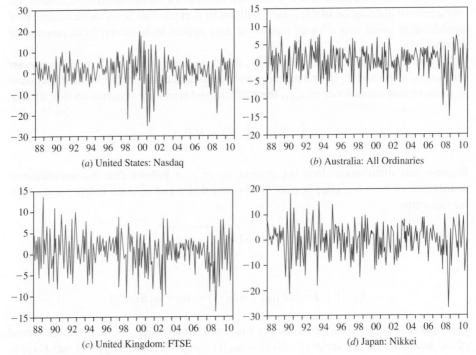

FIGURE **14.1** Time series of returns to stock indices.

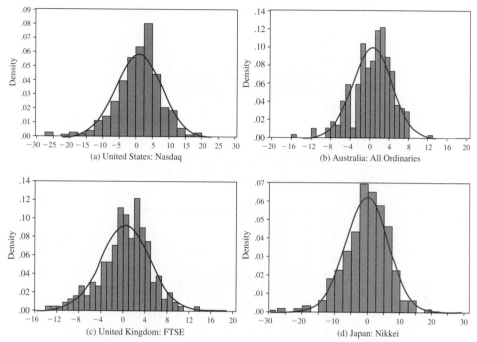

FIGURE **14.2** Histograms of returns to various stock indices.

sample means and sample variances) on top of these histograms. Note that there are more observations around the mean and in the tails. Distributions with these properties— more peaked around the mean and relatively fat tails—are said to be **leptokurtic**.

Note that the assumption that the conditional distribution for $(y_t | I_{t-1})$ is normal, an assumption that we made in (14.2b), does not necessarily imply that the unconditional distribution for y_t is normal. When we collect empirical observations on y_t into a histogram, we are constructing an estimate of the unconditional distribution for y_t. What we have observed is that the unconditional distribution for y_t is leptokurtic.

To illustrate how the ARCH model can be used to capture changing volatility and the leptokurtic nature of the distribution for y_t, we generate some simulated data for two models. In both cases we set $\beta_0 = 0$ so that $y_t = e_t$. The top panel in Figure 14.3 illustrates the case when $\alpha_0 = 1$, $\alpha_1 = 0$. These values imply $\text{var}(y_t | I_{t-1}) = h_t = 1$. This variance is constant, and not time-varying, because $\alpha_1 = 0$. The bottom panel in Figure 14.3 illustrates the case when $\alpha_0 = 1$, $\alpha_1 = 0.8$, the case of a time-varying variance given by $\text{var}(y_t | I_{t-1}) = h_t = \alpha_0 + \alpha_1 e_{t-1}^2 = 1 + 0.8 e_{t-1}^2$. Note that relative to the series in the top panel, volatility in the bottom panel is not constant; rather, it changes over time and it clusters—there are periods of small changes (for example, around observation 100) and periods of big changes (around observation 175).

In Figure 14.4 we present histograms of y_t for the two cases. The top panel is the histogram for the constant variance case where $(y_t | I_{t-1})$ and y_t have the same distribution, namely the noise process $y_t \sim N(0, 1)$ because $h_t = 1$. The bottom panel is the histogram for the time-varying variance case. We know that the conditional distribution for $(y_t | I_{t-1})$ is $N(0, h_t)$. But what about the unconditional distribution for y_t? Again, we can check for normality by superimposing a normal distribution on top of the histogram. In this case, to allow for a meaningful comparison with the histogram in the top panel, we plot the standardized observations of y_t. That is for each observation we subtract the sample mean

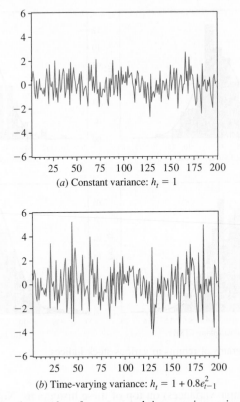

FIGURE 14.3 Simulated examples of constant and time-varying variances.

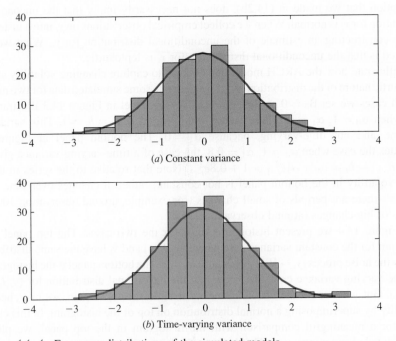

FIGURE 14.4 Frequency distributions of the simulated models.

and divide by the sample standard deviation. This transformation ensures that the distribution will have a zero mean and variance one, but it preserves the shape of the distribution. Comparing the two panels, we note that the second distribution has higher frequencies around the mean (zero) and higher frequencies in the tails (outside ± 3). This feature of time series with ARCH errors—the unconditional distribution of y_t is non-normal—is consistent with what we observed in the stock return series.

Thus, the ARCH model is intuitively appealing because it seems sensible to explain volatility as a function of the errors e_t. These errors are often called "shocks" or "news" by financial analysts. They represent the unexpected! According to the ARCH model, the larger the shock, the greater the volatility in the series. In addition, this model captures volatility clustering, as big changes in e_t are fed into further big changes in h_t via the lagged effect e_{t-1}. The simulations show how well the ARCH model mimics the behavior of financial time series shown in Figure 14.1, including their non-normal distributions.

14.3 Testing, Estimating, and Forecasting

14.3.1 TESTING FOR ARCH EFFECTS

A Lagrange multiplier (*LM*) test is often used to test for the presence of ARCH effects. To perform this test, first estimate the **mean equation**, which can be a regression of the variable on a constant (like 14.1) or may include other variables. Then save the estimated residuals $\hat{e}_t$ and obtain their squares $\hat{e}_t^2$. To test for first-order ARCH, regress $\hat{e}_t^2$ on the squared residuals lagged $\hat{e}_{t-1}^2$,

$$\hat{e}_t^2 = \gamma_0 + \gamma_1 \hat{e}_{t-1}^2 + v_t \tag{14.3}$$

where v_t is a random term. The null and alternative hypotheses are

$$H_0 : \gamma_1 = 0 \qquad\qquad H_1 : \gamma_1 \neq 0$$

If there are no ARCH effects, then $\gamma_1 = 0$ and the fit of (14.3) will be poor, and the equation R^2 will be low. If there are ARCH effects, we expect the magnitude of $\hat{e}_t^2$ to depend on its lagged values, and the R^2 will be relatively high. The *LM* test statistic is $(T-q)R^2$ where T is the sample size, q is the number of $\hat{e}_{t-j}^2$ terms on the right-hand side of (14.3), and R^2 is the coefficient of determination. If the null hypothesis is true, then the test statistic $(T-q)R^2$ is distributed (in large samples) as $\chi^2_{(q)}$, where q is the order of lag, and $T-q$ is the number of complete observations; in this case, $q = 1$. If $(T-q)R^2 \geq \chi^2_{(1-\alpha,q)}$, then we reject the null hypothesis that $\gamma_1 = 0$ and conclude that ARCH effects are present.

To illustrate the test, consider the returns from buying shares in the hypothetical company BrightenYourDay (BYD) Lighting. The time series and histogram of the returns are shown in Figure 14.5 (data file *byd.dat*). The time series shows evidence of time-varying volatility and clustering, and the unconditional distribution is non-normal.

To perform the test for ARCH effects, first estimate a mean equation that in this example is $r_t = \beta_0 + e_t$, where r_t is the monthly return on shares of BYD. Second, retrieve the estimated residuals. Third, estimate (14.3). The results for the ARCH test are

$$\hat{e}_t^2 = 0.908 + 0.353\hat{e}_{t-1}^2 \quad R^2 = 0.124$$
$$(t) \qquad\qquad (8.409)$$

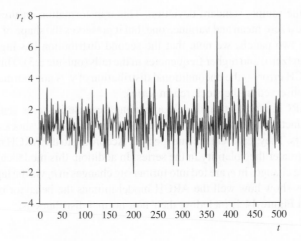

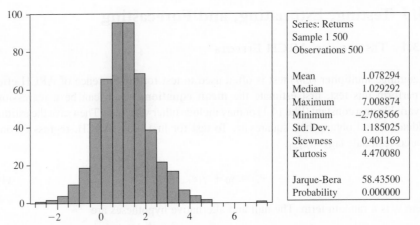

FIGURE **14.5** Time series and histogram of returns for BYD Lighting.

The t-statistic suggests a significant first-order coefficient. The sample size is 500, giving an LM test value of $(T - q)R^2 = 61.876$. Comparing the computed test value to the 5% critical value of a $\chi^2_{(1)}$ distribution $(\chi^2_{(0.95,1)} = 3.841)$ leads to the rejection of the null hypothesis. In other words, the residuals show the presence of ARCH(1) effects.

14.3.2 ESTIMATING ARCH MODELS

ARCH models are estimated by the maximum likelihood method. Estimation details are beyond the scope of this book, but the maximum likelihood method (see Appendix C.8) is programmed in most econometric software.

Equation (14.4) shows the results from estimating an ARCH(1) model applied to the monthly returns from buying shares in Brighten Your Day Lighting. The estimated mean of the series is described in (14.4a), while the estimated variance is given in (14.4b).

$$\hat{r}_t = \hat{\beta}_0 = 1.063 \tag{14.4a}$$

$$\hat{h}_t = \hat{\alpha}_0 + \hat{\alpha}_1 \hat{e}^2_{t-1} = 0.642 + 0.569 \hat{e}^2_{t-1}$$
$$(t) \qquad\qquad\qquad (5.536) \tag{14.4b}$$

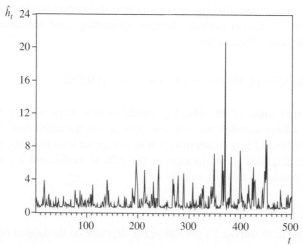

FIGURE **14.6** Plot of conditional variance.

The t-statistic of the first-order coefficient (5.536) suggests a significant ARCH(1) coefficient. Recall that one of the requirements of the ARCH model is that $\alpha_0 > 0$ and $\alpha_1 > 0$, so that the implied variances are positive. Note that the estimated coefficients $\hat{\alpha}_0$ and $\hat{\alpha}_1$ satisfy this condition.

14.3.3 FORECASTING VOLATILITY

Once we have estimated the model, we can use it to forecast next period's return r_{t+1} and the conditional volatility h_{t+1}. When one invests in shares (or stocks), it is important to choose them not just on the basis of their mean returns, but also on the basis of their risk. Volatility gives us a measure of their risk.

For our case study of investing in BrightenYourDayLighting, the forecast return and volatility are

$$\hat{r}_{t+1} = \hat{\beta}_0 = 1.063 \tag{14.5a}$$

$$\hat{h}_{t+1} = \hat{\alpha}_0 + \hat{\alpha}_1(r_t - \hat{\beta}_0)^2 = 0.642 + 0.569(r_t - 1.063)^2 \tag{14.5b}$$

Equation (14.5a) gives the estimated return that—because it does not change over time—is both the conditional and unconditional mean return. The estimated error in period t, given by $\hat{e}_t = r_t - \hat{r}_t$, can then be used to obtain the estimated conditional variance (14.5b). The time series of the conditional variance does change over time and is shown in Figure 14.6. Note how the conditional variance around observation 370 coincides with the period of large changes in returns shown in Figure 14.5.

14.4 Extensions

The ARCH(1) model can be extended in a number of ways. One obvious extension is to allow for more lags. In general, an ARCH(q) model that includes lags $e_{t-1}^2, \ldots, e_{t-q}^2$ has a conditional variance function that is given by

$$h_t = \alpha_0 + \alpha_1 e_{t-1}^2 + \alpha_2 e_{t-2}^2 \cdots + \alpha_q e_{t-q}^2 \tag{14.6}$$

In this case the variance or volatility in a given period depends on the magnitudes of the squared errors in the past q periods. Testing, estimating, and forecasting, are natural extensions of the case with one lag.

14.4.1   THE GARCH MODEL—GENERALIZED ARCH

One of the shortcomings of an ARCH(q) model is that there are $q+1$ parameters to estimate. If q is a large number, we may lose accuracy in the estimation. The generalized ARCH model, or GARCH, is an alternative way to capture long lagged effects with fewer parameters. It is a special generalization of the ARCH model and it can be derived as follows. First, consider (14.6) but write it as

$$h_t = \alpha_0 + \alpha_1 e_{t-1}^2 + \beta_1 \alpha_1 e_{t-2}^2 + \beta_1^2 \alpha_1 e_{t-3}^2 + \cdots$$

In other words, we have imposed a geometric lag structure on the lagged coefficients of the form $\alpha_s = \alpha_1 \beta_1^{s-1}$. Next, add and subtract $\beta_1 \alpha_0$ and rearrange terms as follows:

$$h_t = (\alpha_0 - \beta_1 \alpha_0) + \alpha_1 e_{t-1}^2 + \beta_1 (\alpha_0 + \alpha_1 e_{t-2}^2 + \beta_1 \alpha_1 e_{t-3}^2 + \cdots)$$

Then, since $h_{t-1} = \alpha_0 + \alpha_1 e_{t-2}^2 + \beta_1 \alpha_1 e_{t-3}^2 + \beta_1^2 \alpha_1 e_{t-4}^2 + \cdots$, we may simplify to

$$h_t = \delta + \alpha_1 e_{t-1}^2 + \beta_1 h_{t-1} \tag{14.7}$$

where $\delta = (\alpha_0 - \beta_1 \alpha_0)$. This generalized ARCH model is denoted as GARCH(1,1). It can be viewed as a special case of the more general GARCH (p,q) model, where p is the number of lagged h terms and q is the number of lagged e^2 terms. We also note that we need $\alpha_1 + \beta_1 < 1$ for stationarity; if $\alpha_1 + \beta_1 \geq 1$ we have a so-called "integrated GARCH" process, or IGARCH.

The GARCH(1,1) model is a very popular specification because it fits many data series well. It tells us that the volatility changes with lagged shocks (e_{t-1}^2) but there is also momentum in the system working via h_{t-1}. One reason why this model is so popular is that it can capture long lags in the shocks with only a few parameters. A GARCH(1,1) model with three parameters $(\delta, \alpha_1, \beta_1)$ can capture similar effects to an ARCH(q) model requiring the estimation of $(q+1)$ parameters, where q is large, say $q \geq 6$.

To illustrate the GARCH(1,1) specification, consider again the returns to our shares in BrightenYourDayLighting, which we reestimate (by maximum likelihood) under the new model. The results are

$$\hat{r}_t = 1.049$$

$$\hat{h}_t = 0.401 + 0.492\,\hat{e}_{t-1}^2 + 0.238\,\hat{h}_{t-1}$$

$$(t) \qquad\qquad (4.834) \qquad (2.136)$$

The significance of the coefficient in front of $\hat{h}_{t-1}$ suggests that the GARCH(1,1) model is better than the ARCH(1) results shown in (14.4). Plots of the mean equation and the time-varying variance are shown in Figures 14.7(a) and 14.7(b) respectively.

14.4.2   ALLOWING FOR AN ASYMMETRIC EFFECT

A standard ARCH model treats bad "news" (negative $e_{t-1} < 0$) and good "news" (positive $e_{t-1} > 0$) symmetrically: that is, the effect on the volatility h_t is the same $(\alpha_1 e_{t-1}^2)$. However,

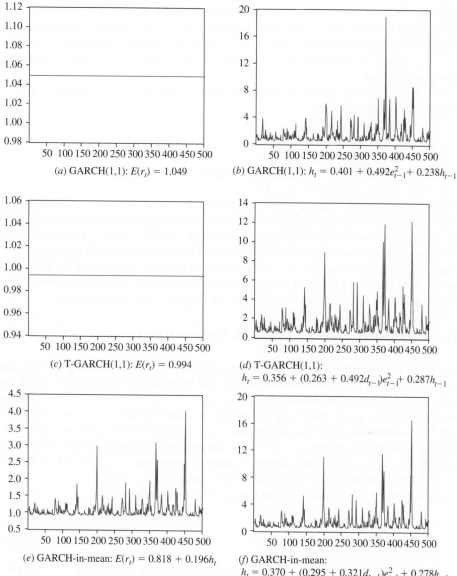

FIGURE **14.7** Estimated means and variances of ARCH models.

the effects of good and bad news may have asymmetric effects on volatility. In general, when negative news hits a financial market, asset prices tend to enter a turbulent phase and volatility increases, but with positive news volatility tends to be small and the market enters a period of tranquility.

The threshold ARCH model, or T-ARCH, is one example where positive and negative news are treated asymmetrically. In the T-GARCH version of the model, the specification of the conditional variance is

$$h_t = \delta + \alpha_1 e_{t-1}^2 + \gamma d_{t-1} e_{t-1}^2 + \beta_1 h_{t-1}$$

$$d_t = \begin{cases} 1 & e_t < 0 & \text{(bad news)} \\ 0 & e_t \geq 0 & \text{(good news)} \end{cases} \qquad (14.8)$$

where γ is known as the asymmetry or leverage term. When $\gamma = 0$, the model collapses to the standard GARCH form. Otherwise, when the shock is positive (i.e., good news) the effect on volatility is α_1, but when the news is negative (i.e., bad news) the effect on volatility is $\alpha_1 + \gamma$. Hence, if γ is significant and positive, negative shocks have a larger effect on h_t than positive shocks.

The returns to our shares in BrightenYourDayLighting were reestimated with a T-GARCH(1,1) specification:

$$\hat{r}_t = 0.994$$

$$\hat{h}_t = 0.356 + 0.263\hat{e}_{t-1}^2 + 0.492d_{t-1}\hat{e}_{t-1}^2 + 0.287\hat{h}_{t-1}$$

$$(t) \qquad\qquad (3.267) \qquad (2.405) \qquad\qquad (2.488)$$

These results show that when the market observes good news (positive e_t), the contribution of e_t^2 to volatility h_{t+1} is by a factor 0.263, whereas when the market observes bad news (negative e_t), the contribution of e_t^2 to volatility h_{t+1} is by a factor $(0.263 + 0.492)$. Overall, negative shocks create greater volatility in financial markets. Figures 14.7(b) and 14.7(d) compare the conditional variance of the symmetric GARCH model with that generated by the T-GARCH model. Note how the T-GARCH model highlighted the period around observation 200 as another period of turbulence (see Figure 14.5 for the time series of the returns).

14.4.3 GARCH-IN-MEAN AND TIME-VARYING RISK PREMIUM

Another popular extension of the GARCH model is the "GARCH-in-mean" model. The positive relationship between risk (often measured by volatility) and return is one of the basic tenets of financial economics. As risk increases, so does the mean return. Intuitively, the return to risky assets tends to be higher than the return to safe assets (low variation in returns) to compensate an investor for taking on the risk of buying the volatile share. However, while we have estimated the mean equation to model returns, and have estimated a GARCH model to capture time-varying volatility, we have not used the risk to explain returns. This is the aim of the GARCH-in-mean models.

The equations of a GARCH-in-mean model are shown below:

$$y_t = \beta_0 + \theta h_t + e_t \tag{14.9a}$$

$$e_t | I_{t-1} \sim N(0, h_t) \tag{14.9b}$$

$$h_t = \delta + \alpha_1 e_{t-1}^2 + \beta_1 h_{t-1}, \quad \delta > 0, \ 0 \le \alpha_1 < 1, \ 0 \le \beta_1 < 1 \tag{14.9c}$$

The first equation is the mean equation; it now shows the effect of the conditional variance on the dependent variable. In particular, note that the model postulates that the conditional variance h_t affects y_t by a factor θ. The other two equations are as before.

The returns to shares in BrightenYourDayLighting were reestimated as a GARCH-in-mean model:

$$\hat{r}_t = 0.818 + 0.196h_t$$

$$(t) \qquad\qquad (2.915)$$

$$\hat{h}_t = 0.370 + 0.295\hat{e}_{t-1}^2 + 0.321d_{t-1}\hat{e}_{t-1}^2 + 0.278\hat{h}_{t-1}$$

$$(t) \qquad\qquad (3.426) \qquad (1.979) \qquad\qquad (2.678)$$

The results show that as volatility increases, the returns correspondingly increase by a factor of 0.196. In other words, this result supports the usual view in financial markets—high risk, high return. The GARCH-in-mean model is shown in Figures 14.7(e) and 14.7(f). Note that the expected mean return is no longer a constant value, but rather has high values (e.g., around observation 200) that coincide with higher conditional variances.

One last point before we leave this section. The first equation of the GARCH-in-mean model is sometimes written as a function of the time-varying standard deviation $\sqrt{h_t}$—that is, $y_t = \beta_0 + \theta\sqrt{h_t} + e_t$. This is because both measures—variance and standard deviation—are used by financial analysts to measure risk. There are no hard-and-fast rules about which measure to use. Exercise 14.8 illustrates the case when we use $\sqrt{h_t}$. A standard t test of significance is often used to decide which is the more suitable measure.

14.5 Exercises

14.5.1 PROBLEMS

14.1 The ARCH model is sometimes presented in the following multiplicative form:

$$y_t = \beta_0 + e_t$$

$$e_t = z_t\sqrt{h_t}, \quad z_t \sim N(0,1)$$

$$h_t = \alpha_0 + \alpha_1 e_{t-1}^2, \quad \alpha_0 > 0, \quad 0 \le \alpha_1 < 1.$$

This form describes the distribution of the standardized residuals $e_t/\sqrt{h_t}$ as standard normal z_t. However, the properties of e_t are not altered.
(a) Show that the conditional mean $E(e_t|I_{t-1}) = 0$.
(b) Show that the conditional variance $E(e_t^2|I_{t-1}) = h_t$.
(c) Show that $e_t|I_{t-1} \sim N(0, h_t)$.

14.2 The equations of an ARCH-in-mean model are shown below:

$$y_t = \beta_0 + \theta h_t + e_t$$

$$e_t|I_{t-1} \sim N(0, h_t)$$

$$h_t = \delta + \alpha_1 e_{t-1}^2 \quad \delta > 0, 0 \le \alpha_1 < 1$$

Let y_t represent the return from a financial asset and let e_t represent "news" in the financial market. Now use the third equation to substitute out h_t in the first equation, to express the return as

$$y_t = \beta_0 + \theta(\delta + \alpha_1 e_{t-1}^2) + e_t$$

(a) If θ is zero, what is $E_t(y_{t+1})$, the conditional mean of y_{t+1}? In other words, what do you expect next period's return to be, given information today?
(b) If θ is not zero, what is $E_t(y_{t+1})$? What extra information have you used here to forecast the return?

14.3 Consider the following T-ARCH model:

$$h_t = \delta + \alpha_1 e_{t-1}^2 + \gamma d_{t-1} e_{t-1}^2$$

$$d_t = \begin{cases} 1 & e_t < 0 \quad \text{(bad news)} \\ 0 & e_t \ge 0 \quad \text{(good news)} \end{cases}$$

(a) If γ is zero, what are the values of h_t when $e_{t-1} = -1$, when $e_{t-1} = 0$, and when $e_{t-1} = 1$?

(b) If γ is not zero, what are the values of h_t when $e_{t-1} = -1$, when $e_{t-1} = 0$, and when $e_{t-1} = 1$? What is the key difference between the case $\gamma = 0$ and $\gamma \neq 0$?

14.4 The GARCH(1,1) model shown below can also be re-expressed as an ARCH (q) model, where q is a large number (in fact, infinity). Derive the ARCH form of a GARCH model using the method of recursive substitution.

$$h_t = \delta + \alpha_1 e_{t-1}^2 + \beta_1 h_{t-1}$$

14.5.2 COMPUTER EXERCISES

14.5 The data file *share.dat* contains time-series data on the Straits Times share price index of Singapore.

(a) Compute the time series of returns using the formula $r_t = 100 \ln(y_t/y_{t-1})$, where y_t is the share price index. Generate the correlogram of returns up to at least order 12, since the frequency of the data is monthly. Is there evidence of autocorrelation? If so, it indicates the presence of significant lagged mean effects.

(b) Square the returns and generate the correlogram of squared returns. Is there evidence of significant lagged effects? If so, it indicates the presence of significant lagged variance effects.

14.6 The data file *euro.dat* contains 204 monthly observations on the returns to the Euro share price index for the period 1988:01 to 2004:12. A plot of the returns data is shown in Figure 14.8(a), together with its histogram in Figure 14.8(b).

(a) What do you notice about the volatility of returns? Identify the periods of big changes and the periods of small changes.

(b) Is the distribution of returns normal? Is this the unconditional, or conditional, distribution?

(c) Perform a Lagrange multiplier test for the presence of first-order ARCH and check that you obtain the following results:

$$\hat{e}_t^2 = 20.509 + 0.237\hat{e}_{t-1}^2, \quad (T-1)R^2 = 11.431$$
$$(t) \qquad\qquad (3.463)$$

Is there evidence of ARCH effects?

(d) Estimate an ARCH(1) model and check that you obtain the following results:

$$\hat{r}_t = 0.879, \quad \hat{h}_t = 20.604 + 0.230\hat{e}_{t-1}^2$$
$$(t) \quad (2.383) \qquad (10.968) \ (2.198)$$

Interpret the results.

(e) A plot of the conditional variance is shown in Figure 14.8(c). Do the periods of high and low conditional variance coincide with the periods of big and small changes in returns?

14.7 Figure 14.9 (see page 532) shows the time series for monthly changes to the $US/$A exchange rate and its histogram for the period 1985:07 to 2010:06 (data file *exrate.dat*).

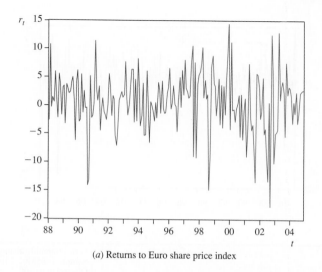

(a) Returns to Euro share price index

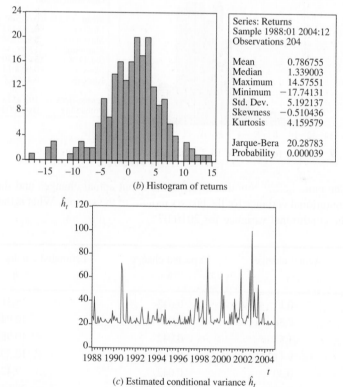

(b) Histogram of returns

(c) Estimated conditional variance $\hat{h}_t$

FIGURE **14.8**   Graphs for Exercise 14.6.

(a) Comment on the unconditional distribution of the series. Is it normal?
(b) Estimate a GARCH(1,1) model and check that you obtain the following results:

$$\hat{s}_t = 0.042, \quad \hat{h}_t = 0.615 + 0.149\hat{e}_{t-1}^2 + 0.800\hat{h}_{t-1}$$
$$(t) \quad (0.269) \qquad (1.511) \quad (1.735) \qquad (8.406)$$

where s denotes the change in the exchange rate. Interpret the results.

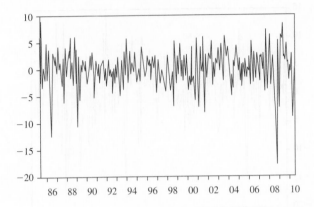

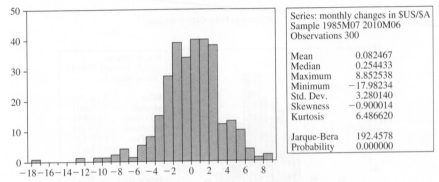

FIGURE **14.9**   Graphs for Exercise 14.7: Changes in $US/$A exchange rate.

(c) The table below contains information about actual changes and the estimated conditional variance for the last six months of the sample. What is the forecast of the conditional variance for 2010:07?

	Actual change s	Expected change $\hat{s}$	Estimated conditional variance $\hat{h}_t$
2010:01	−0.11	0.042	15.31
2010:02	2.88	0.042	12.94
2010:03	1.53	0.042	10.98
2010:04	−9.11	0.042	10.59
2010:05	0.39	0.042	9.42
2010:06	5.29	0.042	20.61
2010:07			

14.8   Figure 14.10 shows the weekly returns to the US S&P 500 for the sample period January 1990 to December 2004 (data file *sp.dat*).

(a) Estimate an ARCH(1) model and check that you obtain the following results:

$$\hat{r}_t = 0.197 \quad \hat{h}_t = 3.442 + 0.253\hat{e}_{t-1}^2$$

$$(t) \quad (2.899) \quad\quad (22.436) \ (5.850)$$

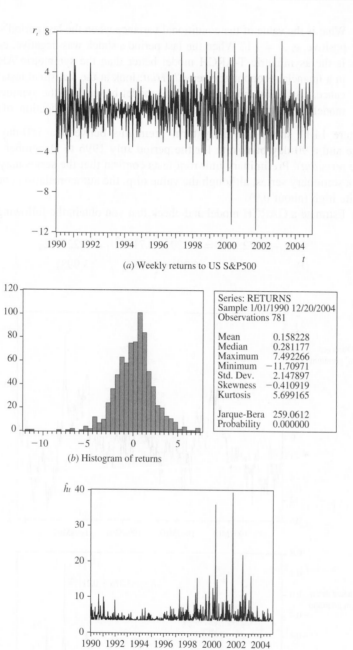

FIGURE **14.10** Graphs for Exercise 14.8.

What is the value of the conditional variance when the last period's shock was positive, $e_{t-1} = +1$? What about when the last period's shock was negative, $e_{t-1} = -1$?

(b) Estimate a T-ARCH model and check that you obtain the following results:

$$\hat{r}_t = 0.147, \quad \hat{h}_t = 3.437 + (0.123 + 0.268 d_{t-1})\hat{e}_{t-1}^2$$
$$(t) \quad (2.049) \quad\quad (22.963) \quad (2.330) \quad (2.944)$$

(c) What is the value of the conditional variance when the last period's shock was positive, $e_{t-1} = +1$? When the last period's shock was negative, $e_{t-1} = -1$?

(d) Is the asymmetric T-ARCH model better than the symmetric ARCH model in a financial econometric sense? (*Hint*: look at the statistical tests for significance.) Is the asymmetric T-ARCH model better than the symmetric ARCH model in a financial economic sense? (*Hint*: look at the implications of the results.)

14.9   Figure 14.11 shows the daily term premiums between a 180-day bank bill rate and a 90-day bank rate for the period July 1996 to December 1998 (data file *term.dat*). Preliminary unit root tests confirm that the series may be treated as a stationary series, although the value of ρ, the autocorrelation coefficient, is quite high (about 0.9).

(a) Estimate a GARCH model and check that you obtain the following results:

$$\hat{r}_t = -2.272, \quad \hat{h}_t = 1.729 + 0.719\hat{e}_{t-1}^2 + 0.224\,\hat{h}_{t-1}$$

$$(t) \qquad\qquad\qquad (6.271)\ (6.282) \qquad (3.993)$$

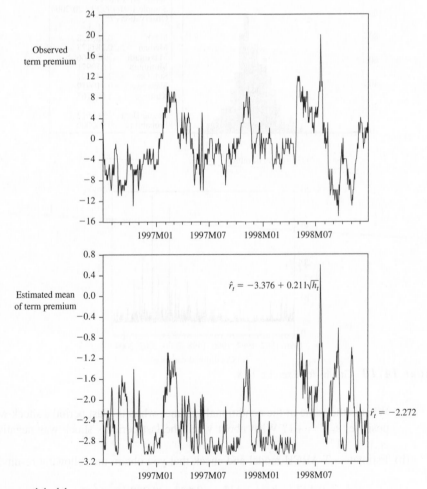

FIGURE **14.11**   Graphs for Exercise 14.9.

(b) Estimate a GARCH-in-mean model and check that you obtain the following results:

$$\hat{r}_t = -3.376 + 0.211\sqrt{h_t}, \quad \hat{h}_t = 1.631 + 0.730\hat{e}_{t-1}^2 + 0.231\,\hat{h}_{t-1}$$
$$(t) \qquad\qquad (2.807) \qquad\qquad (5.333)\ (6.327) \qquad (4.171)$$

What is the contribution of volatility to the term premium?

(c) Is the GARCH-in-mean model better than the GARCH model in a financial econometric sense? (*Hint*: look at the statistical tests for significance.) Is the GARCH-in-mean model better than the GARCH model in a financial economic sense? (*Hint*: look at the implications of the results, in particular the behavior of the term premium.) A plot of the expected term premium estimated for parts (a) and (b) is shown in Figure 14.11.

14.10 The data file *gold.dat* contains 200 daily observations on the returns to shares in a company specializing in gold bullion for the period December 13, 2005 to September 19, 2006.

(a) Plot the returns data. What do you notice about the volatility of returns? Identify the periods of big changes and the periods of small changes.

(b) Generate the histogram of returns. Is the distribution of returns normal? Is this the unconditional or conditional distribution?

(c) Perform a Lagrange multiplier test for the presence of first-order ARCH.

(d) Estimate a GARCH(1,1) model. Are the coefficients of the correct sign and magnitude?

(e) How would you use the estimated GARCH(1,1) model to improve your forecasts of returns?

14.11 The seminal paper about ARCH by Robert Engle was concerned with the variance of UK inflation. The data file *uk.dat* contains seasonally adjusted data on the UK consumer price index (*UKCPI*) for the sample period 1957:06 to 2006:06.

(a) Compute the monthly rate of inflation (*y*) for the sample period 1957:07 to 2006:06 using the formula

$$y_t = 100\left[\frac{UKCPI_t - UKCPI_{t-1}}{UKCPI_{t-1}}\right]$$

(b) Estimate a T-GARCH-in-mean model and check that you obtain the following results:

$$\hat{y}_t = -0.407 + 1.983\sqrt{h_t}$$
$$(t)\ \ (-2.862)\ (5.243)$$

$$\hat{h}_t = 0.022 + (0.211 - 0.221d_{t-1})e_{t-1}^2 + 0.782\,\hat{h}_{t-1}$$
$$(4.697)\ \ (8.952)(-8.728) \qquad\quad (27.677)$$

(c) The negative asymmetric effect (−0.221) suggests that negative shocks (such as falls in prices) reduce volatility in inflation. Is this a sensible result for inflation?

(d) What does the positive in-mean effect (1.983) tell you about inflation in the UK and volatility in prices?

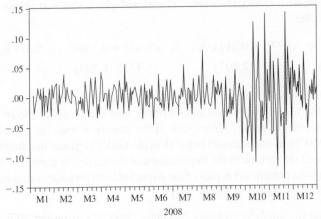

FIGURE **14.12**   Returns to shares in Time Warner.

14.12 The data file *warner.dat* contains daily returns to holding shares in Time Warner Inc. The sample period is from January 3, 2008 to December 31, 2008 (260 observations) and a graph of the returns appears in Figure 14.12.

(a) Estimate a GARCH(1,1) model and an ARCH(5) model. Which model would you prefer, and why?

(b) What is the expected return next period? The expected volatility next period?

(c) Use your preferred model to forecast next period's return and next period's volatility.

(d) Do good news and bad news have the same effect on return? On volatility?

14.13 Consider the quarterly rates of growth contained in *gfc.dat* used in Exercise 13.13. A researcher in the Euro area (this is the group of countries in Europe where the Euro currency is the legal tender) is interested in testing the proposition that growth in the Euro region is affected by its own history, growth in the United States, and shocks to economic activity.

(a) Specify an econometric model for the Euro Area based only on its own history and where the expected effect of shocks on the expected quarterly rate of growth is zero.

(b) Specify an econometric model for the Euro Area based only on its own history and where shocks may come from distributions with zero mean, but time-varying variances.

(c) Specify an econometric model for the Euro Area based on its own history, the history of growth in the United States, and where the expected effect of shocks on the expected quarterly rate of growth is zero.

(d) Specify an econometric model for the Euro Area based on its own history and allow shocks in the Euro area to have an effect of zero on the quarterly rate of growth.

(e) Specify an econometric model for the Euro Area based on its own history, the history of growth in the United States, and where shocks in the Euro area and in the United States have an effect on the expected quarterly rate of growth.

Chapter *15*

Panel Data Models

Learning Objectives

Based on the material in this chapter you should be able to

1. Explain how a data panel differs from either a cross section or a time series of data.

2. Explain the different ways in which individual heterogeneity can be modeled using panel data, and the assumptions underlying each approach.

3. Explain how the fixed effects model allows for differences in the parameter values for each individual cross section in a data panel.

4. Compare and contrast the least squares dummy variable estimator and the fixed effects estimator.

5. Compare and contrast the fixed effects model and the random effects model. Explain what leads us to consider individual differences to be random.

6. Explain the error assumptions in the random effects model, and what characteristic leads us to consider generalized least squares estimation.

7. Describe the steps required to obtain generalized least squares estimates for the random effects estimator.

8. Explain the meaning of cluster-robust standard errors, and describe how they can be used with pooled least squares, fixed effects, and random effects estimators.

9. Explain why endogeneity is a potential problem in random effects models, and how it affects our choice of estimator.

10. Test for the existence of fixed and/or random effects, and use the Hausman test to assess whether the random effects estimator is inconsistent.

11. Explain how the Hausman-Taylor estimator can be used to obtain consistent estimates of coefficients of time-invariant variables in a random effects model.

12. Explain how "seemingly unrelated regressions" are related to one another, and how this knowledge leads to improved estimation.

13. Use your software to estimate fixed effects models, random effects models, and seemingly unrelated regressions for panel data.

14. Test for contemporaneous correlation in a seemingly unrelated regression model.

15. Test cross-equation hypotheses on the coefficients in a seemingly unrelated regression model.

Keywords

Balanced panel
Cluster-robust standard errors
Contemporaneous correlation
Cross-equation hypotheses
Deviations from individual
    means
Endogeneity
Error components model
Fixed effects estimator
Fixed effects model

Hausman test
Hausman-Taylor estimator
Heterogeneity
Instrumental variables
Least squares dummy
    variable model
LM test
Panel corrected
    standard errors

Pooled least squares
Pooled model
Random effects estimator
Random effects model
Seemingly unrelated
    regressions
Time-invariant variables
Time-varying variables
Unbalanced panel

A panel of data consists of a group of cross-sectional units (people, households, firms, states, countries) who are observed over time. We will often refer to such units as individuals, with the term "individual" being used generically, even when the unit of interest is not a person. Let us denote the number of cross-sectional units (individuals) by N, and number of time periods in which we observe them as T. Panel data comes in several different "flavors," each of which introduces new challenges and opportunities. Peter Kennedy[1] describes the different types of panel data sets as

- "Long and narrow," with "long" describing the time dimension and "narrow" implying a relatively small number of cross sectional units
- "Short and wide," indicating that there are many individuals observed over a relatively short period of time
- "Long and wide," indicating that both N and T are relatively large

A "long and narrow" panel may consist of data on several firms over a period of time. A classic example is a data set analyzed by Grunfeld and used subsequently by many authors.[2] These data track investment in plant and equipment by $N = 11$ large firms for $T = 20$ years. This panel is narrow because it consists of only $N = 11$ firms. It is relatively "long" because $T > N$. We use this data set later in the chapter.

Many microeconomic analyses are performed on panel data sets with thousands of individuals who are followed through time. For example, the Panel Study of Income Dynamics (PSID) has followed approximately 8,000 families since 1968.[3] The U.S. Department of Labor conducts National Longitudinal Surveys (NLS) such as NLSY79, "a nationally representative sample of 12,686 young men and women who were 14–22 years old when they were first surveyed in 1979.[4] These individuals were interviewed annually through 1994 and are currently interviewed on a biennial basis." Such data sets are "wide" and "short," because N is much, much larger than T. Using panel data sets of this kind we can account for unobserved individual differences, or **heterogeneity**. Furthermore, these data panels are becoming long enough so that dynamic factors, such as spells of employment and unemployment, can be studied. These very large data sets are rich in information, and require the use of considerable computing power.

---

[1] *A Guide to Econometrics*, 5th edition (2003), MIT Press, Chapter 17.
[2] See Kleiber and Zeileis (2010), "The Grunfeld Data at 50," *German Economic Review*, forthcoming and http://statmath.wu-wien.ac.at/~zeileis/grunfeld/.
[3] See http://psidonline.isr.umich.edu/.
[4] See www.bls.gov/nls/.

Macroeconomists who study economic growth across nations employ data that is "long" and "wide." The Penn World Table[5] provides purchasing power parity and national income accounts converted to international prices for 189 countries for some or all of the years 1950–2007, which we may roughly characterize as having both large N and large T.

Finally, it is possible to have data that combines cross-sectional and time-series data which do not constitute a panel. We may collect a sample of data on individuals from a population at several points in time, but the individuals are not the same in each time period. Such data can be used to analyze a "natural experiment," for example when a law affecting some individuals changes, such as a change in unemployment insurance in a particular state. Using data before and after the policy change, and on groups of affected and unaffected people, the effects of the policy change can be measured. Methods for estimating effects of this type were introduced in Chapter 7.5.

Our interest in this chapter is how to use all available data to estimate econometric models describing the behavior of the individual cross-section units over time. Such data allow us to control for individual differences and study dynamic adjustment, and to measure the effects of policy changes. For each type of data we must take care not only with error assumptions, but also with our assumptions about whether, how, and when parameters may change across individuals and/or time.

15.1 A Microeconomic Panel

Our first example is of a data set that is short and wide. It is typical of many microeconometric analyses that use large data sets with many individuals, coming from the National Longitudinal Surveys (NLS) conducted by the U.S. Department of Labor, which has a database on women who were between 14 and 24 in 1968. To illustrate, we use a subsample of $N = 716$ women who were interviewed in 1982, 1983, 1985, 1987, and 1988. The sample consists of women who were employed, and whose schooling was completed, when interviewed. The data file is named *nls_panel.dat*[6] and contains 3,580 lines of data. Panel data observations are usually stacked, with all the time series observations for one individual on top of the next. The observations on a few variables for the first three women in the NLS panel are shown in Table 15.1. The first column *ID* identifies the individual and *YEAR* represents the year in which the information was collected. These identifying variables must be present so that your software will properly identify the cross-section and time series units. Then there are observations on each of the variables. In a typical panel there are some observations with missing values, usually denoted as "." or "NA". We have removed all the missing values in the data file *nls_panel.dat*. In microeconomic panels the individuals are not always interviewed the same number of times, leading to an **unbalanced panel** in which the number of time series observations is different across individuals. The data file *nls_panel.dat* is, however, a **balanced panel**; for each individual, we observe five time-series observations. A larger, unbalanced panel, is in the file *nls.dat*. Most modern software packages can handle both balanced and unbalanced panels.

In the sections that follow we consider various models and estimators for estimating a wage equation, with dependent variable ln(*WAGE*) and explanatory variables years of

---

[5] See http://pwt.econ.upenn.edu/.

[6] The data in *nls_panel.dat* and *nls.dat* are subsets of the *nlswork.dta* data used by the software Stata as an illustration. See *Stata Longitudinal/Panel Data, Reference Manual, Release 9*, StataCorp, 2005. We thank Stata for permission to use the data for illustration purposes.

Table 15.1 **Representative Observations from NLS Panel Data**

ID	YEAR	LWAGE	EDUC	SOUTH	BLACK	UNION	EXPER	TENURE
1	82	1.8083	12	0	1	1	7.6667	7.6667
1	83	1.8634	12	0	1	1	8.5833	8.5833
1	85	1.7894	12	0	1	1	10.1795	1.8333
1	87	1.8465	12	0	1	1	12.1795	3.7500
1	88	1.8564	12	0	1	1	13.6218	5.2500
2	82	1.2809	17	0	0	0	7.5769	2.4167
2	83	1.5159	17	0	0	0	8.3846	3.4167
2	85	1.9302	17	0	0	0	10.3846	5.4167
2	87	1.9190	17	0	0	1	12.0385	0.3333
2	88	2.2010	17	0	0	1	13.2115	1.7500
3	82	1.8148	12	0	0	0	11.4167	11.4167
3	83	1.9199	12	0	0	1	12.4167	12.4167
3	85	1.9584	12	0	0	0	14.4167	14.4167
3	87	2.0071	12	0	0	0	16.4167	16.4167
3	88	2.0899	12	0	0	0	17.8205	17.7500

education (*EDUC*), total labor force experience (*EXPER*) and its square (*EXPER*^{2}), tenure in current job (*TENURE*) and its square (*TENURE*^{2}), and indicator or dummy variables *BLACK*, *SOUTH*, and *UNION*.

15.2 Pooled Model

A **pooled model** is one where the data on different individuals are simply pooled together with no provision for individual differences that might lead to different coefficients. For an equation with two explanatory variables x_2 and x_3, a pooled model can be written as

$$y_{it} = \beta_1 + \beta_2 x_{2it} + \beta_3 x_{3it} + e_{it} \tag{15.1}$$

The first thing to notice about (15.1) is the two subscripts: i to denote the ith individual and t to denote the tth time period. Thus, y_{it}, for example, represents the tth observation on the dependent variable for the ith individual. Assuming we have T observations on N individuals, the indices i and t are such that $i = 1, 2, \ldots, N$ and $t = 1, 2, \ldots, T$, implying a total of NT observations. For the data set illustrated in Table 15.1, $i = ID$, $t = 1$ for 1982, $t = 2$ for 1983, and so on up to $t = 5$ for 1988, with $N = 716$ and $T = 5$. If a panel is unbalanced, T is different for each individual, and we write $t = 1, 2, \ldots, T_i$; the total number of observations is $\sum_{i=1}^{N} T_i$.

The second thing to notice in (15.1) is that the coefficients (β_1, β_2, β_3) do not have i or t subscripts. They are assumed to be constant for all individuals in all time periods, and do not allow for possible individual heterogeneity. It is this characteristic that leads to (15.1) being called a pooled model. If, in addition, we assume the errors e_{it} have zero mean and constant variance, are uncorrelated over time (t) and individuals (i), and are uncorrelated with x_2 and x_3, then there is nothing special about (15.1) that distinguishes it from the multiple regression model studied in Chapters 5–7. The least squares estimator for ($\beta_1, \beta_2, \beta_3$) has all its desirable properties. It is consistent, and the usual t and F statistics are valid in large samples for hypothesis testing and interval estimation. If we also assume x_2 and x_3 are nonrandom, the least squares estimator is the minimum variance linear unbiased estimator in finite samples. We will focus on large sample properties, however, because it is typically unrealistic to assume x_2 and x_3 are nonrandom, and our sample sizes are usually large. In the panel data set introduced in Section 15.1 each woman is selected at random, implying that ln(*WAGE*), *EDUC*, *EXPER*, *UNION*, etc., are random outcomes, and the total sample size $NT = 3580$ is large. The least squares estimator, when applied to a pooled model, is referred to as **pooled least squares**. The data for different individuals are pooled together, and the equation is estimated using least squares.

For future reference it is useful to write explicitly the error assumptions required for pooled least squares to be consistent and for the t and F statistics to be valid when computed using the usual least squares variance estimates and standard errors. They are

$$E(e_{it}) = 0 \qquad \text{(zero mean)} \tag{15.2}$$

$$\text{var}(e_{it}) = E(e_{it}^2) = \sigma_e^2 \qquad \text{(homoskedasticity)} \tag{15.3}$$

$$\text{cov}(e_{it}, e_{js}) = E(e_{it}, e_{js}) = 0 \quad \text{for } i \neq j \text{ or } t \neq s \text{ (all errors are uncorrelated)} \tag{15.4}$$

$$\text{cov}(e_{it}, x_{2it}) = 0, \quad \text{cov}(e_{it}, x_{3it}) = 0 \quad \text{(errors uncorrelated with } x\text{'s)} \tag{15.5}$$

15.2.1 CLUSTER-ROBUST STANDARD ERRORS

Applying pooled least squares in a way that ignores the panel nature of the data is restrictive in a number of ways. The first unrealistic assumption that we consider is the lack of correlation between errors corresponding to the same individual. If, for a given level of education, experience, education, etc., a woman's wage is higher than average in one year, it is also likely to be higher than average in the other years. Looked at another way, if there are unobservable individual characteristics that by necessity are excluded from the set of explanatory variables, and hence are included in the error term, then those characteristics will lead to similar effects in different years for the same individual.

To relax the assumption of zero error correlation over time for the same individual, we write

$$\text{cov}(e_{it}, e_{is}) = \psi_{ts} \tag{15.6}$$

Notice that this alternative assumption also relaxes the assumption of homoskedasticity because, when $t = s$, we have

$$\text{cov}(e_{it}, e_{it}) = \text{var}(e_{it}) = \psi_{tt}$$

The error variance can be different in different time periods, but is constant over individuals. To avoid confusion with different σ^2's that will be used later, we have introduced another Greek letter "psi" (ψ) to denote the variances and covariances.

Notice that assumption (15.6) does not say anything about the nature of within-individual correlation, just that it is nonzero. It does not assume the correlation is constant over time—an assumption of the random effects model that we consider later in this chapter. Nor does it assume the correlation declines as the errors become further apart in time—an assumption of the stationary time series models considered in Chapter 9.

We continue to assume that the errors for different individuals are uncorrelated. This is a reasonable assumption if the individuals constitute a random sample from some population. Thus, we have

$$\text{cov}(e_{it}, e_{js}) = 0 \text{ for } i \neq j$$

What are the consequences of using pooled least squares in the presence of the hetero-skedasticity and correlation described by (15.6)? The least squares estimator is still consistent, but its standard errors are incorrect, implying that hypothesis tests and interval estimates based on these standard errors will be invalid. Typically, the standard errors will be too small, overstating the reliability of the least squares estimator. Fortunately, there is a way of correcting the standard errors to reflect the more realistic assumption in (15.6). We had a similar situation in Chapters 8 and 9. In Chapter 8 we saw how White's heteroskedasticity-consistent standard errors could be used for assessing the reliability of least squares estimates in a regression model with heteroskedasticity of unknown form. Least squares is not efficient in these circumstances—the generalized least squares estimator has lower variance—but using least squares avoids the need to specify the nature of the heteroskedasticity, and using least squares with White standard errors provides a valid basis for interval estimation and hypothesis testing. The Newey-West standard errors introduced in Chapter 9 served a similar function in an autocorrelated error model. They provided a valid basis for inference using least squares estimates without the need to specify the nature of the autocorrelated error process.

In a similar way standard errors that are valid for the pooled least squares estimator under the assumption in (15.6) can be computed. These standard errors have various names, being referred to as **panel-robust standard errors** or **cluster-robust standard errors**. The time-series observations on individuals are the clusters.

Derivation of cluster-robust standard errors requires some advanced algebra which you can avoid by using standard options in computer software. However, it is useful to gain some understanding and appreciation of how they are calculated. Some details are provided for this purpose in Appendix 15A.

15.2.2 Pooled Least Squares Estimates of Wage Equation

Pooled least squares estimates of the wage equation are displayed in Table 15.2 alongside least-squares standard errors, t-values and p-values, and the corresponding cluster-robust standard errors, t-values and p-values.[7] Looking first at the estimates, we find there is a 7% return to an extra year of education. Overall market experience and job tenure have positive but diminishing effects on ln(*WAGE*). Wages are 12% lower for black workers, and 11% lower for workers living in the South. Union members enjoy wages that are 13% higher. These estimates have their usual partial derivative interpretation—other factors are held constant in each case.

A comparison of the least-squares standard errors with the corresponding cluster-robust standard errors reveals some dramatic differences. Almost all of the cluster-robust standard errors are at least 50% higher than their least squares counterparts and consequently have t-values that are at least 50% lower. Ignoring the within-individual correlation means that the reliability of the pooled least squares estimates is overstated. In this particular example, there is little effect on conclusions about the significance of the estimated coefficients, because the p-values for hypothesis tests of significance are mostly 0.000 (correct to three decimal places) for both sets of standard errors. However, for those coefficients with

---

[7] The cluster-robust standard errors are computed with degrees of freedom correction in Stata 11.0. Some other software packages use different degrees of freedom corrections, which can lead to slightly different cluster-robust standard errors. See Appendix 15A for details.

Table 15.2 **Pooled Least Squares Estimates of Wage Equation**

Variable	Coefficient	Least Squares Standard Errors			Cluster-Robust Standard Errors		
		Std. Error	*t*-value	*p*-value	Std. Error	*t*-value	*p*-value
C	0.47660	0.05616	8.49	0.000	0.08456	5.64	0.000
EDUC	0.07145	0.00269	26.57	0.000	0.00550	12.99	0.000
EXPER	0.05569	0.00861	6.47	0.000	0.01130	4.92	0.000
EXPER^2	−0.00115	0.00036	−3.18	0.002	0.00049	−2.33	0.020
TENURE	0.01496	0.00441	3.39	0.001	0.00712	2.10	0.036
TENURE^2	−0.00049	0.00026	−1.89	0.059	0.00041	−1.18	0.236
BLACK	−0.11671	0.01572	−7.43	0.000	0.02813	−4.15	0.000
SOUTH	−0.10600	0.01420	−7.46	0.000	0.02706	−3.92	0.000
UNION	0.13224	0.01496	8.84	0.000	0.02707	4.88	0.000

p-values greater than 0.000, there are large changes in those *p*-values. That for *TENURE2* changes from 0.059 to 0.236, casting doubt about whether this variable should be included in the equation. Allowing for correlation between the errors for each individual is clearly important; there are individual characteristics that are not completely captured by the included explanatory variables.

15.3 The Fixed Effects Model

In the previous section we saw that one way to recognize the existence of individual characteristics in a panel data model is to allow individual errors in different time periods to be correlated. A second way is to relax the assumption that all individuals have the same coefficients. Extending the model in (15.1) along these lines, we can write

$$y_{it} = \beta_{1i} + \beta_{2i}x_{2it} + \beta_{3i}x_{3it} + e_{it} \tag{15.7}$$

An *i* subscript has been added to each of the subscripts, implying that $(\beta_1, \beta_2, \beta_3)$ can be different for each individual. This model is a legitimate panel data model, but it is not suitable for panels that are short and wide. In the wage equation example, we have 716 individuals, and only five time-series observations on each individual. Thus, to estimate (15.7) with this data set, we would be using only five observations to estimate three coefficients for each individual. The resulting estimates would not be precise, and do not have desirable large sample properties. If (15.7) is extended to include all the explanatory variables in the wage equation, we have more coefficients than time-series observations, making estimation impossible.

A popular simplification of (15.7) from which meaningful estimates can be obtained in short and wide panels is one where the intercepts β_{1i} are different for different individuals but the slope coefficients β_2 and β_3 are assumed to be constant for all individuals. In this case, the model becomes

$$y_{it} = \beta_{1i} + \beta_2 x_{2it} + \beta_3 x_{3it} + e_{it} \tag{15.8}$$

All behavioral differences between individuals, referred to as **individual heterogeneity**, are assumed to be captured by the intercept. Individual intercepts are included to "control" for individual-specific, time-invariant characteristics. A model with these features is called a **fixed effects model**. The intercepts are called **fixed effects**.

As we will see, the term "fixed effects" often relates more to the estimation procedure and to other assumptions that we make than it does to whether the intercepts are fixed or random. In the wage equation example the sample of women is selected randomly, implying that their intercepts are random. However, when estimated within the framework of a fixed effects model, they are treated as nonrandom. In some cases, such as models where the individuals are geographical regions such as states, and all states are included, the intercepts are more clearly "fixed."

We consider two methods for estimating (15.8). These methods are identical in the sense that they give the same estimates, but they differ computationally. One is the **least squares dummy variable estimator** and the other is the **fixed effects estimator**.

15.3.1 THE LEAST SQUARES DUMMY VARIABLE ESTIMATOR FOR SMALL N

One way to estimate the model in (15.8) is to include an intercept dummy variable (indicator variable) for each individual. If the number of individuals is small, this can be done by brute force. In our example $N = 716$ is not small. Including 716 indicator variables, while possible, is tedious. Thus, to illustrate the least squares dummy variable estimator we use the first 10 individuals in the file *nls_panel.dat*. The observations for these 10 individuals have been stored in a new file called *nls_panel10.dat*. We begin by defining 10 dummy (indicator) variables, such as

$$D_{1i} = \begin{cases} 1 & i = 1 \\ 0 & \text{otherwise} \end{cases} \quad D_{2i} = \begin{cases} 1 & i = 2 \\ 0 & \text{otherwise} \end{cases} \quad D_{3i} = \begin{cases} 1 & i = 3 \\ 0 & \text{otherwise} \end{cases}$$

Then (15.8) can be written

$$y_{it} = \beta_{11}D_{1i} + \beta_{12}D_{2i} + \cdots + \beta_{1,10}D_{10i} + \beta_2 x_{2it} + \beta_3 x_{3it} + e_{it} \quad (15.9)$$

The equation for women's wages has more than two explanatory variables, but we confine this discussion to two x's to avoid notational overload.

To make (15.9) consistent with our earlier treatment of indicator variables in Chapter 7, we would specify a constant and nine dummy variables. Each dummy variable coefficient would be equal to the difference between the intercept for its individual and the intercept for the base individual for which we did not specify a dummy variable. The specification in (15.9) is more convenient for our current discussion. However, you should recognize that the two alternatives are just different ways of looking at the same model.

If the error terms e_{it} are uncorrelated with mean zero and constant variance σ_e^2 for all observations—they satisfy the assumptions in (15.2) to (15.5)—the best linear unbiased estimator of (15.9) is the least squares estimator. In a panel data context, it is called the **least squares dummy variable estimator**. Its large sample properties need a special mention. Since N is large and T is small the large sample properties relevant for approximating the finite sample properties of the estimator are those obtained for $N \to \infty$. In this sense, the least squares estimator for the slope coefficients β_2 and β_3 is consistent, but the estimator for the intercepts is not. The intercepts are not estimated consistently because as N gets larger we get more intercepts, not more information on the existing intercepts, and so the distributions of their estimators do not collapse to their true values as is required for consistency. The implications of these results are that inferences about β_2 and β_3 can proceed with a large sample justification, but inferences drawn about the β_{1i} are

Table 15.3 **Dummy Variable Estimation of Wage Equation for $N = 10$**

Variable	Coefficient	Std. Error	t-value	p-value
D1	0.1519	1.0967	0.139	0.891
D2	0.1869	1.0715	0.174	0.863
D3	−0.0630	1.3509	−0.047	0.963
D4	0.1856	1.3435	0.138	0.891
D5	0.9390	1.0978	0.855	0.398
D6	0.7945	1.1118	0.715	0.480
D7	0.5812	1.2359	0.470	0.641
D8	0.5379	1.0975	0.490	0.627
D9	0.4183	1.0840	0.386	0.702
D10	0.6146	1.0902	0.564	0.577
EXPER	0.2380	0.1878	1.268	0.213
EXPER^2	−0.0082	0.0079	−1.036	0.307
TENURE	−0.0124	0.0341	−0.362	0.720
TENURE^2	0.0023	0.0027	0.854	0.399
UNION	0.1135	0.1509	0.753	0.457

$SSE = 2.667190$

conditional on the individuals selected and their x's, and need normally distributed errors in order to be valid.

The results from applying the least squares dummy variable estimator to the wage equation for the first 10 individuals (a total of 50 observations) appear in Table 15.3. The variables *EDUC*, *BLACK*, and *SOUTH* have been omitted. Why? First consider *BLACK*. This variable is an individual characteristic that does not change over time; for each individual it is one or zero in all five time periods. Since individual indicator variables have been included to capture all time-invariant, individual-specific characteristics, the effect of *BLACK* will form part of each indicator variable coefficient, and the variable *BLACK* becomes redundant. If you try to include the variable *BLACK* in the least squares regression, your software will either give you an error message or throw out the variable because of exact collinearity. Exact collinearity occurs because the sum of the all the individual indicator variables for black women will be equal to the variable *BLACK*.

The situation is similar for *EDUC*. Since all women had completed their education at the beginning of the sample, their numbers of years of schooling will not change over time. For each woman *EDUC* is the same in all five years. Thus, the effect of *EDUC* will also be picked up by the coefficients of the indicator variables for each of the women. The source of the collinearity in this case is $EDUC = \sum_{i=1}^{10} EDUC_i \times D_i$ where $EDUC_i$ is the number of years of schooling for the ith woman and D_i is her corresponding individual indicator variable.

The reason for omitting *SOUTH* is slightly different. It turns out that none of the first 10 individuals in the data *nls_panel.dat* had ever lived in the South, and so all values of this variable are zero. It is impossible to measure the effects of living in the South when nobody lives in the South. Later, when we include all individuals, we discover some did live in the South, and that some changed their location during the time defined by the five time-series observations. If nobody changed their location, then the variable *SOUTH* would be similar to *EDUC* and *BLACK*. Its individual effect would be picked up by the coefficients of the

Table 15.4 **Pooled Least Squares Estimates of Wage Equation for $N = 10$**

Variable	Coefficient	Std. Error	t-value	p-value
C	0.6209	1.0172	0.610	0.545
$EXPER$	0.1947	0.1730	1.125	0.267
$EXPER^2$	−0.0049	0.0071	−0.688	0.495
$TENURE$	0.0014	0.0375	0.036	0.971
$TENURE^2$	−0.0009	0.0023	−0.371	0.712
$UNION$	−0.0175	0.1024	−0.171	0.865

$SSE = 5.502466$.

dummy variables. The variable $UNION$ can be included because individuals 2, 3, 8, and 9 changed their union status over the sample time period.

Turning to the estimates in Table 15.3, we find that none of them are significantly different from zero at even a 20% level of significance. Using only 10 individuals has not given us enough information to get reliable estimates. The individual intercepts vary considerably, suggesting that the assumption of different intercepts for different individuals could be appropriate. Since these intercepts have relatively large standard errors, it is advisable to formally test whether they might be all equal, in which case there is no individual heterogeneity. To do so, we set up the following hypotheses:

$$H_0 : \beta_{11} = \beta_{12} = \cdots = \beta_{1,10}$$
$$H_1 : \text{the } \beta_{1i} \text{ are not all equal} \tag{15.10}$$

These $N-1 = 9$ joint null hypotheses are tested using the usual F-test statistic. In the restricted model all the intercept parameters are equal. If we call their common value β_1, then the restricted model is the pooled model

$$\ln(WAGE) = \beta_1 + \beta_2 EXPER + \beta_3 EXPER^2 + \beta_4 TENURE + \beta_5 TENURE^2$$
$$+ \beta_6 UNION + e$$

The pooled least squares estimates of this restricted model are shown in Table 15.4. Again, the standard errors are relatively large, indicating that the estimates are not precise. To test whether there are individual fixed effects, we are interested in the sum of squared errors $SSE_R = 5.502466$, where the subscript "R" is used to indicate this is the restricted model that assumes H_0 is true. The unrestricted sum of squared residuals $SSE_U = 2.667190$ comes from the dummy variable model. With these two values we can construct the F-statistic as

$$F = \frac{(SSE_R - SSE_U)/J}{SSE_U/(NT - K)}$$
$$= \frac{(5.502466 - 2.667190)/9}{2.667190/(50 - 15)}$$
$$= 4.134$$

If the null hypothesis is true, then $F \sim F_{(9, 35)}$. The value of the test statistic $F = 4.134$ yields a p-value of 0.0011; we reject the null hypothesis that the intercept parameters for all individuals are equal. We conclude that there are differences in individual intercepts, and that the data should not be pooled into a single model with a common intercept parameter.

15.3.2 THE FIXED EFFECTS ESTIMATOR

The technique of including a dummy variable for each individual is feasible when the number of individuals is small. However, if we have a very large number of individuals, this approach will not work. Today's typical computer simply cannot handle that computing task quickly and accurately. Luckily there is a fantastic trick that makes estimating the fixed effects model with a large number of individuals relatively easy.

Take the data on individual i:

$$y_{it} = \beta_{1i} + \beta_2 x_{2it} + \beta_3 x_{3it} + e_{it} \quad t = 1, \ldots, T \tag{15.11}$$

Average the data across time, by summing both sides of the equation and dividing by T

$$\frac{1}{T} \sum_{t=1}^{T} (y_{it} = \beta_{1i} + \beta_2 x_{2it} + \beta_3 x_{3it} + e_{it})$$

Using the fact that the parameters do not change over time, we can simplify this as

$$\bar{y}_i = \frac{1}{T} \sum_{t=1}^{T} y_{it} = \beta_{1i} + \beta_2 \frac{1}{T} \sum_{t=1}^{T} x_{2it} + \beta_3 \frac{1}{T} \sum_{t=1}^{T} x_{3it} + \frac{1}{T} \sum_{t=1}^{T} e_{it}$$

$$= \beta_{1i} + \beta_2 \bar{x}_{2i} + \beta_3 \bar{x}_{3i} + \bar{e}_i \tag{15.12}$$

The "bar" notation $\bar{y}_i$ indicates that we have averaged the values of y_{it} over time. Then, subtract (15.12) from (15.11), term by term, to obtain

$$y_{it} = \beta_{1i} + \beta_2 x_{2it} + \beta_3 x_{3it} + e_{it}$$

$$-(\bar{y}_i = \beta_{1i} + \beta_2 \bar{x}_{2i} + \beta_3 \bar{x}_{3i} + \bar{e}_i)$$

$$\overline{\hspace{6cm}} \tag{15.13}$$

$$y_{it} - \bar{y}_i = \beta_2 (x_{2it} - \bar{x}_{2i}) + \beta_3 (x_{3it} - \bar{x}_{3i}) + (e_{it} - \bar{e}_i)$$

In the last line of (15.13) note that the intercept parameter β_{1i} has fallen out. These data are said to be in "deviation from the individual's mean" form, and if we repeat this process for each individual, then we have a transformed model

$$\tilde{y}_{it} = \beta_2 \tilde{x}_{2it} + \beta_3 \tilde{x}_{3it} + \tilde{e}_{it} \tag{15.14}$$

The "tilde" notation $\tilde{y}_{it} = y_{it} - \bar{y}_i$ indicates that the variables are in deviation from the mean form. In Table 15.5 we show the observations for the first three individuals for the variables $y = LWAGE$ and $x_2 = EXPER$. The average of the $T = 5$ years of data on each individual is computed. For example, the average value of $LWAGE$ for the first individual ($i = 1$) over the five-year period was 1.8328. This value is subtracted from each value of $LWAGE$ for individual one. This process is repeated for each variable for each individual. Notice what would happen if one of the variables was time-invariant—for each individual it is constant over time, like $EDUC$ and $BLACK$. The corresponding deviation from means variable would consist completely of zeros, and, as in the dummy variable model, cannot be included.

The advantage from the transformation in (15.14) is that the least squares estimates of the parameters β_2 and β_3 from (15.14) are identical to the least squares estimates from the full dummy variable model shown in (15.9), and they can be obtained without having to include

Table 15.5   **Data in Deviation from Individual Mean Form**

i	t	y_{it}	$\bar{y}_i$	$\tilde{y}_{it} = y_{it} - \bar{y}_i$	x_{2it}	$\bar{x}_{2i}$	$\tilde{x}_{2it} = x_{2it} - \bar{x}_{2i}$
1	1	1.8083	1.8328	−0.0245	7.667	10.446	−2.779
1	2	1.8634	1.8328	0.0306	8.583	10.446	−1.863
1	3	1.7894	1.8328	−0.0434	10.179	10.446	−0.267
1	4	1.8465	1.8328	0.0137	12.179	10.446	1.733
1	5	1.8564	1.8328	0.0236	13.622	10.446	3.176
2	1	1.2809	1.7694	−0.4885	7.577	10.319	−2.742
2	2	1.5159	1.7694	−0.2535	8.385	10.319	−1.935
2	3	1.9302	1.7694	0.1608	10.385	10.319	0.065
2	4	1.9190	1.7694	0.1496	12.038	10.319	1.719
2	5	2.2010	1.7694	0.4316	13.212	10.319	2.892
3	1	1.8148	1.9580	−0.1432	11.417	14.497	−3.081
3	2	1.9199	1.9580	−0.0381	12.417	14.497	−2.081
3	3	1.9584	1.9580	0.0004	14.417	14.497	−0.081
3	4	2.0071	1.9580	0.0491	16.417	14.497	1.919
3	5	2.0899	1.9580	0.1318	17.821	14.497	3.323

$y_{it} = LWAGE_{it}, \quad x_{2it} = EXPER_{it}$.

all the dummy variables. Furthermore, the least squares residuals from (15.14) are the same as the least squares residuals from (15.9).[8]

Writing the fixed effects model in terms of deviations from individual means, as in (15.14), emphasizes another important characteristic of the fixed effects estimator: the coefficient estimates depend only on the variation of the dependent and explanatory variables **within individuals**. Thus, when estimating the effect of experience on wages, for example, it is only the variation in wages and experience over time for each individual that contributes to the estimated coefficients. The variation in wages from different individuals with different levels of experience does not play a role.

15.3.2a   Fixed Effects Estimates of Wage Equation for $N = 10$

In this section we estimate the wage equation for the first 10 individuals using data in the form of deviations from individual means and demonstrate the equivalence of the results with those from the least squares dummy variable estimator. The data file *nls_panel_devn* .dat contains observations on the variables LWAGE, EXPER, EXPER², TENURE, TENURE², and UNION for the first 10 individuals, expressed in terms of deviations from individual means.

The least squares estimates and standard errors from estimating (15.14) are those displayed on the left side of Table 15.6. Notice that the estimates for the coefficients β_2 and β_3 and the sum of squared errors are identical to those in Table 15.3, obtained using the least squares dummy variable estimator. The standard errors are slightly different, however. The difference arises because the estimate of the error variance used by the least squares software when estimating (15.14) is $\tilde{\sigma}_e^2 = SSE/(NT - 5)$ when what is required is $\hat{\sigma}_e^2 = SSE/(NT - N - 5)$. The calculation of $\tilde{\sigma}_e^2$ ignores the loss of $N = 10$ degrees of freedom that occurs when the variables are corrected by their sample means. The correct divisor is $NT - N - 5 = 35$, which is the degrees of freedom in the dummy variable

---

[8] The proofs of these results involve matrix algebra. See William Greene (2008), *Econometric Analysis*, 6th edition, Pearson Prentice Hall, Chapter 3.3.

Table 15.6   **Fixed Effects Estimation of Wage Equation for $N = 10$**

Variable	Using Least Squares Deviation Form		Using Fixed Effects Software Command	
	Coefficient	Std. Error	Coefficient	Std. Error
C			0.4347	1.1452
EXPER	0.2380	0.1656	0.2380	0.1878
$EXPER^2$	−0.0082	0.0070	−0.0082	0.0079
TENURE	−0.0124	0.0301	−0.0124	0.0341
$TENURE^2$	0.0023	0.0024	0.0023	0.0027
UNION	0.1135	0.1330	0.1135	0.1509
	$SSE = 2.66719$		$SSE = 2.66719$	

model, taking into account both the dummy variables and explanatory variables. If we multiply the standard errors from estimating (15.4) by the correction factor

$$\sqrt{(NT - 5)/(NT - N - 5)} = \sqrt{45/35} = 1.133893$$

the resulting standard errors are identical to those in Table 15.3.

When using software designed to carry out fixed effects estimation automatically, these corrections will have already been done. In the right side of Table 15.6 we report the results in the format used by two econometric software packages (EViews 7.0 and Stata 11.0). Note that the coefficient estimates and standard errors are identical to those from the dummy variable model in Table 15.3. The reported constant term C is the average of the estimated coefficients on the cross section dummy variables. That is $C = N^{-1}\sum_{i=1}^{N} b_{1i}$, where the b_{1i} are the least squares estimates of the parameters β_{1i} in (15.9), and are the coefficients of the dummy variables in Table 15.3. Other software may report the results in a different format.

It is usually the case that when estimating panel data models, we are most interested in the coefficients of the explanatory variables and not the individual intercept parameters. Recall that the intercept parameters are the coefficients of the dummy variables and are also called the fixed effects. Although they are typically of lower priority, these coefficients can be "recovered" by using the fact that the least squares fitted regression passes through the point of the means, just as it did in the simple regression model. That is,

$$\bar{y}_i = b_{1i} + b_2 \bar{x}_{2i} + b_3 \bar{x}_{3i}$$

where b_2 and b_3 are the estimates obtained from (15.14) and b_{1i} denotes the estimates of individual specific constants, or fixed effects. Given b_2 and b_3, we can compute the fixed effects as

$$b_{1i} = \bar{y}_i - b_2 \bar{x}_{2i} - b_3 \bar{x}_{3i} \quad i = 1, \dots, N \tag{15.15}$$

Econometric software packages usually make it possible to recover these estimates.

15.3.3   Fixed Effects Estimates of Wage Equation from Complete Panel

The estimates in Tables 15.3, 15.4, and 15.6 were included for illustrative purposes only. Panel-data samples are typically much larger than $N = 10$ and $T = 5$. The need for a larger sample was evident from the large standard errors and the failure to find any coefficient estimates that were significantly different from zero. In this section we improve the precision of estimation by using the complete sample of $N = 716$ individuals.

Also considered in this section is a relaxation of the assumption that the errors e_{it} are uncorrelated over time for each individual. When considering the pooled model in Section 15.2, we argued that unobserved individual characteristics captured by the error term are likely to lead to similar effects in different years for the same individual. This implies that each individual's errors are correlated, an assumption we wrote as $\text{cov}(e_{it}, e_{is}) = \psi_{ts}$. Under this assumption, least squares standard errors are invalid and cluster-robust standard errors should be used. In the fixed effects model time-invariant individual characteristics are included in the fixed effects, and so nonzero values for ψ_{ts} (for $t \neq s$) are less likely. Nevertheless, within-individual error correlations can still remain, in which case cluster-robust standard errors should be used in conjunction with the fixed-effects estimator. In the illustrative example with $N = 10$ individuals we assumed that all e_{it} were uncorrelated—the assumptions in (15.2) to (15.5). For the $N = 716$ individuals considered in this section two sets of standard errors are computed—those which assume completely uncorrelated e_{it}, and cluster robust standard errors to allow for the possibility that e_{it} and e_{is} are correlated.

The estimates, and the two sets of standard errors, t-values and p-values are displayed in Table 15.7.[9] Since some individuals in the sample of $N = 716$ moved into or out of the South during the sample period, it is now possible to include *SOUTH* as a variable. The variables *EDUC* and *BLACK* continue to be omitted because they are exactly collinear with the implied dummy variables. A relevant question to ask is: What impact does including fixed effects to allow for individual heterogeneity have on the coefficient estimates? How do the estimated effects on wages of more experience, longer tenure, living in the South, and belonging to a union change? The answer to this question is given by comparing the pooled least squares estimates in Table 15.2 with those in Table 15.7. What we discover is that ignoring individual heterogeneity leads to coefficient estimates that are much larger in absolute value. For *SOUTH* and *UNION*, this means that their effect on wages is grossly overstated when the fixed effects are omitted. It is less clear how the estimated effects of experience and tenure change because both linear and quadratic terms are included for these variables. Table 15.8 contains a comparison of the two sets of estimates of the percentage change in wages attributable to changes in each of the variables. For experience

T a b l e 1 5 . 7   **Fixed Effects Estimates of Wage Equation for $N = 716$**

Variable	Coefficient	Least Squares Standard Errors			Cluster-Robust Standard Errors		
		Std. Error	t-value	p-value	Std. Error	t-value	p-value
C	1.45003	0.04014	36.12	0.000	0.06149	23.58	0.000
EXPER	0.04108	0.00662	6.21	0.000	0.00921	4.46	0.000
$EXPER^2$	−0.00041	0.00027	−1.50	0.135	0.00037	−1.11	0.268
TENURE	0.01391	0.00328	4.24	0.000	0.00471	2.95	0.003
$TENURE^2$	−0.00090	0.00021	−4.35	0.000	0.00028	−3.21	0.001
SOUTH	−0.01632	0.03615	−0.45	0.652	0.06535	−0.25	0.803
UNION	0.06370	0.01425	4.47	0.000	0.01884	3.38	0.001

---

[9] The cluster-robust standard errors are computed with the degrees of freedom correction in EView 7.0. Some other software packages use different degrees of freedom corrections which can lead to slightly different cluster-robust standard errors. See Appendix 15A.

Table 15.8 **Percentage Marginal Effects on Wages**

Variable	Pooled Least Squares	Fixed Effects Estimator
EXPER	2.81	3.13
TENURE	0.82	0.14
SOUTH	−10.60	−1.63
UNION	13.22	6.37

and tenure the percentage changes are evaluated at the approximate sample means $EXPER = 12$ and $TENURE = 7$. There are some large differences. The wage benefit from being a member of a union has halved from 13% to 6.4%. The negative effect of being in the South has fallen from 10.6% to 1.6%. The marginal effect of experience is slightly larger when the fixed effects are included, but that for tenure declines from 0.82% to 0.14%.

Turning now to the standard errors, t-values and p-values, we find that inferences about what variables are relevant can also be sensitive to whether or not the fixed effects are included. From the results in Table 15.2, there was doubt about whether $TENURE^2$ should be included. The results in Table 15.7 suggest that $EXPER^2$ and $SOUTH$ are possible exclusions. A comparison of the least squares standard errors with the cluster-robust standard errors in Table 15.7 suggests that some within-individual error correlation still remains after including the fixed effects. The differences are not as large as they were in Table 15.2, but ignoring the correlation does lead to smaller standard errors, suggesting that these standard errors overstate the precision of estimation.

15.4 The Random Effects Model

In the fixed-effects model (15.8) we assumed that all individual differences were captured by differences in the intercept parameter. The intercepts β_{1i} were considered to be "fixed" parameters that we could estimate directly using the least squares estimator. In the **random effects model** we again assume that all individual differences are captured by the intercept parameters, but we also recognize that the individuals in our sample were randomly selected, and thus we treat the individual differences as *random* rather than fixed, as we did in the fixed-effects dummy variable model. Random individual differences can be included in our model by specifying the intercept parameters β_{1i} to consist of a fixed part that represents the population average, $\overline{\beta}_1$, and random individual differences from the population average, u_i. In equation form this breakdown is

$$\beta_{1i} = \overline{\beta}_1 + u_i \tag{15.16}$$

The random individual differences u_i, which are called **random effects**, are analogous to random error terms, and we make the standard assumptions about them—namely, that they have zero mean, are uncorrelated across individuals, and have a constant variance σ_u^2, so that

$$E(u_i) = 0, \quad \text{cov}(u_i, u_j) = 0 \quad i \neq j, \quad \text{var}(u_i) = \sigma_u^2 \tag{15.17}$$

If we substitute (15.16) into (15.8) we obtain

$$y_{it} = \beta_{1i} + \beta_2 x_{2it} + \beta_3 x_{3it} + e_{it}$$

$$= (\overline{\beta}_1 + u_i) + \beta_2 x_{2it} + \beta_3 x_{3it} + e_{it} \tag{15.18}$$

In this expression $\bar{\beta}_1$ is a fixed population parameter, and u_i is a random effect. We can rearrange (15.18) to make it resemble a familiar regression equation,

$$
\begin{aligned}
y_{it} &= \bar{\beta}_1 + \beta_2 x_{2it} + \beta_3 x_{3it} + (e_{it} + u_i) \\
&= \bar{\beta}_1 + \beta_2 x_{2it} + \beta_3 x_{3it} + v_{it}
\end{aligned}
\tag{15.19}
$$

where now $\bar{\beta}_1$ is the intercept parameter and the error term v_{it} is composed of a component u_i that represents a random individual effect and the component e_{it} which is the usual regression random error. The combined error is

$$
v_{it} = u_i + e_{it}
\tag{15.20}
$$

Because the random effects regression error in (15.20) has two components, one for the individual and one for the regression, the random effects model is often called an **error components model**.

15.4.1 ERROR TERM ASSUMPTIONS

The assumptions we make for e_{it} are those given in (15.2) to (15.6)—namely, that the e_{it} have zero mean and constant variance σ_e^2 and are uncorrelated over time and individuals so that $\text{cov}(e_{it}, e_{js}) = 0$ for $i \neq j$ or $t \neq s$. They are also assumed to be uncorrelated with the explanatory variables so that $\text{cov}(e_{it}, x_{2it}) = 0$ and $\text{cov}(e_{it}, x_{3it}) = 0$. Further, we assume the individual effects u_i are not correlated with the regression error e_{it}, so that $\text{cov}(u_i, e_{it}) = 0$, and not correlated with the explanatory variables, so that $\text{cov}(u_i, x_{2it}) = 0$ and $\text{cov}(u_i, x_{3it}) = 0$.

Using these assumptions about u_i and e_{it}, we can derive the properties of the combined error term $v_{it} = u_i + e_{it}$. It has zero mean

$$
E(v_{it}) = E(u_i + e_{it}) = E(u_i) + E(e_{it}) = 0 + 0 = 0
$$

and a constant, homoskedastic, variance:

$$
\begin{aligned}
\sigma_v^2 = \text{var}(v_{it}) &= \text{var}(u_i + e_{it}) \\
&= \text{var}(u_i) + \text{var}(e_{it}) + 2\text{cov}(u_i, e_{it}) \\
&= \sigma_u^2 + \sigma_e^2
\end{aligned}
\tag{15.21}
$$

So far these error properties are the usual ones. Differences appear when we consider correlations between the error terms v_{it}. There are several correlations that can be considered.

1. The correlation between two individuals, i and j, at the same point in time, t. The covariance for this case is given by

$$
\begin{aligned}
\text{cov}(v_{it}, v_{jt}) = E(v_{it} v_{jt}) &= E[(u_i + e_{it})(u_j + e_{jt})] \\
&= E(u_i u_j) + E(u_i e_{jt}) + E(e_{it} u_j) + E(e_{it} e_{jt}) \\
&= 0 + 0 + 0 + 0 = 0
\end{aligned}
$$

2. The correlation between errors on the same individual (i) at different points in time, t and s. The covariance for this case is given by

$$
\begin{aligned}
\text{cov}(v_{it}, v_{is}) = E(v_{it} v_{is}) &= E[(u_i + e_{it})(u_i + e_{is})] \\
&= E(u_i^2) + E(u_i e_{is}) + E(e_{it} u_i) + E(e_{it} e_{is}) \\
&= \sigma_u^2 + 0 + 0 + 0 \\
&= \sigma_u^2
\end{aligned}
\tag{15.22}
$$

3. The correlation between errors for different individuals in different time periods. The covariance for this case is

$$
\begin{aligned}
\text{cov}(v_{it}, v_{js}) = E(v_{it}v_{js}) &= E\big[(u_i + e_{it})(u_j + e_{js})\big] \\
&= E(u_iu_j) + E(u_ie_{js}) + E(e_{it}u_j) + E(e_{it}e_{js}) \\
&= 0 + 0 + 0 + 0 = 0
\end{aligned}
$$

What we have shown is that the errors $v_{it} = u_i + e_{it}$ are correlated over time for a given individual, but are otherwise uncorrelated. This is the type of correlation we allowed for when using cluster-robust standard errors. The correlation is caused by the component u_i that is common to all time periods. It is constant over time and, in contrast to the AR(1) error model [Chapter 9.5.2a], it does not decline as the observations get further apart in time. It is given by

$$
\rho = \text{corr}(v_{it}, v_{is}) = \frac{\text{cov}(v_{it}, v_{is})}{\sqrt{\text{var}(v_{it})\text{var}(v_{is})}} = \frac{\sigma_u^2}{\sigma_u^2 + \sigma_e^2} \quad t \neq s \tag{15.23}
$$

The correlation equals the proportion of the variance in the total error term v_{it} that is attributable to the variance of the individual component u_i.

In terms of the notation introduced to explain the assumptions that motivate the use of cluster-robust standard errors

$$
\text{var}(v_{it}) = \psi_{tt} = \sigma_u^2 + \sigma_e^2 \quad \text{and} \quad \text{cov}(v_{it}, v_{is}) = \psi_{ts} = \sigma_u^2 \quad t \neq s
$$

The variance and correlation structure of the random effects model is a special case of the assumptions used for cluster-robust errors, where both the variance ψ_{tt} and the covariance ψ_{ts} are constant over time.

It is convenient to summarize the error term assumptions of the random effects model as follows:

$$
E(v_{it}) = 0 \quad \text{(zero mean)} \tag{15.24}
$$

$$
\text{var}(v_{it}) = \sigma_e^2 + \sigma_u^2 \quad \text{(homoskedasticity)} \tag{15.25}
$$

$$
\text{cov}(v_{it}, v_{is}) = \sigma_u^2 \quad \text{for } t \neq s \quad \text{(errors for individual } i \text{ are correlated)} \tag{15.26}
$$

$$
\text{cov}(v_{it}, v_{js}) = 0 \quad \text{for } i \neq j \quad \text{(errors for different individuals are uncorrelated)} \tag{15.27}
$$

$$
\text{cov}(e_{it}, x_{2it}) = 0, \quad \text{cov}(e_{it}, x_{3it}) = 0 \quad \text{(errors } e_{it} \text{ uncorrelated with } x\text{'s)} \tag{15.28}
$$

$$
\text{cov}(u_i, x_{2it}) = 0, \quad \text{cov}(u_i, x_{3it}) = 0 \quad \text{(random effects uncorrelated with } x\text{'s)} \tag{15.29}
$$

15.4.2 TESTING FOR RANDOM EFFECTS

The magnitude of the correlation ρ in (15.23) is an important feature of the random effects model. If $u_i = 0$ for every individual, then there are no individual differences and no heterogeneity to account for. In such a case the pooled linear regression model (15.1) is appropriate, and there is no need for either a fixed or a random effects model. We are assuming that the error component u_i has expectation zero, $E(u_i) = 0$. If, in addition, u_i has a variance of *zero*, then it is said to be a degenerate random variable; it is a constant with value equal to zero. In this case, if $\sigma_u^2 = 0$, then the correlation $\rho = 0$, and there is no random individual heterogeneity present in the data. We can test for the presence of heterogeneity by testing the null hypothesis $H_0 : \sigma_u^2 = 0$ against the alternative hypothesis $H_1 : \sigma_u^2 > 0$. If the null hypothesis is rejected, then we conclude that there are random individual differences among sample members, and that the random effects model is appropriate. On the other hand, if we fail to reject the null hypothesis, then we have no evidence to conclude that random effects are present.

The Lagrange multiplier (*LM*) principle for test construction is very convenient in this case, because *LM* tests require estimation of only the restricted model that assumes that the null hypothesis is true. If the null hypothesis is true, then $u_i = 0$ and the random effects model in (15.19) reduces to

$$y_{it} = \overline{\beta}_1 + \beta_2 x_{2it} + \beta_3 x_{3it} + e_{it}$$

The best estimator for this model is the least squares estimator. The test statistic is based on the least squares residuals

$$\hat{e}_{it} = y_{it} - \overline{b}_1 - b_2 x_{2it} - b_3 x_{3it}$$

The test statistic for balanced panels is

$$LM = \sqrt{\frac{NT}{2(T-1)}} \left\{ \frac{\sum\limits_{i=1}^{N} \left(\sum\limits_{t=1}^{T} \hat{e}_{it} \right)^2}{\sum\limits_{i=1}^{N} \sum\limits_{t=1}^{T} \hat{e}_{it}^2} - 1 \right\} \tag{15.30}$$

The numerator of the first term in curly brackets differs from the denominator because it contains terms like $2\hat{e}_{i1}\hat{e}_{i2} + 2\hat{e}_{i1}\hat{e}_{i3} + 2\hat{e}_{i2}\hat{e}_{i3} + \cdots$ whose sum will not be significantly different from zero if there is no correlation over time for each individual, and will reflect a positive correlation if there is one. If the sum of the cross-product terms is not significant, the first term in the curly brackets is not significantly different from one, and the term in the curly brackets is not significantly different from zero. If the sum of the cross-product terms is significant, then the first term in the curly brackets will be significantly greater than one, and *LM* will be positive.

If the null hypothesis $H_0 : \sigma_u^2 = 0$ is true, i.e., there are no random effects, then $LM \sim N(0, 1)$ in large samples. Thus, we reject H_0 at significance level α and accept the alternative $H_1 : \sigma_u^2 > 0$ if $LM > z_{(1-\alpha)}$, where $z_{(1-\alpha)}$ is the $100(1-\alpha)$ percentile of the standard normal $[N(0, 1)]$ distribution.[10] This critical value is 1.645 if $\alpha = 0.05$ and 2.326 if $\alpha = 0.01$. Rejecting the null hypothesis leads us to conclude that random effects are present.

----

[10] The original *LM* test due to Breusch and Pagan used LM^2 with the distribution under H_0 as $\chi_{(1)}^2$. Subsequent authors pointed out that the alternative hypothesis for using LM^2 is $H_1 : \sigma_u^2 \neq 0$, and that we can do better by using *LM* as a one-sided $N(0,1)$ test with alternative hypothesis $H_1 : \sigma_u^2 > 0$. Some software, for example Stata, reports LM^2. The danger from using LM^2 is that $LM < 0$ is possible and should not be taken as evidence that $\sigma_u^2 > 0$. The adjustment for a chi-square test at significance α is to use the $100(1 - 2\alpha)$ percentile of the χ^2-distribution. This critical value for an $\alpha = 0.05$ test is 2.706, which is equal to 1.645^2. It should only be used for $LM > 0$.

15.4.3 ESTIMATION OF THE RANDOM EFFECTS MODEL

The random effects model (15.19) has errors with zero expectation, and a constant variance $\sigma_v^2 = \sigma_u^2 + \sigma_e^2$. The complicating factor is a special type of serial correlation—the errors for each cross-sectional unit are intercorrelated with correlation $\rho = \sigma_u^2/(\sigma_u^2 + \sigma_e^2)$. Under these assumptions, the least squares estimator is unbiased and consistent, but not minimum variance. Also, the usual least squares standard errors are incorrect, but they can be "corrected" using cluster-robust standard errors.

The minimum variance estimator for the random effects model is a generalized least squares (GLS) estimator explicitly developed for the assumptions in (15.24)–(15.29). As was the case when we had heteroskedasticity or autocorrelation, we can obtain the generalized least squares estimator in the random effects model by applying least squares to a transformed model. The transformed model is

$$y_{it}^* = \bar{\beta}_1 x_{1it}^* + \beta_2 x_{2it}^* + \beta_3 x_{3it}^* + v_{it}^* \tag{15.31}$$

where the transformed variables are

$$y_{it}^* = y_{it} - \alpha \bar{y}_i, \quad x_{1it}^* = 1 - \alpha, \quad x_{2it}^* = x_{2it} - \alpha \bar{x}_{2i}, \quad x_{3it}^* = x_{3it} - \alpha \bar{x}_{3i} \tag{15.32}$$

The variables $\bar{y}_i$, $\bar{x}_{2i}$ and $\bar{x}_{3i}$ are the individual means defined in (15.12). The transformed error term is $v_{it}^* = v_{it} - \alpha \bar{v}_i$. The key transformation parameter α is defined as

$$\alpha = 1 - \frac{\sigma_e}{\sqrt{T\sigma_u^2 + \sigma_e^2}} \tag{15.33}$$

It can be shown that the v_{it}^* have constant variance σ_e^2 and are uncorrelated. The proof is long and tedious, so we will not inflict it on you.[11]

Because the transformation parameter α depends on the unknown variances σ_e^2 and σ_u^2, these variances need to be estimated before least squares can be applied to (15.31). Some details of how the estimates $\hat{\sigma}_e^2$ and $\hat{\sigma}_u^2$ are obtained can be found in Appendix 15B. Then, least squares is applied to (15.31) with σ_e^2 and σ_u^2 replaced by $\hat{\sigma}_e^2$ and $\hat{\sigma}_u^2$.

From (15.32) we can see that when $\alpha = 1$, the random effects estimator is identical to the fixed effects estimator. For $\alpha < 1$, it can be shown that the random effects estimator is a "matrix-weighted average" of the fixed effects estimator that utilizes only within-individual variation and a "between estimator" which utilizes variation between individuals.[12] Suppose that we are interested in the coefficients showing the effect of experience on wages. In contrast to the fixed effects estimator, the random effects estimator uses both variation in experience and wages over time for each individual, and variation in wages for individuals with different levels of experience.

15.4.4 RANDOM EFFECTS ESTIMATION OF THE WAGE EQUATION

Because the women in our microeconomic data panel were randomly selected from a larger population, it seems sensible to treat individual differences between the 716 women as

---

[11] The details can be found in *Econometric Analysis of Cross Section an Panel Data*, 2nd Edition, by Jeffrey Wooldridge (MIT Press, 2010), p. 326. This text is very advanced and presumes skill with matrix algebra.

[12] Advanced algebra is needed to study the details of this relationship. See, for example, Badi Baltagi (2008), *Econometric Analysis of Panel Data*, 4th edition, John Wiley and Sons, p. 20.

Table 15.9 **Random Effects Estimates of Wage Equation**

Variable	Coefficient	GLS Standard Errors[a]			Cluster-Robust Standard Errors[a]		
		Std. Error	t-value	p-value	Std. Error	t-value	p-value
C	0.53393	0.07988	6.68	0.000	0.08209	6.50	0.000
EDUC	0.07325	0.00533	13.74	0.000	0.00540	13.57	0.000
EXPER	0.04362	0.00636	6.86	0.000	0.00755	5.78	0.000
EXPER²	−0.00056	0.00026	−2.14	0.033	0.00031	−1.83	0.068
TENURE	0.01415	0.00317	4.47	0.000	0.00400	3.54	0.000
TENURE²	−0.00076	0.00019	−3.88	0.000	0.00024	−3.21	0.001
BLACK	−0.11674	0.03021	−3.86	0.000	0.02928	−3.99	0.000
SOUTH	−0.08181	0.02241	−3.65	0.000	0.02833	−2.89	0.004
UNION	0.08024	0.01321	6.07	0.000	0.01547	5.19	0.000

[a]Different software can give standard errors with very slight differences. Those reported are from Stata Version 11.0.

random effects. Recall that the wage equation has dependent variable ln(*WAGE*) and explanatory variables years of education (*EDUC*), total labor force experience (*EXPER*) and its square, tenure in current job (*TENURE*) and its square, and dummy variables *BLACK*, *SOUTH*, and *UNION*. Before carrying out random effects estimation, we test for the presence of random effects using the *LM* test statistic in (15.30). The value of the test statistic is *LM* = 62.1, which of course far exceeds a critical value from the $N(0,1)$ distribution for any reasonable significance level. We conclude that there is strong evidence of individual heterogeneity.

The random effects estimates are given in Table 15.9. Because the random effects estimator utilizes both between and within individual variation, we are able to estimate the effects of years of education and race on ln(*WAGE*). The problem of exact collinearity between these variables and individual dummy variables no longer exists. We estimate that the return to education is about 7.3%, and that blacks have wages about 12% lower than whites, everything else held constant. These effects are not estimable using the fixed effects approach which only utilizes within individual variation. Living in the South leads to wages about 8% lower, and union membership leads to wages about 8% higher, everything else held constant.

Two sets of standard errors, *t*-values and *p*-values are presented in Table 15.9—those using GLS standard errors calculated under the random effects assumptions in (15.24)–(15.29), and those using cluster-robust standard errors which relax assumptions about $\text{var}(v_{it})$ and $\text{cov}(v_{it}, v_{is})$. When we use cluster-robust standard errors in conjunction with pooled least squares or fixed effects estimation, we are replacing the assumptions $\text{var}(e_{it}) = \sigma_e^2$ and $\text{cov}(e_{it}, e_{is}) = 0$ for $t \neq s$ with the more general assumptions $\text{var}(e_{it}) = \psi_{tt}$ and $\text{cov}(e_{it}, e_{is}) = \psi_{ts}$ for $t \neq s$. The cluster-robust standard errors are valid in the presence of heteroskedasticity and correlation within individuals, although the estimators are no longer minimum variance under these circumstances. When we use cluster-robust standard errors with the random effects estimator, we are replacing the assumptions $\text{var}(v_{it}) = \sigma_e^2 + \sigma_u^2$ and $\text{cov}(v_{it}, v_{is}) = \sigma_u^2$ for $t \neq s$ with the more general assumptions $\text{var}(v_{it}) = \psi_{tt}$ and $\text{cov}(v_{it}, v_{is}) = \psi_{ts}$. We are allowing for the possible existence of heteroskedasticity and a less restrictive correlation structure. The random effects estimator will no longer be minimum variance under this less restrictive structure, but the cluster-robust standard errors will be valid. A comparison of the two sets of standard errors in Table 15.9 does not reveal any big differences. With the exception of that for *BLACK*, the cluster-robust standard errors are slightly larger. Similar inferences would be made about the coefficients with the possible exception of that for $TENURE^2$, which would no longer be significantly different from zero using a two-tail test and a 5% significance level.

As a final note, the estimates of the error components (their standard deviations) are $\hat{\sigma}_u = 0.3290$ and $\hat{\sigma}_e = 0.1951$. The estimated correlation in (15.23) is $\hat{\rho} = 0.74$. Thus a large fraction of the total error variance is attributable to individual heterogeneity. The estimate of the transformation parameter α is

$$\hat{\alpha} = 1 - \frac{\hat{\sigma}_e}{\sqrt{T\hat{\sigma}_u^2 + \hat{\sigma}_e^2}} = 1 - \frac{0.1951}{\sqrt{5 \times 0.1083 + 0.0381}} = 0.7437$$

Using this value to transform the data as in (15.32), then applying least squares to the transformed regression model in (15.31), yields the random effects estimates.

15.5 Comparing Fixed and Random Effects Estimators

We have two sets of estimates for the wage equation based on the NLS data. Naturally, we would like to know which one to use and report in our research report. If random effects are present, so that $\sigma_u^2 > 0$, and the assumptions in (15.24)–(15.29) hold, then the random effects estimator is preferred for several reasons. First, the random effects estimator takes into account the random sampling process by which the data were obtained. Second, the random effects estimator permits us to estimate the effects of variables that are individually time-invariant, such as race or gender, and in the NLS data, the years of education. Thirdly, the random effects estimator is a generalized least squares estimation procedure, and the fixed effects estimator is a least squares estimator. In large samples, the GLS estimator has a smaller variance than the least squares estimator.

The greater precision of the random effects estimator and its ability to estimate the effects of time invariant variables are related. As noted earlier, to estimate the effects of the explanatory variables on y, the fixed effects estimator only uses information from variation in the x's and y over time, for each individual. It does not use information on how changes in y across different individuals could be attributable to the different x-values for those individuals. These differences are not picked up by the fixed effects estimator. In contrast, the random effects estimator uses both sources of information.

15.5.1 ENDOGENEITY IN THE RANDOM EFFECTS MODEL

However, there is a potential problem when using random effects estimation, which has one critical assumption that is often violated. If the random error $v_{it} = u_i + e_{it}$ is correlated with any of the right-hand-side explanatory variables in a random effects model, then the least squares and GLS estimators of the parameters are biased and inconsistent. The problem of **endogenous regressors** was first considered in a general context in Chapter 10, where we considered the general problem of using regression analysis when explanatory variables are random. The problem arose again in Chapter 11, when we considered simultaneous equations models. The problem is common in random effects models, because the individual specific error component u_i may well be correlated with some of the explanatory variables. In the NLS wage equation example we considered in the previous section, think about the individual characteristics that are captured by the error component u_i. A person's ability, industriousness, and perseverance are variables not explicitly included in the wage equation, and thus these factors are included in u_i. These characteristics may well be correlated with a woman's years of education completed and her previous job market experience and job tenure. If this is the case, then the random effects estimator is inconsistent; it will attribute the effects of the error component to the included explanatory factors. The assumption $cov(u_i, x_{2it}) = 0$, $cov(u_i, x_{3it}) = 0$ given in (15.29) will be violated.

Another example may help reinforce the idea. Let us consider the problem of estimating a cost function for producing a particular output. Suppose we have a panel of data consisting of time series observations on outputs, costs, and inputs from various production facilities scattered across the country. Each plant has a manager, or management team, whose quality is not always directly measurable. If we estimate a cost function, with cost per unit as the dependent variable, and inputs (labor, materials, energy, etc.) as explanatory variables, then it is very possible that unmeasured managerial qualities, contained in u_i, will be correlated with the explanatory variables. More efficient, better managers may use fewer inputs to produce the same level of output. Such a correlation will cause the random effects estimator to be inconsistent.

15.5.2 The Fixed Effects Estimator in a Random Effects Model

In the panel data context a simple alternative to random effects exists that is consistent in the presence of a correlation between the random error component u_i and any of the explanatory variables x_{kit}. The fixed effects estimator is consistent even in the presence of such correlation. To see why, let us return to the derivation of the fixed effects estimator in Section 15.3.2. The panel data regression (15.19), including the error component u_i, is

$$y_{it} = \overline{\beta}_1 + \beta_2 x_{2it} + \beta_3 x_{3it} + (u_i + e_{it}) \tag{15.34}$$

The first step in fixed effects estimation is to average the panel observations for each individual over time,

$$\overline{y}_i = \frac{1}{T}\sum_{t=1}^{T} y_{it} = \overline{\beta}_1 + \beta_2 \frac{1}{T}\sum_{t=1}^{T} x_{2it} + \beta_3 \frac{1}{T}\sum_{t=1}^{T} x_{3it} + \frac{1}{T}\sum_{t=1}^{T} u_i + \frac{1}{T}\sum_{t=1}^{T} e_{it}$$

$$= \overline{\beta}_1 + \beta_2 \overline{x}_{2i} + \beta_3 \overline{x}_{3i} + u_i + \overline{e}_i \tag{15.35}$$

Subtracting (15.35) from (15.34), term by term, we have

$$y_{it} = \overline{\beta}_1 + \beta_2 x_{2it} + \beta_3 x_{3it} + u_i + e_{it}$$
$$\underline{-(\overline{y}_i = \overline{\beta}_1 + \beta_2 \overline{x}_{2i} + \beta_3 \overline{x}_{3i} + u_i + \overline{e}_i)} \tag{15.36}$$
$$y_{it} - \overline{y}_i = \beta_2(x_{2it} - \overline{x}_{2i}) + \beta_3(x_{3it} - \overline{x}_{3i}) + (e_{it} - \overline{e}_i)$$

which is exactly the same result as in (15.13). The fixed effects transformation, putting the data in deviation from the mean form, *eliminates* the random effect u_i as well as any other time-invariant factors. The least squares estimator of (15.14) is consistent, converging to the true values as $N \to \infty$, whether the random effect u_i is correlated with the regressors or not. In this sense, it is always safe to use the fixed effects estimator to estimate panel data models.

15.5.3 A Hausman Test

To check for any correlation between the error component u_i and the regressors in a random effects model, we can use a **Hausman test**. This test compares the coefficient estimates from the random effects model to those from the fixed effects model. The idea underlying the Hausman test is that both the random effects and fixed effects estimators are consistent if there is no correlation between u_i and the explanatory variables x_{kit}. If both estimators are consistent, then they should converge to the true parameter values β_k in large samples. That is, in large samples, the random effects and fixed effects estimates should be similar. On the other hand, if u_i is correlated with any x_{kit}, the random effects estimator is inconsistent, while the fixed effects estimator remains consistent. Thus, in large samples the fixed effects estimator converges to the true parameter values, but the random effects estimator converges to some other value that is not the value of the true parameters. In this case, we expect to see differences between the fixed and random effects estimates.

Examine the fixed effects and random effects estimates in Tables 15.7 and Table 15.9. Recall that the fixed effects estimator is unable to estimate coefficients on time-invariant variables like *BLACK* and, in the NLS data, *EDUC*. Except for the coefficients on *SOUTH*, the estimates do not seem very different, but as we have learned many times, casual inspection of the values is not a statistical test. The Hausman test in this context can be carried out for specific coefficients, using a t-test, or jointly, using an F-test or a chi-square test. Let us consider the t-test first. Let the parameter of interest be β_k; denote the fixed effects estimate as $b_{FE,k}$ and the random effects estimate as $b_{RE,k}$. Then the t-statistic for testing that there is no difference between the estimators is

$$t = \frac{b_{FE,k} - b_{RE,k}}{\left[\widehat{\mathrm{var}(b_{FE,k})} - \widehat{\mathrm{var}(b_{RE,k})}\right]^{1/2}} = \frac{b_{FE,k} - b_{RE,k}}{\left[\mathrm{se}(b_{FE,k})^2 - \mathrm{se}(b_{RE,k})^2\right]^{1/2}} \tag{15.37}$$

In this t-statistic it is important that the denominator is the estimated variance of the fixed effects estimator minus the estimated variance of the random effects estimator. The reason is that under the null hypothesis that u_i is uncorrelated with any of the explanatory variables, the random effects estimator will have a smaller variance than the fixed effects estimator, at least in large samples. Consequently, we expect to find $\widehat{\mathrm{var}(b_{FE,k})} - \widehat{\mathrm{var}(b_{RE,k})} > 0$, which is necessary for a valid test. A second interesting feature of this test statistic is that

$$\mathrm{var}(b_{FE,k} - b_{RE,k}) = \mathrm{var}(b_{FE,k}) + \mathrm{var}(b_{RE,k}) - 2\mathrm{cov}(b_{FE,k}, b_{RE,k})$$
$$= \mathrm{var}(b_{FE,k}) - \mathrm{var}(b_{RE,k})$$

The unexpected result in the last line occurs because Hausman proved that in this particular case, $\mathrm{cov}(b_{FE,k}, b_{RE,k}) = \mathrm{var}(b_{RE,k})$.

Let us apply the t-test to the coefficients of *SOUTH* in Tables 15.7 and 15.9. Using the conventional (not robust) standard errors, the test statistic value is

$$t = \frac{b_{FE,k} - b_{RE,k}}{\left[\mathrm{se}(b_{FE,k})^2 - \mathrm{se}(b_{RE,k})^2\right]^{1/2}} = \frac{-0.01632 - (-0.08181)}{\left[(0.03615)^2 - (0.02241)^2\right]^{1/2}} = 2.31$$

Using the standard 5% large sample critical value of 1.96, we reject the hypothesis that the estimators yield identical results. Our conclusion is that the random effects estimator is inconsistent, and that we should use the fixed effects estimator, or should attempt to improve the model specification. The null hypothesis will be rejected for any reason that makes the two sets of estimates differ, including a misspecified model. There may be nonlinearities in the relationship we have not captured with our model, and other explanatory variables may be relevant. The p-value of the test is 0.021. Thus, if we had chosen the 1% level of significance, we would have not rejected the null hypothesis.

More commonly, the Hausman test is automated by software packages to contrast the complete set of common estimates. That is, we carry out a test of a joint hypothesis comparing all the coefficients in Table 15.7, except the intercept, to the corresponding estimates in Table 15.9. If there is no correlation between the error component u_i and the values of x_{kit}, then the six variables common to the two tables (*EXPER, EXPER*^{2}, *TENURE, TENURE*^{2}, *SOUTH*, and *UNION*) will have coefficient estimates with similar magnitudes. The Hausman contrast[13] test jointly checks how close the differences between the pairs of coefficients are to zero. The calculated value of this chi-square statistic is 20.73. We are comparing the values of six coefficients, and the test statistic has an asymptotic chi-square distribution with six degrees of freedom. The 5% critical value for this distribution is 12.592, and the 1% critical value is 16.812. On the basis of the joint test, we reject the null hypothesis that the difference between the estimators is zero even at the 1% level of significance. Again this implies that we should use the fixed effects estimator in this case, or revisit the specification of our model.

The form of the Hausman test in (15.37) and its χ^2 equivalent are not valid for cluster-robust standard errors, because under these more general assumptions, it is no longer true that $\text{var}\left(b_{FE,k} - b_{RE,k}\right) = \text{var}\left(b_{FE,k}\right) - \text{var}\left(b_{RE,k}\right)$.

15.6 The Hausman–Taylor Estimator

The outcome from our comparison of the fixed and random effects estimates of the wage equation poses a dilemma. Correlation between the explanatory variables and the random effects means that the random effects estimator will be inconsistent. We can overcome the inconsistency problem by using the fixed effects estimator, but doing so means that we can no longer estimate the effects of the time invariant variables *EDUC* and *BLACK*. The wage return to an extra year of education, and whether or not there is wage discrimination on the basis of race, might be two important questions that we would like to answer.

To solve this dilemma we ask: How did we cope with the endogeneity problem in Chapter 10? We did so by using instrumental variable estimation. Variables known as "instruments," which are correlated with the endogenous variables but uncorrelated with the equation error, were introduced, leading to an instrumental variables estimator that has the desirable property of consistency. The **Hausman-Taylor estimator** is an instrumental variables estimator applied to the random effects model to overcome the problem of inconsistency caused by correlation between the random effects and some of the explanatory variables. To explain how it works consider the regression model

$$y_{it} = \beta_1 + \beta_2 x_{it,exog} + \beta_3 x_{it,endog} + \beta_4 w_{i,exog} + \beta_5 w_{i,endog} + u_i + e_{it} \tag{15.38}$$

We have divided the explanatory variables into four categories:

$x_{it,exog}$: exogenous variables that vary over time and individuals

$x_{it,endog}$: endogenous variables that vary over time and individuals

$w_{i,exog}$: time-invariant exogenous variables

$w_{i,endog}$: time-invariant endogenous variables

---

[13] Details of the joint test are beyond the scope of this book. For a very advanced reference that contains a careful exposition of the *t*-test, the chi-square test, and a regression-based alternative that may be preferable, see *Econometric Analysis of Cross Section and Panel Data,* 2nd Edition, by Jeffrey Wooldridge (MIT, 2010), p. 328.

Equation (15.38) is written as if there is one variable of each type, but in practice there could be more than one. For the Hausman-Taylor estimator to work the number of exogenous time-varying variables $(x_{it,exog})$ must be at least as great as the number of endogenous time-invariant variables $(w_{i,endog})$.

For the wage equation we will make the following assumptions

$$x_{it,exog} = \{EXPER,\ EXPER^2,\ TENURE,\ TENURE^2,\ UNION\}$$
$$x_{it,endog} = \{SOUTH\}$$
$$w_{i,exog} = \{BLACK\}$$
$$w_{i,endog} = \{EDUC\}$$

The variable *EDUC* is chosen as an endogenous variable on the grounds that it will be correlated with personal attributes such as ability and perseverance. It is less clear why *SOUTH* should be endogenous, but we include it as endogenous because its fixed and random effects estimates were vastly different. Perhaps those living in the South have special attributes. The remaining variables—experience, tenure, *UNION*, and *BLACK*—are assumed uncorrelated with the random effects.

Following Chapter 10, we need instruments for $x_{it,endog}$ and $w_{i,endog}$. Since the fixed effects transformation $\tilde{x}_{it,endog} = x_{it,endog} - \bar{x}_{i,endog}$ eliminates correlation with u_i, we have $\tilde{x}_{it,endog}$ as a suitable instrument for $x_{it,endog}$. Also, the variables $\bar{x}_{i,exog}$ are suitable instruments for $w_{i,endog}$. The exogenous variables in (15.38) can be viewed as instruments for themselves, making the complete instrument set $x_{it,exog},\ \tilde{x}_{it,endog},\ w_{i,exog},\ \bar{x}_{i,exog}$. Hausman and Taylor modify this set slightly using $\tilde{x}_{it,exog},\ \tilde{x}_{it,endog},\ w_{i,exog},\ \bar{x}_{i,exog}$ which can be shown to yield the same results. Their estimator is applied to the transformed generalized least squares model from (15.31)

$$y_{it}^* = \beta_1 + \beta_2 x_{it,exog}^* + \beta_3 x_{it,endog}^* + \beta_4 w_{i,exog}^* + \beta_5 w_{i,endog}^* + v_{it}^* \qquad (15.39)$$

where, for example, $y_{it}^* = y_{it} - \hat{\alpha}\bar{y}_i$, and $\hat{\alpha} = 1 - \hat{\sigma}_e / \sqrt{T\hat{\sigma}_u^2 + \hat{\sigma}_e^2}$. The estimate $\hat{\sigma}_e^2$ is obtained from fixed-effects residuals; an auxiliary instrumental variables regression[14] is needed to find $\hat{\sigma}_u^2$.

Estimates for the wage equation are presented in Table 15.10. Compared to the random effects estimates, there has been a dramatic increase in the estimated wage returns to education from 7.3% to 17%. The estimated effects for experience and tenure are similar. The wage reduction for *BLACK* is estimated as 3.6% rather than 11.7%, and the penalty for being in the *SOUTH* is also less, 3.1% instead of 8.2%. The instrumental-variable standard errors are mostly larger, particularly for *EDUC* and *BLACK* where the biggest changes in estimates have been observed. Which set of estimates is better will depend on how successful we have been at making the partition into exogenous and endogenous variables in (15.38), and whether the gain from having consistent estimates is sufficiently large to compensate for the increased variance of the instrumental variables estimators.

15.7 Sets of Regression Equations

So far in this chapter, we have considered methods for estimating panel data models when the panel is short and wide: N is large and T is small. We now turn to a model and estimation

---

[14] Details can be found in the advanced book, Jeffrey Wooldridge (2010), *Econometric Analysis of Cross-Section and Panel Data*, 2nd Edition, MIT Press, pp. 358–361.

Table 15.10 **Hausman–Taylor Estimates of Wage Equation**

Variable	Coefficient	Std. Error	*t*-value	*p*-value
C	−0.75077	0.58624	−1.28	0.200
$EDUC$	0.17051	0.04446	3.83	0.000
$EXPER$	0.03991	0.00647	6.16	0.000
$EXPER^2$	−0.00039	0.00027	−1.46	0.144
$TENURE$	0.01433	0.00316	4.53	0.000
$TENURE^2$	−0.00085	0.00020	−4.32	0.000
$BLACK$	−0.03591	0.06007	−0.60	0.550
$SOUTH$	−0.03171	0.03485	−0.91	0.363
$UNION$	0.07197	0.01345	5.35	0.000

procedures for a panel that is long and narrow: T is large relative to N. If the number of time-series observations is sufficiently large, and N is small, we can estimate separate equations for each individual. These separate equations can be specified as

$$y_{it} = \beta_{1i} + \beta_{2i}x_{2it} + \beta_{3i}x_{3it} + e_{it} \tag{15.40}$$

The i subscript on the β's means that they can be different for each individual. Thus, this model can be used to represent N different equations, one for each individual. There are T observations on each of the N equations. For the short and wide panel considered in earlier sections, T was not sufficiently large to estimate separate equations for each individual. We assumed $\beta_{2i} = \beta_2$ and $\beta_{3i} = \beta_3$; the slope coefficients were the same for all individuals, but the intercept β_{1i} was allowed to vary.

15.7.1 GRUNFELD'S INVESTMENT DATA

The example we use for this section is an old but very famous one. The factors affecting the investment behavior by firms was studied by Grunfeld[15] using a panel of data. His example and data, which is simply referred to in the literature as "the Grunfeld data," have been used many times to illustrate the issues involved in modeling panel data.

Investment demand is the purchase of durable goods by both households and firms. In terms of total spending, investment spending is the volatile component. Therefore, understanding what determines investment is crucial to understanding the sources of fluctuations in aggregate demand. In addition, a firm's net fixed investment, which is the flow of additions to capital stock or replacements for worn-out capital, is important because it determines the future value of the capital stock and thus affects future labor productivity and aggregate supply.

There are several interesting and elaborate theories that seek to describe the determinants of the investment process for the firm. Most of these theories evolve to the conclusion that perceived profit opportunities (expected profits or present discounted value of future

---

[15] Grunfeld, Y. (1958) *The Determinants of Corporate Investment.* Unpublished Ph.D. thesis, Department of Economics, University of Chicago. Grunfeld, Y. and Z. Griliches (1960) "Is Aggregation Necessarily Bad?" *Review of Economics and Statistics*, 42, 1–13.

earnings) and desired capital stock are two important determinants of a firm's fixed business investment. Unfortunately, neither of these variables are directly observable. Therefore, in formulating our economic model, we use observable proxies for these variables instead.

In terms of expected profits, one alternative is to identify the present discounted value of future earnings as the market value of the firm's securities. The price of a firm's stock represents and contains information about these expected profits. Consequently, the stock market value of the firm at the beginning of the year, denoted for firm i in time period t as V_{it}, may be used as a proxy for expected profits.

In terms of desired capital stock, expectations play a definite role. To catch these expectations effects, one possibility is to use a model that recognizes that actual capital stock in any period is the sum of a large number of past desired capital stocks. Thus, we use the beginning of the year actual capital stock, denoted for the ith firm as K_{it}, as a proxy for permanent desired capital stock.

Focusing on these explanatory variables, an economic model for describing gross firm investment for the ith firm in the tth time period, denoted INV_{it}, may be expressed as

$$INV_{it} = f(V_{it}, K_{it}) \tag{15.41}$$

Our concern is how we might take this general economic model and specify an econometric model that adequately represents a panel of real-world data. The data (see *grunfeld11.dat*) consist of $T = 20$ years of data (1935–1954) for $N = 11$ large firms.[16] For expository purposes we will consider only two firms at this point, General Electric and Westinghouse, and we will specify the cross-sectional indicator i to be either *GE* or *WE*. These two firms are similar in the range of products they offer, which includes everything from home appliances to light bulbs. Their observations are stored in the file *grunfeld2.dat*.

In line with (15.40) and (15.41), we specify the following two equations for General Electric and Westinghouse.

$$\begin{aligned}
INV_{GE,t} &= \beta_{1,GE} + \beta_{2,GE}V_{GE,t} + \beta_{3,GE}K_{GE,t} + e_{GE,t} && t = 1935, \ldots, 1954 \\
INV_{WE,t} &= \beta_{1,WE} + \beta_{2,WE}V_{WE,t} + \beta_{3,WE}K_{WE,t} + e_{WE,t} && t = 1935, \ldots, 1954
\end{aligned} \tag{15.42}$$

We will consider various ways of estimating these two investment equations. The choice of estimator depends on what assumptions we make about the coefficients and the error terms. Specifically,

1. Are the *GE* coefficients equal to the *WE* coefficients?

2. Do the equation errors $e_{GE,t}$ and $e_{WE,t}$ have the same variance?

3. Are the equation errors $e_{GE,t}$ and $e_{WE,t}$ correlated?

---

[16] The long history of use of this data is well documented by Kleiber and Zeileis (2010), "The Grunfeld Data at 50," *German Economic Review*, forthcoming. See also http://statmath.wu-wien.ac.at/~zeileis/grunfeld/. They point out a number of errors and inconsistencies that have crept into the data, leading to a number of incorrect versions that have been propagated over time. The file *grunfeld11.dat* is the corrected version kindly supplied by Kleiber and Zeileis. It differs from the earlier version *grunfeld.dat* used in the 3rd edition of this textbook.

Table 15.11 **Pooled Least Squares Estimates of Investment Equations**

Variable	Coefficient	Std. Error	t-value	p-value
C	17.8720	7.0241	2.54	0.015
V	0.0152	0.0062	2.45	0.019
K	0.1436	0.0186	7.72	0.000

$SSE = 16563.00 \quad \hat{\sigma}^2 = 447.65$

15.7.2 ESTIMATION: EQUAL COEFFICIENTS, EQUAL ERROR VARIANCES

The assumption that both firms have the same coefficients and the same error variances can be written as

$$\beta_{1,GE} = \beta_{1,WE} \quad \beta_{2,GE} = \beta_{2,WE} \quad \beta_{3,GE} = \beta_{3,WE} \quad \sigma_{GE}^2 = \sigma_{WE}^2 \tag{15.43}$$

where $\text{var}(e_{GE,t}) = \sigma_{GE}^2$ and $\text{var}(e_{WE,t}) = \sigma_{WE}^2$ denote the two error variances. If, in addition, we assume the errors are uncorrelated, both over time for each firm and between firms, pooled least squares as discussed in Section 15.2 is a suitable estimation technique. No distinction is made between the observations from the two firms. The pooled least squares estimates, standard errors, and t- and p-values are given in Table 15.11. The coefficients of V and K have their expected signs and, under the assumption of equal variances and uncorrelated errors, are significantly different from zero at a 5% level of significance. The standard errors are the conventional ones. We will say more about cluster error variances shortly, noting at this point that the cluster-robust standard errors described in Section 15.2 are not suitable in this case where N is small.

15.7.3 ESTIMATION: DIFFERENT COEFFICIENTS, EQUAL ERROR VARIANCES

If we relax the assumption that both firms have the same coefficients, but retain the assumption that the error variances are the same, then the two equations in (15.42) can be combined using the indicator (dummy) variable format described in Sections 7.1.2 and 7.2.3. Let D_i be an indicator variable equal to one for the Westinghouse observations and zero for the General Electric observations. Specify a model with slope and intercept indicator variables,

$$INV_{it} = \beta_{1,GE} + \delta_1 D_i + \beta_{2,GE} V_{it} + \delta_2 (D_i \times V_{it}) + \beta_{3,GE} K_{it} + \delta_3 (D_i \times K_{it}) + e_{it} \tag{15.44}$$

Equation (15.44) represents a pooled set of 40 observations, and as we learned in Section 7.2.3, it is just another way of writing (15.42) where $\beta_{1,WE} = \beta_{1,GE} + \delta_1$, $\beta_{2,WE} = \beta_{2,GE} + \delta_2$, and $\beta_{3,WE} = \beta_{3,GE} + \delta_3$. The least squares estimates from (15.44) will be identical to the least squares estimates obtained by estimating the two equations in (15.42) separately, although, as we will see, the standard errors will be different. In Table 15.12 we report the dummy variable model estimates.

The small t-values and large p-values on the coefficients for D, $D \times V$ and $D \times K$ suggest that the null hypothesis $H_0 : \delta_1 = 0$, $\delta_2 = 0$, $\delta_3 = 0$ may not be rejected, in which case we do not have evidence to suggest that General Electric's coefficients differ from those of Westinghouse. However, as we discovered in Chapter 6, this hypothesis should be tested using a joint F-test rather than separate t-tests. For this purpose we have $SSE_R = 16563.00$

Table 15.12   **Least Squares Estimates from the Dummy Variable Model**

Variable	Coefficient	Std. Error	t-value	p-value
C	−9.9563	23.6264	−0.42	0.676
D	9.4469	28.8054	0.33	0.745
V	0.0266	0.0117	2.27	0.030
$D \times V$	0.0263	0.0344	0.77	0.448
K	0.1517	0.0194	7.84	0.000
$D \times K$	−0.0593	0.1169	−0.51	0.615

$SSE = 14989.82$ $\hat{\sigma}^2 = 440.877$

from Table 15.11, $SSE_U = 14989.82$ from Table 15.12, and, using the Chow test described in Chapter 7,

$$F = \frac{(SSE_R - SSE_U)/J}{SSE_U/(NT - NK)} = \frac{(16563.00 - 14989.82)/3}{14989.82/(40 - 6)} = 1.189 \qquad (15.45)$$

where $NT - NK$ is the total number of degrees of freedom in the unrestricted model. The p-value for an $F_{(3,34)}$-distribution is 0.328, implying that the null hypothesis of equal coefficients cannot be rejected.

A word of warning is in order at this point. Any t and F-tests performed using the results in Table 15.12 are only valid if the error variances of the two equations are the same and the errors are uncorrelated over time and over the two firms. This result is similar to the consequences of using least squares when the errors are heteroskedastic or autocorrelated. If robust standard errors are not used, hypothesis tests and interval estimates will not be valid. In the next two subsections, we relax, in turn, the assumption of equal variances and the assumption of uncorrelated errors, after which we reconsider the test for equality of coefficients for General Electric and Westinghouse.[17]

15.7.4 ESTIMATION: DIFFERENT COEFFICIENTS, DIFFERENT ERROR VARIANCES

When both the coefficients and the error variances of the two equations differ, and in the absence of contemporaneous correlation that we introduce in the next section, there is no connection between the two equations, and the best we can do is apply least squares to each equation separately. These results are reported in Table 15.13.

Note that the estimates of $\beta_{k,GE}$, $k = 1, 2, 3$ in Table 15.13 are identical to those in Table 15.12, and the estimates of $\beta_{k,WE}$, $k = 1, 2, 3$ in Table 15.13 are given by the estimates of $\beta_{k,GE} + \delta_k$, $k = 1, 2, 3$ in Table 15.12. However, their standard errors are different, a consequence of the fact that the two separate regressions in Table 15.13 allow the variances of the error terms to differ for the two firms, whereas the dummy variable regression in Table 15.12 assumes that the variance of the error term is constant across all 40 observations.

The large difference in the estimates of the error variances in Table 15.13 suggests that the assumption of different error variances is more realistic. We can use the Goldfeld-Quandt test (Chapter 8.2.3) to test the null hypothesis $H_0 : \sigma^2_{GE} = \sigma^2_{WE}$, which we reject at

---

[17] We are omitting the case where the two equations have identical coefficients and different error variances. Details for this case are given in Section 8.4.2.

Table 15.13   **Least Squares Estimates of Separate Investment Equations**

Equation	Variable	Coefficient	Std. Error	t-value	p-value
	C	-9.9563	31.3743	-0.32	0.755
GE	V	0.0266	0.0156	1.71	0.106
	K	0.1517	0.0257	5.90	0.000
	$SSE = 13216.59$		$\hat{\sigma}_{GE}^2 = 777.446$		
	C	-0.5094	8.0153	-0.06	0.950
WE	V	0.0529	0.0157	3.37	0.004
	K	0.0924	0.0561	1.65	0.118
	$SSE = 1773.23$		$\hat{\sigma}_{WE}^2 = 104.308$		

the $\alpha = 0.05$ level of significance ($F = 7.45$, $F_{(0.975, 37, 37)} = 1.92$), leading us to prefer the results in Table 15.13.

15.7.5 SEEMINGLY UNRELATED REGRESSIONS

In the previous section the two investment equations appeared unrelated. They had different coefficients and different error variances, and we estimated them separately. If, in addition, the errors in one equation are uncorrelated with the errors in the other equation, we do indeed have nothing to link the two equations together. Combining the data from the two firms brings no gains. In this section we introduce an assumption about the correlation between the General Electric errors and the Westinghouse errors. This link makes it possible to utilize a joint estimation procedure that is better than separate least squares estimation. The assumption is

$$\text{cov}\left(e_{GE,t}, e_{WE,t}\right) = \sigma_{GE,WE} \quad \sigma_{GE,WE} \neq 0 \tag{15.46}$$

The error terms in the two equations, at the same point in time, are correlated. This kind of correlation is called **contemporaneous correlation**. To understand why $e_{GE,t}$ and $e_{WE,t}$ might be correlated, recall that these errors contain the influence on investment of factors that have been omitted from the equations. Such factors might include capacity utilization, current and past interest rates, liquidity, and the general state of the economy. Since the two firms are similar in many respects, it is likely that the effects of the omitted factors on investment by General Electric will be similar to their effect on investment by Westinghouse. If so, then $e_{GE,t}$ and $e_{WE,t}$ will be capturing similar effects and will be correlated. Adding the contemporaneous correlation assumption (15.46) has the effect of introducing additional information that is not included when we carry out separate least squares estimation of the two equations.

The dummy-variable model (15.44) represents a way to "stack" the 40 observations for the GE and WE equations into one regression. Allowing for the variances of the error terms for the two firms to differ, $\sigma_{GE}^2 \neq \sigma_{WE}^2$, means that the error term e_{it} in the dummy-variable model in (15.44) will be heteroskedastic; it will have variance σ_{GE}^2 when $i = GE$ and variance σ_{WE}^2 when $i = WE$. What happens if we also add the contemporaneous correlation assumption in (15.46)? It means that all 40 errors will not be uncorrelated. We continue to assume that the errors are not serially correlated over time. In other words, the 20 General Electric errors are uncorrelated with each other, and the 20 Westinghouse errors are uncorrelated with each other. However, the first Westinghouse error will be correlated with the first General Electric error, the second Westinghouse error will be correlated with the second General Electric error, and so on. This information cannot be utilized when the equations are estimated separately, but it can be utilized to produce better estimates when the equations are jointly estimated as they are in the dummy variable model.

To improve the precision of the dummy variable model estimates, we use **seemingly unrelated regressions** (SUR) estimation, which is a generalized least squares estimation procedure. It estimates the two investment equations jointly, accounting for the fact that the variances of the error terms are different for the two equations *and* accounting for the contemporaneous correlation between the errors of the *GE* and *WE* equations. There are three stages in the SUR estimation procedure.

1. Estimate the equations separately using least squares.

2. Use the least squares residuals from step (1) to estimate σ^2_{GE}, σ^2_{WE} and $\sigma_{GE,WE}$. The estimates $\hat{\sigma}^2_{GE} = 777.446$ and $\hat{\sigma}^2_{WE} = 104.308$ are given by the usual variance estimates from each equation. The estimated covariance is given by

$$\hat{\sigma}_{GE,WE} = \frac{1}{\sqrt{T - K_{GE}}\sqrt{T - K_{WE}}} \sum_{t=1}^{20} \hat{e}_{GE,t}\hat{e}_{WE,t} = \frac{1}{T-3} \sum_{t=1}^{20} \hat{e}_{GE,t}\hat{e}_{WE,t}$$

$$= 207.587$$

where K_{GE} and K_{WE} are the numbers of parameters in the *GE* and *WE* equations, respectively. The reason for the odd-looking divisor is that in seemingly unrelated regressions the number of variables in each equation might be different, and this is one way to correct for the number of parameters estimated. In this case $K_{GE} = K_{WE} = 3$.

3. Use the estimates from step (2) to estimate the two equations jointly within a generalized least squares framework.[18]

Econometric software includes commands for SUR (or SURE) that automatically perform all three steps.

More insights into the contemporaneous correlation assumption and the estimation procedure can be obtained by recalling the assumption we used earlier when computing cluster-robust standard errors. In earlier parts of this chapter, each individual was treated as a cluster of time-series observations that were correlated within clusters. With the contemporaneous correlation assumption, each time period represents a cluster of observations on individuals (firms). Again, the observations are correlated within clusters. Another difference is that previously, within-cluster correlation was used to correct standard errors for estimation procedures that were optimal under error assumptions more restrictive than those used to get the standard errors. The SUR estimation procedure is optimal under the contemporaneous correlation assumption, so no standard error adjustment is necessary.

Estimates of the coefficients of the two investment functions are presented in Table 15.14. Since the SUR technique utilizes the information on the correlation between the error terms, it is more precise than the least squares estimation procedure. This fact is supported by the standard errors of the SUR estimates in Table 15.14 that are lower than those of the

---

[18] For details, see William E. Griffiths, R. Carter Hill and George G. Judge (1993) *Learning and Practicing Econometrics* Wiley, Chapter 17. A more advanced reference is William Greene (2008) *Econometric Analysis*, 6th edition, Pearson Prentice Hall, Chapter 10.

Table 15.14 **SUR Estimates of Investment Equations**

Equation	Variable	Coefficient	Std. Error	t-values	p-values
	C	−27.7193	29.3212	−0.95	0.351
GE	V	0.0383	0.0144	2.66	0.012
	K	0.1390	0.0250	5.56	0.000
	C	−1.2520	7.5452	−0.17	0.869
WE	V	0.0576	0.0145	3.96	0.000
	K	0.0640	0.0530	1.21	0.236

Note: p-values computed from $t_{(34)}$ distribution.

least squares estimates in Table 15.13.[19] You should be cautious, however, when making judgments about precision on the basis of standard errors. Standard errors are themselves estimates; it is possible for a standard error for SUR to be greater than a corresponding least squares standard error even when SUR is a better estimator than least squares. From an economic standpoint our estimated coefficients for the capital stock and value variables have the expected positive signs. Also, all are significantly different from zero except for the coefficient of capital stock in the Westinghouse equation. This coefficient has a low t value and hence is estimated with limited precision.

Equations that exhibit contemporaneous correlation were called "seemingly unrelated" by University of Chicago econometrician Arnold Zellner when he developed the SUR estimation procedure. The equations seem to be unrelated, but the additional information provided by the correlation between the equation errors means that joint generalized least squares estimation is better than single-equation least squares estimation.

15.7.5a Separate or Joint Estimation?

Is it always better to estimate two or more equations jointly, or are there circumstances when it is just as good to estimate each equation separately?

There are two situations in which separate least squares estimation is just as good as the SUR technique. The first of these cases is when the equation errors are not contemporaneously correlated. If the errors are not contemporaneously correlated, there is nothing linking the two equations, and separate estimation cannot be improved upon.

The second situation is less obvious. Indeed, some advanced algebra is needed to prove that least squares and SUR give *identical* estimates when the same explanatory variables appear in each equation. By the "same explanatory variables," we mean more than variables with similar definitions, like the value and capital stock variables for General Electric and Westinghouse. We mean the same variables with the same observations on those variables. For example, suppose we are interested in estimating demand equations for beef, chicken, and pork. Since these commodities are all substitutes, it is reasonable to specify the quantity demanded for each as a function of the price of beef, the price of chicken, and the price of pork, as well as income. The same variables with the same observations appear in all three equations. Even if the errors of these equations are correlated, as is quite likely, the use of SUR will not yield an improvement over separate estimation.

If the explanatory variables in each equation are different, then a test to see if the correlation between the errors is significantly different from zero is of interest. If a null hypothesis of zero correlation is not rejected, then there is no evidence to suggest that SUR

---

[19] Note that we do not compare the SUR estimates to those in Table 15.12, because the latter incorporate the assumption that the two error variances are equal, a hypothesis that we have rejected.

will improve on separate least squares estimation. To carry out such a test we compute the squared correlation

$$r^2_{GE,WE} = \frac{\hat{\sigma}^2_{GE,WE}}{\hat{\sigma}^2_{GE}\hat{\sigma}^2_{WE}} = \frac{(207.5871)^2}{(777.4463)(104.3079)} = 0.5314$$

The correlation $r_{GE,WE} = 0.729$ (the square root of 0.5314) indicates a strong contemporaneous correlation between errors of the General Electric and Westinghouse investment equations. To check the statistical significance of $r^2_{GE,WE}$, we can test the null hypothesis $H_0 : \sigma_{GE,WE} = 0$. If $\sigma_{GE,WE} = 0$, then $LM = T \times r^2_{GE,WE}$ is a Lagrange Multiplier test statistic that is distributed as a $\chi^2_{(1)}$ random variable in large samples. The 5% critical value of a χ^2-distribution with one degree of freedom is 3.841. The value of the test statistic from our data is $LM = 10.628$. Hence we reject the null hypothesis of no correlation between $e_{GE,t}$ and $e_{WE,t}$, and conclude that there are potential efficiency gains from estimating the two investment equations jointly using SUR.

If we are testing for the existence of correlated errors for more than two equations, the relevant test statistic is equal to T times the sum of squares of all the correlations; the probability distribution under H_0 is a χ^2-distribution with degrees of freedom equal to the number of correlations. For example, with three equations, denoted by subscripts 1, 2 and 3, the null hypothesis is

$$H_0 : \sigma_{12} = \sigma_{13} = \sigma_{23} = 0$$

and the $\chi^2_{(3)}$ test statistic is

$$LM = T\left(r^2_{12} + r^2_{13} + r^2_{23}\right)$$

In the general case of an SUR system with M equations, the statistic becomes

$$LM = T \sum_{i=2}^{M} \sum_{j=1}^{i-1} r^2_{ij}$$

Under the null hypothesis that there are no contemporaneous correlations, this LM statistic has a χ^2-distribution with $M(M - 1)/2$ degrees of freedom, in large samples.

There are many economic problems where we have cause to consider a system of equations. The investment function example was one; estimation of demand functions, like the meat demand functions we alluded to in this section, is another. Further examples are given in the exercises.

15.7.5b   Testing Cross-Equation Hypotheses

In Section 15.7.4 we used the dummy variable model and the Chow test originally discussed in Chapter 7 to test whether the two equations had identical coefficients. That is,

$$H_0 : \beta_{1,GE} = \beta_{1,WE} \quad \beta_{2,GE} = \beta_{2,WE} \quad \beta_{3,GE} = \beta_{3,WE} \tag{15.47}$$

We did not reject H_0, but we issued a caution about this conclusion since the dummy variable model ignored the presence of heteroskedastcity and contemporaneous correlation. It is also possible to test hypotheses such as (15.47) when the more general error assumptions of the SUR model are relevant. Because of the complicated nature of the model, the test statistic can no longer be calculated simply as an F-test statistic based on residuals from restricted and unrestricted models. Most econometric software will perform an F-test and/or a Wald

χ^2-test in a multi-equation framework such as we have here. In the context of SUR equations both tests are large sample approximate tests. The F-statistic has J numerator degrees of freedom and $(MT - K)$ denominator degrees of freedom, where J is the number of hypotheses, M is the number of equations, K is the total number of coefficients in the whole system, and T is the number of time series observations per equation. The χ^2-statistic has J degrees of freedom. For our particular example, we find that $F = 2.92$ with a p-value of 0.0479, using the $F_{(3,34)}$-distribution. The chi-square test statistic is $\chi^2 = 8.77$ with a p-value of 0.0326, using the $\chi^2_{(3)}$-distribution. Thus, from the results of both tests, we reject the null hypothesis of equal coefficients at a 5% significance level.

The equality of coefficients is not the only cross-equation hypothesis that can be tested. Any restrictions on parameters in different equations can be tested. Such restrictions are particularly relevant when estimating equations derived from demand and production theory. Tests for hypotheses involving coefficients within each equation are valid whether done on each equation separately or using the SUR framework. However, tests involving cross-equation hypotheses need to be carried out within an SUR framework if contemporaneous correlation exists.

15.8 Exercises

15.8.1 PROBLEMS

15.1 This exercise uses data from the paper: Zhenjuan Liu and Thanasis Stengos, "Nonlinearities in Cross Country Growth Regressions: A Semiparametric Approach," *Journal of Applied Econometrics*, Vol. 14, No. 5, 1999, pp. 527–538. There are observations on 86 countries, in three time periods, 1960, 1970, and 1980. The authors attempt to explain each country's growth rate (G) in terms of the explanatory variables: POP = population growth, INV = the share of output allocated to investment, $IGDP$ = initial level of GDP in 1960 in real terms, SEC = human capital measured as the enrollment rate in secondary schools. We are considering three cross-sectional regressions, one for each of the years 1960, 1970, and 1980.

$$G_{60} = \alpha_1 + \alpha_2 POP_{60} + \alpha_3 INV_{60} + \alpha_4 IGDP_{60} + \alpha_5 SEC_{60} + e_{60}$$
$$G_{70} = \beta_1 + \beta_2 POP_{70} + \beta_3 INV_{70} + \beta_4 IGDP_{70} + \beta_5 SEC_{70} + e_{70}$$
$$G_{80} = \gamma_1 + \gamma_2 POP_{80} + \gamma_3 INV_{80} + \gamma_4 IGDP_{80} + \gamma_5 SEC_{80} + e_{80}$$

Estimating a three-equation, seemingly unrelated regression system, we obtain the estimated equations

$$G_{60} = 0.0231 - 0.2435 POP_{60} + 0.1280 INV_{60} - 0.0000021 IGDP_{60} + 0.0410 SEC_{60}$$
(se) (0.0195) (0.2384) (0.0333) (0.0000020) (0.0172)

$$G_{70} = 0.0185 - 0.4336 POP_{70} + 0.1870 INV_{70} - 0.0000026 IGDP_{70} + 0.0127 SEC_{70}$$
(se) (0.0313) (0.4029) (0.0397) (0.0000018) (0.0184)

$$G_{80} = 0.0423 - 0.8156 POP_{80} + 0.1155 INV_{80} - 0.0000007 IGDP_{80} + 0.0028 SEC_{80}$$
(se) (0.0265) (0.2997) (0.0297) (0.0000013) (0.0141)

(a) Comment on the signs of the coefficients. Can you explain these signs in terms of the expected impact of the explanatory variables on growth rate?
(b) Does human capital appear to influence growth rate?
(c) The estimated correlations between the errors for the three equations are

$$r_{12} = 0.1084 \quad r_{13} = 0.1287 \quad r_{23} = 0.3987$$

Carry out a hypothesis test to see if SUR estimation is preferred over separate least squares estimation.
(d) Consider the following null hypothesis:

$$H_0 : \alpha_2 = \beta_2 \quad \beta_2 = \gamma_2, \quad \alpha_3 = \beta_3, \quad \beta_3 = \gamma_3, \quad \alpha_4 = \beta_4, \quad \beta_4 = \gamma_4,$$
$$\alpha_5 = \beta_5, \quad \beta_5 = \gamma_5$$

with the alternative hypothesis being that at least one of the equalities being tested is false. What is the economic interpretation of these hypotheses?
(e) The appropriate chi-squared test statistic value (*Hint*: see Section 15.7.5b) is 12.309. Using Table 3 at the end of the book, do you reject the null hypothesis, or not, at the 5% level of significance? Using your statistical software, compute the p-value for this test.
(f) Using the information in (e) carry out an F-test of the null hypothesis in (d). What do you conclude? What is the p-value of this test?

15.2 The system of equations in Exercise 15.1 is estimated with some restrictions imposed on the parameters. The restricted estimations are

$$G_{60} = 0.0352 - 0.4286 \, POP_{60} + 0.1361 \, INV_{60} - 0.0000011 \, IGDP_{60} + 0.0150 \, SEC_{60}$$
(se)   (0.0153) (0.1889)   (0.0206)   (0.0000010)   (0.0100)

$$G_{70} = 0.0251 - 0.4286 \, POP_{70} + 0.1361 \, INV_{70} - 0.0000011 \, IGDP_{70} + 0.0150 \, SEC_{70}$$
(se)   (0.0159) (0.1889)   (0.0206)   (0.0000010)   (0.0100)

$$G_{80} = 0.0068 - 0.4286 \, POP_{80} + 0.1361 \, INV_{80} - 0.0000011 \, IGDP_{80} + 0.0150 \, SEC_{80}$$
(se)   (0.0164) (0.1889)   (0.0206)   (0.0000010)   (0.0100)

(a) What restrictions have been imposed?
(b) Comment on any substantial differences between these results and those in Exercise 15.1.
(c) The null hypothesis $H_0 : \alpha_1 = \beta_1, \beta_1 = \gamma_1$ is tested against the alternative that at least one of the equalities is not true. The resulting chi-square test statistic value is 93.098. Using Table 3 at the end of the book, test the null hypothesis at the 1% level of significance. (*Hint*: see Section 15.7.5b). Compute the p-value for the test.

15.3 Another way to estimate the model in Exercise 15.2 is to pool all the observations and use dummy variables for each of the years 1960, 1970, and 1980.
(a) If you estimate the model this way, what different assumptions are you making about the error terms, relative to the assumptions made for Exercise 15.2?
(b) The results for the estimated dummy variable model appear in Table 15.15. Report the estimated equation. Comment on any differences or similarities with the estimates obtained in Exercise 15.2.
(c) Does RESET suggest the equation is misspecified?

Table 15.15 **Dummy Variable Regression Model for Exercise 15.3**

Dependent Variable: G
Included observations: 258

Variable	Coefficient	Std. Error	t-value	p-value
D60	0.031527	0.014673	2.149	0.0326
D70	0.020514	0.015297	1.341	0.1811
D80	0.002896	0.015794	0.183	0.8546
POP	−0.436464	0.182325	−2.394	0.0174
INV	0.162829	0.020750	7.847	0.0000
IGDP	−1.43E-06	9.42E-07	−1.517	0.1306
SEC	0.014886	0.009759	1.525	0.1284
$R^2 = 0.406$ $SSE = 0.094778$				

Ramsey RESET:
F-value $= 1.207756$ p-value $= 0.300612$

15.4 Consider the model

$$y_{it} = \beta_{1i} + \beta_2 x_{it} + e_{it}$$

(a) Show that the fixed effects estimator for β_2 can be written as

$$\hat{\beta}_{2,FE} = \frac{\sum\limits_{i=1}^{N} \sum\limits_{t=1}^{T} (x_{it} - \bar{x}_i)(y_{it} - \bar{y}_i)}{\sum\limits_{i=1}^{N} \sum\limits_{t=1}^{T} (x_{it} - \bar{x}_i)^2}$$

(b) Show that the random effects estimator for β_2 can be written as

$$\hat{\beta}_{2,RE} = \frac{\sum\limits_{i=1}^{N} \sum\limits_{t=1}^{T} \left[x_{it} - \hat{\alpha} \left(\bar{x}_i - \bar{\bar{x}} \right) - \bar{\bar{x}} \right] \left[y_{it} - \hat{\alpha} \left(\bar{y}_i - \bar{\bar{y}} \right) - \bar{\bar{y}} \right]}{\sum\limits_{i=1}^{N} \sum\limits_{t=1}^{T} \left[x_{it} - \hat{\alpha} \left(\bar{x}_i - \bar{\bar{x}} \right) - \bar{\bar{x}} \right]^2}$$

where $\bar{\bar{y}}$ and $\bar{\bar{x}}$ are the overall means.

(c) Write down an expression for the pooled least squares estimator of β_2. Discuss the differences between the three estimators.

15.8.2 COMPUTER EXERCISES

15.5* The file *liquor.dat* contains observations on annual expenditure on liquor (L) and annual income (X), (both in thousands of dollars) for 40 randomly selected households for three consecutive years. Consider the model

$$L_{it} = \beta_{1i} + \beta_2 X_{it} + e_{it}$$

where $i = 1,2,...,40$ refers to household and $t = 1,2,3$ refers to year; the e_{it} are assumed to be uncorrelated with $e_{it} \sim N(0, \sigma_e^2)$.

(a) Compare the alternative estimates for β_2, and their corresponding standard errors, that are obtained under the following circumstances:

   (i) The different household intercepts are modeled using dummy variables.

   (ii) Only average data are available, averaged over the three years.

   (iii) The β_{1i} are random drawings with mean $\overline{\beta}_1$ and variance σ_u^2.

   Comment on the estimates and their relative precision.

(b) Test the hypothesis that all household intercepts are equal.

15.6 The file *mexican.dat* contains data collected in 2001 from the transactions of 754 Mexican sex workers. There is information on four transactions per worker.[20] The labels *ID* and *TRANS* are used to describe a particular woman and a particular transaction. There are three categories of variables.

  1. Sex worker characteristics: (i) *AGE*, (ii) an indicator variable *ATTRACTIVE* equal to 1 if the worker is attractive, and (iii) an indicator variable *SCHOOL* if she has completed secondary school or higher.

  2. Client characteristics: (i) an indicator variable *REGULAR* equal to one if the client is a regular, (ii) an indicator variable *RICH* equal to one if the client is rich, and (iii) an indicator variable *ALCOHOL* if the client has consumed alcohol before the transaction.

  3. Transaction characteristics: (i) the log of the price of the transaction *LNPRICE*, (ii) an indicator variable *NOCONDOM* equal to one if a condom was not used, and (iii) two indicator variables for location, *BAR* equal to one if the transaction originated in a bar and *STREET* if the transaction originated in the street.

(a) Estimate a fixed effects model with *LNPRICE* as the dependent variable, and as explanatory variables the client characteristics, and the remaining transaction characteristics.

   (i) Why did we omit the sex worker characteristics?

   (ii) What coefficient estimates are significantly different from zero at a 5% level of significance?

   (iii) Gertler, Shah, and Bertozzi argue that the coefficient of *NOCONDOM* is a risk premium. Some sex workers are willing to take the risk of having unprotected sex because of the extra price some clients are willing to pay to avoid using a condom. What is your estimate of the risk premium? Interpret each of the other coefficient estimates. How is the price affected when clients are rich, are regular, and have consumed alcohol? How does the location of the transaction influence the price?

(b) Estimate the model assuming random effects and with the characteristics of the sex workers added to the model. Compare the estimates with those from fixed effects. How have the coefficients of the common variables changed? How do the sex worker characteristics affect the price of commercial sex? How much extra does a client have to pay to have unprotected sex with an attractive secondary-educated sex worker?

---

[20] These data are a subset of those used by Paul Gertler, Manisha Shah, and Stefano Bertozzi in their study "Risky Business: The Market for Unprotected Sex," *Journal of Political Economy*, (2005), 113, 518–550. We are grateful to the authors for permission to use their data and to Manisha Shah for compiling the subset used in this exercise.

(c) Using the *t*-test statistic in (15.37) and a 5% significance level, test whether there are any significant differences between the fixed effects and random effects estimates of the coefficients on *NOCONDOM, RICH, REGULAR, ALCOHOL, BAR*, and *STREET*. If there are significant differences between any of the coefficients, should we rely on the fixed effects estimates or on the random effects estimates? Explain your choice.

(d) Reconsider the random effects model from part (b), but assume that *NOCONDOM* is correlated with the random effects. Why might there be such a correlation? Re-estimate the model using the Hausman-Taylor estimator with *NOCONDOM* treated as endogenous. Compare the results with those obtained in part (b). How much extra does a client have to pay to have unprotected sex with an attractive secondary-educated sex worker?

15.7 This exercise uses data from the STAR experiment introduced in Chapter 7, Sections 7.5.3 and 7.5.4. In the STAR experiment children were randomly assigned within schools into three types of classes: small classes with 13–17 students, regular-sized classes with 22–25 students, and regular-sized classes with a full-time teacher aide to assist the teacher. Student scores on achievement tests were recorded, as was some information about the students, teachers, and schools. Data for the kindergarten classes is contained in the data file *star.dat*.

(a) Estimate a regression equation (with no fixed or random effects) where *MATHSCORE* is related to *SMALL, AIDE, TCHEXPER, BOY*, and *WHITE_ASIAN*. Discuss the results. Do students perform better at math when they are in small classes? Does a teacher's aide improve scores? Do the students of more experienced teachers score higher on math tests? Does gender or race make a difference?

(b) Re-estimate the model in part (a) with school fixed effects. Compare the results with those in part (a). Have any of your conclusions changed?

(c) Test for the significance of the school fixed effects. Under what conditions would we expect the inclusion of significant fixed effects to have little influence on the coefficient estimates of the remaining variables?

(d) Re-estimate the model in part (a) with school random effects. Compare the results with those from parts (a) and (b). Are there any variables in the equation that might be correlated with the school effects?

(e) Using the *t*-test statistic in (15.37) and a 5% significance level, test whether there are any significant differences between the fixed effects and random effects estimates of the coefficients on *SMALL, AIDE, TCHEXPER*, and *WHITE_ASIAN*. What are the implications of the test outcomes? What happens if we apply the test to the fixed and random effects estimates of the coefficient on *BOY*?

(f) Estimate a random effects model omitting *AIDE* and including *TCHMASTERS* and *SCHURBAN*. What do you conclude about the effect of the two new variables on *MATHSCORE*? What happens if you try to get fixed effects estimates of this model?

15.8 Consider the NLS panel data on young women discussed in Section 15.4.3. However, let us consider only years 1987 and 1988. These data are contained in the file *nls_panel2.dat*. We are interested in the wage equation that relates the logarithm of *WAGE* to *EXPER*, its square *EXPER*^{2}, *SOUTH*, and *UNION*.

(a) Estimate the ln(*WAGE*) model by least squares separately for each of the years 1987 and 1988. How do the results compare? For these individual year estimations, what are you assuming about the regression parameter values across individuals (heterogeneity)?

(b) Estimate the ln(*WAGE*) equation using both years of data, pooling them into a single regression. For this estimation, what are you assuming about the regression parameter values across individuals (heterogeneity) and the variance of the error term?

(c) The ln(*WAGE*) equation specified as a fixed effects model that allows for heterogeneity across individuals is

$$\ln(WAGE_{it}) = \beta_{1i} + \beta_2 EXPER_{it} + \beta_3 EXPER_{it}^2 + \beta_4 SOUTH_{it} + \beta_5 UNION_{it} + e_{it}$$

Explain any differences in assumptions between this model and the models in parts (a) and (b).

(d) Estimate the fixed effects model in part (c) and test the null hypothesis that the intercept parameter is identical for all women in the sample. What does this imply about the estimation results in (b)?

(e) Re-estimate the model in part (c) using cluster-robust standard errors. In the context of this sample, explain the different assumptions you are making when you estimate with and without cluster-robust standard errors. Compare the standard errors with those that you obtained in part (d).

(f) Suppose you wish to obtain the results in (d) but do not have access to specialized software for fixed effects estimation. The model in part (c) holds for all time periods t. Write down the model for time period $t - 1$. Subtract this model from the one in part (c). What happens to the heterogeneity term? Using your computer software, create the necessary first differences of the variables, for example, $DLWAGE_{it} = \ln(WAGE_{it}) - \ln(WAGE_{i,t-1})$. Estimate the wage equation using the differenced data, omitting an intercept term. Compare your results to the fixed effects estimates in part (d).

(g) Create a dummy variable that is one for 1988 and zero otherwise. Add it to the specification in part (c) and estimate the resulting model by fixed effects. What is the interpretation of the coefficient of this variable? Is it statistically significant?

(h) Using the differenced data in part (f), estimate the wage equation in part (g), but including an intercept term. What is the interpretation of the intercept?

15.9 Consider the NLS panel data on young women discussed in Section 15.4.3. However, let us consider only years 1987 and 1988. These data are contained in the file *nls_panel2.dat*. We are interested in the wage equation that relates the logarithm of *WAGE* to *EDUC*, *EXPER*, its square *EXPER*^{2}, *BLACK*, *SOUTH*, and *UNION*.

(a) Estimate the ln(*WAGE*) model by least squares separately for each of the years 1987 and 1988. How do the results compare? For these individual year estimations, what are you assuming about the regression parameter values across individuals (heterogeneity)?

(b) Estimate the ln(*WAGE*) equation using both years of data, pooling them into a single regression. For this estimation, what are you assuming about the regression parameter values across individuals (heterogeneity), the variance of the error term, and the correlation between the errors?

(c) Re-estimate the model in part (b) using cluster-robust standard errors with the individuals as clusters. How do the assumptions you are making differ from those in part (b)? Compare the standard errors with those that you obtained in part (b).

(d) Allowing heterogeneity across individuals, the wage equation is

$$\ln(WAGE_{it}) = \beta_{1i} + \beta_2 EDUC_i + \beta_3 EXPER_{it} + \beta_4 EXPER_{it}^2$$
$$+ \beta_5 BLACK_i + \beta_6 SOUTH_{it} + \beta_7 UNION_{it} + e_{it}$$

Explain any differences in assumptions between this model and the models in parts (a) and (b). Explain why the variables $EDUC$ and $BLACK$ have the subscripts i rather than i and t, like the other variables.

(e) Estimate the model shown in part (d) using the fixed effects estimator. Test the null hypothesis that the intercept parameter is identical for all women in the sample. What do you conclude?

(f) Estimate the model shown in part (d) using the random effects estimator. Test the null hypothesis that there are no random effects. What do you conclude?

(g) What is the estimated return on an additional year of education in the random effects model? Is it statistically significant? Construct a 95% interval estimate for this parameter.

(h) Explain why it is possible to estimate a return to education in part (f) but not in part (e).

(i) Using the t-test statistic in (15.37) and a 5% significance level, test whether there are any significant differences between the fixed effects and random effects estimates of the coefficients on $EXPER$, its square $EXPER^2$, $SOUTH$, and $UNION$. If there are significant differences between any of the coefficients, should we rely on the fixed effects estimates or on the random effects estimates? Explain your choice.

15.10 What is the relationship between crime and punishment? This important question has been examined by Cornwell and Trumbull[21] using a panel of data from North Carolina. The cross sections are 90 counties, and the data are annual for the years 1981–1987. The data are in the file *crime.dat*. In these models the crime rate is explained by variables describing the deterrence effect of the legal system, wages in the private sector (which represents returns to legal activities), socioeconomic conditions such as population density and the percentage of young males in the population, and annual dummy variables to control for time effects. The authors argue that there may be heterogeneity across counties (unobservable county specific characteristics).

(a) What do you expect will happen to the crime rate if (i) deterrence increases, (ii) wages in the private sector increase, (iii) population density increases, (iv) the percentage of young males increases?

(b) Consider a model in which the crime rate ($LCRMRTE$) is a function of the probability of arrest ($LPRBARR$), the probability of conviction ($LPRBCONV$), the probability of a prison sentence ($LPRBPRIS$), the average prison sentence ($LAVGSEN$), and the average weekly wage in the manufacturing sector ($LWMFG$). Note that the logarithms of the variables are used in each case. Estimate this model by least squares. (i) Discuss the signs of the estimated coefficients and their significance. Are they as you expected? (ii) Interpret the coefficient on $LPRBARR$.

---

[21] "Estimating the Economic Model of Crime with Panel Data," *Review of Economics and Statistics*, 76, 1994, 360–366. The data were kindly provided by the authors.

(c) Estimate the model in (b) using a fixed effects estimator. (i) Discuss the signs of the estimated coefficients and their significance. Are they as you expected? (ii) Interpret the coefficient on *LPRBARR* and compare it to the estimate in (b). What do you conclude about the deterrent effect of the probability of arrest? (iii) Interpret the coefficient on *LAVGSEN*. What do you conclude about the severity of punishment as a deterrent?

(d) In the fixed effects estimation from part (c), test whether the county level effects are all equal.

(e) To the specification in part (b) add the population density (*LDENSITY*) and the percentage of young males (*LPCTYMLE*), as well as dummy variables for the years 1982–1987 (*D82–D87*). (i) Compare the results obtained by using least squares (with no county effects) and the fixed effects estimator. (ii) Test the joint significance of the year dummy variables. Does there appear to be a trend effect? (iii) Interpret the coefficient of *LWMFG* in both estimations.

(f) Based on these results, what public policies would you advocate to deal with crime in the community?

15.11 Macroeconomists are interested in factors that explain economic growth. An aggregate production function specification was studied by Duffy and Papageor-giou.[22] The data are in the file *ces.dat*. They consist of cross sectional data on 82 countries for 28 years, 1960 to 1987.

(a) Estimate a Cobb-Douglas production function

$$LY_{it} = \beta_1 + \beta_2 LK_{it} + \beta_3 LL_{it} + e_{it}$$

where *LY* is the log of GDP, *LK* is the log of capital, and *LL* is the log of labor. Interpret the coefficients on *LK* and *LL*. Test the hypothesis that there are constant returns to scale, $\beta_2 + \beta_3 = 1$.

(b) Add a time trend variable $t = 1, 2, \ldots, 28$, to the specification in (a). Interpret the coefficient of this variable. Test its significance. What effect does this addition have on the estimates of β_2 and β_3?

(c) Assume $\beta_2 + \beta_3 = 1$. Solve for β_3 and substitute this expression into the model in (b). Show that the resulting model is $LYL_{it} = \beta_1 + \beta_2 LKL_{it} + \lambda t + e_{it}$ where *LYL* is the log of the output-labor ratio, and *LKL* is the log of the capital-labor ratio. Estimate this restricted, constant returns to scale, version of the Cobb-Douglas production function. Compare the estimate of β_2 from this specification to that in part (b).

(d) Estimate the model in (b) using a fixed effects estimator. Test the hypothesis that there are no cross-country differences. Compare the estimates to those in part (b).

(e) Using the results in (d), test the hypothesis that $\beta_2 + \beta_3 = 1$. What do you conclude about constant returns to scale?

(f) Estimate the restricted version of the Cobb-Douglas model in (c) using the fixed effects estimator. Compare the results to those in part (c). Which specification do you prefer? Explain your choice.

(g) Using the specification in (b), replace the time trend variable t with dummy variables *D2–D28*. What is the effect of using this dummy variable specification rather than the single time trend variable?

---

[22] "A Cross-Country Empirical Investigation of the Aggregate Production Function Specification," *Journal of Economic Growth*, 5, 83–116: March 2000. The authors thank Chris Papageorgiou for providing the data.

15.12 This exercise uses the data file *nls_panel.dat* that was introduced in Section 15.1 and carried through as an example in Sections 15.2 to 15.6. We are interested in estimating the equation

$$LWAGE_{it} = \beta_{1i} + \beta_2 EDUC_i + \beta_3 EXPER_{it} + \beta_4 EXPER_{it}^2 + \beta_5 HOURS_{it}$$
$$+ \beta_6 BLACK_i + e_{it}$$

Our primary focus is on estimating the percentage return to education $\phi = 100\beta_2$ and the percentage return to experience for a woman with five years of experience, $\theta = 100(\beta_3 + 10\beta_4)$.

(a) Why is the percentage return to experience for a woman with five years of experience equal to $100(\beta_3 + 10\beta_4)$?

(b) Estimate the model assuming that the intercept β_{1i} is the same for all individuals ($\beta_{1i} = \beta_1$) and that the errors e_{it} are homoskedastic and uncorrelated. Find 95% interval estimates for ϕ and θ.

(c) Estimate the model assuming that the intercept β_{1i} is the same for all individuals ($\beta_{1i} = \beta_1$), computing standard errors consistent with the assumption $\text{cov}(e_{it}, e_{is}) = \psi_{ts}$. Find 95% interval estimates for ϕ and θ. Discuss any differences between these results and those from part (b).

(d) Estimate the model assuming that the intercept β_{1i} is a random variable with mean $\bar{\beta}_1$ and variance σ_u^2, and the errors e_{it} are homoskedastic and uncorrelated. Find 95% interval estimates for ϕ and θ. Discuss any differences between these results and those from parts (b) and (c).

(e) Are there any variables in the model that might be correlated with the β_{1i} in part (d)? Use t tests and an overall χ^2-test to test for correlation between the β_{1i} and the variables in the model.

(f) Re-estimate the model in (d) assuming that *EDUC* and *HOURS* are correlated with the β_{1i}. Find 95% interval estimates for ϕ and θ. Discuss any differences between these results and those from parts (b), (c), and (d).

15.13 This exercise illustrates the transformation that is necessary to produce generalized least squares estimates for the random effects model. It utilizes the data on investment (*INV*), value (*V*), and capital (*K*) in the file *grunfeld11.dat*. The model is

$$INV_{it} = \bar{\beta}_1 + \beta_2 V_{it} + \beta_3 K_{it} + u_i + e_{it}$$

We assume that the random effects assumptions of Section 15.4 hold.

(a) Find fixed effects estimates of β_2 and β_3. Check that the variance estimate that you obtain is $\hat{\sigma}_e^2 = 2530.042$.

(b) Compute the sample means $\overline{INV}_i$, $\bar{V}_i$ and $\bar{K}_i$ for each of the 11 firms. (*Hint*: Regress each of the variables (*INV*, then *V*, then *K*) on 11 indicator variables, one for each firm, and in each case save the predictions.)

(c) Estimate $\bar{\beta}_1$, β_2, and β_3 from the between regression

$$\overline{INV}_i = \bar{\beta}_1 + \beta_2 \bar{V}_i + \beta_3 \bar{K}_i + u_i + \bar{e}_i$$

Check that the variance estimate for $\sigma_*^2 = \text{var}(u_i + \bar{e}_i)$ is $\hat{\sigma}_*^2 = 6328.554$. (*Hint*: Use the predictions obtained in (b) to run the regression. If you do so, you will be using each of the N observations repeated T times. The coefficient estimates will be unaffected, but the sum of squared errors will be $T = 20$ times bigger than it should be, and the divisor used to estimate the error variance will be $NT - K$ instead of $N - K$. You will need to make adjustments accordingly.)

(d) Show that

$$\hat{\alpha} = 1 - \sqrt{\frac{\hat{\sigma}_e^2}{T\hat{\sigma}_*^2}} = 0.85862$$

(e) Apply least squares to the regression model

$$INV_{it}^* = \overline{\beta}_1 x_1^* + \beta_2 V_{it}^* + \beta_3 K_{it}^* + v_{it}^*$$

where the transformed variables are given by $INV_{it}^* = INV_{it} - \hat{\alpha}\,\overline{INV}_i$, $V_{it}^* = V_{it} - \hat{\alpha}\overline{V}_i$, and $K_{it}^* = K_{it} - \hat{\alpha}\overline{K}_i$.

(f) Use your software to obtain random effects estimates of the original equation. Compare the estimates with those you obtained in part (e).

15.14* Consider the three demand equations

$$\ln(Q_{1t}) = \beta_{11} + \beta_{12} \ln(P_{1t}) + \beta_{13} \ln(Y_t) + e_{1t}$$
$$\ln(Q_{2t}) = \beta_{21} + \beta_{22} \ln(P_{2t}) + \beta_{23} \ln(Y_t) + e_{2t}$$
$$\ln(Q_{3t}) = \beta_{31} + \beta_{32} \ln(P_{3t}) + \beta_{33} \ln(Y_t) + e_{3t}$$

where Q_{it} is the quantity consumed of the ith commodity, $i = 1,2,3$, in the tth time period, $t = 1,2,...,30$, P_{it} is the price of the ith commodity in time t, and Y_t is disposable income in period t. The commodities are meat ($i = 1$), fruits and vegetables ($i = 2$), and cereals and bakery products ($i = 3$). Prices and income are in real terms, and all data are in index form. They can be found in the file *demand.dat*.

(a) Estimate each equation by least squares and test whether the equation errors for each household are correlated. Report the estimates and their standard errors. Do the elasticities have the expected signs?

(b) Estimate the system jointly using the SUR estimator. Report the estimates and their standard errors. Do they differ much from your results in part (a)?

(c) Test the null hypothesis that all income elasticities are equal to unity. (Consult your software to see how such a test is implemented.)

15.15 In the model

$$\ln\left(\frac{GAS}{CAR}\right) = \beta_1 + \beta_2 \ln\left(\frac{Y}{POP}\right) + \beta_3 \ln\left(\frac{P_{MG}}{P_{GDP}}\right) + \beta_4 \ln\left(\frac{CAR}{POP}\right) + e$$

GAS/CAR is motor gasoline consumption per car, Y/POP is per capita real income, P_{MG}/P_{GDP} is real motor gasoline price, and CAR/POP is the stock of cars per capita. The data file *gascar.dat* contains 19 time-series observations on the above variables, for the countries Austria, Belgium, Canada, Denmark, France, and Germany, respectively. The data are a subset of those used by Baltagi, B. H. and J. M. Griffin (1983), "Gasoline Demand in the OECD: An Application of Pooling and Testing Procedures," *European Economic Review*, 22, 117–137. Consider a set of six equations, one for each country.

(a) Compare least squares and SUR estimates of the coefficients of each equation. Comment on the signs.
(b) Test for contemporaneous correlation.
(c) Using the SUR-estimated equations:
   (i) Test the hypothesis that corresponding slope coefficients in different equations are equal.
   (ii) Test the hypothesis that $\ln(CAR/POP)$ should be omitted from all six equations.

15.16 The U.S. Secretary of Agriculture asks a staff economist to provide a basis for determining cattle inventories in the Midwest, Southwest, and West. Let $i = 1,2,3$ denote the three regions. The economist hypothesizes that in each region cattle numbers at the end of the year (C_{it}) depend on average price during the year (P_{it}), rainfall during the year (R_{it}), and cattle numbers at the end of the previous year $(C_{i,t-1})$. Because growing conditions are quite different in the three regions, three separate equations are specified, one for each region:

$$C_{1t} = \beta_{11} + \beta_{12}P_{1t} + \beta_{13}R_{1t} + \beta_{14}C_{1,t-1} + e_{1t}$$
$$C_{2t} = \beta_{21} + \beta_{22}P_{2t} + \beta_{23}R_{2t} + \beta_{24}C_{2,t-1} + e_{2t}$$
$$C_{3t} = \beta_{31} + \beta_{32}P_{3t} + \beta_{33}R_{3t} + \beta_{34}C_{3,t-1} + e_{3t}$$

(a) What signs would you expect on the various coefficients? Why?
(b) Under what assumptions about the e_{it} should the three equations be estimated jointly as a set rather than individually?
(c) Use the data that appear in the file *cattle.dat* to find separate least squares estimates for each equation, and the corresponding standard errors.
(d) Test for the existence of contemporaneous correlation between the e_{it}.
(e) Estimate the three equations jointly using the seemingly unrelated regression technique. Compare these results with those obtained in (c) in terms of reliability and economic feasibility.

15.17◆Consider the production function

$$Q = f(K, L)$$

where Q is output, K is capital, and L is labor. Suppose that the function $f(\cdot)$ is a CES or constant elasticity of substitution production function. The elasticity of substitution, which we denote by ω, measures the degree to which capital and labor are substituted when the factor price ratio changes. Let P be the price of output, R be the price of capital, and W the price of labor. If the function $f(\cdot)$ is a CES production function, then the conditions for profit maximization, with errors attached, are

$$\ln\left(\frac{Q}{L}\right) = \gamma_1 + \omega \ln\left(\frac{W}{P}\right) + e_1 \qquad \text{where } e_1 \sim N(0, \sigma_1^2)$$

$$\ln\left(\frac{Q}{K}\right) = \gamma_2 + \omega \ln\left(\frac{R}{P}\right) + e_2 \qquad \text{where } e_2 \sim N(0, \sigma_2^2)$$

Since these equations are linear in γ_1, γ_2, and ω, some version(s) of least squares can be used to estimate these parameters. Data on 20 firms appear in the file *cespro.dat*.

    (a) Find separate least squares estimates of each of the first-order conditions. Compare the two estimates of the elasticity of substitution.

    (b) Test for contemporaneous correlation between e_1 and e_2.

    (c) Estimate the two equations using generalized least squares, allowing for the existence of contemporaneous correlation.

    (d) Repeat part (c), but impose a restriction so that only one estimate of the elasticity of substitution is obtained. (Consult your software to see how to impose such a restriction.) Comment on the results.

    (e) Compare the standard errors obtained in parts (a), (c), and (d). Do they reflect the efficiency gains that you would expect?

    (f) If $\omega = 1$, the CES production function becomes a Cobb-Douglas production function. Use the results in (d) to test whether a Cobb-Douglas production function is adequate.

15.18 The file *rice.dat* contains 352 observations on 44 rice farmers in the Tarlac region of the Phillipines for the eight years 1990 to 1997. Variables in the dataset are tonnes of freshly threshed rice (*PROD*), hectares planted (*AREA*), person-days of hired and family labor (*LABOR*), and kilograms of fertilizer (*FERT*).

    (a) Using a fixed effects estimator where relevant, estimate the production function

$$\ln(PROD_{it}) = \beta_{1it} + \beta_2 \ln(AREA_{it}) + \beta_3 \ln(LABOR_{it}) + \beta_4 \ln(FERT_{it}) + e_{it}$$

under the following assumptions: (i) $\beta_{1it} = \beta_1$, (ii) $\beta_{1it} = \beta_{1i}$, (iii) $\beta_{1it} = \beta_{1t}$, and (iv) β_{1it} can be different over time and farms.

    (b) Comment on the sensitivity of the estimates of the input elasticities to the assumption made about the intercept.

    (c) Which of the estimated models do you prefer? Perform a series of hypothesis tests to help you make your decision.

    (d) For the model estimated in part (a)(iv), find 95% interval estimates for the input elasticities using (i) conventional standard errors and using (ii) cluster-robust standard errors. Comment on any differences.

15.19 Using the data set from Exercise 15.18, consider the model

$$\ln(PROD_{it}) = \beta_{1t} + \beta_{2t} \ln(AREA_{it}) + \beta_{3t} \ln(LABOR_{it}) + \beta_{4t} \ln(FERT_{it}) + e_{it}$$

    (a) Estimate three seemingly unrelated regressions for the years 1995, 1996, and 1997 and report the results.

    (b) What assumptions are you making when you estimate the equations in (a)? How would you interpret what was called contemporaneous correlation in Section 15.3? Is this correlation significant?

    (c) Test the hypothesis that the input elasticities are the same in all three years.

Appendix 15A Cluster-Robust Standard Errors: Some Details

To appreciate the nature of cluster-robust standard errors, we return momentarily to a simple regression model for cross sectional data

$$y_i = \beta_1 + \beta_2 x_i + e_i$$

Using the result $b_2 = \beta_2 + \sum_{i=1}^{N} w_i e_i$, where $w_i = (x_i - \bar{x}) \big/ \sum_{i=1}^{N}(x_i - \bar{x})^2$, in Appendix 8A we showed that the variance of the least squares estimator b_2, in the presence of heteroskedasticity, is given by

$$\text{var}(b_2) = \text{var}\left(\sum_{i=1}^{N} w_i e_i\right) = \sum_{i=1}^{N} w_i^2 \text{var}(e_i) + \sum_{i=1}^{N}\sum_{j=i+1}^{N} 2w_i w_j \text{cov}(e_i, e_j)$$

$$= \sum_{i=1}^{N} w_i^2 \text{var}(e_i) = \sum_{i=1}^{N} w_i^2 \sigma_i^2$$

Because we are assuming a random sample of cross-sectional individuals, $\text{cov}(e_i, e_j) = 0$ for $i \neq j$, leading to the simplification in the second line of the above equation.

Now suppose we have a panel simple regression model

$$y_{it} = \beta_1 + \beta_2 x_{it} + e_{it} \tag{15A.1}$$

with the assumptions $\text{cov}(e_{it}, e_{is}) = \psi_{ts}$ and $\text{cov}(e_{it}, e_{js}) = 0$ for $i \neq j$. The pooled least squares estimator for β_2 is given by

$$b_2 = \beta_2 + \sum_{i=1}^{N}\sum_{t=1}^{T} w_{it} e_{it} \tag{15A.2}$$

where

$$w_{it} = \frac{x_{it} - \bar{\bar{x}}}{\sum_{i=1}^{N}\sum_{t=1}^{T}\left(x_{it} - \bar{\bar{x}}\right)^2}$$

with $\bar{\bar{x}} = \sum_{i=1}^{N}\sum_{t=1}^{T} x_{it} \big/ NT$. The variance of the pooled least squares estimator b_2 is given by

$$\text{var}(b_2) = \text{var}\left(\sum_{i=1}^{N}\sum_{t=1}^{T} w_{it} e_{it}\right) = \text{var}\left(\sum_{i=1}^{N} g_i\right) \tag{15A.3}$$

where $g_i = \sum_{t=1}^{T} w_{it} e_{it}$ is a weighted sum of the errors for individual i. Because we have a random sample, the errors for different individuals are uncorrelated, implying that g_i is uncorrelated with g_j for $i \neq j$. Thus,

$$\text{var}(b_2) = \text{var}\left(\sum_{i=1}^{N} g_i\right) = \sum_{i=1}^{N} \text{var}(g_i) + \sum_{i=1}^{N}\sum_{j=i+1}^{N} 2\text{cov}(g_i, g_j) = \sum_{i=1}^{N} \text{var}(g_i) \tag{15A.4}$$

To find $\text{var}(g_i)$ suppose for the moment that $T = 2$, then

$$\text{var}(g_i) = \text{var}\left(\sum_{t=1}^{2} w_{it} e_{it}\right) = w_{i1}^2 \text{var}(e_{i1}) + w_{i2}^2 \text{var}(e_{i2}) + 2w_{i1} w_{i2} \text{cov}(e_{i1}, e_{i2})$$

$$= w_{i1}^2 \psi_{11} + w_{i2}^2 \psi_{22} + 2w_{i1} w_{i2} \psi_{12}$$

$$= \sum_{t=1}^{2}\sum_{s=1}^{2} w_{it} w_{is} \psi_{ts}$$

For $T > 2$, $\text{var}(g_i) = \sum_{t=1}^{T}\sum_{s=1}^{T} w_{it}w_{is}\psi_{ts}$. Substituting this expression into (15A.4), we have

$$
\text{var}(b_2) = \sum_{i=1}^{N}\sum_{t=1}^{T}\sum_{s=1}^{T} w_{it}w_{is}\psi_{ts}
$$

$$
= \frac{\sum_{i=1}^{N}\sum_{t=1}^{T}\sum_{s=1}^{T} \left(x_{it} - \bar{\bar{x}}\right)\left(x_{is} - \bar{\bar{x}}\right)\psi_{ts}}{\left(\sum_{i=1}^{N}\sum_{t=1}^{T} \left(x_{it} - \bar{\bar{x}}\right)^2\right)^2}
\tag{15A.5}
$$

Recall that $\text{cov}(e_{it}, e_{is}) = E(e_{it}e_{is}) = \psi_{ts}$. A cluster-robust variance estimate is obtained from (15A.5) by replacing ψ_{ts} with $\hat{e}_{it}\hat{e}_{is}$. Thus, a cluster-robust standard error for b_2 is given by the square root of

$$
\widehat{\text{var}(b_2)} = \frac{\sum_{i=1}^{N}\sum_{t=1}^{T}\sum_{s=1}^{T} \left(x_{it} - \bar{\bar{x}}\right)\left(x_{is} - \bar{\bar{x}}\right)\hat{e}_{it}\hat{e}_{is}}{\left(\sum_{i=1}^{N}\sum_{t=1}^{T} \left(x_{it} - \bar{\bar{x}}\right)^2\right)^2}
\tag{15A.6}
$$

The above description of how cluster-robust standard errors are calculated and the logic behind them was done in terms of a model with just one explanatory variable. To describe the robust variance estimator for models with more than one explanatory variable, matrix algebra is required, but the principle is the same.

Finally, you will find that the cluster robust standard errors produced by most software packages apply a degrees of freedom correction to the expression in (15A.6). Unfortunately, they do not all use the same correction factor. For example, Stata 11.0 multiplies the expression in (15A.6) by $(N/(N-1))\times((NT-1)/(NT-K))$. EViews 7.0 multiplies it by $NT/(NT-K)$. In these expressions NT is the total number of observations in a balanced panel and K is the number of parameters being estimated. Note that in the fixed effects model, $K > N$. For unbalanced panels NT is replaced by $\sum_{i=1}^{N}T_i$.

Appendix 15B Estimation of Error Components

The random effects model is

$$
y_{it} = \bar{\beta}_1 + \beta_2 x_{2it} + \beta_3 x_{3it} + (u_i + e_{it})
\tag{15B.1}
$$

where u_i is the individual specific error and e_{it} is the usual regression error. We will discuss the case for a balanced panel, with T time series observations for each of N individuals. To implement generalized least squares estimation we need to consistently estimate σ_u^2, the variance of the individual specific error component, and σ_e^2, the variance of the regression error.

The regression error variance σ_e^2 comes from the fixed effects estimator. In (15.14) we transform the panel data regression into "deviation about the individual mean" form

$$
y_{it} - \bar{y}_i = \beta_2(x_{2it} - \bar{x}_{2i}) + \beta_3(x_{3it} - \bar{x}_{3i}) + (e_{it} - \bar{e}_i)
\tag{15B.2}
$$

The least squares estimator of this equation yields the same estimates and sum of squared errors (denoted here by SSE_{DV}) as least squares applied to a model that includes a dummy variable for each individual in the sample. A consistent estimator of σ_e^2 is obtained by dividing SSE_{DV} by the appropriate degrees of freedom, which is $NT - N - K_{slopes}$, where K_{slopes} is the number of parameters that are present in the transformed model (15B.2)

$$\hat{\sigma}_e^2 = \frac{SSE_{DV}}{NT - N - K_{slopes}} \tag{15B.3}$$

The estimator of σ_u^2 requires a bit more work. We begin with the time-averaged observations in (15.12)

$$\bar{y}_i = \bar{\beta}_1 + \beta_2 \bar{x}_{2i} + \beta_3 \bar{x}_{3i} + u_i + \bar{e}_i \quad i = 1, 2, \ldots, N \tag{15B.4}$$

The least squares estimator of (15B.4) is called the **between estimator**, as it uses variation between individuals as a basis for estimating the regression parameters. This estimator is unbiased and consistent, but not minimum variance under the error assumptions of the random effects model. The error term in this model is $u_i + \bar{e}_i$; it is uncorrelated across individuals, and has homoskedastic variance

$$\text{var}(u_i + \bar{e}_i) = \text{var}(u_i) + \text{var}(\bar{e}_i) = \text{var}(u_i) + \text{var}\left(\sum_{t=1}^{T} e_{it}/T\right)$$

$$= \sigma_u^2 + \frac{1}{T^2}\text{var}\left(\sum_{t=1}^{T} e_{it}\right) = \sigma_u^2 + \frac{T\sigma_e^2}{T^2} \tag{15B.5}$$

$$= \sigma_u^2 + \frac{\sigma_e^2}{T}$$

We can estimate the variance in (15B.5) by estimating the between regression in (15B.4), and dividing the sum of squared errors, SSE_{BE}, by the degrees of freedom $N - K_{BE}$, where K_{BE} is the total number of parameters in the between regression, including the intercept parameter. Then

$$\sigma_u^2 + \frac{\sigma_e^2}{T} = \frac{\widehat{SSE_{BE}}}{N - K_{BE}} \tag{15B.6}$$

With this estimate in hand we can estimate σ_u^2 as

$$\hat{\sigma}_u^2 = \widehat{\sigma_u^2 + \frac{\sigma_e^2}{T}} - \frac{\hat{\sigma}_e^2}{T} = \frac{SSE_{BE}}{N - K_{BE}} - \frac{SSE_{DV}}{T(NT - N - K_{slopes})} \tag{15B.7}$$

We have obtained the estimates of σ_u^2 and σ_e^2 using what is called the Swamy-Arora method. This method is implemented in software packages and is well established. We note, however, that it is possible in finite samples to obtain an estimate $\hat{\sigma}_u^2$ in (15B.7) that is negative, which is obviously infeasible. If this should happen, one option is simply to set $\hat{\sigma}_u^2 = 0$, which implies that there are no random effects. Alternatively, your software may offer other options for estimating the variance components, which you might try.

Chapter 16

Qualitative and Limited Dependent Variable Models

Learning Objectives

Based on the material in this chapter, you should be able to:

1. Give some examples of economic decisions in which the observed outcome is a binary variable.

2. Explain why probit, or logit, is usually preferred to least squares when estimating a model in which the dependent variable is binary.

3. Give some examples of economic decisions in which the observed outcome is a choice among several alternatives, both ordered and unordered.

4. Compare and contrast the multinomial logit model to the conditional logit model.

5. Give some examples of models in which the dependent variable is a count variable.

6. Discuss the implications of censored data for least squares estimation.

7. Describe what is meant by the phrase "sample selection."

Keywords

binary choice models
censored data
conditional logit
count data models
feasible generalized least squares
Heckit
identification problem
independence of irrelevant alternatives (IIA)
index models
individual and alternative specific variables
individual specific variables
latent variables
likelihood function
limited dependent variables
linear probability model
logistic random variable

logit
log-likelihood function
marginal effect
maximum likelihood estimation
multinomial choice models
multinomial logit
odds ratio
ordered choice models
ordered probit
ordinal variables
Poisson random variable
Poisson regression model
probit
selection bias
Tobit model
truncated data

In this book we focus primarily on econometric models in which the dependent variable is continuous and fully observable; quantities, prices, and outputs are examples of such variables. However, microeconomics is a general theory of choice, and many of the choices that individuals and firms make cannot be measured by a continuous outcome variable. In this chapter we examine some fascinating models that are used to describe choice behavior, and which do not have the usual continuous dependent variable. Our descriptions will be brief, since we will not go into all the theory, but we will reveal to you a rich area of economic applications.

We also introduce a class of models with dependent variables that are *limited*. By that we mean that they are continuous, but that their range of values is constrained in some way, and their values not completely observable. Alternatives to least squares estimation must be considered for such cases, since the least squares estimator is both biased and inconsistent.

16.1 Models with Binary Dependent Variables

Many of the choices that individuals and firms make are "either–or" in nature. For example, a high school graduate decides either to attend college or not. A worker decides either to drive to work or to get there using a different means of transportation. A household decides either to purchase a house or to rent. A firm decides either to advertise its product in a local newspaper or it decides not to. As economists we are interested in explaining why particular choices are made, and what factors enter into the decision process. We also want to know *how much* each factor affects the outcome. Such questions lead us to the problem of constructing a statistical model of binary, either–or, choices. Such choices can be represented by a binary (indicator) variable that takes the value 1 if one outcome is chosen and the value 0 otherwise. The binary variable describing a choice is the dependent variable rather than an independent variable. This fact affects our choice of a statistical model.

The list of economic applications in which choice models may be useful is a long one. These models are useful in any economic setting in which an agent must choose one of two alternatives. Examples include the following:

- An economic model explaining why some individuals take a second or third job, and engage in "moonlighting."
- An economic model of why some legislators in the U.S. House of Representatives vote for a particular bill and others do not.
- An economic model explaining why some loan applications are accepted and others are not at a large metropolitan bank.
- An economic model explaining why some individuals vote for increased spending in a school board election and others vote against.
- An economic model explaining why some female college students decide to study engineering and others do not.

This list illustrates the great variety of circumstances in which a model of binary choice may be used. In each case an economic decision maker chooses between two mutually exclusive outcomes.

We will illustrate **binary choice models** using an important problem from transportation economics. How can we explain an individual's choice between driving (private transportation) and taking the bus (public transportation) when commuting to work, assuming, for simplicity, that these are the only two alternatives? We represent an individual's choice by the indicator variable

$$y = \begin{cases} 1 & \text{individual drives to work} \\ 0 & \text{individual takes bus to work} \end{cases} \qquad (16.1)$$

If we collect a random sample of workers who commute to work, then the outcome y will be unknown to us until the sample is drawn. Thus, y is a random variable. If the probability that an individual drives to work is p, then $P[y = 1] = p$. It follows that the probability that a person uses public transportation is $P[y = 0] = 1 - p$. The probability function for such a binary random variable is

$$f(y) = p^y(1 - p)^{1-y}, \quad y = 0, 1 \qquad (16.2)$$

where p is the probability that y takes the value one. This discrete random variable has expected value $E(y) = p$ and variance $\text{var}(y) = p(1 - p)$.

What factors might affect the probability that an individual chooses one transportation mode over the other? One factor will certainly be how long it takes to get to work one way or the other. Define the explanatory variable

$$x = (\text{commuting time by bus} - \text{commuting time by car})$$

There are other factors that affect the decision, but let us focus on this single explanatory variable. *A priori* we expect that as x increases, and commuting time by bus increases relative to commuting time by car, an individual would be more inclined to drive. That is, we expect a positive relationship between x and p, the probability that an individual will drive to work.

16.1.1 THE LINEAR PROBABILITY MODEL

One way to model binary choice is with the linear probability model that was introduced in Chapter 7.4. There we noted several problems with using the linear probability model. It implies marginal effects of changes in continuous explanatory variables are constant, which cannot be the case for a probability model. This feature also can result in predicted probabilities outside the [0, 1] interval. The linear probability model error term is heteroskedastic, so that a better estimator is generalized least squares, as discussed in Chapter 8.6. You should review the earlier sections for the best understanding. Here we briefly summarize the issues for completeness.

In regression analysis we break the dependent variable into fixed and random parts. If we do this for the indicator variable y, we have

$$y = E(y) + e = p + e \qquad (16.3)$$

We then relate the fixed, systematic portion of y, the probability p that $y = 1$, to explanatory variables that we believe help explain the choice probability. We are assuming that the probability of driving is related to the difference in driving times, x, in the transportation example. Assuming that the relationship is linear,

$$E(y) = p = \beta_1 + \beta_2 x \qquad (16.4)$$

The linear regression model for explaining the choice variable y is called the **linear probability model**. It is given by

$$y = E(y) + e = \beta_1 + \beta_2 x + e \tag{16.5}$$

One problem with the linear probability model is that the error term is heteroskedastic; the variance of the error term e varies from one observation to another. The probability density functions for y and e are as follows:

y-Value	e-Value	Probability
1	$1 - (\beta_1 + \beta_2 x)$	$p = \beta_1 + \beta_2 x$
0	$- (\beta_1 + \beta_2 x)$	$1 - p = 1 - (\beta_1 + \beta_2 x)$

Using these values it can be shown that the variance of the error term e is

$$\text{var}(e) = (\beta_1 + \beta_2 x)(1 - \beta_1 - \beta_2 x)$$

If we adopt the linear probability model (16.5), we should use generalized least squares estimation. This is generally done by first estimating the model (16.5) by least squares; then the estimated variance of the error term is

$$\hat{\sigma}_i^2 = \widehat{\text{var}(e_i)} = (b_1 + b_2 x_i)(1 - b_1 - b_2 x_i) \tag{16.6}$$

Using this estimated variance the data can be transformed as $y_i^* = y_i / \hat{\sigma}_i$ and $x_i^* = x_i / \hat{\sigma}_i$, then the model $y_i^* = \beta_1 \hat{\sigma}_i^{-1} + \beta_2 x_i^* + e_i^*$ is estimated by least squares to produce the **feasible generalized least squares** estimates. Both least squares and feasible generalized least squares are consistent estimators of the regression parameters.

   In practice certain difficulties may arise with the implementation of this procedure. They are related to another problem with the linear probability model—that of obtaining probability values that are less than zero or greater than one. If we estimate the parameters of (16.5) by least squares, we obtain the fitted model explaining the systematic portion of y. This systematic portion is p, the probability that an individual chooses to drive to work. That is,

$$\hat{p} = b_1 + b_2 x \tag{16.7}$$

When using this model to predict behavior, by substituting alternative values of x, we can easily obtain values of $\hat{p}$ that are less than zero or greater than one. Values like these do not make sense as probabilities, and we are left in a difficult situation. It also means that some of the estimated variances in (16.6) may be negative. The standard fix-up is to set negative $\hat{p}$ values to a small value like 0.01, and values of $\hat{p}$ greater than one to 0.99. Making these changes will not hurt in large samples.

   The underlying feature that causes these problems is that the linear probability model (16.4) implicitly assumes that increases in x have a constant effect on the probability of choosing to drive,

$$\frac{dp}{dx} = \beta_2 \tag{16.8}$$

That is, as x increases the probability of driving continues to increase at a constant rate. However, since $0 \leq p \leq 1$, a constant rate of increase is impossible. To overcome this problem we consider the nonlinear **probit** model.

16.1.2 THE PROBIT MODEL

To keep the choice probability p within the interval [0, 1], a nonlinear S-shaped relationship between x and p can be used. In Figure 16.1(a) such a curve is illustrated. As x increases, the probability curve rises rapidly at first, and then begins to increase at a decreasing rate. The *slope* of this curve gives the change in probability given a unit change in x. The slope is not constant as in the linear probability model.

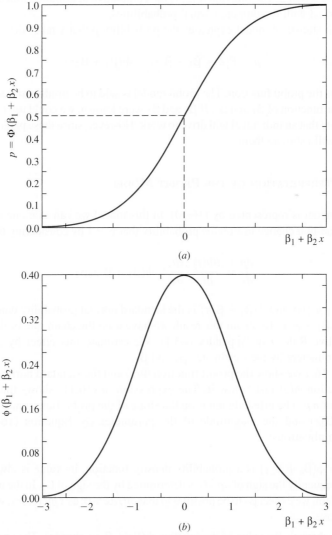

FIGURE **16.1** (*a*) Standard normal cumulative distribution function. (*b*) Standard normal probability density function.

A functional relationship that is used to represent such a curve is the probit function. The probit function is related to the standard normal probability distribution. If Z is a standard normal random variable, then its probability density function is

$$\phi(z) = \frac{1}{\sqrt{2\pi}} e^{-0.5z^2}$$

The probit function is

$$\Phi(z) = P[Z \leq z] = \int_{-\infty}^{z} \frac{1}{\sqrt{2\pi}} e^{-0.5u^2} du \tag{16.9}$$

This integral expression is the probability that a standard normal random variable falls to the left of point z. In geometric terms it is the area under the standard normal probability density function to the left of z. The function $\Phi(z)$ is the cumulative distribution function (*cdf*) that we have worked with to compute normal probabilities.

The probit statistical model expresses the probability p that y takes the value 1 to be

$$p = P[Z \leq \beta_1 + \beta_2 x] = \Phi(\beta_1 + \beta_2 x) \tag{16.10}$$

where $\Phi(z)$ is the probit function. The probit model is said to be **nonlinear** because (16.10) is a nonlinear function of β_1 and β_2. If β_1 and β_2 were known, we could use (16.10) to find the probability that an individual will drive to work. However, since these parameters are not known, we will estimate them.

16.1.3   INTERPRETATION OF THE PROBIT MODEL

The probit model is represented by (16.10). In this model we can examine the **marginal effect** of a one-unit change in x on the probability that $y = 1$ by considering the derivative,

$$\frac{dp}{dx} = \frac{d\Phi(t)}{dt} \cdot \frac{dt}{dx} = \phi(\beta_1 + \beta_2 x)\beta_2 \tag{16.11}$$

where $t = \beta_1 + \beta_2 x$ and $\phi(\beta_1 + \beta_2 x)$ is the standard normal probability density function evaluated at $\beta_1 + \beta_2 x$. To obtain this result we have used the chain rule of differentiation (See Derivative Rule 9 in Appendix A.3.1). We estimate this effect by replacing the unknown parameters by their estimates $\tilde{\beta}_1$ and $\tilde{\beta}_2$.

In Figure 16.1 we show the probit function $\Phi(z)$ and the standard normal probability density function $\phi(z)$ just below it. The expression in (16.11) shows the effect of an increase in x on p. The effect depends on the slope of the probit function, which is given by $\phi(\beta_1 + \beta_2 x)$ and the magnitude of the parameter β_2. Equation (16.11) has the following implications:

1. Since $\phi(\beta_1 + \beta_2 x)$ is a probability density function, its value is always *positive*. Consequently the sign of dp/dx is determined by the sign of β_2. In the transportation problem, we expect β_2 to be positive so that $dp/dx > 0$; as x increases, we expect p to increase.

2. As x changes, the value of the function $\phi(\beta_1 + \beta_2 x)$ changes. The standard normal probability density function reaches its maximum when $z = 0$ or when $\beta_1 + \beta_2 x = 0$.

In this case $p = \Phi(0) = 0.5$ and an individual is equally likely to choose car or bus transportation. It makes sense that in this case the effect of a change in x has its greatest effect, since the individual is "on the borderline" between car and bus transportation. The slope of the probit function $p = \Phi(z)$ is at its maximum when $z = 0$, the borderline case.

3. On the other hand, if $\beta_1 + \beta_2 x$ is large, say, near three, then the probability that the individual chooses to drive is very large and close to one. In this case a change in x will have relatively little effect, since $\phi(\beta_1 + \beta_2 x)$ will be nearly zero. The same is true if $\beta_1 + \beta_2 x$ is a large negative value, say, near -3. These results are consistent with the notion that if an individual is "set" in their ways, with p near zero or one, the effect of a small change in commuting time will be negligible.

The results of a probit model can also be used to predict an individual's choice. The ability to predict discrete outcomes is very important in many applications. For example, prior to approving loans, banks predict the probability that an applicant will default. If the probability of default is high, then the loan is either not approved or additional conditions, such as extra collateral or a higher interest rate, are imposed.

In order to predict the probability that an individual chooses the alternative $y = 1$, we can use the probability model $p = \Phi(\beta_1 + \beta_2 x)$. In the following section we describe how to obtain estimates $\tilde{\beta}_1$ and $\tilde{\beta}_2$ of the unknown parameters. Using these we estimate the probability p to be

$$\hat{p} = \Phi(\tilde{\beta}_1 + \tilde{\beta}_2 x) \tag{16.12}$$

By comparing to a threshold value, like 0.5, we can predict choice using the rule

$$\hat{y} = \begin{cases} 1 & \hat{p} \geq 0.5 \\ 0 & \hat{p} < 0.5 \end{cases}$$

16.1.4 MAXIMUM LIKELIHOOD ESTIMATION OF THE PROBIT MODEL

Suppose we randomly select three individuals and observe that the first two drive to work and the third takes the bus: $y_1 = 1, y_2 = 1$, and $y_3 = 0$. Furthermore, suppose that the values of x, in minutes, for these individuals are $x_1 = 15$, $x_2 = 6$, and $x_3 = 7$. What is the joint probability of observing $y_1 = 1, y_2 = 1$, and $y_3 = 0$? The probability function for y is given by (16.2), which we now combine with the probit model (16.10) to obtain

$$f(y_i) = [\Phi(\beta_1 + \beta_2 x_i)]^{y_i} [1 - \Phi(\beta_1 + \beta_2 x_i)]^{1-y_i}, \quad y_i = 0, 1 \tag{16.13}$$

If the three individuals are independently drawn, then the joint probability density function for y_1, y_2, and y_3 is the product of the marginal probability functions:

$$f(y_1, y_2, y_3) = f(y_1) f(y_2) f(y_3)$$

Consequently, the probability of observing $y_1 = 1$, $y_2 = 1$, and $y_3 = 0$ is

$$P[y_1 = 1, y_2 = 1, y_3 = 0] = f(1, 1, 0) = f(1) f(1) f(0)$$

Substituting the y and x values into (16.13) we have

$$P[y_1 = 1, y_2 = 1, y_3 = 0] = \Phi(\beta_1 + \beta_2(15)) \times \Phi(\beta_1 + \beta_2(6))$$
$$\times [1 - \Phi(\beta_1 + \beta_2(7))] \qquad (16.14)$$
$$= L(\beta_1, \beta_2)$$

In statistics, the function (16.14), which gives us the probability of observing the sample data, is called the **likelihood function**. The notation $L(\beta_1, \beta_2)$ indicates that the likelihood function is a function of the unknown parameters, β_1 and β_2. Intuitively, it makes sense to choose as estimates for β_1 and β_2 the values $\tilde{\beta}_1$ and $\tilde{\beta}_2$ that maximize the probability, or likelihood, of observing the sample. Unfortunately, there are no formulas that give us the values for $\tilde{\beta}_1$ and $\tilde{\beta}_2$ as there are in least squares estimation of the linear regression model. Consequently, we must use the computer and techniques from numerical analysis to obtain $\tilde{\beta}_1$ and $\tilde{\beta}_2$. In practice, instead of maximizing (16.14), we maximize the logarithm of (16.14), which is called the **log-likelihood function**

$$\ln L(\beta_1, \beta_2) = \ln\{\Phi(\beta_1 + \beta_2(15)) \times \Phi(\beta_1 + \beta_2(6)) \times [1 - \Phi(\beta_1 + \beta_2(7))]\}$$
$$= \ln \Phi(\beta_1 + \beta_2(15)) + \ln \Phi(\beta_1 + \beta_2(6)) + \ln[1 - \Phi(\beta_1 + \beta_2(7))] \quad (16.15)$$

The maximization of the log-likelihood function $\ln L(\beta_1, \beta_2)$ is easier than the maximization of (16.14), because it is a sum of terms and not a product of terms. The logarithm is a nondecreasing, or monotonic, function so that the maximum values of the two functions $L(\beta_1, \beta_2)$ and $\ln L(\beta_1, \beta_2)$ occur at the same values of β_1 and β_2, $\tilde{\beta}_1$ and $\tilde{\beta}_2$. The value of the log-likelihood function (16.15) evaluated at the maximizing values $\tilde{\beta}_1$ and $\tilde{\beta}_2$ is very useful for hypothesis testing, which is discussed in Section 16.2.3. Using econometric software, we find that the parameter values that maximize (16.15) are $\tilde{\beta}_1 = -1.1525$ and $\tilde{\beta}_2 = 0.1892$. These values maximize the log-likelihood function, $\ln L(\beta_1, \beta_2)$, and also maximize the likelihood function $L(\beta_1, \beta_2)$. They are the **maximum likelihood estimates**. Any other values of the parameters that we might try will yield a lower value of the log-likelihood function. Plugging these values into (16.15) we obtain the value of the log-likelihood function evaluated at the maximum likelihood estimates, which is $\ln L(\tilde{\beta}_1, \tilde{\beta}_2) = -1.5940$.

An interesting feature of the maximum likelihood estimation procedure is that while its properties in small samples are not known, we can show that in large samples the maximum likelihood estimator is normally distributed, consistent and *best*, in the sense that no competing estimator has smaller variance. The properties of maximum likelihood estimators are fully discussed in Appendix C.8.

We have used only three observations in the numerical illustration above for demonstration purposes only. In practice such maximum likelihood estimation procedures should only be used when large samples are available. In the next section we present another simple example that will demonstrate more aspects of the probit choice model.

16.1.5   A TRANSPORTATION EXAMPLE

Ben-Akiva and Lerman[1] have sample data on automobile and public transportation travel times and the alternative chosen for $N = 21$ individuals. The complete set of data is in the file *transport.dat*. In the data file, *AUTO* is an indicator variable taking the value one if automobile transportation is chosen and zero otherwise. The data set also includes the

---

[1] Moshe Ben-Akiva and Steven Lerman, *Discrete Choice Analysis* (Cambridge, MA: MIT Press, 1985).

variables *AUTOTIME* and *BUSTIME*, which are commuting times, in minutes. The explanatory variable we consider is *DTIME* = (*BUSTIME*−*AUTOTIME*)÷10, which is the commuting time differential in 10-minute increments. The probit model is $P(AUTO = 1) = \Phi(\beta_1 + \beta_2 DTIME)$. The maximum likelihood estimates of the parameters are

$$\tilde{\beta}_1 + \tilde{\beta}_2 DTIME = -0.0644 + 0.3000 DTIME$$
$$(se) \qquad (0.3992) \ (0.1029)$$

The values in parentheses below the parameter estimates are estimated standard errors that are valid in large samples. These standard errors can be used to carry out hypothesis tests and construct interval estimates in the usual way, with the qualification that they are valid in large samples. The negative sign of $\tilde{\beta}_1$ implies that when commuting times via bus and auto are equal so *DTIME* = 0, individuals have a bias against driving to work, relative to public transportation, though the estimated coefficient is not statistically significant. The positive sign of $\tilde{\beta}_2$ indicates that an increase in public transportation travel time, relative to auto travel time, increases the probability that an individual will choose to drive to work, and this coefficient is statistically significant.

Suppose that we wish to estimate the marginal effect of increasing public transportation time, given that travel via public transportation currently takes 20 minutes longer than auto travel. Using (16.11),

$$\frac{\widehat{dp}}{dDTIME} = \phi(\tilde{\beta}_1 + \tilde{\beta}_2 DTIME)\tilde{\beta}_2 = \phi(-0.0644 + 0.3000 \times 2)(0.3000)$$
$$= \phi(0.5355)(0.3000) = 0.3456 \times 0.3000 = 0.1037$$

For the probit probability model, an incremental (10-minute) increase in the travel time via public transportation increases the probability of travel via auto by approximately 0.1037, given that taking the bus already requires 20 minutes more travel time than driving.

The estimated parameters of the probit model can also be used to "predict" the behavior of an individual who must choose between auto and public transportation to travel to work. If an individual is faced with the situation that it takes 30 minutes longer to take public transportation than to drive to work, then the estimated probability that auto transportation will be selected is calculated using (16.12):

$$\hat{p} = \Phi(\tilde{\beta}_1 + \tilde{\beta}_2 DTIME) = \Phi(-0.0644 + 0.3000 \times 3) = 0.7983$$

Since the estimated probability that the individual will choose to drive to work is 0.7983, which is greater than 0.5, we "predict" that when public transportation takes 30 minutes longer than driving to work, the individual will choose to drive.

16.1.6 FURTHER POST-ESTIMATION ANALYSIS

In the previous section we computed the marginal effect of an increase of travel time on the probability of choosing *AUTO* given that travel via public transportation takes 20 minutes longer than auto travel as 0.1037. A 20-minute differential is a scenario in which we might be interested. If particular values of interest are difficult to identify, many researchers evaluate the marginal effect "at the means." In these data, the average time travel differential is $\overline{DTIME} = -0.1224$ (1.2 minutes), and for this value the marginal effect of a 10-minute increase in the time travel differential is 0.1191. The slightly larger effect is consistent with the second point in the Section 16.1.3 discussion. When the mean difference in travel time is near zero, the effect of a change in travel time difference is greater.

Rather than evaluate the marginal effect at a specific value, or the mean value, the **average marginal effect (AME)** is often considered. It is the average of the marginal effects evaluated at each sample data point. That is,

$$\widehat{AME} = \frac{1}{N}\Sigma_{i=1}^{N}\phi(\tilde{\beta}_1 + \tilde{\beta}_2 DTIME_i)\tilde{\beta}_2$$

The average marginal effect has become a popular alternative to computing the marginal effect at the mean as it summarizes the response of individuals in the sample to a change in the value of an explanatory variable. For the current example, $\widehat{AME} = 0.0484$, which is the average estimated increase in probability given a 10-minute increase in bus travel time relative to auto travel time. Because the estimated marginal effect is different for each individual in the sample, we are interested in not only its average value, but also in its variation in the sample. The sample standard deviation of $\phi(\tilde{\beta}_1 + \tilde{\beta}_2 DTIME_i)\tilde{\beta}_2$ is 0.0365, and its minimum and maximum values are 0.0025 and 0.1153.

A second point has to do with the nature of the marginal effect

$$\frac{\widehat{dp}}{dDTIME} = \phi(\tilde{\beta}_1 + \tilde{\beta}_2 DTIME)\tilde{\beta}_2 = g(\tilde{\beta}_1, \tilde{\beta}_2)$$

The marginal effect is an estimator, since it is a function of the estimators $\tilde{\beta}_1$ and $\tilde{\beta}_2$. Based on the discussion of the "delta method" in Appendix 5B.5, which is relevant because the marginal effect is a **nonlinear** function of $\tilde{\beta}_1$ and $\tilde{\beta}_2$, the marginal effect estimator is consistent and asymptotically normal with a variance given by (5B.8). Using this result, we can test marginal effects or compute interval estimates for them. For example, if the time differential is currently 20 minutes, so that $DTIME = 2$, the estimated marginal effect is 0.1037 and the estimated standard error of the marginal effect is 0.0326 using the delta method. Therefore a 95% interval estimate of the marginal effect, using the t-critical value $t_{(0.975,19)} = 2.093$, is [0.0354, 0.1720]. This interval is fairly wide. Recall, however, that the maximum likelihood estimates are based on only 21 observations, which is a very small sample. The details of the calculation of the standard error are given in Appendix 16A.1. We can also evaluate the standard error of the average marginal effect using the delta method. Recall that $\widehat{AME} = 0.0484$. Its standard error estimated using the delta method is 0.0034. Details of this calculation are given in Appendix 16A.2. A 95% interval estimate of the population average marginal effect, using the t-critical value, is [0.0413, 0.0556]. This is much narrower than the previous interval estimate, because we are estimating a different quantity, namely $AME = \frac{1}{N}\Sigma_{i=1}^{N}\phi(\beta_1 + \beta_2 DTIME_i)\beta_2$.

The predicted probability that $AUTO = 1$, given that the commuting time difference of 30 minutes is calculated as $\hat{p} = \Phi(\tilde{\beta}_1 + \tilde{\beta}_2 DTIME) = \Phi(-0.0644 + 0.3000 \times 3) = 0.7983$. This was shown in Section 16.1.5. Note that the predicted probability is a nonlinear function of the parameter estimates. Using the delta method we can compute a standard error for the prediction and, thus, an interval estimate. The calculated standard error is 0.1425, so that a 95% prediction interval, again using the t-critical value $t_{(0.975,19)} = 2.093$, is [0.5000, 1.0966]. Note that the upper endpoint of the interval is greater than one, which means that some of the values are infeasible. This example has been designed to illustrate in a simple problem how probit works. In reality, estimating complicated models like probit and logit, with as few observations as we are using, $N = 21$, is not a good idea. In fact, microeconometric models can have many more parameters and sometimes are estimated using very large data sets.

16.2 The Logit Model for Binary Choice

Probit model estimation is numerically complicated because it is based on the normal distribution. A frequently used alternative to the probit model for binary choice situations is the logit model. These models differ only in the particular S-shaped curve used to constrain probabilities to the [0, 1] interval. If L is a **logistic random variable**, then its probability density function is

$$\lambda(l) = \frac{e^{-l}}{\left(1 + e^{-l}\right)^2}, \quad -\infty < l < \infty \tag{16.16}$$

The corresponding cumulative distribution function, unlike the normal distribution, has a closed form expression, which makes analysis somewhat easier. The cumulative distribution function for a logistic random variable is

$$\Lambda(l) = P[L \le l] = \frac{1}{1 + e^{-l}} \tag{16.17}$$

In the logit model, the probability p that the observed value y takes the value 1 is

$$p = P[L \le \beta_1 + \beta_2 x] = \Lambda(\beta_1 + \beta_2 x) = \frac{1}{1 + e^{-(\beta_1 + \beta_2 x)}} \tag{16.18}$$

This can be expressed in a more generally useful form. The probability that $y = 1$ can be written as

$$p = \frac{1}{1 + e^{-(\beta_1 + \beta_2 x)}} = \frac{\exp(\beta_1 + \beta_2 x)}{1 + \exp(\beta_1 + \beta_2 x)}$$

The probability that $y = 0$ is

$$1 - p = \frac{1}{1 + \exp(\beta_1 + \beta_2 x)}$$

Represented in this way, the logit model can be extended to cases in which the choice is between more than two alternatives, as we will see in Section 16.3.

In maximum likelihood estimation of the logit model, the probability given in (16.18) is used to form the likelihood function (16.14) by inserting "Λ" for "Φ". To interpret the logit estimates, the derivative in (16.11) is still valid, using (16.16) instead of the normal probability density function.

The shapes of the logistic and normal probability density functions are somewhat different, and maximum likelihood estimates of β_1 and β_2 will be different. However, the marginal probabilities and the predicted probabilities differ very little in most cases.

16.2.1 AN EMPIRICAL EXAMPLE FROM MARKETING

In Chapter 7.4.1 we introduced the example of a linear probability model for the choice between Coke and Pepsi. Here we compare the linear probability model to the probit and logit models for this binary choice. The variable *COKE*

$$COKE = \begin{cases} 1 & \text{if Coke is chosen} \\ 0 & \text{if Pepsi is chosen} \end{cases}$$

The expected value of this variable is $E(COKE) = p_{COKE}$ = probability that Coke is chosen. We use the relative price of Coke to Pepsi (*PRATIO*) as an explanatory variable, as well as *DISP_COKE* and *DISP_PEPSI*, which are indicator variables taking the value one if the respective store display is present and zero if it is not. We expect that the presence of a Coke display will increase the probability of a Coke purchase, and the presence of a Pepsi display will decrease the probability of a Coke purchase.

The data file *coke.dat* contains "scanner" data on 1,140 individuals who purchased Coke or Pepsi. The probit and logit models for the choice are

$$p_{COKE} = E(COKE) = \Phi(\beta_1 + \beta_2 PRATIO + \beta_3 DISP\_COKE + \beta_4 DISP\_PEPSI)$$

$$p_{COKE} = E(COKE) = \Lambda(\gamma_1 + \gamma_2 PRATIO + \gamma_3 DISP\_COKE + \gamma_4 DISP\_PEPSI)$$

We have given the logit choice model parameters different symbols to emphasize that they will be different values than those for probit. The estimates are given in Table 16.1.

The parameters and their estimates vary across the models and no direct comparison is very useful, but some rules of thumb exist.[2] Roughly

$$\tilde{\gamma}_{\text{Logit}} \cong 4\hat{\beta}_{\text{LPM}}$$

$$\hat{\beta}_{\text{Probit}} \cong 2.5\hat{\beta}_{\text{LPM}}$$

$$\tilde{\gamma}_{\text{Logit}} \cong 1.6\hat{\beta}_{\text{Probit}}$$

More relevant, however, is the comparison of the predicted probabilities and marginal effects implied by the alternative models. Suppose that *PRATIO* = 1.1, indicating that the price of Coke is 10% higher than the price of Pepsi, and no store displays are present. Using the linear probability model, the predicted probability of Coke choice is 0.4493 with standard error 0.0202. Using probit the predicted probability is 0.4394 with standard error 0.0218, and for logit predicted probability is 0.4323 with standard error 0.0224.

In the linear probability model the marginal effect of *PRATIO* is −0.4009. This does not depend on the values of the variables. For the probit model the average marginal effect (AME) of *PRATIO* is −0.4097 with standard error 0.0616. For the logit model the average marginal effect (AME) of *PRATIO* is −0.4333 with standard error 0.0639. In this example,

Table 16.1   **Coke–Pepsi Choice Models**

	LPM	probit	logit
C	0.89022***	1.10806***	1.92297***
	(0.0653)	(0.1900)	(0.3258)
PRATIO	−0.40086***	−1.14596***	−1.99574***
	(0.0604)	(0.1809)	(0.3146)
DISP_COKE	0.07717**	0.21719**	0.35160**
	(0.0339)	(0.0966)	(0.1585)
DISP_PEPSI	−0.16566***	−0.44730***	−0.73099***
	(0.0344)	(0.1014)	(0.1678)

*Standard errors in parentheses (White robust se for LPM) * p<0.10, ** p<0.05, *** p<0.01.*

[2] T. Amemiya (1981) "Qualitative response models: A Survey," *Journal of Economic Literature*, 19, pp. 1483–1536, or A. Colin Cameron and Pravin K. Trivedi *Microeconometrics Using Stata: Revised Edition* (College Station, TX: Stata Press), p. 465.

the average marginal effects from the probit and logit models are not too different from that implied by the linear probability model. If we examine specific scenarios, then differences appear. For example, suppose $PRATIO = 1.1$, indicating that the price of Coke is 10% higher than the price of Pepsi, and no store displays are present. The marginal effect of $PRATIO$ from the probit model is -0.4519, with standard error 0.0703. For logit the marginal effect of $PRATIO$ is estimated to be -0.4898 with standard error 0.0753.

Another basis for comparison is how well the alternative models predict choice outcomes. For the linear probability model, compute the predicted value $\widehat{COKE}$, then predict consumer choice by comparing this value to 0.5. If $\widehat{COKE}$ is greater than 0.5, we predict the consumer will choose Coke. For the probit model, we estimate the probability of choosing Coke using (16.10). For logit, again use (16.10) with the logistic cdf, Λ, replacing the standard normal cdf, Φ. Using the 0.5 threshold for all three estimation methods, we find that of the 510 consumers who chose $COKE$, 247 were correctly predicted. Of the 630 who chose $PEPSI$, 507 were corrected predicted. In this example, the number of correct predictions is identical for the three estimation methods.

16.2.2 WALD HYPOTHESIS TESTS

Hypothesis tests concerning individual coefficients in probit and logit models are carried out in the usual way based on an "asymptotic-t" test. If the null hypothesis is $H_0 : \beta_k = c$, then the test statistic using the probit model is

$$t = \frac{\tilde{\beta}_k - c}{\text{se}(\tilde{\beta}_k)} \overset{a}{\sim} t_{(N-K)}$$

where $\tilde{\beta}_k$ is the probit parameter estimator, N is the sample size, and K is the number of parameters estimated. The test is asymptotically justified, and if N is large the critical values from the $t_{(N-K)}$ distribution will be very close to those from the standard normal distribution. In smaller samples, however, the use of the t-distribution critical values can make minor differences and is the more "conservative" choice.

The t-test is based on the **Wald principle**. This testing principle is discussed in Appendix C.8.4b. It is common for software packages to have "built-in" Wald test statements (something like "TEST") that are convenient to use. To illustrate, using the probit model, consider the two hypotheses

Hypothesis (1) $H_0 : \beta_3 = -\beta_4$, $H_1 : \beta_3 \neq -\beta_4$

Hypothesis (2) $H_0 : \beta_3 = 0$, $\beta_4 = 0$, $H_1 :$ either β_3 or β_4 is not zero

Hypothesis (1) is that the coefficients on the display variables are equal in magnitude but opposite in sign, or that the effect of the Coke and Pepsi displays have an equal but opposite effect on the probability of choosing Coke. To test hypothesis (1) in a linear model, we would compute

$$t = \frac{\tilde{\beta}_{DISP\_COKE} + \tilde{\beta}_{DISP\_PEPSI}}{\text{se}(\tilde{\beta}_{DISP\_COKE} + \tilde{\beta}_{DISP\_PEPSI})} \overset{a}{\sim} t_{(1140-4=1136)}$$

Noting that it is a two-tail hypothesis, we reject the null hypothesis at the $\alpha = 0.05$ level if $t \geq 1.96$ or $t \leq -1.96$. The calculated t-value is $t = -2.3247$, so we reject the null hypothesis and conclude that the effects of the Coke and Pepsi displays are not of equal magnitude with opposite sign. This test is asymptotically valid because $N-K = 1140-4 = 1136$ is a large sample.

Automatic TEST statements usually generate the chi-square distribution version of the test, which in this case is the square of the t-statistic, $W = 5.4040$. If the null hypothesis is true, the Wald test statistic has an asymptotic $\chi^2_{(1)}$ distribution. Using Table 3 at the end of the book, the 0.95 percentile value for this distribution is 3.841. Using a Wald chi-square test, we reject the null hypothesis if the test statistic value is greater than the critical value. We reach the same conclusion as using the t-test. The link between the t and chi-square test is fully explained in Appendix C.8.4b.

A generalization of the Wald statistic is used to test the joint null hypothesis (2) that neither the Coke nor Pepsi display affects the probability of choosing Coke. Here we are testing two hypotheses, so that the Wald statistic has an asymptotic $\chi^2_{(2)}$ distribution. Using Table 3 at the end of the book, the 0.95 percentile value for this distribution is 5.991. In this case, the value of the Wald statistic is $W = 19.4594$, and thus we reject the null hypothesis (2).

16.2.3   LIKELIHOOD RATIO HYPOTHESIS TESTS

When using maximum likelihood estimators, such as probit and logit, tests based on the likelihood ratio principle are generally preferred. Appendix C.8.4a contains a discussion of this methodology. The idea is much like the F-test in the linear regression model. One test component is the log-likelihood function value in the unrestricted, full model (call it $\ln L_U$) evaluated at the maximum likelihood estimates. This calculation was illustrated in Section 16.1.4. The second ingredient is the log-likelihood function value from the model that is "restricted" by imposing the condition that the null hypothesis is true (call it $\ln L_R$). The likelihood ratio test statistic is $LR = 2(\ln L_U - \ln L_R)$. If the null hypothesis is true, the statistic has an asymptotic chi-square distribution with degrees of freedom equal to the number of hypotheses being tested. The null hypothesis is rejected if the value LR is larger than the chi-square distribution critical value.

To test hypothesis (1) from the previous section, $H_0 : \beta_3 = -\beta_4$, we first obtain the unrestricted probit model log-likelihood value. This value, $\ln L_U = -710.9486$, is reported by econometric software when a probit model is estimated. The restricted probit model is obtained by imposing the condition $\beta_3 = -\beta_4$, leading to

$$\begin{aligned}
p_{COKE} = E(COKE) &= \Phi(\beta_1 + \beta_2 PRATIO + \beta_3 DISP\_COKE + \beta_4 DISP\_PEPSI) \\
&= \Phi(\beta_1 + \beta_2 PRATIO - \beta_4 DISP\_COKE + \beta_4 DISP\_PEPSI) \\
&= \Phi(\beta_1 + \beta_2 PRATIO + \beta_4(DISP\_PEPSI - DISP\_COKE))
\end{aligned}$$

Estimating this model by maximum likelihood probit, we obtain $\ln L_R = -713.6595$. The likelihood ratio test statistic value is then

$$LR = 2(\ln L_U - \ln L_R) = 2(-710.9486 - (-713.6595)) = 5.4218$$

This value is larger than the 0.95 percentile from the $\chi^2_{(1)}$ distribution, 3.841, and thus we reject the null hypothesis (1). Note that the values of the LR and Wald statistics are not the same but are close in this case. The Wald test statistic value is easier to compute, since it requires only the maximum likelihood estimates for the original, unrestricted model. However the likelihood ratio test has been found to be more reliable in a wide variety of more complex testing situations, and it is the preferred test.

To test the null hypothesis (2), $H_0 : \beta_3 = 0$, $\beta_4 = 0$, use the restricted model $E(COKE) = \Phi(\beta_1 + \beta_2 PRATIO)$. The value of the likelihood ratio test statistic is

19.55, which is larger than the $\chi^2_{(2)}$ 0.95 percentile value 5.991. We reject the null hypothesis that neither the Coke nor Pepsi display has an effect on the choice of Coke.

As in the linear regression model, we are interested in testing the overall significance of the probit model. In the Coke choice example, the null hypothesis for this test is $H_0 : \beta_2 = 0,\ \beta_3 = 0,\ \beta_4 = 0$. The alternative hypothesis is that at least one of the parameters is not zero. If the null hypothesis is true, the restricted model is $E(COKE) = \Phi(\beta_1)$. The log-likelihood value for this restricted model is $\ln L_R = -783.8603$, and the value of the likelihood ratio test statistic is $LR = 145.8234$. The test statistic has an asymptotic $\chi^2_{(3)}$ distribution if the null hypothesis is true. The 0.95 percentile value for this distribution is 7.815, so we reject the null hypothesis that none of the explanatory variables help explain the choice of Coke versus Pepsi. Also, like the linear regression model, this "overall" test is reported in standard probit computer output.

16.3 Multinomial Logit

In probit and logit models the decision maker chooses between two alternatives. Clearly we are often faced with choices involving more than two alternatives. These are called **multinomial choice** situations. Examples include the following:

- If you are shopping for a laundry detergent, which one do you choose? Tide, Cheer, Arm & Hammer, Wisk, and so on. The consumer is faced with a wide array of alternatives. Marketing researchers relate these choices to prices of the alternatives, advertising, and product characteristics.

- If you enroll in the business school, will you major in economics, marketing, management, finance, or accounting?

- If you are going to a mall on a shopping spree, which mall will you go to, and why?

- When you graduated from high school, you had to choose between not going to college and going to a private four-year college, a public four-year college, or a two-year college. What factors led to your decision among these alternatives?

It would not take you long to come up with other illustrations. In each of these cases, we wish to relate the observed choice to a set of explanatory variables. More specifically, as in probit and logit models, we wish to explain and predict the probability that an individual with a certain set of characteristics chooses one of the alternatives. The estimation and interpretation of such models is, in principle, similar to that in logit and probit models. The models themselves go under the names **multinomial logit**, **conditional logit**, and **multinomial probit**. We will discuss the most commonly used logit models.

16.3.1 MULTINOMIAL LOGIT CHOICE PROBABILITIES

Suppose that a decision maker must choose between several distinct alternatives. Let us focus on a problem with $J = 3$ alternatives. An example might be the choice facing a high school graduate. Shall I attend a two-year college, a four-year college, or not go to college? The factors affecting this choice might include household income, the student's high school grades, family size, race, and gender, and the parents' education. As in the logit and probit models, we will try to explain the probability that the ith person will choose alternative j,

$$p_{ij} = P[\text{individual } i \text{ chooses alternative } j]$$

In our example there are $J = 3$ alternatives, denoted by $j = 1, 2,$ or 3. These numerical values have no meaning, because the alternatives in general have no particular ordering and are assigned arbitrarily. You can think of them as categories A, B, and C.

If we assume a single explanatory factor, x_i, then, in the multinomial logit specification, the probabilities of individual i choosing alternatives $j = 1, 2, 3$ are

$$p_{i1} = \frac{1}{1 + \exp(\beta_{12} + \beta_{22}x_i) + \exp(\beta_{13} + \beta_{23}x_i)}, \quad j = 1 \tag{16.19a}$$

$$p_{i2} = \frac{\exp(\beta_{12} + \beta_{22}x_i)}{1 + \exp(\beta_{12} + \beta_{22}x_i) + \exp(\beta_{13} + \beta_{23}x_i)}, \quad j = 2 \tag{16.19b}$$

$$p_{i3} = \frac{\exp(\beta_{13} + \beta_{23}x_i)}{1 + \exp(\beta_{12} + \beta_{22}x_i) + \exp(\beta_{13} + \beta_{23}x_i)}, \quad j = 3 \tag{16.19c}$$

The parameters β_{12} and β_{22} are specific to the second alternative, and β_{13} and β_{23} are specific to the third alternative. The parameters specific to the first alternative are set to zero to solve an **identification problem** and to make the probabilities sum to one.[3] Setting $\beta_{11} = \beta_{21} = 0$ leads to the 1 in the numerator of p_{i1} and the 1 in the denominator of each part of (16.19). Specifically, the term that would be there is $\exp(\beta_{11} + \beta_{21}x_i) = \exp(0 + 0x_i) = 1$.

A distinguishing feature of the multinomial logit model in (16.19) is that there is a single explanatory variable that describes the individual, *not* the alternatives facing the individual. Such variables are called **individual specific**. To distinguish the alternatives, we give them different parameter values. This situation is common in the social sciences, where surveys record many characteristics of the individuals, and choices they made.

16.3.2 Maximum Likelihood Estimation

Let y_{i1}, y_{i2}, and y_{i3} be indicator variables representing the choice made by individual i. If alternative 1 is selected, then $y_{i1} = 1$, $y_{i2} = 0$, and $y_{i3} = 0$. If alternative 2 is selected, then $y_{i1} = 0, y_{i2} = 1,$ and $y_{i3} = 0$. In this model each individual must choose one, and only one, of the available alternatives.

Estimation of this model is by maximum likelihood. Suppose that we observe three individuals, who choose alternatives 1, 2, and 3, respectively. Assuming that their choices are independent, then the probability of observing this outcome is

$$P(y_{11} = 1, y_{22} = 1, y_{33} = 1) = p_{11} \times p_{22} \times p_{33}$$

$$= \frac{1}{1 + \exp(\beta_{12} + \beta_{22}x_1) + \exp(\beta_{13} + \beta_{23}x_1)}$$

$$\times \frac{\exp(\beta_{12} + \beta_{22}x_2)}{1 + \exp(\beta_{12} + \beta_{22}x_2) + \exp(\beta_{13} + \beta_{23}x_2)}$$

$$\times \frac{\exp(\beta_{13} + \beta_{23}x_3)}{1 + \exp(\beta_{12} + \beta_{22}x_3) + \exp(\beta_{13} + \beta_{23}x_3)}$$

$$= L(\beta_{12}, \beta_{22}, \beta_{13}, \beta_{23})$$

---

[3] Some software may choose the parameters of the last (Jth) alternative to set to zero, or perhaps the most frequently chosen group. Check your software documentation.

In the last line we recognize that this joint probability depends on the unknown parameters and is in fact the likelihood function. Maximum likelihood estimation seeks those values of the parameters that maximize the likelihood or, more specifically, the **log-likelihood function**, which is easier to work with mathematically. In a real application the number of individuals will be greater than three, and computer software will be used to maximize the log-likelihood function numerically. While the task might look daunting, finding the maximum likelihood estimates in this type of model is fairly simple.

16.3.3   POST-ESTIMATION ANALYSIS

Given that we can obtain maximum likelihood estimates of the parameters, which we denote as $\tilde{\beta}_{12}$, $\tilde{\beta}_{22}$, $\tilde{\beta}_{13}$, and $\tilde{\beta}_{23}$, what can we do then? The first thing we might do is estimate the probability that an individual will choose alternative 1, 2, or 3. For the value of the explanatory variable x_0, we can calculate the predicted probabilities of each outcome being selected using (16.19). For example, the probability that such an individual will choose alternative 1 is

$$\tilde{p}_{01} = \frac{1}{1 + \exp(\tilde{\beta}_{12} + \tilde{\beta}_{22}x_0) + \exp(\tilde{\beta}_{13} + \tilde{\beta}_{23}x_0)}$$

The predicted probabilities for alternatives 2 and 3, $\tilde{p}_{02}$ and $\tilde{p}_{03}$, can similarly be obtained. If we wanted to predict which alternative would be chosen, we might choose to predict that alternative j will be chosen if $\tilde{p}_{0j}$ is the maximum of the estimated probabilities.

Because the model is such a complicated nonlinear function of the parameters, it will not surprise you to learn that the βs are not "slopes." In these models the **marginal effect** is the effect of a change in x, everything else held constant, on the probability that an individual chooses alternative $m = 1, 2$, or 3. It can be shown[4] that

$$\left.\frac{\Delta p_{im}}{\Delta x_i}\right|_{\text{all else constant}} = \frac{\partial p_{im}}{\partial x_i} = p_{im}\left[\beta_{2m} - \sum_{j=1}^{3}\beta_{2j}p_{ij}\right] \qquad (16.20)$$

Recall that the model we are discussing has a single explanatory variable, x_i, and that $\beta_{21} = 0$.

Alternatively, and somewhat more simply, the difference in probabilities can be calculated for two specific values of x_i. If x_a and x_b are two values of x_i, then the estimated change in probability of choosing alternative 1 $[m = 1]$ when changing from x_a to x_b is

$$\widetilde{\Delta p_1} = \tilde{p}_{b1} - \tilde{p}_{a1}$$

$$= \frac{1}{1 + \exp(\tilde{\beta}_{12} + \tilde{\beta}_{22}x_b) + \exp(\tilde{\beta}_{13} + \tilde{\beta}_{23}x_b)}$$

$$- \frac{1}{1 + \exp(\tilde{\beta}_{12} + \tilde{\beta}_{22}x_a) + \exp(\tilde{\beta}_{13} + \tilde{\beta}_{23}x_a)}$$

---

[4] One can quickly become overwhelmed by the mathematics when seeking references on this topic. Two relatively friendly sources, with good examples, are *Regression Models for Categorical and Limited Dependent Variables* by J. Scott Long (Thousand Oaks, CA: Sage Publications, 1997) [see Chapter 6] and *Quantitative Models in Marketing Research* by Philip Hans Franses and Richard Paap (Cambridge University Press, 2001) [see Chapter 5]. At a much more advanced level, see *Econometric Analysis*, 6th edition by William Greene (Upper Saddle River, NJ: Pearson Prentice Hall, 2008) [see Section 23.11.1].

This approach is good if there are certain scenarios that you as a researcher have in mind as typical or important cases, or if x is an indicator variable with only two values, $x_a = 0$ and $x_b = 1$.

Another useful interpretive device is the **probability ratio**. It shows how many times more likely category j is to be chosen relative to the first category and is given by

$$\frac{P(y_i = j)}{P(y_i = 1)} = \frac{p_{ij}}{p_{i1}} = \exp(\beta_{1j} + \beta_{2j}x_i), \quad j = 2, 3 \tag{16.21}$$

The effect on the probability ratio of changing the value of x_i is given by the derivative

$$\frac{\partial(p_{ij}/p_{i1})}{\partial x_i} = \beta_{2j}\exp(\beta_{1j} + \beta_{2j}x_i), \quad j = 2, 3 \tag{16.22}$$

The value of the exponential function $\exp(\beta_{1j} + \beta_{2j}x_i)$ is always positive. Thus the sign of β_{2j} tells us whether a change in x_i will make the jth category more or less likely relative to the first category.

An interesting feature of the probability ratio (16.21) is that it does not depend on how many alternatives there are in total. There is the implicit assumption in logit models that the probability ratio between any pair of alternatives is **independent of irrelevant alternatives (IIA)**. This is a strong assumption, and if it is violated, multinomial logit may not be a good modeling choice. It is especially likely to fail if several alternatives are similar. Tests for the IIA assumption work by dropping one or more of the available options from the choice set and then re-estimating the multinomial model. If the IIA assumption holds, then the estimates should not change very much. A statistical comparison of the two sets of estimates, one set from the model with a full set of alternatives, and the other from the model using a reduced set of alternatives, is carried out using a Hausman contrast test proposed by Hausman and McFadden (1984).[5]

16.3.4 AN EXAMPLE

The National Education Longitudinal Study of 1988 (NELS:88) was the first nationally representative longitudinal study of eighth-grade students in public and private schools in the United States. It was sponsored by the National Center for Education Statistics. In 1988, some 25,000 eighth-graders and their parents, teachers, and principals were surveyed. In 1990, these same students (who were then mostly 10th-graders, and some dropouts) and their teachers, and principals were surveyed again. In 1992, the second follow-up survey was conducted of students, mostly in the 12th grade, but dropouts, parents, teachers, school administrators, and high school transcripts were also surveyed. The third follow-up was in 1994, after most students had graduated.[6]

We have taken a subset of the total data, namely those who stayed in the panel of data through the third follow-up. On this group we have complete data on the individuals and their households, high school grades, and test scores, as well as their post-secondary education choices. In the file *nels_small.dat* we have 1,000 observations on students who

---

[5] "Specification Tests for the Multinomial Logit Model," *Econometrica*, 49, pp. 1219–1240. A brief explanation of the test may be found in Greene (2008), op. cit., p. 847.

[6] The study and data are summarized in *National Education Longitudinal Study: 1988–1994, Descriptive Summary Report With an Essay on Access and Choice in Post-Secondary Education*, by Allen Sanderson, Bernard Dugoni, Kenneth Rasinski, and John Taylor, C. Dennis Carroll project officer, NCES 96-175, National Center for Education Statistics, March 1996.

Table 16.2 **Maximum Likelihood Estimates of PSE Choice**

Parameters	Estimates	Standard errors	*t*-Statistics
β_{12}	2.5064	0.4183	5.99
β_{22}	−0.3088	0.0523	−5.91
β_{13}	5.7699	0.4043	14.27
β_{23}	−0.7062	0.0529	−13.34

chose, upon graduating from high school, either no college (*PSECHOICE* = 1), a two-year college (*PSECHOICE* = 2), or a four-year college (*PSECHOICE* = 3). For illustration purposes we focus on the explanatory variable *GRADES*, which is an index ranging from 1.0 (highest level, A+ grade) to 13.0 (lowest level, F grade) and represents combined performance in English, math, and social studies.

Of the 1,000 students, 22.2% selected not to attend a college upon graduation, 25.1% selected to attend a two-year college, and 52.7% attended a four-year college. The average value of *GRADES* is 6.53, with highest grade 1.74 and lowest grade 12.33. The estimated values of the parameters and their standard errors are given in Table 16.2. We selected the group who did not attend a college to be our base group, so that the parameters $\beta_{11} = \beta_{21} = 0$.

Based on these estimates, what can we say? Recall that a larger numerical value of *GRADES* represents a poorer academic performance. The parameter estimates for the coefficients of *GRADES* are negative and statistically significant. Using expression (16.22) on the effect of a change in an explanatory variable on the probability ratio, this means that if the value of *GRADES* increases, the probability that high school graduates will choose a two-year or a four-year college goes down, relative to the probability of not attending college. This is the anticipated effect, as we expect that a poorer academic performance will increase the odds of not attending college.

We can also compute the predicted probability of each type of college choice using (16.19) for given values of *GRADES*. In our sample the median value of *GRADES* is 6.64, and the top 5th percentile value is 2.635.[7] What are the choice probabilities of students with these grades? In Table 16.3 we show that the probability of choosing no college is 0.1810 for the student with median grades, but this probability is reduced to 0.0178 for students with top grades. Similarly, the probability of choosing a two-year school is 0.2856 for the average student but is 0.0966 for the better student. Finally, the average student has a 0.5334 chance of selecting a four-year college, but the better student has a 0.8857 chance of selecting a four-year college.

The marginal effect of a change in *GRADES* on the choice probabilities can be calculated using (16.20). The marginal effect again depends on particular values for *GRADES*, and we report these in Table 16.3 for the median and 5th percentile students. An increase in *GRADES* of one point (worse performance) increases the probabilities of choosing either no college or a two-year college and reduces the probability of attending a four-year college. The probability of attending a four-year college declines more for the average student than

---

[7] The 5th percentile value of *GRADES* is given as 2.635 which is halfway between observations 50 and 51 in this 1,000-observation data set. While this is a common way to calculate the 5th percentile, it is not the only way. Since 0.05 × 1000 = 50, some software will report the 50th value, after sorting according to increasing value, 2.63. Others may take a weighted average of the 50th and 51st values, such as 0.95 × 2.63 + 0.05 × 2.64 = 2.6305. Thanks to Tom Doan (Estima) for noting this. Standard errors in Table 16.3 are computed via "the delta method," in a fashion similar to that described in Appendix 16A.

Table 16.3 **Effects of Grades on Probability of PSE Choice**

PSE Choice	GRADES	$\hat{p}$	se($\hat{p}$)	Marginal effect	se(ME)
No College	6.64	0.1810	0.0149	0.0841	0.0063
	2.635	0.0178	0.0047	0.0116	0.0022
Two-Year College	6.64	0.2856	0.0161	0.0446	0.0076
	2.635	0.0966	0.0160	0.0335	0.0024
Four-Year College	6.64	0.5334	0.0182	−0.1287	0.0095
	2.635	0.8857	0.0174	−0.0451	0.0030

for the top student, given the 1-point increase in *GRADES*. Note that for each value of *GRADES* the sum of the predicted probabilities is one, and the sum of the marginal effects is zero, except for rounding error. This is a feature of the multinomial logit specification.

As you can see there are many interesting questions we can address with this type of model.

16.4 Conditional Logit

Suppose that a decision maker must choose between several distinct alternatives, just as in the multinomial logit model. In a marketing context, suppose our decision is between three types ($J = 3$) of soft drinks, say Pepsi, 7-Up, and Coke Classic, in 2-liter bottles. Shoppers will visit their supermarkets and make a choice, based on prices of the products and other factors. With the advent of supermarket scanners at checkout, data on purchases (what brand, how many units, and the price paid) are recorded. Of course we also know the prices of the products that the consumer did not buy on a particular shopping occasion. The key point is that if we collect data on soda purchases from a variety of supermarkets, over a period of time, we observe consumer choices from the set of alternatives and we know the prices facing the shopper on each trip to the supermarket.

Let y_{i1}, y_{i2}, and y_{i3} be indicator variables that indicate the choice made by individual i. If alternative one (Pepsi) is selected, then $y_{i1} = 1$, $y_{i2} = 0$, and $y_{i3} = 0$. If alternative two (7-Up) is selected, then $y_{i1} = 0$, $y_{i2} = 1$, and $y_{i3} = 0$. If alternative 3 (Coke) is selected, then $y_{i1} = 0$, $y_{i2} = 0$, and $y_{i3} = 1$. The price facing individual i for brand j is *PRICE*$_{ij}$. That is, the price of Pepsi, 7-Up, and Coke is potentially different for each customer who purchases soda. Remember, different customers can shop at different supermarkets and at different times. Variables like *PRICE* are **individual- and alternative-specific** because they vary from individual to individual and are different for each choice the consumer might make. This type of information is very different from what we assumed was available in the multinomial logit model, where the explanatory variable x_i was **individual-specific**; it did not change across alternatives.

16.4.1 CONDITIONAL LOGIT CHOICE PROBABILITIES

Our objective is to understand the factors that lead a consumer to choose one alternative over another. We construct a model for the probability that individual i chooses alternative j

$$p_{ij} = P[\text{individual } i \text{ chooses alternative } j]$$

The conditional logit model specifies these probabilities as

$$p_{ij} = \frac{\exp(\beta_{1j} + \beta_2 PRICE_{ij})}{\exp(\beta_{11} + \beta_2 PRICE_{i1}) + \exp(\beta_{12} + \beta_2 PRICE_{i2}) + \exp(\beta_{13} + \beta_2 PRICE_{i3})}$$
(16.23)

Note that unlike the probabilities for the multinomial logit model in (16.19), there is only one parameter β_2 relating the effect of each price to the choice probability p_{ij}. We have also included alternative specific constants (intercept terms). These cannot all be estimated, and one must be set to zero. We will set $\beta_{13} = 0$.

Estimation of the unknown parameters is by maximum likelihood. Suppose that we observe three individuals, who choose alternatives one, two, and three, respectively. Assuming that their choices are independent, then the probability of observing this outcome is

$$P(y_{11} = 1, y_{22} = 1, y_{33} = 1) = p_{11} \times p_{22} \times p_{33}$$

$$= \frac{\exp(\beta_{11} + \beta_2 PRICE_{11})}{\exp(\beta_{11} + \beta_2 PRICE_{11}) + \exp(\beta_{12} + \beta_2 PRICE_{12}) + \exp(\beta_2 PRICE_{13})}$$

$$\times \frac{\exp(\beta_{12} + \beta_2 PRICE_{22})}{\exp(\beta_{11} + \beta_2 PRICE_{21}) + \exp(\beta_{12} + \beta_2 PRICE_{22}) + \exp(\beta_2 PRICE_{23})}$$

$$\times \frac{\exp(\beta_2 PRICE_{33})}{\exp(\beta_{11} + \beta_2 PRICE_{31}) + \exp(\beta_{12} + \beta_2 PRICE_{32}) + \exp(\beta_2 PRICE_{33})}$$

$$= L(\beta_{11}, \beta_{12}, \beta_2)$$

16.4.2 POST-ESTIMATION ANALYSIS

How a change in price affects the choice probability is different for "own price" changes and "cross-price" changes. Specifically it can be shown that the own price effect is

$$\frac{\partial p_{ij}}{\partial PRICE_{ij}} = p_{ij}(1 - p_{ij})\beta_2$$
(16.24)

The sign of β_2 indicates the direction of the own price effect.

The change in probability of alternative j being selected if the price of alternative k changes $(k \neq j)$ is

$$\frac{\partial p_{ij}}{\partial PRICE_{ik}} = -p_{ij} p_{ik} \beta_2$$
(16.25)

The cross-price effect is in the opposite direction of the own price effect.

An important feature of the conditional logit model is that the probability ratio between alternatives j and k is

$$\frac{p_{ij}}{p_{ik}} = \frac{\exp(\beta_{1j} + \beta_2 PRICE_{ij})}{\exp(\beta_{1k} + \beta_2 PRICE_{ik})} = \exp[(\beta_{1j} - \beta_{1k}) + \beta_2(PRICE_{ij} - PRICE_{ik})]$$

The probability ratio depends on the difference in prices, but not on the prices themselves. As in the multinomial logit model this ratio does not depend on the total number of alternatives,

Table 16.4a   **Conditional Logit Parameter Estimates**

Variable	Estimate	Standard error	t-Statistic	p-value
PRICE (β_2)	−2.2964	0.1377	−16.68	0.000
PEPSI (β_{11})	0.2832	0.0624	4.54	0.000
7-UP (β_{12})	0.1038	0.0625	1.66	0.096

Table 16.4b   **Marginal Effect of Price on Probability of Pepsi Choice**

PRICE	Marginal effect	Standard error	95% Interval estimate
COKE	0.3211	0.0254	[0.2712, 0.3709]
PEPSI	−0.5734	0.0350	[−0.6421, −0.5048]
7-UP	0.2524	0.0142	[0.2246, 0.2802]

and there is the implicit assumption of the independence of irrelevant alternatives (IIA). See the discussion at the end of Section 16.3.3. Models that do not require the IIA assumption have been developed, but they are difficult. These include the **multinomial probit** model, which is based on the normal distribution, and the **nested logit** and **mixed logit** models.[8]

16.4.3   AN EXAMPLE

We observe 1,822 purchases, covering 104 weeks and 5 stores, in which a consumer purchased 2-liter bottles of either Pepsi (34.6%), 7-Up (37.4%), or Coke Classic (28%). These data are in the file *cola.dat*. In the sample the average price of Pepsi was $1.23, of 7-Up $1.12, and of Coke $1.21. We estimate the conditional logit model shown in (16.23), and the estimates are shown in Table 16.4a.

We see that all the parameter estimates are significantly different from zero at a 10% level of significance, and the sign of the coefficient of *PRICE* is negative. This means that a rise in the price of an individual brand will reduce the probability of its purchase, and the rise in the price of a competitive brand will increase the probability of its purchase. Table 16.4b contains the marginal effects of price changes on the probablity of choosing Pepsi. The marginal effects are calculated using (16.24) and (16.25) with prices of Pepsi, 7-Up and Coke set to $1.00, $1.25 and $1.10, respectively. The standard errors are calculated using the delta method. Note two things about these estimates. First, they have the signs we anticipate. An increase in the price of Pepsi is estimated to have a negative effect on the probability of Pepsi purchase, while an increase in the price of either Coke or 7-Up increases the probability that Pepsi will be selected. Secondly, these values are very large for changes in probabilities because a "one-unit change" is $1, which then represents almost a 100% change in price. For a 10 cent increase in the prices the marginal effects, standard errors and interval estimate bounds should be multiplied by 0.10.

As an alternative to computing marginal effects, we can compute specific probabilities at given values of the explanatory variables. For example, at the prices used for Table 16.4b, the estimated probability of selecting Pepsi is then

$$\hat{p}_{i1} = \frac{\exp(\tilde{\beta}_{11} + \tilde{\beta}_2 \times 1.00)}{\exp(\tilde{\beta}_{11} + \tilde{\beta}_2 \times 1.00) + \exp(\tilde{\beta}_{12} + \tilde{\beta}_2 \times 1.25) + \exp(\tilde{\beta}_2 \times 1.10)} = 0.4832$$

---

[8] For a brief description of these models at an advanced level see William Greene, *Econometric Analysis*, 6th Edition by (Upper Saddle River, NJ: Pearson Prentice Hall, 2008), pp. 831–835.

The standard error for this predicted probability is 0.0154, which is computed via "the delta method." If we raise the price of Pepsi to $1.10, we estimate that the probability of its purchase falls to 0.4263 (se $= 0.0135$). If the price of Pepsi stays at $1.00 but we increase the price of Coke by 15 cents, then we estimate that the probability of a consumer selecting Pepsi rises by 0.0445 (se $= 0.0033$). These numbers indicate to us the responsiveness of brand choice to changes in prices, much like elasticities.

16.5 **Ordered Choice Models**

The choice options in multinomial and conditional logit models have no natural ordering or arrangement. However, in some cases choices are ordered in a specific way. Examples include the following:

1. Results of opinion surveys in which responses can be strongly in disagreement, in disagreement, neutral, in agreement, or strongly in agreement.
2. Assignment of grades or work performance ratings. Students receive grades A, B, C, D, and F, which are ordered on the basis of a teacher's evaluation of their performance. Employees are often given evaluations on scales such as Outstanding, Very Good, Good, Fair, and Poor, which are similar in spirit.
3. Standard and Poor's rates bonds as AAA, AA, A, BBB, and so on, as a judgment about the credit worthiness of the company or country issuing a bond, and how risky the investment might be.
4. Levels of employment as unemployed, part-time, or full-time.

When modeling these types of outcomes, numerical values are assigned to the outcomes, but the numerical values are **ordinal** and reflect only the ranking of the outcomes. In the first example, we might assign a dependent variable y the values

$$y = \begin{cases} 1 & \text{strongly disagree} \\ 2 & \text{disagree} \\ 3 & \text{neutral} \\ 4 & \text{agree} \\ 5 & \text{strongly agree} \end{cases}$$

In Section 16.3 we considered the problem of choosing what type of college to attend after graduating from high school as an illustration of a choice among unordered alternatives. However, in this particular case there may in fact be natural ordering. We might rank the possibilities as

$$y = \begin{cases} 3 & \text{four-year college (the full college experience)} \\ 2 & \text{two-year college (a partial college experience)} \\ 1 & \text{no college} \end{cases} \qquad (16.26)$$

The usual linear regression model is not appropriate for such data, because in regression we would treat the y-values as having some numerical meaning when they do not. In the next section we discuss how probabilities of each choice might be modeled.

16.5.1 Ordinal Probit Choice Probabilities

When faced with a ranking problem, we develop a "sentiment" about how we feel concerning the alternative choices, and the higher the sentiment, the more likely a

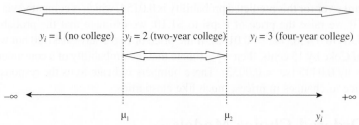

FIGURE **16.2** Ordinal choices relative to thresholds.

higher-ranked alternative will be chosen. This sentiment is, of course, unobservable to the econometrician. Unobservable variables that enter decisions are called **latent variables**, and we will denote our sentiment toward the ranked alternatives by y_i^*, with the "star" reminding us that this variable is unobserved.

Microeconomics is well described as the "science of choice." Economic theory will suggest that certain factors (observable variables) may affect how we feel about the alternatives facing us. As a concrete example, let us think about what factors might lead a high school graduate to choose among the alternatives "no college," "two-year college," and "four-year college" as described by the ordered choices in (16.26). Some factors that affect this choice are household income, the student's high school grades, how close a two- or four-year college is to the home, whether parents had attended a four-year college, and so on. For simplicity, let us focus on the single explanatory variable *GRADES*. The model is then

$$y_i^* = \beta GRADES_i + e_i$$

This model is not a regression model, because the dependent variable is unobservable. Consequently it is sometimes called an **index model**. The error term is present for the usual reasons. The choices we observe are based on a comparison of "sentiment" toward higher education y_i^* relative to certain thresholds, as shown in Figure 16.2.

Because there are $M = 3$ alternatives, there are $M - 1 = 2$ thresholds μ_1 and μ_2, with $\mu_1 < \mu_2$. The index model does not contain an intercept, because it would be exactly collinear with the threshold variables. If sentiment toward higher education is in the lowest category, then $y_i^* \leq \mu_1$ and the alternative "no college" is chosen, if $\mu_1 < y_i^* \leq \mu_2$ then the alternative "two-year college" is chosen, and if sentiment toward higher education is in the highest category, then $y_i^* > \mu_2$ and "four-year college" is chosen. That is,

$$y = \begin{cases} 3 \text{ (four-year college)} & \text{if} \quad y_i^* > \mu_2 \\ 2 \text{ (two-year college)} & \text{if} \quad \mu_1 < y_i^* \leq \mu_2 \\ 1 \text{ (no college)} & \text{if} \quad y_i^* \leq \mu_1 \end{cases}$$

We are able to represent the probabilities of these outcomes if we assume a particular probability distribution for y_i^*, or equivalently for the random error e_i. If we assume that the errors have the standard normal distribution, $N(0, 1)$, an assumption that defines the **ordered probit model**, then we can calculate the following:

$$P(y = 1) = P(y_i^* \leq \mu_1) = P(\beta GRADES_i + e_i \leq \mu_1)$$

$$= P(e_i \leq \mu_1 - \beta GRADES_i)$$

$$= \Phi(\mu_1 - \beta GRADES_i)$$

$$P(y = 2) = P(\mu_1 < y_i^* \le \mu_2) = P(\mu_1 < \beta GRADES_i + e_i \le \mu_2)$$
$$= P(\mu_1 - \beta GRADES_i < e_i \le \mu_2 - \beta GRADES_i)$$
$$= \Phi(\mu_2 - \beta GRADES_i) - \Phi(\mu_1 - \beta GRADES_i)$$

and the probability that $y = 3$ is

$$P(y = 3) = P(y_i^* > \mu_2) = P(\beta GRADES_i + e_i > \mu_2)$$
$$= P(e_i > \mu_2 - \beta GRADES_i)$$
$$= 1 - \Phi(\mu_2 - \beta GRADES_i)$$

16.5.2 ESTIMATION AND INTERPRETATION

Estimation, as with previous choice models, is by maximum likelihood. If we observe a random sample of $N = 3$ individuals, with the first not going to college ($y_1 = 1$), the second attending a two-year college ($y_2 = 2$), and the third attending a four-year college ($y_3 = 3$), then the likelihood function is

$$L(\beta, \mu_1, \mu_2) = P(y_1 = 1) \times P(y_2 = 2) \times P(y_3 = 3)$$

Note that the probabilities depend on the unknown parameters μ_1 and μ_2 as well as the index function parameter β. These parameters are obtained by maximizing the log-likelihood function using numerical methods. Econometric software includes options for both **ordered probit**, which depends on the errors being standard normal, and **ordered logit**, which depends on the assumption that the random errors follow a logistic distribution. Most economists will use the normality assumption, but many other social scientists use the logistic. In the end, there is little difference between the results.

The types of questions we can answer with this model are the following:

1. What is the probability that a high school graduate with $GRADES = 2.5$ (on a 13-point scale, with one being the highest) will attend a two-year college? The answer is obtained by plugging in the specific value of $GRADES$ into the predicted probability based on the maximum likelihood estimates of the parameters,

$$\hat{P}(y = 2 | GRADES = 2.5) = \Phi(\tilde{\mu}_2 - \tilde{\beta} \times 2.5) - \Phi(\tilde{\mu}_1 - \tilde{\beta} \times 2.5)$$

2. What is the difference in probability of attending a four-year college for two students, one with $GRADES = 2.5$ and another with $GRADES = 4.5$? The difference in the probabilities is calculated directly as

$$\hat{P}(y = 3 | GRADES = 4.5) - \hat{P}(y = 3 | GRADES = 2.5)$$

3. If we treat *GRADES* as a continuous variable, what is the marginal effect on the probability of each outcome, given a one-unit change in *GRADES*? These derivatives are

$$\frac{\partial P(y=1)}{\partial GRADES} = -\phi(\mu_1 - \beta GRADES) \times \beta$$

$$\frac{\partial P(y=2)}{\partial GRADES} = [\phi(\mu_1 - \beta GRADES) - \phi(\mu_2 - \beta GRADES)] \times \beta$$

$$\frac{\partial P(y=3)}{\partial GRADES} = \phi(\mu_2 - \beta GRADES) \times \beta$$

In these expressions "$\phi(\cdot)$" denotes the probability density function of a standard normal distribution, and its values are always positive. Consequently the sign of the parameter β is opposite the direction of the marginal effect for the lowest category, but it indicates the direction of the marginal effect for the highest category. The direction of the marginal effect for the middle category goes one way or the other, depending on the sign of the difference in brackets.

There are a variety of other devices that can be used to analyze the outcomes of ordered choice models, including some useful graphics. For more on these see (from a social science perspective) *Regression Models for Categorical and Limited Dependent Variables* by J. Scott Long (Sage Publications, 1997, Chapter 5) or (from a marketing perspective) *Quantitative Models in Marketing Research* by Philip Hans Franses and Richard Paap (Cambridge University Press, 2001, Chapter 6).

16.5.3 An Example

To illustrate, we use the college choice data introduced in Section 16.3 and contained in the file *nels_small.dat*. We treat *PSECHOICE* as an ordered variable with 1 representing the least favored alternative (no college) and 3 denoting the most favored alternative (four-year college). The estimation results are in Table 16.5.

The estimated coefficient of *GRADES* is negative, indicating that the probability of attending a four-year college goes down when *GRADES* increase (indicating a worse performance), and the probability of the lowest ranked choice, attending no college, increases. Let us examine the marginal effects of an increase in *GRADES* on attending a four-year college. For a student with median grades (6.64) the marginal effect is -0.1221, and for a student in the 5th percentile (2.635) the marginal effect is -0.0538. These are similar in magnitude to the marginal effects shown in Table 16.3.

Table 16.5 **Ordered Probit Parameter Estimates**

Parameters	Estimates	Standard errors
β	−0.3066	0.0191
μ_1	−2.9456	0.1468
μ_2	−2.0900	0.1358

16.6 Models for Count Data

When the dependent variable in a regression model is a count of the number of occurrences of an event, the outcome variable is $y = 0, 1, 2, 3, \ldots$ These numbers are actual counts, and thus different from the ordinal numbers of the previous section. Examples include the following:

- The number of trips to a physician a person makes during a year.
- The number of fishing trips taken by a person during the previous year.
- The number of children in a household.
- The number of automobile accidents at a particular intersection during a month.
- The number of televisions in a household.
- The number of alcoholic drinks a college student takes in a week.

While we are again interested in explaining and predicting probabilities, such as the probability that an individual will take two or more trips to the doctor during a year, the probability distribution we use as a foundation is the Poisson, not the normal or the logistic. If Y is a Poisson random variable, then its probability function is

$$f(y) = P(Y = y) = \frac{e^{-\lambda}\lambda^y}{y!}, \quad y = 0, 1, 2, \ldots \tag{16.27}$$

The factorial (!) term $y! = y \times (y-1) \times (y-2) \times \cdots \times 1$. This probability function has one parameter, λ, which is the mean (and variance) of Y. That is, $E(Y) = \mathrm{var}(Y) = \lambda$. In a regression model, we try to explain the behavior of $E(Y)$ as a function of some explanatory variables. We do the same here, keeping the value of $E(Y) \geq 0$ by defining

$$E(Y) = \lambda = \exp(\beta_1 + \beta_2 x) \tag{16.28}$$

This choice defines the **Poisson regression model** for count data.

16.6.1 Maximum Likelihood Estimation

The parameters β_1 and β_2 can be estimated by maximum likelihood. Suppose we randomly select $N = 3$ individuals from a population and observe that their counts are $y_1 = 0, y_2 = 2$, and $y_3 = 2$, indicating 0, 2, and 2 occurrences of the event for these three individuals. Recall that the likelihood function is the joint probability function of the observed data, interpreted as a function of the unknown parameters. That is,

$$L(\beta_1, \beta_2) = P(Y = 0) \times P(Y = 2) \times P(Y = 2)$$

This product of functions like (16.27) will be very complicated and difficult to maximize. However, in practice, maximum likelihood estimation is carried out by maximizing the logarithm of the likelihood function, or

$$\ln L(\beta_1, \beta_2) = \ln P(Y = 0) + \ln P(Y = 2) + \ln P(Y = 2)$$

Using (16.28) for λ, the log of the probability function is

$$\ln[P(Y = y)] = \ln\left[\frac{e^{-\lambda}\lambda^y}{y!}\right] = -\lambda + y\ln(\lambda) - \ln(y!)$$
$$= -\exp(\beta_1 + \beta_2 x) + y \times (\beta_1 + \beta_2 x) - \ln(y!)$$

Then the log-likelihood function, given a sample of N observations, becomes

$$\ln L(\beta_1, \beta_2) = \sum_{i=1}^{N}\{-\exp(\beta_1 + \beta_2 x_i) + y_i \times (\beta_1 + \beta_2 x_i) - \ln(y_i!)\}$$

This log-likelihood function is a function of only β_1 and β_2 once we substitute in the data values (y_i, x_i). The log-likelihood function itself is still a nonlinear function of the unknown parameters, and the maximum likelihood estimates must be obtained by numerical methods. Econometric software has options that allow for the maximum likelihood estimation of count models with the click of a button.

16.6.2 INTERPRETATION IN THE POISSON REGRESSION MODEL

As in other modeling situations, we would like to use the estimated model to predict outcomes, determine the marginal effect of a change in an explanatory variable on the mean of the dependent variable, and test the significance of coefficients.

Prediction of the conditional mean of y is straightforward. Given the maximum likelihood estimates $\tilde{\beta}_1$ and $\tilde{\beta}_2$, and given a value of the explanatory variable x_0,

$$\widehat{E(y_0)} = \tilde{\lambda}_0 = \exp(\tilde{\beta}_1 + \tilde{\beta}_2 x_0)$$

This value is an estimate of the expected number of occurrences observed if x takes the value x_0. The probability of a particular number of occurrences can be estimated by inserting the estimated conditional mean into the probability function, as

$$\widehat{P(Y = y)} = \frac{\exp(-\tilde{\lambda}_0)\tilde{\lambda}_0^y}{y!}, \quad y = 0, 1, 2, \dots$$

The marginal effect of a change in a continuous variable x in the Poisson regression model is not simply given by the parameter, because the conditional mean model is a nonlinear function of the parameters. Using our specification that the conditional mean is given by $E(y_i) = \lambda_i = \exp(\beta_1 + \beta_2 x_i)$, and using rules for derivatives of exponential functions, we obtain the marginal effect

$$\frac{\partial E(y_i)}{\partial x_i} = \lambda_i\beta_2 \tag{16.29}$$

To estimate this marginal effect, replace the parameters by their maximum likelihood estimates and select a value for x. The marginal effect is different depending on the value of x chosen. A useful fact about the Poisson model is that the conditional mean $E(y_i) = \lambda_i = \exp(\beta_1 + \beta_2 x_i)$ is always positive, because the exponential function is always positive. Thus the direction of the marginal effect can be determined from the sign of the coefficient β_2.

Equation (16.29) can be expressed as a percentage, which can be useful:

$$\frac{\%\Delta E(y)}{\Delta x_i} = 100 \frac{\partial E(y_i)/E(y_i)}{\partial x_i} = 100\beta_2\%$$

If x is not transformed, then a one-unit change in x leads to $100\beta_2\%$ change in the conditional mean.

Suppose the conditional mean function contains a indicator variable, how do we calculate its effect? If $E(y_i) = \lambda_i = \exp(\beta_1 + \beta_2 x_i + \delta D_i)$, we can examine the conditional expectation when $D = 0$ and when $D = 1$.

$$E(y_i|D_i = 0) = \exp(\beta_1 + \beta_2 x_i)$$

$$E(y_i|D_i = 1) = \exp(\beta_1 + \beta_2 x_i + \delta)$$

Then, the percentage change in the conditional mean is

$$100\left[\frac{\exp(\beta_1 + \beta_2 x_i + \delta) - \exp(\beta_1 + \beta_2 x_i)}{\exp(\beta_1 + \beta_2 x_i)}\right]\% = 100[e^\delta - 1]\%$$

This is identical to the expression we obtained for the effect of an indicator variable in a log-linear model. See Section 7.3.

Finally, hypothesis testing can be carried out using standard methods. The maximum likelihood estimators are asymptotically normal with a variance of a known form. The actual expression for the variance is complicated and involves matrix expressions, so we will not report the formula here.[9] Econometric software has the variance expressions encoded, and along with parameter estimates, it will provide standard errors, t-statistics, and p-values, which are used as always.

16.6.3 AN EXAMPLE

The Olympic Games are a subject of great interest to the global community. Rightly or wrongly, the attention focuses on the number of medals won by each country. Andrew Bernard and Meghan Busse[10] examined the effect of a country's economic resources on the number of medals won. The data are in the file *olympics.dat*. Using the data from 1988, we estimate a Poisson regression explaining the number of medals won (*MEDALTOT*) as a function of the logarithms of population and gross domestic product (1995 dollars). These results are given in Table 16.6.

Both the size and the wealth of the country have a positive and significant effect on the number of medals won. Using these estimates, the estimated conditional mean number of medals won for the country with median population (5,921,270) and median GDP (5.51E + 09) is 0.8634. If we keep GDP at the median value but raise population to the 75th percentile (1.75E + 07), the estimated mean is 1.0495. And if we keep population at the

---

[9] See J. Scott Long, *Regression Models for Categorical and Limited Dependent Variables* (Thousand Oaks, CA: Sage Publications, 1997), Chapter 8. A much more advanced and specialized reference is *Regression Analysis of Count Data* by A. Colin Cameron and Pravin K. Trivedi (Cambridge, UK: Cambridge University Press, 1998).

[10] "Who Wins the Olympic Games: Economic Resources and Medal Totals," *The Review of Economics and Statistics*, 2004, 86(1), 413–417. The data were kindly provided by Andrew Bernard.

Table 16.6 **Poisson Regression Estimates**

Variable	Coefficient	Std. Error	t-Statistic	p-Value
INTERCEPT	−15.8875	0.5118	−31.0420	0.0000
ln(*POP*)	0.1800	0.0323	5.5773	0.0000
ln(*GDP*)	0.5766	0.0247	23.3238	0.0000

median but raise GDP to the 75th percentile (5.18E + 10), the estimated mean number of medals is 3.1432. Alternatively, we can estimate the mean outcome for a specific county. In 1988 the population in the United Kingdom was 5.72E + 07 and its GDP was 1.01E + 12. The estimated mean number of medals was 26.2131. They in fact won a total of 24 medals.

16.7 Limited Dependent Variables

In the previous sections of this chapter we reviewed choice behavior models that have dependent variables that are discrete variables. When a model has a discrete dependent variable, the usual regression methods we have studied must be modified. In this section we present another case in which standard least squares estimation of a regression model fails.

16.7.1 CENSORED DATA

An example that illustrates the situation is based on Thomas Mroz's (1987) study of married women's labor force participation and wages. The data are in the file *mroz.dat* and consist of 753 observations on married women. Of these 325 did not work outside the home, and thus had no hours worked and no reported wages. The histogram of hours worked is shown in Figure 16.3. The histogram shows the large fraction of women

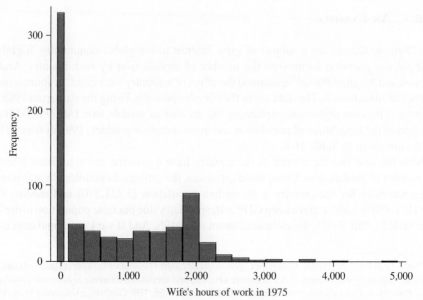

FIGURE *16.3* Histogram of wife's hours of work in 1975.

who did not enter the labor force. This is an example of **censored data**, meaning that a substantial fraction of the observations on the dependent variable take a limit value, which is zero in the case of market hours worked by married women. Other natural examples include variables like charitable giving or damage caused by a hurricane. In these examples a sample of households will yield a large number of households who give nothing or who have no hurricane damage.

In Section 2.2 we explained the type of data generation process for which least squares regression can be successful. Refer back to Figure 2.3. There we show the probability density functions for the dependent variable y, at different x-values, centered on the regression function

$$E(y|x) = \beta_1 + \beta_2 x \tag{16.30}$$

This leads to sample data being scattered along the regression function. Least squares regression works by fitting a line through the center of a data scatter, and in this case such a strategy works fine, because the true regression function also fits through the middle of the data scatter.

Unfortunately, in situations like we have with the supply of labor by married women, when a substantial number of observations have dependent variable values taking the limit value of zero, the regression function $E(y|x)$ is no longer given by (16.30). Instead $E(y|x)$ is a complicated nonlinear function of the regression parameters β_1 and β_2, the error variance σ^2, and x. The least squares estimators of the regression parameters obtained by running a regression of y on x are biased and inconsistent—least squares estimation fails.

If having all the limit observations present is the cause of the problem, then why not drop them out? This does not work, either. The regression function becomes the expected value of y, conditional on the y-values being positive, or $E(y|x, y > 0)$. Once again it can be shown that this regression function is nonlinear and not equal to (16.30).

16.7.2 A Monte Carlo Experiment

Let us illustrate these concepts using a simulated sample of data (*tobit.dat*). Using simulation is an excellent way to learn econometrics. It requires us to understand how the data are obtained under a particular set of assumptions.[11] In this example we give the parameters the specific values $\beta_1 = -9$ and $\beta_2 = 1$. The observed sample is obtained within the framework of an **index** or **latent variable model**, similar to the one discussed in Section 16.5 on the ordered probit model. Let the latent variable be

$$y_i^* = \beta_1 + \beta_2 x_i + e_i = -9 + x_i + e_i \tag{16.31}$$

with the error term assumed to have a normal distribution, $e_i \sim N(0, \sigma^2 = 16)$. The observable outcome y_i takes the value zero if $y_i^* \leq 0$, but $y_i = y_i^*$ if $y_i^* > 0$. In the simulation we

- Create $N = 200$ random values of x_i that are spread evenly (or uniformly) over the interval [0, 20]. We will keep these fixed in further simulations.
- Obtain $N = 200$ random values e_i from a normal distribution with mean zero and variance 16.

---

[11] Peter Kennedy is an advocate of using Monte Carlo experiments in teaching econometrics. See "Using Monte Carlo Studies for Teaching Econometrics," in W. Becker and M. Watts (Eds.), *Teaching Undergraduate Economics: Alternatives to Chalk and Talk*, Cheltenham, UK: Edward Elgar, 1998, pp. 141–159; see also Peter Kennedy (2003) *A Guide to Econometrics*, 5th edition, Cambridge, MA: MIT Press, pp. 24–27.

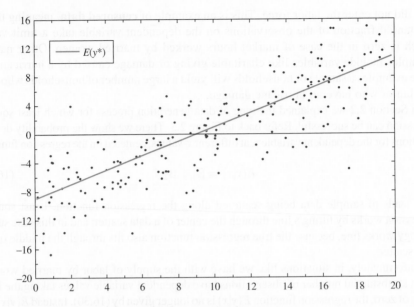

FIGURE **16.4**   Uncensored sample data and regression function.

- Create $N = 200$ values of the latent variable $y_i^* = -9 + x_i + e_i$.
- Obtain $N = 200$ values of the observed y_i using

$$y_i = \begin{cases} 0 & \text{if} \quad y_i^* \le 0 \\ y_i^* & \text{if} \quad y_i^* > 0 \end{cases}$$

The 200 observations obtained this way constitute a sample that is **censored** with a lower limit of zero. The latent data are plotted in Figure 16.4. In this figure the line labeled $E(y^*)$ has intercept -9 and slope one. The values of the latent variable y_i^* are scattered along this regression function. If we observed these data we could estimate the parameters using the least squares principle, by fitting a line through the center of the data.

However, we do not observe all the latent data. When the values of y_i^* are zero or less, we observe $y_i = 0$. We observe y_i^* when they are positive. These observable data, along with the fitted least squares regression, are shown in Figure 16.5.

The least squares principle will fail to estimate $\beta_1 = -9$ and $\beta_2 = 1$, because the observed data do not fall along the underlying regression function $E(y^*|x) = \beta_1 + \beta_2 x = -9 + x$. In Figure 16.5 we show the estimated regression function for the 200 observed y-values, which is given by

$$\hat{y} = -2.1477 + 0.5161x$$
$$\text{(se)} \quad (0.3706) \quad (0.0326) \tag{16.32a}$$

If we restrict our sample to include only the 100 positive y-values, the fitted regression is

$$\hat{y} = -3.1399 + 0.6388x$$
$$\text{(se)} \quad (1.2055) \quad (0.0827) \tag{16.32b}$$

In a Monte Carlo simulation we repeat this process of creating $N = 200$ observations, and applying least squares estimation, many times. This is analogous to "repeated sampling" in the context of experimental statistics. In this case we repeat the process $NSAM = 1,000$

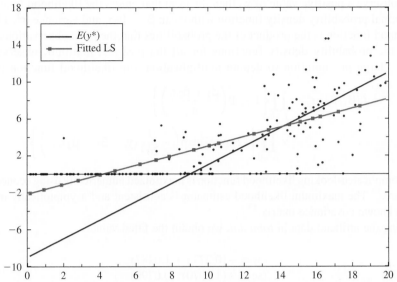

FIGURE **16.5** Censored sample data, and latent regression function and least squares fitted line.

times, keeping the x-values fixed and drawing new error values e, recording each time the values of the estimates we obtain. At the end, we can compute the average values of the estimates, recorded in *tobitmc.dat*, which is the Monte Carlo "expected value,"

$$E_{MC}(b_k) = \frac{1}{NSAM} \sum_{m=1}^{NSAM} b_{k(m)} \qquad (16.33)$$

where $b_{k(m)}$ is the estimate of β_k in the mth Monte Carlo sample.

If we apply the least squares estimation procedure to all the observed censored data (i.e., including observations $y = 0$), the average value of the estimated intercept is -2.0465 and the average value of the estimated slope is 0.5434. If we discard the $y = 0$ observations and apply least squares to just the positive y observations, these averages are -1.9194 and 0.5854, respectively. The least squares estimates are biased by a substantial amount, compared to the true values $\beta_1 = -9$ and $\beta_2 = 1$. This bias will not disappear, no matter how large the sample size we consider, because the least squares estimators are inconsistent when data are censored.

16.7.3 MAXIMUM LIKELIHOOD ESTIMATION

If the dependent variable is censored, having a lower limit and/or an upper limit, then the least squares estimators of the regression parameters are biased and inconsistent. In this case we can apply an alternative estimation procedure, which is called **Tobit** in honor of James Tobin, winner of the 1981 Nobel Prize in Economics, who first studied this model. Tobit is a maximum likelihood procedure that recognizes that we have data of two sorts, the limit observations ($y = 0$) and the nonlimit observations ($y > 0$). The two types of observations that we observe, the limit observations and those that are positive, are generated by the latent variable y^* crossing the zero threshold or not crossing that threshold. The (**probit**) probability that $y = 0$ is

$$P(y = 0) = P(y^* \le 0) = 1 - \Phi[(\beta_1 + \beta_2 x)/\sigma]$$

If we observe a positive value of y_i, then the term that enters the likelihood function is the normal probability density function with mean $\beta_1 + \beta_2 x_i$ and variance σ^2. The full likelihood function is the product of the probabilities that the limit observations occur times the probability density functions for all the positive, nonlimit, observations. Using "large pi" notation to denote multiplication, the likelihood function is

$$L(\beta_1, \beta_2, \sigma) = \prod_{y_i=0} \left\{ 1 - \Phi\left(\frac{\beta_1 + \beta_2 x_i}{\sigma}\right) \right\}$$

$$\times \prod_{y_i>0} \left\{ (2\pi\sigma^2)^{-\frac{1}{2}} \exp\left(-\frac{1}{2\sigma^2} (y_i - \beta_1 - \beta_2 x_i)^2 \right) \right\}$$

This complicated-looking likelihood function is maximized numerically using econometric software.[12] The maximum likelihood estimator is consistent and asymptotically normal, with a known covariance matrix.[13]

Using the artificial data in *tobit.dat*, we obtain the fitted values

$$\tilde{y} = -10.2773 + 1.0487x$$
$$\text{(se)} \quad (1.0970) \quad (0.0790) \tag{16.34}$$

These estimates are much closer to the true values $\beta_1 = -9$ and $\beta_2 = 1$, especially when compared to the least squares estimates in (16.32). Maximum likelihood estimation also yields an estimate of σ (true value equals 4) of 3.5756 with a standard error of 0.2610.

The Monte Carlo simulation experiment results from Section 16.7.2 are summarized in Table 16.7. The column "MC average" reports the average estimates over the 1,000 Monte Carlo samples, as calculated using (16.33). While the least squares estimates based on all the data and the least squares estimates based only on data corresponding to positive y-values are not close to the true values, the Tobit estimates are very close. The standard errors reported in

Table 16.7   **Censored Data Monte Carlo Results**

Estimator	Parameter	MC average	Std. Dev.
Least squares	β_1	−2.0465	0.2238
	β_2	0.5434	0.0351
	σ	2.9324	0.1675
Least squares $y > 0$	β_1	−1.9194	0.9419
	β_2	0.5854	0.0739
	σ	3.3282	0.2335
Tobit	β_1	−9.0600	1.0248
	β_2	1.0039	0.0776
	σ	3.9813	0.2799

---

[12] Tobit requires data on both the limit values of $y = 0$, and also the nonlimit values for which $y > 0$. Sometimes it is possible that we do not observe the limit values; in such a case the sample is said to be truncated. In this case Tobit does not apply; however, there is a similar maximum likelihood procedure, called **truncated regression**, for such a case. An advanced reference is William Greene (2008) *Econometric Analysis*, 6th edition, Pearson Prentice Hall, Section 24.2.3.

[13] The asymptotic covariance matrix can be found in *Introduction to the Theory and Practice of Econometrics*, 2nd edition, by George G. Judge, R. Carter Hill, William E. Griffiths, Helmut Lütkepohl, and Tsoung-Chao Lee (John Wiley and Sons, 1988), Section 19.3.2.

(16.34) are valid in large samples, and we can see that they do reflect the actual variability of the estimates, as measured by their sample standard deviation, labeled "Std. Dev." in Table 16.7.

A word of caution is in order about commercial software packages: There are many algorithms available for obtaining maximum likelihood estimates, and different packages use different ones, which may lead to slight differences (in perhaps the third or fourth decimal) in the parameter estimates and their standard errors. When carrying out important research, it is a good tip to confirm empirical results with a second software package, just to be sure they give essentially the same numbers.

16.7.4 Tobit Model Interpretation

In the Tobit model the parameters β_1 and β_2 are the intercept and slope of the latent variable model (16.31). In practice we are interested in the marginal effect of a change in x on either the regression function of the observed data $E(y|x)$ or the regression function conditional on $y > 0$, $E(y|x, y > 0)$. As we indicated earlier, these functions are not straight lines. Their graphs are shown in Figure 16.6. The slope of each changes at each value of x. The slope of $E(y|x)$ has a relatively simple form, being a scale factor times the parameter value; it is

$$\frac{\partial E(y|x)}{\partial x} = \beta_2 \Phi\left(\frac{\beta_1 + \beta_2 x}{\sigma}\right) \tag{16.35}$$

where Φ is the cumulative distribution function (*cdf*) of the standard normal random variable that is evaluated at the estimates and a particular x-value. Because the *cdf* values are positive, the sign of the coefficient tells the direction of the marginal effect, but the magnitude of the marginal effect depends on both the coefficient and the *cdf*. If $\beta_2 > 0$, as x increases, the *cdf* function approaches one, and the slope of the regression function approaches that of the latent variable model, as is shown in Figure 16.6. The marginal effect can be decomposed into two factors called the "McDonald-Moffit" decomposition:

$$\frac{\partial E(y|x)}{\partial x} = \text{Prob}(y > 0)\frac{\partial E(y|x, y > 0)}{\partial x} + E(y|x, y > 0)\frac{\partial \text{Prob}(y > 0)}{\partial x}$$

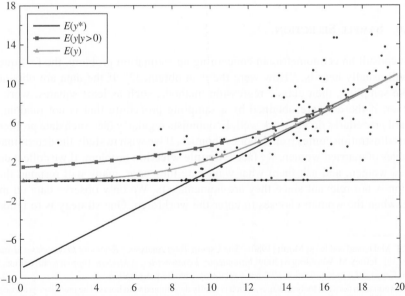

FIGURE 16.6 Censored sample data, and regression functions for observed and positive *y*-values.

The first factor accounts for the marginal effect of a change in x for the portion of the population whose y-data is observed already. The second factor accounts for changes in the proportion of the population who switch from the y-unobserved category to the y-observed category when x changes.[14]

16.7.5   AN EXAMPLE

If we wish to estimate a model explaining the market hours worked by a married woman, what explanatory variables would we include? Factors that would tend to pull a woman into the labor force are her education and her prior labor market experience. Factors that may reduce her incentive to work are her age and the presence of young children in the home.[15] Thus, we might propose the regression model

$$HOURS = \beta_1 + \beta_2 EDUC + \beta_3 EXPER + \beta_4 AGE + \beta_4 KIDSL6 + e \qquad (16.36)$$

where *KIDSL6* is the number of children less than six years old in the household. Using Mroz's data, we obtain the estimates shown in Table 16.8. As previously argued, the least squares estimates are unreliable because the least squares estimator is both biased and inconsistent. The Tobit estimates have the anticipated signs and are all statistically significant at the 0.01 level. To compute the scale factor required for calculation of the marginal effects, we must choose values of the explanatory variables. We choose the sample means for *EDUC* (12.29), *EXPER* (10.63), and *AGE* (42.54) and assume one small child at home (rather than the mean value of 0.24). The calculated scale factor is $\tilde{\Phi} = 0.3638$. Thus the marginal effect on observed hours of work of another year of education is

$$\frac{\partial E(HOURS)}{\partial EDUC} = \tilde{\beta}_2 \tilde{\Phi} = 73.29 \times 0.3638 = 26.34$$

That is, we estimate that another year of education will increase a wife's hours of work by about 26 hours, conditional upon the assumed values of the explanatory variables.

16.7.6   SAMPLE SELECTION

If you consult an econometrician concerning an estimation problem, the first question you will usually hear is, "How were the data obtained?" If the data are obtained by random sampling, then classic regression methods, such as least squares, work well. However, if the data are obtained by a sampling procedure that is not random, then standard procedures do not work well. Economists regularly face such data problems. A famous illustration comes from labor economics. If we wish to study the determinants of the wages of married women, we face a **sample selection** problem. If we collect data on married women, and ask them what wage rate they earn, many will respond that the question is not relevant since they are homemakers. We only observe data on market wages when the woman chooses to enter the workforce. One strategy is to ignore the

---

[14] J. F. McDonald and R. A. Moffit (1980) "The Uses of Tobit Analysis," *Review of Economics and Statistics*, 62, 318–321. Jeffrey M. Wooldridge (2009) *Introductory Econometrics: A Modern Approach*, 4th edition, South-Western Cengage Learning, Section 17.2 has a relatively friendly presentation.

[15] This equation does not include wages, which is jointly determined with hours. The model we propose may be considered a reduced-form equation. See Section 11.2.

Table 16.8   **Estimates of Labor Supply Function**

Estimator	Variable	Estimate	Std. Error
Least squares	*INTERCEPT*	1335.31	235.65
	EDUC	27.09	12.24
	EXPER	48.04	3.64
	AGE	−31.31	3.96
	KIDSL6	−447.85	58.41
Least squares	*INTERCEPT*	1829.75	292.54
$y > 0$	*EDUC*	−16.46	15.58
	EXPER	33.94	5.01
	AGE	−17.11	5.46
	KIDSL6	−305.31	96.45
Tobit	*INTERCEPT*	1349.88	386.30
	EDUC	73.29	20.47
	EXPER	80.54	6.29
	AGE	−60.77	6.89
	KIDSL6	−918.92	111.66
	SIGMA	1133.70	42.06

women who are homemakers, omit them from the sample, then use least squares to estimate a wage equation for those who work. This strategy fails, the reason for the failure being that our sample is not a random sample. The data we observe are "selected" by a systematic process for which we do not account.

A solution to this problem is a technique called **Heckit**, named after its developer, Nobel Prize winning econometrician James Heckman. This simple procedure uses two estimation steps. In the context of the problem of estimating the wage equation for married women, a probit model is first estimated explaining why a woman is in the labor force or not. In the second stage, a least squares regression is estimated relating the wage of a working woman to education, experience, and so on, and a variable called the "inverse Mills ratio," or IMR. The IMR is created from the first step probit estimation and accounts for the fact that the observed sample of working women is not random.

16.7.6a The Econometric Model

The econometric model describing the situation is composed of two equations. The first is the **selection equation** that determines whether the variable of interest is observed. The sample consists of N observations; however, the variable of interest is observed only for $n < N$ of these. The selection equation is expressed in terms of a latent variable z_i^* that depends on one or more explanatory variables w_i, and is given by

$$z_i^* = \gamma_1 + \gamma_2 w_i + u_i, \quad i = 1, \ldots, N \tag{16.37}$$

For simplicity we will include only one explanatory variable in the selection equation. The latent variable is not observed, but we do observe the indicator variable

$$z_i = \begin{cases} 1 & z_i^* > 0 \\ 0 & \text{otherwise} \end{cases} \tag{16.38}$$

The second equation is the linear model of interest. It is

$$y_i = \beta_1 + \beta_2 x_i + e_i, \quad i = 1, \ldots, n, \quad N > n \tag{16.39}$$

A **selectivity problem** arises when y_i is observed only when $z_i = 1$ and if the errors of the two equations are correlated. In such a situation the usual least squares estimators of β_1 and β_2 are biased and inconsistent.

Consistent estimators are based on the conditional regression function[16]

$$E(y_i | z_i^* > 0) = \beta_1 + \beta_2 x_i + \beta_\lambda \lambda_i, \quad i = 1, \ldots, n \tag{16.40}$$

where the additional variable λ_i is the "inverse Mills ratio." It is equal to

$$\lambda_i = \frac{\phi(\gamma_1 + \gamma_2 w_i)}{\Phi(\gamma_1 + \gamma_2 w_i)} \tag{16.41}$$

where, as usual, $\phi(\cdot)$ denotes the standard normal probability density function and $\Phi(\cdot)$ denotes the cumulative distribution function for a standard normal random variable. While the value of λ_i is not known, the parameters γ_1 and γ_2 can be estimated using a probit model, based on the observed binary outcome z_i in (16.38). Then the estimated IMR

$$\tilde{\lambda}_i = \frac{\phi(\tilde{\gamma}_1 + \tilde{\gamma}_2 w_i)}{\Phi(\tilde{\gamma}_1 + \tilde{\gamma}_2 w_i)}$$

is inserted into the regression equation as an extra explanatory variable, yielding the estimating equation

$$y_i = \beta_1 + \beta_2 x_i + \beta_\lambda \tilde{\lambda}_i + v_i, \quad i = 1, \ldots, n \tag{16.42}$$

Least squares estimation of this equation yields consistent estimators of β_1 and β_2. A word of caution, however, as the least squares estimator is inefficient relative to the maximum likelihood estimator, and the usual standard errors and t-statistics produced after estimation of (16.42) are incorrect. Proper estimation of standard errors requires the use of specialized software for the "Heckit" model.

16.7.6b   Heckit Example: Wages of Married Women

As an example we will reconsider the analysis of wages earned by married women using the Mroz (1987) data, *mroz.dat*. In the sample of 753 married women, 428 have market employment and nonzero earnings. First, let us estimate a simple wage equation, explaining ln(*WAGE*) as a function of the woman's education, *EDUC*, and years of market work experience (*EXPER*), using the 428 women who have positive wages. The result is

$$
\begin{aligned}
\ln(WAGE) &= -0.4002 + 0.1095 EDUC + 0.0157 EXPER \qquad R^2 = 0.1484 \\
(t) &\quad (-2.10) \qquad (7.73) \qquad\qquad (3.90)
\end{aligned}
\tag{16.43}
$$

---

[16] Further explanation of this material requires understanding the truncated normal distribution, which is beyond the scope of this book. See William Greene (2008) *Econometric Analysis*, 6th edition, Pearson Prentice Hall, Chapter 24.5.

The estimated return to education is about 11%, and the estimated coefficients of both education and experience are statistically significant.

The Heckit procedure starts by estimating a probit model of labor force participation. As explanatory variables we use the woman's age, her years of education, an indicator variable for whether she has children, and the marginal tax rate that she would pay upon earnings if employed. The estimated probit model is

$$\widehat{P(LFP = 1)} = \Phi(1.1923 - 0.0206AGE + 0.0838EDUC - 0.3139KIDS - 1.3939MTR)$$
$$(t) \qquad\qquad (-2.93) \qquad (3.61) \qquad (-2.54) \qquad (-2.26)$$

As expected, the effects of age, the presence of children, and the prospects of higher taxes significantly reduce the probability that a woman will join the labor force, while education increases it. Using the estimated coefficients we compute the inverse Mills ratio for the 428 women with market wages

$$\tilde{\lambda} = IMR = \frac{\phi(1.1923 - 0.0206AGE + 0.0838EDUC - 0.3139KIDS - 1.3939MTR)}{\Phi(1.1923 - 0.0206AGE + 0.0838EDUC - 0.3139KIDS - 1.3939MTR)}$$

This is then included in the wage equation, and least squares estimation applied to obtain

$$\ln(WAGE) = 0.8105 + 0.0585EDUC + 0.0163EXPER - 0.8664IMR$$
$$(t) \quad (1.64) \quad (2.45) \qquad (4.08) \qquad (-2.65) \qquad\qquad (16.44)$$
$$(t\text{-adj}) \quad (1.33) \quad (1.97) \qquad (3.88) \qquad (-2.17)$$

Two results are of note. First, the estimated coefficient of the inverse Mills ratio is statistically significant, implying that there is a selection bias present in the least squares results (16.43). Second, the estimated return to education has fallen from approximately 11% to approximately 6%. The upper row of t-statistics is based on standard errors as usually computed when using least squares regression. The usual standard errors do not account for the fact that the inverse Mills ratio is itself an estimated value. The correct standard errors,[17] which do account for the first stage probit estimation, are used to construct the "adjusted t-statistics" reported in (16.44). As you can see the adjusted t-statistics are slightly smaller, indicating that the adjusted standard errors are somewhat larger than the usual ones.

In most instances it is preferable to estimate the full model, both the selection equation and the equation of interest, jointly by maximum likelihood. While the nature of this procedure is beyond the scope of this book, it is available in some software packages. The maximum likelihood estimated wage equation is

$$\ln(WAGE) = 0.6686 + 0.0658EDUC + 0.0118EXPER$$
$$(t) \quad (2.84) \quad (3.96) \qquad (2.87)$$

The standard errors based on the full information maximum likelihood procedure are smaller than those yielded by the two-step estimation method.

---

[17] The formulas are very complicated. See William Greene (2008) *Econometric Analysis*, 6th edition, Pearson Prentice Hall, p. 887. There are several software packages, such as Stata and LIMDEP, that report correct standard errors.

16.8 Exercises[18]

Answers to exercises marked * can be found at www.wiley.com/go/global/hill.

16.1 In Section 16.1.5 we present an example of transportation choice. Use the sample data on automobile and public transportation times in *transport.dat* for the following exercises.

 (a) Estimate the linear probability model $AUTO = \beta_1 + \beta_2 DTIME + e$ using least squares estimation. What is the estimated marginal effect of an increase in *DTIME* on the probability of a person choosing automobile transportation given that $DTIME = 2$?

 (b) For each sample observation, calculate the predicted probability of choosing automobile transportation $\widehat{P(AUTO)} = b_1 + b_2 DTIME$. Are all the predicted probabilities plausible?

 (c) Using the error variance in (16.6) compute the feasible generalized least squares estimates of the linear probability model. If a predicted probability is zero or negative, replace it by 0.01; if a predicted probability is greater than or equal to one, replace it by 0.99. Compare these estimates to those from part (a).

 (d) Using generalized least squares, as we have done in part (c), cures the basic deficiency of the linear probability model. True or false? Explain your answer.

 (e) For each of the 21 observations, estimate the probability of choosing automobile transportation using the generalized least squares estimates of the linear probability model. Predict the choice of transportation mode using the rule $\widehat{AUTO} = 1$ if the predicted probability is 0.5 or larger, otherwise $\widehat{AUTO} = 0$. Define a successful prediction to be when we predict that a person will choose the automobile $(\widehat{AUTO} = 1)$ when they actually did $(AUTO = 1)$, OR when we predict that a person will choose public transportation $(\widehat{AUTO} = 0)$ when they did $(AUTO = 0)$. Calculate the percentage of correct predictions in the $N = 21$ cases.

 (f) Compare the percentage of correct predictions from the linear probability model to that for the probit model.

16.2* In Section 16.1.5 we present an example of transportation choice. Use the sample data on automobile and public transportation times in *transport.dat* for the following exercises.

 (a) Estimate the logit model explaining the choice of automobile transportation as a function of difference in travel time (*DTIME*). Compare the parameter estimates and their standard errors to the estimates from the probit model.

 (b) Based on the logit model results, estimate the marginal effect of an increase in *DTIME* given that $DTIME = 2$. Use (16.11) but replace the standard normal density function $\phi(\cdot)$ by the logistic density function $\lambda(\cdot)$ given in (16.16). Compare this result to that for the probit model in Section 16.1.5, where the estimated marginal effect is 0.1037.

 (c) Using the logit estimates, calculate the probability of a person choosing automobile transportation given that the time differential $DTIME = 3$. Compare this value to the probit estimate of the probability of choosing automobile transportation, which is 0.7983.

 (d) For each of the 21 observations, estimate the probability of choosing automobile transportation using the logit model. Predict the choice of transportation mode using the rule $\widehat{AUTO} = 1$ if the predicted probability is 0.5 or larger, otherwise

---

[18] All exercises in this chapter are computer-based.

$\widehat{AUTO} = 0$. Define a successful prediction to be when we predict that a person will choose the automobile ($\widehat{AUTO} = 1$) when they actually did ($AUTO = 1$), OR when we predict that a person will choose public transportation ($\widehat{AUTO} = 0$) when they did ($AUTO = 0$). Calculate the percentage of correct predictions in the $N = 21$ cases.

16.3* Dhillon, Shilling, and Sirmans ("Choosing between Fixed and Adjustable Rate Mortgages," *Journal of Money, Credit and Banking*, 19(1), 1987, 260–267) estimate a probit model designed to explain the choice by homebuyers of fixed versus adjustable rate mortgages. They use 78 observations from a bank in Baton Rouge, Louisiana, taken over the period January 1983 to February 1984. These data are contained in the file *sirmans.dat*. *ADJUST* $= 1$ if an adjustable mortgage is chosen. The explanatory variables, and their anticipated signs, are *FIXRATE* $(+) = $ fixed interest rate ; *MARGIN* $(-) = $ the variable rate $-$ the fixed rate; *YIELD* $(-) = $ the ten-year Treasury rate less the one-year rate; *MATURITY* $(-) = $ ratio of maturities on adjustable to fixed rates; *POINTS* $(-) = $ ratio of points paid on an adjustable mortgage to those paid on a fixed rate mortgage; *NETWORTH* $(+) = $ borrower's net worth.

(a) Obtain the least squares estimates of the linear probability model explaining the choice of an adjustable mortgage, using the explanatory variables listed above. Obtain the predicted values from this estimation. Are the signs consistent with expectations? Are the predicted values between zero and one?

(b) Estimate the model of mortgage choice using probit. Are the signs consistent with expectations? Are the estimated coefficients statistically significant?

(c) Using the probit estimates from part (b), estimate the probability $\hat{p}$ of choosing an adjustable rate mortgage for each sample observation. What percentage of the outcomes do we successfully predict, using the rule that if $\hat{p} \geq 0.5$, we predict that an adjustable rate mortgage will be chosen?

(d) Estimate the marginal effect of an increase in the variable *MARGIN*, with all explanatory variables fixed at their sample means. Explain the meaning of this value.

16.4 Use the data on college choice contained in *nels_small.dat*. These data are discussed in Section 16.3.

(a) Define a variable *COLLEGE* that equals one if a high school graduate chooses either a two-year or a four-year college, and zero otherwise. What percentage of the high school graduates attended college?

(b) Estimate a probit model explaining *COLLEGE*, using as explanatory variables *GRADES*, 13-point scale with 1 indicating the highest grade and 13 the lowest; *FAMINC*, gross family income in $1,000 increments; *FAMSIZ*, number of family members; *PARCOLL* $= 1$ if the most educated parent had a college degree; *FEMALE* $= 1$ if female; and *BLACK* $= 1$ if black. Are the signs of the estimated coefficients consistent with your expectations? Explain. Are the estimated coefficients statistically significant?

(c) Using the estimates in (b), predict the probability of attending college for a black female with *GRADES* $= 5$, *FAMINC* $=$ sample mean, from a household with five members, with a parent who attended college. Repeat this probability calculation with *GRADES* $= 10$.

(d) Repeat the calculations in (c) for (i) a white female and (ii) a white male.

(e) Reestimate the model in (b), but omitting the variables *PARCOLL*, *BLACK*, and *FEMALE*. How are the signs and significance of the remaining coefficients affected?

(f) Test the joint significance of *PARCOLL*, *BLACK*, and *FEMALE* using a likelihood ratio test. [*Hint:* The test statistic is $LR = 2$(log-likelihood of unrestricted model – log-likelihood of restricted model). The test statistic is chi-square with three degrees of freedom if the null hypothesis is true.]

16.5 Use the data on college choice contained in *nels_small.dat*. These data are discussed in Section 16.3. In this exercise you will consider only those students who chose to attend a college, whether a two-year or a four-year college. Within this subsample, define a variable $FOURYR = 1$ if the student attended a four-year college, and zero otherwise.

(a) What percentage of the high school graduates who attended college selected a four-year college? What percentage of those choosing a four-year college are female? What percentage of those choosing a four-year college are black?

(b) Estimate a probit model explaining *FOURYR*, using as explanatory variables *GRADES*, a 13-point scale with one indicating highest grade and 13 the lowest; *FAMINC*, gross family income in $1,000 increments; and *FAMSIZ*, number of family members. Are the signs of the estimated coefficients consistent with your expectations? Explain. Are the estimated coefficients statistically significant?

(c) Reestimate the model in (b) separately for the populations of black students and white students $(BLACK = 0)$. Compare and contrast these results.

16.6 Use the data on college choice contained in *nels_small.dat*. These data are discussed in Section 16.3.

(a) Estimate a multinomial logit model explaining *PSECHOICE*. Use the group who did not attend college as the base group. Use as explanatory variables *GRADES*, *FAMINC*, *FEMALE*, and *BLACK*. Are the estimated coefficients statistically significant?

(b) Compute the estimated probability that a white male student with median values of *GRADES* and *FAMINC* will attend a four-year college.

(c) Compute the probability ratio that a white male student with median values of *GRADES* and *FAMINC* will attend a four-year college rather than not attend any college.

(d) Compute the change in probability of attending a four-year college for a white male student with median *FAMINC* whose *GRADES* change from 6.64 (the median value) to 4.905 (top 25th percentile).

(e) From the full data set create a subsample, omitting the group who attended a two-year college. Estimate a logit model explaining student's choice between attending a four-year college and not attending college, using the same explanatory variables in (a). Compute the probability ratio that a white male student with median values of *GRADES* and *FAMINC* will attend a four-year college rather than not attend any college. Compare the result to that in (c).

16.7 In Section 16.4.3 we considered a conditional logit model of choice among three brands of soda: Coke, Pepsi, and 7-Up. The data are in the file *cola.dat*.

(a) In addition to *PRICE*, the data file contains variables indicating whether the product was "featured" at the time (*FEATURE*) or whether there was a store display (*DISPLAY*). Estimate a conditional logit model explaining choice of soda using *PRICE*, *DISPLAY*, and *FEATURE* as explanatory variables. Discuss the signs of the estimated coefficients and their significance. (*Note:* In this model, do not include alternative specific intercept terms.)

(b) Compute the probability ratio of choosing Coke relative to Pepsi and 7-Up if the price of each is $1.25 and no display or feature is present.

(c) Compute the probability ratio of choosing Coke relative to Pepsi and 7-Up if the price of each is $1.25, a display is present for Coke but not for the others, and none of the items is featured.

(d) Compute the change in the probability of purchase of each type of soda if the price of Coke changes from $1.25 to $1.30, with the prices of the Pepsi and 7-Up remaining at $1.25. Assume that a display is present for Coke, but not for the others, and none of the items is featured.

(e) Add the alternative specific "intercept" terms for Pepsi and 7-Up to the model in (a). Estimate the conditional logit model. Compute the probability ratio in (c) based upon these new estimates.

(f) Based on the estimates in (e), calculate the effects of the price change in (d) on the choice probability for each brand.

16.8 In Section 16.5.1 we described an ordinal probit model for post-secondary education choice and estimated a simple model in which the choice depended simply on the student's *GRADES*.

(a) Using the estimates in Table 16.5, calculate the probability that a student will choose no college, a two-year college, and a four-year college if the student's grades are the median value, *GRADES* = 6.64. Recompute these probabilities assuming that *GRADES* = 4.905. Discuss the probability changes. Are they what you anticipated? Explain.

(b) Expand the ordered probit model to include family income (*FAMINC*), family size (*FAMSIZ*), and the indicator variables *BLACK* and *PARCOLL*. Discuss the estimates and their signs and significance. (*Hint:* Recall that the sign indicates the direction of the effect for the highest category, but is opposite for the lowest category).

(c) Test the joint significance of the variables added in (b) using a likelihood ratio test.

(d) Compute the probability that a black student from a household of four members, including a parent who went to college, and household income of $52,000, will attend a four-year college if (i) *GRADES* = 6.64 and (ii) *GRADES* = 4.905.

(e) Repeat (d) for a "nonblack" student and discuss the differences in your findings.

16.9 In Section 16.6.3 we estimated a Poisson regression explaining the number of Olympic Games medals won by various countries as a function of the logarithms of population and gross domestic product (in 1995 dollars). The estimated coefficients are in Table 16.6.

(a) In 1988 Australia had *GDP* = 3.0E + 11 and a population of 16.5 million. Predict the number of medals that Australia would win. (They did win 14 medals.) Calculate the probability that Australia would win 10 medals or more.

(b) In 1988 Canada had *GDP* = 5.19E + 11 and a population of 26.9 million. Predict the number of medals that Canada would win. (They did win 10 medals.) Calculate the probability that they would win 15 medals or less.

(c) Use the combined data on years 1992 and 1996 to estimate the model explaining medals won as a function of the logarithms of population and gross domestic product. Compare these estimates to those in Table 16.6.

(d) In addition to population and *GDP*, the file *olympics.dat* contains an indicator variable (*SOVIET*) to indicate that a country was part of the former Soviet Union. The variable *HOST* indicates the country hosting the Olympic Games.

Using again the combined data for 1992 and 1996, estimate the Poisson regression model that adds these two variables to the specification. Discuss the results. Are the signs what you expected? Are the added variables statistically significant?

(e) A variable similar to *SOVIET* is *PLANNED*, which includes nonmarket, typically communist countries. Use this variable instead of *SOVIET* and repeat (d). Which model do you prefer, the one with *SOVIET*, or the one with *PLANNED*? Why?

(f) In 2000, the *GDP* (in 1995 US $) of Australia was 3.22224E + 11, and that of Canada was 6.41256E + 11. The Australian population in 2000 was 19.071 million, and that of Canada was 30.689 million. Using these figures, predict the number of medals won by Canada and Australia based on the estimates in part (e). Note that the 2000 games were held in Sydney, Australia. In 2000, Australia won 58 medals and Canada won 14. How close were your predictions?

16.10 Bernard and Busse use the Olympic Games data in *olympics.dat* to examine the share of medals won by countries. The total number of medals awarded in 1988 was 738; in 1992 there were 815 medals awarded, and in 1996, 842 medals were awarded. Using these totals, compute the share of medals (*SHARE*) won by each country in each of these years.

(a) Construct a histogram for the variable *SHARE*. What do you observe? What percent of the observations are zero?

(b) Estimate a least squares regression explaining *SHARE* as a function of the logarithms of population and real GDP, and the variables *HOST* and *SOVIET*. (i) Discuss the estimation results. (ii) Plot the residuals against ln(*GDP*). Do they appear random? (iii) Use your computer software to compute the skewness and kurtosis values of the residuals. How do these values compare to those for the normal distribution, which has skewness of zero and kurtosis of three?

(c) In 2000, the *GDP* (in 1995 US $) of Australia was 3.22224E + 11, and that of Canada was 6.41256E + 11. The Australian population in 2000 was 19.071 million, and that of Canada was 30.689 million. Predict the share of medals won by Canada and Australia based on the estimates in part (b). Note that the 2,000 games were held in Sydney, Australia. In 2000, Australia won 58 medals and Canada won 14 out of the 929 medals awarded. How close were your predicted shares?

(d) Estimate the model described in (b) using Tobit. Compare the parameter estimates to those in (b).

(e)◆ In the Tobit model the expected value of the dependent variable, conditional on the fact that it is positive, is given by an expression like (16.40). Specifically, it is $E(y_i|y_i > 0) = \beta_1 + \beta_2 x_i + \sigma\lambda_i$ where $\lambda_i = \phi(z_i)/\Phi(z_i)$ is the inverse Mills ratio and $z_i = (\beta_1 + \beta_2 x_i)/\sigma$. Use the information in part (c) to predict the share of medals won by Australia and Canada. Are these predicted shares closer to the true shares, or not?

16.11 In Chapter 7.5.3 we examined the Tennessee's Project STAR.[19] In the experiment, children were randomly assigned within schools into three types of classes: small

---

[19] See www.heros-inc.org/star.htm for program description, public use data and extensive literature.

classes with 13–17 students, regular-sized classes with 22–25 students, and regular-sized classes with a full-time teacher aide to assist the teacher. In Chapter 7.5.4b, using the data in *star.dat*, we checked for random assignment of children to the three types of classes using a linear probability model, regressing the indicator *SMALL* (small class) on student characteristics. Let us reconsider this regression using probit rather than the linear probability model. If there is random assignment we should not find any significant relationships.

(a) Estimate a probit model with outcome variable *SMALL* and explanatory variables *BOY, WHITE_ASIAN*, and *BLACK*. Individually test the coefficients of these variables for significance. What do you find? Test the coefficients jointly for significance using the likelihood ratio test. What do you find? Can we reject the null hypothesis that assignment to small classes is done randomly?

(b) Repeat the estimation and testing in part (a) using outcome variables *AIDE* and *REGULAR*. Do you find any evidence that students were not randomly assigned?

(c) Add the variables *FREELUNCH* to the models in (a) and (b) and re-estimate them. Do you find any evidence that there is a systematic pattern between class assignment and this variables?

(d) Add the two variables *TCHWHITE* and *TCHMASTERS* to the models in (c) and re-estimate them. In each, carry out a likelihood ratio test for the joint significance of *TCHWHITE* and *TCHMASTERS*. What do you conclude? In the experiment students were randomized *within* schools but not *across* schools. Does this offer any explanation of your findings? If so, how?

16.12 Mortgage lenders are interested in determining borrower and loan factors that may lead to delinquency or foreclosure. In the file *lasvegas.dat* are 1,000 observations on mortgages for single family homes in Las Vegas, Nevada during 2008. The variable of interest is *DELINQUENT*, an indicator variable $= 1$ if the borrower missed at least three payments (90+ days late), but 0 otherwise. Explanatory variables: are *LVR* $=$ the ratio of the loan amount to the value of the property; *REF* $= 1$ if purpose of the loan was a "refinance" and $= 0$ if loan was for a purchase; *INSUR* $= 1$ if mortgage carries mortgage insurance, 0 otherwise; *RATE* $=$ initial interest rate of the mortgage; *AMOUNT* $=$ dollar value of mortgage (in \$100,000); *CREDIT* $=$ credit score, *TERM* $=$ number of years between disbursement of the loan and the date it is expected to be fully repaid, *ARM* $= 1$ if mortgage has an adjustable rate, and $= 0$ if mortgage has a fixed rate.

(a) Estimate the linear probability (regression) model explaining *DELINQUENT* as a function of the remaining variables. Use White robust standard errors. Are the signs of the estimated coefficients reasonable?

(b) Use probit to estimate the model in (a). Are the signs and significance of the estimated coefficients the same as for the linear probability model?

(c) Compute the predicted value of *DELINQUENT* for the 500th and 1,000th observations using both the linear probability model and the probit model. Interpret the values.

(d) Construct a histogram of *CREDIT*. Using both linear probability and probit models, calculate the probability of delinquency for *CREDIT* $= 500, 600$, and 700 for a loan of \$250,000 (*AMOUNT* $= 2.5$). For the other variables, loan to value ratio (*LVR*) is 80%, initial interest rate is 8%, indicator variables take the value one, and *TERM* $= 30$. Discuss similarities and differences among the predicted probabilities from the two models.

(e) Compute the marginal effect of *CREDIT* on the probability of delinquency for *CREDIT* = 500, 600, and 700, given that the other explanatory variables take the values in (d). Discuss the interpretation of the marginal effect.

(f) Construct a histogram of *LVR*. Using both linear probability and probit models, calculate the probability of delinquency for *LVR* = 20 and *LVR* = 80, with *CREDIT* = 600 and other variables set as they are in (d). Compare and contrast the results.

(g) Compare the percentage of correct predictions from the linear probability model and the probit model, using a predicted probability of 0.5 as the threshold.

(h) As a loan officer, you wish to provide loans to customers who repay on schedule and are not delinquent. Suppose you have available to you the first 500 observations in the data on which to base your loan decision on the second 500 applications (501–1,000). Is using the probit model, with a threshold of 0.5 for the predicted probability the best decision rule for deciding on loan applications? If not, what is a better rule?

16.13 This exercise deals with the loan data described in Exercise 6.12. The "Chow" test was introduced in Chapter 7.2.3 for testing the equality of coefficients in two regressions on subsets of observations. Here we ask a similar question concerning the parameters of the probit model for deliquency for the two subpopulations of borrowers who either have mortgage insurance (*INSUR* = 1) or do not (*INSUR* = 0).

(a) Estimate the probit model for *DELINQUENT* using all explanatory variables except *INSUR* and all observations. Call the value of the log-likelihood function evaluated at the maximum likelihood estimates $\ln L_R$.

(b) Re-estimate the model in (a) using the sample observations for which *INSUR* = 0. Call the value of the log-likelihood function evaluated at the maximum likelihood estimates $\ln L_0$.

(c) Re-estimate the model in (b) using the sample observations for which *INSUR* = 1. Call the value of the log-likelihood function evaluated at the maximum likelihood estimates $\ln L_1$.

(d) Compare the estimates from the models in (a), (b) and (c). What major differences in coefficient signs, magnitudes, and significance do you observe?

(e) Re-estimate the model in (a), including each explanatory variable, *INSUR*, and interactions with *INSUR*. Compare the value of the log-likelihood function from the fully interacted model, call it $\ln L_U$, to $\ln L_0 + \ln L_1$. If you have done things correctly, then $\ln L_U$ should equal $\ln L_0 + \ln L_1$. Can you explain why this must be so?

(f) Carry out a likelihood ratio version of the Chow test by computing $LR = 2(\ln L_U - \ln L_R)$. What is the appropriate critical value for a test at the 5% level of significance? What conclusion do you draw about the subgroups of individuals who do and do not have mortgage insurance? Do the two groups behave in the same way?

16.14 Data on 1,500 purchases of canned lite tuna are in the file *tunafish.dat*. There are four brands of tuna (Starkist–water, Starkist–oil, Chicken of the Sea–water, Chicken of the Sea–oil). The A.C. Nielsen data are available through the University of Chicago's Graduate School of Business.[20] The data file *tunafish_small.dat* is a smaller dataset with 250 purchases. The data are in "stacked" format with four datalines per purchase, one for each tuna brand. The consumer choice is indicated by the indicator variable *CHOICE*. Relevant variables are *NETPRICE* = price minus coupon value,

---

[20] http://research.chicagobooth.edu/marketing/databases/erim/index.aspx.

if used; $DISPLAY = 1$ if product is on display, $FEATURE = 1$ if item is featured, and $INCOME = $ household income.

(a) What is the primary variable-type distinction between the *NETPRICE* and *INCOME*?

(b) What is the sample percentage of purchases for each brand? What do you observe about consumer preferences for these product choices?

(c) Using the conditional logit model, write the probability of choosing each brand using as explanatory variables *NETPRICE, DISPLAY,* and *FEATURE*, plus an alternative specific constant using Starkist packed in water as the base category.

(d) Estimate the model specified in part (c).

(e) For the model in (d) find the marginal effect of *NETPRICE* on the probability of choice of each brand, using for all brands $DISPLAY = FEATURE = 0$. Do these marginal effects have the signs you anticipate? Are the marginal effects statistically significant?

(f) Add the variable *INCOME* to the model specified in (c). Perform a likelihood ratio test of its significance.

(g) For the model in (f) find the marginal effect of *NETPRICE* on the probability of choice of each brand, using for all brands $DISPLAY = FEATURE = 0$ and $INCOME = 30$.

Appendix 16A[21] Probit Marginal Effects: Details

16A.1 STANDARD ERROR OF MARGINAL EFFECT AT A GIVEN POINT

Consider the probit model $p = \Phi(\beta_1 + \beta_2 x)$. The marginal effect of a continuous x, evaluated at a specific point $x = x_0$, is

$$\frac{dp}{dx}\bigg|_{x=x_0} = \phi(\beta_1 + \beta_2 x_0)\beta_2 = g(\beta_1, \beta_2)$$

The estimator of the marginal effect is $g(\tilde{\beta}_1, \tilde{\beta}_2)$, where $\tilde{\beta}_1$ and $\tilde{\beta}_2$ are the maximum likelihood estimators of the unknown parameters. The variance of this estimator was developed in Appendix 5B.5, in (5B.8), and is given by

$$\operatorname{var}\left[g(\tilde{\beta}_1, \tilde{\beta}_2)\right] \cong \left[\frac{\partial g(\beta_1, \beta_2)}{\partial \beta_1}\right]^2 \operatorname{var}(\tilde{\beta}_1) + \left[\frac{\partial g(\beta_1, \beta_2)}{\partial \beta_2}\right]^2 \operatorname{var}(\tilde{\beta}_2)$$
$$+ 2\left[\frac{\partial g(\beta_1, \beta_2)}{\partial \beta_1}\right]\left[\frac{\partial g(\beta_1, \beta_2)}{\partial \beta_2}\right]\operatorname{cov}(\tilde{\beta}_1, \tilde{\beta}_2) \tag{16A.1}$$

The variances and covariances of the estimators come from maximum likelihood estimation. The essence of these calculations is given in Appendix C.8.2. To implement the delta method we require the derivative

---

[21] This appendix contains advanced material.

$$\frac{\partial g(\beta_1, \beta_2)}{\partial \beta_1} = \frac{\partial [\phi(\beta_1 + \beta_2 x_0)\beta_2]}{\partial \beta_1}$$

$$= \left\{ \frac{\partial \phi(\beta_1 + \beta_2 x_0)}{\partial \beta_1} \times \beta_2 \right\} + \phi(\beta_1 + \beta_2 x_0) \times \frac{\partial \beta_2}{\partial \beta_1}$$

$$= -\phi(\beta_1 + \beta_2 x_0) \times (\beta_1 + \beta_2 x_0) \times \beta_2$$

The second line above uses the product rule, Derivative Rule 6. To obtain the final result we used $\partial \beta_2 / \partial \beta_1 = 0$ and

$$\frac{\partial \phi(\beta_1 + \beta_2 x_0)}{\partial \beta_1} = \frac{\partial}{\partial \beta_1} \left[\frac{1}{\sqrt{2\pi}} e^{-\frac{1}{2}(\beta_1 + \beta_2 x_0)^2} \right]$$

$$= \frac{1}{\sqrt{2\pi}} e^{-\frac{1}{2}(\beta_1 + \beta_2 x_0)^2} \left(2 \times -\frac{1}{2} \times (\beta_1 + \beta_2 x_0) \right)$$

$$= -\phi(\beta_1 + \beta_2 x_0) \times (\beta_1 + \beta_2 x_0)$$

The second step uses Derivative Rule 7 for exponential functions. Using similar steps we obtain the other key derivative,

$$\frac{\partial g(\beta_1, \beta_2)}{\partial \beta_2} = \phi(\beta_1 + \beta_2 x_0)[1 - (\beta_1 + \beta_2 x_0) \times \beta_2 x_0]$$

From the maximum likelihood estimation results using the transportation data example we obtain the estimator variances and covariances[22]

$$\begin{bmatrix} \widehat{\mathrm{var}(\tilde{\beta}_1)} & \widehat{\mathrm{cov}(\tilde{\beta}_1, \tilde{\beta}_2)} \\ \widehat{\mathrm{cov}(\tilde{\beta}_1, \tilde{\beta}_2)} & \widehat{\mathrm{var}(\tilde{\beta}_2)} \end{bmatrix} = \begin{bmatrix} 0.1593956 & 0.0003261 \\ 0.0003261 & 0.0105817 \end{bmatrix}$$

The derivatives must be evaluated at the maximum likelihood estimates. For the transportation data used in Chapter 16.1.5, and For *DTIME* $= 2$ ($x_0 = 2$), the calculated values of the derivatives are

$$\frac{\partial g(\beta_1, \beta_2)}{\partial \beta_1} = -0.055531 \text{ and } \frac{\partial g(\beta_1, \beta_2)}{\partial \beta_2} = 0.2345835$$

Using (16A.1), and carrying out the required multiplication we obtain the estimated variance and standard error of the marginal effect

$$\widehat{\mathrm{var}[g(\tilde{\beta}_1, \tilde{\beta}_2)]} = 0.0010653 \text{ and } \mathrm{se}[g(\tilde{\beta}_1, \tilde{\beta}_2)] = 0.0326394$$

16A.2 STANDARD ERROR OF AVERAGE MARGINAL EFFECT

Consider the probit model $p = \Phi(\beta_1 + \beta_2 x)$. For the transportation data example, the explanatory variable $x = DTIME$. The average marginal effect of this continuous variable is

$$AME = \frac{1}{N} \Sigma_{i=1}^N \phi(\beta_1 + \beta_2 DTIME_i)\beta_2 = g_2(\beta_1, \beta_2)$$

---

[22] Using minus the inverse matrix of second derivatives.

The estimator of the average marginal effect is $g_2(\tilde{\beta}_1, \tilde{\beta}_2)$. To apply the delta method to find $\text{var}[g_2(\tilde{\beta}_1, \tilde{\beta}_2)]$, we require the derivatives

$$\frac{\partial g_2(\beta_1, \beta_2)}{\partial \beta_1} = \frac{\partial}{\partial \beta_1}\left[\frac{1}{N}\Sigma_{i=1}^N \phi(\beta_1 + \beta_2 DTIME_i)\beta_2\right]$$

$$= \frac{1}{N}\Sigma_{i=1}^N \frac{\partial}{\partial \beta_1}[\phi(\beta_1 + \beta_2 DTIME_i)\beta_2]$$

$$= \frac{1}{N}\Sigma_{i=1}^N \frac{\partial g(\beta_1, \beta_2)}{\partial \beta_1}$$

The term $\dfrac{\partial g(\beta_1, \beta_2)}{\partial \beta_1}$ we evaluated in the previous section. Similarly, the derivative

$$\frac{\partial g_2(\beta_1, \beta_2)}{\partial \beta_2} = \frac{\partial}{\partial \beta_2}\left[\frac{1}{N}\Sigma_{i=1}^N \phi(\beta_1 + \beta_2 DTIME_i)\beta_2\right]$$

$$= \frac{1}{N}\Sigma_{i=1}^N \frac{\partial}{\partial \beta_2}[\phi(\beta_1 + \beta_2 DTIME_i)\beta_2]$$

$$= \frac{1}{N}\Sigma_{i=1}^N \frac{\partial g(\beta_1, \beta_2)}{\partial \beta_2}$$

For the transportation data we compute

$$\overline{\frac{\partial g_2(\beta_1, \beta_2)}{\partial \beta_1}} = -0.00185 \quad \text{and} \quad \overline{\frac{\partial g_2(\beta_1, \beta_2)}{\partial \beta_2}} = -0.032366$$

Using (16A.1) with g replaced by g_2, and carrying out the required multiplication, we obtain the estimated variance and standard error of the average marginal effect

$$\overline{\text{var}[g_2(\tilde{\beta}_1, \tilde{\beta}_2)]} = 0.0000117 \quad \text{and} \quad \text{se}[g_2(\tilde{\beta}_1, \tilde{\beta}_2)] = 0.003416$$

Appendix *A*

Mathematical Tools

Learning Objectives

Based on the material in this appendix, you should be able to:

1. Explain the relationship between exponential functions and natural logarithms.
2. Explain and apply scientific notation.
3. Define a linear relationship, as opposed to a nonlinear relationship.
4. Compute the elasticity at a point on a function.
5. Explain the concept of a derivative, and its relationship to the slope of a function.
6. Compute the derivatives of simple functions and provide their interpretations.
7. Describe the relationship between a derivative and a partial derivative.
8. Explain the concept of an integral.

Keywords

absolute value	integral	quadratic function
antilogarithm	intercept	rational numbers
ceteris paribus	irrational numbers	real numbers
derivative	linear relationship	relative change
e	logarithm	scientific notation
elasticity	marginal effect	slope
exponential function	natural logarithm	Taylor series
exponents	nonlinear relationship	
inequalities	partial derivative	
integers	percentage change	

We assume that you have studied basic math. Hopefully you understand the calculus concepts of differentiation and integration, though these tools are *not required* for success in this class. In this appendix we review some essential concepts that you may wish to consult from time to time.[1]

---

[1] Summation signs and operations are covered in the Probability Primer that precedes Chapter 2.

A.1 Some Basics

A.1.1 NUMBERS

Integers are the whole numbers, $0, \pm 1, \pm 2, \pm 3, \ldots$. The positive integers are the counting numbers. **Rational** numbers can be written as a/b, where a and b are integers and $b \neq 0$. The **real numbers** can be represented by points on a line. There are an uncountable number of real numbers, and they are not all rational. Numbers such as $\pi \cong 3.1415927$ and $\sqrt{2}$ are said to be **irrational** since they cannot be expressed as ratios, and have only decimal representations. Numbers like $\sqrt{-2}$ are not real numbers. The **absolute value** of a number is denoted $|a|$. It is the positive part of the number: $|3| = 3$ and $|-3| = 3$.

Inequalities among numbers obey certain rules. The notation $a < b$, a is less than b, means that a is to the left of b on the number line, and that $b - a > 0$. If a is less than or equal to b, it is written $a \leq b$. Three basic rules are

$$\text{If } a < b, \text{ then } a + c < b + c$$

$$\text{If } a < b, \text{ then } \begin{cases} ac < bc & \text{if } c > 0 \\ ac > bc & \text{if } c < 0 \end{cases}$$

$$\text{If } a < b \text{ and } b < c, \text{ then } a < c$$

A.1.2 EXPONENTS

Exponents are defined as follows:

$$x^n = xx \cdots x \ (n \text{ terms}) \text{ if } n \text{ is a positive integer}$$
$$x^0 = 1 \text{ if } x \neq 0. \ [0^0 \text{ is does not have meaning and is "undefined."}]$$

Some common rules for working with exponents, assuming x and y are real, m and n are integers, and a and b are rational, are as follows:

$$x^{-n} = \frac{1}{x^n} \text{ if } x \neq 0. \text{ For example, } x^{-1} = \frac{1}{x}$$

$$x^{1/n} = \sqrt[n]{x}. \text{ For example, } x^{1/2} = \sqrt{x} \text{ and } x^{-1/2} = \frac{1}{\sqrt{x}}$$

$$x^{m/n} = \left(x^{1/n}\right)^m. \text{ For example, } 8^{4/3} = \left(8^{1/3}\right)^4 = 2^4 = 16$$

$$x^a x^b = x^{a+b}, \qquad \frac{x^a}{x^b} = x^{a-b}$$

$$\left(\frac{x}{y}\right)^a = \frac{x^a}{y^a}, \qquad (xy)^a = x^a y^a$$

A.1.3 SCIENTIFIC NOTATION

Scientific notation is useful for very large or very small numbers. A number in scientific notation is written as a number between 1 and 10 multiplied by a power of 10. So, for example: $5.1 \times 10^5 = 510{,}000$, and $0.00000034 = 3.4 \times 10^{-7}$. Scientific notation makes handling large numbers much easier, because complex operations can be broken into simpler ones. For example,

$$510,000 \times 0.00000034 = (5.1 \times 10^5) \times (3.4 \times 10^{-7})$$
$$= (5.1 \times 3.4) \times (10^5 \times 10^{-7})$$
$$= 17.34 \times 10^{-2}$$
$$= 0.1734$$

and

$$\frac{510,000}{0.00000034} = \frac{5.1 \times 10^5}{3.4 \times 10^{-7}} = \frac{5.1}{3.4} \times \frac{10^5}{10^{-7}} = 1.5 \times 10^{12}$$

Computer programs sometimes write $5.1 \times 10^5 = 5.1E5$ or $5.1D5$ and $3.4 \times 10^{-7} = 3.4E - 7$ or $3.4D - 7$.

A.1.4   LOGARITHMS AND THE NUMBER e

Logarithms are exponents. If $x = 10^b$, then b is the logarithm of x using the base 10. The irrational number $e \cong 2.718282$ is used in mathematics and statistics as the base for logarithms. If $x = e^b$, then b is the logarithm of x using the base e. Logarithms using the number e as base are called **natural logarithms**. *All logarithms in this book are natural logarithms.* We express the natural logarithm of x as $\ln(x)$,

$$\ln(x) = \ln(e^b) = b$$

Note that $\ln(1) = 0$, using the laws of exponents. Table A.1 gives the logarithms of some powers of 10.

Note that logarithms have a compressed scale compared to the original numbers. Since logarithms are exponents, they follow similar rules:

$$\ln(xy) = \ln(x) + \ln(y)$$
$$\ln(x/y) = \ln(x) - \ln(y)$$
$$\ln(x^a) = a\ln(x)$$

Table A.1   **Some Natural Logarithms**

x	$\ln(x)$
1	0
10	2.3025851
100	4.6051702
1000	6.9077553
10,000	9.2103404
100,000	11.512925
1,000,000	13.815511

For example, if $x = 1000$ and $y = 10{,}000$, then

$$\ln(1000 \times 10{,}000) = \ln(1000) + \ln(10{,}000)$$

$$= 6.9077553 + 9.2103404$$

$$= 16.118096$$

What is the advantage of this? The value of xy is a multiplication problem, which by using logarithms we can turn into an addition problem. We need a way to go backwards, from the logarithm of a number to the number itself. By definition,

$$x = e^{\ln(x)} = \exp[\ln(x)]$$

When there is an **exponential function** with a complicated exponent, the notation **exp** is often used, so that $e^{(\cdot)} = \exp(\cdot)$. The exponential function is the **antilogarithm**, because we can recover the value of x using it. Then,

$$1000 \times 10{,}000 = \exp(16.118096) = 10{,}000{,}000$$

You will not be doing many calculations like these, but the knowledge of logarithms and exponents is quite critical in economics and econometrics.

A.1.5 DECIMALS AND PERCENTAGES

Suppose the value of a variable y changes from the value $y = y_0$ to $y = y_1$. The difference between these values is often denoted $\Delta y = y_1 - y_0$, where the notation Δy is read "change in y", or "delta-y." The **relative change in y** is defined to be

$$\text{relative change in } y = \frac{y_1 - y_0}{y_0} = \frac{\Delta y}{y_0} \tag{A.1}$$

For example, if $y_0 = 3$ and $y_1 = 3.02$, then the relative change in y is

$$\frac{y_1 - y_0}{y_0} = \frac{3.02 - 3}{3} = 0.0067$$

Often the relative change in y is written as $\Delta y / y$, omitting the subscript.

A relative change is a decimal. The corresponding **percentage change in y** is 100 times the relative change.

$$\text{percentage change in } y = 100\frac{y_1 - y_0}{y_0} = \%\Delta y \tag{A.2}$$

If $y_0 = 3$ and $y_1 = 3.02$, then the percentage change in y is

$$\%\Delta y = 100\frac{y_1 - y_0}{y_0} = 100\frac{3.02 - 3}{3} = 0.67\%$$

A.1.6   LOGARITHMS AND PERCENTAGES

A feature of logarithms that helps greatly in their economic interpretation is that they can be approximated very simply. Let y_1 be a positive value of y, and let y_0 be a value of y that is "close" to y_1. A useful approximation rule is

$$100[\ln(y_1) - \ln(y_0)] \cong \%\Delta y = \text{percentage change in } y \qquad (A.3)$$

That is, 100 times the difference in the logarithms is the approximate percentage difference between y_0 and y_1, if y_0 and y_1 are close.

A.1.6a   Derivation of the Approximation

The result in (A.3) follows from the mathematical tool called a Taylor series approximation, which is developed in Example A.3 in Section A.3.1. Using this approximation, the value of $\ln(y_1)$ can be written

$$\ln(y_1) \cong \ln(y_0) + \frac{1}{y_0}(y_1 - y_0) \qquad (A.4)$$

For example, let $y_1 = 1 + x$ and let $y_0 = 1$. Then, as long as x is small,

$$\ln(1 + x) \cong x$$

Subtracting $\ln(y_0)$ from both sides of (A.4), we obtain

$$\ln(y_1) - \ln(y_0) = \Delta \ln(y) \cong \frac{1}{y_0}(y_1 - y_0) = \text{relative change in } y$$

The symbol $\Delta \ln(y)$ represents the "difference" between two logarithms. Using (A.2),

$$100\Delta \ln(y) = 100[\ln(y_1) - \ln(y_0)]$$

$$\cong 100 \times \frac{(y_1 - y_0)}{y_0}$$

$$= \%\Delta y = \text{percentage change in } y$$

A.1.6b   Approximation Error

The approximation (A.3) works well for values of y_1 and y_0 that are close to each other. For example, suppose that $y_0 = 1$. The percentage difference between y_1 and y_0 is

$$\%\Delta y = 100 \times \frac{(y_1 - y_0)}{y_0} = 100(y_1 - 1)$$

The quantity we are approximating is $100\Delta \ln(y) = 100[\ln(y_1) - \ln(1)] = 100 \times \ln(y_1)$ using $\ln(1) = 0$. The percentage error in the approximation is

$$\% \text{ approximation error} = 100\left[\frac{\%\Delta y - 100\Delta \ln(y)}{100\Delta \ln(y)}\right] = 100\left[\frac{(y_1 - 1) - \ln(y_1)}{\ln(y_1)}\right]$$

A few values are reported in Table A.2.

Table A.2 **Log Difference Approximation Errors**

y_1	$\%\Delta y$	$100\Delta \ln(y)\,(\%)$	Approximation error (%)
1.01	1.00	0.995	0.50
1.05	5.00	4.88	2.48
1.10	10.00	9.53	4.92
1.15	15.00	13.98	7.33
1.20	20.00	18.23	9.70
1.25	25.00	22.31	12.04

As you can see, if y_1 and y_0 differ by 10%, then the approximation error is 4.92%. If y_1 and y_0 differ by 20%, then the approximation error is 9.7%.

A.2 Linear Relationships

In economics, and in econometrics, we study linear and nonlinear relationships between variables. In this section, we review basic characteristics of linear relationships. Let y and x be variables. The standard form for a linear relationship is

$$y = mx + b \tag{A.5}$$

In Figure A.1, the slope is m and the y-intercept is b. The symbol Δ represents "a change in," so Δx is read as a "change in x." The slope of the line is

$$m = \frac{y_2 - y_1}{x_2 - x_1} = \frac{\Delta y}{\Delta x}$$

For the straight-line relationship in Figure A.1, the slope m is the ratio of the change in vertical distance (rise) to the change in horizontal distance (run) as a point moves along the line in either direction. The slope of a straight line is constant; the rate at which y changes as x changes is constant over the length of the straight line.

The slope m is very meaningful to economists as it is the **marginal effect** of a change in x on y. To see this, solve the **slope** definition $m = \Delta y/\Delta x$ for Δy, obtaining

$$\Delta y = m\,\Delta x \tag{A.6}$$

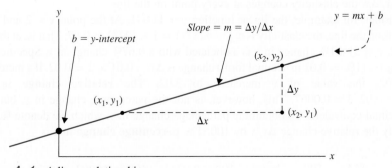

FIGURE *A.1* A linear relationship.

If x changes by one unit, $\Delta x = 1$, then the corresponding change in y is $\Delta y = m$. The marginal effect, m, is always the same for a linear relationship like (A.5), because the slope is constant.

The **intercept** parameter indicates where the linear relationship crosses the vertical axis—that is, it is the value of y when x is zero,

$$y = mx + b = m \times 0 + b = b$$

A.2.1   SLOPES AND DERIVATIVES

Derivatives have an important role in econometrics. In a relationship between two variables, $y = f(x)$, the **first derivative** measures the slope. The slope of the line $y = f(x) = mx + b$ is denoted as dy/dx. The notation dy/dx is a "stylized" version of $\Delta y/\Delta x$, and for the linear relationship (A.5) the first derivative is

$$dy/dx = m \qquad\qquad (A.7)$$

In general, the first derivative measures the change in the function value y given an infinitesimal change in x. For the linear function the first derivative is the constant $m = \Delta y/\Delta x$. The "infinitesimal" does not matter in this case, because the rate of change of y with respect to changes in x is a constant.

A.2.2   ELASTICITY

A favorite tool of the economist is **elasticity**. It is the percentage change in one variable associated with a 1% change in another variable for movements along a specific curve. That is, if we move from one point on a curve to another point on the curve, what are the relative percentage changes? For example, in Figure A.1, what is the percentage change in y relative to the percentage change in x as we move from the point (x_1, y_1) to (x_2, y_2)? For a linear relationship, the elasticity of y with respect to a change in x is

$$\varepsilon_{yx} = \frac{\%\Delta y}{\%\Delta x} = \frac{100(\Delta y/y)}{100(\Delta x/x)} = \frac{\Delta y/y}{\Delta x/x} = \frac{\Delta y}{\Delta x} \times \frac{x}{y} = slope \times \frac{x}{y} \qquad (A.8)$$

The elasticity is seen to be a product of the slope of the relationship and the ratio of an x value to a y value. In a linear relationship, such as Figure A.1, while the slope is constant, $m = \Delta y/\Delta x$, the elasticity changes at every point on the line.

Consider, for example, the linear function $y = 1x + 1$. At the point $x = 2$ and $y = 3$, which is on the line, the elasticity is $\varepsilon_{yx} = m(x/y) = 1 \times (2/3) = 0.67$. That is, at the point $(x = 2, y = 3)$ a 1% change in x is associated with a 0.67% change in y. Specifically, at $x = 2$ a 1% (1% $= 0.01$ in decimal form) change is $\Delta x = 0.01 \times 2 = 0.02$. If x increases to $x = 2.02$, the value of y increases to 3.02. The **relative change** in y is $\Delta y/y = 0.02/3 = 0.0067$. This, however, is not the percentage change in y, but rather the decimal equivalent. To obtain the percentage change in y, which we denote $\%\Delta y$, we multiply the relative change $\Delta y/y$ by 100. The **percentage change** in y is

$$\%\Delta y = 100 \times (\Delta y/y) = 100 \times 0.02/3 = 100 \times 0.0067 = 0.67\%$$

A.3 Nonlinear Relationships

While linear relationships are intuitive and easy to work with, many real-world economic relationships are nonlinear, as illustrated in Figure A.2.

The slope of this curve is not constant. The slope measures the marginal effect of x on y, and for a nonlinear relationship like that in Figure A.2, the slope is different at every point on the curve. The changing slope tells us that the relationship is not linear. Since the slope is different at every point, we can only talk about the effect of small changes in x on y. In (A.6) we replace Δ, the symbol for "a change in," with d, which we will take to mean an "infinitesimal change in." In the linear case when we made this replacement, the slope was given by $dy/dx = m$, where m, was a constant. See (A.7).

However, with nonlinear functions such as that in Figure A.2, the slope (derivative) is not constant, but changes as x changes, and must be determined at each point. Strictly speaking, the slope of a curve is the slope of the **tangent** to the curve at a specific point. To work out the slope at different points on a nonlinear curve, we need some rules for obtaining the derivative dy/dx.

A.3.1 RULES FOR DERIVATIVES

Some rules for finding derivatives are the following:

Derivative Rule 1. The derivative of a constant c is zero. That is, if $y = f(x) = c$, then

$$\frac{dy}{dx} = 0$$

Derivative Rule 2. If $y = x^n$, then

$$\frac{dy}{dx} = nx^{n-1}$$

Derivative Rule 3. If $y = cu$ and $u = f(x)$, then

$$\frac{dy}{dx} = c\frac{du}{dx}$$

Constants can be factored out of functions before taking the derivative.

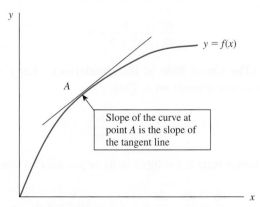

FIGURE *A.2* A nonlinear relationship.

Derivative Rule 4. If $y = cx^n$, using Rules 2 and 3,

$$\frac{dy}{dx} = cnx^{n-1}$$

Derivative Rule 5. If $y = u + v$, where $u = f(x)$ and $v = g(x)$ are functions of x, then

$$\frac{dy}{dx} = \frac{du}{dx} + \frac{dv}{dx}$$

The derivative of the sum (or difference) of two functions is the sum of the derivatives. This rule extends to more than two terms in a sum.

Derivative Rule 6. If $y = uv$, where $u = f(x)$ and $v = g(x)$ are functions of x, then

$$\frac{dy}{dx} = \frac{du}{dx}v + u\frac{dv}{dx}$$

This is called the product rule. The quotient rule, for $y = u/v$, is obtained by inserting v^{-1} for v in the product rule.

Derivative Rule 7. If $y = e^x$, then

$$\frac{dy}{dx} = e^x$$

If $y = \exp(ax + b)$, then

$$\frac{dy}{dx} = \exp(ax + b) \times a$$

In general, the derivative of the exponential function is the exponential function times the derivative of the exponent.

Derivative Rule 8. If $y = \ln(x)$, then

$$\frac{dy}{dx} = \frac{1}{x}, \quad x > 0$$

If $y = \ln(ax + b)$, then

$$\frac{dy}{dx} = \frac{1}{ax + b} \times a$$

Derivative Rule 9 (The Chain Rule of Differentiation).   Let $y = f(u(x))$, so that y depends on u which in turn depends on x. Then

$$\frac{dy}{dx} = \frac{dy}{du} \times \frac{du}{dx}$$

For example, in Derivative Rule 8, $y = \ln(ax + b)$, or $y = \ln(u(x))$ where $u = ax + b$. Then

$$\frac{dy}{dx} = \frac{dy}{du} \times \frac{du}{dx} = \frac{1}{u} \times a = \frac{1}{ax + b} \times a$$

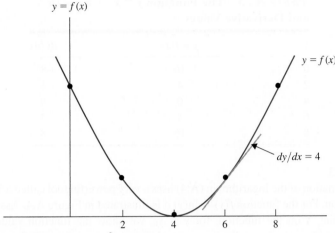

FIGURE **A.3**   The function $y = x^2 - 8x + 16$.

Example A.1

The derivative of $y = f(x) = 4x + 1$ is

$$\frac{dy}{dx} = \frac{d(4x)}{dx} + \frac{d(1)}{dx} = 4$$

Because this function is the equation of a straight line, $y = mx + b$, its slope is constant and given by the coefficient of x, which in this case is 4.

Example A.2

Consider the function $y = x^2 - 8x + 16$, shown in Figure A.3. This quadratic function is a parabola. Using the rules of derivatives, the slope of a line tangent to the curve is

$$\frac{dy}{dx} = \frac{d(x^2 - 8x + 16)}{dx}$$

$$= \frac{d(x^2)}{dx} - 8\frac{d(x^1)}{dx} + \frac{d(16)}{dx}$$

$$= 2x^1 - 8x^0 + 0$$

$$= 2x - 8$$

This result means that the slope of the tangent line to this curve is $dy/dx = 2x - 8$. The derivative and function values are shown for several values of x in Table A.3

Note a few things. First, the slope is different at each value of x. The slope is negative for values of $x < 4$, the slope is zero when $x = 4$, and the slope is positive for values of $x > 4$. To interpret these slopes, recall that the derivative of a function at a point is the slope of the tangent at that point. The slope of the tangent is the **rate of change** of the function—how much $y = f(x)$ is changing as x changes. At $x = 0$, the derivative is -8, indicating that y is falling as x increases, and that the rate of change is 8 units in y per unit change in x. At $x = 2$, the rate of change of the function has diminished, and at $x = 4$, the rate of change of the function is $dy/dx = 0$. That is, at $x = 4$, the slope of the tangent to the curve is zero. For values of $x > 4$, the derivative is positive, which indicates that the function $y = f(x)$ is increasing as x increases.

Table A.3   **The Function $y = x^2 - 8x + 16$**
and Derivative Values

x	$y = f(x)$	dy/dx
0	16	−8
2	4	−4
4	0	0
6	4	4
8	16	8

Example A.3

The approximation of the logarithm in (A.4) uses a very powerful tool called a Taylor series approximation. For the function $f(y) = \ln(y)$ it is illustrated in Figure A.4. Assume that we know the point A on the function: for $y = y_0$, we know the function value $f(y_0)$. The approximation idea is to draw a line tangent to the curve $f(y) = \ln(y)$ at A, then approximate the point on the curve $f(y_1) = \ln(y_1)$ by the point B on the tangent line. For a smooth curve like $\ln(y)$, this strategy works well, and the approximation error will be small if y_1 is close to y_0. The slope of the tangent line at point A, $(y_0, f(y_0) = \ln(y_0))$, is the derivative of the function $f(y) = \ln(y)$ evaluated at y_0. Using Derivative Rule 8, we have

$$\frac{d \ln(y)}{dy}\bigg|_{y=y_0} = \frac{1}{y}\bigg|_{y=y_0} = \frac{1}{y_0}$$

The value of the linear approximation at B is given by geometry. Recall that the slope of the tangent (straight) line is "the rise over the run." The "run" is A to C, or $(y_1 - y_0)$, and the corresponding "rise" is C to B. Then

$$\text{tangent slope} = \frac{d \ln(y)}{dy}\bigg|_{y=y_0} = \frac{\text{rise}}{\text{run}} = \frac{\overline{CB}}{\overline{AC}} = \frac{B - \ln(y_0)}{y_1 - y_0}$$

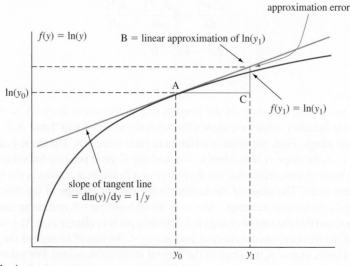

FIGURE $A.4$ Taylor series approximation of $\ln(y)$.

Solving this equation for $B =$ approximate value of $f(y_1)$, we obtain the expression in (A.4),

$$B = \ln(y_0) + \frac{d\ln(y)}{dy}\bigg|_{y=y_0} (y_1 - y_0) = \ln(y_0) + \frac{1}{y_0}(y_1 - y_0)$$

The Taylor series approximation is used in many contexts.

Derivative Rule 10 (Taylor Series Approximation). If $f(x)$ is a smooth function, then

$$f(x) \cong f(a) + \frac{df(x)}{dx}\bigg|_{x=a} (x - a) = f(a) + f'(a)(x - a)$$

where $f'(a)$ is a common notation for the first derivative of the function $f(x)$ evaluated at $x = a$. The approximation is good for x close to a.

A.3.2 ELASTICITY OF A NONLINEAR RELATIONSHIP

Given the slope of a curve, the elasticity of y with respect to changes in x is given by a slightly modified (A.8),

$$\varepsilon_{yx} = \frac{dy/y}{dx/x} = \frac{dy}{dx} \times \frac{x}{y} = slope \times \frac{x}{y}$$

For example, the quadratic function $y = ax^2 + bx + c$ is a parabola. The slope (derivative) is $dy/dx = 2ax + b$. The elasticity is

$$\varepsilon_{yx} = slope \times \frac{x}{y} = (2ax + b)\frac{x}{y}$$

As a numerical example, consider the curve defined by $y = f(x) = x^2 - 8x + 16$. The graph of this quadratic function is shown in Figure A.3. The slope of the curve is $dy/dx = 2x - 8$. When $x = 6$, the slope of the tangent line is $dy/dx = 4$. When $x = 6$, the corresponding value of $y = 4$. So the elasticity at that point is

$$\varepsilon_{xy} = (dy/dx) \times (x/y) = (2x - 8)(x/y) = 4(6/4) = 6$$

A 1% increase in x corresponds to a 6% change in y.

A.3.3 PARTIAL DERIVATIVES

When a functional relationship includes several variables, such as $y = f(x, z)$, the slope depends on the values of x and z, and there are slopes in two directions rather than one. In Figure A.5, we illustrate the partial derivative of the function with respect to x, holding z constant at the value $z = z_0$.

At the point (x_0, z_0) the value of the function is $y_0 = f(x_0, z_0)$. The slope of the tangent line $\overline{CD}$ is the partial derivative.

$$\text{Slope of } \overline{CD} = \frac{\partial f(x, z)}{\partial x}\bigg|_{x=x_0, z=z_0}$$

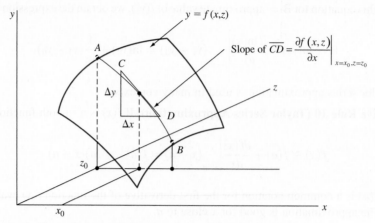

FIGURE **A.5**   Three-dimensional diagram of a partial derivative.

The vertical bar indicates that the partial derivative function is evaluated at the point (x_0, z_0). To find the partial derivative we use the already established rules. Consider the function

$$y = f(x, z) = ax^2 + bx + cz + d$$

To find the partial derivative of y with respect to x, treat z as a constant. Then

$$\frac{\partial y}{\partial x} = \frac{d(ax^2)}{dx} + \frac{d(bx)}{dx} + \frac{d(cz)}{dx} + \frac{d(d)}{dx}$$
$$= 2ax + b$$

Using Derivative Rule 1, the third and fourth terms in the derivative are zero, because cz and d are treated as constants.

A.3.4   THEORY OF DERIVATIVES[2]

Many rules for derivatives can be obtained using limit operations. Consider the curve $y = f(x)$ shown in Figure A.6 on page 645.

Two points on the curve are (x_1, y_1) and (x_2, y_2). The slope of the line segment joining (x_1, y_1) and (x_2, y_2) is

$$\frac{\Delta y}{\Delta x} = \frac{y_2 - y_1}{x_2 - x_1} \tag{A.9}$$

Suppose that (x_1, y_1) remains a fixed point and that we slide the point (x_2, y_2) along the curve towards (x_1, y_1). The slope of the line segment will vary from point to point. For a smooth curve like the one we have shown, as (x_2, y_2) moves closer and closer to (x_1, y_1), the slope of the line segment will change less and less, approaching a limiting value. When this occurs, the limiting value is said to be the **slope of the tangent** at (x_1, y_1), or the slope of the curve at (x_1, y_1).

---

[2] This section contains advanced material.

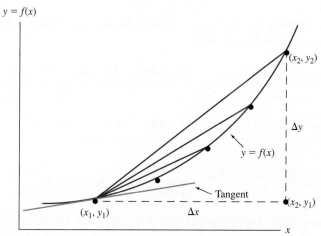

FIGURE $A.6$ The slope of a curve.

The slope of the curve $f(x)$ is the **derivative** of the function $f(x)$, with respect to x, at the point (x_1, y_1). Algebraically, the first derivative is defined as

$$\frac{dy}{dx} = \lim_{\Delta x \to 0} \frac{\Delta y}{\Delta x} \tag{A.10}$$

The notation dy/dx can be thought of as a stylized version of $\Delta y / \Delta x$, with the reminder that the changes in x are infinitesimal.

To calculate the derivative using (A.10), it is convenient to let the stationary point $(x_1, y_1) = (x, y)$ and the moving point $(x_2, y_2) = (x + \Delta x, y + \Delta y)$. Then the derivative of $f(x)$ at (x, y) is

$$\frac{dy}{dx} = \lim_{\Delta x \to 0} \frac{\Delta y}{\Delta x} = \lim_{\Delta x \to 0} \frac{y_2 - y_1}{\Delta x}$$
$$= \lim_{\Delta x \to 0} \frac{f(x + \Delta x) - f(x)}{\Delta x} \tag{A.11}$$

The derivative dy/dx is a function of x, which must be evaluated at specific points in order to obtain the slope of the function at those points.

Example A.4
Consider the function $y = f(x) = 4x + 1$. The slope of this function is

$$\frac{dy}{dx} = \lim_{\Delta x \to 0} \frac{f(x + \Delta x) - f(x)}{\Delta x} = \lim_{\Delta x \to 0} \frac{4(x + \Delta x) + 1 - (4x + 1)}{\Delta x}$$

$$= \lim_{\Delta x \to 0} \frac{4\Delta x}{\Delta x} = \lim_{\Delta x \to 0} 4 = 4$$

The slope of the straight line $y = f(x) = 4x + 1$ is $dy/dx = 4$. The rate of change of the function is constant, since it is a straight line. For each one-unit increase in x, the value of y increases by four units. For a straight line $y = f(x) = mx + b$ with slope m, the derivative is $dy/dx = m$.

Example A.5

The quadratic function $y = f(x) = x^2 - 8x + 16$ is shown in Figure A.3. Applying the derivative formula in (A.11), we have

$$\frac{dy}{dx} = \lim_{\Delta x \to 0} \frac{f(x + \Delta x) - f(x)}{\Delta x} = \lim_{\Delta x \to 0} \frac{\left[(x + \Delta x)^2 - 8(x + \Delta x) + 16 - (x^2 - 8x + 16) \right]}{\Delta x}$$

$$= \lim_{\Delta x \to 0} \frac{\left[x^2 + 2x(\Delta x) + (\Delta x)^2 - 8x - 8\Delta x + 16 - x^2 + 8x - 16 \right]}{\Delta x}$$

$$= \lim_{\Delta x \to 0} \frac{2x(\Delta x) + (\Delta x)^2 - 8\Delta x}{\Delta x} = \lim_{\Delta x \to 0} 2x + \Delta x - 8 = 2x - 8$$

This is the same result obtained in Example A.2 using rules for derivatives.

A.4 Integrals

An integral is an "anti-derivative." If $f(x)$ is a function, we can ask the question, "Of what function $F(x)$ is this the derivative?" The answer is given by the **indefinite integral**

$$\int f(x)\, dx = F(x) + C$$

The function $F(x) + C$, where C is a constant called the **constant of integration**, is an anti-derivative of $f(x)$, because

$$\frac{d[F(x) + C]}{dx} = \frac{d[F(x)]}{dx} + \frac{d[C]}{dx} = f(x)$$

Finding $F(x)$ is an application of reversing the rules for derivatives. For example, using the rules of derivatives,

$$\frac{d(x^n + C)}{dx} = nx^{n-1}$$

Thus, $\int nx^{n-1} dx = x^n + C = F(x) + C$, so in this case $F(x) = x^n$. Many indefinite integrals have been worked out and are tabled in your favorite calculus book and at many websites.

Two handy facts about integrals are as follows:

Integral Rule 1.

$$\int [f(x) + g(x)]\, dx = \int f(x) dx + \int g(x) dx$$

An integral of a sum is the sum of the integrals.

Integral Rule 2.

$$\int cf(x)\, dx = c \int f(x)\, dx$$

Constants can be factored out of integrals.

These rules can be combined so that

Integral Rule 3.

$$\int [c_1 f(x) + c_2 g(x)]\, dx = c_1 \int f(x)dx + c_2 \int g(x)dx$$

Also,

Integral Rule 4 (power rule).

$$\int x^n dx = \frac{1}{n+1}x^{n+1} + C, \text{ where } n \neq -1$$

A.4.1 COMPUTING THE AREA UNDER A CURVE

An important use of integrals in econometrics and statistics is to calculate areas under curves. For example, in Figure A.7, what is the shaded area under the curve $f(x)$?

The area between a curve $f(x)$ and the x-axis, between the limits a and b, is given by the **definite integral**

$$\int_a^b f(x)dx$$

The value of this integral is provided by the **fundamental theorem of calculus**, which says that

$$\int_a^b f(x)dx = F(b) - F(a)$$

Example A.6

Consider the function

$$f(x) = \begin{cases} 2x & 0 \leq x \leq 1 \\ 0 & \text{otherwise} \end{cases} \tag{A.12}$$

This is the equation of a straight line through the origin, as shown in Figure A.8.

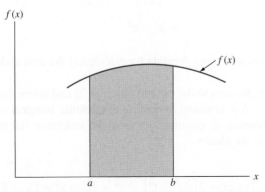

FIGURE $A.7$ Area under a curve.

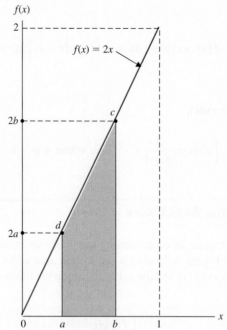

FIGURE $A.8$ Area under the curve $f(x) = 2x, \quad 0 \le x \le 1$.

What is the shaded area in Figure A.8, the area under the line between a and b? The answer can be found using the geometry of triangles. The area of a triangle is half the base times the height, $\frac{1}{2} \times base \times height$. Triangles can be identified by their corners. Let $\Delta 0bc$ represent the area of the triangle formed by the points 0 (the origin), b, and c. Similarly $\Delta 0ad$ represents the area of the smaller triangle formed by the points 0, a and d. The shaded area that represents the area under $f(x) = 2x$ between a and b is the difference between the areas of these two triangles.

$$\text{Area} = \Delta 0bc - \Delta 0ad$$

$$= \left(\frac{1}{2}b\right)(2b) - \frac{1}{2}a(2a) \tag{A.13}$$

$$= b^2 - a^2$$

Equation (A.13) gives us an easy formula for calculating the area under $f(x) = 2x$ falling between a and b.

Using integration, the area under the curve $f(x) = 2x$ and above the x-axis between the limits $x = a$ and $x = b$ is obtained by finding the **definite integral** of $f(x) = 2x$. To use the fundamental theorem of calculus we need the indefinite integral. Use the power rule, Integral Rule 4, we obtain

$$\int 2x\,dx = 2\int x\,dx = 2\left[\frac{1}{2}x^2 + C\right] = x^2 + 2C = x^2 + C_1 = F(x) + C_1$$

where $F(x) = x^2$ and the constant of integration is C_1. The area we seek is given by

$$\int_a^b 2x\,dx = F(b) - F(a) = b^2 - a^2 \tag{A.14}$$

This is the same answer we obtained in (A.13) using geometry.

Many times the algebra is abbreviated, because the constant of integration does not affect the definite integral. You will see for definite integrals

$$\int_a^b 2x\,dx = x^2 \big|_a^b = b^2 - a^2$$

The vertical bar notation means: Evaluate the expression first at b and subtract from it the value of the expression at a.

A.4.2 THE DEFINITE INTEGRAL

Let us take a more general approach to finding the area under the curve $f(x) = 2x$ that will lead to the concept of an integral. Divide the interval $[a, b]$ into n sub-intervals of width $\Delta x = (b - a)/n$ by inserting the $n - 1$ equally spaced points $x_1, x_2, \ldots, x_{n-1}$ between $a = x_0$ and $b = x_n$, as shown in Figure A.9.

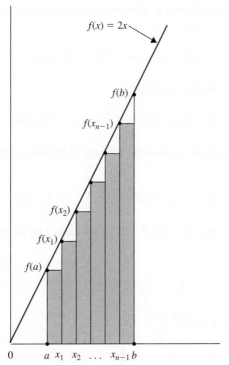

FIGURE **A.9** Area under the curve $f(x) = 2x$, $a \le x \le b$.

The $n-1$ points are

$$x_1 = a + \Delta x$$
$$x_2 = a + 2(\Delta x)$$

$$\vdots$$

$$x_i = a + i(\Delta x)$$ (A.15)

$$\vdots$$

$$x_{n-1} = a + (n-1)(\Delta x)$$

By placing these points we are able to construct n rectangles underneath the line $f(x) = 2x$. The idea is now that we can approximate the area under the curve by summing the areas of the inscribed rectangles. The approximation will be off a little, because we are not counting the little triangular area at the top of each rectangle. However, if we put in many rectangles of narrow width, then the approximation area will be small. The "exact" area will be obtained if we let the number of rectangles go to infinity.

A.4.3   THE DEFINITE INTEGRAL: DETAILS[3]

The area of a rectangle is *height* × *width*. The first and smallest rectangle has width $= x_1 - x_0 = \Delta x$, height $= f(x_0) = 2a$, and area

$$A_1 = f(x_0)\Delta x = (2a)(\Delta x)$$

Similarly, the second rectangle has the same width, and height $f(x_1)$, where x_1 is expressed in (A.15), and it has area

$$A_2 = f(x_1)\Delta x = 2(a + \Delta x)(\Delta x)$$

The area of the last and largest rectangle is

$$A_n = f(x_{n-1})\Delta x = 2[a + (n-1)\Delta x](\Delta x)$$

In order to develop a general expression, it is useful to have a representation for the ith rectangle

$$A_i = f(x_{i-1})\Delta x = 2[a + (i-1)\Delta x](\Delta x)$$

We can approximate the area $A = \Delta 0bc - \Delta 0ad$ by adding up the areas of the n rectangles. This sum, S_n, is

$$S_n = A_1 + A_2 + \cdots + A_n = \sum_{i=1}^{n} f(x_{i-1})\Delta x = \sum_{i=1}^{n} 2[a + (i-1)\Delta x]\Delta x$$

$$= 2a\Delta x \sum_{i=1}^{n} 1 + 2(\Delta x)^2 \sum_{i=1}^{n} (i-1)$$ (A.16)

---

[3] This section contains advanced material.

There are two tricks with summations that now come in handy. First, if c is a constant, then $\sum_{i=1}^{n} c = nc$, so $\sum_{i=1}^{n} 1 = 1 + 1 + \cdots + 1 = n$. Second, $\sum_{i=1}^{k} i = k(k+1)/2$, so

$$\sum_{i=1}^{n}(i-1) = 0 + 1 + \cdots + (n-1) = \sum_{i=1}^{n-1} i = \frac{(n-1)(n)}{2}$$

Using these two expressions, we can simplify the second line of (A.16) as

$$S_n = 2a\frac{(b-a)}{n}n + \frac{2(b-a)^2}{n^2} \cdot \frac{(n-1)(n)}{2}$$
$$= 2a(b-a) + (b-a)^2 \cdot \frac{n-1}{n} \tag{A.17}$$

This sum, S_n, is an approximation to the area under the line $f(x) = 2x$ between the points a and b. The approximation becomes better when more rectangles are used—that is, when n, the number of divisions between a and b, is larger. In fact, the exact area under the graph can be obtained by evaluating the limit of S_n as $n \to \infty$. The only place in (A.17) where n appears is in the last term. The limit of this term is

$$\lim_{n\to\infty} \frac{n-1}{n} = \lim_{n\to\infty} \left(1 - \frac{1}{n}\right) = 1 - \lim_{n\to\infty} \frac{1}{n} = 1 \tag{A.18}$$

Using (A.18) we can take the limit of (A.17) to obtain

$$Area = \lim_{n\to\infty} S_n = \lim_{n\to\infty} \sum_{i=1}^{n} f(x_i)\Delta x = 2a(b-a) + (b-a)^2$$
$$= (b-a)(b+a) = b^2 - a^2$$

This solution is identical to the result in (A.13) using the geometry of triangles and the fundamental theorem of calculus.

A.5 Exercises

Answers to exercises marked * can be found at www.wiley.com/go/global/hill.

A.1*   Let $Q^s = -3 + 1.5P$, where Q^s is the quantity supplied of a good and P is the market price.
(a) State the interpretation of the slope in economic terms.
(b) Calculate the elasticity at $P = 10$ and at $P = 50$, and state their interpretations.

A.2   Suppose the rate of inflation INF, the annual percentage increase in the general price level, is related to the annual unemployment rate $UNEMP$ by the equation $INF = -2 + 6 \times (1/UNEMP)$.
(a) Sketch the curve for values of $UNEMP$ between 1 and 10.
(b) Where is the impact of a change in the unemployment rate the largest?
(c) If the unemployment rate is 5%, what is the marginal effect of an increase in the unemployment rate on the inflation rate?

A.3*   Simplify the following expressions:

(a) $x^{1/2}x^{1/6}$

(b) $x^{2/3} \div x^{7/8}$

(c) $(x^4y^3)^{-1/2}$

A.4 (a) The velocity of light is 186,000 miles per second. Write the velocity of light in scientific notation.

(b) Find the number of seconds in a year and write in scientific notation.

(c) Express the distance light travels in one year in scientific notation.

A.5* Technology affects agricultural production by increasing yield over time. Let $WHEAT_t$ = average wheat production (tonnes per hectare) for the period 1950–2000 ($t = 1, \ldots, 51$) in the Western Australia shire of Chapman Valley.

(a) Suppose production is defined by $WHEAT_t = 0.5 + 0.20 \ln(t)$. Plot this curve. Find the slope and elasticity at the point $t = 49$ (1998).

(b) Suppose production is defined by $WHEAT_t = 0.80 + 0.0004\, t^2$. Plot this curve. Find the slope and elasticity at the point $t = 49$ (1998).

A.6 Forensic scientists can deduce the amount of arsenic in drinking water from concentrations (in parts per million) in toenails. Let y = toenail concentration of arsenic and x = drinking water concentration of arsenic. The following three equations describe the relationship:

$$\ln(y) = 0.8 + 0.4 \ln(x)$$
$$y = 1.5 + 0.2 \ln(x)$$
$$\ln(y) = -1.75 + 20x$$

(a) Plot each of the functions for $x = 0$ to $x = 0.15$

(b) Calculate the slope of each function at $x = 0.10$. State the interpretation of the slope.

(c) Calculate the elasticity of each function at $x = 0.10$ and give its interpretation.

A.7* Consider the numbers $x = 4573239$ and $y = 59757.11$.

(a) Write each number in scientific notation.

(b) Use scientific notation to obtain the product xy.

(c) Use scientific notation to obtain the quotient x/y.

(d) Use scientific notation to obtain the sum $x + y$. [Hint: write each number as a numeric part times 10^6.]

A.8 Consider the function $y = f(x) = 3 + 2x + 3x^2$.

(a) Sketch the curve for values of x between $x = 0$ and $x = 4$.

(b) Find the derivative dy/dx and evaluate it at $x = 2$. Sketch the tangent to the curve at this point.

(c) Compute $y_1 = f(1.99)$ and $y_2 = f(2.01)$. Locate these values (approximately) on your sketch.

(d) Evaluate $m = [f(2.01) - f(1.99)]/.02$. Compare this value to the value of the derivative computed in (b). Explain, geometrically, why the values should be close. The value m is a "numerical derivative," which is useful for approximating derivatives.

Appendix *B*

Probability Concepts

Learning Objectives

Based on the material in this appendix you should be able to:

1. Explain the difference between a random variable and its values, and give an example.

2. Explain the difference between discrete and continuous random variables, and give examples of each.

3. State the characteristics of probability density functions (*pdf*) for discrete and continuous random variables, and give examples illustrating these characteristics.

4. Compute probabilities of events, given the probability density function for a discrete or continuous random variable.

5. Show, geometrically and algebraically, using integration, how to compute probabilities given a *pdf* for a continuous random variable.

6. Use the definitions of expected values for discrete and continuous random variables to compute expectations, given a *pdf* $f(x)$ and a function $g(x)$.

7. Define the variance of a random variable, and explain in what sense the values of a random variable are more spread out if the variance is larger.

8. Use a joint *pdf* for two continuous random variables to compute probabilities of joint events, and to find the (marginal) *pdf* of each individual random variable.

9. Find the conditional *pdf* for one random variable given the value of another and their joint *pdf*, and use it to compute conditional probabilities, the conditional mean, and conditional variance.

10. Define the covariance and correlation between two random variables, and compute these values given a joint probability function.

11. Explain and apply the law of iterated expectations.

12. Find the distribution of a random variable $Y = g(X)$, when $g(X)$ is a strictly increasing or decreasing function, given the probability density function $f(x)$ for the random variable X.

13. Obtain a random number from a probability density function $f(x)$ when its cumulative distribution function $F(x)$ is invertible.

14. Explain in what sense random numbers generated by a computer are random, and in what sense they are not.

Keywords

binary variable	experiment	probability
binomial random variable	*F*-distribution	probability density
cdf	inversion method	function
change-of-variable technique	iterated expectation	pseudo-random numbers
chi-square distribution	Jacobian	random number
conditional *pdf*	joint probability	random number seed
conditional probability	density function	random variable
continuous random variable	marginal distribution	standard deviation
correlation	mean	standard normal
covariance	median	distribution
cumulative distribution	modulus	statistical independence
function	monotonic	strictly monotonic
degrees of freedom	normal distribution	*t*-distribution
discrete random variable	*pdf*	uniform distribution
expected value	Poisson distribution	variance

We assume that you have had a basic probability and statistics course and that you have read the Probability Primer that precedes Chapter 2. If you have not read the Probability Primer, then do so now.

In this appendix we summarize rules of expected values and variances for discrete random variables for easy reference. We then develop similar rules for continuous random variables that will require the use of integral concepts introduced in Appendix A.4. We review the properties of some important discrete and continuous random variables, including the *t*, chi-square, and *F* distributions. Finally, we introduce concepts related to computer generated random numbers.

B.1 Discrete Random Variables

In this section we provide a summary of operations with discrete random variables. See the Probability Primer for examples and general background discussion.

A **random variable** is a variable whose value is unknown until it is observed; in other words, it is a variable that is not perfectly predictable. A **discrete random variable** can take only a limited, or countable, number of values. An example of a discrete random variable is the number of late credit card bill payments last year by a randomly selected individual. A special case occurs when a random variable can only be one of two possible values. A payment is either late or it is not. Outcomes like this can be characterized by a **binary variable**, say *LATE*, taking the value one for late payments and zero for those that are on time. Such variables are also called **indicator variables**, or **dummy variables**.

We summarize the probabilities of possible outcomes using a **probability density function (*pdf*)**. The *pdf* for a discrete random variable indicates the probability of each possible value occurring. For a discrete random variable X the value of the probability density function $f(x)$ is the probability that the random variable X takes the value x, $f(x) = P(X = x)$. Because $f(x)$ is a probability, it must be true that $0 \leq f(x) \leq 1$ and, if X takes n possible values $x_1, \ldots, x_n$, then the sum of their probabilities must be one

$$P(X = x_1) + P(X = x_2) + \cdots + P(X = x_n) = f(x_1) + f(x_2) + \cdots + f(x_n) = 1$$

The **cumulative distribution function (*cdf*)** is an alternative way to represent probabilities. The *cdf* of the random variable X, denoted $F(x)$, gives the probability that X is less than or equal to a specific value x. That is,

$$F(x) = P(X \leq x) \tag{B.1}$$

Two key features of a probability distribution are its center (location) and width (dispersion). A measure of the center is the **mean**, or **expected value**; measures of dispersion are **variance,** and its square root—the **standard deviation**.

B.1.1   Expected Value of a Discrete Random Variable

The **mean** of a random variable is given by its **mathematical expectation**. If X is a discrete random variable taking the values $x_1, \ldots, x_n$ then the mathematical expectation, or **expected value**, of X is

$$\mu_X = E(X) = x_1 P(X = x_1) + x_2 P(X = x_2) + \cdots + x_n P(X = x_n) \tag{B.2a}$$

The expected value, or mean, of X is a weighted average of its values, the weights being the probabilities that the values occur. The mean is often symbolized by μ, or μ_X. It is the average value of the random variable in an infinite number of repetitions of the underlying experiment. Because the probability that the discrete random variable X takes the value x is given by its *pdf* $f(x)$, $P(X = x) = f(x)$, the expected value in (B.2a) can be written equivalently as

$$
\begin{aligned}
\mu_X = E(X) &= x_1 f(x_1) + x_2 f(x_2) + \cdots + x_n f(x_n) \\
&= \sum_{i=1}^{n} x_i f(x_i) = \sum_x x f(x)
\end{aligned} \tag{B.2b}
$$

Functions of random variables are also random. Expected values are obtained using calculations similar to those in (B.2). If X is a discrete random variable and $g(X)$ is a function of it, then

$$E[g(X)] = \sum_x g(x) f(x) \tag{B.3}$$

Using (B.3) we can develop some frequently used rules. If a is a constant, then

$$E(aX) = aE(X) \tag{B.4}$$

Similarly, if a and b are constants, then we can show that

$$E(aX + b) = aE(X) + b \tag{B.5}$$

To see how this result is obtained, we apply the definition in (B.3) to the function $g(X) = aX + b$

$$
\begin{aligned}
E[g(X)] = \sum g(x) f(x) &= \sum (ax + b) f(x) = \sum [axf(x) + bf(x)] \\
&= \sum [axf(x)] + \sum [bf(x)] = a \sum x f(x) + b \sum f(x) \\
&= aE(X) + b
\end{aligned}
$$

In the final step we recognize $E(X)$ from its definition in (B.2), and use the fact that $\sum f(x) = 1$.

If $g_1(X), g_2(X), \ldots, g_M(X)$ are functions of X, then

$$E[g_1(X) + g_2(X) + \cdots + g_M(X)] = E[g_1(X)] + E[g_2(X)] + \cdots + E[g_M(X)] \qquad \text{(B.6)}$$

This rule extends to any number of functions. **The expected value of a sum is always the sum of the expected values.**

A similar rule does not work, in general, for nonlinear functions. That is, $E[g(X)] \neq g[E(X)]$. For example, $E(X^2) \neq [E(X)]^2$.

B.1.2 Variance of a Discrete Random Variable

The **variance** of a discrete random variable X is the expected value of

$$g(X) = [X - E(X)]^2$$

The variance of a random variable is important in characterizing the scale of measurement and the spread of the probability distribution. We give it the symbol σ^2, which is read "sigma squared," or σ_X^2. Algebraically, letting $E(X) = \mu_X$,

$$\text{var}(X) = \sigma_X^2 = E\left[(X - \mu_X)^2\right] = E(X^2) - \mu_X^2 \qquad \text{(B.7)}$$

The variance of a random variable is the *average* squared difference between the random variable X and its mean value μ. The larger the variance of a random variable, the more "spread out" its values are. The square root of the variance is called the **standard deviation**; it is denoted by σ or σ_X. It measures the spread or dispersion of a distribution and has the advantage of being in the same units of measure as the random variable.

A useful property of variances is the following. Let a and b be constants; then

$$\text{var}(aX + b) = a^2 \text{var}(X) \qquad \text{(B.8)}$$

This result is proven in the Probability Primer, Section P.5.4.

Two other characteristics of a probability distribution are its **skewness** and **kurtosis**. These are defined as

$$skewness = \frac{E\left[(X - \mu_X)^3\right]}{\sigma_X^3} \qquad \text{(B.9)}$$

and

$$kurtosis = \frac{E\left[(X - \mu_X)^4\right]}{\sigma_X^4} \qquad \text{(B.10)}$$

Skewness measures the lack of symmetry of a distribution. If the distribution is symmetric, then its *skewness* $= 0$. Distributions with long tails to the left are negatively skewed, and *skewness* < 0. Distributions with long tails to the right are positively skewed, and *skewness* > 0. Kurtosis measures the "peakedness" of a distribution. A distribution with large kurtosis has more values concentrated near the mean and a relatively high central peak. A distribution that is relatively flat has a lower kurtosis. The benchmark value for kurtosis is 3, which is the kurtosis of the *normal* distribution that we discuss later in this appendix (Section B.3.5).

B.1.3 Joint, Marginal, and Conditional Distributions

If X and Y are discrete random variables, then the joint probability that $X = a$ and $Y = b$ is given by the joint *pdf* of X and Y, written as $f(x, y)$, and $P[X = a, Y = b] = f(a, b)$. The sum of the joint probabilities is one, $\sum_x \sum_y f(x, y) = 1$. Given a joint probability density function, we can obtain the probability distributions of individual random variables, which are also known as **marginal distributions**. If X and Y are two discrete random variables, then

$$f_X(x) = \sum_y f(x, y) \text{ for each value } X \text{ can take} \tag{B.11}$$

For discrete random variables, the probability that the random variable Y takes the value y *given* that $X = x$ is written $P(Y = y | X = x)$. This conditional probability is given by the **conditional *pdf*** $f(y|x)$:

$$f(y|x) = P(Y = y | X = x) = \frac{P(Y = y, X = x)}{P(X = x)} = \frac{f(x, y)}{f_X(x)} \tag{B.12}$$

Two random variables are **statistically independent** if the conditional probability that $Y = y$ given that $X = x$, is the same as the unconditional probability that $Y = y$. In this case, knowing the value of X does not alter the probability distribution of Y. If X and Y are independent random variables, then

$$P(Y = y | X = x) = P(Y = y) \tag{B.13}$$

Equivalently, if X and Y are independent, then the conditional *pdf* of Y given $X = x$ is the same as the unconditional, or marginal, *pdf* of Y alone,

$$f(y|x) = \frac{f(x, y)}{f_X(x)} = f_Y(y) \tag{B.14}$$

The converse is also true, so that if (B.13) or (B.14) are true *for every possible pair of x and y values*, then X and Y are statistically independent.

Solving (B.14) for the joint *pdf*, we can also say that X and Y are statistically independent if their joint *pdf* factors into the product of their marginal *pdfs*

$$f(x, y) = f_X(x) f_Y(y) \tag{B.15}$$

If (B.15) is true for each and every pair of values x and y, then X and Y are statistically independent. This result extends to more than two random variables. If X, Y and Z are statistically independent, then their joint probability density function can be factored and written as $f(x, y, z) = f_X(x) \cdot f_Y(y) \cdot f_Z(z)$.

B.1.4   EXPECTATIONS INVOLVING SEVERAL RANDOM VARIABLES

A rule similar to (B.3) exists for functions of several random variables. Let X and Y be discrete random variables with joint *pdf* $f(x,y)$. If $g(X,Y)$ is a function of X and Y, then

$$E[g(X, Y)] = \sum_x \sum_y g(x, y) f(x, y) \tag{B.16}$$

Using (B.16) we can show that

$$E(X + Y) = E(X) + E(Y) \tag{B.17}$$

This follows by using the definition (B.16) and letting $g(X, Y) = X + Y$. Then

$$
\begin{aligned}
E(X + Y) &= \sum_x \sum_y g(x, y) f(x, y) \\
&= \sum_x \sum_y (x + y) f(x, y) \\
&= \sum_x \sum_y x f(x, y) + \sum_x \sum_y y f(x, y) \\
&= \sum_x x \sum_y f(x, y) + \sum_y y \sum_x f(x, y) \\
&= \sum_x x f(x) + \sum_y y f(y) \\
&= E(X) + E(Y)
\end{aligned}
$$

To go from the fourth to the fifth line, we have used (B.11) to obtain the marginal distributions of X and Y, and the fact that the order of summation does not matter. Using the same logic, we can show that

$$E(aX + bY + c) = aE(X) + bE(Y) + c \tag{B.18}$$

In general, $E[g(X, Y)] \neq g[E(X), E(Y)]$. For example, in general, $E(XY) \neq E(X)E(Y)$. If, however, X and Y are statistically independent, then using (B.16), we can also show that $E(XY) = E(X)E(Y)$. To see this, recall that if X and Y are independent, then their joint *pdf* factors into the product of the marginal *pdfs*, $f(x, y) = f(x)f(y)$. Letting $g(X, Y) = XY$, we have

$$
\begin{aligned}
E(XY) &= E[g(X, Y)] = \sum_x \sum_y xy f(x, y) = \sum_x \sum_y xy f(x) f(y) \\
&= \sum_x x f(x) \sum_y y f(y) = E(X) E(Y)
\end{aligned}
$$

This rule can be extended to more independent random variables.

B.1.5   COVARIANCE AND CORRELATION

One particular application of (B.16) is the derivation of the **covariance** between X and Y. Define a function that is the product of X minus its mean times Y minus its mean,

$$g(X, Y) = (X - \mu_X)(Y - \mu_Y) \tag{B.19}$$

The covariance is the expected value of (B.19)

$$\text{cov}(X, Y) = \sigma_{XY} = E[(X - \mu_X)(Y - \mu_Y)] = E(XY) - \mu_X \mu_Y \tag{B.20}$$

If the covariance σ_{XY} of the variables is positive, then when x values are greater than their mean, the y values also tend to be greater than their mean, and when x values are below their mean, then the y values also tend to be less than their mean. In this case the random variables X and Y are said to be **positively** or **directly associated**. If $\sigma_{XY} < 0$, then the association is negative, or inverse. If $\sigma_{XY} = 0$, then there is neither a positive nor negative relationship.

Interpreting the actual value of σ_{XY} is difficult, because X and Y may have different units of measurement. Scaling the covariance by the standard deviations of the variables eliminates the units of measurement, and defines the **correlation** between X and Y:

$$\rho = \frac{\text{cov}(X, Y)}{\sqrt{\text{var}(X)}\sqrt{\text{var}(Y)}} = \frac{\sigma_{XY}}{\sigma_X \sigma_Y} \tag{B.21}$$

As with the covariance, the correlation ρ between two random variables measures the degree of *linear* association between them. However, unlike the covariance, the correlation must lie between -1 and 1. The correlation between X and Y is 1 if there is a perfect positive linear relationship between X and Y and -1 if there is a perfect negative, or inverse, association between X and Y. If there is no *linear* association between X and Y, then $\text{cov}(X, Y) = 0$ and $\rho = 0$. For other values of correlation, the magnitude of the absolute value $|\rho|$ indicates the "strength" of the linear association between the values of the random variables.

If X and Y are independent random variables, then the covariance and correlation between them are zero. The converse of this relationship is *not* true. Independent random variables X and Y have zero covariance, indicating that there is no linear association between them. However, just because the covariance or correlation between two random variables is zero *does not* mean that they are necessarily independent. There may be more complicated nonlinear associations such as $X^2 + Y^2 = 1$.

In (B.17) we found the expected value of a sum of random variables. There are similar rules for variances. If a and b are constants, then

$$\text{var}(aX + bY) = a^2 \text{var}(X) + b^2 \text{var}(Y) + 2ab\text{cov}(X, Y) \tag{B.22}$$

To see this, it is convenient to define a new discrete random variable $Z = aX + bY$. This random variable has expected value

$$\mu_Z = E(Z) = E(aX + bY) = aE(X) + bE(Y) = a\mu_X + b\mu_Y$$

The variance of Z is

$$\begin{aligned}
\text{var}(Z) = E\left[(Z - \mu_Z)^2\right] &= E\left\{[(aX + bY) - (a\mu_X + b\mu_Y)]^2\right\} \\
&= E\left\{[(aX - a\mu_X) + (bY - b\mu_Y)]^2\right\} \\
&= E\left\{[a(X - \mu_X) + b(Y - \mu_Y)]^2\right\} \\
&= E\left[a^2(X - \mu_X)^2 + b^2(Y - \mu_Y)^2 + 2ab(X - \mu_X)(Y - \mu_Y)\right] \\
&= E\left[a^2(X - \mu_X)^2\right] + E\left[b^2(Y - \mu_Y)^2\right] + E[2ab(X - \mu_X)(Y - \mu_Y)] \\
&= a^2\text{var}(X) + b^2\text{var}(Y) + 2ab\text{cov}(X, Y)
\end{aligned}$$

These rules extend to more random variables. For example, if X, Y, and Z are random variables, then

$$\text{var}\,(aX + bY + cZ) = a^2\text{var}(X) + b^2\text{var}(Y) + c^2\text{var}(Z) + 2ab\text{cov}(X, Y)$$
$$+ 2bc\text{cov}(Y, Z) + 2ac\text{cov}(X, Z) \tag{B.23}$$

B.1.6 CONDITIONAL EXPECTATIONS

If X and Y are two random variables with joint probability distribution $f(x,y)$, then the conditional probability distribution of Y given X is $f(y|x)$. We can use this conditional *pdf* to compute the **conditional mean** of Y given X. That is, we can obtain the expected value of Y given that $X = x$. The conditional expectation $E(Y|X = x)$ is the average (or mean) value of Y given that X takes the value x. In the discrete case, it is defined to be

$$E(Y|X = x) = \sum_y yP(Y = y|X = x) = \sum_y yf(y|x) \tag{B.24}$$

Similarly, we can define the **conditional variance** of Y given X. This is the variance of the conditional distribution of Y given X. In the discrete case, it is

$$\text{var}(Y|X = x) = \sum_y [y - E(Y|X = x)]^2 f(y|x) \tag{B.25}$$

B.1.7 ITERATED EXPECTIONS

The **law of iterated expectations** says that the expected value of Y is equal to the expected value of the conditional expectation of Y given X. That is,

$$E(Y) = E_X[E(Y|X)] \tag{B.26}$$

What this means becomes clearer with the following demonstration that it is true in the discrete case. We will use two facts about probability distributions. First, the marginal *pdf* of Y is $f(y) = \sum_x f(x, y)$ and second, the joint *pdf* of X and Y can be expressed as $f(x, y) = f(y|x)f(x)$. Then,

$$E(Y) = \sum_y yf(y) = \sum_y y\left[\sum_x f(x, y)\right]$$
$$= \sum_y y\left[\sum_x f(y|x)f(x)\right]$$
$$= \sum_x \left[\sum_y yf(y|x)\right]f(x) \qquad \text{[by changing order of summation]}$$
$$= \sum_x E(Y|X = x)f(x)$$
$$= E_X[E(Y|X)]$$

In the final expression the $E_X[\ ]$ means that the expectation of the term in brackets is taken assuming that X is random. Thus, the expected value of Y can be found by finding its conditional expectation given X and then taking the expected value of the result with respect to X.

Two other results are shown to be true the same way:

$$E(XY) = E_X[XE(Y|X)] \tag{B.27}$$

and

$$\text{cov}(X, Y) = E_X[(X - \mu_X)E(Y|X)] \tag{B.28}$$

B.2 Working With Continuous Random Variables

Continuous random variables can take any value in an interval. In economics variables like income and market prices are treated as continuous random variables. In Figure P.2 of the Probability Primer, we depict the probability density function for a continuous random variable that ranges between zero and infinity, or $x \geq 0$. Because continuous random variables can take uncountably many values, the probability that any single value occurs in a random experiment is zero. For example, $P(X = 100) = 0$ or $P(X = 200) = 0$. Probability statements for continuous random variables are meaningful when we ask about outcomes within intervals, or ranges. We can ask, "What is the probability that X takes a value between 100 and 200?" These ideas were introduced in Sections P.1 and P.2 of the Probability Primer. There we noted that probabilities like these are areas under a curve that is the probability density function. It would be a good time to review those sections now if the concepts are not fresh in your minds. What we did not discuss in the Probability Primer was how exactly such probabilities are calculated. We delayed that discussion until now, because tools from integral calculus are required.

In this section, we discuss how to work with continuous random variables. The **interpretation** of probabilities, expected values, and variances carries over from what you learned about discrete random variables. What changes is the algebra—summation signs turn into integrals, and this takes a little getting used to. If you have not done so, review the discussion of integrals in Appendix A.4.

B.2.1 PROBABILITY CALCULATIONS

If X is a continuous random variable with probability density function $f(x)$, then $f(x)$ must obey certain properties:

$$f(x) \geq 0 \tag{B.29}$$

$$\int_{-\infty}^{\infty} f(x)dx = 1 \tag{B.30}$$

$$P(a \leq X \leq b) = \int_{a}^{b} f(x)dx \tag{B.31a}$$

Property (B.29) states that the *pdf* cannot take negative values. Property (B.30) states that the total area under the *pdf*, which is the probability that X falls between $-\infty$ and ∞, is one.

Property (B.31a) states that the probability that X falls in the interval $[a,\ b]$ is the area under the curve $f(x)$ between those values. Because a single point has probability zero, it is also true that

$$P(a \leq X \leq b) = P(a < X \leq b) = P(a \leq X < b) = P(a < X < b) = \int_a^b f(x)dx \quad \text{(B.31b)}$$

The **cumulative distribution function**, *cdf*, for a continuous random variable is $F(x) = P(X \leq x)$. Using the *cdf* we can compute

$$P(X \leq a) = \int_{-\infty}^a f(x)dx = F(a) \quad \text{(B.32a)}$$

The *cdf* is obtained by integrating the *pdf*. The integral is an "anti-derivative," so that we can obtain the *pdf* $f(x)$ by differentiating the *cdf* $F(x)$. That is,

$$f(x) = \frac{dF(x)}{dx} = F'(x) \quad \text{(B.32b)}$$

The concept of a *cdf* is useful in many ways, including working with computer software, which includes the *cdf*s of many random variables so that probabilities can be easily computed.

Example B.1
Let X be a continuous random variable with *pdf* $f(x) = 2(1 - x)$ for $0 \leq x \leq 1$. This *pdf* is depicted in Figure B.1.

Property (B.29) holds for x in the interval $[0, 1]$. Furthermore, property (B.30) holds because

$$\int_{-\infty}^{\infty} f(x)dx = \int_0^1 2(1 - x)dx = \int_0^1 2dx - \int_0^1 2xdx = 2x\Big|_0^1 - x^2\Big|_0^1 = 2 - 1 = 1$$

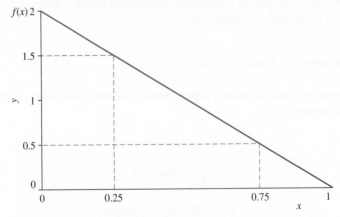

FIGURE **B.1**   Probability density function $f(x) = 2(1 - x)$.

Using Figure B.1, we can compute $P\left(\frac{1}{4} \leq X \leq \frac{3}{4}\right) = \frac{1}{2}$ using geometry. Using integration, we come to the same conclusion:

$$P\left(\tfrac{1}{4} \leq X \leq \tfrac{3}{4}\right) = \int_{1/4}^{3/4} f(x)dx = \int_{1/4}^{3/4} 2(1-x)dx$$

$$= \int_{1/4}^{3/4} 2dx - \int_{1/4}^{3/4} 2xdx = 2x \Big|_{1/4}^{3/4} - x^2 \Big|_{1/4}^{3/4} = 1 - \left(\frac{9}{16} - \frac{1}{16}\right) = \frac{1}{2}$$

The cumulative distribution function is $F(x) = 2x - x^2$ for x in the interval $[0,1]$, so the probability can also be computed as

$$P\left(\tfrac{1}{4} \leq X \leq \tfrac{3}{4}\right) = F\left(\tfrac{3}{4}\right) - F\left(\tfrac{1}{4}\right)$$

Example B.2
Let X be a continuous random variable with *pdf* $f(x) = 3x^2$ for x in the interval $[0, 1]$. Properties (B.29) and (B.30) hold. Because the *pdf* is a quadratic, we cannot use simple geometry to compute $P\left(\frac{1}{4} \leq X \leq \frac{3}{4}\right)$. We must use integration, obtaining

$$P\left(\tfrac{1}{4} \leq X \leq \tfrac{3}{4}\right) = \int_{1/4}^{3/4} f(x)dx = \int_{1/4}^{3/4} 3x^2 dx = x^3 \Big|_{\frac{1}{4}}^{\frac{3}{4}} = \frac{9}{64} - \frac{1}{64} = \frac{1}{8}$$

B.2.2 PROPERTIES OF CONTINUOUS RANDOM VARIABLES

If X is a continuous random variable with probability density function $f(x)$, then its expected value is

$$\mu_X = E(X) = \int_{-\infty}^{\infty} xf(x)dx \tag{B.33}$$

Compare this to the expected value of a discrete random variable in (B.2). An integral has replaced the summation. The interpretation of $E(X)$ is exactly the same as in the discrete case. It is the average value of X that occurs in an infinite number of repetitions of the underlying experiment.

Example B.1 (continued)
The expected value of the random variable in Example B.1 is

$$\int_{-\infty}^{\infty} xf(x)dx = \int_{0}^{1} x \cdot 2(1-x)dx = \int_{0}^{1} (2x - 2x^2)dx = x^2 \Big|_{0}^{1} - \tfrac{2}{3}x^3 \Big|_{0}^{1} = 1 - \frac{2}{3} = \frac{1}{3}$$

The variance of a random variable X is defined as $\sigma_X^2 = E[(X - \mu_X)^2]$. This definition holds for discrete and continuous random variables. In order to compute the variance we use the analog to the rule in (B.3) for continuous random variables,

$$E[g(X)] = \int_{-\infty}^{\infty} g(x)f(x)dx \tag{B.34}$$

Then, letting $g(x) = (X - \mu_X)^2$ we have

$$\begin{aligned}
\sigma_X^2 &= E\left[(X - \mu_X)^2\right] = \int_{-\infty}^{\infty} (x - \mu_X)^2 f(x)dx \\
&= \int_{-\infty}^{\infty} (x^2 + \mu_X^2 - 2x\mu_X)f(x)dx \\
&= \int_{-\infty}^{\infty} x^2 f(x)dx + \mu_X^2 \int_{-\infty}^{\infty} f(x)dx - 2\mu_X \int_{-\infty}^{\infty} xf(x)dx \\
&= E(X^2) + \mu_X^2 - 2\mu_X^2 \\
&= E(X^2) - \mu_X^2
\end{aligned} \tag{B.35}$$

To go from the third line to the fourth line, we use property (B.30) and the definition of expected value (B.33). The end result is that $\sigma_X^2 = E[(X - \mu_X)^2] = E(X^2) - \mu_X^2$ as in the discrete case.

To obtain the variance of the random variable described in Example B.1, we first find

$$\begin{aligned}
E(X^2) &= \int_{-\infty}^{\infty} x^2 f(x)dx = \int_0^1 x^2 \cdot 2(1-x)dx = \int_0^1 (2x^2 - 2x^3)dx \\
&= \tfrac{2}{3}x^3 \Big|_0^1 - \tfrac{2}{4}x^4 \Big|_0^1 = \frac{2}{3} - \frac{1}{2} = \frac{1}{6}
\end{aligned}$$

Then,

$$\operatorname{var}(X) = \sigma_X^2 = E(X^2) - \mu_X^2 = \frac{1}{6} - \left(\frac{1}{3}\right)^2 = \frac{1}{18}$$

B.2.3 JOINT, MARGINAL, AND CONDITIONAL PROBABILITY DISTRIBUTIONS

To make simultaneous probability statements about more than one continuous random variable, we need the **joint probability density function** of the random variables. For example, consider the two continuous random variables $U =$ unemployment and $P =$ inflation rate. Suppose that their joint *pdf* is as depicted in Figure B.2.

The joint *pdf* is a surface and probabilities are volumes under the surface. If the two random variables are nonnegative, then we might ask, "What is the probability that inflation is less than 5% and at the same time unemployment is less than 6%?" That is, what is $P(U \leq 6, P \leq 5)$? Geometrically the answer is that this is the volume under the surface above the rectangle (in the base of the figure) defining the event. Just as an integral is used to

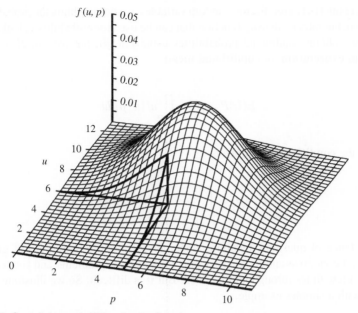

FIGURE **B.2** A joint probability density function.

obtain the area under a curve, a double integral is used to obtain volumes like that shown in Figure B.2. Given the joint *pdf* $f(u, p)$ we can compute the probability as

$$P(U \leq 6, \ P \leq 5) = \int_{u=0}^{6} \int_{p=0}^{5} f(u, p)\, dp\, du$$

If we know the joint *pdf*, can we obtain the marginal *pdf* of one of the random variables? If so, we can answer questions like "What is the probability that unemployment will be between 2% and 5%?" Analogous to (B.11) for discrete random variables, we integrate out the unwanted random variable. That is, the **marginal probability density function** for U is

$$f(u) = \int_{-\infty}^{\infty} f(u, p)\, dp \tag{B.36}$$

Then, for example, $P(2 \leq U \leq 5) = \int_{2}^{5} f(u)\, du$.

We might ask "What is the probability that unemployment will be between 2% and 5% **if** we can use monetary policy to keep the inflation rate at 2%?" This is a question about a **conditional probability**. Given that $P = 2$, what is the probability that $2 \leq U \leq 5$? Or in terms of conditioning notation, what is $P(2 \leq U \leq 5 | P = 2)$. To answer such questions for continuous random variables, we need the **conditional probability density function** $f(u|p)$, which is given by

$$f(u|p) = \frac{f(u, p)}{f(p)} \tag{B.37}$$

Unlike the result (B.12) for discrete random variables, we do not obtain the probability from this division, but rather a density function that can be used for probability calculations. Not only can we obtain conditional probabilities using $f(u\,|\,p)$, but we can also obtain the **conditional expectation**, or **conditional mean**,

$$E(U|P = p) = \int_{-\infty}^{\infty} uf(u\,|\,p)du \tag{B.38}$$

Similarly, the **conditional variance** is

$$\mathrm{var}(U|P = p) = \int_{-\infty}^{\infty} [u - E(U|P = p)]^2 f(u|p)du \tag{B.39}$$

The importance of questions involving unemployment and inflation are of great social importance. Economists and econometricians work on these problems, and you will glimpse the issues a few times throughout this book. But it is difficult. So we illustrate the above concepts with a simpler example.

Example B.3
Let X and Y be continuous random variables with joint *pdf* $f(x, y) = x + y$ for x in [0, 1] and y in [0, 1]. You might test for geometric skills by creating a three-dimensional graph of this joint density function. Is it a valid density function? It satisfies the more general version of property (B.29), because $f(x, y) \geq 0$ for all points $x \in [0, 1]$ and $y \in [0, 1]$. Also the total amount of probability, the volume under the surface, is

$$\int_{y=0}^{1}\int_{x=0}^{1} f(x, y)dx\,dy = \int_{y=0}^{1}\int_{x=0}^{1} (x + y)dx\,dy$$

$$= \int_{y=0}^{1}\int_{x=0}^{1} xdx\,dy + \int_{y=0}^{1}\int_{x=0}^{1} ydx\,dy$$

$$= \int_{y=0}^{1}\left[\int_{x=0}^{1} xdx\right]dy + \int_{x=0}^{1}\left[\int_{y=0}^{1} ydy\right]dx$$

$$= \int_{y=0}^{1}\left[\frac{1}{2}x^2\Big|_{0}^{1}\right]dy + \int_{x=0}^{1}\left[\frac{1}{2}y^2\Big|_{0}^{1}\right]dx$$

$$= \int_{y=0}^{1}\frac{1}{2}dy + \int_{x=0}^{1}\frac{1}{2}dx = \frac{1}{2} + \frac{1}{2} = 1$$

In the third line, we have used a property of multiple integrals. In the Probability Primer, Section P.4, the rule "Sum 9" states that the order of multiple summations does not matter. Similarly, as long as the limits of integration for one variable do not depend on the value of the other, the order of integration does not matter when we have multiple integrals. However, we must keep the integral symbol with its lower and upper limits paired with the variable of integration, indicated by dx or dy. In the first term in the third line above, we have isolated the integral involving x inside the integral involving y. Multiple integrals are evaluated by working from the "inside out." Solve the inside integral with respect to x, and then solve the outer integral with respect to y.

For further practice with double integrals find the probability that X is between zero and $\frac{1}{2}$ while Y is between $\frac{1}{4}$ and $\frac{3}{4}$. This is a joint probability and is computed as follows:

$$P\left(0 \leq X \leq \tfrac{1}{2}, \ \tfrac{1}{4} \leq Y \leq \tfrac{3}{4}\right) = \int_{y=1/4}^{3/4} \int_{x=0}^{1/2} f(x,y)dx\,dy$$

$$= \int_{y=1/4}^{3/4} \int_{x=0}^{1/2} (x+y)dx\,dy$$

$$= \int_{y=1/4}^{3/4} \int_{x=0}^{1/2} x\,dx\,dy + \int_{y=1/4}^{3/4} \left[\int_{x=0}^{1/2} y\,dx\right]dy$$

$$= \int_{y=1/4}^{3/4} \left[\int_{x=0}^{1/2} x\,dx\right]dy + \int_{y=1/4}^{3/4} y\left[\int_{x=0}^{1/2} dx\right]dy$$

$$= \int_{y=1/4}^{3/4} \left[\tfrac{1}{2}x^2\Big|_0^{1/2}\right]dy + \int_{y=1/4}^{3/4} y\left[x\Big|_0^{1/2}\right]dy$$

$$= \tfrac{1}{8}\int_{y=1/4}^{3/4} dy + \tfrac{1}{2}\int_{y=1/4}^{3/4} dy$$

$$= \tfrac{1}{8}\left[y\Big|_{1/4}^{3/4}\right] + \tfrac{1}{2}\left[y\Big|_{1/4}^{3/4}\right] = \frac{1}{8}\times\frac{1}{2} + \frac{1}{2}\times\frac{1}{2} = \frac{5}{16}$$

In the third step of this example, we did not change the order of integration in the second term. This illustrates another feature of working with multiple integrals. When carrying out the "inside" integration with respect to x the value of y is fixed, and because it is fixed it can be factored out in the fourth line, leaving a simpler inside integral.

The marginal *pdf* of X, for $x \in [0, 1]$, is

$$f(x) = \int_{y=0}^{1} f(x,y)dy = \int_{y=0}^{1} (x+y)dy = \int_{y=0}^{1} x\,dy + \int_{y=0}^{1} y\,dy = x\cdot y\Big|_0^1 + \tfrac{1}{2}y^2\Big|_0^1 = x + \frac{1}{2}$$

Technically we should also say that $f(x) = 0$ for $x \notin [0,1]$, but we will generally not explicitly include this extra information. Using similar steps the marginal *pdf* of Y is $f(y) = y + \frac{1}{2}$ for values of y in the $[0,1]$ interval. The marginal *pdf* for X can be used to compute probabilities that X falls in intervals in the domain of X, $x \in [0, 1]$. For example,

$$P\left(\tfrac{1}{2} < X < \tfrac{3}{4}\right) = \int_{1/2}^{3/4} \left(x + \tfrac{1}{2}\right)dx = \int_{1/2}^{3/4} x\,dx + \tfrac{1}{2}\int_{1/2}^{3/4} dx$$

$$= \tfrac{1}{2}x^2 \Big|_{1/2}^{3/4} + \tfrac{1}{2}x \Big|_{1/2}^{3/4}$$

$$= \frac{1}{2}\left(\frac{9}{16} - \frac{1}{4}\right) + \frac{1}{2}\left(\frac{3}{4} - \frac{1}{2}\right)$$

$$= \frac{1}{2} \times \frac{5}{16} + \frac{1}{2} \times \frac{1}{4} = \frac{9}{32}$$

Using the marginal *pdf* of X, we can find its expected value.

$$\mu_X = E(X) = \int_{-\infty}^{\infty} xf(x)dx = \int_0^1 x\left(x + \tfrac{1}{2}\right)dx$$

$$= \int_0^1 x^2 dx + \int_0^1 \tfrac{1}{2}x\,dx$$

$$= \tfrac{1}{3}x^3 \Big|_0^1 + \tfrac{1}{4}x^2 \Big|_0^1 = \frac{1}{3} + \frac{1}{4} = \frac{7}{12}$$

The limits of integration in the first line change from $(-\infty, \infty)$ to $[0,1]$, because for $x \notin [0,1]$, $f(x) = 0$ and the area (probability) under $f(x) = 0$ is zero.

To find the variance of X, we first find

$$E(X^2) = \int_0^1 x^2 f(x)dx = \int_0^1 x^2\left(x + \tfrac{1}{2}\right)dx$$

$$= \int_0^1 x^3 dx + \int_0^1 \tfrac{1}{2}x^2 dx$$

$$= \tfrac{1}{4}x^4 \Big|_0^1 + \tfrac{1}{6}x^3 \Big|_0^1 = \frac{1}{4} + \frac{1}{6} = \frac{5}{12}$$

Then

$$\sigma_X^2 = \text{var}(X) = E(X^2) - [E(X)]^2 = \frac{5}{12} - \left(\frac{7}{12}\right)^2 = \frac{11}{144}$$

The conditional *pdf* of Y given that $X = x$ is

$$f(y|x) = \frac{f(x,y)}{f(x)}$$

In Example, B.3, the conditional *pdf* is

$$f(y|x) = \frac{f(x,y)}{f(x)} = \frac{x+y}{x+\tfrac{1}{2}} \quad \text{for } y \in [0,1]$$

As a specific example,

$$f\left(y \Big| X = \tfrac{1}{3}\right) = \frac{y + \tfrac{1}{3}}{\tfrac{1}{3} + \tfrac{1}{2}} = \frac{1}{5}(6y + 2) \quad \text{for } y \in [0,1]$$

The conditional *pdf* can be used to compute probabilities that Y falls in a given interval. Also, we can compute the **conditional mean** of Y given that $x = 1/3$

$$\mu_{Y|X=1/3} = E\left(Y|X = \tfrac{1}{3}\right) = \int_{y=0}^{1} yf\left(y|X = \tfrac{1}{3}\right)dy$$

$$= \int_{y=0}^{1} y \cdot \tfrac{1}{5}(6y + 2)dy$$

$$= \int_{y=0}^{1} \tfrac{6}{5}y^2 dy + \int_{y=0}^{1} \tfrac{2}{5}y\,dy$$

$$= \tfrac{6}{5}\left(\tfrac{1}{3}y^3 \Big|_0^1\right) + \tfrac{2}{5}\left(\tfrac{1}{2}y^2 \Big|_0^1\right) = \frac{2}{5} + \frac{1}{5} = \frac{3}{5}$$

Note that the conditional expected value is not the same as the **unconditional** expected value $\mu_Y = E(Y) = \tfrac{7}{12}$.

To calculate the **conditional variance**, we first calculate

$$E\left(Y^2 \Big|X = \tfrac{1}{3}\right) = \int_{y=0}^{1} y^2 f\left(y\Big|X = \tfrac{1}{3}\right)dy = \int_{y=0}^{1} y^2 \tfrac{1}{5}(6y + 2)dy = \frac{13}{30}$$

The conditional variance is then

$$\mathrm{var}\left(Y\Big|X = \tfrac{1}{3}\right) = E\left(Y^2\Big|X = \tfrac{1}{3}\right) - \left[E\left(Y\Big|X = \tfrac{1}{3}\right)\right]^2 = \frac{11}{150} = 0.07333$$

The unconditional variance is $\sigma_Y^2 = \mathrm{var}(Y) = \tfrac{11}{144} = 0.07639$. The conditional variance is smaller than the unconditional variance, which will always be the case unless the random variables are independent.

The **correlation** between X and Y is

$$\rho = \frac{\mathrm{cov}(X, Y)}{\sigma_X \sigma_Y}$$

The covariance between X and Y can be calculated using $\mathrm{cov}(X, Y) = E(XY) - \mu_X \mu_Y$. To compute the expected value of XY, we calculate the double integral

$$E(XY) = \int_{y=0}^{1}\int_{x=0}^{1} xyf(x, y)dx\,dy = \int_{y=0}^{1}\int_{x=0}^{1} xy(x + y)dx\,dy$$

$$= \int_{y=0}^{1}\int_{x=0}^{1} x^2 y\,dx\,dy + \int_{y=0}^{1}\int_{x=0}^{1} xy^2\,dx\,dy$$

$$= \int_{y=0}^{1} y\left[\int_{x=0}^{1} x^2\,dx\right]dy + \int_{y=0}^{1} y^2\left[\int_{x=0}^{1} x\,dx\right]dy = \frac{1}{6} + \frac{1}{6} = \frac{1}{3}$$

Then

$$\text{cov}(X, Y) = E(XY) - \mu_X \mu_Y = \frac{1}{3} - \left(\frac{7}{12}\right)\left(\frac{7}{12}\right) = \frac{-1}{144}$$

Finally, the correlation between X and Y is

$$\rho = \frac{\text{cov}(X, Y)}{\sigma_X \sigma_Y} = \frac{-1/144}{\sqrt{11/144}\sqrt{11/144}} = \frac{-1}{11} = -0.09091$$

B.2.4   ITERATED EXPECTATIONS

A useful result, proved in Section B.1.7 for the discrete case, is the **law of iterated expectations**. If X and Y are continuous random variables with joint *pdf* $f(x,y)$, then the expected value of Y can be calculated as

$$E(Y) = E_X[E(Y|X)]$$

This is the same result as in (B.26) for the discrete case. The exact meaning of this expression is best understood by first deriving it and then carrying through an illustration. To establish that this result is true, we proceed as follows:

$$E(Y) = \int_{y=-\infty}^{\infty} yf(y)dy$$

$$= \int_{y=-\infty}^{\infty} y\left[\int_{x=-\infty}^{\infty} f(x, y)dx\right]dy \qquad \text{replacing marginal } pdf$$

$$= \int_{y}\int_{x} yf(x, y)dx\,dy \qquad \text{simplifying integral}$$

$$= \int_{y}\int_{x} y[f(y|x)f(x)]dx\,dy \qquad \text{replace joint } pdf$$

$$= \int_{x}\left[\int_{y} yf(y|x)dy\right]f(x)dx \qquad \text{reverse order of integration}$$

$$= \int_{x} [E(Y|X)]f(x)dx \qquad \text{recognize } E(Y|X)$$

$$= E_X[E(Y|X)] \qquad \text{recognize expectation wrt } X$$

In the last line of the expression, the notation $E_X[\cdot]$ means that we take the expectation of the term in brackets treating X as random. Note that we also replaced the $(-\infty, \infty)$ integral form with a simpler form in line three indicating "over all values" of the variable of integration.

To better understand the iterated expectation expression, for Example B.3 find the **conditional expectation** of Y given that $X = x$, where the value x is not specified:

$$E(Y|X = x) = \int_{y=0}^{1} yf(y|x)dy = \int_{y=0}^{1} y\left[\frac{x+y}{x+\frac{1}{2}}\right]dy$$

$$= \frac{2+3x}{3(2x+1)}$$

Note that the integration over the values of Y, treating x as given, leaves us with a function of x. If we now recognize that x can take any value and is thus random, we can find the expected value of the function

$$g(X) = \frac{2+3X}{3(2X+1)}$$

The law of iterated expectations says that if we take the expectation of $g(X)$, treating X as random, we should obtain $E(Y)$. Just for fun, let's try it.

$$E[g(X)] = \int_{x=0}^{1} \frac{2+3x}{3(2x+1)}f(x)dx$$

$$= \int_{x=0}^{1} \frac{2+3x}{3(2x+1)}\left(x+\frac{1}{2}\right)dx$$

$$= \int_{x=0}^{1} \frac{2+3x}{3(2x+1)}\frac{1}{2}(2x+1)dx = \int_{x=0}^{1} \frac{1}{6}(2+3x)dx$$

$$= \int_{x=0}^{1} \frac{1}{3}dx + \int_{x=0}^{1} \frac{1}{2}x\,dx = \frac{1}{3}x\Big|_{0}^{1} + \frac{1}{4}x^2\Big|_{0}^{1} = \frac{1}{3}+\frac{1}{4} = \frac{7}{12} = E(Y)$$

It works!

Besides being a neat trick, there are a couple of important implications of the law of iterated expectations. First, based on $E(Y) = E_X[E(Y|X)]$, we can see that if $E(Y|X) = 0$, then $E(Y) = E_X[E(Y|X)] = E_X(0) = 0$. If the conditional expectation of Y is zero, then the unconditional expectation of Y is also zero.

Second, if $E(Y|X) = E(Y)$, then $\text{cov}(X, Y) = 0$. To see this, first rewrite $E(XY)$ as

$$E(XY) = \int_x \int_y xyf(x,y)dy\,dx$$

$$= \int_x \int_y xyf(y|x)f(x)dy\,dx$$

$$= \int_x x\left[\int_y yf(y|x)dy\right]f(x)dx$$

$$= \int_x x[E(Y|X)]f(x)dx$$

(B.40)

If $E(Y|X) = E(Y)$, then the last line of (B.40) becomes

$$E(XY) = \int_x x[E(Y)]f(x)dx = E(Y)\int_x xf(x)dx = E(Y)E(X) = \mu_Y\mu_X$$

The covariance between X and Y in this case is

$$\text{cov}(X, Y) = E(XY) - \mu_X\mu_Y = \mu_X\mu_Y - \mu_Y\mu_X = 0$$

An extremely important special case of these two results concerns the consequences of $E(Y|X) = 0$. We have already seen that $E(Y|X) = 0 \Rightarrow E(Y) = 0$. Now we can also see that if $E(Y|X) = E(Y) = 0$, then $\text{cov}(X, Y) = 0$. This result plays an important role in Chapter 10.1.3 in Assumption A10.3[*].

B.2.5   DISTRIBUTIONS OF FUNCTIONS OF RANDOM VARIABLES

As we have noted several times, a function of a random variable is random itself. The question we address in this section is, "What is the probability density function of the new random variable?" For the case of a discrete random variable this problem is not too hard. For example, consider the discrete random variable X that can take the values 1, 2, 3, or 4 with probabilities 0.1, 0.2, 0.3, and 0.4, respectively. Let $Y = 2 + 3X = g(X)$. What is the *pdf* for Y? In this case it is clear. The probability that $Y = 5, 8, 11,$ or 14 corresponds exactly to the probability that $X = 1, 2, 3,$ or 4, respectively, as shown in Table B.1.

What makes this possible is that each value of y corresponds to a unique value of x, and each value of x corresponds to a unique value of y. Another way to say this is that the transformation from X to Y is "one-to-one." This type of relationship is ensured to hold when the function $g(X)$ relating Y to X is either strictly increasing or strictly decreasing. Such functions are said to be **strictly monotonic**. Our function $Y = 2 + 3X = g(X)$ is strictly (monotonically) increasing. This guarantees that if $x_2 > x_1$, then $y_2 = g(x_2) > y_1 = g(x_1)$. Note in particular that we are ruling out the possibility that $y_1 = y_2$.

Determining the distribution of $Y = g(X)$ in the continuous case is a bit more challenging. In the following example, we present the **change-of-variable** technique that applies when the function $g(X)$ is strictly increasing or decreasing.

Example B.4

Let X be a continuous random variable with *pdf* $f(x) = 2x$ for $0 < x < 1$. Let $Y = g(X) = 2X$ be another random variable. We want to compute probabilities that Y falls in certain

Table B.1   **Change of Variable: Discrete Case**

x	$P(X = x) = P(Y = y)$	y
1	0.1	5
2	0.2	8
3	0.3	11
4	0.4	14

intervals. One solution is to compute probabilities for Y based on the probability of the corresponding event for X. For example,

$$P(0 < Y < 1) = P\left(0 < X < \frac{1}{2}\right) = \int_0^{1/2} 2x\,dx = x^2 \Big|_0^{1/2} = \frac{1}{4}$$

Although this is reasonable and relatively simple in this case, it will not always be so. It is preferable to determine the *pdf* of Y, say $h(y)$, and use it to compute probabilities for Y. Since $X = Y/2$, we might be tempted to substitute this into the *pdf* $f(x)$ to obtain $h(y) = 2(y/2) = y$ for $0 < y < 2$. This substitution does not work, however, because

$$\int_{-\infty}^{\infty} h(y)\,dy = \int_0^2 y\,dy = \tfrac{1}{2}y^2 \Big|_0^2 = 2$$

This violates property (B.30) for a probability density function. Furthermore, using $h(y)$ to compute the probability of Y falling in the interval $(0,1)$ produces 0.5, which we know is incorrect.

The problem is that we must adjust the height of $h(y)$ to account for the fact that Y can take values in the interval $(0,2)$ whereas X can take values only in $(0,1)$. In fact, a change in Y of one unit corresponds to a change in X of half a unit. If we adjust $h(y)$ by this factor, we have

$$h(y) = 2(y/2)\left(\tfrac{1}{2}\right) = y/2, \ 0 < y < 2$$

Using this corrected *pdf*, property (B.30) is satisfied:

$$\int_{-\infty}^{\infty} h(y)\,dy = \int_0^2 \tfrac{1}{2}y\,dy = \tfrac{1}{4}y^2 \Big|_0^2 = 1$$

Also, we obtain the correct probability that Y falls in the interval $(0,1)$:

$$P(0 < Y < 1) = \int_0^1 \tfrac{1}{2}y\,dy = \tfrac{1}{4}y^2 \Big|_0^1 = \frac{1}{4}$$

Another perspective on the change-of-variable technique is obtained by examining the integral representation for the probability that Y falls in the interval $(0,1)$:

$$P(0 < Y < 1) = \int_0^1 h(y)\,dy$$

The integral representation of the equivalent X event, showing explicitly the lower and upper limits of the integral, is

$$P(0 < Y < 1) = P\left(0 < X < \frac{1}{2}\right) = \int_{x=0}^{x=1/2} f(x)\,dx = \int_{x=0}^{x=1/2} 2x\,dx$$

Thinking of dx as a small change in X, and noting that $x = y/2$, $dx = dy/2$. Substituting this into the integral above, we have

$$P(0 < Y < 1) = \int_{y/2=0}^{y/2=1/2} 2\left(\tfrac{1}{2}y\right)\left(\tfrac{1}{2}dy\right) = \int_{y=0}^{y=1} \tfrac{1}{2}y\,dy$$

The adjustment factor $1/2$ that we obtained intuitively appears here in the relation of dx to dy. The mathematical name for this adjustment factor is the **Jacobian of the transformation** (actually its absolute value, as we will soon see). Its purpose is to make the integral expression in terms of x equal to that in terms of y. Now we are ready to describe the change-of-variable technique more precisely.

Let X be a continuous random variable with $pdf\, f(x)$. Let $Y = g(X)$ be a function that is strictly increasing or strictly decreasing. This condition ensures that the function is one-to-one, so that there is exactly one Y value for each X value and exactly one X value for each Y value. The importance of this condition on $g(X)$ is that we can solve $Y = g(X)$ for X. That is, we can find an **inverse function** $X = w(Y)$. Then the pdf for Y is given by

$$h(y) = f[w(y)] \cdot \left| \frac{dw(y)}{dy} \right| \tag{B.41}$$

where $||$ denotes the absolute value.

Change of variable technique to find the *pdf* of Y: Step by Step

1. Solve $y = g(x)$ for x in terms of y;
2. Substitute this for x in $f(x)$,
3. Multiply by the absolute value of the derivative $dw(y)/dy$, which is called the Jacobian of the transformation.

The scale factor $|dw(y)/dy|$ is the adjustment factor that makes the probabilities (i.e., the integrals) come out right. In the previous example the inverse function is $X = w(Y) = Y/2$. The Jacobian term is $dw(y)/dy = d(y/2)/dy = \tfrac{1}{2}$, and $|dw(y)/dy| = \left|\tfrac{1}{2}\right| = \tfrac{1}{2}$.

Example B.5

Let X be a continuous random variable with $pdf\, f(x) = 2x$ for $0 < x < 1$. Let $Y = g(X) = 8X^3$ be the function of X in which we are interested. The function $Y = g(X) = 8X^3$ is strictly increasing for the set of values that X can take, $0 < x < 1$. The corresponding set of values that Y can take is $0 < y < 8$. Because the function is strictly increasing, we can solve for the inverse function

$$x = w(y) = \left(\tfrac{1}{8}y\right)^{1/3} = \tfrac{1}{2}y^{1/3}$$

and

$$\frac{dw(y)}{dy} = \tfrac{1}{6}y^{-2/3}$$

Applying the change-of-variable formula (B.41), we have

$$h(y) = f[w(y)] \cdot \left| \frac{dw(y)}{dy} \right|$$
$$= 2\left(\tfrac{1}{2} y^{1/3} \right) \cdot \left| \tfrac{1}{6} y^{-2/3} \right|$$
$$= \tfrac{1}{6} y^{-1/3}, \, 0 < y < 8$$

The change-of-variable technique can be modified for the case of several random variables, X_1, X_2 being transformed into Y_1, Y_2. For a description of the method, which requires matrix algebra, see William Greene (2008) *Econometric Analysis*, 6th edition, Pearson Prentice Hall, pp. 1004–1005.

B.3 Some Important Probability Distributions

In this section we give brief descriptions and summarize the properties of the probability distributions used in this book.

B.3.1 THE BERNOULLI DISTRIBUTION

Let the random variable X denote an experimental outcome with only two possible outcomes, A or B. Let $X = 1$ if the outcome is A and let $X = 0$ if the outcome is B. Let the probabilities of the outcomes be $P(X = 1) = p$ and $P(X = 0) = 1 - p$ where $0 \le p \le 1$. X is said to have a **Bernouilli distribution**. The *pdf* of this Bernoulli random variable is

$$f(x|p) = \begin{cases} p^x (1-p)^{1-x} & x = 0, 1 \\ 0 & \text{otherwise} \end{cases} \tag{B.42}$$

The expected value of X is $E(X) = p$, and its variance is $\text{var}(X) = p(1-p)$. This random variable arises in **choice models**, such as the linear probability model (Chapters 7, 8, and 16) and in binary and multinomial choice models (Chapter 16).

B.3.2 THE BINOMIAL DISTRIBUTION

If X_1, $X_2, \ldots, X_n$ are independent random variables, each having a Bernouilli distribution with parameter p, then $X = X_1 + X_2 + \cdots + X_n$ is a discrete random variable that is the number of successes (i.e., Bernoulli experiments with outcome $X_i = 1$) in n trials of the experiment. The random variable X is said to have a **binomial distribution**. The *pdf* of this random variable is

$$P(X = x|n, p) = f(x|n, p) = \binom{n}{x} p^x (1-p)^{n-x} \text{ for } x = 0, 1, \ldots, n \tag{B.43}$$

where

$$\binom{n}{x} = \frac{n!}{x!(n-x)!}$$

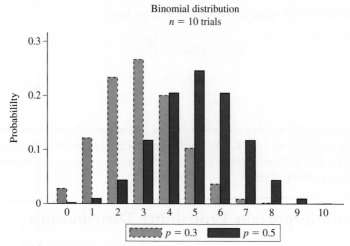

FIGURE **B.3** Binomial distributions for $n = 10$.

is the number of combinations of n things taken x at a time. This distribution has two parameters, n and p, where n is a positive integer indicating the number of experimental trials and $0 \leq p \leq 1$. These probabilities are tedious to compute by hand, but econometric software has functions to carry out the calculations. The discrete probabilities are illustrated in Figure B.3.

The expected value and variance of X are

$$E(X) = \sum_{i=1}^{n} E(X_i) = np$$

$$\text{var}(X) = \sum_{i=1}^{n} \text{var}(X_i) = np(1 - p)$$

A related random variable is $Y = X/n$, which is the proportion of successes in n trials of an experiment. Its mean and variance are $E(Y) = p$ and $\text{var}(Y) = p(1 - p)/n$.

B.3.3 THE POISSON DISTRIBUTION

Whereas a binomial random variable is the number of event occurrences in a given number of experimental trials, n, the Poisson random variable is the number of event occurrences in a given interval of time or space. The probability density function for the discrete random variable X is

$$P(X = x | \mu) = f(x | \mu) = \frac{e^{-\mu} \mu^x}{x!} \quad \text{for } x = 0, 1, 2, 3, \ldots \tag{B.44}$$

Probabilities depend on the parameter μ, and $e \cong 2.71828$ is the base of natural logarithms. The expected value and variance of X are $E(X) = \text{var}(X) = \mu$. The Poisson distribution is used in models involving count variables (Chapter 16), such as the number of visits a person makes to a physician during a year. Probabilities for $x = 0$ to 10 for distributions with $\mu = 3$ and $\mu = 4$ are shown in Figure B.4.

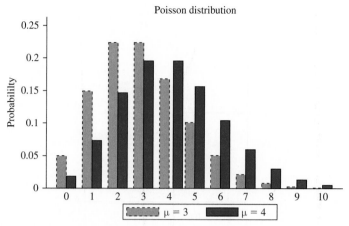

FIGURE **B.4** Poisson distribution.

B.3.4 THE UNIFORM DISTRIBUTION

A continuous distribution that is vastly important for theoretical purposes is the **uniform distribution**. The random variable X with values $a \leq x \leq b$ has a uniform distribution if its *pdf* is given by

$$f(x|a,b) = \frac{1}{b-a} \text{ for } a \leq x \leq b \tag{B.45}$$

The plot of the density function is given in Figure B.5

The area under $f(x)$ between a and b is one which is required of any probability density function for a continuous random variable. The expected value of X is the midpoint of the interval $[a, b]$, $E(X) = (a+b)/2$. This can be deduced from the symmetry of the distribution. The variance of X is $\text{var}(X) = E(X^2) - \mu^2 = (b-a)^2/12$.

An interesting special case occurs when $a = 0$ and $b = 1$, so that $f(x) = 1$ for $0 \leq x \leq 1$. The distribution, shown in Figure B.6, describes one common meaning of "a random number between zero and one."

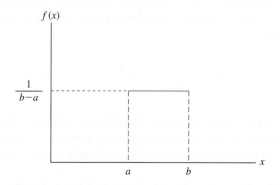

FIGURE **B.5** A uniform distribution.

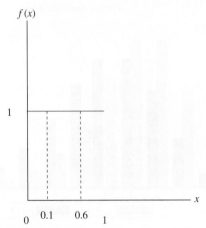

FIGURE *B.6*   A uniform distribution on [0, 1] interval.

The uniform distribution has the property that any two intervals of equal width have the same probability of occurring. That is

$$P(0.1 \leq X \leq 0.6) = P(0.3 \leq X \leq 0.8) = P(0.21131 \leq X \leq 0.71131) = 0.5$$

Picking a number randomly between zero and one is conceptually complicated by the fact that the interval has an uncountably infinite number of values, and the probability of any one of them occurring is zero. What is more likely meant by such a statement is that each interval of equal width has the same probability of occurring, no matter how narrow. This is exactly the nature of the uniform distribution.

B.3.5   THE NORMAL DISTRIBUTION

The normal distribution was described in the Probability Primer, Section P.6. A point not stressed at that time was why we must consult tables, like Table 1 at the end of the book, to calculate normal probabilities. For example, we now know that for the continuous and normally distributed random variable X, with mean μ and variance σ^2, the probability that X falls in the interval $[a, b]$ is

$$\int_a^b f(x)dx = \int_a^b \frac{1}{\sqrt{2\pi\sigma^2}} \exp\left[-(x - \mu)^2 / 2\sigma^2\right] dx$$

Unfortunately this integral does not have a closed-form, algebraic solution. Consequently, we wind up working with tabled values containing numerical approximations to areas under the standard normal distribution, or we use computer software functions in a similar manner.

The normal distribution is related to the chi-square, t, and F distributions, which we now discuss.

B.3.6   THE CHI-SQUARE DISTRIBUTION

Chi-square random variables arise when standard normal random variables are squared. If $Z_1, Z_2, \ldots, Z_m$ denote m *independent* $N(0, 1)$ random variables, then

$$V = Z_1^2 + Z_2^2 + \ldots + Z_m^2 \sim \chi_{(m)}^2 \qquad (\text{B.46})$$

The notation $V \sim \chi_{(m)}^2$ is read as: The random variable V has a chi-square distribution with m **degrees of freedom**. The degrees of freedom parameter m indicates the number of *independent* $N(0,1)$ random variables that are squared and summed to form V. The value of m determines the entire shape of the chi-square distribution, including its mean and variance

$$
\begin{aligned}
E[V] &= E\left[\chi_{(m)}^2\right] = m \\
\text{var}[V] &= \text{var}\left[\chi_{(m)}^2\right] = 2m
\end{aligned}
\qquad (\text{B.47})
$$

In Figure B.7 graphs of the chi-square distribution for various degrees of freedom are presented. The values of V must be nonnegative, $v \geq 0$, because V is formed by squaring and summing m standardized normal $N(0,1)$ random variables. The distribution has a long tail, or is *skewed*, to the right. As the degrees of freedom m gets larger, however, the distribution becomes more symmetric and "bell-shaped." In fact, as m gets larger, the chi-square distribution converges to, and essentially becomes, a normal distribution.

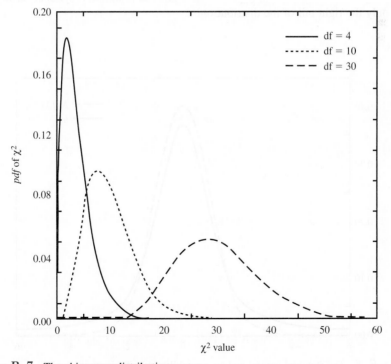

FIGURE **B.7**   The chi-square distribution.

The 90th, 95th, and 99th percentile values of the chi-square distribution for selected values of the degrees of freedom are given in Table 3 at the end of the book. These values are often of interest in hypothesis testing.

B.3.7 THE t-DISTRIBUTION

A t random variable (no upper case) is formed by dividing a standard normal random variable $Z \sim N(0, 1)$ by the square root of an *independent* chi-square random variable, $V \sim \chi^2_{(m)}$, that has been divided by its degrees of freedom m. If $Z \sim N(0, 1)$ and $V \sim \chi^2_{(m)}$, and if Z and V are independent, then

$$t = \frac{Z}{\sqrt{V/m}} \sim t_{(m)} \tag{B.48}$$

The t-distribution's shape is completely determined by the degrees of freedom parameter, m, and the distribution is symbolized by $t_{(m)}$.

Figure B.8 shows a graph of the t-distribution with $m = 3$ degrees of freedom relative to the $N(0,1)$. Note that the t-distribution is less "peaked," and more spread out than the $N(0,1)$. The t-distribution is symmetric, with mean $E(t_{(m)}) = 0$ and variance $\text{var}(t_{(m)}) = m/(m-2)$. As the degrees of freedom parameter $m \to \infty$ the $t_{(m)}$ distribution approaches the standard normal $N(0,1)$.

Computer programs have functions for the *cdf* of t-random variables that can be used to calculate probabilities. Since certain probabilities are widely used, Table 2 at the back of this book, also inside the front cover, contains frequently used percentiles of t-distributions, called **critical values** of the distribution. For example, the 95th percentile of a t-distribution with 20 degrees of freedom is $t_{(0.95, 20)} = 1.725$. The t-distribution is symmetric, so Table 2 shows only the right tail of the distribution.

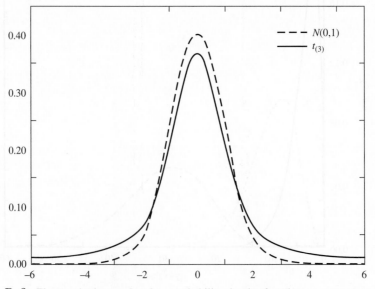

FIGURE **B.8**   The standard normal and $t_{(3)}$ probability density functions.

B.3.8   The F-distribution

An F random variable is formed by the ratio of two independent chi-square random variables that have been divided by their degrees of freedom. If $V_1 \sim \chi^2_{(m_1)}$ and $V_2 \sim \chi^2_{(m_2)}$, and if V_1 and V_2 are independent, then

$$F = \frac{V_1/m_1}{V_2/m_2} \sim F_{(m_1,m_2)} \tag{B.49}$$

The F-distribution is said to have m_1 *numerator degrees of freedom* and m_2 *denominator degrees of freedom*. The values of m_1 and m_2 determine the shape of the distribution, which in general looks like Figure B.9. The range of the random variable is $(0,\infty)$ and it has a long tail to the right. For example, the 95th percentile value for an F-distribution with $m_1 = 8$ numerator degrees of freedom and $m_2 = 20$ denominator degrees of freedom is $F_{(0.95,8,20)} = 2.45$. Critical values for the F-distribution are given in Table 4 (the 95th percentile) and Table 5 (the 99th percentile).

B.4 Random Numbers

In several chapters we carry out Monte Carlo simulations to illustrate the sampling properties of estimators. See, for example, Chapters 3, 4, 5, 10, and 11. To use Monte Carlo simulations we rely upon the ability to create **random numbers** from specific probability distributions, such as the uniform and the normal. The use of computer simulations is widespread in all sciences. In this section we introduce to you this aspect of computing.[1] You should first realize that the idea of creating random numbers using a computer is paradoxical, because by definition random numbers that are "created" cannot be truly random. The random numbers generated by a computer are **pseudo-random numbers** in that they "behave as if they were random." We present one method for generating pseudo-random numbers called the **inverse transformation** approach, or the

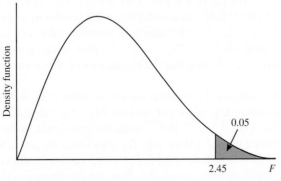

FIGURE **B.9** The probability density function of an $F_{(8,20)}$ random variable.

---

[1] A well-written book on the subject is by James E. Gentle (2003) *Random Number Generation and Monte Carlo Methods,* New York: Springer.

inversion method. This method assumes that we have the ability to generate pseudo-random numbers from the **uniform distribution** (see Sections B.3.4 and B.4.1) on the (0,1) interval. The uniformly distributed random variables are then transformed into random variables with other distributions.

Example B.6

Let U be a random variable with a uniform distribution. It is a continuous random variable with *pdf* $h(u) = 1$ for $x \in (0, 1)$. See Figure B.6 for an illustration. If $Y = U^{1/2}$, then $0 < y < 1$. Furthermore, the square root function is strictly increasing, so that we can apply the change-of-variable technique to find the *pdf* of Y. The inverse function is $U = w(Y) = Y^2$, and the Jacobian of the transformation is $dw(y)/dy = d(y^2)/dy = 2y$. The *pdf* of Y is then

$$f(y) = h[w(y)] \cdot \left| \frac{dw(y)}{dy} \right| = 1 \cdot |2y| = 2y, \quad 0 < y < 1 \tag{B.50}$$

This is a distribution that we have used in Examples B.4 and B.5. The importance of this example is that it shows that we can obtain a random number from the distribution in (B.50) by taking the square root of a random number from a uniform distribution.

Example B.6 leads us towards a general technique, the inversion method, for drawing random numbers from certain distributions. Suppose you wish to obtain a random number from a specific probability distribution, with *pdf* $f(y)$ and *cdf* $F(y)$.

The Inversion Method: Step by Step

1. Obtain a uniform random number u_1 in the (0,1) interval.
2. Let $u_1 = F(y_1)$
3. Solve the equation in step 2 for y_1.
4. The value y_1 is a random number from the *pdf* $f(y)$.

The inversion method can be used to draw random numbers from any distribution that permits you to carry out step 3. The solution is often denoted $y_1 = F^{-1}(u_1)$, where F^{-1} is called the **inverse cumulative distribution function**. The *cdf* function F is said to be **invertible**.

Suppose the target distribution, from which we want a random number, is $f(y) = 2y$, $0 < y < 1$. The *cdf* of Y is $P(Y \leq y) = F(y) = y^2$, $0 < y < 1$. The two distributions are shown in Figure B.10. Set a uniform random number $u_1 = F(y_1) = y_1^2$ and solve to obtain $y_1 = F^{-1}(u_1) = (u_1)^{1/2}$. The value y_1 is a random value, or a **random draw**, from the probability distribution $f(y) = 2y$, $0 < y < 1$. This agrees perfectly with the result in Example B.6, where we showed that the square root of a uniform random variable has this *pdf*.

In Figure B.10(a) suppose the uniform random number is $u_1 = 0.16$. It falls between 0 and 1, along the vertical axis of the *cdf* function $F(y)$. The value $u_1 = 0.16$ corresponds to the value $y_1 = 0.4 = (u_1)^{1/2} = (0.16)^{1/2}$ on the horizontal axis. In the lower panel we see the connection between the *pdf* and the *cdf*. The area under the *pdf* to the left of $y_1 = 0.4$ is the probability $P(0 < Y < 0.4) = 0.16$. For every randomly drawn uniform random number u_i there is a unique corresponding y_i from the distribution $f(y) = 2y$, $0 < y < 1$.

To illustrate, in the file *uniform1.dat* we have 1,000 observations on two independent uniform random variables *U1* and *U2*. [2] Figure B.11 shows the histogram of *U1*. There

---

[2] The file *uniform2.dat* contains 10,000 observations if you prefer a larger sample.

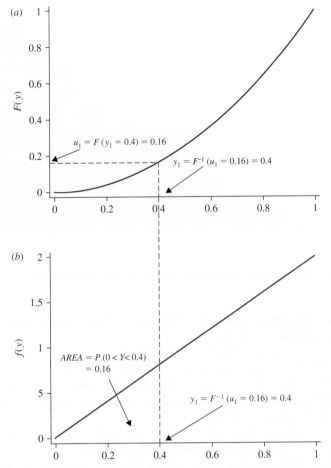

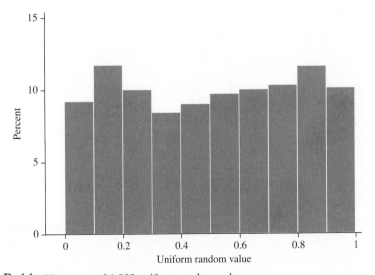

FIGURE **B.10**   (*a*) Cumulative distribution function (*b*) Probability density function.

FIGURE **B.11**   Histogram of 1,000 uniform random values.

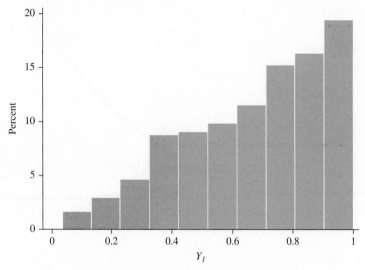

FIGURE **B.12**   Histogram of 1,000 square roots of uniform random values.

are 10 intervals and approximately 10% of the values fall into each, as we would expect for values from a uniform distribution.

Let $Y1$ be the square root of the $U1$ values. The histogram of these values is shown in Figure B.12. It looks like a triangle, doesn't it? Just like the density $f(y) = 2y,\ \ 0 < y < 1$.

As a second example, let us consider a slightly more exotic distribution. The **extreme value distribution** is the foundation of logit choice models that are discussed in Chapter 16. It has probability density function $f(v) = \exp(-v) \cdot \exp(-\exp(-v))$, depicted in Figure B.13. The extreme value *cdf* is $F(v) = \exp(-\exp(-v))$. Despite its complicated-looking form, we can obtain values from this distribution using $v = F^{-1}(u) = -\ln(-\ln(u))$. Using the 1,000 values $U1$ in *uniform1.dat*, we obtain the histogram of values from the

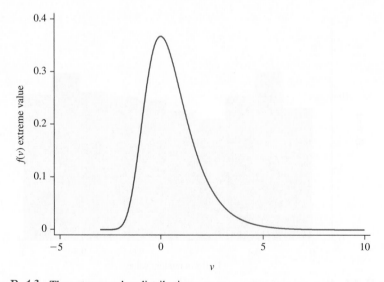

FIGURE **B.13**   The extreme value distribution.

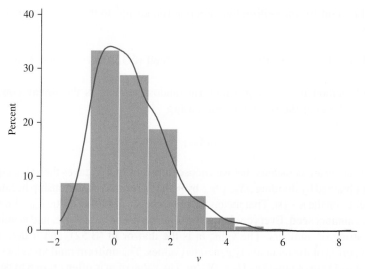

FIGURE *B.14* Histogram of simulated draws from the extreme value distribution.

extreme value distribution shown in Figure B.14.[3] The solid curve superimposed on the histogram looks much like the extreme value density function in Figure B.13.

To summarize, the **inversion method** for generating random numbers from specific distributions depends upon (1) the ability to obtain uniform random numbers and (2) the density having a *cdf* that is invertible. The procedure does not work for joint distributions.

Knowing the inversion method, you can generate random variables from other distributions given a uniform random number generator. Books on statistical distributions[4] have instructions on how to transform uniform random numbers into a wide variety of distributions. A particular method for generating normal random numbers is illustrated in Exercise B.8.

B.4.1 Uniform Random Numbers

The inversion method depends upon the ability to obtain random numbers from a uniform distribution. The generation of "random numbers" when used without modifiers usually means uniform random numbers, which is a field of study in and of itself. As noted earlier, the notion of computer-generated random numbers is illogical. Computers use algorithms to do their work; an algorithm is a formula so that the product is not "random," but randomlike. Computers generate **pseudo-random numbers**. Enter that term into your favorite search engine and you will find many, many links.

One bit of notation that appears in citations is for the mathematical **modulus**, denoted $a \bmod b$. This is shorthand for the remainder resulting from dividing a by b. One method for calculating the modulus is[5]

$$n \bmod m = n - m \operatorname{ceil}(n/m) + m \tag{B.51}$$

---

[3] The solid curve is a kernel density fitted to the data using a Gaussian kernel. See Appendix C.10 for more on kernel densities.

[4] See, for example, Catherine Forbes, Merran Evans, Nicholas Hastings, Brian Peacock (2010) *Statistical Distributions*, 4th edition, John Wiley and Sons, Inc.

[5] www.functions.wolfram.com/IntegerFunctions/Mod/27/01/03/01/0001/.

where **ceil** is short for the **ceiling** function that rounds up[6] to the next integer. To see how this works:

$$7 \bmod 3 = 1 = 7 - 3\text{ceil}(7/3) + 3 = 7 - 3\text{ceil}(2.3333) + 3 = 7 - 3 \cdot 3 + 3 = 1$$

A standard method for creating a uniform random number is the **linear congruential generator**[7]. Consider the recursive relationship

$$X_n = (aX_{n-1} + c) \bmod m \tag{B.52}$$

where a, c, and m are constants that we choose. It means that X_n takes the value equal to the remainder obtained by dividing $aX_{n-1} + c$ by m. It is a recursive relationship because the nth value depends on the $n-1$st. That means we must choose a starting value X_0, which is called the random number **seed**. Everyone using the same seed, and values a, c, and m will generate the same string of numbers. The value m is the divisor in (B.52), and it determines the maximum period of the recursively generated values. The uniform random values falling in the interval $(0,1)$ are obtained as $U_n = X_n/m$. The value of m is often chosen to be 2^{32} when using computers with 32-bit architecture. The values of a and c are critical to the success of the random number generator. Bad choices result in sequences of numbers that are not random. For example, type RANDU into your search engine. This was a popular random number generator in the 1960s (I used it too!) that was later discovered to be very flawed, failing tests of randomness.[8]

To illustrate that the process defined in (B.52) can generate apparently random numbers, we choose $X_0 = 1234567$, $a = 1664525$, $b = 1013904223$, and $m = 2^{32}$ and create 10,000 values, labeled $U1$ in the file *uniform3.dat*[9]. Using a histogram with 20 bins, we would expect 5% of the values in each, and as Figure B.15 illustrates, that is about what we get.

The 10,000 values for $U1$ have sample mean 0.4987197 and variance 0.0820758 compared to the true mean and variance for a uniform distribution of 0.5 and 0.08333. The minimum and maximum values are 0.0000327 and 0.9998433, respectively.

The lessons learned from these exercises are that random numbers are not random, and some random number generators are better than others. Ones that are popularly cited are the Mersenne twister (used in SAS 9.1) and the KISS+Monster algorithm (used by Gauss 10). New ones continue to be developed, and each software provider uses different algorithms which are predominately kept secret, or difficult to discover at any rate.

The third lesson is that you should probably **not** attempt to write your own random number algorithms. Professor Ken Train, an econometrician who has studied computational methods a great deal, says,[10] "From a practical perspective, my advice is the following: unless one is willing to spend considerable time investigating and resolving (literally, re-solving)..." the issues related to designing pseudo-random number routines "... it is probably better to use available routines rather than write a new one." Our advice is to use your software to generate random numbers, but when documenting your work, cite the software used and the software version, as revisions can change results from one version to another.

---

[6] ceil(x) is the smallest integer not less than x.

[7] A description and link to sources is www.en.wikipedia.org/wiki/Linear_congruential_generator.

[8] George Marsaglia developed a series of tests for randomness that are widely used. They are available at www.stat.fsu.edu/pub/diehard/.

[9] The variable $U2$ in this file uses seed 987654321.

[10] *Discrete Choice Methods with Simulation*, 2003, Cambridge University Press, p. 209.

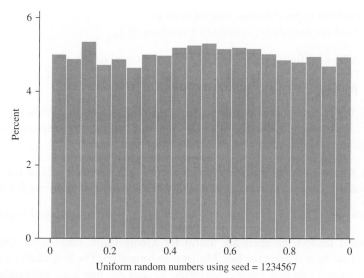

FIGURE **B.15** Histogram of 10,000 generated random values.

B.5 Exercises

Answers to exercise marked * can be found at www.wiley.com/go/global/hill.

B.1* Let X_1, X_2, ..., X_n be independent random variables which all have the same probability distribution, with mean μ and variance σ^2. Let

$$\overline{X} = \frac{1}{n}\sum_{i=1}^{n} X_i$$

(a) Use the properties of expected values to show that $E(\overline{X}) = \mu$.
(b) Use the properties of variance to show that $\mathrm{var}(\overline{X}) = \sigma^2/n$. How have you used the assumption of independence?

B.2 Suppose that Y_1, Y_2, Y_3 is a sample of observations from a $N(\mu, \sigma^2)$ population but that Y_1, Y_2, and Y_3 are *not* independent. In fact, suppose that

$$\mathrm{cov}(Y_1, Y_2) = \mathrm{cov}(Y_2, Y_3) = \mathrm{cov}(Y_1, Y_3) = \frac{\sigma^2}{2}$$

Let $\overline{Y} = (Y_1 + Y_2 + Y_3)/3$.
(a) Find $E(\overline{Y})$.
(b) Find $\mathrm{var}(\overline{Y})$.

B.3* Let X be a continuous random variable with probability density function given by

$$f(x) = -\frac{1}{2}x + 1, \quad 0 \le x \le 2$$

(a) Graph the density function $f(x)$.
(b) Find the total area beneath $f(x)$ for $0 \le x \le 2$.
(c) Find $P(X \ge 1)$ using both geometry and integration.
(d) Find $P(X \le \frac{1}{2})$.
(e) Find $P(X = 1\frac{1}{2})$.

(f) Find the expected value and variance of X.

(g) Find the cumulative distribution function of X.

B.4   Let X be a uniform random variable on the interval (a,b).

(a) Use integration techniques to find the mean and variance of X.

(b) Find the cumulative distribution function of X.

B.5*   Use the recursive relationship in (B.52) with $X_0 = 79$, $m = 100$, $a = 263$, and $c = 71$ to generate 40 values $X_1, X_2, \ldots, X_{40}$. Do the resulting numbers appear random? Is this a good random number generator, or not?

B.6   Let X have a normal distribution with mean μ and variance σ^2. Use the change of variable technique to find the probability density function of $Y = aX + b$.

B.7*   Show that if $E(Y|X) = E(Y)$, then $\text{cov}(Y, g(X)) = 0$ for any function $g(X)$.

B.8   Normal random numbers are useful for Monte Carlo simulations. One way to generate them is using the Box-Muller transformation. The Box-Muller transformation creates two new random variables, $Z1$ and $Z2$, that have independent $N(0,1)$ distributions, using

$$Z1 = \sqrt{-2\ln(U1)}\,\cos(2\pi U2), \quad Z2 = \sqrt{-2\ln(U1)}\,\sin(2\pi U2)$$

(a) Construct a histogram of $Z1$ and $Z2$ obtained by using the 1,000 uniform random values $U1$ and $U2$ in *uniform1.dat* (or the 10,000 values in *uniform2.dat*). Is the distribution of values "bell-shaped"?

(b) Calculate the summary statistics for $Z1$ and $Z2$. Are the sample mean and variance close to zero and one, respectively?

(c) Construct a scatter diagram for $Z1$ and $Z2$. That is, plot $Z1$ (vertical axis) and $Z2$ (horizontal axis) in the x-y plane. Is there any evidence of positive or negative correlation?

B.9*   Let X be a continuous random variable with pdf $f(x) = 3x^2/8$ for $0 < x < 2$. Compute

(a) $P\left(0 < X < \frac{1}{2}\right)$

(b) $P(1 < X < 2)$

B.10   A continuous random variable X is said to have an exponential distribution if its pdf is $f(x) = e^{-x}$, $x \geq 0$.

(a) Plot this density function for $0 \leq x \leq 10$.

(b) The cumulative distribution function for X is $F(x) = 1 - e^{-x}$. Plot this function over the interval $0 \leq x \leq 10$. Is it strictly increasing or decreasing, or are you unsure?

(c) Use the inverse transformation method to draw random values $X1$ from this distribution. Use the 1,000 values for $U1$ in *uniform1.dat* or the 10,000 values for $U1$ in *uniform2.dat*. Construct a histogram of the values you have created. Does it resemble the plot in (a)?

(d) The true mean and variance of X are $\mu = 1$ and $\sigma^2 = 1$. How close are the sample mean and the sample variance to the true values?

B.11   Use the recursive relationship in (B.52) with $X_0 = 1234567$, $m = 2^{32}$, $a = 1103515245$, and $c = 12345$ to generate 1,000 random values called $U1$. Do the resulting numbers appear random? Is this a good random number generator, or not? Choose another seed value and generate another 1,000 values called $U2$. Find the summary statistics and sample correlation for $U1$ and $U2$. Do the values behave as you expect them to, or not?

B.12* Suppose that the joint *pdf* of the continuous random variables X and Y is $f(x, y) = 6x^2y$ for $0 \le x \le 1,\ 0 \le y \le 1$.
  (a) Does this function satisfy the conditions for a valid *pdf*?
  (b) Find the marginal *pdf* of X, as well as its mean and variance.
  (c) Find the marginal *pdf* of Y.
  (d) Find the conditional *pdf* of X given $Y = \frac{1}{2}$.
  (e) Find the conditional mean and variance of X given $Y = \frac{1}{2}$.
  (f) Are X and Y independent? Explain.

B.13 Suppose that X and Y are continuous random variables with joint *pdf* $f(x, y) = \frac{1}{2}$ for $0 \le x \le y \le 2$ and $f(x, y) = 0$ otherwise. Note that the values of X are less than or equal to the values of Y.
  (a) Verify that the volume under the joint *pdf* is 1.
  (b) Find the marginal *pdfs* of X and Y.
  (c) Find $P(X < \frac{1}{2})$.
  (d) Find the *cdf* of Y.
  (e) Find the conditional probability $P(X < \frac{1}{2} | Y = 1.5)$. Are X and Y independent?
  (f) Find the expected value and variance of Y.
  (g) Use the law of iterated expectations to find $E(X)$.

Appendix C

Review of Statistical Inference

Learning Objectives

Based on the material in this appendix you should be able to

1. Discuss the difference between a population and a sample, and why we use samples of data as a basis for inference about population parameters.

2. Connect the concepts of a population and a random variable, indicating how the probability density function of a random variable, and the expected value and variance of the random variable, inform us about the population.

3. Explain the difference between the population mean and the sample mean.

4. Explain the difference between an estimate and an estimator, and why the latter is a random variable.

5. Explain the terms sampling variation and sampling distribution.

6. Explain the concept of unbiasedness, and use the rules of expected values to show that the sample mean is unbiased.

7. Explain why we prefer unbiased estimators with smaller variances to those with larger variances.

8. Describe the central limit theorem, and its implications for statistical inference.

9. Explain the relation between the population "standard deviation" and the standard error of the sample mean.

10. Explain the difference between point and interval estimation, and construct and interpret interval estimates of a population mean given a sample of data.

11. Give, in simple terms, a clarification of what the phrase "95% level of confidence" does and does not mean in relation to interval estimation.

12. Explain the purpose of hypothesis testing, and list the elements that must be present when carrying out a test.

13. Discuss the implications of the possible alternative hypotheses when testing the null hypothesis $H_0 : \mu = 7$. Give an economic example in which this hypothesis might be tested against one of the alternatives.

14. Describe the level of significance of a test, and explain the difference between the level of significance and the p-value of a test.

15. Define Type I error, and its relationship to the level of significance of a test.

16. Explain the difference between one-tail tests and two-tail tests, describing when one is preferred to the other.

17. Explain the difference and implications between the statements "I accept the null hypothesis" and "I do not reject the null hypothesis."

18. Give an intuitive explanation of maximum likelihood estimation, and describe the properties of the maximum likelihood estimator.

19. List the three types of tests associated with maximum likelihood estimation and comment on their similarities and differences.

20. Distinguish between parametric and nonparametric estimation.

21. Understand how a kernel density estimator fits an empirical distribution.

Keywords

alternative hypothesis	likelihood function	sample mean
asymptotic distribution	likelihood ratio test	sample variance
BLUE	linear estimator	sampling distribution
central limit theorem	log-likelihood function	sampling variation
central moments	maximum likelihood	standard error
estimate	estimation	standard error of the mean
estimator	nonparametric estimation	standard error of the estimate
experimental design	null hypothesis	statistical inference
information measure	parametric estimation	test statistic
interval estimate	point estimate	two-tail tests
kernel density estimator	population parameter	Type I error
Lagrange multiplier test	p-value	Type II error
law of large numbers	random sample	unbiased estimators
level of significance	rejection region	Wald test

Economists are interested in relationships between economic variables. For example, how much can we expect the sales of Frozen Delight ice cream to rise if we reduce the price by 5%? How much will household food expenditure rise if household income rises by $100 per month? Questions such as these are the main focus of this book.

However, sometimes questions of interest focus on a single economic variable. For example, an airplane seat designer must consider the average hip size of passengers in order to allow adequate room for each person, while still designing the plane to carry the profit-maximizing number of passengers. What is the average hip size, or more precisely hip width, of U.S. flight passengers? If a seat 18 inches wide is planned, what percent of customers will not be able to fit? Questions like this must be faced by manufacturers of everything from golf carts to women's jeans. How can we answer these questions? We certainly cannot take the measurements of every man, woman, and child in the U.S. population. This is a situation when statistical inference is used. Infer means "to conclude by reasoning from something known or assumed." **Statistical inference** means that we will draw conclusions about a population based on a sample of data.

C.1 A Sample of Data

To carry out statistical inference, we need data. The data should be obtained from the population in which we are interested. For the airplane seat designer this is essentially

Table C.1   **Sample Hip Size Data**

14.96	14.76	15.97	15.71	17.77
17.34	17.89	17.19	13.53	17.81
16.40	18.36	16.87	17.89	16.90
19.33	17.59	15.26	17.31	19.26
17.69	16.64	13.90	13.71	16.03
17.50	20.23	16.40	17.92	15.86
15.84	16.98	20.40	14.91	16.56
18.69	16.23	15.94	20.00	16.71
18.63	14.21	19.08	19.22	20.23
18.55	20.33	19.40	16.48	15.54

the entire U.S. population above the age of two, since small children can fly "free" on the laps of their suffering parents. A separate branch of statistics, called **experimental design**, is concerned with the question of how to actually collect a representative sample. How would you proceed if you were asked to obtain 50 measurements of hip size representative of the entire population? This is not such an easy task. Ideally the 50 individuals will be randomly chosen from the population, in such a way that there is no pattern of choices. Suppose we focus on only the population of adult flyers, since usually there are few children on planes. Our experimental design specialist draws a sample that is shown in Table C.1 and stored in the file *hip.dat*.

A first step when analyzing a sample of data is to examine it visually. Figure C.1 is a histogram of the 50 data points. Based on this figure, the "average" hip size in this sample seems to be between 16 and 18 inches. For our profit-maximizing designer this casual estimate is not sufficiently precise. In the next section we set up an econometric model that will be used as a basis for inference in this problem.

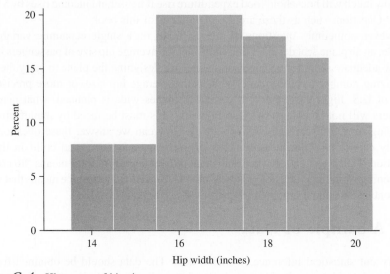

FIGURE *C.1*   Histogram of hip sizes.

C.2 An Econometric Model

The data in Table C.1 were obtained by sampling. Sampling from a population is an experiment. The variable of interest in this experiment is an individual's hip size. Before the experiment is performed we do not know what the values will be, thus the hip size of a randomly chosen person is a random variable. Let us denote this random variable as Y. We choose a sample of $N = 50$ individuals, $Y_1, Y_2, \ldots, Y_N$, where each Y_i represents the hip size of a different person. The data values in Table C.1 are specific values of the variables, which we denote as $y_1, y_2, \ldots, y_N$. We assume that the population has a center, which we describe by the expected value of the random variable Y,

$$E(Y) = \mu \tag{C.1}$$

We use the Greek letter μ ("mu") to denote the mean of the random variable Y, and also the mean of the population we are studying. Thus if we knew μ we would have the answer to the question "What is the average hip size of adults in the United States?" To indicate its importance to us in describing the population we call μ a **population parameter**, or, more briefly, a parameter. Our objective is to use the sample of data in Table C.1 to make inferences, or judgments, about the unknown population parameter μ.

The other random variable characteristic of interest is its variability, which we measure by its variance,

$$\text{var}(Y) = E[Y - E(Y)]^2 = E[Y - \mu]^2 = \sigma^2 \tag{C.2}$$

The variance σ^2 is also an unknown population parameter. As described in the Probability Primer, the variance of a random variable measures the "spread" of a probability distribution about the population mean, with a larger variance meaning a wider spread, as shown in Figure P.3. In the context of the hip data, the variance tells us how much hip sizes can vary from one randomly chosen person to the next. To economize on space, we will denote the mean and variance of a random variable as $Y \sim (\mu, \sigma^2)$ where $\sim$ means "is distributed as." The first element in parentheses is the population mean and the second is the population variance. So far we have not said what kind of probability distribution we think Y has.

The econometric model is not complete. If our sample is drawn randomly, we can assume that $Y_1, Y_2, \ldots, Y_N$ are statistically independent. The hip size of any one individual is independent of the hip size of another randomly drawn individual. Furthermore, we assume that each of the observations we collect is from the population of interest, so each random variable Y_i has the same mean and variance, or $Y_i \sim (\mu, \sigma^2)$. The Y_i constitute a **random sample**, in the statistical sense, because $Y_1, Y_2, \ldots, Y_N$ are statistically independent with identical probability distributions. It is sometimes reasonable to assume that population values are *normally* distributed, which we represent by $Y \sim N(\mu, \sigma^2)$.

C.3 Estimating the Mean of a Population

How shall we estimate the population mean μ given our sample of data values in Table C.1? The population mean is given by the expected value $E(Y) = \mu$. The expected value of a random variable is its average value in the population. It seems reasonable, by analogy, to use the average value in the sample, or **sample mean**, to estimate the population mean. Denote by $y_1, y_2, \ldots, y_N$ the sample of N observations. Then the sample mean is

$$\bar{y} = \Sigma y_i / N \tag{C.3}$$

The notation $\bar{y}$ (pronounced "y-bar") is widely used for the sample mean, and you probably encountered it in your statistics courses. For the hip data in Table C.1 we obtain $\bar{y} = 17.1582$, thus we estimate that the average hip size in the population is 17.1582 inches.

Given the estimate $\bar{y} = 17.1582$ we are inclined to ask, "How good an estimate is 17.1582?" By that we mean how close is 17.1582 to the true population mean, μ? Unfortunately this is an ill-posed question in the sense that it can never be answered. In order to answer it, we would have to know μ, in which case we would not have tried to estimate it in the first place!

Instead of asking about the quality of the *estimate* we will ask about the quality of the *estimation procedure*, or **estimator**. How good is the sample mean as an estimator of the mean of a population? This is a question we can answer. To distinguish between the estimate and the estimator of the population mean μ we will write the estimator as

$$\bar{Y} = \sum_{i=1}^{N} Y_i / N \tag{C.4}$$

In (C.4) we have used Y_i instead of y_i to indicate that this general formula is used whatever the sample values turn out to be. In this context Y_i are random variables, and thus the estimator $\bar{Y}$ is random too.

We do not know the value of the estimator $\bar{Y}$ until a data sample is obtained, and different samples will lead to different values. To illustrate, we collect 10 more samples of size $N = 50$ and calculate the average hip size, as shown in Table C.2. The estimates differ from sample to sample because $\bar{Y}$ is a random variable. This variation, due to collection of different random samples, is called **sampling variation**. It is an inescapable fact of statistical analysis that the estimator $\bar{Y}$—indeed, all statistical estimation procedures— are subject to sampling variability. Because of this terminology, an estimator's probability density function is called its **sampling distribution**.

We can determine how good the estimator $\bar{Y}$ is by examining its expected value, variance, and sampling distribution.

Ta b l e C . 2 **Sample Means from 10 Samples**

Sample	$\bar{y}$
1	17.3544
2	16.8220
3	17.4114
4	17.1654
5	16.9004
6	16.9956
7	16.8368
8	16.7534
9	17.0974
10	16.8770

C.3.1 THE EXPECTED VALUE OF $\overline{Y}$

Write out formula (C.4) fully as

$$\overline{Y} = \sum_{i=1}^{N} \frac{1}{N} Y_i = \frac{1}{N} Y_1 + \frac{1}{N} Y_2 + \cdots + \frac{1}{N} Y_N \tag{C.5}$$

From (P.16) the expected value of this sum is the sum of expected values

$$\begin{aligned}
E(\overline{Y}) &= E\left[\frac{1}{N} Y_1\right] + E\left[\frac{1}{N} Y_2\right] + \cdots + E\left[\frac{1}{N} Y_N\right] \\
&= \frac{1}{N} E[Y_1] + \frac{1}{N} E[Y_2] + \cdots + \frac{1}{N} E[Y_N] \\
&= \frac{1}{N} \mu + \frac{1}{N} \mu + \cdots + \frac{1}{N} \mu \\
&= \mu
\end{aligned}$$

The expected value of the estimator $\overline{Y}$ *is* the population mean μ that we are trying to estimate. What does this mean? The expectation of a random variable is its average value in many repeated trials of an experiment, which amounts to collecting a large number of random samples from the population. If we did obtain many samples of size N, and obtained their average values, like those in Table C.2, then the average of all *those* values would equal the true population mean μ. This property is a good one for estimators to have. Estimators with this property are called **unbiased estimators**. The sample mean $\overline{Y}$ is an unbiased estimator of the population mean μ.

Unfortunately, while unbiasedness is a good property for an estimator to have, it does not tell us anything about whether our estimate $\overline{y} = 17.1582$, based on a single sample of data, is close to the true population mean value μ. To assess how far the estimate might be from μ, we will determine the variance of the estimator.

C.3.2 THE VARIANCE OF $\overline{Y}$

The variance of $\overline{Y}$ is obtained using the procedure for finding the variance of a sum of uncorrelated (zero covariance) random variables in (P.23). We can apply this rule if our data are obtained by random sampling, because with random sampling the observations are statistically independent, and thus are uncorrelated. Furthermore, we have assumed that $\text{var}(Y_i) = \sigma^2$ for all observations. Carefully note how these assumptions are used in the derivation of the variance of $\overline{Y}$, which we write as $\text{var}(\overline{Y})$:

$$\begin{aligned}
\text{var}(\overline{Y}) &= \text{var}\left(\frac{1}{N} Y_1 + \frac{1}{N} Y_2 + \cdots + \frac{1}{N} Y_N\right) \\
&= \frac{1}{N^2} \text{var}(Y_1) + \frac{1}{N^2} \text{var}(Y_2) + \cdots + \frac{1}{N^2} \text{var}(Y_N) \\
&= \frac{1}{N^2} \sigma^2 + \frac{1}{N^2} \sigma^2 + \cdots + \frac{1}{N^2} \sigma^2 \\
&= \frac{\sigma^2}{N}
\end{aligned} \tag{C.6}$$

This result tells us that (i) the variance of $\overline{Y}$ is *smaller* than the population variance, because the sample size $N \geq 2$, and (ii) the larger the sample size, the smaller the sampling variation of $\overline{Y}$ as measured by its variance.

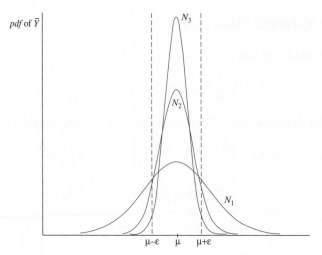

FIGURE C.2   Increasing sample size and sampling distributions of $\overline{Y}$.

C.3.3   THE SAMPLING DISTRIBUTION OF $\overline{Y}$

If the population data are normally distributed, then we say that the random variable Y_i follows a normal distribution. In this case the estimator $\overline{Y}$ also follows a normal distribution. In (P.30) it is noted that weighted averages of normal random variables are normal themselves. From (C.5) we know that $\overline{Y}$ is a weighted average of Y_i. If $Y_i \sim N(\mu, \sigma^2)$, then $\overline{Y}$ is also normally distributed, or $\overline{Y} \sim N(\mu, \sigma^2/N)$.

We can gain some intuition about the meaning and usefulness of the finding that $\overline{Y} \sim N(\mu, \sigma^2/N)$ if we examine Figure C.2.

Each of the normal distributions in this figure is a sampling distribution of $\overline{Y}$. The differences among them are the samples sizes used in estimation. The sample size $N_3 > N_2 > N_1$. Increasing the sample size decreases the variance of the estimator $\overline{Y}$, $\text{var}(\overline{Y}) = \sigma^2/N$, and this increases the probability that the sample mean will be "close" to the true population parameter μ. When examining Figure C.2, recall that an area under a probability density function (*pdf*) measures the probability of an event. If ε represents a positive number, the probability that $\overline{Y}$ falls in the interval between $\mu - \varepsilon$ and $\mu + \varepsilon$ is greater for larger samples. The lesson here is that having more data is better than having less data, because having a larger sample increases the probability of obtaining an estimate "close" or "within ε" of the true population parameter μ.

In our numerical example, suppose we want our estimate of μ to be within 1 inch of the true value. Let us compute the probability of getting an estimate within $\varepsilon = 1$ inch of μ—that is, within the interval $[\mu - 1, \mu + 1]$. For the purpose of illustration assume that the population is normal, $\sigma^2 = 10$ and $N = 40$. Then $\overline{Y} \sim N(\mu, \sigma^2/N = 10/40 = 0.25)$. We can compute the probability that $\overline{Y}$ is within 1 inch of μ by calculating $P[\mu - 1 \leq \overline{Y} \leq \mu + 1]$. To do so we standardize $\overline{Y}$ by subtracting its mean μ and dividing by its standard deviation $\sigma/\sqrt{N}$, and then use the standard normal distribution and Table 1 at the end of the book:

$$P[\mu - 1 \leq \overline{Y} \leq \mu + 1] = P\left[\frac{-1}{\sigma/\sqrt{N}} \leq \frac{\overline{Y} - \mu}{\sigma/\sqrt{N}} \leq \frac{1}{\sigma/\sqrt{N}} \right]$$

$$= P\left[\frac{-1}{\sqrt{0.25}} \leq Z \leq \frac{1}{\sqrt{0.25}} \right]$$

$$= P[-2 \leq Z \leq 2] = 0.9544$$

Thus, if we draw a random sample of size $N = 40$ from a normal population with variance 10, using the sample mean as an estimator will provide an estimate within 1 inch of the true value about 95% of the time. If $N = 80$, the probability that $\overline{Y}$ is within 1 inch of μ increases to 0.995.

C.3.4 THE CENTRAL LIMIT THEOREM

We were able to carry out the above analysis because we assumed that the population we are considering, hip width of U.S. adults, has a normal distribution. This implies that $Y_i \sim N(\mu, \sigma^2)$, and $\overline{Y} \sim N(\mu, \sigma^2/N)$. A question we need to ask is "If the population is not normal, then what is the sampling distribution of the sample mean?" The **central limit theorem** provides an answer to this question.

> **CENTRAL LIMIT THEOREM:** If $Y_1, \ldots, Y_N$ are independent and identically distributed random variables with mean μ and variance σ^2, and $\overline{Y} = \sum Y_i/N$, then
> $$Z_N = \frac{\overline{Y} - \mu}{\sigma/\sqrt{N}}$$
> has a probability distribution that converges to the standard normal $N(0,1)$ as $N \to \infty$.

This theorem says that the sample average of N independent random variables from *any* probability distribution will have an approximate standard normal distribution after standardizing (i.e., subtracting the mean and dividing by the standard deviation), if the sample is sufficiently large. A shorthand notation is $\overline{Y} \overset{a}{\sim} N(\mu, \sigma^2/N)$, where the symbol $\overset{a}{\sim}$ means *asymptotically distributed*. The word **asymptotic** implies that the approximate normality of $\overline{Y}$ depends on having a large sample. Thus even if the population is not normal, if we have a sufficiently large sample, we can carry out calculations like those in the previous section. How large does the sample have to be? In general, it depends on the complexity of the problem, but in the simple case of estimating a population mean, if $N \geq 30$ then you can feel pretty comfortable in assuming that the sample mean is approximately normally distributed, $\overline{Y} \overset{a}{\sim} N(\mu, \sigma^2/N)$, as indicated by the central limit theorem.

To illustrate how well the central limit theorem actually works, we carry out a simulation experiment. Let the continuous random variable Y have a triangular distribution, with probability density function

$$f(y) = \begin{cases} 2y & 0 < y < 1 \\ 0 & \text{otherwise} \end{cases}$$

Draw a sketch of the triangular *pdf* to understand its name. The expected value of Y is $\mu = E(Y) = 2/3$, and its variance is $\sigma^2 = \text{var}(Y) = 1/18$. The central limit theorem says that if $Y_1, \ldots, Y_N$ are independent and identically distributed with density $f(y)$ then

$$Z_N = \frac{\overline{Y} - 2/3}{\sqrt{\dfrac{1/18}{N}}}$$

has a probability distribution that approaches the standard normal distribution as N approaches infinity.

We use a random number generator to create random values from the triangular *pdf*. Plotting 10,000 values gives the histogram in Figure C.3(a). We generate 10,000 samples of sizes $N = 3, 10$, and 30, compute the sample means of each sample, and create Z_N. Their histograms are shown in Figure C.3 (b)–(d). You see the amazing convergence of the

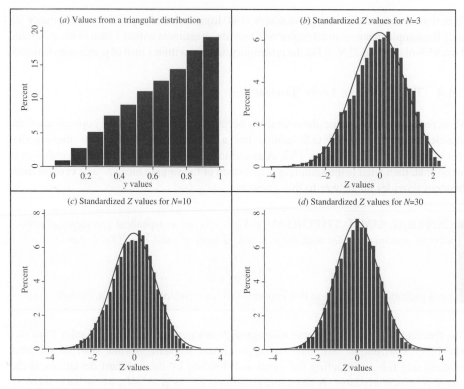

FIGURE C.3   Central limit theorem.

standardized sample mean's distribution to a distribution that is bell shaped, centered at zero, symmetric, with almost all values between -3 and 3, just like a standard normal distribution, with a sample size as small as $N = 10$.

C.3.5 BEST LINEAR UNBIASED ESTIMATION

Another powerful finding about the estimator $\overline{Y}$ of the population mean is that it is the best of all possible estimators that are both *linear* and *unbiased*. A **linear estimator** is simply one that is a weighted average of Y_i's, such as $\tilde{Y} = \sum a_i Y_i$, where a_i are constants. The sample mean $\overline{Y}$, given in (C.4), is a linear estimator with $a_i = 1/N$. The fact that $\overline{Y}$ is the "best" linear unbiased estimator (BLUE) accounts for its wide use. "Best" means that it is the linear unbiased estimator with the smallest possible variance. In the previous section we demonstrated that it is better to have an estimator with a smaller variance rather than a larger one—because it increases the chances of getting an estimate close to the true population mean μ. This important result about the estimator $\overline{Y}$ is true *if* the sample values $Y_i \sim (\mu, \sigma^2)$ are uncorrelated and identically distributed. It does not depend on the population being normally distributed. A proof of this result is in Section C.9.2.

C.4 Estimating the Population Variance and Other Moments

The sample mean $\overline{Y}$ is an estimate of the population mean μ. The population mean is often called the "first moment" since it is the expected value of Y to the first power. Higher moments are obtained by taking expected values of higher powers of the random variable, so the second moment of Y is $E(Y^2)$, the third moment is $E(Y^3)$, and so on. When the random variable has its population mean subtracted, it is said to be *centered*. Expected values of powers of centered random variables are called **central moments**, and they are often denoted as μ_r, so that the rth central moment of Y is

$$\mu_r = E\big[(Y - \mu)^r\big]$$

The value of the first central moment is zero since $\mu_1 = E\big[(Y - \mu)^1\big] = E(Y) - \mu = 0$. It is the higher central moments of Y that are interesting:

$$\mu_2 = E\big[(Y - \mu)^2\big] = \sigma^2$$
$$\mu_3 = E\big[(Y - \mu)^3\big]$$
$$\mu_4 = E\big[(Y - \mu)^4\big]$$

You recognize that the second central moment of Y is its variance, and the third and fourth moments appear in the definitions of skewness and kurtosis introduced in Appendix B.1.2. The question we address in this section is, now that we have an excellent estimator of the mean of a population, how do we estimate these higher moments? We will first consider estimation of the population variance, and then address the problem of estimating the third and fourth moments.

C.4.1 ESTIMATING THE POPULATION VARIANCE

The population variance is $\text{var}(Y) = \sigma^2 = E[Y - \mu]^2$. An expected value is an "average" of sorts, so if we knew μ we could estimate the variance by using the sample analog $\tilde{\sigma}^2 = \Sigma(Y_i - \mu)^2/N$. We do not know μ, so replace it by its estimator $\overline{Y}$, giving

$$\tilde{\sigma}^2 = \frac{\Sigma(Y_i - \overline{Y})^2}{N}$$

This estimator is not a bad one. It has a logical appeal, and it can be shown to converge to the true value of σ^2 as the sample size $N \to \infty$, but it is biased. To make it unbiased, we divide by $N - 1$ instead of N. This correction is needed since the population mean μ has to be estimated before the variance can be estimated. This change does not matter much in samples of at least 30 observations, but it does make a difference in smaller samples. The unbiased estimator of the population variance σ^2 is

$$\hat{\sigma}^2 = \frac{\Sigma(Y_i - \overline{Y})^2}{N - 1} \tag{C.7}$$

You may remember this estimator from a prior statistics course as the "sample variance." Using the sample variance we can estimate the variance of the estimator $\overline{Y}$ as

$$\widehat{\text{var}(\overline{Y})} = \hat{\sigma}^2/N \tag{C.8}$$

In (C.8) note that we have put a "hat" $(\widehat{})$ over this variance to indicate that it is an estimated variance. The square root of the estimated variance is called the **standard error** of $\overline{Y}$ and is also known as the **standard error of the mean** and the **standard error of the estimate**,

$$\mathrm{se}(\overline{Y}) = \sqrt{\widehat{\mathrm{var}(\overline{Y})}} = \hat{\sigma}/\sqrt{N} \qquad (\text{C.9})$$

C.4.2   ESTIMATING HIGHER MOMENTS

Recall that central moments are expected values, $\mu_r = E[(Y - \mu)^r]$, and thus are averages in the population. In statistics the **law of large numbers** says that sample means converge to population averages (expected values) as the sample size $N \to \infty$. We can estimate the higher moments by finding the sample analog and replacing the population mean μ by its estimate $\overline{Y}$, so that

$$\tilde{\mu}_2 = \Sigma(Y_i - \overline{Y})^2/N = \tilde{\sigma}^2$$
$$\tilde{\mu}_3 = \Sigma(Y_i - \overline{Y})^3/N$$
$$\tilde{\mu}_4 = \Sigma(Y_i - \overline{Y})^4/N$$

Note that in these calculations we divide by N and not $N - 1$, since we are using the law of large numbers (i.e., large samples) as justification, and in large samples the correction has little effect. Using these sample estimates of the central moments we can obtain estimates of the skewness coefficient (S) and kurtosis coefficient (K) as

$$\widehat{skewness} = S = \frac{\tilde{\mu}_3}{\tilde{\sigma}^3}$$

$$\widehat{kurtosis} = K = \frac{\tilde{\mu}_4}{\tilde{\sigma}^4}$$

C.4.3   THE HIP DATA

The sample variance for the hip data is

$$\hat{\sigma}^2 = \frac{\Sigma(y_i - \bar{y})^2}{N - 1} = \frac{\Sigma(y_i - 17.1582)^2}{49} = \frac{159.9995}{49} = 3.2653$$

This means that the estimated variance of the sample mean is

$$\widehat{\mathrm{var}(\overline{Y})} = \frac{\hat{\sigma}^2}{N} = \frac{3.2653}{50} = 0.0653$$

and the standard error of the mean is

$$\mathrm{se}(\overline{Y}) = \hat{\sigma}/\sqrt{N} = 0.2556$$

The estimated skewness is $S = -0.0138$ and the estimated kurtosis is $K = 2.3315$ using

$$\tilde{\sigma} = \sqrt{\Sigma(Y_i - \overline{Y})^2/N} = \sqrt{159.9995/50} = 1.7889$$

$$\tilde{\mu}_3 = \Sigma(Y_i - \overline{Y})^3/N = -0.0791$$

$$\tilde{\mu}_4 = \Sigma(Y_i - \overline{Y})^4/N = 23.8748$$

Thus, the hip data is slightly negatively skewed and is slightly less peaked than would be expected for a normal distribution. Nevertheless, as we will see in Section C.7.4, we cannot conclude that the hip data follow a non-normal distribution.

C.4.4 USING THE ESTIMATES

How can we summarize what we have learned? Our estimates suggest that the hip size of U.S. adults is normally distributed with mean 17.158 inches and with a variance of 3.265; $Y \sim N(17.158, 3.265)$. Based on this information, if an airplane seat is 18 inches wide, what percentage of customers will not be able to fit? We can recast this question as asking what the probability is that a randomly drawn person will have hips larger than 18 inches,

$$P(Y > 18) = P\left(\frac{Y - \mu}{\sigma} > \frac{18 - \mu}{\sigma}\right)$$

We can give an approximate answer to this question by replacing the unknown parameters by their estimates,

$$\widehat{P(Y > 18)} \cong P\left(\frac{Y - \overline{y}}{\hat{\sigma}} > \frac{18 - 17.158}{1.8070}\right) = P(Z > 0.4659) = 0.3207$$

Based on our estimates, 32% of the population would not be able to fit into a seat 18 inches wide.

How large would a seat have to be to fit 95% of the population? If we let y^* denote the required seat size, then

$$\widehat{P(Y \leq y^*)} \cong P\left(\frac{Y - \overline{y}}{\hat{\sigma}} \leq \frac{y^* - 17.1582}{1.8070}\right) = P\left(Z \leq \frac{y^* - 17.1582}{1.8070}\right) = 0.95$$

Using your computer software, or the table of normal probabilities, the value of Z such that $P(Z \leq z^*) = 0.95$ is $z^* = 1.645$. Then

$$\frac{y^* - 17.1582}{1.8070} = 1.645 \Rightarrow y^* = 20.1305$$

Thus, to accommodate 95% of U.S. adult passengers, we estimate that the seats should be slightly greater—20 inches wide.

C.5 Interval Estimation

In contrast to a point estimate of the population mean μ, like $\overline{y} = 17.158$, a confidence interval, or interval estimate, is a range of values that may contain the true population mean.

A confidence interval contains information not only about the location of the population mean, but also about the precision with which we estimate it.

C.5.1 Interval Estimation: σ^2 Known

Let Y be a normally distributed random variable, $Y \sim N(\mu, \sigma^2)$. Assume that we have a random sample of size N from this population, $Y_1, Y_2, \ldots, Y_N$. The estimator of the population mean is $\overline{Y} = \sum_{i=1}^{N} Y_i/N$. Because we have assumed that Y is normally distributed, it is also true that $\overline{Y} \sim N(\mu, \sigma^2/N)$.

For the present, let us assume that the population variance σ^2 is known. This assumption is not likely to be true, but making it allows us to introduce the notion of confidence intervals with few complications. In the next section we introduce methods for the case when σ^2 is unknown. Create a standard normal random variable

$$Z = \frac{\overline{Y} - \mu}{\sqrt{\sigma^2/N}} = \frac{\overline{Y} - \mu}{\sigma/\sqrt{N}} \sim N(0,1) \tag{C.10}$$

Cumulative probabilities for the standard normal are given by its cumulative distribution function (see the Probability Primer, Section P.6)

$$P(Z \le z) = \Phi(z)$$

These values are given in Table 1 at the end of this book. Let z_c be a "critical value" for the standard normal distribution, such that $\alpha = 0.05$ of the probability is in the tails of the distribution, with $\alpha/2 = 0.025$ of the probability in the tail to the right of z_c and $\alpha/2 = 0.025$ of the probability in the tail to the left of $-z_c$. The critical value is the 97.5 percentile of the standard normal distribution, $z_c = 1.96$, with $\Phi(1.96) = 0.975$. It is shown in Figure C.4. Thus, $P(Z \ge 1.96) = P(Z \le -1.96) = 0.025$ and

$$P(-1.96 \le Z \le 1.96) = 1 - 0.05 = 0.95 \tag{C.11}$$

Substitute (C.10) into (C.11) and rearrange to obtain

$$P\left(\overline{Y} - 1.96\,\sigma/\sqrt{N} \le \mu \le \overline{Y} + 1.96\,\sigma/\sqrt{N}\right) = 0.95$$

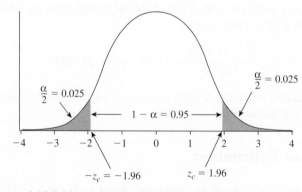

FIGURE **C.4** $\alpha = 0.05$ Critical values for the $N(0, 1)$ distribution.

Table C.3   **30 Values from** $N(10, 10)$

11.939	11.407	13.809
10.706	12.157	7.443
6.644	10.829	8.855
13.187	12.368	9.461
8.433	10.052	2.439
9.210	5.036	5.527
7.961	14.799	9.921
14.921	10.478	11.814
6.223	13.859	13.403
10.123	12.355	10.819

In general,

$$P\left(\overline{Y} - z_c \frac{\sigma}{\sqrt{N}} \le \mu \le \overline{Y} + z_c \frac{\sigma}{\sqrt{N}}\right) = 1 - \alpha \qquad (C.12)$$

where z_c is the appropriate critical value for a given value of tail probability α such that $\Phi(z_c) = 1 - \alpha/2$. In (C.12) we have defined the interval estimator

$$\overline{Y} \pm z_c \frac{\sigma}{\sqrt{N}} \qquad (C.13)$$

Our choice of the phrase interval *estimator* is a careful one. Intervals constructed using (C.13), in repeated sampling from the population, have a $100(1 - \alpha)\%$ chance of containing the population mean μ.

C.5.2   A SIMULATION

In order to use the interval estimator in (C.13) we must have data from a normal population with a known variance. To illustrate the computation, and the meaning of interval estimation, we will create a sample of data using a computer simulation. Statistical software programs contain random number generators. These are routines that create values from a given probability distribution. Table C.3 (*table_c3.dat*) contains 30 random values from a normal population with mean $\mu = 10$ and variance $\sigma^2 = 10$.

The sample mean of these values is $\overline{y} = 10.206$ and the corresponding interval estimate for μ, obtained by applying the interval estimator in (C.13) with a 0.95 probability content, is $10.206 \pm 1.96 \times \sqrt{10/30} = (9.074, 11.338)$. To appreciate how the sampling variability of an interval estimator arises, consider Table C.4, which contains the interval estimate for the sample in Table C.3, as well as the sample means and interval estimates from another 9 samples of size 30, like that in Table C.3. The whole 10 samples are stored in the file *table_c4.dat*.

Table C.4 illustrates the sampling variation of the estimator $\overline{Y}$. The sample mean varies from sample to sample. In this simulation, or Monte Carlo experiment, we know the true population mean, $\mu = 10$, and the estimates $\overline{y}$ are centered at that value. The half-width of the interval estimates is $1.96\sigma/\sqrt{N}$. Note that while the point estimates $\overline{y}$ in Table C.4 fall near the true value $\mu = 10$, not all of the interval estimates contain the true value. Intervals from samples 3, 4, and 6 do not contain the true value $\mu = 10$. However, in 10,000 simulated

Table C.4   **Confidence Interval Estimates from 10 Samples of Data**

Sample	$\bar{y}$	Lower bound	Upper bound
1	10.206	9.074	11.338
2	9.828	8.696	10.959
3	11.194	10.063	12.326
4	8.822	7.690	9.953
5	10.434	9.303	11.566
6	8.855	7.723	9.986
7	10.511	9.380	11.643
8	9.212	8.080	10.343
9	10.464	9.333	11.596
10	10.142	9.010	11.273

samples the average value of $\bar{y} = 10.004$ and 94.86% of intervals constructed using (C.13) contain the true parameter value $\mu = 10$.

These numbers reveal what is, and what is not, true about interval estimates.

- Any one interval estimate may or may not contain the true population parameter value.

- If *many* samples of size N are obtained, and intervals are constructed using (C.13) with $(1 - \alpha) = 0.95$, then 95% of them will contain the true parameter value.

- A 95% level of "confidence" is the probability that the interval estimator will provide an interval containing the true parameter value. Our confidence is in the procedure, not in any one interval estimate.

Since 95% of intervals constructed using (C.13) will contain the true parameter $\mu = 10$, we will be surprised if an interval estimate based on one sample does not contain the true parameter. Indeed, the fact that three of the 10 intervals in Table C.4 do not contain $\mu = 10$ is surprising, since out of 10 we would assume that only one 95% interval estimate might not contain the true parameter. This just goes to show that what happens in any one sample, or just a few samples, is not what sampling properties tell us. Sampling properties tell us what happens in many repeated experimental trials.

C.5.3   INTERVAL ESTIMATION: σ^2 UNKNOWN

The standardization in (C.10) assumes that the population variance σ^2 is known. When σ^2 is unknown, it is natural to replace it with its estimator $\hat{\sigma}^2$ given in (C.7)

$$\hat{\sigma}^2 = \frac{\sum\limits_{i=1}^{N}(Y_i - \bar{Y})^2}{N - 1}$$

When we do so, the resulting standardized random variable has a t-distribution (see Appendix B.3.7) with $(N - 1)$ degrees of freedom,

$$t = \frac{\bar{Y} - \mu}{\hat{\sigma}/\sqrt{N}} \sim t_{(N-1)} \tag{C.14}$$

The notation $t_{(N-1)}$ denotes a t-distribution with $N-1$ "degrees of freedom." Let the critical value t_c be the $100(1-\alpha/2)$-percentile value $t_{(1-\alpha/2,N-1)}$. This critical value has the property that $P[t_{(N-1)} \leq t_{(1-\alpha/2,N-1)}] = 1 - \alpha/2$. Critical values for the t-distribution are contained in Table 2 at the end of the book, and also inside the front cover. If t_c is a critical value from the t-distribution, then

$$P\left(-t_c \leq \frac{\overline{Y} - \mu}{\hat{\sigma}/\sqrt{N}} \leq t_c\right) = 1 - \alpha$$

Rearranging, we obtain

$$P\left(\overline{Y} - t_c \frac{\hat{\sigma}}{\sqrt{N}} \leq \mu \leq \overline{Y} + t_c \frac{\hat{\sigma}}{\sqrt{N}}\right) = 1 - \alpha$$

The $100(1-\alpha)\%$ interval estimator for μ is

$$\overline{Y} \pm t_c \frac{\hat{\sigma}}{\sqrt{N}} \quad \text{or} \quad \overline{Y} \pm t_c \mathrm{se}(\overline{Y}) \tag{C.15}$$

Unlike the interval estimator for the known σ^2 case in (C.13), the interval in (C.15) has center *and* width that vary from sample to sample.

> **REMARK:** The confidence interval (C.15) is based upon the assumption that the population is normally distributed, so that $\overline{Y}$ is normally distributed. If the population is not normal, then we invoke the central limit theorem, and say that $\overline{Y}$ is approximately normal in "large" samples, which from Figure C.3 you can see might be as few as 30 observations. In this case, we can use (C.15), recognizing that there is an approximation error introduced in smaller samples.

C.5.4   A SIMULATION (CONTINUED)

Table C.5 contains estimated values of σ^2 and interval estimates using (C.15) for the same 10 samples used for Table C.4. For the sample size $N = 30$ and the 95% confidence level the t-distribution critical value $t_c = t_{(0.975,29)} = 2.045$. The estimates $\overline{y}$ are the same as in Table C.4. The estimates $\hat{\sigma}^2$ vary about the true value $\sigma^2 = 10$. Of these

Ta b l e C. 5   **Interval Estimates Using (C.15) from 10 Samples**

Sample	$\overline{y}$	$\hat{\sigma}^2$	Lower bound	Upper bound
1	10.206	9.199	9.073	11.338
2	9.828	6.876	8.849	10.807
3	11.194	10.330	9.994	12.394
4	8.822	9.867	7.649	9.995
5	10.434	7.985	9.379	11.489
6	8.855	6.230	7.923	9.787
7	10.511	7.333	9.500	11.523
8	9.212	14.687	7.781	10.643
9	10.464	10.414	9.259	11.669
10	10.142	17.689	8.571	11.712

10 intervals, those for samples 4 and 6 do not contain the true parameter $\mu = 10$. Nevertheless, in 10,000 simulated samples 94.82% of them contain the true population mean $\mu = 10$.

C.5.5 INTERVAL ESTIMATION USING THE HIP DATA

We have introduced the empirical problem faced by an airplane seat design engineer. Given a random sample of size $N = 50$ we estimated the mean U.S. hip width to be $\bar{y} = 17.158$ inches. Furthermore we estimated the population variance to be $\hat{\sigma}^2 = 3.265$; thus the estimated standard deviation is $\hat{\sigma} = 1.807$. The standard error of the mean is $\hat{\sigma}/\sqrt{N} = 1.807/\sqrt{50} = 0.2556$. The critical value for interval estimation comes from a t-distribution with $N - 1 = 49$ degrees of freedom. While this value is not in Table 2, the correct value using our software is $t_c = t_{(0.975,49)} = 2.0095752$, which we round to $t_c = 2.01$. To construct a 95% interval estimate we use (C.15), replacing estimates for the estimators, to give

$$\bar{y} \pm t_c \frac{\hat{\sigma}}{\sqrt{N}} = 17.1582 \pm 2.01 \frac{1.807}{\sqrt{50}}$$
$$= [16.6447, \ 17.6717]$$

We estimate that the population mean hip size falls between 16.645 and 17.672 inches. Although we do not know if this interval contains the true population mean hip size for sure, we know that the procedure used to create the interval "works" 95% of the time; thus we would be surprised if the interval did not contain the true population value μ.

C.6 Hypothesis Tests About a Population Mean

Hypothesis testing procedures compare a conjecture, or a hypothesis, that we have about a population to the information contained in a sample of data. The conjectures we test here concern the mean of a normal population. In the context of the problem faced by the airplane seat designer, suppose that airplanes since 1970 have been designed assuming the mean population hip width is 16.5 inches. Is that figure still valid today?

C.6.1 COMPONENTS OF HYPOTHESIS TESTS

Hypothesis tests use sample information about a parameter—namely, its point estimate and its standard error—to draw a conclusion about the hypothesis. In every hypothesis test, five ingredients must be present:

> **COMPONENTS OF HYPOTHESIS TESTS**
>
> A *null* hypothesis, H_0
> An *alternative* hypothesis, H_1
> A test *statistic*
> A *rejection* region
> A conclusion

C.6.1a   The Null Hypothesis

The "null" hypothesis, which is denoted H_0 (*H-naught*), specifies a value c for a parameter. We write the null hypothesis as $H_0 : \mu = c$. A null hypothesis is the belief we will maintain until we are convinced by the sample evidence that it is not true, in which case we *reject* the null hypothesis.

C.6.1b   The Alternative Hypothesis

Paired with every null hypothesis is a logical alternative hypothesis, H_1, that we will accept if the null hypothesis is rejected. The alternative hypothesis is flexible and depends to some extent on the problem at hand. For the null hypothesis $H_0 : \mu = c$ three possible alternative hypotheses are

- $H_1 : \mu > c$. If we reject the null hypothesis that $\mu = c$, we accept the alternative that μ is greater than c.

- $H_1 : \mu < c$. If we reject the null hypothesis that $\mu = c$, we accept the alternative that μ is less than c.

- $H_1 : \mu \neq c$. If we reject the null hypothesis that $\mu = c$, we accept the alternative that μ takes a value other than (not equal to) c.

C.6.1c   The Test Statistic

The sample information about the null hypothesis is embodied in the sample value of a **test statistic**. Based on the value of a test statistic, we decide either to reject the null hypothesis or not to reject it. A test statistic has a very special characteristic: its probability distribution is completely known when the null hypothesis is true, and it has some other distribution if the null hypothesis is not true.

Consider the null hypothesis $H_0 : \mu = c$. If the sample data come from a normal population with mean μ and variance σ^2, then

$$t = \frac{\overline{Y} - \mu}{\hat{\sigma}/\sqrt{N}} \sim t_{(N-1)}$$

If the null hypothesis $H_0 : \mu = c$ is true, then

$$t = \frac{\overline{Y} - c}{\hat{\sigma}/\sqrt{N}} \sim t_{(N-1)} \tag{C.16}$$

If the null hypothesis is not true, then the t-statistic in (C.16) does not have the usual t-distribution.

REMARK: The test statistic distribution in (C.16) is based on an assumption that the population is normally distributed. If the population is not normal, then we invoke the central limit theorem, and say that $\overline{Y}$ is approximately normal in "large" samples. We can use (C.16), recognizing that there is an approximation error introduced if our sample is small.

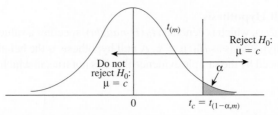

FIGURE C.5   The rejection region for the one-tail test of $H_0 : \mu = c$ against $H_1 : \mu > c$.

C.6.1d   The Rejection Region

The rejection region depends on the form of the alternative. It is the range of values of the test statistic that leads to rejection of the null hypothesis. They are values that are *unlikely* and have low probability of occurring when the null hypothesis is true. The chain of logic is "If a value of the test statistic is obtained that falls in a region of low probability, then it is unlikely that the test statistic has the assumed distribution, and thus it is unlikely that the null hypothesis is true." If the alternative hypothesis is true, then values of the test statistic will tend to be unusually large or unusually small. The terms "large" and "small" are determined by choosing a probability α, called the **level of significance** of the test, which provides a meaning for "an *unlikely* event." The level of significance of the test α is usually chosen to be 0.01, 0.05, or 0.10.

C.6.1e   A Conclusion

When you have completed a hypothesis test, you should state your conclusion, whether you reject the null hypothesis. However, we urge you to make it standard practice to say what the conclusion means in the economic context of the problem you are working on—that is, interpret the results in a meaningful way. This should be a point of emphasis in all statistical work that you do.

We will now discuss the mechanics of carrying out alternative versions of hypothesis tests.

C.6.2   ONE-TAIL TESTS WITH ALTERNATIVE "GREATER THAN" ($>$)

If the alternative hypothesis $H_1 : \mu > c$ is true, then the value of the t-statistic (C.16) tends to become larger than usual for the t-distribution. Let the critical value t_c be the $100(1 - \alpha)$-percentile $t_{(1-\alpha, N-1)}$ from a t-distribution with $N - 1$ degrees of freedom. Then $P(t \le t_c) = 1 - \alpha$, where α is the level of significance of the test. If the t-statistic is greater than or equal to t_c, then we reject $H_0 : \mu = c$ and accept the alternative $H_1 : \mu > c$, as shown in Figure C.5.

If the null hypothesis $H_0 : \mu = c$ is *true*, then the test statistic (C.16) has a t-distribution, and its values would tend to fall in the center of the distribution, where most of the probability is contained. If $t < t_c$, then there is no evidence against the null hypothesis, and we do not reject it.

C.6.3   ONE-TAIL TESTS WITH ALTERNATIVE "LESS THAN" ($<$)

If the alternative hypothesis $H_1 : \mu < c$ is true, then the value of the t-statistic (C.16) tends to become smaller than usual for the t-distribution. The critical value $-t_c$ is the 100-percentile $t_{(\alpha, N-1)}$ from a t-distribution with $N - 1$ degrees of freedom. Then $P(t \le -t_c) = \alpha$, where α

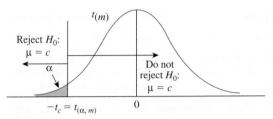

FIGURE **C.6**   Critical value for one-tail test $H_0 : \mu = c$ versus $H_1 : \mu < c$.

is the level of significance of the test as shown in Figure C.6. If $t \le -t_c$, then we reject $H_0 : \mu = c$ and accept the alternative $H_1 : \mu < c$. If $t > -t_c$, then we do not reject $H_0 : \mu = c$.

> **MEMORY TRICK:** The rejection region for a one-tail test is in the direction of the arrow in the alternative. If alternative is ">", then reject in right tail. If alternative is "<", reject in left tail.

C.6.4   TWO-TAIL TESTS WITH ALTERNATIVE "NOT EQUAL TO" ($\neq$)

If the alternative hypothesis $H_1 : \mu \neq c$ is true, then values of the test statistic may be unusually "large" or unusually "small." The rejection region consists of the two "tails" of the t-distribution, and this is called a two-tail test. In Figure C.7, the critical values for testing $H_0 : \mu = c$ against $H_1 : \mu \neq c$ are depicted. The critical value is the $100(1 - \alpha/2)$-percentile from a t-distribution with $N - 1$ degrees of freedom, $t_c = t_{(1-\alpha/2, N-1)}$, so that $P(t \ge t_c) = P(t \le -t_c) = \alpha/2$.

If the value of the test statistic t falls in the rejection region, either tail of the $t_{(N-1)}$ distribution, then we reject the null hypothesis $H_0 : \mu = c$ and accept the alternative $H_1 : \mu \neq c$. If the value of the test statistic t falls in the nonrejection region, between the critical values $-t_c$ and t_c, then we do not reject the null hypothesis $H_0 : \mu = c$.

C.6.5   EXAMPLE OF A ONE-TAIL TEST USING THE HIP DATA

Let us illustrate by testing the null hypothesis that the population hip size is 16.5 inches, against the alternative that it is *greater* than 16.5 inches. The following five-step format is recommended.

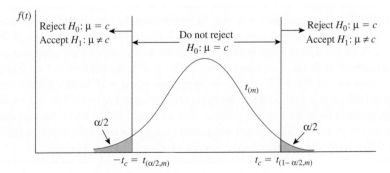

FIGURE **C.7**   Rejection region for a test of $H_0 : \mu = c$ against $H_1 : \mu \neq c$.

1. The null hypothesis is $H_0 : \mu = 16.5$. The alternative hypothesis is $H_1 : \mu > 16.5$.

2. The test statistic $t = (\bar{Y} - 16.5)/(\hat{\sigma}/\sqrt{N}) \sim t_{(N-1)}$ *if the null hypothesis is true.*

3. Let us select the level of significance $\alpha = 0.05$. The critical value $t_c = t_{(0.95,49)} = 1.6766$ for a t-distribution with $N - 1 = 49$ degrees of freedom. Thus we will reject the null hypothesis in favor of the alternative if $t \geq 1.68$.

4. Using the hip data, the estimate of μ is $\bar{y} = 17.1582$, with estimated variance $\hat{\sigma}^2 = 3.2653$, so $\hat{\sigma} = 1.807$. The value of the test statistic is

$$t = \frac{17.1582 - 16.5}{1.807/\sqrt{50}} = 2.5756.$$

5. *Conclusion:* Since $t = 2.5756 > 1.68$, we *reject* the null hypothesis. The sample information we have is *incompatible* with the hypothesis that $\mu = 16.5$. We accept the alternative that the population mean hip size is greater than 16.5 inches, at the $\alpha = 0.05$ level of significance.

C.6.6   EXAMPLE OF A TWO-TAIL TEST USING THE HIP DATA

Let us test the null hypothesis that the population hip size is 17 inches, against the alternative that it is *not equal to* 17 inches. The steps of the test are

1. The null hypothesis is $H_0 : \mu = 17$. The alternative hypothesis is $H_1 : \mu \neq 17$.

2. The test statistic $t = (\bar{Y} - 17)/(\hat{\sigma}/\sqrt{N}) \sim t_{(N-1)}$ *if the null hypothesis is true.*

3. Let us select the level of significance $\alpha = 0.05$. In a two-tail test $\alpha/2 = 0.025$ of probability is allocated to each tail of the distribution. The critical value is the 97.5 percentile of the t-distribution, which leaves 2.5% of the probability in the upper tail, $t_c = t_{(0.975,49)} = 2.01$ for a t-distribution with $N - 1 = 49$ degrees of freedom. Thus, we will reject the null hypothesis in favor of the alternative if $t \geq 2.01$ or if $t \leq -2.01$.

4. Using the hip data, the estimate of μ is $\bar{y} = 17.1582$, with estimated variance $\hat{\sigma}^2 = 3.2653$, so $\hat{\sigma} = 1.807$. The value of the test statistic is $t = (17.1582 - 17)/(1.807/\sqrt{50}) = 0.6191$.

5. *Conclusion:* Since $-2.01 < t = 0.6191 < 2.01$ we *do not reject* the null hypothesis. The sample information we have is *compatible* with the hypothesis that the population mean hip size $\mu = 17$.

WARNING: Care must be taken here in interpreting the outcome of a statistical test. One of the basic precepts of hypothesis testing is that finding a sample value of the test statistic in the nonrejection region does not make the null hypothesis true! Suppose another null hypothesis is $H_0 : \mu = c^*$, where c^* is "close" to c. If we fail to reject the hypothesis $\mu = c$, then we will likely fail to reject the hypothesis that $\mu = c^*$. In the example above, at the $\alpha = 0.05$ level, we fail to reject the hypothesis that μ is 17, 16.8, 17.2, or 17.3. In fact, in any problem there are many hypotheses that we would fail to reject, but that does not make any of them true. The weaker statements "we do not reject the null hypothesis" or "we fail to reject the null hypothesis" do not send a misleading message.

C.6.7 THE p-VALUE

When reporting the outcome of statistical hypothesis tests it has become common practice to report the p-**value** of the test. If we have the p-value of a test, p, we can determine the outcome of the test by comparing the p-value to the chosen level of significance, α, *without* looking up or calculating the critical values ourselves. The rule is

> p-**VALUE RULE:** Reject the null hypothesis when the p-value is less than, or equal to, the level of significance α. That is, if $p \leq \alpha$ then reject H_0. If $p > \alpha$, then do not reject H_0.

If you have chosen the level of significance to be $\alpha = 0.01, 0.05, 0.10$, or any other value, you can compare it to the p-value of a test and then reject, or not reject, without checking the critical value t_c.

How the p-value is computed depends on the alternative. If t is the calculated value (not the critical value t_c) of the t-statistic with $N - 1$ degrees of freedom, then

- if $H_1 : \mu > c$, $p = $ probability to the right of t
- if $H_1 : \mu < c$, $p = $ probability to the left of t
- if $H_1 : \mu \neq c$, $p = $ *sum* of probabilities to the right of $|t|$ *and* to the left of $-|t|$

The direction of the alternative indicates the tail(s) of the distribution in which the p-value falls.

In Section C.6.5 we used the hip data to test $H_0 : \mu = 16.5$ against $H_1 : \mu > 16.5$. The calculated t-statistic value was $t = 2.5756$. In this case, since the alternative is "greater than" ($>$), the p-value of this test is the probability that a t-random variable with $N - 1 = 49$ degrees of freedom is greater than 2.5756. This probability value cannot be found in the usual t-table of critical values, but it is easily found using the computer. Statistical software packages, and spreadsheets such as Excel, have simple commands to evaluate the *cumulative distribution function* (*cdf*) (see the Probability Primer, Section P.2) for a variety of probability distributions. If $F_X(x)$ is the *cdf* for a random variable X, then for any value $x = c$, $P[X \leq c] = F_X(c)$. Given such a function for the t-distribution, we compute the desired p-value

$$p = P\left(t_{(49)} \geq 2.576\right) = 1 - P\left(t_{(49)} \leq 2.576\right) = 0.0065$$

Given the p-value, we can immediately conclude that at $\alpha = 0.01$ or 0.05 we reject the null hypothesis in favor of the alternative, but if $\alpha = 0.001$ we would not reject the null hypothesis.

The logic of the p-value rule is shown in Figure C.8. If 0.0065 of the probability lies to the right of $t = 2.5756$, then the critical value t_c that leaves a probability of $\alpha = 0.01$ ($t_{(0.99,49)}$) or $\alpha = 0.05$ ($t_{(0.95,49)}$) in the tail must be to the left of 2.5756. In this case, when the p-value $\leq \alpha$, it must be true that $t \geq t_c$, and we should reject the null hypothesis for either of these levels of significance. On the other hand, it must be true that the critical value for $\alpha = 0.001$ must fall to the right of 2.5756, meaning that we should not reject the null hypothesis at this level of significance.

For a two-tail test, the rejection region is in the two tails of the t-distribution, and the p-value must similarly be calculated in the two tails of the distribution. For the hip data,

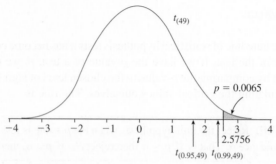

FIGURE *C.8*   *p*-value for a right-tail test.

we tested the null hypothesis $H_0 : \mu = 17$ against $H_1 : \mu \neq 17$, yielding the test statistic value $t = 0.6191$. The *p*-value is

$$p = P[t_{(49)} \geq 0.6191] + P[t_{(49)} \leq -0.6191] = 2 \times 0.2694 = 0.5387$$

Since the *p*-value $= 0.5387 > \alpha = 0.05$, we do not reject the null hypothesis $H_0 : \mu = 17$ at $\alpha = 0.05$ or any other common level of significance. The two-tail *p*-value is shown in Figure C.9.

C.6.8   A COMMENT ON STATING NULL AND ALTERNATIVE HYPOTHESES

A statistical test procedure cannot prove the truth of a null hypothesis. When we fail to reject a null hypothesis, all the hypothesis test can establish is that the information in a sample of data is *compatible* with the null hypothesis. On the other hand, a statistical test can lead us to *reject* the null hypothesis, with only a small probability, α, of rejecting the null hypothesis when it is actually true. Thus rejecting a null hypothesis is a stronger conclusion than failing to reject it.

The null hypothesis is usually stated in such a way that if our theory is correct, then we will reject the null hypothesis. For example, our airplane seat designer has been operating under the assumption (the maintained or null hypothesis) that the population mean hip width is 16.5 inches. Casual observation suggests that people are getting larger all the time. If we are larger, and if the airline wants to continue to accommodate the same percentage of the population, then the seat widths must be increased. This costly change should be undertaken only if there is statistical evidence that the population hip size is indeed larger. When using a hypothesis test we would like to find out whether there is statistical evidence against our current

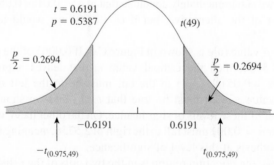

FIGURE *C.9*   The *p*-value for a two-tail test.

"theory," or whether the data are compatible with it. With this goal, we set up the null hypothesis that the population mean is 16.5 inches, $H_0 : \mu = 16.5$, against the alternative that it is greater than 16.5 inches, $H_1 : \mu > 16.5$. In this case, if we reject the null hypothesis, we have shown that there has been a "statistically significant" increase in hip width.

You may view the null hypothesis to be too limited in this case, since it is feasible that the population mean hip width is now smaller than 16.5 inches. The hypothesis test of the null hypothesis $H_0 : \mu \leq 16.5$ against the alternative hypothesis $H_1 : \mu > 16.5$ is exactly the same as the test for $H_0 : \mu = 16.5$ against the alternative hypothesis $H_1 : \mu > 16.5$. The test statistic and rejection region are exactly the same. For a one-tail test you can form the null hypothesis in either of these ways.

Finally, it is important to set up the null and alternative hypotheses before you analyze or even collect the sample of data. Failing to do so can lead to errors in formulating the alternative hypothesis. Suppose that we wish to test whether $\mu > 16.5$ and the sample mean is $\bar{y} = 15.5$. Does that mean we should set up the alternative $\mu < 16.5$, to be consistent with the estimate? The answer is no. The alternative is formed to state the conjecture that we wish to establish, $\mu > 16.5$.

C.6.9 TYPE I AND TYPE II ERRORS

Whenever we reject—or do not reject—a null hypothesis, there is a chance that we may be making a mistake. This is unavoidable. In any hypothesis testing situation, there are two ways that we can make a correct decision and two ways that we can make an incorrect decision.

CORRECT DECISIONS

The null hypothesis is *false* and we decide to *reject* it.

The null hypothesis is *true* and we decide *not* to reject it.

INCORRECT DECISIONS

The null hypothesis is *true* and we decide to *reject* it (a Type I error).

The null hypothesis is *false* and we decide *not* to reject it (a Type II error).

When we reject the null hypothesis we risk what is called a Type I error. The probability of a Type I error is α, the level of significance of the test. When the null hypothesis is true, the t-statistic falls in the rejection region with probability α. Thus hypothesis tests will *reject* a true hypothesis $100\alpha\%$ of the time. The good news here is that we can control the probability of a Type I error by choosing the level of significance of the test, α.

We risk a Type II error when we do not reject the null hypothesis. Hypothesis tests will lead us to fail to reject null hypotheses that are false with a certain probability. The magnitude of the probability of a Type II error is not under our control and cannot be computed, because it depends on the true value of μ, which is unknown. However, we do know that

- The probability of a Type II error varies inversely with the level of significance of the test, α, which is the probability of a Type I error. If you choose to make α smaller, the probability of a Type II error increases.
- If the null hypothesis is $\mu = c$, and if the true (unknown) value of μ is *close* to c, then the probability of a Type II error is high.

- The larger the sample size N, the lower the probability of a Type II error, given a level of Type I error α.

An easy to remember example of the difference between Type I and Type II errors is from the U.S. legal system. In a trial, a person is presumed innocent. This is the "null" hypothesis, the alternative hypothesis being that the person is guilty. If we convict an innocent person, then we have rejected a null hypothesis that is true, committing a Type I error. If we fail to convict a guilty person, failing to reject the false null hypothesis, then we commit a Type II error. Which is the more costly error in this context? Is it better to send an innocent person to jail, or to let a guilty person go free? It is better in this case to make the probability of a Type I error very small.

C.6.10   A Relationship between Hypothesis Testing and Confidence Intervals

There is an algebraic relationship between two-tail hypothesis tests and confidence interval estimates that is sometimes useful. Suppose that we are testing the null hypothesis $H_0 : \mu = c$ against the alternative $H_1 : \mu \neq c$. If we fail to reject the null hypothesis at the α level of significance, then the value c will fall within a $100(1 - \alpha)\%$ confidence interval estimate of μ. Conversely, if we reject the null hypothesis, then c will fall outside the $100(1 - \alpha)\%$ confidence interval estimate of μ. This algebraic relationship is true because we fail to reject the null hypothesis when $-t_c \leq t \leq t_c$, or when

$$-t_c \leq \frac{\overline{Y} - c}{\hat{\sigma}/\sqrt{N}} \leq t_c$$

which when rearranged becomes

$$\overline{Y} - t_c \frac{\hat{\sigma}}{\sqrt{N}} \leq c \leq \overline{Y} + t_c \frac{\hat{\sigma}}{\sqrt{N}}$$

The endpoints of this interval are the same as the endpoints of a $100(1 - \alpha)\%$ confidence interval estimate of μ. Thus for any value of c within the confidence interval, we do not reject $H_0 : \mu = c$ against the alternative $H_1 : \mu \neq c$. For any value of c outside the confidence interval, we reject $H_0 : \mu = c$ and accept the alternative $H_1 : \mu \neq c$.

This relationship can be handy if you are given only a confidence interval and want to determine what the outcome of a two-tail test would be.

C.7 Some Other Useful Tests

In this section we very briefly summarize some additional tests. These tests are not only useful in and of themselves, but also illustrate the use of test statistics with chi-square and F-distributions. These distributions were introduced in Appendix B.3.

C.7.1   Testing the Population Variance

Let Y be a normally distributed random variable, $Y \sim N(\mu, \sigma^2)$. Assume that we have a random sample of size N from this population, $Y_1, Y_2, \ldots, Y_N$. The estimator of the population mean is $\overline{Y} = \Sigma Y_i/N$, and the unbiased estimator of the population variance is $\hat{\sigma}^2 = \Sigma(Y_i - \overline{Y})^2/(N-1)$. To test the null hypothesis $H_0 : \sigma^2 = \sigma_0^2$, we use the test statistic

$$V = \frac{(N-1)\hat{\sigma}^2}{\sigma_0^2} \sim \chi^2_{(N-1)}$$

If the null hypothesis is true, then the test statistic has the indicated chi-square distribution with $N-1$ degrees of freedom. If the alternative hypothesis is $H_1 : \sigma^2 > \sigma_0^2$, then we carry out a one-tail test. If we choose the level of significance $\alpha = 0.05$, then the null hypothesis is rejected if $V \geq \chi^2_{(0.95,N-1)}$, where $\chi^2_{(0.95,N-1)}$ is the 95th percentile of the chi-square distribution with $N-1$ degrees of freedom. These values can be found in Table 3 at the end of this book, or computed using statistical software. If the alternative hypothesis is $H_1 : \sigma^2 \neq \sigma_0^2$, then we carry out a two-tail test, and the null hypothesis is rejected if $V \geq \chi^2_{(0.975,N-1)}$ or if $V \leq \chi^2_{(0.025,N-1)}$. The chi-square distribution is skewed, with a long tail to the right, so we cannot use the properties of symmetry when determining the left- and right-tail critical values.

C.7.2 TESTING THE EQUALITY OF TWO POPULATION MEANS

Let two normal populations be denoted by $N(\mu_1, \sigma_1^2)$ and $N(\mu_2, \sigma_2^2)$. In order to estimate and test the difference between means, $\mu_1 - \mu_2$, we must have random samples of data from each of the two populations. We draw a sample of size N_1 from the first population, and a sample of size N_2 from the second population. Using the first sample we obtain the sample mean $\overline{Y}_1$ and sample variance $\hat{\sigma}_1^2$; from the second sample we obtain $\overline{Y}_2$ and $\hat{\sigma}_2^2$. How the null hypothesis $H_0 : \mu_1 - \mu_2 = c$ is tested depends on whether the two population variances are equal or not.

Case 1: Population variances are equal   If the population variances are equal, so that $\sigma_1^2 = \sigma_2^2 = \sigma_p^2$, then we use information in both samples to estimate the common value σ_p^2. This "pooled variance estimator" is

$$\hat{\sigma}_p^2 = \frac{(N_1 - 1)\hat{\sigma}_1^2 + (N_2 - 1)\hat{\sigma}_2^2}{N_1 + N_2 - 2}$$

If the null hypothesis $H_0 : \mu_1 - \mu_2 = c$ is true, then

$$t = \frac{(\overline{Y}_1 - \overline{Y}_2) - c}{\sqrt{\hat{\sigma}_p^2 \left(\frac{1}{N_1} + \frac{1}{N_2}\right)}} \sim t_{(N_1 + N_2 - 2)}$$

As usual, we can construct a one-sided alternative, such as $H_1 : \mu_1 - \mu_2 > c$, or the two-sided alternative $H_1 : \mu_1 - \mu_2 \neq c$.

Case 2: Population variances are unequal   If the population variances are not equal, then we cannot use the pooled variance estimate. Instead, we use

$$t^* = \frac{(\overline{Y}_1 - \overline{Y}_2) - c}{\sqrt{\frac{\hat{\sigma}_1^2}{N_1} + \frac{\hat{\sigma}_2^2}{N_2}}}$$

The exact distribution of this test statistic is neither normal nor the usual t-distribution. The distribution of t^* can be approximated by a t-distribution with degrees of freedom

$$df = \frac{(\hat{\sigma}_1^2/N_1 + \hat{\sigma}_2^2/N_2)^2}{\left(\dfrac{(\hat{\sigma}_1^2/N_1)^2}{N_1 - 1} + \dfrac{(\hat{\sigma}_2^2/N_2)^2}{N_2 - 1}\right)}$$

This is one of several approximations that appear in the statistics literature, and your software may well use a different one.

C.7.3   TESTING THE RATIO OF TWO POPULATION VARIANCES

Given two normal populations, denoted by $N(\mu_1, \sigma_1^2)$ and $N(\mu_2, \sigma_2^2)$, we can test the null hypothesis $H_0 : \sigma_1^2/\sigma_2^2 = 1$. If the null hypothesis is true, then the population variances are equal. The test statistic is derived from the results that $(N_1 - 1)\hat{\sigma}_1^2/\sigma_1^2 \sim \chi_{(N_1-1)}^2$ and $(N_2 - 1)\hat{\sigma}_2^2/\sigma_2^2 \sim \chi_{(N_2-1)}^2$. In Appendix B.3.8 we define an F random variable, which is formed by taking the ratio of two independent chi-square random variables that have been divided by their degrees of freedom. In this case, the relevant ratio is

$$F = \frac{\dfrac{(N_1 - 1)\hat{\sigma}_1^2/\sigma_1^2}{(N_1 - 1)}}{\dfrac{(N_2 - 1)\hat{\sigma}_2^2/\sigma_2^2}{(N_2 - 1)}} = \frac{\hat{\sigma}_1^2/\sigma_1^2}{\hat{\sigma}_2^2/\sigma_2^2} \sim F_{(N_1-1, N_2-1)}$$

If the null hypothesis $H_0 : \sigma_1^2/\sigma_2^2 = 1$ is true then the test statistic is $F = \hat{\sigma}_1^2/\hat{\sigma}_2^2$, which has an F-distribution with $N_1 - 1$ numerator and $N_2 - 1$ denominator degrees of freedom. If the alternative hypothesis is $H_1 : \sigma_1^2/\sigma_2^2 \neq 1$, then we carry out a two-tail test. If we choose level of significance $\alpha = 0.05$, then we reject the null hypothesis if $F \geq F_{(0.975, N_1-1, N_2-1)}$ or if $F \leq F_{(0.025, N_1-1, N_2-1)}$, where $F_{(\alpha, N_1-1, N_2-1)}$ denotes the 100α-percentile of the F-distribution with the specified degrees of freedom. If the alternative is one-sided, $H_1 : \sigma_1^2/\sigma_2^2 > 1$, then we reject the null hypothesis if $F \geq F_{(0.95, N_1-1, N_2-1)}$.

C.7.4   TESTING THE NORMALITY OF A POPULATION

The tests for means and variances we have developed began with the assumption that the populations were normally distributed. Two questions immediately arise. How well do the tests work when the population is not normal? Can we test for the normality of a population? The answer to the first question is that the tests work pretty well even if the population is not normal, so long as samples are sufficiently large. How large must the samples be? There is no easy answer, since it depends on how "nonnormal" the populations are. The answer to the second question is yes, we can test for normality. Statisticians have been vitally interested in this question for a long time, and a variety of tests have been developed, but the tests and underlying theory are very complicated and far outside the scope of this book.

However, we can present a test that is slightly less ambitious. The normal distribution is symmetric and has a bell shape with a peakedness and tail thickness leading to a kurtosis of three. Thus we can test for departures from normality by checking the skewness and kurtosis from a sample of data. If skewness is not close to zero, and if kurtosis is not close to three, then we reject the normality of the population. In Section C.4.2 we developed sample measures of skewness and kurtosis

$$\widetilde{skewness} = S = \frac{\tilde{\mu}_3}{\tilde{\sigma}^3}$$

$$\widetilde{kurtosis} = K = \frac{\tilde{\mu}_4}{\tilde{\sigma}^4}$$

The **Jarque–Bera** test statistic allows a joint test of these two characteristics,

$$JB = \frac{N}{6}\left(S^2 + \frac{(K-3)^2}{4}\right)$$

If the true distribution is symmetric and has kurtosis three, which includes the normal distribution, then the JB test statistic has a chi-square distribution with two degrees of freedom if the sample size is sufficiently large. If $\alpha = 0.05$, then the critical value of the $\chi^2_{(2)}$ distribution is 5.99. We reject the null hypothesis and conclude that the data are nonnormal if $JB \geq 5.99$. If we reject the null hypothesis, then we know the data have nonnormal characteristics, but we do not know what distribution the population might have.

For the hip data, skewness and kurtosis measures were estimated in Section C.4.3. Plugging these values into the JB test statistic formula we obtain

$$JB = \frac{N}{6}\left(S^2 + \frac{(K-3)^2}{4}\right) = \frac{50}{6}\left((-0.0138)^2 + \frac{(2.3315 - 3)^2}{4}\right) = 0.9325$$

Since $JB = 0.9325$ is less than the critical value 5.99, we conclude that we cannot reject the normality of the hip data. The p-value for this test is the tail area of a $\chi^2_{(2)}$-distribution to the right of 0.9325,

$$p = P\left[\chi^2_{(2)} \geq 0.9325\right] = 0.6273$$

C.8 Introduction to Maximum Likelihood Estimation[1]

Maximum likelihood estimation is a powerful procedure that can be used when the population distribution is known. In this section we introduce the concept with a very simple but revealing example. Consider the following "Wheel of Fortune" game. You are a contestant faced with two wheels, each of which is partly shaded and partly nonshaded (see Figure C.10). Suppose that after spinning a wheel, you win if a pointer is in the shaded area, and you lose if the pointer is in the nonshaded area. On wheel A 25% of the area is shaded so that the probability of winning is $1/4$. On wheel B 75% of the area is shaded so that the probability of winning is $3/4$. The game that you must play is this. One of the wheels is chosen and spun three times, with outcomes WIN, WIN, LOSS. You *do not* know which wheel was chosen, and must pick which wheel was spun. Which would you select?

---

[1] This section contains some advanced material.

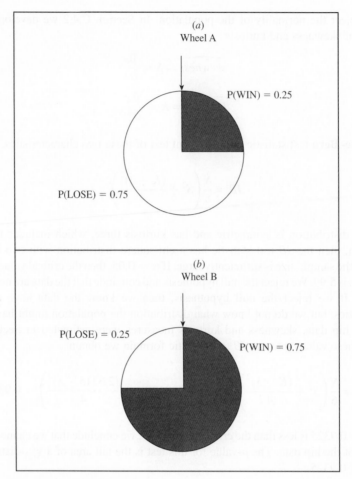

FIGURE $C.10$ Wheel of fortune game.

One intuitive approach is the following: let p denote the probability of winning on one spin of a wheel. Choosing between wheels A and B means choosing between $p = 1/4$ and $p = 3/4$. You are estimating p, but there are only two possible estimates, and you must choose based on the observed data. Let us compute the probability of each sequence of outcomes for each of the wheels.

For wheel A, with $p = 1/4$, the probability of observing WIN, WIN, LOSS is

$$\frac{1}{4} \times \frac{1}{4} \times \frac{3}{4} = \frac{3}{64} = 0.0469$$

That is, the probability, or **likelihood**, of observing the sequence WIN, WIN, LOSS when $p = 1/4$ is 0.0469.

For wheel B, with $p = 3/4$, the probability of observing WIN, WIN, LOSS is

$$\frac{3}{4} \times \frac{3}{4} \times \frac{1}{4} = \frac{9}{64} = 0.1406$$

The probability, or likelihood, of observing the sequence WIN, WIN, LOSS when $p = 3/4$ is 0.1406.

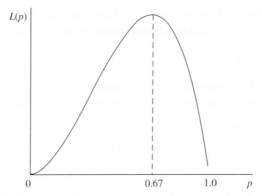

FIGURE **C.11**   A likelihood function.

If we had to choose wheel *A* or *B* based on the available data, we would choose wheel *B* because it has a higher probability of having produced the observed data. It is more *likely* that wheel *B* was spun than wheel *A*, and $\hat{p} = 3/4$ is called the **maximum likelihood estimate** of *p*. The **maximum likelihood principle** seeks the parameter values that maximize the probability, or likelihood, of observing the outcomes actually obtained.

Now suppose *p* can be any probability between zero and one, not just $1/4$ or $3/4$. We have one wheel with a proportion of it shaded, which is the probability of WIN, but we do not know the proportion. In three spins we observe WIN, WIN, LOSS. What is the most likely value of *p*? The probability of observing WIN, WIN, LOSS is the likelihood *L* and is

$$L(p) = p \times p \times (1 - p) = p^2 - p^3 \tag{C.17}$$

The likelihood *L* depends on the unknown probability *p* of a WIN, which is why we have given it the notation $L(p)$, indicating a functional relationship. We would like to find the value of *p* that maximizes the likelihood of observing the outcomes actually obtained. The graph of the likelihood function (C.17) and the choice of *p* that maximizes this function is shown in Figure C.11. The maximizing value is denoted as $\hat{p}$ and is called the maximum likelihood estimate of *p*. To find this value of *p* we can use calculus. Differentiate $L(p)$ with respect to *p*,

$$\frac{dL(p)}{dp} = 2p - 3p^2$$

Set this derivative to zero:

$$2p - 3p^2 = 0 \Rightarrow p(2 - 3p) = 0$$

There are two solutions to this equation, $p = 0$ or $p = 2/3$. The value that maximizes $L(p)$ is $\hat{p} = 2/3$, which is the maximum likelihood estimate. That is, of all possible values of *p*, between zero and one, the value that maximizes the probability of observing two wins and one loss (the order does not matter) is $\hat{p} = 2/3$.

Can we derive a more general formula that can be used for any observed data? In Appendix B.3.1 we introduced the Bernouilli distribution. Let us define the random variable

X that takes the values $x = 1$ (WIN) and $x = 0$ (LOSS) with probabilities p and $1 - p$. The probability function for this random variable can be written in mathematical form as

$$P(X = x) = f(x|p) = p^x(1 - p)^{1-x}, \quad x = 0, 1$$

If we spin the "wheel" N times we observe N sample values $x_1, x_2, \ldots, x_N$. Assuming that the spins are independent, we can form the joint probability function

$$
\begin{aligned}
f(x_1, \ldots, x_N|p) &= f(x_1|p) \times \cdots \times f(x_N|p) \\
&= p^{\Sigma x_i}(1 - p)^{N - \Sigma x_i} \\
&= L(p|x_1, \ldots, x_N)
\end{aligned}
\tag{C.18}
$$

The joint probability function gives the probability of observing a specific set of outcomes, and it is a generalization of (C.17). In the last line we have indicated that the joint probability function is algebraically equivalent to the **likelihood function** $L(p|x_1, \ldots, x_N)$. The notation emphasizes that the likelihood function depends upon the unknown probability p *given* the sample outcomes, which we observe. For notational simplicity we will continue to denote the likelihood function as $L(p)$.

In the "Wheel of Fortune" game, the maximum likelihood estimate is that value of p that maximizes $L(p)$. To find this estimate using calculus we use a trick to simplify the algebra. The value of p that maximizes $L(p) = p^2(1 - p)$ is the same value of p that maximizes the **log-likelihood function** $\ln L(p) = 2\ln(p) + \ln(1 - p)$, where "ln" is the natural logarithm. The plot of the log-likelihood function is shown in Figure C.12. Compare Figures C.11 and C.12. The maximum of the likelihood function is $L(\hat{p}) = 0.1481$. The maximum of the log-likelihood function is $\ln L(\hat{p}) = -1.9095$. Both of these maximum values occur at $\hat{p} = 2/3 = 0.6667$.

This trick works for all likelihood and log-likelihood functions and their parameters, so when you see maximum likelihood estimation being discussed it will always be in terms of maximizing the log-likelihood function. For the general problem we are considering, the log-likelihood function is the logarithm of (C.18)

$$\ln L(p) = \sum_{i=1}^{N} \ln f(x_i|p)$$

$$= \left(\sum_{i=1}^{N} x_i\right)\ln(p) + \left(N - \sum_{i=1}^{N} x_i\right)\ln(1 - p) \tag{C.19}$$

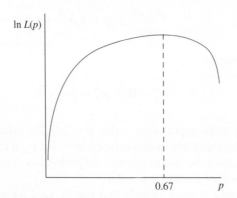

FIGURE $C.12$ A log-likelihood function.

The first derivative is

$$\frac{d \ln L(p)}{dp} = \frac{\sum x_i}{p} - \frac{N - \sum x_i}{1 - p}$$

Setting this to zero and replacing p by $\hat{p}$ to denote the value that maximizes $\ln L(p)$ yields

$$\frac{\sum x_i}{\hat{p}} - \frac{N - \sum x_i}{1 - \hat{p}} = 0$$

To solve this equation, multiply both sides by $\hat{p}(1 - \hat{p})$. This gives

$$(1 - \hat{p})\sum x_i - \hat{p}(N - \sum x_i) = 0$$

Finally, solving for $\hat{p}$ yields

$$\hat{p} = \frac{\sum x_i}{N} = \bar{x} \tag{C.20}$$

The estimator $\hat{p}$ is the **sample proportion**; $\sum x_i$ is the total number of 1s (wins) out of N spins. As you can see, $\hat{p}$ is also the sample mean of x_i. This result is completely general. Any time we have two outcomes that can occur with probabilities p and $1 - p$, then the maximum likelihood estimate based on a sample of N observations is the sample proportion (C.20). This estimation strategy can be used if you are a pollster trying to estimate the proportion of the population intending to vote for candidate A rather than candidate B, a medical researcher who wishes to estimate the proportion of the population having a particular defective gene, or a marketing researcher trying to discover whether the population of customers prefers a blue box or a green box for their morning cereal. Suppose in this latter case that you select 200 cereal consumers at random and ask whether they prefer blue boxes or green. If 75 prefer a blue box, then we would estimate that the population proportion preferring blue is $\hat{p} = \sum x_i/N = 75/200 = 0.375$. Thus, we estimate that 37.5% of the population prefers a blue box.

C.8.1 Inference with Maximum Likelihood Estimators

If we use maximum likelihood estimation, how do we perform hypothesis tests and construct confidence intervals? The answers to these questions are found in some remarkable properties of estimators obtained using maximum likelihood methods. Let us consider a general problem. Let X be a random variable (either discrete or continuous) with a probability density function $f(x|\theta)$, where θ is an unknown parameter. The log-likelihood function, based on a random sample $x_1, \ldots, x_N$ of size N, is

$$\ln L(\theta) = \sum_{i=1}^{N} \ln f(x_i|\theta)$$

If the probability density function of the random variable involved is relatively smooth, and if certain other technical conditions hold, then in large samples the maximum likelihood estimator $\hat{\theta}$ of a parameter θ has a probability distribution that is approximately normal, with expected value θ and a variance $V = \text{var}(\hat{\theta})$ that we will discuss in a moment. That is, we can say

$$\hat{\theta} \overset{a}{\sim} N(\theta, V) \tag{C.21}$$

where the symbol $\overset{a}{\sim}$ denotes "asymptotically distributed." The word "asymptotic" refers to estimator properties when the sample size N becomes large, or as $N \to \infty$. To say that an estimator is asymptotically normal means that its probability distribution, which may be unknown when samples are small, becomes approximately normal in large samples. This is analogous to the central limit theorem we discussed in Section C.3.4.

Based on the normality result in (C.21) it will not surprise you that we can immediately construct a t-statistic and obtain both a confidence interval and a test statistic from it. Specifically, if we wish to test the null hypothesis $H_0 : \theta = c$ against a one-tail or two-tail alternative hypothesis, then we can use the test statistic

$$t = \frac{\hat{\theta} - c}{\operatorname{se}(\hat{\theta})} \overset{a}{\sim} t_{(N-1)} \tag{C.22}$$

If the null hypothesis is true, then this t-statistic has a distribution that can be approximated by a t-distribution with $N - 1$ degrees of freedom in large samples. The mechanics of carrying out the hypothesis test are exactly those in Section C.6.

If t_c denotes the $100(1 - \alpha/2)$-percentile $t_{(1-\alpha/2, N-1)}$, then a $100(1 - \alpha)\%$ confidence interval for θ is

$$\hat{\theta} \pm t_c \operatorname{se}(\hat{\theta})$$

This confidence interval is interpreted just like those in Section C.5.

REMARK: These asymptotic results in (C.21) and (C.22) hold only in large samples. We have indicated that the distribution of the test statistic can be approximated by a t-distribution with $N - 1$ degrees of freedom. If N is truly large, then the $t_{(N-1)}$-distribution converges to the standard normal distribution $N(0, 1)$ and the $100(1 - \alpha/2)$-percentile value $t_{(1-\alpha/2, N-1)}$ converges to the corresponding percentile from the standard normal distribution. Asymptotic results are used, rightly or wrongly, when the sample size N may not be large. We prefer using the t-distribution critical values, which are adjusted for small samples by the degrees of freedom correction, when obtaining interval estimates and carrying out hypothesis tests.

C.8.2 THE VARIANCE OF THE MAXIMUM LIKELIHOOD ESTIMATOR

A key ingredient in both the test statistic and confidence interval expressions is the standard error $\operatorname{se}(\hat{\theta})$. Where does this come from? Standard errors are square roots of estimated variances. The part we have delayed discussing until now is how we find the variance of the maximum likelihood estimator, $V = \operatorname{var}(\hat{\theta})$. The variance V is given by the inverse of the negative expectation of the second derivative of the log-likelihood function,

$$V = \operatorname{var}(\hat{\theta}) = \left[-E\left(\frac{d^2 \ln L(\theta)}{d\theta^2} \right) \right]^{-1} \tag{C.23}$$

This looks quite intimidating, and you can see why we put it off. What does this mean? First of all, the second derivative measures the curvature of the log-likelihood function. A second

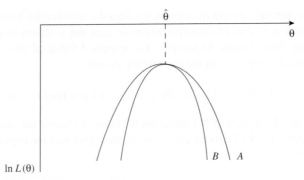

FIGURE **C.13** Two log-likelihood functions.

derivative is literally the derivative of the derivative. A single derivative, the first, measures the slope of a function or the rate of change of the function. The second derivative measures the rate of change of the slope. To obtain a maximum of the log-likelihood function, it must be an "inverted bowl" shape, like those shown in Figure C.13.

At any point to the left of the maximum point, the slope of the log-likelihood function is positive. At any point to the right of the maximum, the slope is negative. As we progress from left to right the slope is *decreasing* (becoming less positive or more negative), so that the second derivative must be negative. A larger absolute magnitude of the second derivative implies a more rapidly changing slope, indicating a more sharply curved log-likelihood. This is important. In Figure C.13 the two log-likelihood functions A and B have the same maximizing value $\hat{\theta}$. Imagine yourself a climber who is trekking up one of these mountains. For which mountain is the summit most clearly defined? For log-likelihood B, the summit is a sharp peak, and its maximum is more easily located than that for log-likelihood A. The sharper peak has less "wiggle room" at the summit. The smaller amount of wiggle room means that there is less uncertainty as to the location of the maximizing value $\hat{\theta}$; in estimation terminology, less uncertainty means greater precision, and a smaller variance. The more sharply curved log-likelihood function, the one whose second derivative is larger in absolute magnitude, leads to more precise maximum likelihood estimation, and to a maximum likelihood estimator with smaller variance. Thus the variance V of the maximum likelihood estimator is inversely related to the (negative) second derivative. The expected value "E" must be present because this quantity depends on the data and is thus random, so we average over all possible data outcomes.

C.8.3   THE DISTRIBUTION OF THE SAMPLE PROPORTION

It is time for an example. At the beginning of Section C.8 we introduced a random variable X that takes the values $x = 1$ and $x = 0$ with probabilities p and $1 - p$. It has log-likelihood given in (C.19). In this problem the parameter θ that we are estimating is the population proportion p, the proportion of $x = 1$ values in the population. We already know that the maximum likelihood estimator of p is the sample proportion $\hat{p} = \sum x_i / N$. The second derivative of the log-likelihood function (C.19) is

$$\frac{d^2 \ln L(p)}{dp^2} = -\frac{\sum x_i}{p^2} - \frac{N - \sum x_i}{(1-p)^2} \tag{C.24}$$

To calculate the variance of the maximum likelihood estimator we need the "expected value" of expression (C.24). In the expectation we treat the x_i values as random because these values vary from sample to sample. The expected value of this discrete random variable is obtained using (P.9) in the probability primer:

$$E(x_i) = 1 \times P(x_i = 1) + 0 \times P(x_i = 0) = 1 \times p + 0 \times (1 - p) = p$$

Then, using a generalization of (P.16) (the expected value of a sum is the sum of the expected values and constants can be factored out of expectations) we find the expected value of the second derivative as

$$E\left(\frac{d^2 \ln L(p)}{dp^2}\right) = -\frac{\sum E(x_i)}{p^2} - \frac{N - \sum E(x_i)}{(1 - p)^2}$$

$$= -\frac{Np}{p^2} - \frac{N - Np}{(1 - p)^2}$$

$$= -\frac{N}{p(1 - p)}$$

The variance of the sample proportion, which is the maximum likelihood estimator of p, is then

$$V = \text{var}(\hat{p}) = \left[-E\left(\frac{d^2 \ln L(p)}{dp^2}\right)\right]^{-1} = \frac{p(1 - p)}{N}$$

The asymptotic distribution of the sample proportion, which is valid in large samples, is

$$\hat{p} \overset{a}{\sim} N\left(p, \frac{p(1 - p)}{N}\right)$$

To estimate the variance V we must replace the true population proportion by its estimate,

$$\hat{V} = \frac{\hat{p}(1 - \hat{p})}{N}$$

The standard error that we need for hypothesis testing and confidence interval estimation is the square root of this estimated variance:

$$\text{se}(\hat{p}) = \sqrt{\hat{V}} = \sqrt{\frac{\hat{p}(1 - \hat{p})}{N}}$$

As a numerical example, suppose a cereal company CEO conjectures that 40% of the population prefers a blue box. To test this hypothesis, we construct the null hypothesis $H_0 : p = 0.4$ and use the two-tail alternative $H_1 : p \neq 0.4$. If the null hypothesis is true, then the test statistic $t = (\hat{p} - 0.4)/\text{se}(\hat{p}) \overset{a}{\sim} t_{(N-1)}$. For a sample of size $N = 200$ the critical value from the t-distribution is $t_c = t_{(0.975, 199)} = 1.96$. Therefore we reject the null hypothesis if the calculated value of $t \geq 1.96$ or $t \leq -1.96$. If 75 of the respondents prefer a blue box, then the sample proportion is $\hat{p} = 75/200 = 0.375$. The standard error of this estimate is

$$\text{se}(\hat{p}) = \sqrt{\frac{\hat{p}(1 - \hat{p})}{N}} = \sqrt{\frac{0.375 \times 0.625}{200}} = 0.0342$$

The value of the test statistic is

$$t = \frac{\hat{p} - 0.4}{\text{se}(\hat{p})} = \frac{0.375 - 0.4}{0.0342} = -0.7303$$

This value is in the nonrejection region, $-1.96 < t = -0.7303 < 1.96$, so we do not reject the null hypothesis that $p = 0.4$. The sample data are compatible with the conjecture that 40% of the population prefer a blue box.

The 95% interval estimate of the population proportion p who prefer a blue box is

$$\hat{p} \pm 1.96\,\text{se}(\hat{p}) = 0.375 \pm 1.96(0.0342) = [0.3075, 0.4425]$$

We estimate that between 30.8% and 44.3% of the population prefer a blue box.

C.8.4 ASYMPTOTIC TEST PROCEDURES

When using maximum likelihood estimation, there are three test procedures that can be used, with the choice depending on which one is most convenient in a given case. The tests are *asymptotically equivalent* and will give the same result in large samples. Suppose that we are testing the null hypothesis $H_0 : \theta = c$ against the alternative hypothesis $H_1 : \theta \neq c$. In (C.22) we have the *t*-statistic for carrying out the test. How does this test really work? Basically it is measuring the distance $\hat{\theta} - c$ between the estimate of θ and the hypothesized value c. This distance is normalized by the standard error of $\hat{\theta}$ to adjust for how precisely we have estimated θ. If the distance between the estimate $\hat{\theta}$ and the hypothesized value c is large, then that is taken as evidence against the null hypothesis, and if the distance is large enough, we conclude that the null hypothesis is not true.

There are other ways to measure the distance between $\hat{\theta}$ and c that can be used to construct test statistics. Each of the three testing principles takes a different approach to measuring the distance between $\hat{\theta}$ and the hypothesized value.

C.8.4a The Likelihood Ratio (*LR*) Test
Consider Figure C.14. A log-likelihood function is shown, along with the maximum likelihood estimate $\hat{\theta}$ and the hypothesized value c. Note that the distance between $\hat{\theta}$ and c is also reflected by the distance between the log-likelihood function value evaluated at the maximum likelihood estimate $\ln L(\hat{\theta})$ and the log-likelihood function value evaluated at

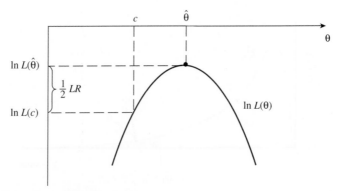

FIGURE *C.14*   The likelihood ratio test.

the hypothesized value $\ln L(c)$. We have labeled the difference between these two log-likelihood values $(1/2)\,LR$ for a reason that will become clear. If the estimate $\hat{\theta}$ is close to c, then the difference between the log-likelihood values will be small. If $\hat{\theta}$ is far from c, then the difference between the log-likelihood values will be large. This observation leads us to the **likelihood ratio statistic**, which is twice the difference between $\ln L(\hat{\theta})$ and $\ln L(c)$,

$$LR = 2[\ln L(\hat{\theta}) - \ln L(c)] \tag{C.25}$$

Based on some advanced statistical theory, it can be shown that if the null hypothesis is true, then the LR test statistic has a *chi-square* distribution (see Appendix B.3.6) with $J = 1$ degree of freedom. In more general contexts J is the number of hypotheses being tested and it can be greater than 1. If the null hypothesis is not true, then the LR test statistic becomes large. We reject the null hypothesis at the α level of significance if $LR \geq \chi^2_{(1-\alpha, J)}$, where $\chi^2_{(1-\alpha, J)}$ is the $100(1 - \alpha)$ percentile of a chi-square distribution with J degrees of freedom, as shown in Figure C.15. The 90th, 95th, and 99th percentile values of the chi-square distribution for various degrees of freedom are given in Table 3 at the end of the book.

When estimating a population proportion p the log-likelihood function is given by (C.19). The value of p that maximizes this function is $\hat{p} = \sum x_i / N$. Thus, the maximum value of the log-likelihood function is

$$\begin{aligned}
\ln L(\hat{p}) &= \left(\sum_{i=1}^{N} x_i\right) \ln \hat{p} + \left(N - \sum_{i=1}^{N} x_i\right) \ln(1 - \hat{p}) \\
&= N\hat{p} \ln \hat{p} + (N - N\hat{p}) \ln(1 - \hat{p}) \\
&= N[\hat{p} \ln \hat{p} + (1 - \hat{p}) \ln(1 - \hat{p})]
\end{aligned}$$

where we have used the fact that $\sum x_i = N\hat{p}$. For our cereal box problem, $\hat{p} = 0.375$ and $N = 200$, so we have

$$\ln L(\hat{p}) = 200[0.375 \times \ln(0.375) + (1 - 0.375)\ln(1 - 0.375)]$$
$$= -132.3126$$

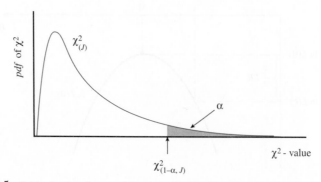

FIGURE C.15   Critical value from a chi-square distribution.

The value of the log-likelihood function assuming $H_0 : p = 0.4$ is true is

$$\ln L(0.4) = \left(\sum_{i=1}^{N} x_i\right)\ln(0.4) + \left(N - \sum_{i=1}^{N} x_i\right)\ln(1 - 0.4)$$

$$= 75 \times \ln(0.4) + (200 - 75) \times \ln(0.6)$$

$$= -132.5750$$

The problem is to assess whether -132.3126 is significantly different from -132.5750. The *LR* test statistic (C.25) is

$$LR = 2[\ln L(\hat{p}) - \ln L(0.4)] = 2 \times \left(-132.3126 - (-132.575)\right) = 0.5247$$

If the null hypothesis $p = 0.4$ is true, then the *LR* test statistic has a $\chi^2_{(1)}$-distribution. If we choose $\alpha = 0.05$, then the test critical value is $\chi^2_{(0.95,1)} = 3.84$, the 95th percentile from the $\chi^2_{(1)}$ distribution. Since $0.5247 < 3.84$ we do not reject the null hypothesis.

C.8.4b   The Wald Test

In Figure C.14 it is clear that the distance $(1/2) LR$ will depend on the curvature of the log-likelihood function. In Figure C.16 we show two log-likelihood functions with the hypothesized value c and the distances $(1/2) LR$ for each of the log-likelihoods. The log-likelihoods have the same maximum value $\ln L(\hat{\theta})$, but the values of the log-likelihood evaluated at the hypothesized value c are different.

The distance $\hat{\theta} - c$ translates into a larger value of $(1/2) LR$ for the more highly curved log-likelihood, *B*, so it seems reasonable to construct a test measure by weighting the distance $\hat{\theta} - c$ by the magnitude of the log-likelihood's curvature, which we measure by the negative of its second derivative. This is exactly what the Wald statistic does:

$$W = (\hat{\theta} - c)^2 \left[-\frac{d^2 \ln L(\theta)}{d\theta^2} \right] \tag{C.26}$$

The value of the Wald statistic is larger for log-likelihood function *B* (more curved) than log-likelihood function *A* (less curved).

If the null hypothesis is true, then the Wald statistic (C.26) has a $\chi^2_{(1)}$-distribution, and we reject the null hypothesis if $W \geq \chi^2_{(1-\alpha,1)}$. In more general situations we may test $J > 1$ hypotheses jointly, in which case we work with a chi-square distribution with J degrees of freedom, as shown in Figure C.15.

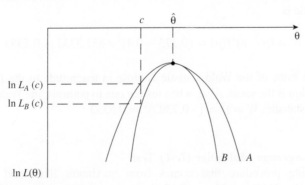

FIGURE **C.16**   The Wald statistic.

There is a linkage between the curvature of the log-likelihood function and the precision of maximum likelihood estimation. The greater the curvature of the log-likelihood function, the smaller the variance V in (C.23) and the more precise maximum likelihood estimation becomes, meaning that we have more **information** about the unknown parameter θ. Conversely, the more information we have about θ, the smaller the variance of the maximum likelihood estimator. Using this idea we define an information measure to be the reciprocal of the variance V,

$$I(\theta) = -E\left[\frac{d^2 \ln L(\theta)}{d\theta^2}\right] = V^{-1} \tag{C.27}$$

As the notation indicates the information measure $I(\theta)$ is a function of the parameter θ. Substitute the information measure for the second derivative in the Wald statistic in (C.26) to obtain

$$W = (\hat{\theta} - c)^2 I(\theta) \tag{C.28}$$

In large samples the two versions of the Wald statistic are the same. An interesting connection here is obtained by rewriting (C.28) as

$$W = (\hat{\theta} - c)^2 V^{-1} = (\hat{\theta} - c)^2 / V \tag{C.29}$$

To implement the Wald test, we use the estimated variance

$$\hat{V} = [I(\hat{\theta})]^{-1} \tag{C.30}$$

Then, taking the square root, we obtain the t-statistic in (C.22),

$$\sqrt{W} = \frac{\hat{\theta} - c}{\sqrt{\hat{V}}} = \frac{\hat{\theta} - c}{\mathrm{se}(\hat{\theta})} = t$$

That is, the t-test is also a Wald test.

In our blue box–green box example, we know that the maximum likelihood estimate $\hat{p} = 0.375$. To implement the Wald test we calculate

$$I(\hat{p}) = \hat{V}^{-1} = \frac{N}{\hat{p}(1 - \hat{p})} = \frac{200}{0.375(1 - 0.375)} = 853.3333$$

where $V = p(1 - p)/N$ and $\hat{V}$ were obtained in Section C.7.3. Then the calculated value of the Wald statistic is

$$W = (\hat{p} - c)^2 I(\hat{p}) = (0.375 - 0.4)^2 \times 853.3333 = 0.5333$$

In this case the value of the Wald statistic is close in magnitude to the *LR* statistic and the test conclusion is the same. Also, when testing one hypothesis, the Wald statistic is the square of the t-statistic, $W = t^2 = (-0.7303)^2 = 0.5333$

C.8.4c   The Lagrange Multiplier (*LM*) Test
The third testing procedure that comes from maximum likelihood theory is the Lagrange multiplier (*LM*) test. Figure C.17 illustrates another way to measure the distance

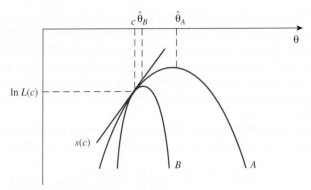

FIGURE C.17   Motivating the Lagrange multiplier test.

between $\hat{\theta}$ and c. The slope of the log-likelihood function, which is sometimes called the *score*, is

$$s(\theta) = \frac{d \ln L(\theta)}{d\theta} \tag{C.31}$$

The slope of the log-likelihood function depends on the value of θ, as our function notation $s(\theta)$ indicates. The slope of the log-likelihood function at the maximizing value is zero, $s(\hat{\theta}) = 0$. The *LM* test examines the slope of the log-likelihood function at the point c. The logic of the test is that if $\hat{\theta}$ is close to c then the slope $s(c)$ of the log-likelihood function evaluated at c should be close to zero. In fact testing the null hypothesis $\theta = c$ is equivalent to testing $s(c) = 0$.

The difference between c and the maximum likelihood estimate $\hat{\theta}_B$ (maximizing $\ln L_B$) is smaller than the difference between c and $\hat{\theta}_A$. In contrast to the Wald test, more curvature in the log-likelihood function implies a smaller difference between the maximum likelihood estimate and c. If we use the information measure $I(\theta)$ as our measure of curvature (more curvature means more information), the Lagrange multiplier test statistic can be written as

$$LM = \frac{[s(c)]^2}{I(\theta)} = [s(c)]^2 [I(\theta)]^{-1} \tag{C.32}$$

The *LM* statistic for log-likelihood function A (less curved) is greater than the *LM* statistic for log-likelihood function B (more curved). If the null hypothesis is true, *LM* test statistic (C.32) has a $\chi^2_{(1)}$-distribution, and the rejection region is the same as for the *LR* and Wald tests. The *LM*, *LR*, and Wald tests are asymptotically equivalent and will lead to the same conclusion in sufficiently large samples.

In order to implement the *LM* test we can evaluate the information measure at the point $\theta = c$, so that it becomes

$$LM = [s(c)]^2 [I(c)]^{-1}$$

In cases in which the maximum likelihood estimate is difficult to obtain (which it can be in more complex problems) the *LM* test has an advantage because $\hat{\theta}$ is not required. On the other hand, the Wald test in (C.28) uses the information measure evaluated at the maximum likelihood estimate $\hat{\theta}$,

$$W = (\hat{\theta} - c)^2 I(\hat{\theta})$$

It is preferred when the maximum likelihood estimate and its variance are easily obtained. The likelihood ratio test statistic (C.25) requires calculation of the log-likelihood function at both the maximum likelihood estimate and the hypothesized value c. As noted, the three tests are asymptotically equivalent, and the choice of which to use is often made on the basis of convenience. In complex situations, however, the rule of convenience may not be a good one. The likelihood ratio test is relatively reliable in most circumstances, so if you are in doubt, it is a safe one to use.

In the blue box–green box example, the value of the score, based on the first derivative shown just below (C.19), evaluated at the hypothesized value $c = 0.4$ is

$$s(0.4) = \frac{\sum x_i}{c} - \frac{N - \sum x_i}{1 - c} = \frac{75}{0.4} - \frac{200 - 75}{1 - 0.4} = -20.8333$$

The calculated information measure is

$$I(0.4) = \frac{N}{c(1 - c)} = \frac{200}{0.4(1 - 0.4)} = 833.3333$$

The value of the LM test statistic is

$$LM = [s(0.4)]^2 [I(0.4)]^{-1} = [-20.8333]^2 [833.3333]^{-1} = 0.5208$$

Thus, in our example, the values of the LR, Wald, and LM test statistics are very similar and give the same conclusion. This was to be expected, since the sample size $N = 200$ is large, and the problem is a simple one.

C.9 Algebraic Supplements

C.9.1 Derivation of Least Squares Estimator

In this section we illustrate how to use the least squares principle to obtain the sample mean as an estimator of the population mean. Represent a sample of data as $y_1, y_2, \ldots, y_N$. The population mean is $E(Y) = \mu$. The least squares principle says to find the value of μ that minimizes

$$S = \sum_{i=1}^{N} (y_i - \mu)^2$$

where S is the sum of squared deviations of the data values from μ.

The motivation for this approach can be deduced from the following example. Suppose you are going shopping at a number of shops along a certain street. Your plan is to shop at one store and return to your car to deposit your purchases. Then you visit a second store and return again to your car, and so on. After visiting each shop you return to your car. Where would you park to minimize the total amount of walking between your car and the shops you visit? You want to minimize the *distance* traveled. Think of the street along which you shop as a number line. The Euclidean distance between a shop located at y_i and your car at point μ is

$$d_i = \sqrt{(y_i - \mu)^2}$$

The squared distance, which is mathematically more convenient to work with, is

$$d_i^2 = (y_i - \mu)^2$$

To minimize the total squared distance between your parking spot μ and all the shops located at $y_1, y_2, \ldots, y_N$ you would minimize

$$S(\mu) = \sum_{i=1}^{N} d_i^2 = \sum_{i=1}^{N} (y_i - \mu)^2$$

which is the sum of squares function. Thus the least squares principle is really the least *squared distance* principle.

Since the values of y_i are known given the sample, the sum of squares function $S(\mu)$ is a function of the unknown parameter μ. Multiplying out the sum of squares, we have

$$S(\mu) = \sum_{i=1}^{N} y_i^2 - 2\mu \sum_{i=1}^{N} y_i + N\mu^2 = a_0 - 2a_1\mu + a_2\mu^2$$

For the data in Table C.1 we have

$$a_0 = \Sigma y_i^2 = 14880.1909, \quad a_1 = \Sigma y_i = 857.9100, \quad a_2 = N = 50$$

The plot of the sum of squares parabola is shown in Figure C.18. The minimizing value appears to be a bit larger than 17 in the figure. Now we will determine the minimizing value exactly.

The value of μ that minimizes $S(\mu)$ is the "least squares estimate." From calculus, we know that the minimum of the function occurs where its slope is zero. The function's

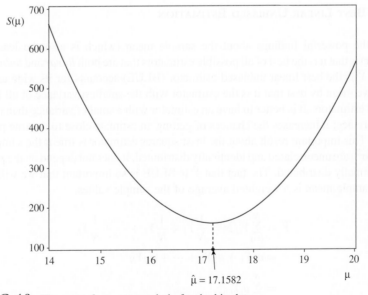

FIGURE *C.18*   The sum of squares parabola for the hip data.

derivative gives its slope, so by equating the first derivative of $S(\mu)$ to zero and solving, we can obtain the minimizing value exactly. The derivative of $S(\mu)$ is

$$\frac{dS(\mu)}{d\mu} = -2a_1 + 2a_2\mu$$

Setting the derivative to zero determines the least squares estimate of μ, which we denote as $\hat{\mu}$. Setting the derivative to zero,

$$-2a_1 + 2a_2\hat{\mu} = 0$$

Solving for $\hat{\mu}$ yields the formula for the least squares estimate,

$$\hat{\mu} = \frac{a_1}{a_2} = \frac{\sum\limits_{i=1}^{N} y_i}{N} = \bar{y}$$

Thus, the least squares estimate of the population mean is the sample mean, $\bar{y}$. This formula can be used in general, for any sample values that might be obtained, meaning that the least squares estimator is

$$\hat{\mu} = \frac{\sum\limits_{i=1}^{N} Y_i}{N} = \bar{Y}$$

For the hip data in Table C.1

$$\hat{\mu} = \frac{\sum\limits_{i=1}^{N} y_i}{N} = \frac{857.9100}{50} = 17.1582$$

Thus, we estimate that the average hip size in the population is 17.1582 inches.

C.9.2   BEST LINEAR UNBIASED ESTIMATION

One of the powerful findings about the sample mean (which is also the least squares estimator) is that it is the best of all possible estimators that are both *linear* and *unbiased*. The fact that $\bar{Y}$ is the best linear unbiased estimator (BLUE) accounts for its wide use. In this context we mean by best that it is the estimator with the smallest variance of all linear and unbiased estimators. It is better to have an estimator with a smaller variance than one with a larger variance; it increases the chances of getting an estimate close to the true population mean μ. This important result about the least squares estimator is true *if* the sample values $Y_i \sim (\mu, \sigma^2)$ are uncorrelated and identically distributed. It does not depend on the population being normally distributed. The fact that $\bar{Y}$ is BLUE is so important that we will prove it.

The sample mean is a weighted average of the sample values,

$$\bar{Y} = \sum_{i=1}^{N} Y_i/N = \frac{1}{N}Y_1 + \frac{1}{N}Y_2 + \cdots + \frac{1}{N}Y_N$$
$$= a_1 Y_1 + a_2 Y_2 + \cdots + a_N Y_N$$
$$= \sum_{i=1}^{N} a_i Y_i$$

where the weights $a_i = 1/N$. Weighted averages are also called linear combinations, so we call the sample mean a **linear estimator**. In fact, any estimator that can be written like $\sum_{i=1}^{N} a_i Y_i$ is a linear estimator. For example, suppose the weights a_i^* are constants different from $a_i = 1/N$. Then we can define another linear estimator of μ as

$$\tilde{Y} = \sum_{i=1}^{N} a_i^* Y_i$$

To ensure that $\tilde{Y}$ is different from $\overline{Y}$, let us define

$$a_i^* = a_i + c_i = \frac{1}{N} + c_i$$

where c_i are constants that are not all zero. Thus,

$$\begin{aligned}
\tilde{Y} &= \sum_{i=1}^{N} a_i^* Y_i = \sum_{i=1}^{N} \left(\frac{1}{N} + c_i\right) Y_i \\
&= \sum_{i=1}^{N} \frac{1}{N} Y_i + \sum_{i=1}^{N} c_i Y_i \\
&= \overline{Y} + \sum_{i=1}^{N} c_i Y_i
\end{aligned}$$

The expected value of the new estimator $\tilde{Y}$ is

$$\begin{aligned}
E[\tilde{Y}] &= E\left[\overline{Y} + \sum_{i=1}^{N} c_i Y_i\right] = \mu + \sum_{i=1}^{N} c_i E[Y_i] \\
&= \mu + \mu \sum_{i=1}^{N} c_i
\end{aligned}$$

The estimator $\tilde{Y}$ is not unbiased unless $\sum c_i = 0$. We want to compare the sample mean to other linear and unbiased estimators, so we will assume that $\sum c_i = 0$ holds. Now we find the variance of $\tilde{Y}$. The linear unbiased estimator with the smaller variance will be best.

$$\begin{aligned}
\mathrm{var}(\tilde{Y}) &= \mathrm{var}\left(\sum_{i=1}^{N} a_i^* Y_i\right) = \mathrm{var}\left(\sum_{i=1}^{N} \left(\frac{1}{N} + c_i\right) Y_i\right) = \sum_{i=1}^{N} \left(\frac{1}{N} + c_i\right)^2 \mathrm{var}(Y_i) \\
&= \sigma^2 \sum_{i=1}^{N} \left(\frac{1}{N} + c_i\right)^2 = \sigma^2 \sum_{i=1}^{N} \left(\frac{1}{N^2} + \frac{2}{N} c_i + c_i^2\right) = \sigma^2 \left(\frac{1}{N} + \frac{2}{N} \sum_{i=1}^{N} c_i + \sum_{i=1}^{N} c_i^2\right) \\
&= \sigma^2/N + \sigma^2 \sum_{i=1}^{N} c_i^2 \qquad \left(\text{since } \sum_{i=1}^{N} c_i = 0\right) \\
&= \mathrm{var}(\overline{Y}) + \sigma^2 \sum_{i=1}^{N} c_i^2
\end{aligned}$$

It follows that the variance of $\tilde{Y}$ must be greater than the variance of $\overline{Y}$, unless all the c_i values are zero, in which case $\tilde{Y} = \overline{Y}$.

C.10 Kernel Density Estimator

As econometricians, we work with data that are drawings from unknown distributions. For example, Figure C.19 shows the empirical distributions of two datasets, presented here as histograms. The variables X and Y are in the file *kernel.dat*. The problem before us is to estimate the density functions that yielded the observations. Knowledge about the distributions is important for statistical inference.

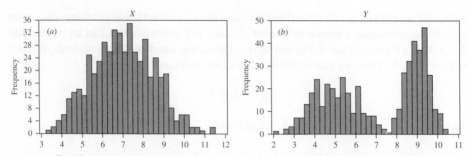

FIGURE C.19   Histograms of Variables (*a*) unimodal variable *X* (*b*) bimodal variable *Y.*

There are two main ways to estimate the distribution. We can use a parametric density estimator, or we can use a nonparametric kernel density estimator. In the **parametric approach**, we rely on density functions with well-defined functional forms characterized by parameters. For example, the normal probability density distribution $f(\cdot)$ has a specific functional form defined by two parameters—the mean μ and the standard deviation σ:

$$f(x|\mu, \sigma) = \frac{1}{\sigma\sqrt{2\pi}}\exp\left(-\frac{1}{2}\left(\frac{x-\mu}{\sigma}\right)^2\right)$$

Once we have estimates of the mean and the standard deviation, $\hat{\mu}$ and $\hat{\sigma}$, we plug these into the normal density function formula to obtain

$$\widehat{f(x)} = \frac{1}{\hat{\sigma}\sqrt{2\pi}}\exp\left(-\frac{1}{2}\left(\frac{x-\hat{\mu}}{\hat{\sigma}}\right)^2\right)$$

Figure C.20 shows our application of this approach; the generated normal density functions are superimposed onto the histograms of the data. We have applied this parametric approach in the discussion about the Central Limit Theorem (C.3.4) and in discussion about ARCH models (Chapter 14).

The histogram of the variable *X*, on the left in Figure C.20, is unimodal, and the normal distribution appears to fit the shape of the data well. In contrast, the histogram of the variable *Y* on the right in Figure C.20 is bimodal, and the normal distribution is a poor representation of the underlying density function. We could try fitting the data with other parametric distributional forms, but rather than do that, let us adopt a nonparametric kernel density estimator to capture the shape of the data in a smooth continuous form.

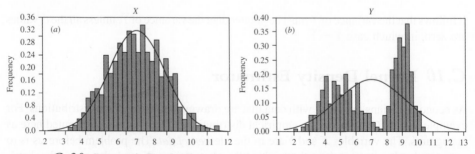

FIGURE C.20   Parametric Density Estimator (*a*) unimodal variable *X* (*b*) bimodal variable *Y.*

Nonparametric methods do not require specific functional forms (e.g., the normal distribution formula) to generate the distribution. Instead, smoothing functions, called **kernels**, are used to "fit" the shape of the distribution of the data.

The logic of the nonparametric approach can be grasped intuitively by thinking about how we set up histograms. Figure C.21 shows two histograms for the dataset Y. The one on the left has nine bins (i.e., the rectangles in the histogram) with bin width = 1 whereas the one on the right has many bins each with bin width = 0.1. The histogram with less bins has the higher frequency per bin as more observations fall into the larger bin width. More specifically, if x_k is the midpoint of the kth bin and h is the bin width, the range of values in the bin is $x_k \pm h/2$, and the frequency count n_k is the number of observations which falls in that range. The sum of all frequencies equals the sample size n, while the sum of the areas equals nh, since each area is $n_k h$ and $\Sigma_k n_k = n$. Note, too, that the shapes of the histograms are similar, but that the one with the larger bin width is "smoother" (fewer spikes and dips).

We can think of the histogram as a density function estimator $\widehat{f(x)}$, where x takes values over the domain of x and

$$\widehat{f(x)} = \frac{1}{nh} \sum_{i=1}^{n} 1(A_i)$$

The expression $1(A_i)$ is an **indicator function** taking on the value of 1 if A_i is true; A_i is the condition that x_i is in the same bin as x. For example, suppose we wish to find $\widehat{f(x)}$ for an x that lies in the kth bin. Then, A_i is true for all x_i such that $x_k - h/2 < x_i < x_k + h/2$. Thus, in the kth bin, $\sum_{i=1}^{n} 1(A_i) = n_k$, and the histogram density estimator for all x in the kth bin is $\widehat{f(x)} = n_k/nh$. The divisor nh ensures that the bin areas sum to one.

Now consider another density estimator where, instead of having a number of a predetermined bins with midpoints x_k, we consider a bin with midpoint x and count the number of observations in the range $x \pm h/2$. If we repeat this process for all values of x, we can picture it as creating an infinite number of overlapping bins along the domain of x. In this case the density estimator is given by

$$\widehat{f(x)} = \frac{1}{nh} \sum_{i=1}^{n} 1\left(x - \frac{h}{2} < x_i < x + \frac{h}{2} \right) = \frac{1}{nh} \sum_{i=1}^{n} 1\left(-\frac{1}{2} < \frac{x_i - x}{h} < \frac{1}{2} \right)$$

In practice, as you sum over the observations, the indicator function ensures that you only "count" the relevant observations. However, this density function will not be smooth, because each observation is given a weight of either zero or one—that is, it is either in or out, according to the condition specified in the indicator function.

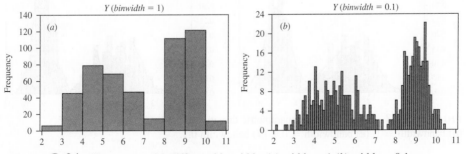

FIGURE **C.21** Histograms with different bin widths (a) width = 1 (b) width = 0.1.

Suppose we now replace this simple counting rule with a more sophisticated weighting function known as a **kernel**:

$$\widehat{f(x)} = \frac{1}{nh} \sum_{i=1}^{n} K\left(\frac{x_i - x}{h}\right)$$

where K is a kernel, h is a smoothing parameter called the **bandwidth**, and x is any value over the domain of possible values. There are many kernel functions; one of them is Gaussian and is described as follows:

$$K\left(\frac{x_i - x}{h}\right) = \frac{1}{\sqrt{2\pi}} \exp\left(-\frac{1}{2}\left(\frac{x_i - x}{h}\right)^2\right)$$

Figure C.22 shows the application of this kernel estimator to variable Y in *kernel.dat* with four different bandwidths. Note how the shape of the density function is controlled by the bandwidth. The smaller the bandwidth, the better the fit, but there is a tradeoff between the number of "humps" captured and the smoothness of the fit. Intuitively, decreasing the bandwidth is like decreasing the bin width in the histogram, and the kernel is like a "counter"—but one which puts less weight on observations that are further away from the point being evaluated. (Imagine moving from the histogram on the right in Figure C.21 to the one on the left as you increase the bandwidth, and then imagine the use of the kernel to smooth the bars.) The kernel (Gaussian) density function with bandwidth equal to 0.4 appears to have captured the bimodality in the data.

There is a vast literature about the optimal choice of bandwidth as well as extensions of the nonparametric methods to regression analysis. Useful references include Pagan, A.

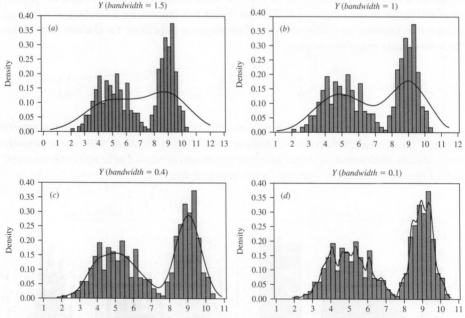

FIGURE C.22 Fitting with a nonparametric density estimator (*a*) bandwidth = 1.5, (*b*) bandwidth = 1, (*c*) bandwidth = 0.4, (*d*) bandwidth 0.1.

and Ullah, A., *Nonparametric Econometrics*, Cambridge University Press, 1999; and Li, Q and Racine, J. S. *Nonparametric Econometrics: Theory and Practice,* Princeton University Press, 2007.

C.11 Exercises

Answers to exercises marked * can be found at www.wiley.com/go/global/hill.

C.1 Suppose $Y_1, Y_2, \ldots, Y_N$ is a random sample from a population with mean μ and variance σ^2. Rather than using all N observations, consider an easy estimator of μ that uses only the first two observations

$$Y^* = \frac{Y_1 + Y_2}{2}$$

(a) Show that Y^* is a linear estimator.
(b) Show that Y^* is an unbiased estimator.
(c) Find the variance of Y^*.
(d) Explain why the sample mean of all N observations is a better estimator than Y^*.

C.2 Suppose that Y_1, Y_2, Y_3 is a random sample from a $N(\mu, \sigma^2)$ population. To estimate μ, consider the weighted estimator

$$\tilde{Y} = \frac{1}{2}Y_1 + \frac{1}{3}Y_2 + \frac{1}{6}Y_3$$

(a) Show that $\tilde{Y}$ is a linear estimator.
(b) Show that $\tilde{Y}$ is an unbiased estimator.
(c) Find the variance of $\tilde{Y}$ and compare it to the variance of the sample mean $\overline{Y}$.
(d) Is $\tilde{Y}$ as good an estimator as $\overline{Y}$?
(e) If $\sigma^2 = 9$, calculate the probability that each estimator is within one unit on either side of μ.

C.3* The hourly sales of fried chicken at Louisiana Fried Chicken are normally distributed with mean 2,000 pieces and standard deviation 500 pieces. What is the probability that in a nine-hour day more than 20,000 pieces will be sold?

C.4 Starting salaries for economics majors have a mean of $47,000 and a standard deviation of $8,000. What is the probability that a random sample of 40 economics majors will have an average salary of more than $50,000?

C.5* A store manager designs a new accounting system that will be cost-effective if the mean monthly charge account balance is more than $170. A sample of 400 accounts is randomly selected. The sample mean balance is $178 and the sample standard deviation is $65. Can the manager conclude that the new system will be cost effective?

(a) Carry out a hypothesis test to answer this question. Use the $\alpha = 0.05$ level of significance.
(b) Compute the *p*-value of the test.

C.6 An econometric professor's rule of thumb is that students should expect to spend two hours outside of class on coursework for each hour in class. For a three-hour-per-week class, this means that students are expected to do six hours of work outside class. The professor randomly selects eight students from a class, and asks how many hours they studied econometrics during the past week. The sample values are 1, 3, 4, 4, 6, 6, 8, 12.

(a) Assuming that the population is normally distributed, can the professor conclude at the 0.05 level of significance that the students are studying on average more than six hours per week?

(b) Construct a 90% confidence interval for the population mean number of hours studied per week.

C.7 Modern labor practices attempt to keep labor costs low by hiring and laying off workers to meet demand. Newly hired workers are not as productive as experienced ones. Assume that assembly line workers with experience handle 500 pieces per day. A manager concludes that it is cost-effective to maintain the current practice if new hires, with a week of training, can process more than 450 pieces per day. A random sample of $N = 50$ trainees is observed. Let Y_i denote the number of pieces each handles on a randomly selected day. The sample mean is $\bar{y} = 460$, and the estimated sample standard deviation is $\hat{\sigma} = 38$.

(a) Carry out a test of whether or not there is evidence to support the conjecture that current hiring procedures are effective, at the 5% level of significance. Pay careful attention when formulating the null and alternative hypotheses.

(b) What exactly would a Type I error be in this example? Would it be a costly one to make?

(c) Compute the p-value for this test.

C.8* To evaluate alternative retirement benefit packages for its employees, a large corporation must determine the mean age of its workforce. Assume that the age of its employees is normally distributed. Since the corporation has thousands of workers, a sample is to be taken. If the standard deviation of ages is known to be $\sigma = 21$ years, how large should the sample be to ensure that a 95% interval estimate of mean age is no more than four years wide?

C.9 Consider the discrete random variable Y that takes the values $y = 1, 2, 3$, and 4 with probabilities 0.1, 0.2, 0.3, and 0.4, respectively.

(a) Sketch this *pdf*.

(b) Find the expected value of Y.

(c) Find the variance of Y.

(d) If we take a random sample of size $N = 3$ from this distribution, what are the mean and variance of the sample mean, $\bar{Y} = (Y_1 + Y_2 + Y_3)/3$?

C.10 This exercise is a low-tech simulation experiment related to Exercise C.9. It can be a group or class exercise if desired. Have each group member create a set of 10 numbered, identical, slips of paper like the following table.

1	2	2	3	3
3	4	4	4	4

(a) Draw a slip of paper at random and record its value, preferably entering each number into a data file for use with your computer software. Draw a total of 10 times, each time replacing the slip into the pile and stirring them well. Compare the average of these values to the expected value in Exercise C.9(b). Draw 10 more values with replacement. What is the average of all 20 values?

(b) Calculate the sample variance of the 20 values obtained in part (a). Compare this value to the true variance in Exercise C.9(c).

(c) Draw three slips of paper at random, with replacement. Calculate the average of the numbers on these $N = 3$ slips of paper, $\overline{Y} = (Y_1 + Y_2 + Y_3)/3$. Repeat this process at least $NSAM = 20$ times, obtaining $NSAM$ average values, $\overline{Y}_1, \overline{Y}_2, \ldots, \overline{Y}_{NSAM}$. Calculate the sample average and sample variance of these $NSAM$ values. Compare these to the expected value and variance of the sample mean obtained in Exercise C.9(d).

(d) Enter the $NSAM$ values $\overline{Y}_1, \overline{Y}_2, \ldots, \overline{Y}_{NSAM}$ into a data file. Standardize these values by subtracting the true mean and dividing by the true standard deviation of the mean, from Exercise C9(d). Use your computer software to create a histogram. Discuss the central limit theorem and how it relates to the figure you have created.

(e) Repeat parts (c) and (d) using $NSAM$ samples of more than $N = 3$ slips of paper, perhaps five or seven. How do the histograms compare to the one in part (d)?

(f) Discuss the terms "sampling variation" and "sampling distribution" in the context of the experiments you have performed.

C.11 At the famous Fulton Fish Market in New York City, sales of whiting (a type of fish) vary from day to day. Over a period of several months, daily quantities sold (in pounds) were observed. These data are in the file *fultonfish.dat*.

(a) Using the data for Monday sales, test the null hypothesis that the mean quantity sold is greater than or equal to 10,000 pounds per day against the alternative that the mean quantity sold is less than 10,000 pounds. Use the $\alpha = 0.05$ level of significance. Be sure to (i) state the null and alternative hypotheses, (ii) give the test statistic and its distribution, (iii) indicate the rejection region, including a sketch, (iv) state your conclusion, and (v) calculate the p-value for the test. Include a sketch showing the p-value.

(b) Assume that daily sales on Tuesday (X_2) and Wednesday (X_3) are normally distributed with means μ_2 and μ_3, and variances σ_2^2 and σ_3^2, respectively. Assume that sales on Tuesday and Wednesday are independent of each other. Test the hypothesis that the variances σ_2^2 and σ_3^2 are equal against the alternative that the variance on Tuesday is larger. Use the $\alpha = 0.05$ level of significance. Be sure to (i) state the null and alternative hypotheses, (ii) give the test statistic and its distribution, (iii) indicate the rejection region, including a sketch, (iv) state your conclusion, and (v) calculate the p-value for the test. Include a sketch showing the p-value.

(c) We wish to test the hypothesis that mean daily sales on Tuesday and Wednesday are equal against the alternative that they are not equal. Using the result in part (b) as a guide to the appropriate version of the test (Section C.7), carry out this hypothesis test using the 5% level of significance.

(d) Let the daily sales for Monday, Tuesday, Wednesday, Thursday, and Friday be denoted as X_1, X_2, X_3, X_4, and X_5, respectively. Assume that $X_i \sim N(\mu_i, \sigma_i^2)$, and that sales from day to day are independent. Define total weekly sales as $W = X_1 + X_2 + X_3 + X_4 + X_5$. Derive the expected value and variance of W. Be sure to show your work and justify your answer.

(e)◆ Referring to part (d), let $E(W) = \mu$. Assume that we estimate μ using

$$\hat{\mu} = \overline{X}_1 + \overline{X}_2 + \overline{X}_3 + \overline{X}_4 + \overline{X}_5$$

where $\overline{X}_i$ is the sample mean for the ith day. Derive the probability distribution of $\hat{\mu}$ and construct an approximate (valid in large samples) 95% interval estimate for μ. Justify the validity of your interval estimator.

Appendix D

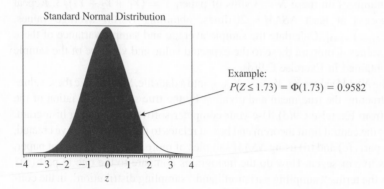

Standard Normal Distribution

Example:
$P(Z \le 1.73) = \Phi(1.73) = 0.9582$

Table 1 **Cumulative Probabilities for the Standard Normal Distribution**
$\Phi(z) = P(Z \le z)$

z	0.00	0.01	0.02	0.03	0.04	0.05	0.06	0.07	0.08	0.09
0.0	0.5000	0.5040	0.5080	0.5120	0.5160	0.5199	0.5239	0.5279	0.5319	0.5359
0.1	0.5398	0.5438	0.5478	0.5517	0.5557	0.5596	0.5636	0.5675	0.5714	0.5753
0.2	0.5793	0.5832	0.5871	0.5910	0.5948	0.5987	0.6026	0.6064	0.6103	0.6141
0.3	0.6179	0.6217	0.6255	0.6293	0.6331	0.6368	0.6406	0.6443	0.6480	0.6517
0.4	0.6554	0.6591	0.6628	0.6664	0.6700	0.6736	0.6772	0.6808	0.6844	0.6879
0.5	0.6915	0.6950	0.6985	0.7019	0.7054	0.7088	0.7123	0.7157	0.7190	0.7224
0.6	0.7257	0.7291	0.7324	0.7357	0.7389	0.7422	0.7454	0.7486	0.7517	0.7549
0.7	0.7580	0.7611	0.7642	0.7673	0.7704	0.7734	0.7764	0.7794	0.7823	0.7852
0.8	0.7881	0.7910	0.7939	0.7967	0.7995	0.8023	0.8051	0.8078	0.8106	0.8133
0.9	0.8159	0.8186	0.8212	0.8238	0.8264	0.8289	0.8315	0.8340	0.8365	0.8389
1.0	0.8413	0.8438	0.8461	0.8485	0.8508	0.8531	0.8554	0.8577	0.8599	0.8621
1.1	0.8643	0.8665	0.8686	0.8708	0.8729	0.8749	0.8770	0.8790	0.8810	0.8830
1.2	0.8849	0.8869	0.8888	0.8907	0.8925	0.8944	0.8962	0.8980	0.8997	0.9015
1.3	0.9032	0.9049	0.9066	0.9082	0.9099	0.9115	0.9131	0.9147	0.9162	0.9177
1.4	0.9192	0.9207	0.9222	0.9236	0.9251	0.9265	0.9279	0.9292	0.9306	0.9319
1.5	0.9332	0.9345	0.9357	0.9370	0.9382	0.9394	0.9406	0.9418	0.9429	0.9441
1.6	0.9452	0.9463	0.9474	0.9484	0.9495	0.9505	0.9515	0.9525	0.9535	0.9545
1.7	0.9554	0.9564	0.9573	0.9582	0.9591	0.9599	0.9608	0.9616	0.9625	0.9633
1.8	0.9641	0.9649	0.9656	0.9664	0.9671	0.9678	0.9686	0.9693	0.9699	0.9706
1.9	0.9713	0.9719	0.9726	0.9732	0.9738	0.9744	0.9750	0.9756	0.9761	0.9767
2.0	0.9772	0.9778	0.9783	0.9788	0.9793	0.9798	0.9803	0.9808	0.9812	0.9817
2.1	0.9821	0.9826	0.9830	0.9834	0.9838	0.9842	0.9846	0.9850	0.9854	0.9857
2.2	0.9861	0.9864	0.9868	0.9871	0.9875	0.9878	0.9881	0.9884	0.9887	0.9890
2.3	0.9893	0.9896	0.9898	0.9901	0.9904	0.9906	0.9909	0.9911	0.9913	0.9916
2.4	0.9918	0.9920	0.9922	0.9925	0.9927	0.9929	0.9931	0.9932	0.9934	0.9936
2.5	0.9938	0.9940	0.9941	0.9943	0.9945	0.9946	0.9948	0.9949	0.9951	0.9952
2.6	0.9953	0.9955	0.9956	0.9957	0.9959	0.9960	0.9961	0.9962	0.9963	0.9964
2.7	0.9965	0.9966	0.9967	0.9968	0.9969	0.9970	0.9971	0.9972	0.9973	0.9974
2.8	0.9974	0.9975	0.9976	0.9977	0.9977	0.9978	0.9979	0.9979	0.9980	0.9981
2.9	0.9981	0.9982	0.9982	0.9983	0.9984	0.9984	0.9985	0.9985	0.9986	0.9986
3.0	0.9987	0.9987	0.9987	0.9988	0.9988	0.9989	0.9989	0.9989	0.9990	0.9990

Source: This table was generated using the SAS® function PROBNORM.

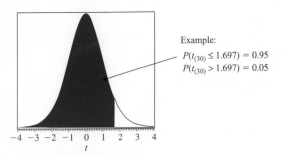

Example:
$P(t_{(30)} \leq 1.697) = 0.95$
$P(t_{(30)} > 1.697) = 0.05$

Table 2   Percentiles of the *t*-distribution

df	$t_{(0.90,\text{df})}$	$t_{(0.95,\text{df})}$	$t_{(0.975,\text{df})}$	$t_{(0.99,\text{df})}$	$t_{(0.995,\text{df})}$
1	3.078	6.314	12.706	31.821	63.657
2	1.886	2.920	4.303	6.965	9.925
3	1.638	2.353	3.182	4.541	5.841
4	1.533	2.132	2.776	3.747	4.604
5	1.476	2.015	2.571	3.365	4.032
6	1.440	1.943	2.447	3.143	3.707
7	1.415	1.895	2.365	2.998	3.499
8	1.397	1.860	2.306	2.896	3.355
9	1.383	1.833	2.262	2.821	3.250
10	1.372	1.812	2.228	2.764	3.169
11	1.363	1.796	2.201	2.718	3.106
12	1.356	1.782	2.179	2.681	3.055
13	1.350	1.771	2.160	2.650	3.012
14	1.345	1.761	2.145	2.624	2.977
15	1.341	1.753	2.131	2.602	2.947
16	1.337	1.746	2.120	2.583	2.921
17	1.333	1.740	2.110	2.567	2.898
18	1.330	1.734	2.101	2.552	2.878
19	1.328	1.729	2.093	2.539	2.861
20	1.325	1.725	2.086	2.528	2.845
21	1.323	1.721	2.080	2.518	2.831
22	1.321	1.717	2.074	2.508	2.819
23	1.319	1.714	2.069	2.500	2.807
24	1.318	1.711	2.064	2.492	2.797
25	1.316	1.708	2.060	2.485	2.787
26	1.315	1.706	2.056	2.479	2.779
27	1.314	1.703	2.052	2.473	2.771
28	1.313	1.701	2.048	2.467	2.763
29	1.311	1.699	2.045	2.462	2.756
30	1.310	1.697	2.042	2.457	2.750
31	1.309	1.696	2.040	2.453	2.744
32	1.309	1.694	2.037	2.449	2.738
33	1.308	1.692	2.035	2.445	2.733
34	1.307	1.691	2.032	2.441	2.728
35	1.306	1.690	2.030	2.438	2.724
36	1.306	1.688	2.028	2.434	2.719
37	1.305	1.687	2.026	2.431	2.715
38	1.304	1.686	2.024	2.429	2.712
39	1.304	1.685	2.023	2.426	2.708
40	1.303	1.684	2.021	2.423	2.704
50	1.299	1.676	2.009	2.403	2.678
∞	1.282	1.645	1.960	2.326	2.576

Source: This table was generated using the SAS® function TINV.

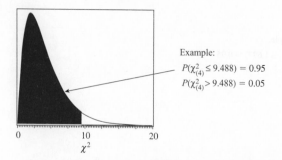

Example:
$P(\chi^2_{(4)} \leq 9.488) = 0.95$
$P(\chi^2_{(4)} > 9.488) = 0.05$

Table 3 Percentiles of the Chi-square Distribution

df	$\chi^2_{(0.90,df)}$	$\chi^2_{(0.95,df)}$	$\chi^2_{(0.975,df)}$	$\chi^2_{(0.99,df)}$	$\chi^2_{(0.995,df)}$
1	2.706	3.841	5.024	6.635	7.879
2	4.605	5.991	7.378	9.210	10.597
3	6.251	7.815	9.348	11.345	12.838
4	7.779	9.488	11.143	13.277	14.860
5	9.236	11.070	12.833	15.086	16.750
6	10.645	12.592	14.449	16.812	18.548
7	12.017	14.067	16.013	18.475	20.278
8	13.362	15.507	17.535	20.090	21.955
9	14.684	16.919	19.023	21.666	23.589
10	15.987	18.307	20.483	23.209	25.188
11	17.275	19.675	21.920	24.725	26.757
12	18.549	21.026	23.337	26.217	28.300
13	19.812	22.362	24.736	27.688	29.819
14	21.064	23.685	26.119	29.141	31.319
15	22.307	24.996	27.488	30.578	32.801
16	23.542	26.296	28.845	32.000	34.267
17	24.769	27.587	30.191	33.409	35.718
18	25.989	28.869	31.526	34.805	37.156
19	27.204	30.144	32.852	36.191	38.582
20	28.412	31.410	34.170	37.566	39.997
21	29.615	32.671	35.479	38.932	41.401
22	30.813	33.924	36.781	40.289	42.796
23	32.007	35.172	38.076	41.638	44.181
24	33.196	36.415	39.364	42.980	45.559
25	34.382	37.652	40.646	44.314	46.928
26	35.563	38.885	41.923	45.642	48.290
27	36.741	40.113	43.195	46.963	49.645
28	37.916	41.337	44.461	48.278	50.993
29	39.087	42.557	45.722	49.588	52.336
30	40.256	43.773	46.979	50.892	53.672
35	46.059	49.802	53.203	57.342	60.275
40	51.805	55.758	59.342	63.691	66.766
50	63.167	67.505	71.420	76.154	79.490
60	74.397	79.082	83.298	88.379	91.952
70	85.527	90.531	95.023	100.425	104.215
80	96.578	101.879	106.629	112.329	116.321
90	107.565	113.145	118.136	124.116	128.299
100	118.498	124.342	129.561	135.807	140.169
110	129.385	135.480	140.917	147.414	151.948
120	140.233	146.567	152.211	158.950	163.648

Source: This table was generated using the SAS® function CINV.

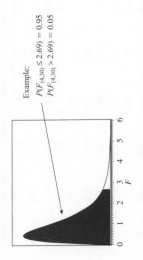

Example:
$P(F_{(4,30)} \leq 2.69) = 0.95$
$P(F_{(4,30)} > 2.69) = 0.05$

Table 4 **95th Percentile for the *F*-distribution**

v_2/v_1	1	2	3	4	5	6	7	8	9	10	12	15	20	30	60	∞
1	161.45	199.50	215.71	224.58	230.16	233.99	236.77	238.88	240.54	241.88	243.91	245.95	248.01	250.10	252.20	254.31
2	18.51	19.00	19.16	19.25	19.30	19.33	19.35	19.37	19.38	19.40	19.41	19.43	19.45	19.46	19.48	19.50
3	10.13	9.55	9.28	9.12	9.01	8.94	8.89	8.85	8.81	8.79	8.74	8.70	8.66	8.62	8.57	8.53
4	7.71	6.94	6.59	6.39	6.26	6.16	6.09	6.04	6.00	5.96	5.91	5.86	5.80	5.75	5.69	5.63
5	6.61	5.79	5.41	5.19	5.05	4.95	4.88	4.82	4.77	4.74	4.68	4.62	4.56	4.50	4.43	4.36
6	5.99	5.14	4.76	4.53	4.39	4.28	4.21	4.15	4.10	4.06	4.00	3.94	3.87	3.81	3.74	3.67
7	5.59	4.74	4.35	4.12	3.97	3.87	3.79	3.73	3.68	3.64	3.57	3.51	3.44	3.38	3.30	3.23
8	5.32	4.46	4.07	3.84	3.69	3.58	3.50	3.44	3.39	3.35	3.28	3.22	3.15	3.08	3.01	2.93
9	5.12	4.26	3.86	3.63	3.48	3.37	3.29	3.23	3.18	3.14	3.07	3.01	2.94	2.86	2.79	2.71
10	4.96	4.10	3.71	3.48	3.33	3.22	3.14	3.07	3.02	2.98	2.91	2.85	2.77	2.70	2.62	2.54
15	4.54	3.68	3.29	3.06	2.90	2.79	2.71	2.64	2.59	2.54	2.48	2.40	2.33	2.25	2.16	2.07
20	4.35	3.49	3.10	2.87	2.71	2.60	2.51	2.45	2.39	2.35	2.28	2.20	2.12	2.04	1.95	1.84
25	4.24	3.39	2.99	2.76	2.60	2.49	2.40	2.34	2.28	2.24	2.16	2.09	2.01	1.92	1.82	1.71
30	4.17	3.32	2.92	2.69	2.53	2.42	2.33	2.27	2.21	2.16	2.09	2.01	1.93	1.84	1.74	1.62
35	4.12	3.27	2.87	2.64	2.49	2.37	2.29	2.22	2.16	2.11	2.04	1.96	1.88	1.79	1.68	1.56
40	4.08	3.23	2.84	2.61	2.45	2.34	2.25	2.18	2.12	2.08	2.00	1.92	1.84	1.74	1.64	1.51
45	4.06	3.20	2.81	2.58	2.42	2.31	2.22	2.15	2.10	2.05	1.97	1.89	1.81	1.71	1.60	1.47
50	4.03	3.18	2.79	2.56	2.40	2.29	2.20	2.13	2.07	2.03	1.95	1.87	1.78	1.69	1.58	1.44
60	4.00	3.15	2.76	2.53	2.37	2.25	2.17	2.10	2.04	1.99	1.92	1.84	1.75	1.65	1.53	1.39
120	3.92	3.07	2.68	2.45	2.29	2.18	2.09	2.02	1.96	1.91	1.83	1.75	1.66	1.55	1.43	1.25
∞	3.84	3.00	2.60	2.37	2.21	2.10	2.01	1.94	1.88	1.83	1.75	1.67	1.57	1.46	1.32	1.00

Source: This table was generated using the SAS® function FINV.

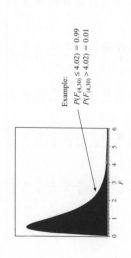

Example:
$P(F_{(4,30)} \leq 4.02) = 0.99$
$P(F_{(4,30)} > 4.02) = 0.01$

Table 5 99th Percentile for the F-distribution

v_2/v_1	1	2	3	4	5	6	7	8	9	10	12	15	20	30	60	∞
1	4052.18	4999.50	5403.35	5624.58	5763.65	5858.99	5928.36	5981.07	6022.47	6055.85	6106.32	6157.28	6208.73	6260.65	6313.03	6365.87
2	98.50	99.00	99.17	99.25	99.30	99.33	99.36	99.37	99.39	99.40	99.42	99.43	99.45	99.47	99.48	99.50
3	34.12	30.82	29.46	28.71	28.24	27.91	27.67	27.49	27.35	27.23	27.05	z26.87	26.69	26.50	26.32	26.13
4	21.20	18.00	16.69	15.98	15.52	15.21	14.98	14.80	14.66	14.55	14.37	14.20	14.02	13.84	13.65	13.46
5	16.26	13.27	12.06	11.39	10.97	10.67	10.46	10.29	10.16	10.05	9.89	9.72	9.55	9.38	9.20	9.02
6	13.75	10.92	9.78	9.15	8.75	8.47	8.26	8.10	7.98	7.87	7.72	7.56	7.40	7.23	7.06	6.88
7	12.25	9.55	8.45	7.85	7.46	7.19	6.99	6.84	6.72	6.62	6.47	6.31	6.16	5.99	5.82	5.65
8	11.26	8.65	7.59	7.01	6.63	6.37	6.18	6.03	5.91	5.81	5.67	5.52	5.36	5.20	5.03	4.86
9	10.56	8.02	6.99	6.42	6.06	5.80	5.61	5.47	5.35	5.26	5.11	4.96	4.81	4.65	4.48	4.31
10	10.04	7.56	6.55	5.99	5.64	5.39	5.20	5.06	4.94	4.85	4.71	4.56	4.41	4.25	4.08	3.91
15	8.68	6.36	5.42	4.89	4.56	4.32	4.14	4.00	3.89	3.80	3.67	3.52	3.37	3.21	3.05	2.87
20	8.10	5.85	4.94	4.43	4.10	3.87	3.70	3.56	3.46	3.37	3.23	3.09	2.94	2.78	2.61	2.42
25	7.77	5.57	4.68	4.18	3.85	3.63	3.46	3.32	3.22	3.13	2.99	2.85	2.70	2.54	2.36	2.17
30	7.56	5.39	4.51	4.02	3.70	3.47	3.30	3.17	3.07	2.98	2.84	2.70	2.55	2.39	2.21	2.01
35	7.42	5.27	4.40	3.91	3.59	3.37	3.20	3.07	2.96	2.88	2.74	2.60	2.44	2.28	2.10	1.89
40	7.31	5.18	4.31	3.83	3.51	3.29	3.12	2.99	2.89	2.80	2.66	2.52	2.37	2.20	2.02	1.80
45	7.23	5.11	4.25	3.77	3.45	3.23	3.07	2.94	2.83	2.74	2.61	2.46	2.31	2.14	1.96	1.74
50	7.17	5.06	4.20	3.72	3.41	3.19	3.02	2.89	2.78	2.70	2.56	2.42	2.27	2.10	1.91	1.68
60	7.08	4.98	4.13	3.65	3.34	3.12	2.95	2.82	2.72	2.63	2.50	2.35	2.20	2.03	1.84	1.60
120	6.85	4.79	3.95	3.48	3.17	2.96	2.79	2.66	2.56	2.47	2.34	2.19	2.03	1.86	1.66	1.38
∞	6.63	4.61	3.78	3.32	3.02	2.80	2.64	2.51	2.41	2.32	2.18	2.04	1.88	1.70	1.47	1.00

Source: This table was generated using the SAS® function FINV.

Index

Elasticity

$$\eta = \frac{\text{percentage change in } y}{\text{percentage change in } x} = \frac{\Delta y / y}{\Delta x / x} = \frac{\Delta y}{\Delta x} \cdot \frac{x}{y}$$

$$\eta = \frac{\Delta E(y)/E(y)}{\Delta x / x} = \frac{\Delta E(y)}{\Delta x} \cdot \frac{x}{E(y)} = \beta_2 \cdot \frac{x}{E(y)}$$

Least Squares Expressions Useful for Theory

$$b_2 = \beta_2 + \Sigma w_i e_i$$

$$w_i = \frac{x_i - \bar{x}}{\Sigma(x_i - \bar{x})^2}$$

$$\Sigma w_i = 0, \quad \Sigma w_i x_i = 1, \quad \Sigma w_i^2 = 1/\Sigma(x_i - \bar{x})^2$$

Properties of the Least Squares Estimators

$$\text{var}(b_1) = \sigma^2 \left[\frac{\Sigma x_i^2}{N\Sigma(x_i - \bar{x})^2} \right] \quad \text{var}(b_2) = \frac{\sigma^2}{\Sigma(x_i - \bar{x})^2}$$

$$\text{cov}(b_1, b_2) = \sigma^2 \left[\frac{-\bar{x}}{\Sigma(x_i - \bar{x})^2} \right]$$

Gauss-Markov Theorem: Under the assumptions SR1–SR5 of the linear regression model the estimators b_1 and b_2 have the *smallest variance of all linear and unbiased estimators* of β_1 and β_2. They are the Best Linear Unbiased Estimators (BLUE) of β_1 and β_2.

If we make the normality assumption, assumption SR6, about the error term, then the least squares estimators are normally distributed.

$$b_1 \sim N\left(\beta_1, \frac{\sigma^2 \Sigma x_i^2}{N\Sigma(x_i - \bar{x})^2}\right), b_2 \sim N\left(\beta_2, \frac{\sigma^2}{\Sigma(x_i - \bar{x})^2}\right)$$

Estimated Error Variance

$$\hat{\sigma}^2 = \frac{\Sigma \hat{e}_i^2}{N - 2}$$

Estimator Standard Errors

$$\text{se}(b_1) = \sqrt{\widehat{\text{var}(b_1)}}, \quad \text{se}(b_2) = \sqrt{\widehat{\text{var}(b_2)}}$$

t-distribution

If assumptions SR1–SR6 of the simple linear regression model hold, then

$$t = \frac{b_k - \beta_k}{\text{se}(b_k)} \sim t_{(N-2)}, \quad k = 1, 2$$

Interval Estimates

$$P[b_2 - t_c \text{se}(b_2) \le \beta_2 \le b_2 + t_c \text{se}(b_2)] = 1 - \alpha$$

Hypothesis Testing

Components of Hypothesis Tests
1. A *null* hypothesis, H_0
2. An *alternative* hypothesis, H_1
3. A test *statistic*
4. A *rejection* region
5. A conclusion

If the null hypothesis $H_0 : \beta_2 = c$ is *true*, then

$$t = \frac{b_2 - c}{\text{se}(b_2)} \sim t_{(N-2)}$$

Rejection rule for a two-tail test: If the value of the test statistic falls in the rejection region, either tail of the t-distribution, then we reject the null hypothesis and accept the alternative.

Type I error: The null hypothesis is *true* and we decide to *reject* it.

Type II error: The null hypothesis is *false* and we decide *not* to reject it.

p-value rejection rule: When the p-value of a hypothesis test is *smaller* than the chosen value of α, then the test procedure leads to *rejection* of the null hypothesis.

Prediction

$$y_0 = \beta_1 + \beta_2 x_0 + e_0, \ \hat{y}_0 = b_1 + b_2 x_0, \ f = y_0 - \hat{y}_0$$

$$\widehat{\text{var}(f)} = \hat{\sigma}^2 \left[1 + \frac{1}{N} + \frac{(x_0 - \bar{x})^2}{\Sigma(x_i - \bar{x})^2} \right], \text{se}(f) = \sqrt{\widehat{\text{var}(f)}}$$

A $(1 - \alpha) \times 100\%$ confidence interval, or prediction interval, for y_0

$$\hat{y}_0 \pm t_c \text{se}(f)$$

Goodness of Fit

$$\Sigma(y_i - \bar{y})^2 = \Sigma(\hat{y}_i - \bar{y})^2 + \Sigma \hat{e}_i^2$$

$$SST = SSR + SSE$$

$$R^2 = \frac{SSR}{SST} = 1 - \frac{SSE}{SST} = (\text{corr}(y, \hat{y}))^2$$

Log-Linear Model

$$\ln(y) = \beta_1 + \beta_2 x + e, \ \widehat{\ln(y)} = b_1 + b_2 x$$

$100 \times \beta_2 \approx \%$ change in y given a one-unit change in x.

$$\hat{y}_n = \exp(b_1 + b_2 x)$$

$$\hat{y}_c = \exp(b_1 + b_2 x) \exp(\hat{\sigma}^2 / 2)$$

Prediction interval:

$$\exp\left[\widehat{\ln(y)} - t_c \text{se}(f)\right], \ \exp\left[\widehat{\ln(y)} + t_c \text{se}(f)\right]$$

Generalized goodness-of-fit measure $R_g^2 = (\text{corr}(y, \hat{y}_n))^2$

Assumptions of the Multiple Regression Model

MR1 $y_i = \beta_1 + \beta_2 x_{i2} + \cdots + \beta_K x_{iK} + e_i$

MR2 $E(y_i) = \beta_1 + \beta_2 x_{i2} + \cdots + \beta_K x_{iK} \Leftrightarrow E(e_i) = 0.$

MR3 $\text{var}(y_i) = \text{var}(e_i) = \sigma^2$

MR4 $\text{cov}(y_i, y_j) = \text{cov}(e_i, e_j) = 0$

MR5   The values of x_{ik} are not random and are not exact linear functions of the other explanatory variables.

MR6 $y_i \sim N[(\beta_1 + \beta_2 x_{i2} + \cdots + \beta_K x_{iK}), \sigma^2]$
$\Leftrightarrow e_i \sim N(0, \sigma^2)$

Least Squares Estimates in MR Model

Least squares estimates $b_1, b_2, \ldots, b_K$ minimize
$$S(\beta_1, \beta_2, \ldots, \beta_K) = \Sigma(y_i - \beta_1 - \beta_2 x_{i2} - \cdots - \beta_K x_{iK})^2$$

Estimated Error Variance and Estimator Standard Errors

$$\hat{\sigma}^2 = \frac{\Sigma \hat{e}_i^2}{N - K} \quad \text{se}(b_k) = \sqrt{\widehat{\text{var}(b_k)}}$$